Dr. File Finder's Guide to Shareware

The Boston Computer Society

One Center Plaza

Boston,

Massachusetts

02108

Mike Callahan
Nick Anis

Osborne **McGraw-Hill**

Berkeley New York St. Louis San Francisco
Auckland Bogotá Hamburg London Madrid
Mexico City Milan Montreal New Delhi Panama City
Paris São Paulo Singapore Sydney
Tokyo Toronto

Osborne **McGraw-Hill**
2600 Tenth Street
Berkeley, California 94710
U.S.A.

Osborne **McGraw-Hill** offers software for sale. For information on software, translations, or book distributors outside of the U.S.A., please write to Osborne **McGraw-Hill** at the above address.

Dr. File Finder's Guide to Shareware

1234567890 DOC 99876543210

ISBN 0-07-881646-7

The manuscript for this book was prepared and submitted to Osborne **McGraw-Hill** in electronic form. The acquisitions editor for this project was Jeffrey Pepper, the technical reviewer was John Ribar, and the project editor was Judith Brown.

Text design by Marcela Hancik and Stefany Otis, using Zaph for text body and display.

Cover art by Graphic Eye, Inc. Color separation by Colour Image; cover supplier, Phoenix Color Corporation. Screens produced with InSet, from Inset Systems, Inc. Book printed and bound by R.R. Donnelley & Sons Company, Crawfordsville, Indiana.

This book is printed on recycled paper.

For deeply personal reasons, this book is primarily dedicated to the memory of my father, the late Edward T. Callahan. It is also dedicated to my mother, Joan M. Callahan, Carl H. MacCallum, and to Carol, Melaina, and Kadee. For obvious reasons, it is also dedicated to Shareware—and all who *share* in the dream.

CONTENTS

One Center Plaza

Boston,

Massachusetts

02108

Long before the introduction of the IBM PC, users were already on the lookout for low-cost software alternatives. No one can say for sure who originated the concept of Shareware or user-supported software. For purposes of this book Andrew Fluegelman and Jim Button popularized the modern notion of Shareware. Over time one guy has emerged as *the* Shareware expert among Shareware experts. He's the guy who other experts ask questions. I think it's a personal coup that I got him to write this book. His name is Michael Callahan, and he's affectionately known as "Dr. File Finder" to those who use his services.

There are over 85,000 programs available through Shareware. As a resource it's one heck of a cache of code. Besides application areas like word processing, electronic spreadsheets, database management, and finance there are thousands of useful utility programs that can save you time, money, and frustration. There are Shareware enhancements for many of the best-selling commercial programs too.

You'll find that *Dr. File Finder's Guide to Shareware* will be one of the best sources for all the information you'll need to start taking advantage of free and low-cost software.

Dr. File Finder visits thousands of bulletin boards and frequents the online services, transferring Shareware files. He's been called the "Johnny Appleseed of Shareware." You'll find Doc's tips and program insights along with product background and history invaluable.

While Shareware catalogs typically offer brief descriptions of dated programs and other Shareware books may limit their coverage to only a few of the key programs, *Dr. File Finder's Guide to Shareware* offers in-depth, insightful coverage of more programs than anyone else. The book's program descriptions go beyond the typical rehash of documentation. Doc has talked to the authors, read the documentation, and installed and used the programs, which explains the richness of the book's 22 file categories in the 17 file chapters.

There are also chapters covering the Shareware libraries of key online information services like GEnie and CompuServe, along with assorted telecommunications tips and even detailed discussions of programs and commands to use with care. Throughout the 1000-odd pages of text you'll be treated to a personalized guided tour. Doc will take you to his favorite haunts and even give you his "top forty" Shareware picks. Samples of many of the best programs are also provided.

So why hasn't someone done this before? Who has the time? File Finder does this full-time, so nobody can compete with him. That's why we chose him to develop this newest Dvorak book selection. I hope it becomes a permanent addition to your book collection.

John C. Dvorak
Berkeley, California

ACKNOWLEDGMENTS

Writing a book like *Dr. File Finder's Guide to Shareware* is a lot of work. Once a chapter is written there is a whole process that has to take place before you see it the way it appears now. Lots of people pitch in and help out and we'd like to thank all of them for doing such an outstanding job. The technical editor was John Ribar who gave some good input. John was also the one who inadvertently caused us to see that my word processor was somehow losing pages. Special thanks to Judith Brown and Bob O'Keefe for getting the book through the system. Big thanks also go to Juliette Anjos, Audrey Baer Johnson, Pat Mannion, and Ann Kameoka for all their hard work, and to everyone on the copyedit staff for a great job.

Thanks to Emily Rader, Lisa Kissinger, and Kendal Anderson for all of the time and effort they put in. Many thanks to that nice lady at the switchboard, Osborne McGraw-Hill. I assume that's what her name is because that's what she always says when she answers the phone. (*smile*) Seriously, "Thanks, Ann!" My deepest personal thanks to Editor-in-Chief, Jeff Pepper, who was the steady hand at the helm. I actually caught him in his office on 23 occasions—a new record. (And I'll bet Jeff didn't think I was *really* keeping track.)

Very special and personal thanks to Laura Sackerman. Laura did the "tech" edits and "queries" with me over the phone and often brought a much-needed change of pace to my day. Believe me, that meant a lot to me on many days. I owe Laura a dinner at the very least.

A very sincere and personal thank you to John Dvorak. I naturally want to thank John for his support of the project, but most of all for his friendship. We talk on the phone about programs and computers and they are some of the most enjoyable discussions that I ever get into. So, thanks John, for being a friend *and* for supporting this project. *Now* I have it in the order that is most important to me.

Many thanks to my dear friend Professor Rae M. Barent for her insights, support, and for being there to help out anytime she was needed. Her expertise with databases was very helpful in doing Chapter 18. Sincere personal thanks to my very good friend Professor Donald E. Bodley, Chair Professor of Real Estate and Finance at Eastern Kentucky University, for his expertise and assistance on the chapter on business and finance, Chapter 21.

Appreciative smiles to my daughter, Melaina Callahan, for helping to sort through thousands of bulletin board numbers so that Appendix C could be nicely formatted. Another appreciative smile (why am I being so appreciative? they got paid $2 an hour) to my daughter, Kadee Callahan, for sorting and filing disks and manuals. I have an advantage over Nick Anis when it comes to kids. Mine could help out with the mail or around the house or even cook dinner. All his could do was try to cut down on the number of dirty diapers they generated and take longer naps.

We both have to give a lot of thanks to our families. I want to thank mine just for understanding why I had to be down in "The Cave" so many hours a day every day, and also for pitching in and helping take care of things that needed to be done. Having spent a week at my coauthor's house, I *know* that he has to thank his family. For one thing, they put up with his jokes. John Dvorak and I have been talking about hiring a joke writer for Nick—he needs some very new material. Nick's family also supports his crazy hours. They support his craziness just as my family supports mine, and support is important. Many thanks with much love.

A truly special acknowledgment goes to Craig Menefee, who came to our aid at some critical times during work on the book. A real big salute to Brian Miller and Tess Heder of Channel 1, for their help in finding what has to be the widest selection of text files that we've ever seen—some of these are discussed in Chapter 22. Another big thanks to the Mahoneys at EXEC-PC for all of their help and support. A big thanks to John Erikson and Dave Krause, of Erik Labs, for their help and input on the section on BiModem in Chapter 7. Thanks fellas. Talking about file transfer protocols, I really want to thank Chuck Forsberg for clarifying the chronological order in which certain protocols appeared, and for some other great facts as well. A very special note of thanks to Peter Young, of the Interface Group, for his support of this book and of the world of telecommunications.

Thanks to Jack Rickard, publisher of *Boardwatch* magazine, for providing some interesting insights on the industry. The "master" himself, Vern Buerg, was a great help in providing clarification on some of the historical events in Shareware. A tip of the hat to John Friel, author of Qmodem, for his insights and valuable perspectives on file transfer protocols and tele-communications features and functions in general. (I just know that I'm going to forget someone . . . and me with the eidetic memory yet.) A hearty slap on the back to all the folks at PKWARE, especially Phil Katz and Douglas Hay, for keeping us up-to-date on developments in the area of file compression—it was greatly appreciated.

Thanks from both of us to Debby and Brad Schepp for providing some of their research material on CompuServe. Kudos are also due to Matthew Thomas, author of the MPt protocol, for his comments on streaming protocols in Chapter 7. Although I've thanked all of them personally, I'd like to publicly thank Barry Simon, Mark "Sparky" Herring, John Friel, and Sammy Mitchell for their candid remarks on their lives in and out of Shareware in Chapter 2. Many thanks to Rich Levin for making sure we were right on the money about viruses in Chapter 24. We're very grateful to Fred Clark and David Terry, of Clark Development Corporation, for the PC Board system that they provided for our use during the course of the project.

A personal thank you to Barry Simon, just for being my friend and always willing to listen. That's what friends are for, and I won't forget that. Our gratitude to Jim Button and Deedee Wallace, of ButtonWare, for providing accurate background on the history of Shareware and lots of other help besides. Personal thanks to Bob Wallace, of Quicksoft, for his views and perspectives on Shareware, both in the very beginning and as it is today. Another big note of thanks to Nelson Ford, of the Public Software Library, for his help with the history of Shareware and for all his support in general. Thanks to Richard Peterson and Sandy Shupper of PC-SIG for their support and for providing information on the world of disk vending. I have to thank the programmers who allowed their pro-grams to be available through this book, namely: John Friel, Dave Frailey, John Knauer, Terry Tomkow and Peter K. Schotch, Robert Blaine, Steven Calwas, Jim Dodgen, and Norm Patriquin. They created special versions to make sure that all of the programs would fit on the disks. Thanks guys! If you like their programs as much as we do, please register them.

A lot of companies also pitched in and gave their support and service to the project. In particular we'd like to thank: Neal Carmichael and Stan Kalisher at Northgate Computer Systems for all of their assistance with equipment and support. Real big thanks to Peter Reyman, Gary Bailer, and Bob Kramer of Panasonic. Bob, in particular, was a great help in answering all of my questions about the Panasonic dot matrix and laser printers. I can't say enough good things about all the people at GRiD Systems Corporation, especially Bob Goligowski and Jim Detar. A special thank you is due to Maynard Kealiher at the GRiD establishment in Denver for his outstanding help and support. Thanks to the people at NEC who provided their excellent MultiSync 3D monitor for testing all the VGA programs and making writing easier on my eyes. Speaking of VGA, a real big thank you to Jonathon Vall and the rest of the gang at Willow Peripherals for their special VGA-TV card. Being a creature of The Wires I want to extend a special thank you to Karen Novak at U.S. Robotics. Karen and the other fine folks at U.S. Robotics were always there to answer a question. We're very grateful to Quarterdeck Office Systems for providing me with DESQview, Qemm, and Manifest, so that programs discussed could be used under DESQview and multitasking. Thanks gang! Another big thank you to Sterling Software for providing me with the best backup program I've ever seen—their DMS/Intelligent Backup—a real lifesaver in several instances, and a time-saver as well.

A section full of thank yous for this book would not be complete without mentioning Shareware program authors. Their great enthusiasm over the book was truly inspiring. As news about this book spread, I was literally flooded with programs to look at. The record was 73 programs in a 5-day period, and I'd often get 10 to 12 programs a day. I had to start taking my daughters, Melaina and Kadee, to the post office with me just to carry out the mail. This very personal expression of support and excitement was very gratifying to me. (And yes, I tested and used *every* program.) So, thanks folks! for taking the time and effort to *share* your Shareware offerings with me. If you sent something and haven't heard from me, you will. Doing a book this size doesn't leave much time for letter writing. I'll get to it shortly.

Thanks to John Bean for doing a great job on the installation program for the disks that come with the book. Way to go, John! We especially want to thank *anyone* we forgot to thank. If we forgot you, it was strictly an oversight and we'll make it up to you in the future. To everyone who helped make this book possible, Nick and I extend our sincere thanks.

Dr. File Finder (Michael E. Callahan)
Nick Anis, Jr.

Our primary goal is to bring you a definitive guide to Shareware software. Another goal is to help you save time and money in obtaining Shareware software by sorting through the 85,000-plus Shareware programs that are available and describing, in detail, some of the best programs in a wide variety of categories. We believe that we've done a good job and that you are going to find this book interesting and informative. It is our hope that you'll recommend this book to your friends, family, and anyone else who is missing out on what Shareware has to offer. We sincerely hope that *Dr. File Finder's Guide to Shareware* becomes an important part of your computer library.

ABOUT THIS BOOK

This is *not* a Shareware catalog. You *will* learn about Shareware—what it is, how it works, and why you should want to make it work. You'll learn about the history of Shareware software and about the people who started a great marketing idea rolling. You'll also read the candid comments of some successful Shareware authors. In the course of the book you'll also learn about disk vendors, user groups, commercial online networks, and bulletin boards—all ways for you to obtain Shareware programs. We'll take you online and guide you step by step through the process of logging onto a bulletin board. You'll learn about file transfer protocols; not just what they are, but about their history, how they work, and which ones are the best to use in different circumstances.

Then there are the programs. Seventeen chapters that cover some of the *best* programs available in Shareware in over twenty different categories. The programs are described in great detail and most often accompanied by figures that show what a program's screens look like. We've helped to narrow the choices so you can save time and money. You'll also have all the information you need to contact the authors of any of the programs discussed here. When you've read this book, you'll know about Shareware: how to obtain it, how to go online with confidence, and how to recognize some of the best programs.

To give you even more value for the price of the book, you'll find special offers on many of the programs that are discussed. You'll find offers from manufacturers as well as offers from online services for free connect time. The disk that comes with the book is packed with some excellent Shareware programs.

HOW THIS BOOK IS ORGANIZED

The book is divided into four main sections with a fifth section containing the appendixes. The first section, "Examining Shareware and Freeware," gives you a definition of Shareware. It also includes the history of Shareware, interviews with program authors, and tells you about PC user groups and disk vendors. You'll also read about the major commercial networks.

The second section, "Getting Ready to Operate Online," gets you into the vast world of telecommunications. This section is geared to give you some confidence and handy tips. Terms are defined so that they are easy to understand. This section gradually progresses from the simple to the more complex. Compressed files are also covered in this section.

The third section, "Major Operations Online," starts where the second section left off. It looks at file transfer protocols, uploading, downloading, and storing programs on disk. Some extra tips and tricks are also provided—things that you might spend years learning the hard way.

Part Four, "The Best of Shareware—A Prescription for Success," is the start of the section on Shareware programs. The seventeen chapters in this section describe, in detail, some of the very best programs available in Shareware. Finally, the appendixes cover everything from the hardware and software configurations used while running all of the programs discussed in the book, to providing you with a large list of bulletin board numbers. At the very back of the book you'll find the coupons with the special offers.

CONVENTIONS USED IN THIS BOOK

To make *Dr. File Finder's Guide to Shareware* easier to read, the following conventions are used throughout the text:

- When a new term is defined, that term appears in *italic*.

- Text for you to type in is shown in **boldface**.

- Keys for you to press are shown in small capital letters; for example, ENTER.

- Key combinations for you to press appear in small capital letters connected by a hyphen; for example, ALT-C. This means you should press the two keys simultaneously.

PROGRAMS INCLUDED WITH THE BOOK

Here is a brief listing of the programs available through the book. Many of these programs are discussed in some detail in Chapter 17 and in other chapters on the particular subject.

On the Enclosed Disk

Blackbeard   This editor features full mouse support, multiple windows, and much more. Blackbeard is described in Chapter 10. This is the complete program and its documentation is generated automatically.

dCOM   Directory Commander is an excellent DOS shell and a powerful menu program as well. dCOM is discussed in Chapter 17. You'll find that the documentation was abbreviated so that the program itself would fit on the disk. You should have plenty of information for getting dCOM up and running. To get a copy of the documentation, call *any* of the BBSs listed in Appendix C as places where you can leave me a message. I will make sure that a copy of dCOM's documentation is on those boards. Look for the file DCOMTDOC.ZIP. Download it using the same guidelines described for Qmodem in the next section.

DOC 1.0   DOC is the custom program that was written for me by John Knauer for keeping track of programs that I store on disks. DOC is described in detail in Chapter 8. DOC isn't fancy, but it gets the job done, and it's fast and efficient.

IFF 5.0A   IFF is a great program with lots of power for enhancing batch files or just providing information about your system. IFF is discussed in Chapter 15. Use it to create menus and much more.

Programs Available Free from PC-SIG

Qmodem 4.2   Qmodem is an excellent, full-featured communications program; in my opinion, the *best* telecommunications program in Shareware. Qmodem is discussed in Chapter 11. In order to bring you Qmodem, we had to leave out the documentation. Qmodem has context-sensitive help throughout the program so you should be able to get it up and running with no problems. To get the documentation, first configure some of Qmodem using ALT-N. Don't forget Qmodem's Modem Configuration Menu, which will help you set your modem for use with Qmodem. When you've finished making changes, select Exit and be sure to Save your changes.

The first time you load Qmodem, it creates a dialing directory. You access this by pressing ALT-D. You'll find that there are phone numbers already listed for all of the Qmodem regional distribution centers. Now, select the one closest to you by highlighting it with the cursor. Then use CRTL-R to revise the entry. Set the baud rate to what is appropriate for your modem. Databits should be set to 8 and stopbits should be set to 1. Duplex is "F" for Full. Be sure parity is set to "N" for None. When you are done making changes, press F10 to save them. Now you're ready to call that BBS. Once you get logged on, look for the file QM42#4.ZIP. This .ZIP file contains the full documentation for Qmodem. Download this file using the protocol of your choice. Tell the system what protocol you want to use, give it the filename, and the system will tell you to begin your transfer. Hit PGDN and select the protocol that you have chosen to start the transfer on your side. If you select Zmodem on the board that you are connected to, Qmodem will start the download for you automatically! If you need help with logging onto a BBS, go back and take a look at Chapter 5. Chapters 6 through 8 cover advanced topics and Chapter 8 tells all about downloading. I hope you'll enjoy using Qmodem. If you have problems getting the documentation, call The Forbin Project BBS and ask a question—you'll get lots of help!

BackMail 1.10 BackMail is a complete mail and file transfer system that works totally in the background. BackMail is discussed in Chapter 17. Try it out and give a copy to your friends or co-workers. It's a handy way to exchange messages without interrupting what you're doing.

DX Directory eXtended is a powerful DOS command line program that can do many things. DX is discussed in Chapter 17. This program also comes with abbreviated documentation. You'll find a full copy on any of the boards marked in Appendix C as BBSs where you can leave me notes. Just look for the file DXDOC.ZIP.

Anarkey 3.0 Anarkey is a great DOS command line editor with AKAs and much more. Anarkey is described in Chapter 17. Once again a few of the files that ordinarily come with the Anarkey package had to be left out in order to fit the program on the disk. You do have all of the things you need to use the program. If you should want a full copy of the complete file, one has been made available for you. As with Qmodem and dCOM, call any of the boards listed in Appendix C as places where you can leave me messages. Look for the file ANARKEY3.ZIP and follow the download instructions given earlier.

PPrint PPrint is a great all-around printing utility no matter what kind of printer you have. PPRINT is described in Chapter 15. Whether you have a daisy wheel, dot matrix, or laser printer, you'll find that PPrint can really help with your printing needs. More printer definition files can be found on the Patri-Soft BBS—the number is in the documentation.

HOW TO INSTALL THE PROGRAMS

You *cannot* boot your computer with the disks. Boot your computer as always, and then put the disk in drive A. You will be able to install all of the programs either on a hard disk *or* on floppy disks. If you are at the DOS prompt on a hard disk drive C, you can enter

```
C>A:INSTALL
```

Or you can change to drive A by entering

```
C>A:
```

and then type in:

```
A>INSTALL
```

From this point on, the Install program will present you with options and guide you through the process of installing the programs. You can select from either a hard disk or floppy disk installation. Naturally, a hard disk installation is the best option to choose. The Install program will create directories on your hard disk and programs will be unpacked to the proper directories. Just follow the prompts that the Install program gives you. From time to time you'll be asked to change disks. Just insert the proper disk when you are prompted to do so. This install process has been extensively tested so you should have no problems with it. It is our sincere hope that you will enjoy the programs provided.

Look for a coupon in the back of the book for a way to get more of the programs that are discussed in the book. These disks all come with a similar Install program to make the job of installing the programs much easier for you. Most of all . . . Enjoy!

This book was written to give you a definitive guide to Shareware—what it is, how to obtain it, and how it can best serve you. If you've *never* heard of Shareware, this book will open up a whole new world for you; an exciting world where you'll find you can save money while still accomplishing the things you want to do on your PC. If you've never been online, you'll learn how to go online and get around with confidence. If you *are* familiar with Shareware, the information contained here will give you a new perspective and broaden your outlook. Even if you've been around for awhile, you'll find a wealth of information in these pages. From program descriptions to the history of spreadsheets, it's all in here. Whether a newcomer or an old-timer, you'll look at some of the very best programs that are available in Shareware. You'll find a disk containing some excellent software and over 50 money-saving coupons included in the book. There are coupons for everything from discounts on programs discussed in the book to free online time. If you want information on Shareware, you've come to the right place!

LEARN MORE ABOUT COMPUTING

Here is a selection of other excellent books from Osborne/McGraw-Hill that will help you build your skills and maximize the power of the Shareware you have selected.

If you're looking for a handy intermediate-level book that covers popular Shareware programs, see *The Shareware Book: Using PC-Write, PC-File, & PC-Calc*, by Ramon Zamora, Frances Saito, and Bob Albrecht. This fast-paced, hands-on guide quickly covers the basics of all three programs (PC-Write Version 3.0, PC-File+ Version 3.0, and PC-Calc+ Version 2.0) before discussing intermediate techniques and even some advanced topics, including how to integrate them for greater performance.

If you're looking for the best way to get started in telecommunications or how to get more out of the online services available today, see *Dvorak's Guide to PC Telecommunications*. This book/disk package, written by the internationally recognized computer columnist John C. Dvorak with programming whiz Nick Anis, shows you how to instantly plug into the world of electronic databases, bulletin boards, and online services. The package includes an easy-to-read comprehensive guide plus two diskettes loaded with outstanding free software.

Dvorak's Guide to Desktop Telecommunications, Special Edition, also by John C. Dvorak and Nick Anis, is a special edition of *Dvorak's Guide to PC Telecommunications* that does not include disks. Written to cover all computer makes and models, this book is a comprehensive, easy-to-use guide to getting the most from telecomputing.

You can become a hard-disk jockey with *Glossbrenner's Complete Hard Disk Handbook*, by Alfred Glossbrenner and Nick Anis. This comprehensive volume covers everything from buying a hard disk to installing, loading, organizing, and "tweaking" it for optimum performance. This book/disk package also includes two 5.25-inch disks that are packed with tutorials, software tools, and utilities.

## PART ONE

Examining Shareware and Freeware

## CHAPTER ONE

Shareware: A Definition

While there are many topics to discuss and share with you about Shareware, first you need to understand exactly what *Shareware* is. Like any consumer, you need a working definition to help you distinguish true Shareware programs from programs that fall under different definitions. Over the years, the issue has become confused by an infusion of terms like "Freeware," "SourceWare," "Demoware," "Teleware," and others. It's no wonder that at this point most people respond to the question, "What is Shareware?" by saying, "Oh, it's FREE software!" Since Shareware is *not* free and was never intended to be free, let's look at what Shareware really is.

DEFINING SHAREWARE

In simplest terms, Shareware is a marketing concept. It's a way for a programmer to engage in commerce and make money just as commercial software companies do. In this respect, Shareware is commercial software marketed differently. Shareware doesn't have the flash of fancy packaging, nor does it have copy protection devices. There are no huge advertising budgets to support or thousands of employees to pay. Because of the things it doesn't have, Shareware doesn't have the extra *cost* all these extras require. Shareware is copyrighted and/or patented, and it is protected under the same copyright laws as any other copyrighted work or product in the United States.

There are many differences between commercial software and Shareware, but one difference has been the hallmark of Shareware from the very beginning. The basic idea is this: you can try it before you buy it! This is not the case with commercial software. Once you buy any commercial package and leave the store, it's yours, for better or worse. Shareware authors, on the other hand, release their programs with an element of trust, saying in effect, "If you like my program, I expect that you will pay me for it. If you don't like it, you're not obligated to pay me anything." What could be better? Thus, a good, basic definition for Shareware is that Shareware is copyrighted software that you are allowed to try out, without restrictions, before you decide to buy it. If you use it, you are expected to pay for it. If you don't use it, you can erase it and move on to something else. It is marketed by way of disk vendors, user groups, bulletin boards, and commercial online services. These groups and services will be discussed in detail in later chapters.

WHAT IS SHAREWARE AND WHAT IS NOT?

The world of Shareware can provide you with a wide variety of good programs. From utilities and applications to games and graphics, Shareware has it all. It's estimated that there are well over 75,000 Shareware programs available. Each day that number increases. Many programs call themselves Shareware. Using our basic definition of Shareware, you can begin to look at what is considered to be true Shareware. You can also examine programs that are not Shareware and develop an understanding of why they aren't. Why can't some programs be considered Shareware? For the most part, it's because they don't live up to the generally accepted definition of what Shareware is. To give you a better understanding of this sometimes confusing topic, let's look at what's available. In the process, you will learn which programs are Shareware and which are not.

The Public Domain

One group of programs loosely classified under the heading of Shareware are those labeled *public domain*. These programs are not copyrighted, and the author does not make any request for compensation. Quite often these programs will contain a small documentation file where the author explains how to use the program. Many times, somewhere in this documentation, the author may make a statement to the effect, "I hereby donate this program to the public domain." Such programs are totally free. You can use them, abuse them, and have a clear conscience. What kinds of programs can you find that are in the public domain? The variety is amazing. Many well-known Shareware authors have written small utility programs that they have donated to the public domain.

Another source of public domain programs are average computer users. For example, if computer users have a task to perform, and if they have some programming experience, they can write a program to do it. In many cases these people will simply donate their program to the public domain. This allows others who want to perform the same task to use the program. There are many excellent programs in the public domain and, as defined, all of them are absolutely free. One might ask, "Why then, if some programs are not copyrighted and no fee is involved, are they sometimes classified under the term Shareware?" These programs are confused with Shareware primarily because they are fully functioning programs that can be used without restriction. Not all programs can make that claim. Let's take a look at yet another grouping of programs that is available.

Freeware—Public Domain with a Difference

There are other programs that can be found that generally fit the definition of Shareware. In today's world of Shareware, they are called *Freeware* programs. Like Shareware programs, these programs are copyrighted and the author retains the rights to the program. The documentation will say that you are free to use the program without compensating the author for it. Thus, the program is totally free just like public domain programs. While these programs do not require any monetary compensation, they have something that public domain programs do not. By legally retaining the rights to the program, the author reserves something special—the right to change one's mind. Sometimes, programs that were originally released as Freeware are later re-released by the author as Shareware. One example of this would be the new Lynx file transfer protocol by Matthew Thomas. The first two versions (versions 3.00 and 3.01) were released as Freeware. The program was copyrighted, but there was no request for a registration fee. With the third release of Lynx, version 3.02, the author reconsidered and released that version as Shareware.

As a user, what does this mean to you? Quite simply, it means that you can continue to use versions 3.00 and 3.01, released as Freeware, for as long as you want without ever sending in a registration fee. On the other hand, if you wanted to use versions 3.02 and beyond and take advantage of any improvements, upgrades, and so on, you would be expected to register because version 3.02 was released under the Shareware concept.

When you *register* a Shareware program with its author, you send the author's requested fee and are entitled to all of the benefits described in the author's documentation. Such benefits include future upgrades to the program and any support policy that the author has defined. Thus, programs that are released as Freeware are loosely classified under the heading of Shareware because they are copyrighted, the author maintains the rights to the program, and you are free to use the full program without restrictions. The one major difference from true Shareware is that no compensation is expected. Another difference is that the author generally won't provide support or help with the program in case you have a problem—what can you expect for free?

Crippleware—A Lame Alternative

While public domain programs and Freeware can be loosely considered Shareware, one variety of software that is not Shareware is called *Crippleware*. As the name implies, these programs are crippled so that some of their functions work only partially or not at all.

Let's look at a few examples: You have what appears to be a good database program, only to find that you can make 50 entries and no more! How about a really nice hard disk backup and restore program? You try it out and back up your hard disk, only to find that in order to restore it you must pay a registration fee for the program. Another example might be an editor that you load and use to write a message only to discover that you cannot save your work to disk. These programs all call themselves Shareware and all of them are actual programs.

The basic definition of Shareware says that one of the best features of Shareware is that you can try it before you buy it. Under the circumstances just mentioned, how can you truly evaluate the program when portions of it have been disabled? With the database example, you can't find out how fast it would sort through 500 entries because you can only enter 50! If you can't see just how a program functions and how it might meet your needs, how can you make an informed decision? While it doesn't seem possible, bear in mind that these Crippleware programs evolved as a way to encourage users to register. Some program authors felt that people would register just to get the fully functioning program. This idea, however, is not in keeping with the true meaning of the Shareware concept. At this writing, there are relatively few Crippleware programs. The reaction of users has been negative. Thus, most program authors have come up with more subtle ways of encouraging you to pay for their product.

Expireware—"Honey, This Program Won't Work"

Another class of programs that incorrectly bills itself as Shareware is something that can be called *expireware*. These programs generally work well, but only for a certain length of time. One day, the software just dies on you. What the programmer has done is put a timer into the program. Some expireware programs use a timer that is based on how many times you run the program. Others expire on a specific date. In the first case, you may get to run the program 100 times before it stops working. In the second case, you may start using the program in mid-July and on August 1 it won't work anymore. The philosophy behind these expireware programs is similar to that behind Crippleware programs: it is hoped that this will encourage you to register the program with the author.

Of the two timing systems, the programs that count the number of times you use them are slightly more fair than those that just arbitrarily expire on a certain date. Why? Because the ones that count how many times you load the program are at least giving you a chance to use it. It doesn't matter when you obtained the program. With the programs that include timers based on a set date, the author has no idea when you started using the program. You may have gotten the program just two days before it is set to expire. In any case, no matter what timing system is used, expireware is not truly Shareware because it limits fair evaluation of the program. In every other sense, expireware programs meet the definition of Shareware.

Demoware—Commercial Software Takes a Shot

In an attempt to capitalize on the success of many Shareware programs, some commercial software companies have released programs that are called *Demoware*. For the most part, these programs—and the word "program" is used in its most basic sense—are nothing more than flashy advertisements for the real program. In the majority of cases, you can start up the Demoware program and just sit back and watch. You'll see some impressive things that the program can do, fancy colors and graphics, windows popping up all over the screen like magic, and much more. What it amounts to is a demonstration of the uses of the actual program, which means a Demoware program is really an animated commercial. There is nothing wrong with the idea behind Demoware. These commercial software companies are trying to give you a preview of what their programs can do. It should be made clear however that this is only a demonstration.

To be totally accurate, there are some Demoware programs that do allow you to interact with the program. In this context, they can be considered Demoware versions of Crippleware. The only difference is that these programs are crippled versions of regular commercial software. You may want to try a Demoware program if you have an interest in the actual program. For example, a writer might want to download a demo version of ForComment, a writer's productivity tool. It could give the writer the opportunity to look at it and decide if he or she wanted to buy it. There are Demoware versions of popular programs such as WordPerfect, WordStar 5.5, Ask Sam, the FoxBase database, and several other commercial products. Some bulletin boards disagree with the idea of Demoware and have asked that commercial software companies not upload Demoware onto their systems. However, Demoware can be found on many bulletin board systems, and on the commercial online networks.

Antiqueware—"Evaluate This, Register for What?"

There is yet another variety of program that claims to be Shareware that, for lack of a better term, can be called *antiqueware*. The idea is a simple

DOCTOR'S NOTE

Recently, some Shareware authors have been talking about creating demonstration programs for a specific purpose. These authors are thinking of better ways to show users how their programs work, especially with some of the larger programs. In this respect, these demonstrations would act as a supplement to the documentation and allow users to review the functions of the program, letting them know what they should be seeing. John Friel, the author of Qmodem, a fine communications program, included some demonstration programs in his release of Qmodem 4.0. This allowed users to view parts of the software before they actually tried the program. Users may see more Shareware authors using demonstration programs to help make their programs easier to use. These demos will be included in the actual program and should not be confused with Demoware programs, which are programs unto themselves.

one. The program author puts out a version of a program that may be several years old and is the only version you can look at unless, of course, you register. This is like asking someone to pay for a 1992 car when all they can go by is the 1989 model. The 1992 model may have lots of new features, but you can't try them or see them; you just have to use your imagination. Thus, antiqueware programs are Shareware only in the respect that they are copyrighted programs, and the author requests a registration if you use the program. Hmm . . . you might be thinking to yourself, you are using an old version of a program that doesn't let you try all the features that may be available in the newest version. In effect, it isn't truly Shareware because you can't try out the program you are expected to register for before you buy it. There aren't a lot of antiqueware programs around, but you should be aware of them.

To finish up this discussion of what is and is not Shareware, it's important to provide you with some general guidelines to cover those programs that use different terms to describe themselves. While it's good to be original and different, sometimes this can cause confusion, especially where the topic of Shareware is concerned. In response to this confusion, some Shareware authors have come up with names other than Shareware to describe their software distribution method.

For example, Samuel Smith, an excellent programmer and the author of many useful programs, calls his products SourceWare. Sam does this because he believes in including his source code with each of his programs. Another company, Alethic Software, produces an excellent background mail and file transfer system called BackMail and they market it under the term Teleware. (BackMail is on one of the disks that are available through this book.) If you have a credit card, you can call in via modem and register Alethic's program. While you are connected to their toll free number, your Shareware version is actually converted into the registered version. Thus, they came up with Teleware because everything can be handled via online telecommunications. There are other such examples, but the point is that both Sam Smith's SourceWare and Alethic's Teleware are Shareware programs.

Some Guidelines for Identifying Shareware

To resolve any possible confusion that might be caused just because you find a program that doesn't call itself Shareware, here are some basic guidelines you can use. Almost without exception, all programs being marketed under the Shareware concept will have all or most of the following items mentioned in the program or its documentation.

- Copyright declaration
- License agreement
- Request for registration
- Upgrade policy
- Support policy
- Optional printed manual
- Source code

The *copyright declaration* states, "This is a copyrighted program. . ." and that all of the author's rights are legally protected. All Shareware programs are copyrighted and the author will make this very clear.

The *license agreement* gives the terms under which you are expected to use the software. It will often say how long the author feels is an adequate time for you to use and evaluate the program. It will generally include the terms for distribution, such as if you can give copies to friends, send it to bulletin board systems, and so on. The license agreement may also tell you that you can use the program and distribute it freely as long as you do not alter or remove any of the files that you found in the original package and do not charge for the copies. If you've registered for a program you should never distribute your registered copy, but you can allow others to try out unregistered copies of a program.

The *request for registration* tells you what amount of money the authors expect you to send them in order to become a registered user of the program. Each author will tell how to register his or her program. Some work only by mail. Others can accept credit cards or they may have their own bulletin boards that you can call to register. Regardless of the means available, if you like the program and plan on using it, then take the time to register it!

The *upgrade policy* varies from program to program. Many authors will state right from the beginning what their policy is regarding program upgrades. Some offer unlimited upgrades, others give two free upgrades, and so on. If no upgrade policy is stated, you may want to contact the author and find out what their upgrade policy is. Most Shareware authors are very generous when it comes to upgrades.

The *support policy* will also tend to vary. Some programs require more support than others. Depending on their function, some won't require any support. The authors should state from the outset what their policy is regarding technical support for the program. Many handle support by exchange of messages on bulletin boards or commercial online networks. Some will provide telephone support. Still others may offer a variety of support methods and allow you to chose the one that you prefer, depending on how much help you think you'll need with the program. In these cases, the support may result in an extra charge that is determined by the kind of support that you request. As noted earlier, some programs don't require any support and, therefore, none may be offered.

The five items mentioned above are things that you can generally expect to find in the typical Shareware package. Another thing that might be mentioned is whether or not a printed manual comes with your registration or if a printed manual is an option. The author might also offer the source code for the program for an additional fee. Using these general guidelines, you can look at a program, and regardless of whether it says it is CodeWare, ZappoWare, or anything else, you'll know that you are dealing with a Shareware program. Make a point to read the documentation and any other text files that come with the main program files. If you notice that the author mentions that the program will "time out," you have an expireware program on your hands. If you find that certain functions of the program don't work, you've latched onto a piece of Crippleware. In cases like these, the decision to try these programs, of course, is up to you. You can generally do much better, and your best bet is to look for something else. Hopefully, these basic definitions and guidelines will help you as you seek out true Shareware, some of the *best* software available.

How Shareware Should Work

In defining Shareware, it was said that in its simplest form, Shareware is just a different way of marketing software. There are many excellent programmers around who write some truly great software. Let's examine a typical Shareware author.

In many cases Shareware authors are people who work full-time jobs, but who love to write programs. They may put hundreds of hours into a program, working late at night, on weekends, and on their days off. In some cases, it may take several years to get the program the way they want it to be. Now, what can they do with it? Unlike the big commercial software companies who have huge advertising budgets, Shareware authors can't afford to take out advertisements in the major computer magazines. Because they work full time, they can't afford to take off from work to go out and sell the program. They may know that they have a top-of-the-line program, but how can they market it? The answer is Shareware! Shareware is an alternative way of marketing their software.

When the authors of these programs decide to release them under the Shareware concept, they are trusting you to be honest and fair. They include a notice of copyright, telling you that they own the program. A license agreement clearly tells you the terms under which you can use the program and tells you what the author's obligations are to you. Open up any manual for a commercial program and you'll see the same thing! The major difference between the Shareware program and the commercial program is that you have to buy the commercial program before you can open up the manual and read the terms.

The Shareware author, on the other hand, is trusting you by letting you look at the whole program before you pay for it. All the Shareware author asks is that after you have had a fair length of time to evaluate it, that you register it if you continue to use the program, and thereby pay the author for his or her work just as you expect to be paid for work you do. Most of us wouldn't like it very much if our bosses said, "Well, let me think about the work you've done for a little while longer, and then maybe I'll pay you for it." That isn't the way things are supposed to be in the working world.

How should the Shareware concept work? In all honesty, it's quite simple. You obtain a program, you read the documentation, read the license agreement, and then you use the program. Put the program through its paces, do all the things that you expect it to do, and see how well it works for you. Software is a matter of taste and what one person likes, another may not. If you find that you really like the program, that it does exactly what you want and need, just follow the author's instructions for registering. It's just that simple, as simple as picking up your paycheck for the work you've done. By registering, you are sending the program author his or her paycheck for the fine work that they have done. Think about it.

At the same time it is only fair that you should be able to expect certain things from a Shareware program. Perhaps the most important is a good, fully functioning program. If the program is a TSR (terminate and stay resident) then you should be able to expect that it is "well-behaved." This means that it should not cause problems when used along with other programs that you run. Bear in mind that if you load several TSRs, there is always a chance of conflict! Try changing the order the TSRs are loaded in and see if that clears things up.

You should also be able to expect clear and concise documentation. The documentation should give you enough solid information so you can run the program. All of the features of the program should be covered. The author should discuss any special requirements for installing the program on your system. The program author doesn't know if you are a novice user or a "power user." When it comes to program documentation, Shareware authors should assume nothing! This is to say that they should work from the idea that everyone who gets the program is a novice. If authors do work from that point of view, the novice will be able to understand how to use the program. Power users can skip what they don't need to read, and still run the program. If you find that you just don't understand the documentation, you have several options. You can seek help from others, but where? At PC user groups, on bulletin boards, or on commercial online networks. Another option is to try another shareware author's program. So, while a Shareware author has the right to expect certain things of you, you also have the right to expect a program that works for you.

How You Can Make Shareware Work

You can make Shareware work by simply holding up your end of the deal by registering for the programs that you use. Shareware is a good deal, but only you can make it work. To put it into perspective, ask yourself how many long hours you would work without pay. How long would you continue to support a product for a few people if you had little or no money coming in? What would your incentive be to improve the product? Your answer to those questions will probably give you a good idea of how many Shareware authors feel. Shareware is sometimes referred to as user-supported software. Users give it support when they pay for the programs they use.

Another way to make Shareware work is to give copies of the Shareware programs that you use to some of your friends, relatives, and co-workers. Let them see what a great program you've found. More and more businesses are looking at Shareware programs as an alternative to expensive commercial programs. There have been cases where businesses have switched from a commercial program to a Shareware program, not only because it was much less expensive, but because it was a better program.

Shareware programs are also starting to proliferate within many colleges and universities for the same reason. By registering for programs and telling others about them, you help to make the Shareware concept work for all of us.

Why You Should Make Shareware Work

There are many reasons why you should help to make the Shareware concept work. To begin with, there are some truly excellent and unique programs in Shareware. By registering, users give the authors the incentive they need to make existing programs even better. Another factor is that, in general, the authors of Shareware programs tend to offer better support than do their commercial counterparts. Because there is a closer relationship, Shareware authors tend to listen to the input of users. There are many Shareware authors who have added new functions and features to their programs simply because a good number of their registered users requested them.

Of the many advantages to Shareware, there are two factors that stand a bit above the others. The first is that you can try out a Shareware program before you buy it. The second is the price! Let's face it, you can read advertisements for commercial programs, you can read reviews about them, but when it gets right down to it, there is nothing quite as good as trying it out for yourself. Then, when it comes to price, Shareware is the best value around for the money. For example, a commercial database program that is very powerful could cost around $600. On the other hand, there are Shareware database programs that can be registered for a fee of about $60 and are just as powerful as the commercial program. The Shareware program is easier to use, and support is just a phone call away. In talking with friends and other users online, we sometimes talk about our "dust collectors." These are the commercial programs we bought that, for one reason or another, did not really do what we thought they would. Ultimately, they ended up on a shelf, collecting dust. With Shareware you don't have that problem. You can try out 20 editors until you find the one that suits you. Then you can erase the others and only register the one you want to use. No muss, no fuss, and no dust!

THE ASSOCIATION OF SHAREWARE PROFESSIONALS (ASP)

The ASP, or Association of Shareware Professionals, was founded in 1987 by a group of Shareware authors. One of the first things the ASP did was to draw up a set of standards or code of ethics that all members must abide by. For example, the ASP stipulates that a program cannot be limited in *any* way (in other words it must be a fully functioning program) and that it can only have one promotional screen. This screen can only appear once each time you load the program and it may not appear again.

Another stipulation found in the ASP code of ethics is that every member must actively respond to each and every registration and that each must offer at least 90 days of support for their product. By maintaining standards such as these, the ASP hopes to firmly establish the position of Shareware as a very viable alternative to the software found in the traditional market. The ASP stresses professionalism and has even set up a means whereby registered users can complain if they feel that they are not being treated fairly. The ASP's ombudsman can be contacted in such cases. For the most part, however, the ombudsman is seldom if ever used. ASP members are firmly behind the Shareware concept and endeavor to make sure that each customer is satisfied. There is no promise that every program produced by an ASP author is the best that can be found, but you can be sure that at least the author abides by the ASP guidelines. Every ASP member uses the following logo, seen in Figure 1-1, in their documentation file.

The ASP currently has 160 members who are program authors and 80 members who are disk vendors. Those seeking to become a member of the ASP must first submit an application. Each application is reviewed carefully to make sure that the program meets the standards of the ASP. One way to get an application is to log onto CompuServe. (How to access CompuServe will be explained in Chapter 4, which focuses on commercial online networks.)

In talking with former ASP President, Barry Simon, he said, "Just so readers will know, even if ASP gets its own forum, we'll take the *share* GO word with us. We'll also keep section 9 for potential authors. In this way, the commands needed to get into the ASP section will remain the same! Sections 8 and 9, part of IBMJR, are our public sections. Program authors can feel free to drop by and look around."

To help you better understand the ASP and its goals, here is a quote from the ASP's official statement of purpose.

"ASP, the Association of Shareware Professionals, was formed in April 1987 to strengthen the future of Shareware (user-supported software) as an alternative to commercial software. Its members, all of whom are programmers who subscribe to a code of ethics or are non-programmers sincerely interested in the advancement of Shareware, are committed to the concept of Shareware as a method of marketing.

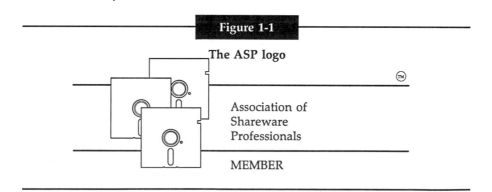

Figure 1-1

The ASP logo

Association of
Shareware
Professionals

MEMBER

"The ASP's primary goals are

- To inform users about Shareware programs and about Shareware as a method of distributing and marketing software

- To encourage broader distribution of Shareware through user groups and disk dealers who agree to identify and explain the nature of Shareware

- To assist members in marketing their software

- To provide a forum through which ASP members may communicate, share ideas, and learn from each other

- To foster a high degree of professionalism among Shareware authors by setting programming, marketing, and support standards for ASP members to follow."

As a potential help to anyone who might be interested in joining the ASP, you will find the membership requirements listed below. These policies should also be of interest to non-programmers since they clearly define what the ASP stands for. Once again, they are quoted from the official ASP literature provided by Barry Simon.

ASP Membership Requirements

The following are the general standards that all ASP authors (full members) have agreed to follow. Each was passed by at least a two-thirds vote of those members voting and is binding on all authors. They consist of a support policy, a policy on payments, a policy on no crippled software, an ombudsman policy, and some other miscellaneous items.

ASP Software Support Policy

1. All ASP members' Shareware products must provide support (included in the purchase price) for a minimum of three months from the date of registration. If the support is by telephone, there may be a limitation on both the total connect time and the period after purchase during which it is available without additional cost so long as the connect time is at least 30 minutes during the required

three months. Support may be provided for a fee after this initial period has elapsed. The support policy must be clearly stated in the Shareware documentation.

2. Support during the initial period may be one or more of the following:

   • Mail support

   • Telephone support (if this is the only support provided, at a minimum an answering machine must be available four hours per day; this support may be limited to 30 minutes of connect time at the option of the author)

   • For communications products, or ones associated with a communication product by BBS or major communications service

   • By any alternate method approved by the Board of Directors by a two-thirds vote (of those directors voting)

3. The minimum level of support required by this policy involves answering questions and fixing serious bugs during the minimum three-month period. For problems involving a specific hardware or software environment or feature, the author may choose not to modify the program. In that case, if the report is within three months after purchase, then the author shall offer to refund the user's purchase price.

4. Any money sent to an author to register an unsupported product shall be promptly returned with an explanation that the product in question is no longer supported.

5. Known incompatibilities with other software or hardware and major or unusual program limitations are noted in the documentation that comes with the Shareware (evaluation) program.

ASP Registration Payment Policy

1. The documentation must clearly describe how to register the product and what goods and/or services the user will receive for registering.

2. Fees must be expressed in fixed monetary amounts. Voluntary payments or contributions may not be solicited, although phrasing such as "if you use and like this product, please register" is allowed.

3. Multiple levels of registration may be set, as long as each level individually satisfies the previous two requirements.

ASP Policy on No Crippling

The principle behind Shareware is "try before you buy." ASP believes that users have a right to try a fully functioning Shareware program in their regular computing environment. Accordingly, ASP authors agree that

1. The executable files (and/or items linked in with executables) in their Shareware and registered versions will be the same (with the exceptions noted in the next section).

2. All the program's features will be fully documented.

3. Registration encouragement procedures which in the judgment of the Board are either unreasonable or unprofessional are not allowed.

Exceptions to a strict interpretation of this policy are as follows:

- To save disk space, tutorial and additional explanatory material may be left out of the Shareware documentation.

- The Shareware version may have registration encouragement procedures absent from the registered version (or that can be disabled with a code provided only to registered users).

- The registered version may include sample files not included in the Shareware version.

- If source code is offered with the registered version, it may be withheld from the Shareware version.

- The author may provide two Shareware versions: a full version and a small version that the author designates as the version to be distributed under normal circumstances (for example, language tools in C only available in one model). The full Shareware version must be available from some public source (possibly for a small distribution fee) and may be copied for trial purposes. The small version's documentation must clearly describe how users may obtain the full Shareware version.

- The author may provide an enhanced retail version of the program so long as it is not (in the opinion of 60% of the Board of Directors) merely an attempt to circumvent the no crippling policy.

- Registered users may be provided bonus utilities unrelated to (and that do not change) the basic functionality of the program.

- Registered users may be given utilities that provide a convenience but are not essential.

- Exceptions approved by the ASP board of directors by a 60% vote of those voting.

ASP Ombudsman Policy

1. The board shall set up the office of ombudsman and appoint someone to that position. The ombudsman's sole role shall be to mediate disputes between ASP members and their customers. The ombudsman shall report to the board situations in which he feels board action or knowledge is appropriate.

2. All ASP members and vendor associate members are required to cooperate with the ombudsman when approached by him/her.

3. If the ASP logo or name is used by any full member in any ads/documentation, and so forth. in connection with any Shareware program, then that member shall include the following statement with their Shareware programs:

"This program is produced by a member of the Association of Shareware Professionals (ASP). ASP wants to make sure that the Shareware principle works for you. If you are unable to resolve a Shareware-related problem with an ASP member by contacting the member directly, ASP may be able to help. The ASP ombudsman can help you resolve a dispute or problem with an ASP member, but does not provide technical support for members' products. Please write to the ASP ombudsman at P.O. Box 5786, Bellevue, WA 98006 or send a CompuServe message via easyplex to ASP ombudsman 70007,3536"

4. This statement is only required if the ASP name is otherwise used by the author and it is only required in programs and/or versions distributed as Shareware. It can be in any file provided with the Shareware version of the program. In addition, members are free to include it in printed documents, ads, and other mailings if they wish.

5. The first sentence may be replaced by "<Member's name> is a member of the Association of Shareware Professionals (ASP)." If an author's company is a company member, then the company name may be used instead of <member's name> if the policy applies.

6. If the ASP logo or name is used by any ASP approved vendor in any ads, catalogs, and so forth, that vendor must include the following statement with the catalogs and newsletters and is encouraged to include it with all disks sold:

"Company X is an approved vendor and associate member of the Association of Shareware Professionals (ASP). ASP wants to make sure that the Shareware principle works for you. If you are unable to resolve a Shareware-related problem with an ASP member by contacting the member directly, ASP may be able to help. The ASP ombudsman can help you resolve a dispute or problem with an ASP member, but does not provide technical support for members' products. Please write to the ASP ombudsman at P.O. Box 5786, Bellevue, WA 98006 or send a CompuServe message via easyplex to ASP ombudsman 70007,3536."

ASP Miscellaneous Standards

- The program has been thoroughly tested by the author and should not be harmful to other files or hardware if used properly.

- Any discussion of the Shareware concept and of registration requirements is done in a professional and positive manner.

- The program author will respond to people who send registration payments, as promised in the program's documentation. At a minimum, the author will acknowledge receipt of all payments.

- The author will keep the ASP apprised of changes in mailing address and of any changes in the status of his programs.

ASP VENDOR.DOC

This is NOT an official requirement but ASP members are requested to place any restrictions on redistribution in a file called VENDOR.DOC. While ASP approved vendors are asked to be on the lookout for restrictions elsewhere, they are only responsible for checking out a VENDOR .DOC file.

A Word About Non-ASP Members

At this point it's necessary to say a word on behalf of the vast number of program authors who do not belong to the ASP. To begin with, the ASP is a relatively new organization. Of the thousands of programmers who write Shareware just in the United States, only a very small percentage (160 authors currently) belong to the ASP. Why? One reason is that many Shareware authors are single-person companies. They may not feel the need to belong to a professional organization. At the same time, they may not want to adhere to the policies of the ASP. Another large group of Shareware authors already provides the same kind of services and benefits offered by the ASP. Thus, they may feel that it does not benefit them to join. The main point to make here is this: the ASP is made up of a group of good program authors who subscribe to a code of ethics, but not all good program authors who subscribe to a code of ethics belong to the ASP.

As long as you truly understand this statement you will have gotten the point. Keeping this statement in mind, you can fairly evaluate Shareware. Using the material quoted earlier, you can look at a program by an ASP author and know that it will meet certain requirements. At the same time, you should be able to look at any program by a non-ASP author and evaluate it. The ASP is an excellent organization, but don't misunderstand the situation by thinking that all of the best programmers automatically became members of the ASP when it was formed. They didn't.

THE DOCTOR'S CREED

In this chapter we've discussed what programs are truly Shareware and what kinds of programs are not. We've talked about Freeware, public domain software, Crippleware, antiqueware, expireware, and more. Hopefully you have been given a better perspective on how Shareware authors feel when people do not register and pay them for the work they've done. The primary reason that authors cripple their programs or make them expire is because they become discouraged when users don't register. Only *you* can make the Shareware concept work, and this chapter has tried to point out why.

Shareware offers you an excellent alternative to the commercial software that you buy in your local retail store. There is almost limitless variety, and Shareware can have a place both in home use and in the business environment. You can't beat the price, and you get the added benefit of being able to try the program before you buy it. This gives you the flexibility of trying out many programs until you find the one that *best* suits your own personal needs.

Do I use any commercial software? Yes, I do, and in recent years I have been asked to test and evaluate many commercial programs. I am, however, very selective about the programs that I buy. In the years that I have spent wandering "The Wires" (my term for the entire realm of telecommunications, for it does indeed take place within a maze of wires, does it not?), I have learned one thing, if nothing else. It has become my creed, for it has been proven to me over and over again. "Virtually everything you need can be found in Shareware!" Yes, there are some exceptions, and I will go over those later in this book. In looking at the programs on my own system, I can say that over 99 percent of the programs that I use are Shareware. In the course of this book I hope to tell you the various ways to get Shareware programs and which ones are the best ones to get. I plan to narrow down that list of over 75,000 Shareware programs so that *you* can benefit from the time, effort, and yes, money, that I have invested in seven years of using, testing, and evaluating software.

The programs described in Chapter 10 through Chapter 26 are among the very best that can be found. For example, I may have used over 50 different text editors, but in Chapter 10 I will describe only the best that I have found. In this way you can benefit from my experience and save yourself a great deal of time, money, and frustration. I want you to know that when I recommend a certain program it is because I have tested and used all of the programs that are available in that same category. By the time this book is released, my personal collection of Shareware will exceed one gigabyte! So, with that, let's move on and see how Shareware got its start, and then, how to get it!

## CHAPTER TWO

The Founding Fathers

In Chapter 1, you got a general definition of what Shareware is, how it should work, why you should want to make it work, and how to distinguish those programs that are really Shareware. Like so many things, Shareware started off as just an idea. Oddly enough, what we now call Shareware was called something totally different when the Shareware concept was first conceived. Three men had roughly the same idea at almost the same time. They became the "founding fathers" of what we now call Shareware. Now that you have a better idea of what Shareware is, it's time to take a brief look at its history, and learn about the men who were there at the very beginning. You'll also learn about some popular Shareware authors, their views on Shareware, and why they feel they are successful with it. They'll also discuss where they feel Shareware is heading in the future. Now, let's go back to the beginning.

THE VERY BEGINNING

To help clear up some inconsistencies, you will look at the beginnings of Shareware from two perspectives. First, you will look at how Shareware was first used as a *concept*, regardless of what it was called. Once that is established, you'll see how the use of the actual term *Shareware* came into use and how this chronology varies slightly from the first. For two programmers, Andrew Fluegelman and Jim Button, the idea of letting people try their software before they paid for it came at almost the exact same point in time. Let's begin in California with Andrew Fluegelman.

The Shareware Concept Coming Together

Andrew Fluegelman created a communications program called PC-Talk. Fluegelman started out by marketing his program in an unusual way. He would give people the program and then simply request that if they liked it and used it, they should pay for it. For the time, late 1981, this was certainly a different way of doing business. Fluegelman, however, was not alone in this unique idea.

Around the same time that Fluegelman was producing PC-Talk, Jim Button, another programmer in Washington state, was doing something similar. Button had written what was initially a mailing label program that he called Easy-File. It later evolved into a full database system. Like Fluegelman, Button gave his software away, but included a request that users share the program with others. He also requested a "donation" if they liked the program. It can be debated as to which of these men actually came up with the idea first, but does it really matter? What does matter is that both of them came up with the idea of letting people try their software before they paid for it. Another factor, and possibly the most important, is that Fluegelman and Button got together and decided to complement the efforts of each other.

Fluegelman and Button Join Forces

How did they come to meet? Ironically, a person who was evaluating Button's Easy-File also had a copy of Fluegelman's PC-Talk. This user noted that both programs had a similar request for a donation and for sharing the program with others. When Button heard about this coincidence, he got curious.

Button contacted Fluegelman and the two talked at length about their method of marketing software. In an effort to help each other out, three things were agreed upon.

- Each referenced the other's programs in their documentation.
- Button changed his program's name to PC-File, to better fit in with PC-Talk.
- Both men set a voluntary donation price of $25.

One difference was that Fluegelman marketed his software under the term Freeware while Button used the term *user supported software*. These events occurred in late 1982.

A Variation on a Theme

In early 1983, Bob Wallace, who had just left Microsoft, started his own company called Quicksoft. Wallace had written a basic word processing program called PC-Write. Using a distribution method similar to that of Fluegelman and Button, he started referring to his product as Shareware. At the time, it was almost unheard of to start a commercial company and then market a product via the Shareware concept. In addition to what Fluegelman and Button were doing, Wallace added an interesting new twist.

Wallace also requested a donation for PC-Write, but offered an added incentive for doing so. As with PC-Talk and PC-File, users of PC-Write were encouraged to share the program with others. What was the incentive to register PC-Write? Getting a commission! Let's say that you paid for the program. When you did, you got a serial number you could put on the opening screen. Now, for example, let's say that you gave copies of PC-Write, complete with your serial number, to five friends. If one of them decided to pay for the program, they would be asked for the serial number that appeared on the opening screen. In this case, since it would be your serial number, you would get paid a commission. Does the commission idea work? Based on my own personal experience, I'd say yes. I paid $75 for my first copy of PC-Write. Since that time I have received around $500 in commissions. The commission idea is an interesting twist that has worked out well for Bob Wallace, Quicksoft, and registered users of PC-Write.

A Good Idea, but What Do We Call It?
By late 1983, Fluegelman, Button, and Wallace were all distributing software under a similar concept. The premise was the same. A person could

try out the software and if they liked it they were asked to pay for it. Users were also encouraged to pass the program around to friends, family, and associates. You'll note, however, that each one was calling it something different. For Fluegelman it was Freeware. Button called it user supported software and Wallace was calling it Shareware. There are reasons why Button and Wallace did not go with Fluegelman's term, but that will be discussed later. For now, suffice it to say that Fluegelman copyrighted the term Freeware, and thus, no one else could use it. Users of the early PCs were looking for a standardized term to refer to this new form of marketing. It took some doing, but eventually, they got it.

Arriving at a Standard

Around the same time, another man stepped into the picture. His name is Nelson Ford. Ford is a programmer and a highly respected member of the PC community. Ford is also the founder of the Public Software Library (PSL). The PSL is an excellent source for obtaining Shareware programs on disk. In 1983, Ford was doing a small publication on software. Well aware of the problem with using the copyrighted term Freeware, he decided to run a contest and let users suggest a word that could be used in its place—and the winner was? *Shareware!* This caused some concern for Ford, who knew that Shareware was already being used by Wallace. He decided to talk with Wallace about it. I spoke with Wallace and he recalled the incident for me.

"Yes, I remember that I had started using the term Shareware before Nelson ran his contest. After the contest, Nelson and I talked about it. He (Nelson) said he knew that I had been using the term Shareware, but would I mind if he used it too. I hadn't tried to copyright it so I told Nelson to go ahead. At the time it just seemed like a good idea to have some continuity. . .a term that people could relate to."

Other program authors now had a standardized term that they could use to market their software. Thus, the use of the word Shareware is credited to Wallace. Since that time, many other program authors have marketed their software under the Shareware concept. Of the original "founding fathers," Button became the next one to begin using the term Shareware with his programs. To be historically correct, Button's PC-File was released after Fluegelman's PC-Talk, but before Wallace's PC-Write. At the same time, Wallace was the first to use the term Shareware with his product. Button, on the other hand, was releasing his program under the term user supported software, and adopted Shareware later.

You should now have a better understanding of how the marketing concept that we call Shareware today got started and how the actual term came into use. To give you more insight, the next few sections will give you brief biographies of the three "founding fathers" and fill you in on their backgrounds. Some of the information has already been mentioned, but this was done to give you a fuller perspective of the events and circumstances that molded what we now call Shareware.

ANDREW FLUEGELMAN

Andrew Fluegelman was a successful attorney and also the editor of *PC World* magazine. In 1982, Fluegelman wrote a telecommunications program called PC-Talk. He copyrighted PC-Talk, and then released it to the public. The program became very popular because it offered many features other programs did not. Fluegelman decided to market his software with a new twist. His concept was that if people liked the software and used it, they would be asked to pay for it. He decided he should have a catchy name for this marketing idea. The name that Fluegelman came up with was Freeware.

Today, the term Freeware means something totally different, but there's a reason why it does. Because of the popularity of PC-Talk, Fluegelman decided to copyright the term Freeware. Around the same period of time, a few other programmers were considering using the same marketing technique as Fluegelman. Because the term Freeware was copyrighted, however, they could not use it for selling their programs. At the time, this caused a minor stir among programmers. They had to come up with a different term to use. Because of this, the term Freeware has come to take on a new meaning. In today's market, a Freeware program is one where no contribution is requested or expected by the program's author.

Fluegelman met with another programmer by the name of Jim Button. Strictly by chance, Button had had a similar idea and had been marketing his new database under the term user supported software. Fluegelman got together with Button and established a means for helping to promote each other's product. PC-Talk gained tremendous popularity, and for a time it was *the* communications program to use.

As editor of *PC World* magazine, Fluegelman did a rave review of Button's PC-File in May 1983. This gave PC-File the extra attention that it so richly deserved. Fluegelman was a driving force in this new area of software distribution and marketing for several years. His program, PC-Talk, continued to prosper and is still in use by some people today.

BOB WALLACE

As one of the founders of the Shareware concept, Bob Wallace has played an important role in the development of Shareware. Wallace willingly shared information about his background and his philosophy about Shareware in a talk I had with him. In several instances, I've quoted him.

Born in 1949 in Washington, D.C., Wallace first became interested in computing at the age of 12. He decided then to become a programmer.

"I still find personal computing wonderfully exciting," Wallace says. He emphasizes the personal in personal computing. "It's great having that much power at your fingertips. But if it's somebody else's computer, you have to do what they tell you to do." His interest led him to Brown University in 1967, where he worked with Professors Andries van Dam and Ted Nelson on the first hypertext editing systems. In 1974, he received a B.S. in Computer Studies at the University of Washington. He founded the Northwest Computer Society in 1976, worked at the first Seattle computer store from 1976 to 1978, and ran the first Seattle Personal Computer Fair in 1977.

In 1978, he became the ninth employee at Microsoft, where he worked as architect of the MS-Pascal compiler. Perhaps it was inevitable that someone allergic to "doing what they tell you to do" would form his own company. Wallace left Microsoft in 1983. With $15,000 he had saved, he started Quicksoft, to develop a word processing package for the IBM PC called PC-Write. Wallace decided to use a new approach to marketing software, for which he coined the term Shareware. People were encouraged to copy and share the software for evaluation. Users who had adopted the software were encouraged to pay for it. He explains his reasoning for using Shareware.

"Not knowing much about marketing, I knew I could do something people would like, but I wasn't sure I could explain why they would like it. Shareware lets the software explain itself." And "word-of-disk" promotion takes a much smaller bite out of a startup budget than advertising. "I also chose Shareware because I wanted to reach a lot of people," Wallace says. "You can look at that in two ways. One, I wanted a high market share for PC-Write. Market share was one key to Microsoft's success. But I also wanted to serve a lot of people. My philosophy is that I want to make a living, not a killing."

The first version of PC-Write was released in August 1983. Wallace designed the program, as well as the marketing, to support end users. "A word processor should help people express their ideas," he says. "It shouldn't get in the way—that's one reason speed is very important. Plus, creating a document is a very individual process, so being able to customize your word processor is important." Quicksoft's mission is to help people create documents. "Helping people write furthers the creation of new ideas. This has two important results. First, it helps people express themselves; it empowers the individual. Second, written expression advances civilization; writing is the tool that permits the evolution of science, medicine, and culture. So, by publishing PC-Write, we're empowering people and advancing society." "And on a further level," Wallace says, "helping the creative process is very important to me. In addition to publishing PC-Write, we are trying to build a company and a culture where individual expression can be integrated in working toward a common goal."

Wallace is also active in helping other software entrepreneurs. From 1983 through 1988, he ran a monthly software marketing group. In 1985, he became active on the board of the Washington Software Association, a trade association of Washington state software companies. He was WSA's chairman for the 1986-1987 term. Quicksoft now employs over 30 people and does over $2 million a year in business, with over 45,000 registered users.

JIM BUTTON

Jim Button first got interested in computers as a hobby in the 1970s. His first personal computer was one that he and his son, John, built in the basement of their home. This machine was so simple, compared to the machines of today, that the only way Button could program anything was to use machine language. The first program Button wrote was one that kept a list for making mailing labels, but he didn't stop there.

When the first Apple computer was released, Button bought one and immediately reprogrammed his mailing label program using the new

Applesoft BASIC. It was in this same time period that Button started to expand the functionality of the program—turning it into a fully functional database program. While he was working on his program, Easy-File, at night and on weekends, Jim Button was an employee of IBM during the day. When the first IBM PC was released in 1981, Button once again was ready to make a change for the sake of his hobby. Having bought the new IBM, it took him only a few days to convert his program over to IBM BASIC.

From that point on, Button continued to enhance his program and give it away to friends and coworkers. Gradually, the program gained some popularity, at least in the area around Seattle, Washington. Little did Button know, at the time, that the program he wrote in his basement would someday be spread throughout the U.S. and the world.

In 1982, Button met Andrew Fluegelman. As a result of that meeting, Button ended up changing the name of his program from Easy-File to PC-File. (PC-File version 5.0 will be discussed in Chapter 18.) The review of PC-File that Fluegelman published in the May 1983 edition of *PC World* magazine helped open the way for Button and PC-File. The review helped make more people aware of PC-File. Swamped with orders, working full-time for IBM, and trying to keep improving the program became difficult. He had founded ButtonWare, Inc. in September of 1982. In 1984, Button finally quit his job at IBM and went into the software business full-time.

Today, ButtonWare, Inc. has annual sales exceeding $2 million. Over the last few years the product line has been expanded from one program to eight. Such programs as PC-Calc, PC-Type, and others are all products of ButtonWare. It is estimated that ButtonWare products have over 700,000 users, and they have become known for their moderate price, excellent user interface, and great support.

CURRENT HEROES IN SHAREWARE

As you wander around The Wires, you may notice that there are people whose names are mentioned more frequently than others when Shareware is being discussed. Since these names have a higher recognition factor among users, you might think, "Oh, another program by him. He writes good software."

The term "hero" is not used in the traditional sense, but rather in the sense that these people are respected for their work in the Shareware community, and for the contributions that they have made and continue to make. Many users are curious about the backgrounds of these people and would like to know more about them. Were they all born with computers in their laps? Do they all have degrees in computer science? How do they feel about Shareware and where do they think it is going in the future? As Shareware authors, how do they view the Shareware concept?

An Inside Look

You're going to get an inside look at what some well-known and successful Shareware authors think about the Shareware concept. I spoke with Barry Simon, Mark "Sparky" Herring, John Friel, and Sammy Mitchell. To keep it consistent, I asked each of them to talk about the following:

- Their background in computers and programming
- How they view the Shareware concept
- Where they see Shareware going in the future
- Personal comments, feelings, and advice

DOCTOR'S NOTE

Since I have worked with all the programmers who participated in these interviews, I wanted them to speak freely and without interruptions from me while they were talking. Thus, I gave them the general questions at the very beginning of our talk, and they understood the basic purpose of the interview. None of them knew what had been said by the others. All of the interviews were recorded on tape as they spoke. What follows is an exact transcript of what each person said. The only things that were edited were pauses for thought, words like "um" and "uh," and any other words, sounds, or personal remarks exchanged between us that would not add to the content of the interviews. Thus, you are reading what each person had to say, exactly as they said it. Any instances where I inserted a question will be shown in bold-faced type.

BARRY SIMON

Barry Simon is a past president of the Association of Shareware Professionals (ASP) and the co-author, with Rick Wilson, of such programs as STACKEY, BATUTIL, EOI, and CTRLALT. Here is what Barry had to say about his background, his views on Shareware, and where he sees it going.

"I had my training as a research scientist and am currently a professor at Cal Tech [California Institute of Technology], as is Rick Wilson, my co-author of CTRLALT and STACKEY. We became fascinated with the technology and what it could do about five years ago. We started fooling around, and CTRLALT 1.0 was the result. We are still both professors at Cal Tech and spend most of our time doing that, but we have gotten involved in the Shareware scene.

"STACKEY was actually Nelson Ford's doing. There were, at the time, two other keyboard stacking programs around that I'm aware of. There was a program called FAKEY, which was around on many bulletin boards, that was from SEA, the makers of ARC. The other program was KEYFAKE, which was a *PC Magazine* utility. Until very recently, *PC Magazine* policies were such that the program could not be posted anywhere or sold as Shareware or on Shareware disks.

"Then, the author of ARC happened to contact me because of a review I had written, and he told me that FAKEY was not supposed to be on bulletin boards. He said that it was a bonus program for registered users of ARC and not in any sense 'shareable.' When I posted this information on CompuServe, the program was immediately pulled. I got a message from Nelson [Ford], who said, 'This means that there is no good keyboard-stuffer. How about if you guys do something about that?' I discussed it with Rick, and we decided that it was an interesting project. Thus, STACKEY 1.0 was a direct result of what Nelson did. We got enough feedback to upgrade it to version 2.0, and I hope it will be further enhanced with the release of 3.0 sometime soon.

"We don't have a great interest in becoming full-time Shareware authors. Some people do—they have full-time jobs they aren't so interested in. We are both academic scientists and continue to do lots of research."

When did you and Rick first study programming?

"Study programming? We don't study programming. Rick, who has actually done the majority of the release programming so far, picked up a well-known book on assembly language by Dan Rolands. He learned a bit of assembler from that and the rest of what he has done has essentially been self-taught. It does make the code spaghetti-like occasionally, but he's also incredibly careful about making things tight. He can see a little bit of disassembly in someone else's program and say, 'Why did he do that? He could have used such-and-such an instruction instead and saved three clock cycles and four bytes.' Rick really is a stickler for making things as tight as possible, but he certainly never had any formal training.

"On both CTRLALT and STACKEY, my involvement was in product design rather than the actual coding—particularly STACKEY, which was based almost entirely on my initial scheme for STACKEY 1.0. I added lots of ideas and independent things. This design isn't quite how the program works; it's on a lower level—what interrupts to use, how to handle various things, and so on. I've done quite a bit of Turbo Pascal programming since—some utilities and the new packages and all of BATUTIL are mine—and I also didn't really have any formal training. Much of the learning was a first cut of the CTRLALT PLUS installation code, which has still not seen the light of day. BATUTIL was using a lot of what I knew about how systems work.

"There are several aspects of Shareware that make it particularly attractive for someone like [Rick] Wilson and me, who are willing to commit the time to do a professional job, who want to have creative control, but are not willing to make it a full-time occupation. I suspect that we could find someone who would publish CTRLALT PLUS. In fact, though, we would lose control—at least we fear we would—over how the product worked and how it operated. So we prefer it being Shareware, and we accept the fact that some people won't register, and that the shipping will be done by a support group. We have no problem doing support—either by mail, which we do now, or as we much prefer, on CompuServe. I much prefer this to having a product that in the end, you just don't feel is being handled right. There's just too much of a chance of that happening. From the point of view of someone who wants to keep control, Shareware is great.

"Bill Machrone (editor-in-chief of *PC Magazine*) uses the phrase *guerrilla marketing,* and I think that's a great term. The startup costs for a commercial program that has any chance of success are enormous. It's a very noisy market; it's one of the reasons that some computer magazines do as well as they do. It's almost impossible to get the attention of the user without spending a lot of money on ads, or something similar, if you're going the commercial route. The BBS system is magnificent, particularly with people like you [Dr. File Finder] going out and finding good programs and talking about them.

"While I think that you are unique in scope, there are other people who do the same thing on a much smaller scale. So, if you have a good program, you don't have to spend a lot on advertising and you don't have to charge a lot, and the user gains also. The startup cost for Shareware, in terms of money, is really not large at all. Whereas commercially, you can have the best program in the world and there may be nothing you can do about it. That doesn't mean that the effort involved in a successful Shareware program is small. The time and the work required to ensure that you have a well-crafted product need to be at least as great as with a commercial product. But with a commercial product, if you find the right niche, even if it's not very good, people will buy it and find out later it's not very good. So you almost have to work harder to get a good Shareware program out there.

"Even if you have a good Shareware program, you can't just post it on bulletin boards and assume that it'll take off. You have to work at it— you've got to make sure the right people see it. You've got to find the right people in the press and get their attention, but it still means the initial monetary startup is not that large. I know of some successful Shareware authors who now have a big enough operation that they work at it full-time and are doing very well, but they started out working at night.

"I can think of one guy in particular. I know because I was reviewing one of his Shareware products. He was up until two o'clock in the morning and did most of his Shareware work between the time his kids went to bed and when he finally collapsed. It's just a full-time job. He quit his regular job, and he's been writing some commercial programs in addition to his Shareware to make extra money. It's a bootstrap operation, and he couldn't have done it without taking an enormous gamble. From the author's point of view it's a tremendously attractive method because of control and a low monetary cost, in spite of the time that must be spent.

"People write junk in an hour and post it and have it spread on the bulletin boards. That hurts Shareware a lot, so I want to emphasize that to write good Shareware is as time-consuming as having to worry about business issues. It's not a time saver for a program's author, but it is a money saver for users. From the users' point of view, it has a lot of benefits.

"Software is a complex set of ideas and tools that may or may not match a user's tastes. Even if the program is non-buggy and well-designed, there will certainly be users out there who will find a program is just unusable for them. Given this situation, the ability to try out a program in your own environment, without having to pay for it, is one advantage of Shareware to the user.

"A second advantage to the user is the fact that prices tend to be lower, although they are not as low as they once were. Some of the biggest Shareware firms have lots of fixed costs involving permanent staff, which affect their prices. In addition, there are people publishing inexpensive utilities at prices not much higher than Shareware programs.

"There is still a price advantage—there's no question. It's still true that at the high end of the market, talking about a word processor for example, 50 percent of the retail price is going to the distribution channel. Of the remaining 50 percent that goes to the software company, around 25 to 30 percent is going to marketing costs—things like advertising. The remaining 25 to 30 percent goes to the company's profit, research and development, and the cost of support.

"In most cases, Shareware authors are only concerned with that last 25 percent. They may have some cost in marketing, they may do some advertising, but they don't generally have distribution channel costs, which means that Shareware prices tend to be lower.

"A third advantage of Shareware is that rather narrowly focused utilities can be offered, even though there isn't enough of a market to push them commercially. The companies that do put out commercial utilities of that sort often just stop supporting them. They don't really have to stop supporting them. They just don't upgrade them. This is true of even relatively popular utilities, like keyboard macro programs. I don't know of a single commercial macro program that has been upgraded in the last three years, with the exception of SmartKey, which was upgraded a year ago. But just as it was upgraded, the company declared bankruptcy.

"Other utilities either aren't available or, the ones that are commercially available, aren't comparable to what you can get in the Shareware market. Users therefore get things via Shareware that they might not get otherwise because the markets aren't big enough. So, there really are a lot of benefits for both the Shareware user and the Shareware author.

"I see Shareware continuing to grow and thrive. It's always going to have the small share of the overall market—partly because the overall market is oriented toward corporate users, where Shareware does have some impact, but not that much. The total Shareware market is estimated now at between $15 and $30 million a year. Given that Microsoft is close to a billion dollars a year, that's a small share of the market. The market is still big enough to keep quite a few successful authors producing Shareware programs for users. I don't see that ending.

"I see new platforms out there—Windows, OS/2—and it's quite clear that the Shareware community will move to those platforms, because as the users move, so will the Shareware authors."

MARK "SPARKY" HERRING

Mark Herring is the originator of Qmail, the innovative approach to obtaining, reading, replying to, and sending mail on PC Board bulletin board systems. Nicknamed "Sparky," Herring also wrote the software for the original PCB-Echo mail conferences, as well as the new QNET netmail software. Here are Sparky's comments on his background and the way he views the Shareware concept.

"I got interested in computing in my senior year of high school in 1976. I was failing my analytics class, and they offered a two week computer course. I decided to take that course because it would get me out of the analytics class for two weeks. I was failing miserably until suddenly, one day, like Helen Keller at the water pump, computers started to fall into place for me—as in what this command did and what that command did. I took off with it and eventually I was at the top of my class.

"I left computers for a while and became a disk jockey. Later, in 1979, I decided to go back to computing. I've worked as a freelance consultant in the Memphis area since 1979. I logged onto my first bulletin board in March of 1979. From that time on I've just been on them all the time.

"As far as Qmail is concerned, it really came about in the fall of 1987, when a friend of mine named Dan Mazchek had to move from Memphis to Wharton, Texas. Dan was very lonely in Wharton because there were no bulletin boards around him. I thought I might try out this idea I had in 1985, where instead of just reading messages online, the system would gather them all up very quickly, and you could download them. I wrote the original Qmail in October of 1987, for him [Dan], so he could keep up with what was going on in Memphis very cheaply.

"About the same time, I was developing the software for the PCB-Echo, which is an echo mail system for PC Board bulletin board systems. All of the sysops started showing an interest in Qmail for their own users, because their systems were getting tied up all the time by people reading messages online. One thing led to another, and I developed Qmail and released it in April of 1988. Just over 520 bulletin boards have purchased the system."

What are your general feelings about the Shareware concept, as a means of selling software?

"I think that Shareware fails pretty badly when it comes to the games and little utilities, because there isn't much incentive for registration. I believe that's really the key to making Shareware successful—there must be a perceived value, otherwise there's no incentive for the user to send the registration in. The original Qmail Reader, released in April 1988, was released as Shareware. By the time we had 80 doors online, we had only 12 readers registered. I decided at that point that I could either use a carrot or a stick to get people to register. I could say, 'You aren't registered; why are you still using my product?' or I could produce a better version of the reader that is given to users as a thank-you for their registration.

"That's how Qmail Deluxe was born. In the first three months that Qmail Deluxe was in existence, I believe 500 copies were registered. That proved to me that there must be an incentive in order for Shareware to work. If you have a word processor, telecommunications, or database program—in other words, serious products—they stand a much better chance of being registered than an adventure game or a utility. Games don't seem to make it because by the time the user has played the game enough to enjoy it and register it, he's burned out on it and ready to move on to the next one.

"Shareware, I think, has a very good future, but it's *always* commercial. I think a lot of people have a misconception about that—that there's some difference between Shareware and commercial, and there really shouldn't be. Shareware is just a different means of distributing commercial software. So, as people play around with the distribution means, whether we register the Shareware directly with a store, or whether it's sent through the mail, remember that all Shareware authors are just trying to find the best way to make money. It's the way we make our living."

What would you recommend to someone thinking about creating Shareware?

"I recommend that they focus on application programs. As far as I know, Qmail was the first program of its type—instead of spending an hour online reading 50 messages, you can spend five minutes online and get 300 messages, and read them when you're not connected to the bulletin board. That was a niche market that exploded for me. It was new and exciting and it really took off. Someone told me once that it was like the Lotus 1-2-3 of bulletin boards—it was at the right place at the right time."

People have asked me, so I'll ask you. How did you get the nickname "Sparky?"

"A Radio Shack computer center manager gave me that nickname in 1979, and it stuck with everybody but me—I hated it. I never could shake it. I decided in 1982 when I needed a company name that I needed something unique, so I said 'All right, I'll take the name—I'll name it Sparkware,' and ever since that time it's always stuck. It worked out well."

Do you feel you've become successful with Shareware?

"Yes, I make my living off of it. I do still have a few consulting contracts from old accounts, but I don't take any new ones. Shareware has worked out well for me."

JOHN FRIEL

John Friel is the author of the increasingly popular communications program, Qmodem. A successful Shareware author, John has his home and office near Cedar Rapids, Iowa. Here are Friel's candid comments about his background in programming, the development of Qmodem, his feelings about Shareware, and where he see's it going in the future.

"I started out with computers when I was in seventh grade. My mom worked for an engineering design firm, and they had a minicomputer, an IBM, that they used in-house. It ran small programs, design-type stuff. I used to go down there after school and say 'Hi' to my mom. There was a guy named Ken Cox who ran the computer, and he was a real nice guy. One day I was down there, and I was looking around, and I was really fascinated by this computer stuff. He [Ken] brought me in and said, 'Hey, do you want to play a game with the computer?' I said 'Sure!' So, he said that he was going to tell the computer that I was going to pick a number between 1 and 100. Then he said the computer would ask me three questions, and when I answered the three questions the computer would tell me what number I'd picked. I said, 'No way! It can't do it!'

"I thought of my number and even wrote it down because I knew that the computer couldn't see it. The computer asked me to divide my number by a certain number and give it the remainder, and I did. Then the computer asked me to divide the number by a different number, so I did, and then again for the third time. We punched out the cards, and Ken let me type on the keypunch and punch in my answers. Ken put it in this deck, ran it through the computer, and out came this big spool of paper. On the paper it told me what my number was. So I said, 'Wow! That's neat; let's do it again.' And the computer was right every time. That got me started. I just had to know how that computer could know my number.

"In the second semester of seventh grade, I started taking this really simple Learning Fortran class—it was an elective. We got to use the University of Northern Iowa's (UNI) big computer, and we could pull our own cards out of a deck to make our programs. The teacher would collect them and the next week we'd get the answers to our program. Well, I 'aced' that. I caught on to that real fast. I just kept fooling with the computers and when I couldn't get access, I'd go to my math teachers. I'd tell them that I'd like to work on more challenging problems and could I include them with seventh grade electives and they said it was all right. So, I did a lot of that on my own.

"About 1978, Radio Shack announced the TRS-80, one of the first home computers. I immediately went down and bought one—since I got one of the earliest ones, they had to order it for me. I was thrilled because it had 4K of memory and BASIC built in. I just couldn't get enough of that. I can remember going to my dad for a loan, because I didn't have enough money from my job after car payments. My dad was getting interested and had been watching me play around with this computer. I remember borrowing $76 so I could get the 16K memory upgrade for the TRS-80. To me that was a big thing because I had all this memory. I had completely filled up the 4K and was running out of room and I had to have 16K. It just went on from there and I expanded to 32K, and I bought a disk drive and then I bought several more.

"After I got out of high school, I was going to go to UNI and get my programming degree. All that time, even during high school, I was doing programming for the university on the side. I didn't get paid for it, but I was doing programming for them on their Hewlett-Packard HP-2000, the multiuser machine. In the interim, the university had connected all the schools in the Blackhawk County area, some 30 to 40 schools, using DECWRITERs (a high-speed printer terminal). They had set up accounts so you could call in at 300 baud and use their interactive system. We made some incredible systems programs that we'd run so we could have a chat, like a CB simulator. We called it 'PA Bell,' and several other students and I would go to the university late at night and use their online terminals. We wrote this system on the HP-2000 so we could chat with other people. The people at the university couldn't believe it when we put an online E-mail system on the HP-2000. They liked that and we had a lot of fun working on it.

"I got out of high school, and I had applied that summer to John Deere. That's the big thing in town, the John Deere tractor works. I didn't have any plans for the summer. I had my schedule for college and I was going to go to school in the fall. About six weeks before school started, the people at John Deere called me and asked if I wanted to come in for an interview, so I said yes. I went in and interviewed for the position of computer operator at the component works. I didn't know if I would get it or not, especially since I was just out of high school, and I was basically self-taught on the TRS-80 and the HP-2000.

"About a week later they called back and said I had the job if I wanted it. Well, no one turns down a job making ten dollars an hour to go in and play with a computer that you'd do for free anyway. At the time, this was the ultimate computer system, so I took the job. I figured that after a couple of years, I'd get John Deere to help pay for my degree in computer science. Well, that never came about.

"I worked at John Deere for about four years, and then I got promoted out of operations into the systems programmer position. All the time that I had been working for them as an operator, I'd been studying the manuals and I'd learned COBOL, FORTRAN, and BAL. While I was in operations, I revised our system for loading jobs, which was all done with cards when I got there. It was like taking 100,000 programs that were all in cards and converting them. We had this super powerful computer with all this disk space, and we were still using cards and I said, 'There has got to be a better way.' We got rid of every deck of cards. Everything was online. With online screens, we could program things daily, weekly, monthly, and so on. In fact, John Deere is still using this same system, that I wrote, today.

"While I was at John Deere as an operator, I purchased my first IBM PC clone, which had 640K and two disk drives. Even at that point, the PC was not really strong at John Deere—everything was mainframes. Qmodem started as a lark, because when I bought my PC that wasn't what I bought it for. What I wanted to do was run a bulletin board on it.

So, I bought my first Qubie 2400 baud modem, and I brought up RBBS-PC as my first bulletin board out of my house. At the time, for communications, I used PC-Talk—version 3, I believe it was. After using PC-Talk for a while, I started thinking that I could rewrite it and do it even better. I had just gotten a copy of Turbo Pascal version 2. I started to figure out how to write a communications program. After I finished it, I just took the 'Q' off of the Qubie modem, stuck the word 'modem' after it, and that's how Qmodem came about.

"Ben Blackstock, in Cedar Rapids, Iowa, owned the nearest bulletin board. It should be noted that the Hawkeye PC Users Group, which is still in existence today, wrote the first RBBS-PC program. They are actually the 'founding fathers' of it. They wrote versions 1 through 9, and then released it to public domain. That's when Tom Mack and John Martin picked it up, and they took it farther than it had ever been before. So, RBBS-PC's real home is 35 miles away from me, in Cedar Rapids, Iowa. Anyway, I would call Ben Blackstock's board and upload new versions of this program I had written. This is when it only used about 20K of RAM. Everyone started leaving suggestions. It got so that there would be lots and lots of mail, and I would put out new versions of Qmodem almost daily. I kept trying to add all these new features that people were suggesting. All the time I was looking at PC-Talk and thinking, 'Well, that was a nice feature; I think people are going to want this . . . .'

"In the back of my mind I kept telling myself that I had to have something that was at least as good as PC-Talk but a whole lot faster—it had to be the only thing people would use. That was my goal, and it was just for the fun of it. Finally, the mail was so overwhelming that I put up my own bulletin board again, this time with two lines. I set up an RBBS, like Ben Blackstock had. I would take my own calls, then take the board down at night to work on Qmodem, and then put it back up.

"That went on for about a year and a half until I had something that had the file transfer protocols and the ANSI support, and it would do all sorts of nifty things. Somebody said that I should start charging for it and make it Shareware like Andrew [Fluegelman] had. I thought that wasn't a bad idea, so I started out asking for $10. I really didn't expect to make money on this thing; I was doing it for the *fun* of it. I had a good paying job, and life was great. To me, it was just fun programming. In 1984, about a year and a half after I'd made Qmodem Shareware, Loren Jones got a copy of Qmodem on his board in Fargo, North Dakota, which was one of the bigger bulletin boards around. He called me and said he thought the program was great and that he was going to send me something for it. He sent me a check for $10, and that was the first money I made on Qmodem.

"That year I made a grand total of $20. Of course, being single, that bought me a lot of beer, and I went out with the guys and had a good time. So, every time one of those checks would come, I'd run to the bank, cash the check, and go out and have a party. My friends just couldn't believe that somebody just sent me a check out of the blue. I'd write the names down and send them a letter of thanks. At this time I figured it was going to amount to $30 or $40 a year—some pocket change.

"The next year it grew. I think I made over $600. It finally got to the point where I was making more money from Qmodem than I was work-ing as a systems analyst at John Deere. This period occurred right around version 2.0 of Qmodem. That's when I made the jump.

"When I wrote version 3.0, I was in Minneapolis, I was no longer working for John Deere, and I was self-employed. I made a full-time job out of Qmodem instead of working two jobs. That brings us up to today. I've got an office and employees. I run an eight node bulletin board system, using state-of-the-art modems and hardware and it's a full-time job."

You are obviously successful with Shareware. Are there any reasons why you think it has been successful for you, when it often isn't for other Shareware authors?

"Shareware, of course, has worked for me and is working quite well. I think that there are a couple of key reasons why. One is that my program is more of an application than it is a utility, that you would use once and put down for a week or a month before using again. I think I got into Shareware at the right time. You hear of people being at the right place at the right time—I think Qmodem was at the right place at the right time. Modems suddenly hit the market and people said, 'Boy, we can communi-cate with big services, like CompuServe and GEnie.' I know myself that I thought it was neat—I could talk to people all over the world with a phone call, and of course a wallet full of money. I thought that it was a hot market and that it was going to get big—and it did.

"I think the smaller utility programs and other Shareware actually promoted the use of Qmodem. That's because they had to have another program to get at the data. I'm the catalyst—the one between all the utilities and all the other Shareware and all of the other things that are out there. So people may be downloading a hundred utilities that they may use a few times a year, but if they are using Qmodem, they are using it a lot.

"I think, in some respects, Shareware works better for communications programs than any other type of Shareware. You're going to see a lot of editors, but unless you are a writer, you aren't going to use them every day. But anyone who has a modem, regardless of what application they're looking for, still has to use a communications program to get at it. That's why I think communications authors in particular have been more successful over the years than editor, spreadsheet, or database program authors. There are exceptions, like PC-Write and PC-File, but in their case, I think they were at the right place at the right time. The key to success is finding a niche or a market that you can expand—basically overtaking the market and still being acceptable.

"I don't think Qmodem would have been successful had I not been accessible and always updating the program. Of course, dedication comes in there too. There are thousands of hours put into Qmodem—technical support and running a bulletin board system so it's easy for people to get at me. I think if I had ignored some of these people, or not been as responsive as I was, Qmodem wouldn't be where it is today. I'm sure of it!

"As I said, if you get in the limelight and people are using your product all the time, you are more likely to get a registration than you are with a utility program. That's not to say that utility programs don't have value, because they do. I don't think we need a program that shows a directory listing in different colors—there are a million of those. If you ask for $5 for them, I can pretty much guarantee you won't get it. Those kinds of utilities people don't need. I would suggest that if authors want recognition for their programs, they release them to the public domain and give away the source code. Then they can ask for something if someone wants to modify or use it. I've seen more public domain programs get into the 'Hall of Fame of Utilities' that don't ask for money, than ones that do. Let's face it. If it takes you five minutes to write a program, don't expect to get rich off of it. If it's something that does something different from everybody else's program and people can't do without it, then you might become a Shareware success story."

Where do you see Shareware going in the future?

"I think it's been stalemated lately, because we've been talking about the same utility doing the same thing, the same way. That's because the basic IBM PC and operating system hasn't changed in the last seven years.

Now, when you suddenly start talking about Windows getting popular and OS/2 getting popular, you're going to see people adjusting to enter these markets. Then, if someone were to take that one utility that shows the directory in different colors, and write it for OS/2, and take advantage of Presentation Manager and add some whistles and bells—if that's one of the first on the market—you can expect it to be a hot seller.

"You can expand on that. Suddenly it's a new market—a new area to go to. Without changing the hardware, any major change will be to the operating system, and that opens up the marketplace. That's how Shareware is going to keep expanding as the software and the computers expand. When computers get into a rut, like the IBM PC has been for the last seven years, there's little room to move. Everyone starts catching up. If you're the first one to be creative and adapt to the operating system, you're going to stay in front, or get to the front if you weren't there already. Yes, Shareware is going to continue, and I think it's going to get better because the operating systems are getting better. The market may have stagnated for the last couple of years, but I think you're going to see a big jump when these new operating systems catch on."

Do you have any personal comments or advice that you'd like to give to young programmers?

"Sure, and that is, if you are going to dedicate yourself to being a programmer, doing Shareware in particular, make sure you have a real life too. Don't let the program control you. I've seen 15- and 16-year-olds writing 24 hours a day on their computers. That's missing the boat. You should be experiencing life too. There's nothing wrong with doing some good programming, or maybe even doing an all-nighter or two, but make sure you've got friends and you're in touch with the rest of the world. That's important later in life, and I think people should realize what's around them. Don't let the computer take over."

People often wonder where you came up with your company name, "The Forbin Project." I know, but do you want to tell everyone?

"Yes. I'm a science fiction fan, and my favorite movie was 'Colossus: The Forbin Project,' where a computer took over the world. I don't see myself as taking over the world, but I do have high hopes for Qmodem in the future as well. You can rest assured that if Qmodem ever takes over the world, I'll unplug it."

SAMMY MITCHELL

Sammy Mitchell is the author of the very popular Shareware editor, QEdit. Since 1984, he has been constantly upgrading and improving QEdit. In March 1990, SemWare, Mitchell's company, released the first TSR version of QEdit. Here are Mitchell's comments about his programming background, his venture into Shareware, how he views Shareware as a marketing technique, and where he sees it going in the future.

"In 1980, I graduated from college, with a major in computer science and visions of compilers, operating systems, and relational databases dancing in my head. A month later, I got a job in the real world, maintaining COBOL business applications. I was not even writing and developing, just more or less keeping things up-to-date. The company was a very large IBM mainframe shop, with hundreds of programmers. It was very different from what I had planned and wanted to do. I tried long and hard to get into a program development group, but my requests were always denied. To placate my desire to program, I became proficient in s370 assembly language and wrote dozens of productivity aids for use by the other programmers. Of course this wasn't my job, so I could only do this type of work at night and on weekends. I was getting a little tired of just maintaining programs; I wanted to create programs.

"I decided the best place for me, in this company at least, would be in the systems programming department. Maybe they actually let systems programmers write programs! So that is the direction I headed. By 1983, after campaigning and fighting for three years, trying to get a position in systems programming, I finally gave up. I went out and got a job at another large company, but this time in systems programming. Now, maybe I'd get to write some programs, and in assembly at that! Things were definitely looking up—at least as far as I was concerned.

"By early 1984, I realized that this new job was not as challenging as I had hoped it would be. I ended up doing mostly operating system maintenance, applying put tapes, and doing general troubleshooting. I really wanted to write and develop software, but it seemed I could not find anybody to pay me to do it. I hung in there as long as I could, but it was getting discouraging. So, in October of that year, I took a job on the side writing some software for an IBM PC. What fun that turned out to be! At last someone was willing to pay me to program.

"By 1985, I knew that I was bitten with the microcomputer bug. It was great fun being able to control the whole machine, and not just where the operating system vendor allowed you to roam. I saved my money and bought an IBM PC-XT to pursue more on-the-side projects. By mid-year, I had decided what I was going to do to keep myself happy. I decided to start a consulting company, specializing in VM/CMS, MVS, and MS-DOS on the IBM PC. Bobbi, my wife, brave soul that she is, did not balk at the idea.

"In May 1985, I quit my cushy, safe, well-paid job to go out on my own. QEdit started to come to life around this period of time. During 1984 and 1985, I wrote a couple of applications that needed some way of allowing the user to edit and maintain simple ASCII configuration files. So I wrote a simple full-screen text editor that I included with those applications. I had never written a text editor before, and doing the original version taught me much that I would use later on. It was very primitive, but still much easier to use than DOS's EDLIN.

"By now I had learned that companies large enough to be running MVS or VM/CMS were also large enough to employ consultants from consulting companies, so I got very little mainframe consulting work. The vast majority of my consulting was with smaller companies using PCs. During this time, I had purchased several text editors to use in my programming on the PC, and a couple of the compilers I had bought also included editors. Of course, being the opinionated rebel that I am, I was not crazy about any of them, and since I spent a large portion of my time using a text editor, much of my programming time was spent in frustration. Why were these editors so slow? Why did they have static key assignments, instead of letting you define your own key-to-command bindings? Why would they allow you to edit only one or two files at a time? And why were they so huge? I guess you could say that the real birth of QEdit as most people know it today came out of this frustration that I experienced with these other editors.

"A friend of mine had used the little editor that I had written, and he routinely commented on how fast it was. That got me thinking. Maybe I should do some more work on my editor, and then I could use it. It should not take too much longer, I thought. Making the editor fast was the hard part. Allowing for multiple files and configurable keystrokes should be easy. I started adding features to the little editor. By July 1985, I was using my own editor to write all my software, and things could not have been better.

"Some friends and I decided that the editor I had produced was a very useful tool, and maybe someone else would like to use it also. Plus, maybe I could make some money on this thing. I wrote and/or called several software publishers, but understandably, none were even the slightest bit interested. There did not seem to be much of a market for yet another text editor in the crowded world of MS-DOS software. Around this same time I discovered the wonderful world of electronic bulletin board systems, and this really interesting marketing concept called Shareware.

"Shareware *was* a revolutionary marketing concept. Basically, Shareware boiled down to a user being able to try out software before buying it. If they did not continue to use the program, they were under no obligation to pay for it. No up-front payment, and nothing to return to worry about. I thought it was a great idea! They can get these fully functional 'tryout' copies from bulletin boards for the cost of a phone call, or for a small copying fee from disk vendors, such as Nelson Ford's 'Public (Software) Library,' Public Brand Software, or PC-SIG.

"I'd had some personal experiences with Shareware and it appealed to me. I really liked the Shareware concept and what it stood for. I had registered eight Shareware programs that I was using, including a communications program, a file archiver, and a file manager. The quality and support of these products was as good or better than the commercial products that I owned. I decided that Shareware might be a good route for my editor. I did not expect much out of it, but at least it might help further my consulting business. Who knows, maybe I would get to write a magazine article and become famous. I decided that in any event I had nothing to lose. I spent the next several months writing documentation, rewriting documentation, and rewriting the documentation some more.

"By November 1985, I was ready for my first Shareware release of QEdit. I had tested and retested the software, and I refused to even look at the documentation again. It was time! I uploaded my QEdit, which was the name Bobbi and I had decided on, to several dozen bulletin boards. The very next day I got a call from an extremely conscientious sysop. His name was Gerhard Barth, and he was the sysop of the TaMiami BBS in Florida. Apparently, QEdit did not work on his color monitor. With his help, I tracked down the problem. Version 1.00A was out just a day after version 1.00.

"Then, a very exciting thing happened. I got two orders for QEdit in December of that year, just a few weeks after I had released it. It was a very good feeling to be paid for a Shareware product. In most shops that I have consulted and worked in, there was always lots more software available than had been paid for. And this was commercial stuff. Can you imagine those same people paying for Shareware? I cannot! So I was very excited, indeed!

"By 1986, I realized that fun was fun, but I had to start making some money. I could not let my wife be the only bread-winner forever. So, 1986 became my year of contract programming. I worked very hard building up my consulting business. I also continued to work on enhancing QEdit. I actually had 200 orders that year. I could not believe it. I was extremely pleased. I began to wonder how many orders I would get if I could devote my full energies to working on the program. At the time, though, that was just a dream, but it is fun to dream. At that same time, Bobbi started actively helping me by doing the accounting and keeping up with orders for QEdit sales, plus, as she keeps reminding me, she also helped with shipping orders.

"Through 1987 I continued to build my consulting business, but I found myself wanting to spend more and more time working on QEdit. It was a very frustrating decision to deal with. I really did like my consulting business, and it did make me money. But I also loved being in the Shareware business, enhancing and updating QEdit, and trying my hand at marketing (I admit that I was lousy at it). I also enjoyed supporting my users. In 1987, I had over 500 orders. While not enough to live on, the income was significant.

"After wrestling with the situation for several months, Bobbi and I decided QEdit was worth a gamble. I would let the consulting business cool, while I worked away on a new version of the editor. If it did not significantly increase sales, I would go back to consulting full-time. If it did significantly increase sales, I would support QEdit full-time. So, from May 1987 until February 1988, I worked night and day on the new version of QEdit. I usually worked 10 to 12 hours a day, six days straight. And I was keeping my fingers crossed all the time because it was a big gamble to take.

"After ten grueling months, version 2.0 was finally ready. In late February, I started sending out update notices to my current users, and uploading QEdit 2.0 to my favorite bulletin boards. The results were dramatic. My phone rang off the hook. Sales doubled. I was getting several phone calls a day from users just wanting to tell me how pleased they were with the program. Then something happened I had not planned for. I was spending a great deal of time taking orders, doing technical support, packaging orders, making trips to the UPS office and the post office, working up site license agreements, and doing the host of other things that must go on in a successful software business. Eventually, I ran out of time to program. I was finally making enough money to support QEdit full-time, but there was no time left to actually work on QEdit. That was not good in the fast-paced microcomputer software market, and the text editor market in particular. It is an extremely crowded market, with dozens of additional entries each year. Without regular updates, QEdit would not sell for long.

"Things were getting out of hand, and I was getting farther and farther behind. The promised new version was hopelessly delayed. I tried talking Bobbi into quitting her job and coming to work with me full-time, but she was in the middle of an important project that she felt obligated to see through to the end. She also had a guaranteed salary, and it was not quite as scary if one of us was financially stable. What I really needed was someone to help me process orders and do technical support, and someone to help me run the day-to-day affairs of the business.

"In July 1988, SemWare made its third major decision, which was to hire outside help. Oh, in case you missed it, or I didn't make it clear, the first decision was to release QEdit as Shareware, and the second was to gamble and spend a year writing version 2.0. We hired Kyle Watkins, Bobbi's brother, to help out with orders and technical support, and Steve Lynch, Bobbi's sister's husband, to help out with everything. Kyle had previously had his own storm window business, and Steve had been a programmer and then a manager at UNISYS. That's when things really started looking up!

"By December 1988, we had a new release ready for shipment. Steve had worked long and hard redoing our manual. It looked great! Now we had quality documentation to go along with a quality product. Finally, QEdit's documentation was as good as it could be. In 1989, sales almost immediately doubled again with the release of the new version. The fancy looking manual and shrink-wrapping really paid off. We started getting lots of new sales in the corporate market, and our overseas orders gradually started to climb. This time I wanted to be ready.

"We hired a friend of ours, Elyce Cobb, to come in and help part-time with order processing. When Elyce left, we convinced Camille Lassetter (a graduate of Clemson University) to come to work for us. By now there were five of us at SemWare—myself, Steve, and Kyle full-time, and Bobbi and Camille part-time. My father-in-law, Bob, started looking for an office we could move into. Little did he know then that we were gradually planting the seeds to bring him out of retirement.

"In July 1989, we moved into a real office. SemWare finally made it out of the living room. Bobbi finally came to work with me full-time, after slaving away part-time since the start. Camille came on board full-time, as did Bob. He's still not quite sure how he started working again, but we are glad he is. We also hired one of our most reliable beta testers, Tim Farley, to help us out with additional programming and technical support. Then, the impossible happened. We were mentioned in *PC Magazine* by John Dvorak. We released a new version. We did a mass mailing to our users. And we released an OS/2 version.

"All of this happened in the third quarter of 1989, and our sales again had a tremendous surge. We did not take the upsurge in stride, but we adjusted quickly, thanks to the availability of additional help, Camille's endurance, and Bob's and Steve's planning and re-engineering of our order processing facilities. We have a very bright and creative group, and we sometimes even plan, thanks to Steve's and Bobbi's constant pushing.

"That brings us up to the present, and we have lots of things in store for 1990. We have hired a marketing agency. It seems that we have not even scratched the surface of the PC community. Our biggest problem is that we are unknown. But we are working on that! We have created a TSR version of QEdit, and we have a new release of the base version to go along with it. Both the MS-DOS and OS/2 versions have been updated, as well as the German version. We are also considering doing a UNIX version. We have hired another programmer—this time Steve's wife—and Bobbi's sister, Cindy.

"Sales keep on climbing. We must be doing something right. Based on feedback from our customer comment cards, 40 percent of our users purchased QEdit on someone else's recommendation. We are proud of that. We are working hard to keep our users happy. We have installed a two-line support bulletin board and outfitted it with two 9600 baud HST modems. We have three phone lines available for orders and technical support, and we have recently installed a fax. We work hard at supporting our users, and it continues to pay off. The future looks bright for QEdit.

"As far as the future of Shareware, I think the future looks good. I think more and more companies will probably be coming into Shareware.

As far as the new operating systems and machines, I think some Shareware companies, of course, will be able to go into those areas—the ones that have money and have been successful. For smaller Shareware ventures, it will be harder to go into those areas just because of the startup capital necessary. But I think, generally, Shareware authors tend to react much more quickly to new environments than commercial companies, because of the lack of red tape, and so on, that you have to go through with a larger company."

Do you have any advice for prospective Shareware authors?

"Yes. Mainline utilities seem to do better, just because the user is using them more often. Something a user doesn't use often doesn't encourage him or her to pay for it. Also, the appearance of the software and the entire package, to me, is very important. It's important that everything appear professional, especially the documentation. The product should be very easy to use. With so many Shareware products out there and so much available, it's easy to get rid of things that are hard to use or don't make any sense. I think it's really important that when a program is first started, users find it fairly easy to use and easy to get into."

Do you feel that Shareware has worked for you?

"Yes, we feel that Shareware has worked for us, simply because we don't have a million dollars to plunk down on an ad campaign. Shareware only costs us thousands of dollars a month, which we can afford. So it's worked very well for us because, for a modest investment, we are able to write software for a living—which is what we love to do."

THE FINAL ANALYSIS

This chapter has dealt with the very beginnings of Shareware—its history and its "founding fathers". We covered the three pioneers—Andrew Fluegelman, Jim Button, and Bob Wallace—and the enterprising, hardworking people like Barry Simon, Mark Herring, John Friel, and Sammy Mitchell. From the early 1980s and into the 1990s, Shareware has been and continues to be a viable alternative to more expensive commercial packages. Shareware is a marketing concept that allows someone who is a good programmer to try his or her hand at making money with it. With a good program and the support of users, like you, Shareware can provide top quality programs for years to come. Shareware authors tend to be more flexible and responsive than their commercial counterparts. Without your support, however, Shareware will fade from view and once it does, it will not return.

Putting Shareware into Perspective

I'd like to paraphrase something that was said to me by a successful Shareware author, regarding Shareware.

Shareware is *not* a religion. It's just a way for programmers to try to make a living doing what they like to do. You don't have huge advertising budgets, or copy protection, or salaries to pay, so you can charge a lower price than the commercial equivalent. Some people expect too much from Shareware. They expect not only a great program at a very low price, but they expect free upgrades for life—and a laser printed manual. The majority of big commercial companies don't give free upgrades. Be realistic in what you expect—that goes for the Shareware author as well as the user. To produce a *quality* product and support it, you have to dedicate yourself to the program. To do that, you have to take a gamble that people will support the product with their registrations. People just have to keep in mind that many of us are not doing this as a hobby. We enjoy writing software and if we get paid for our work, we keep on writing software. If we don't get that support, we stop and have to go back to what we were doing before. It's as simple as that.

I hope that you have gained some new insights into the Shareware industry—both by learning about its history and from reading the candid remarks of programmers who have become successful doing Shareware. Now, let's move along and begin to find out about the different ways in which you can obtain Shareware.

## CHAPTER THREE

PC User Groups and Disk Vendors

This chapter will examine two closely related resources for public domain and Shareware disks—PC user groups and disk vendors. These two distribution avenues augment The Wires, extending the reach of the online world and helping Shareware and PD (public domain) programming stay robust and vital. Since user groups came into being long before Shareware disk vendors, let's start with them.

USER GROUPS

Computer user groups have probably done more for computer literacy in our society than any other single influence. They've been the salvation of countless students in trouble with computer courses. User groups have helped scores of small companies with good products survive in a setting of raging competition. They've become friendly libraries of technical knowledge and central outlets for the best of the Shareware and public domain breed of programs.

Computer user groups were there at the birth of the microcomputer industry and have played a central role ever since as computer technology has unfolded. Their aggressive role has shaped vendor policies and guided product development, even as they steered users toward the best of the new hardware and software products. These groups have provided invaluable feedback to engineers, programmers, and vendors, and have helped to give coherent direction to the breathtaking pace of change and innovation typical in the microcomputer industry.

While the online world is freewheeling and boisterous, like a friendly sort of anarchy, user groups offer more organized centers where authors, users, and vendors can come together to share interests and trade expertise, tips, programs, and gossip. The best of these groups are a cross between a social club and a university, a kind of floating computer show where some very good, creative thinking takes place. It's easy to get hooked on the stimulating atmosphere in these computer "guild halls."

The emphasis within groups has changed since the early days of these groups. Businessmen and professionals have joined the enthusiastic amateurs, changing the flavor quite a bit at times. Also, many groups have shifted from a heavy, almost hobbyist emphasis on hardware to a stronger focus on software. New hardware is still well covered in the larger groups, and such groups may get contributions of products or promotional presentations from hundreds, or even thousands, of manufacturers.

The Will of the People

User groups are essentially a natural extension of the free market principles Americans have come to know. They may not directly determine vendors' products and policies, but they are gaining more strength and influence each day. They are taken very seriously by key vendors. Because user groups have been so effective, they've grown considerably over the past 15 to 20 years. Specialized groups have developed, such as users within large corporations and government organizations. Some of these specialty groups have purchasing clout that vendors find irresistible, making such groups a gold mine for product testing.

The parent organizations often lean heavily on product evaluations by the specialty groups, and vendors are eager to cooperate. If you're part of such an organization, your user group is where you can probably see (and play with) the leading edge in computer technology.

User groups that you can join simply because you're interested have come to enjoy similar influence. In order to maintain their growth and vitality, many groups now generate income by selling public domain and Shareware disks and by renting exhibit space to manufacturers and publishers. Vendors are eager to cooperate because they want the visibility. They often leap at the chance to put their products at the focus of user group meetings attended by hundreds or even thousands of knowledgeable potential customers.

Many vendors then use the feedback from such meetings to polish and improve their products, so the information flows both ways. Some Shareware companies move on to become purely commercial vendors, but many of the best find enough success with Shareware that they stay in that market, continually upgrading and seeking direct feedback from user groups. Sometimes, Shareware companies that try the professional route later decide the extra marketing expense isn't justified by the profit and return to Shareware status.

Whether Shareware or commercial software, their products can be found at user group meetings. It's small wonder these groups have grown in size and influence over the years. As a result, groups that originally started by seeking information for their members have themselves become dispensers of expert information. Their judgments are well respected because they have no axes to grind; their only interest is in comparing and understanding the strengths and weaknesses of competing products. Do you want an unbiased, expert opinion on a product? Would you find it useful, perhaps, to test a new piece of hardware without a salesperson hanging over your shoulder, babbling its virtues? A user group may be just what you're looking for

In the Beginning

Gary Kildall (author of the program CP/M) joined with Gordon Eubanks (CEO of Symantec) and others around 1974 to start one of the earliest PC user groups, the Home Brew Computer Club in what was to become the famous Silicon Valley, south of San Francisco. The Home Brew Computer Club was one of the very first groups visited by Steve Wozniak and Steve Jobs to demonstrate their new Apple computer. The club itself developed from an interest in the Altair computer, one of those early, grand S100-Bus computers that paved the way for practical desktop computing. The Home Brew Computer Club was part of the revolution that swept small computing and changed it from the hobbyist's toy to an essential piece of business equipment. During the period of technological milestones like the Cromemco Z80, WordStar, and VisiCalc, there was a highly charged environment that helped produce many of today's products and advances in technology.

The Association of PC User Groups estimates that there are over 206,000 members in 300 to 500 DOS-based PC user groups at this writing. These figures are very much on the conservative side. Fog International, an umbrella organization, has a list of some 1,900 user groups worldwide, including non-DOS-based groups and specialized computer groups.

The largest single user group, the Boston Computer Society, claimed about 30,000 members at the beginning of 1990. There are at least 20 other clubs nationwide with 850 members or more. On the other hand, one user group in the Midwest has a membership numbering exactly six. Current members are worried about the threat of new members because they meet at a local restaurant and the table can only accommodate six! Should their membership explode to eight or ten, maybe someone will send them a nice folding table and some quarters for the juke box. . . .

Some Key User Groups

Below is a partial listing of some key user groups and their estimated memberships early in 1990.

> Boston Computer Society (MA) 30,000
> Fog International Computer Users Group (Daly City, CA) 19,000
> Capitol Users Group (Washington, DC) 8,900
> Houston Area League - PC (TX) 8,500
> Chicago Computer Society (IL) 2,400
> Central Kentucky Computer Society 2,000
> Philadelphia Area Computer Society (PA) 1,800
> Pasadena IBM PC User Group (CA) 1,500
> Pinellas IBM PC Users Group (FL) 1,500
> Sacramento PC User Group (CA) 1,200
> North Orange County Computer Club (CA) 1,000
> Orange Coast IBM PC User Group (CA) 890
> PC Users Group of Boca Raton (FL) 500
> Utah Blue Chip Society 400

Dues for most computer user groups average $20 to $35 a year. The average member has belonged to a group for about two and a half years, if it is maintaining a healthy growth rate.

DOCTOR'S NOTE

User groups range from memberships the size of a small city to grassroots congregations that would be comfortable together on a fishing trip. Somewhere out there is a user group just right for you! So how do you find the right one in your area? Finding a group with the "right stuff" won't be too difficult, though you won't find many groups listed in the yellow pages. With 1,500 groups—at least 500 of them MS-DOS groups—in the United States, they can't all be listed in this book. But here are some ways to locate a user group near you:

- Ask your computer store. Store personnel often know the local computer "activists" and may be able to point you to just the group you need.

- Go online! Call a BBS (bulletin board service) near you. (You should be able to find one you can call in Appendix C.) Ask the *sysop* (sysop stands for System Operator—the person in charge of the system), or sign onto a GEnie RoundTable or a CompuServe special interest group (SIG) and just put the question out there for all to read. Chances are somebody in your area will reply to your note with a name or a number to call.

- Call your local city or county government and ask about locally registered non-profit organizations. If there's a club of any size near you, chances are it will be registered.

- Look in the *Computer Shopper*, a huge monthly tabloid magazine found in the racks at larger supermarkets, bookstores, and computer outlets. Now owned by Ziff-Davis Publishing, *Computer Shopper* includes a large list of user groups located not only in the U.S. but worldwide. The list may be only a fraction of the hundreds of known user groups, but it is as accurate and current as possible. (Incidentally, *Computer Shopper* also carries a huge assortment of full-page ads from just about every clone vendor and most of their grandmothers. There are more healthy clone makers out there than you have probably ever dreamed existed!)

- Contact the Association of PC User Groups at 1101 Connecticut Avenue N.W., Washington, D.C. 20036, (703) 425-9896 Voice, (408) 439-9367 BBS, and 319-7899 MCI Mail. They've been growing fast, and the chances are very good that any group near you of medium or large size is already registered with them.

- Write to the Fog International Computer Users Group, the source of the *Computer Shopper* list. Fog International has the most current list,

DOCTOR'S NOTE *(Continued)*

since groups must update their information every three months or be dropped. Fog's list includes some 1,900 groups worldwide, 1,500 of them inside the U.S. and at least 500 for DOS-based machines. Groups are classified by location, computer brand, and primary group interest. For a list of groups near you, send a self-addressed, stamped envelope to Fog International, P.O. Box 3474, Daly City, CA 94015. Tell them where you live and any special computing interests you have. They'll send a list of user groups in your area (and a list of local BBSs, too, if you ask) or a list of groups that share your special interests. Incidentally, you can also reach Fog on CompuServe (71561,570), by Round-Table (RT) on GEnie (OFFICE.fog), or as FOG on MCI.

The BCS—Biggest in the World

The Boston Computer Society (or BCS), a non-machine specific user group founded in 1977 by two enthusiastic youngsters, is now widely considered the largest user group in the world. It has more than 28,000 members who each pay $45 in annual dues, and has a yearly budget approaching $2 million!

BCS offers 40 publications, 80 SIGs, and enough influence to attract the interest and support of every key vendor in the industry. Its monthly schedule is packed with more than 100 club activities tailored for members ranging from the total neophyte to the seasoned expert. The BCS's paid and volunteer staffers negotiate phones ringing off the hook and maintain all forms of member and vendor contact. Although there's a lot going on all the time, BCS's atmosphere is generally one of fellowship and community service, and everyone seems to get along fine. Try that in any other organization of this size!

Mitchell Kapor, founder of Lotus Development Corporation, and Daniel (Dan) Bricklin, co-creator of the pivotally important spreadsheet program VisiCalc and creator of Dan Bricklin's Demo program, have long been active in the BCS. It's a place for movers and shakers, but anyone's welcome to join the fun, and a visit there can be quite an experience.

From Humble Beginnings

In 1977, Jonathan Rotenberg, then 13 years of age, started BCS with co-founder Richard Gardner. They held five meetings before Gardner took off to join a commune in Austria. That left the budding organization in the care and keeping of Master Rotenberg, who persevered out of love for the project and a dash of 13-year-old stubbornness.

At first, young Rotenberg had trouble collecting the annual $5 dues from the handful of early BCS members. Originally headquartered in Rotenberg's bedroom at his parents' home in Boston, it soon became upscale by moving to a local McDonald's restaurant where milk shakes and fries were right at hand. Today, BCS headquarters is an office building in downtown Boston.

Early member Gary Haffer recalls: "In the early days, when we held meetings at McDonald's, Jonathan didn't have a driver's license. He wasn't old enough to go to bars, so we'd meet at the corner restaurant near a bus stop."

In 1978 the BCS sponsored an all-day fair with seminars, workshops, and demonstrations. They called it Home/Business Computers '78. During this seven-hour show, BCS membership soared from 60 to 240 and the club has never looked back. Horatio Alger, move over!

Seeds of Success

One reason for the club's success is its continuing ability to attract new members and volunteers. Another factor is its non-machine specific approach, which helps BCS be many things to many people, and lets it adapt to the rapid-fire changes that seem never to relent in the field of microcomputing. Like microcomputing itself, BCS was originally small. It had a clear focus—to get computing into the hands of the masses. Today, the computer industry is as large as it is diverse, and the same can be said of BCS. Its membership now includes teachers, lawyers, doctors, hobbyists, students and professors, office workers, retired professionals, computer novices, expert technicians, and engineers.

BCS was originally a purely volunteer organization. Today it has 12 full-time paid staff members and a 14-member board of directors. The board makes major decisions while daily business is handled by staffers and some 500 or more active volunteers who donate from 15 to 60 hours weekly. For a club with 28,000 members, the operation is a model of good government and management. "This is the type of place where you can say, 'I want to be an editor,' and presto!—you're an editor," notes Les Squires, a BCS member active in the Business User Group.

BCS services now encompass all one would expect of a well established user group including meetings, training, extensive Shareware library, online BBSs, and even an information hotline. It gets donations of equipment from industry leaders such as Apple, Compaq, IBM, and others. In fact, like most user groups it would like to operate entirely with donated equipment and goods—and it comes pretty close to achieving that ideal.

The Technological Vanguard

Vendors who donate products to BCS can benefit greatly from the exposure they receive. For the price of a product or two a vendor can get its message to nearly all of BCS's 28,000 members. As a result, BCS members often get hands-on experience with the very newest of major software and hardware innovations, long before they hit the streets.

BCS has become a beta tester for many new products, giving members an opportunity to help developers debug their products, suggest better ways to get things done, and influence the entire course of a product's development. New product debuts often attract a crowd of thousands at the general membership meetings. New hardware and software unveiled at those meetings sometimes produces an atmosphere of excitement that reminds old-timers of the new automobile model unveilings in Detroit 30 years ago. Vendors with poorly designed products, or products not competitive with today's best offerings, may be well advised to avoid the scrutiny of the BCS membership. Their feedback isn't always positive, and they're not shy about stating their opinions.

Sometimes You Win, Sometimes You Lose

Not all BCS activities have been a dashing success. In August 1984, the BCS entered a two-year agreement that gave each member access to Western Union's Easy Link electronic mail service. Members also received special documentation, free access, and a $25 credit for any other Western Union service.

Although Western Union invested over $300,000 to set up this agreement, the project was a dismal failure. In 1984, E-mail failed to take off in the marketplace, and it did just as poorly at BCS. Many feel that E-mail suits business users better than it does casual or home users. Indeed, Western Union has since changed the focus of its business to reflect this.

Western Union did gain a few thousand customers from this experiment, and both the BCS and Western Union feel it was a valuable learning experience. In fact, it was a $300,000 learning experience. Wow—and some of us thought our university tuition was expensive!

Setting a Good Pace

The BCS is truly a flagship computer user group, with members and staff committed to the club's continued success. They're not afraid to take chances, to explore the leading edge and report back to the rest of us. Their concern with spreading the word and encouraging the growth of microcomputing on an individual, human scale has never flagged.

For all these reasons and more, the BCS will probably keep attracting new members indefinitely. The BCS has become a model and inspiration for user groups throughout the world. They'll keep presenting exciting product debuts and informative demonstrations, and their friendly influence will abide for a long time to come.

How a Group Gets Started

User groups are started by people hungry for knowledge and information about microcomputing. The club's members become each other's resources. Although a group may be the brainchild of a single person, there is usually a core group of people who become responsible for a club's success. In any volunteer organization, 90 percent of the work is done by 10 percent or less of the total membership. User groups are no different.

What does make them different is that the entire field is changing so rapidly that no single, dominant clique has taken charge. Newcomers arrive every day, and the technology changes at a breathless pace. If you want to keep the membership list, you're likely to be the membership director the very next day! If you have a better idea for a SIG, bring it up at a meeting and the project will probably be yours for the asking. Too bad the rest of life isn't always that open to new ideas.

Where to Start and How Long It Takes

Generally it takes about a year to get a new user group off the ground and running. During this development period, new user groups typically operate in someone's home where there is little or no overhead. As membership increases, dues start to come in, and the club may migrate to public facilities with meeting rooms or low-cost commercial meeting facilities.

As membership grows and funds accumulate in the kitty, the group develops its own personality and areas of expertise. Things are now on track and well settled. The first, feisty period of initial growth is over, and the group settles into a steady, continuing growth phase as it stakes out areas of interest and acquires a solid group identity. At this point, your group will be registering with user group umbrella organizations such as Fog International Computer Users Group and the Association of PC User Groups.

Throughout most of these first few years, your group will most likely depend completely upon good ol' American volunteerism — the willingness of interested people to volunteer their time to make a project work. In fact, volunteerism at some of the user group giants like BCS and the Houston Area League (HAL) is still the key to their success.

Volunteerism is not a one-way drain on the volunteers, however. Many user group volunteers go on to successful careers using the experience they gained in the friendly user group environment. The computer industry can be a fierce and hostile place for newcomers, but at your home user group the old adage "you get out what you put in" rings true. Volunteerism does have its drawbacks. You'll have to constantly attract new members and new volunteers or growth will stop and you can wither away. Volunteers burn out after a year or two of service and must be replaced by a fresh crop. Replacing them is getting harder nowadays, as the original user group hobbyists give way to more business-oriented, purely professional members who just don't have the time.

Sufficient staffing is a problem for the bigger groups, and by the time your new group needs to face it, you'll probably have enough money in the bank to hire a small staff to coordinate things and take up the slack. And by the way, when that happens, you'll know for sure you've arrived!

Principle PC User Group Activities

PC user groups have five primary activities:

- **General Membership Meetings** Each month there is a general membership meeting. These typically last three to four hours and

DOCTOR'S NOTE

Marching to a Foggy Different Drummer

When people hear about Fog International Computer Users Group, they tend to visualize the name as FOG and figure the letters stand for something. Or, if they hear Fog is located in Daly City, California, just outside of San Francisco and one of the foggiest cities in the lower 48 states, they may figure that's reason enough for the unusual name. Actually, neither assumption is correct. According to Gale Rhoades, Fog's Executive Director, when the founders sat down in the summer of 1981 to start a computer users group, someone at the table remarked that every time he sat down at one of the little demon machines he felt a fog descend in his brain. Thus, was Fog International born. Originally a CP/M-oriented group, many of Fog's members, including Rhoades, remain vocal partisans of the tight, economical brand of programming associated with the early, memory-cramped CP/M machines. Ask her and she'll wax enthusiastic about the products of CP/M-graduate Shareware programmers like Vern Buerg of LIST.COM and Bob Wallace of PC-Write. "Under CP/M you didn't have any choice," Rhoades observes, "but once you've learned to write in that tight programming style it's hard to let go of the practice."

Nowadays, Fog International is both an umbrella organization and (excuse the expression) a stand-alone user group. As an umbrella organization, Fog maintains lists of user groups and BBSs that are second to none. In early 1990, their roster included 1,900 groups worldwide, and their list is as up-to-date as a list like this can possibly be. "If a group hasn't updated its description in the past three months, we drop them from the list," says Rhoades. "The same goes for BBSs."

As a result, if their list isn't the most complete of all it is certainly the most accurate. That's why publications like *Computer Shopper* use Fog to update their own user group lists. As an independent user group, Fog carries out just about all normal user group functions except those that require holding a general membership meeting in one place. So you won't find product unveilings there. But they communicate with their estimated 19,000 members via a 100-page monthly magazine named *Computer Help*. ("That's because we give help to people in the real world, people who sometimes feel computer fogbound," Rhoades says.) They're also very active on the GEnie computer network (as the OFFICE.FOG RoundTable, or RT), so they're ideal for people who can't attend meetings for one reason or another. They also have their own BBS at (415) 755-8315. If you'd like to

DOCTOR'S NOTE *(Continued)*

Marching to a Foggy Different Drummer

join, membership is $40 a year and includes extensive support, access to a huge software library, special announcements, member-level BBS access, and a subscription to *Computer Help*. Fog International is non-machine specific and covers MS-DOS, CP/M, Apple, and interesting orphans like Osborne, Kaypro, Morrow, and various grand old S100-Bus machines. When you join, tell them Dr. File Finder sent you!

---

are attended by about a quarter of total club membership. Few membership meetings attract more than 300 current members unless the group is holding a special event, such as a major product unveiling.

- **Special Interest Groups (SIGs)**   A typical user group may have 10 to 15 SIGs or even more. SIGs generally meet once a month, separately from the general membership meeting. SIG membership levels may range from 10 to 75 people, depending upon the size of the user group itself, how specialized the special interest is, and so forth. SIGS are one of the best sources for specific information on topics like desktop publishing, major software applications like WordPerfect or Lotus, new products of significance like the new, more affordable laser printers, and more. The Shareware SIGs in some groups are among the most dynamic and freewheeling of all!

- **Newsletter**   Usually monthly, the newsletter is often bulk mailed to all members just before the next general membership meeting and may include the minutes from the last meeting. It may also contain Shareware and PD software reviews, general computer news, information about upcoming club events, reports on SIG meetings, announcements, technical columns, letters from members, and more.

- **Library**   A typical group may have a software library with 3,000 disks and sell copies to their members at 50 percent less than what they charge non-members. Updated library catalogs may go out to members as frequently as four times a year. Often, several disks in particular will be hot items, based on members' reviews and word of mouth. The library will often be set up at a table and be open for business during meeting breaks and after the meeting is over. The profit generally goes toward covering costs of maintaining the library, acquiring more software and, if anything is left over, to fatten the club's treasury.

- **BBS** A group might have two public and one members-only BBS call-in nodes, each of which handles 24 calls a day. Bulletin board membership, which may be available separately from user group membership, may number about 1,500. Club members often get special board privileges such as longer access, unlimited downloading, and so forth.

Other Typical Group Activities

Groups generally have monthly Board of Directors meetings that may or may not be open to the general membership. In either case, the minutes are often published in the monthly newsletter. Usually there are 10 to 15 directors and officers responsible for setting general club policy and making the major decisions affecting a club's future. A set of bylaws or a constitution must often be incorporated and governed by the laws of the state where the club is located. Most clubs have unique bylaws, tailored to their specific interests.

General elections of officers or directors are usually annual events. Special events may include key vendor presentations of new products, equipment or software swap meets, and parties or other purely social events.

DISK VENDORS—FRIENDS OR FOES?

When the first public domain and Shareware disk vendors went into action, there was widespread suspicion that they were being unethical. There they were, charging the public several dollars per disk for public domain and Shareware programs—and not paying one red cent to the hard-working authors of those programs! Worse, they sometimes left the impression that no further fee was necessary, even for Shareware. A lot of people were pretty unhappy with the vendors for a while.

But since those early, sometimes tainted days, Shareware authors have formed the Association of Shareware Professionals (ASP). In turn, the ASP has reached agreement with vendors on ways to distribute Shareware programs using practices the authors themselves endorse. A lot of misun-derstandings were straightened out. Nowadays, a very effective way for Shareware authors to distribute their work is through disk vendors. The better vendors actively promote Shareware programs in their literature and catalogs, giving the author personal credit and making it clear which programs offered are PD and which will require a later Shareware regis-tration fee if kept and used.

As you might imagine, attitudes toward disk vendors have softened as a result. In fact, authors often go out of their way to send their new releases and updates to established vendors. The extra visibility can be an important aid to their success.

When asked about disk vendors, Shareware author Jim Button recently replied: "When Shareware started we really didn't think about disk ven-dors . . . they just sort of started up one day. My firm doesn't object to these people charging a modest fee for distributing a disk. In fact, disk vendors probably help promote Shareware more than anybody. We would like to see Shareware disk vendors continue to improve and update their catalogs and libraries, and make it clear to their customers how Shareware works."

How Vendors Got Started

The first public domain and Shareware disk vendors probably got the idea of selling disks from computer clubs, which were doing a brisk business selling disks to club members. No doubt a member or two of some club, watching that action, figured the same thing might work as a commercial venture, and were they right! Some computer user group members be-came defectors and went into business for themselves. There was consid-erable controversy when one or two former computer club librarians broke from the club and started selling what many believed to be the identical library through their new disk vendor business. But in the computer world things move fast. You don't hear much about club defec-tions anymore.

In the process of trying a commercial approach, the early disk vendors started a gold rush of sorts. Once they started popping up in computer magazine ads, a horde of would-be entrepreneurs got the bug to sell disks themselves. How could they lose? The programs were PD or Shareware, floppy diskettes don't cost much, and you could advertise the programs as being free. What a deal! A lot of jostling went on. Sometimes an aspiring disk vendor would recruit a friend or two with some operating capital, who was willing to do a fair share of disk collecting and copying. In fact, many of today's Shareware disk vendors got their start when a friend told them about the idea.

Many disk vendors are now staunch supporters of Shareware. They may even have begun distributing disks in order to help promote Shareware while offsetting the expense of maintaining a comprehensive personal library. But let's face it—the promise of good profits with limited cash investment was a major contributing factor to the growth of Shareware disk vendors. If you think about it, there's nothing wrong with that.

Many small disk vending enterprises are still operating, but there are some giants as well. While the little guys operate out of their living room or garage, the big guys are likely to occupy large warehouses teeming with activity. It all depends upon their size and their marketing prowess.

The Cost of Doing Business

A vendor's staff may consist of a husband and wife team or even just one highly motivated individual who doesn't mind juggling 250 diskettes per hour and dealing with mailing labels stuck to the printer's platen. But the big vendors are likely to have a staff numbering 40 people and duplication equipment ranging from PC clones to high speed dedicated disk duplicators with autofeed mechanisms. One popular duplication system is the ALF Quick Copy unit which has two drives, copies most any disk format in about 25 seconds, is simple and easy to learn, has error detection controls and indicators, and sells for about $1,200. That's a major investment, but it pays off if a vendor has considerable volume.

Another direct cost lies in the acquisition of a reasonably dependable computer, but it doesn't have to be fast and can be found cheap in the used equipment market. You'd need a printer, perhaps a used nine-pin dot matrix capable of printing mailing labels. And you'd need to keep it supplied with ribbons and labels. (If you're going upscale, Avery has come out with its own line of custom laser printer labels.) With LabelPro software, grinding out mailing labels by the hundreds is a breeze.

You'll need blank diskettes. At this writing, bulk 48 TPI 5.25-inch diskettes average 20 to 28 cents. Sleeves run 3 to 8 cents each. Labels may cost anywhere from 1 to 10 cents each. Finally, the best Shareware disk vendors maintain toll-free order lines that may average 200 calls per day, at an average cost to the vendor of about $2.50.

Demand Fluctuations, Problems, and Solutions

The industry-wide average disk order is for eight disks and returns are less than two percent. Disk exchanges account for another two percent. At this writing there has been a tremendous resurgence in demand for computer games, while demonstration disks attract the least number of orders. Demand is seasonal, running high in the winter months but slowing down during summer.

A major problem faced by successful disk vendors is employee theft. Employees have been known to pilfer entire vendor libraries and go into competition with their former employer, using the ex-boss's disks and catalog. Since the whole point is that PD and Shareware programs are there for anyone to distribute, it's hard to press charges. But you can bet that tempers sometimes run high!

Customers can also be a demanding lot. They often expect 24-hour toll-free technical support for a disk they paid $3 for, and are reluctant to use a toll number for technical support, even assuming the vendor can afford a technical support staff. Sometimes being a disk vendor calls for a thick skin. Published notices that tech support isn't provided don't help much, so vendors sometimes tell their order clerks to claim the tech support people "are in a different building... sorry we can't transfer you from here...." Why not just say that this line is an order line only? It's not so unreasonable when you consider the average toll-free call costs $2.50, and the disks ordered rarely bring in more than $5 each!

Some disk vendors have reported receiving program disks infected with computer viruses, the new scourge sent to us by rogue hackers. A few of these virus reports have been confirmed, but no evidence could be found of a single incident where a virus has made it past a disk vendor's screening process and into circulation among customers. Almost all vendors now check their master disks for viruses, using one of several virus screening programs. Reputable vendors also fire up the software themselves before copying it to make sure all required files are supplied. In the process, they ensure that it is not commercial software and that it works the way it should. Some disk vendors now even check their disks for errors and bad sectors. They may also include menu systems, file listers, and READ.ME type instruction files. These steps help make Shareware easier to begin and more reliable, especially for buyers who are not too sure about how to get started at first.

Turning a Vendor into a Distribution Channel

When disk vendors start, they begin to accumulate their library by downloading and purchasing disks from others. Once they become established, Shareware authors will contact them directly with new programs or new program upgrades. Vendors are now a significant force in Shareware marketing. And, because it's a fiercely competitive market, the prices are kept to an absolute practical minimum.

Vendors can be a great source of new programs, even if you use The Wires or belong to a user group. Well-established disk vendors may receive hundreds of disks from authors each year. Many of us may not realize that vendors perform a very time-consuming, complex, and expensive service for what is actually not a lot of money, all things considered.

Vendors are a very efficient and economical source for public domain and Shareware programs. They maintain libraries of thousands of disks, offer free or low cost catalogs, collect, test, categorize, duplicate, distribute, and often even support the Shareware they distribute. When you think about it, where else can you get so much service for $1.50 to $3.00 per disk? And if you subtract 40 cents or so per disk as the vendor's direct material cost, their fee is even less.

It is hard to grasp that despite the low fees, many disk vendors actually have toll-free phone lines, offer technical support and customer service, and even replace or exchange disks you don't like while charging an average of only $3 each. Remarkable! One reason they can do so much for so little is that they don't have to pay direct royalties for the programs they distribute. Commercial software distributors pay big bucks for each product they carry, but Shareware disk vendors can download a program from a BBS or even buy disks from another disk vendor, copy away, and presto—they have a new title for their collection.

They're NOT Always Angels

Unfortunately, some disk vendors still forget they are only authorized to charge a modest fee for distribution. They are not authorized to sell the programs on the disk. One reason disk vendors do so much volume is that end users sometimes mistakenly believe the $3 vendor's price per disk covers purchase of the programs instead of just their duplication and distribution.

Unscrupulous vendors can feed into this misunderstanding in an attempt to increase sales volume. The ASP attempts to expose such operators, but doesn't always succeed. Users who want Shareware to remain a successful marketplace will do well to avoid such sharks and stick with ethical vendors.

We need to keep in mind that disk vendors get paid for each disk they send out, while Shareware authors must rely on the honor system to get a fair registration fee. How many disk vendors would there be if they shipped disks for, say, 50 cents, and then sat back and waited for satisfied customers to voluntarily mail in the remaining $2.50? This, in effect, is what a Shareware author does. Shareware authors spend months and even years writing a program and documentation. When they release their work as Shareware they must rely on voluntary registrations to start rolling in. Sometimes the registrations just trickle in or don't come at all. Other times they come in a flood. But the whole time, the disk vendors are collecting their $3 nick. Help them stay honest by sticking with vendors who are up front about how Shareware operates. Buy from vendors who name program authors and include the suggested registration amounts in their catalogs. They're the vendors who will help keep Shareware alive and kicking—and everybody will benefit.

Picking a Vendor

With fierce competition the name of the game among disk vendors, it is the buying public who is sitting in the catbird seat. Consumers have an incredible range of choices among vendors. How can users pick the right vendor when their mailboxes fill up with catalogs just weeks after sending in the first coupon or calling in the first order?

You might have a favorite specialized disk vendor who offers custom collections or program insights such as Glossbrenner's Choice, 699 River Road, Yardley, PA 19067, (215) 736-1213, operated by Shareware expert, Alfred Glossbrenner.

You can learn a great deal about most disk vendors by checking the size of their catalog, availability of a toll-free number, and how up-to-date the programs in their catalog are. Even if it's a toll call to your nearest BBS, you're well advised to go online periodically just to keep up on the latest releases of software you want to try. There's nothing like waiting a week to try your new Shareware database, version 2.0, only to find out right after it arrives that version 4.3 was released months ago! Of course, you may never trust that particular disk vendor again, but the damage has already been done.

So go online and look for the latest version of the program you want, even if you don't intend to download it. Then look in vendor catalogs for specific information. What version are they offering? If they don't say, you're inviting disappointment. If the version number is out of date, be sure to ask the order clerk specifically which version they're sending before you order. Catalogs can be out of date, but the order clerk should know. There are other little touches that set really good disk vendors apart from the rest. Order a program disk and take a good look at what you get

- Is the program you bought the latest release? If it's not, the vendor is not doing his or her job—or they're fobbing off old disks already in stock instead of updating them. Change vendors.

- Did the vendor spend the extra five cents on quality sleeves and diskettes? A month or a year down the line you'll grow to appreciate the quality difference. The bottom line is, higher quality means longer life and greater reliability.

- Check the label. Is it clear at a glance exactly what you've received, or does it have a vague "PD Database" sort of label? Good vendors won't leave you wondering what you're holding when you pick up the disk again a few weeks later.

- Is the diskette almost empty? Some vendors leave as much as 75 percent empty real estate on their disks. It's like a milk shake filled only to the fill line, instead of dripping over the top—it's just not as satisfying! They rationalize it by saying it's confusing to send more files. One vendor tells customers who complain, "We believe in filling your order exactly." Forget it. They're just going for maximum bucks. Try other vendors until you find one who'll send you disks that are more fully packed. One of your best prizes may turn out to be the little utility program a vendor threw in to help fill out a disk. Finding those small gems can turn into a very large part of the fun.

- Does your new diskette have any bad sectors? This can happen during shipment, but that's not often the case. Unfortunately, many vendors don't bother to check before shipping. Sure, they'll replace a diskette that wasn't properly copied. But who needs the grief— and the delay? Use a vendor who checks.

- In the same vein, some vendors are starting to use formatting programs that don't put that cryptic "NON-SYSTEM DISK—ABORT, RETRY, IGNORE?" message on the screen when your visiting nephew tries to boot a new game disk. Both Norton's Safe Format program and the PCFORMAT program included with PC Tools put a clear message on the screen, telling your nephew how to handle the problem. The versatile Shareware program Format Master from New-Ware will tell your nephew to change disks after explaining why. Vendors who use such formatting routines show a touch of real class. Stick with them.

- Good vendors won't use subdirectories on their disks, unless they also include an install program of some sort.

- A good vendor won't use archive techniques (which produce .ARC, .ZIP, .PAK, or .LZH files) unless the results are self-extracting or include the necessary program to do the extraction plus a very clear READ.ME-type file explaining what to do.

- Look out for programs that require another program in order to run, especially programs in BASIC, graphics files like GIF pictures that require special viewing, or template files for specific commercial applications like 1-2-3 or dBASE. Some of these may not be compatible with proprietary versions of DOS such as those used by Compaq and AST computers. Templates are useless without the parent application. Vendors who don't warn you aren't doing their job.

BBS, User Group, or Disk Vendor?

PC user groups and disk vendors are closely related sources for public domain and Shareware disks. Most clubs are non-profit, while disk vendors are commercial enterprises—but each has its strengths. A user group is probably the only place where you can talk to other users face to face (sometimes even the program's author) about the programs. And you can telephone a disk vendor, usually at no charge, to order up a dozen disks for less than what it would cost you to download from an online service like CompuServe or GEnie or even a BBS that is a one- or two-message unit call from your computer.

Still, nothing beats the speed and convenience of downloading files from an online BBS. And if you have any questions, chances are you can put them directly to the sysop. If it's a good board, you'll get an answer even if the sysop has to put a message out on The Wires for the author.

When you get right down to it, the BBS is always my own first choice, and that's where you can always find the Doc, in The Wires! In Appendix C, I'll specify certain bulletin boards where you can send messages to me and always get an answer as you travel The Wires.

## CHAPTER FOUR

Commercial Online System Libraries

In the last chapter you learned about obtaining Shareware from PC user groups and disk vendors. Another excellent source of Shareware is the commercial online networks. All of them maintain libraries of Shareware that you can download. There are many other things that you can do on commercial online networks. This chapter will tell you a little bit about what is available on the bigger commercial networks. The commercial online networks that will be discussed are

- GEnie
- CompuServe
- BIX
- Delphi
- EXEC-PC
- Channel 1

You'll see not only what can be obtained from the various online libraries of Shareware programs, but also some of the other online activities in which you might want to participate. More detailed information about the actual process of going online will be discussed in Chapters 5 through 9. If you're ready, let's take a look at what the commercial online networks have to offer.

SPECIAL DOCTOR'S NOTE

This chapter on commercial online networks is dedicated to the memory of Shari Bellamy. Although I never met her face-to-face, we had many enjoyable talks on the GEnie network before she died suddenly in February 1990. Shari enjoyed telecommunicating and helping out on GEnie. Only in her thirties, Shari's enthusiasm was contagious and she loved talking with people online. While she will be sorely missed, she will not be forgotten by those who knew and loved her. Since she loved the atmosphere online, this chapter is for her.

At this point I feel that I should make a comment about *online friendships*. For those who do not venture into the wonderful world of telecommunications, it is often difficult to understand how people become friends with people around the world whom they have never met. I am not one to use the word "friend" lightly. To me, it is a special word. In the course of my time online, I have developed some strong and lasting friendships. Some of these people I have been proud to call "friend" for many years, even though we have never met. I feel as close to them as I do to some people that I have known face-to-face for a long time.

When dealing with people in an online environment you do not have external factors to influence you. You must base your opinion of other people on their words and thoughts. Things like sex, race, height, weight, and so on do not figure into the picture. If you are honest in all of your dealings online, the friendships you form will be just as real, and just as lasting, as the other friendships you make in your life.

For those of you new to telecommunications, this may seem strange or perhaps almost unbelievable. To the old-timers—you'll understand. Thus, I want to take the time to thank my *very* special friends: Don Bodley, Rae Barent, Bob Brody, Ray Majewski, John Knauer, Bonnie Barber, and Dave Blackett—just for being there—and for being special, each in his or her own way.

While I can't name them all, I also want to thank the countless programmers I have worked with, people like: Barry Simon, John Friel, John

SPECIAL DOCTOR'S NOTE *(continued)*

Newlin, Dave Krause, John Erickson, Matt Thomas, Rob Brenner, Shane and Sandi Stump, Tom Smith, Bruce Barkelew, Tom Rawson, Rex Conn, Terry Tomkow, Mark Herring, John Brooks, and all the others, who know who they are, for becoming my friends in the course of working together online.

NETWORK PROS AND CONS

There are two ways to build a software collection using modems and The Wires—bulletin board systems (BBSs) and the large commercial networks. Since most local BBSs are free and offer message systems (which will be discussed in Chapter 8), there wouldn't seem to be much reason to pay a commercial network for the privilege of hooking up. Some of them can cost $50 an hour or more. Who needs it?

The answer is probably nobody does, if getting software is the only concern. But if you want the software along with nearly free support from experts, a choice among sometimes dozens of competing programs, a selection of specialized software libraries that boggles the mind, and a chance to exchange messages with people from all over the world, the fact is, you only get that kind of service on a commercial network.

An Information Revolution

Distinctions between local and nonlocal areas are becoming increasingly blurred as technology marches on. We're living through an information revolution caused by low-cost connection services like PC Pursuit and StarLink. The original local BBSs are not all that local anymore, and this free flow of information has caused a renaissance in programming.

The mix of nonlocal callers has changed the "small-town" atmosphere of the original local BBS, but you'll find nothing beats the cosmopolitan flavor of a large network. The large networks are meeting places of the mind. One of the most impressive programming feats I know of was pulled off by a 16-year-old boy who got his training over The Wires, on The Source. (The Source, which was one of the most interactive of the networks at the time, was bought out by CompuServe in 1989 and no longer exists.)

One of the boy's first programs was made possible by a few people from different parts of the country, who had never met face-to-face, but chipped in some money to buy him some equipment. The result was an expanded-memory RAM disk program that has never been bested in terms of either speed or economy of DOS memory required to run it. You can still find it on BBSs all over the country as NJRAMD.ZIP. That "boy" isn't a boy any more, and his name is Mike Blaszczak. He goes by the name of "Nifty James" and all of his programs start with "NJ." I was very proud to be one of the people to donate money so that a brilliant young programmer like "Nifty" could forge ahead.

CompuServe and GEnie are the two biggest networks at this writing. When you log on to the file library at either of those services, it's like logging onto 2-3,000 local BBSs all at once. Both CompuServe and GEnie cross all regional, city, state, and even national boundaries. CompuServe even has a special group or *forum* reserved for people calling in from Europe.

So, although your data doesn't care if you're sending it to the BBS down the block or to Reginald Smythe in London, you're more likely to meet Reginald on CompuServe than on Bobby's Neighborhood Trading Post BBS. Note that I'm not belittling Bobby's Trading Post — far from it! You're more likely to find me trading programs with Bobby than spending hours on CompuServe. It's more to my liking. But that's strictly a personal feeling. Do I subscribe to any commercial networks? (*smile*) I am on GEnie, CompuServe, BIX, Delphi, Plink, EXEC-PC, and Channel 1 — and I visit all of them regularly.

A Matter of Support and Provenance

On GEnie or CompuServe, there's a strong likelihood that programs you select were uploaded by the author of the program, not by Bobby's friend Michael across the street. Much as I like both Bobby and Michael, there's much to be said in favor of getting your programs from the authors themselves. For one thing, you know who to ask for help when something goes wrong. You're more likely to meet the program's author on a network.

You may run across an author on a bulletin board; some famous authors like Vern Buerg even run their own BBSs. But the fact is that CompuServe has the greatest concentration of author-uploaded files in the world.

DOCTOR'S NOTE

To some people, tightly focused networks like BIX and PCMAGNET are vital. It's a big world out there, and as with hotels and other services, we may just want the one we're used to, or that fits our needs or desires perfectly. If your area only supports 1200 bps and you're used to 2400, you may have to pick and choose among packet switching networks; or you may switch from CompuServe to Delphi, which pays your Tymnet charges.

For people who have many questions to ask, a BBS often doesn't do the job. Do you want to find some answers to a problem with DESQview? On a BBS, there may be five or ten people familiar with the program. On a network, you're likely to find a huge group of users, and some of them may be technicians from the vendors themselves.

Do you need serious business information? A commercial network is the only way to go. Do you need to contact the original author or conduct international business? These are some things you simply cannot do outside the networks.

Most of all, you need the networks to hear a truly different perspective on what concerns you. After all, on a network like GEnie or CIS, everyone's from out of town, even you!

Cost Analysis May Be Surprising

In terms of cost effectiveness, the international networks do not always stand up well to analysis. CompuServe, though accessed in most places by a local phone call, will cost you $6 to $12 an hour to use. A local message unit phone call, on the other hand, weighs in at about 15 cents a minute, or $9 per hour. With a special calling plan, it would be even cheaper. If you sign on at 9600 bps or higher, your reduced downloading time can make the networks look terribly expensive!

The first trick is to find out the true cost basis. AT&T, U.S. Sprint, MCI, and other such companies refuse to offer electronic access to their long-distance phone rate databases. They claim they're more than happy to tell you their rates if you talk to an operator; otherwise, forget it. This makes automated cost-tracking ahead of time nearly impossible.

This may change. It may have to, with the Integrated Digital Service Network visible on the horizon, not to mention the development of the call data standard (the CDS will be discussed in Chapter 6). Until then, there's not much you can do to change the policies of the big phone companies.

What are your remedies? You can try to guess the cost, based on past calls to another number in the same area code. You will probably not be very far off. Better yet, call the operator. In Chapter 6, you'll learn more about costs and how you can minimize them. For now, let's take a look at some of the commercial online networks. You can take a peek at just some of the things they have to offer.

GENIE—COMING ON STRONG

Not as well known as CompuServe and with a smaller membership base, GEnie is a lot friendlier for the new user, in my opinion. It's also about one-third cheaper than "the big guy," CompuServe, during non-prime time hours (6 P.M. to 8 A.M. in your local time zone). GEnie became operational in October 1985 and is now nearing 200,000 individual subscribers throughout the United States and in selected cities in Canada and Japan. It calls itself the fastest growing information service in the U.S.

To sign up for GEnie, dial 800-638-8369 inside the U.S. In Canada, call the customer service number to get your nearest local access number if the numbers for Canada are not local to your area.

GE Information Services, Dept. 02B
401 North Washington Street
Rockville, MD 20850

301-340-4000 (Voice)
800-638-9636 (Customer Service)
416-858-1230 (Toronto)
514-333-1117 (Montreal)
403-232-6121 (Calgary)
604-437-7313 (Vancouver)

The GEnie network is made up of what are called RoundTables, each with its own software library, bulletin board, and real-time conference area. These cover a wide range of interests from genealogy to home business to games to investment counseling. In addition, each of the major types of computer systems—IBM, Macintosh, Apple, Atari, Amiga, and so on—has its own RoundTable (RT), with discussion areas and a file library. Many commercial giants are represented on GEnie: Ashton-Tate, Borland, and Hayes, to name a few.

Since we're focusing on Shareware, I'll confine my discussion to software libraries attached to various RTs and, since each library is different, to the kinds of programs you might find in a representative library of each group. Given the number of RoundTables, each with its own library, the number of files available is staggering. We only have room here to present a small sample to whet your appetite. The best way to find files in your own areas of interest is to simply go exploring.

Types of Libraries

GEnie has a software library for every type of computer, each with over 10,000 files. Amiga and Atari users will find 15,000-plus programs in those libraries. Macintosh users will find a similar number in the Macintosh software library. At last count, there were well over 16,000 files in the IBM library. Here are some GEnie RTs that can keep you busy exploring for many happy hours.

The IBM RoundTable

For a DOS PC user, the IBM RoundTable is the heart of GEnie. The latest versions of Vern Buerg's LIST, all of the compression programs from LHarc to ARC to PKZIP, the editors, word processors, spreadsheet programs, graphics programs, utilities that will do everything but change your bed—they're all here. You will find Shareware from the "giants" like Bob Wallace, Barry Simon, John Friel, Jim Button—just about the entire ASP guild. In addition, you will find programs uploaded by less well-known authors.

Since IBM-compatible programs are the main focus of this book, you'll find references to IBMs throughout this description of GEnie. At this point, it's enough just to say, at the opening screen, type **IBM**. You'll go right to this RT, at the center of the GEnie IBM world. Enter **3** to get the libraries. Then take a deep breath, dive in, and have a wonderful time!

The Borland RoundTable

Juan Jimenez, sysop of the Borland RT, has this to say:

"The vast majority of the files we receive are related to Borland's programming language products, with most of the current emphasis on Turbo C and Turbo Pascal. We do get a lot of other files, particularly files with programming utilities, editors, and so on, but since the RT was originally a programming-language-only area, my assumption is that the emphasis has stuck.

"We have a contest every single month of the year and give away prizes of free programming or toolbox products to four users; so that seems to draw more programming-language-related files than anything else. (Once we had a monster contest where only one person won the prize for the most uploads, but that person walked away with $1500 worth of Borland products.)

"When I was given the task of running the RT, I wanted to make it a valuable resource for users of Borland language products. The programming language areas of the library are dedicated to archives with source code, which make a very valuable and large reference area from which to draw examples of working source. I am a great believer that most programmers learn by example (I learned that way) and that belief extends into how I run the RoundTable."

The Home Office/Small Business (HOSB) RoundTable

In addition to machine-specific RTs and program-specific RTs, GEnie has a large number of RoundTables that cater to specialized interests. Thus, a user who is interested in investing can visit the Schwab RT; a user interested in writing and getting published, the Writers Ink RT; a user interested in aviation, the AVRT; a user interested in Japanese culture and communicating with users from that country, the Japan RT—to name just a few. Each of these has its own specialized library with files of interest to those users.

You'll find one example of such specialization in the Home Office/ Small Business (HOSB) library. Here, you can find demos of many commercial business and financial programs along with user-uploaded Shareware, all in some way related to operating a successful small business from the home. The Shareware programs cover resume writing, managing personnel, managing time, accounting, taxes, and practically everything you would need to start up and run a successful small business.

The HOSB library, like most of the other special interest libraries, contains a large number of text files: resumes, lists of business-oriented BBSs, guides to writing business plans, information on taxes, and many more. One of the most active areas is the resume section in which users upload text files of their resumes for consideration by prospective employers. Since the HOSB is not machine-specific, there are libraries for Macintosh, PC, Amiga, and Atari ST Shareware.

The Genealogy RoundTable

Another specialized library is the Genealogy library, representative of various leisure time RTs. The majority of uploads to this library are text files concerning the family histories of users, but the library also includes public domain and Shareware programs for working with genealogical data like family trees. It is also rich in supplementary programs to use with commercial genealogy software, such as Roots III for the PC, and some of the more popular utilities.

If you're on a quest for family history, you can find an inexpensive Shareware program to handle 2,000 records, or get demo versions of commercial programs built for 200,000 records. The advantage of these specialized libraries is that Macintosh users and PC users, for example, can both find Shareware programs that address their particular needs without having to visit separate libraries and without having to wade through tens of thousands of programs in the machine-specific libraries. Of course, a program with universal appeal, such as Vern Buerg's LIST, can be found in most of the specialty libraries.

Authors of genealogy programs supported in the Genealogy RT include

- Howard Nurse (Roots III - IBM)

- Steve Vorenberg (Family Roots - IBM, Apple, Commodore)

- Tony Lucich (MacGENE)

- Greg Kopchak (It's All Relative - Atari ST)

- Steve Barker (Generation Gap - Atari ST)

- Bob Mosher (FTC-MORE - IBM)

• John Steed (Brother's Keeper - IBM)

The first three are commercial programs. The last four are Shareware; copies of these and other Shareware programs are in Library 8 of the Genealogy RoundTable.

The Games RoundTable

In a typical Games software library, you will find a wealth of leisure time activities. One library, Scorpia, has over 1,700 files consisting of Shareware game programs. Here, you can find the latest in adventure role-playing games, strategy games, word games, and so on.

In addition, GEnie has a number of RTs dedicated to specific games like checkers and chess. If you want the latest in three-dimensional chess programs or tips on how to play these games, you can find them just by looking.

These few software libraries are not even the tip of the iceberg. I just wanted to offer you a sample, but I hope the sample is diverse enough to give you some idea of the range of files available on GEnie.

How to Access GEnie

GEnie can be accessed by any good communications program through GEnie's own local access numbers or, in the rare city or in rural areas where no access number is available, through PC Pursuit (PCP) and Telenet.

To call GEnie using PC Pursuit, dial into the local PCP access number, log into a PCP city, and then have the PCP hookup dial the GEnie node. When it answers, log on just as you would when dialing direct.

To call GEnie direct, dial your local access number. When the connection is established (either by a light on the modem or a "CONNECT" followed by the baud rate on screen), type **HHH** and press ENTER within two to three seconds. At the U# prompt, enter your user ID and password separated by a comma. That will take you to GEnie's top menu. From there, it is a simple matter to move to the various areas GEnie refers to as "pages" by typing **M** followed by the page number at any GEnie prompt. Figure 4-1 shows the Main Menu of GEnie, located at page 1. To return here from any prompt, you would simply type: **M1** and press ENTER.

Figure 4-1

GEnie's Main Menu

```
GEnie           TOP          Page   1
      GE Information Services

  1. GEnie Users' RT  2. Index - Info
  3. Billing/Setup    4. GE Mail & Chat
  5. Computing        6. Travel
  7. Finance          8. Shopping
  9. News            10. Games
 11. Professional    12. Leisure
 13. Reference       14. Logoff

Enter #, or <H>elp?
```

Moving Around on GEnie

Starting from the Main Menu page of each RoundTable, GEnie's libraries are almost always menu option 3. Option 1 is the Bulletin Board (where messages are left). Option 2 is the Real-Time Conference, where users can chat on a real-time basis, meaning that what you type in appears immediately on the screens of everyone participating in the conference. Scheduled "speakers" also appear in option 2 conferences.

Option 3 is where files that can be downloaded are almost always located. This makes it very easy to remember. "GEnieus," the user RT, may be on page 150 and Writers on page 440, with Aviation on page 410 and Scorpia, the games RT, on page 805, but the libraries for each will still be option 3. Of course, the type of files you find depends on the Round-Table you visit.

Advanced Navigation

There are quicker ways of getting around GEnie than the menu options, helpful as those are. After you've visited a few times and gotten used to the system, you'll start getting impatient with the menus. Faster ways are detailed in the GEnie manual that you receive when you register, but here are some pointers for now.

The letter "M" represents moving, so you can *stack* your commands by specifying **M** plus the page number plus the menu option number. If you want to get to the HOSB library, for example, and you already know that HOSB is on page 370, you can type **M 370;3** to go directly to the HOSB library. You can even enter that page number when you log on, right after you enter your user ID and password:

```
U#=xyz12345,guru2,370;3
```

Another easy way to get to the libraries is to remember that in almost every RT, the libraries are located at the RT page plus 1. Thus SFRT, the Science Fiction RoundTable, is at 470; its library is at 471. Scorpia is at 805, its library is at 806, and so on. This lets you add the number of the library function that you need. For example, to check recent uploads on Scorpia, type **M 806;11.** This moves you to page 806, the Scorpia library, and picks option 11 on the menu, which is Check New Uploads.

More Standard Menu Choices

Inside an RT library, option 11 is always Check New Uploads. That's handy. Similarly, option 2 is always Directory of Files, option 5 is Upload File, and option 6 is Download File. If you wanted to upload a file to the HOSB RT from anywhere else on GEnie, for example, you could simply type **M371;5** and follow the prompts from there.

Using page numbers to navigate around GEnie is an easy way to maneuver, because every GEnie RT menu, as has been noted, is the same. Figure 4-2 shows a typical RoundTable menu.

Words, Not Numbers

If remembering page numbers is not your strong suit, every GEnie RT can also be reached by means of a mnemonic, associated word. Thus, if you type **INVEST**, you'll go directly to Schwab. Typing **IBM** takes you directly to the IBM RT. From those top RT areas, you can then follow the menus down to their library, or wherever else you want to go.

Aladdin—A Personal GEnie Navigator

As easy as navigating GEnie is once you get used to it, the program, Aladdin, makes it even easier. Owned by the GEnie Network, Aladdin is

---

Figure 4-2

The HOSB RT menu—a typical RT menu

```
GEnie          HOSB        Page 370
    Home Office/Small Business RT
        Library: ALL Libraries

1. HOSB RoundTable Bulletin Board
2. HOSB Real-Time Conference
3. HOSB Libraries
4. About The HOSB
5. How to use the Bulletin Board..
6. Announcements

7. Feedback to the SysOp

8. Executive Desk Register

Enter #, <P>revious, or <H>elp?
```

```
ANSI   ONLINE  38400 8N1   [Home]=Menu   HDX 8 LF X J J CP LG 1 PR 00:01:54
```

---

free. There is a special Aladdin support forum located at page 110. To get there from any GEnie prompt, type **M110.** You will find that Aladdin makes using the GEnie Network a pleasure.

At one time, Aladdin was a Shareware program. Then it was taken over by the sysops of the IBM RoundTable, and it became a commercial program. The registration fee was $59. Aladdin really does make it easy to use GEnie. It automates many common procedures and saves you time and money. Why would GEnie start giving it away for free? Because the people at GEnie want your online experience to be pleasurable. So the GEnie Network bought the rights to the program and decided that anyone who wanted to use it could have it free of charge. The file containing Aladdin is usually called ALAD???.ZOO or ALAD???.EXE. The ??? denotes the version number. ALAD???.EXE is a self-extracting file. This means that the file will automatically unpack itself. Although other services also provide users with front-ends to ease the task of getting around the system, Aladdin has long been considered just about the best. This can always change, of course. By way of comparison, CompuServe recently introduced a graphics-oriented front-end program called the CompuServe

Information Manager (CIM). CompuServe has long had a very good text-oriented front-end called TAPCIS. The point is—nothing ever stays still for long on The Wires.

At this point, many consider Aladdin the best. When you download it, you can select either a self-extracting LHarc form or a compressed ZOO form. At this writing, Aladdin has not yet been ported to systems other than the PC, but plans are in place to produce Macintosh and Amiga versions.

If you download Aladdin and have any questions or problems, all you have to do is visit the Aladdin Support Forum. People there will be happy to answer your questions and help solve your problems. Aladdin is very easy to set up, so you should have few, if any, problems. The program has built a long track record of responsiveness to users and continued improvements over time. Give it a try—you'll like it!

What Are Some of Aladdin's Features?

Aladdin basically serves as an automated way to use your GEnie time. It checks your mail and your favorite RTs for new messages and files, downloading them automatically if you like, so you can deal with them later, offline. When you're finished, you can either log off or, if you choose, stay online in terminal mode.

You can reply to mail or messages offline with Aladdin's own editor, save captured mail or messages to a file either automatically or manually, or print them out. You can check libraries for new files or search for prespecified files. You can also mark up to 10,000 files for batch downloading via ZModem, which Aladdin makes available as a built-in protocol. The program also handles uploading files to RTs of your choice. You can use the program to start new topics and keep lists of categories and topics in each RT, files in the libraries, and GEnie page numbers and mnemonics. You can import your lists into database programs. It will also keep a log of programs you've downloaded so you won't accidentally download the same file twice.

In short, almost anything that you can do online, this program allows you to do offline. Aladdin will automatically keep track of the time that you spend on GEnie and the approximate amount of money you've spent so there are no surprises at the end of the month. Aladdin is perfect for just about anyone who plans on spending any amount of time on GEnie, participating in conferences, and so forth. It's text-oriented, fast, fully automated—you really owe yourself a chance to try it out.

Getting the Files

Selecting option 2, the Directory of Files, from any software library menu will give a brief description of the files found there. All libraries give the same basic information in these descriptions:

- Identification number of the file
- Filename
- File type (whether binary or text)
- GEmail address of uploader
- Date uploaded
- Size in bytes
- Number of times the file was downloaded
- Library in which it is found

You can search the libraries by filename, file ID number, uploader, and date of upload. Do you want a list of files authored by Norm Patriquin and uploaded to IBM RT after December 1989? Just ask.

GEnie supports Xmodem-1K, Xmodem (CRC), Ymodem-G, and Zmodem file transfer protocols for downloading. However, since GEnie uploads are entirely free during non-prime time—6:00 P.M. to 8:00 A.M. in your local time—GEnie supports only Xmodem uploads at this writing.

GENIE'S LIVEWIRE CHAT LINES

I realize that no discussion of online networks would be complete without talking about the *CB simulators*. The major networks all have some form of CB simulator, even though that area may be called by a different name. What, you may ask, is a CB simulator? As the name implies, it's like an online form of CB (citizen's band) radio. There are channels or lines where people from all over the country, and the world, can "talk" in real time.

Of all the CB simulators, it is my personal opinion that GEnie's Live-Wire Chat Lines is the best. Why? Because it offers more than just talk. There are online games that people play together. There are special discussions on topics of interest, such as substance abuse, abortion, women's rights, the singles scene, and much more. People can go to Chat Lines and interact with others in new and different ways. The Chat Lines sysop, BonBon, actively participates and is constantly striving to add new things that are of interest to the users. Because new things are added regularly, it never gets dull. So, since I want you to at least be aware of the CB simulators on all of the networks, I will discuss the one that I feel is a cut above the rest, and the one that I frequent myself.

Recreation and More

GEnie's LiveWire Chat Lines offers a wide variety of online games that users can play together. These generally take place on Channel 38, but other channels are sometimes used as well. It's great to do a listing of Channel 38 and see the names of people from New York, California, Alaska, Hawaii, Maine, and virtually every other state, all playing Trivia or some other game at the same time. Games are all scheduled in advance,

---

Figure 4-3

Chat Lines' welcome screen

```
SATURDAY, MARCH 10:
(All Times Eastern)
- - - - - - - - - - - - - - - - - -
     Chat Lines Tonight!

 7:00pm: SUBSTANCE ABUSE SUPPORT GROUP with Bo on Channel 10. (SCR=SAS)
 8:00pm: CONTROVERSY with Susan & Talisman Warrior on Channel 14!
         Tonight: Abortion - Where do you stand?
 9:00pm: ROMANCE with Maiden America on Channel 13! LOVELINK tonight!!
10:00pm: REMEMBER WHEN with Lady Jane and Maiden America on Channel 10!
         Tonight: You know you've been online a *long* time when...
11:00pm: VITAMIN R: Rock n Roll with Egg on Channel 11!
         Tonight: Desert Isle Disks - You can bring only 2!
 1:00am: THE LIVING ROOM with BonBon and Wendy Sue on Channel 10!
 6:00am: BREAKFAST CLUB with Loki on Channel 13! Free toast!
- - - - - - - - - - - - - - - - - -
LiveWire Games On Channel 38:
------------------------------
11:00am: Brunch Trivia with -Z-
 2:00pm: True or Bull with Rikki Tikki Tavi
 3:30pm: WordFoundry with Andy
 5:00pm: Stars with Jasmine
 7:00pm: Trivia with Ankh
 9:00pm: Chain Gang with Ambush Bug
10:45pm: Gallows with Night Owl
12:30am: TitleWave with Shron

Please Note: Rules & Instructions for LiveWire Games can be found in the
LiveWire Exchange (Page 400;7) - Category 12. The Game times will not change,
however the scheduled game may change without notice.
```

---

so you'll know when to log on for your favorite. Figure 4-3 shows the opening screen that you see when you first enter Chat Lines.

As you can see, the games scheduled for that night are listed on the banner. Special events or discussions are also listed. All times given are eastern standard time. By seeing this banner the first time you enter Chat Lines each day, you can decide if there is something that you want to come back for, be it a game or a discussion topic that interests you. It's a lot of fun playing the games—not only can you have some fun with the game, but you can interact with other people playing it. Figure 4-4 shows a game of TitleWave in progress on Channel 38 of GEnie's Chat Lines.

The people playing the game are from all over the United States and they play TitleWave in teams that are randomly assigned as a person joins the game. In Chat Lines, each person uses a *handle,* which can be changed at will with the /HAN NAME command. The GEMail ID remains the same unless you specifically ask GEnie to change it for you. It's interesting to note that the software that runs these games was not written by GEnie, but by GEnie subscribers!

In the TitleWave game, for example, it automatically detects when someone new enters the channel and sends you a message telling you

---

Figure 4-4

A game of TitleWave in progress in Chat Lines

```
<TitleWave> ~~ Hiya Mac-Attack!  For TitleWave rules type:  /SEM 42 !RULES
<TitleWave> ok, bons!
<TitleWave> ~~ <Wabbit & Seapuppy>  YOU ARE UP!  Do you want it?
<Noman Gilinde ErCrabion> Hi macster
<x1.5> Hiya, Mattack-Ac.
<Wabbit & Seapuppy> .CO!
<Crab Fingers> What for is he taking pictures?
<Noman Gilinde ErCrabion> hewwo, wabbit
<BonBon> Hi., Mac!! :D
<TitleWave> ~~ +++++++++++++++++++++++++++++++++++++++++++++++++++++++++++++
<TitleWave> ~~ TEAM 2...Jellyfish  your turn
<TitleWave> ~~ <Wabbit & Seapuppy> is up.
<TitleWave> ~~
<TitleWave> ~~ >>> Song:    1    2    3    4    5   <<<
<TitleWave> ~~ +++++++++++++++++++++++++++++++++++++++++++++++++++++++++++++
<-(* LeeAnn *)-> love/
<Wabbit & Seapuppy> NOT ME
<TitleWave> ~~ ======== <Wabbit & Seapuppy>'s clue for the Jellyfish ========
<TitleWave> ~~          NOT ME
<TitleWave> ~~
<-(* LeeAnn *)-> you/
<CaveFish> you/
<Portuguese Man O' Windy> you/
<TitleWave> ~~ +++++++++++++++++++++++++++++++++++++++++++++++++++++++++++++
  SCROLL-BACK  ↑↓ PgUp PgDn  [F1]Help [S]ave [C]lear [ESC]Exit  Queued 451
```

what to do. The person running the game is using the handle TitleWave so he's easily identified. All the rules and instructions for the games can be downloaded from the Chat Lines software library, or you can go to Category 12, at page 400;7. For help with anything in Chat Lines, you can enter **CHATHELP** at any GEnie prompt.

How Chat Lines Works

From any GEnie prompt, you can go to Chat Lines by entering **M400.** This takes you to the Chat Lines menu. If you are in menu mode, you'll see that there is a help section, a section for rules for the games, a section for reserving a handle, and more. GEnie has two Chat Clubs available that can really save you money if you enjoy using Chat Lines.

Option 4 on the Chat Lines menu takes you into Chat Lines. In command mode, you could enter **M400;4** at any prompt to go directly there. When you enter Chat Lines, you are assigned a job number, which is used as a way for others to send you personal messages, and so on, while you are in Chat Lines. If you exit Chat Lines and go to GEMail, your job number may be different when you return.

The commands used to navigate around Chat Lines, or to find out who is where, are quite simple. Unlike the commands used on the rest of GEnie, Chat Lines commands begin with the / character. A list of commands appears in Table 4-1.

Some of the commands, like /NOS, /MON, /PRI, and others, are basically either on or off. Using /SEN, you can send a private message to any other person in Chat Lines. You just use the format **/SEN ##** *message,* where ## is the job number of the person you want to receive the message. For example, if Buffalo Bob is job number 30, then to send a message to him, that only he can see, you'd enter something like:

```
/sen 30 Hi Bob! How's it going tonight??
```

On the other hand, a command like /STA has three uses, as shown below.

/STA	Displays listing of the names of the people on the same channel
/STA *	Displays names of all of the people on every channel in Chat Lines
/STA ##	Displays everyone on a channel, where ## is a channel number; for example, /STA 38 shows everyone on Channel 38

Table 4-1

GEnie's Chat Lines Command Summary

Command	Description
/HELp	List of commands
/BLA	Add blank line
/BYE	Log off and hang up
/CAL *jj*	Call on job *jj*
/CHA *cc*	Move to channel *cc*
/ECHo	Echo to sender on
/EXIt	Return to menu
/HAN *hh*	Change handle to *hh*
/MON *cc*	Monitor channel *cc*
/QUIt	Return to menu
/PRI *jj*	Go private with JOB *jj*
/SCR *k*	Scramble, w/ key *kkkk*
/SEN *jj m*	Sends job *jj*, message *m*
/SHOw *hh*	Show job of handle *hh*
/SQU *jj*	Squelch job *jj* - 4 max
/STA *cc*	See users on channel *cc*
/TIMe	Display time and day
/USErs	See number of users
/WHO *jj*	See handle of JOB *jj*
/XBL	Exit the blank line mode
/XECho	Exit the echo mode
/XMO	Exit the monitor mode
/XNO	Exit the nosend mode
/XPR	Exit private mode
/XSC	Exit scramble mode
/XSQ	Exit squelch
/NOS	Don't allow messages

The /USE command shows you what channels are in use and how many people are on each one. The /PRI command puts you and one other person into private mode, where no one else can see what you are saying. This is used so that people can have private conversations while in Chat Lines. The commands are simple, but if you're new and having trouble, there are always people around who are more than willing to help out. Just ask! We were all new at one time or another.

Interesting Discussions

Another excellent feature of GEnie's Chat Lines is the discussions on topics of interest. People can join the discussions and give their viewpoints — and listen to the viewpoints of others. These "formal" discussions always have someone as a moderator to help keep the conversation on the topic. Besides formal discussions, people on any given channel may start to talk about or debate any subject that happens to come up. Figure 4-5 shows a discussion on a channel in Chat Lines.

As you can see, using a CB simulator like GEnie's Chat Lines is a very different experience from exchanging messages via electronic mail. I can make a statement in Chat Lines, from my home in Colorado, and get an immediate response from someone else who may be 2,000 miles away — an invigorating experience, and one I think you'll enjoy.

Overview of CB Simulators

This has been a brief look at some of the things that transpire on GEnie's Chat Lines. The commands used on the simulators of other networks will

---

Figure 4-5

An online discussion in GEnie's Chat Lines

```
L 1      C 1     I W     396k     c:\dnld\fig4-5.txt
<nancy> Have you finished your book yet? I'm anxious to get it.

<=Guitarman=> Almost. It will be in stores in August

<Traveler> I used those Zmodem parameters you gave me, Doc...
<=Guitarman=> Yes? And how did they work for you?
<Traveler> and they did the trick. Thanks.
<*-Jack-*> The Zmodem here on genie seems to work pretty well

<=Guitarman=> Yes, Jack...it does. I get around 220 CPS at 2400 baud
which is good. Much better than using Xmodem.

<nancy> I set up Zmodem and it seems to work fine for me too
<*-Jack-*> Doc? Any hot tips on programs? <grin>

<=Guitarman=> Oh, look for some new things from Phil Katz.. soon.
<DYNAMO> Hi everyone! What are you folks talking about?
<Diana> Oh, I got my new 386 and it's a beauty....

<Traveler> I have to run. See all of you later!

=[ Keystrokes Queued 0 ]======[ Split Screen ]=================
Just talking about miscellaneous things right now, Dynamo
```

be similar. For more talk about computers and technical matters, you may want to try out the simulator on BIX, called CBix. An entire book could be dedicated to the CB experience, but I wanted to give you just an idea of what goes on and how it works. GEnie's LiveWire Chat Lines offers variety, games you can participate in, scheduled discussions, and friendly people. Each night of the week there is a special welcome discussion on Channel 13, at 10:00 P.M. EST, just for new users. Now, that's something special not found elsewhere. If you are online to GEnie and go to Chat Lines, look for me. My handle is < =Guitarman= > —you can just say "Hi," or you can ask me questions about anything. (You can also reach me by sending me mail; my mail ID is DR-FF.) Come and check it out; it is something that you have to experience for yourself.

What Does GEnie Cost?

One reason for GEnie's success is the fact that it was designed by its owner, General Electric, to keep an enormous computing network busy during slack hours. With nothing to lose (it was dead time anyway), they were motivated to keep rates down. With low rates that appeal to the individual user, GEnie burst upon the scene like gangbusters. They haven't changed their philosophy—they still appeal to individuals by charging low rates.

Basic rates to access GEnie in the U.S. during non-prime time hours, plus all day on weekends and national holidays, are $5 an hour for 300 bps, $6 an hour for 1200 bps, and $10 an hour for 2400 bps. The prime time rate is $18 an hour for all three bps speeds. So for individual users, it's pretty much a nighttime service. There are no monthly minimum charges. The sign-up fee is only $29.95 and includes a $10 usage credit, a GEnie User's Manual, and a subscription to GEnie's *LiveWIRE* magazine.

COMPUSERVE INFORMATION SERVICE (CIS)

Since its introduction in 1979, CompuServe Information Service has become the world's largest online information service. More than 550,000 members can access the service by a local phone call in most U.S. cities and in more than 100 foreign countries. Callers can pick and choose among more than 1,400 different information resources, a menu so rich that some find it intimidating. Don't worry, though; there's always help available at the press of a button.

CompuServe Information Service, Inc.
5000 Arlington Centre Boulevard
Columbus, OH 43220

617-457-8600
800-848-8990 (Customer Service)
617-457-8650 (Ohio residents and outside the U.S.)

Finding Your Local Access

Inside the U.S., use a touchtone phone to call 800-848-8199 to reach a CompuServe voice mail system that will give you the nearest local access number for 300, 1200, or 2400 baud modems. Don't be put off if the number is not particularly close; when you log on to CompuServe for the first time, you can type **GO PHONES** at any prompt to get more complete information and a closer access number.

A comprehensive and detailed users guide with step-by-step instructions for all areas of CompuServe is part of a membership kit available at Waldenbooks, Radio Shack, Sears, ComputerLand, and other computer stores. The kit assigns an initial password and user ID to get you onto the system.

You can also buy a membership kit by phone, using a VISA or Master-Card credit card. Call the 800 number given above and follow the voice mail system directions.

Cost—Not Cheap

At this writing, CompuServe connect rates are identical for 1200 and 2400 baud modems. It doesn't make sense not to take advantage of the cheap 2400 baud modems now available. If you're going to spend much time on

CompuServe, a 2400 baud modem will pay for itself very quickly. Besides connect charges, you'll have to pay access surcharges even on Compu-Serve's own data carrier network. It's only 30 cents an hour, but Delphi, for example, pays your Tymnet connection charges for you; and your local BBS is free.

CompuServe is no great price bargain. A subscriber base of over a half-million people makes CompuServe the heavyweight of networks. CompuServe is certainly doing something right, to remain so big for so long. It could be that at their service level, minor price differences don't count much.

See the tables below for CompuServe charges, current at this writing, for access from within the contiguous United States. For detailed informa-tion on access from Canada, Alaska, Hawaii, and other places, enter **GO RATES** at any CompuServe prompt.

Connect Rates (per connect hour)

Baud	Prime Daytime $/ Hour	Standard Evening $/Hour
up to 300	$ 6.00	$ 6.00
450*	$ 6.00	$ 6.00
1200*	$12.50	$12.50
2400*	$12.50	$12.50
4800*	$32.50	$29.00 (hardwired network connection only)
9600*	$47.50	$44.00 (hardwired network connection only)

*Not available from all locations

Communications Surcharges (contiguous United States)

Phone Access Surcharge	Prime Daytime $/Hour	Standard Evening $/Hour
CompuServe	$ .30	$ .30
Telenet	$12.00	$ 2.00
Tymnet	$12.00	$ 2.00
CSC	$50.00	$50.00
LATA Net-works	$ 6.00	$ 2.00

Forums: The Starting Point

CompuServe's special interest forums let members attend online conferences, exchange information, and benefit from the expertise and enthusiasm of others. More than 150 forums cover such diverse topics as humor,
rock music, auto racing, and science fiction. These forums hold tens of
thousands of public domain and Shareware programs. Over 125 software
and hardware companies provide direct customer support for their products online in forums. These include commercial houses like Borland,
Lotus, Microsoft, and 3Com; Shareware houses include Quicksoft, Magee,
and Datastorm, as well as individual program authors.

CompuServe is a computer user's beehive. Incredible activity and
information sharing go on around the clock. Don't miss your chance to
thread your way through the CompuServe maze—it's not difficult and the
rewards are great.

In this book we'll concentrate on IBMNET, which is an entire cluster of
forums with scores of libraries, every one devoted to DOS-based software
and hardware. That alone is too much to cover completely in a single
chapter, so be aware that it's just the tip of the iceberg. Apple computer
users have their own net called MAUG, just as big as the IBM net. There
are many individual vendor forums, besides the Shareware and other
vendors that offer support in the IBMNET Vendor A and Vendor B
forums.

As with the world's great libraries, it could take a single person several
lifetimes to cover everything on CompuServe. Then they'd have to start
over because CompuServe is an entire electronic universe. Things change
faster than you can keep up with. If you range The Wires, you owe
yourself at least a shot at the CompuServe experience.

Where the Forum Idea Started

In ancient Greece, teachers, tradesmen, and those wanting their services
gathered in a central meeting place called the Agora. Later, when the
Romans borrowed from Greek culture, the Agora became known as the
forum. CompuServe claims its electronic forums simulate the original
Greek experience, but in a different century, in a different language, and
using a different medium, of course—at so much per hour. In this sense,
it's not quite like the original, but the similarities to traditional centers of
human interaction are not hard to see in the more than 150 forums
available here. It's the biggest *E-ride* network of all, to borrow another

dated metaphor. Each forum combines an electronic bulletin board for messages, a library of reference material and software, and the capability for live online group conferencing. These latter-day forums, like their ancient namesakes, are dynamic meeting places. They just take full advantage of modern technology and billing procedures.

How CompuServe Forums Work

Forums provide members with three ways to communicate. First, there are message boards on which to post messages, ask questions, carry on discussions, and list items of interest. Next, online conferencing lets members communicate in real time by typing messages on their computer keyboards. The discussions get lively.

Finally, and most important to a Shareware downloader, there are the libraries—and what libraries they are! Don Watkins, senior sysop for IBMNET, says he isn't even sure how many DOS-based files the IBMNET forums hold. When asked (via CompuServe E-mail, of course!) how many there might be on the entire system, Don replied:

"I couldn't even venture a guess since I only do the IBMNET forums. That doesn't include about 100 other forums that are heavily or exclusively DOS-based, such as Ashton-Tate, Microsoft, Lotus, Midi, Pics, Borland, Novell, Datastorm, Aldus, Software Publishing, Ventura and I'm sure a lot more that I can't recall offhand.

"I can't speak for those other forums, but in IBMNET we've stressed getting authors online and getting files directly from the author. Right now, all our files are uploaded by the author, or by someone representing the author because the author doesn't have an account or modem, or we contacted the author.

"We look for quality rather than quantity. The big advantage of getting the files from the author is that they're usually around for support [not always; some definitely drop off] and updates [again, not always]. Additionally, most of the ASP members stress online support and the ASP ombudsman as a strong selling point."

If you get the impression from Don Watkins that IBMNET libraries are big, you're right. They are huge. Perhaps EXEC-PC has larger DOS-based software collections (we'll get to them in just a bit). I don't know of any collection outside CompuServe where only the authors themselves, or their known representatives, do the uploading. You can't get a much better guarantee against hacked or illegal programs, and if you get stuck by a program, you can ask the author what went wrong.

DOCTOR'S NOTE

CompuServe is widely regarded as the premier testing ground for Shareware authors who want to gauge the market for their products, so I asked noted husband and wife author team Brad and Deb Schepp about downloading from CIS. The Schepps' book, *The Complete Guide to CompuServe,* is also from Osborne/McGraw-Hill. Their reply is quoted below.

"There are many advantages to downloading Shareware from CompuServe. One is that the software is certain to be virus-free. The sysops check every file before posting, and on IBMNET, all the files are uploaded by the authors or their representatives. Another reason to go through CompuServe is the tremendous support Shareware users can get there.

"Since Shareware authors upload their own programs to the system, they usually stick around to support the product afterward. That way they're double winners—they're posted on the largest information service in the world, and they get fast, accurate feedback from the marketplace.

"TAPCIS program author Howard Benner is a case in point. He acts as sysop of the Shareware program's support forum. Benner says his program, which automates the use of CompuServe, would never have the number of international users it does without the TAPCIS forum. Thanks to the forum, he's able to provide support 24 hours a day, every day of the year—something that many users have said they appreciate. Consider the alternatives for an international user—mail support takes too long, and telephone support is prohibitively expensive. Benner says they need online support every bit as much as they need an automated program to keep costs down.

"Knowing that the author can be contacted if there's a problem does a lot to increase the user's comfort. In addition, an online message is usually much less expensive than a phone call. As for authors, especially in the case of some startup operations, they may be holding down another job (or two) and are not always available by phone."

For a complete tour of CompuServe, be sure to look for Brad and Deb Schepp's book, which will be published in September 1990.

Note: With regret, we note that Howard Benner passed away in June 1990.

IBMNET sysop Don Watkins likes dealing with ASP members, and it's easy to understand why. While ASP software is not in any way guaranteed or rated, Watkins says he has no need to ferret out crippled programs when the files come from ASP members. The ASP also has an ombudsman on CompuServe to resolve disputes between users and vendors. Watkins says the ombudsman has not had to step in yet, but it's good knowing the ombudsman is there.

Free Reference Material: GO PRACTICE

If you're new to CompuServe, the first place to visit is the Free Practice forum. Enter **GO PRACTICE** at any prompt. It's a normal forum in all respects, with all the universal areas including a file library—but CompuServe doesn't charge you a dime for the time you spend there. The file library contains a wealth of help files, all designed to help you speed your way around the system.

The first item on any forum's Main Menu is "Instructions," and the documents kept there are worth reading, but they're the same in all forums. So go to the Free Practice forum for them. You'll find excellent material on how best to use any CompuServe forum in the Free Practice Forum. The Instructions menu in the Free Practice Forum is shown here:

```
The Free Practice Forum Instructions Menu

Instructions are available for:
 1 Overview
 2 Messages
 3 Libraries
 4 Conferencing
 5 Announcements
 6 Member directory
 7 Options
 8 Miscellaneous
 9 Complete HELP facility
10 Forum Reference Card
11 Forum User's Guide
```

You can't go wrong for the price, and three entries in particular are worth capturing to disk and printing out. They are the Complete HELP facility, the Forum Reference Card, and the Forum User's Guide. Armed with these three documents, you'll be able to get around and do pretty much anything you need to while in the various IBMNET forums.

Accessing a Forum

To go anywhere on CompuServe, you enter a one-word destination preceded by the word "GO." To get started with IBM forums, for example, you enter **GO IBMNET.** Figure 4-6 shows you the IBMNET menu.

Select option 2, "Top 10 Help Files," from the IBMNET menu and read number 2, LIB.HLP, and number 11, DOWN.HLP. These files tell you everything you need to know to find the file you want, with little or no wasted time. They also tell you how to start with no file transfer protocol on your machine. They explain how to read but not download a BASIC program called MAKCIS.BAS (in the IBMNEW Forum—see below), and run it to create a program you can use to download a fancier program. That's what used to be known as a bootstrap operation!

Other tricks abound in the help files, so if you're not absolutely sure of what you're doing, take time to capture these files to disk, and then print them out and read them. You'll save a lot of frustration, confusion, and wasted time. And time is money, especially when you're online.

Figure 4-6

The IBMNET main forum menu

```
CompuServe              IBMNET

 1 Overview/Survey/Suggestion Box
 2 Top 10 Help Files

 3 New User's/Fun Forum
 4 Hardware Forum
 5 Software Applications Forum
 6 Systems/Utilities Forum
 7 Programming Forum
 8 Communications Forum
 9 Bulletin Board Forum
10 PC Vendor A Forum
11 PC Vendor B Forum

Enter choice or <CR> for more !

12 File Finder
13 IBM PC Junior Forum
14 PC Expert/IBM Message Threads
15 IBM European Users Forum
16 IBM/Special Needs Forum

Last page, enter choice !
```

Sign On and Say Hello

When you select a forum for the first time, you'll get a menu offering information about membership, the forum administrators, announcements, and late-breaking news. The entry to join a forum is always option 8. Since the IBMNET forums cost nothing extra, press 8, which gets you to the menu for the forum. The opening menu for the IBMNEW Forum is shown in Figure 4-7.

At this point, it's good manners to select number 2, "Messages," and leave a short message (including your ID number) for the sysop. In most instances, sysops have special help files and will be more than happy to lead you to them. At $12.50 per hour, anything that saves time is a bonus. The sysops know this and will help all they can—but first you have to tell them you're there and want the help.

Navigation Aids

Once you know your way around, you can decide whether to do without the menu system. Many longtime CompuServe users never switch out of the menu system, because it works well and they're used to it.

Figure 4-7

IBMNET Forum menu

```
IBM New Users Forum Menu

 1 INSTRUCTIONS

 2 MESSAGES
 3 LIBRARIES (Files)
 4 CONFERENCING (0 participating)

 5 ANNOUNCEMENTS from sysop
 6 MEMBER directory
 7 OPTIONS for this forum

Enter choice !
```

`ANSI   ONLINE  38400 8N1  [Home]=Menu   FDX 0 LF X J F CP LG  PR 00:02:21`

However, just as GEnie has Aladdin to make life easier for users, there are three separate systems for navigating around CompuServe. That's not counting the in-house telecommunications program, Professional Connection III, which has graduated from a clunky, patchwork program to one of considerable power. All these programs are *tweaked* (tested and reprogrammed so they work with maximum efficiency on CompuServe). If you expect to spend much time in CompuServe, you could benefit by using one of them.

The programs described below can ease your use of this huge system. The first two, AutoSIG and TAPCIS, can fully automate your sessions. The program signs on, scans the forums or other areas you tell it to, and signs back off without a moment lost. You can then read your mail, compose replies, and decide what files to download and which news items to read. With that done, you send the autopilot program back onto the network, where it does your bidding at maximum speed. There's never a pause or a miskeyed word; you took care of the time-consuming tasks offline. Less time equals less cost.

AutoSIG

This venerable CompuServe navigation program has the distinction of being not only one of the oldest network autopilots but also free. It's a product by a well-known program author, Vern Buerg. It lacks bells and whistles and fancy screens. If you only sign on to CompuServe every third week or so, you'll hardly need it. But AutoSIG has its own forum, with a lot of scripts already prepared by its enthusiasts. The AutoSIG Forum abounds with tips on using the system to the best advantage. To get this program, enter **GO AUTOSIG** from any prompt. Then join in, and examine AutoSIG's file library.

TAPCIS

TAPCIS, which is fancier than AutoSIG, is available as Shareware. Like AutoSIG, TAPCIS has its own support forum with technical support provided year-round. Registration is $79 and includes a 182-page manual, a $15 online usage credit, and an unconditional 90-day guarantee of satisfaction.

TAPCIS is a good, strong program, with a somewhat "techie" feel. Installing it takes some time because you have to specify exactly what you want it to do, and CompuServe gives you a lot of choices. If you're a regular visitor, however, TAPCIS is worth having. It'll pay for itself very quickly. You'll know it because TAPCIS even keeps track of your current month's CompuServe bill. Enter a dollar sign and it'll tell you how far over or under budget you are. TAPCIS is so automated you can let it run unattended for long, late-night downloads if you trust your area's phone system. The number for placing credit card orders is 800-USA-GROUP.

CompuServe Information Manager (CIM)

Released in 1990, CompuServe Informaion Manager (CIM) has much promise. It does many of the same things as AutoSIG and TAPCIS, but without full automation. Instead, CIM (pronounced "sim") is designed as an easy front-end for users who are not very sophisticated about the system.

CIM lets you create a menu of "favorite places." You select destinations by using a mouse and a pull-down menu. CIM maintains your electronic address book, follows message threads, and does many other session chores without much effort. CIM even gives you a graphic "tree" of message threads. You can follow the branches with your cursor and click a mouse button to tell CIM which messages to read.

CIM is quite elegant, although there are some problems. Early users complain that the program seems jerky and slow. The reason for this is that CIM trades data with CompuServe in binary packets, like a file transfer protocol, instead of in a steady ASCII stream. The packet-by-packet approach makes CIM twitch a bit, visually. CompuServe technical reps claim, however, that timing tests show CIM to be as fast as a "normal" telecommunications program.

CIM takes a novel approach to interacting with the service. As modems become faster and information technology improves, CIM could easily become the standard others will try to imitate. At this writing, it costs $24.95 and includes a $15 usage credit. The net cost of $9.95 might make the program worth getting just to try it. (But be aware that it's like paying to be a beta tester and bug reporter!) CIM is available by typing **GO ORDER** at any prompt.

The IBMNET Libraries: Software Treasure for the Taking

The IBMNET forums are a real treasure trove for users of DOS-based computers. Each forum has its own set of libraries, many of them huge. To make navigating a little easier, they are broken into smaller chunks by area of interest. Because it's first on the list, we'll show the libraries in the IBMNEW Forum below. To get this listing, select option 3, "Libraries (Files)" from the forum's Main Menu to get the Libraries menu, shown in Figure 4-8.

There are so many libraries just in the main IBMNET forums that they're best seen in a chart. Later in this chapter, I'll summarize the libraries in each of the different IBMNET forums. You'll then have an idea of where files are located. There's considerable file overlap, especially with programs like LIST.COM and PKZIP, which have no single home. Sometimes, one library's file version will be older than another's. It pays to explore a bit.

Catalog of ASP Programs

A catalog listing of ASP programs is available, if you're looking for Shareware. ASP members make hundreds of Shareware programs available on CompuServe, and they're all listed in the file CATLOG.ARC in Library 8 of the IBM Applications Forum.

Updated monthly, the CATLOG.ARC includes the CompuServe filename, the cost for registering the program, the forum and library location where you'll find the latest version, and a brief description of the program. Each file includes the CompuServe ID for the person (usually the

---

Figure 4-8

The IBMNEW Library menu

```
IBM New Users Forum Libraries Menu

Libraries Available:
 0 New Uploads [N]
 1 Download Help [N]
 2 Library Tools [N]
 3 Adventures [N]
 4 Music [N]
 5 Fun Graphics [N]
 6 Gen Fun & Games [N]
 7 Ask the Sysops [N]
 8 Village Inn [N]
 9 Sports/Chance [N]

Enter choice !
```

author) who uploaded the file. If you're looking for the best in professional Shareware programs, CATLOG.ARC may well be CompuServe's most valuable single resource for you.

Browsing for Summary Files

In every library with a New Uploads section, you can find a summary file with one-line descriptions of every file in the forum. This list is updated monthly but can be kept up-to-date after the first time you download it by downloading only the changes. The navigation aids mentioned earlier will help you update the last summary list by incorporating the new monthly information into your file.

All new files are held in Library 0 for their first 30 days prior to being assigned to their topical libraries. This assists you in finding the latest and best programs without going through multiple libraries. However, these files haven't all been tested by the sysops. There may be problems with them; there may even be rogue programs. It's best to use Library 0 only to download the summary file for the rest of the libraries. Let the rest of them "age."

To find the summary file, select Library 0 and then select BROWSE. When you are prompted for a keyword, type **SUMMARY.** Most such summary files are compressed and require a protocol, but if the file extension is .DES, you can simply READ the file and capture it to disk. Here is the report as captured in early 1990, for the IBM Applications Forum. The file was found by selecting option 3, "Libraries," then Library option 0, "New Uploads," and finally the word BROWSE. The specified keyword was "summary:"

```
[76702,1102]
APPSUM.ZIP/binary       01-Feb-90 57366        Accesses: 412
Title   : summary catalog of all files in IBMAPP
Keywords: LIBRARY DIRECTORY SUMMARY BRIEF DESCRIPTIONS COMBINED
One-line descriptions of files in Libs 1-8,10-13 as of Feb 1,
1990. Updates (including separate change file) are prepared
approximately monthly.  If you want all the summaries, you may
find it easier to download this file.  If you only want some of
the summaries, you can download files APxxxx.DES in your favorite
Libs.  This binary file must be downloaded with a protocol.
```

Using a keyword with the BROWSE option is a much faster way to find out what files a library holds than trying to look through them one by one, or recording a directory listing and trying to figure out what the cryptic six-letter CompuServe filenames mean.

A summary file with a .THD extension indicates a message THreaD from the bulletin board—a series of notes and replies—that the sysop thought interesting enough to put in the library for users who missed it the first time. The MY entries indicate the month and year a file was uploaded. For example, 98 is September 1988, D9 is December 1989, and so forth. With a little practice, you'll get used to it. As you can see, it would be easy to go broke, browsing among such riches!

Libraries in the IBMNET Forums

IBMNET consists of several subgroupings. Each is an individual area that you can visit. For your reference, the forums directly under IBMNET are

IBMAPP	IBM Applications
IBMBBS	IBM Bulletin Board
IBMCOM	IBM Communications
IBMHW	IBM Hardware
IBMNEW	IBM New Users
IBMPRO	IBM Programming
IBMSPC	IBM Special Needs
IBMSYS	IBM Sys/Utilities
IBMJR	IBM PC jr

Each of the forums can be reached by typing **GO** followed by the abbreviation for the forum you want. For example, if you wanted to go to the IBM Communications Forum, you would enter at the prompt (the prompt is !):

```
!GO IBMCOM
```

Each of these forums contains different kinds of files. Figure 4-9 shows you the file library listings for IBMAPP, IBMCOM, and IBMSPECIAL.

As you can see, IBMAPP contains applications programs. This is where you would go to find text editors, .GIF file viewers, business applications,

Figure 4-9

Library contents of IBMAPP, IBMCOM, and IBMSPC

IBM Applications	IBM Communications	IBM/Special Needs
0 New Uploads	0 New Uploads	1 General Information
1 Text Editors	1 AutoSig	2 Software
2 Word Processing [A]	2 Comm Util	3 Hardware
3 DBMS [A]	3 Comm	4 Special Needs
4 Personal Acct [A]	4 FAX [C]	5 Parents
5 Business Acct [A]	5 Ask the	6 Teacher Talk
6 Business Apps [A]	6 Hot Topics	7 Admin. Net
7 Gen. Apps [A]	7 Modems/Comm Hdw	8 Developers
8 Demos [A]	8 Village Inn	9 Beginner's Corner
9 Hot Topic [A]	9 Script/Nav Pgms	10 IBM Bits & Bytes
10 Graphics [A]	10 Protocols	11 Conferences
11 Education [A]	11 Local Area Nets	12 Dealer Talk
12 Desktop Pub [A]		13 Recreation & Games
13 Tech/Engr/Sci [A]		14 Bilingual Tech
		15 Kid to Kid

word processors, and so on. IBMCOM is dedicated to communications. This is where you'd find protocol drivers like DSZ, OZBEXT, and others. You'd also look in IBMCOM for the latest releases of communications programs and utilities. IBMSPC is a general area, with information for parents, teachers, developers, and beginners. There's a lot of valuable information in here. Figure 4-10 displays the libraries for IBMHW, IBMNEW, and IBMPRO. These figures have been included to save you some time if you decide to go exploring within IBMNET.

The IBMHW area contains files that are specifically related to hardware. IBMNEW has a range of files, and the sysops attempt to keep files that might be of interest to new users. IBMPRO is the programmers area, and its libraries specialize in things that are of interest to programmers. If you're interested in programming, this is the spot to visit. Figure 4-11 shows you the IBMBBS, IBMSYS, and IBMJR library listings.

You can find bulletin board-related things in IBMBBS. IBMSYS is where you'll find all of the system utilities, such as DOS utilities, macro programs, desktop organizers, and much more. In IBMJR you'll find a variety of programs, plus the areas for the ASP. Now, let's take a look at some of the other things that are grouped underneath the primary area of IBMNET.

Figure 4-10

The libraries of IBMHW, IBMNEW, and IBMPRO

IBM Hardware	IBM New Users	IBM Programming
0 New Uploads [H]	0 New Uploads [N]	0 New Uploads
1 Disk/Disk Utils [H]	1 Download Help [N]	1 Assembler
2 Printer Utils [H]	2 Library Tools [N]	2 OS Services
3 Video [H]	3 Adventures [N]	3 C [P]
4 Gen. Hardware [H]	4 Music [N]	4 BASIC [P]
5 PC-AT [H]	5 Fun Graphics [N]	5 Other Languages
6 Laptops [H]	6 Gen Fun & Games [N]	6 Debugging/Tools
7 Compatibles [H]	7 Ask the Sysops [N]	7 DBMS Dev.
8 Classifieds [H]	8 Village Inn [N]	8 Demos [P]
9 PS/2 [H]	9 Sports/Chance [N]	9 Job Exchange
10 Mainframe HW/SW [H]		10 DataCompression [P]
		11 APL [P]

Figure 4-11

The IBMBBS, IBMSYS, and IBMJR libraries

IBM Bulletin BOard	IBM Sys/Utilities	IBM PC Junior
0 New Uploads	0 New Uploads [S]	0 General Info
1 BBS Programs	1 DOS Utilities [S]	1 Software
2 BBS Utilities [B]	2 OS/2 Utilities [S]	2 Hardware
3 BBS Doors [B]	3 General Utils [S]	3 Tips&Techniques[J]
4 BBS Management [B]	4 Multitasking [S]	4 Communications [J]
5 Standards [B]	5 DOS Shells/Mgrs [S]	5 Entertainment [J]
6 BBS Hardware [B]	6 File Utilities [S]	6 Graphics [J]
7 BBS Listings [B]	7 Desktop Utils [S]	7 Sysop's Desk [J]
8 BBS Notices [B]	8 Demos [S]	8 ASP Program Info
	9 Hot Topic [S]	9 Potential Authors

Other IBMNET Resources

No description of CompuServe's library resources would be complete without a tip of the hat to vendors and others who support users through forums here. If you go to these areas, you'll see more selections listed online than are shown in this book. The areas not shown here are restricted for beta testing and the like. You can try to select them, but you won't get in.

Vendors A and B Forums

The list of vendors who provide support for their products through CompuServe is long one. The original Vendors forum proved so popular that the network added a second one. As vendors get bigger, they often split off into their own forums; so the Vendors A and B forums tend to change from month to month. Vendors who used the A and B forums in IBMNET to support their products early in 1990 are listed below. Type **GO PCVENA** or **GO PCVENB** and choose option 3, "Libraries," to get an updated list:

```
PC Vendor A Forum Libraries      PC Vendor B Forum Libraries
1 ButtonWare                     1 Quarterdeck
2 Mansfield Software             2 Primavera Systems
3 Enable Software               3 Korenthal Assocs.
4 Broderbund                     4 Personics Corp.
5 TOPS                           5 Quicksoft
6 Magee Enterprises              6 TurboPower Software
7 Custom Technologies            7 ChipSoft, Inc.
8 Knowledge Garden               8 DacEasy
9 Mustang Software               9 Vestronix
10 Toshiba Laptops              11 PDC Prolog
11 MathSoft
12 Foresight Corp.
```

PC Expert

The PC Expert section is a huge database of commonly asked questions and their answers. You might check this section if you're having problems, and not only for problems with CompuServe. They cover hard disk problems, memory chips, and dozens of other areas. CompuServe has so many users there's a very good chance that, if a few people have had the same problem, you'll find the solution in this area. It's also a great place just for browsing, to broaden your knowledge about computers. To access the PC Expert section, type **GO PCE**.

IBM File Finder

IBM File Finder is not to be confused with this author, but it has a similar mission—to help you find the file you need in any of several dozen DOS file libraries. The search is not limited to IBMNET forum libraries, which is a plus. IBM File Finder is always a very good place to start looking, if you're not exactly sure where to find something you need. You may want to note that keyword searches will only be successful if the keywords you use are very specific—so think carefully about the keywords that you want to use for searching.

If you want the very latest version of LIST, for example, File Finder will list the many versions that are available on CompuServe at any given time, together with their locations. If your query turns up too many "hits," you can narrow the search by changing your criteria. You can search by topic, file submission date, forum name, file type, file extension, filename, or the uploader's user ID.

At the time of this writing, IBM File Finder can search for files in the following forums:

Ashton Tate	Lotus Spreadsheets
IBM Applications	IBM Hardware
Borland Programming A	Borland Programming B
IBM Communications	IBM New Users
Lotus Stand-Alone	Microsoft Applications
IBM Programming	IBM Systems
WordPerfect Support Group A	Microsoft Systems
Borland Applications	Crosstalk
IBM PC jr	IBM Bulletin Board
WordPerfect Support Group B	Novell A Forum

PCMAGNET: PC Magazine Jumps In

As if their own libraries weren't profuse enough, CompuServe also administers the online libraries of *PC Magazine,* a publication much read by technically oriented computer users. *PC Magazine* publishes wonderful little utility programs each month and makes them available through CompuServe's computers. Just enter **GO PCMAGNET** and you'll "gateway" right inside.

PCMAGNET offers the complete set of *PC Magazine* utilities, dating back to 1985. If you choose the forums rather than the utilities database, you will find more than 30 forum libraries available, based on the CompuServe system, because that's what most users are familiar with. These utilities are fine programs and well worth adding to your collection.

PCMAGNET also offers the utility documentation that some people find more teasing than fulfilling. The reason? When the utilities are published in the magazine, a lot of space is devoted to explaining exactly how each one works, but the online document is from a single half-page summary printed with each article, to be inserted into the reader's DOS manual. They have a disconcerting habit of referring you to the main article just when things get interesting. They are, however, superb utility programs. If you sign on to CompuServe a lot, eventually you'll want to visit PCMAGNET, if only to browse the more than 30 forum libraries available there.

The Ultimate Information Supermarket

Wandering around CompuServe can be a bit like impulse shopping in the biggest supermarket in town. Before you know it, your basket's full, you've gone over budget by several hundred dollars, and the exit's nowhere in sight. A lot of people thrive on it. The advantages are enormous. With a subscriber base of more than 550,000 companies and individuals, it's a good bet that if someone you're trying to reach has an account anywhere, it's with CompuServe. You can ask questions in the middle of the night, go to bed, and wake up to a whole message thread of answers. If you can't find what you want in one library, try another, or another, or another. In short, if there's nothing here for you—you might be the only such person anywhere on The Wires.

Of course, sometimes a tighter focus is required, or you may want a more businesslike approach to information brokering. There are alternatives to both the fastest growing (GEnie) and the biggest (CompuServe) information utilities. These alternatives will be described briefly in the next few pages.

BIX – THE BYTE INFORMATION EXCHANGE

BIX, which stands for the Byte Information Exchange, specializes in online conferencing for business computer users and computer professionals. Like its parent, *BYTE* magazine, BIX has a very technical flavor and is definitely weighted toward users who are knowledgeable (even sophisticated) about computers. If this puts you off, you might want to start with one of the other services described in this chapter.

On the other hand, the BIX listing areas are chock full of files, many of them with source code, organized like GEnie into areas of interest. Since there are no hourly fees other than your local access costs through Tymnet, you can just sign on and download to your heart's content.

DOCTOR'S NOTE

Like the other online services, BIX has its own command set. Some users find it *intuitive,* meaning it's easy to use without a lot of struggle, while others do not. But it is different from the other services. Whether you find the command system easy to use or not, you will most likely want to leave the newcomer's default menus as soon as you can. BIX was originally designed not to use a menu system at all, and the menu system shows it. It helps until you know the system better, but you won't want to stay with it for long.

The best thing to do is wait until your user manual arrives so you don't waste a lot of time stumbling around. BIX sends out the manual within days after you sign up, and it's worth the wait. If you just can't wait, there's a complete manual online. Follow the procedure described in this section to download the section of interest to you. Print it out and study it before signing back on. It will save you lots of time and connect charges in the long run.

The BIX Background

BIX is actually the electronic component of *BYTE* magazine. It was founded in November 1985 by then-Editor-in-Chief, Phil Lemmons, and former Managing News Editor, George Bond. It's really an online conferencing system with a heavy slant toward the print magazine's primary readership, computer-using professionals. Given its focus on computers and the related sciences, BIX has become a gathering place for more than 30,000 hardware and software engineers, system designers, independent consultants, technology buffs, and computer industry celebrities. That makes it a terrific way to access some of the world's greatest experts in any computer field you can think of.

BIX offers what amounts to a global information community, with users logging in from six continents. It's common to find yourself exchanging information with individuals from Australia, Iceland, and anywhere in between. You'll also run into message exchanges in the French and German languages, plus C, LISP, Pascal, ADA, and other computer programming languages.

BIX users, who call themselves "BIXen," have access to such features as private electronic mail with binary file capability, program listings of uploads and downloads, a daily microcomputer industry newswire, an online chat facility, and more than 150 focus areas, called conferences.

Cost: Flat Fee, Not Hourly

BIX is a subscription-based service; there are no hourly usage fees or surprise costs. BIX does not charge a registration fee but has an annual $156 subscription fee, charged in $39 quarterly installments. That's $13 a month, and if you spend a lot of time on The Wires, it quickly turns into a real bargain. If you're just an occasional browser, however, BIX may not be for you. Unlike GEnie and CompuServe, there is no free access network. Signing on via Tymnet costs an additional $2 an hour outside of peak hours, though flat-rate Tymnet accounts are available at $15 a month. If you live in the Boston area, dialing into BIX is cheaper—BIX has direct-dial numbers that handle speeds up to 9600 baud, free of any extra charges. In Boston, even if you spend only one to two hours a month online to BIX, you're getting a real bargain.

How to Register and Log On

Register for BIX online, not through the mail. Holders of American Express, MasterCard, or VISA credit cards can register and use BIX immediately. Prepayment and invoiced accounts are also available. There is no registration fee.

BIX is accessible from within the United States, some of its territories and possessions, and major Canadian cities through local Tymnet numbers. If you don't know the number for your area, call Tymnet at 800-336-0149. A computerized voice mail system will lead you to the nearest Tymnet access number. For direct access in the Boston area or by PC Pursuit, use your modem to call 617-861-9767 and enter the word **BIX** at the opening prompt. For more information, call the BIX Customer Service Line at 1-800-227-2983 between 8:30 A.M. and 11 P.M. EST on weekdays. In New Hampshire and outside the U.S. or Canada, call 603-924-7681.

Signing On to BIX

As a new BIXen, you are defaulted into a menu mode, which tides you over until your two BIX user manuals arrive. One BIX manual explains menus; the other covers the command interface. The menu manual comes with a disk-based tutorial. The manuals, included free with your membership, are mailed within days of registration. You can also download the manual directly, if you're in a hurry. Do get the manual; without it, you'll quickly feel hopelessly lost.

Most BIXen get their BIX bearings using menus but soon change to the command interface. The menu system will seem slow to you, once you get the hang of it. For beginners, however, it's a real blessing not to be confronted with the lonely command prompt, which used to be your only greeting. If the menus aren't enough, you can get help at any system prompt by entering ?; or you can send BIXmail to "helper" and get a very fast response.

The Main Menu

The Main Menu that you see at logon has three primary areas: electronic mail, conferences, and listings. Other areas, such as CBix, are there just to support your BIX habit. For downloading files, you'll be interested in "Listings," option 3. The BIX Main Menu is shown in Figure 4-12.

First, you need to look at what most BBSs call your profile—the protocol you want to use, how many lines on your screen between pauses, and so on. To set these variables, choose "Individual Options," option 7 on the Main Menu. It will present you with a list of choices, such as screen length.

Figure 4-12

The BIX Main Menu

```
BIX Main Menu

 1  Electronic Mail
 2  Conference Subsystem
 3  Listings
 4  CBix
 5  MicroBytes - Industry News Briefs
 6  Subscriber Information
 7  Individual Options
 8  Quick Download
 9  Command Mode (abandon menus)
10  Logoff (bye)

Enter a menu option or ? for help:
```

If you set your screen length to 0, you'll get rid of those annoying ".More.." prompts, but until you get used to the listings area, it's better to put up with them. They give you an opportunity to back out of whatever you're doing, whether it's a long file listing or a long message.

If you want to stop what you're doing, simply type in the word **No** or the letter **Q** at any prompt including ".More..," and you'll be sent right back to the previous menu.

The BIX Manual—Online in USER.MANUAL

Unless you've received your manual already, the first thing to do on BIX is to join the conference called USER.MANUAL. When you see a listing of topics, read the message called "CONTENTS" to see what's available. Then capture the chapters that interest you to disk, print them out, and read. It's worth the study, because BIX can get pretty confusing without a road map.

USER.MANUAL also has a topic called "Listings," where you can download BIXDEMO.ARC to get an offline BIX tutorial. Download it using one of the available protocols. If you have trouble, select OPTIONS in the "Listings" area and change to another protocol. Both the online manual and the BIXDEMO.ARC tutorial are BIX's way of making life a little easier on the beginner. Take advantage of their thoughtfulness.

The BIX Listings Subsystem

The BIX Listings subsystem is where you find files and programs for downloading. It consists of a general area and conference-specific areas. You can download files from, or upload files to, most areas. When you upload, your time on the system is free because you're contributing to the system, although Tymnet access charges will still apply.

In the BIX Listings you'll find source code for most *BYTE* articles, beginning with September 1984. There is also a wide assortment of public domain and Shareware files. There are separate divisions for specific brands of computers, language types, operating systems, and areas of interest. Sub-areas contain files for applications, leisure, and utilities.

Listing the Files
To get a list of all the files in your selected area, enter the command **LIST ALL.** To search for a file, enter the command **LIST NAME**, followed by as much of the name as you know. The LIST NAME command can incorporate the wildcards * and ?.

Listing from Sub-Areas
To see a list of sub-areas within a main Listings area, use the Sub-area option 2 command. When it prompts for a sub-area name, type ? to see a list scroll down the screen. When the list ends, BIX will prompt you again for a sub-area name; type the name you want. Incidentally, if programming is one of your interests, you can find a huge amount of source code in these *BYTE* issue Listing areas. There's no better way to learn than by looking at other programmers' source code for programs that work.

Listing from a Specific Conference
From the Main Menu, select option 2. This will give you a list of machine-specific conferences. Enter the name of the conference where you want to go, and then select the Listings area. Once there, you can choose option 1

to select a particular file area, or type **?** for a list of various file areas in that conference. They're organized by technical area, function, machine, interest area, and so forth.

For example, in the IBM.PC conference, you'll find file areas on IBM AT, DOS, PC, OS/2, and Utilities. If you're looking for a specific file, take a look at all available areas by picking sub-areas, and then take a guess at where your file might be. If you want to return to the BIX Main Menu from any prompt on BIX, you can enter **MM**.

Getting Help

If you're really stuck and haven't yet received your user's manual, read the online manual in the USER.MANUAL conference. (Type **JOIN USER .MANUAL DIGEST** for a table of contents.)

For immediate questions, you'll be better off using the online help files. Simply type **HELP** plus the name of the command to get general help on that topic. The command, HELP, or ? by itself will give you a list of options. If you don't know what to ask, you can enter **HELP HFILES** for a list of commands for which help is available.

Finally, for a listing of BIX commands and subcommands, type **HELP COMMANDS.** If you can't find your answers online or in the user manual, and you've already taken the Learn conference tutorial, drop a mail note to "helper." Someone from BIX will reply within the next day or so.

BYTE Information Exchange (BIX)
One Phoenix Mill Lane
Peterborough, NH 03458-9990

603-924-9281
800-227-1983 (Customer Service, U.S. and Canada)
603-924-7681 (New Hampshire, outside continental U.S.)

DELPHI—SHAREWARE AND MORE

Delphi offers an online alternative developed along the lines of a community. Delphi's members, who select their own user names, freely communicate among themselves while online. Human interaction makes the experience enjoyable, while Delphi's array of services makes it worthwhile. Services include

- Databases of downloadable software (both Shareware and freeware) for nearly all types of computers

- Electronic mail, conference, and public messaging

- Business news, investment advice, and commodity and stock quotes

- Multi-player games with tournaments and prizes

- Newswires, encyclopedias, and other reference resources

- Travel information and reservations and shopping services

Delphi Index

From the Main Menu, you can read the Delphi Index (shown partially, below). This feature gives you the mnemonic for reaching any area on the system. The index for the letter "P" is shown because it contains GR PC, a short form for the PC Compatibles/IBM SIG. Once you get used to the way Delphi works, you won't have to use anything but the short form to reach your favorite places. The mnemonics also let you get anywhere in the system using automatic scripts.

```
TRAV PARS - PARS TravelShopper
USING SET - Password change
USING PAST - Past Bills
GR PC - PC Compatibles Group
PEOPLE - People Profiles
LIB PERS - Personal Advisor
ENT PERS - Person to Person SIG
ENT POK - Poker Showdown (Multi-Player Game)
NEWS UPI - Political News
GR PORT - Portable Place SIG
USING PRE - Premium Services (listings and rates)
BUS PRESS - Press Releases: BusinessWire
BUS NEWS - Prime/Mortgage Rates
PEOPLE - Profiles
USING SET - Prompt modes
```

Groups and Clubs: A Home for Shareware

To find most of the Delphi Shareware, start from the Groups and Clubs menu, reached directly from Delphi's Main Menu. Like most Main Menu items, two letters are enough to specify the desired item. To reach the Groups and Clubs menu, enter **GR**.

```
GROUPS and CLUBS Menu:

Amiga SIG                OS9 On-Line
Atari SIG                PC Compatibles/IBM
Apple ][ & ///           Portable Place
Aviation SIG             Science Fiction Sig
Business Forum           ST-Log
Close Encounters         Tandy PC SIG
Color Computer           TI Intl Users Net
Commodore SIGs           Theological Network
C*SIX                    ViP - Video & Photo
GameSig                  Wang Users SIG
Hobby Shop               Writers Group
Macintosh ICONtact       HELP
Micro Art - MANIAC       EXIT
Music City
```

The PC Compatibles/IBM SIG Database

From the Main Menu, enter **GR PC** to get to the PC Compatibles/IBM SIG. Delphi will give you a menu of available areas, shown here.

```
Menu of Available Areas

Announcements          PCM Magazine Services
Conference             Topic Descriptions
Databases              Who's Here
Entry Log              Workspace
Forum (Messages)       Help
MAIL (Electronic)      Exit
Member Directory       Classified Ads
Poll                   Questions & Feedback
Set Preferences        Tandy SIG PORTAL
```

If you now enter **DATA**, the system will show you a menu of databases available:

```
Databases Available Menu:

General Information    Utilities
Archives               Demo Programs
Business               Soft Sector Magazine ($)
Education              PCM Magazine ($)
Home & Games           Tandy Specific
Programming            Sanyo Specific
Telecommunications     IBM PC Specific
```

Directory of Software

You can now see which entries are available to download by entering **DIR**, which will display files in most-recently-added order. However, since the database topics have many software entries, it is usually a good idea to use the SEARCH command before typing DIR. This limits the selection. After you type SEARCH, you will be asked to supply a keyword. If you don't know which keyword to use, enter two question marks, pressing ENTER after each question mark.

The first ? will display generic help information. The second will display a list of available keywords and the number of entries each keyword will select. Showing you the number of entries for each keyword is a great enhancement because it lets you "look before you leap." Touches like that are common on Delphi, which is one of the most user-friendly of the information services.

Once you've entered a keyword, type **DIR** and you will see a listing of available entries. Following is a sample listing, which shows some of the games that are available.

```
PC Compatibles Partial Games Listing


SWAMPKILLER EVERGLADE SIMULATION      PROG    29-FEB-1990
GAMANIAC
SPACE DODGER - VERSION 3000           PROG    28-FEB-1990
SRIDE23
CHESS ABC                             PROG    28-FEB-1990
BFISCHER
```

```
CARDSHARKSTER POKER              PROG    24-FEB-1990
AMARILLOS
GAME COMPOSING HINTS             TEXT    21-FEB-1990
GAMANIAC
PCPOLO                           PROG    19-FEB-1990
RALPHL
```

Reading More Information on Files

To find out more about one of the entries, use the READ command. It will tell you the kind of files in the entry, the size, and whether or not it's Shareware, and it will give you some explanatory or descriptive information. For example, if you are interested in chess, you could type **READ CHESS**.

Descriptions can take up an entire screen and provide very extensive information about what you're considering downloading. They can save you a lot of wasted download time—another example of Delphi's good manners and consideration.

Downloading Your Selection

If you want an item, simply type **DOWNLOAD**. Delphi will ask which transfer method you wish to use, Xmodem, Windowed Xmodem, Ymodem, Ymodem Batch, or Kermit. Of these, Ymodem or Ymodem Batch will perform best. To make the download as short and inexpensive as

---

DOCTOR'S NOTE

In Chapter 5 you'll be taking a good look at compressed files and the different kinds of file compression utilities that are available. In that chapter, you will learn about the controversy over the ARC format, developed by System Enhancement Associates, and the ZIP format, developed by PKWARE. It is interesting to note that Delphi users have taken steps so that they can voice their opinion on this issue. In a continuing poll since April 1989, Delphi users have voted roughly 88 to 12 percent in favor of using Phil Katz's ZIP compression rather than System Enhancement Associates' ARC format. When you vote in a Delphi poll you're invited to comment, and the

DOCTOR'S NOTE *(continued)*

comments in the ZIP versus ARC poll are revealing—Delphi users (like BBS users) don't pull any punches when they express their opinions. The Delphi ZIP versus ARC poll is an example of what I mean when I refer to the "PC community"—everyone has a voice in it.

possible, most files are compressed. Delphi uses both ARC and ZIP compression programs, but the required decompression utilities are all available online.

Often, programs consist of more than one file. For example, there may be a program file, a data file, and a documentation file, all separately downloadable. When you use the READ command, if there are multiple files, they will be listed together as a group, each one preceded by a file number. When you type **DOWNLOAD**, simply specify the number of the file you wish to download.

Submitting Files to Delphi

If you write your own Shareware or have some favorite Shareware programs in their original distribution form, you might consider submitting them to Delphi. The time you spend on Delphi submitting software is free, and your Shareware will be available to thousands of people who regularly log on to Delphi.

Putting On the Brakes

If you find yourself in the middle of something that's taking much longer than you expected, either CTRL-O or BREAK can get you through much faster by suspending screen output. In other words, your modem's bps speed limit is suspended, so Delphi can speed through whatever it's doing and return you to the menu.

Delphi's Rates

Delphi charges the same rates for access at 300, 1200, and 2400 bps, so you are not penalized for downloading Shareware at high speed. The prime time connect charge (7 A.M. to 6 P.M. weekdays) is 29 cents a minute ($17.40 an hour). At all other times, the rate is 12 cents a minute ($7.20 an hour).

These rates include access via Tymnet or SprintNet—there is no hourly access charge, as with other services. That puts Delphi among the lowest-cost services in the country. If you plan to use Delphi frequently, it gets even better. You can join Delphi's Advantage Plan (which commits you to $24 of usage per month) and get the lowest rates in the industry: 21 cents a minute ($12.60 an hour) prime time, and 8 cents a minute ($4.80 an hour) non-prime time.

Special Delphi Membership Offer
As a reader of this book, you can join Delphi and save $20. For $29.95, you will receive a lifetime membership, the 300-page book, *Delphi: The Official Guide,* and credit for two evening hours of usage. See the back of this book for instructions.

Delphi
General Videotex Corporation
3 Blackstone Street
Cambridge, MA 02139

617-491-3393
800-544-4005 (Customer Service)
617-491-3393 (Massachusetts and outside continental U.S.)

EXEC-PC—THE BBS THAT GREW AND GREW

EXEC-PC began in 1983 in a Shorewood, Wisconsin basement, when Bob Mahoney found himself spending too much time getting software from other people's BBSs. Mahoney decided to start his own BBS, one with a business software slant. In doing so, he hoped to accomplish two things— provide a distribution point for business-oriented public domain and Shareware programs, and cure his modem addiction. He called it the "Business Knowledge Exchange" when he opened his electronic doors using an IBM PC, a single-line 1200 bps modem, and a whopping 30 megabyte hard disk.

Mahoney already had a superb collection of very useful programs, and he wasn't concerned about "download ratios" and other such judgmental criteria for using his BBS. The word got around faster than anyone could have believed.

How It Grew

Mahoney often found himself straggling into his day job in the morning with only a few hours of sleep. "My boss said to me one morning, 'Bob, you don't look so good,' and I said, 'Yeah, but I've been getting $400 a day in the mail'," Mahoney recalls. Something clicked. He quit his job shortly after that and has never looked back.

One incoming line led to many more, and within a year Mahoney was running the largest BBS in the world, with the biggest DOS software library ever assembled for modem callers. By the end of the third year the Mahoneys had nurtured EXEC-PC into a giant.

In 1989, the Mahoneys moved to an office outside Milwaukee, where by 1990 they were using networked 386s supplied with 600 phone lines in a three-inch-thick cable. With three and a half tons of air conditioning equipment to manage the heat, they could take more than 150 incoming calls at once (scheduled to increase to 300 by mid-1991). Their file transfer rates went as high as 19,200 bps.

Mahoney reports that his winter home heating bills have gone up 30 percent since EXEC-PC removed the electronic heat sources from his home's basement. But at least the lights don't dim anymore, and the power lines across their yard don't buzz and hum into their sleep at night the way they used to.

There's a History in the Files

Mahoney and his wife still consider EXEC-PC a BBS, but to many it seems more like a private national archive for software and PC history. EXEC-PC holds more than 70,000 public domain and Shareware titles. Many prominent software authors use EXEC-PC as their central distribution outlet, so new versions of popular programs often appear here first. If you're interested in PC history, you can come here for original source material. Text files from bygone days divulge rumors of a hush-hush IBM machine under development code-named "Peanut" (it eventually became the ill-fated PCjr). Subscribers gossiped about pending IBM XT and AT machines and about scheduled new releases of DOS. They speculated on future directions in operating systems, netware, and product upgrades—you name it. The Mahoneys don't delete such material; they just add more storage.

Want a stroll down Computer History Lane? It's all on EXEC-PC, still going, still growing. It's what has made The Mahoney Collection justly famed for its quality and size.

A Comfortable Place to Call

Despite its size and stature, EXEC-PC maintains a comfortable BBS feeling. Bob Mahoney is chief librarian, and he likes the BBS flavor. That's how he ran the mini-online service in his basement and people liked it—no sense in changing it. Tracey Mahoney, a former interior designer, now handles bookkeeping and administrative chores. There are no other employees, and you'd better believe it's a full-time job for both Mahoneys. But they insist on keeping EXEC-PC a personal project, refusing to let it bloat into a mega-corporation. The Mahoneys want their customers to be able to reach them personally when they need them.

Using EXEC-PC

When you log on to EXEC-PC you'll find simple menus. They're layered logically, unlike some online services. You can turn off the menus with a simple command when you become familiar with the system. Then you can issue multiple commands on a single command line, which saves much online time. And help is always available by typing ?. An excellent online tutorial is also available.

EXEC-PC is designed for people interested in software uploads and downloads. For $60 a year, you get seven hours a week to download all the software you can handle, with no download ratio or other restrictions. Users download more than 200,000 files a month, calling from as far away as Iran, Greece, Uganda, Hong Kong, the Soviet Union, and 31 other countries. The system is a mother lode of quality software, so it's not surprising that foreign visitors find it worth the expense to come here and browse.

Software Libraries

EXEC-PC has seven hefty software libraries. The Free Collection is available to anyone; you don't have to be an EXEC-PC subscriber to download.

The Free Collection has telecommunications utilities and various text files. Other libraries feature software for the Macintosh, Amiga, Atari ST, and UNIX/XENIX computers.

The Mahoney Software Collection and the PC-SIG Collection are the stars of the show. The Mahoney Collection houses 100,000 software titles, almost all of them uploaded by subscribers and authors. The PC-SIG collection includes some 30,000 popular IBM PC Shareware and public domain programs from the PC-SIG software distributor.

How did the collection grow so fast, with no "free" local access like the net maintained by CompuServe? For one thing, uploads are better than free—they're credited as bonus time on board. When you upload a file, EXEC-PC grants you extra access time at a rate of four to one. Spend ten minutes uploading a program, get forty extra minutes to download other files.

BBS users are no fools. Subscribers post more than a thousand new programs on EXEC-PC each month, at least partly because of the generous upload bonus. (More discussion about downloads and uploads in chapters to come.) The benefits flow in both directions. On a typical day you'll find all kinds of new goodies, enough to make you want to go out and search for something they don't have yet. Find one to upload and you'll have time to download the new ones that you want. EXEC-PC can be wonderfully addictive!

Rogues and Vandals Keep Out

Mahoney has not had much trouble with viruses and other antisocial programs, but he does advise subscribers to wait for new software to "age" a bit before downloading it. With the volume of new software arriving every day, the two-member staff doesn't have time to test it all for booby-traps. If you wait, braver souls can try it and ring the alarms if necessary. Mahoney does test (on a separate computer) any software that looks suspicious, but this is not systematic. On rare occasions when a wolf in sheep's clothing gets in, it's only a matter of days before someone alerts the Mahoneys. The Mahoneys then purge both the software and the uploader from the system.

Finding the Right Program

EXEC-PC's searching and scanning features make it easy to find software. Enter a keyword or phrase such as *database* or *accounting,* and EXEC-PC will scan 10,000 file entries in less than a second, displaying "hits" as it finds them. You can limit the search by age of upload, use *and/or* arguments, or just get a list of files posted since the last time you visited the system. EXEC-PC is centered around those who like to download, especially if your aim is to get in, get on, and get out fast.

To save phone costs, you can download EXEC-PC's complete software directory and use W. Charles Taylor's Maximum Overkill, a sophisticated search program designed especially for the EXEC-PC library lists. Taylor's program is Shareware, and you can download it from the EXEC-PC Free Collection. It's the best way to get started. Once you've located files you want, query the board for a detailed description. Then queue up your selections and download them nonstop using Zmodem, Ymodem Batch, or any batch-download function your telecommunications program supports. You'll find yourself back home with new treasures in no time!

Message Facilities

Early in this chapter we mentioned that if you need network-level access to authors, international users, serious business information, and so forth, you need a network. That pronouncement can now be qualified a bit.

If Bob Mahoney is right and EXEC-PC is just a large bulletin board system, he's broken the "it takes a network" rule. The software library may be the soul of EXEC-PC, but its message section is just as energetic. Public conference topics range from UNIX to OS/2, from Microsoft Windows to computer-aided design (CAD). The participants are likely to be recognized experts in their fields. Many program authors support their programs here. If you have a question dealing with computers, you can ask it on EXEC-PC and get straight answers.

Non-software conferences run the gamut from financial investments to the wacky "Bull Roar and More." You'll find the normal BBS bar stool regulars, including old-timers who reminisce about the days when hard disks made proper crashing sounds when they crashed. Many regulars consider the brittle electronic oasis they call "Bob's Place" as basic to life as their computers and breathing.

EXEC-PC's message system is very easy to use. Full screen menus guide the way but don't interfere when you read or reply to messages. Press a key at any time to see a *conference tree* showing where you are. You can read messages in date order, follow conversations, and mark messages for later retrieval. You can also join and unjoin conferences.

EXEC-PC's ease of use and its many electronic office-oriented features make it popular among business E-mail users. Why? EXEC-PC was business-oriented from the start. Various businesses rent private message and file areas to communicate with customers, clients, or satellite offices. It's another example of how the Mahoneys manage to ignore the distinctions between commercial networks and local, friendly BBSs.

The Road Ahead

EXEC-PC is a "home brew" system. It is not something whose parts can be purchased at a store or ordered through a catalog. All boards, chips, cables, and chassis were hand-wired by the Mahoneys themselves. Tracey Mahoney dropped in 60 megabytes worth of RAM chips and Bob hand-tooled the many custom cables and power harnesses. The basement version of EXEC-PC had a power backup of four golf cart batteries, but the new one uses 12-volt marine batteries supplemented by three standard computer power backup devices. The board has a whopping 6.7 gigabytes of hard disk storage and an additional 1,000 megabytes of CD-ROM storage. It crunches data at a brisk 75 million instructions per second without a belch.

Bob Mahoney's office is down the hall from the bulletin board's *clean room*, where the system's computers are kept in a special environment. Three 80386 PCs adorn his work area and an ARCnet computer network links them to the brains of EXEC-PC and to the PCs on Tracey Mahoney's desk. Bob Mahoney spends at least half of his time answering electronic mail from subscribers. In winter, when the BBS teems with housebound computer addicts, he gets about 150 messages a day from customers and answers them all himself. He balks when people suggest hiring someone to help with the mail. "Answering subscribers' questions directly and helping them with their technical questions is the one personal touch that I will never permit EXEC-PC to lose," Mahoney says.

Tracey Mahoney takes the voice phone calls. She jokes that she is EXEC-PC's sole human interface with the outside world. From her spacious, windowed office she commands bookkeeping and advertising, processes subscriptions, keeps statistics on the online service and customer activity, and conducts market research.

The Mahoneys foresee a day when EXEC-PC will be linked into other electronic messaging networks like USENET and Echomail, but they don't have any definite plans. The system grew by itself in the first place, and the finest art of all is sometimes just to tend the vine and let the growth take care of itself.

EXEC-PC, Inc.
P.O. Box 57
Elm Grove, WI 53122

414-789-4200 (Voice)
414-789-4202 (Data)

(EXEC-PC has 150 phone lines and growing, and uses 300 to 38,400 baud with Level 5 MNP error correction. It is accessible via Starlink, PC Pursuit, and direct dial.)

CHANNEL 1—THE SHAREWARE NETWORK

We've seen how low-cost high-speed modem use has blurred the difference between local and nonlocal data transfer. Local area networks (LANs) and high-speed 386 machines are doing the same thing to distinctions between BBS and networks. By now the difference between the two lies partly in your point of view.

The EXEC-PC is a BBS because Bob and Tracey Mahoney say it is. On the other hand, husband and wife team Brian Miller and Tess Heder of Cambridge, Massachusetts, make no bones about it—their Channel 1 is a network. Channel 1 is a LAN and microcomputer-based interactive information service that does many of the same things as the giant services, but faster and with more flexibility.

Shareware Networking in Practice

The way Miller and Heder have set it up, you sign onto the network as a new user, and after postcard verification, you get a trial membership that lasts three months. If you like it, register your membership and keep coming back. Otherwise, you haven't lost a thing. Now that is a great approach!

Registration gives you access to some nice features including interactive games and some restricted conferences. The trial membership is not the equivalent of crippleware, however, since you have full access to most features. Your trial membership lets you on the system for 26 minutes a day, and you can gain more time by uploading new, quality files.

Uploading also gives you minute-for-minute extra time during that session, and if you don't use it all, you can "deposit" it in an account and draw on it the next time you log on. A nice touch. More neighborhood BBSs should do this.

You can extend your free trial membership if you're either a heavy uploader or program author, or if you partake mostly in the conferences. Even then, if you like the system, since it's a Shareware network, registering will keep the Shareware concept alive and well.

When You First Sign On

Registering your Shareware membership is its own validation, but if you choose a "try it out" membership, the initial sign-on screens will lead you through the simple operation. To get your trial membership, you need to fill out a questionnaire, read a couple of required How It Works-type bulletins, and then be validated by postcard, which is sent out the next day.

While you're on, take time to download the file CHAN1HLP.ZIP, which contains all the Channel 1 help files and command references. You can also go to the Tutor Door and take a helpful, educational tour of the system.

Some Nice Touches

As if starting a fully interactive information utility on a Shareware basis weren't already pretty innovative, Channel 1 has some unusual ways of making your time more productive. One of the best is the F V command. It lets you look into compressed files and read the documents before downloading. This can save time and frustration by giving you all you need to make an informed choice about whether or not to download a program.

The variable-rate membership plan is another Channel 1 grace note. For $20 you get an hour a day for two months, with a 100-file download limit; or for $80 you can get an hour a day for a year, with a 600-file download limit. The higher-ticket memberships come with access via private phone lines, which pretty much guarantees no busy signals. To make things better for members, Channel 1 has different modems running on different lines. Thus, whether you have a U.S. Robotics HST, a Hayes 9600, or a 2400 MNP modem, there is a special line you can call to get the best performance. That kind of thing impresses me because it shows true concern for the members. Miller and Heder don't take a "what you see is what you get" attitude, but go out of their way to provide the very best system possible for all of the people who access Channel 1.

The Shareware Conferences
Channel 1 is the only PC Board system to carry all of the following Echomail systems: RelayNet, InterLink, and SmartNet. It has support conferences for Qmodem, Boyan, QEdit, Telix, PKWARE, Telemate, 4DOS, RoboComm, Qmail, and EZ-READER. It also has support conferences for Shareware and Shareware review. In all, there are over 120 conferences on Channel 1, and that number is going to double in the near future. Conferences are a big part of the online activity on Channel 1, and I'd recommend that you stop by and participate. These conferences are both national and international in scope, so you can just as easily have a question answered by someone in Japan as you can from someone in New Jersey. The scope of the conferences available is staggering. Let's take a look.

Pick a Topic—Any Topic
The conferences on Channel 1 don't just deal with computers, programs, and other computer related topics—not by a long shot. There are conferences on music, chess, cuisine, law, magic, and lots more. I'm so impressed with the list of conferences that are available that I want you to see that list. Here it is:

Help	Small/Home Business
TeX (with files)	Stocks
CAD (with files)	Modems/Telecomm
Amiga (with files)	Politics
Fractals/Chaos	XYWrite
Microsoft (files)	Legal Discussion
Store	Deadheads
ANSI Graphics	Windows
Programs	Robocomm
Around Boston	Cuisine

Relationships	UpLink
Adult (files)	Qmail
Games (DOORs)	Database
Science	DSZ
Grapevine/Jobs	Handicap
Conversations	Qmodem
Online Services	Hayes
Macintosh (files)	C-Language
Desk Top Publishing	Pascal
Teens	QBasic
Software Reviews	AI
Hard Disk	EZ-READER
LAN/Networks	Astronomy
Virus Information	Engineers
Unixnet	Writers
Languages/Programmi	Netusers
Nat'l Amiga	Job Bank
Forum	Religion
Ads	New Age
Popular Music	Astrology
Science Fiction	VGA/EGA
Books	Prodoor
Weather	TPascal
Doors	OS/2
Magick	Boyan
Medical	IBM
MainFrame	WordPerfect
OOPS	Tandy
Relay Feedback	Laptop
Telix	R:Base
USR/HST	1-2-3
PKware	Batch
DESQview	StarTrek
Computer Tech	Music2
Finance	Jokes
Telemate	Shareware
4DOS	Chess
Qedit	Recovery
Space Tech.	Pets
Mozart	Video
Gay Issue	Women
Men	Comics
MIDI	Admin. 1

Take a good look at the list and see if there isn't something that interests you. Conferences such as these are excellent places to share knowledge, ask questions, and just interact with other people with similar interests. You can get help with your computer, but if you like talking about Mozart, there's a conference for that too.

The conferences on Channel 1 are excellent. If you are looking for an inexpensive way to access a wide range of conferences—to gain knowledge or just to express your opinions—consider giving Channel 1 a call and signing up. You'll be getting input from people around the country and around the world. Channel 1 is great forum for the exchange of ideas.

The Files

Channel 1 features 35,000 files in 48 different directories, which are constantly updated. The collection is carefully maintained, and anything you download will be the latest version, not the one that went out of date a month ago. Miller and Heder check every file with the latest version of John McAfee's virus detection program, SCAN. Also, they offer that file as a free download, meaning it doesn't count against your time or file download limits. SCAN is updated frequently as the population of little virus monsters increases, so this is a good way to keep updated. In all, there are over 2.5 gigabytes of files and programs on Channel 1. I think you'll find what you're looking for—and if not, leave me a note and I'll find it for you and upload it.

If you have a large appetite for files and want it all now, you can still take advantage of Channel 1's careful library maintenance. Tape backups of various popular categories are available for $99 each. The tapes are written with a Colorado Memory 40/60 meg (DC2000) backup system using Quarter Inch Cartridge Committee QIC-40 standard format drives.

Note: These tapes are not compatible with Irwin drives, but they are compatible with tape backup systems that use QIC standard formats.

At this writing, the Channel 1 categories available on tape include

- Science and Engineering directory (30 megs)

- C-Language directory (35 megs)

- GIF and Pictures directory (40 megs)

- Education directory (A-L) (28 megs)

- Education directory (M-Z) (26 megs)
- Finance and Business directories (38 megs)
- DOS/System 1 and 2 directories (38 megs)

This list gives you a feel for the size of this carefully quality-controlled library system.

A Great Place to Advertise

If you are a small business owner, a computer consultant, or a freelance programmer, or provide another service, you know the importance of advertising. The problem is that advertising can be very expensive. Channel 1 offers a good alternative. You can advertise on Channel 1 for reasonable rates and reach people around the world. It's a smart investment. After all, reaching people is the whole idea behind advertising. Channel 1 allows you to choose the method of advertising that best suits your needs.

Pick the Plan that Suits You

Channel 1 is a fast-growing videotex and data transfer telecommunications service that is accessed by many people from different walks of life each day. Many of them may be looking for just the service that you offer. On Channel 1 you have the perfect audience. Think about the following facts:

- All callers use a personal computer and a modem
- They represent a targeted audience for your services
- They can find out about your products while they are online
- Most use computers at work and for play at home
- They are prime buyers of computer software, hardware, and other related services
- The average annual household income of PC owners is $54,000

Channel 1 is a very busy place, with over 8,000 regular callers and an average of over 1,200 calls per day! Brian Miller told me that business is growing at a rate of approximately 400 regular callers per month. Channel 1 is a great way to reach a large number of people from around the country and the world, and to do so at reasonable rates. Let's look at the various ways that you can advertise on Channel 1.

Advertising Rates That Are Fair

To better serve a wide variety of advertising needs, Channel 1 offers three types of advertisements—an Ad Bulletin, a Business Card, and a Logoff Message. Following are the rates for each and what each provides.

Ad Bulletins These may be displayed from the main Bulletin menu, which is seen by all new callers and is reviewed by regular callers as well. The minimun size is one full screen and the cost to you is $150 per month for one screen. If you feel that you need more coverage, you can add additional screens for $50 each. A screen contains 23 lines, and each line is 76 characters wide. There is an ASCII (noncolor) and an ANSI (color) version of each ad. You can prepare the screens yourself and upload them to the system, or Channel 1 will prepare your text for you, in both formats.

Business Card Listing Channel 1 also offers a smaller ad that they call a business card. A new bulletin contains business cards for those offering products and services. These might be of particular interest to programmers and consultants. Like the full-screen ads, the business cards are shown in both ASCII and ANSI formats. Each card is eight lines and costs $35 per month. They are a great way to make other callers aware of what you have to offer.

Logoff Advertisement The last type of ad available is called a logoff ad, and it is a notice on the Logoff screen. This type of ad is seen by every caller when they log off. This type of ad might be better suited to a large company or for someone promoting a special event or activity. Since these ads are special in nature, there are only four slots available at any given time. The cost is $750 per month, or you can have one for a week for $200.

    Channel 1's ads offer interesting and beneficial ways of advertising and reaching a large number of people. If this is of interest to you and you have any questions, just leave a Comment to SysOp on the system which will be forwarded to Tess Heder, or you can just leave a regular mail message for her. You can also call voice at 617-864-0741. How do you pay for the ad? Easy. You can pay for it online with VISA, MasterCard, or American Express card by using Script 7, or mail your payment to them.

Note to Non-Bostonians

It may seem extreme to call across country to a LAN-based mini-network for your files. If you have a 300 or 1200 bps modem, you're right. But if you have a high-speed modem, the numbers come out better. (I'll go into detail on costs and charges in some of the next chapters.) This is one network that does not charge you by the hour, by the speed of your modem, or by what you're doing on the system. With cross-country U.S. Sprint rates hovering around 13 cents a minute late at night, if you use a fast modem you could come out well ahead by calling Channel 1 direct instead of logging into a larger network at 2400 baud and $12 an hour. Check your local calling rates if you're interested. AT&T also has its Reach Out America plan. You'll find that it's quite economical. If it looks that way to you too, give Channel 1 a try. The Doc recommends it.

DOCTOR'S NOTE

If you get the idea that I think Channel 1 is an excellent system, you're right! Why do I think so? Because there is something *special* about the place—an atmosphere that makes you feel very comfortable and "at home." I've been on a lot of systems—systems where you are greeted by a list of what I call sysop rules—wherein the sysop demands that you do certain things, or else. Or else what? You can't access their system? I understand the frustrations of being a sysop—I am a sysop, but I also know that no one twisted my arm to put up a system.

Channel 1—with nearly 3 gigabytes of software available, 250 interesting conferences, special offers so you can get files on tape, online newsletters, and much more—demands nothing. The atmosphere is pleasant and warm, the screens are colorful, and you are even greeted by music. There is a simple set of clearcut guidelines for what you *can* do if you would like to become a member of the system. These are the signs of an excellent system and one where people care.

Your sysops and hosts, Brian Miller and Tess Heder, obviously care about what they are doing. Is Channel 1 a network? I guess that depends on

DOCTOR'S NOTE *(continued)*

how you define a network. Do you go by the number of phone lines, the number of callers, or how high the prices are? The term "network" has several different meanings. In general, a network is a group of computers that are hooked together and share things. Well, not only are the computers that make up Channel 1 hooked together and sharing things, but the service that they provide shares things with you. You can go online and download files, upload files, or read the news. To me, Channel 1 is a network and a lot more.

If you have a high-speed modem, you will get more on Channel 1, for every online dollar you spend, than you will anyplace else. Do yourself a favor—check it out!

Channel 1 Communications
P.O. Box 338
Cambridge, MA 02238

617-864-0100
617-354-8873
Separate high-speed access numbers:
617-354-0470 Telebit T2500
617-354-3137 HST 9600/14400
617-354-2505 HST Dual Std. V.32
617-354-6155 Microcom 9600
617-354-5776 Hayes V9600

Channel 1 offers free trial memberships with a 4 to 1 download/upload ratio required. The full registration is $20 to $80, with variable time/download maximums. You can register by modem with VISA, Master-Card, or American Express or by sending a check by mail. A $20 minimum gives you 60 minutes a day for two months with a 100 file download limit. Read their bulletins for other options.

SUMMING UP COMMERCIAL NETWORKS

The big commercial networks like GEnie and CompuServe are excellent places to exchange information, meet new people who are interested in the same things you are, and much more. They offer a vast range of services—from stock prices and airline tickets to online information databases. The conferences on the commercial networks can put you in touch with large numbers of people who may be having the same problems you are—and give you ideas for solutions. Because of all of the things that they have to offer, your online life will not be complete if you don't avail yourself of at least one of the commercial systems.

In discussing the commercial networks, I've had to mention costs, and this was done as a service to you. This is not meant to discourage you from using the online networks. I use them myself daily. Rather, you should be aware of the costs so you can make informed decisions.

In Part Two, you are going to get some tips on how to maximize your time online and save both time and money. There are little tricks that will help you access commercial networks in an efficient manner, so you can get the most out of the money you do spend. The commercial online networks offer a multitude of benefits. You should check them out and take full advantage of them. It's an environment like no other and you will be enriched by the experience.

Keeping these things in mind, let's move on to Part Two and get ready to go online—whether it be to commercial online networks or bulletin boards.

Getting Ready to Operate Online

## CHAPTER FIVE

Online Basics

In Chapter 3 you read about obtaining Shareware programs, and help, from PC user groups. You also learned a bit more about disk vendors and how you can obtain Shareware programs from them. Chapter 4 discussed what is available on some of the larger commercial online networks and what can be found in their file libraries. Over the next several chapters you will become familiar with going *online*. By using your computer, a modem, a communications program, and a phone line, the entire realm of The Wires will open up for you.

In order to take full advantage of user group bulletin boards, commercial online networks, and the estimated 15,000 bulletin boards in the U.S, you need to feel comfortable going online. This chapter will guide you through the basics and the most common problems, gradually getting you up to speed. All of this is designed to help you to save time and money, and also to take away some of the mystique and a mistaken belief that only power users can be good at telecommunications. That just isn't so. People aren't born to be power users; it's something you learn. You, too, can go online with confidence, knowing what to do and how to do it. You'll learn what it takes some users years to figure out for themselves, if ever.

This discussion will start out by talking about compressed files. In general, all of the files that are found on commercial online services or bulletin boards will be compressed in one way or another. Once that subject has been thoroughly covered, you can move on and really get into the online basics!

A DISCUSSION OF COMPRESSED FILES

When program authors decided to distribute their programs using the Shareware concept, they started putting their programs on disk. A disk would contain all of the files necessary to run the program. It would also include documentation, data files, and information regarding registration. When Shareware authors ventured into the world of commercial networks and bulletin boards, however, something else was needed. If a program consisted of several files it would be awkward to put all of the files online. Even if they were online, how would the user get them? How could you transmit a .COM file, which is a program file containing machine language commands in binary format, to a user who did not have a means of receiving binary data?

What Are Compressed Files?

As the name implies, compressed files are programs that have been made smaller than they were originally. Programmers devised ways to pack the contents of a file using algorithms that would compress it. The initial attempts accomplished the goal, but did not achieve a very high rate of compression.

When it came to programs, online systems were faced with two basic problems. First of all, they needed a way to keep all of the files associated with a certain program together. Secondly, they needed a way to make

DOCTOR'S NOTE

In the early days of microcomputers, programs were much smaller. A variety of factors influenced this. In general, computers had one-tenth of the DOS (Disk Operating System) RAM (Random Access Memory) they have today. DOS RAM is that portion of the total RAM directly accessible to DOS. Today, most computers have at least 640K of DOS RAM. The first personal computers had only about 64K of DOS RAM. Disk space was much more expensive. Quite often a program would consist of only a .COM file and a documentation file. To make programs available online, programmers came up with what was called a *hex transfer*. All that was needed were two small conversion programs. One would convert a .COM file into hexadecimal numbers. The user would open a *capture buffer* and collect the flow of hexadecimal numbers. When the transfer was completed, the user closed the buffer. The documentation could also be easily captured in a separate buffer.

Once offline, the user could use a second program that would convert the file containing the hex numbers back into the original .COM file. This method worked fairly well, and for a period of time this system was all there was. Files in hex format were not compressed, but rather, they were expanded. As computers and programs began to get more complex, other means had to be devised for getting programs to potential buyers. The answer? Compressed files.

the programs take up less space. Both of these problems were solved through the use of compressed files. Over the last several years the percentage of compression has improved tremendously. In many cases, text files can be made 70 percent smaller than their original form. It is interesting to note that different file types will compress to varying degrees. Straight ASCII text files, for example, will compress the most, while .EXE and .COM files, which are in binary format, will compress less. Later on, you'll see just why this is important to you, as well as to the online systems that provide the files and programs. For now, you can examine the variety of file compression programs that exist, starting from the beginning and going through all of the compression programs that are available today.

Squeeze Programs

One of the earliest solutions to the file space problem was *squeezed* files. In general, all squeezed files could be easily identified because the second letter of their filename extension was a "Q." The way the squeeze programs worked, a "Q" would replace the second character of a file's extension. An .EXE file would become .EQE, a .DOC file would become a .DQC file, and so on. A file with the name, "RAMBO.EQE" would be an .EXE file that had been squeezed. A variety of squeeze utilities became available. What did they do? You guessed it! They squeezed a file down so that it was smaller.

Around this same period of time, Ward Christianson invented the Xmodem protocol. This made the transfer of binary data possible. Xmodem's development will be discussed more fully in Chapter 7. The Xmodem protocol, however, did allow users to transfer squeezed files and was extremely efficient on the machines of the time. The majority of users were communicating with 300 baud modems. A person with a 1200 baud modem was a real speedster. (See "What Is Baud?" later in this chapter for more information on this term.) Even though the rate of compression was not very great with squeezed files, it did make a slight difference in the time it took to transfer a file. Squeezed files also reduced the amount of space that a program took up on disk. After successfully downloading a squeezed program to your machine from a remote machine, you could then unsqueeze it.

Libraries

Going a step beyond squeezed files, the *library utility* entered the scene. All library files had a file extension of .LBR. The original LBR library utility was developed by Gary Navrisoff and was called LU. Vern Buerg wrote some individual LBR utilities (LUE, LUT, LUU, LUX) and pushed for a standard among library programs. Buerg also incorporated automatic squeezing and unsqueezing (SQeeze was still quite popular) in his LBR utilities. This was a revolutionary idea and made .LBR files even more useful. Another programmer, Paul Homchick, picked up where Navrisoff left off. Tom Jennings, author of the FIDO bulletin board system, also put out a version of LU. With such utilities readily available, library files became very popular and widespread. Each .LBR file was indeed a little library of programs. All of the files that belonged to a program could be put into one .LBR file. Besides being able to just unpack a library file, you could also delete files that were in it, or add others. In addition, you could view the files that the .LBR file contained—certainly a big improvement over using hex files and capture buffers! Library files became very popular, along with squeezed files. For several years they provided the only way to group files together and make them smaller. The .LBR files remained popular until late 1985 and early 1986. Today, you can still find a few .LBR files available. If you do, Vern Buerg's LUE220.COM is an excellent utility for extracting and expanding .LBR files.

Archives—a Better Way

In April 1985, a company called System Enhancement Associates, or SEA, released a new file compression program. The program was called *ARC*. ARC is a copyright of SEA. Using truly innovative file compression algorithms, ARC provided a better way to compress files. Going well beyond the capabilities of the squeeze or library utilities, ARC could compress files into a much smaller size. Within a short period of time, ARC became the standard for data compression. Files with the extension of .ARC soon replaced the now less efficient .LBR and .?Q? files. All .ARC files were known as "archives."

Another feature pioneered by SEA was the *self-extracting* file. This was a very useful and necessary development. Necessary? Sure! Think about it. If you were a relatively new user, how could you unpack ARC20.ARC if you didn't have a copy of ARC already? The fact is that you couldn't. The people at SEA developed a way of putting all of the ARC program files into an executable (.EXE) file. When you run the .EXE file all of the ARC program files extract themselves from the file. Using the single ARC.EXE file you can manipulate any .ARC file. You can add files to it, delete files from it, update files that are already in it, and much more. Figure 5-1 shows of all of the things that ARC can do with an .ARC file.

This list is generated simply by going to the DOS prompt and typing

```
C>ARC
```

and pressing ENTER. Figure 5-1 was produced by ARC version 6.02. The ARC utility dominated the file compression scene for years. All bulletin boards and commercial online networks stored programs in ARC files. Other programmers wrote utility programs to aid in the use of ARC. Quite naturally, still others began to wonder if file compression could be improved even further. Could files be made even smaller and could it be done faster?

Figure 5-1

Listing of ARC's capabilities and uses

```
ARC - Archive utility, Version 6.02, created in January of 1989
Copyright 1985-89 by System Enhancement Associates, Inc.; ALL RIGHTS RESERVED

Usage: ARC {amufdxerlvtcp}[wbmsnzvo5][g<password>] <archive> [<filename> ...]

Where: a = add files to archive        m = move files to archive
       u = update files in archive     f = freshen files in archive
       d = delete files from archive  x,e = extract files from archive
       r = run files from archive      t = test archive integrity
       l = list files in archive       v = verbose listing of files
       c = convert entry to new packing method
       p = copy files from archive to standard output

       w = suppress warning messages   b = retain backup copy of archive
       m = move files to archive       s = suppress compression (store only)
       n = suppress notes and comments z = include subdirectories in archive
       o = overwrite existing files when extracting
       5 = produce only level 5 compatable archives

       g = Encrypt/decrypt archive entry

Please refer to the program documentation for complete instructions.

C>
```

ARC à la Buerg

Vern Buerg, the author of several popular utility programs, decided to give file compression a try. With a license from SEA, Buerg began to create his own series of ARC programs. Using a different approach from that used by SEA, Buerg created individual utility programs. Each performed a certain function on an .ARC file. Whereas SEA's ARC.EXE file could perform all of the functions that could be done with an .ARC file, Buerg broke down those functions into smaller programs. Buerg's ARCE, for example, could be used only for extracting files from an archive. His ARCA was used for creating an archive or for adding files to an existing one. ARCV could be used to show a listing of all of the files contained within an archive. There was one noticeable difference between Buerg's utilities and the original ARC program from SEA. Buerg's ARCA made .ARC files that were a little smaller and were compressed faster. At this point, however, the search for better and faster file compression was far from over.

The Phil Katz ARC Programs

While Vern Buerg and the people at SEA were continuing to develop their file compression programs, another program author, Phil Katz, entered the scene. Katz began by introducing two new programs, PKARC and PKXARC, under the company name of PKWARE. PKARC handled all functions that would be associated with creating or modifying .ARC files. PKXARC, on the other hand, handled all things that were concerned with unpacking archives.

PKWARE'S PKARC also created an archive that had the now standard .ARC extension. The amazing thing about the Katz utilities was that they were *fast!* As if that weren't enough, his PKARC also achieved a substantially better rate of compression. The online community badly needed to conserve disk space. Just as companies like Lotus and WordPerfect Corporation changed their file formats to meet changing needs, PKWARE determined that it was time for something new. If the rate of compression was going to be increased, something innovative was going to have to be done. Up to this point, PKWARE'S PKARC/PKXARC were totally compatible with both SEA's ARC and the programs by Buerg. Then PKWARE came out with two new programs.

The two programs were called PKPAK and PKUNPAK. The PKPAK program still produced an archive with the extension of .ARC, but Phil Katz had added something new. It was a new method of compression that Katz called *squashing*. The addition of squashing made PKPAK and PKUNPAK incompatible with SEA's ARC and Buerg's ARCE. Why was PKUNPAK incompatible? The answer is that ARC and ARCE could not unpack any archives that had been created with PKPAK.

Naturally, this created some confusion. All of the programs created archives that had a file extension of .ARC. A user, however, could not tell if a file had been created with ARC, ARCA, or PKPAK. If you were using Buerg's ARCE and downloaded an .ARC file that had been created with PKPAK, you could not unpack it. In the eyes of some, the standard had been violated, but at the same time the speed and percentage of compression had been improved. There was confusion and dissension in the PC community, and it was about to get worse.

System Enhancement Associates eventually brought a legal action against PKWARE in 1988. One of the issues in the action was PKWARE's use of SEA's copyrighted term "ARC." An agreement that resulted, which seemed to favor SEA, was that PKWARE and Phil Katz could no longer produce any utility that used the term "ARC." There was a strong reaction to this in the online community. Some bulletin board sysops were angered by the decision while others were concerned. There was a great deal of discussion and debate on systems across the country. Many users felt that SEA's action was bad for the online community. The fact that Katz had been using the term "ARC" for several years prior to the suit, without objection, may have influenced their feelings. In any event, Phil Katz emerged in a short time, fulfilling the requirements of the legal settlement and meeting the needs of users as well. The action taken by SEA and the agreement that resulted were to have a far greater effect than anyone realized at the time.

ZOO—Another Approach

Another program author jumped into the file compression arena with a program called ZOO. The ZOO program, created by Rahul Dhesi, does not attempt to adhere in any way to the ARC standard established by SEA. ZOO can create, extract, and update .ZOO files. It can also delete files from within a .ZOO file, add comments, and so on. All compressed files created by this program have the extension of .ZOO.

Several other utility programs have been created for working with .ZOO files. OOZ is a small program that only extracts programs from within .ZOO files. ATOZ is a utility that will convert ARC, LBR, and SQU (squeezed) files into the ZOO format. The current version of ZOO is 1.41. To date, the ZOO utility has not met with a great deal of acceptance among users.

PAK—the Middle of the Road

In October of 1988, a compression utility called PAK was released. Produced by NoGate Consulting of Grand Rapids, Michigan, PAK was a middle-of-the-road alternative. PAK can handle files created by ARC and PKPAK.

In early 1990, PAK was revised so that it could also handle .ZIP files. (For more on .ZIP files, see "Katz Returns and Zips Up the Competition" later in this chapter.) In an interview, Mike Newhouse of NoGate Consulting was asked about the beginnings of PAK. Newhouse said, "PAK started out as a utility that we wrote strictly for ourselves. We used it in-house and were quite pleased with it. In late 1988 we decided that PAK might have some commercial potential. We didn't really want to compete with anyone, but simply offered what we felt was a good program."

While PAK has only done fairly well in the bulletin board community, it's experiencing success in the commercial market. The authors also offer a "Programmer's Tool Kit" that sells for $75. Newhouse explained about the tool kit by saying, "Essentially, the Tool Kit is a library of routines that can be linked into an application. In this way, programmers can include the compression and decompression routines without having to rely on any stand-alone program. We even include sample source code so that a programmer can easily see how it is done."

As you might have guessed, all files created with PAK have an extension of .PAK. NoGate also offers a full-screen version of PAK that allows you to manipulate archived files. The utility is called PAKF and it sells for $30. One feature separates PAK from ARC, ARCE, PKUNPAK, and PKUNZIP. PAK is the only one that can unpack files created by any of the other programs. PAK also has an excellent percentage of compression. This fact makes PAK worth watching as its authors continue to improve it.

LHarc—An Entry from Japan

LHarc is a compression utility that was brought over from Japan. The program creates files with an extension of .LZH. LHarc gives up a little speed in favor of greater compression. One feature of LHarc has made it especially popular in the PC community—LHarc can create self-extracting files—but so can ARC, PKPAK, and PAK. The big difference with the LHarc files is a matter of size.

The other utilities create self-extracting files that are substantially larger than the original compressed file. LHarc, on the other hand, generally creates a self-extracting file (often called an .SFX file) that is only about 1K larger than the original. For this reason, a moderate percentage of systems have converted over to .SFX files created by LHarc.

Another consideration is that with .SFX files the user does not need any decompression program to unpack the file. This has many people keeping a watchful eye on LHarc to see what directions it will take in the future. LHarc is a program in the public domain.

Katz Returns and Zips Up the Competition

In early 1989, Phil Katz released his new file compression programs, PKZIP and PKUNZIP. Files created with this utility have an extension of .ZIP. Katz's new utilities became an immediate success. By late 1989, they had achieved a compression percentage equal to or greater than LHarc. At the same time, none of the other utilities could match the speed of the ZIP programs.

At this point, .ZIP files dominate the majority of bulletin boards in the United States. Commercial online networks have their own policies regarding what compression methods they will accept. There are many utility programs available for converting .ARC files into .ZIP files. The ZIP programs by Phil Katz are fast, efficient, and very popular. This discussion of file compression programs brings us to 1990s. What will the future hold? In the world of Shareware, anything is possible.

DOCTOR'S NOTE

I'd like to talk just for a moment about what I've come to call the "ARC to ZIP phenomenon." I mentioned that many bulletin board sysops were upset by SEA's legal action against Phil Katz. Everyone knew that Katz was working on a new file compression utility. The .ARC file dominated nearly all systems.

What happened when PKZIP and PKUNZIP were released was like nothing I'd ever seen before. I had never seen such a mass movement toward one particular program. On the same day that PKZIP and PKUNZIP were released, I visited at least 50 BBSs that had already converted all of their files from .ARC to .ZIP format. Many systems notified their users that only .ZIP files would be accepted for uploads. Still others would accept .ARC files but would run a utility that would convert the .ARC file into a .ZIP file.

The major reason was a show of support for Phil Katz. A secondary reason was disk space. On my own bulletin board I converted all .ARC files to .ZIP files and saved 21 megabytes of disk space! Dozens of utilities appeared to support ZIP. Phil Katz's new program was literally an overnight success.

How to Use Compressed Files

In the previous section you learned about the history of file compression programs and a bit about what they do. Now, how do you use them? While each is a little different, they all have some similarities. Without exception, you can find out the commands any of the compression utilities use simply by entering the program name at the DOS prompt. Figure 5-2 is an example of the display that is provided by PKUNZIP.

Another similarity is exhibited in some of the basic commands. An *a* means to add a file to the compressed version, an *m* means to move the file, a *t* means to test for accuracy, and so on. To highlight some of the similarities, here are some sample command lines. Each one is doing exactly the same thing. See for yourself as all of the files with the .BAT extension are added into a compressed file called BATFILE.

```
C>ARC a BATFILE *.BAT
C>PKZIP-a BATFILE *.BAT
C>LHARC a BATFILE *.BAT
C>PAK a BATFILE *.BAT
```

Figure 5-2

PKUNZIP's built-in command listing

```
PKUNZIP (tm)    FAST!    Extract Utility    Version 1.02    10-01-89
Copyright 1989 PKWARE Inc. All Rights Reserved. PKUNZIP/h for help

Usage: PKUNZIP [options] zipfile [d:outpath\] [file...]
Options are:
  -c[m] = extract to screen [with more]  -t = test zipfile integrity
  -d = create directories stored in ZIP  -l = display software license
  -n = extract only newer files          -o = overwrite existing files
  -q = enable ANSI in comments           -s<pwd> = unScramble with password
  p[a,b,c][1,2,3] = extract to printer [Asc mode,Bin mode,Com port] [port #]
  -j<H,S,R> = mask off Hidden/System/Readonly attributes upon extraction
  -J<H,S,R> = don't mask off Hidden/System/Readonly attributes
  -v[b,c,d,e,n,p,s,r] = view ZIP(s) [Brief listing/sort by Crc/Date/Ext
     /Name/Percentage/Size/sort Reverse (descending) order]
zipfile = ZIP file name, wildcards *,? ok. Default extension is .ZIP
file    = Name(s) of files to extract. Wildcards *,? ok. Default is ALL files.

If you find PKUNZIP fast, easy, and convenient to use, a registration of $25
would be appreciated.  If you send $47 or more you will receive, when
available, the next version of the PKZIP, PKUNZIP, and PKSFX programs.
Please state the version of the software that you currently have.  Send
check or money order to:  PKWARE, Inc.
                          7545 N. Port Washington Rd.
                          Glendale, WI 53217
C>
```

What would you end up with? BATFILE.ARC, BATFILE.ZIP, BATFILE.LZH, and BATFILE.PAK. While there are similarities, each compression program does have commands that are unique. LHarc, for example, uses a command parameter to turn an .LZH file into a self-extracting .EXE or .COM file. For example:

```
C>LHARC s BATFILE.LZH
```

PAK on the other hand, uses two special command line switches to make a .PAK file into a self-extracting file, as follows:

```
C>PAK c BATFILE.PAK /EXE
```

Either way the net result is the same. You have a self-extracting file. Once you learn the commands for a certain file compression program, they will become second nature. There are also several programs available that automate the handling of compressed files. These programs allow you to move from one format to another without having to know all of the individual commands. These programs will be discussed in more detail in Part Four.

Which Program to Use?

There was a time a few years ago when you could pick just one file compression program. Today, that is not the case. On my own system I have PKZIP/PKUNZIP, LHarc, and PAK. Why? Because PKUNZIP can't unpack an .ARC file. Neither PKUNZIP nor PAK can unpack an .LZH file.

Since different systems keep programs in various formats, you have to be prepared to be able to unpack them. A user can pick the compression utility that he or she likes best and will use to store files. Being realistic, however, you still have to have some of the other utilities. If your personal choice is PKZIP and PKUNZIP and these are the only utilities you have, what happens if a program you want is packed in .LZH format, or .ARC or .PAK? Thus, as you prepare to go online, some of the first programs you'll need to obtain are some of the various file compression programs.

Why You Should Use Compression Programs

There are four main reasons why it benefits you to use file compression programs. They are

- Compressed files keep like files together

- Compressed files save disk space

- Compressed files save time during file transfers

- Compressed files save you money

By using a file compression program, you can keep related files together. For example, by putting all the budget worksheets from your spreadsheet program for one year into one file, and by calling it something like 1991WKS.ZIP, you make it easy to identify, and you know that all of your files are in one place.

Business and personal correspondence, recipes, and much more can all be placed in compressed files that hold similar data. When you pack files together they take up less room. For example, a user with four files totaling 531,662 bytes could use PKZIP to pack them all together, and the resulting .ZIP file would only use 269,664 bytes—nearly half as much space as the four separate files!

Keep in mind that the programs contained in a compressed file are unusable. The whole purpose of file compression programs is to make them take up less space. If you are cramped for space on your hard disk, you can easily remedy the problem. Examine the files on your system and find those that are seldom if ever used. Pack them up and move them off to a floppy disk. Label the disk and you'll always know where those files and programs are.

Another way that compressed files can help you is in evaluating Shareware programs. How? Let's say that you obtain a menu program for your hard disk. You've set it up, configured the colors, created menus, and so on. Now, you've found another menu program that you want to look over and compare to the first. Save yourself some time and effort. Pack up the menu program you've been looking at and put it on a floppy disk. You can try out the second menu program and see how it measures up against the first. If you find that you liked the first one better, you're prepared. All you have to do is copy the compressed file back to your hard disk and unpack it. All of the work you did setting it up is not lost.

When it comes to obtaining good Shareware online, time is money. The smaller a file is the less time it will take you to download it. The same is true for doing uploads. If a program is packed it will take you much less time to send it. This is one reason why you want to carefully consider which file compression program you use. All of the compression programs offer varying degrees of compression.

The size of the file is also very important depending on what speed modem you have. If you are using 2400 baud or below, you want to be very conscious of file size. Using files that are compressed saves you money in several ways. By packing files, they will take up much less space on floppy disks. That means you use fewer disks. Transferring files that are compressed takes much less time which also saves you money.

In the long run you'll find that compressing programs will be of benefit to you. Now that you've taken a thorough look at compressed files let's move on and investigate the process of going online.

COMMUNICATION CONFUSION

Each day, 1.5 million people fire up their modems and go online to commercial networks and bulletin boards. For the experienced user it may seem as easy as saving a file or clearing the screen. For novices, however, it can often be a totally bewildering experience. Telecommunications is a whole new world, filled with its own terminology and jargon. People stumble online without really understanding what they are doing or how they arrived where they did. They are immediately bombarded by a stream of prompts, questions, and decisions to make. That is, of course, if they are lucky.

If they aren't so lucky they may be met by a stream of "garbage characters" that make no sense at all. The end result is confusion. Everyone was a novice at one time or another and it isn't easy. Confusion isn't fun and you're supposed to be having fun. Let's take a brief look at why it can be so confusing.

What's There to Be Confused About?

The novice to telecommunications is faced with many new things all at once. New hardware, new software, and new terms and ideas. Let's take a look at just a few terms: RS-232, Xon, CTS, flow control, databits, baud, Xoff, RTS, parity, DTR, stopbits, NAK, ARQ, MNP, ACK, and CPS. Already it sounds like something from a sci-fi movie or a medical convention. No, you do not put Rice Krispies in a "serial port" and RTS does not mean "Relief To Seals." If you guessed that "MNP" is an additive in toothpaste then you guessed wrong. These few things are just the tip of the iceberg.

The online networks are all set up a bit differently and so are bulletin boards. It takes time to figure these things out and as I said before, time is money. It is estimated that the average new user to telecommunications wastes between 60 percent to 80 percent of the time they spend online. Why? Because there doesn't seem to be a good source to find out the things you need to know—no guide to tell you what you really need to understand and what you can just skip over. You can, however, eliminate most of this "communication confusion."

Telecommunications can be fun for you. You can go online so it will benefit you while being cost-effective. All of the terms mentioned above, and many more, will be explained. Not in "techie" terms but in a way that you'll understand and be able to use. You're going to journey through The Wires and receive lots of information as well as visual examples. You'll understand what you're doing and know what to look for. Let's get started because lots of good Shareware programs are waiting out there.

What You Will Need

If you've already bought the things you need to go online, then this section might clarify some things for you. If you haven't, perhaps this will give you a better idea of what you'd like to get.

Your first decision should be what type of modem you want to use. There are internal modems and external modems. In each of these categories there are error-correcting, MNP modems and non-MNP modems. MNP stands for *Microcom Networking Protocol*, and what it means is that the modem itself is capable of doing error checking. Prior to MNP all error checking was done strictly by software. MNP greatly enhances performance.

Another consideration is what speed of modem you want. The higher the modem's speed, the less time you will spend transferring files. Price may also be a consideration, and high speed modems are more expensive than slower modems. If you select an external modem you will also need a *serial card* (also called a serial port). A typical serial card is shown in Figure 5-3.

This is the same type of card that you would need in order to use a serial printer. With an external modem and serial card you will also need an *RS-232* cable. If you choose an internal modem, the serial card and cable aren't necessary. A standard RS-232C cable is shown in Figure 5-4. This is the cable used on the majority of modem-serial card connections.

You'll also need some good communications software. The communications software is your window into the world of telecommunications so you will want to select one that does everything you need it to. The best Shareware communications programs will be covered in Chapter 11.

Of course, you'll also need a phone line to hook your modem into. Many people who use communications fairly often generally wind up getting an extra phone line that is dedicated to their modem. Once you've had a few files trashed because someone picked up an extension and

Figure 5-3

A typical serial card

Figure 5-4

Serial port RS-232 connector

started dialing, the idea of a separate phone line makes more sense. You'll know if you need to have an extra line installed. Your first big decision—what kind of modem to buy?

Internal Versus External Modems

In order to give you a clear idea of the differences between internal and external modems, the features of each will be described. All terms will be fully explained. After examining both types of modems, the pros and cons will be summarized for you.

An internal modem is a completely self-contained unit. It comes on a card that fits into one of your machine's expansion slots. It may also have a small speaker attached to it. Some internal modems have a series of *DIP switches* that are used to change some of the modem's basic settings. DIP switches will be explained a little later. Figure 5-5 shows a typical internal modem.

In order to install an internal modem all you have to do is

1. Remove the computer's outer cover.

2. Find an empty expansion slot and remove the metal cover plate.

3. Insert the modem card firmly into the expansion slot.

4. Secure it with a screw.

5. Replace the computer cover.

6. Plug the phone line into the modem.

An external modem is generally a low, rectangular box that sits near your computer. Across the front are a series of lights that will be ex-

---

Figure 5-5

Typical internal modem

---

plained fully in a moment. Nearly all external modems have speakers and DIP switches. A U.S. Robotics 9600 HST external modem is shown in Figure 5-6.

In order to install an external modem all you have to do is

1. Remove the computer's outer cover.

2. Find an empty expansion slot and remove the metal cover plate.

3. Insert the serial card firmly into the expansion slot.

4. Secure it with a screw.

5. Replace the computer cover.

6. Connect one end of the RS-232 cable to the serial card and the other end to the modem.

7. Connect the phone line to the modem.

Figure 5-6

The U.S. Robotics 9600 HST

As you can see, when it comes to installing either type of modem, it is basically the same. The only real difference is that the external modem uses the RS-232 cable. Either way, you use one expansion slot. You may already have a serial card installed and not know it. How can you tell? Look and see if there is a card installed in your computer that looks like the picture in Figure 5-3. If it is a serial card it will have a 25-pin female connection protruding from the back of your computer. Internal modems tend to be slightly less expensive than external modems. With an internal modem you also don't have the added expense of a serial card or an RS-232 cable.

In the long run, the difference in cost is probably negligible. If you are on a budget and can't afford the slightly higher cost of an external modem, then an internal modem will serve you well. If possible buy a name brand because many of the very cheap internal modems tend to be unreliable. With that said, let's take a look at the lights on an external modem and explain what they mean.

Lights on the External Modem

The lights on the front of an external modem tell you the status of various functions. (I use a U.S. Robotics 1440 Dual Standard, which is an external modem.) For the purposes of this discussion, however, the lights on a U.S. Robotics 9600 HST will be described.

The 9600 HST is an error-correcting, or MNP, modem. In Figure 5-7 you'll notice that each of the lights has two letters underneath it, except one, that has three.

When a light is on it glows bright red. When it is off you see nothing. Under certain circumstances some lights will blink on and off and will be explained later. Going from left to right, what each of the letter designations stands for will be covered.

HS	High Speed
AA	Auto Answer
CD	Carrier Detect
OH	Off Hook
RD	Receive Data
SD	Send Data
TR	Terminal Ready
MR	Modem Ready
RS	Ready to Send
CS	Clear to Send
ARQ	Error Correction
AL	Analog Loopback

Figure 5-7

Diagram of HST modem lights

HS   AA   CD   OH   RD   SD   TR   MR   RS   CS   ARQ   AL

HS (high speed)   The HS light, when lit, tells you that your modem is set for its highest speed.

AA (auto answer)   When you've set your modem to answer the phone, the AA light will be on. If the AA light is off, your modem will not answer the phone line.

CD (carrier detect)   The CD light tells you when your modem has detected the carrier sent out by another modem. The CD light will stay on as long as a carrier is maintained. If it goes out, you know that you've lost your connection.

RD (receive data)   The RD light will pulse or blink anytime you're receiving data. This applies when you're connected to an online network or bulletin board and just reading messages, and also when transferring files.

SD (send data)   The SD light works in a similar way anytime that your modem is sending data to the modem you are connected to. If you are online and hit the ENTER key you will see a flicker from the RD light.

TR (terminal ready)   The TR light indicates that your terminal program is loaded and ready to operate. This light will be off as long as there is no terminal software loaded.

MR (modem ready)   The MR light indicates that the modem itself is ready. The MR light also indicates that the modem is receiving power. If the MR light is off, be sure to check the connection of the power supply on the modem and the plug into the wall. As an example, if a user were in a word processor, the MR light would be on, but the TR light would be off. This means that the modem is getting power and that it's ready to go, but that no terminal is now functioning. If you were to load Qmodem (the communications program from John Friel and his company, The Forbin Project), the TR light would immediately come to life. That's because Qmodem would make the terminal ready.

RS (ready to send)   The RS light indicates that a modem is *ready to send*. Again, if Qmodem was loaded, the RS light would be on.

CS (clear to send)   The CS light tells you that your modem knows that it is *clear to send*. The CS and RS lights are most active when one MNP modem is talking with another during a file transfer.

ARQ (error-correction)   The ARQ light indicates that error-correction is in effect. Thus, if you were to connect to another MNP modem, the ARQ light would come on. If you connect to a non-MNP modem, the ARQ light remains off.

AL (analog loopback)   The AL light is used for doing self-tests with the modem. Note that the AL light stands for *analog loopback*. What this really means is that the U.S. Robotics modem is capable of testing itself, by looping back, without having to connect to another modem.

Since it is only used if you are running tests on your modem, the AL light is generally off. Please note that not all external modems will have all of these lights. Non-MNP modems will not have an ARQ light for example and others will not have a HS light. A more complex example was used so that you would be ready for almost anything.

DOCTOR'S NOTE

Over the years, I've learned to watch the lights on my modem. The lights can give you information about what's really going on. I can tell if a file transfer is starting to fail or if I'm on a bad line and may lose the connection. I can tell if a file transfer has gone into a loop and I should break the connection. On one occasion, my monitor went out just as I was logging onto a BBS. Using just the modem lights and my knowledge of the prompts that the BBS sends, I continued my logon procedure and then uploaded a message to the message area. It's equivalent to flying on instruments only.

You can learn many things by paying attention to the lights on the modem. This is just one reason why I personally prefer an external modem. For those of you who have an internal modem there are several good Shareware programs that will give a representation of the modem lights on your screen. I'll mention these in Chapter 11. As we continue our journey through The Wires, I'll describe all of the circumstances that I mentioned above and many other tricks I've picked up. Then you'll know what to look for, too!

DIP Switches

It was mentioned that some internal modems have DIP switches and that nearly all external modems have them. The one obvious disadvantage of DIP switches on an internal modem is that they are hard to get to. You have to remove the cover of the machine, and in many cases you have to pull out the modem card to reach them. The DIP switches on external modems generally tend to be on the back. The modem manufacturer will usually have the switches set to what are called the factory defaults. Your communications software should tell you if you need to change any of these defaults.

Each switch controls a given function of the modem and determines how the modem will respond. Various modem manufacturers may arrange the switches in a different order. Keep in mind that it isn't the switch number that matters, but what the function is. Thus, auto answer is auto answer whether it's switch 1 or switch 5.

DIP switches generally operate just the opposite of light switches. DIP switches are either on or off, but many communications programs refer to them as being up or down. Up usually means off and down means on. The DIP switches on the U.S. Robotics 9600 HST will be discussed, with an explanation of what each switch means. The average setting of each switch will also be covered. The switches are

Data Terminal Ready
Verbal or Numeric Result Codes
Result Code Display
Command Mode Local Echo
Auto Answer
Carrier Detect Override
Single/Multiple Phone Installation
Command Set Recognition
Normal Mode Escape Code
Power-On Software Defaults

What Do They Mean? *Data Terminal Ready,* or DTR, gives the modem its status and makes it aware of what's going on. In most cases you would want DTR to be normal and not forced. By leaving DTR normal, the modem and the serial card determine the true status of the modem.

Result Codes can be either *numeric* or *verbal.* When set to numeric the modem returns a number. If you connected to another modem at 1200 baud and had the result codes set to numeric, the modem would return the number 5. When result codes are verbal, the modem would return, "CONNECT 1200." With most communications programs you'll want the result codes to be verbal.

This brings us to *Result Code Display.* This switch determines whether or not the result codes are displayed on the screen. Most communications programs like to have the result codes displayed.

Switch 4 determines whether or not you see the commands that you send to the modem. *Command Mode Local Echo* tells the modem whether or not you want commands like *ATZ* (reset modem) shown on the local screen. Generally, you can have this set so that commands to the modem are not shown. It's really a matter of personal preference.

Switch number 5 on the HST is *Auto Answer.* With the switch in the down position, auto answer is suppressed. This means that the modem will only answer the phone when your software package (or you) have told it to. In the up position this switch would cause your modem to answer the phone on the first ring. It's best to have auto answer suppressed.

The *Carrier Detect Override* switch is similar in function to the DTR switch. You can either have "true" carrier detect or forced carrier detect. As with DTR, it is better to let the modem and serial card determine whether or not there is really a carrier present or not. On the 9600 HST you would have this switch, number 6, in the up position. This would let carrier detect be true and not forced.

Switch number 7 is *Single/Multiple Phone Installation.* If you have an average phone line you would leave this switch in the up position.

Command Set Recognition tells the modem whether or not to use the accepted AT command set. Nearly all modems in use today utilize the AT command set and it should be described in your modem manual. On the HST this switch would be down, telling the modem to use the AT command set.

Normal Mode Escape Code is used to determine if your modem hangs up the phone. The generally accepted escape code is three plus signs in a row, followed by a carriage return. The hangup command on most communications programs uses this same idea. You want your modem to use this convention so, in the case of the HST, switch 9 would be up. With the switch down, the modem does not hang up.

Switch 10 is *Power-On Software Defaults* and it is a function of the U.S. Robotics HST modem. It tells the HST whether or not to load its defaults from NRAM (non-volatile RAM) or from ROM. Your modem may have a switch similar to this one.

DOCTOR'S NOTE

This is a good place to mention something special about DIP switches. In general *up* means *off* and *down* means *on*. Often, however, the modem has a different idea of what on and off are than you might. Here's a good example. On the HST, switch 5 is Auto Answer. For the most part you don't want to have the modem picking up the phone on the first ring. For one thing, this would be very irritating to anyone calling in to talk with you.

So, you want to have auto answer turned off. That means that switch 5 should be up, right? Wrong! The way a modem looks at this is that you are turning off the suppression of auto answer. Does that make sense? By turning this function off, you are telling the modem to answer the phone.

Many users find this a bit confusing at first. Read the manual that comes with your modem. It will tell you what it considers to be on or off for any given DIP switch. To help you to see the total picture, Table 5-1 shows you all of the DIP switch settings for the U.S. Robotics 9600 HST and what the up and down settings really mean to the modem.

Now you've gotten your modem set up, your DIP switches set, and your communications program loaded. The next step is to configure your communications program so you can go online. Your documentation may

Table 5-1

Dip Switch Settings for the U.S. Robotics 9600 HST

Switch	Function	Up Position	Down Position
1	Data Terminal	DTR is normal	DTR is forced
2	Result Codes	Verbal codes	Numeric codes
3	Result Code Display	Not displayed	Results dsplayed
4	Command Mode Echo	Commands echoed	Commands not echoed
5	Auto Answer	Modem answers	Answer suppressed
6	Carrier Detect	Normal detect	Forced detect
7	Phone Installation	Regular phone	Multiple lines
8	Command Set	No command set	AT command set
9	Normal Mode Escape	Hangs up phone	No hangup
10	Software Defaults	Loads NRAM set	Loads ROM settings

seem a bit confusing. It talks about things that you might not know about, including parameters and scripts and transfer protocols. Scripts? You don't want to write a play, you want to go online.

The majority of problems that new users experience simply come from a lack of understanding. The documentation may clearly say, "Set this to that..." but you may not understand what *this* is doing. This book is intended to help eliminate, or at least minimize, some of these early problems for you. Once you understand the terms, setting up your communications program will be much easier.

SETTING UP YOUR COMMUNICATIONS PROGRAM

Many new users of telecommunications have problems setting up their communications program. Why? Primarily because they are faced with making decisions using terms that they don't really understand. Baud, parity, Xon, Xoff, flow control, CTS, RTS, and others. If you don't really know what a term refers to, how can you decide what to set it at? You might see a message "Xon Received" and think that an oil tanker just hit your house.

The next difficulty that most users face is actually going online. It's like your first day in high school. The building is huge, you can't find the rooms, the seniors seem to be speaking Greek, and you are swamped with new things. Once you've been around for a while, these early problems just disappear. The same is true with telecommunications.

Parameters—the Key to Connecting

When two modems connect to each other, via a carrier, they *talk* to each other. Rather than talking about the weather, they find out how the other guy is set up. What baud rate? What parity? How many stopbits and databits? Is this an MNP modem? It's like saying "Knock, knock. Who's there?" The modems exchange what is called a *handshake*. In order to communicate with each other the basic settings, or *parameters*, have to be in sync. If you call into a bulletin board at 9600 baud, for example, and the BBS is using a 2400 baud modem, you will have a conflict.

During the handshake, your modem determines that the other modem is at a lower baud rate and so your modem drops down to 2400 baud. Baud is one parameter that modems can negotiate.

With some of the others, the modems either have to match exactly or you'll see nothing but garbage characters. Also referred to as "junk characters," this refers to graphics characters above ASCII 127. You might ask, "How am I supposed to know what parameters every other modem is using?" A good question. Fortunately, there are certain parameter settings that are used on most systems. The exceptions to these "ideal parameters" are rare. Before we find out what the best settings are, let's learn what all these different terms really mean.

What Is Baud?

Depending on your modem, you'll see that you can use 300, 1200, 2400, or 9600 baud. So, what is baud? A good analogy might be to ask, "What are miles per hour?" You could drive your car at 3, 12, 24, or 96 m.p.h. Going 24 m.p.h., you would get to a destination twice as fast as someone else who was going 12 m.p.h.

Baud, therefore, can be thought of as a way of measuring speed. It is also a measurement of the rate that data will be transferred from one machine to another. Technically, baud is a measurement of the *modulation rate* of the modem. The modulation rate is simply a reference to the number of signal changes that can be done per second. If you are at 9600 baud, your modulation rate is 9600.

You may also have heard the term *bps*. This stands for *bits per second* and it is used to determine the *data rate*. There is a very common misconception among modem users that data rate and baud are the same thing. With the technology that is used in today's high speed modems, it is very seldom that the baud rate is equal to the bps. Bits per second can be determined by taking the baud rate (1200, 2400, and so on) and multiplying it by the number of databits that are transmitted with each signal. The answer that you get is your true data rate and that is the best estimate of your speed.

When it comes to speed, few people use 300 baud modems today because they are simply too slow. Many bulletin boards do not allow 300 baud users to access their systems for the very same reason.

Here's an example of what is meant by slow. Assume that you connected to another modem at 300 baud. You want to download a 30K file. That's 30,000 characters. At its very best, the 300 baud modem will transfer 30 *characters per second* (*cps*). That means that it would take you at least 16.6 minutes to download the 30K file. At 1200 baud you could download the very same file in just over four minutes. The transfer time decreases as the baud rate increases. Thus, at 9600 baud and transferring 1100 cps, you could download the same file in approximately 30 seconds.

Modems that support high baud rates cost more. Just keep in mind that the extra money that you spend for a faster modem will be made up many times over by spending less time online. Just using an average of 20 cents per minute for a long-distance call, the 1200 baud transfer would cost you about 80 cents, whereas the 300 baud transfer would cost about $3.30. So, on the transfer of just one 30K file, you would save $2.50 over the cost of transferring the same file at 300 baud—something to think about.

What Is Flow Control?

Flow control is a means of monitoring the flow of data from one machine to another through a modem. If one machine is sending faster than the receiving machine can accept it, flow control steps in to slow down the process until the receiving machine catches up. There is software flow control and hardware flow control. MNP modems can use both types of flow control. Non-MNP modems can only use software flow control.

What Are Xon and Xoff?

Xon and *Xoff* are methods of software flow control that your computer has built right in. Have you ever used CTRL-S to stop a screen from scrolling off the top? If so, what you did was send an Xoff to your computer. In effect, you told it, "Hey! The flow of data is too fast. Hang on a second."

When you hit CTRL-S again, or CTRL-Q on some machines, you are sending an Xon. This tells your machine that it can continue. Communications programs use Xon/Xoff flow control in much the same way. By having Xon/Xoff toggled on, the machine won't become overloaded and lose data in the process. Users of high speed modems often have Xon/Xoff toggled off, allowing CTS/RTS hardware flow control to handle things.

What Are CTS and RTS?

CTS and RTS are methods of hardware flow control. This method is used by MNP, error-correcting modems. You'll recall that CTS stands for clear to send and that RTS means ready to send. With MNP modems, you would want to have CTS/RTS toggled on. This is especially true with the high speed 9600 baud modems. How does this work? During a file transfer your modem is communicating with the modem on the other end. Your modem sends a signal each time that it is ready to send, and the other modem will respond and say whether it is clear to send. In downloading a file while using CTS/RTS flow control, you will note that your RD and CS lights become synchronized. Why? Because when it's clear to send, it's also time to receive data. Thus, they will blink on and off in unison. After each CTS, your modem will send another RTS to tell the other modem that it's ready for more.

What Is Parity?

Parity represents the parity of the serial port (also called the COM port). Parity can be set for *even, odd, none, mark,* and *space.* The default for DOS is even parity. In communications programs these settings are identified by their first letters. When going online, your parity would show up as E, O, N, M, or S. Parity is just a parameter that modems check when they do a handshake. If you call into a system with your parity set to none and the system is set at even, you'll see only garbage (high bit) characters. Of the five types of parity mentioned, the most commonly used are none and even. This will be covered in more detail shortly.

What Are Databits?

To look at it simply, databits represent the number of bits of data contained in a transmission. The number is either 7 or 8. In DOS, the default is 7. Once again, these parameters have to match. If you call in at 8 databits and the other modem is set to 7 databits, what do you think you'll see? Right! Garbage characters. There are ways around this, and these methods will be discussed at the end of this section.

What Are Stopbits?

As with databits, the number of stopbits can only have certain values. In the case of stopbits it is either 1 or 2. This tells the number of stopbits in each transmission. The number of stopbits most commonly used in communications is 1. Think of the *stopbit* as the period at the end of a sentence. The period tells you that the sentence stops here. The stopbit serves the same purpose in modem communications. By adding the number of databits to the number of stopbits, the length of each transmission is known. Let's say that you set your databits to 8 and your stopbits at 1. We could represent this as:

| 1 | 2 | 3 | 4 | 5 | 6 | 7 | 8 | . |

Each number represents a databit, while the period at the end is the stopbit. The system knows what to expect and handles the data accordingly. If each system is set up differently, one set for 8 databits, 1 stopbit and the other set for 7 databits, 1 stopbit, then a conflict occurs.

What Is Duplex?

Duplex is a term that confuses many new users. They hear people talking about "being at full duplex" and it means nothing to them. Duplex is also referred to as *echo*. Duplex determines how or if the keystrokes you enter while in your communications program will be echoed. Under almost all conditions you will want to be set at full duplex. If you switch to half duplex, then each character you enter will be echoed back to you. If you typed in "goodbye" you would see "ggooooddbbyyee" on your screen. When you are in full duplex mode, the remote computer will echo your keystrokes and there is no local echo. If you ever think that you are starting to have double vision, just check and make sure you are set to full duplex.

The Ideal Parameters

You should now have a better understanding about all the terms discussed. These are all things that you will encounter when you set up your communications program. When someone asks you, "What are your parameters?" they are specifically asking about four things. Baud, databits, parity, and stopbits. To tell them that you were at 2400 baud with parity set to none, databits set to 8 and stopbits set to 1, you could abbreviate it to: 2400,8,N,1. No one would slap your wrists if you said 2400,N,8,1 either. This is a generally accepted format for giving your parameters.

There are two basic sets of parameters that are used most often. These are 7,E,1 and 8,N,1. Ironically, commercial online networks default to 7,E,1 while nearly all bulletin board systems default to N,8,1. With only a few exceptions, all file transfers must be done at 8,N,1. Systems that have you log on at 7,E,1 will automatically switch to 8,N,1 when you begin a file transfer and then switch you back when it's over. Also, even though the commercial systems default to 7,E,1 you can log onto them at 8,N,1. You may be thinking that there is a contradiction here because it was said earlier that the parameters had to match. They do, and in many cases the software on some systems can cause the system to change its parameters to yours. To demonstrate what happens, here is an example with Compu-Serve. CompuServe is set to 7,E,1 and you are set to 8,N,1. Figure 5-8 illustrates what occurs. Note that the first thing you see is a string of garbage characters, the ones mentioned before. Why? Because you are set at 8,N,1 and CompuServe is set at 7,E,1. What that junk really says is "User ID:12345,321," which is the logon prompt and response.

Now, here is the part where the system handshake comes in. Note the perfectly clear "Password:" prompt. Why can you read that and not the "User ID" prompt? Because when you sent the user ID, CompuServe detected that you were at 8,N,1. It made the switch to 8,N,1 so by the time the password prompt shows up, it can be read. Keep in mind that not all system software will do this. With bulletin boards in particular you'd

Figure 5-8

Logging onto CompuServe with parameters 8,N,1

User ID: Password:

Script file "CIS.SCR" at level 1. [ESC] to ABORT

better be at 8,N,1 or be prepared to learn to read the garbage characters. Using 8,N,1 is recommended. It'll be much easier. :) The :) is an *emoticon:* a network and BBS convention for showing a smile. There are others, and they will be shown as you go along.

Logging On

Once you have your communications program set up you are ready to go online. Each communication program has a *dialing directory*. For each system you call, you'll be entering certain information—the system name, baud rate, parity, databits, and stopbits—that the communications program uses. Depending on the communications program you may also be able to enter your password, a default file transfer protocol, and even a special note about that system.

Appendix C contains the numbers of some very good bulletin boards that you can call. You might want to put some of them in your dialing directory. Qmodem by John Friel and The Forbin Project is included on one of the disks you can receive free by sending in the coupon at the back of the book. Qmodem is a widely used communications program and you'll probably like it too. Try it out and if you like it be sure to register. Once you've made some entries in your dialing directory you're ready to go online. The next section will give you some idea of what to expect.

What You Will See

Generally, the first prompt you'll see will ask you if you want graphics. If you have a color monitor you may want to answer yes. Many sysops spend a great deal of time creating some interesting and colorful screens. If you don't have color, then just answer no to this prompt. Figure 5-9 shows you this prompt as it appears on PC Board systems.

When you've answered this prompt, the first thing you'll see is a *welcome screen*. This is a screen that shows the name of the system, the sysop's (system operator) name, and some other information. The next prompt you'll get will ask for your name. Since you've never called in before, the system will know that you are a new caller. On PC Board systems you'll be asked if you want to reenter your name or continue to log on as a new user. Since you probably entered your name correctly you'd enter a **C** to continue. Figure 5-10 shows the welcome screen of Dr. File Finder's Black Bag and these first prompts.

Figure 5-9

Prompt for graphics on PC Board BBS software

```
CONNECT 2400 / 12-31-89 (15:47)
(Error Correcting Modem Detected)

Dr. File Finder's Black Bag
PCBoard (R) - Version 14.1/E3 - Node 2

Do you want graphics (Enter)=no? y
```

ANSI   ONLINE   19200 8N1   [Home]=Menu   FDX 8 LF X ↵ ↓ CP LG ↑ PR 00:00:22

Basic Information

Once you've decided to enter **C** to continue, the system will ask you some questions. Often you will see another screen that gives you information on what to do next. On some systems, this screen will give you the rules, a bulletin, or it may not be there at all. Figure 5-11 shows the screen that appears on The Black Bag.

All bulletin boards require that you give them certain basic information. In most cases this is not even controlled by the sysop, but is a function of the BBS software itself. You'll be asked for your city and state, your home and work phone numbers, and possibly what kind of computer you are using. Figure 5-12 shows the things you are asked when logging onto a PC Board system as a new user.

Answer the questions honestly. Use your real name. If you don't have a work phone number or you don't want anyone to have it for some reason, then just enter your home number twice. It is most likely that you will never get a call from a BBS sysop. The information is requested just so the sysop can have access to it. It's been known to happen when a sysop has a system crash that he or she took the time to call all of their users to tell them that the system would be down for a while. So, don't

Figure 5-10

Welcome screen from The Black Bag and first prompts

```
The System That Will Become A Network!

                           24 Hours/Day   ┌──┐  300/1200/2400
                           901/753-7213   │DRFF│  Use 8-N-1
                           110 Megabytes On-Line - 2 Nodes

 -==Real Names Only==-              -==MS/PC DOS Software==-

 SysOp and Guardian of "The Wires"......................Dr. File Finder
 Co-SysOp................................................Ray Majewski
What is your first name? Nancy
 What is your last name? Newuser

NANCY NEWUSER not found in USER's file.
(R) to re-enter your name or (C) to continue logon as a new user? C
 ◆ ANSI   ONLINE  19200 8N1  [Home]=Menu   FDX 8 LF X LF CP LG ↑ PR 00:01:03
```

be afraid to answer honestly. In a moment you'll learn about some questions that you might not want to answer along with some options.

You've finished supplying the basic information. The next thing you may see on a PC Board system is the *System News*. These are news messages from the sysop to the regular users of the BBS.

Statistical Information

The first time you log onto any bulletin board system you are a new user. As such, you will often see things that you will never see again no matter how many times you call that system. That's because new users are often asked to supply some additional information or to read certain bulletins, and so on. Each sysop handles new callers differently. Many want to get more information about you. In most cases this is strictly for statistical purposes. It gives the sysops a better profile of the kind of users that are on their system.

Figure 5-11

Extra information screen telling you how to proceed

```
Welcome to DR. FILE FINDER'S BLACK BAG!! I'm glad that you called and
I hope that you will enjoy The Black Bag!

First, please access the Newuser Questionnaire. This simply helps me to
maintain the system better. Answer all questions. Upgrade will be totally
automatic! The time you spend in the Newuser Upgrade door does NOT count
against your time on the board, so take your time, read the information,
answer the few questions and you'll be all set. THEN...

Please look around and evaluate the system. You will have access to
all of the features on the system, with the exception of doing uploads.
For a recent list of files on The Black Bag, download FILELIST.ZIP.

Evaluate the system and decide if you'd like to become a part of it. Your
comments and/or questions are ALWAYS welcome!!

                           Dr. File Finder~~~~~~~~~~~~
                           --== SysOp ==--
```

Would you like to register with us (Enter)=yes? y

` ANSI   ONLINE   19200 8N1   [Home]=Menu   FDX 8 LF X ↓↑ CP LG ↑ PR 00:01:41 `

Figure 5-12

Logging onto a PC Board system as a new user

```
                      (------------)
Password (One word please!)? .....
                      (------------)
Re-enter password to verify? .....

                      (----------------------)
City and State calling from? Somewhere, US

                      (--------------)
Business or data phone # is? 111-567-4321

                      (--------------)
  Home or voice phone # is? 111-234-9876

                      (------------------------------)
Brand of CPU you are using? 12 MHz AT clone
```

` ANSI   ONLINE   19200 8N1   [Home]=Menu   FDX 8 LF X ↓↑ CP LG ↑ PR 00:02:56 `

You may be asked your age and your profession, if you are a student, how many BBSs you call, and so on. You may see a list of system rules, or be asked to enter a door that will automatically upgrade you. A *door* is a way to run another program from the main BBS software. When you enter a door you are actually moving from one program (the BBS software) into another program (the door). Since it is similar to moving from one room to another these programs have come to be called doors. On the Dr. File Finder system, new callers enter a door where all they have to do is read some information about the system. They answer four short questions and then they are upgraded, their expiration date is set, and their time limit is increased.

Thus, many sysops use functions like this because it cuts down on the work of maintaining the system. To give you a feel for what this is like, you can continue your logon to The Black Bag. Figure 5-13 shows you the first menu that new callers see on The Black Bag.

Note that you only have three choices. Some sysops prefer to show you the full PC Board menu, but lack most of the functions. This method is used on The Black Bag to make it easy for new callers. You can log off, leave a comment, or you can enter the door and be upgraded. We'll enter the door just so you can see what happens when you come back out of it. The information that new callers read won't be shown. It's really just four screens that describe how the system works. After each screen the new caller enters a **Y** to show that he or she has read it. If you ever call into The Black Bag system, you can read it for yourself. Figure 5-14 shows you the welcome that you get when you've entered the door.

After reading the four screens, the new caller to my system is asked to answer four simple questions.

- Street address
- Type of computer and modem in use
- Age
- Occupation (those in school are asked to enter "Student")

The instant those questions are answered, the door program performs several functions that upgrade the caller's status. The information that was provided is written to a file. This method is good for the new caller because it makes things very simple. Since the door upgrades you, you can continue your call and look around the system, download files, play door games, and the like. On some systems you are asked to answer a

Figure 5-13

Main menu for new callers on The Black Bag

```
DR. FILE FINDER'S BLACK BAG NEWUSER COMMAND MENU

FOR AUTOMATIC UPGRADE, PLEASE ANSWER NEWUSER QUESTIONNAIRE. TYPE "OPEN;20"

  C)omment to Doc          G)oodbye            OPEN a DOOR
    Send a comment to        Logoff of the       Use this command to
    the SysOp                system              access Newuser upgrade.
                                                 Enter OPEN;20

WELCOME NEWUSER!! The Newuser upgrade questionnaire is VERY brief. The
time you spend in the Door is 'Free'. Just read the material presented,
answer ALL questions completely and upgrade is AUTOMATIC!! This process
makes it easier to maintain the system. Just enter 'OPEN;20 '. There
are a few brief questions. When you emerge, you will have access to all
functions on Dr. File Finder's Black Bag. Thanks for your cooperation!
```

(21 min. left) Main Board Command? DOOR;20

`ANSI  ONLINE  19200 8N1  [Home]=Menu   FDX 8 LF X ↵ ↵ CP LG ↑ PR 00:04:19`

Figure 5-14

Welcome screen of the new caller upgrade door

```
Welcome to DR. FILE FINDER'S BLACK BAG and the NEWUSER AUTOMATIC UPGRADE
DOOR! This will be short and simple and will only take a few minutes. The
time you do spend in this Door, will NOT count against your time on the
system, so take your time and just read the information provided and also
answer the questions completely. Then what happens??

1. You will emerge with your access raised and you will be able to access
   all functions on the board with the exception of uploads.

2. You can read bulletins, download freely, read messages, join the
   Conferences, etc. Have fun and just evaluate the system. DR. FILE
   FINDER'S BLACK BAG is a system RUN by it's MEMBERS. See if you'd
   like to join US! Your comments and/or questions are ALWAYS welcome!

                          Dr. File Finder~~~~~~~~~~~~
                          --== SysOp ==--
Type 'Y' to continue.
```

Welcome to NewUser Upgrade Door. (Yes/No/Redisplay)? Y

`ANSI  ONLINE  19200 8N1  [Home]=Menu   FDX 8 LF X ↵ ↵ CP LG ↑ PR 00:04:53` questionnaire, and then you have to wait until the sysop reads it before you can be upgraded. The method used here helps you out on your very first call and it also does some things to help the Doctor out. Figure 5-15 shows you the main menu that you see when you exit the upgrade door.

As you can see, there is quite a difference in relation to the first menu you saw when you were a new caller. No muss, no fuss, and the time you spend in the door doesn't even count against the time you have on the system.

As you go from BBS to BBS you will find that new callers are handled in many different ways. Some systems are totally open. You just answer a few of the basic questions and you are done. The number of bulletin board systems that are totally open has been steadily decreasing over the last few years. Sysops provide a service just as commercial online networks do. You are a guest in their home, and they feel that they'd like to know a little bit more about the people who visit their BBS. You may encounter systems that can't be upgraded until you mail something to the sysop. On others, you will get access, but your access level will depend on the number of files that you download as compared with the number of files you upload. (This will be covered in Chapter 8.)

Figure 5-15

Main menu after using the new caller upgrade door

```
┌─────────────────────────────────────────────────────────────┐
│            DR. FILE FINDER'S BLACK BAG - COMMAND MENU          │
├─────────────────────┬─────────────────────┬───────────────────┤
│  Message Commands    │    File Commands     │  Utility Commands │
├─────────────────────┼─────────────────────┼───────────────────┤
│  C)omment to Doc     │  D)ownload a File    │  H)elp Functions  │
│  E)nter a Message    │  F)ile Directories   │  M)ode (Graphics) │
│  K)ill a Message     │  L)ocate Files (Name)│  P)age Length     │
│  Q)uick Message Scan │  N)ew Files (Date)   │  T)rans. Protocol │
│  R)ead Messages      │  U)pload a File      │  U)*NOT AVAILABLE* │
│  Y)our Personal Mail │  Z)ippy DIR Scan     │  W)rite User Info. │
│                      │                      │  X)pert On/Off     │
│  -= Other Commands =-│  OPEN a DOOR         │                   │
│                      │  CHAT with NODE      │  O)perator Page   │
│  A)bandon a Conference│ B)ulletin Listings  │  S)cript Questionnaires│
│  J)oin a Conference  │  G)oodbye (Hang Up)  │  I)nitial Welcome │
└─────────────────────┴─────────────────────┴───────────────────┘
(22 min. left) Main Board Command?
```

ANSI   ONLINE 19200 8N1 [Home]=Menu   FDX 8 LF X U CP LG PR 00:08:22

There are also a growing number of boards that charge a modest fee. These are generally called *subscription* or *registered* systems. The initial information you will see tells you if a system is a subscription system. The main thing to remember is that new callers are generally required to do certain things to gain higher access. It's up to you whether or not you want to comply.

How and What to Answer

At this point, it would be a good idea to make you aware of some questions that may be asked, just so you'll know about them in advance. You've seen the prompts for basic information that you'll see on PC Board BBSs. You also have a good idea about the normal kind of additional information that some sysops request, primarily for statistical purposes. You now know that each BBS will require different things of new callers. These things are typical and are to be expected. In other words, the kind of things I've mentioned are normal on bulletin boards. There comes a point, however, when you may have to think about some of the questions that you are being asked to answer.

A Rule and When to Break It

Before getting into this, it's necessary to preface the remarks with a general rule. It is never a good practice to simply hang up while you are connected to a system. On BBSs you can *hang* the system, making it unavailable to other callers. In some door programs you can actually damage the door program and cause a loss of data. On commercial networks hanging up can also cause problems. In some rare instances you can leave a "shadow" of yourself there. This means that the system doesn't know that you have left and so you are still being charged. It is not the fault of the system if you hang up and don't log off properly. On all systems, whether bulletin board or commercial systems, you should always log off properly.

With that said, you should be aware of the fact that some BBSs may ask you to answer some unusual questions. I have logged onto many systems. I know from experience that there are specialized systems for almost any subject you can think of. I have logged onto boards that were religiously oriented, sexually oriented, and racially oriented. A sysop who asks you to supply your age, your occupation, or if you are a student for statistical purposes is one thing. You may well see questions that are not so mild. For your enlightenment, I will give you a few actual examples. I have logged onto systems where I was asked to answer the following questions:

Do you practice devil worship?
Are you gay or bisexual?
What race are you?
Do you believe in white supremacy?
What religion are you?
How much money do you make a year?
Do you like to have group sex?

These actual examples should give you the idea.

While sysops may have the right to ask you certain basic questions, they have no right to ask you to answer questions such as those listed above. Questions such as these may be your first clue that you have inadvertently logged on to a specialized board. Do you want to tell a BBS sysop something about yourself that you wouldn't tell your neighbors? On a conventional BBS, your race and religion don't matter. Your sexual preferences are your own business. In general, if you begin to feel awkward or uncomfortable, it's time you got out of there.

If you cannot find any way to get out of the questionnaire, you have two options. Either complete the questionnaire with answers that mean nothing or break the rule just given, and hang up. There are always exceptions to every rule and this would be one of them. Can you avoid such a situation? One way is to pay close attention to the welcome screen that is shown on nearly all systems. Look at it carefully and read what it says. It just may give you a clue that you have arrived someplace where you don't want to be. If you see references to race, religion, the devil, and so on, you may just want to log off right then. Each individual's reaction to these specialized systems will depend on his or her own personal beliefs and philosophy. But you should be aware that some systems like these *do* exist. Other bulletin board systems contain questions that are perfectly normal, but the demands that the sysop makes are not! On one BBS, users are told that in order to obtain higher access they would have to mail a photocopy of their driver's license to the sysop. Demands like these are totally unreasonable. Use your own judgment. If a sysop has rules and requirements that seem particularly strict or unusual, you may not want to be there. There are over 10,000 BBSs in the United States. The number of specialized or unusually strict boards are very few in number. You can afford to go look someplace else.

Another exception to the rule about hanging up can occur if you find yourself stuck on a system. With bulletin board software you may encounter times when you simply cannot get back to the command line prompt. If you can't do that, you can't log off normally. This sometimes happens when a file transfer aborts. In a case like that, rather than politely staying online while your phone bill grows, it would be appropriate to disconnect by hanging up. With that said, let's move on and learn some more about going online.

## CHAPTER SIX

Attaining Mastery

In the last chapter, you took a look at the history of file compression programs and examined the choices available—programs like ARC, ARCE/ARCA, PAK, ZOO, LHarc, and PKZIP/PKUNZIP. You'll have to select the programs you prefer and get accustomed to using them. Terms like baud, parity, databits, stopbits, and flow control should no longer be the abstract concepts they may have been before. These things don't have to be as mysterious as they often sound. You should also be familiar with internal and external modems. With external modems, you should feel fairly comfortable with the meaning of the modem lights and the DIP switch settings. You also got an idea of what it's like to go online with a BBS as a new user.

These things give you a start—the basics. You might now ask, "Now that I'm logged on, what do I do?" That's a good question because you have more new things to think about. There are menus, prompts, lists of files, different file transfer protocols, message areas, and more. To make matters more than a bit confusing, each online network is a bit different.

Each bulletin board can be set up differently by its sysop. If you are to obtain good Shareware programs, and do it efficiently, you need one thing—confidence!

GAINING CONFIDENCE

In order to save yourself time and money, it isn't enough to just know how to set up your modem. It isn't enough just to be able to configure your communications program. These both represent giant steps forward for you, but they won't save you time and money. Once you get online you need to know what to do. You need to know what to look for. It also helps if you know what it's going to cost you and how *you* can reduce those costs. You should be able to go online with all of the confidence that you need. There's no need for a BBS to be a strange and mysterious place. You shouldn't feel terrified at the thought of using any of the commercial networks. There's also no need for the time you spend online to be wasted time. What might appear to be a very simple thing can cost you money. What it boils down to is that you need some experience. You may be saying, "Oh great! Where do I go out and buy experience?" If you are reading this, you already have. There are three major drawbacks to getting your experience firsthand:

- It can be very frustrating.
- It can be very time-consuming.
- It can get to be very expensive.

You can avoid these drawbacks. In the course of this chapter, you will find things that will save you time and money while giving you confidence. You won't even have to turn on your modem. As in the previous chapter, you'll get a peek at what to expect so you will know what to look for. You'll be able to venture online and know what to do and how to do it. Toward the end of the chapter, you'll find out about the different ways that you can call into online systems. You'll see what the costs are and be able to make an informed decision about which method(s) you want to use. If you're ready, let's start gaining some confidence!

Using Log Files

All of the communications programs discussed in Chapter 11 have certain functions in common. One of the functions concerns *log files*. This is the ability to log or record an online session onto a disk file. When you open a log file, everything that occurs is recorded. Every prompt from the system and every response you make goes into the file.

Why would you want to create log files? Because when you are offline you can see precisely what happened. One important benefit of log files is that you can see exactly what the prompts from the system were. A *prompt* is a message telling you that the system requests input. Memory can sometimes play tricks on you. What you think you saw may not be what was actually there. Did the prompt say "Enter your Password:" or did it say "Enter Your Password:?"

Why is this so important? Because another feature that is shared by all of the communications programs discussed in Chapter 11 is that they all have *script languages*. By using these specialized languages you can create scripts that will automate the things that you want to do online. In writing scripts, it is important to know *exactly* what the prompts are. Automation, using scripts, will save you time. Scripts will be discussed in more detail a little later on.

Log files let you review your online session and let you plan ahead. You will see examples of "typical" systems in this chapter. Since some systems will vary, here's a suggestion. Before you log onto a new system for the first time, open a log file. Depending on the communications program, this will be called "Session Log," "Capture Log," or something similar. Remember to close the log file when you are finished recording. (Otherwise it will be recording until you exit the program.)

Systems using the same bulletin board software will tend to have the same prompts. As with most things, however, there will always be exceptions. If you log onto one of the exceptions, your log file will show you what is different. For example, one Qmodem script is all you might need for logging onto almost every PC Board system in the country. For the few that are exceptions, you will need to make special script files. Using the information contained in the log file, you can easily adapt your script files. Log files have other uses that let you plan ahead and save time. You'll see some of these uses mentioned in the sections that follow.

Planning Ahead

When you have to write a term paper for school or an important business letter, it helps if you plan ahead. People generally proceed in a certain order:

1. You plan what it is you want to accomplish.

2. You do some research on things you don't know.

3. You do a rough draft to organize your ideas.

4. You go on to accomplish your goal.

In going online, whether to a commercial network or a bulletin board, it also helps if you plan ahead. Let's say that you want to go online to GEnie. You want to see if you'd like to download any of the new files uploaded to the IBM RT in the last month. That's what you want to accomplish. The trick is to do it as quickly and efficiently as possible. The uninformed user would do it one way and would waste a great deal of time. You are going to be informed, however, so you are going to do it the easy way. Read the following scenario and note what transpires.

Typically, users log onto GEnie and use the menus to get into the IBM RT file area. They use another menu selection to look at the new files. Figure 6-1 shows you part of the file listing.

The scan in Figure 6-1 was done on January 2, 1990. The listing showed all of the new files from January 2, 1990 back to December 1, 1989. The actual list was 24 times longer than what you see in Figure 6-1. From start to finish, at 1200 baud, the list took 3 minutes and 31 seconds to display on the screen. The list goes by fairly quickly and scrolls off the top of the screen. It's hard to read the filenames and descriptions, and many users look at the listing again and again. All the while the time (and money) are ticking away.

Users may jot down a few filenames on a piece of paper, and just as they are about to download a file they hear, "Honey, it's time for dinner!" So they log off, planning to come back later. After dinner, they log onto GEnie again, and once again they follow the menus back to the IBM RT. Now where is that piece of paper they wrote the filenames down on? Well, it's here somewhere but can't be found. Time to scan the new files again. After a few repeats of what they did the first time they logged on, they find the files that they want. They download them and log off. Most of the time (and money) spent was wasted. How are you, a user with confidence, going to do it differently?

Figure 6-1

New files listing on GEnie

No.	File Name	Type	Address	YYMMDD	Bytes	Access	Lib
16826	SCDATA88.89	X	TRADEWIND	900102	23940	12	9
	Desc: Scorecast data through 01/02/90						
16790	GOGAME.LZH	X	MARK.BUTLER	891230	80640	5	7
	Desc: Popular Japanese game - go						
16789	QPACS30.ARC	X	R.WILLIAMS5	891230	107100	4	3
	Desc: Quick Personal Accounting System						
16785	GNESRT10.LZH	X	M.WILDEN1	891230	27720	3	5
	Desc: GEnie RoundTable message file sorter						
16783	VDE150.LZH	X	C.BIEDA1	891230	94500	6	5
	Desc: Pure-ASCII editor; WordStar commands						
16781	P-ROBOT2.ARC	X	D.MALMBERG	891230	160020	2	7
	Desc: Version 2 of Pascal Programming Game						
16780	LIBFILES.LZH	X	HOMCHICK	891230	342720	13	1
	Desc: Directory listing, see description.						
16779	PANEMUL.ARC	X	D.W.B.	891230	8820	8	5
	Desc: Panasonic printer mode select prog.						
16778	LIBNEW.ARC	X	HOMCHICK	891230	6300	23	1
	Desc: New files in LIBFILES this week						
16777	LIBFILE2.LZH	X	HOMCHICK	891230	185220	1	1
	Desc: Partial listing, see description.						
16776	LIBFILE1.LZH	X	HOMCHICK	891230	158760	2	1
	Desc: Partial listing, see description.						

You start your logon to GEnie. After you've been there a few times you'll probably have a script that will do it for you. You may even have one that will automatically take you to the IBM RT file area. For now, however, you are going to open a log file. Remember those? :)   Like most users, you're going to use the menus to get to the IBM RT new files area. You'll start the listing and lean back in your chair. When the listing is done, you'll log off and close your log file. Total time online for you was 5 minutes 18 seconds, of which 3 minutes and 31 seconds was spent listing the files. No wasted time, and you have a copy of the list on your machine.

You can use a program like Vern Buerg's LIST to look at the log file and take your time looking over the file listing from GEnie. When files are scrolling by it's very difficult to really take a good look. You spent just a little bit over five minutes online and you came away with a copy of the listing. You can decide exactly what files you want to download, if any, and then go back and just download them. The typical user spent at least four times longer online without even doing a download. If they want to go back and look for another program it will be necessary to scan the list again. You, on the other hand, used a log file and have a copy of the list.

Another function of communications programs, called a *screen dump,* should be mentioned here. A screen dump is used to capture the contents of the current screen to disk. If what you need is on the current screen, you could use a screen dump. When you first venture online, however, use a log file.

Note: Things that you do offline cost you nothing but time. All things that you do while online cost you both time and money. Therefore, do as many things as possible offline.

Online Help

All of the commercial online networks and all bulletin board software has some online help. Although it varies from system to system, you can usually get help by entering a ? at a prompt. Figure 6-2 shows part of a help screen relating to messages on a Wildcat! bulletin board system.

When you first log onto a system, you are naturally going to be

---

Figure 6-2

Some online help on a Wildcat! BBS

```
┌─────────────────────────────────┐
│       Main Menu Help Screen     │
└─────────────────────────────────┘



BULLETIN MENU - When the "B" option is selected, the file
called BULLETIN.BBS isdisplayed. The Bulletin menu could be considered
a sub-menu of sorts, in that it presents you with the options of reading
one or more bulletins by selecting a bulletin number, re-listing the
bulletins that are available for display, or simply returning to the
MAIN menu. If any bulletins have been updated since your last logon ,you
will be presented a listing of those bulletins by number.

COMMENTS TO SYSOP - This choice enables you to enter a
private message to the system operator. WILDCAT! makes these comments an
integral part of the message base for easy reply by the sysop, if
desired. All comments are automatically directed to a separate message
folder (Folder "Z") for easy reference.  This is the easiest method of
 - More - [C]ontinue, [S]top, [N]onStop:
◆ ANSI   ONLINE  19200 8N1  [Home]=Menu    FDX 8 LF X ♪ ♪ CP LG ↑ PR 00:02:14
```

confused by some of the commands. In addition, there are generally some extended commands for advanced users. Until you learn the meaning of the commands it is wise to take advantage of the online help. You'll waste more time trying to figure it out for yourself.

Once again, here is where a log file can be a big help. A typical user would log onto the system, and each time the user had a problem he or she might use the help. The user might also fumble around for quite a while trying to figure things out. Assuming the user did use the help, he or she might look at the same help listings over and over again. You, on the other hand, have logged on with a log file open. If you use the online help, it will be saved in the log file. Later, when you are offline, you can study the help screens and make yourself more familiar with the commands and what they do. This will give you greater confidence the next time you log onto that system or one like it.

When you have been online for some time, you may encounter new things. When that happens, open a log file and capture the information.

DOCTOR'S NOTE

One approach to maximizing your time online would be to capture all of the help screens on a particular system during one session. For example, on a PC Board system you might make a log file called PCBHELP.LOG. If you have a printer, you could print out the log file and then delete it. Make another one for Wildcat! systems and call it WILDHELP.LOG. If you don't have a printer, keep the log files on your system until you don't need them anymore. You could do the same thing with other bulletin board software. The commercial online networks like GEnie and CompuServe also have help available. Since these networks are much more extensive than bulletin boards, you might want to keep an ongoing log file for help on each network.

As you explore these vast networks and find you need help, you can open your log file and save the new information. Each time you find yourself adding to a log file, take some time when you get offline to study it. A good thing to note here is that the log files created by communications programs are always appended to. In other words, you could have a file in the HELP directory called GENIEHLP.LOG that already had data in it. If you were online you could open a log file and call it C:\HELP\ GENIEHLP.LOG and the new information would automatically be appended to the end.

Online help can serve you well, but there is no sense in reading it over and over while you are online. This only wastes your time and money.

Using Menus

For users new to telecommunications, menus are wonderful things. On bulletin board systems, they show you the commands that you can use. On online networks, they help guide you through the maze to find the things you want. Once again, if you have a log file open the first time you log onto a system, you'll be able to look at the menus more closely offline. You'll also be able to learn more of the commands. This is much more effective than trying to learn them as you go while online. It's cheaper, too! Figure 6-3 is the main menu of the typical Wildcat! BBS.

You can use this example to learn some of the Wildcat! commands before you ever go online. From the main menu, entering **M** will take you to the message area. An **F** will take you into the files area. As you can see, for the most part all commands are *mnemonic*. The term mnemonic refers to memory. It's a device to assist you in recalling information. You will find that mnemonics are used in many Shareware programs as well. In

---

Figure 6-3

Main menu of a typical Wildcat! BBS

```
                          MAIN MENU
    B ulletin Menu
    F ile Menu
    M essage Menu         1st Called: 04-01-88
    N ewsletter           Time: 10:38a
    S tatistics           # of Calls: 213         C omment / Sysop
    V erify a User        Security Index: 80      G oodbye, Log Off
    H elp Level           ———— BBS ————           I nitial Welcome
    D oor Menu            # of Messages: 55       U serlog Listing
    W ho is On-line       # of Files: 586         ? Command Help
                          # Users: 1443           R egister Product
                          # of Calls: 39575       Y our Settings
                                                  P age the Sysop
                                                  T alk to Nodes


    Caller: Mike Callahan      Time On-line: 1      Time Remain    58
```

```
◆ ANSI  ONLINE  19200 8N1  [Home]=Menu   FDX 8 LF X F D CP LG ↑ PR 00:01:40
```

this example, mnemonics are used by making the command letter the same as the first letter of the function you are trying to access. If "F" is for files area and "M" is for message area, what letter in the message area do you think lets you read messages? Yes, it would be an "R."

Figure 6-4 is the typical main menu of a PC Board BBS. Note that the PC Board system also uses mnemonics to assist you. If you use a log file the first time you log onto such a system, you will get copies of all of the various menus, screens, and so on. It's important that you learn the commands needed for various systems. Why? Because while menus are a terrific help when you first go online, they also take up time. Depending on your baud rate it can take quite a while for a menu to be displayed on your screen. This is true on both commercial networks and on bulletin boards. All bulletin boards have what is called an *expert mode*. Online networks have a *command mode*. When you are in expert mode on a BBS you don't see any menus. The same holds true when you are in command mode on an online network. In order to talk about both expert mode on BBSs and command mode on commercial networks at the same time, the term *advanced mode* will be used to represent both of them in the following examples.

Figure 6-4

Main menu of a typical PC Board BBS

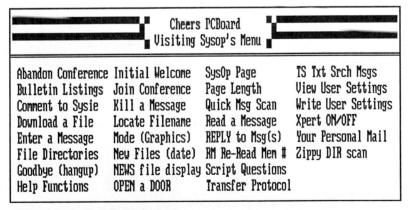

The reason you should learn the available commands on bulletin board systems you visit is so you can get into advanced mode. This will allow you to save time and money. On a big online network like Compu-Serve it can take you a while to get from one area to another if you follow only menus. You have to wait for each menu to be displayed before you can pick the next selection. Step by step you move closer to the place where you want to be. All the while, however, the clock is ticking. If you are in advanced mode, you can move to the same place with one simple command. That saves time and, of course, time is money.

Figure 6-5 shows a mock menu system. It doesn't really exist on any of the online networks, but you can pretend that it does. The goal is to get from the main menu to the Zippo Software section.

As you can see, you have to follow the chain of menus until you finally get to your goal. If this were CompuServe, you could simply type **GO ZIPPO** at a prompt and you would be there. Note that each menu has a page number. If this were GEnie, you could just type **M950** and you'd also be at the Zippo Software section. The advantage is obvious. You bypass all of those other menus and prompts and go straight to your destination. Creating log files when you first start going online makes it easier to do these kinds of things.

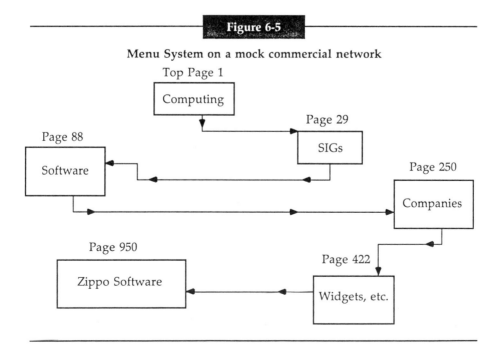

Figure 6-5

Menu System on a mock commercial network

DOCTOR'S NOTE

It has occurred to me that there might be some confusion about my references to using log files. Initially, I said that you should open a log file when you first access a new system. I am not advocating that you open a log file every time you go online. Appendix C contains the phone numbers of some very good bulletin board systems. In each case, it indicates what kind of bulletin board software the system runs—PC Board, Wildcat!, Opus, and so on.

While certain screens and menus from various BBSs are included, it is impossible to include all of the screens that exist on every kind of system. So, when I say to open a log file "the first time you access a new system," I am referring to the BBS software. The first time you call a PC Board system, open a log file so you can capture menus, help screens, and other things that have been discussed. With very few exceptions, and most of those only cosmetic, all PC Board systems will have similar prompts, menus, and the like. If you capture the online help screens from one PC Board system, they will apply to all PC Board systems. The first few times you log onto a Wildcat! system, GEnie, or CompuServe, you'll want to open a log file.

As you spend more time online, you'll find other useful things to use log files for—take electronic mail for example. When users log onto a BBS and see that they have messages waiting for them, a majority will stay online, answering each message. They may spend 40 minutes of long-distance time in the process. Then they log off. You already know of a better way. Use a log file. Read your messages, which will be stored in the file. If reading messages was all you came online to do, you can be off in less than five minutes.

Now, safely offline with the only clock that's ticking the one on the wall, you can take your time answering each message. You can use an editor and name your files REPLY1.TXT, REPLY2.TXT, and REPLY3.TXT. (A bit later you'll find out what to do with your reply files. You'll send them to the system using an *ASCII upload.*) For now let's just say that you can go back to the same system, send your three replies, and be off again in under five minutes. Already you can see how much time you've saved over the users who reply to their mail online. PC Board systems have a means of handling mail that is even faster and will be discussed shortly. For now, let's move on to look at some other ways to speed things up online.

Keyboard Macros

Some of you may use a *keyboard macro* program. These are programs like Newkey, Summacs, Ratkey, SuperKey, and ProKey. If you do, you know that a macro records a series of keystrokes. Once recorded, you can play back the macro any time you want. Macros save time because many keystrokes can be saved in one macro. With keyboard macro programs you can put in pauses, wait for some variables, and have different types of fields. Communications programs have built-in macro functions, too. You could assign your name to one macro and your password to another. (I have four macros I use for putting different signatures on messages.) Because a macro will store many keystrokes, they can be very useful when you are online. Many communications programs let you assign 40 macros or more. Figure 6-6 shows just the function key macros that I have assigned in Qmodem.

Note the macro for F2. Qmodem has a variable for passwords. By making "$PASSWORD" my F2 macro, I can have a different password on every system I call. How? When I log onto a system and it asks for my password, I can press F2. The password variable reads the password that I

Figure 6-6

Some of the Doc's Qmodem macros

```
══════════════════════ Function Key Assignment ══════════════════
          Definitions for Normal F-keys
F1   Dr. File Finder ^M░░░░░░░░░░░░░░░░░░░░░░░░░░░░░░░░░░░░░░░░░░░░░
F2   $PASSWORD^M
F3   @SCRIPT SWITCH.SCR
F4   @SCRIPT HST2TERM.SCR
F5   @SCRIPT CLEAR.SCR
F6   AT &M4 &W^M
F7   @SCRIPT LOG.SCR
F8   @SCRIPT LOG2.SCR
F9   @CLRSCR
F10
F11
F12

  Valid Edit Keys    :   INS - Insert mode Toggle    ↑ - Field Up
                         DEL - Delete Character       ↓ - Field Down
                          ← - Character Left         ^← - Word Left
                          → - Character Right        ^→ - Word Right
  Special Characters :   ^M = [ENTER]                ^~ = ½ second delay
```

```
░░░░ Edit Function Key Entries    [F10] to Save    [ESC] to Abort changes ░░░░
```

have assigned for that system out of Qmodem's dialing directory. In this way I can have one macro that can have an infinite number of values. I've mentioned log files quite a bit and F7 and F8 show you that I practice what I preach. F7 is assigned to execute a Qmodem script called LOG.SCR. When scripts are discussed, you'll have a copy of LOG.SCR to use. Qmodem macros can be used to execute any number of scripts or commands. Note that F6 is used to send a command to the modem. F8 closes a log file for you with one keystroke. Macros save you time and energy because you can record a long sequence of keystrokes once and never have to do it again.

In Qmodem, you can also assign a macro that will execute any of the commands in Qmodem's script language. While macros are very helpful for miscellaneous commands, there is something better you can use for logging on—something much more powerful and automatic for doing things online—script files.

CREATING AND USING SCRIPT FILES

As noted earlier, all of the communications programs discussed in Chapter 11 have script languages. Scripts can be simple and used only for logging you onto a system. They can also be quite complex and perform many different functions depending on conditions that exist. You can even create your own menu interfaces using these very versatile languages.

Note: All of the example scripts in this section and throughout the book are written using the script language in Qmodem by John Friel and The Forbin Project. Scripts that perform the same functions can be written using the script languages used by most of the communications programs described in Chapter 11.

Scripts automate the things you do online and this saves you time. You can create scripts that will handle electronic mail for you, download a list of files, capture a list of files, and much more. The first thing that most people use a script for is logging on. Let's take a look and see how this is done with Qmodem.

Making a Logon Script

Qmodem has a special feature that really makes it easy to create a logon script for any system that you call. It's called the *Quick Learn* script function. Quick Learn will actually make the script for you. Several other communications programs have a similar feature, including Procomm and Telemate.

Let's say that you are about to call your first PC Board system. In Qmodem, you use the dialing directory and enter all of the requested information. When you are prompted for a script name, put in something like **PCB.SCR** or **PCBOARD.SCR**. I know, you don't have a script yet, but you will! Now that all the information is in, save it by using F10. When you start to dial the system you'll notice that a "Q" appears alongside the dialing directory entry. Why? Because you gave a script name that doesn't exist. Qmodem senses that and automatically turns on the Quick Learn function. The communications programs that have an "auto learn" function always let you know when it is active. As you connect to the board and respond to each prompt, the information is being stored and made into a script. When you've gotten to the point where you want the script to stop, use ALT-Q to turn off the Quick Learn function.

Figure 6-7 shows you what you get when you use Qmodem's Quick Learn to create a logon script. You now have a script that will automatically log you onto that system. Can you make it so that you can use that script on almost every PC Board? Sure you can. Load PCB.SCR into an editor. Move down to the point where the script sends your password. Delete your password for that system and change it so it says

```
Send $PASSWORD
```

Just as with the password macro that was discussed, your script will now read the password out of the dialing directory. You can have a different password on each system. When the script encounters the $PASSWORD variable it will send the appropriate one for each system. Logon scripts make it fast and easy to access both bulletin boards and online networks.

Making More Complex Scripts

In the last section, while discussing macros, a macro was mentioned that executes a script called LOG.SCR. Figure 6-8 gives you the script commands that make up LOG.SCR.

Figure 6-7

Logon script created with Qmodem's Quick Learn

```
;
; QuickLearn Script generated at 11:57:12 on 01-09-90
: May require editing before use.
;
Graphics ANSI
TurnON    8_BIT
TurnOFF   LINEFEED
TurnOFF   XON/XOFF
TurnON    NOISE
TurnON    MUSIC
TurnON    SCROLL
TurnOFF   PRINT
TurnOFF   ECHO
TurnOFF   SPLIT
TurnOFF   BS_DEL


TimeOut   30      ; Set Waitfor for 30 seconds

Waitfor   "o you want graphics (Enter)=no?"
Delay     100
Send      "y q^M"

Waitfor   "s your first name? ^[[1;33;40m"
Delay     100
Send      "Rae^M

Waitfor   "your last name? ^[[1;33;40m"
Delay     100
Send      "Barent^M"

Waitfor   "(Dots will echo)? ^[[1;33;40m"
Delay     100
Send      "violot^M"

Waitfor   "(Enter) to continue? ^[[1;33;40m"
Delay     100
Send      "^M"

Waitfor   "1;33;40m(H)elp, More? ^[[1;33;40m"
Delay     100
Send      "n^M"

Waitfor   "st Read' (Enter)=yes? ^[[1;33;40m"
Delay     100
Send      "n^M"

Waitfor   ") Main Board Command? ^[[1;33;40m"
Delay     100
Exit
```

What this does is put a nice-looking little box on your screen that prompts you to "Enter Capture File Name:." You can enter any name you like, but there is an extra option. First you have to make one minor alteration to Qmodem's configuration. With Qmodem loaded, use ALT-N to bring up the *configuration menu.* Now select **O** for *Options.* The next thing to do is to pick **C** for *Characters.* The first item is *Date Separation* and it will show a / . Hit ENTER and an ASCII table will appear. You'll note that

---

Figure 6-8

LOG.SCR for opening a log file and naming/dating it

```
top:
STRING SATTR CAPNAME
ASSIGN SATTR $ATTR
GETSCR
CLRSCR
COLORBG 0
COLORFG 12
BOX 15,20,60,22
CLRSCR
COLOR 2
DISPLAY "Enter Capture File Name: > "
COLOR 14
GET 0 12
if "$0" = " " USEDATE

USENAME:
ASSIGN CAPNAME "$0"
GOTO DO_IT

USEDATE:
ASSIGN CAPNAME "$DATE.LOG"
GOTO DO_IT

DO_IT:
TURNOFF CAPTURE
Capture C:\DNLD\$CAPNAME
PUTSCR
COLOR $SATTR
```

a box will highlight the / character. Using the LEFT ARROW key, move two char acters to the left. That should put you over the dash (-). Select the dash by hitting ENTER. Use ESC to exit. Be sure to save your changes before you exit the configuration.

Now your LOG.SCR will also acccpt dates. If you just hit ENTER when prompted to "Enter Log File Name:" the log file will use today's date. For example, if you hit F7, see the prompt, and hit ENTER, a capture file called 01-04-90.LOG would be created if it were January 4, 1990.

LOG.SCR, shown in Figure 6-8, lets you have some flexibility when you open log files. You can use names that mean something to you. In some instances, you may want to put everything you log on a given day into a .LOG file with that date. Now you have a way to do both. The script also puts your log files in a directory that you specify. Just use an editor and copy LOG.SCR exactly as it is written. There is one change that you will want to make. Look at the label "DO_IT:" and you'll see the following line:

```
Capture C:\DNLD\$CAPNAME
```

This sends all File Finder log files to the C:\DNLD directory on the hard disk. Change this so your log files will go where you want them to go on your system.

An ASCII Upload Script

Earlier, it was explained how you could save time reading messages by capturing them to a log file. With that done you can log off and reply to each message while offline. The example given involved naming the replies to three messages as REPLY1.TXT, REPLY2.TXT, and REPLY3.TXT. An *ASCII upload* is a means of sending non-binary data to the other system. In other words, you are sending ASCII text. You could use a script to make this process faster and easier as well. Figure 6-9 shows the Qmodem script commands that prompt for an ASCII filename and then do the upload. This same type of script could be written in the script language of other communications programs—for example, Procomm, Telix, and Boyan.

Figure 6-9

An ASCII upload script—ASC-UP.SCR

```
top:
STRING SATTR
ASSIGN SATTR $ATTR
GETSCR
CLRSCR
COLORBG 0
COLORFG 12
BOX 15,20,60,22
CLRSCR
COLOR 2
DISPLAY "Enter ASCII File Name: > "
COLOR 14
GET 0 12
UPLOAD A C:\DNLD\$0
PUTSCR
COLOR $SATTR
```

This script puts a box on your screen, just above the command line and prompts you to:

```
Enter ASCII File Name: >
```

Enter the name of the file, REPLY1.TXT, for example. When you hit ENTER the script automatically starts the upload of the file. To do this effectively, you first have to start the message on the bulletin board system. You have to enter the name of the person who will receive the message, the subject, whether it's private, and so on. When you get to line number one of the message, that's when you start the ASCII upload of your message. Figure 6-10 shows what your screen would look like on a PC Board system at the point where you are ready to start your upload.

You would follow the same basic procedure on any bulletin board system or commercial network. Enter the necessary information first and when you get to the first line of the message, send your file. By capturing messages to a log file you save time. You can take all the time you want to reply offline. Then, by sending your replies via an ASCII upload you save still more time. You now have copies of LOG.SCR and ASC-UP.SCR to assist you in doing this with Qmodem.

Figure 6-10

The start of an ASCII upload on PC Board

```
█
(77 min. left) Main Board Command? e

              (-------------------------)
        To (Enter)=`ALL'? SYSOP
    Subject (Enter)=abort? ASCII UPLOADS
Message Security (H)=help?

    Enter your text. (Enter) alone to end. (72 chars/line, 99 lines maximum)
    (----------------------------------------------------------------------)
  1:
```

```
◆ ANSI   ONLINE  19200 8N1  [Home]=Menu   FDX 8 LF X ♪ ♫ CP LG ↑ PR 00:03:29 ▓
```

Creating Advanced Scripts

At first the type of script you will probably use most often will be the logon script. As you gain more confidence, however, you may find that you want to do more advanced things with scripts. If you find that you are having problems writing them yourself, you have several options. One thing you can do is look on bulletin boards or the commercial online networks. Many users like to share their scripts by sending them to bulletin boards and networks. You just might find one that does what you are trying to do. Another good option is to ask for help in the conferences on BBSs and online networks. You may be pleasantly surprised to see how many people are willing to give you some help. By looking at scripts created by others and testing them, you can get a better idea of how the script language works.

Most people who share their scripts put comment lines on the side. This tells you what the script is doing at any particular time. By paying attention to these comments you'll gain a better understanding of the script language yourself. Scripts can be used to create menu interfaces for use on bulletin boards and commercial networks. Such menus generally depend on what is called *conditional branching*. Sounds complicated, but all it means is that the script will branch off in different directions depending on certain conditions. Here is a very brief example of conditional branching in a Qmodem script:

```
GET 0 12
IF $0 = "Messages" MAIL
ELSE GOTO FILES
```

What is this saying? The "GET 0 12" tells the script to get the first 12 characters of what comes in next and to assign that to the variable 0. The "IF $0 = "Messages" MAIL" says that if what came in was the word "Messages," the script should jump to the label "MAIL." This label would most likely do something to capture any new mail. The "ELSE GOTO FILES" says that if what came in was not "Messages," the script should jump to the label "FILES." The FILES label might start a section of the script that would capture a list of new files. The script is branching depending on what the conditions are. If you have messages, you want to go there. If not, you want to go to the files area. As you see more examples of scripts, they will make more and more sense to you.

Scripts Used by Big Business

Scripts aren't used just to access bulletin boards and commercial networks. Many businesses use scripts to perform necessary tasks. John Ferebee, a Qmodem alpha tester and an employee of New York Telephone, said this about Qmodem scripts used by his company. "We use Qmodem scripts to pull massive downloads seven days a week from VAX machines. The scripts download the data and then shell out to DOS and compute the data into formats we need. Then they go back for more. These VAX downloads run about 2 to 3 megabytes per night and run from 7:00 P.M. until 6:30 A.M. The scripts, with some help from John Friel, are about 12K in size and work totally unattended seven days a week. We use most of his script commands for some fancy stuff and we have never had a failure. This is really something if you know anything about VAXs."

As you can see, scripts can be used to do a simple logon or to do complex tasks. The Qmodem script language will be discussed in more detail in Chapter 11.

Prepared Files

The last thing to discuss is preparing files offline. Earlier it was noted how you can save a great deal of time and money by replying to mail messages offline. You have the example of capturing your messages to a log file, writing your replies offline, and then sending them using an ASCII upload. There are certain things that you need to consider when preparing a file for ASCII upload. To avoid problems you should

- Know the maximum line width of the system you are sending to

- Know the maximum number of lines allowed for a message

PC Board and Wildcat! BBSs can have messages that are 72 characters wide; other BBS software will only allow 65 characters. If you format a message for 72 characters and try sending it to a system that only accepts 65 characters, what you get is a messy looking ASCII upload. Why? Because the lines wrap when they get to the 66th character. Your neatly formatted paragraphs will be reduced to rubble.

The second consideration when preparing a file for ASCII upload is the maximum number of lines allowed per message. Some systems, like Wildcat!, allow for 150 lines. On PC Board BBSs the maximum number allowed is 99 lines, but this can be reduced by the sysop. A few bulletin boards allow as few as 18 lines for a message. The commercial online networks, on the other hand, give you an almost unlimited number of lines. Even so, it wouldn't be advisable to try ASCII uploading your 400 page novel as a message.

If you keep these factors in mind when you are replying to messages offline, your ASCII uploads will go smoothly. They'll also look nice. If you should make a mistake and end up with a really messy looking message, *do not* try to fix it online. All you'll do is waste a lot of time. It's much better to abort the message and log off. You can fix the message offline and then go back and send it. The key is to save time. Sending files that you've prepared offline, via ASCII uploads, will be your best bet on nearly all bulletin board systems. If you use either GEnie or CompuServe extensively, you may want to consider using one of the products that were developed especially for them. These programs, like TAPCIS for CompuServe and Aladdin for GEnie, are designed for handling mail specifically on these systems.

The Qmail Door on PC Board

In October 1987, Mark "Sparky" Herring introduced a new concept of handling mail on PC Board systems. What Mark released was the *Qmail Door,* and it has become quite popular. As of this writing, the Qmail Door is on over 500 PC Board systems around the country.

What does the Qmail Door do? For starters it allows PC Board systems to have far more conferences than are normally possible. Each individual user can configure the Qmail Door and select only the conferences that they want to read and reply to. Each time users go into the Qmail Door they can download a packet that contains all of the new mail since they were last logged on. The packet can also contain a list of any new files on the system, updated bulletins, and so on. A user can also elect to download only messages directed to them or to read all new messages. The Qmail Door utilizes several different file transfer protocols. Here again, each user can configure the Door to use the available protocol that they prefer. Figure 6-11 shows the main menu of the Qmail Door.

The packet that users download is compressed, making it much smaller. These files all have an extension of .QWK. Each system that uses

---

Figure 6-11

Main menu of the Qmail Door on PC Board

Main System Menu

```
CLS     Clears your screen
HELP    Help with system commands
C       Configure the Qmail Door
D[p]    Download messages (optional protocol)
G       Logoff and disconnect from PCBoard
M       Toggle graphics mode
O       Chat with the sysop
Q       Quit Qmail Door and return to PCBoard
U[p]    Upload replies (optional protocol)
X       Expert mode toggle
```

(73 min. left) Qmail Command?

ANSI   ONLINE 19200 8N1 [Home]=Menu   FDX 8 LF X ♪ ♫ CP LG ↑ PR 00:06:29

the Qmail Door has its own code name. This lets you use Qmail on several PC Board systems without getting your mail packets confused. For example, a packet from The Black Bag would be called BLKBAG.QWK, while one from the Cheers PC Board would be called CHEERS.QWK. Using the Qmail Door you can go on a PC Board system and download your packet and log off.

When he released the Qmail Door, Mark Herring also released a special Qmail Reader. The Qmail Reader unpacks your packet and gives you the feeling that you are actually on the BBS. You see the welcome screen, the news, the bulletins, and so on. You can then read and reply to all of your messages. When you're done, you exit the Reader and it packs up your replies. Each reply file has the code of the BBS that it's intended for with an extension of .REP. Using the same examples used above you'd have a BLKBAG.REP file or a CHEERS.REP file. You simply return to the board where the replies are to be sent and go back into the Qmail Door.

Once there you upload your reply packet and log off. On many PC Board systems you can go on and get your messages through the Qmail Door and be off in two minutes. Using the latest Qmail Reader, QPRO, I take my time answering my mail. When I'm done, I go back and upload my replies. Once again, this generally takes only a couple of minutes. The Qmail Door and Reader are real time savers! If you use a PC Board system that doesn't have the Qmail Door, encourage the sysop to install it.

Since the release of the Qmail Door in 1987, several other program authors have released programs that utilize the Qmail Door. One of these is EZ-READER by Eric Cockrell. EZ-READER can use the mail packets produced by the Qmail Door. It can unpack .QWK files and create .REP files that are compatible with Qmail. Another program that utilizes the Qmail Door is RoboComm by Dan Parsons. RoboComm automates the access of the Qmail Door on any number of PC Board systems. Please note that RoboComm is not capable of reading the mail packets, but only makes it easier to obtain them.

At the present time in 1990, other bulletin board systems, such as Wildcat!, are working on doors that will have a function similar to that of the Qmail Door. It is anticipated that these doors will produce Qmail compatible data. If they do, Mark Herring's Qmail Reader, QPRO, and Eric Cockrell's EZ-READER could be used with mail packets from these systems. The Qmail Door, or clones of it on other systems, will save you time and money in handling your online mail. Watch for them and use them wherever possible. Let's go on to talk briefly about some common problems that you'll encounter.

COMMON ONLINE PROBLEMS

As you venture out into The Wires and gain more confidence, you will still have occasional problems. Script files that you write may not work perfectly the first time. If that happens to you, don't worry about it. The more you work with them the better you'll get. Even experienced users sometimes have to spend some time refining a complex script. There is another common problem with scripts, especially logon scripts.

Scripts that Die Suddenly

Since you are bound to encounter this problem during your time online, you should be aware of it. Let's say that you have a logon script for a particular bulletin board. This script has worked perfectly for over six months. One day you go to log onto this system and you connect just fine. This is the point where your trusty script takes over. This time it doesn't. You find yourself sitting there staring at the first prompt. You escape from the script and log on manually.

What happened? If it's a system you frequent regularly, when it happens you'll know what's wrong. What happened is that the system has changed the prompts. The sysop may have put up a new type of software or a new kind of user interface. If it isn't one of those things then perhaps items are being displayed in a different order. Maybe the system used to ask you about messages first and then bulletins. Now the order is reversed. The key to all this is one basic fact: all script languages depend on the script reacting to specific incoming data.

This data must be exactly what the script has been told to look for. If the script contains the command, "Waitfor 'Command?'" and it gets "Main Board," the script does nothing. Why? Because it's still waiting for the prompt "Command?". When your existing script dies because the prompts on a system have changed, all you can do is make a new script. If you erase the old one from disk, Qmodem's Quick Learn function will make a new one the next time you log onto that system. By the time you have more experience with scripts, you may very well be able to go in and change your existing script to meet the changes. Just remember that if a script has worked fine for some time and it suddenly stops, the prompts from the system may have changed.

Line Noise

While you are online, some of your biggest problems can be caused by what users generally refer to as *line noise.* Line noise can be caused by several different things. How can you tell if you are having line noise? To begin with you'll *see* it. If the line noise is mild you will see an occasional garbage character on your screen. As mentioned earlier, garbage characters are the ones above ASCII 127, part of the IBM graphics character set. If line noise is bad, you'll get "bursts" of garbage characters on your screen. At it's very worst, line noise can be so bad that you'll have to disconnect from a system because you can't really do anything. There are two major causes of line noise. These are

- Interference from the phone system
- Electrical interference around the modem

Although things have improved somewhat over the last several years, many phone companies are still using some archaic equipment. This old equipment is one source of line noise. In the case of many phone systems, not all of their equipment is old, only portions of it. If you connect to a system and experience line noise, try logging off. Now call back in again. If you're lucky you'll have gotten a new line and the line noise will be gone. When dealing with different dialing services like Telenet, Tymnet, PC Pursuit, and others, you may occasionally get connected to a bad node. This may be a node that has older modems or it may be connected to a bad phone line itself.

Once again, my advice is to disconnect and try calling again. In many cases this will eliminate your problem. In dealing with such services you might want to call their support number and inform them that a particular node seems to have a problem. In most cases, the service in question will investigate the matter and correct it. A word of caution: line noise can damage any data that you send or receive. If you are experiencing line noise and can't get rid of it, postpone any file transfers until you have a clean line. There are a few exceptions to this which will be discussed in the next chapter.

The second major source of line noise comes from in and around your modem. Electrical interference from household appliances may be one source. One way to avoid this is to have your modem, and your computer, for that matter, on a separate circuit in your house. When you do

DOCTOR'S NOTE

One final note on line noise is a personal observation. Although it hasn't been documented, to the best of my knowledge, I believe that severe weather also causes line noise. Having spent a great deal of time online, I've noted that the occurrence of line noise increases during bad weather. Particularly during snow, sleet, and thunderstorms. Ice on the phone lines will also cause some problems. In transferring data between friends, I've noted that we've had the most problems when one of us is having bad weather. Just something for you to keep in mind.

this, the kids can use the popcorn popper and not cause a problem with your file transfers. Try to arrange it so your computer and modem share a common ground. Always keep the phone cord that goes to the modem away from all of the other cables and cords that run from your computer. This helps to prevent any electrical interference from being transferred to the phone line. You may also want to check the integrity of the phone jack to make sure that there isn't a short.

How can you do this? One easy way is to connect the modem line to a phone. While you're at it, use the same phone cord that connects the modem to the jack. Pick up the receiver and move the phone cord around. If you hear clicks or even brief moments of silence, you probably have a short. Now, change cords and try it again. If you don't hear any clicks or static, the short is most likely in the cord that goes to your modem. If you still hear clicks, then it is most likely the phone jack. If you are still having problems with line noise, you may need to check to see where the phone line runs through your house. It could be running across the 220 line that runs to your electric stove.

Since a modem is an electronic device that must be approved by the Federal Communications Commission (FCC) it can be affected by other electronic devices. Use common sense and you'll be able to track down the cause of your line noise and eliminate it.

Aborted Transfers

One major effect of line noise is that it can cause file transfers to abort. Some file transfer protocols are much more resistant to line noise than others. The next chapter will go over all of the most popular file transfer protocols and tell you which are the most resistant to line noise. There are few things more frustrating than receiving 200K of a 300K file, only to have it abort. There are three transfer protocols—Zmodem, BiModem, and MPt—that can recover from an aborted download.

There are other factors that can cause a file transfer to abort. Sometimes, on multiple line bulletin boards, if one node locks up, it causes all nodes to lock up. This would mean that your file transfer would freeze and you'd have to disconnect. You will be able to keep your aborted downloads to a minimum. Now, let's look into an important factor—costs.

DIFFERENT WAYS OF CONNECTING

There are several different ways that you can access bulletin boards and commercial networks. Some have advantages over others. In order to help you save money, let's go into some of the different methods available and discuss what they cost. This will give you some idea of the best ways for you to call various systems, including:

- Direct dial—local and long distance
- Network nodes
- Telenet and PC Pursuit
- Tymnet and StarLink

You'll also learn about surcharges, special online charges, and connect time. The new Call Data Standard or CDS, which will ultimately tell you the best and least expensive ways for you to dial the systems you want to call, will be discussed.

Direct Dial

First, let's look at local calls. There are two types of local charges, unlimited and metered. In an unlimited setup, you are charged a set fee no matter how many local calls you make (and no matter how long you talk). You might benefit from this type of plan if you make a lot of local modem calls. In a metered setup, you are charged a few cents for each local call you make. Generally, you pay a penny or two less per call if you dial after

5:00 P.M. or on weekends. This is a good option for people who make just a few modem calls each month, or who might only call BBSs when the local rates are low.

There are also unit calls where you pay so much per minute. For example, for a user to call a GEnie node in Denver from rural Colorado, it costs 14 cents a minute at night and 17 cents a minute during the day. These are generally calls where you have to dial the number 1 first. During the day, this adds up to $10.20 an hour before any taxes are added. One thing to keep in mind as you learn about network nodes, Telenet and Tymnet, is whether or not these services are local calls for you. If not, you may have to seek alternatives. More examples will be given as we go along.

Dialing direct via long distance can get expensive. If you make most of your calls at night, AT&T's Reach Out America plan can save you money. I know because I use it myself. You can call AT&T toll free at 800-222-0300 to find out more about this plan. If you make most of your calls during the day and spend at least $100 a month, AT&T's ProWATS might be of help to you. To find out more you can call 800-222-0400. If you use a high-speed modem and only make a small or moderate number of modem calls per month, these plans can really benefit you. With 2400 baud or below you may want to look not only at the plans from AT&T or the long-distance carrier of your choice, but into some of the other options available.

Operators usually say long-distance calls are charged by the mileage between you and the other line. However, if you know the cost for one number in a given area code, you can pretty much use that figure for all numbers in that area code. Operators will usually supply you with two complete sets of phone rate data for a given area code or toll prefix. Try not to ask for more data in a single call. Remember, operators have to help other customers too.

Network Nodes

GEnie and CompuServe each has its own network of phone lines that are located in cities throughout the United States. Each of these numbers is called a node. Thus, if you access GEnie through one of its own phone numbers, you are calling via a *GEnie node.* With both services there is no extra charge for using one of their nodes to gain access. These nodes, or phone lines, are maintained by the individual networks. If you ever have a problem with a GEnie or CompuServe node, just call their support lines and report it. CompuServe's customer support number is 800-848-8990. The GEnie customer support line is 800-638-9636.

The first thing you have to find out is if the nearest node is a local call. If you aren't certain, your local operator can tell you. If it's a toll call to the nearest CompuServe node, you're going to want to check out another way of calling. GEnie is only available through its own nodes, which may pose a problem for those who live in rural areas.

Telenet and PC Pursuit

Telenet is a nationwide packet switching network. It handles data transmissions for large businesses as well as individuals. Telenet also has its own system of phones in cities around the country. Each Telenet phone number is also called a node. If your local CompuServe node is not a local call for you, perhaps the nearest Telenet number is. CompuServe can be accessed through Telenet. There is a $2 per hour surcharge for calling CompuServe through Telenet. Figure 6-12 shows the surcharge rates for calling CompuServe via Telenet.

In 1986 Telenet started a new service called PC Pursuit. PC Pursuit allows you to dial many cities across the United States for a set fee of $30 per month for 30 hours. If you wish, you can pay $50 for 60 hours. After you've exhausted your time, you then pay a flat rate of $3 for each additional hour.

PC Pursuit is used at night, starting at 6:00 P.M. and is a great way to call many places and avoid the long-distance charges. It works like this. Let's say you are in Atlanta and you want to call Boston. You call your local Telenet node and enter the code for Boston and the number that you want to call. Telenet connects you to Boston through its lines; then you're just a local call away from the number you want to call. You can call any number in a target city, whether it's a bulletin board, an online network, or a friend's computer. If you start calling a fair number of systems you may want to look into Telenet's PC Pursuit. For information, call 800-336-0437.

Tymnet and StarLink

Tymnet is another packet switching network similar to Telenet. Tymnet also has its own network of nodes around the country. You can access

---
Figure 6-12

CompuServe's Telenet surcharge rates

```
CompuServe (FREE)    BIL-155

                 Prime/  Std/
Telenet(R)       Daytime Evening
from:            $/Hour  $/Hour
_____
contiguous U.S. $12.00  $ 2.00
Alaska          $15.00  $15.00
Hawaii          $14.00  $14.00
Puerto Rico     $11.00  $11.00
```

```
Communications surcharges apply when the respective
communications network is used for connection. Each location has the
option of dialing through the above communications networks. All rates
EXCLUDE long distance and other telephone company charges (e.g. message
units).

In addition to connect time charges, members are also billed for the
supplemental network surcharges for each session on the Information
Service.

Last page!
```

CompuServe through Tymnet. This is an alternative for you if there is not a CompuServe or Telenet node that are local calls, but a Tymnet number that is. Figure 6-13 shows a listing of the communications surcharge for accessing CompuServe via Tymnet.

In 1989 Tymnet started a service called StarLink that is similar to PC Pursuit. You can sign up for StarLink while you're online. Their BBS number is 505-881-6964. When you log on for the first time, you'll be prompted for a user ID or to enter **new** if you are new. It's really very easy to do and the instructions are clear. If you have further questions, their support number is 505-881-6988. Once you have signed up for

StarLink, you access it through local Tymnet nodes. You dial into your local node and send a code that tells StarLink what city you want to dial.

One difference between StarLink and PC Pursuit is that with StarLink you must make sure that the number you want to call is a local call from the Tymnet outdial in that city. For example, let's say you are in Detroit and want to call a bulletin board in Memphis. You call a local Tymnet node and hook into StarLink. You send the access code for Memphis and the next thing you know you are connected to a Tymnet *outdial* (it dials out) in Memphis. The Tymnet (StarLink) outdial will display what the local phone exchange is. In this case that would be the exchange in Memphis.

At this point, the BBS must be a local call away from that Tymnet outdial in Memphis. For calling different systems, just ask the BBS sysop if the BBS is a local call from the local Tymnet outdial. I have found StarLink to be an excellent service and a real money saver. It runs very smoothly and there is no noticeable decrease in your speed or performance. This is an important fact because on some services there is a noticeable slowdown. There is a one time $35 startup fee. After that, you are charged a $10 service fee each month. From then on your charge for

---

Figure 6-13

CompuServe surcharges for access via Tymnet

```
CompuServe (FREE)      RIL-157


                    Prime/  Std/
TYMNET(R)           Daytime Evening
from:               $/Hour  $/Hour
```

	Prime/ Daytime $/Hour	Std/ Evening $/Hour
contiguous U.S.	$12.00	$ 2.00
Alaska (via		
ALASKA/NET)	$10.00	$ 5.50
Hawaii	$12.00	$12.00
Hawaii (via		
Western Union)	$14.00	$14.00
Puerto Rico	$11.00	$11.00
Canada	$ 9.00	$ 9.00

DOCTOR'S NOTE

If you are in a remote area, none of the alternatives mentioned may help you. I'll point out one option that many people are not aware of called a *foreign exchange*. Your local phone company can install a foreign exchange in your home. Using my example of calling Denver from rural Colorado, I had the phone company install a telephone exchange so that Denver would be a local call from that number. That line is now my data line.

The cost of the installation of a foreign exchange varies, but it is generally around $400. If you pay an average of $7 an hour for a toll call, the foreign exchange pays for itself in just 57 hours. From that point on, it is saving you a lot of money. It is something to think about if all the other options I've discussed won't do you any good because of your location. Once you have a foreign exchange you can take advantage of GEnie and CompuServe nodes, Telenet, PC Pursuit, Tymnet, and StarLink. It's worth looking into if all other options are closed to you.

---

using StarLink is just $1.50 per hour in the continental United States, and there is no limit on the number of hours you use. This is the non-prime time rate. Non-prime time begins at 7:00 P.M. and ends at 6:00 A.M. The prime time rate is $14 per hour.

I highly recommend StarLink as a means of cutting your online costs. It also lets you access a large number of systems across the country. Give it a try.

Special Charges and Connect Time

On some of the commercial networks there is an extra charge for accessing certain areas or using certain services. These areas are clearly marked so that you'll know. On CompuServe, for example, all services that require an extra charge are marked with a dollar sign ($). If you should ever stumble into one of these areas accidentally, just exit it immediately. Call customer service and they will take care of the charge. Another thing for you to keep track of is your connect time. CompuServe charges $12.50 per hour for both day and night access. Added to this would be any communications surcharges and/or special charges.

GEnie charges $18 per hour during the day. At night the connect charge varies depending on your baud rate. It is $5 per hour for 300 baud, $6 per hour for 1200 baud, and $10.50 per hour for 2400 baud. One way to keep track of not only your phone bill but your connect time is to use QANALYST in conjunction with Qmodem. Qmodem is included on one of the disks you can receive free by sending in the coupon at the back of this book. QANALYST can be found on many bulletin boards, CompuServe, and GEnie.

CALL DATA STANDARD — COMING SOON

If you use a modem, you've probably wondered if there was a way you could tell the cost of the calls you made. Well, you may soon have that information at your fingertips. Experts from around the nation worked to develop new standards for communications software. They wanted to set up guidelines so programs can keep an accurate log of their modem, fax, and voice phone usage activities. These new guidelines are known as the Call Data Standard (CDS).

There is a growing need for people and companies to track their telephone expenses when they use a modem, but few products today can provide such information. The problem is that communications programs store a call activity log any way they wish, if they store such information at all. The Call Data Standard will establish order in an area where there is no standard. It will affect any program that accesses a phone line to do its job. This includes even external protocol programs and bulletin board systems.

Let's talk about what CDS can do for you. You could choose any phone bill analyzer program, for example, and it would automatically work with any communications software. What's more, a communications program could actually talk to a phone bill analyzer. You could press a key to learn the cost of a call while you're still online with another person or computer. The Call Data Standard makes it all possible. The companies behind TAPCIS and Pibterm have already said they will include CDS in a future version. The Procomm Plus people were impressed with CDS, and Qmodem expects to add the power of instantaneous phone cost information to its next major release.

Barry Simon, former president of the Association of Shareware Professionals, is excited about the Call Data Standard. "The people on the inside know it will be easy to implement," he said. "I expect a great many products will be upgraded to conform to CDS. And then you can expect to see a lot of new products come on the Shareware and retail markets."

CDS was so hot while it was under development that the team received its own private meeting area on the CompuServe network so experts all over the country could get involved. "CDS is something the industry has badly needed for a long time now—a standard means of reporting communications usage," said Chip Rabinowitz, owner of Innovative Data Concepts, a consulting firm. Chip leads the TesSeRact Development Team, a group pushing for industry standards in RAM-resident programs. Rabinowitz plans to encourage his clients to look for CDS support when they purchase software for their modems.

How Does CDS Work?

The Call Data Standard is little more than some file formats and guidelines on how to read and write them. A *call history file*, for example, will hold details about your modem usage. It is a text file, so you'll be able to read it or print it out. There will be rigid instructions on how to write details in the file. This will make it easy for a communications program to store information about a call, and it will make it easy for a phone bill analyzer to read the file. Another file stores important information about the cost of phone calls. The data covers a call for any time of the day, any day of the week, even holidays. You'll be able to store cost details for unique telephone numbers, or for phone prefixes, or for whole area codes.

If you log onto a network like CompuServe or GEnie, you'll be able to enter *host service* cost information separate from any phone company charges. The *phone rate file* is also a text file, but it isn't something you can easily read. It's a text file so you can easily transmit it to other computers. Thus, someone who uses a Commodore Amiga computer could give you a copy of his or her CDS phone rate data file for your IBM PC. The CDS development team wants to make this a standard for all types of computers, not just for DOS machines. The Call Data Standard is currently making its way through the communications software industry. It should only be a matter of time before people will someday come to expect CDS support from any modem, fax, or voice software they purchase.

Suppose you use two different communications programs. One may be for general purposes, the other for an information service like GEnie. How can you tell the total amount of money you spent on modem phone calls? The Call Data Standard will let each communications program speak the same language. You can store information for each telephone call in the same files. If you want to see a sample phone bill, you run a phone bill analysis program that reads CDS files. It doesn't matter what program you use so long as it recognizes CDS. Another interesting feature of CDS is its ability to allow programs to interactively communicate with each other.

If you wanted to see how much the current call was costing you, you could press a key and the information would be displayed on the screen. What your communications program will do is query a phone bill analyzer about the call in progress. The phone bill analyzer calculates what you've already spent and sends this information back to your communications program. You'll get real-time feedback about the cost of a phone call placed by modem. The Call Data Standard is coming soon and it will be a tremendous help to all of us. Watch for it.

SUMMING IT ALL UP

In the course of this chapter the focus has been on how to save you both time and money while you obtain good Shareware programs, exchange messages, and the like. Now it's time to briefly sum up before moving on to new things. What are the main things you need to be aware of?

- Log files
- Automation
- Various calling options
- Expert mode
- Online help
- Doing things offline

By using log files during your early online sessions, you can save a great deal of time. You'll capture all of the prompts as well as any menus or help screens that you look at. When you automate your sessions with macros or scripts, you speed things up and make better use of your online time. Checking out all of the various calling options will allow you to go online for the least amount of money possible. Evaluate your own needs and pick the method that's best for you. When you use expert (advanced) mode, rather than menus, you cut down on the time you spend online and can access things faster. Taking advantage of online help and capturing it for later review gives you more confidence during future online sessions.

Finally, the more things you can do while offline, the better! Answering your mail offline and then sending it via ASCII uploads will greatly reduce the time you spend online. Taking advantage of the Qmail Door on PC Board systems will help even more. Reading the contents of log files and studying things like menus and help screens offline will also save you money. All the while you will be gaining more personal experience and building up more confidence. Planning out exactly what you want to do will make your sessions shorter and more productive. Going online can be fun and educational. You'll learn from other users, and before long you may find yourself giving advice. For now, it's time to move on and begin to find out more about getting the good Shareware programs.

## PART THREE

Major Operations Online

## CHAPTER SEVEN

Protocols

From the beginning of civilization, humans have needed ways to efficiently exchange information. Whether it was pounding on drums, yelling from mountaintops, or using smoke signals, humans have always found a way to get information from one place to another. As human beings have become more sophisticated and technologically oriented, they've found much better ways of communicating.

Transferring data in the early days of computers could be compared to sending smoke signals. Your data would get there, but only if a strong wind didn't come up. Remember the hex transfers discussed in Chapter 5 and how they were accomplished? Believe it or not these worked fairly well most of the time. There was one big problem with capturing hexadecimal numbers in a capture buffer. If you got hit by one little burst of line noise, your transfer was ruined. There was no way to check a file for errors during transmission. You only found out that the file was bad when you tried to use it. At that time, modem speeds were very slow, so a corrupted file cost a lot of time and money. Errors could creep into a file and there was no way for the user to know. As data and programs became more complex, this became totally unacceptable. As has been the case throughout history, people were able to come up with a workable solution to the problem at hand — file transfer protocols.

FILE TRANSFER PROTOCOLS

In order to be sure that data being transferred was intact, there had to be a way to check for errors as a file was received, and a way to compare the copy to the original to make sure that they were identical. Today there are many file transfer protocols available. Several new ones have been developed in just the last few years. The process of transferring files from one machine to another is becoming faster and more efficient all the time. Because all of the protocols used are capable of detecting errors within a file and seeing that the errors are fixed, they are called *error-correcting* protocols.

Most Shareware communications programs have certain protocols in common. Protocols are classified as being either internal or external. *Internal* file transfer protocols are built into the communications program. *External* protocols, on the other hand, are handled by programs that run separately from the communications software. Which protocol is best? That depends on a variety of factors such as the kind of system you are on, the type of modem, the modem speed, the amount of line noise, and so on.

In the course of this chapter you will learn a little bit about the history and evolution of file transfer protocols. For your own benefit you should understand how the most popular protocols work. You'll see performance comparisons that will help you judge which are the most effective. As you venture into The Wires you'll have protocols that are your favorites, while others you'll use only when you have to. Most importantly, you'll know how they work and which might be best in different situations.

Xmodem — The Beginning

Back in the days of the CP/M machines, Ward Christianson wrote a transfer protocol called *Modem7*. With the arrival of the MS/PC DOS machines, Christianson modified his code and created *Xmodem*. Xmodem was the first error-correcting protocol for DOS-based machines. Many of the file transfer protocols that have been developed since have adapted the code of the original Xmodem. How does Xmodem work? It takes a file and breaks it up into 128 byte *blocks*. A file that is 12,288 bytes in size would contain 96 blocks.

With some protocols blocks are called *packets*. Xmodem sends one block at a time. After each block is sent it waits for the receiving side to send an *ACK,* which stands for "acknowledgment." When the ACK is received the next block is sent. Blocks are compared using a *checksum.* (See the Doctor's Note for more on checksum.) When Xmodem sends a block it includes a checksum for that block. When the receiver gets the block it checks to see if the checksum arrived at is the same. If everything matches, the ACK is sent and the sender transfers the next block. If there is an error, the receiver sends a *NAK* which means "not acknowledged." When a NAK is received, the sender automatically sends the block again. With an external modem you can watch this process on the modem's lights.

If you are uploading a file, you will see your SD light (send data) go on, and then off. You'll then see a flicker on your RD (receive data) light. That flicker is the ACK (or NAK) being received. Then the SD light will glow again and the RD light will flicker. (Watching the two lights is similar to watching a ping pong ball going back and forth.) This continues until the entire file is transferred. Due to this typical pattern, Xmodem was called a *send and wait* protocol. At the time it was released, Xmodem was a boon to those using telecommunications. Binary data could now be transferred easily and Xmodem spread quickly. Even today, when many more sophisticated protocols are available, Xmodem is still the most popular. It is included in every communications program described in Chapter 11, as well as every type of bulletin board software.

Xmodem does have its problems. One of them is the wait. With a file containing 1,024 (1K) bytes, and assuming that there are no errors, Xmodem waits for an ACK eight times. To give a fair comparison, all statistics shown in tables that follow were gathered using the same file. All of the tests were done on the same system and during one connection for each baud rate. Table 7-1 shows how Xmodem does while transferring the 12K test file at different baud rates.

Note that even at 9600 baud—eight times faster than 1200 baud—Xmodem performs only about two times better than it did at 1200 baud. This fact is primarily due to the wait that is encountered. Protocols that follow the same pattern as Xmodem have also come to be called send and

Table 7-1

Xmodem Performance on 12K File at Different Speeds

Baud	CPS	Elapsed Time
1200	81 cps	2 min. 25 sec.
2400	150 cps	1 min. 19 sec.
9600	193 cps	1 min. 01 sec.

wait protocols. Another problem with Xmodem is that the checksum method of error checking is not totally efficient. This gave rise to another variation of Xmodem.

Xmodem CRC—A Small Step Forward

Xmodem CRC is identical to Xmodem in almost every way. The one way that it differs is in the way it performs the error checking on the blocks.

DOCTOR'S NOTE

There is a difference between the checksum method and the CRC error-checking approach. With checksum, each block is calculated and a value for that block is determined. Since the checksum is based on numbers, it is possible for one block to be short and for another block to disguise the error. How? By being too long by just enough to make up for the original error in the short block. It would appear that the file has no errors while, in fact, it does.

With the introduction of CRC, the possibility of an error sneaking through is greatly reduced. Because Xmodem CRC, for example, uses a two byte CRC, it makes it close to impossible for a block with an error to get past unnoticed or uncorrected. In order for an error to get through, another block would have to be transmitted that would compensate for the previous error in both of the bytes that are checked. The chances of this happening are very, very small. The newer *streaming* protocols, like Zmodem, use a 32 byte CRC that makes it virtually impossible for an error to get past the protocol. Thus, while a checksum is better than no check at all, the CRC method is much more reliable.

CRC stands for *cyclical redundancy check.* This method, using a two byte CRC is much more effective than the one byte checksum method of the original Xmodem.

Xmodem CRC first came into use around 1985. Although it isn't any faster than Xmodem, it does more to ensure that data transmitted will be error free. Table 7-2 shows you statistics gathered by downloading the same file used with Xmodem. If you compare the figures in Table 7-2 to those in Table 7-1, you'll see that the cps (*characters per second*) transferred, and the elapsed times are almost identical. Thus, while Xmodem CRC does not really improve overall performance from the standpoint of speed, it *does* have better error correction.

After Xmodem CRC was released, some communications programs included it while others retained the older Xmodem checksum. This gave rise to a flavor of Xmodem that is sometimes called *auto Xmodem.* All this really does is have the capability of detecting what type of Xmodem the other side is using. For example, if you were on a bulletin board and your communications program only had regular Xmodem, the system would use Xmodem. If you had Xmodem CRC, on the other hand, the system would use that. As files became larger, programmers started looking at speed and tried to develop ways to make Xmodem (and Xmodem CRC) faster.

1K-Xmodem—Reducing the Number of Blocks

Chuck Forsberg originally wrote *1K-Xmodem* in an attempt to speed things up. 1K-Xmodem uses blocks that are 1,024 bytes in size. 1K-Xmodem

Table 7-2

Performance of Xmodem-CRC at Different Speeds

Baud	CPS	Elapsed Time
1200	80 cps	2 min. 26 sec.
2400	151 cps	1 min. 18 sec.
9600	192 cps	1 min. 02 sec.

is an improvement over Xmodem and Xmodem CRC because the protocol has to wait eight times less often for an ACK or a NAK. 1K-Xmodem provided the first real improvement in speed. Table 7-3 shows how 1K-Xmodem performed on the same file used previously.

Note the improvement over Xmodem and Xmodem CRC even at 1200 baud. At 2400 baud the cps count doubles and at 9600 baud it more than triples. 1K-Xmodem does improve speed, but still has drawbacks. Other than the fact that it uses 1K blocks, 1K-Xmodem is identical in every way to its two predecessors—Xmodem and Xmodem CRC. None of the three transmit the name of the file or its date and time. Another drawback to the Xmodem family is that you cannot send more than one file at a time. It is much more efficient and cost effective if you can upload or download files in a *batch*. In other words, you use less time if you type in the names of five files you want to download, and then start your file transfer protocol. When you have to download files one at a time, you waste time! None of the Xmodem protocols discussed so far has the ability to allow you to upload or download a group of files. The last thing that you need to know for now about 1K-Xmodem is that sometimes it is mistakenly called *Ymodem*. Ymodem is a totally different protocol. Ymodem will be covered next, followed by a commentary on the confusion between Ymodem and 1K-Xmodem.

Ymodem—The Real McCoy

In 1981, Chuck Forsberg created Ymodem. Like 1K-Xmodem, Ymodem uses 1K blocks, but that's where the similarity ends. Forsberg gave Ymodem the ability to send the filename, the date, and the time. It also

---

Table 7-3

Performance of 1K-Xmodem at Various Speeds

Baud	CPS	Elapsed Time
1200	104 cps	1 min. 59 sec.
2400	208 cps	0 min. 59 sec.
9600	699 cps	0 min. 19 sec.

has CRC error checking. Overall it performs about the same as 1K-Xmodem. Table 7-4 shows how Ymodem performed while downloading the 12K file at different speeds.

In comparison with Christianson's Xmodem at 9600 baud, Ymodem can transfer files from 50 to 65 percent faster. When it comes to characters per second, Ymodem beats Xmodem by a factor of three or more. Another feature of Ymodem is that it can send multiple files—a batch. This is a vast improvement over 1K-Xmodem and the rest of the Xmodem family. When it was initially released, users got their first taste of being able to do batch file transfers. One minor drawback to Ymodem is that it is not very resistant to line noise. On even moderately noisy lines, Ymodem will experience errors easily, and a transfer can drag on forever until it aborts. Chuck Forsberg calls this protocol *true Ymodem* for reasons that will be clear in a moment.

Kermit—A Step Forward, a Step Back

The *Kermit* protocol was started as a project at Columbia University in New York. The primary author was Frank da Cruz, and since he began working on Kermit in the early 1980s there have been many other contributors. Following the same direction as Ymodem, Kermit took a step forward from the Xmodem protocols. Kermit can send filenames, dates, and times. It can also send multiple files and it has improved error checking. When you begin a Kermit file transfer, the two sides "negotiate" the transfer and decide how things will proceed.

Kermit was designed so it could be run on large mainframe computers as well as microcomputers. The blocks used with Kermit are called

---

Table 7-4

Performance of Ymodem at Various Speeds

Baud	CPS	Elapsed Time
1200	104 cps	1 min. 54 sec.
2400	203 cps	0 min. 57 sec.
9600	703 cps	0 min. 20 sec.

DOCTOR'S NOTE

For quite a few years there has been confusion over Ymodem and 1K-Xmodem. Some programmers tended to treat the two protocols as if they were the same thing. They are not. The biggest problem occurred on bulletin board systems.

Early on, a BBS sysop might have wanted to improve his or her system by adding a new transfer protocol. As a programmer, the sysop would write the protocol and install it into the BBS software. What was written was actually 1K-Xmodem but the sysop called it Ymodem. This didn't cause too many problems at first, but as time went on things got worse. Some systems would have a protocol listed as Ymodem and it would be a *true Ymodem* as created by Chuck Forsberg. Other systems would have a listing for Ymodem that was in fact 1K-Xmodem. The two protocols do not work together. You cannot send a file using Forsberg's Ymodem to a host that is trying to receive it with 1K-Xmodem. It's as if they are speaking foreign languages to each other.

Some bulletin board software, like RBBS-PC for example, tried to clear up the problem. They began calling Forsberg's Ymodem, *Ymodem Batch* and 1K-Xmodem, *Ymodem*. Quite naturally, many users were still confused. Many assumed that you used Ymodem when you just wanted to transfer one file, and Ymodem Batch when you wanted to transfer multiple files. For a time, one never knew when going from system to system exactly what Ymodem would be.

In the last two years, there has been a movement to correct this long-standing error. Today, on nearly all BBSs and in most communications programs, the two protocols are clearly distinguished. Both PC Board and Wildcat! systems will show a selection for Ymodem and one for 1K-Xmodem. You'll note that Qmodem also lists them as individual protocols, as they should be. In Qmodem, you select **Y** for Chuck Forsberg's Ymodem and **O** for 1K-Xmodem.

Another example can be found on GEnie. GEnie download protocols list 1K-Xmodem, letting users know that this is not Ymodem. If you select 1K-Xmodem on a system, and then pick Ymodem in your communications program, you'll be wasting your time.

Just remember that 1K-Xmodem is nothing more than Xmodem that uses 1K blocks. Ymodem, on the other hand, uses CRC error checking, sends filename, time, date, and can be used to do batch file transfers. At this point the problem has pretty much been resolved.

packets, and they vary in size. The size of the packet is one of the things negotiated at the very beginning. Kermit also offers a small degree of file compression. Kermit took a step forward with many of these innovations. At the same time, Kermit took a small step backwards. In order for it to work on mainframe computers, special considerations had to be made. These considerations tended to make Kermit slower than Xmodem! As an example, if Xmodem transfers a file at 80 cps, Kermit transfers the same file at about 55 cps. This rate seems to be acceptable on mainframe computers, but not on bulletin boards or commercial networks. Kermit is constantly upgraded and improved.

In case you are curious about its name, Jim Henson, creator of the Muppets, allowed the copyrighted name of Kermit the Frog to be used. This was done to help legally protect the protocol. Since Kermit is a public domain protocol, if anyone were to try to capitalize on it, they would be infringing on Henson's copyright of the name Kermit. Columbia University collects any modifications to the Kermit source code. The source code is available from Columbia University for a fee. While Kermit has found its niche in the world of mainframe computers, it needed something added before it could become popular on BBSs. What Kermit needed was *windows*.

Sliding Windows (Super) Kermit

In 1985, Jan van der Eijk released a protocol that he called *Super Kermit*. Jan had added a technique called windowing to the Kermit protocol. Without getting too complicated, there are two types of windowing—*sliding windows* and *fixed windows*. Van der Eijk added sliding windows to his Super Kermit. The author of Super Kermit explains it this way: "Just think of a carousel or perhaps a lazy Susan that is spinning around. The main thing is to envision it as a process that is always moving. Packets leave the carousel (or lazy Susan) and don't wait to see if they are acknowledged. The carousel keeps on spinning. When there is a bad packet there is always a time when the carousel will come back around and the packet can be sent again. Since the protocol doesn't care about the order the packets are received in, you can send it back anytime. Essentially, this is how Sliding Windows Kermit works."

Because it doesn't have to wait for ACKs and NAKs, it is faster than both Kermit and Xmodem. On the average, van der Eijk's Super Kermit is at least one-third faster than Xmodem. The windowing makes Super Kermit more efficient than Xmodem but less efficient than the streaming protocols that will be discussed shortly. Today, Super Kermit can be found on many RBBS-PC bulletin boards and on some other systems around the country. It is also an integral part of the TCOMM bulletin board system, for which van der Eijk also wrote the software.

DOCTOR'S NOTE

All of the transfer protocols discussed so far have either been send and wait or windowing protocols. Overall, Xmodem CRC and Kermit improved on the error-checking capabilities of protocols. Ymodem, 1K-Xmodem, and Super Kermit improved significantly on the performance of the original Xmodem. They did this not only by incorporating good error checking, but by increasing the speed. Many felt that speed could be increased still further. Chuck Forsberg was a pioneer in this area and led the way for many of the faster protocols that have come to life in the last few years. I tend to consider the protocols that have been discussed thus far as the protocols of the past. Yes, they were good and served a valuable purpose at the time, but they have since been replaced by things that are better.

The men who developed these early protocols should be applauded for their enormous contributions. They truly deserve recognition from all of us for their efforts. Ward Christianson deserves recognition for making that "one giant leap for mankind" with his Xmodem protocol. Others expanded on and improved his ideas, coming up with new ideas in the process. Progress, however, is a funny thing. What is in today may very well be the old way tomorrow. Eventually progress pushes us forward, and most of us "go with the flow."

If given the choice between making your morning coffee in a kettle over a fire or using an electric coffee maker, most of us would just laugh. But it wasn't all that long ago when making coffee over the fire was the only way to do it. So it is with file transfer protocols. Using a U.S. Robotics 9600 HST and transferring a file with Xmodem is just like making coffee over a fire. At that speed you'd get about 200 cps with Xmodem while with one of the newer protocols you could be getting six times that much! The protocols discussed next are all quite fast and efficient. They are the protocols of the future and of the present. Keep them in mind when you go online to BBSs. They'll save you lots of time and money.

Zmodem—The One to Beat

Chuck Forsberg released Zmodem in 1986. Zmodem is a program of many "firsts." Zmodem was the first to introduce what Forsberg calls *crash recovery*. What does this mean? It means that if a file transfer aborts for any reason, you can start it right where it left off. Until the release of Zmodem, if a file transfer failed, you were out of luck. Zmodem allows you to restart either an upload or download that has aborted.

Another first for Zmodem was that it was the first true streaming file transfer protocol. *Streaming protocols* send all of the data in a continuous stream and do not wait for ACKs from the receiver. Contained in the data are error codes that the receiver checks. If there is an error, the receiver will tell Zmodem to send the data in question again. The Zmodem protocol is perhaps the most resistant to line noise. In extreme cases, Zmodem even has the ability to fall back to a smaller block size in an attempt to accomplish the transfer. Table 7-5 shows how Zmodem performed while transferring the test file at different speeds.

Zmodem is dramatically faster than all of the other protocols discussed so far. It should be noted that Zmodem tends to start out at a slower rate, building up to a maximum. Because the test file was only 12K in size, the results for Zmodem at 9600 baud are a bit deceiving. With a larger file, say 100K, Zmodem would normally have done around 1,090 cps. Zmodem is fast, efficient, and tough. On a "dirty" line, if you can't complete a transfer using Zmodem, you might as well give up. Zmodem is driven by Chuck Forsberg's DSZ.COM (there is also an .EXE version) and can support other protocols besides Zmodem. The registered version supports Ymodem-G, 1K-Xmodem/G, Ymodem, Xmodem, 1K-Xmodem, and others. I'd encourage you to register a copy of DSZ. It will be one of the best investments you make.

Table 7-5

Performance of Zmodem at Various Speeds

Baud	CPS	Elapsed Time
1200	111 cps	1 min. 45 sec.
2400	224 cps	0 min. 51 sec.
9600	894 cps	0 min. 14 sec.

DOCTOR'S NOTE

It is important that you have a clear understanding of what *cps* really means. To begin with, many people are unsure as to what factors influence how the cps rate is calculated. Some protocols seem to start out with high cps readings, but by the time the transfer is finished the cps rate is fairly low. In addition, as was just noted with Zmodem, the cps rate for streaming protocols is generally slower on small files and much faster on large ones. There is a reason for this. I asked Matt Thomas, author of the Lynx protocol and now the MPt protocol, if he would like to clarify a few things for you. Here's what Thomas had to say regarding cps determination.

"The cps (characters per second) efficiency rating that most external protocols report to their users can be somewhat misleading, if not properly understood. Here are three reasons why you may be questioning cps rates, and the causes for each anomaly.

1. The cps rates that are reported by a particular protocol are physically impossible to reach without some sort of data compression, or an increase in baud rate.

"It is quite a simple task for a computer (or a human) to calculate a cps rate for a single file, given the proper formula:

$$cps = bytes \div seconds$$

"In this formula, bytes must be replaced by the actual number of bytes in the transferred file, and seconds must be replaced by the total number of seconds that elapsed during the actual transfer of file data. If these criteria are met, cps will return the computer's best estimate of the actual throughput during the protocol session.

"There have been reports that some external protocol drivers are miscalculating the cps rates that they are reporting to the user. If you see transfer rates that are consistently questionable, try timing some transfers with a stopwatch. Using the simple formula shown above, make your own best guess at how the protocol is actually performing.

2. Some protocols show very high cps rates at the beginning of a transfer, then rates that slowly diminish, and suddenly nose-dive right at the end.

DOCTOR'S NOTE *(continued)*

"This is not the fault of the protocol, but rather a misconception of how the protocol communicates with the serial port. Most external protocols use buffers to store information that comes and goes through the serial port. What we're concerned with is the transmit buffer. This area in memory holds outgoing information while it waits its turn to be transmitted through the serial port. When the protocol wants to send information, the data is first placed in this ring buffer, and then spooled out the serial port at a specified baud rate by an interrupt driven process.

"As soon as the protocol puts data in this buffer, it assumes that the data has been sent, and includes it in the calculation for average cps. The protocol will put data into this buffer at lightning speeds (much faster than any serial port operates) until the buffer is full. This is why cps rates are very high (sometimes impossibly high) at the start of a transfer. As the data is spooled from the buffer out the serial port, the protocol feeds more information in until the entire file has been sent. At this point, most protocols will wait for some type of acknowledgment that the receiver has gotten all data successfully. The severe drop in cps readings occurs while the sender waits for this response. The reason is that even though the protocol thinks all data has been sent, in reality, part of the file is still in the transmit buffer until it is spooled to the COM port. While it is being spooled, the timer keeps ticking, and the calculated cps rate dips.

"Because of these anomalies in cps readings during a transfer, it is best to judge the performance of a protocol on the final reading, which can usually be logged into a disk file for your inspection, or by using the formula mentioned earlier, and making your own calculations.

   3. I seem to get very good cps rates on long files, but on short ones, the cps rates are somewhat low.

The most probable reason for this phenomenon is that the ratio of protocol overhead data to actual file data is higher on short files.

"Every protocol introduces a certain amount of overhead to the data being transmitted. Examples of this overhead are start-of-packet characters, end-of-packet characters, CRC bytes, block numbers, and so on. Since this data cannot be counted in the cps calculation as part of the file, its presence lowers throughput efficiency. On longer files, the ratio of protocol data to file data is low. Some protocols start with short subpackets, and gradually lengthen them. Longer subpackets introduce less protocol overhead."

I hope this has cleared up some questions regarding cps readings, and why they can vary so widely between protocols and various file lengths.

The MNP Protocols

We discussed MNP (Microcom Networking Protocol) error-correcting modems in Chapter 5. Nearly all BBS software and communications programs now have protocols that support these modems. The thing to remember about MNP modems is that *they* do the error checking. With the other file transfer protocols that have been discussed, it is the protocol itself that does the error checking. When using MNP modems, the protocol serves more as an interface to the modem and the user. The protocol screen shows you how much of the file has been transferred, how many characters per second you are averaging, and so on. Remember, however, that it's the modem that actually does the transfer and error checking. These special MNP protocols can only be used by MNP modems.

Ymodem-G and 1K-Xmodem/G

Both Ymodem-G and 1K-Xmodem/G work in the same way. At the start of a transfer the modems exchange the header information, which includes filename, date, and so on. They also exchange the CRC. After this is accomplished these protocols send the data in a steady stream, one block following another. Thus, both Ymodem-G and 1K-Xmodem/G are streaming protocols. Unlike Zmodem, the modems perform all of the error checking that is done. Please note that there is no provision for recovering from an error. If the receiving modem encounters an error, both sides abort and the transfer is over. The higher the modem speed the more likely this is to occur.

It should be pointed out that with today's MNP modems, like the U.S. Robotics MNP modems, for example, it is very rare for a transfer to abort. You could use either of the G protocols 50 times a day, every day for six months and never have a transfer abort. At 9600 baud both Ymodem-G and 1K-Xmodem/G yield very high cps ratings. Table 7-6 gives you an idea of how these protocols did with the 12K test file. As with Zmodem, on a file of this size neither protocol got up to its highest speed before the file transfer was done.

With the U.S. Robotics 9600 HST connected to a 12 MHz AT, transfers that approach 1,200 cps are not uncommon. The G protocols are both excellent protocols, but you should be aware of their sensitivity. If the line you are on is obviously noisy it might be better to go with protocols like Zmodem, MPt, or BiModem. If you buy a high speed MNP modem, however, keep both Ymodem-G and 1K-Xmodem/G in mind for some really *fast* file transfers.

Table 7-6

Performance of 1K-Xmodem/G and Ymodem-G at Various Speeds

Baud	CPS	Elapsed Time
1K Xmodem/G		
1200	119 cps	1 min. 38 sec.
2400	228 cps	0 min. 50 sec.
9600	878 cps	0 min. 13 sec.
Ymodem-G		
1200	117 cps	1 min. 42 sec.
2400	226 cps	0 min. 52 sec.
9600	896 cps	0 min. 11 sec.

THE LATEST PROTOCOLS

While none of the protocols that have been discussed so far can be called oldtimers, the ones that follow are relative newcomers. Along with Zmodem, Ymodem-G, and 1K-Xmodem/G, these protocols use streaming and all have excellent error correction. At the time of this writing, none of the protocols that follow have been in use online for more than a year. Watch for these and learn to use them. As always, if there is a registration fee and you are using the protocol, be sure to register your copy.

Jmodem

In 1988, Richard Johnson of Colorado released a new protocol called *Jmodem*. The protocol has some interesting features. It maintains the file size, uses a 16 bit CRC for error checking, and also uses data compression. Because it can receive data while writing the previous block to disk, Jmodem transmits data almost continuously. Jmodem also has flow control built right in.

One of the peculiarities of Jmodem is that it uses blocks that vary in size. On the average file transfer where you encounter few or no errors, Jmodem will increase the block size up to a maximum of 8,192 bytes. The initial releases of Jmodem were very easily affected by line noise, but subsequent versions have improved on this greatly. When the protocol begins a transfer, the block size is 512 bytes. Each time a block is received correctly, Jmodem increases the size of the next block by 512 bytes, until it reaches the 8,192 byte maximum. If errors start to become a problem, however, the size of the blocks start to drop, going down by 512 byte increments. The transfer times with Jmodem are quite fast. Table 7-7 gives you an idea of the speed of Jmodem.

As you can see, Jmodem performs quite nicely compared to the other protocols. For this reason, Jmodem has gained popularity among quite a few users and is often found on Wildcat! bulletin boards as well as some other systems.

MPt—A Changing Protocol with a Changing Name

The MPt protocol is a Shareware file transfer protocol driver, authored by Matt Thomas. At the time of this writing, the MPt protocol has only been out for about a week. In view of that, I spoke with Matt Thomas in order to get some of the details about MPt. MPt began as a major revision of Thomas's Lynx protocol. Lynx was developed during the summer of 1988 and released as *Lynx: A Full Streaming/Compression/CRC-32 Batch File Transfer Protocol*.

In this early stage, the Lynx driver was released with two pages of documentation and no license fee. Within a relatively short period of time, Lynx became very popular and began appearing as a standard protocol on many bulletin boards. Lynx was extremely fast at both 1200 and 2400 baud, yielding approximately 118 cps at 1200 baud and 236 cps at 2400 baud.

Table 7-7

Performance of Jmodem at Various Speeds

Baud	CPS	Elapsed Time
1200	114 cps	1 min. 32 sec.
2400	228 cps	0 min. 49 sec.
9600	940 cps	0 min. 13 sec.

In the spring of 1989, six months after releasing Lynx, Thomas received his first "long-distance" feedback about the protocol. An RBBS sysop who discovered that Lynx had potential, started making suggestions for improvement. Thomas started work on Lynx 2.00 immediately. Through the summer of 1989, Thomas revised Lynx to add handshaking, the ability to handle more files, and the ability to display a color status window. Thomas determined that it was time to make Lynx a Shareware product.

Lynx 3.00 was released at the end of August 1989 as a Shareware product. A $15 registration fee got the user a disk with the latest version of Lynx and a license to use all future versions of the Lynx protocol. By October, Thomas discovered that when he designed Lynx, he didn't put in much room for expansion. While Lynx was very fast at 1200 and 2400 baud, it slowed down at 9600 baud. This was disconcerting to users who had first tried Lynx at lower baud rates and had gotten such exciting results. While Lynx performed at nearly maximum potential at 1200 and 2400 baud, it slowed down to about 890 cps at 9600 baud.

Adding some of the features that users wanted would mean releasing a version of Lynx that would not "talk" to older versions. Instead of doing this, Thomas designed a new protocol, and in January of 1990, he released Puma 1.00 as a Shareware product. The program was released as Puma until April 1990, when an apparent copyright problem arose. At this time, Thomas changed its name to MPt. Let's take a look at some of the changes that can be found in MPt.

The MPt protocol is designed to be very dynamic. All present and future versions of MPt will talk to each other by negotiating with *feature flags* to determine what new features can be used during a transfer. Currently, MPt offers features similar to Lynx, such as RLE compression, full streaming data flow, hardware handshaking, and other features found in similar protocols. MPt, however, can be expanded to support additional compression techniques like Lempel-Ziv-Welch and Splay Tree encoding. (In other words, the data could be made even smaller.) Thomas said that a chat mode may be implemented in a future version as well.

Note: RLE, for *Run Length Encoding,* compression occurs when the program detects a group of bytes that are the same, and it sends them as a group rather than sending each byte separately.

The MPt protocol generally transfers data with CRC error-detecting information at 1K byte intervals in the data stream. This allows the receiver to test the integrity of the data in 1,024 byte chunks. If any data is found to be garbled, the MPt receiver will alert the sender to resynchronize. The sender will begin transmitting data at the point in the file where the error occurred. If repeated errors occur, the sender will transmit data with CRC information appearing more often in the data stream, adjusting the interval to 512, 256, 128, or 64 bytes.

This technique, combined with the continuous transmission of data, as opposed to a send and wait protocol, provides a reliable and fast mode of data transfer on clean lines as well as noisy lines. For commuting files directly from one PC to another PC, over a serial cable, MPt was found to consistently exceed the efficiency of other protocols tested on a 115,200 bps link.

MPt also has something that has been missing in protocol drivers since they first appeared: a full-screen, color display that is fast and compatible with most multitasking subsystems. MPt uses direct video memory access for screen displays, unless a recognized multitasker is present. In this case, MPt writes screen data into a buffer that multitaskers use to manage display updates. This removes the possibility of screen *bleed-through* when running multiple programs that share the same screen.

MPt also includes a setup program that makes command line operation much simpler. COM ports, baud rates, and other defaults can be preconfigured with the setup program. MPt can then be run with a simple command line, without a lot of confusing parameters.

MPt will optionally log file transfers in two formats. The first is an enhancement to the single line format that was originally specified by Chuck Forsberg in DSZ. Many communications programs will refer to a "DSZ LOG" feature and this is what they are referring to. The second logging feature is the CDS (Call Data Standard) logging format (discussed in Chapter 6), which has been implemented in MPt in anticipation of its eventual popularity in interfacing communications programs and external protocols.

MPt can resume a file transfer that was interrupted by excessive line noise, *lost carrier* (you "lose carrier" when your modem becomes disconnected from the host modem), or other factors. This means that when the MPt receiver detects that the file to be received is already present in the receiver's path, but is not complete, a request can be made for the sender to begin transmission at the beginning of the missing portion of the file. This avoids sending the same data twice. Along with Zmodem and BiModem, MPt is the only other protocol that has this feature, which Chuck Forsberg dubbed crash recovery. MPt is very stable and very fast. Table 7-8 gives you an idea of how fast MPt is at different baud rates. Again, it should be pointed out that on a 12K file a streaming protocol like MPt does not get up to its maximum transfer speed.

Table 7-8

MPt Performance on a 12K File at Different Speeds

Baud	CPS	Elapsed Time
1200	119 cps	1 min. 34 sec.
2400	236 cps	0 min. 48 sec.
9600	1,000 cps	0 min. 12 sec.

BiModem

Over the years, file transfer protocols have grown with moderate increments in performance. BiModem, however, is a new file transfer protocol that takes a quantum leap in performance. It takes advantage of the fact that most modems can send and receive information concurrently. That's right, it will send a file while it is *receiving* one. After all, good communication consists of the exchange of information, not just a unidirectional dissemination of it. Imagine the savings if you could cut your communications bill in half. Figure 7-1 shows BiModem sending and receiving at the same time.

BiModem is as efficient as possible. The protocol can attain transfer speeds with up to a 98 percent efficiency each way. (Some overhead is required to ensure accuracy.) BiModem is *very* fast besides being very accurate. Table 7-9 shows how BiModem did using the 12K test file while doing a download only.

As you can see, BiModem is very fast at 1200 and 2400 baud. At 9600 baud BiModem is dazzling. Depending on the type of 9600 baud connection, BiModem can give up to 2,300 cps! It was written in assembler so even the slowest XT can take advantage of it. In addition, it is DESQview and DoubleDos aware so if you are using it on an AT or 386 there is a lot of processor power left for other tasks.

File accuracy is ensured by using a modified 32 bit CRC, a 32 bit Filesum, and for even more accuracy, you can elect to verify each file sent. The verify technique can also be used to refresh files. This technique compares files and sends only the information that has changed. This allows large database files to be updated in minutes instead of hours. For example, say you have a business and there is a branch office in another city. You have a large client file that is added to each day. The file on your

---
Figure 7-1

Sending and receiving at the same time with BiModem

```
Executing BM.BAT
S┌──────────────[BiModem - (C) Copyright Erik Labs 1988,89]──────────────
b│ (901)753-7213 Dr. File Finders Black Bag ◆ #1 In our Book! E.L.    v1.20
 ├──────────────────────┬──────────────────────────────┬──────────────
 │ Sending   SKEY30.ZIP │ Receiving scanv57.zip        │ Summary
 │ Bytes      336325  4078│ Bytes       49273     4060  │   8138
 │ Time         5:55    18│ Time           52       16  │     22
 │ Bytes/Sec   947.3 226.5│ Bytes/Sec   947.5    253.7  │  369.9
 │ Err Count          0│ Err Count                0  │     0
 │ Last Err           │ Last Err                    │
 ├──────────────────────┴─────────[Text]────────────┴──────────────
 │
 │
 │
 │
 │
 │
 │ Ray.....you there?
 │
 │
 │
 └═════[Alt/A-Add, Alt/S-Kill Send, Alt/R-Kill Receive, Esc-Terminate]═════
```

---

machine is identical to the file at the branch at the start of each day. At the end of the day, however, the copy at the branch office has new information in it because new clients were entered. Let's say that it's a one megabyte file. Using BiModem, the copy on your machine could be updated quickly. The branch would upload a copy to your machine. BiModem would recognize that the file exists and scan it. Rather than replace the entire one megabyte file each evening, it would only upload the parts that were new or different! What a savings in time and money.

Table 7-9

Performance of BiModem at Various Speeds

Baud	CPS	Elapsed Time
1200	116 cps	1 min. 42 sec.
2400	224 cps	0 min. 46 sec.
9600	912 cps	0 min. 16 sec.

BiModem, like most of the other transfer protocols, splits up the file being sent into blocks. It uses a rather complex method to determine the block size based on transfer performance. Initially, it uses 1K blocks. If there are no errors, it jumps up to 2K blocks, and finally up to 4K blocks. If there are errors during the transmission, it cuts the block size in half. This includes the retransmitted block that was in error. If errors persist, it will continue halving all the way down to 16 byte blocks. As soon as the line clears up, it will double the block size, but since the line may not be trustworthy it will only go back up to 1K blocks.

Most protocols use some form of time out to control the possibility of receiving a short block. Short blocks can occur on noisy lines. Some delay is required because the transfer may be occurring over a network, and it could be a case of the network waiting for enough characters to send. In other words, the network may be blocking its data at a different size. Xmodem, for instance, uses approximately two seconds for its time-out value. That's a lot of time, especially at 9600 baud. BiModem uses a very complex method. Since BiModem sends blocks back to back (not waiting for acknowledgment of the first block before it sends the second), a short block rarely occurs. If it was caused by noise, what happens instead is that part of the second block is initially considered as being part of the first block. In an effort to resynchronize the blocks, BiModem will scan through the buffer to find a properly formatted block header. It will then consider that point as the start of the next block. This will prevent most short blocks from occurring; however, on an extremely noisy line it can still happen. If it does, BiModem will wait for a period of time based on the characters per second being transmitted successfully.

In addition to allowing bidirectional file transfers, BiModem allows you to chat with the operator at the other end. Since many of us are relatively slow typists, this typically reduces throughput by only about 1 to 2 percent. What this means is that chatting with the person on the other side has only a minor effect on the speed of the transfer. You might get a few characters per second less, but so what? A human being simply can't type fast enough to have any major effect on BiModem's perfor-mance. Even the character repeat function of your system will only reduce it by 2 percent. Talking with the other person can be fun and productive. You can discuss business, the files you are sending, and so on. If, during your discussion, you discover that you forgot to send a file, no problem—you just add it to the list while the transfer is taking place. Never again will you have to invoke the transfer program a second time just because you forgot one file.

BiModem is flexible because multiple directories can be searched to locate file requests. You can even use star names (TEST*.*) across these directories. It will double-check to ensure the same file doesn't get sent twice because it matches multiple star name comparisons, and determines if a file exists in multiple directories. Since all this happens at Assembler speed, there is no perceivable search time involved. You have complete control over which directories can be searched and the order they are searched. In addition, you can establish password protection for any file you want. Your friends can send you password protected files that only you can see.

Don't worry if you happen to lose your connection. Like Zmodem and MPt, BiModem can recover from an aborted file transfer. There are three different file recovery methods available. You can specify that loss of connection will delete the file, rename it to an aborted file directory, or just retain it. If you choose either of the last two options, the transfer can restart where it left off.

File date and time handling is also under your control. If you want the file to reflect the date and time it was received, you can still have file recovery because of the ability to rename an aborted transfer to a different directory. Duplicate file receipts can also have their filename reflect the version.

BiModem comes complete with a series of support programs. These programs can be executed individually or through a custom menu program. The following is a brief description of the support programs.

For most users, BiModem will work straight out of the box, but some users may want to change the defaults. BiConfig is the program used to modify the way you want BiModem to function. This includes everything from screen colors to COM port addresses. Three of the other utilities that come with BiModem make it easy for you to exchange the files that you want. You may never have to type a filename again. These three support programs are provided to help eliminate this:

- BiMark is provided to assist users in selecting files to send. It displays the files in a directory and allows you to mark which ones you want sent. It is capable of walking the directory structure of your disk and even changing drives.

- BiList allows you to mark files you wish to receive from a previously downloaded list of available files.

- BiHot is a hot key program that can be invoked at any time to assist you in marking a file you wish to receive. For instance, if you are signed on to a bulletin board and you were listing the files available, you can call up BiHot to tag the files as they appear on your screen.

BiPath is another program available to edit the lists (or actually *type* filenames if you prefer).

Transfer lists can be built even before you connect to another PC. BiMark and BiList can be used offline in this manner. A special program called BiSelect allows you to select which transfer list you want to use. You can select a transfer list based on filename or users' phone numbers. For instance, let's say you only call someone once a week, and then throughout the week whenever you come across something you want to send to that person, you can add it to their phone number list and forget about it. The next time you are connected to that person, BiModem will remember for you and send all the files you thought of during the week.

There is also a mini-terminal emulator supplied. This is a special purpose terminal emulator that monitors the communications line for the BiModem connection string, and when it sees it, it automatically brings up BiModem. This program is connected to the menu as *Remote BiModem*. There is also a menu entry called *Host BiModem*. Using these two entries is all you need in order to connect from one terminal emulation program to another. One or both users create their lists of files to send or receive; then one side invokes Remote BiModem and it will wait for the other side to invoke Host BiModem. It's that simple.

I have BiModem set up in my Qmodem Host Mode. BiModem works on standard modems over telephone lines, telephone networks, communications satellites, or direct connect. When two PCs are directly connected using a null modem, transfer rates of up to 115.2K baud can be attained in both directions. Due to the wide use of telephone networks such as PC Pursuit, extra attention was paid to ensure consistent results.

John Erickson, one of the BiModem authors, had this to say about recent developments with BiModem. "BiModem can be used with any communications program which permits execution of an external program. It is currently available as an internal protocol in GT POWER by P & M Software Company, and Wildcat! BBS by Mustang Software, Inc. Many bulletin board interfaces are also available. We are continually working on additional interfaces, and a developer's interface kit is available on our BBS. BiModem is priced at $25. Laser-printed documentation is available for $7.50 per copy. All you have to do is call our BBS and answer the registration information, responding as a sysop, and answer the questions about your BBS. This information will be listed publicly on the BBS, and we will provide you with a $15 discount on each BiModem registration that will be used exclusively on your BBS."

BiModem is available from Erik Labs, 3431 W. Thunderbird Rd., Suite 13-311, Phoenix AZ 85023. They can be reached at 602-942-5403, or on their bulletin board system at 602-979-5720.

SUMMING IT ALL UP

This chapter has looked at the evolution of the most popular file transfer protocols, starting with Ward Christianson's Xmodem and going all the way through to the bidirectional power of BiModem. Not every file transfer protocol that exists has been discussed, but the chapter did touch on the ones you will encounter most often. Table 7-10 gives a summary of how each of the protocols discussed performed while transferring the 12K test file.

The early protocols opened up new horizons for the transfer of data. The newer streaming protocols have greatly enhanced not only the speed but the accuracy of data transfer. Bear in mind when you look at Table

Table 7-10

Summary of Protocol Performance on a 12K File

Protocol	1200 Baud	2400 Baud	9600 Baud
Xmodem	81	150	193
Xmodem CRC	80	151	192
1K-Xmodem	104	208	699
Ymodem	104	203	703
Super Kermit	103	198	680
Zmodem	111	224	894
G Protocols	118	227	890
Jmodem	114	228	940
MPt	119	236	1,000
BiModem	116	224	912

DOCTOR'S NOTE

Just a word about the various bulletin board interfaces for BiModem. Steve Lea, of SoftLea Developments, wrote the first door for doing BiModem transfers on PC Board systems. Lea's product, BI-DOOR, allows sysops to display a menu of file areas and allows users to view the lists of files available. His BBS number is 503-582-4860. I personally applaud Lea's efforts because he recognized the potential of BiModem and began to support it immediately. BI-DOOR can easily support multiple nodes on PC Board systems. I recommend BI-DOOR, and it's what I use on Dr. File Finder's Black Bag.

Jimmy Pearson, of "the ByteBrothers" came out with another BiModem door for PC Board called "BROdoor." BROdoor is very well done. The first release was a single node version. In January 1990, Pearson released a multiple node version of BROdoor. He can be reached at the Data Warp BBS, 918-455-5544. BiModem is already an integral part of Wildcat! BBSs. It can also be set up quite easily on OPUS systems. Information for doing that can be obtained on the BiModem support BBS.

If you use a BBS with any regularity, encourage the sysop to install the appropriate interface for BiModem. BiModem is the protocol of the 90s, but whether it becomes accepted or not depends on *you*. Once you've seen for yourself what BiModem can do, you have to support it with your registrations. You can help the proliferation of BiModem by encouraging sysops to install it on their systems.

BiModem's ability to both send and receive files at the same time can actually double the total throughput of your modem. What do I mean by this? If you were at 1200 baud and using Zmodem, you would average around 112 cps. The theoretical maximum (100 percent) for a 1200 baud modem is 120 cps. Take the same case using BiModem. You are downloading a file at around 118 cps but you can also be sending a file at 118 cps. In actuality, your modem is handling 236 cps while using BiModem. That's nearly twice the maximum for a 1200 baud modem. Give BiModem a try. The first time you see files moving in two directions at the same time it will absolutely floor you. It's really something to behold. More will be said on BiModem in the next chapter when downloading and uploading are discussed.

7-10 that this reflects just one transfer of a specific file at each baud rate. The results for Xmodem, Xmodem CRC, 1K-Xmodem, Ymodem, and Super Kermit are fairly indicative. The cps (characters per second) rate is what one would expect it to be for these protocols. The results for Zmodem, the G protocols, Jmodem, MPt, and BiModem are typical for the size of the file that was used, but not representative of how they would do on larger files. To give you a better comparison for these streaming protocols, the transfer of a larger file would be more helpful.

Table 7-11 shows how the streaming protocols did while downloading a 243K (248,593 byte) file. The file was downloaded with a U.S. Robotics Dual Standard modem. The connection was made to another Dual Standard and both modems were operating at 38,400 bps.

As you can see there is quite a difference in the cps rate when using a Dual Standard with a large file. With a U.S. Robotics 9600 HST the G protocols averaged around 1,145 cps, Zmodem around 1,120 cps, and Jmodem approximately 1,110 cps. Using BiModem and downloading only, it would have gotten around 1,150 cps with a 9600 HST.

Modifying both the transfer protocol variable and the modem speed variable can make a *big* difference. Because the condition of local phone lines can vary, the expected cps rate for each protocol at different baud rates can fluctuate. You'll find that you might consistently get 1,120 cps with Zmodem at 9600 baud on one board, and always get around 1,050 on another. The protocol hasn't changed, but some of the equipment variables have. These would include:

- The status of the phone lines to which the BBS is connected

- The speed of the machine on which the BBS operates

- The amount of activity on the BBS at the time of download

Table 7-11

Performance of Streaming Protocols on a 243K File

Protocol	1200 Baud	2400 Baud	9600 Baud
Zmodem	115 cps	230 cps	1,094 cps
G Protocols	119 cps	238 cps	1,145 cps
Jmodem	114 cps	230 cps	1,118 cps
MPt	118 cps	237 cps	1,124 cps
BiModem (MMP)	118 cps	237 cps	1,138 cps

Table 7-12			

Average Protocol Ranges

Protocol	1200 Baud	2400 Baud	9600 Baud
Xmodem	45-82 cps	140-150 cps	175-205 cps
Xmodem CRC	45-85 cps	138-155 cps	180-205 cps
1K-Xmodem	92-108 cps	198-218 cps	670-710 cps
Ymodem	94-112 cps	188-210 cps	690-710 cps
Super Kermit	90-108 cps	182-220 cps	675-708 cps
Zmodem	104-116 cps	214-232 cps	960-1,100 cps
G Protocols	112-119 cps	224-237 cps	992-1,148 cps
Jmodem	108-116 cps	224-232 cps	930-1,120 cps
MPt	110-119 cps	220-238 cps	980-1,130 cps
BiModem (MNP)	112-119 cps	222-238 cps	988-1,150 cps

On a multinode bulletin board, transfers may be slower when several nodes are in use at the same time. A system running on a slower machine will not send data as quickly, and the condition of local phone equipment can vary. Table 7-12 does not take into consideration any factors such as line noise causing multiple errors. To give you more information to work with, Table 7-12 gives the general cps range for each protocol under *average* conditions. This information should help you obtain files as quickly and inexpensively as possible no matter where you go in The Wires.

## CHAPTER EIGHT

Moving the Files

In the last chapter you learned some of the history of file transfer protocols and how the various protocols work. The difference between the early send and wait protocols and the more modern streaming protocols is truly amazing. In this chapter you are going to put that knowledge into use and take a look at actually moving the files once you get online.

This chapter will also cover storage concerns—what to do with the compressed files that you download, how to keep track of them, and how to find them in a flash. Downloading a file gives you instant access to a program that you want to try. Uploading a file to a system gives you a chance to share a good program with others and adds to the value of the system. Let's hit The Wires and check out not only how to get, but how to share those good programs that are out there.

ONLINE UPS AND DOWNS

The millions of people who go online to BBSs and commercial networks do so for many reasons. They exchange electronic mail, meet friends on

CB simulators, ask questions in conferences, and discuss things in forums. On bulletin boards they play "Door" games, and on commercial networks they can get the latest stock quotes. For a majority of users, the lure of The Wires comes from the fact that they can download good Shareware software. Since you should always be aware of what this is going to cost you, there are several things to consider. As mentioned in Chapter 3, there are four ways of obtaining Shareware and public domain software:

- PC user groups

- Disk vendors

- Commercial online networks

- Bulletin boards

By taking advantage of user groups or disk vendors, you don't have to download anything. You simply pay the fee for disks that you want. My personal preference has always been the commercial networks and bulletin boards. Let's take a look at downloading first, and some of the things that you have to consider.

DOWNLOADING FILES— THINGS TO CONSIDER

One factor to consider in downloading is that the commercial networks charge *connect time* while bulletin boards do not. At non-prime time, which is generally after 6:00 P.M., the connect time charge for GEnie at 1200 baud is $6 per hour. On CompuServe the rate is $12.50 per hour plus any communications surcharges. With bulletin boards, while there is no connect time charge, there are cost considerations for a long-distance call.

In addition to considering what the connect time or long-distance charges are, you have to give some thought to the size of the file or files that you want. You also have to consider the speed at which you will be able to transfer the data. Only by weighing these factors can you hope to obtain a program at the lowest possible cost.

A Basic Example of Download Cost

To highlight the importance of considering file size and transfer speed, an example is in order. To start out simply, let's say that the file you want to download is 250K, and that you are connected to a commercial network at 1200 baud. (For now, it doesn't matter which commercial network.) Using Xmodem at 1200 baud you would average around 80 cps. Based on this rate, it would take you approximately 52 minutes to download the 250K file. On GEnie, this would cost you about $5.20 and on CompuServe it would cost you roughly $10.80.

To make a fair comparison, let's look at the cost of a long-distance call to a bulletin board. The call originates in Denver, Colorado and connects to a BBS in Lexington, Kentucky. The cost for dialing after 11:00 P.M. (according to AT&T) is 14 cents for the first minute and 15 cents for each additional minute, plus tax. Using the same transfer time of 52 minutes at 1200 baud, the long-distance call would cost $7.94, plus tax. That's $2.76 more than it would have cost you on GEnie, but $2.86 less than it would cost you on CompuServe. Thus far, at 1200 baud, it would be cheapest to download the file from GEnie. Two other important variables enter the picture: maximum modem speed and the transfer protocol used.

Altering the Variables

The example above used 1200 baud as the modem speed and Xmodem as the transfer protocol. If you have a 1200 baud modem, you can't do anything about the speed, but you can do something about the file transfer protocol that you use. The vast majority of bulletin board systems offer Chuck Forsberg's Zmodem, as do GEnie, BIX, and EXEC-PC. Using Zmodem on the same 250K file, you would average around 112 cps. Just by changing protocols you reduce your transfer time from 52 minutes to approximately 37 minutes. The cost of downloading the file from GEnie would now be $3.70 and the cost of the long-distance call would be reduced to $5.54.

Using Zmodem at 2400 baud, you could transfer the file from the bulletin board in only 18 minutes, based on an average of 224 cps. Taking the example all the way, how would you do if you used Zmodem at 9600 baud? If you averaged 1,090 cps, you could download the file in 3.8 minutes with a long-distance charge of only about 59 cents, plus tax.

As you can see, changing the protocol variable alone will help save you money. Using Zmodem, MPt, BiModem, or one of the G protocols can make a big difference. If you have the ability to alter the speed variable as well, you can really save a lot of money. Table 8-1 was calculated using nighttime rates for both GEnie and long-distance service. While the transfer times and charges are approximate, they are close enough to give you an idea. The long-distance rate used is for a call between Denver, Colorado and Lexington, Kentucky.

Download Time Estimates

When you go to download a file from a bulletin board, the system gives you an estimated time it will take to download. Depending on the type of bulletin board software, these estimated times can be pretty far off. Over the last few years both bulletin board software and communications programs have gotten much better at estimating the time, but there are still discrepancies. This is especially true at 1200 or 2400 baud and less true at 9600 baud.

Only a few years ago, if you were online at 1200 baud, you could count on a download taking at least four times longer than the system said it would. Even today, bulletin boards will give you a time that is not

---

Table 8-1

Time and Cost Comparison While Altering the Variables

	GEnie			Bulletin Board Systems (BBS)		
Protocol	**1200**	**2400**	**9600**	**1200**	**2400**	**9600**
Xmodem	52 min. 80 cps $5.20	27 min. 150 cps $3.70	Not available	52 min. 80 cps $7.79	27 min. 150 cps $4.04	21 min. 200 cps $3.14
1K-Xmodem	40 min. 104 cps $4.00	20 min. 208 cps $2.00	Not available	40 min. 104 cps $5.99	20 min. 208 cps $2.99	6 min. 700 cps $0.89
Zmodem	37 min. 111 cps $3.70	18 min. 224 cps $1.80	Not available	37 min. 111 cps $5.54	18 min. 224 cps $2.69	4.6 min. 900 cps $0.74

DOCTOR'S NOTE

Only you will know what your options are. If you have a high-speed, MNP modem and utilize the faster protocols, you can get software quite inexpensively. By using a plan from AT&T like "Reach Out America," you can save even more. Another factor that hasn't been discussed is the amount of time that you actually spend online. If you have a 1200 baud modem and only go online occasionally, the cost of downloading a large file will not be as significant to you.

On the other hand, if you really get hooked, you could spend a moderate-sized fortune. There are countless stories floating around The Wires of husbands trying to explain to wives, or vice versa, about the $1,000 phone bill and the $500 bill for connect time on an online network. In the example given, only one 250K file was used. There are quite a few programs, like spreadsheets, word processors, and so on, that may consist of two or three 200K to 300K files.

As a quick example, if you were using 1200 baud and had to download three 250K files using Xmodem, it would cost you around $25! At 9600 baud it would cost you under $2. In a case like this, you might want to consider several alternatives. You could get the three program files from a disk vendor or from a PC user group for much less than $25. Another alternative is to purchase a high-speed modem. I highly recommend both the U.S. Robotics 9600 HST and Dual Standard. I use them both myself.

Downloading is the greatest because you have the program you want right now, but it can get expensive. Analyze your activity, use the fastest protocols you can, and whenever possible use the highest baud rate that your modem supports. Finally, keep in mind that when it comes to getting programs, bulletin boards have two distinct advantages over commercial networks.

- They support a higher range of baud rates, namely 9600 baud

- They offer faster file transfer protocols

The commercial networks are wonderful places and offer a great many things, but for getting software online, BBSs are best because they are the fastest and least expensive way. Remember, you can also cut your cost by using services like StarLink and PC Pursuit at lower baud rates.

very accurate. For example, I just did a batch download of four files using Ymodem-G. The total for the four files was 486,312 bytes, and the system said that it would take 4 minutes and 27 seconds to complete. In fact, it took 7 minutes and 4 seconds to complete the download. At 1200 and 2400 baud the variance would be even greater.

So, how can you have a better idea of how long it is really going to take? Calculate it yourself. Obviously, each transfer protocol is going to perform a little differently on different systems, various phone lines, and so on. About the best you can do is to establish a base criterion for each protocol at given baud rates and work from there. For example, let's say that you determine that in most cases Xmodem will transfer 80 cps at 1200 baud. You now have a place to work from. How long would it take you to transfer the same four files that were mentioned above?

To calculate the time, you first take the total number of bytes. In this case that is 486,312. Now, divide that number by 80, the number of characters per second that you expect to get. The answer would be 6,078.9 seconds. To find out the exact time in minutes, divide the 6,078.9 by 60. The answer comes to 101.31 minutes (or 1 hour 41 minutes). This estimate will be fairly close to what you'll really get, assuming that your rate is around 80 cps. Here's that formula so it's clear and easy to read.

(Total bytes ÷ Expected cps) ÷ 60 seconds = Estimated transfer time

You might be thinking, "How can I know what to expect from each protocol if I haven't used all of them or haven't used them often enough to come up with an average cps rate?" Good question! Figure 8-1 contains the source code for a program written in BASIC for this book by my friend, Professor Donald E. Bodley. You can make a copy of the program using your BASIC interpreter.

Note: A compiled QuickBASIC version of Bodley's program will be on a disk I'm offering along with some other great programs. You can obtain them by dropping a card, found in the back of the book, in the mail.

How does the program work? All you have to do is tell the program the number of bytes you want to transfer. The program will show you estimated times at 1200, 2400, and 9600 baud for the following protocols:

- Xmodem

- 1K-Xmodem

- Ymodem

FIGURE 8-1

A program that estimates download times for various protocols

```
CLS
DEFINT A-Z

FOR i = 1 TO 8
   FOR j = 1 TO 3
     READ cps(i, j)
   NEXT j
NEXT i

FOR k = 1 TO 8
  READ protocol$(k)
NEXT k

COLOR 11: PRINT CHR$(201); STRING$(78, CHR$(205)); CHR$(187)
          PRINT CHR$(186); STRING$(78, " "); CHR$(186)
          PRINT CHR$(186); STRING$(78, " "); CHR$(186)
          PRINT CHR$(186); STRING$(78, " "); CHR$(186)
          PRINT CHR$(200); STRING$(78, CHR$(205)); CHR$(188)

COLOR 10:
      LOCATE 2, 3: PRINT "TRANSFER TIME CALCULATOR - Popular Transfer Protocols Compared"
COLOR 15:
      LOCATE 3, 18: PRINT "The PROF-BBS - Lexington, KY - FidoNet 108/111 - 606/269-1565"
      LOCATE 4, 10: PRINT "Copyright 1990 - Don Bodley, SysOp - Contributed to the Public Domain"
      PRINT : PRINT : PRINT

BEGIN:

COLOR 11: LOCATE 7, 66: PRINT STRING$(10, " ")
      LOCATE 7, 4: PRINT ">>> Enter Size of File to be Downloaded in bytes or 0 to Exit: ";

COLOR 15: INPUT "", size!
      IF size! = 0 THEN GOTO ALLDONE

FOR x = 1 TO 8
   FOR y = 1 TO 3
      speed(x, y) = (size! \ cps(x, y)) + 5
      mins(x, y) = speed(x, y) \ 60
      secs(x, y) = speed(x, y) MOD 60
   NEXT y
NEXT x

COLOR 15: PRINT : PRINT
PRINT "  +---------------+-----------------+-----------------+-----------------+"
PRINT "  | PROTOCOL      |    1200 baud    |    2400 baud    |    9600 baud    |"
PRINT "  +---------------+-----------------+-----------------+-----------------+"
FOR P = 1 TO 8
PRINT "  |               |                 |                 |                 |"
NEXT P
PRINT "  +---------------+-----------------+-----------------+-----------------+"

COLOR 10:
FOR x = 1 TO 8
   LOCATE 12 + x, 6: PRINT USING "\          \"; protocol$(x)
   LOCATE 12 + x, 21: PRINT USING "### min. ## sec."; mins(x, 1); secs(x, 1)
   LOCATE 12 + x, 39: PRINT USING "### min. ## sec."; mins(x, 2); secs(x, 2)
   LOCATE 12 + x, 57: PRINT USING "### min. ## sec."; mins(x, 3); secs(x, 3)
NEXT x

COLOR 11: PRINT : PRINT : PRINT "   >>> Press Any Key to continue... ";
      WHILE INKEY$ = "": WEND
      LOCATE 22: PRINT STRING$(78, " ");
      GOTO BEGIN

ALLDONE:
   CLS : END

' average protocol time in cps
```

FIGURE 8-1

A program that estimates download times for various protocols (*continued*)

```
DATA 80,114,180
DATA 108,221,890
DATA 108,222,890
DATA 114,234,1090
DATA 116,236,1120
DATA 117,235,1120
DATA 117,235,1120
DATA 116,236,1115
DATA Xmodem,1K-Xmodem,Ymodem,Zmodem,MPt,Ymodem-G,1K-Xmodem/G,BiModem
```

- Zmodem

- MPt

- Ymodem-G

- 1K-Xmodem/G

- BiModem

The program contains tables of average cps rates for each protocol at different baud rates. The tables were compiled over many years, using all of the protocols under a wide range of conditions. You enter in the total number of bytes for each program that you want to download in that session. The program will make all of the calculations and give you the estimated transfer time. In some cases the tables were intentionally figured a bit on the low side, to take into account various online situations. Overall, you should find that it will give you fairly accurate estimates.

What Protocol Where?

The online commercial networks give you a choice of transfer protocols, as do bulletin boards. If you are to download files at the lowest possible cost, you'll want to use the fastest protocol available. This is true no matter what baud rate you use. You've seen that just by altering the file transfer protocol variable alone, your cost can be greatly reduced. Here are some recommendations for protocols to use when calling different places.

GEnie

GEnie offers Xmodem, 1K-Xmodem, and Zmodem. Use Zmodem to obtain maximum performance. Some communications programs have Zmodem built in. With others, you have to utilize Forsberg's DSZ program and run it as an external protocol. DSZ can be found on bulletin boards and commercial networks. It always has a filename such as DSZ1203.ZIP, which means it is the release of the third of December. Put the DSZ.COM file in a directory that is in your DOS PATH.

You'll need to make two batch files, one for sending and one for receiving. DSZ has several command line switches and options. Here are a couple of sample batch files that you can use with DSZ for Zmodem transfers. ZDOWN.BAT is for downloads.

```
ZDOWN.BAT
dsz pB2048 handshake both rz
```

The "pB2048" establishes a buffer for the file transfer. "Handshake both" tells DSZ to use software and hardware handshaking. The "r" is for receive and the "z" is for Zmodem. DSZ is case sensitive, so type it exactly as it is written. ZUP.BAT is for doing uploads.

```
dsz pB2048 handshake both sz %3 %4 %5 %6 %7 %8 %9
```

In this example, the "s" tells DSZ to send. The %3 through %9 variables allow you to upload multiple files. Attach these batch files to your communications program as it instructs you to; then you're ready to go. As you learn more about DSZ, you may want to alter these batch files to better suit the needs of your own system.

Note: DSZ is *case sensitive!* If you copy the batch files listed above, be sure to copy them exactly as they are shown. DSZ expects some of its parameters to be in lowercase and others in uppercase. For more information read the DSZ documentation.

If you are online to GEnie and don't have Zmodem set up, use 1K-Xmodem. While you're at it, download the latest copy of DSZ.

CompuServe

Because of the way CompuServe is set up, only certain protocols will work well with it. Figure 8-2 shows a list of protocols that you can use on CompuServe.

Selection number 6, "CompuServe QB (B w/send ahead)," is the best protocol to use on CompuServe. Its full name is *CompuServe Quick-B,* and it uses 1K blocks, and like Zmodem, MPt, and BiModem, it has the ability to recover from an aborted file transfer. At 1200 baud, the CompuServe Quick-B protocol gives you approximately 116 cps. At 2400 baud it averages about 238 cps. The other possible selections—for example, Xmodem or Kermit—are just too slow. Some communications programs have the Quick-B protocol built in, while others do not. If the communications program that you use does not have *CIS (CompuServe Information Service)* Quick-B, you'll need an external protocol driver. I recommend a program called OZBEXT, written by Steve Sneed. The filename on bulletin boards will generally reflect the release number. For example, at the time of this writing the current release of OZBEXT is 13.2F. The file might be found as OZBX132F.ZIP. Some systems will have it listed simply as OZBEXT.ZIP and the version number will be contained in the description. OZBEXT can be obtained on CompuServe by entering **GO IBMCOM** at any prompt. When you get to the IBM Communications Forum, select item number 3, Libraries. When the library listing is displayed select number 10, Protocols.

Figure 8-2

Transfer protocol selection on CompuServe (CIS)

```
1 READ this file
2 DOWNLOAD this file
3 DESCRIPTION
4 RETURN to library menu


Enter choice or <CR> for next !2
Library Protocol Menu

Transfer protocols available -

1 XMODEM
2 CompuServe B+ and original B
3 CompuServe A
4 DC2/DC4 (Capture)
5 YMODEM
6 CompuServe QB (B w/send ahead)
7 Kermit

0 Abort transfer request

Enter choice !
```
```
◆  ANSI   ONLINE   38400 8N1  [Home]=Menu   FDX 8 LF X ♪ ♫ CP LG ↑ PR 00:03:43
```

You would then pick number 1, Browse, where you will be prompted for a keyword to search on. Type in **OZBEXT** and the system will locate the current version for you. If you are independently wealthy, you can select Kermit or Xmodem for CompuServe file transfers, but otherwise go with the CompuServe Quick-B protocol.

BIX

BIX, the *Byte Information Exchange*, offers several protocols for downloading. BIX supports Xmodem, Kermit, Ymodem, and Zmodem for downloads. If you have it available, use Zmodem for your downloads. For uploads, BIX offers Xmodem, Ymodem, and Kermit. If you are going to do uploads on BIX, use Ymodem. In the cases of both Xmodem and Ymodem, BIX offers both plain and CRC error-checking versions. You can tell BIX which you prefer (always go with the CRC error checking). To select Ymodem with CRC error checking, you would enter **YMODEM.C** when indicating the upload protocol.

Delphi

Delphi is another fine commercial network that has a good library of files available for you to download. Delphi offers Xmodem, windowed Xmodem, Ymodem, Ymodem Batch, and Kermit. For doing downloads or uploads on Delphi, your best choice would be either Ymodem or Ymodem Batch. You can use Ymodem Batch for transferring more than one file or Ymodem for transferring a single file. Why these two? Primarily because Xmodem and Kermit are both slower and windowed Xmodem tends to be unstable.

EXEC-PC

Not all that long ago, EXEC-PC was totally renovated for the purpose of installing Zmodem. This was done because so many users requested it. If you subscribe to EXEC-PC, take advantage of its Zmodem implementation. Zmodem is by far the fastest and most accurate of all the protocols available on EXEC-PC.

Channel 1

Channel 1 also offers Zmodem, and it should be your protocol of choice if you subscribe to Channel 1. Keep in mind that the idea is not just to get the programs you want, but to get them as quickly and inexpensively as possible. If a commercial network offers Zmodem, take advantage of it.

Bulletin Board Systems

Bulletin board systems support various protocols. Some older systems will only give you three choices: Xmodem, ASCII, or none at all—not much of a selection. Since binary files cannot be sent using ASCII, you'd have to select Xmodem. Many RBBS-PC systems offer Super Kermit. If you want to set up the Super Kermit protocol, look for a file called PCKERM21.ZIP. Keep in mind that the original version of Kermit is also floating around on BBSs. This version is known as CKermit or MS Kermit and that would not be the one you want. Why not? The original Kermit is about one-third slower than Xmodem, while Super Kermit is about two to three times faster than Xmodem.

A large number of BBSs provide Zmodem. Assuming that you don't have an MNP modem (where you might want to use one of the G protocols), Zmodem would be the protocol of choice. Even if you do have an MNP modem, Zmodem will often get the job done when other protocols will fail; for example, when there is line noise present. Many bulletin boards are also installing MPt and BiModem. Jmodem is found on quite a few Wildcat! systems. All of these protocols offer excellent throughput. What if you visit a system that offers Jmodem, Zmodem, MPt, and BiModem? Then you have to select the one that you prefer based on your experience or your personal preferences.

Batch Downloads

Some transfer protocols are not capable of handling more than one file at a time. 1K-Xmodem/G is a classic example, as is Xmodem. Protocols like "true Ymodem," Zmodem, MPt, Jmodem, Ymodem-G, and BiModem can transfer files in batches. Many PC Board BBSs use Samuel Smith's ProDoor, which allows you to download as many as 50 files in one session. Whenever possible, try to do your file transfers in a batch. Why? One reason is it will save you time. Let's take a look at doing downloads on a PC Board system and assume that you are using ProDoor.

To begin, tell the system that you want to do a download. ProDoor prompts you to select a file transfer protocol. Figure 8-3 shows what this looks like.

Once you've selected a protocol, you have to enter the name of the file that you want to download. If you are doing a single file transfer, you start your download. When your transfer is completed, the system deter-

DOCTOR'S NOTE

"Software is a matter of taste. What one person likes, another person won't!" This statement is one that I've found to be very true. People do, however, tend to expect software to perform certain basic functions. Jmodem, Zmodem, MPt, the G protocols, and BiModem are all streaming protocols. They all yield high cps rates. They all have good error checking. Zmodem, MPt, and BiModem also have the extra feature of *crash recovery* so that you can save an aborted download. BiModem has some additional features that make it especially versatile. These will be discussed in just a moment. For one reason or another, some of these protocols may appeal to you more than others. MPt, for example, has a very colorful and informative screen, while Zmodem does not. Jmodem doesn't try to be fancy; it's just fast. BiModem let's you "chat" with a person on the other end, and none of the others can do that. Telling you my preferences wouldn't mean a great deal, because "software is a matter of taste."

When it comes to downloading, overall performance should be the primary consideration, whether it looks nice while it does it or not. You will establish your own favorites. There are other protocols that I have not discussed, which you may want to check out for yourself; for example, SEAlink by System Enhancement Associates and Super8K by Crater Rim Software. There is also a new protocol from Europe called Cmodem. You have the tools necessary to evaluate such protocols for yourself. Time file transfers with a stopwatch to make sure that the cps ratings the protocol gives you are accurate. Try the protocol on several systems to see if its performance is consistent. You know about the ones that are currently the best and can judge for yourself about the rest.

---

mines if it was successful or not, and then returns you to the ProDoor main prompt. If you want to get another file, you have to go through the whole process again.

Here is where batch file transfers can save you time. Each time you start a file transfer, the protocol engines on each side have to get synchronized. Every time a transfer is completed, the system does a check to see if it was successful. Finally, you are always returned to the main system prompt.

When you do a batch download, you only have to tell the system once that you are downloading. Once the protocols get synchronized for the

---

Figure 8-3

ProDoor protocol prompt on PC Board

```
IMPROVED COMMANDS:
   (J N), (J S), (REPACK), (F U), (R T), (Y), (Q Y), (QQ Y)

Plus many other changes!  See (?) help messages for details.

Number of Downloads: 139 (3128k total, 0k today)
Number of Uploads:   188 (29648k total)
Earned K Bytes:       22463
Total K Bytes Avail: 32462

>>> There is mail for you Sysop!  Check conference 9.
>>> Use the (J S) command to find conferences with personal mail waiting.
        (This message is valid ONLY if you read ALL your mail in ProDoor)

(1 used, 499 left) [Main Board] Command? d

      (Z) Zmodem Batch              (P) Zmodem Batch (PCP)
      (R) Zmodem Resume Aborted D/L (Y) Ymodem Batch
      (O) Xmodem-1K (Old Ymodem)    (C) Slow Xmodem/CRC
      (K) Slow Kermit Batch         (W) Window Xmodem
   => (F) Qmodem-1K-G (Full flow)   (G) Ymodem-G (registered dsz only)
      (L) Lynx

Protocol: (Enter)=F?
 • ANSI   ONLINE  38400 8N1  [Home]=Menu   FDX 8 LF X ↓ ↑ CP LG ↑ PR 00:01:31
```

---

first file they stay that way, and there is a steady progression from one file to the next. The system only has to check for the success of the downloads one time. Just as 1K-Xmodem was faster than Xmodem because it checked for blocks less often, batch transfers help to streamline the download process. You are eliminating a series of repetitive steps. Figure 8-4 shows the start of a batch download in ProDoor.

Note that ProDoor estimates the time for each individual file transfer and subtracts that time from the amount you have available. It then gives you a total estimated time for the batch transfer. Once you start it, you can just sit back and wait for all of the files you've requested to be transferred. You've gotten all of the files you wanted all at once, and saved time and money besides.

Now that you have the programs that you want to look at, what do you do with them and what things should you look for? Let's take a look.

Figure 8-4

Beginning a batch download in ProDoor

```
   (K) Slow Kermit Batch            (W) Window Xmodem
=> (F) Qmodem-1K-G (Full flow)      (G) Ymodem-G (registered dsz only)
   (L) Lynx

Protocol: (Enter)=F? z

Download Zmodem Batch.

Wildcards are Okay, .ZIP is assumed.
Enter up to 50 filespecs.  End the list with a blank line.

(1064k, 496 min. left) Filespec 1: vpic224.zip   Checking ...
(VPIC224.ZIP) not found on disk!

(1064k, 496 min. left) Filespec 1: vpic24.zip   Checking ...
   63k,   5.0 min.  VPIC24.ZIP - Ok

(1001k, 491 min. left) Filespec 2: pmpsconv.zip   Checking ...
   14k,   1.2 min.  PMPSCONV.ZIP - Ok

(987k, 490 min. left) Filespec 3: psxxx.zip   Checking ...
   21k,   1.7 min.  PSXXX.ZIP - Ok

(966k, 488 min. left) Filespec 4:
```
`ANSI  ONLINE  38400 8N1  [Home]=Menu  FDX 8 LF X ↓ ↑ CP LG ↕ PR 00:06:09`

STORAGE CONCERNS

Once you download a program, you'll want to unpack it and start using it. You'll also want to read the documentation and any other text files that accompany it. If you have a hard disk, you can put the program into a directory of its own. This will, of course, depend on the type of program. It's also wise to keep a copy of the compressed file, just in case one of the program files on your hard disk gets corrupted. That means moving it off to a floppy disk.

   As you download and file away more and more programs, you'll run into a common problem. How do you keep track of what you've got? How can you find a particular program without sifting through countless disks? Let's examine these issues in detail and get some answers to these questions and concerns.

Unpacking Compressed Files—
What to Look for

A Shareware program generally consists of files that make up the actual program, along with a documentation file, usually with an extension of .DOC. Some Shareware authors will give the documentation a file extension of .MAN for manual. There might also be an order form in a file called ORDER.FRM. If it's a relatively small program, there may not be a .DOC file. If there isn't too much to explain about a program, you may just find a file called either README, README.1ST, or READ.ME.

Pay close attention as you unpack a compressed file. If you see any errors like "BAD CRC," then the file you have is corrupted. There are programs that are designed to fix corrupted .ARC and .ZIP files, but these aren't always successful. If it's a .ZIP file, you can use PKZIPFIX.EXE to try to reclaim the file. This may work depending on how badly the file is corrupted. If you get error messages while the file is unpacking and find it can't be fixed, you may have to download it again.

Once you've unpacked a compressed file, take the time to look over the text files that accompany it—the .DOC and README-type files. Many of the problems that arise from running new programs stem from the fact that the program's documentation wasn't read. The so-called *manual on a disk* will tell you if you need to modify your CONFIG.SYS file or add an environment variable and other things that may be necessary for the program to run properly.

Always be a little bit leery of a compressed file that comes with nothing but a .COM or .EXE file inside. Even a program donated to the public domain generally has a short READ.ME file in it. Many *hackers*, who pirate commercial programs, will pack up the file without any documentation. If there is only one file, as a precaution you might want to take a look inside it before running it. Use Vern Buerg's LIST program and see if there is anything out of the ordinary inside the file. Do a search for words like "FORMAT" or "DEL."

If you want to be extremely cautious, you may want to run one of the virus-checking programs against the file. Use something like John McAfee's SCAN program, which is constantly upgraded.

Note: In 99.9 percent of the cases, these files will be just fine, or at least that has been my personal experience. If what you find when you run the program isn't a legitimate Shareware program, it will probably be a hacked or pirated commercial program. Just be aware that it is extremely unusual to find a lone .COM or .EXE file inside of a .ZIP, .ARC, or other compressed file.

Storing Files for Backup

Once you've unpacked the file, read the documentation, and perhaps run the program a few times, you'll want to keep a copy of the compressed file for a backup. The best thing to do is to move the compressed file to a floppy disk. Moving files randomly to a floppy disk, however, can waste a lot of space on the floppy disk. Try doing this instead. Make a subdirectory on your hard disk called C:\HOLDING, C:\HOLD, or whatever name means something to you. Move the compressed files that you've obtained to this temporary holding area. Once you've got a fair sized list of programs in your holding area, it's time to move them off to floppies.

Find a program called FILL, by Jean LaLonde. The current version is 3.0 and the usual filename is FILL30.ZIP. What does FILL do? It analyzes all of the files that you want to move to floppies and determines all of the sizes. It will then "fill" each floppy disk to its maximum potential, not wasting a single byte if possible. In many cases a disk that was filled with FILL will have zero bytes free. By using FILL you will

- Get as many programs on a disk as possible
- Use fewer disks for storing compressed programs
- Have to buy fewer floppy disks

It's amazing how much disk space you can waste if you just move programs to floppies by yourself. Unless you want to use a calculator and figure out which files to put on which disks, FILL will do it all for you and much faster.

Now that you have some of your compressed files on floppies for backup, you will run into the next problem. How can you remember which program is on which disk?

Remembering Where You Put Your Files

As you accumulate more programs, there will be times when you'll want to find the backup of a certain one. Perhaps you want to give it to a friend or upload it to a bulletin board. The goal is to be able to find any program

DOCTOR'S NOTE

I've heard rumors in The Wires that inexpensive floppy disks will "gum up" your floppy drives, cause them to deteriorate, and so on. That has not been my experience. I buy 360K floppy disks in lots of 100 for 25 cents each. I purchase the 5.25-inch high-density disks for 49 cents each in lots of 50. The 3.5-inch high-density disks cost me 89 cents each in lots of 25. I have used thousands and thousands of these disks and have never had any problems with my floppy drives. My one computer has been running these disks for seven years and it still works just fine. I would say that on the average I may have one bad disk in every 1,000 that I use. I cringe when I see disks in stores selling for $40 for a box of 10 disks. For $40 I could get approximately 80 1.2 meg disks. That's 96 megabytes of storage.

The company I use is MEI/Micro Center and their toll-free number is 800-634-3478. They also carry a wide range of printer ribbons, disk boxes, and other supplies at very reasonable prices. As far as inexpensive disks causing problems with floppy drives, I have never had any problems. A $4 floppy disk can become corrupted as easily as one that costs 25 cents.

---

that you have as quickly and easily as possible. People accomplish this goal in a variety of ways. The worst case scenario is the person who deletes each compressed file right after unpacking it. That certainly does save on storage (*smile*), but that's about all it saves on.

Note: (*smile*) is but one of many things used on online systems to display emotions in your messages—in this case, a smile.

If anything should happen to one of the unpacked program files, the program must be downloaded again—not the best solution. Disks can be purchased cheaply enough, so you can easily store compressed files that you download without a great deal of expense.

Once you've moved a program (contained in a compressed file) to a disk, you'll want to be able to find it again. One way is to take advantage of any one of several excellent Shareware disk-cataloging programs. Let's talk about them just briefly for now. These programs will be covered more extensively in Part Four.

Disk-Cataloging Programs

Two of the most popular Shareware disk-cataloging programs are CAT-DISK and WSS INDEX. There are several others that are also available. These programs help you catalog your disks in an efficient manner. Each floppy disk to be cataloged must have a *volume label* because this is how the program keeps track of the disks. You can also enter *keywords* so you can search for programs that have similar functions.

In effect, these programs are really just databases that keep track of the files on your backup disks. They are, however, specialized databases that are specifically designed for disk cataloging. Figure 8-5 shows the main menu of CATDISK and all the functions that it has.

You can both add and delete from the CATDISK database. You can enter a description for each file, even for each file within a compressed program. The program will also put on the volume labels for you so you

Figure 8-5

Main screen of CATDISK

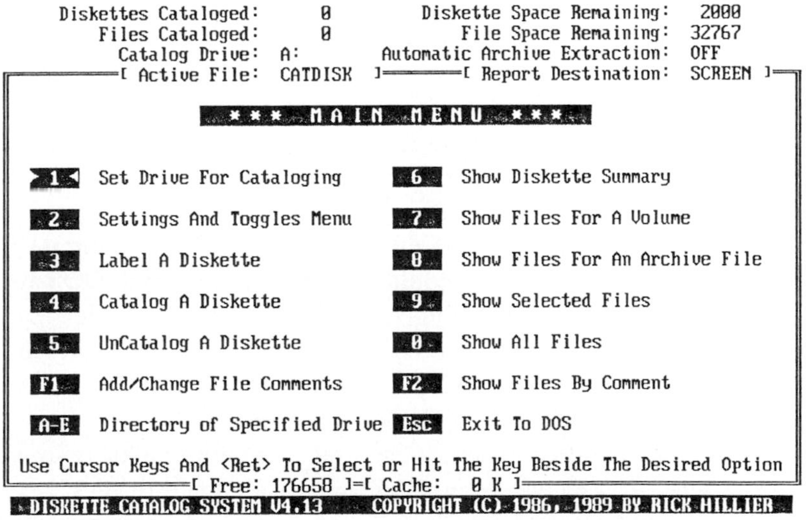

```
Diskettes Cataloged:     0        Diskette Space Remaining:   2000
   Files Cataloged:      0            File Space Remaining:  32767
    Catalog Drive:  A:        Automatic Archive Extraction:  OFF
         =[ Active File:  CATDISK  ]======[ Report Destination:  SCREEN ]=

              *** M A I N  M E N U ***


    1   Set Drive For Cataloging      6   Show Diskette Summary

    2   Settings And Toggles Menu     7   Show Files For A Volume

    3   Label A Diskette              8   Show Files For An Archive File

    4   Catalog A Diskette            9   Show Selected Files

    5   UnCatalog A Diskette          0   Show All Files

   F1   Add/Change File Comments     F2   Show Files By Comment

   A-E  Directory of Specified Drive Esc  Exit To DOS

Use Cursor Keys And <Ret> To Select or Hit The Key Beside The Desired Option
         =[ Free: 176658 ]=[ Cache:    0 K ]=
  DISKETTE CATALOG SYSTEM V4.13     COPYRIGHT (C) 1986, 1989 BY RICK HILLIER
```

don't have to leave the program. While I recognize the excellence of such programs and the functions they provide, I personally prefer something more simple and direct.

The Doc's Method

Because the goal is to be able to find out what disk has a certain program on it and do it quickly, I opted for my own system of cataloging programs. Now, before describing it for you, I want you to promise not to laugh. Keep in mind that I was relatively new to this kind of thing back then. The end result worked very well and still does; it was just a bit tedious getting there.

What I did first was to fill my floppy disks with programs I had gathered. Then I would give each one a volume label. Because .ARC files were prevalent at the time, the disks were labeled in numerical sequence, like ARC-250, ARC-251, and so on. Once they were labeled, I would put each disk into drive A one at a time (it gets crowded if you try two at once), and I would execute the following command from the DOS prompt:

```
C>DIR A: >> C:\TEXT\ARCHIVE.DAT
```

In this way the directory of each disk would be placed in the C:\TEXT\ARCHIVE.DAT file. Since the *redirection symbol*, > >, was used, the next disk's directory would be appended to the end of the file. When I was finished with the disks, I would use an editor, strip out the time field, and put the appropriate label name in its place—for example, ARC-252.

Yes, it was very tedious, but the end result was worth it. Using a DOS command line editor, I created a synonym called LA, which translated to "LIST C:\TEXT\ARCHIVE.DAT." I would use Buerg's SORTF program to sort ARCHIVE.DAT alphabetically. I could be online and drop to DOS and execute LA. Buerg's LIST would bring up the ARCHIVE.DAT file and I could search for a filename that I wanted. I could know, for example, that DSZ1128.ARC was on disk ARC-112 in a matter of seconds. Figure 8-6 shows part of what my ARCHIVE.DAT file looks like.

Over the years this file has grown to be huge, containing a listing of all my files and what disks they are on. With over a gigabyte of files, I can still use my LA synonym and find any program in just seconds. I can easily check to see if I have the most recent version of a program or if I need to download one that I see online. This system fills all of the basic needs in that

- It keeps track of all stored files

- It tells you exactly what disk each file is on

- It enables you to find any file quickly, even while online

The idea was good, it's just that the implementation wasn't: fortunately, a friend stepped in to smooth things out.

A Custom Cataloging Program—Just for You

One night on my bulletin board, a friend logged on. His name is John Knauer, author of IFF 5.0A, TURBO_FLIP_UM, and several other programs. He is known by his friends as "CT John," because he hails from Connecticut. CT and I started chatting and he asked me how I kept track of all of the thousands of programs I have in storage. I told him what I just described to you. A few days later there was a note on my board from CT saying that he had sent me a special program he'd written. It turned out to be a program called "DOC," and it automated my method of

Figure 8-6

A look at the format of ARCHIVE.DAT

```
LIST     139              12-02-89 14:52 ● ARCHIVE.DAT
DOG101A.ZIP     35788   08-21-89   ARC-6
DOODLE.ZIP      16222   08-22-89   ARC-19
DOS31PT.ZIP      5283   08-21-89   ARC-11
DOS31USE.ZIP     6288   08-22-89   ARC-20
DOS32FIX.ZIP    11167   08-21-89   ARC-11
DOS32V4.ZIP      5400   08-21-89   ARC-11
DOSCALL.ZIP      1164   03-27-86   ARC-11
DOSEDIT.ZIP      5131   02-03-86   ARC-11
DOSMODEM.ZIP     4362   08-21-89   ARC-11
DP12.ZIP        18869   08-22-89   ARC-18
DPATH30.ZIP      7352   03-10-86   ARC-11
DRAGONS.ZIP     18135   08-22-89   ARC-18
DRLIST.ZIP      14360   08-22-89   ARC-19
DSZ1220.ZIP     52140   08-23-89   ARC-43
DTC.ZIP         38129   08-22-89   ARC-18
DUP.ZIP         46260   08-23-89   ARC-44
DURASCRN.ZIP    41311   08-23-89   ARC-44
DV-HELP.ZIP     75457   08-22-89   ARC-16
DWPSETUP.ZIP     3687   08-21-89   ARC-11
DX-211.ZIP      47851   08-23-89   ARC-66
DYNAMIND.EXE   102400   08-23-89   ARC-72
DZAML121.ZIP    22917   08-23-89   ARC-68
E88-V402.ZIP    43251   08-22-89   ARC-18
Command▶                  Keys: ↑↓←→ PgUp PgDn F10-exit F1-Help
```

keeping track of programs on disk. No more stripping out the time field, no more editing, nothing. It was remarkably fast and easy!

For this book I asked CT if I could include a copy of DOC on the disk that comes with it. CT laughed and said, "I wrote that program for you, Doc, and you said with your memory you didn't need a place to put in any file descriptions. Most other people might like to be able to do that." The next thing I knew, CT had modified the original DOC program, so you can use it to catalog *your* disks if you like. You can also enter a short description of each file or put keywords in that area instead. Figure 8-7 gives you a peek at the listing that DOC produces.

In this example, some of the lines have descriptions, while others are using keywords instead. A copy of DOC is included on one of the disks that comes with this book. All you have to do is run DOC and put your filled floppy disks into the floppy drive that you specify. Then, tell DOC the name of the file that you want to store your listings in. This feature allows you to have separate listings; perhaps one for those disks containing source code, one for general program files, one for utilities, and so on. DOC will read the disk, and then prompt you for a *disk name* for each

---

Figure 8-7

A listing of the DOC program

```
LIST       1      23     02-04-90 11:21 ♦ ZIPFILES.DAT
ALT124.LZH   285935  08-10-89  ZIP-914 ALT 1.24 - Task switching and more
AM436.EXE    154044  08-27-89  ZIP-915 ARCMASTER 4.36 REG. from John Newlin
CARDGAME.ZIP  28838  00-00-80  ZIP-907 GAME CARDS VGA EGA MOUSE
CGB12.ZIP     96241  09-11-89  ZIP-910 EDUCATION GRADES TEACHER
EMSIM.ARC     12288  08-23-89  ZIP-915 EMS SIMULATE DISK LIM 4.0
FV119.ZIP      5703  08-26-89  ZIP-915 FILE VIEW ver. 1.19 by Vern Buerg
LOG205.ZIP    92000  09-09-89  ZIP-909 Log time/cost. Print reports. Excellent
MENUKEY.ZIP   49152  09-14-89  ZIP-907 Language for writing mouse menus
MICROSPL.ZIP 207104  09-01-89  ZIP-911 SPELL CHECK CORRECT
PCFDB1.ZIP   330752  09-10-89  ZIP-912 PC FILE DB Disk 1 of 3 ButtonWare
PCFDB2.ZIP   349104  09-10-89  ZIP-913 PC FILE DB Disk 2 of 3
PCFDB3.ZIP   134144  09-10-89  ZIP-911 PC-FILE-DB Disk 3 of 3
PCFDBMS.ZIP   19505  09-11-89  ZIP-909 PC-FILE-DB mouse driver
PCW302A.ZIP  201728  08-30-89  ZIP-910 PC Write 3.02 Disk 1 of 3
PCW302C.ZIP  231168  08-30-89  ZIP-914 PC Write 3.02 Disk 3 of 3
PKII-124.COM  63072  06-07-89  ZIP-915 Powerkit II v.1.24 by John Brooks
PWMOUS.ZIP     7106  09-10-89  ZIP-907 MOUSE WRITE MENU MS
SD-160.ZIP    61440  09-21-89  ZIP-908 StupenDOS ver. 1.60 w/mouse support
SHEZ47.EXE    84992  09-20-89  ZIP-909 ARC ZIP MANIPULATE FILES
STAR14.ZIP    66560  08-12-89  ZIP-915 Starport 1.4 - Automates STARLINK- GOOD
TDRAW320.ZIP 163675  05-17-89  ZIP-909 ANSI DRAW ANIMATION COLORS
WORDFIND.ZIP  28672  09-13-89  ZIP-907 GAME PUZZLES WORDS SOLVE
ZIPTV20.ZIP   33792  09-09-89  ZIP-908 ZIPTV 2.0 for ProDoor file viewing
Command►    *** Top-of-file ***       Keys: ↑↓→← PgUp PgDn F10=exit F1=Help
```

disk. You could use ZIP-001, ARC-100, and so on. As long as the disk itself is labeled, it doesn't matter if the floppy has a volume label or not. DOC will then prompt you for a brief description of each file on the disk. When you've finished one disk you can go on and do more or you can quit at any time.

I hope that you'll enjoy it. This program has served me well for several years and I thank Knauer (CT John) for taking the time to write it for me and modify it for you. Now that you have a means of keeping track of the files you've downloaded, it's time to move on. Let's take a look at uploading files to commercial networks and bulletin boards.

UPLOADING FILES — THINGS TO CONSIDER

There was a time, not long ago, when all of the commercial online networks continued to charge you connect time even when you were uploading a file to their system. Gradually, the networks changed their attitude about uploads. They realized that when a user took the time to upload a file, they were making a positive contribution to the system, making it just a little bit richer.

Today, all of the major online networks offer free uploads. When you begin an upload, the timer stops until the upload is completed. Upload a 500K file on CompuServe or GEnie at 1200 baud and it doesn't cost you a penny to do it. Bulletin board systems also have ways of giving credit to users who upload. When the subject of uploads comes up, however, many users shrug their shoulders and say, "Upload? Why should I bother?" Let's take a look at why you should.

Why You Should Upload Files

The vast majority of people who go online are interested in obtaining good Shareware and public domain programs. Because of this they do a lot of downloading. There is a standing joke among bulletin board sysops about users and the D key. In the file section of almost any bulletin board system, the D key stands for "download." Sysops watch a parade of users log on and head straight for the trusty D key. After a while, it gets to be a point of irritation for sysops. Stop and think about it for just a minute. You like to download programs from bulletin boards, but how do you think those programs got there in the first place?

Most sysops can't spare the time, or the expense, to go out and search other systems for new programs. They have to depend on users to send up a new file now and then. Obviously, someone took the time to do some uploads or there would be very little there for you to download. In essence, an upload, as the online networks finally decided, is a contribution to the system. It's a way of sharing with others just as they have shared with you. It makes the system better and, in a way, more valuable. From another angle, it's a way of saying thanks, not only to the sysop, but to the other users, for the things that they have provided for you.

Some users voice the argument, "I don't have anything to upload that the system doesn't already have!" That is a valid point because some users don't download that often and some systems are very active. Other users just don't take the time. The next time you go to press that infamous D key, stop and ask yourself, "Isn't there a Shareware program I've got that I like that I can share with these folks?"

What Kind of Things to Upload

If you visit a number of bulletin boards or any of the online networks, eventually you'll find that you have a program that other systems don't yet have. If it's a program that you think is really good, upload it to a few systems. You may find a program that you are really excited about. If a program makes you want to tell your spouse, "Hey, honey, this program does exactly what we've been looking for!," chances are good that someone else might be looking for the very same thing. Try uploading those kinds of programs to other places.

If you are one of those users who doesn't download a lot of files and often find that you truly don't have anything new to upload, there is still something you can do. Try writing a message about a Shareware program that you do have that you really like. Sharing your message with others makes them aware of a program that they may not have noticed before. Shareware is something that all of us can participate in together. Shareware is

- Users sharing with users
- Users supporting Shareware authors
- Authors supporting their products and making improvements

Whether you share a new file that you upload to a system or a note about a program that you really like, you have made a contribution. Take that extra moment or two and upload a file or a message—and help make the "share" in Shareware mean something. On bulletin boards there are often other things to consider before you upload a file.

Bulletin Board Considerations

As discussed in Chapter 5, each sysop sets up the system independently. Each sysop will have his or her own rules and policies, and as a user you must abide by them. Much of the activity on bulletin boards centers around programs. On some systems, new users cannot download until they have uploaded something. On other BBSs, a new user can download and upload freely on the very first call. Rules and policies about file transfers will vary from system to system. Some sysops run the system based on ratios. Let's take a look at this.

Download-to-Upload Ratios

Many bulletin boards use a system that hinges on *download-to-upload ratios.* In other words, the sysop sets up what they think is a reasonable ratio. Some bulletin board software can actually adjust your security level based on what this ratio is. Other systems will automatically turn off your download privileges when you reach the established ratio. For example, if a system has a download-to-upload ratio of 10 to 1, you can download 10 programs for every 1 that you upload. If you download 10 and haven't uploaded any, you may suddenly find that you can't download anything else until you upload a file. Why is this done? To encourage and ensure that some "new blood" will be uploaded to the system on a regular basis.

Since it's a well-known fact that people like to download files, one way to encourage them to upload a file now and then is to interrupt their ability to download. Any bulletin board system that is using download-to-upload ratios will have it clearly stated in their bulletins. The ratio will vary from system to system, being as low as 5 to 1 or as high as 20 to 1. Some bulletin boards don't have any ratios at all and this is especially true on subscription boards. If you use a system that utilizes download-to-upload ratios, you'll often find that your access or security level goes up depending on how many programs you upload. This often encourages people to upload so they can get programs that may require a higher security level.

PC Board software allows sysops to have something similar to a download-to-upload ratio, but it works on the number of bytes exchanged. For example, a PC Board sysop can set up a system so that all users with a security level of 10 can download 200K per day. If you exceed that number in any given day (actually the system won't let you exceed it), you'd have to upload a file. For each upload you get a credit of so many bytes. Some users view this as being more fair than the straight download-to-upload ratio system. Why? Because with the ratio system if the ratio is 10 to 1, you might download ten 3K files. Another user might download ten 300K files. At the point where you've only downloaded 30K and the other user has downloaded 3 megabytes, both of you would have to upload a file.

Using the total number of bytes seems to make it fair for all users. As you travel in The Wires you'll find some bulletin boards that don't require any uploads and a few systems that don't even allow uploads. Another thing that you'll have to consider about uploads is that sysops sometimes have rules about what you can upload. This really means that they have rules about what kind of files they will accept.

Sysop Rules Regarding Uploads

As mentioned before, sysops determine how they want their system to be run. For one reason or another, sysops sometimes state that only files in a certain format can be uploaded. One example is that many bulletin boards will only accept files that have been packed with Phil Katz's PKZIP. If you try uploading a file with an extension other than .ZIP (for example, .ARC, .ZOO, or .PAK), there are a couple of things that might happen.

One is that you'll be able to do the upload just fine, but then you'll get a note from the sysop asking you not to do it again. If it's a system that gives credit for uploads, you may not get credit for it. Another possibility is that the system will give you a message saying that the file extension you are trying to upload is not acceptable.

On the other hand, a bulletin board sysop may not care about what compressed format an uploaded file is in, but he or she may care about what type of program it is. There is a BBS in North Carolina called NoGames RBBS. There are 624 megabytes of files on the NoGames RBBS and not one game. Obviously, the name of the board is appropriate. There are applications, utilities, GIF (Graphics Interface Format) files, and much more, but the sysop does not want games on his system. At the same time, there are specialized boards that want only game programs uploaded.

The PROF BBS in Lexington, Kentucky is an excellent system devoted primarily to real estate and finance. Professionals and students of real estate and finance can find a wide variety of files and programs that deal with everything from treasury bills to taxes. There are also good discussions and echo mail conferences that center around the theme of the system (see the following Doctor's Note for more about echo mail).

Since the board has a theme and a purpose, there are certain kinds of programs that the sysop does not want uploaded. To leave room for programs that focus on the purpose of the board, the sysop asks that users not upload games (unless they are educational games) or GIF, READMAC, and ADULT THEME files. Figure 8-8 gives you an example of how a sysop might tell you what should not be uploaded, and it's the screen that is seen on the PROF BBS.

If a sysop asks that you not upload certain types of files, abide by the rules. One thing that you should never do is upload any copyrighted software unless it is Shareware. This is a rule that is posted on nearly all bulletin boards. The retail programs that you buy in stores do not belong on bulletin board systems or commercial online networks. It is against the

---

Figure 8-8

Pre-upload screen from PROF BBS

```
================================================================================
       Thank you, Dr., for getting ready to upload to The PROF-BBS!
================================================================================
        Please keep in mind this system ONLY has room for:
            * Business, Finance, Education and Real Estate Related Files
            * Helpful Communications Programs and Utilities
            * Graphics Programs and Utilities on the System Theme

    * DO NOT UPLOAD:
              GAMES - unless they are CLEARLY educational
              COPYRIGHTED PROGRAMS - unless they are ShareWare
              GIF, READMAC or ADULT THEME FILES

    * ALL UPLOADS MUST BE IN .ZIP, .LZH, or SELF EXTRACTING FORMAT
      any other archiving extension are subject to deletion - Thanks!

    Thanks for your cooperation in maintaining the PURPOSE of the System!
                                            --- Don Bodley/SysOp
  - More - [C]ontinue, [S]top, [N]onStop:
```

```
* ANSI   ONLINE   38400 8N1   [Home]=Menu    FDX 8 LF X ♪ ♫ CP LG ↑ PR 00:01:28
```

DOCTOR'S NOTE

Some bulletin board systems have echo mail or netmail conferences. What is *echo mail* or *netmail?* It's a way for many bulletin board systems to exchange messages with each other. Most often, bulletin boards in a given geographical area will form a network and establish conferences of interest to users. Messages that are entered into these conferences are exchanged with all of the other systems in the network at a specified time during the night. In this way, you can get input from a larger group of users on any particular subject. You enter your note on the local system that you call, but you may get replies from users on systems several miles away or even across the country.

Netmail (derived from the idea of a network of systems) is a great way to exchange ideas and obtain information. Usually, netmail is exchanged in the early morning hours, around 3:00 A.M. eastern standard time. If you ever call a system and get a message like "Currently Doing NetMail—Please Call Back Later," you'll know what it means. The concept of netmail was first implemented on the FIDO bulletin board software.

law for you to upload them and it's also against the law for the system to have them online. If you think it's a good idea to get some upload credits by uploading WordPerfect 5.1 or the latest release of Lotus, think again. Another thing to consider when getting ready to upload a file is duplication of a file that already exists on a system.

Duplicate Files

When you go to upload a file to a bulletin board, you'll want to make sure that you aren't duplicating a file that is already on the system. Most bulletin board software will tell you that a file is already there if the filenames match exactly. Figure 8-9 shows what this would look like on a PC Board system.

Unfortunately, for one reason or another, some users like to rename files. If they downloaded a file that the program author called OZBX132F.ZIP, they might decide to rename it OZBEXT.ZIP. Something to keep in mind is that programs are often given certain names for a reason. Using the current example, there have been many releases of OZBEXT by Sneed. The reason "132F" was included in the original filename was so that users could tell what version of OZBEXT it was. The

Figure 8-9

Duplicate file message on PC Board

```
Scan Message Base Since 'Last Read' (Enter)=yes? n

(197 min. left) Qmodem (1) Conference Command? door;3
Insufficient security for DOOR (PRODOOR)

(197 min. left) Qmodem (1) Conference Command? j;28

Alpha (28) Conference Joined

Scan Message Base Since 'Last Read' (Enter)=yes? n

(197 min. left) Alpha (28) Conference Command? door;3
Insufficient security for DOOR (PRODOOR)

(197 min. left) Alpha (28) Conference Command? u

Filename to Upload (Enter)=none? beta.zip
Checking file transfer request. Please wait ...
(BETA.ZIP) duplicates a current board file.

Filename to Upload (Enter)=none?
```
ANSI   ONLINE   38400 8N1   [Home]=Menu   FDX 8 LF X ♪♫ CP LG ↑ PR 00:00:39

idea is to save people time and money. Why download a program if you already have that version of the program? This naming convention is used by many program authors. Look at the following list of actual examples.

```
SD161.ZIP
AM445REG.ZIP
DSZ0122.ZIP
IFF50A.ZIP
```

Note that each filename has numbers in it. The numbers are meant to tell users the version number of the program. The four programs listed are StupenDOS 1.61, the registered version of ArcMaster 4.45, Forsberg's DSZ release of January 22, 1990, and IFF 5.0A. If you download SD161.ZIP and rename it STUPNDOS.ZIP, no one knows what version of Stupen-DOS it is. Yes, you could include the version number in your description when you upload it, but many people don't do that. In addition, descriptions on a BBS aren't a part of the file. If you download STUPNDOS.ZIP,

DOCTOR'S NOTE

It's very easy to get caught up in downloading programs. For some people, the more they have the more they want. At the same time, these same people often do not like having to maintain download-to-upload ratios. Because of this, some users intentionally rename files and upload them to bulletin board systems. Why? To get upload credits or to maintain their download-to-upload ratio. Rather than uploading a new program that the system doesn't have, they give a new name to a file that is already on the system. The bulletin board software can only go by the filename and not what is in it. Thus, the upload is accepted.

Speaking from personal experience, it is very frustrating and irritating to download what you think is a new program, only to find that it's one that you already have. It's very disappointing and also a complete waste of time and money. If everyone did this, you could never be sure what you were downloading. Some bulletin board software allows you to look at the contents of a packed file. If you see a file that you are interested in, but the name or description looks vaguely familiar, look at the files that are inside it. This might save you some time. Smith's ProDoor has a function whereby you can actually read the text files found inside a packed file. This might also help you determine if this is a file that you already have.

In your dealings online, try to be fair to yourself and others. If you don't have anything new to upload, wait until you do. The programs that you want to download will still be there. On BBSs where the sysop is not very attentive, I've seen as many as 20 copies of the same program, all with different names. So, the practice of giving a new name to a file and uploading it wastes disk space, time, and money. Be considerate of your fellow users and your local sysop. The first time you download a file that you already have, simply because the name was changed, you'll understand what I mean.

and then upload it to another system, the version number won't show up unless you remember to put it in your description of the file. Thus, it's better for everyone concerned if the version number remains a part of the filename.

How to Do Things to Your Advantage

Whether you are downloading or uploading, you want to go online knowing what you plan on doing. In this way you can spend as little time online as possible, and get the most benefit from that time. A large number of bulletin boards and the commercial online networks keep lists of all the files and programs they have. In most cases, this will be a compressed file that you can download. BBS sysops will often post the name of this file in a bulletin or at the top of the file area menu. You might see something like "For a complete listing of all files on The Goose Egg BBS, download EGGFILES.ZIP." Other typical names are FILELIST .ZIP, AREALIST.ZIP, DIR1.ZIP, and LISTING.ZIP.

If you are new on a system, or if you haven't visited a particular BBS in quite a while, go online and download this listing file. Then you can log off. Now you can unpack the file and take your time looking at it. Use Buerg's LIST to look at it, load it into your editor, or even print it. (Some of these lists are very long, so you may not want to print them.) You can take your time deciding what files you want to download from the system and what programs you have that you could upload.

Make a list of the programs that you want to download and upload. Then, when you get online you'll be ready for action. Log on at the highest modem speed you have available. Pick one of the faster streaming protocols. Whenever possible, do batch downloads and uploads. Taking a little bit of time while you are offline to decide what you want to do will pay for itself many times over when you get online. There is a special case in which you can optimize your time online even further and do the most for your money. Let's check it out.

The Best of Both Worlds: Full Duplex Protocols

In the world of real estate, a duplex is a house that is divided into two halves. A family can live in each half of the duplex. In telecommunications, *duplex* refers to the echoing of characters through the modem, but it is also slightly more than that. A modem is a *full duplex* device that uses a given band width, somewhat like a radio station. All of the file transfer protocols that were discussed in Chapter 7, with one exception, use only a small portion of the modem's band width. The exception is BiModem.

BiModem, by John Erickson and Dave Krause of Erik Labs, utilizes nearly the entire band width of a full duplex modem. This is what gives BiModem the capability of both sending and receiving files at the same time. Since BiModem can give you this capability, it can also save you time. How? Let's say, for example, that you are on a system that has

BiModem and you want to download a 100K file. If you'd like to upload an 80K file to the system, you can do so and the upload will cost you nothing! Why not? Because in using BiModem, you are doing the download and the upload simultaneously. Since the 80K file that you want to upload is slightly smaller than the 100K file that you want to download, the upload will complete just a little before the download. You've accomplished two things that you wanted to do in the same time frame.

Looking at it from yet another way, let's say that the download was going to take 3 minutes, and that the upload was going to take 2.8 minutes. Completed separately, this would total 5.8 minutes. Using BiModem, both transfers would only take as long as it takes to transfer the biggest file. In this case, that would be 3 minutes, and you just saved 2.8 minutes and did the upload besides! Over a period of time, using BiModem to download and upload files simultaneously can save you a great deal of time and money. You might want to get a copy of BiModem and register it. Then you can take advantage of BiModem's bidirectional abilities on systems that offer BiModem as a protocol. If a BBS that you call frequently doesn't have BiModem, encourage the sysop to install it. As mentioned earlier, BiModem can be installed easily on a wide range of BBS software. Doing two things at the same time can save you time and money. Let's investigate some other ways of doing this.

Multitasking and File Transfers

It is often said that "there is only so much time in a day," and it's so very true. Sometimes, it seems as if there just aren't enough hours in the day to get everything done. As noted above in the discussion of BiModem, being able to do several things simultaneously saves you time. This is time that you can dedicate to completing other things that need to be done. Until only a short time ago, multitasking was something that was out of reach.

With the advent of 386-based machines and better software for multitasking, new ways of saving time have opened up for all of us. If you have to do a report for work, download a program to augment that report, and check for messages in a support conference on one of the online networks, you can start to feel the crunch. Let's look at two options, both of which involve multitasking, that can help you to save time and get more accomplished.

Using True Multitasking

Today's 386 machines are providing new ways to handle memory, in addition to offering much greater speed. With improved software that can handle large amounts of memory, multitasking has become a viable alternative for many users.

Using a Northgate 386-20 MHz machine and Quarterdeck's DESQview 2.25, I just downloaded a 243K file while I was writing the last paragraph. :) Utilizing the speed of the Northgate machine and the four megabytes of RAM on my machine, plus DESQview's ability to divide up the memory into "windows," I can have several things going at once—my word processor in this window and Qmodem in another. The file transfer, completed at 38,400 bps, was only about 100 cps off from what I would have normally expected. Thus, I was able to accomplish two things at the same time. I got a file that I had to pick up and I completed a paragraph. Even better, it was all done with no noticeable difference in the performance of either task. If you have a 386 machine, or intend to buy one, the amount of time it can save you is one thing to consider. Doing file transfers while multitasking can help you be more productive and save you time and money. Think about it.

Programs That Work in the Background

If you don't have a 386 machine, or any means of doing multitasking, you needn't despair. The ingenuity of Shareware authors is amazing. An alternative to multitasking is making use of programs that can do file transfers in the *background*. A program is considered to be in the background when it can be loaded and perform work while you use another program. These small communications programs do their work in the background, freeing up your machine for other things. They can help you go online and transfer files while you are doing something else. There are a few good ones in Shareware, and a few in the retail arena. The Shareware programs that you might want to try will be discussed in detail in Part Four. For now, let's take a quick look at how these programs work.

Communications programs that work in the background load as TSR (terminate and stay resident) programs. One thing that you need to be conscious of is how much RAM they use. These programs have their own dialing directories where you can enter numbers that you want to call.

The newer ones support 9600 baud. You can tell the program to start dialing a particular bulletin board, and then exit back to another program.

The background communications program will happily dial the BBS while you use an editor, spreadsheet, or any other program. When it connects to the BBS, it lets you know. At that point, you can toggle to the background and log on. You can start a file transfer, and then go back to what you were doing. The background program will signal you when the transfer is done. You can then toggle to it and log off of the BBS. All very simple and very neat. It also lets you get more done in a given amount of time. These programs that work in the background are something that you may want to consider if you find that you have lots of things to do and not enough time to do them.

BRINGING IT ALL TOGETHER

A lot of material has been covered in this chapter and those preceding it. To summarize briefly, remember that the focus is on the following things:

- Knowing your equipment and software
- Gaining more confidence each time you go online
- Planning your activities before going online
- Doing things as efficiently as possible
- Taking advantage of scripts, macros, and capture files
- Using the highest baud rate possible
- Making use of the faster, more accurate streaming protocols
- Doing batch downloads and uploads
- Using multitasking or background programs for more productivity

This is just a quick summary, but it highlights some of the key things to keep in mind. Now, it's time to move on and see about some tricks and tips that you can use online.

## CHAPTER NINE

Techno-Hints from the Doctor's Black Bag

In the preceding chapters you examined the process of going online. You had the opportunity to see how using log files can help you learn the systems you plan on visiting. The use of macros and scripts were looked at so you can save time when accessing online systems. Actual screen captures of bulletin board logons were used so you'd have a better idea of what to look for. All of these things were meant to help you by providing you with the benefit of some experience. Unlike the typical user, you can venture online with some confidence. The most popular file transfer protocols were also discussed in detail, and you got an idea of what you can expect from each. In the last chapter you took a good look at uploading, downloading, and how you can cut costs and save time. You should have enough examples to allow you to master these techniques in a relatively short period of time.

At this point, you should have a pretty good idea of what it's like when you go online. Some things, however, you generally only find out about through personal experience. This chapter is going to deal with some of those things that you only find out about with actual hands-on experience—some tips, tricks, and techniques that might save you some aggravation someday.

TIDBITS PICKED UP OVER TIME

Some things that occur online happen so rarely that it may be quite some time before you'd ever encounter them. In some cases this might be only a matter of months, but in others, it might be a matter of years. Among other things, this chapter is going to share some tips and tricks picked up over the years that I've been online. Some may prove useful to you and some may not. You will, however, at least have the benefit of knowing about them in advance. Some of the tips are things that you'd normally only learn the hard way.   :-)   (*Another form of emoticon.*)

A few of the tricks are things that I discovered by doing some experimentation. In a few cases, I can't tell you why they work; I can only tell you that they do. In general, the idea is to give you some extra knowledge that you probably would pick up eventually on your own. Learning it the hard way does not help you the first 25 times it happens. ;) (*That's an online wink.*) This will save you some time and effort. To begin with, for those with external modems, let's explore some of the things you can learn just by watching the modem lights. For those of you with internal modems, use one of the programs mentioned in Chapter 5 that puts a simulation of the modem lights on your screen, and you can use these tips too.

WATCHING THE MODEM LIGHTS

Your modem, via the serial port, is your window to the world when you are online. By watching the lights of your modem, you can see if your modem is *ready* (the MR light), if your modem is *clear to send* (the CS light), and if your terminal program is *loaded* (the TR light). When you start to dial a system, you can see that the phone is off the hook by taking note of the OH light. When you finally connect, you can know it immediately just by seeing the *carrier detect* (the CD light) come on. Yes, these are the basics, but the lights on your modem can tell you so much. In some cases—when I'm trying to determine the nature of a problem, for example—I don't look at my monitor at all. Instead, I have my eyes focused on the modem lights. Here are some situations where knowing what the lights mean can help you out.

The Unstable Phone Line

Let's say that you're online and entering a message to an online friend. You are typing along when all of a sudden you notice that the last few characters entered didn't show up on the screen. Immediately check the status of the modem lights. On an MNP modem, you may note that the ARQ light and the TR light are slowly going off and then coming back on. On a non-MNP modem, just the TR light will flicker off, and then return. This is an indication that the phone connection that you have with the system is not stable. The instability may be caused by power fluctuations on the host's side. Whatever the cause, I've found that 80 percent of the time when you note this phenomenon on the modem lights, you will be disconnected—maybe not immediately, but within five minutes.

This is not a good time to start a file transfer unless you are using one of the protocols that can recover files from an aborted download. These protocols are Zmodem, MPt, and BiModem. What might be best is to try to finish your note, and then log off. This phenomenon took quite a while to analyze, but now I have it well documented. Watch for it—the modem lights will tell you.

The Aborted Transfer Loop

Every so often, while performing a file transfer, you'll have a transfer *blow up* on you. A blow-up can occur in several ways. One way is for the transfer to abort and fill your screen with graphics characters, or what are commonly called garbage characters. Since I haven't had much luck capturing any from my screen, here are some garbage characters created for you to admire.

εεΣφÇÇÇÇÇ•£ü¥£β∞∞Ξ ε∩ ±αμμΦΦ╬╣ Æ╝ ╫▓ÇÇ

You may also hear beeps and sputtering noises, the screen may clear and then be filled again, and so on. What this means is that the host is still trying to send. The host is clearing out its buffer, so to speak. On the majority of BBSs, you can hit CTRL-X eight to ten times, which often shuts down the protocol on the other side. Don't worry. If nothing else, it will eventually stop by itself. You might want to think of this as "aborted transfer fireworks" since that's what it looks like. Pounding on your keyboard won't help. :> (*Yet another form of emoticon used by people online. This one always reminds me of the Grinch.*) There is another way that transfers can abort that is totally silent and more of a problem.

What I've come to call the *aborted transfer loop* is a situation that you can see on your modem lights. Imagine that you are online looking at a screen. No key that you hit has any effect. If you look at your modem lights, you'll notice that the receive data (RD) and send data (SD) lights are *both* on and fluttering violently back and forth. It's like big time wrestling in the modem community. Data is being sent, and at the same time, received. In effect, you are going nowhere. The data is in a loop, and loops can go on forever. If you find yourself caught in an aborted transfer loop, it is one of the rare cases where it is acceptable to disconnect by hanging up. Unless you are really enjoying the battle between your RD and SD lights, hanging up is the only alternative. Once again, your modem lights will tip you off. Unless you are doing a bidirectional BiModem transfer, your RD and SD lights will never be *fully* lit simultaneously.

You're Connected but Nobody's Home

Now imagine that you are calling a local bulletin board. Since you call there fairly often, you have a logon script. You make your call and connect just fine. You can tell that by looking at the modem lights. Besides, your communications program agrees. Just the same, nothing happens. Your script doesn't do anything and the screen is blank. Wait about 30 seconds, and then abort your script.

Take a look at your modem lights and you'll see that all the proper lights are lit. The CD and OH lights are lit, telling you that your modem is detecting a carrier and that your modem is off hook. You should be connected and you probably are. Try entering a carriage return while watching the modem lights. You may or may not see your SD light flicker each time you hit the ENTER key. On some systems, you may need to hit the

SPACEBAR. Try hitting alternate carriage returns and the SPACEBAR. You may still get no response from the other side. What's the problem?

You've connected to the bulletin board, but the bulletin board isn't there. You may say, "But the modem answered the phone!" Yes, but a modem is a piece of hardware. It has been told to answer the phone. (Using a program found on BBSs called MODCMD16.ZIP, I can tell my modem to answer the phone while I'm at the DOS prompt.) What has happened, in most cases, is that the BBS software is not loaded. You connected to a modem that isn't connected to any software that tells it what to do.

This often occurs when a sysop takes down the system to do maintenance and does not *busy out* the modem. In other cases, some problem may have caused the BBS software to exit, leaving the modem online and ready to answer. This is another case where you can disconnect with a clear conscience, by hanging up the phone. After all, you weren't connected to a system, just its modem. When your modem lights tell you that you are connected and you get no response from the other side, you've connected with a system but nobody's home.

THE HARD DISK THAT WON'T BOOT

One day you turn on your computer and get that awful message "boot failure." You try again and get the same response. If you've been around computers for a while you may think, "No problem, I'll boot from a floppy, and then figure out what's wrong with the hard disk!" A good idea, but in this instance you find that the computer won't boot from a floppy. It ignores the floppy and tries to read the hard disk. What's the problem? The most obvious one is that the master boot record (MBR), found on Track 0, is trashed. You suddenly feel sick, as you realize that you have been slack in backing up the hard disk. You've got tons of new files on that hard disk and now they are lost forever—or are they?

There is a solution that often works. At the moment, your hard disk is trying to boot but there seems to be a hitch. The MBR is corrupted, but that doesn't mean the file allocation table (FAT) is. It's the FAT that keeps track of all of the files and subdirectories on the hard disk, not the MBR. You've got to find a way to get the hard disk over that hump. One way to do this is to borrow a hard disk similar to your own. Disconnect the "dead" hard disk and connect a good one. Now, boot the computer until you get to the DOS prompt. With the machine still running, disconnect the good hard disk and hook up your dead one.

Warning: Do *not* put your hands near the power supply. Do *not* poke around at the nifty chips that are inside the machine. Your focus should be *only* on the cables that connect the hard disk controller to the hard disk. Start poking around and you can get a nasty jolt!

The odds are very good that you will now be able to access the information on your dead hard disk. Back up the hard disk to floppies as quickly as possible. Why does this usually work? Only because it is the MBR that is defective and not the file allocation tables. Once the disk is past the problem of booting, by using a good hard disk, the data is still there and accessible. You might want to keep this tip in mind—it's better than losing all your data. Better yet, back up your hard disk at regular intervals.

The Instant DOS PATH

There are occasions when people with hard disk systems boot from a floppy. When they do, they often find that they can't access many of the programs on their hard disk. Why not? Because they didn't have a DOS PATH statement, and DOS doesn't know where to look for the programs. Typing the PATH in manually can get very tedious. There's an easy way to remedy this problem once and for all.

The next time you boot normally and have your full PATH set, just do this:

```
C>PATH > RESET.BAT
```

What this is doing is sending a copy of your current PATH to the file RESET.BAT. The > sign is a means of *redirecting output.* So, instead of the content of your PATH going to the screen, it is redirected to the file RESET.BAT. Now, the next time you boot from a floppy and find that you have no PATH to work with, all you have to do is type **RESET** at the C prompt and press ENTER, and you'll have the full PATH that you normally have. You can name the file anything you want that you'll remember, but don't call it PATH.BAT or it won't work.

INSTANT HOST MODE

Most of the communications programs discussed in Chapter 11 have a *host mode*. This is an interface that allows your friends, family, and business associates to access your computer. Many of the host modes allow your callers to not only transfer files, but to leave messages as well. Did you know that in a pinch, you don't really need a host mode in order to connect with someone? In case you should ever find yourself in a position where you need an instant host mode, here's how to do it.

Let's say your boss calls one morning and needs a report from you immediately. Your boss is getting ready to catch a plane to an important meeting. Your communications program has a host mode but you've never set it up or used it. Tell your boss to call your computer via modem, using parameters of 8,N,1. Now, get to your computer and load your communications program.

The first thing you'll want to do is set your communications program to *half duplex*. Why? Because duplex determines *local echo*, and if you're at *full duplex*, you won't be able to see what you type to your boss after he connects. Once he does connect, tell him to switch to half duplex as well. Using Qmodem, use ALT-E to switch from full to half duplex.

The next thing you want to do is turn on *line feeds*. Why? Because with line feeds off, as they normally are, each item you type to your boss will be written over by his replies. (When you hit ENTER, the cursor goes back to the beginning of the line and not down a line.) That can make things hard to read and a bit confusing. In Qmodem, use SHIFT-TAB to turn on line feeds. Now when you use ENTER, the cursor will move down one line each time. Your instant host mode is ready to go. There are now just two more things to take care of. One is making your modem answer the phone. The other will be negotiating the file transfer.

When your boss calls in, you'll have to make the modem answer the phone. There are two ways that you can do this. If you have an external modem, you'll see the RD light glow when the phone rings. You'll also see "RING" on your screen. When that happens, simply type **ATA** and press ENTER, and your modem will answer the call. Another way is to type in **AT S0=1** and press ENTER. This will tell your modem to answer on the first ring.

When your boss is connected, you'll see a message on your screen, such as "CONNECT 1200 . . .". You can say hello and ask him if he's ready to do the file transfer. You must determine which transfer protocol you are going to use, because both of you must use the same one. You then have to decide when to start the transfer. When someone is downloading from you, you are uploading to them. Once you've decided on a protocol, you can type something like, **OK, start it now!** At that moment, you can begin an upload of the file while your boss begins a download. The protocol will synchronize and you'll be off and running. That's all there is to it. When the transfer is done, you can say goodbye and then break the connection by using your communications program's hangup command.

Summarizing Instant Host Mode

While a built-in host mode is nice, it isn't absolutely necessary in order for someone else to connect to your modem. The steps you need to take to set up an instant host mode can be easily summarized.

1. Set your communications program to half duplex.
2. Turn on line feeds.
3. Set the modem to answer, using either **AT S0=1** or **ATA**.
4. When the connection is complete, decide on a protocol to use.
5. If someone downloads from you, you are uploading to them.
6. If someone uploads to you, you are downloading from them.
7. Start the protocol as close to the same time as possible.
8. When finished with your session, use the hangup command.

Believe it or not, there may be times when you will have to use the instant host mode, and now you know how to do it.

THE RESTORE THAT DOESN'T

If you look on your DOS disks, you'll see that DOS comes with its own BACKUP and RESTORE programs. You can use these to back up your hard disk and restore it. Any good book on DOS or a regular DOS manual will tell you how to use these two programs in an effective manner. Here's one command that they probably won't mention.

If you enter a command such as

```
C>RESTORE C:
```

you will trash all of the files on your hard disk! This is not exactly what you had in mind. Since most manuals don't mention it, why am I? Because people often like to experiment. After all, it is perfectly normal to enter

```
C>FORMAT A:
```

so it is logical to enter **RESTORE C:**. But don't do it.

RECOVERING A SUPER KERMIT TIMEOUT

If you find yourself using the Super Kermit protocol—often the best choice on many RBBS-PC systems—this next trick may help you out. If you are doing a Super Kermit transfer, you may on occasion start seeing some "Packet Re-sent" messages. This is often due to a dirty phone line. If enough packets have to be re-sent, you will eventually start to get "Timeout" messages from Super Kermit. If you glance at your modem lights, you'll note that the RD and SD lights are not lit. There may be, however, an occasional flicker. This flicker is the protocol trying to reestablish synchronization. If the protocol doesn't synchronize and enough timeouts occur, the transfer will abort.

At this point, just hit any function key. If you are watching the modem lights, you may suddenly notice some activity from the RD and SD lights. Try hitting a function key again. Based on my own experience, over 80 percent of the time the transfer will recover from the timeout and complete successfully. Why? I have no idea! I've talked about this with Jan van der Eijk, author of Super Kermit, and he can't explain it either. It may be because hitting the function key stimulates the protocol and makes the two sides start talking again. In any case, it works over 80 percent of the time. Does it matter which function key you use? Not that I can tell and I've tried all of them, but my favorite is F10. :) So, if you are in the middle of a Super Kermit file transfer that is "timing out," try hitting a function key. You have nothing to lose and everything to gain.

WAITING FOR PARITY ERRORS

On some machines you may find that you start getting the dread "parity error" message. Getting this error once or twice isn't so bad, but when you get it often it is cause for concern. Often it means having to check out your entire system to find out what the problem is. There is one thing that you can do to save yourself some time and perhaps eliminate the problem entirely.

Check your system configuration (usually done with a SETUP or CMOS program) and see if your machine is set for a "0 wait state." If it is, try setting the wait state to 1 instead of 0. Then run your machine for a while. Reboot it several times; run programs and see if the "parity error" message comes back. In some cases, setting the wait state from 0 to 1 will eliminate the parity errors completely. It certainly is worth a try, and if it solves the problem it has saved you a lot of time.

ADDING PROTOCOLS TO COMMUNICATIONS PROGRAMS

In addition to the large, full-featured communications programs that will be discussed in Chapter 11, there are also some very good small communications programs available. In general, these smaller programs don't have all of the so-called "bells and whistles" that the bigger programs have. These smaller programs have become popular with some users, however, because they use less RAM and fit well into a window in DESQview, Omniview, and so on. In many cases they don't have file transfer protocols that are *internal*. This means that you have to use *external* protocol drivers and batch files to do file transfers. Some of the most popular external protocol drivers are

- DSZ by Chuck Forsberg
- BiModem by Erik Labs (John Erickson and Dave Krause)
- MPt by Matt Thomas
- Megalink by Paul Meiners
- Jmodem by Richard B. Johnson

Of all of these, DSZ is the most complex because it can be used to implement several different transfer protocols. Using DSZ you can implement Xmodem, true Ymodem, 1K-Xmodem/G, Ymodem-G, and Zmodem. While the others are all excellent, they tend to be easier to set up because they are covering only one protocol. Since so many users have problems with setting up the various DSZ protocols, I'm going to give some sample batch files.

Note: Some of the protocols available via DSZ are only available with the registered version—Ymodem-G, for example. If you use DSZ, please register it.

Batch Files for 1K-Xmodem/G

If you are using one of the smaller communications programs and have an MNP modem, you will want to be able to use the G protocols. Here are batch files for using 1K-Xmodem/G:

```
1KXGDOWN.BAT
dsz pB2048 handshake both rx -c -k -g %3

1KXGUP.BAT
dsz pB2048 handshake both sx -k -g c:\dnld\%3
```

In both of the batch files for 1K-Xmodem/G, notice the *pB2048* parameter. This sets up a buffer for DSZ. On slower machines, below 8 MHz for example, you may want to change this to pB4096. This slightly larger buffer helps the protocol to run smoother and faster on slower machines. On faster machines, you would not want to make this buffer any larger than the pB2048. Notice that in 1KXGUP.BAT, I specified the c:\dnld\ directory as the directory where the file to be uploaded will be located. The %3 parameter represents the filename. Also, when using DSZ, it is perfectly acceptable to abbreviate "handshake both" to "ha bo." Remember that DSZ is case-sensitive. Thus, in pB2048 the "p" must be lowercase and the "B" must be uppercase.

Batch Files for Ymodem-G

If you want to use DSZ to implement Ymodem-G, you must have a registered copy of DSZ. The batch files for downloading and uploading would look like this:

```
YG-DOWN.BAT
dsz pB2048 handshake both rb -g -b
```

```
YG-UP.BAT
dsz pB2048 handshake both sb -k -g *.*   OR
```

```
dsz pB2048 handshake both sb -k -g %3 %4 %5 %6 %7 %8 %9
```

In the download batch file, you don't need to specify a filename or a filename parameter. This is because the sending system automatically passes the filename to the protocol. In YG-UP.BAT there are two alternatives because Ymodem-G is a batch protocol. In the first example, if you use a *.* then Ymodem-G will send every file in the designated upload directory. In the second example, the % parameters would be replaced by filenames that you supply on the command line like the example that follows:

```
YG-UP TEST1.ZIP TEST2.PAK TEST3.ARC TEST4.LZH TEST5.ZOO
```

You already have batch files for Zmodem that were provided in Chapter 7. To help round out your DSZ arsenal, let's add one more protocol.

True Ymodem Batch Files

If you recall from Chapter 7, true Ymodem sends 1,024 byte blocks. Unlike the old 1K-Xmodem, however, it also passes the filename, time, and date. True Ymodem is also a batch file transfer protocol. The batch files for downloading and uploading would look like this:

```
Y-DOWN.BAT
dsz pB2048 rb -k -p
```

```
Y-UP.BAT
dsz pB2048 sb -k *.*
```

Armed with these sets of batch files that utilize DSZ, plus BiModem, MPt, Jmodem, and Megalink, you'd be ready to do file transfers almost anywhere. While you can use Ymodem on CompuServe, I'd recommend getting OZBEXT by Steve Sneed so you could use the CompuServe Quick-B protocol.

PERSONALIZED FORMAT AND EXCESS FAT

In the wake of so-called *Trojan horse* programs and viruses, many users are concerned about their data. Many of these destructive programs attempt to damage data in one of two ways. One way is to format the hard disk and another is to damage the file allocation table (FAT). Let's take a look at what you can do to help eliminate the threat of an unwanted format.

Modifying Format—Warning Included

A program that has been designed to destroy your data by formatting the hard disk generally depends on one fact—your hard disk contains the DOS program FORMAT.COM. It does help to have it there so you can format floppy disks, doesn't it? At the same time, there is nothing that says it has to be named FORMAT.COM. Thus, there is something that you can do.

- Make FORMAT.COM *invisible* to harmful programs
- Set up a way to be notified if something is trying to format a disk

To begin with, rename FORMAT.COM to something that means something to you. You can name it X271GY.COM, ZZA299BY.COM, or even OHBABY.COM. DOS doesn't really care what the name is because what the program does remains the same. Now make a tiny batch file called FORMAT.BAT. The contents would be

```
CLS
TYPE FORMAT.TXT
```

The next thing to do is use your text editor to prepare a small text file called FORMAT.TXT. The contents might be

```
WARNING ---- WARNING ---- WARNING ---- WARNING
Some program on the system is trying to access the DOS program,
FORMAT.COM. Check out the system immediately.
```

Now when an outside program tries to use the FORMAT command, your FORMAT.BAT file will run, and it will type your warning message to the screen.

Note: Renaming FORMAT.COM will make the program inaccessible to programs like DOS shells, menus, and so forth. For formatting all types and sizes of diskettes, I'd recommend using something like John Newlin's FORMAT MASTER, which is faster, more efficient, and much more flexible than the DOS FORMAT command.

Having Excess FAT

Since the file allocation table (actually there is more than one) keeps track of what is on your disk and where, a program that destroys the FAT doesn't have to destroy individual program files or format the disk. With the FAT destroyed, none of the files that you have are accessible. You might think of it as a hard disk lobotomy. Is there anything you can do about that? Sure!

You are making backups of the files on your system regularly, so why not make a backup of your FAT? Without a viable FAT, your backups aren't worth the disks they're written on. There are several good Shareware programs that will make backups of the file allocation table. In addition, there are some good commercial programs like the Mace Utilities, Norton Commander, and others that will give you the same protection. Many of these programs can be included in your AUTOEXEC.BAT file so that your FAT is backed up each time you boot your computer. The Shareware programs that can assist you with this will be discussed in Part Four. By investing only a few seconds, you can save yourself a lot of aggravation.

SLOW MACHINES AND FAST MODEMS

This is about a problem that could drive you absolutely nuts, and if you didn't know exactly what the problem was you might never get rid of it. Let's say that you have an XT class machine and have been using a 2400 baud modem. Everything has always worked smoothly for you, and you've had only a few problems with file transfers. Then, one day, you decide to buy a high-speed MNP modem. Excited, you hook it up and log onto a BBS at 9600 baud. Much to your surprise you find that every protocol you try to use is coming back with errors. Zmodem gives you so many serial input errors (SIEs) that your cps rate is around 200 cps. The G protocols abort almost immediately. Even trusty old Xmodem gets so many errors that it aborts. Your first thought may be, "Something is wrong with the modem." You're partly right and partly wrong. What is the problem?

There's nothing physically wrong with the modem, but there is a problem with the interaction between the modem and your machine. Because they send data so fast, high-speed modems tend to be a bit sensitive. If you analyze your system, odds are that you have a keyboard macro program loaded, or some other program that grabs keyboard or timer interrupts. While these programs would not cause any problem on a machine with a faster clock, they do interfere enough with a slower machine and a high-speed modem to cause a problem. While the modem is trying to exchange data at the fastest rate possible, an offending program moves at the speed of a timer tick, and that is the cause of the transfer errors. What can you do about it?

When I first discovered this problem, there was nothing I could do except remove any offending program(s). This could be a difficult choice if it were a program you really liked. At the same time, there is no point in having a high-speed modem if the errors caused by programs bring you back to 2400 baud rates. However, there is a simpler solution.

I discussed the problem with Barry Simon, program author and past president of the Association of Shareware Professionals (ASP). Once the cause of the problem was known, Barry came up with a tiny terminate and stay resident (TSR) program that he called EOI. EOI only uses about eight bytes of memory and is loaded immediately before your communications program. Once it's loaded the problem disappears. To date, EOI has been tested with machines having a clock speed of 4.77 MHz while using a U.S. Robotics 9600 HST. There have been no transfer errors, or to put it more accurately, there have been no transfer errors associated with the clock interrupt problem. Some errors can always occur during any transfer regardless of the type of equipment you have. So, if you have a slower machine and a fast modem, look for EOI on bulletin boards and the commercial online networks. It will solve the problem for you without sacrificing any of the programs you like to use.

MAXIMIZING YOUR BBS TIME

This tip will be especially helpful to those of you with 1200 and 2400 baud modems. Let's say that you log on to a BBS, and you're allowed 40 minutes on the system. Normally, you may not spend much time on the system, but today there are some programs that you want to get. In order to maximize the time you have, just do the following.

Find the biggest file that you want to download during this session. There may be five or six that you want to get, but pick the one that is the largest. Now start to download that file. When you do, the system will tell you how long it thinks the transfer will take. As was noted earlier, nearly all BBS software will underestimate this time. Abort the transfer before it starts. Why? Because all you wanted to find out was how long the system thinks it will take to download the largest file you want. For this example, let's say that the system said it would take seven minutes.

Now you can go about your business and download the smaller files. Read mail, look at new bulletins, upload a file, and so on. When you see that your time remaining is down to about eight minutes, begin the download of that largest file. Since you have eight minutes left, and the system thinks the download will only take seven minutes, it will let you start the download. Once started, the system will not log you off until the transfer completes! During a file transfer, the protocol, not the BBS software, is in control of the situation. Thus, even if the transfer takes 20 minutes, the system will let the download complete, even though you only had eight minutes left. You will be logged off the system the instant the transfer is completed. In this example, instead of 40 minutes, you managed to squeeze out 53 minutes. I do not advocate doing this all the time, only when there is a program you really want, and your time is going to run out.

SAY GOOD-BYE EARLY

When you go online to bulletin board systems, you may find yourself pressed for time. You may have messages to read or send and some files that you want to download. Take care of your messages first, and then get ready to do your file transfers.

More and more bulletin board software is giving you the option of telling the system that you want to log off when your file transfers are done. As was discussed earlier, pick a protocol that will let you do a batch file transfer. When you start your transfer, tell the system good-bye. At that point you can go off and eat dinner, read the paper, or balance your checkbook. When the file transfer is complete, the system will automatically log you off. This ability to tell a system that you want to say good-bye when file transfers are completed is one of the handiest innovations to come along. It saves you time and money, and it saves you from having to sit and watch each file transfer.

BEWARE OF THE DEADMAN'S SWITCH

Nearly all online systems, both commercial networks and bulletin boards, can sense when there is no activity from your keyboard. After a given length of time with no keyboard activity, the system will automatically log you off. In some cases, on commercial networks for example, the system may knock you back to the previous menu first. If another interval goes by without any keyboard activity from you, then it will log you off. Let me clarify. Say that you are online to GEnie and using Chat Lines, GEnie's excellent CB simulator, which is a fun place to talk with other users and play online games like Trivia, WordFoundry, and so on. (I visit there often, and if you come online to GEnie's Chat Lines, look for me and say "hi"—my reserved handle is < = Guitarman = >.)

If you sit there long enough, watching a conversation and not typing anything, you will suddenly be bounced out to the Chat Lines main menu. The system will watch for keyboard input from you, and if it doesn't get any after approximately eight minutes, GEnie will politely log you off. This is done as a courtesy to save you unnecessary connect time (or phone charges) in case you should fall asleep at the keyboard or have a sudden emergency, or some other event occurs that makes you leave the keyboard in a hurry. Think of it as a safety net that's there for your protection.

There are programs in Shareware that are designed to help you override this *safety net*. They are reminiscent of the *deadman's switch* that used to be on trains. What the programs do is send a carriage return or some string of characters every few seconds. The effect is that you can simulate keyboard input when you aren't at the keyboard. This is handy if you're online chatting or have to leave the room for a while, and don't want to be logged off.

A problem, however, is that these programs have to be loaded before your communications program. All of those I've seen are difficult or impossible to shut off once they are activated. If you forget you have one of these programs loaded (easy to do) and fall asleep at the keyboard, you will not be automatically logged off by the system. You've effectively cut your safety net and you will have to pay the price. Avoid this kind of program. It is far better to have to log back on to a system than to have to pay the price if a deadman's switch program keeps you logged on when you don't want to be. Another adverse effect of these programs is that they will cause errors with file transfers. Your best bet is to stick with the safety net.

This concludes this section, and it is my hope that some of these little tricks and tips will be of help to you in the future. Now, let's take a look at some of the best programs in Shareware and see what they're all about.

## PART FOUR

The Best of Shareware — A Prescription for Success

## CHAPTER TEN

Word Processors and Text Editors

The first question that a new user usually asks after getting comfortably connected to a bulletin board or commercial online network is, "What is the best text editor?" The answer is almost always, "There isn't any *best*. Text editors are like cars—they come in all shapes, sizes, and colors. What is best for user A is not always best for user B. Everyone has a favorite. Out of every ten people you ask, nine will give a different answer to the question. Some will swear by Galaxy; some never use anything but Edwin; others insist that QEdit is the top of the line, and so on. Let's start at the top and take a look at what is available and how to make a decision.

DOCTOR'S NOTE

This chapter will discuss some of the better and more full-featured text editors and word processors that are available in Shareware. There are many text editors available. Some are very simple and may have been written in a few hours. In some cases all they can do is let you type in text and save it as a file. For writing messages offline, notes to friends, or letters to businesses, you need something more. The basic problem is that since there are so many editors available you can't possibly know what you're getting. Bulletin board and online network descriptions tend to be very brief.

There are over 80 editors in my collection of Shareware programs. I have used all of them, or tried to, and many of them are not worth the time it took to download them. With some, I had to reboot to exit the program, while others had no help, no colors, and no real features. You could waste a lot of time and money downloading text editors that won't do what you need them to do. The goal here is to give you an idea of some of the best editors and word processors that are available in Shareware in an effort to save you the expenditure of time, energy, and money. There isn't enough room to cover every good or even decent text editor available, but the ones described in this chapter are all solid and dependable. They offer the features that most users want and give you some names to look for when you go online looking for a text editor or word processor. I would like to thank my friend, Rae Barent, a sysop in the Home Office/Small Business Round-Table on GEnie, for her help in the final testing of the programs reviewed in this chapter.

A BRIEF OVERVIEW OF EDITORS

To begin with, and to add to the confusion, there are really two different kinds of text editors: stand-alone programs and text editors attached to other programs. Many different kinds of programs, Shareware or commercial, have a rudimentary text editor available. Some of these have very few features and are useful for little more than making notes to yourself within the program or adding a note to some section of the program. Some programs come very close to being full-fledged text editors with a full range of features. After a quick check of my own system, I found that, aside from QEdit, PC-Write, and Galaxy, which I will discuss later, I have several programs that include text editors of various sizes and capabilities. My telecommunications program, Qmodem 4.2 for example, includes an editor for reading and writing messages offline or for quickly updating script files.

In addition, several other types of programs, although primarily designed for other tasks, have text editors with varying degrees of sophistication. For example, dCOM is an excellent file and directory management program, while Alt is a program to utilize expanded memory and maximize DOS memory by swapping into partitions. Other examples include Managing Your Money, a financial management program, and PC-File DB, a database program. All include some sort of text editor. Of the programs mentioned, all of them are Shareware with the exception of Managing Your Money, which is commercial.

Choosing an Editor

How do you choose which of the stand-alone text editors is best for you? It all depends on your needs. If you like working with a number of different files at once, then you need an editor like QEdit, which can open eight windows. If you have an off-beat printer, then you might want PC-Write, which supports more different printers than any of the other editors and has font support. If, on the other hand, all you want is a cheap, effective text editor to write offline messages for transmitting to a BBS or network, then Edwin or Blackbeard might be more than adequate.

The second question that the new user asks is, "If I already have a good word processor, do I still need a text editor?" The answer to that is a definite maybe. Any of the sophisticated retail (read non-Shareware) word processors will do everything that a text editor will do and a lot more besides, but at a much higher cost. For any kind of major writing project where presentation is a key factor, a word processor is a necessity. For small jobs, and especially for handling any ASCII text file, text editors tend to be faster to access, easier to use, and a lot more flexible. For example, to read and reply to E-mail using WordPerfect, you would need to import the file into WordPerfect format, reset certain defaults, and then export the file in ASCII text. It's a lot easier just to read the file into a text editor.

The Evolution of Text Editors
Text editors began life as programmers' tools to work around the inadequacies and complexities of EDLIN, the DOS line editor. Because programmers wrote editors, often for themselves, these text editors often

included functions that made writing program code easier. Input from users caused them to start including some of the features found in word processors. As time went on, they acquired more and more features until some, like PC-Write, are classed as being word processors more than text editors. Because PC-Write reads and writes files only in ASCII text, it is often thought of as a text editor, although it really should be considered a Shareware word processor. Now, let's go on to see what features and functions most users want in an editor.

The Most Popular Features

All of the better text editors, whether part of another program or free-standing, have certain features in common: word wrap; the use of ASCII text rather than a dedicated format; windowing; search and replace; and the standard editing, filing, and printing functions. Oddly enough, although WordPerfect has replaced WordStar as the industry leader, almost all text editors use the WordStar command set. This has the advantage of enabling a user of Galaxy, for example, to switch to QEdit with very little inconvenience.

To summarize, some of the most sought after features that cut across all text editors and Shareware word processors are

- Editing functions
- Blocking text
- WordStar command set
- Search and replace
- File handling
- Windowing
- Macros
- Drop to DOS
- Paragraph reformatting

First of all, let's take a look at all of these functions in text editors in general. This will help you to fairly evaluate other text editors in the future. Once that's accomplished, we'll move on to examine more closely the text editors and word processors that were selected for this chapter.

Editing Functions

The basic editing function is the ability to move the cursor more than a single space. Generally, using a combination of CTRL and ALT keys with either letter keys or function keys, most editors allow you to move your cursor immediately to the beginning, end, top, or bottom of a page, document, or screen. In addition, almost all of the better text editors have keystroke combinations that will enable you to delete a line, a word to the right of the cursor, a word to the left of the cursor, or to the end of the line. You can also insert a blank line, split a line, or reformat the paragraph. These features can all be used in *insert mode,* in which a character is inserted in a line or word and the rest of the word moves to the right, or in *strikeover mode* (sometimes called *overwrite* or *typeover*), in which the character is replaced by the newly typed character.

You can set your margins so you begin at the extreme left margin or at any place on the line. You can toggle word wrap on or off so you do away with carriage returns at the end of lines. You can set tabs at any position on the line. Usually the default setting is five spaces. Once these options are set to your satisfaction, the program will generally remember the settings so the next time you access the program the settings are all there for you.

To summarize the editing commands: The character-left command moves the cursor left one character at a time until it reaches column 1; then it stops. The character-right command moves the cursor right, even beyond the end of the text. It does not stop until it reaches the maximum line length at 999 characters. Horizontal scrolling of the screen occurs whenever the cursor passes the left or right border of the screen. Word left and word right move one word with each command. Words are separated by spaces, common punctuation, and the beginning and end of lines. Line scrolling works in the expected manner. Page up and page down scroll by one line less than the full screen. For windows covering less than the full screen, scrolling is based on the window size, not the full screen size.

Blocking Text

Blocking text is another useful editing function. Usually, blocked text is displayed in a different color, or in reverse video or brighter text on a monochrome monitor. Once the text has been blocked, the block can be moved, copied, deleted, or written out as a new file. But before you can edit a block, you must mark it first. Put the cursor at the place where you want the block to begin. Press the designated key or select Block Begin from a pull-down menu. There will be some indication on your screen that blocking is in effect. Now, move the cursor to the end of the text you want to block. Press the designated key or select the Block End option from a pull-down menu. Since the basic principle of blocking text is cut and paste, you usually have to cut the block from where it is and paste it down into a new location.

One thing to remember is that when you *copy* a block you don't move it from its original location; you duplicate it in a new location. When you *move* a block, you delete it from its original location and paste it into its new location. You can block only one section at a time. If you want to move three paragraphs, skipping a sentence at the end of each, you would have to mark each one separately and move it separately. QEdit uses what it calls Scrap Buffers, which can be named and used to store blocked text. These are discussed later in the section "Macros."

The WordStar Command Set

I've mentioned the WordStar commands quite a bit in talking about text editors. Some editors use only these commands. Some, like QEdit, can be configured to use them, and they are included as the default key combinations. Some editors use them with other ALT, CTRL, and SHIFT combinations. Table 10-1 shows these WordStar commands.

These commands work for Edwin, Galaxy, QEdit, and the majority of the other text editors.

Table 10-1

The WordStar Command Set

Basic Cursor Movements

Character left	LEFT ARROW	CTRL-S
Character right	RIGHT ARROW	CTRL-D
Word left	CTRL-LEFT ARROW	CTRL-A
Word right	CTRL-RIGHT ARROW	CTRL-F
Line up	UP ARROW	CTRL-E
Line down	DOWN ARROW	CTRL-X
Scroll up	CTRL-UP ARROW	CTRL-W
Scroll down	CTRL-DOWN ARROW	CTRL-Z
Page down	PGDN	CTRL-C
Page up	PGUP	CTRL-R

Table 10-1

The WordStar Command Set (*continued*)

Quick Movements

Top of window	CTRL-PGUP	CTRL-Q CTRL-R
Bottom of window	CTRL-PGDN	CTRL-Q CTRL-C
Cursor to left side	HOME	CTRL-Q CTRL-S
Cursor to right side	END	CTRL-Q CTRL-D
Top of screen	CTRL-HOME	CTRL-Q CTRL-E
Bottom of screen	CTRL-END	CTRL-Q CTRL-X
Up to equal indent	CTRL-J CTRL-B	
Down to equal indent	CTRL-J CTRL-E	
Go to line	CTRL-Q CTRL-N	
Go to column	CTRL-O CTRL-C	
Go to window	CTRL-O CTRL-Q	
Previous cursor position	CTRL-Q CTRL-P	

Insertion and Deletion

Undo last deletion	ESC	CTRL-Q CTRL-U
Restore line	CTRL-Q CTRL-L	
Smart tab	CTRL-I	
Insert control character	CTRL-P	
New line	CTRL-M	
Insert line	CTRL-N	
Delete current character	DEL	CTRL-G
Delete left character	CTRL-H	CTRL-BACKSPACE
Delete right word	CTRL-T	
Delete line right	CTRL-Q CTRL-Y	
Delete line	CTRL-Y	
Delete line (no undo)	CTRL-DEL	

Find and Replace

Find pattern	CTRL-Q CTRL-F
Find and replace	CTRL-Q CTRL-A
Search and apply macro	CTRL-Q CTRL-M
Find next	CTRL-L

Files and DOS Interface

Invoke DOS shell	CTRL-O CTRL-I
Append block to file	CTRL-K CTRL-A

Table 10-1

The WordStar Command Set (*continued*)

Files and DOS Interface (*continued*)

Save and exit to menu	CTRL-K CTRL-D
Abandon file	CTRL-K CTRL-Q
Read file into window	CTRL-K CTRL-R
Save and continue edit	CTRL-K CTRL-S
Write block to file	CTRL-K CTRL-W
Save and exit to DOS	CTRL-K CTRL-X

Windows

Add window	CTRL-O CTRL-A	
Grow current window	CTRL-O CTRL-G	
Shrink current window	CTRL-O CTRL-S	
Switch windows	CTRL-O CTRL-O	
Show help window	CTRL-J CTRL-H	F1
Zoom current window	CTRL-O CTRL-Z	

Blocks

Begin block	CTRL-K CTRL-B	F7
End block	CTRL-K CTRL-K	F8
Top of block	CTRL-Q CTRL-B	
Bottom of block	CTRL-Q CTRL-K	
Copy block	CTRL-K CTRL-C	
Move block	CTRL-K CTRL-V	
Delete block	CTRL-K CTRL-Y	
Toggle block display	CTRL-K CTRL-H	
Mark current word	CTRL-K CTRL-T	

Macros

Load macros from disk	CTRL-J CTRL-R
Write macros to disk	CTRL-J CTRL-W
Toggle macro record	CTRL-J CTRL-T

Toggles and Status

Show version number	CTRL-J CTRL-V	
Show available memory	CTRL-O CTRL-M	
Toggle insert mode	CTRL-V	INS
Toggle auto-indent mode	CTRL-Q CTRL-I	

Table 10-1

The WordStar Command Set (*continued*)

Text Processing

Toggle case	CTRL-O CTRL-T
Lowercase	CTRL-O CTRL-L
Uppercase	CTRL-O CTRL-U
Set right margin	CTRL-O CTRL-R
Reformat paragraph	CTRL-B
Toggle word wrap	CTRL-O CTRL-W
Abort command (1 char)	CTRL-U

DOCTOR'S NOTE

You may be asking yourself why so many editors use the WordStar command set. There are several reasons why this is so common. To begin with, WordStar was one of the first truly popular word processors on the market. Because of this fact, many computer users grew up learning and using the WordStar commands. Then Borland International released SideKick, one of the first popular pop-up programs. The SideKick editor also used the Word-Star commands. One thing that is so handy about them is that in most cases, you don't have to move your fingers from the area of the "home" keys to execute special commands. You can delete an entire line with CTRL-Y or delete the character to the right with CTRL-G. This fact tends to make editing much easier, so the WordStar commands became quite popular.

Another factor that has contributed to the popularity of the WordStar command set is one that most people don't often think of. When Borland International created Turbo Pascal, they made it so that Turbo Pascal's editor also uses WordStar commands. There are many programmers who write programs using Turbo Pascal. When some of these Turbo Pascal programmers created editors, it probably seemed perfectly natural to give their editors WordStar commands. Thus, for a variety of reasons, the WordStar command set is quite popular and is found in many different editors.

Search and Replace

All good text editors allow you to search for a character string. A character string is a word or group of words. You can tell the program to replace a character string automatically with another string, or with nothing at all, with or without asking you first. You can usually search both backward or forward from the cursor position. Most search and replace functions are case insensitive. That means that if you're looking for "Text" it will find "TEXT" or "Text" or "teXt," or any combination of upper- and lowercase letters. A typical search and replace menu, such as the one found in Blackbeard, is shown in Figure 10-1.

Let's take a look at PC-Write's search and replace method. The keystrokes will vary from editor to editor, but the functions will be basically identical.

To enter search and replace mode, you press F9. The top line now shows the following:

Esc F9:Find "." F10:Replace "."

Figure 10-1

Find and Replace menu from the Blackbeard editor

Type the text you want to find at the cursor in the Find area. If you just want to do a search, press ENTER. If you want to replace the found string with another, press F10 now, enter the replacement in the Replace area, and then press ENTER. To search forward through the text, press either the + key on the numeric keyboard, F12 if you have an enhanced keyboard, or CTRL-L. For a backward search, the keys are the − key, F11, or CTRL-O.

To search for text with the option to either replace or not, press the + or the − key. Then press F10 to replace, or the + or − key again to find the next occurrence of the text without replacing this one. If you press F10, the text will be replaced here and in all subsequent locations automatically.

In searching for and replacing every occurrence automatically without being prompted, you have several options. To limit the replacement to only part of your text, you can mark the part as a block or box. Figure 10-2 shows what the PC-Write top menu looks like in editing mode.

To start from the beginning of the file, press SHIFT-+ or ALT-+. This will bring up a new top menu. F9 will limit automatic replacement to the

---

Figure 10-2

PC-Write's top menu

```
Esc:Menu PusH Wrap+Se- R:F 68%    10/1587  Read "A:\chap10.txt"          N
  F1:System/help  F3.Copy/mark    F5.Un-mark     F7.Paragraph    F9:Find-text
  F2:Window/ruler F4.Delete/mark  F6.Move/mark   F8.Lower/upper  F10.Replace
0---+---T1----+-T--2----T---3--T-+----4T---+---T5----+-T--6---R
all they can do is let you type in text and save it as a file.
For writing messages offline, notes to friends, or letters to
businesses, you need something more. The basic problem is that
since there are so many editors available you can't possibly know
what you are getting. Bulletin board and online network descrip-
tions tend to be very brief. There are over eighty (80) editors
in my collection of Shareware programs. I have used all of them,
or tried to, and many of them are not worth the time it took to
download them. With some I had to reboot to exit the program,
while others had no help, no colors, and no real features. You
could waste a lot of time and money downloading text editors that
will not do what you need them to do. The goal here is to give
you an idea of some of the best editors and word processors that
are available in Shareware in an effort to save you the expendi-
ture of time, energy, and money.  There isn't enough room to
cover every good or even decent text editor available, but the
ones described in this chapter are all solid and dependable. They
offer the features that most users want and give you some names
to look for when you go online looking for a text editor or word
processor.  I would like to thank my friend, Rae Barent, a sysop
in the Home Office/Small Business Round Table on GEnie, for her
```

marked block of text. To *unreplace* a piece of text, the cursor should be placed just after the replaced text. Press ALT-F10. The top menu now reads

Esc:Cancel F9:Repeat-replace F10:Unreplace

Press F10 and the text is unreplaced.

PC-Write has a few other unique search and replace features that will be discussed in the section devoted to the program, but these are the ones that are similar in function, if not in keystroke, to all other text editors.

File Handling

To edit a file using a text editor, you can do one of two things. You can enter the name of the file on the command line; for example, **q test.txt** will start QEdit and bring up the file called TEST.TXT automatically. You can either choose a preexisting file from a directory listing once you are in the program or enter a filename when prompted. Some programs will only prompt for a filename before you try to quit; others will ask for one at the beginning. Some editors, QEdit for one, will allow you to enter more than one filename.

If you are using Edwin, for example, whenever you are prompted for a filename, you can enter the name of a drive, directory, or wildcard file specification. Edwin will pop up a window showing the matching files, and you can select one via the UP ARROW and DOWN ARROW keys and the ENTER key. Figure 10-3 displays the editing selection menu for QEdit.

Windowing

Windowing means simply that you can work with more than one file, or copy of a file, at the same time. The program usually has a zoom mode, which allows the current window to grow to fill the full screen, hiding any other files until zoom is toggled again. You can switch back and forth between windows, making changes and saving edited files. The number of windows that a text editor can open will vary. Galaxy can open up to ten windows. Figure 10-4 shows Galaxy with two windows open and a different file in each window.

Edwin opens as many as six windows. QEdit also lets you view parts of files in windows, as well as whole files, and opens as many as eight windows. QEdit can show the same file eight times or show eight different files.

Figure 10-3

The editing menu for QEdit

Figure 10-4

Two windows open in Galaxy

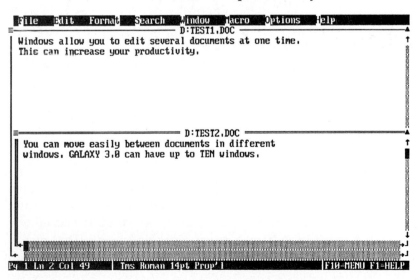

The ability to refer to and copy text from a number of different files makes programming much easier. All block operations can be performed across windows, as well as within a single window. Usually, the screen is divided into horizontal strips. Each window can consist of a variable number of rows, from a minimum of 2 text lines to a maximum of 23. Windows can be created, sized, and deleted dynamically. To remove windows, use the file Save or Abandon command. When a window is added, the current window is split in half to make space for the new window. The current window must be at least seven lines tall for this operation to be successful. When the window is split, you will probably be prompted for a new filename. Note that the filename can contain a complete DOS drive and pathname. If you specify a filename that matches that of an existing window, the new window will be linked to the existing one. In this way, you can have two or more views onto a single file. Edits made in one window will simultaneously appear in the other.

The Grow and Shrink window commands make the current window one line taller or shorter for each invocation of the command. The Switch windows command moves the cursor to the next window down the screen. The Zoom window command allows you to focus on a single window when you have a number of windows on screen. Using the Zoom command causes the current window to fill the entire screen. Any other windows are hidden, but their text remains in memory. While the Zoom state is active, an indicator will be made visible on the window status line. To go back to the original multiwindow screen, simply execute the Zoom command again. Alternately, saving or abandoning the file in the Zoom window will restore the other windows to the screen. You cannot open additional windows when the Zoom command has filled the screen with a single window.

Macros

A macro is a shorthand way of doing anything. If you find that you are frequently entering the same series of commands or keystrokes—for example, a signature line for messages to a favorite bulletin board—you can assign all the commands and keystrokes to a single key combination, SHIFT-F9 say, and the next time you finish your message and want to enter your signature line, all you have to do is press SHIFT-F9. Most text editors that have macro editors also have a macro recording mode. That means you can set the record mode on and go through and save the keystrokes you want as a macro. The macro is then created. The steps to create a macro in QEdit, for example, which has one of the better macro editors, are very simple.

1. Place the cursor where you want to begin entering the series of keystrokes.

2. Press the Macro Record (CTRL-M) key combination. An "R" will appear on the status line that indicates macro recording is on.

3. Press the key that you want to assign to the commands and keystrokes. The key must be *configurable;* that is, it cannot be reserved for one of QEdit's functions, and it cannot have already been used for a macro you have defined.

4. Enter the series of commands and keystrokes. The commands can be DOS commands as well as QEdit commands. The "R" still appears on the status line.

5. Press CTRL-M again. This automatically turns macro recording off, and the "R" will no longer show on the status line. The macro is now created and assigned to the key that you specified in step 3.

To use your new macro, just position the cursor properly and press the assigned macro key.

QEdit keeps the macro in a scrap area that can be accessed with CTRL-ENTER. Once you exit the program, the new macro is lost unless you have saved it. To save a macro, you press the Macro Write (ESC, M, W) command. You will be prompted for a macro filename to write. This new macro file will appear in your DOS directory and can be retrieved using the Macro Read (ESC, M, R) command. You will then be prompted for a filename to read. Enter the name of the previously saved macro file and QEdit will load the file. With QEdit, you can also configure a key sequence that will automatically load the macro file for you. Figure 10-5 shows part of QEdit's CONFIG.DAT file and its macros.

Edwin's macro record mode is also a convenient way to create macros, but macros may also be loaded via the default macro file EDWIN.MAC, which automatically loads into memory when the editor is started, or edited with the macro editor. The EDWIN.MAC file includes macros for indenting and unindenting text and inserting standard Pascal constructs (procedure, function, program, and register set) into a program. In addition, a full blown macro editor is incorporated into the installation program EDWINST. This macro editor can be used at any time to generate new macro files.

The macro editor operates in two modes. The command mode reserves several keys to aid in the function of the editor. One interesting feature of Edwin is that if you have SuperKey or another memory-resident macro

Figure 10-5

Macro lines found in the QEdit CONFIG.DAT file

```
^f1      macro_begin macro_read "c:\file\qed1.mac" return
^f2      macro_begin find pause 'i' return
^f3      macro_read
^f4      macro_write
^f5      save_file
^f6      find_replace
^f7      find
^f8      repeat_find
^f9      unkill
^f10     change_file_name
```

processor installed, pressing any key combinations defined as macros for that processor will insert that macro into the Edwin macro. Neither Edwin nor EDWINST take over the keyboard at such a low level as to inhibit other macro processors.

You can develop macros in two ways. First, within the editor, you can turn on a recording mode. This simply keeps a record of all of your keystrokes until the recording process is turned off. When recording is complete, you will be prompted for a macro number in which the keystrokes will be stored. Second, a macro editor is frequently included with the program. You can use this editor to edit previously recorded macros or to develop new macros from scratch. The macros developed in this way are stored in files, and then loaded into the text editor for use there.

Drop to DOS

Almost all text editors allow you to invoke a DOS shell from within the editor. After executing this command, you will find yourself at the standard DOS prompt. For this command to be successful, two factors are required. First, a copy of COMMAND.COM must be available in the drive and directory specified by the COMSPEC parameter in your DOS environment. Second, sufficient free memory must be available. From the DOS prompt, you can run any command or program you normally would, with a few exceptions. For example, you should never install a memory-resident program from within a shell. Doing so will most likely cause a system crash. Another thing to remember is that if you change directories within the shell, you should return to the directory in which the shell was invoked. Otherwise, when you return to the editor, files you save will probably be written to the wrong directory. An exception to this rule occurs when you have opened files using their complete pathnames rather than using DOS shorthand to refer to the current directory.

Paragraph Reformat

Sometimes, in using an editor, you will add a few words to a line and find the line is now longer than 80 characters and runs off the end of the screen. Most text editors will not automatically wrap text in a paragraph when you've done this. To fill the current right margin, starting from the current line and continuing until it encounters a blank line, which is generally considered the end of a paragraph, you will have to use a special key—most often the combination CTRL-B.

In addition, each text editor discussed in this chapter has certain features that make it unique. These features will be discussed in the individual sections. As an experiment, each section has been written using the text editor under discussion. Thus, the section on Galaxy is written with Galaxy, the section on Edwin is written with Edwin, and so on. Then, all sections were imported into WordPerfect 5.1. The editors are discussed in alphabetical order.

BLACKBEARD

Like all of the text editors discussed in this chapter, Blackbeard is Shareware, which means that you are free to use and distribute it in any way you want for a $20 donation. It is primarily designed for professional programmers to edit programs and documentation, but it performs all the normal editing operations you would expect of any text editor, including cutting and pasting, block operations, and so on. Blackbeard is *user-configurable*. This means you can redefine key bindings and set various editing options and colors. Some other features include *on the fly* keystroke macros that can be saved and recalled, automatic indenting for block structured languages like C and Pascal, an ASCII table, and a versatile cut and paste facility that includes column cut and paste.

Unique Functions

One of Blackbeard's most exceptional features is its windowing capability. The windows can be individually sized. You can have up to ten windows, and each can support the same or a different file. Blackbeard is also one of the only editors that allows you to have vertical windows as well as horizontal windows. Most editors only allow for horizontal windows. Colors can be configured for each individual window, which is one way for you to know which window you are in. A single keystroke moves you from window to window. In addition to being able to drop to DOS, a window to DOS can be opened allowing you to enter DOS commands.

No Manual Required

Blackbeard is designed to be easy to use without the assistance of a manual. It has excellent context-sensitive help screens, which can be updated with a file called BBMAN.EXE to reflect changes in the Option/ Setup menu. These help screens are accessed with ALT-H. Figure 10-6 shows the help screen that you see in Blackbeard when you press ALT-H.

Pressing ENTER from the help menu provides a list of features; select a number and a new help screen will pop up. This is a rather unique feature among editors, and is very handy. You can scan through the

---

Figure 10-6

The Blackbeard main help screen

```
126─────────────────────Help-(αH)──────────────────────
The Blackbeard help facility is available for status line prompts
and menu selections.  It is context sensitive.  To view any help
message enter the number of the desired help message.

Help can be invoked with a ALT-H from anywhere (menus and
prompts) Use ESC to exit from help screen.  Prompt help screens
let you view the help while responding to the prompt.

if you press ENTER from this help message you will get a complete
list of help screens that you may select from; go ahead and look
around.  Some help screens of interest early on are:

        0   running blackbeard
       87   direct and menu execution of commands
      223   configuration (environment SET commands)

Please note that the manual is generated from the BB.HLP and
does not contain any additional information.

Use the ESC key to pop up BlackBeard menus
```

Help number:

numbers and find exactly the topic you need help with. Figure 10-7 shows you Blackbeard's numbered help screen, which pops up when you press ENTER from the main help screen.

Easily Accessible Menus—and More

Blackbeard is a high-performance text editor with simple word processing features like word wrap, paragraph reformat, text formatting, and line drawing using the IBM extended graphics characters. Blackbeard includes intelligent screen paging, a feature activated by pressing PGDN three times. This displays the third page of a document without displaying the intervening pages. Blackbeard can also edit large files.

Functions can be activated with pop-up menus by direct execution of keystrokes (combinations of ALT, SHIFT, CTRL, or function keys). Menu selections can be activated by cursor movement, mouse, or first letter, and all menu entries have online help (ALT-H). Blackbeard alone among the text editors also provides full mouse support, and comes with drivers and menus for the Mouse Systems mouse. Support for the Microsoft mouse is built in. Using a mouse, you can access every function of Blackbeard. You can switch between windows, mark blocks, cut and paste, and save files. Figure 10-8 shows the Cut and Paste menu for Blackbeard.

Figure 10-7

The Blackbeard numbered help screen

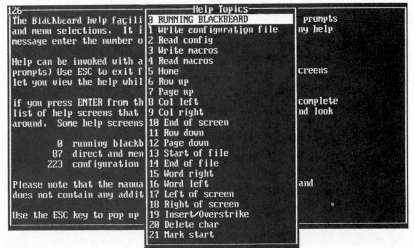

Enter to select help topic

Figure 10-8

The Blackbeard Cut and Paste menu

```
┌─Cut & Paste───┐
│Mark start   F1│
│Mark end     F2│
│Grab         F3│
│Cut          F4│
│Shift left   F5│
│Shift right  F6│
│Copy         F7│
│Paste        F8│
│Unmark       F9│
│Paste window F10│
│Clear paste  ^F9│
│Print Region   │
└───────────────┘
```

[1] Line   6 Col 10 < W N> Kill   1 Paste   1 C:\DNLD\OSBORNE.DOC   1

Note: Blackbeard not only allows for cutting and pasting full-sized blocks, but also for columns. This is a great feature if you have a lot of columns of numbers in your documents that you want to move around.

Blackbeard as a TSR Editor

Blackbeard can be installed as a resident program, allowing you to pop in and out, with the editor remembering where you were. Blackbeard can remember the last file edited and the cursor location, using the Save/Restore option, and will automatically pull up the last file edited. While it uses a fair amount of DOS RAM, this TSR feature can be very useful.

Print Formatting and Fonts

Printing out documents is an essential task associated with any text processing system. Blackbeard performs the editing tasks very well. The

Blackbeard formatter is a simple-to-use, "do-what-I-tell-you," text processor. It takes any text file and produces clean printed output. It is also a powerful formatter for producing technical documents.

A separate manual describes how to use the formatter. To run the Blackbeard document formatter, type **BBF** or **BBF** followed by the filename of the document to be formatted. (BBF does not include a pop-up directory of files to format yet.) BBF will format your document and write it to the standard output device—commonly, the screen. To send the output to the printer, run Blackbeard with the following command:

BBF *filename* >prn

This redirects output to the printer. You could also redirect the output to a filename by substituting a filename for **prn**. The default format is to print two blank lines at the top of the page, followed by the filename (used for the title). Then, two more blank lines are printed, followed by text lines as they appear in the file (with no formatting except that tabs are converted to spaces, fonts are replaced if enabled, and spaces are inserted if a left margin is used).

The Use of Fonts

The formatter can also perform font translation. It does this by recognizing font designators in your text file. A font designator begins with the ASCII font character, followed by another ASCII character for the font number.

When fonts are enabled, the font designations are replaced by the escape sequence required for the printer, as defined in the Blackbeard font file. When the formatter starts up, it looks for a font file. Blackbeard looks in the current subdirectory for a file named BB.FNT. (This file defines the font-to-escape sequence relationship.) If there is not a file named BB.CFG in the current subdirectory, Blackbeard will look in the DOS environment for the symbol BBFNT. If it is found, Blackbeard will use the filename supplied with the symbol. This will let you keep one font file and use Blackbeard from any disk or directory. To set BBFNT, place the following command in your AUTOEXEC.BAT file:

```
SET BBFNT=C:\BB.FNT
```

> ## DOCTOR'S NOTE
>
> The α symbol is used in Blackbeard to represent the ALT key. Thus, αQ would stand for ALT-Q. This is the alpha character and is ASCII 224 decimal. You can make it too. Just hold down your ALT key, and then use your numeric keypad. While holding down the ALT key, enter 224. When you release the ALT key, the α character will appear. You can use this technique to enter any graphics character. All you have to do is hold down the ALT key while you enter the number of the character you want.
>
> For example, the beta character is ASCII 225 decimal, and it looks like this: β. The symbol for one-fourth is ASCII 172 decimal. To make this, hold down the ALT key while you enter 172 on the numeric keypad.

The font file looks like the following:

```
0   18          18        (normal = 10 CPI)
1   27,45,1      27,45,0   (underline)
2   27,69        27,70     (bold)
3   27,69        27,70     (italic)
4   27,69        27,70     (subscript)
5   27,69        27,70     (superscript)
6   15           18        (compressed)
7   14           20        (double)
8   27,58        27,58     (12 CPI)
```

The first number is the font number. The second set of numbers defines the "on" sequence for that font number. The third set of numbers defines the "off" sequence for that font number. The rest of the line is ignored and can be used for comments. A comma separates numbers of a set. Spaces separate sets from sets.

The following is a list of Blackbeard keystrokes:

^Q-	Tab left	αI	Insert file
αQ	Line drawing	αP	Adjust special ^T
αW	Write file	αA	Settings
αE	Expand LNG	αS	Repeat search reverse
αR	Repeat replace	αD	Delete block
αT	Change case	αF	Repeat find

αU	Undo	αG	Switch to file
αH	Help	RIGHT ARROW	Column right
αJ	Break and next line	END	End of screen
αK	Join line	DOWN ARROW	Row down
αL	Last DOS command	PGDN	Page down
αZ	Abort	INS	Insert/Overstrike
αX	Execute named macro	DEL	Delete character
αC	Center line	⌂F1	Mark column start
αV	Name macro	⌂F2	Mark column end
αB	Bullet off	⌂F3	Grab column
αn	Reread file	⌂F4	Cut column
αM	Delete macro	⌂F5	Remove column
F1	Mark start	⌂F6	Replace column
F2	Mark end	⌂F7	Copy column
F3	Grab	⌂F8	Paste column
F4	Cut	⌂F9	Clear paste
F5	Shift left	⌂F10	Change case region
F6	Shift right	^F1	Window 1
F7	Copy	^F2	Window 2
F8	Paste	^F3	Window 3
F9	Unmark	^F4	Window 4
F10	Paste window	^F5	Window 5
HOME	Home	^F6	Window 6
UP ARROW	Row up	^F7	Window 7
PGUP	Page up	^F8	Window 8
LEFT ARROW	Column left	^F9	Window 9
CTRL-F10	Window 10	^B	Bullet
αF1	DOS window	^C	ASCII chart
αF2	Exit to DOS	^D	Delete line
αF3	Do command	^E	End of line
αF4	Kill window	^F	Find
αF5	Switch to window	^G	Goto
αF6	Select	BACKSPACE	Backspace
αF7	Expand	TAB	Tab
αF8	Frame/Move	^J	Return
αF9	Color/B&W	^K	Break line

αF10	Select color	^L	Insert line
^LEFT ARROW	Word left	RETURN	Return and insert line
^RIGHT ARROW	Word right	^N	New file
^END	Right of screen	^0	Tab left
^PGDN	End of file	^P	Adjust paragraph
^HOME	Left of screen	^Q	Insert special character
α1	Backup file	^R	Find and replace
α2	Show bindings	^S	Search reverse
α3	Insert number	^T	Transpose
α4	Repeat key	^U	Undelete line
α5	Edit screen	^V	Define macro
α6	Goto start marker	^W	Delete to end-of-line
α7	Set delimeters	^X	Execute macro
α8	Ruler	^Y	Yank line
α0	LNG window	^Z	Exit
CTRL-PGUP	Start of file		
^A	Options		

These are the default keystrokes, which are also called "key bindings." All key bindings can be configured to suit your taste. You do this by editing the BBKEYS.TXT file and making the changes that you want. You then compile it with the Key Binding Compiler that comes with the editor. The Blackbeard editor is on the disk bundled with this book.

Jim Dodgen
Blackbeard
P.O. Box 638
San Bernardino, CA 92402
$20 registration fee

EDWIN

If you are looking for the most editor for the money, then Edwin, for the price of a $10 donation, is worth considering. Edwin is a programmer's editor, written by Kim Kokkonen of Turbo Power Software. Based on the

Borland Editor Toolbox, it offers all of the features that the other editors offer: multiple editing windows and buffers, block moves between windows, undeletion, online help, Pascal structure editing, macro recording and playback, the ability to drop to DOS from the editor, and the ability to handle files whose size is limited only by available RAM. Like many editors, Edwin uses the WordStar commands by default, but these are fully configurable.

Edwin's Features

Edwin started as a WordStar clone (more accurately, as a Turbo Pascal editor clone). It is strictly a text editor, designed primarily for programmers. It, therefore, has minimal word processing features. The word processing features were added to Edwin to satisfy the needs of programmers to write simple documentation or comments that are embedded in a program. (As I mentioned at the beginning of the chapter, I am using Edwin's editor to write this section explaining the features of Edwin.)

When Edwin is started, you will see a simple main menu. It allows you to change the default drive or directory, invoke a DOS shell, or edit a file. You will return to this menu whenever all files are closed and you have not chosen to return to DOS. Edwin can also be started by naming the files to edit on the DOS command line. Up to three files may be specified on the command line:

EDWIN [*file1*] [*file2*] [*file3*]

Each filename may include an optional drive and pathname.

One major benefit of Edwin is the ability to open windows on multiple files. This version of Edwin can open up to six windows at once. Windows can be added, sized, and closed at any time during an edit session. If two windows refer to the same file, changes made in one of the windows will automatically appear in the other. A window Zoom command causes the current window to fill the entire screen, while leaving any other open windows hidden in the background.

Editing with Edwin

The top line of the Edwin editing screen is always reserved for command prompts, editor status information, and error messages. You will also note that a + sign appears at the left edge of this command line whenever a multi-key command has been partially entered. Edwin reserves one line at the top of each window for status information about that window. This line includes the following:

- Current filename
- Current line number
- Current column number
- Number of characters from the cursor to the beginning of the file

If word wrap mode is selected, the right margin value is displayed. In addition, Edwin displays a flag for insert or overwrite mode, a flag for auto-indent mode, a flag showing that the macro recording is active, and a flag indicating that a file must be saved. The save flag indicates that the file has been changed since it was last stored to disk. A save is never required until you exit the editor, but intermediate saves will protect your work from hardware or software crashes. If the current filename is longer than will fit in the area reserved for it, the leading portion of the name will be truncated. The term *flag* means that Edwin shows you that a certain status is in effect. For example, if a file has been altered, but not saved, a * will appear next to the filename. That would be the *save flag*. If indent is on, an *I* would appear on the status line, and so on. In this way, you can always glance at the status line and know what features are toggled on or off.

The maximum line length of files in Edwin is 999 characters. Lines exceeding this length will be broken when the file is read into the editor. The maximum number of lines in any file is 32,767. Memory requirements will see to it that you never reach this limit.

Configurable Key Commands and Help

If you know WordStar commands, you'll be able to start using Edwin immediately. If you're uncomfortable with the WordStar commands, the keyboard is fully reconfigurable. The Fast Install option enables you to reconfigure a great number of keys at once, since it sequentially prompts for each entry. It is the desirable method if you are reconfiguring many keys from the WordStar version. The installation program in Edwin called EDWINST, automatically generates a help file matching the current keyboard installation.

Help Updates Itself

What makes Edwin so unique is what it does with the help file. One of the commands that is reconfigurable during keyboard installation is the one for the help key. If any keys are chosen for this command, EDWINST will write a fairly large help file (EDWIN.HLP), which is loaded into memory when Edwin runs. The full help file uses about 15K of RAM space while Edwin runs. If you don't want help, or if you need to regain the 15K of space, you can delete the keystroke definitions for the Help command. In this case, EDWINST will write a minimal help file using less than 1K of RAM space.

The help facility treats the help file just like any other file or window. Pressing the Help command sequence, or F1, opens a new window, reads the help file from the installed directory, and lets you do any Edwin commands within that file. Note that you can modify the file if you see fit. Figure 10-9 shows the help screen for Edwin.

By default, Edwin is configured for online help. Pressing F1 opens a window onto a summary of commands and macros. The help window is just like any other Edwin window. You can scroll around in it, search for keywords, and even change it if you wish. Use the Quit File (CTRL-K Q) command to close the help window.

Figure 10-9

The Edwin help screen

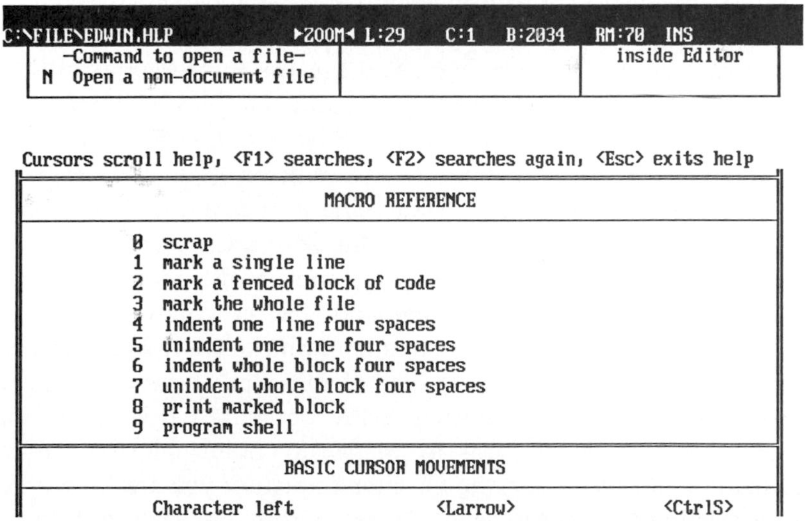

```
C:\FILE\EDWIN.HLP          ►ZOOM◄ L:29    C:1    B:2034    RM:70  INS
   -Command to open a file-                          inside Editor
 N  Open a non-document file


Cursors scroll help, <F1> searches, <F2> searches again, <Esc> exits help
┌─────────────────────────────────────────────────────────────────────┐
│                         MACRO REFERENCE                               │
├─────────────────────────────────────────────────────────────────────┤
│      0  scrap                                                         │
│      1  mark a single line                                           │
│      2  mark a fenced block of code                                 │
│      3  mark the whole file                                          │
│      4  indent one line four spaces                                 │
│      5  unindent one line four spaces                               │
│      6  indent whole block four spaces                              │
│      7  unindent whole block four spaces                            │
│      8  print marked block                                          │
│      9  program shell                                                │
├─────────────────────────────────────────────────────────────────────┤
│                      BASIC CURSOR MOVEMENTS                           │
│      Character left              <Larrow>              <CtrlS>        │
└─────────────────────────────────────────────────────────────────────┘
```

Aborting, Searching, and Replacing

Edwin has what they call an Abort command. Pressing the Abort command sequence at any time in the editor will cause the current operation to be stopped. This will be especially useful during find and replace operations, command prompts, file reads or writes, or other lengthy editor operations that you wish to halt prematurely.

The various find and replace commands in Edwin accept modifiers to the searching behavior, as follows:

U	Search in uppercase (matching is not case sensitive)
B	Search backward (toward the top of file)
W	Match whole words only
G	Search throughout entire file (globally)
M	Search in marked block only
N	No prompts before replacement

Edwin editing operations occur in the memory of your computer. Until a file is saved to disk, there is no permanent record of your edits.

File Handling

Whenever Edwin prompts you for a filename, you can ask it for a directory of available files. To look at all files in the current directory, simply press ENTER. Alternatively, you can enter any combination of drive, pathname, and DOS wildcards. After you do this, Edwin will pop up a window showing all the matching files. You can use the cursor arrows to scroll through this list. When you find a file you want, press ENTER. If none of the files is what you want, press ESC. Edwin offers the option of abandoning any edits you have done. A save indicator (see "Editing with Edwin") will appear in the window status line to indicate that you have unsaved edits. If you attempt to abandon a file with unsaved edits, Edwin will prompt for confirmation. You can merge another file into the current one via the Read File into Window command. The new file is read in at the current cursor position. After this command finishes, Edwin leaves the block markers surrounding the newly read file. Similarly, you can write a portion of the current file to another file with the Write Block command. The Append Block command adds to an existing file, while the Write Block command will always start the file from scratch. If you ask to write a block to an existing file, Edwin will require confirmation before it overwrites it. During an append block operation, Edwin uses logic to avoid embedded ^Z characters in the resulting file. You can also use the Write Block command to print a file from within the editor. Simply mark a block and write it to a file named PRN, LPT1, or LPT2.

Macros and Blocks

In Edwin, marked blocks can be of use in find and replace macro operations, as well as some text processing commands. Sometimes you will find it useful to have these features available. Such commands operate over the complete region of a marked block of text if any block is marked and visible, and if the cursor is currently within the block. Note that the Toggle Case command is the safest to use, since its actions can be undone simply by repeating the command.

Miscellaneous Features

There are a few things to watch out for in using Edwin. As mentioned previously, Edwin operates with all available system memory. If you attempt to read a file that exceeds memory capacity, Edwin will read in as much as it can fit and then send an error message stating that the entire file cannot be read. Continuing from this point is very dangerous. If you save the file, you will overwrite the complete file with a partial version, and lose the remainder. Also, if Edwin's "Expand tabs on read" installation option is active, any tabs in the file will be lost when the file is rewritten to disk. Another warning found in the manual is this:

> Edwin incorporates a DOS critical error handler. This serves to keep DOS' annoying "Abort, Retry, Ignore" from overwriting the editor screen. Instead Edwin's own error message will appear whenever you attempt to write to a drive that isn't ready or to print to an unselected printer. In the case of the unselected printer, there may be a substantial delay before the error message appears. Have no fear, this is the printer timeout period normally allowed for long printer operations like form feeds. If the EDWIN.ERR file is not available when Edwin starts up, error messages will appear as numbers rather than text. Refer to the EDWIN.ERR file for the correspondence between the numbers and text. If you don't like the text for a particular message, edit the EDWIN.ERR file to change it to something more desirable. Be sure to follow the format of the existing file if you do so. Similarly, you can edit the EDWIN.MSG file to change various command prompts of the editor. Unlike the ERR file, the MSG file must be found at startup, or the editor will not continue.

Kim Kokkonen
Turbo Power Tools
404-438-8608 (9:00 A.M. - 5:00 P.M. PST)
72457,2131 CompuServe ID
$10 donation

GALAXY WORD PROCESSOR

Over the years I have watched Galaxy evolve as a program. It had humble beginnings as the Galaxy Editor. It is based on the editor included in the Turbo Pascal Editor's Toolkit. The interface has been improved and more features added, such as mouse support. The last version of the Galaxy Editor was 2.43. When I contacted the people at Omniverse about including the Galaxy Editor in this book, I was told that something new was in the works. It was then that I learned about the new and exciting Galaxy word processor. Let's take a look at what's available in this new version of Galaxy. It's not just an editor anymore.

Overview of Galaxy 3.0

The cover of the new manual proclaims, "Friendly... Powerful... Blindingly Fast...". I still have my vision, but I must say the new Galaxy word processor is all the things it claims. Friendly? Yes, commands can be issued from the keyboard or with a mouse and they are clear and concise. Online help is available at all times. Blindingly fast? Yes, whether it's moving around inside a document or searching for text, the new Galaxy is very fast. Is it "powerful?" That, perhaps, is almost an understatement. If you never saw Galaxy before, you'll be suitably impressed. If you have used earlier versions of Galaxy, you have some surprises in store.

Galaxy now comes with a 100,000 word spelling checker and a 220,000 word thesaurus created by Microlytics. You can now enter descriptive lines, including title, subject, author, and operator. In addition, you can add keywords to help you search and find out the date and time that a document was last changed. You can create *style sheets,* so you can have documents with many different formats simply by calling up the proper style sheet. What else is new? A tutorial system, automatically numbered footnotes, powerful macros, multiple documents, and windows that can be sized and moved. The interface is reminiscent of Microsoft Windows or Presentation Manager. All in all it's a very comprehensive package. Let's take a closer look at some specific features.

Many Ways to Format

Galaxy gives you many ways to format your text. There are special formatting areas for characters, paragraphs, sections, and the entire document. Under character formatting you can choose from a selection of fonts. You can also set text attributes like bold, italics, and normal. With paragraph formatting you can control text alignment, line spacing, and indenting. Section formatting lets you handle things like margins, headers, footers, and page numbering. Lastly, you can use document formatting to set paper size, location of footnotes, and other things that affect the entire document. Figure 10-10 shows the Character Formatting dialogue box from Galaxy.

Note: You can have a wide range of fonts and print styles, including proportional and compressed.

Style Sheets

When you get a particular kind of format set up, you can save it as a style sheet. Here again, Galaxy gives you some interesting options. Let's say

---

Figure 10-10

The Character Formatting dialogue menu in Galaxy

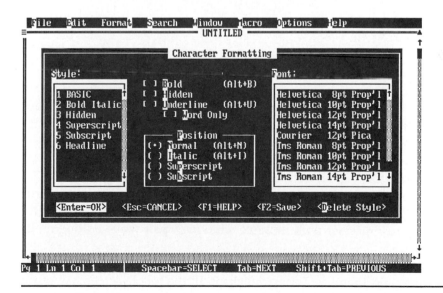

that you had created a certain format for your basic writing—with certain margins, page numbering, and so on. Perhaps you'd like to have another style sheet just like this one but using a different style of print; for example, bold italic. Galaxy allows you to save style sheets not only with a name but with a style number as well. Thus, you could call one "MY-STYLE 1," with the basic style of print, and call another "MYSTYLE 2," for the bold italic print. Style sheets give you tremendous flexibility and also save you time. Once you've set up a format, you can save it and use it again and again. Style sheets really add to the power of Galaxy.

Window Action

The old Galaxy editor had windows, but not like the windows that you can have in the new Galaxy word processor. From the pull-down menu, "Window," you have the following options:

- New
- Zoom
- Close
- Move
- Size
- DOS Shell
- Run Program

The New command opens up another window. Zoom causes the current window to fill the entire screen, no matter how many windows you have open. With Close you can get rid of any windows you don't need any longer. The next two commands let you alter the position and size of the windows that you open. Using the Move command, you can place a window anywhere you want on the screen. With Size you can make the window any size you choose. The DOS Shell command takes you to DOS so that you can execute DOS commands, while Run Program lets you run other programs while you are within Galaxy. Figure 10-11 shows the Galaxy word processor with multiple windows open while editing multiple files.

You can easily move between windows, select the one you want to work with, and then use Zoom to make it fill the whole screen. All of the

Figure 10-11

Multiple windows and documents in Galaxy

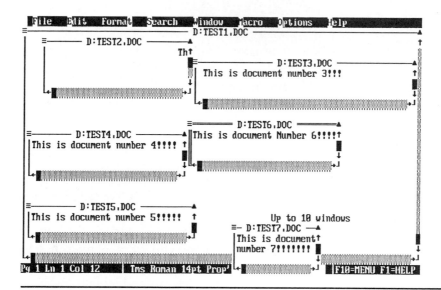

other windows remain—hidden underneath. You can also cut and paste text between windows. Thus, Galaxy lets you edit multiple documents or several copies of the same document and exchange text among them quickly and efficiently.

Printer Support

Galaxy supports a wide range of printers, both dot matrix and laser. In all, 350 different printers are supported. In testing the program, I printed documents on both the Panasonic KX-P1124, 24-pin dot matrix printer and the Panasonic KX-P4450 laser printer, using a variety of fonts. The results were text that was clear and well-defined. To further enhance the quality look of your documents, Galaxy offers

- Microjustification
- Proportional spacing
- Bold print
- Underlining

- Italics

- Superscripts

- Subscripts

These are the kinds of features usually found only in the more expensive commercial word processors. So, if you are looking for a word processor that supports a variety of printers and a wide selection of fonts and printing options, Galaxy may be the program you want to look at first.

Help Is Everywhere

Galaxy gives you help every step of the way. For starters, it comes with a Learn feature that guides you through the program. It's like taking a tour of the program—a big help for all users.

The dialogue boxes are set up logically, so commands that belong together are together. This makes it easier for you to maneuver and to take care of business quickly. Galaxy also has an Undo function that lets you take back your last action. For example, if you accidentally delete a line of text, you can undo the deletion with a single keystroke.

A special attraction of Galaxy is it's context-sensitive help system, which is available throughout the program. All you do is highlight a command that is in question and press F1. The help system also has a complete index. Say you are getting help with Character Formatting and decide that you want help with something else. From inside the help screen you can press F1 again, and you'll get a complete index of help topics that are available. Scroll through the index, select the topic you want, and you go right to that section of help. Figure 10-12 shows you what the index within the help system looks like. No other Shareware word processor gives you such a complete and easily understandable help system.

High-Priced Features in a Low-Cost System

Galaxy has some high-priced features for its low cost. For example, you can get special legal, medical, and even foreign language dictionaries. Tell Galaxy to automatically back up your document every so many minutes—and it will. It also includes network support, macros, global search and replace, and support for expanded memory. Using expanded memory you

Figure 10-12

Galaxy's Help Index from within a help screen

can edit files that are as large as 8 megabytes. How much is 8 megabytes—a file about 8 times bigger than the portion of this book that you've read so far.

Summing Up Galaxy

Galaxy has the features, the speed, the help, and the power that you need to write a book or a note to your mother. It's more than just user friendly, it's "writer friendly." It has the printer support and the formatting functions to make your documents look good. It's easy to learn and easy to use. I'm not the only one who thinks so, because Galaxy is used by the following companies or groups:

- 3M Corporation
- Hewlett-Packard
- AT&T
- Rockwell International

- U.S. Army Corps of Engineers
- MCI
- United Auto Workers
- The United Nations
- NASA

Steve Schauer, Bob Foster, and Gordon Wanner
Omniverse
P.O. Box 1570
Port Townsend, WA 98368
800-365-7627
206-385-6667 (BBS; 24 hours)
$99.95 registration fee, includes printed manual and support

PC-WRITE

To call PC-Write a text editor is stretching things a bit. In truth, it is a full-function Shareware word processor. The only thing it has in common with other text editors is that it saves in ASCII rather than in a dedicated word processing format. Included with PC-Write's downloaded version is a complete tutorial that allows you to familiarize yourself with the major editing functions of PC-Write, and a Quick Guide, which is a fairly comprehensive manual for registered and nonregistered users alike. The Quick Guide also provides instructions for customizing PC-Write.

Getting Started with PC-Write

There are a number of different ways to get started in PC-Write. The simplest is to type **ED** at the DOS prompt. You will then see an opening menu with several choices. Figure 10-13 shows this opening screen.

Press F6 and then either edit the default WORK.DOC file, create a new file, or press F8 for a directory list of files to choose from (you will be prompted for the directory). You can either load the file immediately by pressing ESC or make a backup of it first. Another way to get started is to type **ED** and a filename at the DOS prompt.

Figure 10-13

Figure 10-13

PC-Write's opening screen

```
(To get these options later when you are editing, press the F1:System/help key)

┌──────────────────────────────────────────────────────────────────────┐
│                                                                        │
│     Welcome to PC-Write, Version 3.03, by Quicksoft!                   │
│                                                                        │
│     Please press one of the following function keys:                   │
│                                                                        │
│  ┌──┐                                                                   │
│  │F1│ Help.....Give information about PC-Write operations and features. │
│  └──┘                                                                   │
│  ┌──┐                                                                   │
│  │F2│ Exit.....Return back to DOS, saving the file you were working on. │
│  └──┘                                                                   │
│  ┌──┐                                                                   │
│  │F6│ File.....Enter the name of a file to edit or create.             │
│  └──┘                                                                   │
│  ┌──┐                                                                   │
│  │F7│ Print....Enter the name of a file to print.                      │
│  └──┘                                                                   │
│  ┌──┐                                                                   │
│  │F8│ Dir......Get a directory of disk files, pick one to edit or print.│
│  └──┘                                                                   │
│                                                                        │
└──────────────────────────────────────────────────────────────────────┘
```

You can include drive and path specifications. If you want to skip the step where you are asked if you want to make a backup, add /e after the filename. If you want to make a backup without having to be prompted, add /s. Other *switches* allow you to edit a read-only file on a network, pause each time PC-Write reads a control file, and so on. Once you have finished, there are almost as many different ways to save files and exit as there are to create and retrieve files.

When you first enter PC-Write, you will see a clean screen with a status line at the top. This status line has two functions: it gives you the status of the program—whether you are in word wrap or in automatic formatting mode, and so on—and it displays messages and prompts. Figure 10-14 shows what this screen looks like.

Features of PC-Write

The message "Esc:Menu" reminds you that you must press the ESC key to bring up the Main Menu. The remainder of the status line will vary

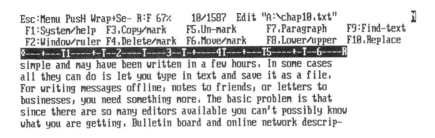

Figure 10-14

PC-Write's status line

depending on what options you have selected in PC-Write. Keyboard-Status gives you the current keyboard status and the cursor shape that goes with that status. The status can be one of the following: Over, OVER, and over (all strikeover modes) and Push, PUSH, and push (all insert modes with cursors of varying sizes). Edit-Status tells you what kind of reformatting mode is operating. Unlike text editors, PC-Write will automatically reformat paragraphs.

In addition, the keyboard status line will tell you if you are currently merging text, if you have marked a block of text anywhere in the document, if you are in boxing mode, or if you are recording a macro, among other things.

Spell-Status indicates the toggles for the spell checker. You can do a quick check of a word with the + key, or activate the spell checker menu line with ALT-2. Here you have, in addition to the usual options, a Guess option, which will give a choice of possible correct spellings. Move the highlighted box to the correct choice, press F10, and the word is automatically inserted. In addition, F7 will cause PC-Write to let out a little beep when you type a word incorrectly. You can add words to the master list by creating a user list and merging it with the master list. You can also scan a file for the next word that is not in the master list or user list, and scan backward or forward.

PC-Write also has a shorthand mode. That means that you can make a file of commonly used words or phrases and assign them abbreviations using the format "abbreviation:replacement." Then bring up shorthand mode from the Spell Check menu, type the abbreviation, type any key that is *not* a letter, DEL, BACKSPACE, or INS, and the abbreviation will be replaced by the word.

In addition to the status markers, other information shows up on the status line: the percentage of computer memory available for editing; the line number that the cursor is on, followed by the total number of lines (*nn/nn*); and the page number, which is always 1.

Page breaks can be inserted for printing purposes, but as the Quick Guide warns, "If there are page breaks in the file, you must repage after any editing to make sure these numbers are correct."

The File Save status marker has several options. "Read" appears when you first load a file and means that you have made no changes yet. Once you make a change, "Read" changes to "Edit," and when you exit, your changes are saved automatically. If these words are in uppercase, you are in read-only mode. You can still make changes, but in order to save them you will have to rename the file. If the words are in lowercase, you are locked onto a network. The final item on the editing status line is the full path and name of the file you are working on.

Handling Files

The top line also serves as a way of accessing the other menus and a place to respond to PC-Write prompts for a filename or other text. The list of features is almost endless. File management functions give you the following options:

- Rename files

- Change drives or directories

- Copy files from one directory to another

- Delete files

- Open and close windows and move around within windows

- Split files

- Merge files

- Move text from one file to another using windows

PC-Write has blocking ability, but it also has what it calls *boxing*. The difference between a block and a box is that a block is a continuous range of text while a box is a rectangular area of text. This is handy if you want to move a column of figures, for example, from one place to another without moving a second column. Both boxes and blocks can be moved, copied, or deleted. More than that, however, a vertical box the entire length of the file can be created with a single keystroke and boxed areas can literally be boxed—you can draw a frame around them.

Headers, footers, indexes, pagination, tables of contents, footnotes, typewriter mode—the extras that text editors do not provide—PC-Write provides them all. In addition, PC-Write has printing capabilities that the others do not have, and supports an almost unbelievable number of printers. The customer support offered by Quicksoft is second to none, and the people are not only knowledgeable, but friendly. PC-Write is an excellent program, and I wouldn't be without it.

Bob Wallace
Quicksoft
219 First Ave. N. #224
Seattle, WA 98109
206-282-0452 or 800-888-8088
$99, includes manual and support

PC-TYPE

PC-Type, a text editor from ButtonWare, is somewhat unique in that it does not use the WordStar commands. Instead, it uses a combination of function keys for the most used functions such as deleting or adding a line; saving a file; exiting to DOS; exiting the program; and either saving or not saving a file. At the bottom of an essentially clear screen are letters that indicate which options are toggled on. For example, "XWI" means that a carriage return will bring the cursor to a new line, that word wrap is active, and that insert mode is on. Other ALT key combinations mirror some of the function keys. There are also a series of command line options and a help screen to explain what they mean. Figure 10-15 shows the help screen for the command line options.

Features of PC-Type

ESC will move the cursor to the command line and any DOS command can then be entered. You can use the command line to load, print, or edit a new file without dropping to DOS. Specify the line number of the file so

Figure 10-15

PC Type's command line help

```
Esc: Help off, cancel.  F1: Help off, to last menu.  Arrows: Select Help topic
Basic editing    Deleting text    Formatting       Page layout      Shortcuts
Auto-numbering   DOS commands     Headers/footers  Paragraph style  Shorthand
Box operations   Dot lines        Index/contents   Printer setup    Spell checker
Change margins   Enhancing text   Margins/tabs     Printing         Status line
Characters       Entering text    Marking text     Problem solving  Switching files
Columns          File conversion  Measuring        Recording keys   Typewriter mode
Control files    File management  Merging          Repaging         Windows
Copy/move text   Find/replace     Misc.operations  Ruler lines      Support service
Cursor moves     Footnotes        Page elements    Shell to DOS     Shareware
B A S I C   E D I T I N G

Using help screens
Use the four arrow keys, Home, End, and Tab key to select a topic.
Use the PgUp and PgDn keys to scroll a long help screen, like this one.
Shifted PgUp and PgDn keys scroll a screenfull at once.

File Operations
1. Create or load a file    A>ED filename
2. Enter text               type on keyboard
3. Save the text to disk    Press F1 F3
4. Edit the text            Bksp, Del, Ins
5. Print the file           Press F1 then F7
6. Save the file, exit      Press F1 then F2
                                                              More:PgDn
```

you can then work with only part of a file. PC-Type can also do math calculations within your text. Like PC-Write, PC-Type has to be considered more of a full word processor than merely a text editor. A great many things can be configured by the user.

Configurable Options
You can elect to configure all of the colors used by PC-Type as well as the type of graphics port used. The default for tabs, imported files, and date options can also be user configured. Set up the default printer configuration that you want, along with things like default box characters, file handling, and time options. All of these things allow you to make PC-Type function exactly the way you want it too.

Graphs and Mail-Merge
You can also do graphs in PC-Type. You must, of course, have a printer that can support the printing of graphs. PC-Type can create pie, vertical bar, scatter, line, and horizontal graphs. The program helps you set up

column titles and so forth, so your presentation looks truly professional; you can even highlight parts of the graph.

Mail-merge is another feature of PC-Type. By using the data contained in a database, such as PC-File DB, or any comma-delimited file, you can create highly personalized letters and mailing labels.

A Host of Other Features

What other things does PC-Type have? A complete spell checker, context-sensitive help, the ability to draw boxes around your text, and the ability to work with up to ten files in four windows at one time. PC-Type is also designed to work hand-in-hand with other fine ButtonWare products—specifically PC-File DB, PC-Calc+, and PC-File+, as well as with any data that is in ASCII format. You can also create up to 25 macros within PC-Type to help make your work a little easier and less repetitive.

Jim Button
ButtonWare, Inc.
P.O. Box 5786
Bellevue, WA 98006
800-J-BUTTON (800-528-8866)
$59.95 + $5.00 shipping and handling

QEDIT

SemWare's QEdit, written by Sammy Mitchell, was mentioned earlier in this chapter in the discussion about text editors. QEdit provides all of the features of a good text editor and is moderately priced. For $57.95, you can get the latest update of the program and a manual; or, if you prefer, you can get the manual on disk, with the program, for $45.50. What makes QEdit outstanding is the extent to which you can configure it to suit yourself. In fact, SemWare will even provide a customized configuration for you. The current version of QEdit is version 2.10.

Lots of Things You Can Customize

You don't have to customize QEdit; you can use the default settings and never bother with the QCONFIG program. You can make a new configuration file with a new name and save it, as well as the original Q.EXE file, and switch back and forth between them. If you choose to configure the Q.EXE file, the first thing you should do is make a backup of the original .EXE file. Then type **qconfig** at the DOS prompt, and when asked for the program name, press the ENTER key. You will then see the Configuration menu. Figure 10-16 shows what the Main Menu of QCONFIG looks like.

Choose the category you want to reconfigure by typing the first letter of the menu item, and respond to the options within each category. You can either change the option or keep the old one. After you finish with one category, you will be returned to the menu, and can then select another category to customize. You can customize as much or as little as you wish. Then you can save the changes or, if you want everything to revert to the defaults, just press N when asked if you want to save, and the changes will not be saved.

Advanced Options

You can tell QEdit to test for certain conditions: the presence of EGA or VGA adapters, or the presence of an enhanced keyboard, enabling the use of the F11 and F12 keys on a 101-key keyboard. You can change the cursor size, change the number of rows shown on the screen, and make other technical changes. For example, you can change the amount of memory that is reserved from DOS, what code is generated by the ALT numeric keypad, or load a file at a specific line number from the DOS command line.

Figure 10-16

Main Menu of QCONFIG

```
A:\>qconfig
Configuration program for: QEdit v2.08  July, 1989.
Enter program name to config, <CR> for Q.EXE :
Enter new name for Q.EXE, <CR> for Q.EXE :

Configuration choices,
Choose One of the Following by pressing the indicated Key:

A)dvanced options
C)olors/screen
G)eneral options
H)elp install
K)eys
P)rinter options
Q)uit
S)ave changes and quit
T)ab settings
```

Colors/Screen Option

With the Colors/Screen option, you set the colors when using a color monitor. If you have a monochrome monitor, you can still tell QEdit to use normal, highlighted, underlined, and reverse video values for marking blocks of text, for error messages, for the status line, and so on. There are several other options that are covered here. You can move the status line from the top to the bottom, enclose it in a box or not, and indicate what character you want to use to separate the information. Here is where you tell QEdit to restore you to your original screen after exiting the program.

General Options

General options are primarily for editing, but they invoke some of the special editing functions of QEdit. The usual options include: toggling word wrap on or off and setting the default margin for it; toggling insert mode on or off; and toggling auto-indent mode. Another option is the ability to load or list files when a wildcard specification is encountered from either the command line or from inside the program. You can choose to load, for instance, all files with the extension .DOC, or simply get a listing so you can choose from the list. This is where you would select the default search and replace options.

Some options are unique to QEdit, such as starting QEdit in matching mode, in which double quotes, parentheses, and square brackets all have their matching character automatically entered; adding a CTRL-Z end-of-file marker; or displaying "***End of File**."

Help Screen

QEdit allows you to design your own help screen if you don't wish to use the QEdit help screen that is already loaded. You create a text file and list all of the information you want to be able to pull up with Quick Help (F1). Save this and, using the Help option in QCONFIG.EXE, enter the name of the file.

Keys

When it comes to customizing the keyboard, QEdit allows for a lot of creativity. QEdit supports the enhanced IBM keyboard and allows you to configure all 101 keys as well as the ALT, CTRL, and function keys. Included with the program is a file called QCONFIG.DAT, which contains the default settings for the keyboard and can be edited either with a text editor or with QCONFIG.EXE. The configuration can be a single key followed by a command, a macro, or a multiple command.

You can also assign a command to a twokey. A *twokey* is two distinct keystrokes, for example CTRL-K B, which could be assigned the command Exit. On bulletin boards and the commercial online networks you can find configuration files for QEdit that will make it emulate WordPerfect, Brief, WordStar, and other popular commercial editors and word processors. Using QCONFIG.EXE, you can also configure the printer commands.

Additional Features of QEdit

There are other features that make QEdit different from most of the other editors. They include the ability to load multiple files from the DOS command line with or without wildcard characters; a pull-down file list for easy selection; and closing brackets and parentheses, which are useful for programming, but also helpful for writing in general.

QEdit uses pull-down menus that are accessed by pressing ESC and then moving across a Main Menu bar at the top of the screen, or by typing the initial letter of the submenu. Figure 10-17 shows QEdit's Main Menu with the File submenu pulled down.

Figure 10-17

The QEdit menu with the File submenu pulled down

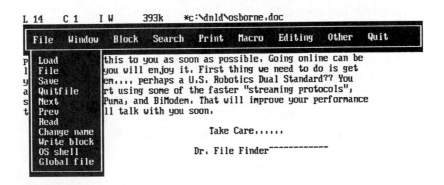

After you become more familiar with the program, you can use the CTRL, ALT, and function keys. There is a lot of flexibility and speed, and an editor that you can configure any way you want.

The TSR Version of QEdit—QTSR

In March 1990, SemWare released a full version of QEdit that can be loaded as a TSR program. This special version of QEdit can be loaded in several different ways, depending on your system configuration. It is best, however, if you have expanded memory (EMS) or a fast hard disk. At this time, QTSR is only available to registered users of QEdit. I talked with Sammy Mitchell, and he said that a Shareware release is planned for QTSR sometime in the future. Let's take a look at what QTSR does.

Making the Most of QTSR

You can load QTSR as a regular TSR program, but this would not really be efficient. Loaded as such, QTSR would require approximately 60K of DOS RAM for itself, and then as much RAM as you could allocate to handle the largest sized file you would need to edit. Thus, if you wanted to be able to edit a 40K file, for example, QTSR would take up 100K of DOS RAM in its resident state. Where QTSR really shines, however, is if you have EMS. Utilizing EMS, QTSR will only use 9K of DOS RAM, while the rest of the program *swaps* in and out of expanded memory. What does this mean? When QTSR is not active, the remainder of the program is held in expanded memory. The moment you press the hot key, the program is moved into current memory. You can configure the hot key that calls QTSR, using its own configuration program, QTCONFIG. If you have extended memory (XMS), you can use a DOS utility like HIMEM .SYS to allow you to use QTSR. If you don't have EMS or XMS, you can configure the resident version of QEdit so that it swaps to disk. This is a viable option if you have a fast hard disk. If your hard disk is extremely slow, you could still use this option, but it would take several seconds for QTSR to swap back and forth. The resident version of QEdit can use the same key definitions as your standard version of QEdit.

Sammy Mitchell
SemWare
730 Elk Cove Court
Kennesaw GA 30144-4047
404-428-6416 (9 A.M. - 5 P.M. EST)
404-641-8968 (BBS)

WORDMASTER

Wordmaster, a full-function Shareware word processor, has an easily accessed, easy-to-use menu system that gives you both visual cues to the basic commands and a complete context-sensitive help system. Press F1, and a menu appears at the top of the screen that gives the basic options. Figure 10-18 shows what this looks like.

These options can be used by either typing the first letter or moving the highlighted cursor bar and pressing ENTER. If you have one set of commands showing, and want to move to the next one, just use the LEFT ARROW or RIGHT ARROW key. Pressing F1 will bring up a help screen for any of the options. In addition, the keystroke command for that option appears above the menu line. This is a feature that helps you learn the individual commands more easily.

Easily Accessible Functions

Any of Wordmaster's functions can be accessed either through the menu or directly from the keyboard. For example, if you want to edit a file, you

Figure 10-18

The Wordmaster top menu

eyboard Command:

```
 File   Window   Text   Block   Goto   Search   Options   Misc
```

        This is just a note to inform you that all is going well. I
plan on sending this to you as soon as possible. Going online can be
lots of fun and you will enjoy it. First thing we need to do is get
you a better modem.... perhaps a U.S. Robotics Dual Standard?? You

can press F1, choose **F**, choose **O**, or move the cursor bar to Open file and press ENTER. From the keyboard, you would just press F10. You would then enter the name of the file to be edited or press ENTER for a list of files after entering the path.

One special feature of Wordmaster is that if you enter just the first letter of a filename, Wordmaster will retrieve the closest file beginning with that letter. You could begin each of your filenames with a different letter (A, B, C, for example) and save the trouble of typing in the full filename. Of course, an existing document can be loaded from the DOS command line by typing **WM filename** (it may be necessary to give the full path if the file is in a different directory than the Wordmaster files).

When you enter Wordmaster for the first time, the name of the file showing in the upper left-hand corner will be NEWFILE. To name the file, you can go into the Files menu and choose the Name option. When you have finished working with one file, you can choose a second one with the Change option from the Files menu. Both of these options can also be invoked from the keyboard as can any menu option. If you intend to use Wordmaster a great deal, you will find that it speeds things up if you learn the control and function commands rather than relying on the menu.

Lots of Good Features

Since the menu is fairly easy to use, let's discuss some of the features of Wordmaster by referring to the keyboard commands. Wordmaster has two Undelete functions. F2 will restore a line to the status it had when you entered the document. This will undo deletions made with the CTRL-END key combination. CTRL-Q will restore lines deleted with the CTRL-Y command. (CTRL-END deletes everything on the line to the right of the cursor; CTRL-Y deletes the whole line that the cursor is on, no matter where the cursor is placed.)

Wordmaster also has two DOS commands. CTRL-F1 will open a window that gives you a DOS command line from which you can execute any program or command without leaving Wordmaster, provided there is sufficient RAM. SHIFT-F1 opens a window that shows the current directory and allows you to change to another directory or subdirectory.

ALT-F1 and F1 are the two Help commands. ALT-F1 brings up a help menu in the center of the screen and gives the keyboard commands for all the functions. Figure 10-19 shows the ALT-F1 help menu screen.

Figure 10-19

The Wordmaster ALT-F1 **help index screen**

```
┌─── Help Sections ───┐
│ Help and status      │
│ Cursor movement      │
│ Quick movement       │
│ Insert and delete    │
│ Search and replace   │
│ Files                │
│ Windows              │
│ Blocks               │
│ Text commands        │
│ Tabs                 │
│ Utilities            │
│ Settings and toggles │
│ Spell checking       │
│ Macros               │
│ Printing             │
│ Function keys        │
└──────────────────────┘
```

F1 activates the full set of help screens. If you select, for example, the File menu and then press F1 again, more help is available. This is a truly innovative approach in text editors. Figure 10-20 shows you what this would look like.

The search and replace functions of Wordmaster are a bit more flexible than most. In addition to the usual capabilities of doing a search backward or forward, and ignoring case in searches, you can search only within a marked block. Wordmaster provides all of the expected block functions, and your searches are not limited to a single word but can be any sequence of letters or numbers.

All the Right Stuff

Wordmaster supports macro creation and playback, and windowing. With Wordmaster you can open multiple windows. Any change made to a file in one window will be reflected in all of the windows in which the file is opened. If you delete something from a file in window 1, the deletion will show up as well in the same file in window 4. Unlike most text editors,

---

Figure 10-20

Additional help with a file in Wordmaster

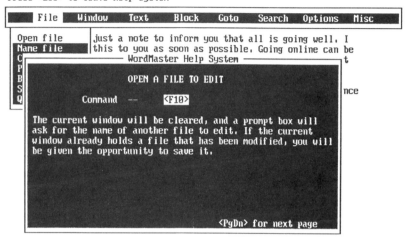

```
Press <Esc> to leave help system

┌─────┬──────────────────────────────────────────────────────┐
│ File│ Window   Text    Block    Goto   Search  Options  Misc│
├─────┴──────────────────────────────────────────────────────┤
│ Open file    │just a note to inform you that all is going well. I │
│ Name file    │this to you as soon as possible. Going online can be│
│ C  ┌─────────────── WordMaster Help System ──────────────┐ t
│ P  │                                                      │
│ B  │            OPEN A FILE TO EDIT                        │
│ S  │                                                      │  nce
│ Q  │     Command  --       <F10>                           │
│    │                                                      │
│    │ The current window will be cleared, and a prompt box will │
│    │ ask for the name of another file to edit. If the current  │
│    │ window already holds a file that has been modified, you will │
│    │ be given the opportunity to save it.                 │
│    │                                                      │
│    │                                                      │
│    │                                                      │
│    │                                                      │
│    │                      <PgDn> for next page            │
│    └──────────────────────────────────────────────────────┘
```

Wordmaster will allow you to insert printer commands into the text so that you can print in compressed, bold, underlined, double-strike, super-script, or subscript fonts, depending on your printer's capabilities. Included with the program are several printer drivers. These can be edited to suit your particular printer.

There are quite a few print format commands that can be accessed with the ALT-F1 Help command. These include setting the page number and moving it to a position other than the default upper right-hand corner, eliminating page numbers entirely, and defining the headers and footers and setting the margins for these. Margins can be set for the document itself by resetting the defaults in the options. Wordmaster needs to have the high bits stripped in order to import its files, and this too can be toggled on or off.

All of the default settings in Wordmaster can be reconfigured either from the menu or by keyboard commands. You can toggle word wrap, justification, auto-indent, pagination, and the size of the cursor. If you have a monitor that can handle it, you can toggle to a 43-line screen display. Wordmaster has a set of unique system commands. CTRL-S-I displays information about the current file as well as the operating system. CTRL-S-M displays the available RAM. CTRL-S-P lets you set the page length. CTRL-S-S sets the path where the support files are found. As you can see, there is a logic to the keys that are used for these as for all keyboard commands, which makes them much easier to remember. Unfortunately, Wordmaster does not have a built-in spell checker and thesaurus, but does make use of Borland's Turbo Lightning. I spoke with Wordmaster's author, William Farrar, and he said he was hoping that version 2.0 will have its own spell checker and allow the user to configure the key sequences.

William M. Farrar
Masterworks
P.O. Box 116
McCleary, WA 98557
$20

SUMMARY

These examples are by no means all of the text editors and Shareware word processors that are available. What I have tried to do is show the ways in which these programs are similar and highlight some of their unique features. What each individual wants from a text editor will vary, whether it be mouse support, lots of help screens, complete keyboard configurability, or just a simple program to write a few offline messages. Whatever your needs, there is a text editor to suit you. The text editors and word processors described here are among the best. The way to decide which one you like is to try several, and then make a decision. When you do decide, be sure to register the program with its author— you'll be glad you did.

## CHAPTER ELEVEN

Communications Programs and Utilities

In Chapters 5 through 9 you examined the process of going online. The online environment is an excellent place to obtain not only good Shareware programs, but to interact with other users and exchange information as well. In order to do this effectively, you'll need a good communications program. The program best for you depends in part on your needs. If you are only going online to transfer files, then you may not need a full-featured communications program. On the other hand, if you want to send and receive messages, participate in online conferences, utilize CB simulators to talk with other users, and take advantage of all of the resources available online, then you'll want a program that can make your life easier.

This chapter will examine the very best communications programs available in Shareware while also looking at some of the most popular and useful utilities. Let's begin by taking a look at communications programs in general.

COMMUNICATIONS PROGRAMMING—OVERVIEW

In simple terms, a communications program is just an interface, but it's a highly complex interface. As part of the program's routine chores, it must serve as an interface for:

- Your computer
- Your modem
- Your serial port
- The host serial port
- The host modem
- The host computer
- The software running on the host

You can see that a communications program must handle all of these things and do it gracefully, while giving you a pleasant environment. Jan van der Eijk, author of the Super Kermit protocol, once called communications programming "the black art of programming." Van der Eijk used this reference because in many ways communications programming is a bit mysterious.

The programmer must blend together the proper ingredients, using a touch of this and a bit of that, and sometimes the results are still difficult to explain. This means having to go back to add a dash of something else, and then trying it again. Because the interface is so complex and there are so many factors to take into account, the process of writing a good communications program can be a lengthy one. Ultimately, you end up with a useful tool for taking full advantage of all the resources online.

A Gradual Evolution

During the time I've been online, I have watched with curiosity as communications programs evolved. A version of Qmodem or Procomm from five years ago would astound you if you compared it to the versions that will be discussed in this chapter. Five years ago the average person online was using a 300 baud modem. There was no Zmodem or BiModem or MPt. MNP modems were "things of the future." At that time a file transfer was an arduous task.

Today, using a high speed modem, you can download a file in 3 minutes that would have taken you 90 minutes at 300 baud. As machines and modems became faster, communications programs had to change. As the faster streaming protocols entered the scene, communications programs had to change again. At the same time, the number of things that a person could do online gradually increased, thereby putting more demand on the programs used to access online services and bulletin boards.

The communications programs of today are highly complex pieces of software, pulling a variety of factors together and giving you information in an intelligent and useful manner. The goal of this chapter is to take a good look at seven of the best full-featured communications programs in Shareware and two smaller communications programs.

You will examine their similarities and differences so you can make an informed choice, or at least have a good place to start.

Programs to Be Discussed

In no special order, the communications programs to be discussed in this chapter are

- Qmodem 4.2
- Procomm 2.4.3
- Telix 3.12
- GT Power Comm 15.1
- Boyan Deluxe
- Zcomm 17.59
- Telemate 2.0B

You will also get a look at two smaller communications programs that may be of interest to you. These are Commo 4.30 and Chatterbox 1.0. All of these communications programs are good. Because they are good they have many functions that are similar, and those functions will be discussed first. At the same time, each one has certain features that make it unique. In the end, you will choose the one that best meets your needs and seems best to you. Having used all of them, I hope to be able to give you an accurate picture of each one. Let's take a look at some of the features these fine programs have in common. As you move along you will see the menu of commands for all of the programs in this chapter.

File Transfer Protocols

File transfer protocols are an integral part of all of the full-featured communications programs. Each program has a basic core of protocols that are internal. In addition, all of them offer some way of adding external protocol drivers, such as Zmodem, BiModem, MPt, SEAlink, and others. The ability to add the file transfer protocols that you want helps to make the program more flexible and allows you to add protocols that suit

DOCTOR'S NOTE

To give you a better idea of my perspective on these programs, a little history is in order. I mentioned that I had used all of the programs to be discussed, and I would like to clarify that. I have used all of the programs that are discussed in Part Four and thousands more besides. The programs I've selected to describe in detail are the best I could find in each category. In all cases, programs were used on my system and tested extensively while being compared to other programs that perform the same functions.

As to the programs in this chapter, I am currently an alpha tester for Qmodem and I beta-tested Telix 3.11. Prior to that I was a beta tester for Datastorm Technologies and tested Procomm from version 1.9 through Procomm Plus. I have followed the development of Boyan, GT Power Comm, and Telemate from the moment they appeared on the Shareware scene. Zcomm, Commo, and Chatterbox are all programs that I have used and tested extensively.

In no case did I use any of the programs for a period of less than six months. In fact, there have been times when I had five or more communications programs on my system at the same time while I tested and evaluated them. At this writing, all nine programs are on my system and fully functional. Thus, when I say that I have used a program, I do not mean loading it once or twice, but rather keeping a program on my system and utilizing all of its features and functions until I know each program's capabilities.

your needs.

Each of the programs discussed includes different internal protocols. The popular external protocol drivers can be found on bulletin boards and online networks. For your benefit, here is a listing of the most popular external protocols and the filename that is most often used. I will give them an extension of .ZIP, but keep in mind that the extension may vary depending on where you find the file. It could also be .ARC, .PAK, .LZH, and so on.

Zmodem	DSZXXXX.ZIP (where XXXX is the release date)
MPt	MPT100.ZIP
BiModem	BIMOD122.ZIP (1.22 is the most recent)
SEAlink	CLINK120.ZIP
Jmodem	JMOD33.ZIP (current release is 3.3)
Super8K	SK&JXXXX.ZIP (XXXX is the release date)
Megalink	MLINK16.ZIP
OZBEXT	OZBEXT.ZIP or OZBEX???.ZIP (??? is version number)
Super Kermit	PCKERM21.ZIP
Kermit	CKERMXXX.ZIP (XXX is release number)

By paying attention to the release date and/or version numbers that are included in the filename, you will know if you have the most recent version of any of these protocol drivers. Since the protocols that are internally supported by each of these communications programs vary, they will be considered when each program is discussed individually. Figure 11-1 shows the menu of commands for Qmodem.

Script Languages

Scripts have become an important part of communications programs, and all programs have their own script languages. The script language used by Procomm is called ASPECT and is copyrighted. All Procomm script files have an extension of .ASP for this reason. Of the seven programs discussed, five have script languages that are in "English." By this I mean that the scripts use easily identifiable words like "send," "waitfor," "exit," and so on, rather than something that looks more like a programming language. These five are Qmodem, Procomm, GT Power Comm, and

Figure 11-1

Qmodem's command menu

```
========================= COMMAND MENU =========================
------------- BEFORE -------------        ------------- TOGGLES -------------
Alt-D  Phone Book       Alt-G  Term Emulation    Alt-0  Session Log
------------- DURING -------------                Alt-1  Backspace DEL/^H
Alt-C  Clear Screen     ^Home  Capture File       Alt-5  Host Mode
Alt-F  Execute Script   ^End   Send BREAK         Alt-8  Hi-Bit Strip
Alt-Q  QuickLearn       PgUp   Upload Files       Alt-9  Printer Echo
Alt-S  Split Screen     PgDn   Download Files     Alt-B  Beeps & Bells
Alt-T  Screen Dump                                Alt-E  Half/Full Duplex
↑      Scroll Back                                Alt-I  Order Information
------------- AFTER -------------                 Alt-M  ANSI Music
Alt-H  Hangup Modem     Alt-X  Exit Qmodem        Alt-U  Scrollback Record
                                                  Alt-Z  XON/XOFF Flow Ctrl
------------- SETUP -------------                 Alt-=  DoorWay Mode
Alt-A  Translate Table  Alt-N  Configuration      Alt--  Status Lines
Alt-J  Function Keys    Alt-P  Change Baud Rate   ShTab  CR/CRLF Mode
Alt-K  Change COM Port                            Alt-2  80x25 (EGA/VGA)
                                                  Alt-4  80x43/50 (EGA/VGA)
------------- DOS -------------                   ------------- COPYRIGHT -------------
Alt-L  Change Drive     Alt-V  View/Edit File     The Forbin Project, Inc.
Alt-O  Change Directory Alt-W  List Directory     Post Office Box 702
Alt-R  DOS Shell        Alt-Y  Delete File        Cedar Falls, IA  50613
================ Qmodem SST Version 4.2 BETA  Compiled 03/18/90 ================
        Select a function,  [F1] for Help  -or-  [Esc] to TERMINAL Mode
```

Telemate. The scripts in Telemate are compiled just before they are executed so they run faster, but the script terminology is in "English." In general, many users find these script languages easier to learn and to work with.

The other three programs—Zcomm, Telix, and Boyan—use script languages that are a little different. Because they are different, let's take a brief look at how they differ from the script languages based on readily identifiable words. Figure 11-2 is a display of the menu of commands for GT Power Comm.

Telix's SALT Language

The Telix script language is called SALT. To the casual observer it looks very much like the C programming language. The Telix script language is very powerful and extremely flexible. Telix scripts are also compiled before execution, which means that the elements of the script are manipulated into an executable form. You might imagine it like this: If you write a program in BASIC, you run it with the BASIC interpreter that comes with DOS. Because the program has to be run through the interpreter, it

Figure 11-2

Menu of commands for GT Power Comm

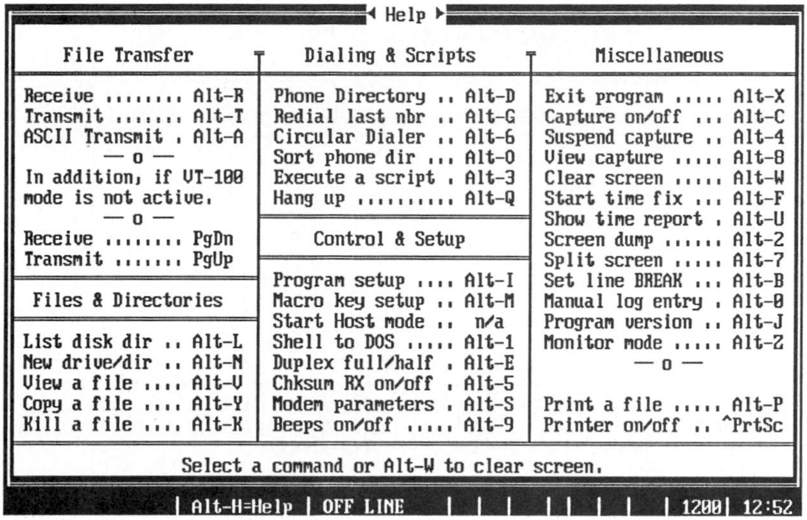

```
◀ Help ▶
┌─────────────────────────────────────────────────────────────────┐
│    File Transfer    ┬   Dialing & Scripts   ┬     Miscellaneous   │
├─────────────────────┼───────────────────────┼─────────────────────┤
│ Receive ........ Alt-R │ Phone Directory .. Alt-D │ Exit program ..... Alt-X │
│ Transmit ....... Alt-T │ Redial last nbr .. Alt-G │ Capture on/off ... Alt-C │
│ ASCII Transmit . Alt-A │ Circular Dialer .. Alt-6 │ Suspend capture .. Alt-4 │
│        — o —           │ Sort phone dir ... Alt-O │ View capture ..... Alt-8 │
│ In addition, if VT-100 │ Execute a script . Alt-3 │ Clear screen ..... Alt-W │
│ mode is not active,    │ Hang up .......... Alt-Q │ Start time fix ... Alt-F │
│        — o —           │                          │ Show time report . Alt-U │
│ Receive ........ PgDn  │    Control & Setup       │ Screen dump ...... Alt-2 │
│ Transmit ....... PgUp  │                          │ Split screen ..... Alt-7 │
│                        │ Program setup .... Alt-I │ Set line BREAK ... Alt-B │
│   Files & Directories  │ Macro key setup .. Alt-M │ Manual log entry . Alt-8 │
│                        │ Start Host mode ..  n/a  │ Program version .. Alt-J │
│ List disk dir .. Alt-L │ Shell to DOS ..... Alt-1 │ Monitor mode ..... Alt-Z │
│ New drive/dir .. Alt-N │ Duplex full/half . Alt-E │        — o —           │
│ View a file .... Alt-V │ Chksum RX on/off . Alt-5 │                          │
│ Copy a file .... Alt-Y │ Modem parameters . Alt-S │ Print a file ..... Alt-P │
│ Kill a file .... Alt-K │ Beeps on/off ..... Alt-9 │ Printer on/off .. ^PrtSc │
├────────────────────────────────────────────────────────────────┤
│          Select a command or Alt-W to clear screen.             │
├────────────────────────────────────────────────────────────────┤
│ Alt-H=Help │ OFF LINE   │ │ │  │ │ │  │ 1200│ 12:52 │
└────────────────────────────────────────────────────────────────┘
```

runs at a given speed. If you take the same BASIC program and compile it using a BASIC compiler, the program can run many times faster. Why? Because the essence of the program, the actual commands, have been compiled down into a more readily usable form.

The same process happens with Telix script files. They are written and then compiled so that Telix can execute them faster. Some people have a problem with the programming-oriented SALT language. The author of Telix is currently working on a script generator for the SALT language. Figure 11-3 shows you the command menu for Telix.

The Zcomm Script Language

Similar to the script language in Telix, the language used by Zcomm is closer to a programming language than it is to plain English. Zcomm is a powerful communications program with a powerful script language. Zcomm does, however, come with a built-in "TurboLearn" script generator. Using the TurboLearn function, you can automatically create logon scripts with Zcomm. If you want to get into scripts that do conditional branching and other more complex functions, however, you will need to

---

Figure 11-3

Command menu for Telix

```
                  Telix v3.12 Command Summary

             Main Functions                    Other functions

Dialing directory..Alt-D  Queue Redial #s....Alt-Q   Local echo........Alt-E
Send files.........Alt-S  Receive files......Alt-R   DOS command.......Alt-V
Exit Telix.........Alt-X  Run script (Go)....Alt-G   Run editor........Alt-A
Comm Parameters....Alt-P  cOnfigure Telix....Alt-O   Screen Image......Alt-I
Key defs./macros...Alt-K  Terminal emulation.Alt-T   Printer on/off...Ctrl-@
Capture on/off.....Alt-L  Scroll Back........Alt-B   Chat Mode.........Alt-Y
DOS Functions......Alt-F  Jump to DOS shell..Alt-J   Translate Table...Alt-W
Hang-up modem......Alt-H  Clear screen.......Alt-C   Add LF on/off.....S-Tab
Usage Log on/off...Alt-U  Misc. functions....Alt-M   Send BREAK........C-End
                                                     DOORWAY mode......Alt-=

        Select function or press Enter for none.

Copyright 1986-89 by Exis Inc., P.O. Box 130, West Hill, ON  CANADA  M1E 4R4

   Time .. 12:54:05   Online .... No    │  Capture ... Off
   Date .. 03-19-90                     │  Printer ... Off
   Baud .. 38400      Terminal .. ANSI-BBS │ Script ....
   Comm .. N,8,1      Port ...... COM1   │  Reg. Key .. TELIX.KEY
   Echo .. Off        Add LF .... Off    │  Dial Dir .. TELIX.FON
```

---

study Zcomm's script language. I used Zcomm for over a year and found that the scripts created with the TurboLearn script generator were more than adequate for my needs.

The Boyan Script Language

The script language found in the Boyan communications program is unique among script languages. It is not written in plain English nor is it similar to a programming language. Rather, the Boyan script language is based on macros. There are many regular macros that you can define, as you can with all of the other programs in this chapter, but the script language macros are predefined within Boyan. For example, use the macro command \ME, which looks like this,

```
\ME"Calling GEnie To Check For Mail"
```

to put the following message on the screen:

```
Calling GEnie To Check For Mail
```

The macro language of Boyan is extensive and handles everything from communications parameters to downloading. The macros can even accept variables for use in other places in a script. Some Boyan macro commands can execute other macro commands. Thus, the Boyan macro script language is comprehensive and quite versatile. It is unlike many others because of the way it is structured. Figure 11-4 shows Boyan's command menu.

Programs with Script Generators

Six of the seven communications programs discussed have script generating functions. Generally, these script generators all work in the same manner. The script generator in Boyan, however, is different in that it works out of the *scroll-back buffer* (a way to capture information). In principle, Boyan's script generator accomplishes the same goal as the others. How do script generators work? You start the Learn function and begin calling an online system. The script generator monitors everything

---

Figure 11-4

Boyan's command menu

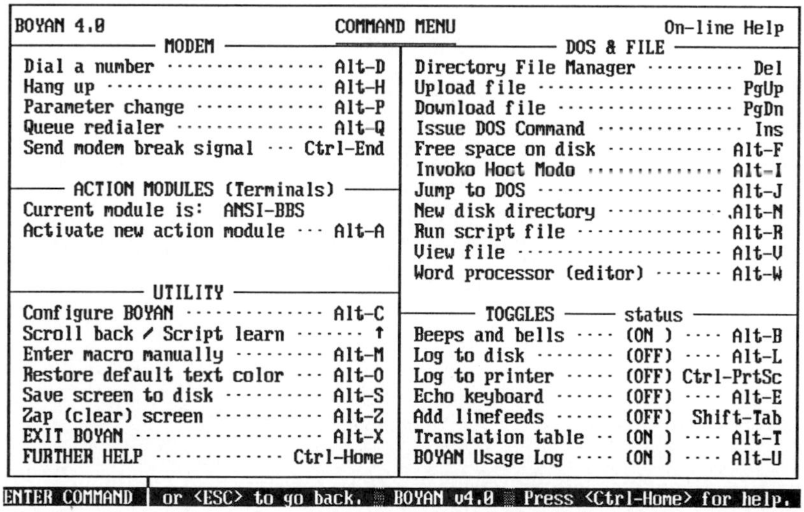

```
BOYAN 4.0              COMMAND MENU              On-line Help
———— MODEM ————              ———— DOS & FILE ————
Dial a number ··············· Alt-D   Directory File Manager ·········· Del
Hang up ····················· Alt-H   Upload file ···················· PgUp
Parameter change ············ Alt-P   Download file ·················· PgDn
Queue redialer ·············· Alt-Q   Issue DOS Command ··············· Ins
Send modem break signal ··· Ctrl-End  Free space on disk ············ Alt-F
                                      Invoke Host Mode ·············· Alt-I
———— ACTION MODULES (Terminals) ————  Jump to DOS ··················· Alt-J
Current module is:  ANSI-BBS          New disk directory ············.Alt-N
Activate new action module ··· Alt-A  Run script file ··············· Alt-R
                                      View file ····················· Alt-V
                                      Word processor (editor) ······· Alt-W
———————— UTILITY ————————
Configure BOYAN ············· Alt-C   ———— TOGGLES ———— status
Scroll back / Script learn ········ ↑  Beeps and bells ···· (ON )  ···· Alt-B
Enter macro manually ········ Alt-M   Log to disk ········ (OFF)  ···· Alt-L
Restore default text color ··· Alt-O  Log to printer ····· (OFF) Ctrl-PrtSc
Save screen to disk ········· Alt-S   Echo keyboard ······ (OFF)  ···· Alt-E
Zap (clear) screen ·········· Alt-Z   Add linefeeds ······ (OFF)  Shift-Tab
EXIT BOYAN ·················· Alt-X   Translation table ·· (ON )  ···· Alt-T
FURTHER HELP ············· Ctrl-Home  BOYAN Usage Log ···· (ON )  ···· Alt-U

ENTER COMMAND | or <ESC> to go back.  BOYAN v4.0  Press <Ctrl-Home> for help.
```

that occurs. This includes all prompts from the system and your responses to them. When you are finished, a script is created for you.

It should be mentioned that since these script generators monitor everything that occurs, it is always wise to bring them up in an editor and look at them. You may find that a burst of line noise was intercepted. If this is the case, it could stop the script from working properly. At the same time, you should be aware that the script generators will pick up ANSI escape codes found on bulletin boards with color graphics. These codes should be left in the script, even if they look like garbage characters to you, because that is what the script generator "saw" and that is what it will be looking for the next time. Here is a line captured by Qmodem's QuickLearn function while logging onto a Wildcat! BBS with ANSI graphics enabled.

```
Waitfor  "[0;1;33;40m]NonStop: ^[[0;1;33;40m"
```

ANSI sequences like "[0;1;33;40m]" display the "NonStop" prompt in bright yellow. This is what the QuickLearn function picked up, and this is what the resulting script will expect to see when it is used. Other ANSI sequences will have a similar format, even though the numbers involved may vary, depending on what color is being displayed. Leave these things in the script that was created. Qmodem, Procomm, Telemate, Boyan, and Zcomm all have script generating functions that can greatly simplify things for you. Figure 11-5 shows the menu of commands used by Procomm 2.4.3.

Information Gathering Capabilities

Other features that all of these communications programs have in common include

- Capture logs
- Screen dumps
- Scroll-back buffers

All of these features allow you to gather information while you are online. Capture logs, screen dumps, and scroll-back buffers are used to

DOCTOR'S NOTE

Something you should know about the scripts created by some script generators is that short "wait" periods are automatically installed. Let's use Qmodem and Procomm as examples. In a script created by Procomm's script generator, there will be a "PAUSE 1" between every line. With Qmodem's QuickLearn script generator, a "Delay 100" is put between every line. For example, in a logon script created by QuickLearn you would see this:

```
Waitfor "Password:"
Delay 100
Send "Yipeee^M"
```

A script created with Procomm would look similar except that "Delay 100" would be replaced with "PAUSE 1." It has been my experience, after much experimentation, that automatically generated waits aren't really necessary. If they are, I haven't found a machine speed that requires them. I've tested this theory out on a 4.77 MHz machine, a Tandy 1000 SX running at 7 MHz, a GRiD 386 laptop at 12.5 MHz, and the Northgate 386 20 MHz, and the lack of a delay or pause does not make a difference. If anything, the scripts run faster than before and just as accurately.

For years I've always removed these waits that are inserted by script generators without any problems. Keep in mind that this is simply an observation and not a criticism of the script generators themselves. :) When you look at a newly generated script with an editor, you may want to remove these extra waits while you are looking the file over. A "PAUSE 1" 60 times is equal to a minute. When you're online a minute costs you money, so why wait if you don't have to?

capture information in a variety of ways so you can review it when you are offline. Each of the programs discussed here handles these functions a little differently and the same function may be called by different names. Because of this, I will describe each program's capture functions separately. Figure 11-6 shows a menu that was devised for Zcomm by a Zcomm user. It is now bundled with the product.

GT Power Comm 15.1 — Capture Features

GT Power Comm, by Paul Meiners and P&M Software, combines the functions of a capture log and a scroll-back buffer. That is to say that in its

---

Figure 11-5

Menu of commands for Procomm 2.4.3

```
╔══════════════════════════════════════════════════════════════════╗
║                       P r o C o m m    H e l p                     ║
╟────────────────────────────────────────────────────────────────────╢
║                                                                     
║     MAJOR FUNCTIONS        UTILITY FUNCTIONS        FILE FUNCTIONS  
║                                                                     
║   Dialing Directory . Alt-D   Program Info ...... Alt-I   Send files ...... PgUp
║   Automatic Redial... Alt-R   Setup Screen ...... Alt-S   Receive files ... PgDn
║   Keyboard Macros ... Alt-M   Kermit Server Cmd . Alt-K   Directory ...... Alt-F
║   Line Settings ..... Alt-P   Change Directory .. Alt-B   View a File .... Alt-V
║   Translate Table ... Alt-W   Clear Screen ...... Alt-C   Screen Dump .... Alt-G
║   Editor ............ Alt-A   Toggle Duplex ..... Alt-E   Log Toggle .... Alt-F1
║   Exit .............. Alt-X   Hang Up Phone ..... Alt-H   Log Hold ...... Alt-F2
║   Host Mode ......... Alt-Q   Elapsed Time ...... Alt-T
║   Chat Mode ......... Alt-O   Print On/Off ...... Alt-L
║   DOS Gateway ...... Alt-F4   Set Colors ........ Alt-Z
║   Command Files .... Alt-F5   Auto Answer ....... Alt-Y
║   Redisplay ........ Alt-F6   Toggle CR-CR/LF .. Alt-F3
║                               Break Key ........ Alt-F7
╚══════════════════════════════════════════════════════════════════╝
```

DATASTORM TECHNOLOGIES, INC.

Figure 11-6

Sample menu created for Zcomm

```
          >>> ZComm Function Key Menu <<<

Alt-N  EMERGENCY EXIT, 'Nuke It' to get out of trouble/escape a command

   F1  Exit Circular Buffer          F2  Enter Circular Buffer
   F3  OPEN Capture file             F4  Send ASCII Text
   F5  Send Kermit Upload            F6  Send Zmodem Upload      <<BEST>>
   F7  Receive CrcXmodem Download    F8  Send CrcXmodem Upload
   F9  Press for THIS HELP SCREEN    F10  Flashup Help Processor
   Alt-1  Get DOS Command prompt     Alt-2  Get ZCOMM Command prompt

   sF3  Show some ZComm color choices  sF4  Use Turbolearn Script Writer
   sF5  Search for dialing entry       sF6  <not defined>

   aF1  AutoLog APCO´ (300 baud)       aF2  AutoLog APCO (1200 baud)
   aF3  CLOSE Capture file             aF4  CIS DEMO at 1200 baud
   aF5  Call PC Magazine's BBS         aF6  Enter HOST MODE operation
   aF7  Sign name on-line              ALT-F9  Edit PHODIR.T SCRIPT

        TO CALL OTHER BBSs: enter 'call name' where name is a label

   Stop Redialing ---- press <CR>     Hangup w/o pgm exit - enter 'bye'
   PgUp into Buffer; <CR> to return    -> EXIT hit F1 then -- enter 'off'
   (F9=Menu) d:/zcomm->
```

natural state, there is no scroll-back unless you open up a *capture file*. Once you've initiated the capture, you can look at what's currently stored in it. GT's combination scroll-back/capture file lets you search for text strings. This is a handy feature if you are trying to find a particular piece of data.

When you finish your session, you can close the capture file. At that time you are prompted if you want to save the contents or not. If you want to save the contents, give the file a name and it will be saved to disk for your later review. If not, the capture file, and hence the scroll-back, will be deleted. The size of the capture buffer is determined by the user.

Qmodem 4.2 — Several Ways to Capture Data

Qmodem 4.2 by John Friel and his company, The Forbin Project, offers all three information-gathering functions. As mentioned earlier, you can open a capture log and let it have a default name, for example CAPTURE .LOG, or you can give each one a unique name. When you are finished, you can simply close the capture file and save it to disk. If, at a later time, you open a capture file and use the same name as an existing capture file on disk, Qmodem will automatically append any new data to the end of the existing file.

For those times when you only have one screen full of data that you want to capture to a file, Qmodem also offers a screen dump command. As with the capture log feature, the screen dump can have a default filename or you can name each one separately. This feature is particularly handy for capturing a note or message off the screen. It's also very fast and quite efficient.

Qmodem also has a scroll-back buffer and you can configure its size. For example, I have mine set to hold 1,500 lines. That is a lot of data that you can look back at while you are online. While in Qmodem's scroll-back buffer you have two options available to you. You can clear the buffer and start fresh, or you can save the entire contents of the buffer to a file on disk. In many cases you could automatically use just the scroll-back buffer to save the contents of an online session without having to open up a capture log. All you have to do is remember to save the contents of the scroll-back buffer before you exit the program, while the data you want is still in it.

In addition, Qmodem also has a *session log* that you can toggle off and on. This log keeps track of each call you make, the time it started, file transfers you make, the number you called, and so on. While this log does not track things that you *see* online, it does track everything that you *do* online.

Procomm 2.4.3 — Capture Functions

Procomm, by Datastorm Technologies, has a capture log facility that lets you capture incoming data and save it to disk. There is also a function that allows you to put the current capture file on hold. When you are ready, you can take off the hold and the capture continues. This is just like closing the file, reopening it, and appending new data to the end. Procomm offers a screen dump feature whereby you can dump the contents of one screen to a file on disk. Procomm also has a scroll-back buffer that allows you to view information that has scrolled off the screen.

Zcomm Capture Abilities

Zcomm, by Chuck Forsberg and Omen Technologies, captures data and allows you to bring it up later for review. If you want to start fresh, you can have Zcomm "rewind" the capture buffer to the beginning. The data contained in the capture area can also be saved to a disk file.

Boyan's Capture Functions

The Boyan communications program, written by Justin Boyan, has several means of capturing data. There is a capture log you can open and label with a filename. Boyan has a screen dump feature as well, which is good for getting one screen of data. The scroll-back feature in Boyan has some interesting features. For one, you can go into the scroll-back buffer and mark a region of text. You can send this region to the printer or to a file. As was mentioned, the scroll-back buffer is also the place where Boyan generates logon scripts.

Capture Abilities of Telix

Telix has a scroll-back buffer and a capture log. The size of the scroll-back buffer is configurable. For example, you can set it to capture 50K of data. While you are in the scroll-back buffer you can search for text. You can also save an image of what is in the buffer, but only the part that you can see. This, in effect, is the same as a screen dump. You can open up a capture log in Telix and give it a unique name. If you like, you configure it so the log is opened each time you load the program.

Telemate 2.0 — Capture Functions

Telemate is a relative newcomer to the Shareware scene and already it has made an impression on users because of its many interesting features. (Figure 11-7 shows Telemate's command menu.) Like the others, Telemate gives you the ability to open up a capture log and give it a unique name. What is really spectacular about Telemate, however, are the functions of its scroll-back buffer.

As with Qmodem, you define the number of lines Telemate's scroll-back will have. Like GT Power Comm, Telemate lets you search for data in the scroll-back buffer. At the same time, like Boyan, Telemate lets you mark blocks of text within the scroll-back buffer. Thus, Telemate's scroll-back buffer gives you the configurability of Qmodem, the search capability

---

Figure 11-7

Command menu of Telemate

```
≡  Window  Dial  Terminal  Edit  View  Back  Macro  Options          1:17:55pm
┌──────────────────────────────── Help ────────────────────────────────┐
│     Line 202   Col 1   Total 502              TM.HLP             HELP  █
│  Terminal                                                             ║
│  ────────                                                             ║
│                                                                       ║
│  Send (upload) files to remote system  . . . . . . . . . . . . [PgUp] ║
│  Receive (download) files from remote system . . . . . . . . . [PgDn] ║
│  Capture received text to log file  . . . . . . . . . . . . .  [Alt L]║
│  Execute script file . . . . . . . . . . . . . . . . . . . . . [Alt S]║
│  Learn script file . . . . . . . . . . . . . . . . . . . . . . [Alt N]║
│  Paste text from clipboard . . . . . . . . . . . . . . . . . . [Alt P]║
│  Quote text from clipboard . . . . . . . . . . . . . . . . . . [Alt Q]║
│  Copy the content of terminal to image file  . . . . . . . . . [Alt I]║
│  Chat mode . . . . . . . . . . . . . . . . . . . . . . . . . . [Alt C]║
│  Originate mode  . . . . . . . . . . . . . . . . . . . . . . . [Alt G]║
│  Answer mode . . . . . . . . . . . . . . . . . . . . . . . . . [Alt A]║
│  Hang up phone . . . . . . . . . . . . . . . . . . . . . . . . [Alt H]█
├─────────────────────────────── Status ───────────────────────────────┤
│   Name:                                  Script: Off                  │
│   Memo:                                File Log: Off                  │
│   Alarm:                             Printer Log: Off                  │
│   Port: COM1                     Date:  3-19-1990    Online: 00:00:00  │
│   Para: 38400N81, ANSI           Time:  1:17:55pm   Offline: 00:00:34  │
└───────────────────────────────────────────────────────────────────────┘
```

of GT Power Comm, and the marking functions found in Boyan, plus much more. The blocks that you mark can be sent to a printer or disk, but that's not all. You can mark a block and paste it into Telemate's "clipboard." From there, you can edit it if you like. For answering messages on bulletin boards and commercial online networks, Telemate also has a Quote feature.

Let's say you read a message on a BBS. The message is in the scroll-back buffer. You go in, mark the message, and paste the block into the clipboard or into Telemate's editor. When responding to mail on online systems, a common convention is to quote some lines from the original message so it's easier to know what your message is referring to. Telemate's Quote feature lets you mark the lines you want to quote in the scroll-back buffer. It will automatically put the > sign next to each quoted line. (The > indicates that it is a quote from another message.) You can then either paste the block into the editor or send it right into a message while you are online. These functions make Telemate's scroll-back buffer the most versatile capture feature of all the programs discussed.

Other Common Features

In addition to the features already discussed, such as script languages and capture features, all of the full-featured communications programs share other functions as well. So as not to confuse you with a lot of meaningless commands, I will simply point out the features. In this way you'll know some of the other features that these programs have in common and not be bogged down with commands for all of the programs.

Drop to DOS

Each of the communications programs gives you some way to *shell to DOS* while leaving the connection intact if one exists. This allows you to execute other programs, look for files, move things around, and so on. Of the seven programs, six have a specific key sequence that lets you drop to DOS. Zcomm does not have a predefined command, but you can easily create a macro that performs this function.

Qmodem has the most unique way to drop to DOS because it offers what is called the "Optimum Shell." If you have this feature toggled on in

Qmodem and have expanded memory (EMS), Qmodem itself is swapped to EMS and occupies only 4K of DOS RAM. If you don't have expanded memory, Qmodem will swap out to disk. The net result is that you have all of your DOS RAM available for doing something else, minus just 4K for Qmodem. Since this is a shell to DOS, in all cases you simply type **EXIT** to return to the communications program.

Keyboard Macros

You can define a macro to enter your name, password, or any other string of characters that you type frequently. The macro functions in all of the programs are fairly similar, and they help you save keystrokes when you are online. The nice thing about the macro functions in communications programs is that they:

- Are easy to create

- Execute instantly

- Don't conflict with the program

Conflict with programs is important because some keyboard macro programs, like Newkey and SuperKey, will cause conflicts with communications, especially at high speeds. Thus, you will find the internal keyboard macro functions a very useful feature while you are online.

Colors, Emulations, and More

By now you may have gotten the idea that the best communications programs have many features in common. Perhaps this is what makes them the best—they all have the features that the majority of users want.

In addition to all of the features already mentioned, all seven of the full-featured communications programs share still other features. All of them allow you to configure the colors for use on color monitors. Each program offers a varying range of *terminal emulations,* such as ANSI, VT-52, VT-100, and others. Terminal emulations allow you to emulate other types of keyboards while using the program. This is a handy feature if you have to access mainframe computers. All of the programs give you some way to redial a list of numbers over and over again.

Another common feature is *split-screen mode*, which is used while chatting with others online. If you use one of the CB simulators, like Chat Lines on GEnie, you'll want to use split-screen mode. This keeps the

DOCTOR'S NOTE

I would like to make note of the contributions made by Philip R. Burns, the author of Pibterm. Burns wrote Pibterm in 1983. Pibterm is the only communications program that has always had all of its Turbo Pascal source code released along with it. Burns encouraged others to use his source code and to improve on it, and share those new features with others. Here is a quote from one of the files that comes with Pibterm.

```
"You should distribute the program without any changes you have made,
and then a SEPARATE version with any changes you've made. You should
clearly mark the changes in some sort of documentation file, as well
as in the source files you change.  I also suggest that you add a line
to the initial output of Pibterm indicating your name and the date of
your modification.
```

```
"You may use the source code and modify it as you please for NON-
COMMERCIAL APPLICATIONS ONLY.  You may NOT use the code in developing
commercial applications without my permission. I encourage you to
extend this program and add interesting new features.  I also encour-
age you to upload these changes to your local BBSs in order to share
your work with others.  What I do NOT want is for you to rip off this
code as if it were yours and sell it for a profit.  That's not nice."
```

The source code for the last release of Pibterm can be found under the filenames PIBT41S1.ARC, PIBT41S2.ARC, PIBT41S3.ARC, and PIBT41S4.ARC (file extension may vary). Because of the author's willingness to share his work, many communications programmers gleaned ideas from the source code of Pibterm—ideas for communication routines, window functions, and much more. Since there will be no further releases of Pibterm, I do not discuss the program in this chapter. I did, however, want to acknowledge Burns' contributions. His fine program and his willingness to share his source code have had an impact on the communications programs that we see and use today. His efforts give real meaning to the "share" in Shareware.

text you are entering in a window on the bottom and all the input from the remote side in a window at the top. In this way, what you are writing never gets wiped away by incoming data sent by someone else. Having looked at some of the major functions shared by all of these excellent communications programs, let's take a look at them individually and see the unique features each has to offer.

QMODEM 4.2–PACKED WITH FEATURES

Qmodem 4.2 is a dynamic communications program that has all of the features and functions that you'd want for going online. John Friel is dedicated to not only giving Qmodem the capabilities that users want, but to making those capabilities the best they can be. He will fine-tune a file transfer protocol to get just 10 cps more out of it. Over the course of the last year, many new and innovative things have been added to Qmodem and more will be added in the very near future. Let's take a look at some of the things that make Qmodem stand apart from other communications programs.

Maximum Configurability

Qmodem's configuration program is separate from the rest of the program. This gives you the flexibility to make changes quickly. Using the configuration portion of Qmodem, you can set the colors you want, the modem parameters, the default names for capture, screen dump, and scroll-back files, parameters for Host Mode, and much more. Figure 11-8 shows the main configuration menu of Qmodem, with the Toggles menu pulled down.

Because of its flexibility, Qmodem can easily be configured to fit a wide range of hardware setups. Whether you have an XT with a 1200 baud modem or a 386 and a U.S. Robotics Dual Standard, Qmodem can be configured so that it runs at maximum efficiency on your system. If you have EMS, Qmodem can use its overlay file, but it doesn't have to if you don't want it to. A truly unique feature in Qmodem is its *modem configuration* abilities.

Modem Configuration

Many users have problems setting up their modem to run correctly with a communications program. How should the DIP switches be set? What

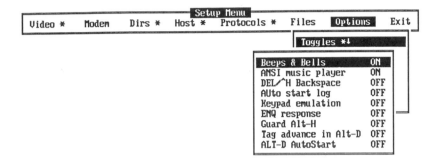

Figure 11-8

Qmodem configuration menu with Toggles pulled down

commands should go in the modem initialization string? Using Qmodem's Quick Modem Configuration option, Qmodem will set up your modem for you. Figure 11-9 shows the first part of Qmodem's Quick Modem Configuration function.

You can scroll through the list of modems and find the type you have, or one that is very much like it. When you select a modem, Qmodem automatically shows you how the DIP switches should be set. If commands can be saved to NRAM (non-volatile RAM), such as with many MNP modems, Qmodem will send the appropriate commands to the modem and write them to the modem's memory. Qmodem guides you through the modem installation and sets it up correctly.

Qmodem's Transfer Protocols

As noted earlier, Qmodem, like the other communications programs, comes with certain transfer protocols that are internal. Qmodem offers the following internal protocols:

- ASCII

- Xmodem

- Xmodem CRC

- Xmodem Relaxed

- Xmodem-1K

- Ymodem Batch

- Zmodem Batch

If you have an MNP modem you also have

- 1K-Xmodem/G

- Ymodem-G Batch

The internal protocols that come with Qmodem are all very solid and function at their maximum capabilities. The internal Zmodem is the best I

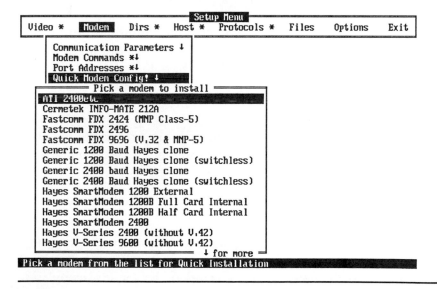

Figure 11-9

Qmodem's Modem Configuration function

have tested, even when compared to Zmodem powered by DSZ. In addition to this range of internal protocols, Qmodem also allows you to add up to ten external file transfer protocols, such as BiModem, MPt, SEAlink, Jmodem, and others. You can also use these external protocol "slots" to run other programs from within Qmodem. So, when it comes to file transfer protocols, Qmodem has you covered with a fine selection of internal protocols and the ability to add the external protocols of your choice. Now, when it comes to doing batch uploads, Qmodem really does have a unique feature.

Qmodem's Batch Entry Window

In general, communications programs let you set one default upload directory. When you go to do an upload, you are presented with a small window where you can enter perhaps four filenames. This poses a problem if you want to use Zmodem, for example, to do a batch upload of, say, 40 files. Qmodem 4.2 has eliminated this problem. When you are going to do an upload using any of the batch protocols, you are presented with Qmodem's Batch Entry window or BEW. Figure 11-10 shows what this window looks like with some sample filenames entered.

Note that the first section uses your standard default upload directory, which in my case is C:\DNLD. In this area alone, you can enter 24 filenames to upload. If a file does not exist, Qmodem lets you know. In addition, the next two levels let you specify other directories from which to upload files. When you've selected a directory, you can press F2, and you will see a listing of that directory. All you have to do is move through the directory listing and pick the files you want to upload.

What proves to be a real time and money saver is that you can prepare this screen while you are offline and save it. When you go online to do your batch upload, the instant you go to start the upload, the window appears exactly as you created it. All you have to do to start the upload is hit F10. When you are finished, you can press F4 to clear your BEW.

Constantly Improving

Qmodem is a communications program that is constantly improving. Features like the built-in modem configuration, the BEW, and the extremely flexible configuration menu are just a few of the many new

Figure 11-10

Qmodem's Batch Entry window

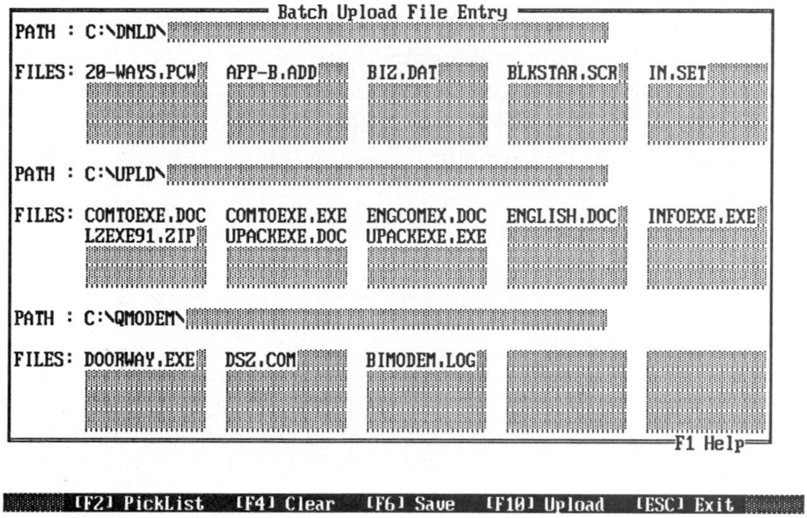

```
═══════════════════════════ Batch Upload File Entry ═══════════════════
PATH : C:\DNLD\
FILES: 20-WAYS.PCW    APP-B.ADD    BIZ.DAT     BLKSTAR.SCR   IN.SET




PATH : C:\UPLD\
FILES: COMTOEXE.DOC   COMTOEXE.EXE ENGCOMEX.DOC ENGLISH.DOC  INFOEXE.EXE
       LZEXE91.ZIP    UPACKEXE.DOC UPACKEXE.EXE



PATH : C:\QMODEM\
FILES: DOORWAY.EXE    DSZ.COM      BIMODEM.LOG



                                                           ─F1 Help─
    [F2] PickList   [F4] Clear   [F6] Save   [F10] Upload   [ESC] Exit
```

features that have been added to Qmodem. Some others include: the ability to add a personal note to each dialing directory entry; the ability to edit a script file from the dialing directory; recognition of the 16550A UART, a FIFO (first in first out) buffer, and recognition of the enhanced keyboard.

Qmodem 4.2—Just for You

A copy of the basic Qmodem 4.2 files is on the disks you can have by mailing the coupon at the back of this book. Normally, Qmodem comes packed in five different files. The files include the documentation, sample scripts, and much more. You'll receive the full version of Qmodem 4.2, its online help, and the modem configuration. To take full advantage of all Qmodem's features, get the other files that normally come with it.

When you load Qmodem, it creates a phone directory file. The first time you load Qmodem, take a look in the dialing directory. You'll find that it already includes the names and phone numbers of all of the

Qmodem distribution sites located around the country. All of these systems will have the current release of Qmodem and its associated files. You may, however, want to change the baud rate to the one in use on your system. If you want to edit any of the dialing directory entries—for example, to change the baud rate—just highlight the entry you want to change and use CTRL-R. You can make your changes, and then press F10 to save them. If you have any questions about Qmodem, don't hesitate to send me a message, either on The Forbin Project bulletin board, or on one of the boards indicated in Appendix C.

John Friel
The Forbin Project
P.O. Box 702
Cedar Falls, IA 50613
319-232-4516
319-233-6157 (BBS)
$50 registration, disks, and manual; VISA/MasterCard accepted

PROCOMM 2.4.3—THE SHAREWARE VERSION

Procomm 2.4.3 is distributed by Datastorm Technologies and is a fine communications program. The authors, Tom Smith and Bruce Barkelew, have brought Procomm up from a basic communications program to one that is top-notch. In March 1990, Datastorm Technologies established its own support forum on CompuServe. There are now actually two distinct versions of Procomm that you can find in The Wires. To avoid confusion, let me explain briefly.

At one time, Procomm was strictly a Shareware product and could only be found on bulletin boards, commercial networks, and through PC user groups and disk vendors. With the release of Procomm Plus, the program became "commercial" in the sense that Procomm Plus can now be found in stores. Procomm Plus is not available through normal Shareware channels. Procomm 2.4.3 is, and it's an excellent communications program. You can also find a version of what is called Procomm Plus Test Drive on bulletin boards and commercial networks. This is a version of Procomm Plus that will let you see some of its features, but since there is no real documentation, you are for the most part on your own.

In keeping with the theme of this book, you will examine Procomm 2.4.3, which is the true Shareware version of Procomm. Thus, you can try out Procomm 2.4.3, and if you like it, you can get Procomm Plus either directly from Datastorm or from your local software store. Let's take a look at some of the things that Procomm 2.4.3 offers. From this point on, I'll simply refer to it as "Procomm" and leave off the 2.4.3.

Procomm's Transfer Protocols

Procomm has a moderate range of internal file transfer protocols. Some of the ones that are included were not discussed in Chapter 7 "Protocols. " I will discuss them briefly in a moment, but first, here is the listing of the protocols that are available.

- Xmodem

- Kermit

- Telink

- Modem7

- Ymodem

- Ymodem Batch

- ASCII

- CompuServe Quick-B

- Wxmodem

- Ymodem-G

- Ymodem-G Batch

Modem7 and Telink are older protocols and are simply variations of Xmodem. Telink is a batch protocol and is found primarily on FIDO bulletin board systems. Wxmodem is *Windowed Xmodem,* which is also a variation on Xmodem. Using a windowing technique, similar to that used in Super Kermit, Wxmodem gives you faster transfers than does Xmodem.

Wxmodem can be found on some bulletin boards, often on Wildcat! and RBBS systems. Note that Procomm has the CompuServe Quick-B protocol built in and also offers two G protocols for those with high-speed MNP modems.

Procomm's CompuServe Quick-B protocol detects when you start a file transfer on CompuServe and automatically starts the transfer for you. The Kermit implementation in Procomm is unusual. You may recall that there are two variations of Kermit: the regular Kermit protocol, which is slower than Xmodem, and the Super Kermit version, which is two to three times faster. Procomm gives you both in one selection. If you are on a system that only offers the regular Kermit and you select that for a file transfer, Procomm will use regular Kermit. However, if the system offers the faster Super Kermit variety, Procomm will detect it and will automatically switch into Super Kermit mode. This list of protocols will serve you well on virtually any system you might want to call. What about adding external protocols? There is a way to add them.

Adding External Protocols

By default, Procomm uses ALT-A as the editor key—a holdover from when there were no streaming protocols like Zmodem, MPt, and BiModem. ALT-A was used so you could attach your favorite editor and use it while Procomm was loaded. However, you can use ALT-A to run any program.

For adding external protocols to Procomm, I would recommend the excellent Power Node by Jimmy Pearson and the Byte Brothers. Power Node will let you add Zmodem, BiModem, Jmodem, and other streaming protocols to Procomm's arsenal. The latest version of Power Node, at this writing, is version J and it can be found online as BBPOWERJ.ZIP. Once you have Power Node, you can add it to Procomm as the editor and you'll have all of the flexibility you need for doing file transfers.

Procomm's Command Files

Earlier, I mentioned that the script language for Procomm, called ASPECT, is copyrighted. To be more precise, the ASPECT script language was copyrighted for Procomm Plus and the script files all have filename extensions of .ASP. Prior to Procomm Plus, as in Procomm 2.4.3, the files that created scripts were called "command files," and they have a file-name extension of .CMD. An interesting feature in Procomm is that you can bring up a screen that shows all of your .CMD files. You can then use the cursor keys to move to the one you want, or type in a command filename in a separate window. Figure 11-11 shows what this looks like in Procomm.

As you can see, this makes it easy to find the exact script that you are looking for, and then execute it. While the script language used in Procomm is very good, the ASPECT language used in Procomm Plus is much more powerful and greatly increases your capabilities.

The Setup Menu

Procomm has a Setup menu where you can configure the program to use your selected defaults. You can access this menu in Procomm by using

---
Figure 11-11

Procomm's Command File windows

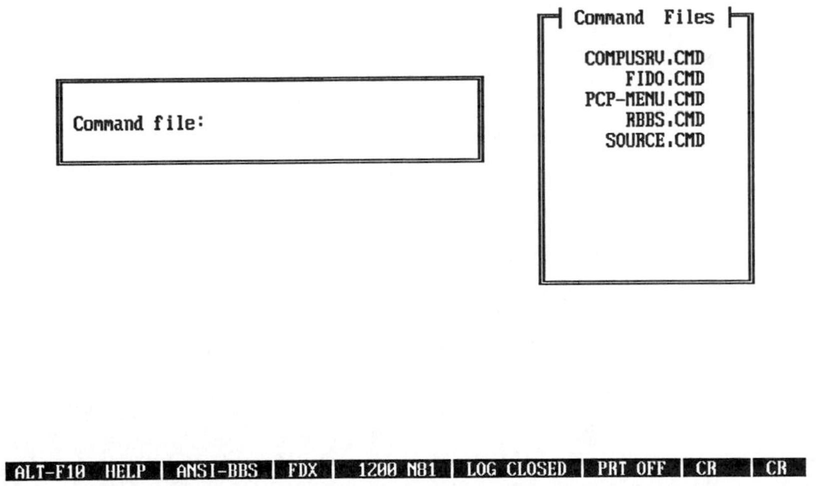

```
                                        ┌─┤ Command  Files ├─┐
                                        │                    │
                                        │  COMPUSRV.CMD      │
                                        │     FIDO.CMD       │
                                        │  PCP-MENU.CMD      │
 ┌──────────────────────────────┐       │     RBBS.CMD       │
 │                              │       │   SOURCE.CMD       │
 │ Command file:                │       │                    │
 │                              │       │                    │
 └──────────────────────────────┘       │                    │
                                        │                    │
                                        │                    │
                                        └────────────────────┘
```

```
 ALT-F10  HELP │ ANSI-BBS │ FDX │ 1200 N81 │ LOG CLOSED │ PRT OFF │ CR │  CR
```

ALT-S. The colors used throughout the program can be set by you from a separate configuration, accessed by using ALT-Z. The Setup menu allows you to set things such as a default download directory, modem parameters, default names for capture logs, and much more. Figure 11-12 shows the opening screen of Procomm's Setup menu.

You'll note that there are selections for "KERMIT SETUP" and "ASCII TRANSFER SETUP." The Kermit area is used to alter certain parameters used by the Kermit protocol. In normal use, you will not need to alter anything in this area. The same holds true for the menu selection for ASCII. Using this area, you could reconfigure the parameters used for doing ASCII uploads and downloads. Once again, the default parameters are adequate for most uses. When you use the Setup menu, make sure you save it before you exit. If you forget and exit without saving your changes, the changes will be lost. The Setup menu in Procomm Plus is quite similar, but has more options. Procomm Plus, for example, allows you to add external protocols.

Figure 11-12

Procomm's Setup menu

---| SETUP MENU |---

1) MODEM SETUP

2) TERMINAL SETUP

3) KERMIT SETUP

4) GENERAL SETUP

5) HOST MODE SETUP

6) ASCII TRANSFER SETUP

S) SAVE SETUP TO DISK

OPTION ➞   ESC▶ Exit

Procomm 2.4.3 Overview

Procomm is a full-featured communications program with all of the basic features that you need to go online effectively. It does not, however, have all of the extras that come with Procomm Plus. To quote a portion of the opening screen that is displayed when Procomm 2.4.3 is loaded

```
PROCOMM PLUS takes all of the features of Procomm and adds a greatly
expanded script language, additional terminal emulations, more file trans-
fer protocols, expanded "point and shoot" dialing directories, keyboard
re-mapping, user setable COM ports, enhanced Host Mode with electronic
mail, context sensitive help, 375 page manual, voice technical support, and
much more.
```

If you are new to telecommunications, you may be content with Procomm 2.4.3; it has all the things you need. If you are so inclined, you might want to take a look at the "test drive" version of Procomm Plus. This will give you a better idea of what is contained in the commercial version of Procomm and allow you to make an informed decision. Procomm is a well-established communications program that has stood the test of time and has received an Editor's Choice award from *PC Magazine.*

Tom Smith and Bruce Barkelew
Datastorm Technologies
P.O. Box 1471
Columbia, MO 65205
314-474-8461
$75 registration for disks, manual, and voice support; also available at various software stores

ZCOMM—POWER ORIENTED

Zcomm is a product of Omen Technology and Chuck Forsberg. Unlike all of the other programs discussed here, Zcomm does not have colorful, pop-up menus—it has no menus at all. It does support color, EGA, and VGA graphics adapters. Some Zcomm users have written menu scripts that can be run with the program and some of these are included with the latest releases of Zcomm. Zcomm's focus is on power and it is the baby brother of Professional YAM (Pro-YAM). Pro-YAM is even more powerful than Zcomm. Let's take a brief overview of what Zcomm can do.

Underneath the Hood

At first glance, if you look at Zcomm's almost blank screen, you might think that Zcomm is a simple program. Nothing could be further from the truth. Behind that deceiving screen—underneath the hood, if you will—is a powerful communications engine with many built-in features. Zcomm's own documentation says, "If you want a flashy program, you've come to the wrong place."

Zcomm's focus is on functions, not flash. Zcomm has an extremely powerful script language. It has file transfer protocols that are built in and are designed to function at maximum capacity. It has its own TurboLearn script generator. It has all of the features that the others do—and that's what's so deceiving about it. It doesn't look like it does.

Zcomm's Protocols

Essentially, Zcomm is controlled by the contents of one file, PHODIR.T. This file holds your dialing directory, protocols, scripts, and much more. Zcomm is the originator of the Auto Zmodem Download. If you are connected to a bulletin board or commercial network and start a Zmodem file transfer, Zcomm will start up the protocol on your side automatically. You don't have to do a thing.

The same is true for the CompuServe Quick-B protocol. It's just there—waiting to start a download if it detects the right signals from the host system. Super Kermit is also built in and automatic. In addition, via macros that are stored in the PHODIR.T file, you can add any of the file transfer protocols supported by DSZ. These include

- Xmodem
- Xmodem CRC
- True Ymodem
- Zmodem
- Ymodem-G
- 1K-Xmodem/G

DOCTOR'S NOTE

I used Zcomm for about a year. I will never forget the first time I was on CompuServe while I was using it. I was still getting the feel of the program and was still a little unsure about some things. I went to start a download from CompuServe and decided that I would figure out how to get the CompuServe Quick-B protocol going when the time came.

I started the transfer and was trying to remember what I had to do to get my side going, when to my amazement, Zcomm started the transfer all by itself. As it turned out, I didn't have to do anything. Zcomm detected the transfer request from CompuServe and just started it up all by itself. That is what I mean by Zcomm being deceiving. It has power, but it isn't found on a menu or a list.

Are the protocols stable? You bet. Remember that Chuck Forsberg invented Ymodem, Zmodem, and the G protocols. You might ask about adding external protocols like BiModem, MPt, Jmodem, and so on. These can be added to Zcomm via a macro that goes to DOS and runs something like Power Node. Zcomm, all by itself, has all of the protocols you need, and you can add others if you wish.

An Overview of Zcomm

Zcomm is particularly appealing to programmers and power users. It has scripts, macros, screen capture, a scroll-back buffer, internal protocols that automatically start, and much more. You can change directories from the command prompt of the program and do it just as if you were in DOS. You can then use the DIR command to see what's in the current directory. When you use DIR, Zcomm automatically estimates the time it would take to send all of the files in that directory—using your currently defined baud rate and Zmodem. Figure 11-13 shows this feature using the C:\UPLD directory as an example.

Do you want to find an estimate of how long it will take to send one file? Just change to the directory you want and type

```
DIR BBPOWERJ.ZIP
```

Figure 11-13

Zcomm directory with transfer time estimate

```
(F9=Menu) c:/upld-> dir
./            ../             comtoexe.doc   comtoexe.exe   engcomex.doc
english.doc   engupack.doc    infoexe.exe    lzexe.doc      lzexe91.zip
readme.eng    upackexe.doc    upackexe.exe
13 Files 88 K  1.7 Minutes Xmsn Time at 38400 Baud
Drive c: has 17547264 Chars Free Current Directory is /UPLD
(F9=Menu) c:/upld->
```

Zcomm will show you a directory listing for just that one file and will also estimate how long it would take to transfer it.

By editing the PHODIR.T file, you configure the way Zcomm sets up your modem, and the parameters for some common modem configurations are included in the file. Scripts can call on subroutines, which make them very flexible. Zcomm has online help that is available at the touch of a key and the help is quite extensive.

A Matter of Taste
Because it is so complex, Zcomm often puzzles both new users and old-timers alike. That's no reason not to give Zcomm a try. As with all software, some people love it while others are awed by it. The thing that I want to make very clear is that Zcomm is an excellent communications tool. It has the basic features that all the others have and several that the others do not have. It simply presents all of these things in an interface unlike that used by the others. If you want a communications program that has menus, bells, and whistles, Zcomm is not for you. On the other hand, if you don't care about or need those things and want a truly powerful communications program, Zcomm is just the thing.

Chuck Forsberg
Omen Technology, Inc.
P.O. Box 4681
Portland, OR 97208
503-621-3746 (BBS)
503-621-3735 (Fax)
$40 registration fee (includes typeset manual and disk; custom three-ring binder $10)

GT POWER COMM

The author of GT Power Comm is Paul Meiners and it is distributed by his company, P&M Software. There are currently two versions of GT Power Comm. One version is a complete terminal program with a superior Host Mode. For those who don't need a Host Mode, there is a second version called GTO, which has the terminal portion only. Depending on what your needs are, you can select the version of GT Power Comm that's right for you. Loaded with features, GT Power Comm will serve you well in carrying out your online business. First, let's take a look at its array of file transfer protocols.

GT's Transfer Protocols

Like the other programs in this chapter, GT Power Comm has certain protocols that are internal. Figure 11-14 shows the download protocols available as seen in GT Power Comm.

Figure 11-14

GT Power Comm's Protocol menu

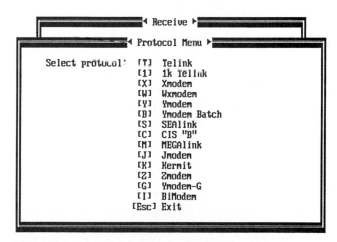

| ◄ Receive ► |
| ◄ Protocol Menu ► |

```
Select protocol:  [T]  Telink
                  [1]  1k Telink
                  [X]  Xmodem
                  [W]  Wxmodem
                  [Y]  Ymodem
                  [B]  Ymodem Batch
                  [S]  SEAlink
                  [C]  CIS "B"
                  [M]  MEGAlink
                  [J]  Jmodem
                  [K]  Kermit
                  [Z]  Zmodem
                  [G]  Ymodem-G
                  [I]  BiModem
                 [Esc] Exit
```

| Alt-H=Help | OFF LINE | | | | | | | 1200 | 12:53 |

By now, most of these should look fairly familiar to you. Telink and Telink 1K are variations of Xmodem, as mentioned previously, and Telink is found primarily on FIDO bulletin board systems. One that you may not have encountered before is selection S, SEAlink. This is a protocol developed by System Enhancement Associates, the creators of ARC. Various bulletin boards around the country have SEAlink available as a protocol. You'll note that GT Power Comm has the CompuServe Quick-B protocol built in, along with Ymodem, Ymodem Batch, Xmodem, and Wxmodem. Megalink is a protocol developed by Meiners, the author of GT. It can also be found on some systems as a protocol choice.

It should be pointed out that options J through I are *not* internal protocols, even though they appear on the menu. In order for you to use Jmodem, Kermit, Zmodem, Ymodem-G, and BiModem, you must have the external protocol drivers associated with each. GT has simply done you the favor of putting them on the menu in advance. All of these protocol drivers can be found on commercial networks and bulletin boards. Thus, with its own internal protocols and the five external protocols that you can add, GT Power Comm gives you many options for transferring files.

GT's Host Mode

When a Host Mode was added to GT Power Comm, it did not stop there as a system with just the basic necessities. Included were features like being able to leave and read messages, transfer files, and page the host. Unlike the Host Modes in other communications programs, GT's was designed to be set up as a full bulletin board system. In fact, there are some fairly large BBSs across the country that are set up using the Host Mode of GT Power Comm. Do I really mean that it can be just like a bulletin board system? You bet! Here's just a quick review of some of the things it offers.

With GT's Host Mode you can have multiple security levels, online bulletins, script questionnaires, a full range of upload and download directories configured by you, and much more. You can set up welcome screens, provide the file transfer protocols of your choice, and do most of the things that you see on systems running regular bulletin board software.

GT's Host Mode is not as flexible or configurable as something like PC Board or Wildcat! BBSs, but it is quite impressive, especially when you consider that it is running off a communications program. You can configure the system to be as simple or as complex as you like. The version of GT that has the Host Mode has more files associated with it and therefore takes up much more disk space. If you don't feel you need such a feature, you can get the terminal-only version, which is quite a bit smaller.

On the other hand, if you would like to run a small to mid-size BBS and don't want the added expense of purchasing regular bulletin board software, then the version of GT Power Comm with Host Mode might be just what you are looking for. You could have your communications program and your BBS all in one package.

Summing Up GT Power Comm

If you are trying to select a communications program, you will find that GT Power Comm will do all the things you need to do while you are online. It has good transfer protocols and capture facilities, and an excellent Host system. The script language is fairly flexible and the program runs well. As with all Shareware programs, if you try out GT and decide that you like it, be sure to register it with the author.

Paul Meiners
P&M Software
3104 E. Camelback #503
Phoenix, AZ 85016
602-285-9914 (Voice)
602-285-1146 or 713-772-2090 (Modem)
$70 registration fee; $20 to upgrade; VISA/MasterCard are accepted

BOYAN — SOLID COMMUNICATIONS

The current release of Boyan is version 4.0. Its author, Justin Boyan, wrote the first version when he was 16 years old and it was impressive even then. As he got older, the program got better, so today's version is a smooth, full-featured program. You can easily change directories, check for the amount of free disk space, or edit a file by attaching the editor of your choice to Boyan's ALT-W key. You've already taken a brief look at

Boyan's macro script language, which is versatile and works well. Boyan is extremely popular at many colleges and universities around the country. How does Boyan stand in relation to the file transfer protocols available? Let's take a look.

Boyan's Transfer Protocols

Like several other communications programs, Boyan offers you some basic transfer protocols that are internal, and then lets you add the external protocols of your choice. Figure 11-15 shows the Upload Protocol window in Boyan.

You'll note that Boyan has Xmodem, CRC-Xmodem, and Relaxed Xmodem. Relaxed Xmodem is simply a variation of Xmodem that has some timing changes, which can often be used on CompuServe. It also has 1K-Xmodem, which, you'll recall, is just Xmodem using 1K blocks. With Ymodem you get a batch transfer protocol and for those with MNP modems there's G-Ymodem (also called Ymodem-G). ASCII is used to send text files to the remote system. Boyan has a special feature in its

---
Figure 11-15

Boyan's Upload Protocol window

```
┌──────────────────UPLOAD FILES───────────────────┐
│                                                  │
│..................................................│
│·PROTOCOL: ▶▨·····································│
│..................................................│
│···············[X] Xmodem·······················│
│···············[C] CRC-Xmodem····················│
│···············[R] Relaxed-Xmodem················│
│···············[1] 1k-Xmodem·····················│
│···············[Y] Ymodem························│
│···············[G] G-Ymodem······················│
│···············[A] ASCII·························│
│···············[M] Message Upload················│
│..................................................│
│..................................................│
│..................................................│
│..................................................│
│..................................................│
│..................................................│
│..................................................│
│..................................................│
└──────────────────────────────────────────────────┘
```

Press <ESC> to abort.   ▌ BOYAN v4.0 ▌ Press <Ctrl-Home> for help.

Message Upload option. Sometimes, when uploading messages to bulletin boards with an ASCII upload, you can get into problems. Boyan's Message Upload feature lets you enter the name of the file, and then it allows you to indicate what kind of prompt the system is using. For example, if each line of a message on a particular system starts with a >, you can tell Boyan to look for that character. It then knows exactly where each line begins. This Message Upload feature works quite well.

Adding External Protocols

Boyan lets you add up to nine external protocols from a special section in the configuration menu. An interesting feature is that several of the most popular external protocols are already inserted for you. Figure 11-16 shows what this external protocol menu looks like.

How do you make them work? It's easy. Note that the names of the protocol drivers are shown in the one column, for example, DSZ.COM and PCKERMIT.EXE. When you put DSZ.COM where Boyan can find it,

Figure 11-16

External Protocol window of Boyan

CONFIGURATION AREA X

#	Protocol Name	Menu Letter	External File	Prompt for DL-name?
0	Kermit	K	PCKERMIT.EXE	NO
1	Compuserve-B	B	OZBEXT.EXE	NO
2	Sealink	S	CLINK.EXE	NO
3	megaLink	L	MLINK.COM	NO
4				NO
5	Zmodem	Z	DSZ.COM	NO
6	ymOdem-batch	O	DSZ.COM	NO
7				NO
8				NO
9				NO

<Ctrl-Home>=help <ESC>=abort

Protocol # to configure (0-9): ▓ BOYAN v4.0 ▓ Press <Ctrl-Home> for help.

you'll automatically be able to have Zmodem and Ymodem Batch. As with many other functions in Boyan, the external protocols are activated by macros, but Boyan has the necessary macro information already entered for you, as you can see in Figure 11-16. This makes it very easy for even new users to set up external protocols.

Some Other Good Features

Boyan has a good Host Mode so your friends and family can call into your machine. It also has a split-screen mode, called Gossip, for use on CB simulators. The online help in Boyan is excellent and it follows you wherever you go. If you go to one section and need help, you can generally get even more help just by pressing CTRL-HOME. This is something to consider if you are relatively new to telecommunications and think you're going to need help along the way.

Justin Boyan has taken the time to give you a lot of help and many examples, even in setting up macros. The documentation is good and relatively easy to understand. The documentation is also filled with many examples in an effort to help you understand exactly how each function works and what it does. These features are important and worth noting. Boyan has another unusual feature in its Directory File Manager. Let's take a quick look at what it can do.

Boyan's Directory File Manager

The Directory File Manager is activated by using the DEL (delete) key. When you activate it, you give yourself access to a number of functions that you can use to manipulate files. Figure 11-17 shows you what the Directory File Manager display looks like.

In the box on the right side of the screen is a display of my C:\DNLD directory. Note that across the bottom you have a number of commands available to you. I'll explain them briefly.

Newdir lets you quickly change to a new directory. Upload lets you tag a file for uploading. You are often prompted to enter the filename of a file that you want to upload. Using the Send command, you can highlight the file that you want to upload and send it out the modem to the host system. You never have to type it in at all.

If you highlight a file and use the Info command, it will tell you its size and how long it will take to transfer it at your currently set baud rate. The Free command will show you the total amount of free disk space on any

---

Figure 11-17

Boyan's Directory File Manager

```
► ..              ◄
COMTOEXE.DOC
COMTOEXE.EXE
ENGCOMEX.DOC
ENGLISH .DOC
ENGUPACK.DOC
INFOEXE .EXE
LZEXE   .DOC
LZEXE91 .ZIP
README  .ENG
UPACKEXE.DOC
UPACKEXE.EXE
```

```
CMDS:↑↓←→|Newdir|Upload|Send|Info|Free|View|Word|Exec|Cpy|Del|Ren|Ctrl-Home=help
43,975 bytes ≈ 0:00:16 send (38400b) ▌ BOYAN v4.0 ▌ Press <Ctrl-Home> for help.
```

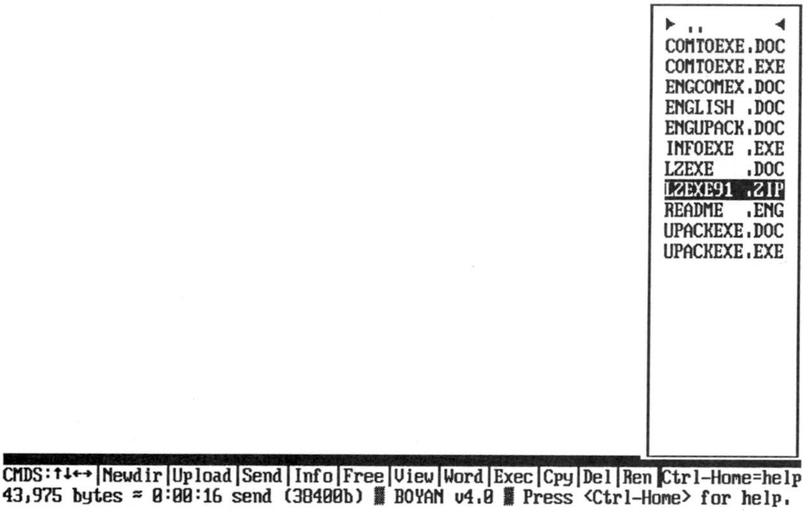

drive that you have, while the View command will let you look at any text file. This is very handy if you want to do a last minute check to make sure you are sending the right message to the right person. The Word command will bring up your editor, and the Exec function will actually run another program from within Boyan, assuming you have enough memory.

Using the Directory File Manager you can also copy, delete, or rename files on your system, using the Cpy, Del, and Ren functions, respectively. These are very powerful features that give you a great deal of control and information without ever having to leave the communications program.

A Good Look at Boyan
Overall, Boyan is a well-written communications program that has many fine features, excellent help, and a nice presentation. It is fully configurable, so you can set the colors you want, the macros, external protocols,

and much more. It has good capture facilities, a Host Mode, and all of the things that you need to enjoy the online experience. The macro script language is quite flexible and gives you a wide range of options.

Boyan also has a Usage Log, which keeps track of all of your online activity. As noted above, the Directory File Manager gives you control over the files on your entire system and provides you with useful functions and information. Over the years, Boyan has become popular not only among college students, but with many others as well. If you're looking for a good communications program, with everything you need and lots of built-in help, you might want to check out Boyan.

Justin Boyan
9458 Two Hills Court
Columbia, MD 21045
919-682-4225 (BBS)
$40 registration fee

TELIX 3.12

Telix is written by Colin Sampaleanu and is distributed by his company, Exis. Over the last one to two years, Telix has become very popular with quite a few users. Like other programs previously discussed in this chapter, Telix contains all of the elements that many people consider essential when going online. It has good capture features, a usage log to keep track of online activity, some terminal emulations, and compiled scripts.

As noted earlier, Telix's SALT script language is very powerful, but many users find it difficult to use. Fortunately, it is the nature of people on The Wires to share things, so Telix scripts can be found on many bulletin board systems. Perhaps its greatest strength is the fact that it has quite a range of internal file transfer protocols. Let's take a look at this arsenal.

The Telix Internal Protocols

While Telix allows you to add up to four external protocols, it has some very popular protocols built right in. It was the first communications program, other than Zcomm, to have Auto Zmodem Download. Figure 11-18 shows the Download Protocol menu of Telix.

The first thing you might notice is that Telix automatically shows you the amount of space you have free on your default drive. Like the other programs, it has an ASCII protocol for sending text files, as well as Xmodem, Telink, and Modem7 for transferring files on older bulletin board systems. The built-in CIS (CompuServe) Quick-B protocol is also quite handy. Unlike any of the others, Telix also has the Kermit protocol built in, as well as having a built-in version of SEAlink.

You also have the 1K-Xmodem protocol and Ymodem Batch to help round out the basic file transfer needs. Telix finishes up by including three of the streaming protocols, namely, G-1K-Xmodem, YmodEm-g, and Zmodem. (G-1K-Xmodem is the same as 1K-Xmodem/G and YmodEm-g is the same as Ymodem-G.) This is quite an assortment of internal protocols. Plus, you still have room to add four external protocols, such as BiModem, MPt, Jmodem, or others. This makes transfer protocols Telix's strong suit.

Figure 11-18

The Download Protocol menu of Telix

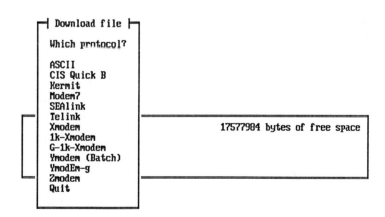

```
┤ Download file ├

Which protocol?

ASCII
CIS Quick B
Kermit
Modem7
SEAlink
Telink
Xmodem                          17577904 bytes of free space
1k-Xmodem
G-1k-Xmodem
Ymodem (Batch)
YmodEm-g
Zmodem
Quit
```

Alt-Z for Help | ANSI-BBS | 38400·N81 FDX | | | | Offline

Miscellaneous Options

Telix has some interesting options; for example, you can toggle the screen display between 80 × 25, 80 × 43, and 80 × 50. This assumes, of course, that you have a video graphics card that supports these modes. Telix also has an option that allows you to send a modem initialization string to the modem or the commands that set the modem to auto answer mode.

Like a few of the other communications programs—Qmodem for example—Telix has a doorway mode that you can toggle on and off. What is this for? Many bulletin board sysops run a program called DOORWAY, written by Marshal Dudley. DOORWAY is an excellent program for running almost any .COM or .EXE file as a *door* program. Sysops often use DOORWAY as a "remote drop to DOS." As a sysop, you could call into your system from a remote location and use DOORWAY to drop to DOS to move files, do maintenance, and so on. How does doorway mode help you? It helps because when you toggle it on, the keys that you enter on your keyboard are accepted by the remote system. For example, it you dropped to DOS on your BBS and brought up a maintenance program that required you to use F10 to access the user database, you could do it with doorway mode toggled on. Thus, doorway mode is a popular feature among bulletin board sysops because it lets them do things from remote that they could not do otherwise.

Checking Out Telix

If you are interested in Telix, you will find that it will give you all of the things you need to operate in The Wires. It has an impressive list of internal protocols, many options can be configured by the user, and it runs smoothly and efficiently. It keeps its own usage log (if you want it to), captures things to disk, and has keyboard macros and a powerful script language. Telix is a good, all-purpose communications program that will serve you well.

Colin Sampaleanu
Exis, Inc.
P.O. Box 130, West Hill
Ontario, Canada M1E 4R4
416-289-4641
416-289-4645 (Fax)

416-439-8293 (BBS)
$39 U.S. / $44 Canadian registration fee

TELEMATE

Telemate is one of the most interesting communications programs to come along in quite some time. From the very first version, it was packed with innovative ideas and concepts. For a brand new program it is clearly exceptional. Do I mean for this statement to detract from the other programs discussed? Not at all! Keep in mind that other programs like Qmodem, Procomm, Boyan, Zcomm, and GT Power Comm have all been around for several years.

As time has gone by, they have matured—added functions that were not necessary before. For example, at one point programs like Qmodem and Procomm had no need for the G protocols, because there were no MNP modems. When there was a need, those protocols were added. When you are the "new kid on the block," you can benefit from the experiences of those who have gone before you. As a new program, Telemate started out with features that had been added to other communications programs over the years. At the same time, however, Telemate offers some features that are different from the others, and these are what will be discussed here. Telemate's first release boasted "multitasking," so let's take a look at what this means.

Multitasking in Telemate

Generally, when you are doing a file transfer, even in a DESQview window, you can't do anything else—at least in that window. This is not true with Telemate. The author of Telemate, Tsung Hu (who uses the name "Winfred" in messages), has designed what he calls a "multitasking kernel" that is used in Telemate. Thus, you can do something else while doing a file transfer. For example, you can bring up Telemate's editor and write a note at the same time that you are downloading a file. Figure 11-19 shows this type of multitasking being done in Telemate.

In Figure 11-19, I've popped up the editor while a transfer is going, but you can do other things as well. Add a number to your dialing directory, write a message that you want to send, make up a macro—just

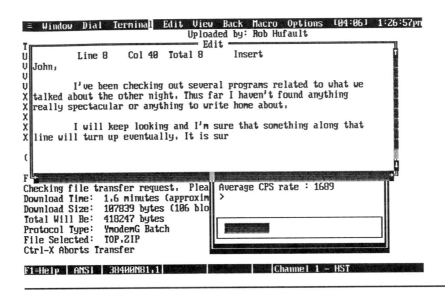

Figure 11-19

Multitasking in Telemate—editing and downloading

about anything you want. This is a useful feature because you can make use of what otherwise might have been wasted time. Telemate also features a good list of internal protocols, so let's look at those.

Telemate's Protocols

Telemate has a good selection of internal protocols for you to use. For fast transfers it has Zmodem, SEAlink, and Ymodem-G. For use on older systems it also has Telink, Ymodem, Xmodem, Modem7, and Relaxed Xmodem. Batch Ymodem and ASCII are also a part of its protocol list, as is the CIS Quick-B protocol. Telemate also allows you to have up to four external protocols, which are run from batch files supplied with the program. The batch files take care of BiModem, Jmodem, Kermit, and MPt. This is a good assortment of file transfer protocols for you to use. Don't forget that in order to implement any of the external protocols, you'll need to get the protocol drivers from bulletin boards or commercial networks.

Various Other Features

Another interesting feature in Telemate is that the entire program is "mouseable." You can configure it for the Mouse Systems mouse or the Microsoft mouse. Anything that you need to do within the program can be done with a mouse—from saving your configuration options to starting a script. We already discussed Telemate's interesting scroll-back buffer that allows you to mark text, and then cut it, paste it, or "quote" it.

Telemate also includes a View function that lets you look at any file on your system while you are online. Figure 11-20 shows the View screen in place while the program is dialing a number.

As you can see, the View screen is popped up over the dialing directory and if you wanted, you could pop up the Edit window or one of the others over the top of that. This interesting new program also has doorway mode, chat mode, and a way to toggle both originate and answer modes. The alarms in Telemate are also a bit different from other programs in that they are portions of songs. There are twenty songs available ranging from the "Addams Family" theme to the William Tell

---

Figure 11-20

Viewing a file while dialing in Telemate

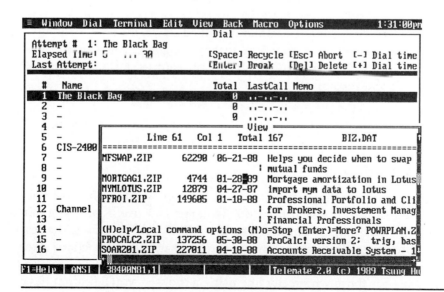

Overture. If you want to hear more of the song :) you can just set a long alarm time.

Window Functions and More

Telemate is made up of a series of windows that can be opened at the same time. The windows are

- Terminal

- Back (Scroll-Back)

- Edit

- Dial

- View

- Macros

Each window can be resized to suit your tastes and when necessary you can zoom a window so it fills the entire screen. You can also move the windows around the screen if you don't like their default positions, and you can save those positions to your basic configuration file. Telemate will come up with the windows exactly where you put them. The Telemate editor has quite a few good features. Figure 11-21 shows the Telemate editor with its menu of commands pulled down.

For an editor within a communications program, you can see that Telemate's editor gives you a fair number of features, including cut and paste, search and replace, and more.

Testing Telemate

Telemate is an interesting new communications program with some very innovative features. If you have EMS, Telemate can use it, and you can define how much EMS it can use. The more EMS Telemate uses, the less DOS RAM it uses. Telemate allows you to pop up other functions over existing functions and use them while you are online. It is mouse-compatible—for those who really like using a mouse—you'll seldom have

Figure 11-21

The Telemate editor and its menu

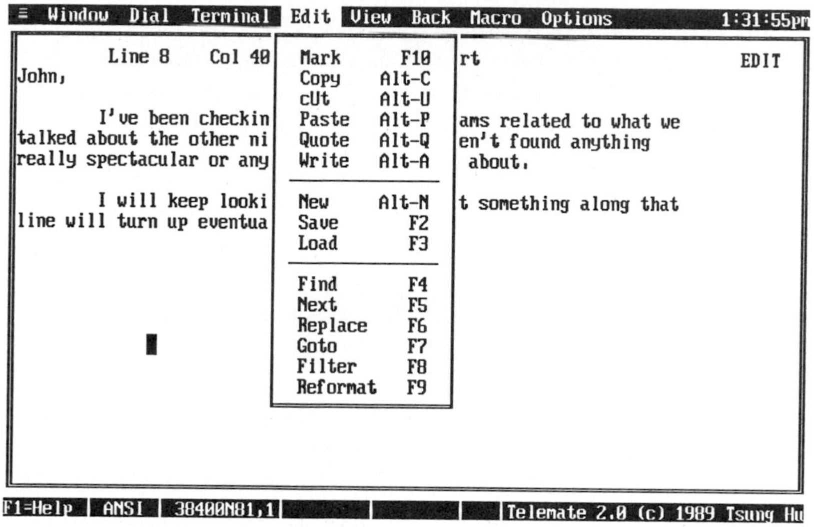

```
≡ Window  Dial  Terminal  Edit  View  Back  Macro  Options         1:31:55pm
 ┌──────────────────────┬─────────────────┬──────────────────────────────┐
 │      Line 8    Col 40 │ Mark      F10   │ rt                      EDIT │
 │John,                  │ Copy     Alt-C  │                              │
 │                       │ cUt      Alt-U  │                              │
 │       I've been checkin│ Paste    Alt-P  │ ams related to what we       │
 │talked about the other ni│ Quote   Alt-Q  │ en't found anything          │
 │really spectacular or any│ Write   Alt-A  │  about.                      │
 │                       │                 │                              │
 │       I will keep looki│ New      Alt-N  │ t something along that        │
 │line will turn up eventua│ Save      F2   │                              │
 │                       │ Load      F3   │                              │
 │                       │                 │                              │
 │                       │ Find      F4   │                              │
 │                       │ Next      F5   │                              │
 │                       │ Replace   F6   │                              │
 │              ▮        │ Goto      F7   │                              │
 │                       │ Filter    F8   │                              │
 │                       │ Reformat  F9   │                              │
 │                       └─────────────────┘                              │
 │                                                                        │
 │                                                                        │
 │                                                                        │
 │F1=Help │ ANSI │ 38400N81,1 │         │      │ Telemate 2.0 (c) 1989 Tsung Hu│
 └────────────────────────────────────────────────────────────────────────┘
```

to touch a key. Telemate has automatic script learn and its scripts are compiled immediately prior to execution.

As with any new program (or some older ones for that matter), the first two versions of Telemate were a little bit "buggy," but version 2.00 seems to be relatively bug-free. If it sounds interesting to you, give it a try. If you use it, be sure to register with the author. He has even more new things planned for Telemate in the future.

Tsung Hu
10530 Keating Crescent
Windsor, Ontario, Canada N8R 1T5
$40 U.S. / $48 Canadian registration fee

This concludes our discussion of the larger, full-featured communications programs. I'd like to state again that all of the communications programs discussed so far are good programs. They all have many features that are similar and some that are unique. The ones that you like and end up using will depend on your tastes and your needs. You certainly won't lose by trying any of these programs. That's part of what Shareware is all about—trying it before you buy it! If you try a program and don't find it to your liking, try one of the others. When you do find one that suits you, be sure to register.

Let's move on now and take a look at two smaller communications programs that might be of interest to some of you. After that, I'll just briefly mention a few utility programs that you may want to get to make your life online more productive.

TWO SMALLER COMMUNICATIONS PROGRAMS

Often, for just transferring files or sending a message, you may not need all of the features found in a full-sized communications program. You need just the basics—something to get you online, send your message, and get you back off again. There are several small communications programs available that don't have all of the features found in the programs discussed so far. They don't use as much RAM either.

I've selected two programs to take a look at—for different reasons. The first is called Commo. It is small, compact, and yet fairly powerful. Commo can be used in a DESQview window that is 180K or less. The other program is called Chatterbox, and it is also small. Chatterbox has some features that I've never seen in any other communications program.

If you are short of RAM, running on a laptop computer, or just want to run a program that will accomplish a few basic tasks, one of these two programs might be just the thing for you. Let's move on and examine these two compact communications programs.

COMMO—SMALL YET POWERFUL

There are several factors that make Commo a powerful little program. To begin with, Commo has a built-in macro processor that allows you to automate tasks such as logging on to BBSs or downloading files. You can think of this as a way of replacing the script languages found in the larger programs. You can also assign macros to function keys and use them to send information to the host, start another macro, or do just about anything you want. You can even attach a macro to a dialing directory number, just like you would a script file. Since Commo has a built-in editor, you can alter your macros quickly and not have to leave the program—a nice feature in such a small program.

Power You Wouldn't Expect

The author of Commo, Fred Brucker, has packed a lot of features into a program that only uses about 35K of RAM. In testing it, I was able to run Commo and DSZ in a DESQview window that was only 120K in size. You might want to allow for more—just in case you want to do some other things. Commo is, however, what programmers call "DESQview aware," meaning that it recognizes DESQview and behaves accordingly. That's not all though, because Commo can also handle ANSI graphics, up to four serial ports, and it can do ASCII uploads.

In addition, Commo can have a capture log that saves data to disk; you can do a screen dump, or send data to a printer. There is also online help available. Figure 11-22 shows Commo's context-sensitive help screen.

You can look up the information you want simply by pressing **T** and then the topic number. If that isn't enough, Commo also has a chat mode and a doorway mode, just like some of the larger programs. You can shell to DOS, dial multiple numbers, toggle the sound on and off, or send a break signal to the modem.

Configurability

By using Commo's built-in editor, you can edit and configure Commo's configuration file, macros, and dialing directory. Most of the program's other features are also easily configurable. For example, you can configure the addresses of the COM ports. Commo will support up to 115,200 bps, depending on your machine; it also can detect the 16550A UART. A very interesting feature is that the program will also put up a display of the modem lights on its status line, so you can see their activity.

Commo—The Bottom Line

As you can see, for a small program Commo offers quite a few solid features—especially for a program that can run in just 35K of RAM. For

---

Figure 11-22

Commo's help screen

```
▓▓▓▓▓▓▓▓▓▓▓▓ {COMMO} (tm) Help  ↑ ↓  PgDn PgUp  [Esc] to exit ▓▓▓▓▓▓▓▓▓▓▓▓

 Type "T" to view a topic.   ┌───────────────┐   You may need to scroll down
 Then enter topic number.    │ Main Help Menu │   to see all the menu items.
                             └───────────────┘

 HOW TO USE HELP ············· 99   Alt-1  Capture File Options ····· 15
                                    Alt-2  Print Log ················ 16
 Alt-A  ASCII Upload ············ 1  Alt-3  Sound Control ············ 17
 Alt-B  Send Break Signal ······· 2  Alt-4  ANSI Emulation ··········· 18
 Alt-C  Clear Terminal Screen ··· 3  Alt-5  AutoBaud Detect ·········· 19
 Alt-D  Dialing Directory ······· 4  Alt-6  Local Echo ··············· 20
 Alt-G  Configuration File ······ 5  Alt-7  Chat Mode ················ 21
 Alt-I  Screen Image Save ······· 6  Alt-8  Signal Lights Display ···· 22
 Alt-L  Communication Parameters  7  Alt-=  Doorway Mode ············· 23
 Alt-M  Macro Processor ········· 8
 Alt-O  Initialize Modem ········ 9  How to Register {COMMO} ········· 24
 Alt-P  Send Current Password ·· 10  Uploading / Downloading ········· 25
 Alt-Q  Hang Up Modem ·········· 11  Using the Internal Editor ······· 26
 Alt-S  Shell to DOS ··········· 12  Searching for Text in Files ····· 27
 Alt-U  Multi Number Dial ······ 13  What is on the Status Line ······ 28
 Alt-X  Exit from {COMMO} ······ 14  Error Message Explanations ······ 29

 {COMMO} (tm) Help  (C)Copyright 1989,1990 Fred P. Brucker  All Rights Reserved
▓▓▓▓▓▓ [H] how to use help  [M] for main menu   [T] to select topic ▓▓▓▓▓▓
▓▓▓▓▓▓ [E] for edit help    [S] for text search  [A] to search again ▓▓▓▓▓▓
```

---

file transfers, all you need is a copy of DSZ, but Commo can also handle BiModem, MPt, Jmodem, and other external protocols. These protocols are set up in the macro editor, and the macro commands are fully described in the documentation. For such a tiny program, Commo has many features, making it ideal for those who only want a small communications program or who don't have enough RAM for a larger one. Take a look at Commo; you'll be impressed.

Fred P. Brucker
P.O. Box 9103
Santa Rosa, CA 95405
$25 check or money order to register

CHATTERBOX

Chatterbox is a fascinating communications program written by Mark Wilden. Wilden originally wrote the program for himself, but as friends saw it, they wanted copies too. While Chatterbox has several good features, it will be of particular interest to those who use CB simulators, like those found on GEnie and CompuServe. Chatterbox has some features that I have never seen in any other communications program. Unlike Commo, Chatterbox is not yet DESQview aware, but personally, I find Chatterbox so helpful and so refreshing that I gladly unload DESQview in order to use Chatterbox if I am going online to chat. You might like it too.

Chatterbox Conventional Features

Chatterbox has some of the features offered by the larger communications programs. For example, you can log a session to a disk file. The program also lets you define macros for the ten function keys. You can set all of the screen colors by using ALT-U. In addition, you can shell to DOS, so that you can move files, or do other routine things while online. Don't want to shell to DOS? That's all right—by using ALT-Y you can issue any DOS command and not have to leave the program at all. Chatterbox lets you attach the editor of your choice so you can edit messages or other files. What about file transfers? Yes, Chatterbox gives you those too.

Chatterbox File Transfers

All you need to do file transfers with Chatterbox is a copy of DSZ.COM. Place DSZ either in the same directory as Chatterbox or somewhere in your DOS PATH. Using ALT-F from within the program, you can select from the following protocols:

- Zmodem

- Ymodem

- 1K-Xmodem

- Xmodem CRC

- Xmodem

That's all you have to do. The commands that drive the protocols are all internal. You just select the protocol that you want and take off. Chatterbox also lets you upload messages quite smoothly.

Some Other Features

Besides the things already mentioned, Chatterbox lets you toggle the local echo (duplex) on and off. You can get a help screen by using ALT-Z, shown in Figure 11-23.

In its dialing directory you can add, change, find, erase, or move dialing directory entries. Using ALT-P, you can set your communications parameters like baud, parity, databits, and stopbits. Since Chatterbox was designed with the commercial networks in mind, the maximum baud rate is currently 2400.

The configuration menu lets you indicate your highest baud rate, what COM port you are using, if you have a tone or pulse phone, if you want fast screen updating, and your choice of editor. By using ALT-V, you can automatically edit your default script file. Chatterbox also has an interesting script language that works extremely well. More about scripts in a moment—first let's take a look at the very special features that Chatterbox has for chatting online.

Figure 11-23

Chatterbox help screen

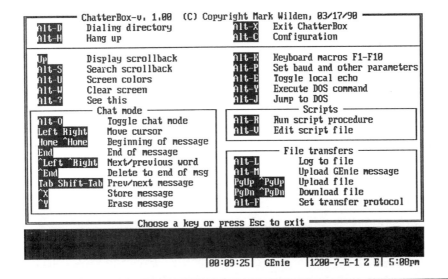

Chatterbox's Chat Features

Let's say you are going online to chat on GEnie's Chat Lines. That is where I first found Wilden and Chatterbox. The program will use a script to dial in and log you on. A script for doing just that comes with the program, and the script will even check to see if you have mail. Once you enter **Chat Lines**, you can put Chatterbox into chat mode by pressing ALT-O. Here is where some of the program's unique functions start to come into play.

While online in Chat Lines, people can send you private messages via a function called /SEN, which was mentioned in Chapter 4. Wilden created a script that you can run from inside the Chat window. You start the script with ALT-R and it stays active until you stop it. What does this little SEN script do? Anytime someone sends you a private message, you hear a beep, and the first line of that message is highlighted for you. For those who spend time chatting, this is an excellent feature, because you can't miss a private message. Another fantastic feature is the scroll-back function in Chatterbox (see Figure 11-24).

Figure 11-24

The "live" scroll-back in Chatterbox

```
Active users on Channel 38
Job State Chan Sta Handle                 GE Mail
   2   MD   38    N Ambush Bug             M.YOUNG9
   3   VA   38    N Zeroy                  R.RANDALL5
   5   NY   38    N Gary 7                 S.FULK
   7   CO   38    N =Guitarman=            DR-FF
  11   FL   38    N D'Artagnan             S.RICHBOURG
  14   NY    1    M Bo                     RASMITH
  15   CA   38    N Click & Clack          STC
  16   NJ   38    N ANKH                   AYJAY
  18   MA   38    N RODEO BLUE             J.OCONNELL6
  19   MD   38    N Loki                   PENNI
<D'Artagnan> sigh... (choke)
<Ambush Bug> Different Ambush Bug maybe?
<ANKH> ~~ New Game started: 'Volume II
                                        ' Edition.
<ANKH> ~~ No !JOINing necessary!
          Use cursor keys to view, Alt-S to search, or Esc to exit
<D'Artagnan> nopee.. there's only one ambush bug :)
** <TRIV> was <ANKH>
<Zeroy> aw, i wanna join
                        |00:07:20| GEnie   |1200-7-E-1 Z E| 5:06pm
ousand in special offers..for hardware and software
/sta
```

This is no normal scroll-back function. In every other communications program while you are looking at the scroll-back buffer, you cannot do anything else. Not so with Chatterbox. You use the UP ARROW key to display the scroll-back, and you can see what has gone on but you can continue typing. You can respond to a message and answer it in detail because you can look at it while you answer it. You can also search the scroll-back, while you type, to find a piece of text, a person's name, or whatever you want to look for. You have to experience it to believe it. It's excellent programming.

If you type in a line and decide that you don't want to send it just now—no problem. You can use CTRL-X to store the line for later retrieval. In addition, Chatterbox has a series of commands that makes it easier to chat online. You can delete to the end of a message or move to the beginning of a message, to the next word, the previous word, and so on. It really makes online chats much more enjoyable and it's great for use in online conferences.

Chatterbox Summary

Chatterbox is a small communications program with some good standard as well as innovative features that make it an excellent tool for chatting online. It is ideal for those who want to go online for mail or download an occasional file from an online network. For online chats and conferences it's excellent and worth using just for that purpose as I do. Its live scroll-back feature is tremendously handy, not only for those who are responding to a message, but for new users as well. Think of it. You can get a help listing from the system, and then look at it while you type in the commands. So, if these features sound like something you'd like to experience, give Chatterbox a try.

Mark Wilden
P.O. Box 926
Oakhurst, CA 93644
$10 registration fee

COMMUNICATIONS UTILITIES

There are many utility programs designed to function, in one way or another, with communications programs. Just a few of the categories of communications utilities would include

- Dialing directory editors
- Dialing directory sorters
- Usage log analyzers
- Protocol drivers
- Protocol interfaces
- Dialing directory converters
- StarLink accessory programs
- PC Pursuit accessory programs
- Modem enhancement programs
- Script files
- Script generators
- Host modes

This listing should provide you with the general idea, even though it's only a partial list of what's available, covering a multitude of programs. Space doesn't allow for evaluation of programs in all of these and other categories. So, as a compromise, I will give the names of some of the better programs that you can find and may want to get.

Some programs can only be used with a certain communications program. Programs marked with *** (three stars) are not only excellent, but ones that I recommend registering for. Rather than describe, in detail, only a few communications utilities, I would much rather give you a list of programs that might be of help to you.

Protocol Drivers and Interfaces

There are certain protocol drivers that have become almost a *must* for doing efficient, high-speed file transfers. These protocols are proliferating quickly and are appearing on more and more systems daily. File extensions may vary.

*** DSZ by Chuck Forsberg - Registration: $20
Usually found as DSZ????.ZIP, where ???? is release date

*** MPt by Matthew Thomas - Registration: $25
Usually found as MP???.ZIP, where ??? is version number

*** BiModem by Eric Labs - Registration: $25
Usually found as BIMOD???.ZIP, where ??? is version number

*** Jmodem by Richard Johnson - public domain
Usually found as JMOD???.ZIP, where ??? is version number

*** OZBEXT by Sam Sneed
Usually found as OZBX???? where ???? is version number

*** Power Node by Jimmy Pearson - Registration: $25
Usually found as BBPOWER?.ZIP, where ? is release letter

*** ICEX by Wayne Wolf - Registration: $25
Usually found as ICEX????.ZIP where ???? is version number

Other programs that you may want to look at are

Super8K by Sal Manaro
Usually found as SK&J????.ZIP, where ???? is release date

SEAlink by System Enhancement Associates
Usually found as CLINK???.ZIP, where ??? is version number

Megalink by Paul Meiners
Usually found as MLINK??.ZIP, where ?? is version number

POE by Mark "Sparky" Herring (Freeware)
Usually found as POE120.ZIP (protocol interface)

Miscellaneous Utilities

Registration for the following programs will depend upon whether or not you are using a particular communications program and whether you find the program to be useful. Thus, I will not recommend each one but will simply say, "If you use it, register for it."

Telix Phone Editor
Usually found as TFE_???.ZIP, where ??? is version number

Qmodem Phone Editor
Usually found as QFE_???.ZIP, where ??? is version number

ProFonEdit - Dialing directory editor
Usually found as PFEPL???.ZIP, where ??? is version number

CVTFON - Dialing directory converter
Usually found as CVTFON??.ZIP, where ?? is version number

STARDIAL - a StarLink dialing aid
Usually found as STARDIAL.ZIP

STAR14 - A StarLink dialing aid
Usually found as STAR14.ZIP

Qanalyst - Qmodem phone log and cost analyzer - Rob Rosenberger
Usually found as QANA-???.ZIP, where ??? is version number

Minihost - a stand-alone host system
Usually found as MINIHOST.ZIP,

FSTHST - a utility for maximizing USR 9600 HSTs
Usually found as FSTHST??.ZIP, where ?? is version number

Just a Sample of What's in The Wires

For those of you who haven't frequented any bulletin boards, here is a short list of some of the communications utilities that are available in The Wires.

DOCTOR'S NOTE

In various places throughout the rest of this book, you will find actual bulletin board listings. The entries are shown exactly as they appear on the bulletin board. They have not been edited in any way to correct grammar, spelling, or abbreviations. When you go online, these are the kinds of lists you will see.

ANSWER2.ARC	15280	Electronic Answering Machine to answer
APILOT15.ZIP	77824	Great shell for adding external protocols.
AT-DTR.ARC	1640	Program to control modem from DOS.
BBPOWERI.ZIP	128114	ByteBros. Powernode BBS file transfer tool kit.
BEXE_210.ZIP	223096	BinkleyTerm Mailer/Term prog.
BGFTD200.ZIP	146432	Background file transfer system v2.0.
BI_DOR14.ARC	43170	Set up BIMODEM on PC Board 14.x.
CALLCTRL.ZIP	1520	Disable call waiting
CISHELP.ARC	75770	CompuServe resident HELP.
CKERM4E.ZIP	330557	C-kermit Ver 4E(72) 04/89, full C src.
COMPORTS.ARC	32856	Allows DOS to use COM3 & COM4.
CT.ARC	85134	Track time/cost on computer services,CIS,etc..
FLASHLIN.ZIP	45824	MNP protocol in software
FSTHST21.ZIP	16287	FASTHST v2.1:configures USR HST Modems
HAYES.ARC	3853	A good reference command list for Hayes modem.
MDR22.ZIP	42790	Diagnostices for your modem.
MNPCON.ZIP	8246	Information about MNP protocol.
MODEMD22.ZIP	42475	Version 2.2 of Modem Doctor.
OZBX132B.ARC	62091	Latest OZBEXT, CIS B and B+ protocols
PCB141.ZIP	7718	Info on the 14.1 release of PCBoard;
PCBUD102.ARC	26959	Qmodem/PCBOARD script generator
PCLOG.ARC	50911	Log program from GT software.
PCPDIRED.ARC	97591	Edit Procomm Plus Telephone Directory.
PCPMAN.ARC	30944	Unofficial PCPursuit Manual.
PROTOCL2.ARC	35840	Larry Jordan describes Kermit, Xmodem & Ymodm.
QANA-203.ZIP	151552	Qmodem v4.1 phone bill estimator v2.03.
QFE_403.ZIP	103489	QFE: THE Qmodem .FON processor v 4.03.
QMFONUT.ARC	11899	Converts QMODEM.FON to ASCII & back.
RCOMMV21.ARC	48123	RCOMM v2.1; TSR; resident communications
ROBO20-B.ZIP	126377	RoboComm v2.0 Automated Comm. prg 2/2
RSTUTOR.ARC	106449	RS232 communications tutor in color.
SDIAL200.ZIP	62387	Stardial v2.00: Starlink auto-dialing
SK&J1202.ZIP	143872	Sal Manaro's latest external protocol
STAR14.ZIP	61411	STARPORT v1.4: dialer for Starlink;
TAP.ARC	146124	Tapcis v5.1c.1 automates CIS forum
TAPDOC.ARC	110564	Documentation for TAPCIS 5.1b.
TELEDISK.ARC	58038	Transfer any diskette into/from a file
TFE_210.ZIP	52222	Full-screen editor for Telix FON files.
TIMSET53.ZIP	100352	Set CPU clock to Naval Observatory
TOPBRD6B.ARC	11554	List of TOP US BBSs.
TYMNET.ZIP	14610	Listing of Tymnet access numbers
WHATLN20.ZIP	36511	Use 1 phone for modem, FAX and Voice.
WINDSZ.ARC	4440	Use DSZ under Microsoft Windows.

```
XYW-DIAL.ARC    12980   Telephone Dialer (voice) for XyWrite
ZCOMUPL.ARC      1576   Auto upload script for zcomm.
ZDOC0113.ZIP    25289   Guide to the DSZ Zmodem Driver
ZMDMOV.ARC      21734   Overview of ZMODEM protocol by Forsberg.
```

This listing is only the tip of the iceberg. As you move around and explore, you'll find utilities to work with your system and with the communications program of your choice. When in doubt as to what you need, or if you have problems—ask questions! You may be surprised by how much help you'll get.

SOME FINAL THOUGHTS

This chapter has looked at some of the best full-featured communications programs in some detail. All of them are very good programs. If you aren't already using a communications program, the information contained here may be of help to you. If you are using a communications program, perhaps this chapter will make you curious about some of the others that are available.

Your choice of a utility program will depend upon personal preference and need, and there is always advice on the right utility for you available on bulletin boards and commercial networks. We'll leave communications programs behind and move on to look at another group of programs—the file utilities.

## CHAPTER TWELVE

File Utilities

The world of Shareware is fairly bursting with utility programs. The tremendous variety and scope of what these countless utility programs do is staggering. These many utilities vary in size from the very small to some that are quite large—programs that strip the "high bits" out of WordStar documents, alter file attributes, enhance the power of batch files, speed up the keyboard, and more.

This is an area where Shareware authors shine, having created wonderful utility programs that you won't find in any store. A large number of utility programs are totally free, belonging in the public domain. Commercial software companies can't afford to market such programs, no matter how useful they are. While the commercial arena seriously lacks good utility programs, these programs abound in Shareware and in the public domain. It seems that no matter what the task, someone has written a good utility program to do it. The only place you can find this wide variety of utility programs is through PC user groups and disk vendors, and on commercial networks and bulletin boards. So vast are their numbers that an entire book this size could be dedicated to just the existing utilities.

For years system operators have struggled with categorizing utility programs into a logical order and breaking them into subdivisions. The task is not an easy one. Let's take a moment to examine the realm of utility programs.

PROBLEMS CATEGORIZING UTILITY PROGRAMS

One of the biggest problems in categorizing utility programs is that they are functionally so varied. Some programs can be classified more easily because they perform a very specific task. A program that increases the typing rate of your keyboard can be easily called a keyboard utility, and one that sends codes to your printer is clearly a printer utility. Other programs, however, don't fit so easily into a niche.

Another problem is that different people give the categories different names. Should a utility that consists of "words of wisdom" be classified as a *general, miscellaneous, unclassified,* or *educational* utility? These examples are all actual file area names on bulletin boards. People do their best to classify these programs, but it's a next to impossible task. Even if you know what utility program you want, you may have to hunt through a system to find it.

One thing to keep in mind is that on almost all systems you can search on a word that is part of the filename or the description. This is generally the fastest way to find those hard-to-classify utility programs.

Putting Utilities in Groups

There are so many excellent utility programs that preparing for this chapter was not an easy job. Grouping some programs is fairly clear cut, but classifying others is a judgment call. Utilities of interest to most

DOCTOR'S NOTE

The number and variety of utility programs can be overwhelming at times. Almost any program that isn't a specific *application* program can be lumped into the classification of a utility program, and there seems to be a utility for almost everything. As you encounter problems in working with your computer, here is something to keep in mind—the odds are very good that someone else has encountered the same problems. The odds are also very good that someone with some programming skills wrote a utility program addressing these problems.

For example, look in Chapter 11 at the utilities that exist just for communications programs. There are utilities to sort dialing directories, create scripts, track usage, run external protocols, and many more. Many of these programs were created because someone wanted a program that would perform a specific task and couldn't find one that did. Utilities are also written to solve problems, or to enhance certain programs. Others are written to stand alone, which means that they don't depend on any other program in order to do what they do.

In general, utilities are designed to enhance something. You will find the widest possible selection on bulletin boards. The following is a partial listing of some actual file area names on bulletin boards. Keep in mind that all of these categories contain nothing but utility programs for that particular subject.

Communications utilities
Word processing utilities
Screen utilities
Keyboard utilities
Programming utilities
General, Miscellaneous, and
Unclassified utilities

DOS utilities
System utilities
Disk utilities
Hard disk utilities
Printer utilities
Sysop utilities

If you get the idea that there are a lot of utility programs, you're right! If you want or need a utility program, hit The Wires. Check out the utility sections on bulletin boards and you might be surprised to find exactly what you need.

people, which are those that are more clearly defined, will be discussed in Chapter 15. These include

- DOS utilities
- Keyboard utilities
- Printer utilities
- General utilities

Utility programs in these areas are easier to classify, because the functions are more specific. General utilities will cover some interesting programs that aren't easily classified.

In this chapter we will examine the category of file utilities, what they are, and how they work.

Defining File Utilities

To call your attention to as wide a range of utility programs as possible, I created the "file utility" grouping. This is not a classification that you will find on most systems, but it allows me to tell you about a greater variety of programs. For the purposes of this chapter, file utilities will be considered programs dealing with "files" on any level.

The programs that will be discussed here will have a wide range of functions. One thing that they will all have in common is that they all do something *with* or *to* files, such as move, categorize, alter, enhance, and so on. In this way, you will examine a larger number of utilities with varying functions.

PROFESSIONAL MASTER KEY

Professional Master Key has often been called a Norton Utilities clone since it can do many of the things that the commercial program does. Professional Master Key, hereafter called PMK, has a menu interface that lets you use all of its functions easily. In addition to the main program, several utilities are included that are quite useful. All of the programs included in the PMK package can be used from a main or master menu. Figure 12-1 shows you the master menu interface of the PMK utilities.

The main PMK module is a whole series of utilities in itself. The menu lets you access all of the extra utility programs that come with PMK.

Figure 12-1

Master menu screen of Professional Master Key

```
┌─────────────────────────────────────────────┐  Professional Master Key
│   Move the highlighted bar with ↑ or ↓       │  Fill Disk
│       to select the desired program.         │  File Sort
│                                              │  UnFormat
│   Type in any needed options/parameters.     │  Zero Disk
│     Press *ENTER* to run the program.        │  Zero File
└─────────────────────────────────────────────┘  Quit PMK Master Menu
╔══════════════ Professional Master Key ═══════════════════════════╗
║ - Look at and modify any sector or file available on any MS-DOS disk. ║
║ - Search for text strings or hexadecimal data anywhere on the disk.   ║
║ - Show a graphic map depicting disk and file fragmentation.           ║
║ - Modify a file's attributes:  Read-Only, Hidden, System, and Archive.║
║ - Quickly find the location of any file anywhere on a disk.           ║
║ - Undelete any file or sub-directory that can be recovered.           ║
║                                                                       ║
║ PMK [/Mono ON : OFF : AUTO] [/Bios ON : OFF] [d:]                     ║
║   PMK /Bios ON B:          -- display using BIOS; set working drive to B:║
║                                                                       ║
║ Options                                                               ║
║   /Mono (Toggle monochrome).          ON = no color.  OFF = show color.║
║   /Bios (Toggle direct screen writing) ON = use BIOS. OFF = direct.   ║
║   d: (Set working drive).                                             ║
║ ─────────────────────────────────────────────────────────────────── ║
║ PMK                                                                   ║
╚══════ Copyright 1990 by Public Brand Software, all rights reserved. ══╝
```

When you highlight a specific program, the main portion of the screen displays a description of what the utility does and all of its command line options. At the bottom of the screen, you can enter the command line options you want to use. You can use all of the PMK programs without the menu if you like. Let's take a brief look at what comes in the PMK package and then look at each of the utilities.

The Professional Master Key Package

The main PMK program is a series of utilities that lets you manipulate files, disks, and even each individual sector on a disk. You can "edit" sectors and thereby change their contents, as well as erase, rename, and unerase files. The utility programs in the PMK package allow you to do the following:

- Access any system, hidden, or read-only files

- Show a map of disk usage and free space

- Show what area any file occupies on a disk

- Erase any file, even hidden, system, or read-only files

- Rename any file or directory

- Change the file attributes of any file or subdirectory

- Unerase any file

- Physically sort files on disk in any order

- Totally wipe a file from a disk

- Totally wipe a disk *clean*

- Unformat an accidentally formatted drive

It's an impressive set that provides much of what the more expensive commercial programs provide. Figure 12-2 shows the main menu of the PMK module and the options that are available.

All of the functions are listed clearly on the left side of the screen, while a description of the function is shown on the right. This is a

---

Figure 12-2

PMK's main menu display

```
┌──────────── Professional Master Key, version 3.1 ────────────┐
│          Select a function by moving the highlighted bar with ↑, ↓, or    │
│          the first letter in the function name, and pressing «ENTER».       │
│  ─────────────────────────────────────────────────────────────  │
│                                                                  │
│  Alter Files .... Alter any directory or file's attribs, date, or time.  │
│  Change Disk .... Change the working drive to any available drive.        │
│  Disk Edit ...... Examine and/or modify the current drive's sectors.      │
│  Erase Files .... Erase any file that exists on the current drive.        │
│  File Edit ...... Examine and/or modify any file on the current drive.    │
│  Information .... Display information about the current drive's data.      │
│  Locate Files ... Find any file anywhere on the current drive.            │
│  Map Disk/Files . Show a visual map of the space used the disk & files.   │
│  Quit .......... Exit Professional Master Key and return to DOS.          │
│  Rename Files ... Rename any file or directory on the current drive.      │
│  Undelete Files . Undelete any file or directory on the current drive.    │
│  ─────────────────────────────────────────────────────────────  │
│                                                                  │
│                   The working drive is C:                        │
│                                                                  │
│  ==== Public Brand Software  P.O. Box 51315  Indianapolis IN  46251 ====  │
│  ──────── Copyright 1990 by Public Brand Software, all rights reserved. ──│
└──────────────────────────────────────────────────────────────────┘
```

powerful program, so let's take a closer look at the PMK module itself and what it can do.

PMK Module Functions

PMK is fast, efficient, and easy to use. It has a host of features and its menu format gives you easy access so you can do the things you want to do without a lot of bother. All of the colors that are used are configurable. Using an install program that comes in the package, you can let all the modules use the same colors or set different colors for each one. You can bring up the PMK module either from the master menu or from the DOS prompt by typing **PMK** at the C prompt and pressing ENTER.

Here is a list of the features of the PMK module, from Figure 12-2.

- Alter Files

- Change Disk

- Disk Edit

- Erase Files

- File Edit

- Information

- Locate Files

- Map Disk/Files

- Quit

- Rename

- Undelete Files

To help you better understand the power that PMK offers, let's briefly examine what each of these functions does. You'll see that PMK lets you do a lot of things, both to files and to the physical disk as well.

Alter Files   By selecting this option you can easily change any file's date, time, or file attributes. For example, say you have a program that creates quite a few hidden files as part of its work. By using the Alter feature, you can quickly turn off the hidden attribute so that the files can be seen.

There are times when you may want a certain group of files to all have the same time and date. With PMK you can do this easily.

Change Disk   This command allows you to change the current drive. This includes changing to and from the hard disk or floppy drives. After PMK is loaded, it scans your system and knows exactly how many drives you have. You could examine the contents of a floppy on your drive A as easily as you could your hard disk, or drive C, by simply changing drives.

Disk Edit   The Disk Edit function is a very powerful feature. It should only be used if you know exactly what you are doing, since it lets you edit or change the physical contents of any sector of your disk. There is no sector of the disk that cannot be accessed from PMK's Disk Edit function. This means that you can access important areas like the boot sector, the file allocation tables (FAT), and any other part of the disk. If you are new to computers, or aren't sure of what you are doing, avoid using this function until you *do* know.

If you should make random changes to the boot sector, for example, and then save them, you could cause serious problems. Whenever you alter something, you will be asked if you want to save your changes before exiting. If you have *any* doubts at all, then do not save them. Figure 12-3 shows PMK's Disk Edit feature, showing the boot sector of a C drive.

If you look at Figure 12-3, you'll see several things. First, the screen is divided into two parts. The left side of the screen is a *hexadecimal* display and the right side is in ASCII. Looking at the right side, notice that you can see the names of the DOS system files—MSDOS.SYS and IO.SYS. What may look like random characters really contains some special information. This is an area where you don't want to start experimenting.

Note: Disk Edit can be a very handy tool. Think of Disk Edit as allowing you to look at a disk on the microscopic level. Each little "hex" grouping on the screen is like a molecule that helps to make up the total fabric of your disk. If you cut that fabric, you may not be able to patch it back together again. It cannot be stressed enough that it must be used with caution.

Erase Files   Have you ever been unable to erase a file and have DOS flash an error message like "Access Denied"? Using PMK's Erase feature, you can erase *any* file, no matter how stubborn it might be. This includes hidden, system, and read-only files. If you encounter a file or files that DOS or other utilities can't seem to erase, PMK will be able to do it.

Figure 12-3

Disk Edit showing the boot sector

```
══════════════════════ Disk Editing ══════════════════════
EB3C904D 53444F53 342E3000 02040100 02000200 00F84100 .<.MSDOS4.0..........A.
1A000500 1A000000 E6030100 800029CA 14301A4D 41535445 ............).0.MASTE
52204649 4C454641 54313620 2020FA33 C08ED0BC 007C1607 R FILEFAT16   .3....I..
BB780036 C5371E56 1653BF3E 7CB90B00 FCF3A406 1FC645FE .x.6.7.U.S.>I........E.
0F8B0E18 7C884DF9 894702C7 073E7CFB CD13727C 33C03906 ....I.M..G...>I...rI3.9.
137C7408 8B0E137C 890E207C A0107CF7 26167C03 061C7C13 .It....I.. I..I.&.I...I.
161E7C03 060E7C03 D200A350 7C891652 7CA3497C 89164B7C ..I....I....PI..RI.I!..KI
B82000F7 26117C8B 1E0B7C03 C348F7F3 0106497C 83164B7C . ..&.I...I..HI.....I!..KI
00BB0005 8B16527C A1507CE8 87007220 B001E0A1 0072190B ......RI.PI...r ....rI.
FBB90B00 BEDB7DF3 A6750D0D 7F20BEE6 7DB90B00 F3A67418 ......}..u....}.....t.
BE937DE8 510032E4 CD165E1F 8F040F44 02CD1958 5858EBE8 ..}.Q.2..^....D..XXX..
BB0007B9 0300A149 7C8B164B 7C505251 E83A0072 E6B001E8 .......II..KIPRQ.:.r....
5400595A 5872C905 010003D2 00031E0B 7CE2E20A 2E157C8A T.YZXr...........I.....I.
16247C8B 1E497CA1 4B7CEA00 007000AC 0AC07429 B40EBB07 .$I..I!.KI...p....t)....
00CD18EB F23B1618 7C7319F7 36187CFE C20B164F 7C33D2F7 .....;..Is..6.I....0I3..
361A7C88 16257CA3 4D7CF8C3 F9C3B402 8B164D7C B106D2E6 6.I..%I.MI.......MI....
0A364F7C 8BCA86E9 8A16247C 8A36257C CD13C30D 0A4E6F6E .60I.....$I.6%I.....Non
2D537973 74656D20 6469736B 206F7220 6469736B 20657272 -System disk or disk err
6F72200D 0A526570 6C616365 20616E64 20707265 7373206E or..Replace and press an
79206B65 79207768 656E2072 65616479 0D0A0049 4F202020 y key when ready...IO
20202053 59534D53 444F5320 20205359 53000000 00000000    SYSMSDOS   SYS.......
00000000 000055AA                                     ......U.
 Editing disk C: sector 0.  Cursor at offset 0 (Hex 0)
 Press F1 for help ═══════════════════════════════Standard══24 wide══
```

File Edit   File Edit is very similar to the Disk Edit feature except that you are editing the contents of individual files on your disk and not the actual sector of your disk. You can search for text within a .COM or .EXE file and even change screen displays. Here again, if you don't know what you are doing, you could end up with a program that won't work. If you want to try out the File Edit function, here are a few words of advice: never work on the original file, but work on a copy instead. For example, if you want to edit a file called INTACT.EXE, copy it first under another filename called TEST.EXE. You would do this like so:

```
C>COPY INTACT.EXE TEST.EXE
```

You could then use PMK to edit TEST.EXE. If the changes work, then you could always copy TEST.EXE to INTACT.EXE. If they don't work, you at least still have the original copy of INTACT.EXE. As with Disk Edit, use the File Edit feature with care and caution. It can be a great tool for manipulating the contents of files, but it can also make a program disfunctional. If you always work on a copy, the only thing you have to lose is time if you make a mistake.

Information   This function gives you complete information about the current drive, whether it be the hard disk or a floppy. It shows the total space available, the percentage free, and much more. Figure 12-4 shows the information provided about my drive C.

Note that it also tells you where the FAT sectors start, the size of each sector, and any bad sectors that exist on the disk.

Locate Files   This feature lets you locate files anywhere on the disk. You can enter a specific filename or you can use the DOS wildcards "*" and "?". PMK scans your entire disk and can find a file very quickly. This is a great feature for finding the exact location of a file. When PMK finds a file it displays the directory, the filename, the size, the date, the time the file was created or last altered, and even file attributes like hidden, system, and so on. In terms of time, the Locate Files portion of PMK is *very* fast.

Map Disk/Files   This shows you a graphical presentation or map of your disk. It shows you what sectors are being used, which are bad, what percentage of the disk is free, and much more. You can also use this feature to find out the exact location of a file.

Figure 12-4

The Information function of PMK

```
┌══════════════ Professional Master Key, version 3.1 ══════════════┐
│  ┌═══════════════════ Information On Drive C: ═══════════════════┐ │
│  │                                                              │ │
│  │  Disk capacity information...                                │ │
│  │        32  Megabytes total disk capacity possible.           │ │
│  │        15  Megabytes disk capacity available (49% free).     │ │
│  │                                                              │ │
│  │  Disk logical dimensions...                                  │ │
│  │       512  Bytes in each sector.                             │ │
│  │     66530  Sectors existing on the entire disk.              │ │
│  │     66368  Data Sectors possible for file usage on the disk. │ │
│  │         4  Data Sectors exist in each Data Cluster.          │ │
│  │     16592  Data Clusters possible for file usage on the disk.│ │
│  │         1  Reserved Sector(s) at the beginning of the disk.  │ │
│  │         2  FAT copies available, each using 65 sectors.      │ │
│  │       512  Files allowed in the Root Directory.              │ │
│  │                                                              │ │
│  │          Start of all FAT sectors:     sector     1          │ │
│  │          Start of the Root Directory:  sector   131          │ │
│  │          Start of all Data Sectors:    sector   163          │ │
│  │                                                              │ │
│  └══════════════════════════════════════════════════════════════┘ │
│  ==== Public Brand Software  P.O. Box 51315  Indianapolis IN  46251 ==== │
│  ══════ Copyright 1990 by Public Brand Software, all rights reserved. ══════ │
└──────────────────────────────────────────────────────────────────┘
```

Quit   This option lets you quit PMK. If you called the main PMK module from the master menu, then you will be returned to the menu. On the other hand, if you started PMK from the DOS prompt, you will be returned to DOS. If you hit F10 from the PMK menu, you will be asked if you want to quit, or you can select Quit directly.

Rename Files and Directories   With this feature you can rename any file on your system, regardless of its file attribute. To rename a file, just highlight it and press ENTER, and you will be prompted to enter the new filename. You can rename any of the directories that branch off from the root directory too. First, highlight the directory and press ENTER, and PMK will ask you for the new name. To rename any subdirectories below the first level, select the parent directory of the subdirectory that you want to rename. For example, let's say you have a C:\EDIT\ARTICLE directory and you want to rename the "ARTICLE" subdirectory "BOOK." The C:\EDIT directory is the *parent* directory for the ARTICLE subdirectory, so you would select the C:\EDIT directory. From there, highlight the ARTICLE subdirectory and rename it.

Undelete Files   We all sometimes make mistakes while working on the computer. As you begin to delete a group of files, the word "Oops" escapes your lips—or perhaps something stronger. Never fear, for PMK also has an Undelete feature. Files that you delete are still there; it's just that the first character of their filename has been replaced and the File Allocation Table doesn't recognize them anymore.

Using PMK's Undelete function, you can go in and unerase a file that you accidentally deleted. Keep in mind that with any undelete program, one of the most important factors in being able to recover the file is that you do not write anything to disk before you try to undelete the file. If you write something to disk, it may very well be written to a part of the disk that the deleted file used to occupy. This cuts down dramatically on your chances of recovering a file. With care, PMK's Undelete will work for you in a majority of cases.

The Extra Utilities of PMK

The many capabilities contained in the PMK module would be more than enough for any utility program to offer, but PMK's authors decided they wanted to give you more. The extra features include the ability to totally unformat an accidentally formatted disk, a way to erase a disk so completely that no data can be recovered, the option of doing the same thing to a single file, and more. Let's take a quick look at these extras that come with PMK.

The Fill Disk Utility

With PMK's Fill Disk utility, you can write a message of your choice on all of the free sectors on a disk. It does *not* disturb any existing data. This same feature can be used to *zero* all unused sectors, which means to remove all traces of data that existed in those areas. Fill Disk can be used in many ways, for example, to "mark" your hard disk with your social security number, your name and address, or anything allowing you to positively identify the disk if it was stolen. If you work with data that is sensitive or very personal, Fill Disk can be used to make sure that all old data is completely removed from the system.

UnFormat

This is another safety feature offered by the higher priced commercial products. If you use UnFormat at regular intervals it will save you from losing most of your files and data in case you accidentally format your hard disk. If you should do this, UnFormat will help you to restore your hard disk to the condition it was in before the accidental formatting occurred.

Full Screen File Sort

The File Sort utility of PMK lets you rearrange the order of filenames on a disk in any order that you choose. It can sort filenames in ascending or descending order. It can also sort by name, extension, date, time, or size. You can move files individually, so that files in any directory are in exactly the order you want them to be. File Sort also has a Pack option. When you use the Pack feature, the files are not only sorted, but all files that have been erased are removed from the directory.

The Zero Disk Utility

This is not like Fill Disk, which fills a disk with characters of your choosing and will not touch any existing data. Zero Disk removes *all* traces of *all* data from a disk. It does not skip over anything in its efforts to completely scrub the disk clean. If you are getting rid of a used hard disk and want to make sure the next owner has no idea of what you ever had on the disk, then Zero Disk is the answer. On a smaller level, you can do something similar with Zero File.

The Zero File Utility

If you have one or several files you want removed from your system completely, then Zero File is the answer. This utility makes it impossible to recover any portion of a file. Files erased by DOS or other utilities can often be recovered—if not completely, then partially. Zero File removes all traces of a file's current data from your disk. Not even one byte of a file removed by this utility can be recovered.

The Tiny Edit Program

The PMK package also includes a small text editor that can be used to edit batch files and other small files. The editor is very small with no bells and whistles, but is effective for what it's designed for. It's tiny enough that you can fit it easily on a floppy disk with other files, or on a laptop, or use it on your system for very simple editing tasks.

Summing Up Professional Master Key

The Professional Master Key program and its package of utilities provide a lot of power. Some may ask, "Why isn't it considered to be a DOS shell?" Primarily because it doesn't have many of the features considered standard on all good DOS shell programs (discussed in Chapter 14). On the other hand, it does have many features that DOS shells do not, and it would make a wonderful addition to your collection of Shareware utility programs.

Public Brand Software
P.O. Box 51315
Indianapolis, IN 46251
800-426-3475, 800-727-3476 in Indiana
317-856-7571 in Indianapolis
$35 registration includes printed manual, phone support, notice of updates, and latest version

PCOPY

Norm Patriquin is the author of many useful and popular utility programs. PCOPY is a file copy/move utility that has a list of options a mile long. All of these options give you tremendous flexibility when copying or moving files. PCOPY is very useful for copying files to other areas of a hard disk or moving them off to a floppy disk. You can set up and define criteria for PCOPY to match before it copies a file. This is not a "mindless" copy program that just copies and never asks a question. PCOPY will do *exactly* what you instruct it to do—checking for existing files, file dates, and much more. Let's look at some of PCOPY's options.

PCOPY Thinks for You

PCOPY is a smart utility. It was designed to help you and to even anticipate your needs. The COPY command of DOS is very limited, and it can do little more than copy a file from one place to another. It never questions what you tell it to do, and that would be good enough if humans never made mistakes. If you use DOS COPY to copy a file to drive X, even if there is a file there by that name already, DOS will proceed to overwrite it. PCOPY, however, has an option that will ask you if you want to *rename* the other file and give it a version number. This will save you the needless frustration of copying one file over another and finding out that your original data is now lost forever.

PCOPY will also let you move files between directories and drives. When you move a file, it is similar to copying it from one place to another, and then deleting it from the original area. PCOPY has some very intelligent options related to moving files as well.

PCOPY will let you use the DOS wildcards (? and *) when copying or moving files. I've said that PCOPY is "smart" and it is. For example, if you try to copy a file to a subdirectory that does not exist, PCOPY will actually ask you if you want it to create the directory.

Patriquin has created PCOPY to handle a variety of tasks at one time, eliminating the need to specify a string of DOS commands that would accomplish the same thing.

Many Options with PCOPY
PCOPY is loaded with options, some of which you might never need, but the important thing is that they are available in case you do. An easy way

to remember the options is to make up special batch files for different functions with PCOPY. If you use a DOS command line editor that allows for aliases, like Anarkey or CED, for example, you can create special commands that incorporate the PCOPY commands that you want to use for different tasks. Here are some of the available options taken from PCOPY's documentation.

- Copies files to and from any disk or directory

- Allows you to save older versions of files with new names before replacing them

- Moves files by copying them or renaming them to the new location

- Deletes the original file if /X is specified

- Creates target directories if needed

- Makes sure the DOS archive flag is set correctly for each file as it is moved

- Preserves the DOS date and time for each file moved

- Allows you to pause in processing at any time by pressing any key

- Provides file selection and processing control options to tailor the move function to the user's needs

- Allows commands to be tested, ensuring that commands are as specified by the user

- Copies updated files to a special disk or directory

- If there is not sufficient space on the current target disk, PCOPY will allow placing another disk in the drive to continue processing; this allows for copying groups of files larger than disk size to other computers

- Starts with a specific file in a directory

- Ends with a specific file in a directory

- Processes files based on the date stored in its directory entry

- Warns you before overlaying a file unless specific parameters indicating otherwise are specified

- Checks target disk for available space before starting to copy files, saving wasted time

- Provides status on the progress of a command
- Runs with windows or using standard DOS screen output
- Formats floppy disks by pressing F3 at any prompt
- Processes one directory, a single directory subtree, or all directories on a disk

These are just some of the options PCOPY gives you. You can copy files based on date, copy whole directories, or even back up your hard disk using PCOPY. Patriquin tried to think of everything to provide you with a safe and very flexible tool for copying and moving files.

Sizing Up PCOPY

PCOPY is an extremely effective and efficient utility for copying and moving files. It provides options that no other utility offers. It also makes copying simple, fast, and perhaps most importantly, safe.

For those who prefer to work from a command line, PCOPY has a command mode. It can also be run in a windows mode, which allows you to see everything that is going on. Figure 12-5 shows PCOPY copying files in the windows mode.

All of Patriquin's utility programs have the same standards of excellence that are found in PCOPY and he offers good support. If you are looking for a top of the line copy/move program with multiple options, look no further than PCOPY.

Norm Patriquin
Patri-Soft
P.O. Box 8263
San Bernardino, CA 92412
714-369-9766 (BBS)
800-242-4775 (Orders only)
Accepts MasterCard and VISA
For $20 you will receive a registered version of PCOPY with all bonus features activated, plus a disk of the most recent copies of all Patriquin utilities. For $45 you will receive a fully registered version of *all* the Patriquin utilities and a bound manual of documentation for the set. Add $4 shipping and handling for MasterCard and VISA orders.

Figure 12-5

PCOPY copying files in windows mode

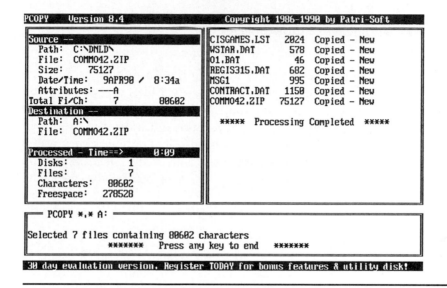

FIND DUPLICATES

Find Duplicates by John Bean is a utility that will search all of your drives and display a list of duplicate files. In the course of using a computer, it's easier than you think to end up with multiple copies of one program on your system, especially for those with several hard disks. I have a friend who was having difficulty understanding why his hard disk seemed to be filling up so fast. Using Find Duplicates, he found eight copies of PKZIP/PKUNZIP on his system. He used Find Duplicates to delete the extra copies and just kept one copy in his DOS PATH. Let's take a look at what Find Duplicates does and how it can help you keep your system organized and free from multiple program copies.

Giving You All the Information

After Find Duplicates searches all drives you specify, locating duplicate files, it displays the results on your screen. Figure 12-6 shows what the Find Duplicates screen looks like. At this point you have several options available to you. You can

- Tag files for deletion

- Print out a list of duplicate files

- View the contents of duplicate files

These options give you flexibility in dealing with duplicates. In some cases, you may *want* duplicates of certain files — text files, for example. You can move through the listing and tag files you want to delete while leaving others alone. Perhaps you want to print out a copy of the duplicates and study it before making any decisions. This option is very useful on systems that have very large hard disks with many files. Lastly, you have the option to look inside some of the files before you decide to delete them or not.

Figure 12-6

The display of Find Duplicates

Find Duplicates, Version 4.01 by JB Technology Inc.- EVALUATION COPY

```
File Name    Location              Size      Date      Time
AUTOSAVE.EXE C:\QEMM\             11562   03/04/88  13:16.20
AUTOSAVE.EXE D:\                  11562   03/04/88  13:16.20

BUD2.ARK     C:\MYM\BUSINESS\         2   01/30/84  20:06.04
BUD2.ARK     C:\MYM\PERSONAL\         2   01/29/90  14:05.22

BUDGET.ARK   C:\MYM\BUSINESS\     56749   11/30/89  23:24.14
BUDGET.ARK   C:\MYM\PERSONAL\         2   01/29/90  14:00.12

BUDGET.DB    C:\MYM\BUSINESS\     20032   01/20/90  14:00.50
BUDGET.DB    C:\MYM\PERSONAL\    157579   04/09/90  07:06.18

CIS.SCR      C:\QMODEM\SCRIPTS\    1123   02/20/89  21:10.00
CIS.SCR      D:\TMATE\SCRIPTS\      197   03/18/90  21:35.24

COMPOUND.DB  C:\MYM\BUSINESS\      5205   12/08/89  17:03.30
COMPOUND.DB  C:\MYM\PERSONAL\      5205   12/08/89  17:03.30
```

F1-Help   F10-Erase Tagged Duplicates   Esc-Exit Program

Command Line Options

Find Duplicates has some command line options listed here:

/BW	Forces display to black and white
/D	Defines drives to be searched
/DISK	Saves information to disk
/VW	Defines a viewing program
/RO	Finds read-only files

Find Duplicates automatically detects if you have a color monitor. If you should want the display to be in black and white, you can force the program to use it by using the /BW command.

The /D option defines disk drives you want searched. Take, for example, the following command line that would tell the program to search drives C and D.

```
C>FD /D=C,D
```

You can use a parameter *ALL*, which will have Find Duplicates search every drive that you have, including floppy drives. The command would look like this:

```
C>FD /D=ALL
```

If you use this command, the program will begin with drive A and work its way down.

The */DISK* parameter is available only in the registered version of the program. What is it for? Normally, the data gathered by Find Duplicates is stored in RAM. If you have a very large system you could use the */DISK* parameter to have the list stored to disk.

The */VW* parameter lets you define the program to be used for viewing duplicate files. Find Duplicates comes with a program called VIEW.COM,. If you prefer to use Vern Buerg's LIST, for example, on the command line, you would enter

```
C>FD /D=C,D /VW=LIST.COM
```

Find Duplicates would search drives C and D and would use LIST for viewing files.

The last command line option is /RO, and this is used for finding read-only files. You may choose to include any or all of these options on the Find Duplicates command line.

Summing Up Find Duplicates

For managing hard disks and eliminating wasted space, you can't beat the Find Duplicates utility. Many bulletin board sysops use this fine program to ensure against multiple copies of a program in various file areas. Find Duplicates is fast, efficient, and gives you the option of removing or keeping duplicate files. It's a good addition to any system that has one or more hard disks. Try it!

John E. Bean
JB Technology, Inc.
28701 N. Main Street
Ridgefield, WA 98642
206-887-3442 for questions or to place an order
$15 registration
Registered users receive a printed manual, a disk with the latest version of Find Duplicates, and the /DISK option activated.

DFF

DFF is a good file finding utility that is very fast. It's offered free by Daniel Doman, who has written several other excellent utility programs. DFF can search one or more drives for a variety of filenames. It can even work on network drives. Figure 12-7 shows what DFF displays on the screen.

In timing it against other file finding utilities on a 66 megabyte hard disk, DFF consistently averaged better times. It should be noted that the abilities of any such utility will depend in part on the directory structure of your hard disk. If your subdirectory structure is quite complex, then any file finding utility is going to take longer than if your directory structure was simple.

In testing DFF, a similar program took 4.60 seconds to find a particular file, but DFF took about 2.50 seconds. Your results may vary, but DFF was much faster than similar utilities that come with various commercial packages.

Figure 12-7

DFF in action finding all .BAT files

```
        MAKEZIP2.BAT              59 Bytes    Dec 22, 1989   2:00:00a
        MAKEZIP3.BAT             107 Bytes    Dec 22, 1989   2:00:00a
        MLINK-D.BAT              30 Bytes    Dec 22, 1989   2:00:00a
        MLINK-U.BAT              33 Bytes    Dec 22, 1989   2:00:00a

D:\UTIL
        LOVE.BAT                 56 Bytes    Oct 10, 1988  12:02:02a
        PTHSET.BAT               42 Bytes    Jan 27, 1990   2:51:11a
        01.BAT                   46 Bytes   April  9, 1990  12:22:06a

D:\UPI\GRASP
        RUN.BAT                  17 Bytes    Dec 18, 1989   1:40:14p

D:\WYNFILE
        README.BAT              397 Bytes    Dec  1, 1989  12:00:00a

D:\XTGOLD
        BAT.BAT                   3 Bytes    Oct 13, 1989   5:00:00p
        COM.BAT                   3 Bytes    Oct 13, 1989   5:00:00p
        EXE.BAT                   3 Bytes    Oct 13, 1989   5:00:00p

Total Files Found ->83    Total Bytes ->15,487

c:\>
```

DFF's Command Line Options

As it searches for files, DFF displays the subdirectory it is in, so you always know its current status. On a Northgate 386, for example, the search process is so fast it's hard to see.

DFF follows certain conventions and also has some command line parameters that can alter how it works. For example, DFF searches for a file from the root directory of the current drive. You can search one particular path if you like, and in that case, DFF will only search *that* path. For example, let's say you have a directory called C:\BUSINESS with directories under it. You would enter

```
C>DFF C:\BUSINESS\*.WKS
```

DFF would find every *.WKS file in every directory located under the C:\BUSINESS directory. Here are the possible command line parameters available with DFF:

/D	Searches all drives starting with the current drive
/C	Searches all drives and starts with drive C
/Dx	Searches all drives beginning with drive x
/M{#}	Limits matches to one
/N	Non-stop action (DFF does not pause after a full screen)
/Q	Quiet mode (DFF does not show the search in progress)

An interesting feature is that you can redirect DFF's output to a file and it will still display the search on the screen. Thus, you could enter something like:

```
DFF /D F*.* > SEARCH.LST
```

DFF would display the search on the screen while sending the same information to the file SEARCH.LST.

In summary, DFF is an excellent file finding program and is free to the general public.

Daniel Doman
DannySoft, Inc.
166 East 96th Street
New York, NY 10128
212-427-1805 BBS
No registration fee

LIST

Vern Buerg's LIST may well be the most popular Shareware program ever written. With LIST you can search for text within a file, filter out "high bit" characters, use a mouse, and much more. With the release of version 7.0 of LIST, Buerg introduced LIST PLUS. Since many users are familiar with LIST, let's take a look at LIST PLUS and see what it can do.

The Power of LIST PLUS

Like the original versions of LIST, LIST PLUS allows users to easily view files. Figure 12-8 shows what LIST PLUS displays when loaded from the root directory on drive C.

Figure 12-8

LIST PLUS loaded in the root directory

```
LIST - File Selection        1 of 39       Path: C:\*.*
↓DCOM          <DIR>    02-20-90 13:33   4DOS206  .EXE    63393   03-07-90 03:00
↓DNLD          <DIR>    02-20-90 13:34   4START   .BAT      103   03-22-90 21:17
↓DOS           <DIR>    02-20-90 13:34   ALIASES            1794   04-08-90 00:12
↓DRFFBK        <DIR>    02-20-90 13:35   AUTOEXEC .BAT      588   04-08-90 22:12
↓DU            <DIR>    02-20-90 13:35   BURNDEV  .SYS     2595   04-13-89 12:16
↓FASTBACK      <DIR>    02-20-90 13:07   COMMAND  .COM    37557   12-19-88 00:00
↓GETIT         <DIR>    04-07-90 14:28   CONFIG   .SYS      179   03-20-90 17:28
↓HDM           <DIR>    03-24-90 17:43   DO-ONCE  .DAT      135   03-20-90 17:36
↓LIGHT         <DIR>    04-05-90 03:51   DOS      .HLP    87328   03-07-90 03:00
↓MEMO          <DIR>    02-20-90 13:40   GREET    .COM      563   05-22-86 01:53
↓MYM           <DIR>    02-20-90 13:45   HELP     .EXE    44944   03-07-90 03:00
↓PRNSHP        <DIR>    02-20-90 13:47   IO       .SYS    33337   12-19-88 00:00
↓QEMM          <DIR>    02-20-90 13:48   KBFIX3   .COM     7200   12-16-88 22:16
↓QMODEM        <DIR>    02-20-90 13:48   MENU     .COM     2540   01-15-88 12:00
↓TEXT          <DIR>    02-20-90 13:49   MSDOS    .SYS    37376   04-19-89 00:38
↓TST1          <DIR>    04-07-90 13:58   WSHL     .BAT       39   03-27-90 15:02
↓UPLD          <DIR>    02-20-90 16:21
↓UTL           <DIR>    03-13-90 07:16
↓WORK          <DIR>    02-20-90 13:55
↓WP50          <DIR>    02-20-90 13:55
↓WSHELL        <DIR>    03-20-90 16:03
4DLOAD   .BAT      32    04-08-90 16:03
4DOS     .COM   10042    03-07-90 03:00
List Copy Del Edit Move Path Ren Sort Tag Untag ViewArc  1-6  F1=Help  Esc=Exit
```

In this example, LIST PLUS is set to display data in two columns. You can set the program to display from one to six columns. In single-column mode, LIST PLUS shows you the directory or filename, the extension, the size, the date, the time, and the file attribute. You can vary the display mode and set that feature so LIST PLUS always loads with that default. This doesn't mean you can't change the display. For example, you may prefer the single-column mode in most cases and set LIST PLUS to come up in that mode. However, you can toggle between any of the other modes without affecting your default. Here is a listing of LIST PLUS features:

- List
- Copy
- Delete
- Edit
- Move
- Path

- Rename

- Sort

- Tag

- Untag

- ViewArc

Let's take a closer look at some of these features.

File Handling Features
In addition to having all the great file handling features associated with LIST, LIST PLUS provides even more. LIST PLUS lets you navigate around your computer system without having to leave the program. Edit files with the editor of your choice, dial a phone number, and even run other programs from LIST PLUS.

Changing Directories in LIST PLUS   LIST PLUS uses a down-arrow to designate subdirectories. If you highlight one of these arrows and press ENTER, you will go into that directory. If the directory you are in is a subdirectory, there will be an up-arrow. If you select the up-arrow you will go into the directory one level above. These features allow you to easily move around your hard disk from within LIST PLUS.

Copying Files
You can copy a file to a new subdirectory by highlighting the file you want to copy and pressing the ENTER key. LIST PLUS will prompt you for the new path to copy the selected file to. Type the path, **C:\DNLD**, for example, and press the ENTER key. The file will be copied. LIST PLUS lets you tag and untag files, including *all* of the files in a directory for copying to another directory. You can use the tag and untag options with other features in LIST PLUS as well.

Deleting Files
LIST PLUS lets you delete any file in the current directory by highlighting or tagging the file to be deleted and pressing ENTER. The program will

always prompt you to make sure that you want to delete one or a group of files.

Moving Files

You can move any file in the current directory to any other directory. Select the file that you want to move by highlighting or tagging it and hitting ENTER. LIST PLUS will then prompt you for a path where you want the files to be moved. Enter the path and the file or files will be moved to the target directory.

Changing the Path This LIST PLUS feature is another way to move around the system from within the program. As previously mentioned, you can highlight directories from within the program and move around your system. The path command lets you switch to any other directory by typing in the path, for example,

```
C:\WORK\EDIT
```

You will be in the C:\WORK\EDIT directory and LIST PLUS will show you the contents on the screen.

You Can Rename, Too!

To rename files, highlight the file you want to rename. The program will prompt you for a new filename. After you've entered it, LIST PLUS will prompt you to make sure that you are certain. Respond with a **Y** if you're sure or with an **N** if you've changed your mind.

Sorting Filenames You can always change the order in which filenames are displayed. Select the Sort option and choose sorting by:

- Filename

- Extension

- Date

- Size

- No sort at all (natural order)

You can toggle back and forth until you get the sort order that you want.

The ViewArc Function

This function lets you view the contents of any packed or compressed file, even self-extracting files. To use this feature, you must have another utility created by Vern Buerg. The program is File View (FV), and it must be in your DOS PATH. It's handy for seeing what is inside of .ZIP, .ARC, .LZH, .PAK, and self-extracting .COM and .EXE files. FV can be found as FV???.ZIP (extension may vary), where ??? is the version number.

Invoking Programs

The word "invoke" can help you remember that by using the I key, you can run programs from within LIST PLUS. Highlight any .COM, .EXE, or .BAT file and then press I. The program will run, assuming you have enough memory. When the run is complete, you will be returned to LIST PLUS.

The Ability to Edit

Over the years, people using LIST have often wished they could select a file and then *edit* it. By attaching the editor of your choice to LIST PLUS, you can edit any file. To do this, create a batch file called EDIT.BAT. Highlight the program you want to edit and press E. You'll find yourself in your favorite editor. After exiting, you'll be returned to LIST PLUS. Make sure both LIST PLUS and EDIT.BAT are in your DOS PATH.

Want to Dial the Phone?

You can dial phone numbers with your modem using LIST PLUS. You can be within any document and use the phone dialing feature, assuming the phone number you want to call is within the document. You use CTRL-T and LIST PLUS prompts you to highlight the number you want to call. Move the cursor to the first digit of the phone number and press ENTER. Press the SPACEBAR and your modem will dial the number. Pick up the phone and be ready to talk. You can use CTRL-H to hang up the modem. If you use LIST PLUS, you might find it handy to keep an ASCII file with just names and phone numbers in it. When you want to dial a number, you can just bring up the file with LIST, find the number you want to call, and dial it.

Listing the Features of LIST PLUS

One could go on listing all of the features and extras found in LIST PLUS. Buerg has taken an already great program and gone many steps beyond that, giving LIST PLUS a lot of power. Buerg still packages the regular version of LIST (just for file viewing), as well as a small version of LIST (for those with less RAM), along with LIST PLUS.

Buerg holds true to the best concepts that make Shareware what it is. He *lives* the concept by *sharing* his products with users. He does not demand payment, but asks for a donation in any amount, with $20 suggested. In the information section at the end of this discussion, there is a quote of Buerg's request for payment. LIST is a unique program and LIST PLUS is amazing. You won't find programs of their caliber in the commercial market.

Vernon D. Buerg
139 White Oak Circle
Petaluma, CA 94952
707-778-8944 (BBS and public node)
Request: "If you are using LIST and find it of value, your gift in any amount ($20 suggested) will be greatly appreciated. Please make checks payable in U.S. dollars to Vernon D. Buerg. For use by corporations and other institutions, please contact me for a licensing arrangement."

CON > FORMAT — CONCURRENT FORMATTER

Con>Format can do its work and not intrude on what you are doing with your machine. Edit a document, view a file, do whatever you need to do, and Con>Format will format disks while you do it. Let's examine exactly what Con>Format does.

Formatting with Con > Format

This program is a TSR utility that waits in memory until you want to use it. You can determine what key sequences are used to make Con > Format pop up. At that time, the program opens a window and asks which drive you would like to format on and what kind of format. Once you've supplied this information, all evidence of Con > Format disappears. The only time you see it is when a format is completed.

   Con > Format formats disks on 5.25- and 3.5-inch diskette drives. It can format for 180K, 360K, 720K, 1.2 meg and 1.44 meg diskettes. The program and the formatting are compatible with all DOS versions from 2.0 through 4.01. The program has some built-in safety features. For example, if a program you are using tries to access a disk drive while Con > Format is formatting a disk, Con > Format will delay the process until the format is complete. You are notified when this happens. As soon as the format is completed, you can remove the formatted disk and insert the disk that the calling program is looking for. If you're tired of watching the screen while you format disks, then don't. (*smile*) Take a look at Con > Format and do something else while your disks are formatting.

Sydex
153 North Murphy Avenue
Sunnyvale, CA 94086
$15 registration by check or money order
You receive the most recent version of the program and technical support. Printed manual is $3 extra. Some extra utilities are included. Please indicate what product you are ordering and if you want a 3.5-inch, 720K disk. Customers outside the U.S. should add $5 for airmail shipping. Updates are $5 to cover shipping

MORE ON FILE UTILITIES

This chapter describes a few very good file utilities. There are so many that it would be impossible to cover them all. Here is a listing of some other good utilities you might want to look for.

ALTER22.ZIP	2368	ALTER 2.2 - Change file attributes.
ASKEY.ZIP	13646	Finds KEY words in text files.
BOOTHRU.ZIP	2420	Alters a floppy, so Drive C will boot.
CDISK361.ZIP	113615	CDISK 3.61 - EXCELLENT Disk Cataloger
CN.ZIP	14348	Rename files using wildcards. Great!
COMPARE.ZIP	30337	Compare two text files. Send to printer.
CPUB.ZIP	27268	Excellent Encryption/Decryption program
DATE.ZIP	4403	Manipulate file dates with options!
DATEDEL.ZIP	8686	Delete files by range of dates.
DELZ.ZIP	2421	A controlled 'delete' utility.
DISKMOD5.ZIP	6494	DISK MODIFIER -peek inside files!!
DISKOKAY.ZIP	2497	Checks to see if floppy is OK.
DR.ZIP	17669	PC Mag's excellent DIR utility.
FAT.ZIP	15111	Lets you look at the contents of the FAT
FATBACK.ZIP	5468	Backs up your File Allocation Table.
FILECAT1.ZIP	89577	Excellent file cataloguing system.
FILL30.ZIP	37628	FILL v3.0 Maxmize File Backups
FMOVE2.ZIP	6640	Fastest MOVE program in all the world.
HIDE.ZIP	6215	Change file attributes!
JLSWEEP.ZIP	12379	Performs functions across your hard disk
NEW-MOVE.ZIP	2395	Moves files quickly and easily.
NEW.ZIP	6416	Tells what files are new on your system
NJATTRIB.ZIP	13875	Attribute program - Change files/dirs.
PALERT.ZIP	18407	Checks disk for free space. GOOD!
PDEL33C.ZIP	30777	Patriquins Delete Utility. Many options
PURGEV15.ZIP	12654	Cleans up your hard disk of extra files.
QDR33D.ZIP	7795	Vern Buerg's Quick Disk Reformater
QSCAN.COM	2560	QSCAN -scan files for a matching line.
QSORT.ZIP	17143	QSORT is an enhanced SORT utility.
RN.ZIP	37181	System directory, file manager. PC MAG
SDIR.COM	3328	Sorts directory by size,ext,etc. Good.
SFILE.ZIP	5414	Searches for a file, even in archives!
SINCE2.ZIP	10964	Specify a date,it shows you any new file
SORTDISK.ZIP	2005	Physically sorts a disk by extension
SRCH82.ZIP	32077	SEARCH version 8.2 by Art Hill.
TCFM.ZIP	41816	File Manager written in Turbo C.
VFILE.ZIP	8247	Good file manager utility.

As noted, these are just a few file utilities that exist—many more await you out in The Wires. Other programs worth taking a good look at include

- **Copy Master** Found as CM???.ZIP, where ??? is the version number. This is a copy/move program by John Newlin and New-Ware.

- **PSEARCH** Found as PSRCH??.ZIP, where ?? is the version number. This utility searches for text within files.

- **PALERT** Found as PALERT.ZIP, it alerts you on disk space.

- **PATTR** Found as PATTR.ZIP, it alters file attributes.

- **PDAILY** Found as PDAILY.ZIP, it does .BAT files selectively on boot. It can run things once a week, once a month, and so on.

- **CATDISK** Found as CDISK???.ZIP, where ??? is the version number. It is an excellent disk cataloging program.

- **DIREDIT** Found as DREDIT??.ZIP, where ?? is the version number. This utility physically sorts files in the order you want and rewrites the disk.

- **EZ FORMAT** Found as EASY??.ZIP where ?? is the version number. EZ FORMAT is actually several format utilities: a menu version, a fast command line version, and even one especially designed for use with DESQview.

We'll leave utility programs for now, but examine many more in Chapter 15. Let's move on and take a look at hard disk backup programs and menus.

## CHAPTER THIRTEEN

Hard Disk Backup and Menu Programs

This chapter is going to take a look at two different kinds of programs. Both types deal with hard disks and aid you in using them more easily and efficiently. The first type of program that you'll examine are hard disk backup and restore programs. The number of very good programs of this type is rather limited in Shareware, but they do exist.

The second type of program that you'll look at are hard disk menu programs. There are a large number of these in Shareware, exhibiting a wide range of features and functions. Hard disk backup and restore programs help keep the data on your hard disk secure by always giving you something to fall back on. Hard disk menu programs make it easy for both power users and new users to easily access all of the programs and files on a hard disk.

LIFE INSURANCE FOR YOUR DATA

Having a hard disk can make the use of your computer a great deal easier. It also makes it faster and puts many programs within your reach in an instant. At the same time, there are some extra things you must consider. If one floppy disk goes bad, you've lost the contents of that one disk. If you have a problem with your hard disk, on the other hand, it's like losing the contents of many floppy disks.

One thing to remember when you have a hard disk is that the programs kept on the disk must be backed up regularly. If you have a hard disk and don't back it up, you will find out why you needed to only after it's too late. For most people, losing everything on their hard disk only has to happen once to convince them that doing a backup is a good idea. Restoring everything that was contained on your hard disk by using compressed files stored on floppy disks is an irritating and frustrating process. To make the process of backing up and restoring your hard disk easier, faster, and simpler, special programs have been developed. Let's talk about them in general terms first.

Hard Disk Backup and Restore Programs

All versions of DOS come with two programs that can assist you in duplicating the files that you keep on your hard disk. These are BACKUP.COM and RESTORE.COM. The programs are fairly efficient, but have limited options. The files that you put on floppy disks using BACKUP.COM are useless unless they are put back with RESTORE.COM.

Because backing up your hard disk is a chore that should be done often, programmers have come up with ways to make it more efficient and more selective. There are several good commercial programs available, but you pay the price. Some of the better Shareware programs are good, and in many cases the programs are absolutely free. The most important thing to remember is that you need to get in the habit of backing up your hard disk.

A Necessity Born Out of Frustration

A 40 megabyte hard disk holds the equivalent of 110 360K floppy disks. That is a lot of information. Your hard disk may contain customized batch files, commercial and Shareware programs, data from work, and much more. Using a hard disk system without making backups regularly is like driving a car without brakes or skydiving without a reserve parachute.

Think about all of the things that you keep on your hard disk. A good hard disk backup program will put copies of all that data on floppy disks.

Then, if you have a problem, you can easily restore 1 file or 50. Let's say that you back up your hard disk on the first of each month. During the course of the month, you will very likely put some new programs on your hard disk. Text files will change and data may be added to other files. Some backup programs allow you to do interim backups as well. An interim backup only backs up new files or files that have changed since the original backup. If nothing else, consider doing a full backup at least once a month, and then do interim backups during the month.

If you back up just once a month, you can still lose a lot of data. How? Say you add to a file every day for 20 days. If something happens to your disk, the one backup that you made will contain *none* of that data. If you do interim backups, at least you will only lose part of that new data. The hard disk backup and restore programs discussed here were picked because they are easy to use and allow you to do interim backups. Let's take a look.

Archive 3.0 — Fast and Free

On bulletin boards and commercial networks you will commonly find the Archive 3.0 program as ARCHVE30.ZIP (the extension may vary). I have tested Archive 3.0 with DOS versions 2.1, 3.1, 3.2, and 3.3. Archive can only be used with drive A.

Archive is menu driven and allows for several possibilities when doing backups. You can do a full backup of the disk, or select specific directories or specific files to back up. The same is true of its restore procedure. You can also back up files based on a date that you specify. Archive 3.0 is Freeware and there is no registration. There have been two versions of this fine program, but no one is really sure who wrote it. There is no documentation and it comes packed by itself. The program consists of a single file, ARCHIVE.EXE. Figure 13-1 shows the main Backup menu of Archive.

Note that you can tag either entire directories or just individual files. You can toggle back and forth using the TAB key. Thus, in Figure 13-1, rather than back up every file in the root directory, I used the TAB key, and the cursor moved over to the side where the files are listed. In this way you can tag one file and not another. The files that I tagged are marked with a diamond.

If you stay on the directory side and use "T" for "Tag," tagging a directory tags every file in it. If you have just one file that you don't want

---

Figure 13-1

The Backup menu of Archive

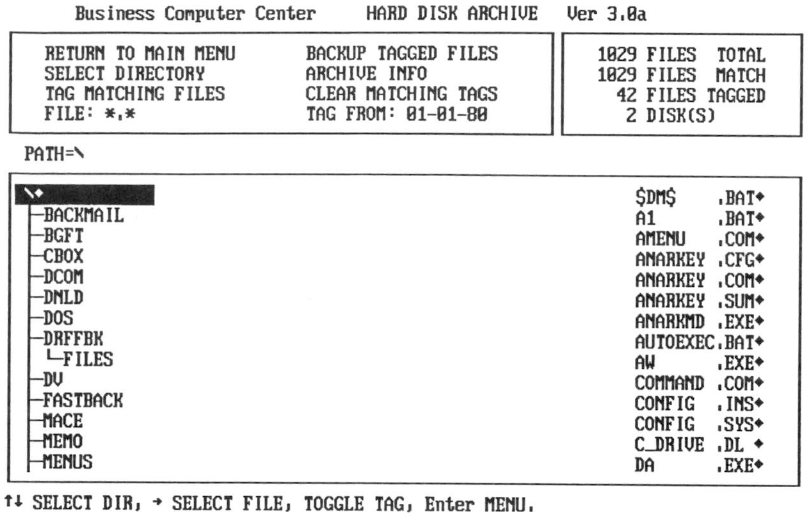

```
Business Computer Center    HARD DISK ARCHIVE    Ver 3.0a
┌─────────────────────────────────────────────────┐ ┌──────────────────┐
│ RETURN TO MAIN MENU    BACKUP TAGGED FILES       │ │ 1029 FILES  TOTAL│
│ SELECT DIRECTORY       ARCHIVE INFO              │ │ 1029 FILES  MATCH│
│ TAG MATCHING FILES     CLEAR MATCHING TAGS       │ │   42 FILES TAGGED│
│ FILE: *.*              TAG FROM: 01-01-80        │ │    2 DISK(S)     │
└─────────────────────────────────────────────────┘ └──────────────────┘
PATH=\
┌────────────────────────────────────────────────────────────────────┐
│ \◆                                          $DM$      .BAT◆          │
│ ├─BACKMAIL                                  A1        .BAT◆          │
│ ├─BGFT                                      AMENU     .COM◆          │
│ ├─CBOX                                      ANARKEY   .CFG◆          │
│ ├─DCOM                                      ANARKEY   .COM◆          │
│ ├─DNLD                                      ANARKEY   .SUM◆          │
│ ├─DOS                                       ANARKMD   .EXE◆          │
│ ├─DRFFBK                                    AUTOEXEC  .BAT◆          │
│ │ └─FILES                                   AW        .EXE◆          │
│ ├─DV                                        COMMAND   .COM◆          │
│ ├─FASTBACK                                  CONFIG    .INS◆          │
│ ├─MACE                                      CONFIG    .SYS◆          │
│ ├─MEMO                                      C_DRIVE   .DL ◆          │
│ ├─MENUS                                     DA        .EXE◆          │
└────────────────────────────────────────────────────────────────────┘
↑↓ SELECT DIR, → SELECT FILE, TOGGLE TAG, Enter MENU.
```

---

to back up, tag the entire directory, and then use TAB to move to the file side of the screen. Now you can highlight that one file and untag it. In the upper right-hand corner of the screen you can see where Archive keeps track of how many files exist, how many have been tagged, and how many disks it will take to back up the tagged files. To date, the estimate has never been wrong. If it says you'll need 24 disks, you can count on needing exactly 24.

Interim Backups

Archive performs another handy function by formatting disks for you as it goes along. Doing a full backup is easy. Just move to the directory screen and tag the root directory. This tags *all* the directories (and files) below the root.

You can do an interim backup in several ways. You could go through and manually tag all of the files that you know have changed since your last full backup. The most efficient way, however, is to use Archive's date function. You can tell the program to back up any files that are new or that have been altered since a certain date. Do not put your interim backups on the same disks as your full backup. Keep a separate set of disks that you use only for interim backups. In this way, your original full backup is always intact and any changes are kept on the interim backup disks.

Restoring Files Is Just as Easy

Archive is not colorful, but it is fast and efficient. It gives you some flexibility in backing up your hard disk. Restoring your files is basically the same as doing the backup. If you want to restore all of the files, you can tag the root directory and all files will be tagged. If you only need to restore a few files, you can do that too. Use TAB to move over to the file side of the screen and tag the files that you want restored. Archive will prompt you to put in the appropriate disks. It's that easy. Archive will serve you well by allowing you to do full backups, interim backups, and restore files as needed. To top it all off, it's free.

Point & Shoot Backup/Restore

Point & Shoot Backup/Restore (P&SBR) is an excellent program with a good user interface. P&SBR is a product of Kurt Diesch and his company, Applied Micro Systems Technology (AMST). This is one of the better hard disk backup programs and offers great flexibility for the user. You can configure the colors that the program uses to suit your taste. One exceptional feature of P&SBR is that it allows you to maintain up to ten predefined backup patterns. You can give each of your specialized configurations a unique name. If you wanted to back up all of your word processing files once a week, for example, you could make a configuration called WP-BAKUP. This configuration might only back up those directories and files that hold your word processing information. The program offers several other interesting options. Figure 13-2 shows the menu of P&SBR.

Fast and Flexible

P&SBR supports 360K, 1.2 meg, 720K, and 1.4 meg disks. You can also ask the program to calculate the number of disks needed to do the backup,

---

Figure 13-2

The main screen of P&SBR

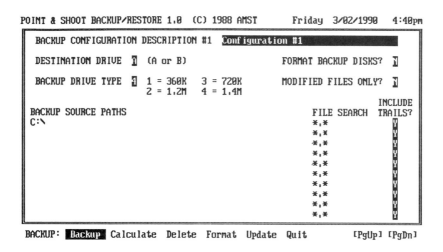

```
POINT & SHOOT BACKUP/RESTORE 1.0  (C) 1988 AMST       Friday  3/02/1990   4:40pm
┌──────────────────────────────────────────────────────────────────────────┐
│  BACKUP CONFIGURATION DESCRIPTION #1  Configuration #1                      │
│                                                                            │
│  DESTINATION DRIVE  A  (A or B)          FORMAT BACKUP DISKS?  N            │
│                                                                            │
│  BACKUP DRIVE TYPE  2  1 = 360K  3 = 720K  MODIFIED FILES ONLY?  N          │
│                        2 = 1.2M  4 = 1.4M                                   │
│                                                            INCLUDE          │
│  BACKUP SOURCE PATHS                            FILE SEARCH  TRAILS?        │
│  C:\                                               *.*          Y           │
│                                                    *.*          Y           │
│                                                    *.*          Y           │
│                                                    *.*          Y           │
│                                                    *.*          Y           │
│                                                    *.*          Y           │
│                                                    *.*          Y           │
│                                                    *.*          Y           │
│                                                    *.*          Y           │
│                                                    *.*          Y           │
└──────────────────────────────────────────────────────────────────────────┘
  BACKUP:  Backup  Calculate  Delete  Format  Update  Quit      [PgUp] [PgDn]

  BACKUP - Proceed with backup according to current configuration
```

---

based on the capacity of the floppy disks that you'll be using. From my experience in using the program, I know that it would take me 60 360K disks, or only 18 1.2 meg disks, to back up my C drive. Figure 13-3 shows you this calculation, based on using 1.2 meg floppy disks.

A nice feature about the ten possible backup configurations is that you can set P&SBR so that:

- All specified files are backed up

- Files meeting a certain specification are backed up

- Only modified files are backed up

P&SBR also shows you a directory tree to assist you in selecting directories you want to back up. Unlike some other programs, P&SBR will keep files intact while backing up, unless a file is so large that it can't fit on one disk. This program works well, and offers you the option of formatting disks as the program does its backup work.

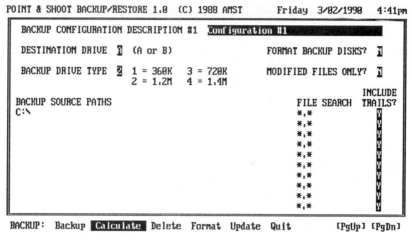

Figure 13-3

P&SBR disk calculations

Custom Restoration

When it comes to restoring files, P&SBR gives you some options that other programs don't. For example, you can elect to restore a program to a path different from the one where the back up was made. Many programs will not allow this. To give you an extra feeling of confidence, the program will also prompt you if it encounters a file that has been modified since the backup, or if it finds a duplicate file. As with the backup procedure, you can also restore only selected files. P&SBR offers some excellent options that make it easy to restore an entire hard disk or just a few files.

System Configuration In order to use P&SBR you will need a system with the following configuration: a DOS version of 2.0 or above and at least 256K of free memory. The program can be run with monochrome, CGA, EGA, or VGA displays. The program supports both 5.25-inch and 3.5-inch disks, both regular and high density. If you need a good hard disk backup and restore program, P&SBR is one to look for. The program can usually be found with a filename of P&SBR10.ZIP. For information or to register, write to:

Kurt H. Diesch
Applied Micro Systems Technology
P.O. Box 1596, Welch Avenue Station
Ames, IA 50010
$35 registration fee includes full support and printed documentation

Diskpack—Command Driven

The programs described thus far both use menus as an interface for doing hard disk backup and restore. To provide you with an alternative method, command line options rather than a menu, there is Diskpack. Diskpack is a product of Biologic Software and is run from the DOS prompt. Many users prefer this method to using a menu-driven program. Diskpack is fast and uses its own compression techniques. The compression factor means that you use fewer disks. On the average, Diskpack can back up ten megabytes of data in approximately four minutes. Let's take a look at some of Diskpack's command line options and what they allow you to do.

/?	Display help
/A	Do not change the archive bit so DOS knows it has been backed up
/B	Beep when prompted to insert a disk
/C[[d:][path]filename.[ext]]	Create a catalog containing the file-names of files backed up using speci-fied drive, path, and filename
/Dmm-dd-yy	Back up files modified on or after spec-ified date
/H	Include hidden files in backups
/I	Display registration information
/M	Back up files modified since the last backup
/P	Display a (y/n)? prompt before copying each file
/S	Back up subdirectory files in addition to current directory
/V	Display a verbose description of backup in progress
/W	Prompt user to press a key before reading source files

Using various combinations of these commands, you can have Diskpack back up your hard disk in a variety of ways. You can back up all files or only files that have been modified. You have the option of basing your backup on files modified on or after a certain date. In addition, you can tell Diskpack to back up subdirectories, prompt you before copying a file, beep at you when you need to insert a new disk, and much more. Here is an example:

```
C>DISKPACK *.* A:/S/V
```

This command would have Diskpack back up all of the files in the current directory and all files in any subdirectories below the current directory to drive A. It would also give you a verbose listing of all of the files that are being backed up. To begin backing up your entire hard disk, you would want to start in the root directory using the following command:

```
C>DISKPACK C:\*.* A:/S/V/C
```

This command line tells Diskpack to back up all files in the root directory of drive C. The /S also informs Diskpack to back up all the subdirectories of drive C. The /V will let you see a verbose listing of the files that are being backed up. Lastly, the /C will create a catalog of the files that are backed up, using the default filename DISKPACK.CAT in the current directory. You can have various backup routines by putting the Diskpack commands that you want in batch files. Thus, you could have one batch file for doing a full backup, one for doing interim backups, and so on.

To give you an idea of what Diskpack displays on the screen, let's work with an example. Let's say you have a directory on drive C called C:\WORK. Beneath that, you have a subdirectory called EDIT; so it's the C:\WORK\EDIT directory. Figure 13-4 shows what you will see if you type in the following command line:

```
C>DISKPACK *.* A:/S/V
```

Notice that Diskpack gives a verbose listing and also backs up not only the C:\WORK directory, but the C:\WORK\EDIT directory as well. In using Diskpack to back up your hard disk, always use the /C option. By doing

Figure 13-4

Diskpack at work

```
DISKPACK REG     3285 03-07-88  10:49p
DRESTORE EXE    31096 03-19-88   8:52a
DRESTORE HLP     3867 03-07-88  10:40p
README   BAT       55 03-19-88   8:57a
        11 File(s)   12343296 bytes free

C:\WORK!1>
>diskpack *.* A:/S/U
Biologic Diskpack, Version 2.1
Copyright (C) Biologic Company 1987,1988.  All rights reserved.
\WORK\DISKPACK.ZIP
\WORK\DISKPACK.DOC
\WORK\DISKPACK.EXE
\WORK\DISKPACK.HLP
\WORK\DISKPACK.REG
\WORK\DRESTORE.EXE
\WORK\DRESTORE.HLP
\WORK\README.BAT
\WORK\EDIT\REGISTER.FRM
\WORK\EDIT\SELLSHWR.TXT

insert backup disk 1 in drive A:
files in the target drive will be erased
press any key when ready
```

so, you have a record of all of the files that have been backed up and a point of reference. Diskpack will default to a filename of DISKPACK.CAT, or you can give the file a unique name. Now let's take a brief look at how Diskpack restores files.

Selective Restore Capabilities
For restoring programs to the hard disk, the Diskpack program comes with another program called DRESTORE. Using command line parameters similar to the ones used by Diskpack, you can restore files to your hard disk in a variety of ways. Here are just a few of the DRESTORE parameters:

/D	Display filenames only
/P1	Display a (y/n)? prompt before restoring a hidden file
/P2	Display a (y/n)? prompt before restoring every file
/R	Restore files
/S	Restore subdirectory files
/V	Give a verbose listing of the restore process

By using these commands, DRESTORE allows you to restore an entire hard disk or just certain files. DRESTORE is not as fast as Diskpack, in part because the files have to be decompressed before they can be restored. Here is a command line that would restore the entire hard disk:

```
C>DRESTORE C:\*.*/S
```

This command tells DRESTORE to restore all of the files on drive C. The /S tells it to restore all subdirectories as well. By using the command /P2, you could selectively restore files to any subdirectory. The /V option would have DRESTORE show you what it was doing on the screen as it was doing it. To find out what backup disk a particular file is on, you can print out the file DISKPACK.CAT, but only if you told Diskpack to create one by using the /C option.

Diskpack 2.0 is fast, efficient, and uses compression so programs take up less space and fewer disks. If you want a fast, command-driven hard disk backup and restore program, Diskpack may be what you are looking for. The Shareware version of Diskpack will work without restrictions. DRESTORE, however, will not do a restore, but it will verify that the backup was accurate. Upon registration, Biologic Company will send the registered version as quickly as you need it.

Biologic Company
11982 Coverstone Hill Circle, Suite 1622
Manassas, VA 22110
703-368-2949 (Voice)
$49 + $3 shipping and handling; site licenses available

HARD DISK MENU PROGRAMS

There are those who live and die by menus, as well as those who wouldn't have one on their system for any money. If you are in the first group, you probably already have a menu system that you're comfortable with, and maybe nothing in this chapter will convince you to change. If you are in the second group, perhaps nothing is going to convince you that menus are for you. (If that's the case, you can skip this chapter and go on to the next one.)

There is a possibility, however, that there may be something of interest here for both groups. If you have never considered menus, you might be pleasantly surprised at the ease of access to your programs, speed in starting programs, and lack of difficulty in setting up most menu programs. By using a menu you can: switch to your word processing subdirectory, start the program, retrieve a specified file, and send a command line parameter to instruct the program to use expanded memory. When you're finished, you can return to your menu to select another program. All this can be done with only one or two keystrokes.

Using a menu, you can lock people out of selected directories by password-protecting them. On the other hand, you can also make it easy for relatives (who may not be computer-literate) to access your financial records in case of an emergency. You can set up a menu of DOS commands that will copy files to another drive, format disks, or do a full system backup of your hard drive.

The World of Menus

Many menu programs go beyond their primary function and offer disk management systems of one kind or another. Some have links to your choice of text editor. AUTOMAXX, for example, links to ARC to compress files from the menu program. Menu program utilities can include information about your system, the amount of free RAM, and currently loaded TSRs. Those that offer mouse support make the running of programs even quicker. Since all of the menu programs allow some way of dropping to DOS, you need only include in your menu those programs and activities that you use often, running new programs and infrequently used programs from the DOS command line.

The following menu programs should give you a representative sampling of the dozens that are available. In the last one to two years, there has been a dramatic increase in the number of Shareware menu programs available. I regret that more of them cannot be covered in this chapter.

Once a menu is set up, using it is simply a matter of moving a highlighted bar or pressing a number or letter for the entry. The emphasis in each section will be on how to set up the menus, with a description of what features they have in common, and what specific features each one has. Please note that for all of these programs I've given the price for a single copy. All of them have multiple-copy, site license, and corporate license prices available. Contact the author or company for current prices on special license agreements.

PowerMenu 3.0

PowerMenu is an easy-to-use, easy-to-set-up menu that requires only 2.5K of RAM when running programs. It stays in the background and comes with a preset menu and submenu that include many utilities needed for maintaining PowerMenu. Utilities include the ability to reindex your menus and submenus, and commonly used DOS utilities, such as FOR-MAT, COPY, DIR, and so forth.

Setting up PowerMenu is fairly simple. When you run the install program, PowerMenu will read your hard disk and install many of your programs for you. For other entries you may wish to make, begin install-ing each menu and submenu with INS and close with ESC. The menu entries are composed of a series of fields much like a database record. The menu entry fields are

- **Title field** This field has the name you want to appear on the Main Menu, for example, Communications.

- **Directory field** The directory field is where the program is located.

- **Command name field** This field has the FILENAME.EXT needed to run the program. PowerMenu will run all .BAT, .COM, and .EXE files, as well as DOS commands such as COPY, MOVE, and so on.

- **Parameters field** This field has optional command line parameters, for example, /r to tell WordPerfect to run in expanded memory.

- **Password field** If this field is not blank, PowerMenu will prompt for a password. This is optional and may be left blank.

- **Pause field** A "Y" in this space will tell PowerMenu to pause before returning to the Main Menu.

- **Prompt for Parameters** A "Y" will tell PowerMenu to prompt the user for command line parameters, for example, a filename to load into a text editor.

To create submenus, you need only put [**MENU**] in the Directory field and an eight-letter name in the Command name field. The square brackets must be included. Figure 13-5 shows PowerMenu's display of multiple levels of menus and submenus.

General Features

As you can see from the menus, 10,000 entries are possible in four levels of submenus. You can include both applications and DOS commands in any menu or submenu, and each menu and submenu from the Main Menu down can be password-protected with different passwords for each. In that way, people can have access to only certain areas of your hard disk. You can fine-tune it as much as you like.

In addition to a help screen to remind you of the few key combinations you need to edit the menus (for example, ALT-F4 will shell to DOS), you can use a text editor to write a custom designed help screen for each

---

Figure 13-5

Multilevel menus in PowerMenu

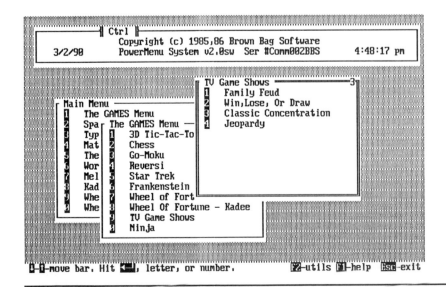

menu and menu entry. You can decide that your password to access GEnie is "whatever" and attach it to the function key whose number matches the menu entry.

Special Features of PowerMenu

DiskMan is a file management system that operates either from the Options menu of PowerMenu, which is accessed by pressing F2, or by pressing F5 at the main screen. It provides information about your hard disk and the directories, subdirectories, and files and allows you to manipulate them. Figure 13-6 shows the DiskMan screen.

The general information about the disk provided by PowerMenu includes the volume label, the total number of bytes, the number of bytes in use, the number of bytes available, and the percentage·of disk space remaining. The information about the files includes the byte size and the date and time of creation.

On the right side of the screen are listed the functions for manipulating files and directories. You can sort directories alphabetically by filename, alphabetically by file extension, by file date and time, or by file size.

Figure 13-6

DiskMan screen from PowerMenu

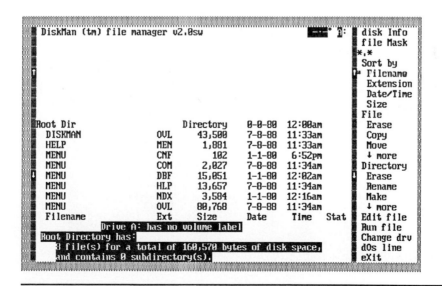

The program also lets you erase, move, or copy files from one directory to another; erase, make, or rename directories; edit files; run programs; or change the file attributes so that you can work with hidden or read-only files. You can mark files so that you can operate on a single file or a group of files.

PowerMenu Utilities   As part of the main program, PowerMenu includes a Utilities menu, accessed by F2. Figure 13-7 shows the Utilities menu. On this menu, System Info allows you to retrieve information about your system that includes the number of serial ports, the kind of computer, the amount of RAM, and so on. RAM Status tells you how much RAM is free after all TSRs are loaded. Printer Status tells you if your printer is on or off. Map of Progs lists all TSRs, their addresses, and how much RAM they are using. New Date and Time Set let you change the date or time if you made a mistake or neglected to enter the information when you booted. Colors lets you choose the colors for the menu.

In summary, PowerMenu has a number of very nice features. The PowerMenu system manages up to 10,000 separate programs from easily-accessed pop-up menus, and it automatically installs many popular pro-

---

Figure 13-7

The PowerMenu Utilities menu

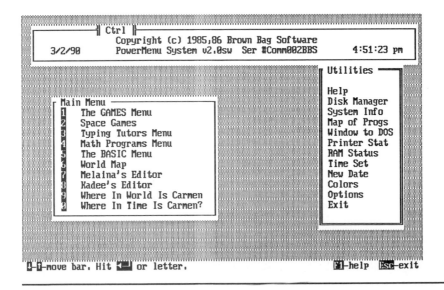

grams in the proper places on the menus (particularly handy if you are a novice at setting up menus). It also has an integral DiskMan File Manager that is similar to XTree (the DOS shell), giving you instant access to a host of information about your system, memory status, printer status, and other related functions, and it includes password protection.

Brown Bag Software
2155 S. Bascom Avenue #114
Campbell, CA 95008
408-559-4545
$89.95 registration fee

AUTOMAXX 2.36

AUTOMAXX is a menu program that has several interesting features and is relatively popular.

Setting up AUTOMAXX is a bit more complicated than setting up PowerMenu. AUTOMAXX entries are based on a series of DOS commands kept in an AUTOMAXX.DAT file, which is in ASCII text, and can be edited with any good text editor. AUTOMAXX uses special characters (shown below) as first characters for each line, telling AUTOMAXX how to build its menus.

%	Menu title
*	Menu option description
+	DOS command
>	Title of menu to display
.	Comment
#	End of file

A sample AUTOMAXX.DAT file is included with the program to provide a guide for building your own menus. You may find, however, that you need a working knowledge of DOS commands to edit the .DAT file.

The maximum length of each line is 50 characters; the maximum number of menus is approximately 50. You can have only eight options per menu, but you can *nest* menus by preceding a submenu title with an asterisk (or "star"). (Nesting means that you can have multiple levels of menus below the Main Menu. For example, the Main Menu could have eight submenu titles and each submenu could have eight sub-submenu titles.) The utilities are accessed from the Main Menu screen by pressing /, which brings up a menu bar at the top of the screen. You can toggle between black and white and color modes and swap between monochrome and CGA screens. You can also change the directory, enter the file management utility or drop to DOS, and get information about your operating system, the system memory, or the ports and the logical drives. It's also possible to switch to another drive from the menu bar or execute a command line prompt such as a batch file, a program, or a DOS command. You can also reset your screen.

AUTOMAXX's DOS shell has some unusual features not found in most menu programs. For example, with a single keystroke, by pressing A, you can archive a tagged file using SEA's ARC.EXE. As another example, by pressing W you can find out where a file is on any drive on your system. From the shell, you can activate a pop-up calculator and a pop-up calendar. You can make a backup copy with a .BAK extension of a highlighted file. AUTOMAXX also allows you to send a text file to a selected printer, which you have set up using the options in the Print menu. If you rename your printer file AUTOMAXX.PRT, it will load automatically when the printer option is selected the first time.

In addition, the File Manager has all of the usual features found in file management with a few extra touches: switching directories is made easier because a list of directories appears at the bottom of the screen. You only have to move the highlighted bar to select one, or touch the first letter of the directory name (the same is true for copy and move operations). Tagging files has the additional option of allowing you to tag files before or after the one the bar is on, and sorting files can be done in ascending or descending order. The Filter option allows you to select the specifications for file searches so that you can, for example, display only .EXE files.

In short, while AUTOMAXX is not quite as easy to set up as some of the other menus since it requires a working knowledge of DOS commands, it does have some rather unique file-management capabilities and offers printer capabilities that none of the others do.

William P. Smith
The Computer Enhancement Group
11711 Whittier Road
Mitcheville, MD 20716
$35 registration fee

Menu Commando II

Anyone who acknowledges the help of eight cats in writing a program displays a sense of humor that bodes well for a user-friendly menu program. Sandi and Shane Stump's Menu Commando is certainly that. It's also the first of the menu programs discussed that offers mouse support. Menu Commando can be configured so that a separate, blinking mouse cursor appears on your screen, and you can use your favorite mouse to activate the menu commands. While a menu program in itself saves time in activating programs, the use of a mouse can make the savings in time and effort even more worthwhile.

The number of menu entries is almost infinite. The Main Menu and all other menus accept 26 entries, each of which can, itself, be a menu. Each of the submenus for each menu entry can be a menu, and so on with no apparent limits. If you do have a menu structure with many levels of submenus, you will particularly like the Menu Tree feature. It displays all of the menus and submenus in a tree structure in a vertical window on the left side of the screen, and the programs in any highlighted menu or submenu in a vertical window on the right.

This is a very handy feature for fine-tuning the logical structure of the menu. You can move, add, or delete menu entries, or switch to Programs and delete, add, or move — all from the Menu Tree. This allows you to always have a picture of the entire structure in front of you, which is a truly distinctive feature, and I have seen nothing to equal it in any other menu program.

Menu Commando Setup

Setting up Menu Commando is very simple. To set up a menu entry, enter on a template the name of the entry and, if you wish, the access level and password for that entry. Passwords can be assigned to menus, programs, users, and Menu Commando commands. Setting up a program entry is surprisingly easy considering what can be included. Again, you will be working with a template that prompts you for responses. Filling in the path and the filename is simplified because Menu Commando will pop up directories, and once a path is chosen, display a list of executable files in that directory. All you have to do is move the cursor bar and press ENTER. You can enter command line prompts or have Menu Commando ask for them. What is different is the Run Mode option. With the Run Mode option you tell Menu Commando to either run in swap mode, where it will use about 7K of memory, or in batch mode, where it will only use 96 bytes. Menu Commando is not TSR; it swaps out to EMS, if available, or to a disk. At the top of the Main Menu screen is a set of pull-down menus, activated with F2. These command menus give you a variety of options, functions, and configurations.

Excellent Security System

The contents of the Setup menu depend on the program mode. Menu Commando can be set up either as a single-user menu system, which does not require the entering of passwords or names, or as a multiuser system, with program protection including security levels and passwords that can be assigned not only to users but to menus, programs, and menu command lines.

In multiuser mode, everyone who has access to the menu is assigned a security level and a password that must be entered at the Log On screen—something like logging on to a bulletin board. One person is designated as the PC-Coordinator (sort of like a sysop). The PC-Coordinator defines the operating environment, the menu structure, the program entries, and the name, security level, and password for each user. This is set up from the first option in the Setup menu, which is Accounting Setup. Figure 13-8 shows the setup template used to establish each user in a multiuser mode of operation.

In addition to limiting access to the menus and programs, you can also limit access to the Run menu, which allows the user to drop to DOS. Even if you use Menu Commando in single-user mode, you can still password-protect the Setup, Run, and Quit menus by using the Privilege option in the Setup menu. Of course, you can also protect individual menus and programs.

If you don't want anyone to access your computer, you can *blank* your monitor and lock up the keyboard with the Alt— menu. If you blank the

Figure 13-8

Menu Commando user setup

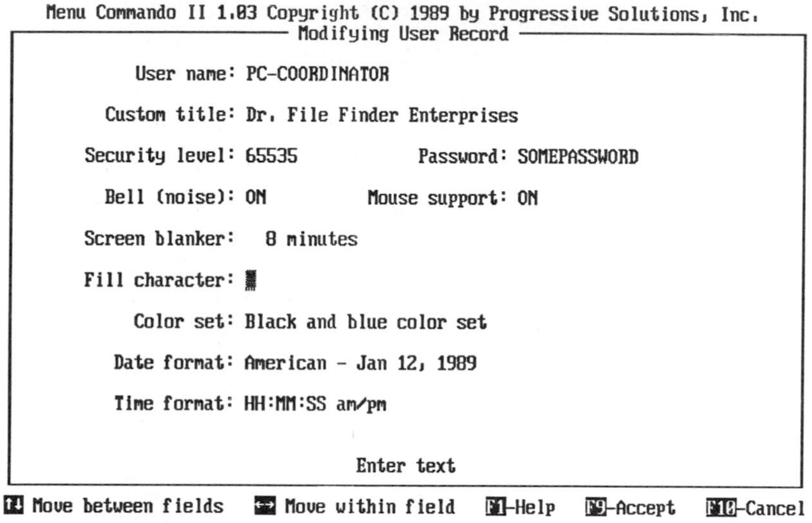

```
Menu Commando II 1.83 Copyright (C) 1989 by Progressive Solutions, Inc.
─────────────────────── Modifying User Record ───────────────────────

        User name: PC-COORDINATOR

      Custom title: Dr. File Finder Enterprises

    Security level: 65535          Password: SOMEPASSWORD

      Bell (noise): ON        Mouse support: ON

    Screen blanker:   8 minutes

    Fill character: █

        Color set: Black and blue color set

      Date format: American - Jan 12, 1989

      Time format: HH:MM:SS am/pm


                         Enter text
```

↕ Move between fields   ↔ Move within field   F1-Help   F9-Accept   F10-Cancel

screen, the date and time will show, and move randomly to a different location every 30 seconds. To lock the keyboard, choose a password (which can be different every time) and enter the password to unlock the keyboard.

Run and Utility Options

The other two command line menus are Run and Utility. The Run menu offers the option of dropping to DOS or just pulling up a DOS command line. The Utility menu has a lot of interesting features. Like PowerMenu's Utility menu, it allows you to change the date and time, and view a memory map and a system hardware report.

In addition to those utilities, Menu Commando also allows you to view and label your hard disk drives; format disks; pull up a file editor; and display a tree of any drive, where you can make directories, remove directories, move to a new directory, and so on. Figure 13-9 shows the display of Menu Commando's Tree function.

The most interesting utility in Menu Commando is the File Locator. You can, for example, search for a list of all files on drive C with a .TXT

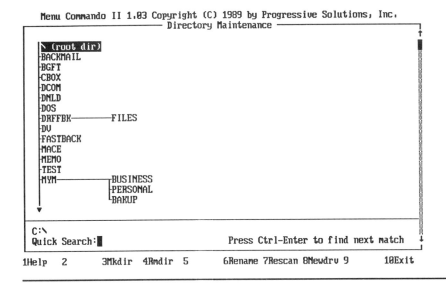

Figure 13-9

Menu Commando's tree display

extension or a .DOC extension. You have space for about a dozen choices and can exclude certain files. Figure 13-10 shows Menu Commando's File Locator in action.

Some Excellent Features

The extensive use of fill-in templates makes Menu Commando an extremely easy-to-set-up and easy-to-use menu program. Mouse support, the small amount of RAM it uses, and the sophisticated security system it employs make it a very worthwhile menu program. Menu Commando also keeps a detailed user log that can keep track of who used the system, what programs were run, and the amount of time spent. This feature can be helpful for tax purposes, seeing if your children really used the math program, or just tracking how you use your computer. Figure 13-11 shows a segment of the user log.

The program authors, Sandi and Shane Stump, not only offer excellent support, but are open to suggestions from users.

Figure 13-10

Finding all the .DOC and .TXT files with Menu Commando's File Locator

```
Menu Commando II 1.03 Copyright (C) 1989 by Progressive Solutions, Inc.
                          Located Files
 DRFILE1 .TXT      1,664   1-14-90   10:01p  C:\BGFT              ↑
 CB      .DOC     34,341   8-12-89   02:28a  C:\CBOX
 FILES2  .TXT      5,597   2-21-90   11:47p  C:\DMLD
 README  .TXT     14,148  10-12-88   09:13p  C:\DOS
 FORM    .DOC      8,588   6-24-89   09:57a  C:\TEMP
 REGISTER.DOC     11,445   6-26-89   10:11a  C:\TEMP
 TELEMATE.DOC    172,292  12-22-89   02:00a  C:\TMATE
 TMSCRIPT.DOC     74,611  12-22-89   02:00a  C:\TMATE
 QHELP   .TXT      2,052   3-01-90   02:40a  C:\UPLD
 QMAC    .DOC     28,970   2-26-90   02:10a  C:\UPLD
 QM      .DOC      5,577   2-26-90   02:10a  C:\UPLD
 DISKPACK.DOC     23,571   3-10-88   11:57a  C:\WORK
 CHARACTR.DOC     42,223  11-06-89   12:00p  C:\WP50
 DRFFBOOK.TXT      4,096  11-21-89   10:35p  C:\DRFFBK\FILES
 OUTLINE .TXT      6,278  12-03-89   04:06p  C:\DRFFBK\FILES
 TIMELINE.TXT      3,059  12-10-89   09:43p  C:\DRFFBK\FILES
 SELLSHWR.TXT     28,928  12-06-89   00:59a  C:\WORK\EDIT
 RESUME  .DOC      8,286  12-21-89   03:00p  C:\WORK\EDIT
 NOTE    .TXT      7,307   2-21-90   10:37p  C:\WORK\EDIT
 CITIZEN .TXT      4,741  12-29-89   02:13a  C:\WP50\MISC
 INFO    .TXT      1,468   9-05-89   07:30a  C:\WP50\OSBRN        ↓
                          1 / 23
1Help   2       3       4       5       6       7       8       9       10Exit
```

Figure 13-11

The Usage Log of Menu Commando

```
Menu Commando II 1.03 Copyright (C) 1989 by Progressive Solutions, Inc.
  Mar 4, 1990          Dr. File Finder Enterprises          01:52:53 pm
  PC-COORDINATOR                                       Station #:0000000001
                          Drowco Usage Log
User: DOC                          LogOn:  3/03/90 01:06  LogOff : 01:10  ↑
Appl: Picem 2.0B          Stat:    Proj#: None            Elapsed: 00:03

User: DOC                          LogOn:  3/03/90 01:10  LogOff : 01:18
Appl: BlockOut            Stat:    Proj#: None            Elapsed: 00:07

User: DOC                          LogOn:  3/03/90 01:18  LogOff : 01:52
Appl: 688 Attack Sub      Stat:    Proj#: None            Elapsed: 00:34

User: DOC                          LogOn:  3/03/90 02:13  LogOff : N/A
Appl: Log-On              Stat:    Proj#: None            Elapsed: N/A

User: DOC                          LogOn:  3/03/90 02:13  LogOff : 02:14
Appl: StupedDOS 1.61      Stat:    Proj#: None            Elapsed: 00:00

User: DOC                          LogOn:  3/03/90 02:14  LogOff : 02:15
Appl: FormatMaster        Stat:    Proj#: None            Elapsed: 00:01  ↓
                          78 / 103
1Help   2       3       4       5Totals 6       7Export 8       9Print  10Exit
```

Sandi and Shane Stump
Progressive Solutions, Inc.
1321 Klondike Street
San Antonio, TX 78245
512-670-1061
512-670-0954 or 713-955-7211 (BBS)
$50 registration fee

The Instant Access Menu System (IAMS 2.6)

Instant Access is a menu system that lives up to its name. It is instantly configurable and, once configured, instantly accesses 400 applications. A Functions menu, to the right of the Main Menu on the opening screen, gives you the options to invoke a Note Pad; call up your own favorite editor; drop to DOS; toggle AutoExecute, a Mini-Log, and Blank Screen; and configure the menu system. Figure 13-12 shows the opening menu screen of Instant Access.

Some Strong Features

The Note Pad that IAMS pops up is a handy tool for jotting down reminders, comments on the menu entries, or lists of frequently used phone numbers. It supports a few editing commands like blocking, insert/ overwrite, reformatting, and insertion and deletion of characters and lines. If you feel the need for a more full-function text editor, IAMS allows you to instantly access either the default text editor, Turbo Editor, or an editor you choose by entering its name and path in the Configurations menu.

While in the Configurations menu, you can also decide if you want to have IAMS save a Mini-Log, which is a log for time tracking. Dates and times an application was entered and exited and the name of the application are listed in ASCII text in a MINILOG.TXT file. Here is a brief sample of what the log looks like.

```
**  08:58:17 : 02/25/90  Beginning an IAMS session.

    >> 08:59:35 : 02/25/90 | Enter Application
    ## Application         | IAMS Configuration Program.
    << 09:11:16 : 02/25/90 | Exiting Application
```

```
>> 09:24:12 : 02/25/90 | Enter Application
## Application           | Text Editor
<< 09:24:39 : 02/25/90 | Exiting Application

>> 09:49:37 : 02/25/90 | Enter Application
## Application           | IAMS Configuration Program.
<< 09:52:55 : 02/25/90 | Exiting Application

>> 09:53:08 : 02/25/90 | Enter Application
## Application           | IAMS DOS Shell.
<< 09:54:19 : 02/25/90 | Exiting Application
```

Instant Access' AutoExecute

The most notable feature of IAMS is the AutoExecute function. You can select this feature from the Functions menu. After you select a letter for the program you want to execute automatically, you are presented with a template with six prompts. Enter the time in military time, and the date

---

Figure 13-12

Opening menu of Instant Access

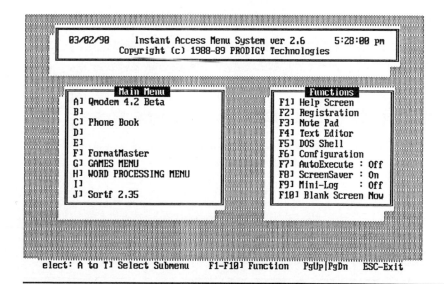

you want the program to run, or **Everyday,** if you want the program to execute at the same time every day. Enter the name of the program or any name you want to give it. Now you can do one of two things: you can enter a path and a FILENAME.EXT for the program and command line parameters, or leave those items blank and after the program pops up in the listing, press F3 and import the data from your already configured menu selection. Figure 13-13 shows the Auto Execution screen.

Patrolling Itself

Another interesting feature of IAMS is its self-checking procedures. When you start the program, IAMS will run a check to see if all of the necessary files to be run are present. If they are, you will then be presented with the Main Menu. Otherwise, any missing files will be listed and the program will exit. You can then run the Configuration program, tell IAMS where to find the missing files, or have it create the ones needed.

IAMS will also check for correct paths and program names when you set these up as menu entries. If, in entering the path or command line for a menu entry, you make an error, IAMS will inform you with "Path not

Figure 13-13

Auto Execution screen of IAMS

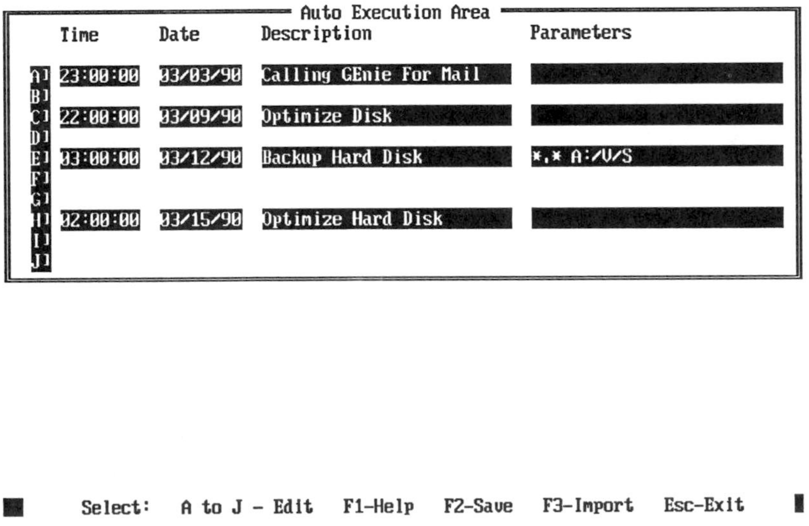

```
┌──────────────── Auto Execution Area ────────────────┐
│    Time      Date    Description          Parameters │
│ A] 23:00:00  03/03/90 Calling GEnie For Mail         │
│ B]                                                    │
│ C] 22:00:00  03/09/90 Optimize Disk                  │
│ D]                                                    │
│ E] 03:00:00  03/12/90 Backup Hard Disk    *.* A:/U/S  │
│ F]                                                    │
│ G]                                                    │
│ H] 02:00:00  03/15/90 Optimize Hard Disk             │
│ I]                                                    │
│ J]                                                    │
└──────────────────────────────────────────────────────┘

    Select:  A to J - Edit   F1-Help   F2-Save   F3-Import   Esc-Exit
```

found" or "File not found." If you get an "Illegal Path" or "Illegal (character)" message, that means the drive letter, colon, or backslash has been omitted from the path, or that you have a wildcard or illegal syntax in the filename.

If you have done everything correctly, you will get "Path found," or "File found," or "Internal." The last message means you have entered a DOS command that is acceptable. If you enter the filename incorrectly and have the correct path, a window will pop up with a list of files in that directory from which you may choose. In setting up your menu for the first time, you can go into the Configuration program, set up all of the Main Menu entries, and then set up the programs in each submenu.

Program Security Functions

The Password configuration section lets you assign a password to every aspect of IAMS. You can have a different password for each of the 20 menus; a password for the DOS shell, the text editor, the AutoExecute section, and the Configuration program; and a password for limiting access to DOS entirely.

IAMS is probably the most diligent of all the menu programs in checking that the files it needs are where they are supposed to be, and that entries are made correctly. The AutoExecute feature makes IAMS unique.

Tony Gentile
Prodigy Technologies
14611 Carmel Ridge Road
San Diego, CA 92128
$25 registration fee

Hard Disk Menu (HDM IV 1.2)

Hard Disk Menu has the highest number of optional features of all of the menu systems discussed in this chapter. Like IAMS, it has an Automatic Execution feature. Like Menu Commando II, it offers mouse support. The primary menu system consists of up to 100 menu files with 10 menu pages each. Each page has 10 entries, for a total of 10,000 possible entries to choose from. Not only can each entry start a program or execute a DOS command, but it can run any type of batch file. Add to this the capability of adding 10 macros to each menu file and a telephone dialing facility, and you have quite an impressive program. HDM's functions are activated in two ways: through Menu Action and through pull-down menus. Figure 13-14 shows HDM's opening menu screen.

Menu Actions

Let's begin by looking at HDM's Menu Action functions. A Menu Action can be anything that can be put in a batch file, including the execution instructions to start an application, DOS functions, macros, parameters, and so on. Each step in a batch file is separated in the Menu Action by a tilde (~). Thus, a batch file to start your text editor might look like this:

```
C:
CD \QEdit
Q TEXT.FIL
```

Figure 13-14

HDM's opening menu

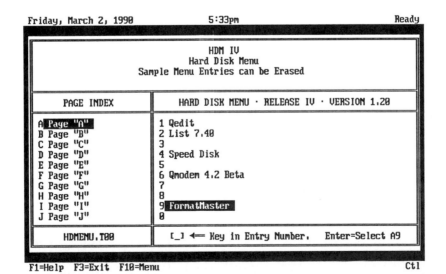

The Menu Action line would read: C:~CD\QEDIT~Q TEXT.FIL~. To make adding or editing a menu entry easier, HDM has an Auto-Build function that presents you with a template to fill in the steps and convert them to a Menu Action. You can include a macro; add other batch files; add beeps; add a {CK *drive letter*}, which will check to see if the drive is ready; add a Dial command to tell your modem to dial a phone number; add a command to switch to another menu; and have HDM check for the presence of a user and send a personal message to that user. Some of these are self-explanatory; let's examine some of the others.

HDM Macros and More

Macros are numbered from 0 to 9 with an ampersand (&) in front of the number. Inserting **&9** in a Menu Action line would cause the corresponding macro to be sent to DOS for execution. Perhaps the example given in the documentation will make this clearer.

```
Menu number nine contains:
C:~{(} \*{?Enter extension}}dir \dir1%1~dir \dir2%1~dir \dir-3%1~dir \dir4%1~dir \dir5%1~

First the user is asked to enter a file estension. If EXE is
entered, the menu action becomes:

{&9 \*.EXE}dir \dir1%1~dir \dir2%1~dir \dir3%1~dir \dir4%1~dir \dir5%1~

Next &9 is replaced by C:~ and %1 is filled with first macro parameter, \*.EXE

C:~dir \dir1%1~dir \dir2%1~dir \dir3%1~dir \dir4%1~dir \dir5%1"

Finally, all the %1's are replaced with the contents of the first
macro parameter, so it looks like this:

C:~dir \dir1\*.EXE~dir \dir2\*.EXE~dir \dir3\*.EXE~dir \dir4\*.-EXE~dir  \dir5\*.EXE

HDM now removes the tildes and passes the lines to DOS for execution.
```

The tilde is used in Menu Action to represent ENTER and is replaced by a carriage return and a line feed when the Menu Action is passed to DOS for execution.

The Dial and User Functions   The two unique Menu Action functions are the Dial function and the User function. The Dial function can be used to set up a telephone directory and automatic phone dialing directory if you have a Hayes-compatible modem. You would simply set up a new Menu file as your phone directory, and each page could then represent a different company or bulletin board or individual that you want dialed. You could set up a page for a company and have each entry on that page represent a different individual in that company. You would activate it as you would any other menu entry. The Menu Action would be {DIAL 1(800) 555-5555}. A message would flash on your screen telling you to pick up the phone and press a key. This disconnects the modem and frees you to talk on the phone.

The User function will display the name of the user in a Menu Action. For example, the Menu Action might read:

```
TYPE {?Dear {USER}, please check the download directory for the
new file you wanted.}~
```

Then, when Rae logs on, she will see this:

```
Dear Rae, please check the download directory for the new file
you wanted.
```

Pull-Down Menus

The second way in which HDM's functions are activated is through a set of pull-down menus at the top of the screen, accessed with F10. These provide an entirely different set of functions from those provided by the Menu Actions.

The first of these functions is called Menu, and it allows you to add, change, delete, or copy menu entries. If any of the entries are password protected, you must enter the proper password to manipulate the entries. Page, the next option, does the same things with pages, once you provide the proper password, if necessary.

Password-Protecting Your Menus   Password protection is handled in the next selection, Security. Here you can add, change, or delete password protection for all Main Menu entries in the current menu file, for access to the pull-down menu line. From this menu you can also log a user off so that another user could log on—a handy feature if HDM is set up for multiple users. You can also set a master password, which will override any other password. With the master password you can get around forgotten passwords or passwords that others have set up. Security is the pull-down menu that has the option to set all passwords and remove them.

HDM Global and Local Functions

The next two options are Local and Global operations. Local operations affect only the currently displayed menu and include: displaying the Menu Action for any highlighted menu description; changing the borders used in the menus and changing the colors of the Main Menu; toggling between displaying the date and time, the top menu bar, or both; changing the titles that will appear at the top of the current menu file; and switching the positions of the Main Menu and the page index. The most important of the Local operations is accessing the Macro menu so you can add, delete, or change any of the ten macros for the current menu file.

The Global options affect all menus and include: changing the rate at which the cursor blinks, the horizontal and vertical sensitivity or speed of the mouse, the communications parameters, and the length of time before the screen blanks. The most important function in this option is the Timed Execution feature. This option allows you to set up menu entries that will run automatically from any menu file, based on the day of the week, or month, and the time of day. In order for this to work, you have to be in the HDM at the set time. A window will open and you can enter the menu file number, the entry number (which consists of the letter and number that designate the entry), a **w** or **m** for weekly or monthly, the days of the week or the month, and the time you want the entry to run. Figure 13-15 shows the Timed Execution window.

The HDM Help System

HDM has the most extensive help screens of any of the menu programs examined thus far. Figure 13-16 shows HDM's Help menu. All in all, HDM IV is a menu program filled with features, functions, and help.

Jim Hass
P.O. Box 447
Richfield, OH 44286-0447
216-659-9489 (Voice)
$50 registration fee

Figure 13-15

HDM's Timed Execution window

```
Friday, March 2, 1990                5:35pm              Timed execution

┌─────────────────────────────────────────┐┌──────────────────────────┐
│ FILE ENTRY  DAYS·OF·WEEK·OR·MONTH   TIME  ││                          │
│                                           ││be Erased                 │
│    02 │ A1 │ M  1              3:00am      │└──────────────────────────┘
│    06 │ A1 │ W  4              2:30am      │┌──────────────────────────┐
│                                           ││ RELEASE IV · VERSION 1.20│
│                                           │└──────────────────────────┘
│                                           │
│                                           │
│                                           │
│ Enter=Change  Esc=Cancel  F2=Save  Del=Del.│
├───────────────────────┬───────────────────┤
│ I Page "I"            │ 9 FormatMaster     │
│ J Page "J"            │ 0                  │
├───────────────────────┼───────────────────┤
│    HDMENU.T00         │ [_] ⟵ Key in Entry Number.   Enter=Select A9│
└───────────────────────┴───────────────────┘

F1=Help  F3=Exit  F10=Menu                              Ctl
```

Figure 13-16

HDM's Help menu

```
Friday, March 2, 1990                5:36pm                    HELP

┌───────────────────────┬─────────────────────────────────────────┐
│ A How to use HELP     │      How to use the Help System       F1 │
│ B Installation notes  │                                          │
│ C HDM Startup options │ A list of topics is displayed in the left window.│
│ D How to use MAIN MENU│ A description of the highlighted topic is shown│
│ E MAIN MENU Keyboard  │ in the right window.  Active keys are listed below:│
│ F How to use TOP MENU │                                          │
│ G TOP MENU Keyboard   │ Up Arrow, BackSpc, PgUp Key:  Go up one. │
│ H MENU Pull Down      │ Down Arrow, Space, PgDn Key:  Go down one.│
│ I PAGE Pull Down      │        Home Key, - Key:  Go to beginning.│
│ J SECURITY Pull Down  │         End Key, + Key:  Go to end.      │
│ K LOCAL Pull Down     │     Letter Key (A-U):  Go directly to topic.│
│ L GLOBAL Pull Down    │        Escape Key:  Return from Help.    │
│ M EXIT Pull Down      │           F3 Key:  Exit from HDM to DOS. │
│ N Menu Action contents│                                          │
│ O Menu Action examples│                                          │
│ P Menu Functions      │ This is a user supported program.  You are my best│
│ Q Common keys & Mouse │ distributor.  Please give a copy of HDM to your│
│ R Useful Editing Keys │ friends, upload it to your local bulletin board,│
│ S Menu Error Messages │ or take a copy to your PC users group for the disk│
│ T Pricing Structure   │ librarian.  Thank you for your help.  Jim Hass.│
│ U HDM Copyright Notice│                                          │
└───────────────────────┴─────────────────────────────────────────┘

Esc=Cancel  F3=Exit                                           Ctl
```

The System Manager

The System Manager is such a security-conscious menuing system that you can't even try it out until you have first set up a security ID for yourself. It allows up to 12 nested submenus to be activated at one time, with ten selections per menu, so that hundreds of programs can be entered in the menus.

The menu selections are activated by batch files you create. These can contain up to ten DOS batch mode commands and can include parameter prompts indicated by entering a %# as part of the batch file. The opening screen indicates the amount of free RAM available and a calculator and calendar can be popped up. The System Manager uses only 80K for itself, leaving the rest of DOS RAM for running applications.

Creating Menus

When you first try to create a menu, you will be prompted for the name of the menu. This is a filename with an .MDF extension that will be saved in the default directory. If you've already started one that you need to edit, select it from a Pop-Up directory by highlighting an .MDF file and having it pop into the prompt area. You are then asked to choose a title for the menu, which is the name that will appear on the menu screen centered at the top of the menu. You could, for example, call it "Word Processors." Next, you will be prompted for the information to complete the menu entry:

- Description is the name displayed on the menu.

- Security Level is the lowest level allowable.

- Batch Commands are the actual statements that are executed to run the program.

- Help Message is a user-defined help screen for that entry.

The Batch Command is really a small batch file that you write. In it you might tell the program to: change to your D drive, and then change directories to your word processing program directory; run the word processing program with parameters; and then change back to the original drive and directory, and return you to the Main Menu.

To create submenus, instead of entering batch commands, you enter the name of a submenu followed by the .MDF extension. You can treat the submenu as a primary menu or as a submenu. If you want to keep it as a submenu, you have to put a RETURN as the batch file for an entry marked "Return to Main Menu." In creating any menu, always make sure that you include an option to exit the program.

Some Special Features

One of the System Manager's special features is its ability to handle command line parameters. At any point where you might need to enter a command line parameter for a DOS command or for a program, you can use ALT-P and a window will pop up for you to enter the parameters. You can also use F8, and a directory will pop up so you can retrieve a filename into the parameter line window.

Vinnie Murdico
954 Ambassador Drive
Toms River, NJ 08753
$25 registration fee

PCMENU

PCMENU also operates on batch files, but in this case, a single batch file that contains all of the entries. The authors call it a "menu for people who don't want lots of bells and whistles, and who need something small, fast, and very easy to use." PCMENU is all that.

To set it up, you create an ASCII text file that contains a series of batch files and menu choices, which are essentially a listing of the batch files. The advantage to PCMENU is that you can group together all of those batch files you now store in a directory of their own—or have scattered throughout your system. PCMENU lets you group them either in one menu text file, or a related group of submenu files.

To make it even easier, the authors have included a sample file with all of the headers already in place. All you have to do is put in the label names that will appear in the three-column menu listing in the first column, and then fill in the commands in another column by indenting or tabbing them. Only the items in the first column will be displayed when PCMENU is started. The commands create a batch file, which then goes into a file called PC_EXEC.BAT created by PCMENU. PCMENU, once it is set up, takes up very little storage space on your disk and requires almost no RAM to run.

There are a few extra touches, to be sure. Using a / as the last command will cause PCMENU's batch file to return you to the menu when you exit the application. You can add a password to an entry by simply adding a comma plus the password, with no spaces after the item name. If you have a group of entries you wish to password-protect, you add a **.p=password** in the far left column. To end the grouping enter a **.p=**. Any single-entry password would not be affected. A third option is to create an Administrator Password with **.a=** in the far left column followed by a password. This will bypass individual item passwords.

By and large, PCMENU delivers exactly what it promises—a fast, simple, easy way to run all of the programs on your system.

Bob Trevithick and Rich Kiss
Bob Trevithick: 409 Woodhill Apts.
Newark, NY 14513
315-331-1700
Rich Kiss: 518-370-7529
GEnie Addresses: R.TREVITHICK and R.W.KISS

XMENU

Xmenu is another menu system that offers few bells and whistles. When you start XMENU you are presented with an uncluttered screen that lists the date and time, the version number of XMENU, the page of the particular menu you are on, and a list of menu selections that you have entered.

In order to make changes or additions to the menu, the documentation instructs you to use ALT-M. This brings up a Maintenance menu at the bottom of the screen, from which you add, delete, or edit entries on the particular menu you are looking at. XMENU saves each of its menus and submenus as separate files with the extension .MNU. You are allowed ten entries per page, but you can have up to 99 pages for each menu. For

---

Figure 13-17

The ALT-M screen of XMENU

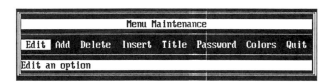

```
                          Main Menu
Date: Mar 2, 1990                        Page 1 of 1
Time: 05:37:38                           Version 2.10


          1.  Lattice Compiler
          2.  Electronic Spread Sheets
          3.  Word Processing
          4.  Norton Utilities
          5.  Games
          6.  Utilities
          7.  DOS Utilitys




┌──────────────────────────────────────────────────┐
│              Menu Maintenance                      │
├──────────────────────────────────────────────────┤
│ Edit  Add  Delete  Insert  Title  Password  Colors  Quit │
├──────────────────────────────────────────────────┤
│Edit an option                                      │
└──────────────────────────────────────────────────┘
```

---

each of those you can create a new menu, which is saved with the .MNU extension. Thus, your first entry in the Main Menu can be a menu entry called Communications. You would then select it and press ENTER, and a Communications submenu would be ready for you to make entries. After making your entries, you would be prompted to save the menu. XMENU would create the new .MNU file called COMM.MNU.

You can combine menu entries and DOS entries in any menu. To make a menu entry, you enter a name in the indicated space. To create an executable entry, you choose "D" for DOS entry and you can enter up to 50 DOS commands. Leaving a DOS entry line blank takes you to the next prompt, which asks for the name of a Help file that you can later create using any text editor. Figure 13-17 shows the ALT-M menu.

Keeping Track of Time

If you start XMENU with a /L parameter, XMENU will keep track of the date, time, and activity and save them to a default file called XMENU .LOG. Here is an example of what the log looks like:

```
2/26/90 09:15:54 XMENU log file opened
2/26/90 09:16:10    START mym personal
2/26/90 09:16:15    ENDED (rc=0)
2/26/90 09:16:24    START C:
2/26/90 09:16:25    ENDED (rc=0)
2/26/90 09:16:25    START cd \roots3\rae
2/26/90 09:16:29    ENDED (rc=0)
2/26/90 09:16:29    START r.bat
2/26/90 09:16:55    ENDED (rc=0)
2/26/90 09:17:02 XMENU log file closed
```

While XMENU doesn't offer much more than password protection for each menu and application, it works well enough and fast enough so any added features you might want could easily be set up as a menu. For example, included with the program is a sample (NORTON.MNU) that has all of the Norton Utility commands on only three pages. This is a short and sweet menu program that is ideal for the user who just wants a simple but effective menu system that offers some security.

Gary Wood
540 Lakeview Road N.
Little Rock, AR 72116
$25 registration fee

Automenu 4.5

Automenu allows an unlimited number of menu selections. It shares a number of features with other full-function menu programs, such as:

- Password protection
- Mouse support
- Timed, unattended execution of a menu selection
- Ability to run on networks
- Ability to accept user input for parameters
- Submenus
- Ability to remove itself from memory before a program is run

- Context-sensitive help screens

- Screen blanking

- Built-in editor

- AUTOMAKE, which makes it easier to create and edit Menu Definition Files

- On-screen display of time, date, keyboard status, and available RAM

In addition, Automenu makes use of a proprietary Menu Definition Language (MDL) to make menu creation easier for those unfamiliar or uncomfortable with DOS commands. It also has the ability to swap between monochrome and CGA, and to encrypt menu files. Let's examine a few of these in more detail.

Menu Definition Files
Menu Definition Files (MDF) are data files in which the Automenu menus are stored. Automenu provides an editor specifically for constructing and editing these files, called AUTOMAKE, which will check the syntax of the MDF and return error messages if necessary. It also provides the means for encrypting the menu files. It is indicated on the main screen as "Menu-Building Facility." The screen that appears when this facility is invoked is divided into six sections, most of which are automatically filled in by AUTOMAKE. All you need to enter is the filename, a title if it is a new file, and program-selection information introduced by a function symbol. These are the same symbols used by AUTOMAXX.

Where AUTOMAKE differs is that it will present you with a sample menu to use in constructing your own. What you are doing is constructing a batch file, which then activates the program selection from the menu. One of the nice features of Automenu is that you can nest menus using an @ sign preceding the name of the MDF you want to load. You can add @AUTOMENU.MDF at the end of each related .MDF file that will return you to the Main Menu after the application executes. You can also add explanations of each menu entry by using a ? in your Menu Definition. This could introduce something like: "Please insert a blank disk in Drive A:," or "Run this program with a /r for EMS." Similarly,

Figure 13-18

The Main Menu of Automenu

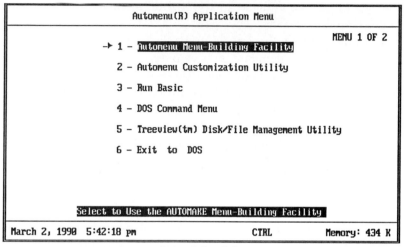

certain commands either keep Automenu resident (!) or remove it from RAM before a program executes (+). Figure 13-18 shows the Main Menu of Automenu.

Menu Format in Automenu

While Automenu is primarily batch-file driven, you can also make direct commands using - or = for pausing or not pausing—that is, for responding to the message, "Press a key to continue." These are mostly DOS commands.

Function symbols are also used to include other Automenu special features in MDFs. The ^ is the symbol for passwords. Multiple passwords can be included in a single menu entry. The example given in the documentation demonstrates how to prevent other users from formatting disks:

```
%TEST MENU   (The name of the menu)
*Format Drive A: (The menu entry)
^OK (First password)
```

```
^BOSS (Second password)
-Format A: (Direct command with no pause after completion)
#END (The mandatory closing statement for all entries)
```

Another set of unique and useful commands involves the use of the right and left angle brackets. The right angle bracket (>) outputs a message to the user, while the left angle bracket (<) allows the user to input a response such as a filename, a drive letter, or a "Y" or "N" for Yes or No. You validate the choices by using the %# DOS variable where # can be any number from 1 to 9. Timed executions are also added to menu selections with a specific symbol ([) preceding the time value. All of your timed executions would be in one MDF, which can contain as many as 128 items and load an additional MDF for another 128. The number thus becomes limitless.

Customizing Automenu

Most of the customizing of Automenu is done through the flexibility of the MDF, but there are a few other areas that can be customized to suit you. Colors, date and time formats, screen blanking, and mouse support are all toggled using an auxiliary program called AUTOCUST.

While the use of arbitrary symbols in sending commands to the program might seem intimidating at first, once you get used to using them by starting off with fairly simple menu files, working up to increasingly complex ones becomes less daunting. This is an excellent menu system that offers a wide range of features and great flexibility.

Marshall Magee
Magee Enterprises, Inc.
P.O. Box 1587
Norcross, GA 30091
76004,1541 and 70167,2200 CompuServe IDs
404-368-0710 (Fax-24 hours)
404-446-6611 (Phone)
404-446-6650 (BBS-24 hours)
$50 registration fee

Let's move on now to another type of program that seems to be becoming more and more popular—the DOS shell program.

## CHAPTER FOURTEEN

DOS Shell Programs

Sometimes, it seems that the more you use your computer, the more complex using it can become. For example, you first start with an AUTO-EXEC.BAT file that might only contain a few items such as TIME, DATE, and maybe a PATH. As you learn more about the way your computer works, your AUTOEXEC.BAT file starts to expand.

The same is true of a CONFIG.SYS file. Many new users don't even have one. When you finally create one, it may only contain lines for FILES and BUFFERS. Later, you begin to fill it with device drivers and other statements that help set up your machine in a way that's more to your liking. You move from the simple to the complex. The same is true for files and programs.

You may start out with a floppy-based system, but soon you must have a hard disk to store your programs. You then find that you need a bigger drive. Your hard disk may soon become a maze of directories, subdirectories, and files. Navigating through this jungle can often be tricky—and a bit tedious.

Some people, like myself, like working from the DOS prompt. By using things like macros, "synonyms," and batch files, you can do a lot of things. Others, however, never get to the point where they like working with DOS. Eventually, even a fair number of those who like working from the DOS prompt get tired of it. As a result, DOS shell programs were created. In this chapter, we'll examine some good DOS shell programs, but before that, let's take a look at what DOS shells are and what they do.

WHAT IS A DOS SHELL?

In simplest terms, a *DOS shell* is an interface between the user and the operating system. The shell gathers up information about the system, and then presents it to the user in a way that makes more sense. The user can see things more clearly from this enhanced point of view.

A DOS shell allows you to look around, find what you need, and get things done. DOS shells may appeal to you or they may not. Let's take a look at some of the things that DOS shell programs have in common with each other.

A Room with a View

The first task of a DOS shell is to give you an overview of your system by letting you see all your directories and subdirectories—something you can't do from the DOS prompt. DOS shells lay out a map of your system at your fingertips. They do this by showing you a tree display of your system, beginning with the root directory followed by all of the directories and subdirectories that branch off of it. Figure 14-1 shows an example of this tree-structured directory system.

As you can see, this kind of presentation allows you to see all your directories at a glance. In this example, you can easily see that the MYM directory has two subdirectories branching off of it, BUSINESS and PERSONAL. If you were at the DOS prompt, in the DNLD directory, you couldn't see that kind of branching. So, DOS shells give you an overview of your entire system. The next thing they give you is mobility.

Gaining Some Mobility

Now that you can see the directories on your system, you need to be able to travel easily between them. DOS shells allow you to move between

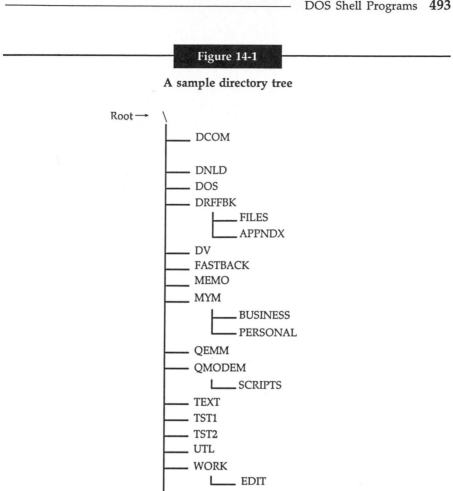

Figure 14-1

A sample directory tree

directories by using either the cursor keys, a mouse, or both. In many cases, the tree display will appear on one side of the screen, while the files in a currently highlighted directory will appear on the other side. Even at this early stage, a DOS shell has provided you with two things: the ability to view everything that is contained on your system and a way to move around.

Now you can easily move from one directory to another, scan the files that are in that directory, and then move on to another one. With this enhanced view of your system, you can now easily perform operations on files that might have been a chore when you were working from the DOS prompt. What are some of the operations that DOS shells help you to perform? Let's take a look.

Moving Files Easily

DOS shells make it a bit easier to handle the files on your system. For example, let's say that you want to move some files from one directory to another. All you have to do is move to the desired directory, tag the files that you want to move, and inform the shell where to send them. You could tag all of the files in one directory and move them to another. Such operations are very easy when you are using a good DOS shell program. By using the same concepts, you can perform other operations on files as well.

Copying Files

Just as you can use a DOS shell to move program files around your system, you can also have the shell program copy files from one place to another. Let's say that you want to send a friend a disk containing some good Shareware utilities that you use on your own system. With a DOS shell, you can quickly move to the desired directory, tag the files you want, and have those files copied to a disk in drive A.

You might also want to copy files from one area on your hard disk to another. As a "safety net," many DOS shells will warn you if you are about to overwrite an existing file. That gives you a chance to change your mind. If you were using the DOS COPY command, you wouldn't get a second chance.

Deleting Files

Another operation that DOS shells make easier is deleting files. You can move to the directory that you want and clearly see all the files it contains. You can then tag the ones you want to delete. Once again, most DOS shells will prompt you and ask if you are sure that you want to delete the file(s) you tagged. Here again, you get a second chance.

Do you want to delete all of the files in one directory? Many shell programs give you an option of being able to tag all of the files in the selected directory at one time. Thus, with one keystroke or one click of a mouse button, you can tag any number of files for deletion. When you go to perform this mass deletion, you'll still get that prompt asking you if you are sure. This "tag all" feature can be useful for copying and moving files as well.

A good DOS shell makes it easy to move, copy, and delete files. This can be done either individually, several files at a time, or a whole directory at once. One benefit is that you can clearly see what files you are tagging before executing an operation. What other functions do DOS shells provide? Let's examine them a bit closer.

Other File Operations

Since DOS shells are intended to make life easier, many of them give you the ability to do other things with the files on your system. Some shell programs provide more options than others. All of the DOS shells to be discussed in this chapter offer a range of different functions. There are other changes to files that you can make besides just copying, moving, or deleting them. For example, nearly all DOS shells provide you with the ability to rename, execute, and change the attributes of a file. Let's look briefly at these features.

Renaming Files

It's often handy to be able to rename a file. While DOS allows you to have files with the same name, as long as they are in different directories, this can sometimes cause problems. One common problem among computer users is that they accidentally erase one version of a file by copying another version with the same name over it.

You might be thinking, "Don't most shell programs warn me if I tried to copy a file with the same name over another one?" That's right, they do. If you try to overwrite a file, you'll be warned and can stop the operation. If you still want to copy a file into a directory containing a file with the same name, you are going to have to rename one of the files. Most DOS shell programs allow you to rename files easily, and you can see all the filenames so you aren't as likely to try a name already in use.

Executing Programs in Shells

Another feature of DOS shells is that you can execute other programs right from the shell. In most cases, any .COM, .EXE, or .BAT file can be run from the shell, and you'll return to the shell when you exit the program! Assuming you know what the executable files on your system do, you could look at this as a menu system without the menus. Perhaps an example is in order.

Let's say that you are in your shell program and you want to run a communications program called HOCK. All you'd have to do is move to the HOCK directory and highlight the HOCK.EXE file. With some shells you can just press ENTER and the program will run. With others you use a special Execute command. In any event, you leave the shell and end up in HOCK. When you are finished, exit the program, and you are returned to the shell.

You could do this with almost every program on your system, depending on how much memory the program requires and how much the shell program uses. There are quite a few people who run almost everything from their DOS shell and seldom, if ever, visit the DOS prompt.

Changing File Attributes

All files can have various *attributes,* and there may be times when you want to change them. What are attributes? Without going into too much detail, a file's attributes determine how the file is handled by the system. The possible attributes are

- Archive

- Hidden

- System

- Read-Only

When a file is altered in any way, its *archive bit* is turned on. This is one way that hard disk backup programs can determine which files need to be backed up. (Many can also determine the date or time a file was created or modified.) When a file is backed up, its archive bit is turned off. Another example is the system files that work together with COMMAND .COM. These are MSDOS.SYS and IO.SYS. These files happen to have three different file attributes. They are *hidden, system,* and *read-only* files.

Why would you want to change a file's attributes? Let's say that your shell program lets you see hidden files, but places a special mark next to them to let you know that they *are* hidden files. You may have a program that creates hidden files for swapping out tasks or other reasons. You can't delete a hidden file because the system pretends it isn't there. If the DOS shell you are using lets you change file attributes, you can change hidden files to archive files, allowing you to delete them. Since there are other programs that can alter file attributes, some DOS shells will give you this ability and others will not.

Thus far, you've seen that DOS shells can have some benefits for you. They give you a good overview of your system; the mobility to move around it rapidly; and the ability to manipulate files by moving, copying, deleting, renaming, executing, and changing file attributes. You've also seen how shell programs give you the power to tag multiple files so you can perform several functions in one operation. What else do some DOS shells offer?

Handling Compressed Files

Due to the popularity of compressed files, some newer DOS shells include the ability to work with them. Among the programs discussed in this chapter are several that can work with compressed files, making things easier for you.

Some shell programs allow you to tag files you want packed into a compressed file. You also have the ability to extract the contents of a compressed file, view its contents, or test the file for integrity. The ability to handle a compressed file from within a shell gives you just a bit more flexibility. At the same time, however, there are programs like ArcMaster by John Newlin, Shez by Jim Derr, and PKZMENU by Doug Hay that perform many different functions on packed files.

If you should decide to use a DOS shell and it does not support the handling of compressed files, don't despair. The ability to handle compressed files should not be of primary concern when selecting a shell program. Since there are other good Shareware programs that can take care of this, concern yourself instead with the shell program's overall ease of use.

Miscellaneous Functions

Depending on the program, DOS shells provide several other functions as well. Since each program varies somewhat, you will have to select the one with the features most important to you. Ease of use is also a consideration, as well as the way in which data is presented. Various DOS shells may offer some of the following features:

- Ability to attach the editor of your choice
- Ability to add a file viewer such as LIST
- Ability to create a list of programs you can run
- Ability to configure a certain compression utility to use with the shell

If you want to use a DOS shell, and I say "if" because not all people like them, there are several to choose from. The ones that will be examined in this chapter are among the very best, based on ease of use, presentation, number of functions, and other factors to be discussed.

Giving You Statistics

Another feature that most DOS shells provide is statistics on your system. As I mentioned earlier, a DOS shell gathers up information about your system and presents it in an interesting and informative manner. These programs keep track of statistics in many ways, including

- Total disk space available
- Total disk space free
- Amount of disk space occupied by files
- Total amount of memory
- Total amount of free memory
- Time and date
- Name and size of currently highlighted file
- Attribute of currently highlighted file
- Attributes of all files in current directory

As you can see, these statistics give you information about your system at a glance. To find out the same information at the DOS prompt, you would have to do a CHKDSK, run a utility that shows file attributes, and install a TSR clock. Still there would be some things that you couldn't find out. As with menu programs, people either hate DOS shells or they love them. If nothing else, you owe it to yourself to at least try them.

Having taken a quick look at some of the things that DOS shells can do and the services they provide, it's time to examine some of the better DOS shell programs available.

HARD DISK DIRECTOR

The Hard Disk Director is an excellent DOS shell billed as a "complete program, file, and directory manager." The Director comes in several modules providing a wide range of hard disk management possibilities. In addition, there is a complete menu system that you can run from the shell. Director is a comprehensive package that enables you to have full control over your system, no matter how many drives you have. There is a configuration program allowing you to customize default settings such as colors, the default directory, the editor and file viewer of your choice, and much more.

The programs that make up the Director can be used from the keyboard using function and cursor keys, or you can use any Microsoft-

---

DOCTOR'S NOTE

At one point, I could never have imagined myself using any kind of DOS shell program. I tested them and evaluated them, but they were not for me. It's strange how our ideas change the more we experience. Today, while I still like working from the DOS prompt, I can at least see the usefulness of DOS shells. They speed up many operations, especially if you work with a lot of files. By using a mouse and a DOS shell that supports one, you can whip around between directories—moving, copying, and deleting files. You know how much disk space and memory you have free at any given moment. You can quickly make new subdirectories and remove old ones.

Five or six years ago I made the statement, "I can do anything as fast or faster from the DOS prompt as someone else can from a shell." I know now that I was wrong. There is a time and place for everything, and depending on your needs, there may be a place for a DOS shell on your system as well.

compatible mouse. Since this "program" is really a series of programs, let's take an overview of the entire package and then look at each of the modules individually.

An Overview of Director

While other shell programs generally consist of a main program and perhaps some associated auxiliary files, Director is a series of individual programs. The executable programs that come in the Director package are as follows:

DL.EXE	The primary shell program for directories and files
DB.EXE	A file management tool for individual directories
DA.EXE	A complete drive management system
DM.EXE	A hard disk menu system
DCONFIG.EXE	The configuration program

Each of these modules provides a slightly different function, but when used together they give you dynamic control over the files and subdirectories on your system. DL is a full-featured shell showing you the tree structure of your hard disk. You can change directories and tag files for moving, copying, or deletion.

Besides renaming files, you can hide files that are normally visible or "unhide" files that are normally hidden. A special feature of DL is that you can copy or move whole directories to another drive. Figure 14-2 shows what the DL display looks like.

DB is a stripped down version of DL and is great when you want to work from the DOS prompt. (DB will be discussed in more detail later in this chapter.) The DA module lets you manage all of the files on a drive, showing the files and providing some valuable options. DM provides a nice menu system, which will be discussed in detail shortly. First, let's take a quick look at how you can configure all of the programs that make up Director.

Configurability Options

The configuration program that comes with Director, DCONFIG.EXE, gives you the opportunity to configure each of the other Director modules, individually or all at the same time. It allows you, for example, to use one color scheme in DL and another in DB. You might also set other

Figure 14-2

The DL tree display

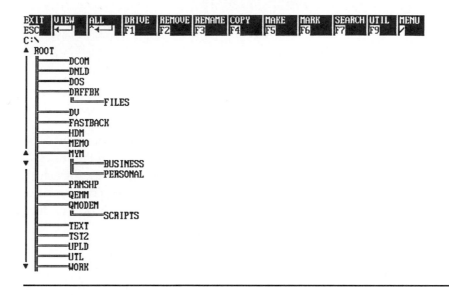

options differently. On the other hand, if you want consistency, you can configure all of the modules together.

Director can be brought up from anywhere on your system. You can add the editor of your choice as well as a file viewing program. Other configurable options include telling Director how many lines a screen can display, whether to add command line arguments to any programs that are run, and if Director should save a copy of the tree to disk. If you use a mouse, you can tell Director you want a scroll bar present. Other options you can configure include

- Printing the IBM extended character set
- Warning about overwriting other files
- Sending a form feed to the printer after printing
- Creating a default method for sorting file listings
- Parking the hard disks after a given length of time
- Blanking the screen after so many minutes of inactivity
- Configuring all the colors used by Director

Thus, DCONFIG allows you to set up Director the way you want it, using the defaults that you set. If at any time you change your mind or get different equipment, you can always run DCONFIG again and alter your previous choices.

Since DL is the heart of Director, let's take a closer look at some of the things that it can do.

DL—The Heart of Director

While the complete Director package is made up of several program files, DL is the main program and the full DOS shell. As you saw in Figure 14-2, DL gives you a full tree display and allows you to choose the directory that you want to work with. When a directory is displayed, you get quite a bit of information about the files it contains. Figure 14-3 shows the files in the C:\UPLD directory and what DL tells you about them.

Figure 14-3

A directory listing in DL

EXIT	VIEW	EDIT	COPY	DELETE	RENAME	MOVE	SORT	MARK	RUN IT	UTIL	MENU
ESC	⟵	⌂⟵	F1	F2	F3	F4	F5	F6	F7	F9	✓

File	Type	Size	Date	Time	Attr
▲ 4DLOAD.BAT	Batch File	32	4-03-1990	11:48 PM	Arc
4DOS.COM	Program	10042	3-07-1990	3:00 AM	
4DOS286.EXE	Program	63393	3-07-1990	3:00 AM	
4START.BAT	Batch File	183	3-22-1990	9:17 PM	
ALIASES		1906	4-03-1990	11:48 PM	Arc
AUTOEXEC.BAT	Batch File	609	3-20-1990	5:33 PM	
BURNDEV.SYS		2595	4-13-1989	12:16 PM	
COMMAND.COM	Program	37557	12-19-1988	0:00 AM	
CONFIG.SYS		179	3-20-1990	5:20 PM	
DO-ONCE.DAT		135	3-20-1990	5:36 PM	
▲ DOS.HLP		87328	3-07-1990	3:00 AM	
▼ FRESNO.FNT		4096	6-03-1988	7:41 AM	
GREET.COM	Program	563	5-22-1986	1:53 AM	
HELP.EXE	Program	44944	3-07-1990	3:00 AM	
IO.SYS		33337	12-19-1988	0:00 AM	Sys R/O
KBFIX3.COM	Program	7280	12-16-1988	10:16 PM	
LOD.COM	Program	4353	2-08-1989	11:55 PM	
MENU.COM	Program	2540	1-15-1988	12:00 PM	
MSDOS.SYS		37376	4-19-1989	8:30 AM	Sys R/O
NEW-WARE.LOG		737	4-01-1990	9:54 AM	
QEMM.SYS		54072	1-04-1990	12:49 PM	
▼ RUNFILE.COM	Program	3500	12-20-1989	11:14 AM	

| C:\ | | | | Marked 0 | | | | Total 402096 |

Note that DL gives you the filename, but if DL knows that a certain file is a program, for example, it states that. If it knows that another file is a document of some sort, it makes note of that as well as any batch files. DL displays the file size, its creation date, and the time the file was created or last updated.

Lastly, DL shows you what file attribute each file possesses. Please note that in this case "Arc" stands for the archive file attribute and not the fact that the file is a certain type of compressed file. Notice in Figure 14-3, the file IO.SYS, and how Director tells you that it is a "system, read-only" file. With all of the files in a directory clearly displayed, you now have many options, depending on what you want to do.

Viewing a File

You can view the highlighted file by selecting the View option. If you didn't configure a special program for this feature, using DCONFIG, don't worry. Director comes with its own internal viewer. This is an excellent feature for looking at program documentation, batch files, and so on.

The Edit Function

To edit a batch file, exit from the viewer and select the Edit option. Director will bring up your favorite editor, and it will automatically load the file that you have highlighted. When you are finished editing, save your work as usual and you'll be returned to DL. You can edit your CONFIG.SYS or AUTOEXEC.BAT file quickly and never leave Director.

What if you want to edit a new file? If you have an editor like QEdit, you could highlight any text file, and then use the Edit function. Once inside QEdit, you could open another window and create your new file. DL doesn't care what you do in the editor once you're in it; it just waits for you to exit. Another option is to hook up your editor in Director's menu module, which will be discussed later.

Copying, Deleting, Renaming, and Moving

Director also gives you a full range of possibilities for managing your files. You can copy files individually, or in groups, to any directory on your system—even on another drive. The same can be done with deleting or moving files. You can tag all of the files in a directory and perform the same function on all of them at the same time. You can copy, delete, or move whole groups of files in one quick step. Renaming a file is a snap. All you have to do is highlight the file you want to rename, and then select the Rename function. Type in the new name and presto—it's changed.

An exciting feature of DL is that you can actually copy or move an entire directory from one drive to another. To do this, tag the directory you want and select Copy. Because you've tagged a directory, and not files, Director will ask you if you want to copy or move the directory. Select which you want and you'll be prompted for where you want the directory to go. It's quite convenient for moving a directory to another drive.

Sorting, Marking, and Running Programs

Using the Sort function, you can sort the directory by:

- Filename

- Extension

- Date

- Size

You can also ask that the directory be unsorted. Files can be tagged or marked individually, or you can mark all of the files in a given directory. Director also lets you unmark files, one at a time or as a group. It's very fast to mark all of the files, and if there are two files that you don't want to perform a function on, for example, you can quickly unmark them individually.

To execute a program from Director, highlight any executable file, such as any .EXE, .COM, or .BAT file. Select the Run-It option and the program will run from Director. When you exit the program, you will be returned to Director.

Utilities and Menu

Director has a few handy utilities that you can access via the Util function. Figure 14-4 shows the options this feature gives you.

Statistics shows you how many files are in the current directory and how much space they occupy. It also shows you what percentage of your total disk is occupied, how many of the files in that directory need to be

Figure 14-4

Director's Utility menu statistics

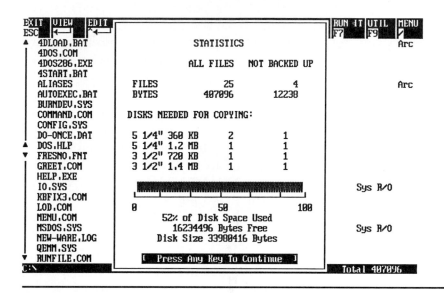

backed up, and how many disks you'd need to do it for 360K, 720K, 1.2 meg, and 1.44 meg disks. You can also print a file listing or just the text of any text file. The Attributes selection lets you change the file attributes of one file or as many files as you have marked. The File Spec selection lets you enter the file specification that you want, for example, *.DOC. In this case, only files with an extension of .DOC would appear in the directory list. This is great for use in a crowded directory when you want to focus your attention on only certain kinds of files. Lastly, Director gives you an option to Go To DOS so you can do something else. Director is a complete DOS shell program that gives you a lot of options, but there's more in the total package.

A Nifty Change Directory

One added function of DL is that even when it's not loaded, it can be of help to you at the DOS prompt. Many people love Norton's Change Directory (NCD). Director's DL can do the same thing as NCD. If you were at the DOS prompt and wanted to go to the C:\TEST1 directory, all you'd have to enter is this:

```
C>DL TE
```

DL scans its list of directories and immediately goes to the first directory that matches the information you supplied, in this case TE. If you had a C:\TEMP directory, DL would take you there because it comes first alphabetically. If you know your directory structure, you can avoid going to the wrong directory simply by supplying one more character:

```
C>DL TES
```

You would then go immediately to the C:\TEST1 directory, making it very easy to quickly move around the system, even when you aren't in Director. This feature can also be used to go to a directory on another drive. For example, to go to the D:\GAMES directory from the root directory of drive C, you would enter

```
C>DL D: GAM
```

As a final touch, you can also have Director come up in a specified directory anywhere on the system, displaying the file listing of that directory. To bring up Director in the C:\MYM directory, you would enter

```
C>DL ! C:\MYM
```

Director provides you with some very handy ways to move around your system, even when you aren't inside the main program.

DB — A Small Director

Even those who like to use a DOS shell most of the time will sometimes need to work from the DOS prompt. DL's companion program, DB, is excellent for this. Let's say you are at the DOS prompt in the C:\DNLD directory. Instead of entering **DIR** you can enter **DB**. Figure 14-5 shows what the DB display looks like.

DB is like a miniature DL — it gives you all the functions of DL, but for a single directory. You can mark, delete, and move files, look at the statistics, and so on. DB can be run from the command line with a file specification. For example:

```
C>DB *.COM
```

In this case, DB would appear with a directory listing containing only the .COM files in that directory. This is an excellent tool for managing the files in one directory at a time. My own C:\DNLD directory often gets crowded, and I use DB to quickly move files off to other "work" directories, erase files that are no longer needed, or to view text files. If you're the kind of person who doesn't like DOS shells, the Director package is worth having for the convenience of using DB to work with directories.

DA—Complete Drive Control

Ever want to take a look at all of the files on a drive at one time? The DA portion of Director allows you to do just that. DA scans the entire drive and brings up a listing of every file, using your default sort preference. Figure 14-6 shows DA's listing of my C drive.

Figure 14-5

DB's directory display

```
EXIT  VIEW   EDIT   COPY   DELETE RENAME MOVE   SORT   MARK   RUN IT UTIL   MENU
ESC   |←—    |←—    F1     F2     F3     F4     F5     F6     F7     F9     /
▲  $DM$.BAT     Batch File      36   3-24-1990   12:08 PM
   AW.EXE       Program       8198   3-01-1986    8:44 AM
   BURNOUT.COM  Program        168  12-14-1987   11:01 AM
   C_DRIVE.DL                 1292   4-03-1990    7:16 AM
   DA.EXE       Program      60616   4-03-1990    8:37 AM                Arc
   DB$$$.BAT    Batch File       0   4-03-1990   11:56 PM                Arc
   DB.EXE       Program      43364   4-03-1990    8:37 AM                Arc
   DCONFIG.EXE  Program      36518   2-14-1990    5:17 PM
   DESCRIPT.ION                267   4-03-1990    8:34 AM   Hid          Arc
   DL$$$.BAT    Batch File       0   4-03-1990   11:55 PM                Arc
▲  DL.EXE       Program      67948   4-03-1990    8:37 AM                Arc
▼  DLBASE.EXE   Program      26911   2-21-1990   11:41 AM
   DLWP.COM     Program      11710   2-21-1990   11:49 AM
   DM$$$.BAT    Batch File      76   3-23-1990    2:44 PM
   DM.EXE       Program      36504   4-03-1990    8:37 AM                Arc
   DM.MEN                      715   3-25-1990   10:36 AM
   DOCPLUS.EXE  Program      24773  12-03-1989   10:27 AM
   DRFF.KEY                    101   3-28-1990    5:40 PM
   DX.EXE       Program      30471   8-12-1989    1:07 AM
   D_DRIVE.DL                  760   4-03-1990    7:31 AM                Arc
   FF.EXE       Program      13865   1-30-1989   11:53 AM
▼  FILL.EXE     Program      25003   8-06-1988   10:03 AM
C:\UTIL                              Marked 0          Total 887989
```

Figure 14-6

DA's complete disk listing

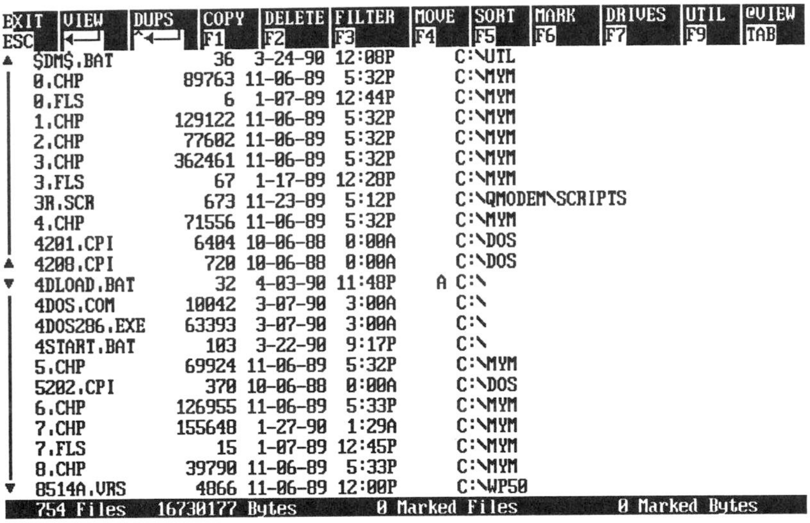

```
EXIT  VIEW    DUPS    COPY  DELETE FILTER  MOVE  SORT  MARK  DRIVES  UTIL  QVIEW
ESC   ◄───┐   ┌─►◄─┐  F1    F2     F3      F4    F5    F6    F7      F9    TAB
▲   $DM$.BAT      36  3-24-90 12:00P      C:\UTIL
    0.CHP      89763 11-06-89  5:32P      C:\MYM
    0.FLS          6  1-07-89 12:44P      C:\MYM
    1.CHP     129122 11-06-89  5:32P      C:\MYM
    2.CHP      77602 11-06-89  5:32P      C:\MYM
    3.CHP     362461 11-06-89  5:32P      C:\MYM
    3.FLS         67  1-17-89 12:20P      C:\MYM
    3R.SCR       673 11-23-89  5:12P      C:\QMODEM\SCRIPTS
    4.CHP      71556 11-06-89  5:32P      C:\MYM
    4201.CPI    6404 10-06-88  0:00A      C:\DOS
▲   4200.CPI     720 10-06-88  0:00A      C:\DOS
▼   4DLOAD.BAT    32  4-03-90 11:48P    A C:\
    4DOS.COM   10042  3-07-90  3:00A      C:\
    4DOS286.EXE 63393 3-07-90  3:00A      C:\
    4START.BAT   103  3-22-90  9:17P      C:\
    5.CHP      69924 11-06-89  5:32P      C:\MYM
    5202.CPI     370 10-06-88  0:00A      C:\DOS
    6.CHP     126955 11-06-89  5:33P      C:\MYM
    7.CHP     155648  1-27-90  1:29A      C:\MYM
    7.FLS         15  1-07-89 12:45P      C:\MYM
    8.CHP      39790 11-06-89  5:33P      C:\MYM
▼   8514A.VRS   4866 11-06-89 12:00P      C:\WP50
  754 Files   16730177 Bytes      0 Marked Files      0 Marked Bytes
```

The listing shows which directory each file occupies, and its file attribute, date, time, and size. DA will also sort items by PATH so all files from one directory are together in the listing. This provides you with a way to review all the files on one drive at the same time. The DA program can also handle drives with large partitions. I tested it on both a 33 meg hard disk and a 66 meg hard disk. It is a superior feature for total management of all of the files on one drive.

The Director Menu System

Director also comes with its own menu system. While small and unpretentious, the menu program, DM.EXE, can handle a large number of menu entries. You can even have submenus. The menu can be activated from either the DL or the DB module of the program.

While it is not intended to have any of the extra features that a full-blown menu program offers, the Director menu is quite useful. You can have it prompt you for command line parameters, whether you want the program to return to the menu, or to make another submenu listing.

You can park the hard disk heads from within the menu, add or change menu entries, and then return to the calling program.

Being Direct About Director

The Hard Disk Director is a DOS shell and a lot more. Its modules give you tremendous flexibility in managing your system, whether it's from the tree portion of DL, an individual directory using DB, your entire disk using DA, or running programs from the DM menu. It is obvious that the author, Dan Baumbach, cares about the program and has worked very hard to give it a wide range of functions while keeping it bug free. The main Director module, DL, is excellent by itself, but the added modules give you a great deal of power and control over everything on your system. I highly recommend the Hard Disk Director—it's an excellent program.

Dan Baumbach
Helpware
100 Bayo Vista Way #6
San Rafael, CA 94901
415-453-9779 (Voice)
$35 registration includes printed manual & support; MasterCard and VISA accepted

STUPENDOS—SOME EXTRAS INCLUDED

StupenDOS is a DOS shell that offers all the features one would expect in a good shell program plus a few more. Coincidentally, while I was writing up StupenDOS, the author, Douglas Hay, released a new version with even more features. StupenDOS can be used with the cursor and function keys or with a mouse. It also has pull-down menus. Figure 14-7 shows the main display of StupenDOS as seen from my root directory.

Note that the left side of the screen shows a directory display of your hard disk. If you start the program in the root directory it will display all of the subdirectories off of the root and any files in the root directory. If

---

Figure 14-7

The main screen of StupenDOS

```
Dos    Sort    Tag    More    File    Zip    setuP    eXit          11:57:01 PM
↑=C:\
■ CSERVE          <DIR>   4-03-90   9:09p   │ tag all  │ File 0001 of 0043
  DCOM            <DIR>   2-20-90   1:33p   │ clr all  │
  DNLD            <DIR>   2-20-90   1:34p   │ new dir  │ Bytes Free      16222208
  DOS             <DIR>   2-20-90   1:34p   │ eXecute  │
  DRFFBK          <DIR>   2-20-90   1:35p   │          │ Total Tagged          0
  DV              <DIR>   2-20-90   1:35p   │          │ Bytes Tagged          0
  FASTBACK        <DIR>   2-20-90   1:07p   │ copy a:  │
  HDM             <DIR>   3-24-90   5:43p   │ copy b:  │ Total Deleted         0
  MEMO            <DIR>   2-20-90   1:40p   │          │ Bytes Deleted         0
  MYM             <DIR>   2-20-90   1:45p   │ A:   B:  │
  PRNSHP          <DIR>   2-20-90   1:47p   │ C:   D:  │ ←,→ = Pull Down Menus
  QEMM            <DIR>   2-20-90   1:48p   │          │
  QMODEM          <DIR>   2-20-90   1:48p   │          │ Press F10 for HELP
  TEXT            <DIR>   2-20-90   1:49p   │          │ Filespec: *.*
  TST2            <DIR>   3-20-90   1:32a   │          │
  UPLD            <DIR>   2-20-90   4:21p   │          │ Eclipse Technologies
  UTL             <DIR>   3-13-90   7:16a   │          │ 7733 N. 80th Street
  WORK            <DIR>   2-20-90   1:55p   │          │ Milwaukee, WI 53223
  WP50            <DIR>   2-20-90   1:55p   │          │
  WSHELL          <DIR>   3-20-90   4:03p   │ LAST     │ Mouse Installed 02 53
↓
StupenDOS - Ver 1.92p    Copyr. 1990 Eclipse Technologies  All rights reserved.
F1-Copy F2-Move F4-Delete F5-driVe F7-Tree F8-tYpe F9-mOre F10-Help
```

StupenDOS is in your PATH, you can start it from any directory of your system and still have it display the root directory. Simply enter

```
C>SD C:\  <ENTER>
```

This tells the program to load and to start in the root directory of drive C. If you leave out the backslash (\), and just use C:, the program will load and display your current directory.

Setting Up StupenDOS

StupenDOS has excellent features and the program's author has taken great pains to let you set up the program exactly the way you want it. From your choice of editor to what .GIF file viewer you use, you can configure it in StupenDOS. I've always liked programs that provide some flexibility in customizing the program and this one has lots of flexibility. Figure 14-8 shows you the Setup window found in StupenDOS.

Figure 14-8

The Setup window of StupenDOS

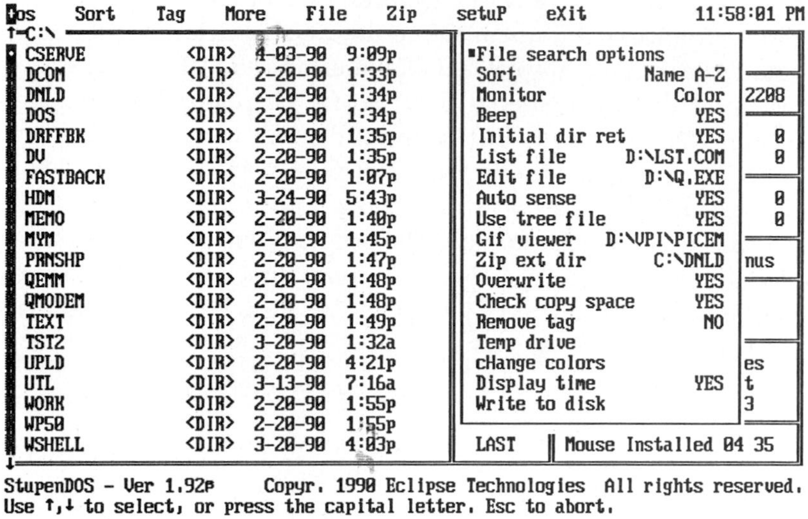

```
Dos    Sort    Tag    More    File    Zip    setuP    eXit        11:58:01 PM
┌─C:\
▌CSERVE      <DIR>  4-03-90   9:09p    ┌─■File search options
 DCOM        <DIR>  2-20-90   1:33p    │ Sort              Name A-Z
 DNLD        <DIR>  2-20-90   1:34p    │ Monitor            Color    2208
 DOS         <DIR>  2-20-90   1:34p    │ Beep                 YES
 DRFFBK      <DIR>  2-20-90   1:35p    │ Initial dir ret      YES       0
 DV          <DIR>  2-20-90   1:35p    │ List file      D:\LST.COM      0
 FASTBACK    <DIR>  2-20-90   1:07p    │ Edit file      D:\Q.EXE
 HDM         <DIR>  3-24-90   5:43p    │ Auto sense           YES       0
 MEMO        <DIR>  2-20-90   1:40p    │ Use tree file        YES       0
 MYM         <DIR>  2-20-90   1:45p    │ Gif viewer   D:\VPI\PICEM
 PRNSHP      <DIR>  2-20-90   1:47p    │ Zip ext dir       C:\DNLD     nus
 QEMM        <DIR>  2-20-90   1:48p    │ Overwrite            YES
 QMODEM      <DIR>  2-20-90   1:48p    │ Check copy space     YES
 TEXT        <DIR>  2-20-90   1:49p    │ Remove tag            NO
 TST2        <DIR>  3-20-90   1:32a    │ Temp drive
 UPLD        <DIR>  2-20-90   4:21p    │ cHange colors                 es
 UTL         <DIR>  3-13-90   7:16a    │ Display time         YES       t
 WORK        <DIR>  2-20-90   1:55p    │ Write to disk                 3
 WP50        <DIR>  2-20-90   1:55p    │
 WSHELL      <DIR>  3-20-90   4:03p    │ LAST  ║ Mouse Installed 04 35
└
StupenDOS - Ver 1.92p   Copyr. 1990 Eclipse Technologies  All rights reserved.
Use ↑,↓ to select, or press the capital letter. Esc to abort.
```

You can configure the sort order, the editor, whether the program should overwrite existing files, and much more. You can set the colors used by the program, which recognizes EGA and VGA graphics cards. You can even put it in 50 line mode if you like, using a wide range of colors. Several of the options, (File search options for example), have submenus with still more options. This gives you maximum control over how StupenDOS "views" your system.

Some Unique StupenDOS Features

StupenDOS can do all the things you'd want a good DOS shell program to do such as:

- Create and remove directories
- Move, copy, delete, rename, and execute files
- Tag single files, tag all files, and untag files
- Change file attributes

- Find, edit, and view files

- Set sort order

The program, however, provides features that other DOS shell programs do not. You can tell StupenDOS to do a global delete of all *.BAK files on your system. It will display a .GIF file using the .GIF file viewer of your choice, and there is a special selection for changing the date/time stamp of a file. You can execute DOS commands from within the program or drop to DOS if you like, leaving StupenDOS in memory.

Another useful feature is that you can tag a group of files, and then tell the program to make a list for you. The program will prompt you for a filename for the list and you can specify a drive, directory, and filename. In addition, StupenDOS can readily handle .ZIP files. Let's examine that facet of the program.

Manipulating Packed Files

One way in which StupenDOS can handle files created with PKWARE's PKZIP is through the powerful program PKZMENU. (PKZMENU will be discussed in detail in Chapter 16.) StupenDOS has a built-in interface and you can select from it off a pull-down menu. Even if you don't have PKZMENU, however, StupenDOS lets you

- Unzip a .ZIP file

- Zip up all tagged files

- View the contents of a .ZIP file

In the Setup menu, you can specify a directory where all .ZIP files will be unpacked. In other words, you can tell the program that no matter where a .ZIP file is when you unpack it, you want all of the extracted files to go to the C:\WORK directory. You could, for example, use the "Zip tagged files" option, to pack up all of your spreadsheet files for 1989 and put them into a .ZIP file.

When you select this option you are presented with a screen that lets you select which PKZIP options you want to use. Do you want to add the files? Do you want to move the files? The choices are up to you. Figure 14-9 shows you what this options screen looks like.

Figure 14-9

ZIP options in StupenDOS

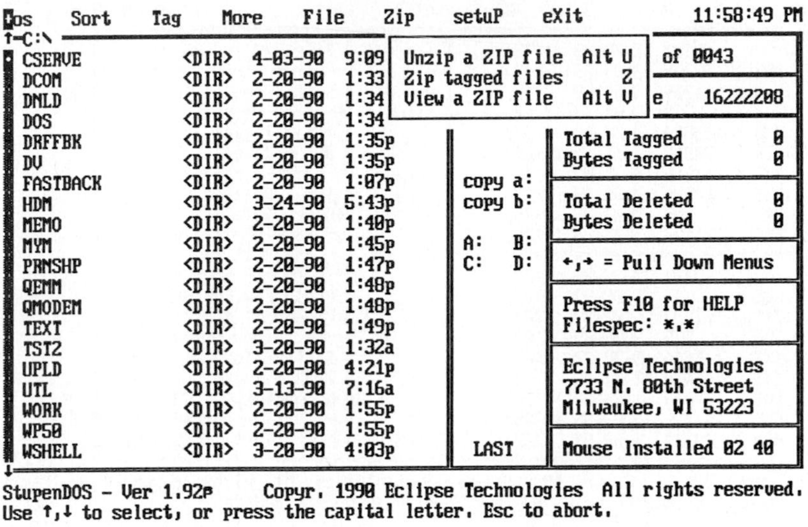

```
Dos   Sort   Tag   More   File   Zip   setuP   eXit        11:58:49 PM
↑=C:\
█ CSERVE        <DIR>  4-03-90  9:09│ Unzip a ZIP file  Alt U │ of 0043
  DCOM          <DIR>  2-20-90  1:33│ Zip tagged files     Z  │
  DNLD          <DIR>  2-20-90  1:34│ View a ZIP file   Alt V │e   16222208
  DOS           <DIR>  2-20-90  1:34│
  DRFFBK        <DIR>  2-20-90  1:35p│               ║ Total Tagged       0
  DU            <DIR>  2-20-90  1:35p│               ║ Bytes Tagged       0
  FASTBACK      <DIR>  2-20-90  1:07p│ copy a:       ║
  HDM           <DIR>  3-24-90  5:43p│ copy b:       ║ Total Deleted      0
  MEMO          <DIR>  2-20-90  1:40p│               ║ Bytes Deleted      0
  MYM           <DIR>  2-20-90  1:45p│ A:   B:       ║
  PRMSHP        <DIR>  2-20-90  1:47p│ C:   D:       ║ ←,→ = Pull Down Menus
  QEMM          <DIR>  2-20-90  1:48p│               ║
  QMODEM        <DIR>  2-20-90  1:48p│               ║ Press F10 for HELP
  TEXT          <DIR>  2-20-90  1:49p│               ║ Filespec: *.*
  TST2          <DIR>  3-20-90  1:32a│               ║
  UPLD          <DIR>  2-20-90  4:21p│               ║ Eclipse Technologies
  UTL           <DIR>  3-13-90  7:16a│               ║ 7733 N. 80th Street
  WORK          <DIR>  2-20-90  1:55p│               ║ Milwaukee, WI 53223
  WP50          <DIR>  2-20-90  1:55p│               ║
  WSHELL        <DIR>  3-20-90  4:03p│ LAST          ║ Mouse Installed 02 40
↓
StupenDOS - Ver 1.92p   Copyr. 1990 Eclipse Technologies  All rights reserved.
Use ↑,↓ to select, or press the capital letter. Esc to abort.
```

Simply select the options you want, give the .ZIP file a name, add any additional options, and tell the program to go to work. It's simple and effective, and stupenDOS has even more to add to this superior flexibility.

Two Are Better than One

Version 2.0 of StupenDOS lets you have two windows on the screen at the same time. This means you can be viewing and working in two different directories and, if you like, on two different drives simultaneously. You can tag files for moving on one screen, switch to the other window and tag files for deletion, and move back and forth at will. You also have complete control over the size of each window. Make one very small and make the other quite large. You could move files and be looking at both the source directory and the target directory at the same time. Figure 14-10 shows you the StupenDOS display while viewing two directories on two different drives simultaneously.

Figure 14-10

Using two windows in StupenDOS

```
Dos    Sort    Tag    More    File    Zip    setuP    eXit          12:01:58 AM
↑=D:\GAMES
  ..              <DIR>  2-20-90  1:43p      tag all    │ File 0001 of 0023
  688    .BAT       299  3-04-89  7:40p      clr all    │
  688    .PAK     64000  3-04-89  7:40p      new dir    │ Bytes Free    16209920
  688    .PAL       768  3-04-89  7:40p      eXecute    │
  7STUD  .EXE    103824  4-05-89  1:53p                 │ Total Tagged         0
  7STUD  .HLP     20962  2-14-89 11:21a                 │ Bytes Tagged         0
  7STUD  .INF     11666  4-26-89  6:46p      copy a:    │
  ALFA   .PAK     64000  3-04-89  7:40p      copy b:    │ Total Deleted        0
  ALFA   .PAL       768  3-04-89  7:40p                 │ Bytes Deleted        0
  BANANOID.CMP    21400 11-27-89 12:00a      A:   B:    │
↕=C:\TST2                                           ↕  C:   D:    │ ←,→ = Pull Down Menus
  ..              <DIR>  3-20-90  1:32a                 │
  ASB    .COM       619  5-08-89  1:02p                 │ Press F10 for HELP
  ASBDOC .TXT      1537  5-08-89  1:02p                 │ Filespec: *.*
  ASBE   .COM       598  5-08-89  1:02p                 │
  CHANGES.TXT      6444  5-08-89  1:02p                 │ Eclipse Technologies
  FILES  .TXT      2450 12-27-88  3:25p                 │ 7733 N. 80th Street
  INSTALL.BAT       636  1-09-89 11:05a                 │ Milwaukee, WI 53223
  PAS    .EXE    154736  4-03-90 10:09p A               │
  PAS    .HLP     39329  5-08-89  1:02p      LAST       │ Mouse Installed 15 05
↕
StupenDOS - Ver 1.92p    Copyr. 1990 Eclipse Technologies  All rights reserved.
F1-Copy F2-Move F4-Delete F5-driVe F7-Tree F8-tYpe F9-mOre F10-Help
```

The top window shows the D:\GAMES directory, and the C:\TST2 directory is in the lower window. You can tag files in both windows without having to change windows. The cursor will pass from the top window into the bottom window and back again. To execute a function—for example, moving a group of tagged files—you do change windows using ALT-W, so the active window is where you will do some work. This exciting feature gives you more power over your system.

Stupendous StupenDOS

StupenDOS is an extremely powerful and flexible DOS shell program providing all the features you would expect, plus a series of extras that increase its overall power and usefulness. It is totally configurable to meet your specifications, handles .ZIP files, has an interface to PKZMENU, and you can operate in two places at one time.

This is a program that was good from the beginning and has gotten progressively better. The interface is easy to understand and use. The ability to use a mouse throughout the entire program makes it fast and simple to use. If you are looking for a good DOS shell, you might want to take a look at StupenDOS.

Douglas Hay
Eclipse Technologies
7733 N. 80th Street
Milwaukee, WI 53223
$35 registration includes free upgrade; please include version you are using when you register

SCOUT AND SCOUT-EM

Scout is a TSR DOS shell that is loaded with features, functions, and capabilities. Scout is a product of John Newlin and his company, New-Ware. New-Ware also produces ArcMaster, CopyMaster, and FormatMaster. Scout and its sister program, Scout-EM, are both very powerful. The only difference between them is that Scout-EM can use expanded memory

---

Figure 14-11

The main display of Scout

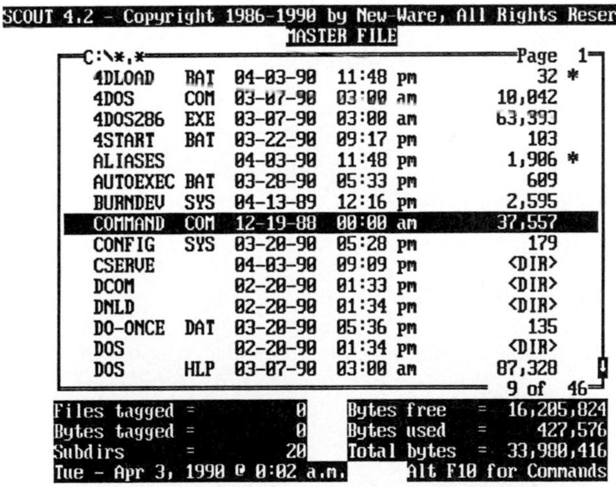

```
SCOUT 4.2 - Copyright 1986-1990 by New-Ware, All Rights Reserved
                          MASTER FILE
   ┌─C:\*.*─                              ─Page  1─┐
     4DLOAD    BAT  04-03-90  11:48 pm         32 *
     4DOS      COM  03-07-90  03:00 am     10,042
     4DOS286   EXE  03-07-90  03:00 am     63,393
     4START    BAT  03-22-90  09:17 pm        103
     ALIASES        04-03-90  11:48 pm      1,906 *
     AUTOEXEC  BAT  03-20-90  05:33 pm        609
     BURNDEV   SYS  04-13-89  12:16 pm      2,595
     COMMAND   COM  12-19-88  00:00 am     37,557
     CONFIG    SYS  03-20-90  05:28 pm        179
     CSERVE         04-03-90  09:09 pm      <DIR>
     DCOM           02-20-90  01:33 pm      <DIR>
     DNLD           02-20-90  01:34 pm      <DIR>
     DO-ONCE   DAT  03-20-90  05:36 pm        135
     DOS            02-20-90  01:34 pm      <DIR>
     DOS       HLP  03-07-90  03:00 am     87,328
                                        ─ 9 of  46─
   Files tagged =            0   Bytes free  =   16,205,824
   Bytes tagged =            0   Bytes used  =      427,576
   Subdirs      =           20   Total bytes =   33,980,416
   Tue - Apr 3, 1990 @ 0:02 a.m.     Alt F10 for Commands
```

(EMS) and much less DOS RAM. Because Scout is a TSR, or memory resident program, it has one distinct advantage over every other DOS shell program: it can be used from *anywhere*. In Figure 14-11 you can see the main display of Scout, while viewing my root directory.

Scout can be used just as easily from within an applications program as it can be when you are at the DOS level. If you are in a multitasking environment, like Quarterdeck's DESQview, you could have a DOS shell in a window by itself. If you are not in a multitasking environment, you could call a DOS shell from a menu program or from the DOS prompt. With Scout, however, you can have all the functions no matter where you are on your system and no matter what you are doing.

A Closer Look at Scout

Besides having all of the things that you'd want in a DOS shell, Scout provides many more capabilities. Borrowing from the actual Scout documentation (which is very well written), here is a partial list of Scout's features.

- Move, copy, and delete individual files
- Move, copy, and delete tagged files
- Rename files, directories, and volume labels
- Create and remove directories and volume labels
- Change file attributes
- Sort files in five different ways
- Specify ascending or descending sorts
- Define your own hot keys
- Format 3.5 and 5.25-inch diskettes
- Search entire disk for files
- Print directory listing of files
- Print graphic directory tree
- Send printer control codes to printer
- Print a text file (formatted or unformatted)

- Browse (line by line) through a text file
- Search a text file for a specified string
- Go directly to a line number in a text file
- Change drive\directory with single keystroke
- Change drives
- Move files across drives
- List unused space on all drives
- View monthly calendar
- View ASCII table
- Automatically tag files for move, copy, delete
- Pop up graphic screen images
- Print graphics screen image
- Save captured text screen image to text file
- View system memory allocation
- Reset file archive bits
- Copy (back up) updated files
- Set system date/time
- Set file date/time
- CRC during file copying
- Built-in mouse support
- Network capability

In addition, Scout can be used in a network environment. You can also run programs from within Scout using two different program menus.

Scout Configuration Options

Scout and Scout-EM come with their own configuration program that lets you customize the program in many ways. Figure 14-12 shows you the configuration menu.

Figure 14-12

The Scout Configuration menu

```
SCOUT Main Configuration Menu

┌─────────────────────────────────────────┐
│ Assign Overlay File Path                 │
│ Assign SCOUT Activation Key              │
│ Assign Default File Mask Keys            │
│ Assign Directories to Function Keys      │
│ Assign Printer Codes                     │
│ Set Printer Margins                      │
│ Define Program Menu                      │
│ Assign Default Sort                      │
│ Set Floppy Drive Parameters              │
│ File Copy Date/Time Setting              │
│ Set Prime Key                            │
│ Set CGA Snow Avoidance                   │
│ Define Ctrl-X Program Menu               │
│ Save Configuration to .BIN file          │
│ Retrieve Configuration .BIN file         │
│                                          │
│ Quit With Option to Save                 │
└─────────────────────────────────────────┘
```

Specify DOS directory path where the SCOUT overlay (.000) file will reside.

Note that you can set the key sequence that activates Scout, set margins for printing, and even set printer codes for your printer. The Assign Directories to Function Keys option lets you quickly change to certain directories with the touch of a function key. You could set F1 to move you to the C:\DNLD directory, set F2 to move you to the C:\UTL directory, and so on. Any time you are in the main Scout display, you could simply press F1 and be in the C:\DNLD directory. It's a convenient feature for rapidly changing to some of your most commonly used directories.

You can also define a Program menu that will automatically execute programs for you, set the default method of sorting, tell Scout what kind of floppy drives you have, and much more. When finished, you can save this information so Scout always comes up exactly as you want it. If at any time your system changes or you find that you have new needs, you can always run the configuration program again. You can also change many of the defaults that you've set from within the program. Let's take a look at some of the things that make Scout unique.

Unique Features in Scout

As noted, Scout/Scout-EM has the full range of features expected in a good DOS shell program. It is a complete system for managing the files and directories on your system. In addition to these standard features, however, Scout has some interesting extras. For example, not only can you have Scout view a text file, but you can tell it to start at a certain line within that text file. You can also search through a text file to find a specific string. Scout can also find any file on your system.

Since Scout/Scout-EM is a TSR, you can pop it up over anything, including graphics screens, something that many TSR programs cannot accomplish. With Scout, not only can you print files, but you can also print graphics screens. Scout is always there, whether you are at the DOS prompt, in your editor, or in your favorite communications program. You can move files, change file attributes, and much more and never leave your primary applications program.

Saving You Precious RAM

The standard version of Scout uses approximately 160K of DOS RAM. Scout-EM, on the other hand, is capable of using expanded memory. If you use Scout-EM, the program will only use 5K of your conventional memory and the rest will be stored in expanded memory. Imagine a resident DOS shell with the power and features of Scout that only uses 5K of RAM. Best of all, both versions are offered as Shareware, so you can try out both of them. If you have expanded memory on your system, you'll be most interested in Scout-EM; if not, Scout is the version you'll want to see.

Scout is generally found in a file called SCOUT??.ZIP, where ?? is the version number. You may find a self-extracting version named SCOUT?? .EXE. Scout-EM can be found as SCT-EM??.ZIP and also as a self-extracting file called SCT-EM??.EXE. The current version as of this writing is version 4.2.

The Scoop on Scout

If you're looking for an excellent DOS shell program that hosts a multitude of features, you may well want to check out either Scout or Scout-EM. If you like using a DOS shell and have expanded memory, Scout-EM is an excellent choice. It gives you instant access from anywhere on your system. Both Scout and Scout-EM have everything you could want in a shell program plus a lot more. Another factor is that the author, John Newlin, constantly upgrades his programs to make them the very best that they can be.

You can register for the program in three different ways—via mail, voice phone, or on the Shareware Products bulletin board, using VISA or MasterCard. When you register you wait one business day and then go online and download the current registered version. The latest program version, supporting files, and documentation are mailed to all registrants regardless of the registration method. New-Ware also offers superior support for all of its products.

John Newlin
New-Ware
8050 Camino Kiosco
San Diego, CA 92122
619-455-6225 (Voice)
619-455-5226 (BBS)
$30 registration for Scout or Scout-EM; VISA/MasterCard accepted; registered users get access to a special 9600 baud phone line.

POINT AND SHOOT HARD DISK MANAGER

The Point and Shoot (P&S) Hard Disk Manager is actually two programs in one. Not only is it a DOS shell program, but it's a complete menu program as well. I've discussed the possibility of running a DOS shell program from a menu program, but this program gives you both.

As a menu program, P&S Hard Disk Manager offers you some of the best features of menu programs. At the same time, it offers you the most common features wanted in a good DOS shell. One must keep in mind that a combination program like this may not give you all the features found in a program dedicated to just one task. In other words, you should not expect it to have all of the features offered by a program that is a dedicated menu system. It may also not have some of the little extras that are offered by programs exclusively written as DOS shells. Since it does have the most commonly sought features of both a menu and a shell program, many users may find that P&S meets their needs quite well. First, let's take a brief look at its menu capabilities.

More Than Enough Menus

P&S Hard Disk Manager lets you define up to 300 menu items. For many users, this would be more than enough. Since the program is not a TSR, it does not use any RAM when programs are executed. This is not always the case with some DOS shells that let you execute programs. P&S makes sure all your available RAM is there for programs. Your menu entries may also allow for optional command line parameters, another option that is not always offered by some DOS shells when you execute programs. Figure 14-13 shows the menu entry screen.

You can run any .COM, .EXE, or .BAT file from the P&S menus. Note that if you run batch files from the menu, the last line must contain "PS"

Figure 14-13

Point and Shoot menu entry screen

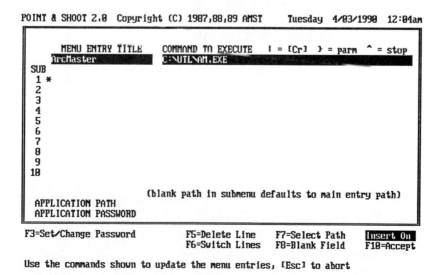

```
POINT & SHOOT 2.0  Copyright (C) 1987,88,89 AMST    Tuesday  4/03/1990  12:04am

      MENU ENTRY TITLE    COMMAND TO EXECUTE   | = [Cr]  } = parm   ^ = stop
      ArcMaster                C:\UTL\AM.EXE
SUB
  1 *
  2
  3
  4
  5
  6
  7
  8
  9
 10
                    (blank path in submenu defaults to main entry path)
   APPLICATION PATH
   APPLICATION PASSWORD

F3=Set/Change Password       F5=Delete Line    F7=Select Path    Insert On
                             F6=Switch Lines   F8=Blank Field    F10=Accept

Use the commands shown to update the menu entries, [Esc] to abort
```

in order to return to the main program, P&S. Both the menu and shell portions of the program are seen on the same screen. You don't have to toggle to another area to see one or the other. Figure 14-14 shows you the main display of P&S Hard Disk Manager.

Note that the menu portion occupies the top half of the screen, while the shell commands of the program occupy the bottom half. From this area you can execute one of the shell commands or a menu option. The P&S Hard Disk Manager also has some other interesting features. Let's take a look at what they are.

These Features Are Standard

For your convenience, the program has a calculator and a perpetual calendar. You can use the calculator to quickly solve basic math problems. Using the calendar, you can look ahead for a date in the future or look back for a date in the past. P&S also lets you recall your last ten DOS

Figure 14-14

Main display of Point and Shoot

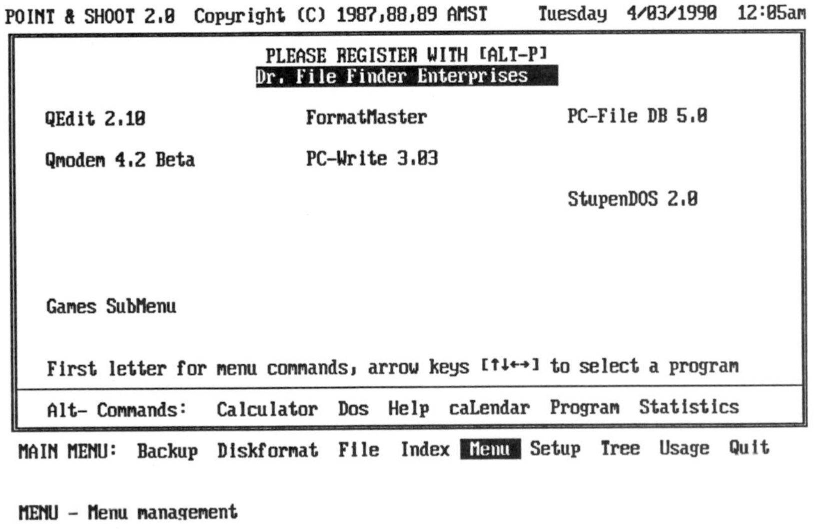

```
POINT & SHOOT 2.0  Copyright (C) 1987,88,89 AMST      Tuesday  4/03/1990  12:05am
┌──────────────────────────────────────────────────────────────────────┐
│                      PLEASE REGISTER WITH [ALT-P]                       │
│                     Dr. File Finder Enterprises                        │
│                                                                        │
│   QEdit 2.10              FormatMaster              PC-File DB 5.0      │
│                                                                        │
│   Qmodem 4.2 Beta         PC-Write 3.03                                │
│                                                                        │
│                                                    StupenDOS 2.0        │
│                                                                        │
│                                                                        │
│                                                                        │
│   Games SubMenu                                                        │
│                                                                        │
│   First letter for menu commands, arrow keys [↑↓←→] to select a program│
│  ┌──────────────────────────────────────────────────────────────────┐ │
│   Alt- Commands:   Calculator  Dos  Help  caLendar  Program  Statistics│
└──────────────────────────────────────────────────────────────────────┘
  MAIN MENU:  Backup  Diskformat  File  Index  Menu  Setup  Tree  Usage  Quit

  MENU - Menu management
```

commands, which is a handy feature. P&S can format all sizes of floppy disks, it lets you define colors, and it has a built-in screen blanker and mouse support.

One interesting feature of the menu system is that it has password protection and facilities for maintaining a usage log. This is a nice feature for tax purposes or finding out who is running what programs. You can set up user IDs for any number of users and even print reports on usage. The usage function gives you the following options:

- Change Password
- Fixup Databases
- Timelog Database
- User Database

By using these functions you can change your password, fix corrupted usage databases, and monitor system use by time or user. In addition, P&S has an interface to the P&S Backup and Restore program, written by the same author. (It was discussed in Chapter 13.) P&S Hard Disk Manager is not only a menu and a DOS shell, but it has added features, making it fairly versatile.

P&S Hard Disk Manager—The Shell

As a DOS shell program, P&S has all the standard features you would expect from a good shell program, including:

- Changing the file attributes of any file
- Editing text files with a built-in editor or one of your choice
- Moving, copying, renaming, or deleting files
- Sorting files by name, extension, date, or size
- Finding files
- Printing text files
- Viewing any text file
- Making, deleting, or renaming directories
- A tree structured directory

You can also hide or unhide directories and look at two lists of files at the same time. P&S also has an undelete function so that you can unerase files that you accidentally deleted—a nice lineup of capabilities.

Sizing Up P&S Hard Disk Manager

The P&S Hard Disk Manager is a good menu system and a good DOS shell program combined in one package. It has some of the best essential features of both classifications of programs. If you only want a DOS shell or only a menu program, P&S may not be for you. If you contemplate using both types of programs, P&S offers you a good mix—giving you the best of both worlds in one relatively compact and efficient package.

Kurt H. Diesch
Applied Micro Systems Technology
P.O. Box 1596, Welch Ave. Station
Ames, IA 50010
$45 registration fee

THE SWISS ARMY SHELL

From the name of the program, you can tell the Swiss Army Shell is a lot of tools in one program. The phrase "Swiss Army" conjures up pictures of screw drivers, saw blades, and cork screws in one small knife handle. In this respect, the program's name is quite appropriate. It does have a large number of tools to help you manipulate the files on your system. It gives you all the capabilities discussed at the beginning of this chapter in reference to DOS shells, including an overall view of your system, mobility, and the power to tag, untag, delete, copy, move, and rename. The Swiss Army Shell, or SAS, can handle up to 15 logical drives. Let's take a look at what else it can do.

Swiss Army Shell Extras

SAS can use expanded memory or disk to swap things out. This allows you to run larger application programs from within the shell. You can define an editor of your choice, as well as a program for viewing files, and then tell the program if you want swapping to take place or not. SAS has an easy-to-use interface and can be controlled from the keyboard or with a mouse. Figure 14-15 shows the main display of the Swiss Army Shell.

Note that the directory tree is on the left, the files in that directory are displayed on the right, and statistics appear at the bottom. Across the top are the pull-down menu selections, each of which offers a range of options. In addition to configuring an editor and a file viewer, you can also configure

- Your favorite word processor

- Your favorite colors for each window

- Up to ten DOS command lines for later execution

- Whether you want to confirm exiting the program

- Whether you want to transfer each program you use to EMS or disk

Figure 14-15

Swiss Army Shell's main display

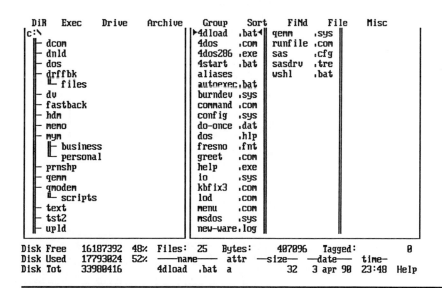

SAS also handles .ZIP files and you can configure certain options for that. Figure 14-16 shows you the options available for working with compressed files.

These options give you the ability to manipulate .ZIP files without ever having to leave the shell. SAS is fast and efficient and a very complete package. If you are looking for a good DOS shell that has some extra tools for convenience, you might want to check out the Swiss Army Shell.

Steven C. Lee
304 Pierson Drive
Trussville, AL 37173
205-836-9311
BBS Mail: The ST BBS
CompuServe Mail: 71076,1216
$20 registration includes free upgrade

Figure 14-16

The SAS Archive options

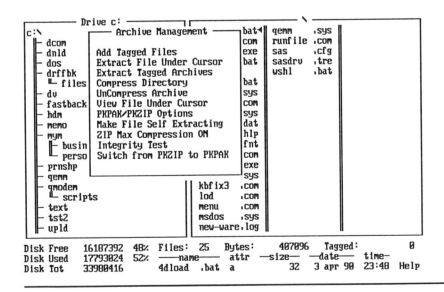

SUMMARIZING DOS SHELLS

This concludes our look at DOS shell programs and what they can do. All of the programs discussed in this chapter are very good and offer certain features that are similar. At the same time, each offers some features that are unique. The ones described here give you a starting point. There are many shell programs, with varying interfaces and features. The one that is ultimately right for you is the one that offers the most features you want. Others that you might want to look at include

- The Still Rivers DOS Shell found as SR???.ZIP, where ??? is the version number

- Cliff's Directory Program found as CDP-SW.ZIP. This is the only other TSR shell program that I found and it's quite good. It uses 9K of RAM if you have expanded memory

- DOSamatic found as DSM???.ZIP, where ??? is the version number

- Disk Scanner found as DS???.ZIP, where ??? is the version number

- Minshell found as MINSHELL.ZIP

Let's move on now and take a look at the wide world of utility programs. There's a lot more to explore in The Wires.

## CHAPTER FIFTEEN

Utilities

In Chapter 12 you were introduced to some interesting utility programs that were classified as file utilities. These programs, in one way or another, manipulate files. You looked at a complex program, Professional Master Key, that can perform many file operations on your system and can even alter sectors on your hard disk. At the same time, you examined Norm Patriquin's PCOPY, which copies and moves programs around your system "intelligently," giving you countless options.

As noted previously, commercial companies can't afford to market such programs, yet people need and want utility programs to enhance other software or hardware. Before we dive into this chapter, which will cover DOS, keyboard, printer, and general utilities, let's take a closer look at the constantly expanding world of utility programs.

THE NEED TO IMPROVE

The question, "Why are there so many utility programs?" has several answers. Some utility programs were written because of the shortcomings of DOS. Many users were dissatisfied with DOS's very tiny keyboard buffer, its inability to blank the screen, a typematic rate that made you feel like you were typing in mud, and many other irritating inadequacies. People are seldom satisfied with the way things are. Humans, by nature, have a need to improve their material culture, particularly their tools and resources. This tendency applied to computers is one reason for the unending flow of utility programs.

Covering All the Bases

With so many handy utility programs available, it is difficult for one chapter to do this topic justice. Four major program categories will be discussed. You'll look at some fine examples from each category. It's hoped that this sampling of utility programs will provide you with at least an overview of this topic. Let's move on and examine utility programs, beginning with DOS, or operating system, utilities.

DOS AND SYSTEM UTILITIES

For our purposes, a DOS utility is any program that takes something that DOS does and enhances its function. On some bulletin boards and commercial online networks, the term DOS utilities is interchangeable with system utilities. The functions of the utilities span many different areas. Here are some DOS utilities that you might find useful.

SORTF

SORTF is another fine program by Vern Buerg. This DOS utility is meant to replace the SORT program included with a standard DOS disk. There are several benefits to using SORTF:

- You can sort files larger than 63K
- You can sort much faster than with DOS SORT
- Files with fixed length records can be sorted
- Up to 16 fields can be sorted

SORTF has command line parameters similar to those used by the DOS SORT program. You can sort a file on multiple fields so that the output file is exactly as you want it. Its command line format would be similar to:

```
C>SORTF OLDFILE.TXT NEWFILE.TXT
```

This would take the contents of OLDFILE.TXT and sort it alphabetically to NEWFILE.TXT. If you want to perform complex sorting, SORTF has command line parameters to do it.

SORTF Command Line Options

If you want to sort on specific fields, you can use SORTF to do it quickly and neatly. SORTF will sort both logical and fixed length records. A *logical* record is simply one that ends with a carriage return and a line feed. A *fixed length* record, on the other hand, can contain all types of data, including carriage returns. The one major difference is that with a fixed length record, *every* record is exactly the same size, while logical records can vary in size. Information can be sorted in either ascending or descending order and you can switch between the two within the same file. Here are some of the command line options of SORTF.

/C   Tells SORTF that keys are not case sensitive
/Q   Stops you from seeing messages from SORTF
/R   Reverses sorting order
/K   Creates an output file of sorted data that includes a 5-byte information prefix
/L   Tells SORTF that the file has fixed length records
/+   Gives location of field and sorts in ascending order
/−   Gives location of field and sorts in descending order

Let's say you have a file that is packed with names and phone numbers and you want to sort them by area code. The file contents might look like this:

```
John Andrews              1-555-232-1898
```

The first number of the area code is in column 36. To sort on the area code you would give the following command:

```
C>SORTF PHONE.DAT PHONE2.DAT /+36
```

This tells SORTF to sort the file PHONE.DAT, based on the number in the 36th column, in ascending order, and to write the results to a file called PHONE2.DAT.

Sorting with SORTF

Not only is SORTF faster than the DOS SORT program, but it can sort through files that are much larger, and through a larger number of fields. The file containing SORTF also contains an .OBJ file allowing you to call SORTF easily from a QuickBASIC program. The number of records you can sort depends on how much memory you have. The average number is about 40,000 records. For example, if your records were 80 bytes in size, you could sort a file 3.2 megabytes in size.

If you're looking for an excellent program to replace the hampered SORT program included with DOS, SORTF is fast and very efficient.

Vernon D. Buerg
139 White Oak Circle
Petaluma, CA 94952
707-778-8944 BBS
70007,1212 CompuServe ID
$15 donation recommended (any amount accepted)

FormatMaster

FormatMaster is a program by John Newlin that has formatting diskettes down to a science. You configure the program so it meets the needs of your particular system. There are many defaults you can save and turn on and off. In this way, the program always comes up knowing what kind of drives you have and what options you want as defaults.

To make FormatMaster as versatile as possible, Newlin included some interesting options to make your life easier. The main screen of Format-Master is shown in Figure 15-1. Since there are quite a few options for you to choose from, let's go over them quickly so you can appreciate the features that this fine program has.

Enter DOS

While using FormatMaster you can drop to DOS, which is a handy feature if you are in the middle of formatting diskettes and need information from another part of your system. When you are finished with your task at the DOS prompt, type **exit** to return to FormatMaster.

Transfer System

Disks used only for data cannot be used to boot your computer. However, you may want to make a system disk that you can boot from. When you toggle the Transfer System option, the DOS system files and COMMAND .COM will be copied to a diskette as you format it.

Add Volume Label

There are times when you may want to add a volume label to one of your disks. It often helps to know what is on a disk when you do a DIR command. FormatMaster gives you an easy way to add a volume label by allowing you to toggle this feature on or off.

Cycle Format and Double Cycle

The task of formatting disks can be tedious. Here again, FormatMaster comes through with two very interesting options. One is the Cycle Format

---

Figure 15-1

Main screen of FormatMaster

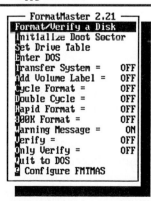

Format/Verify a 5¼" or 3½" floppy diskette.

```
┌─ FormatMaster 2.21 ─┐
│ Format/Verify a Disk │
│ Initialize Boot Sector │
│ Set Drive Table │
│ Enter DOS │
│ Transfer System =   OFF │
│ Add Volume Label =  OFF │
│ Cycle Format =      OFF │
│ Double Cycle =      OFF │
│ Rapid Format =      OFF │
│ 360K Format =       OFF │
│ Warning Message =    ON │
│ Verify =            OFF │
│ Only Verify =       OFF │
│ Quit to DOS │
│ Configure FMTMAS │
└─────────────────────┘
```

option. Let's say you have one floppy drive and a stack of 360K diskettes to format. With the Cycle Format toggled on, you can format disks one right after another by answering any prompts when you start the first disk. From that point on, when one disk is finished all you have to do is enter a **Y** if you want to do another one or an **N** if you want to stop. This really speeds the process by eliminating answering the same prompts over and over. If you have two floppy drives, you can elect to use the Double Cycle option. This will automatically alternate between disk drives so a disk is always being formatted. While one disk is formatting in drive A, you can be labeling one that was just formatted in drive B.

Rapid Format and 800K Format
A quick way of formatting disks that have been formatted previously is to use the Rapid Format option. It's good way of cleaning the disk surface. The 800K format can be used on machines that have 1.2 meg 5.25-inch floppy drives. When you toggle this feature on, you can format a regular 360K floppy to hold 800K, over twice as much as it normally holds. Since the BIOS on machines varies, the FormatMaster package comes with a TSR program to help overcome problems on machines that might have trouble with the 800K format.

Verify or Only Verify
While formatting disks you can toggle the Verify option on so the entire operation is verified by DOS. This will cause the format to take a little longer than if Verify was off. The Only Verify option can be used to check the integrity of a disk before you use it.

On Track with FormatMaster

FormatMaster is the most complete disk formatting program I have seen. It is configurable, loaded with time- and money-saving options, and quite fast. Options that you configure as defaults can always be changed quickly while using the program. If you want an excellent program for formatting disks, check out FormatMaster.

John Newlin
New-Ware
8050 Camino Kiosco
San Diego, CA 92122

619-455-6225 (Voice)
619-455-5226 (BBS)
$25 registration; MasterCard and VISA accepted

Back Off!

Back Off!, by John Bean, is a program that can eliminate backup files or file groups by searching for common file extensions like .BAK, .TMP, and .~BA. Here's what Back Off! can do for you.

Saving Wasted Space

Many programs make backup files, which can be very helpful in case your original file is corrupted. Once you are finished, however, you might be surprised to find out how much disk space is being devoted to backups of original files. The most common extension is .BAK, but there are many other possibilities. Back Off! lets you define and search for up to 30 filename extensions. Figure 15-2 shows you the main display of Back Off!

Since different programs create backup files with different extensions, Back Off! lets you edit the list of extensions that it searches for. You can add or delete extensions and give each a description, which helps remind you what program created the file. As you'll note in Figure 15-2, you can also use the DOS wildcards when defining extensions.

Back Off! is capable of searching on multiple hard drives. When Back Off! begins searching, it scans the drive(s) you've specified and finds all files matching the extensions you defined. The list of files is placed on the screen, allowing you to tag files you want to delete. You can also use ALT-T to tag all of the files, and then F10 to delete them. The registered version of Back Off! can be run from a batch file and will automatically erase all matching files.

Another feature found only in the registered version is a command line parameter that lets you specify a filename with extensions meant for deletion. This feature allows you to use one set of extensions on drive C, for example, while using a different set of extensions on drive D. You can even print out your extensions list so you can review it more easily. Additionally, Back Off! has an easy-to-work-with interface and automatically knows if you have a color monitor. This is a very handy utility for eliminating unnecessary files and conserving disk space.

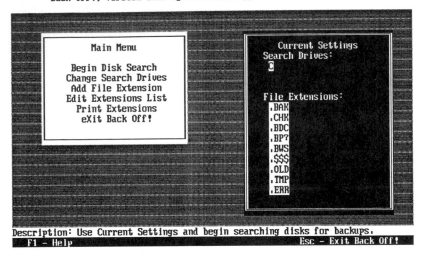

Figure 15-2

Main display of Back Off!

Back Off!, Version 1.20 by JB Technology Inc. - EVALUATION COPY

John E. Bean
JB Technology, Inc.
28701 N. Main Street
Ridgefield, WA 98642
206-887-3442 (Voice)
$15 registration

IFF—Enhanced Batch Files

The multitude of functions that can be performed with batch files are often overlooked by many users. If you look in a DOS reference manual you'll see a section completely devoted to special commands used in batch files. IFF, by John Knauer, gives even more power to batch files and has some other capabilities as well. What can IFF do? IFF can

- Tell you if a drive door is open
- Tell you how much disk space is free

- Tell you if you have EMS
- Respond to yes or no questions
- Create menus with many options
- Detect if a disk has been formatted

IFF has been used by several colleges and universities to set up CAI (Computer Aided Instruction) classes using its menu functions. IFF can also check dates and days of the week, search a list for a particular filename, and find out what the last available drive is on your system. It can take a regular batch file and make it into a super batch file.

Some of the Power of IFF

There are other batch file enhancer programs, but generally they perform only one function. IFF, however, combines many different functions into one small package. The IFF.EXE file is only 19K. IFF works by analyzing a DOS error level, which is set depending on what you have IFF doing. Here is a sample IFF batch file that generates a menu.

```
REM turn echo off and clear the screen
ECHO OFF
CLS
REM START heading label.  present a small menu using ECHO's and call
REM IFF with a limit of 0-3 for a response
:START
    CLS
    ECHO      START YOUR FAVORITE PROGRAM
    ECHO      YOUR OPTIONS ARE
    ECHO .
    ECHO      1 - YOUR SPREADSHEET
    ECHO      2 - YOUR DATABASE
    ECHO      3 - YOUR WORD PROCESSOR
    ECHO .
    ECHO      0 - END
    IFF P 3
REM check the return code in ERRORLEVEL.
    IF ERRORLEVEL 3 GOTO WORD
    IF ERRORLEVEL 2 GOTO DATA
    IF ERRORLEVEL 1 GOTO SPREAD
    GOTO END
```

```
REM SPREADsheet heading label.  Show the user what they chose.
:SPREAD
    ECHO YOU CHOSE YOUR SPREADSHEET
    PAUSE
    GOTO START
REM DATAbase heading label.  Show the user what they chose.
:DATA
    ECHO YOU CHOSE YOUR DATABASE
    PAUSE
    GOTO START
REM WORD_processor heading label.  Show the user what they chose.
:WORD
    ECHO YOU CHOSE YOUR WORDPROCESSOR
    PAUSE
    GOTO START
REM END heading label.  If they press #0 then we're here and ending.
:END
```

This batch file would give you a simple menu from which you could run programs. There is another IFF option allowing you to create more complex menus. Overall, IFF is an excellent utility program that gives tremendous power and flexibility to your batch files. You'll find IFF included on the disk that comes with this book, along with sample batch files. Give IFF a try and see all the things it can do.

John Knauer
P.O. Box 747
Brookfield, CT 06804
$20 partial registration includes a diskette of the current version of IFF and one upgrade to the next major version of IFF.
$25 full registration includes a diskette and printed manual for the current version of IFF as well as a diskette and printed manual for the next major version of IFF when it becomes available.

Some Special Mentions

Other DOS utilities worth mentioning are listed below. Look for these programs from disk vendors, user groups, online networks, and bulletin boards.

- **GSETUP**   GSETUP, by Juan Jimenez, is an excellent CMOS setup utility that lets you manipulate your CMOS configuration without rebooting. Generally found as either GSETUP.ZIP or GSETUP??.ZIP, where ?? is the version number.

- **DYNABOOT**   DYNABOOT, by Matt Palcic, allows you to have multiple AUTOEXEC.BAT and CONFIG.SYS files so that you can reboot with a different configuration and do it easily. The program is menu-driven and very easy to use.

- **CED**   CED, by Chris Dunford, is an excellent DOS command line editor and the first to offer synonyms. Synonyms allow you to create your own set of commands that can perform many complex functions. If you like CED, register for PCED, the commercial version, which is even more powerful.

- **NJRAMD**   NJRAMD, by Nifty James (Mike Blaszczak), is the best RAM disk driver for use with EMS (expanded memory) that I've found. Create any size RAM drive in EMS and it only uses 720 bytes of DOS RAM.

Keep in mind that if you need a utility function, someone has probably written a program to do it. If you can't find what you need, send me a note on GEnie (mail ID, DR-FF) or to one of the bulletin boards marked in Appendix C. For now, let's take a look at a few keyboard utilities.

KEYBOARD UTILITIES

Keyboard utilities perform a variety of functions. For the most part, however, they will fall into one or more of the following categories:

- Increase the default keyboard buffer and/or manipulate it

- Speed up the default typematic rate

- Help redefine the keys in one way or another

With these features in mind, it's easier to cover keyboard utilities than it is some of the other groupings. If you take a close look at the keyboard utilities available on online networks and bulletin boards, or through disk vendors and user groups, you'll find that most of them fit into one or more of these classifications. Let's take a quick look at each of these categories.

The Keyboard Buffer

In DOS, the first major problem with the keyboard buffer is its small size. When you start typing, if you don't press ENTER you'll start hearing beeps from your machine telling you the keyboard buffer has been filled. The DOS default is about 15 keystrokes, which is not long enough. Why not? Let's say you wanted to change into a directory called C:\MAIN\EDIT\ ARTICLE. You won't be able to get to it using the DOS default keyboard buffer. You can type in this much,

```
C>CD \MAIN\EDIT\A
```

and DOS doesn't allow you to enter any more characters, so you must change to that directory in smaller steps.

A larger keyboard buffer lets you "stuff" the buffer with keystrokes to send to a program. There are many utilities that are designed to enlarge and utilize the keyboard buffer.

The Typematic Rate

Another keyboard setting is the default typematic rate. The typematic rate governs how long a key is depressed before it starts to repeat and, once it does start to repeat, how often it will repeat. Quite a few programs have been written to give you some control over the typematic rate, the repeat rate, and some other features as well. For example, a program may include the ability to reverse the SHIFT and CAPS LOCK keys, enlarge the buffer, or other related tasks, even if the primary function is to alter the typematic rate.

Redefining the Keyboard

There are many programs that redefine the keyboard. Keyboard macro programs are one way, but there are others. For example, you can redefine the keyboard by using ANSI escape sequences. Other programs redefine the keyboard by altering what specific keys do, such as making the CTRL key become the SHIFT key, or displaying on screen when the CAPS LOCK or NUM LOCK key is on. There are some versions of BIOS used on clone machines that can alter the keyboard. Programs have been written to change keyboards back to their original state. There are countless programs for redefining function keys, the CTRL and SHIFT keys, the numeric keypad, and others.

Let's examine how a few programs that perform some of the functions noted above, notably those that work with the keyboard buffer, increase the typematic rate, and help to redefine the keys on your system.

KBFIX—A Keyboard Enhancer

KBFIX, by Skip Gelbrech, is an all-around keyboard enhancement program. The last version was released in 1986, yet it still works well even on 386 machines and performs several functions while using only 2.5K of RAM. KBFIX will expand the size of the keyboard buffer to 160 bytes, which is more than enough for typing ahead. It also offers several ways of adjusting the default typematic rate of your keyboard. You can adjust the rate itself, the repeat rate, and even the duration of the pause between repeats. In addition, you can tell KBFIX how many characters should be inserted into the keyboard buffer for each repeat. The documentation suggests some basic default settings. By experimenting you can set KBFIX just the way you want it. What other functions does KBFIX perform?

Altering Some Keys

Ever forget you have the CAPS LOCK key on, and then press the SHIFT key? What you get is a lowercase letter. KBFIX has an option allowing you to bypass this minor problem. If you toggle this option on, you will get an uppercase letter even if you do press the SHIFT key while CAPS LOCK is on. There is another toggle whereby the first character entered will be uppercase and all others will be lowercase when CAPS LOCK is on and if SHIFT is depressed. This, in effect, is like turning the CAPS LOCK off. KBFIX will also tell you when any of your locking keys are toggled on.

Keeping Track of Things

You can decide exactly where on the screen you want KBFIX to appear, assuming you have toggled a feature that will cause it to display information. For example, if you have KBFIX show you the state of the locking keys, you can place that display anywhere on screen that is convenient for you. You can also have KBFIX generate a beep any time a locking key is toggled on. As an extra option you can control the pitch of the beeps that KBFIX generates. KBFIX will also prevent snow on older CGA monitors by controlling the timer interrupt.

Summing Up KBFIX

KBFIX can handle most common keyboard deficiencies and can be found in the public domain. It can even be loaded into high memory with no problems. If you want a good all-around keyboard enhancer that only uses a small amount of RAM, KBFIX might be your answer.

Skip Gilbrech
90 Lexington Avenue #10-G
New York, NY 10016
71445,534 CompuServe ID

STACKEY

STACKEY is a program by Barry Simon and Rick Wilson. The original version acted as simply a keyboard stuffer, which puts keystrokes into the keyboard buffer, and then passes them along to the programs. How can this be useful? As an example, earlier versions of QEdit did not have an option for loading macro files from the command line. Macros were instead assigned to a function key sequence and loaded once inside QEdit. STACKEY, on the other hand, allows you to use a batch file containing STACKEY commands that load QEdit, a file to be edited, and a macro file. Let's take a brief look at what else STACKEY can do.

STACKEY—Multiple Uses

One of STACKEY's most basic functions is its ability to duplicate almost any key on the keyboard, including BACKSPACE, arrow keys, TAB, HOME, and many more. Figure 15-3 shows one of the STACKEY help screens that displays some of its key codes.

STACKEY can duplicate many of the more unusual key combinations in addition to alphanumeric and function keys. STACKEY can pause, wait, and flush the keyboard buffer, and it has a special code to be used with DESQview. The STACKEY code D1 is the same as toggling the DESQ key in DESQview. For example, here is a simple batch file called O1.BAT, for "open 1."

```
stackey D1
stackey "O"
stackey "BD" CR
```

The O1.BAT file tells STACKEY to pull up the DESQview menu. It then tells DESQview to open a window and load the *BD* or Big DOS program. You could also replace the BD with a *%1* and load any program you've defined in DESQview, by putting the appropriate DESQview menu keys on the command line. You could also include STACKEY commands to zoom the new window.

Figure 15-3

STACKEY help display showing key codes

```
STACKEY Version 3.0  Help:CODES SUMMARY    c(o) B. Simon & R. Wilson, 1990

UA - Up Arrow        ES - Escape              PS - Print Screen
DA - Down Arrow      BS - Backspace           CP - Ctrl-PrtSc
LA - Left Arrow      CB - Ctrl-Backspace      TA,TB - Tab
RA - Right Arrow     SP - Space               ST,BT - Shift Tab
PU - Page Up         CR - Enter (Carriage Return)  DL  Delete
PD - Page Down       LF - Ctrl-Enter (Line Feed)   IN - Insert
HM - Home            FF - Form Feed           DQ - " Double quote
EN - End             PH,WR - "Phony" keystrokes  SQ - ' Single quote
G+,N+ - Grey Plus
G*,N* - Grey *       ┌─────────────────────────────────────────────┐
G-,N- - Grey Minus   │ 'Enhanced' keyboard combos: AB,AC,AE,AT,CT,K/,K* │
N. - decimal point   │  K-,K+,KC,K0-9,K.^/,^*,^-,^+,^0,^5,^2,^0,^.,GE │
N0,...,N9 - keypad   │  GC,G1-4,G6-0,G.                             │
                     └─────────────────────────────────────────────┘
H! - Flush hotkey    WB - Wait for Buffer empty   CA - Ctrlalt Plus
H* - Flush scan      WH - Wait for restart hotkey D1,D2 - Desqview
H- - Stop hotkey     WK - Wait for any key        DL - Desqview Learn
H+ - Restart hotkey  WS - Wait for specific key   Qn - Carousel
SC - Scan for text   BE - Script beeps            TE - Tesseract
SS - Scan silently   ME,MP - Popup messages       SH - Shift Mask

Commands: PgUp/Dn,↑,↓,Home,End,<G>oto,<S>earch,<Esc>=Exit.    Page  3 of 17
```

STACKEY Utilities Mode

While STACKEY is excellent for passing keystrokes to programs, it also has a utilities mode that lets you perform some interesting functions. For example, you can reboot your computer, toggle between monitors, change screen modes, send a file to the printer, and set colors. Figure 15-4 shows the STACKEY Utilities Mode help screen.

Note that STACKEY can also swap LPT1 and LPT2 or COM1 and COM2, set the number of lines to 25, 43, or 50, and much more. If you want to execute a function at a specific time, you can even tell STACKEY to delay processing until a given time. In addition to having links to DESQview, STACKEY has specific commands for use with Software Carousel or the TesSeRact TSR utilities, and for calling up SideKick or Primetime. STACKEY has the added benefit of making it easier to use these other programs. STACKEY can also set the EGA/VGA palettes, put messages on the screen in color, and make many other chores much easier.

Figure 15-4

STACKEY'S Utilities Mode help screen

```
STACKEY Version 3.0  Help:UTILITIES MODE    c(o) B. Simon & R. Wilson, 1990

The following commands are done by the non-resident part of STACKEY
 {BOOT}         Warm reboot              {Wait=nnn}    Real time pause
 {BOOT=c}       Cold reboot              {UNtil=HH:MM} Real time holds
 {MONitor=x}    x=Color, Mono, Switch    {Keywait}     Wait for input
 {MODe=n}       Switch to screen mode n  {Enterwait}   Wait for <Enter>
 {UMode=n}      Switch w/o checking      {Abortwait}   Abort on Y
 {LInes=n}      n=25,43,50 text lines    {^abortwait}  Abort on N
 {CUrsor=x}     x=+/- cursor on/off      {HAlt}        Absolute abort
 {CUrsor=m,n}   cursor scan lines n to m {DUMPP}       screen dump to printer
 {Prn}          Swap LPT1 and LPT2       {DUMPF=x}     screen dump to file x
 {COmm}         Swap COMM1 and COMM2     {DUMPL=x}        with CR/LF's
 {BEep=nn,mm}   nn=1/pitch; mm=duration  {DUMPOF=x}       with overwrite
 {LO=xy} Locks on/off(x=+/- y = N,C,S,I) {DUMPOL=x}       with both


The following commands done by the resident part of STACKEY are utilities
 P-/P+          Disable/Reenable Shift PrtScr (PrintScreen)
 Z-/Z+          Slowdown/Speedup of CPU (some clones only)
 +N/+C etc      Turn on/off various lock combos
 [...]          Color commands (see specific help on colors)


Commands: PgUp/Dn,↑,↓,Home,End,<G>oto,<S>earch,<Esc>=Exit.        Page  7 of 17
```

The BATUTIL Package

STACKEY comes packaged with another program called BATUTIL, which works with your batch files giving them color, music, and more. In my opinion, STACKEY and BATUTIL are must-have utilities. On bulletin boards or online networks you'll find the STACKEY/BATUTIL package in two files. The executable programs are in SKEY30.ZIP, and the full documentation for both programs is in SK30DOC.ZIP. Take a good look at STACKEY. It's an excellent utility that gets progressively better with each release.

Barry Simon and Rick Wilson
CTRLALT Associates
260 South Lake Avenue, Suite 133
Pasadena, CA 91101 (support address)

Support Group, Inc.
P.O. Box 130
McHenry, MD 21541 (registration address)
800-872-4768
$39 registration for STACKEY and BATUTIL includes printed manual and 90-day money back guarantee; MasterCard, VISA, American Express, Discover Card, and purchase orders accepted.

Newkey

Newkey is several programs rolled into one, but its primary function is as a keyboard macro program. It can also act as a screen blanker, provide keyboard enhancement, speed up the typematic rate, and increase the size of the keyboard buffer. When you consider features, functions, price, and RAM usage, Newkey, by Frank Bell and FAB Software, is the best program of its kind available anywhere. There is no commercial program that can match its low RAM and EMS usage or its price. No other Shareware macro program offers so much. Let's examine Newkey and some of its many features.

The Functions of Newkey

There are three different versions of Newkey. The full-sized Newkey program has a pop-up menu that you can activate by using ALT-/. This version of Newkey even has an excellent cut and paste function. Figure 15-5 shows the pop-up menu of the full version of Newkey.

By using this menu you can load, save, and merge various macro files. You can change Newkey defaults such as colors, keystrokes, and parameters. Newkey will also recognize the 101-key enhanced keyboard. Note from Figure 15-5, that you can access the cut and paste function, and Newkey shows how many characters are left free for macro definitions. If you have expanded memory, the full version of Newkey uses 37K of DOS RAM and two pages of the EMS. Other full-function macro programs use between 50K to 60K of RAM and can't use expanded memory.

Before going on to discuss the other two versions of Newkey, let's examine what you can do with Newkey macros.

The Newkey Macros

Newkey can handle both fixed and variable field macros. With a *fixed* field macro, you tell Newkey that you only want a fixed number of characters entered. For example, let's say you have a macro that will move files from

---

Figure 15-5

Newkey pop-up menu

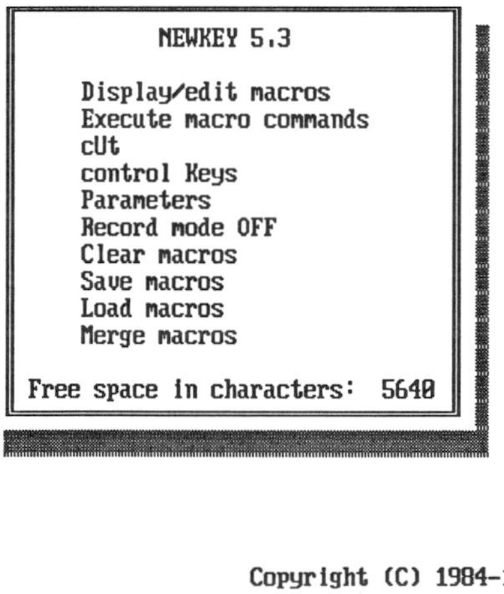

```
        NEWKEY 5.3

   Display/edit macros
   Execute macro commands
   cUt
   control Keys
   Parameters
   Record mode OFF
   Clear macros
   Save macros
   Load macros
   Merge macros

Free space in characters:  5648
```

Copyright (C) 1984-1989 Frank A. Bell

your C drive to another drive. You could use a fixed field to enter only the drive letter of the destination drive. The instant you enter that character, the macro resumes.

With a *variable* field macro, you set Newkey to wait until the user hits ENTER before carrying out the rest of the macro. This gives you the flexibility of entering filenames of various lengths. Newkey macros can wait for a specified period of time before continuing execution. Here's a listing of just some of Newkey's capabilities.

- Defines almost any key

- Creates menu macros

- Creates display macros

- Translates nested keys

- Displays the macro directory

- Displays macros

- Utilizes a full-featured macro editor

- Changes any macro

- Copies or moves one macro to another

- Moves keyboard buffer into macro

- Loads, merges, and saves macro files from within other applications

- Watches your keystrokes and when they match a macro name, automatically plays back the macro; no special hot key to enter, no wasted keystrokes

- Defines your own date and time templates and fills them in for you

- Uses Newkey's pop-up features in graphics mode

- Works with IBM's new enhanced keyboard

- Guards macros from accidental deletion

- Deactivates macros

- Utilizes disk wait during macro playback

- Provides enhanced compatibility with other programs

- Sounds a beep during macro definition

- Provides optional cursor change during macro definition/playback

- Provides slow typing mode
- Provides the capability to make a macro call itself
- Defines a macro within a macro
- Provides multi-character macro naming
- Calls Newkey from its own macros
- Supports DOS 2.0 pathnames

Newkey can create display and menu macros. Once a *display* macro is defined it will put a box on the screen. This can be used to prompt for a filename or request other information. This information can then be used by another macro. A *menu* macro puts a menu of macro selections on screen. Like a typical menu program, the Newkey menu lets you select from any of the defined macros. One selection might load your word processor, another might load a game, and so on. This is a great alternative for those who want to pick items off a list, but who don't want all the features associated with menu programs.

Modules for Every Need

For those who don't need the pop-up menu, there is an intermediate version of Newkey. The executable program is named NEWKEYSM.EXE. The "SM" stands for small. This variety of Newkey does not have the pop-up menu or cut and paste, but it has all of the other powerful features Newkey offers. Unlike the larger module, NEWKEYSM only uses 22K of DOS RAM and one page of expanded memory. Even with this smaller size it can still use features like the display and menu macros. The Newkey package comes with a menu program called NEWKEYSP.EXE, which is very similar to the built-in menu contained in the large Newkey program. Figure 15-6 shows the display of NEWKEYSP.

By comparing this display to the one shown in Figure 15-5, you'll see they are very similar. If you want this menu to pop up, create a Newkey macro that will call the program. You still have easy access to the menu program for editing and saving macros and more. If you don't need a cut and paste utility, you can easily use this mid-sized version of Newkey.

The Smallest Newkey Module

If you simply want some very powerful macro capabilities and don't need the cut and paste or the display/menu macros, then you can use the

---

Figure 15-6

Newkey's NEWKEYSP display showing parameters

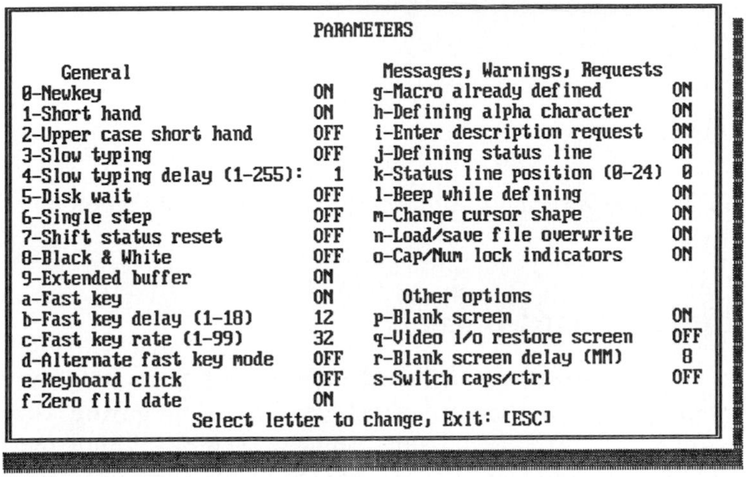

```
                        PARAMETERS

      General                    Messages, Warnings, Requests
0-Newkey               ON      g-Macro already defined         ON
1-Short hand           ON      h-Defining alpha character      ON
2-Upper case short hand OFF    i-Enter description request     ON
3-Slow typing          OFF     j-Defining status line          ON
4-Slow typing delay (1-255):  1 k-Status line position (0-24)  0
5-Disk wait            OFF     l-Beep while defining            ON
6-Single step          OFF     m-Change cursor shape            ON
7-Shift status reset   OFF     n-Load/save file overwrite       ON
8-Black & White        OFF     o-Cap/Num lock indicators        ON
9-Extended buffer      ON
a-Fast key             ON          Other options
b-Fast key delay (1-18) 12     p-Blank screen                   ON
c-Fast key rate (1-99) 32      q-Video i/o restore screen      OFF
d-Alternate fast key mode OFF  r-Blank screen delay (MM)        8
e-Keyboard click       OFF     s-Switch caps/ctrl              OFF
f-Zero fill date       ON
              Select letter to change, Exit: [ESC]
```

---

smallest version of Newkey. The executable program is called NEWKEY VS.EXE. The "VS" is for very small, and the program only uses 16K of DOS RAM and one page of expanded memory. It can use all Newkey macros except the display and menu macros. This module can also access NEWKEYSP, so you still have access to a Newkey menu. There is no other keyboard macro program that gives you the power of Newkey's macros while using only 16K of RAM. NEWKEYVS is a good choice if you don't want to use some of the enhanced features of Newkey.

Overview of Newkey

Newkey is an extremely powerful, flexible, and valuable program that provides you with superior macro capabilities and other keyboard enhancement features as well. Its display and menu macros give you creative control if you want to use the program to its fullest. Newkey's smaller modules give you fewer options, depending on what you need. If all you need are powerful macros, NEWKEYVS might be for you. The slightly larger NEWKEYSM will still allow you to use the display and menu macros. After comparing all the competing commercial and Shareware programs in this category, Newkey stands above the rest.

Frank Bell
FAB Software
P.O. Box 336
Wayland, MA 01778
508-358-6357
$43 registration; MasterCard or VISA, check or U.S. currency accepted

Leaving the Keyboard Behind

You've looked at a few excellent keyboard utilities, but there are many other well-written programs that can assist you in reconfiguring your keyboard, expanding the keyboard buffer, and much more. You'll have very little trouble finding a program to do what you want it to do, based on your needs and your machine configuration. Now let's take a look at some very good general printing utilities.

PRINTING UTILITIES—WHERE TO BEGIN?

As you might imagine, there is no shortage of programs when it comes to printing utilities. There are countless utilities to configure different brands of printers, and a vast number of auxiliary utilities created for performing a variety of printer functions. For example, there are programs to send fonts to laser printers, to print on two sides of a sheet of paper, and a host of others. As the number and types of printers have increased, so have the number of printer-oriented utilities. As with the other categories of utility programs, it is difficult to decide what programs to talk about. To make this chapter as helpful as possible to the largest number of people, a few excellent broad-spectrum printer utilities will be covered. Rather than discuss utilities that focus on a few brands of printers, this chapter will cover utilities that can be used on many different printers.

Something for Everyone

Almost without exception, you can find utilities specifically written for your printer. There are specific utility programs for printers by Panasonic, Epson, Hewlett-Packard, Okidata, Fujitsu, Citizen, Toshiba, Cordata, Canon, Roland, IBM, and others. In addition, there are utilities that are specific for different models of all these different brands. These programs alone could generate a very long list, but there's more.

There are scores of font files for laser printers, utilities that aid you in viewing, editing, and creating fonts, print spoolers, programs to swap the printer ports, support for various programs like Print Shop, First Publisher, and more. By now, you'd have a huge list, but you've only touched the tip of the iceberg. If you want to use your printer for something special, there is a utility program that will do what you want.

Being General Rather Than Specific

With a better understanding of just how many printer utilities there are, you can see that trying to cover all of them would be an impossible task. To cover the utilities used by only some brands of printers would be unfair. The utilities discussed here are all excellent and are designed to work with a wide range of printers. So, whether you have a daisy wheel, dot matrix, or a laser printer, you'll be able to try out these utilities.

PPRINT—The Printing Specialist

PPRINT is another fine utility by Norm Patriquin. What makes PPRINT so interesting is that it can be used with just about any brand or type of printer. PPRINT not only aids you in making your document look the way you want it to, but it has many other options as well. You can include headers or footers, pause at the end of each printed page, and more. The program uses command line parameters to accomplish its tasks. PPRINT can work with dot matrix, laser, and even daisy wheel printers. To get a listing of all of PPRINT's parameters, you can just enter the

DOCTOR'S NOTE

I'd like to make a special note here for those of you who have daisy wheel printers. For many years I used daisy wheel printers since most publishers would not accept dot matrix printing. In scanning lists of printer utilities, you will find very few that specifically mention daisy wheel printers, but don't despair. You'll find that you can use many of the utility programs written for dot matrix printers. Many printer utilities will have an option for a generic printer. If you have this option, select it. If this option is not available, then pick one for a dot matrix printer.

I've found that many printer programs include a selection for Epson printers, and this is your next best choice. You won't be able to use any of the specialized printing commands like Emphasized, Compressed, and so on, but you will be able to take advantage of special formatting. When in doubt, experiment a little. You won't hurt your printer and you may find something that will do what you want. Don't let the lack of a daisy wheel-specific program throw you. I've done some pretty fancy printing on daisy wheel printers using utilities designed for dot matrix printers. If you don't give them a try, you'll never know what you might be missing.

program name at the DOS prompt. In his documentation, Patriquin says that PPRINT has so many parameters that you should only learn the ones you need. Let's take a look at some of the more common command line parameters used with PPRINT.

Flexible Printing

One of the things that is so appealing about PPRINT is its flexibility. It helps you format your text as it's being printed. Here are just some of the command line parameters that can be used with PPRINT.

/B:*fn*	Begin printing with *filename*
/CO:*n*	Print *n* copies of each file
/ML:*nn*	Maximum input lines printed from each file
/MP:*nn*	Maximum pages printed for each file
/ND	Ignore duplicate input lines
/SL:*n*	Restart printing beginning with input line number *n*
/SP:*n*	Restart printing beginning with page number *n*

/TS:*xx*	Only print lines containing text *xx*
/DS	Double space print lines
/F	Print page footers with filename/date/page
/FP	Print footers with page number only
/G	C language source print option, 'if' guides
/HD	Heading with filename/date/time/page number
/HP	Heading with page number only
/HT	Prompt for heading text information
/HT:*cc*	Heading text on command (/HT:Head_Line)
/LC	Line compress, compress multiple spaces to one
/LJ	Left justify each line
/LM:*n*	Left margin characters
/LP:*n*	Lines per page, 59 assumed
/LQ	Print letter quality
/N	Print line number on each line

From these command line examples you can see that PPRINT provides a great deal of control over how your document will look. You can set up batch files for printing tasks that include the parameters you want. You can set margins and page length, number pages, make multiple copies, and include footers. Other options that are available include setting different typefaces for dot matrix and laser printers, setting top and bottom margins, viewing the lines sent to the printer, and more.

Giving You What You Need

PPRINT is a solid printing utility. Depending on the type of printer you have, you'll be able to take advantage of specific PPRINT parameters; but everyone will be able to use some of the features of this fine program. I believe that PPRINT is such a good overall printing utility that I've included a copy of it on the free disks you can receive by mailing in the coupon at the back of this book. Check it out and if you like it, be sure to register.

Norm Patriquin
Patri-Soft
P.O. Box 8263
San Bernardino, CA 92412
800-242-4775 (orders only)
$15 registration only

$30 registration and manual
$45 registration includes all utilities and manual
MasterCard and VISA accepted

ZAPCODE — Printer Control

ZAPCODE is a printer utility that can be used as a stand-alone program or as a TSR. You use ZAPCODE to send various codes to your printer, for example, the command that will make your printer start underlining. When you are finished, call up the program and send the code to stop underlining. While the program comes with definition files for different printers, the beauty of ZAPCODE is that you can create your own definition files for your particular printer. As a TSR, or resident program, ZAPCODE uses approximately 15K of RAM plus up to 10K more depending on the size of your printer definition file. ZAPCODE has a built-in editor for editing the .PMF, or printer make file, that it uses.

Truly Configurable Printing

ZAPCODE can be used by any printer as a result of two factors:

- It uses printer codes
- It can edit .PMF files

If you look in your printer's manual, you will find a section listing various printer codes. It might show that sending the decimal number 13 will generate a *line feed* or that decimal 12 will send a *form feed*. Using this information, you can create a ZAPCODE .PMF file for your printer. Figure 15-7 shows the main screen of ZAPCODE, with the selections available for the Panasonic KX-P1124 printer.

In the editor mode, you can define all the options shown on the screen. Using the printer manual as a reference, define as few or as many options as you like. The ZAPCODE editor lets you enter a selection name, a description, and then the codes that perform that task. Figure 15-8 shows the editor mode of ZAPCODE.

Totally Configurable

You'll find that unlike utilities created for a specific printer, ZAPCODE lets you configure it. You can include only the options you use most

Figure 15-7

ZAPCODE selection display

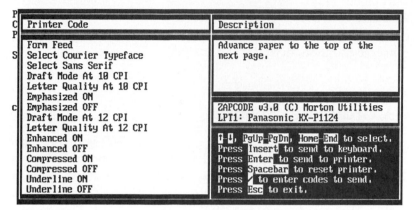

Figure 15-8

ZAPCODE's editor mode

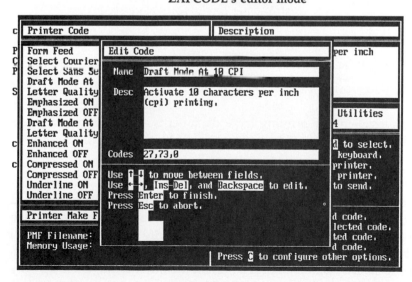

frequently. If you don't have multitasking capability, it's convenient to have a small TSR printer utility you can pop up as you need it.

Morton Utilities
81-887 Tournament Way
Indio, CA 92201
$9.95 license and registration
$19.95 license, registration, diskette, and manual

DMP—A Great Print Spooler

DMP is an extremely versatile spooler for printing. DMP is a true *print spooler*, meaning that it takes and saves all of the printer output to disk or some other form of nonsystem memory. Nearly all so-called spoolers available grab a good-sized chunk of your DOS RAM to do their work. DMP, on the other hand, uses only 12K to 13K of RAM. The spooler portion can use disk, extended memory, expanded memory, or any combinations of these. Not only is DMP efficient at what it does, but it does its job using the very minimum of your system's resources. Some of DMP's features include:

- Support for serial printers
- An option to print to a disk file rather than to the printer
- An internal buffer that can be altered
- Spooling to any disk recognized by DOS
- Ability to work with a wide range of printers

DMP is excellent for printing large documents and getting your DOS prompt back as fast as possible. Let's take a look at what DMP can do.

Start Printing and Move On

The main idea behind a print spooler is to take your printer output and spool it into files or buffers, freeing your machine so you can use it while the spooler takes care of the print job. The majority of programs that call themselves spoolers simply don't do a good job. If they do, it's at a high cost to your main system memory. DMP, on the other hand, takes up only 13K of RAM. Let's say that you've told DMP to spool to drive D, which is a 300K RAM drive. You tell DMP to print a 200K file. There is a slight pause and suddenly you have your DOS prompt back and the printer starts printing. On drive D, you'll see many small temporary files. This is what DMP has made of your 200K text file. As each portion is printed, the temporary file containing that text is deleted. DMP continues to print the document while you are free to do something else.

Helping Your Printer Besides

In addition to doing a great job spooling your printer output, DMP can also assist your printer. For example, if your printer does not send form feeds, DMP has a command that will simulate form feeds for you. You can also utilize formatting functions like setting the left print margin, telling DMP to skip perforations, assigning a default page length, and much more. You can load DMP with some default parameters, but they can be changed by typing in new parameters. To cancel a printing job, at the DOS prompt enter

```
C>DMP /SK
```

All of your print buffers will be cleared instantly. If the phone rings and you simply want to pause the printing, use a /S- parameter to temporarily stop DMP.

I believe that you'll find DMP to be an excellent addition to your software library and an extremely useful printing utility. The program's author, Terry McGuire, also sells a printer utility based on DMP, called LaserZ. For those with PostScript printers, LaserZ will provide some special functions. Here are a few extra features that LaserZ provides.

For PostScript printers
   Selectable fonts and print size
   Emulation for Epson or Diablo to PostScript
   Print-screen for text screens
   Full IBM extended character set
For all printers
   Fast output for laser, dot matrix and other printers
   Select LPT 1,2,3 or serial port output and switch between printers any time
   Print to disk file option

Versatile character conversion, tab expansion, margins, and page alignment options

LaserZ can be ordered from the author when you register for DMP. I've used LaserZ, and it is also an excellent program.

Terry McGuire
DMP Software
1223 Wilshire Blvd., Suite 199
Santa Monica, CA 90403
$18 Registration
73210,2531 CompuServe ID

Grab Plus

Grab Plus is a TSR envelope printer and database with many imitators. You can pull up Grab Plus at any time and snatch an address off the screen. You can also edit the address, alter the size of the envelope to be used, and more. Figure 15-9 shows the main screen of Grab Plus.

Figure 15-9

Main screen of Grab Plus

```
he120rpn.d.jp    19204   8-21-89
readme            7389  12-27-89
ro120rpn.d.jp    19507   8-21-89
    387,072 bytes in 15 file(s)
 18,208,768 bytes free

d:\grabplus>grab
GRAB The Memory Resident Envelope Printer Versi
Copyright (c) 1986, 1987, 1988 & 1989 by Paul M

GRAB loaded. Press <Alt>Z to call up GRAB.

After GRAB is popped up, its command keys are:
    To print address from under marker block: <A
    To edit address from under marker block & pr
    To call up manual entry address window: <Alt
    To toggle the printing of the return address
    To toggle the printing of small size envelop
    To toggle between primary & alternate return
    To enter a comment line that will print unde
    To edit the return address before printing:

To uninstall GRAB type GRAB /R
```

```
Use arrow keys to move the
marker to cover the address.
F7 & F8 to change length, F9
to decrease size and F10 to
increase the size of marker.
Print large size envelopes.
Do not print return.
Print landscape mode.
<ESC>      Abort the process.
<F2>       Not active.
<Alt>X     Print the address.
<Alt>E     Edit the address.
<Alt>C     Enter the address.
<Alt>R     Toggle return.
<Alt>S     Toggle size.
<Alt>A     Toggle primary/alt.
<Alt>I     Comment = Empty.
<Alt>Y     Edit return addr.
F1Key Toggle Help On/Off
```

Note that you can enter an address manually, edit your return address, and enter a comment to print. Some time after Grab Plus had been on the market as Shareware, several commercial companies released similar programs with functions inferior to Grab Plus, and with prices that weren't competitive either. Let's take a look at how to use Grab Plus.

The Functions of Grab Plus

Let's say for a moment that you run a small business. You type letters to clients yourself because you can't afford a secretary. You've just finished a letter and now must get it ready for mailing. As you may have discovered by now, printing envelopes is not an easy task, even for a sophisticated word processor. Just pop up Grab Plus and move its box so that it encloses the address on the letter you've just typed. After adjusting the size, use ALT-X, and the address on your document will be sent to the envelope. You don't even have to be in an editor or word processor. With Grab Plus you can "grab" an address out of a database while online, or any place you happen to be, and it uses only about 6K of RAM.

A Database to Call On

If you plan on doing a lot of correspondence, you might want to do a group of envelopes all in one sitting. Grab Plus makes this task simpler since it comes with its own database where you can keep names, addresses, and phone numbers of people you correspond with. You can add entries, find names, and even export the entire database to an ASCII file. Figure 15-10 shows the main screen of the Grab Plus database.

You can import data into the database as well. I've used Grab Plus on both my Panasonic KX-P1124 dot matrix printer and on the Panasonic KX-P4450 laser printer and had great results. It also worked well with a daisy wheel printer. This is a very useful program that takes some of the drudgery out of doing envelopes.

Paul Mayer
ZPAY Payroll Systems
3516 Ruby Street
Franklin Park, IL 60131
312-671-3364
$29.95 registration plus $2 shipping and handling includes printed manual

---

DOCTOR'S NOTE

With the number of laser printers steadily increasing, there is a growing interest in soft fonts. *Soft fonts* are files that define different print styles and can be downloaded to laser printers. This gives you flexiblity when printing documents from DOS or your word processor. Over the years, the name Gary Elfring has become synonymous with fonts. His font utilities are excellent, and in my opinion, better than their commercial counterparts.

Do the Elfring Soft Fonts work on all laser printers? Elfring answered this question by saying, "To date, the fonts have worked on every laser printer we have tried with the exception of the NEC." The Elfring Soft Fonts and utilities will be of interest to the majority of laser printer users. Let's take a look at some of the programs produced by Elfring.

Figure 15-10

The Grab Plus database screen

```
                    GRABDB  Data Base Utility

Title (Mr., Mrs, etc.): Mr.

Last Name: John

First Name: Dvorak

Company: Osborne:McGraw-Hill

Street Address 1: 1234 YouThinkI'dTell?

Street Address 2:

City: Somewhere              State: CA    Zip: 12345-5432

Phone No: (555) 123-4567  Ext:    Tag fields: 1=  2=  3=  4=  5=


   Delete   Next   Previous   Edit   Quit   Help   Tags
Quit this menu and move to ADD/FIND menu

F7, F8 & F9 Keys ARE Now Active - Tag field set to: *
```

Download and TSR Download

To use soft fonts, you need a program that will download them to the laser printer. This is similar to downloading a file with a modem because you are taking the font file from the disk and putting it in the printer. Elfring has produced a program called Download that performs this task quite well. Simply tell Download the name of the font file you want to use, the printer port, whether it's to be a temporary or permanent font, and whether it's a primary or secondary font. Download sends the font file to the printer and you are ready to print with the selected print style. Elfring Soft Fonts also produce a wide variety of fonts for use with laser printers. I use them on my Panasonic KX-P4450 laser printer and the results are beautiful. You can choose from fonts such as:

- Times Roman
- Broadway
- Century Schoolbook
- Flourish
- Greek
- Script
- Helvetica

All of these come in various sizes. Download works very well, and now there is a TSR version of Download, so your fonts are just a keystroke away.

The TSR Version of Download

For those who want instant access to their font files, the TSR version of Download is a convenient choice, using only 40K of DOS RAM. If you use the hot key, a screen pops up showing all the available fonts you have. When you highlight a font, its definition is shown in plain English, with no programming code to decipher. Figure 15-11 shows this display.

The listing of font files may look cryptic. On the very bottom of the display, however, the highlighted font files' definition is easy to understand. Using TSR Download, you can select one font or several to be downloaded to your laser printer. Another feature is a printer control

Figure 15-11

TSR Download font display

```
Copyright 1989, 1990 by Elfring Soft Fonts, Version 1.9c
Shareware version, register your copy today!
TSR Download is now loaded into memory.
Use Ctrl-Alt-D to activate. Remove with dl -r.

c:\utl>
                   ═══ Shareware TSR Download ═══
       BW100RPN.USP HEL18RS.USP  SC120RPN.USP TR120BPN.USP
       CE120RPN.USP HU100BPN.USP SM100RPN.USP TR120IPN.USP
       CS100RPN.USP HU100IPN.USP TR100BPN.USP TR120RPN.USP
       FL120RPN.USP HU100RPN.USP TR100IPN.USP TR12B.SFP
       GR100RPN.USP HU120BPN.USP TR100RPN.USP TR12I.SFP
       HEL12B.USP   HU120IPN.USP TR10B.SFP    TR12R.SFP
       HEL12I.USP   HU120RPN.USP TR10I.SFP    TR180BPN.USP
       HEL12R.USP   HU180BPN.USP TR10R.SFP    TR18B.SFP
       Broadway, 18 point, normal port LJ
```

menu that lets you send default settings to the printer. It can also be used to reset the printer, put it in landscape mode, and so on. Figure 15-12 shows you the Printer Control menu found in TSR Download.

Figure 15-12

Printer Control menu in TSR Download

```
Copyright 1989, 1990 by Elfring Soft Fonts, Version 1.9c
Shareware version, register your copy today!
TSR Download is now loaded into memory.
Use Ctrl-Alt-D to activate. Remove with dl -r.

c:\utl>
              ═══════ Printer Control ═══════
         Form Feed           66 lines/page
         Reset printer        4 lines/inch
         Remove soft fonts    6 lines/inch
         Default font         8 lines/inch
         10 cpi              12 lines/inch
         16.67 cpi           16 lines/inch
         Landscape mode      Manual Feed
         Portrait mode       Tray Feed
```

TSR Download lets you change fonts quickly, load multiple fonts, and reset the printer. Extra font files are also available from Elfring Soft Fonts. Both Download and TSR Download are excellent programs for use with laser printers, but Elfring Soft Fonts offers another program called Laser Font, for use with word processors.

Laser Font

If you've ever tried to define soft fonts for some of the better word processors, you know that it can be quite a job. Elfring has developed a way to do it that is so easy you won't believe it. The Laser Font package can be used with WordPerfect 5.0, WordPerfect 5.1, Microsoft Word 5.0, and PC-Write 3.0x. Let's use WordPerfect as an example.

The Laser Font package comes with a printer definition file that contains 21 fonts. With easy to follow directions, you use the WordPerfect PTR program to transfer the Elfring fonts from his definition file to yours by following a few simple steps. If you've tried to do it yourself, you will appreciate how easy Elfring has made it to add fonts to these major word processing programs. These fonts also work with Ventura Publisher and Aldus Pagemaker. There is also a Deskjet Font package for those with the Hewlett-Packard Deskjet printer. If you use one of these word processing programs and have a laser printer, you must try the Laser Font or Deskjet Font package from Elfring Soft Fonts.

Compact Font Technology

Compact Font Technology is a combined effort of Gary Elfring, Rubicon Publishing, and *BYTE* magazine. Working to improve the way fonts are used, this technology compresses font files so that they don't occupy as much disk space. The average rate of compression results in a font file one-ninth its original size. Smaller font files compress by about one-fourth of their size. Larger font files can be compressed to take up as little as one-seventeenth of their original space. Compressed fonts also load much faster than conventional fonts. These new fonts will soon be part of the TSR Download package.

Finalizing the Fonts

If you have a laser printer, you may want to check out the quality programs and fonts produced by Elfring Soft Fonts. Both the programs and fonts are of superior quality. The TSR Download utility makes it easy to access font files. At the same time, the Laser-Deskjet Font programs make it a snap to install fonts into some of the major word processors. The package comes with utilities that display and print your fonts so you can see exactly what they look like in print. These are excellent programs and fonts for laser printers.

Gary Elfring
Elfring Soft Fonts
P.O. Box 61
Wasco, IL 60183
708-377-3520
$35 registration fee for Download and TSR Download
$25 registration fee for LaserJet Font Package
$25 registration fee for Deskjet Font Package
Registration includes catalog of latest programs, fonts, and full telephone support.

4PRINT

4PRINT is a utility for laser printers that works with the Hewlett-Packard line of laser printers and all compatible lasers such as the Panasonic KX-P4450. 4PRINT is a utility that helps you:

- Save paper

- View up to four pages of a document at once

- Create your own manuals

- Print wide spreadsheets easily

4PRINT uses a special font included in the package to print smaller text. It scans the document to be printed, calculates pages, and prints sideways on the page. Using 4PRINT, for example, you can get two pages of a document on one sheet of paper. 4PRINT also has an option allowing you to print on both sides of a piece of paper. It is then possible to print four pages on one sheet. You can use it to print a document so it takes up fewer pages and you can see more of the document at one time. Let's look at more 4PRINT features.

Plenty of Choices with 4PRINT

Besides printing several pages on one sheet of paper, 4PRINT provides you with many choices, depending on your needs and your equipment. The program can print any ASCII text file as well as WordStar documents. Figure 15-13 shows the command line options of 4PRINT.

You can have 4PRINT add line numbers, indent the right side, send files to another device, change the font being used, and print multiple copies of a document. This is an excellent laser printer utility for both businesses and individuals.

Summing Up 4PRINT

I recommend 4PRINT to anyone who uses a laser printer. You can use the program to create your own manuals and put them into "IBM-style" binders. If you are in business, 4PRINT can help you save money and be more productive. Programmers will find it excellent for printing

---

Figure 15-13

4PRINT's command line option display

```
4PRINT Version 3.20-R  HP LaserJet Multiple ASCII File Printing Utility
Copyright (C) 1989 Korenthal Associates, Inc.     All rights reserved.
  Usage: 4print [options] filespec [more filespecs or options]
Options: -m  manual feed for reverse side I -u  runs unattended (no prompts)
         -f  prints front side only       I -b  (or -r) prints back side only
         -s  prints document single-sided I -t  truncates long lines (no wrap)
         -w  prints WordStar (tm) files   I -z  bypasses end of file characters
         -e  allows printing escape codes I -c  forces new line for CR chars
         -d  duplex mode (LaserJet II-D)  I -pr proportional font handling
         -wide  doc/spreadsheet, 165 cols I -tiny  internal font; 110/230 cols
         -x<number> number of copies      I -tab<number>  tab width (default=8)
         -ft prints T-frame, -f0 = no frame (see manual for other frame styles)
         -tt prints titles at top of page; -tb at bottom, -ta alternates titles
         -h<string>   sets header (see manual for description of header string)
         -n[<number>] adds line numbers (-np numbers each page from line 1)
         -i<number>   causes every line to be indented <number> spaces
         -ri<number>  indents right side only (to create IBM-style binders)
         -o<name>     specifies output file or device (default=prn:)
         -p<number>-<number> prints range of pages, inclusive (see manual)
         -q[<number>] quick prints (no scan pass); max page # may be specified
         -#<number>   prints using font previously downloaded as <number>
         -[<string>   uses font with specified characteristics ("["=Esc)
   Note: After each pass, you can force printer to manual feed by pressing "M".
```

out and reviewing source code for programs. This is a program that anyone with a laser printer should seriously consider getting.

Jim Korenthal
Korenthal Associates, Inc.
230 West 13th Street
New York, NY 10011
212-242-1790 (Voice)
212-242-2599 (Fax)
76164,237 CompuServe ID
$35.85 registration fee plus $4 shipping & handling; MasterCard, VISA, and purchase orders accepted

While some good printer utilities have been covered thus far, as with all categories of utilities, there are many more to choose from. If there is something you want to do with a printer you can probably find a program to do it. There are also utility packages that aid in the use of commercial programs like Print Master, PFS: First Publisher, Print Shop, and others. For now, let's move on and look at a few interesting "general" utilities.

UTILITIES THAT ARE HARD TO CATEGORIZE

In the course of this chapter you've seen some specific utility programs for DOS, for keyboards, and for printing. Because of their functions, these programs are relatively easy to put into groups. Not all utility programs are as easy to categorize. User group librarians, disk vendors, and BBS sysops struggle to put some utilities into a meaningful category. How do you categorize a program that gives you Rodney Dangerfield jokes, or one that provides exciting events on this date in history? It's not easy to do. With that in mind, we'll call this section *general* utilities since the functions are quite varied.

A Few Examples

General utilities range from programs that display screens filled with useful information to tools that can save you time and keystrokes. For example, you might find the program REMIND helpful, which will interrupt you when running a program like WordPerfect to notify you it's time to have lunch with your spouse.

If you are looking for a chuckle, the program RODNEY may amuse you by randomly generating some of Rodney Dangerfield's jokes each time you run it.

The program TODAY provides some useful information. You can run it by typing **TODAY**, and it will provide a listing of historic events corresponding to today's date. You can also enter any date and get the same result. Here's what happened on coauthor Nick Anis's birthday:

```
G:\PCB>today
TODAY/PC  V1.0 (c) 1986 by Patrick Kincaid
Good afternoon!  It's 12:15pm on Wednesday May 2, 1990

Happy Birthday to...
    In 1837 Henry Martyn Robert, author of "Robert's Rules of
Order"
    In 1904 Bing Crosby, crooner
    Say Happy Birthday to the Sysop Today... and Thank Ya
On this day...
    In 1925 Kezar Stadium in Golden Gate Park opens.
    In 1939 Lou Gehrig sets record for being in most consecutive
games (2130).
    In 1946 Prisoners revolt at Alcatraz, 5 die.
Reminder...
Pay the mortgage!
And remember...
    The Doc wishes you a good day
```

Here is a listing for the Doc's birthday:

```
G:\PCB>today 0610
TODAY/PC  V1.0 (c) 1986 by Patrick Kincaid
Good afternoon!  It's 12:22pm on Sunday June 10, 1990

Happy Birthday to...
    In 1904 Frederick Loewe, Composer
    In 1949 Michael E. Callahan, Friend of Shareware
On this day...
    In 1772 Burning of the Gaspee, British revenue cutter by Rhode
    Islanders
```

```
In 1869 The 'Agnes' arrives in New Orleans with the 1st ever
  shipment of frozen beef.
In 1898 US Marines land at Cuba in Spanish-American War.
In 1954 PBS reaches San Francisco: KQED (Channel 9) starts
  broadcasting.
In 1977 Apple Computer ships its first Apple II.
National Day, celebrated in Portugal.
And remember...
  Happy birthday Doc!
```

Dunford and Graham

Two of the elders of miscellaneous Shareware and Freeware utilities are Chris Dunford and Keith Graham. Both have created enough of these little gems to write a book. Here are two of my favorites.

CONCOPY by Chris Dunford

CONCOPY performs the task of copying to a disk file the information DOS sends to your screen or console device. CONCOPY is also useful for recording DOS commands as they are entered and providing a history of your DOS commands. It also gives you a learn mode to create batch files. In addition, it's a security tool providing you with a record of your system's activity. Here's the syntax for CONCOPY:

CONCOPY [d:][path]file[.ext] [command]

If you don't include a command when you run CONCOPY, such as "CONCOPY temp.dat," CONCOPY will still be active, but you'll have to access the DOS prompt to execute DOS programs and commands. As you run commands, batch files, and programs, the information sent to the screen will also be sent to a disk file.

CONCOPY in program mode terminates when you exit the program. In DOS mode, CONCOPY terminates when you type **EXIT** at the DOS prompt.

CONCOPY captures the information sent to the console device using standard DOS services. Like DOS's output redirection, data written directly to the screen using BIOS services, or by accessing screen memory, will not be copied to the file.

MOREDIR

MOREDIR by Keith Graham changes the boot table directory count for floppy diskettes. The directory count default of 112 can be changed from 16 to 255. Reducing the count to 16 will make an additional 4K of floppy disk space available for file storage.

When you run MOREDIR, a diskette's FAT won't be changed. However, MOREDIR does erase a disk and clear the volume label, so it's better to use freshly formatted diskettes. Flagged bad sectors will still remain bad, so if you are trying to fill a disk to the limit, use one free of defects. The format for running MOREDIR is

MOREDIR *n:xxx*

where *n*: is the diskette drive and *xxx* is the number of directory entries desired from 16 to 255.

MOREDIR accesses your diskette with interrupt 13h and will destroy data if used improperly. This program is only for floppy disks and will not work on hard drives. Systems that have older DOS or BIOS versions may have problems reading these disks.

SOME OTHER INTERESTING UTILITIES

HI.EXE is a 47K EXE program that clears the screen and displays a cute message. My favorite is "Don't worry if you are a kleptomaniac. You can always take something for it." Besides wisecracks, there are also famous quotes and computer related comments. Many Shareware users add HI to their AUTOEXEC.BAT file, and it's commonly found on bulletin board systems.

DECEIVE by Carl Burtner is a program designed for the employee who wants to protect him- or herself from a strict supervisor. DECEIVE will help you avoid getting caught by your boss while in the middle of a great game, balancing your checkbook, or updating your resume, without rebooting your system and calling even more attention to yourself.

You can use DECEIVE to take a screenshot of the work you are supposed to be doing—for instance, a spreadsheet session—and then you can start up your game.

When the need arises, DECEIVE allows you to pause the program and instantly display the screen of your choice. With the push of a key, that incriminating arcade game can be transformed into a spreadsheet, word processor, or anything you desire.

LCG/Remind—Reminders with Meaning

There are many so-called reminder programs that remind you of things you have to do, appointments, and so on. What makes LCG/Remind different from others is that it can give you information so you can make a decision about what you want to do. You can use the program to display information, recommend a particular action, or run any program on a regular schedule. It's great for reminding you to back up your hard disk, for example.

What LCG/Remind Can Do

LCG/Remind lets you ask multiple choice questions. You can also have it ask simple yes or no questions from within your batch files. The authors recommend using the program from within your AUTOEXEC.BAT file. It will determine when you last ran your backup program. If it is time for a new backup, a message will appear asking you whether to automatically run the backup program of your choice. It will also give you facts on which you can base your decisions to back up or not. Here are some of the things that LCG/Remind can do:

- It determines when your disk was last backed up by examining the date of log files created by your backup software. If your software doesn't create these files, LCG/Remind will maintain them.

- You can set the number of days before triggering a reminder message, or you can set it to trigger on specific days of the week or month.

- You can set it to only trigger for a specified time of day.

- Triggering can be initiated or prevented based on the total size of files that need to be backed up or the amount of free space on your hard disk.

- The reminder message can be customized. Foreign language support allows for yes or no responses in any language.

- The name of the file containing a message can be specified on the command line, as can the file whose date is being examined. This allows the program to be used to trigger a number of different events based on different date files.

- LCG/Remind sets DOS error levels to reflect whether it was triggered and displays the answer, allowing for maximum flexibility in system design, and absolute minimum memory use.

- You can specify how long you want a message or question displayed.

- You can specify the color of the pop-up windows, their borders, and the title line.

As you can see, LCG/Remind gives you a lot of flexibility in creating reminders that give you options while providing you with some specific information.

Giving You Some Facts

The message file used by LCG/Remind is just a straight ASCII text file. LCG/Remind, however, gives you ways to include some valuable information when that file is displayed. Here is a listing of what you can include in the text file. Each % option puts different information into the display.

%n   The number of days since the last backup
%d   The date of the last backup
%c   The position of the cursor; also the signal that the message contains a question
%f   The number of files matching the /pa: specification
%k   The size in kilobytes of files matching the /pa: specification
%p   The percent of the disk specified in the /df: switch that is full

Placing the % parameters in your message file can give you some facts to work with. You can decide if you want to do a backup or not. For example, Figure 15-14 shows an LCG/Remind display that uses several of these % parameters. It shows you how many days it's been since your last backup, what day that was, and the size in kilobytes of the files that need to be backed up.

LCG/Remind is more than just a simple reminder program. It has many useful purposes and provides many options that can be exercised from batch files. It would be well worth your time to check out LCG/Remind.

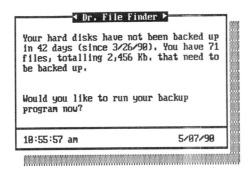

Figure 15-14

The informative display of LCG/Remind

Levin Consulting Group
P.O. Box 62050
Cincinnati, OH 45262
73277,2356 CompuServe ID
Regina.Levin GEnie Mail
$12.95 registration fee

BRINGING UTILITIES TO A CLOSE

The world of Shareware is so filled with utility programs of every possible type that you've only seen a few of the more interesting and beneficial programs. The Wires are filled with countless utilities that can make your life easier or add a little humor to your day. As was mentioned earlier, if you find that there is something you want to do, the odds are good there is already a utility program that will do it. For now, we'll bring our discussion of utility programs to a close and move on to examine some programs that deal with file compression.

## CHAPTER SIXTEEN

Compression Programs and Utilities

In these times of ever increasing amounts of data, file compression utility programs have an important function. They help to conserve disk space and reduce the time it takes to transmit data via modem. Compression programs have evolved from relatively simple utilities into fairly complex tools. The compression programs of today contain data on volume labels and subdirectories, for example. Data can be encrypted, comments included, and you can even extract a file to the printer. When discussing file compression programs, two features in particular are always the focus of attention. These are

- Compression percentage
- Speed of compression

There seem to be two schools of thought when it comes to compression programs. One group wants the greatest amount of compression possible, regardless of speed. The other is willing to sacrifice a bit of compression in favor of speed. With so much interest in speed, including faster machines, hard disks, and modems, many people lean toward compression utilities that are faster. After all, you can buy more disk space, but not more time. Another point of view is to look for a happy medium between percentage of compression and speed.

This chapter will examine the more popular file compression programs in use today. It will discuss them as products and compare their performances. You'll also look at some programs designed to make it easier to work with a variety of compression formats and compressed files in general.

THE STATE OF THE ART

In the early days of microcomputers there were squeezed files and there were library files. These both fulfilled a basic need by:

- Keeping like files together in one file

- Decreasing the total size of all files

For a time this was all that was needed or expected. ARC then arrived on the scene, the product of System Enhancement Associates, or SEA. ARC could compress data into smaller files than any of the squeeze or library utilities. ARC became the standard for file compression. The .ARC files, and utilities to support the .ARC file format, dominated the scene.

Vern Buerg, one of the pioneers in the earlier compression methods, began to dabble with .ARC files. With a license from SEA, Buerg created ARCE and ARCA, used to extract and create ARC format files, respectively. People noticed that ARCE and ARCA were slightly faster than the original ARC utility. Buerg established that the algorithms being used for compression could be improved upon. You could have compression that was as good or better than that achieved by the standard and still have greater speed. The performance of Buerg's utilities started others thinking along the same lines. The seeds of change had been planted.

The Only Constant Is Change

At about this time, a young programmer by the name of Phil Katz, with a company called PKWARE, produced some ARC-compatible utilities. The utilities were called PKARC and PKXARC and were slightly faster than the programs of Vern Buerg. Katz worked incessantly on his programs in an effort to achieve greater speed and better compression. In January 1989 he changed the name of his ARC-compatible programs to PKPAK and PKUNPAK. By then it was well known that programs by PKWARE were not only faster, but achieved better compression than the programs of Buerg or SEA.

At this point, PKWARE introduced a new compression method that was called *squashing*. While it optimized both speed and compression, it made PKPAK and PKUNPAK incompatible with the ARC standard. ARC had been the constant and now squashing was about to change that.

Changing of the Guard

With the introduction of squashing, there was some dissent in the PC community. Many people liked the increased compression and the greater speed of the latest PKWARE releases. The problem was that Buerg's ARCE and SEA's ARC could not unpack .ARC files created with Katz's new compression algorithm. SEA took PKWARE to court over a copyright matter. The result was that PKWARE and Katz could no longer use the file extension .ARC.

Meanwhile, a company called NoGate Consulting released a new compression program called PAK. PAK was compatible with both the programs of Buerg and SEA, but the reverse was not true. Although PAK could create files with an .ARC extension, these files could not be unpacked by ARC or Buerg's ARCE. If all of this weren't enough, another compression program called ZOO entered the picture, which was not compatible with any of the others and did not try to be. Fairly popular in the UNIX world, ZOO never gained great popularity among DOS users. Enough users have tried it, however, to confuse things even further.

Files created with all of these programs are found on bulletin boards and online networks. To be prepared, you needed a copy of PAK for unpacking any .PAK files, a copy of ZOO to unpack .ZOO files, and a copy of PKXARC to decompress any files created with that utility. You might also need a copy of ARC or ARCE/ARCA just for insurance.

The Variable Becomes the Constant

In 1989, PKWARE released a new utility that created files with an extension of .ZIP. Phil Katz's PKZIP and PKUNZIP gained immediate popularity. ZIP was fast and also had very good compression. Bulletin board sysops gravitated to it, often converting all of their existing .ARC files to .ZIP files overnight. ZIP utility programs flooded The Wires and the switch to ZIP was on. Since .ZIP files were quite a bit smaller than .ARC files, sysops were saving megabytes of disk space by converting their files to .ZIP files.

A short time after the initial release of PKZIP and PKUNZIP, another compression utility was introduced. A public domain program called LHarc was brought over from Japan. LHarc achieves very good compression, but cannot match the speed of PKZIP. What LHarc does best is create self-extracting files, and many people are using it for this purpose. Today, the majority of compressed files are in .ZIP format. PKWARE, at one time a variable in the world of compression programs, has now become the constant.

Looking at Compression Utilities

The rest of this chapter will examine and compare the major file compression programs—ARC, ZIP, PAK, LHarc, and ZOO. Keep in mind that these five programs perform better on certain types of files, like documentation and ASCII files, which tend to compress better than binary files. ZIP, PAK, and LHarc are all very close in compression levels. Performance will vary according to circumstances, such as the kind of files being compressed.

You will also look at the creation of self-extracting files and how the programs compare in this respect. The last portion of this chapter will deal with utilities that were created to make using compressed files easier.

Test Descriptions

Before looking at each of the compression programs, you should have an understanding of the tests that were performed. The tests were designed to show you how well each program did while compressing various types of file formats, and each test was timed. ARC, ZIP, PAK, and LHarc were also tested to compare the results when used to create self-extracting files. A brief description of each test is included in this section.

Test 1 was done using two large files. One file was an executable, or .EXE, file in binary format. The other was a large documentation (.DOC)

DOCTOR'S NOTE

In preparing this chapter, I did some tests with each of the compression programs that will be discussed here. I used each program to pack up different types of files and used a stopwatch to time the process. As you read about each individual program, you will see tables that show how that particular program performed on the tests. After all of the programs have been examined, there are tables summarizing the performance of all of the programs for each of the tests. Why am I telling you this? (*smile*) So you don't keep looking back to see how the previous program did on a particular test. All of the results will be displayed together at the end of the discussion. I want you to look at the data and draw your own conclusions about which compression program you would like to use. Be sure to keep in mind that one set of tests only gives you an idea as to how a program performs. Under different conditions, using different files, some programs might do better and some might do worse. The tests done for this chapter, however, will give you a fairly accurate picture of each program's average performance.

file composed of straight ASCII text. The .EXE file was 293,449 bytes and the .DOC file was 228,331 bytes, for a total of 521,762 bytes. The test gives an indication of how each program performs while packing two large but different types of files.

Test 2 consisted of compressing five ASCII text files that varied in size. The total size of the five files was 454,517 bytes. Text files generally compress more easily than binary files. This test shows how each compression program performs when compressing strictly text files.

Test 3 was done using five files that were all binary in structure. There were three .EXE files and two .COM files. The total for all five files was 435,285 bytes. Since binary data is more difficult to compress, this test gives an indication of how each program performs.

Test 4 was done to compare how ARC, PAK, LHarc, and ZIP do when creating binary files. The test consisted of five files, three that were binary and two that were straight ASCII text. The total for the five files was 326,749 bytes. In each case, each utility was used to create a compressed file in its own format. The size of the resulting compressed file was noted. Each program was then used to convert the compressed file into a self-extracting (SFX) file. This test was not timed, but was meant to serve as a comparision of how the utilities perform when creating self-extracting files. The size of the resulting SFX file was also noted.

ARC—SEVERAL FIRSTS

ARC, from SEA, was the first of the modern file compression utilities. ARC came onto the scene in 1985, quickly replacing the squeezed files and library files that had been previously used.

ARC quickly dominated the scene and many utilities were written by other authors to use with ARC. Their programs could merge two .ARC files, view their contents, and so on. ARC also offered many options that were not available before. ARC became the standard that all other compression programs were measured by. A listing of all of the ARC commands is seen in Figure 16-1.

To get this listing yourself, all you have to do is switch to the directory that contains your ARC program file, type in **ARC** at the C> prompt, and press ENTER.

Figure 16-1

Command line options of ARC 6.02

```
ARC - Archive utility, Version 6.02, created in January of 1989
Copyright 1985-89 by System Enhancement Associates, Inc.; ALL RIGHTS RESERVED

Usage: ARC {amufdxerlvtcp}[wbmsnzvo5][g<password>] <archive> [<filename> ...]

Where: a = add files to archive        m  = move files to archive
       u = update files in archive     f  = freshen files in archive
       d = delete files from archive   x,e = extract files from archive
       r = run files from archive      t  = test archive integrity
       l = list files in archive       v  = verbose listing of files
       c = convert entry to new packing method
       p = copy files from archive to standard output

       w = suppress warning messages   b  = retain backup copy of archive
       m = move files to archive       s  = suppress compression (store only)
       n = suppress notes and comments z  = include subdirectories in archive
       o = overwrite existing files when extracting
       5 = produce only level 5 compatable archives

       g = Encrypt/decrypt archive entry

Please refer to the program documentation for complete instructions.
```

The single ARC.EXE file is used to pack, unpack, view the contents of files, and much more. Some subsequent utilities use two modules—one for doing the packing and related chores and another for unpacking.

ARC was also the first compression program to create self-extracting files. With a self-extracting file, the receiver does not need any particular utility in order to unpack it. A self-extracting file unpacks itself. You can download an SFX file, unpack it, and then repack the contents with the compression program of your choice.

ARC is an excellent utility and offers good compression. Now, let's take a look at how ARC performed on the tests.

ARC Test Performance

ARC version 6.02 was used in the following tests. ARC had a very good time in processing the two large files, one binary and one ASCII. Figure 16-2 shows ARC's performance on Test 1.

ARC also did fairly well on Test 2, compressing the five ASCII text binary files. In Test 2, ARC had good compression and finished in only slightly over 30 seconds. Figure 16-3 shows the results for ARC on Test 2.

Figure 16-4 shows how ARC did on Test 3, which consisted of compressing five binary files. It's interesting to note that ARC did much the same as it did in Test 1, even though the total amount to be compressed in Test 3 was less. This helps to illustrate the point that binary files are more difficult to compress.

Figure 16-2

ARC's performance on Test 1

TEST 1

Compressing 1-.EXE 1-.DOC File

| Compressing A Total Of 521,762 bytes |
| Resulting File Size: 325,349 bytes |
| Total Elapsed Time: 00:44:06 |

ARC 6.02

Figure 16-3

Performance of ARC on Test 2

TEST 2

Compressing 5 ASCII Text Files

| Compressing A Total Of 454,517 bytes |
| Resulting File Size: 192,658 bytes |
| Total Elapsed Time: 00:30:35 |

ARC 6.02

Lastly, Figure 16-5 shows the performance of ARC on Test 4 in creating a self-extracting file. The .ARC file was approximately 8K smaller than the resulting self-extracting file. This difference is the average amount added to the file size when creating an SFX file with ARC.

ARC 6.02 did well on all of the tests, getting the most compression on Test 2, the ASCII text files. If you use the program, please register for it.

System Enhancement Associates, Inc.
21 New Street
Wayne, NJ 07470
Contribution requested; a program disk and printed manual are supplied with contribution of $50 or more. This also includes 30 days of support, which may be extended by purchasing a maintenance contract from SEA. Site licenses and commercial distribution licenses are available.

Figure 16-4

Results for ARC on Test 3

TEST 3

Compressing 5 Binary Files

| Compressing A Total Of 435,285 bytes |
| Resulting File Size: 326,749 bytes |
| Total Elapsed Time: 00:42:28 |

ARC 6.02

Figure 16-5

Creating an SFX file with ARC

```
        TEST 4

Creating A Self-Extracting File

┌─────────────────────────────────────────┐
│  Compressing A Total Of 349,282 bytes    │
├─────────────────────────────────────────┤
│  Size Of Compressed File:  184,612 bytes │
├─────────────────────────────────────────┤
│  Size of .SFX File was:    192,328 bytes │
└─────────────────────────────────────────┘

           ARC 6.02
```

PKWARE'S ZIP UTILITY

Since their initial release in 1989, there have been three versions of PKZIP and PKUNZIP. The first release was version 0.92 and the second was version 1.02. In March 1990, PKWARE released version 1.10. Release 1.10 had several improvements, including a facility for registered users to verify that all files contained in a .ZIP file have remained unchanged from the time they were packed. This is an excellent feature for verifying that the contents have not been tampered with. PKZIP has many command line options to meet a wide range of needs. Figure 16-6 shows the command listing for PKZIP. To obtain this listing, switch to the directory that holds your PKZIP program, type in **PKZIP**, and press ENTER.

You'll note that PKZIP's options allow you to store the directory name, include ASCII comments, pass on a volume label, and much more. PKUNZIP is used for extracting .ZIP files and for tasks like extracting documentation to the screen or testing the integrity of a .ZIP file. Figure 16-7 shows the command summary screen for PKUNZIP.

This summary is obtained the same way you get the summary for PKZIP—simply enter **PKUNZIP** at the DOS prompt. Each command is discussed in detail in the program's documentation.

ZIP—The Popular Favorite

From the moment it was released, the ZIP utilities from PKWARE gained tremendous popularity. As noted earlier, the majority of files found on bulletin boards and on some online networks are in .ZIP format. PKZIP

Figure 16-6

Command line options of PKZIP

```
Usage: PKZIP [-b[path]] [options] zipfile [@list] [files...]
Options summary - consult the PKWARE documentation for additional information
  -x<filespec!@list> = eXclude filespec(s)        -z = add zipfile comment
  -d = delete files             -f = freshen files      -i = add changed files
  -l = display license info     -u = update files      -m[u,f] = move files
  -a = add files                -b = create temp zipfile on alternate drive
  -c = add/edit file comments   -C = add comments to new files only
  -k = keep same ZIP date       -o = set ZIP date to latest file
  -q = enable ANSI comments     -s<pwd> = Scramble files with password
  -r = recurse subdirs          -$[drive] = save volume label
  -t[mmddyy] = Compress files on or after specified date (default=today)
  -e[x,i,s] = use maXimal compression/Implode only/Shrink only
  -<p!P> = store pathnames ! p=recursed into ! P=specified & recursed into
  -<w!W><H,S> = ! w=include ! W=don't include ! Hidden/System files
  -<J!J><H,S,R> = ! J=mask ! J=don't mask ! Hidden/System/Readonly attributes
  -v[b,c,d,e,n,p,s,r,t] = view ZIP [Brief listing/show Comments/sort by -
    Date/Ext/Name/Percentage/Size/sort Reverse/Technical (long) listing]
zipfile = ZIP file name.  Default extension is .ZIP
file    = Names of files to compress. Wildcards *,? ok. Default is ALL files.
@list   = listfile containing names of files to add or view etc.
```

has become so popular because it offers the best speed while delivering a high compression rate. With certain types of files, PKZIP may take slightly longer than a program like ARC, but this difference is offset by greater compression of the file. Although .ZIP files are dominating the current online scene, you will still find .ARC files and .ZOO files. It seems that LHarc and PAK are predominantly used for creating self-extracting .EXE files. Overall, the majority of files are in .ZIP format. Let's see how PKZIP performed on the four tests.

PKZIP Test Performance

PKZIP version 1.10 was used for the test. On Test 1 PKZIP demonstrated the amount of compression it can attain. The results for Test 1 are seen in Figure 16-8.

Note that PKZIP compressed the files by more than 50 percent of their original size. If you are trying to save on disk space or cut down on file transfer time, this amount of compression is very important. The results of Test 2 are shown in Figure 16-9.

Figure 16-7

Command line options of PKUNZIP

```
PKUNZIP (R)   FAST!   Extract Utility   Version 1.1   03-15-90
Copr. 1989-1990 PKWARE Inc. All Rights Reserved. PKUNZIP/h for help
PKUNZIP Reg. U.S. Pat. and Tm. Off.

Usage: PKUNZIP [options] zipfile [d:outpath\] [file...]
Options summary - consult the PKWARE documentation for additional information
  -c[m] = extract to screen [with more]      -t = test zipfile integrity
  -d = create directories stored in ZIP      -l = display software license
  -n = extract only newer files              -o = overwrite existing files
  -q = enable ANSI in comments               -s<pwd> = unScramble with password
  -f = extract only newer & existing files   -$ extract volume label if in ZIP
  -p[a,b,c][1,2,3] = extract to printer [Asc mode,Bin mode,Com port] [port #]
  -<J!J><H,S,R> = ! J=mask ! J=don't mask ! Hidden/System/Readonly attributes
  -e[c,d,e,n,p,s] = extract files in CRC/Date/Ext/Name/Percentage/Size order
  -v[b,c,d,e,n,p,s,r] = view ZIP(s) [Brief listing/sort by CRC/Date/Ext
    /Name/Percentage/Size/sort Reverse (descending) order]
zipfile = ZIP file name, wildcards *,? ok. Default extension is .ZIP
file    = Name(s) of files to extract. Wildcards *,? ok. Default is ALL files.
```

As you can see, PKZIP managed approximately 70 percent compression of the five ASCII text files. This fact helps keep program files smaller, because program authors know their text files, like documentation, will compress quite well. Figure 16-10 shows how PKZIP did on Test 3.

The phenomenal PKZIP got approximately 50 percent compression of the five binary files and did it in just over 36 seconds. Finally, we get to

Figure 16-8

Test 1 performance of PKZIP

```
        TEST 1

  Compressing 1-.EXE 1-.DOC File
```

Compressing A Total Of 521,762 bytes	
Resulting File Size:	233,435 bytes
Total Elapsed Time:	00:58:82

```
        PKZIP 1.10
```

Figure 16-9

PKZIP performance on Test 2

TEST 2

Compressing 5 ASCII Text Files

| Compressing A Total Of 454,517 bytes |
| Resulting File Size: 141,266 bytes |
| Total Elapsed Time: 01:02:73 |

PKZIP 1.10

Test 4. PKZIP uses an extra program, ZIP2EXE.EXE, to convert .ZIP files into self-extracting files. (This program is included in the PKZIP/PKUNZIP package.) Figure 16-11 gives PKZIP's statistics for Test 4. The self-extracting .EXE file is about 12K larger than the original .ZIP file that was created. This is about the average amount of "overhead" added when using PKZIP and ZIP2EXE to create an SFX file.

ZIPing Right Along

The PKWARE utility has become the most popular compression utility. Whether you decide to use the PKWARE programs or not, you will need a copy in order to unpack many files you will receive by either downloading or other means. It's an excellent compression utility that is constantly being improved.

Figure 16-10

Test 3 statistics for PKZIP

TEST 3

Compressing 5 Binary Files

| Compressing A Total Of 435,285 bytes |
| Resulting File Size: 238,026 bytes |
| Total Elapsed Time: 00:36:34 |

PKZIP 1.10

Figure 16-11

PKZIP statistics for Test 4

```
TEST 4

Creating A Self-Extracting File
┌─────────────────────────────────────────────┐
│ Compressing A Total Of 349,282 bytes         │
├─────────────────────────────────────────────┤
│ Size Of Compressed File:  137,218 bytes      │
├─────────────────────────────────────────────┤
│ Size of .SFX File was:    158,882 bytes      │
└─────────────────────────────────────────────┘
           PKZIP 1.18
```

Phil Katz
PKWARE, Inc.
7545 North Port Washington Road
Glendale, WI 53217
414-352-3670 (Voice)
414-352-7176 (BBS)
414-352-3815 (Fax)
$47 registration; MasterCard and VISA; site licenses available

PAK—A COMPROMISE?

PAK is a product of NoGate Consulting. While PAK does not attempt to match the speed of the PKWARE products, it does a very good job of file compression. On a personal note, I have observed that PAK does not seem to be used a great deal for creating files that have the typical .PAK extension. I have noted, however, that a good number of self-extracting files are created with PAK. Unlike ARC and PKZIP, PAK does not require another utility program to create SFX files. Figure 16-12 shows the many command line options available with PAK.

You can see that the top section contains the available commands while the bottom section contains all of PAK's many options. PAK can be considered a compromise program because it has good compression, often equaling PKZIP, and better speed than some of the others. While not as fast as PKZIP, it does quite well, but it has not gained wide acceptance. The authors of PAK say that the majority of their business is in the

Figure 16-12

PAK commands and options

```
Commands:
 A  Add files to archive          M  Move files to archive
 U  Update archive files          F  Update duplicate files
 E  Extract files from archive    X  Move files from archive
 D  Delete files                  L  List files
 V  List files                    P  Display files
 T  Test files                    C  Convert files
 R  Revise remarks                H  Revise archive header
Options:
 SEC   Security envelope verify    C    use Crunching compression
 S     use Squashing compression   CR   use Crushing compression
 G     Garble with password        M    Move files
 R     with Remarks                H    With archive header remark
 D     Duplicate files only        P    Pack archives
 SN    Sort by Name                ST   Sort by time
 SS    Sort by Size                SE   Sort by extension
 S-    no sort                     WA   Write over Always
 WP    Prompt Write over           WO   Write over Older
 WN    Never Write over            L    Use last date in archive
 T     set Temporary path          HEX  Print in hex format
 MORE  Pause after each page       REM  Rename archive to .PAK
 PATH  Use Path                    I    Include subdirectories
 EXE   Create Self-extracting file
```

commercial sector, with a modest percentage coming from individual users. Let's see how PAK did on the four tests.

Running Some Tests with PAK

Test 1 shows that PAK can compress almost as well as PKZIP, while lagging behind in speed. The results of Test 1 are seen in Figure 16-13.

As for compression, PAK was within 2K of the figure attained by PKZIP. You can see that PAK offers an excellent rate of compression. Test 2 shows you how different factors can affect performance. The results are shown in Figure 16-14.

In this test, PAK was about two seconds faster than PKZIP, but the resulting file was about 5K larger. As expected, PAK did very well in compressing the text files. Test 3 also has some interesting results, which are shown in Figure 16-15.

In compressing the binary files, PAK was within 1K of PKZIP, both of which did much better than ARC. The one difference is that PAK took

---

Figure 16-13

PAK statistics for Test 1

TEST 1

Compressing 1-.EXE 1-.DOC File

| Compressing A Total Of 521,762 bytes |
| Resulting File Size: 235,435 bytes |
| Total Elapsed Time: 01:13:04 |

PAK 2.10

---

about 22 seconds longer to achieve these results. Finally, in Test 4, PAK shows how well it did in creating a self-extracting file. These statistics are seen in Figure 16-16.

You'll note that the resulting SFX file is about 8K larger than the .PAK file that was created. This is the average amount of difference when creating a self-extracting file with PAK. In this one test, PAK and PKZIP came out with files that were only 271 bytes different in size.

Overview of PAK

PAK is a very good compression program even though it has not received wide support in the PC community. It offers good compression with a wide variety of file formats and does quite well in making self-extracting files. There is also a full screen version of PAK, called PAKF, which will be described later. The latest release of PAK can also pack and unpack ZIP format files, giving it added flexibility and appeal. With this addition, PAK

Figure 16-14

Statistics for PAK on Test 2

TEST 2

Compressing 5 ASCII Text Files

| Compressing A Total Of 454,517 bytes |
| Resulting File Size: 146,575 bytes |
| Total Elapsed Time: 01:00:66 |

PAK 2.10

Figure 16-15

PAK performance on Test 3

```
        TEST 3

   Compressing 5 Binary Files

┌─────────────────────────────────────────┐
│ Compressing A Total Of 435,285 bytes     │
├─────────────────────────────────────────┤
│ Resulting File Size:  239,389 bytes      │
├─────────────────────────────────────────┤
│ Total Elapsed Time:  00:58:12            │
└─────────────────────────────────────────┘

           PAK 2.10
```

is the only compression utility that can unpack the formats of two other utilities. If you use PAK, please be sure to register it with its authors.

NoGate Consulting
P.O. Box 88115
Grand Rapids, MI 49518
616-455-6270 (Voice)
616-455-5179 (BBS)
$15 registration

ZOO — PUBLIC DOMAIN

ZOO, while very popular in the world of UNIX, has never really caught on with DOS users. A version of ZOO has also been ported over to the

Figure 16-16

Test 4 statistics for PAK

```
         TEST 4

  Creating A Self-Extracting File

┌─────────────────────────────────────────┐
│ Compressing A Total Of 349,282 bytes     │
├─────────────────────────────────────────┤
│ Size Of Compressed File:  141,130 bytes  │
├─────────────────────────────────────────┤
│ Size of .SFX File was:  149,731 bytes    │
└─────────────────────────────────────────┘

           PAK 2.10
```

Figure 16-17

ZOO command line options

```
Usage: zoo {acDeglLPTuUvx}[aAcCdEf InmMNoOpPqu1:/,@n] archive file
("zoo h" for help)

Novice usage:  zoo -cmd archive[.zoo] file...  where -cmd is one of these:
-add -extract -move -test -print -delete -list -update -freshen -comment
```

Amiga line of computers. ZOO is in no way compatible with any of the other file compression utilities. Its compression ability is similar to that of ARC while its speed is somewhere between that of PKZIP and PAK. Figure 16-17 shows the command line options for ZOO.

You can see that ZOO does not offer as many options as some of the other compression programs. ZOO does offer an expert command mode and a novice command mode. Files in the ZOO format can be found on some bulletin boards and on the GEnie network. For this reason, you may want to obtain a copy of the ZOO utility in case you encounter a program you want that is packed in the ZOO format.

Testing ZOO

On Test 1, both ZOO and ARC were very close in file size and time. The results are seen in Figure 16-18. The compression time, as compared to ARC, was less than one second faster, but ZOO did make a compressed file that was approximately 11K smaller than ARC did. The results on Test 2 were very much the same, as seen in Figure 16-19.

Figure 16-18

ZOO results on Test 1

```
        TEST 1

Compressing 1-.EXE 1-.DOC File
```

Compressing A Total Of	521,762 bytes
Resulting File Size:	314,370 bytes
Total Elapsed Time:	00:43:42

```
    ZOO 2.01
```

Figure 16-19

ZOO performance on Test 2

TEST 2

Compressing 5 ASCII Text Files

Compressing A Total Of 454,517 bytes
Resulting File Size: 181,513 bytes
Total Elapsed Time: 00:30:28

ZOO 2.01

Here again, when compared to ARC, file size and time were very close when using ZOO. Ironically, the size variance was once again almost exactly 11K, and the time difference was just one hundredth of a second! This same pattern can be seen by looking at the results of Test 3, shown in Figure 16-20.

Once again, ZOO matches fairly well with ARC in both speed and amount of compression. Test 4 was not done using the ZOO utility. To create self-extracting files, ZOO requires a totally separate utility called SEZ. The three copies I obtained of SEZ were all inoperable.

Be aware that the ZOO compression program and its source code, written by Rahul Dhesi, are available in the public domain. There is also a utility program called OOZ, which is used just to extract ZOO files.

Figure 16-20

Statistics for ZOO on Test 3

TEST 3

Compressing 5 Binary Files

Compressing A Total Of 435,285 bytes
Resulting File Size: 321,591 bytes
Total Elapsed Time: 00:43:56

ZOO 2.01

LHARC—COMPRESSION FROM JAPAN

LHarc was created in Japan by a programmer who, for reasons of simplification, goes by the name Yoshi. The author's full name is Haruyasu Yoshizaki. The original documentation is in Japanese but a translation was quickly supplied.

LHarc achieves very good rates of compression at the sacrifice of speed. In the Shareware world, LHarc has become most popular for the low overhead of its self-extracting files. Version 2.0 of LHarc is in the works and promises to maintain the level of compression while improving speed. LHarc, like ZOO, is also in the public domain, so there is no registration fee. Figure 16-21 shows the commands and switches used by LHarc.

The documentation includes other commands that can be used with LHarc. For example, LHarc self-extracting files can display a message to the user before the actual unpacking begins. It can even give the user the option of aborting the unpacking procedure.

Figure 16-21

LHarc commands and switches

```
LHarc  version 1.13c           Copyright (c) Haruyasu Yoshizaki, 1988-89
=============================================== 05/31/89 ===
              <<< High-Performance File-Compression Program >>>
===============================================================================
usage: LHarc [<command>] [[{/I-}{<switch>[-I+I2I<option>]}},...] <archive_name>
             [[<drive_name>:}I{<home_directory_name>\}] [<path_name> ...]
-------------------------------------------------------------------------------
 <command>
   a: Add files to archive          u: Update files to archive
   f: Freshen files in archive      m: Move new files into archive
   d: Delete files from archive     e,x: EXtract files from archive
   p: disPlay files in archive      l,v: View List of files in archive
   s: make a Self-extracting archive t: Test integrity of archive
 <switch>
   r: Recursively collect files     w: assign Work directory
   x: allow eXtended file names     m: no Message for query
   p: distinguish full Path names   c: skip time-stamp Check
   a: allow any Attributes of files v: View files by another utility
   n: display No indicator          k: Key word for AUTOLARC.BAT
   t: archive's Time-stamp option
===============================================================================
You may copy or distribute without any donation to me. Nifty-Serve  PFF00253
(See the User's Manual for detailed descriptions.)      ASCII-pcs   pcs02846
```

Testing LHarc

On Test 1, LHarc got a level of compression that was nearly as good as that obtained with PKZIP and PAK. Its time was closer to that of PAK, while running about 21 seconds behind PKZIP. The results are seen in Figure 16-22.

The compression percentage is quite good but sacrifices some speed in performance. If speed is not a concern, LHarc may be for you. LHarc's performance on Test 2 shows similar findings. Figure 16-23 gives the statistics for Test 2.

Once again, LHarc was very close to the level of compression offered by PKZIP and PAK. When it came to Test 3, LHarc actually did slightly better than PAK in level of compression and only took about seven seconds longer. LHarc's performance on Test 3 is seen in Figure 16-24.

Obviously, LHarc does quite well with binary data. Finally, when it comes to creating self-extracting files, LHarc has an advantage over the other utilities. Test 4 is the area where LHarc really shines, as seen in Figure 16-25. In this test, LHarc outperformed both PKZIP and PAK. An interesting thing to note is that LHarc adds the least overhead when generating an SFX file. The original .LZH file was larger than either the .ZIP or the .PAK file. The resulting difference is due to the fact that LHarc only adds between 1K and 2K when creating a self-extracting file. This is why it has become so popular as a means of creating SFX files.

Looking at LHarc

There is no question about the compression abilities of the LHarc utility. If you are not concerned with speed, LHarc will suit you nicely. It gets

---

Figure 16-22

Performance of LHarc on Test 1

```
        TEST 1

Compressing 1-.EXE 1-.DOC File
┌─────────────────────────────────────────┐
│ Compressing A Total Of 521,762 bytes     │
├─────────────────────────────────────────┤
│ Resulting File Size:  239,737 bytes      │
├─────────────────────────────────────────┤
│ Total Elapsed Time:  01:19:21            │
└─────────────────────────────────────────┘
        LHARC 1.13C
```

Figure 16-23

LHarc statistics for Test 2

TEST 2

Compressing 5 ASCII Text Files

Compressing A Total Of 454,517 bytes
Resulting File Size: 151,661 bytes
Total Elapsed Time: 01:29:53

LHARC 1.13C

Figure 16-24

Test 3 performance of LHarc

TEST 3

Compressing 5 Binary Files

Compressing A Total Of 435,285 bytes
Resulting File Size: 238,026 bytes
Total Elapsed Time: 01:05:92

LHARC 1.13C

Figure 16-25

Test 4 performance of LHarc

TEST 4

Creating A Self-Extracting File

Compressing A Total Of 349,282 bytes
Size Of Compressed File: 142,919 bytes
Size of .SFX File was: 144,214 bytes

LHARC 1.13C

---

consistently good performance when packing files of various formats and adds very little overhead to self-extracting files. This is one program to keep an eye on.

SUMMARIZING THE COMPRESSION TESTS

The test results of all of the compression programs will be summarized through the following tables. Keep in mind that this is only one set of tests and is not intended to be a comprehensive study. The tests should give you an overall indication of how each utility performs with various file formats, how well it compresses, and how fast it is. You must decide which utility you want to use based on your needs and tastes. Figure 16-26 gives the summary of Test 1, which consisted of packing a large text and a large binary file.

Test 2 consisted of packing five ASCII text files. Figure 16-27 gives the summary of Test 2. The next summary compares how the utilities did when compressing binary files. Figure 16-28 summarizes the results of Test 3. Lastly, Test 4 shows how the programs did when creating self-extracting files. Figure 16-29 gives this summary.

As noted in Chapter 5, while you can decide what compression utility you want for personal use, it is hard to get by with just one utility, since

---
Figure 16-26

Summary of Test 1

Compressing 1–.EXE 1–.DOC File Compressing A Total Of 521,762 bytes		
Compression Type	Resulting File Size:	Total Elapsed Time:
ARC 6.02	325,349 bytes	00:44:06
ZOO 2.01	314,370 bytes	00:43:42
PAK 2.10	235,435 bytes	01:13:04
LHARC 1.13C	239,737 bytes	01:19:21
PKZIP 1.10	233,435 bytes	00:58:02

Summary of Test 2

Compressing 5 ASCII Text Files Compressing A Total Of 454,517 bytes		
Compression Type	Resulting File Size:	Total Elapsed Time:
ARC 6.02	192,658 bytes	00:30:35
ZOO 2.01	181,513 bytes	00:30:20
PAK 2.10	146,575 bytes	01:00:66
LHARC 1.13C	151,661 bytes	01:29:53
PKZIP 1.10	141,260 bytes	01:02:93

files are found in all of the formats discussed and you may need to unpack any one of them. Decide on the one you like best, but be prepared to deal with the others.

Let's move on and look at some programs that are designed to make your use of compressed files easier.

Summary of Test 3

Compressing 5 Binary Files Compressing A Total Of 435,205 bytes		
Compression Type	Resulting File Size:	Total Elapsed Time:
ARC 6.02	326,749 bytes	00:42:20
ZOO 2.01	321,591 bytes	00:43:56
PAK 2.10	239,389 bytes	00:58:12
LHARC 1.13C	238,026 bytes	01:05:92
PKZIP 1.10	238,026 bytes	00:36:34

Figure 16-29

Summary of Test 4

Creating A Self-Extracting File Compressing A Total Of 349,282 bytes		
Compression Type	Resulting File Size:	Size Of SFX File:
ARC 6.02	184,612 bytes	192,328 bytes
PAK 2.10	141,130 bytes	149,731 bytes
LHARC 1.13C	142,919 bytes	144,214 bytes
PKZIP 1.10	137,218 bytes	150,002 bytes

PKZMENU — LOOKING AHEAD

As of this writing PKZMENU has not yet been released, but is in beta testing. The program is by Douglas Hay, the author of StupenDOS (discussed in Chapter 14) and is distributed by PKWARE. PKZMENU provides an excellent interface for working with .ZIP files. Figure 16-30 shows the main display of PKZMENU, showing all of the .ZIP files in the D:\HOLD directory.

The program can be controlled from the keyboard and provides mouse support. Across the top you'll note the headers for various pull-down menus. To give you just an idea of what the program can do, let's briefly cover some of the functions found in the pull-down menus.

The Setup Menu

The Setup menu of PKZMENU gives users complete control over how the program looks, how it functions, and so on. You can configure the colors, the sort options, what type of monitor you have, and much more. To simplify matters, here is a list of the Setup menu options.

Sort	Extract directory
Monitor	Zip options
Color selection	Printer setup
Beep	Time on screen
Return to startup	Use mouse
386 instructions	Virus checking
Virus program	List file

You can see that PKZMENU provides many configurable options. If you have a 386 machine, PKZMENU will handle data accordingly. You can also configure the printer, the mouse, and the directory where .ZIP files are unpacked. PKZMENU even gives you the option of doing virus checking and lets you use the virus checking program of your choice. Let's take a closer look at the Zip Options menu, which allows you to easily handle .ZIP files.

Figure 16-30

Main display of PKZMENU

```
Extract    Tag    Sort   Misc    setuP    eXit                5:30:50
↑ Drive: D:\HOLD
  ..✓                                        <DIR>  02-20-90   02:07p
  ANYTIME.ZIP                                38045  04-12-90   12:42a
  BO120.ZIP                                  40171  04-12-90   12:42a
  BURN231.ZIP                                15516  04-12-90   12:42a
  COMM042.ZIP                                74926  04-12-90   12:42a
  DHAYPCKG.ZIP                              143324  04-12-90   12:42a
  DVORAK.ZIP                                   360  01 12 90   12:42a
  FD401.ZIP                                  44868  04-12-90   12:42a
  HOWLONG.ZIP                                26503  04-12-90   12:42a
  LZEXE91.ZIP                                43975  04-12-90   12:42a
  NB21C.ZIP                                  58925  04-12-90   12:42a
  NJFIND.ZIP                                 33429  04-12-90   12:42a
  PCREG.ZIP                                 128198  04-12-90   12:42a
  PMK31.ZIP                                 222508  04-12-90   12:42a
  REMCTL53.ZIP                               42262  04-12-90   12:42a
  UNLZEXE.ZIP                                 9118  04-12-90   12:42a
  VDE152.ZIP                                 91625  04-12-90   12:42a
↓
┌─────────────────────────────────────────────────────────────────┐
│ Extract directory : C:\DNLD                                       │
├──────────────────┬──────────────────┬────────────────┬───────────┤
│ File 0001 of 0018│ Tagged Files 0000│ Bytes Tagged 0 │MODE:EXTRACT│
└──────────────────┴──────────────────┴────────────────┴───────────┘
PKZMENU Ver 0.90e  Ser#102   Copyright 1990 by PKWARE Inc - All rights reserved
```

Configuring PKZMENU to Suit You

Using the Zip Options selection, you can tell the program the options you want to see, such as comments, or if you want pathnames displayed, and so on. Figure 16-31 shows the options available.

You can save all choices to disk and alter them later. You can set up the menu so when you tag a .ZIP file, the contents of that file are automatically shown to you on the screen. It's also possible to tell PKZMENU whether to overwrite or not, to create directories, or to set up a temporary drive. You can also read the documentation inside of a file using a program like LIST. All of these features make PKZMENU a very powerful program for working with .ZIP files. From the Extract menu you can test the integrity of all .ZIP files and send tagged files to the printer. There are no commands to remember and you can set up the program so it always uses the defaults you've selected.

Optimum Performance with PKZMENU

PKZMENU provides tremendous flexibility. It is fast, efficient, and gives you optimum performance. PKZMENU offers a host of options, toggles,

---

Figure 16-31

The Zip Options of PKZMENU

```
Extract    Tag    Sort    Misc    setuP    eXit                    5:31:52
↑ Drive: D:\HOLD
█ ..✓
  ANYTIME.ZIP                         ┌─────────────────────────────────────┐
  B0120.ZIP                           │ Sort           Name A-Z  0-90  02:07p │
  BURN231.ZIP                         │ Extract dir.    C:\DNLD  2-90  12:42a │
  COMM042.ZIP                       ■ │ Monitor           Color  2-90  12:42a │
  DHAYPCKG.ZIP                      ■ │ ▪ Zip options            2-90  12:42a │
  DVORAK.ZIP                        ✓ │ ┌───────────────────────┐       :42a │
  FD401.ZIP                         ✓ │ │ • Expand zip files    │       :42a │
  HOWLONG.ZIP                       ✓ │ │ • Sort inners         │       :42a │
  LZEXE91.ZIP                       ✓ │ │ ✓ Comments displayed  │       :42a │
  NB21C.ZIP                         ✓ │ │ ✓ Pathnames displayed │       :42a │
  MJFIND.ZIP                        • │ │ • Volume label creation       :42a │
  PCREG.ZIP                           │ │ ✓ More (console)      │       :42a │
  PMK31.ZIP                           │ │ • Overwrite           │       :42a │
  REMCTL53.ZIP                        │ │ • Never               │       :42a │
  UNLZEXE.ZIP                         │ │ • Directory creation  │       :42a │
  VDE152.ZIP                          │ │   Inner display  size,time,date :42a │
                                      │ │   Temporary drive     │       :42a │
                                      │ ▪ Zip file extensions   │       :42a │
↓─────────────────────────────────────────────────────────────────────────
│ Extract directory : C:\DNLD
├───────────────────────┬───────────────────┬──────────────┬──────────────
│ File 0001 of 0018     │ Tagged Files 0000 │ Bytes Tagged 0 │ MODE:EXTRACT
Press ←┘ to invoke the highlighted selection.  Press W to write setup
```

switches, and configurable parameters. Keep in mind that the version listed for this book is a beta version. Other features will be added to make PKZMENU an indispensable tool for working with .ZIP files.

Douglas Hay
PKWARE, Inc.
7545 North Port Washington Road
Glendale, WI 53217
414-352-3670
$35 registration plus $3.50 shipping and handling

PAKF—FULL SCREEN PAK

PAKF is a full screen version of the PAK utility discussed earlier. PAKF utilizes a menu interface, letting you work more easily with archived files. PAKF allows you to view the contents of files, create new .PAK files or self-extracting .EXE files, and much more.

Like PKZMENU, which works only with .ZIP files, PAKF only supports files that are in its own format—either .PAK files or .ARC files created with ARC or ARCA. PAKF will make it easier for you to create compressed files with the PAK format. You can elect to copy (add) files to a new archive or move them into a compressed file. When you move a file into a compressed file it is erased from the disk. If you add a file, the original stays on the disk.

You Choose the Options

PAKF has an options menu allowing you to set up and save program defaults. For example, if you want PAKF to always generate self-extracting files, it can be set in the options menu. You can also set features like the packing method to be used, a temporary path, and so on.

As you can see, the options menu lets you configure everything from colors to compression method and then allows you to save your choices. If you use PAK or think you would like to, you might want to take a look at PAKF. It will simplify your work with .PAK and .ARC files.

NoGate Consulting
P.O. Box 88115
Grand Rapids, MI 49518
616-455-6270
$30 registration entitles you to both PAKF and PAK

SHEZ—COMPRESSED FILE TOOL

Shez is a complex shell program that works with many of the different compressed file formats. Shez can handle .ZIP, .PAK, .LZH, .ARC, and .ZOO files. If you have the utilities that create these various formats, Shez lets you convert files from one format to another. You can extract or create compressed files, view their contents, read documentation within compressed files, and much more. Shez comes with a full configuration program allowing you to configure colors, work with a mouse, and establish file formats. Figure 16-32 shows the main display of Shez.

Figure 16-32

Main menu display of Shez with Miscellaneous menu down

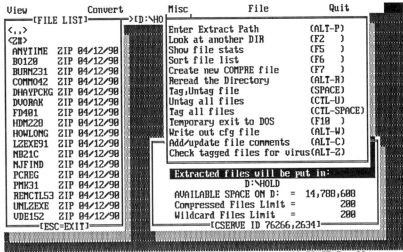

Shez can be used from the keyboard or with a mouse. It can be used to convert a .ZIP file, for example, into a self-extracting file. Shez has pull-down menus that give you access to all of its many features, making it a complete program for dealing with compressed files. Let's examine some of the features that can make your life easier.

Creating Compressed Files

Shez can create, unpack, and convert compressed files of varying formats. Creating new compressed files, for example, is a snap with Shez. You can create a new compressed file by using the F7 key to show the directory display window, or you can pick from the compressed file window using the C command. When you do this, a window pops up and prompts you to enter the name of the compressed file you want to create.

Depending on how you configured the program, you can enter any number of compressed file extensions. If you configured Shez to use .ARC, .ZIP, and .PAK files, you will have to tell it which kind of compressed file to make. From that point, you either add or move files into your new file. Shez will also prompt you for a password, for example, used to encrypt a compressed file, or for other kinds of input when unpacking files.

Since you've seen the variety existing among compression programs, let's take a look at how Shez handles converting between several compression formats.

Using Shez for Conversions

Depending on how you configure the program, Shez can handle all of the following compression programs:

- ARC
- PKZIP/PKUNZIP
- PAK
- LHarc
- ZOO

It can also convert files between different formats. How would you do this with Shez? Let's say that you have downloaded some .PAK format files and want to convert them into .ZIP format. There are several ways to do this, but there is one way that is recommended in the documentation. To convert the .PAK files you would load Shez from DOS with the following command:

```
C>SHEZ *.PAK
```

Shez comes up and only displays files you want to convert. Highlight one of the files, and then use ALT-V, which gives you the conversion menu. Shez prompts you for the new format, so you'd enter a **Z** to convert the .PAK file to a .ZIP file. Shez will also ask if you want the original file to be erased after the conversion is complete. You can answer either Yes or No.

If you wanted to, you could mark all of the files for conversion at the same time. Highlight them, and then press the SPACEBAR to tag them. In this instance you would use CTRL-V instead of ALT-V. CTRL-V is the command for converting all tagged files. Shez will convert all of the .PAK files into .ZIP files. You can also tell Shez to delete old files when you are finished.

Setting the Environment for Shez

Shez has certain environment variables that you can set. Environment variables provide a program with information about itself, help the program to find its own files, and so on. Common features like the DOS PATH and PROMPT are also part of your system's environment. When you set environment variables for Shez, it will always know your specified defaults. You can set the following environment variables for Shez.

- Mono
- BIOS
- Shezwork
- Shezex
- Shezcmt

The Mono environment variable tells Shez not to use color, but to use monochrome mode instead. The BIOS variable tells Shez to use your computer's BIOS for screen writes and not to write directly to the screen. In the case of the Mono and BIOS variables, you would set each with a **Y** if you wanted it on. For example, if you wanted Shez to be in monochrome mode, you would put the following line in your AUTOEXEC.BAT file.

```
SET MONO=Y
```

The Shezwork variable tells Shez that you want it to work only in a certain directory. Please note that if you don't set this environment variable, Shez will create a directory of its own, and then remove it when you exit the program. To set the Shezwork variable, you first have to create the directory before loading Shez. Secondly, no other program can use this directory. Lastly, you must make sure that all files are removed from this directory before you exit Shez. Why? When you exit Shez, the program will delete every file in that directory—even hidden files.

The Shezex variable tells Shez where you want all files to be unpacked. To always have files unpacked to a C:\DNLD directory, for example, you would put the following line in your AUTOEXEC.BAT file.

```
SET SHEZEX=C:\DNLD
```

With Shezex set, Shez will always know where you want extracted files to go. The last environment variable you can set is Shezcmt, which allows you to specify a default comment file for use when you are adding comments to compressed files.

Shez has been designed to make working with compressed files as easy as possible. With so many different file formats available, Shez gives you the power to manipulate different types of compressed files in a way that best suits you. Shez even has support for the anti-virus program SCAN. This particular option can be set in the configuration program. Figure 16-33 shows the file menu of Shez.

If you handle a lot of compressed files, especially with varying formats, a program like Shez can really simplify your work. To appreciate Shez, you have to see it for yourself. The program is updated and improved frequently and is very complete.

Jim Derr
California Software Design
P.O. Box 15248
Santa Rosa, CA 95402
707-538-8710 (BBS)
76266,2634 CompuServe ID
$25 registration; site licenses available

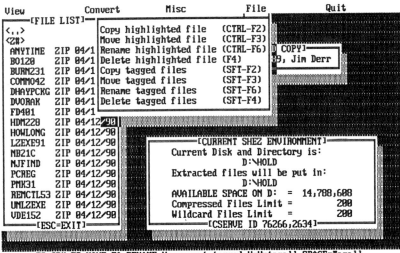

Figure 16-33

The File menu of Shez

ARCMASTER—BY NEW-WARE

ArcMaster, written by John Newlin, was actually the first program to provide a complete interface for working with compressed files. Over the last few years it has evolved to handle the increasing variety among file compression programs. ArcMaster can still deal with the last versions of PKWARE's PKPAK and PKUNPAK. Currently, ArcMaster works with all of the following compression programs.

- ARC

- PKPAK/PKUNPAK

- ARCA/ARCE

- PKZIP/PKUNZIP

- PAK

- LHarc

ArcMaster does not handle files in the .ZOO format. ArcMaster does support LIST, which can be used to read program text files and documentation. Figure 16-34 shows the main display of ArcMaster with its menu popped up.

Let's take a closer look at how ArcMaster works.

Working with ArcMaster

ArcMaster can be used with a combination of cursor and function keys and offers full mouse support. When using ArcMaster, everything moves from the left window to the right window. You can have the same directory displayed in both windows. You set defaults for the two windows in the configuration program. You can also set the directories when the program loads. For example, to work with files in your C:\WORK directory and have them moved to the C:\DNLD directory, enter the following when you load ArcMaster:

```
C>AM C:\WORK C:\DNLD
```

Figure 16-34

ArcMaster main display with menu toggled

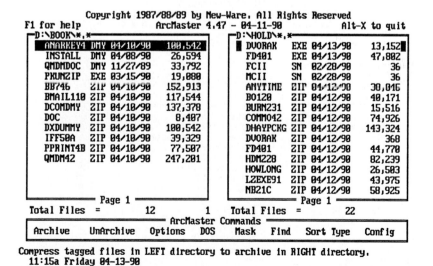

Compress tagged files in LEFT directory to archive in RIGHT directory.
11:15a Friday 04-13-90

After the program is loaded, the left window displays the files in the C:\WORK directory, and the right window shows the C:\DNLD directory. ArcMaster easily converts between any of the formats you are supporting. Want to convert an .LZH file to a .ZIP file? Tag the .LZH file, let ArcMaster know you want the default compression method to be ZIP, and ArcMaster quickly does the conversion.

ArcMaster's Online Help

ArcMaster has complete and detailed context-sensitive help throughout the program. There is also an index of help topics. You can be anywhere in the program and use F1 to activate the help system. Figure 16-35 shows ArcMaster's index of help topics.

With built-in help like this, it doesn't matter if you are using the Archive menu selection or the Config option; you can just press F1 and get immediate help. For those who don't have a mouse, the various key combinations are shown in the help system as well.

Figure 16-35

ArcMaster's help system index

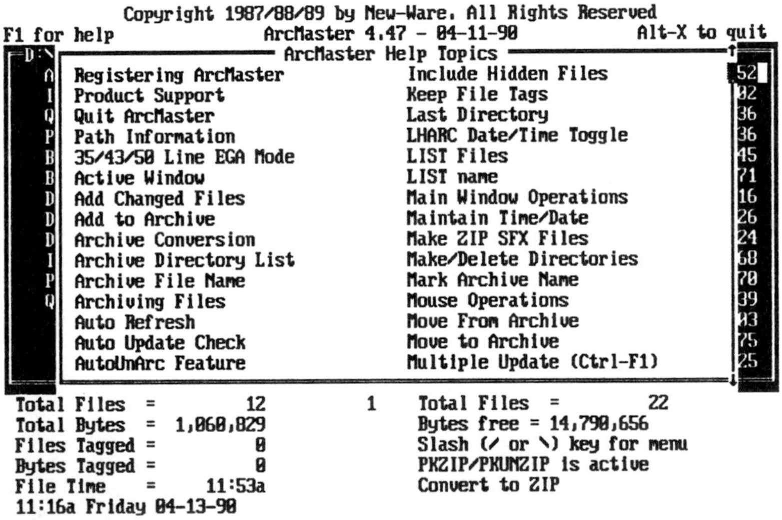

```
                Copyright 1987/88/89 by New-Ware. All Rights Reserved
F1 for help                  ArcMaster 4.47 - 04-11-90              Alt-X to quit
┌─D:\──────────────────── ArcMaster Help Topics ─────────────────────────┐
│ n  Registering ArcMaster        Include Hidden Files            52│
│ I  Product Support              Keep File Tags                  82│
│ Q  Quit ArcMaster               Last Directory                  36│
│ P  Path Information             LHARC Date/Time Toggle          36│
│ B  35/43/50 Line EGA Mode       LIST Files                      45│
│ B  Active Window                LIST name                       71│
│ D  Add Changed Files            Main Window Operations          16│
│ D  Add to Archive               Maintain Time/Date              26│
│ D  Archive Conversion           Make ZIP SFX Files              24│
│ I  Archive Directory List       Make/Delete Directories         68│
│ P  Archive File Name            Mark Archive Name               70│
│ Q  Archiving Files              Mouse Operations                39│
│    Auto Refresh                 Move From Archive               43│
│    Auto Update Check            Move to Archive                 75│
│    AutoUnArc Feature            Multiple Update (Ctrl-F1)       25│
└────────────────────────────────────────────────────────────────────────┘
Total Files  =        12     1   Total Files  =        22
Total Bytes  = 1,060,829         Bytes free = 14,790,656
Files Tagged =         0         Slash (/ or \) key for menu
Bytes Tagged =         0         PKZIP/PKUNZIP is active
File Time    =    11:53a         Convert to ZIP
11:16a Friday 04-13-90
```

Constantly Improving—Adding Features

ArcMaster doesn't sit still for long. Author John Newlin is always upgrading the program, fixing bugs, and adding features that have been requested by users. ArcMaster gives you a way to work with a variety of compression formats quickly and easily. In this time of multiple compressed file formats, a program like ArcMaster can really be a lifesaver.

John Newlin
New-Ware
8050 Camino Kiosco
San Diego, CA 92122
619-455-6225 (Voice)
619-455-5226 (BBS)
$35 registration; MasterCard and VISA accepted

SUMMING IT ALL UP

This chapter has covered the major file compression programs available. Tests were done with each program under a variety of conditions to give you an idea of how each performs. While only one set of tests was used, their results are indicative of each program's average performance.

You also looked at programs that make it easier for you to work with compressed files. Programs like PKZMENU and PAKF are specifically oriented around a given file format. At the same time, programs like Shez and ArcMaster are geared to handle a variety of formats and can convert between them. These are all excellent programs, so take your time and evaluate the options.

For now we'll leave the world of compression programs and utilities and move on to take a look at some special programs.

## CHAPTER SEVENTEEN

Special Programs

The number of programs marketed under the Shareware concept continues to grow each day. It is estimated that there are around 80,000 Shareware programs, but that number is steadily increasing. This doesn't include new releases, or updates of existing programs. Innovative new programs are being written by authors who have never been heard from before. Many of these authors are quite young—in their teens or early twenties. They are moving out and testing the waters of the Shareware market. As more program authors decide to try out the Shareware concept, the number of existing Shareware programs will continue to grow. As the number of programs available grows, you will have an increasingly better selection of Shareware programs to choose from. Before you examine some programs that are special in many ways, let's take a look at Shareware software in general.

BE FAIR TO SHAREWARE

Because it is often misunderstood, Shareware software often gets a bum rap from uninformed or inexperienced users. You'll hear comments like, "Shareware software just doesn't do what I want it to do..." or "Shareware programs can't be as good as commercial programs. . . ." If a Shareware program isn't doing what you want it to do, perhaps you are looking at the wrong program. In any given category there are many programs to choose from. Yes, there are really good Shareware programs and there are others that aren't so good. This is true among commercial programs as well. One of the purposes of this book is to make you aware of some of the better Shareware programs, to help save you time, money, and frustration.

There is no reason why Shareware programs can't be as good as commercial programs. Shareware programs *are* commercial programs— they are just being marketed in a different manner. It is true that Shareware programs don't have some of the things that retail commercial programs have: they don't have high prices, copy protection, expensive packaging, budgets for advertising, and middlemen to pay. There are inferior programs in the commercial market just as there are inferior programs in Shareware. The difference is that when you buy an inferior commercial program, you are stuck with it for good. If you find an inferior Shareware program, on the other hand, all you have to do is erase it and look for another one. In almost every case, you can find a Shareware program that will do what you want, and it will be cheaper than any of its commercial counterparts. Every now and then, you may even run across a Shareware program that is really special, a program that sets itself apart from the rest.

SOME SPECIAL PROGRAMS

This chapter is going to look at some programs that I think are a little bit *special*. Each one is special for different reasons. Perhaps it performs a function that no other program performs. Maybe it does something better than any other program of its type. A few of them are special just because they do what they do so well. Some of them could have been discussed in other chapters, but I felt that they were too exceptional for that. You may find that you like them too, or you may not. Remember, software is a matter of taste. I use all of them because they do a better job than other programs or provide things that other programs don't.

4DOS—What DOS Might Have Been

4DOS has been described as being "what DOS should have been." In vendor catalogs, in user group libraries, and on bulletin boards and commercial networks, you'll find 4DOS listed as "a COMMAND.COM replacement." You may also see it listed as "a really good shell program." Many people wonder how 4DOS can be considered a "shell" program. Tom Rawson, one of the coauthors of 4DOS, had this to say about the shell question.

"The biggest problem is that there have come to be two different definitions for the term *shell*. First you have the technical and historical definition of the term and then you have what might be called a *visual shell*. The technical definition of a shell is that it is a command interpreter—something that can run programs. What most people have come to know as a shell is the visual shell variety. They display directories and files and give users options to delete, tag, move, and so on. 4DOS is a shell based on the technical definition of the word, which is still defined that way in the UNIX world. 4DOS is a command interpreter, and as such, it is a shell."

The programs discussed in Chapter 14 would all fall under the visual shell category. 4DOS is a shell program that is intended to replace COMMAND.COM, the interpreter that comes with DOS. Because 4DOS is such a complex and unique program, you'll look at just some of the many things that it provides. This is an overview of a system that gives you many of the things that DOS might have given you if anyone had thought of them at the time.

Online Help

One very interesting feature of 4DOS is that it comes with its own online help system. If you want help with DOS, you'll need to buy a book, or maybe several. Not so with 4DOS. When 4DOS is installed, all you have to do is press F1 to bring up the main Help screen. Help can be utilized with the keyboard or a mouse. Select the 4DOS command that you need help with, and you'll be provided with command syntax and examples. Figure 17-1 shows the main Help screen of 4DOS.

Do some of these 4DOS commands look unfamiliar to you? If so, it's because 4DOS not only serves as a COMMAND.COM replacement, but it also has enhanced commands of its own. Unlike DOS, 4DOS gives you built-in help at the touch of a key.

Enhanced Commands

4DOS has taken some of the standard DOS commands and enhanced them so they are better and more efficient. When working with files, DOS lets you copy and delete files, for example. When you delete a file or group of files in DOS, all that happens is that the cursor moves down to a new prompt. What did you just delete? What if you made a mistake and accidentally deleted a file that you didn't want to delete? With DOS you have no way of knowing. DOS doesn't tell you anything; it just does it. The DEL command is just one command that 4DOS has enhanced. Figure 17-2 shows what you see when you delete some files with 4DOS installed.

4DOS tells you what it is deleting. It shows you the names of the files that you have told it to erase. Now, if you've accidentally erased a file, you know it, and you can try to unerase the file. The 4DOS COPY command gives you similar information. It shows you what files you are copying and where you are copying them to. You can have 4DOS prompt you if it is going to overwrite another file.

You can't move a file with DOS because there is no such command. 4DOS, on the other hand, does have a MOVE command. Like the 4DOS COPY and DEL commands, the MOVE command shows you what it's doing. Figure 17-3 shows the MOVE command in action. Once again, you

---

Figure 17-1

The main Help screen of 4DOS

```
══════════════════ 4DOS 3.0 HELP ══════════════════
┌──────────────────────────────────────────────────┐
│ (c) 1990   COLOR      FIND      MODE      SETDOS   │
│ -HELP-     COMP       FOR       MORE      SETLOCAL │
│ -KEYS-     COPY       FORMAT    MOVE      SHARE    │
│ -MOUSE-    CTTY       FREE      PATH      SHIFT    │
│ -EDITING-  DATE       GLOBAL    PAUSE     SORT     │
│ -VARS-     DEL        GOSUB     POPD      SUBST    │
│ ?          DELAY      GOTO      PRINT     SWAPPING │
│ ALIAS      DESCRIBE   GRAFTABL  PROMPT    SYS      │
│ ASSIGN     DIR        HISTORY   PUSHD     TEE      │
│ ATTRIB     DIRS       IF        QUIT      TEXT     │
│ BACKUP     DISKCOMP   IFF       RD        TIME     │
│ BEEP       DISKCOPY   INKEY     REM       TIMER    │
│ BREAK      DRAWBOX    INPUT     REN       TREE     │
│ CALL       DRAWHLINE  JOIN      RENAME    TYPE     │
│ CANCEL     DRAWVLINE  KEYSTACK  RESTORE   UNALIAS  │
│ CD         ECHO       LABEL     RETURN    UNSET    │
│ CDD        ENDLOCAL   LIST      RMDIR     VER      │
│ CHCP       ERASE      LOG       SCREEN    VERIFY   │
│ CHDIR      ESET       MD        SCRPUT    VOL      │
│ CHKDSK     EXCEPT     MEMORY    SELECT    XCOPY    │
│ CLS        EXIT       MKDIR     SET       Y        │
└──────────────────────────────────────────────────┘
```

Figure 17-2

Display showing 4DOS deleting files

```
c:\dnld>dir

 Volume in drive C is MASTER FILE
 Directory of  c:\dnld\*.*
.              <DIR>      2-20-90  13:34
..             <DIR>      2-20-90  13:34
asp2.rep        1771      5-06-90  20:42
dmp.nte          897      5-06-90  10:29
figs21.txt       193      5-07-90  14:53
heads21.txt     1208      5-07-90  14:50
poker.dat       1998      5-06-90  19:53
      10,240 bytes in 7 file(s)
   19,224,576 bytes free

c:\dnld>del *.*
c:\dnld\*.* : Are you sure ? (Y/N) : Y
Deleting c:\dnld\heads21.txt
Deleting c:\dnld\figs21.txt
Deleting c:\dnld\dmp.nte
Deleting c:\dnld\asp2.rep
Deleting c:\dnld\poker.dat

c:\dnld>
```

can see what files you are moving and where you are moving them to. If you've made an error, you know about it.

Better Batch Commands

DOS batch files can be very powerful. 4DOS batch files can knock the socks off of DOS batch files. 4DOS batch files are totally compatible with DOS batch files, but there are some extra 4DOS batch file commands that can make batch files do spectacular things. Take a look at these extra batch file commands.

- **BEEP** Beep the speaker at the specified frequency and for the specified duration.

- **CALL** Execute nested batch files without loading a secondary copy of the command processor.

- **CANCEL** Terminate nested batch file processing.

- **DELAY**   Wait for the specified period of time before continuing batch processing.

- **DRAWBOX/DRAWHLINE/DRAWVLINE**   Draw boxes, horizontal, and vertical lines in single or double widths, in your choice of colors. These commands automatically make connectors when crossing other lines.

- **GOSUB/RETURN**   Call subroutines within a batch file.

- **IF**   Allow many new comparison tests, (including less than, greater than, and so on) and tests for memory, disk, and display type.

- **IFF/THEN/ELSEIFF/ELSE/ENDIFF**   Allow for nested IF/THEN/ELSE tests in batch files and aliases and support all of the new IF tests.

- **INPUT/INKEY**   Input variables from the keyboard while in a batch file, with an optional timeout period.

- **KEYSTACK**   Send keystrokes to a program, as if entered from the keyboard.

- **QUIT**   Exit the current batch file.

Figure 17-3

Moving files with 4DOS

```
Now In The Download Directory!

c:\dnld>dir

Volume in drive C is MASTER FILE
Directory of  c:\dnld\*.*
.             <DIR>      2-28-98  13:34
..            <DIR>      2-28-98  13:34
dcominfo.doc   8891      8-25-89  12:12
ed.dat         4833      5-07-98  14:29
graphic.log   26985      4-16-98   7:38
pianoman.nte    859      5-03-98  15:52
scroll.sav     9911      5-04-98  11:32
     53,248 bytes in 7 file(s)
  19,236,864 bytes free

c:\dnld>move *.* \tst1
c:\dnld\dcominfo.doc -> c:\tst1\dcominfo.doc
c:\dnld\graphic.log -> c:\tst1\graphic.log
c:\dnld\pianoman.nte -> c:\tst1\pianoman.nte
c:\dnld\scroll.sav -> c:\tst1\scroll.sav
c:\dnld\ed.dat -> c:\tst1\ed.dat
     5 file(s) moved

c:\dnld>
```

- **SCREEN**   Position the cursor and (optionally) display text.

- **SCRPUT**   Position the cursor and display text in specified colors.

- **SETLOCAL/ENDLOCAL**   Define a local environment within a batch file, saving the original environment, disk, and directory, and restoring them when finished.

- **SHIFT**   Optionally specify how many positions to shift, including reverse shifts.

- **TEXT/ENDTEXT**   Display a block of text.

Without the aid of any other utilities, you can do amazing things with your batch files. You can create menus that are in color, surrounded by boxes, and wait for the user to input something. Based on that input, you can have all kinds of conditional branching, you can generate a beep if the user makes an error, and much more. 4DOS can also have special batch files with a .BTM (batch to memory) extension, and these execute several times faster than regular batch files. It's easy to see that the extra 4DOS batch file commands give you endless possibilities.

DOS Command Editor and Aliases

Many people like to use a DOS command line editor and one that provides the ability to create your own commands. 4DOS has these functions built right in. You can use the cursor keys to recall DOS commands that you've issued in the past. As for the 4DOS alias function, it can be used to do many things. An alias can include multiple commands, can include variables like %1, and can even call another alias. Let's say you wanted a simple command to copy files from drive A to the directory of your choice on drive C. We'll call the alias ACC for "A: Copy to C:;" and it would look like this:

```
ALIAS ACC copy a:\%1 c:\%2
```

With this alias defined, it is now easy to copy any file(s) from drive A to any directory on drive C. For example, if you wanted to copy all of the .DAT files from drive A to your C:\DNLD directory, here is what you would enter:

```
C>ACC *.DAT DNLD
```

4DOS aliases can be used extensively to turn a complex set of commands into just a few keystrokes. You can have multiple commands in one alias as well. Each command is separated by the default symbol, ^, but you can change this if you like. Here is an example of an alias that loads a file into PC-Write.

```
ALIAS PCW D: ^ cd \PCWRT ^ CLS ^ ED %1
```

If, at the command line, you entered

```
C>PCW TEST.DAT
```

this alias would switch to your D drive, change to the D:\PCWRT directory, clear the screen, and load PC-Write with the file TEST.DAT. If you just entered **PCW**, it would do everything, and PC-Write would ask you to supply a filename to edit. That's getting a lot done in a few keystrokes. 4DOS aliases can be as complex or simple as you want them to be.

Scanning 4DOS Features

4DOS is easy on system memory and can utilize EMS as well. It uses less than 4K of RAM for its resident portion and less than 1K if you use XMS swapping. Thus, 4DOS doesn't hog your RAM, but rather it tries to use as little as possible. Another interesting feature of 4DOS is that you can create your own executable file extensions. What does this mean? Normally, you can only execute files that have extensions of .BAT, .COM, or .EXE (with 4DOS you can execute .BTM files also). 4DOS allows you to define additional extensions and the programs they should invoke. For example, you could set it up so that when you enter any file with the extension of .DOC, your editor would spring to life.

Ever forget what a particular program does? 4DOS has a DESCRIBE function that helps you out. 4DOS allows you to provide descriptions for each of your files and directories. These descriptions are displayed with the filenames whenever you use the SELECT or DIR command. In addition, if you rename, copy, move, or erase a file, the description goes right along with it.

4DOS also gives you the ability to enter multiple commands on one line. Need to alter your PATH or any other environment variable? 4DOS allows you to edit any environment variable, add to the PATH, change where your DSZLOG goes, and more. Monochrome, CGA, EGA, and VGA display adapters are all supported. 4DOS can also deal with any number of columns and lines per screen. Thus, you can be in 80 × 60 mode with no problem. How much more can one program have?

Some Exciting Extras   4DOS has its own logging capabilities. If you turn the log on, it will track every program that you use on your system. Another unique feature is that 4DOS has a built-in timer function. You can use this to time how long a program takes to execute, how long it takes to compile a QuickBASIC program, or anything else you like. You can start the function by simply entering **Timer On** at the 4DOS prompt. If you like, you could redirect this to a file so you have a record of it. When you are finished timing, you can enter **Timer Off**, and the function will show you the total elapsed time. If you send it to a file, the file will contain the start time, stop time, and total elapsed time. 4DOS also has its own built-in file viewing capability, called LIST. Using this function, you can look at text, search for text in the file being viewed, and also print it.

Pulling It All Together

4DOS is a complete package that offers many enhancements over DOS. Many commands have parameters that you can set to customize the display. 4DOS has powerful batch files, aliases, online help, command line editing and recall, a timer, a file lister, a log function, and enhanced commands that provide you with more information. Even though version 3.0 was just released in April, 1990, the beta test group is already working on more new functions. If you haven't given 4DOS a try, you owe it to yourself to do so. This is a very special program in every sense of the word.

Rex Conn and Tom Rawson
J.P. Software
Box 1470
East Arlington, MA 02174
617-646-3975 (Voice)
617-646-0904 (Fax)
73577,243 CompuServe ID

$50 registration includes:

A disk with the latest version of 4DOS, registered to you

One copy of the printed and bound 4DOS manual

A free upgrade to the next version of 4DOS (future upgrades will be available for downloading from a wide variety of sources; if you do not have a modem, there will be a minimal processing charge to obtain an upgrade on diskette)

Technical support via electronic mail or telephone

A subscription to the 4DOS newsletter

BackMail

BackMail is primarily a mail program that functions in the background while you work in the foreground. It can also transfer files. It is a complete point-to-point mail system that has valuable uses among individuals or in a business setting. Using only 34K of DOS RAM, BackMail sits in the background waiting to work for you. It can save you time, money, and lots of irritation. BackMail eliminates phone tag with friends and associates. It gives you the ability to handle mail messages and files in the least amount of time necessary. You can pop it up, write a quick message, tell BackMail who to send it to, and go back to work. Here's a more in-depth look at how BackMail works.

The BackMail Concept

BackMail is called a *point-to-point* mail system because it delivers mail and files from one point to another. It has many options that are configurable. You can configure the availability time of your individual BackMail. Other BackMail systems will honor the times that you have set. Your BackMail maintains a dialing directory of the people you call. Your BackMail is keyed to the phone number you assign it. The phone number is your BackMail address. If an unknown caller calls into your BackMail, you can easily add their information to your dialing directory (the first time anyone calls your BackMail, they are called an *unknown caller*). With BackMail, you don't get an answering machine; you don't get put on hold; you simply enter your message and tell BackMail who you want it to go to. You can tag a file that you want to send to someone and BackMail will handle that too. You can go back to doing what you were doing, knowing that the messages you've written will be handled by BackMail.

BackMail will not forget about a message. If it can't get through, it will try later. You may not catch someone on the phone, but you will catch them with BackMail when they sit down at their computer. You can configure BackMail for the times you want it to be available for receiving mail. Let's say you put in an availability time of 8:00 A.M. to 10:00 P.M. When you exchange mail with other BackMails, their dialing directories are automatically updated with your information. When others send BackMail to you, their BackMail will know that it can't send any before 8:00 A.M.

Features and Functions of BackMail

With BackMail you can keep old messages for later review or delete them. You can forward a note to other BackMail users. In addition, BackMail is configurable in many ways, from the colors it uses to what your BackMail header will display. It works with all Hayes-compatible modems and registration is easy. How easy? You use BackMail to call a toll-free number with your registration and credit card information. Your Shareware version is automatically upgraded during that phone call.

BackMail really makes personal communication easy and hassle-free. I like it so well that a copy is included on the disks you can send for with the coupon at the back of the book. Try it out and if you like the idea, register your copy. Give a copy to your friends who have computers and exchanging mail with them will become much easier.

Using BackMail in Business

To give you an idea of how BackMail works, let's use an example. You and three friends start a business. You are in New York and the others are in Chicago, Denver, and Los Angeles. You are on an important project, so you have to keep each other up to date. You are each in a different time zone. Let's call your partners C, D, and L to match the cities they are in. You could play telephone tag with them all day, but you are going to use BackMail. You start working and decide you want Ms. L to know about something as soon as she wakes up. You hit a hot key and up pops the BackMail menu. Figure 17-4 shows the BackMail menu.

You enter a note to Ms. L and then go back to work. Working in the background, BackMail calls Ms. L's computer and delivers the message,

Figure 17-4

BackMail's pop-up menu

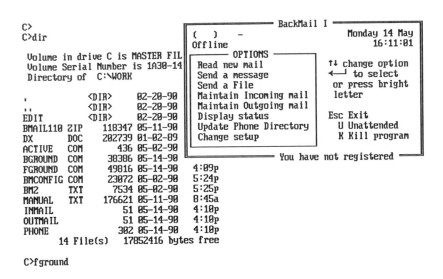

picking up a file that she left for you at the same time. When Ms. L gets up and goes to her machine, she sees a message on her screen, "You Have New Mail Waiting," so she pops up her BackMail, finds your message, reads it, and decides that Mr. D should know about this too. All she has to do is forward your note. BackMail increments the header—it shows who originated the message and who the receiver was. If a message is forwarded several times, the person receiving it will always know who the original sender was and who else has seen the note. When Mr. D gets the message, he reads it and sends a message of his own off to Mr. C. Figure 17-5 shows the editing screen of BackMail.

Ms. L takes care of what was in your message, pops up her BackMail, and sends a message to you. The beauty of BackMail is that the four of you can work on a project, keep each other informed, and yet do it in the minimum amount of time. You can use your computer while BackMail handles the messages and files in the background. You can save time and money by avoiding needless chatter. When you have to let any of your partners know something, you can just BackMail it to them in a note.

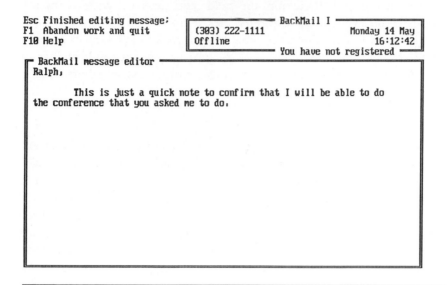

Figure 17-5

The editing screen of BackMail

```
Esc Finished editing message:         ━━ BackMail I ━━
F1  Abandon work and quit     ┌─────────────────────────────────┐
F10 Help                      │ (303) 222-1111      Monday 14 May│
                              │ Offline                 16:12:42 │
                              └──── You have not registered ─────┘
 ┌─ BackMail message editor ──────────────────────────────────────┐
 │ Ralph,                                                          │
 │                                                                 │
 │         This is just a quick note to confirm that I will be able to do │
 │ the conference that you asked me to do.                         │
 │                                                                 │
 │                                                                 │
 │                                                                 │
 │                                                                 │
 │                                                                 │
 │                                                                 │
 │                                                                 │
 │                                                                 │
 │                                                                 │
 │                                                                 │
 │                                                                 │
 └─────────────────────────────────────────────────────────────────┘
```

They can respond directly back to you, forward your note to one of the other partners, or do both. In many ways, BackMail is like having a paperless fax.

In the example just used, it could just as easily be you and three friends keeping in touch, with no business involved. BackMail would, however, be excellent for use by large businesses. Why? Because BackMail recognizes telephone extensions. Thus, a company might have one main number and 2,000 extensions. No problem. By using BackMail you could cut down on office noise. A person working at a computer on the fifth floor could BackMail a memo to a person on the second floor. That person could forward multiple copies of the memo to other BackMails located all around the building. Employees wouldn't miss important messages from other employees because their BackMail would catch them while they were away from their machine. They would come back to see that "You Have New Mail Waiting" message.

If you have clients you need to get information from each day, BackMail could handle that too. Set up a BackMail on your client's machine. Using BackMail you can put a message or file on hold so the message or file does not get sent unless the receiver calls you. In this way, your clients would not have to pay for exchanging the information with you. They could put their file on hold and one of your company BackMails could call in once a day to pick it up. If you have a business, you might want to consider using BackMail to make mail exchange more time and cost efficient. BackMail is already in use by several branches of the U.S. Armed Forces, government agencies, businesses, and individuals.

A Hub and a Daemon

Alethic Software, the makers of BackMail, is currently working with another company to develop some interesting additions for use with BackMail. A BackMail hub is being developed and will be available by the time you read this. A *hub system* can be used as a central message point for BackMail users. For example, I could call a hub and leave a message for John Smith. When John Smith calls into the hub, it will recognize him and send him all mail that is marked for him. A hub system would be useful to businesses and other organizations that have many computers using BackMail, but where all of the computers are not always manned—for example, companies that have several shifts. If you are working and the person you want to send a message to has gone home for the day, you could direct your message to the hub. The intended receiver of your message might be in the habit of always checking the hub for new BackMail messages. When they returned the next morning and checked the hub, they would receive your message. The hub will open up many possibilities for the expanded use of BackMail.

Another project that Alethic Software is working on is called a *daemon*. This is being developed due to popular demand from government agencies and some corporations. The daemon is a special version of BackMail that performs one specific function. It is told to pop up every so often, for example, once a month, and send a specified file to a certain location. Then it disappears until the next time it is scheduled to perform. It cannot receive mail or do anything else; it simply sends the data and retreats. The daemon will be available by the time you read this.

BackMail in Your Future

The BackMail concept of point-to-point mail is rapidly catching on. Businesses are finding that BackMail cuts down on the use of paper and eliminates the need for expensive interoffice messaging systems. BackMail received an Editor's Choice award from *PC Magazine* and is catching the eye of many corporations, the government, and individuals. It's a great way to handle projects that use the networking approach. BackMail and the concept of point-to-point mail are becoming very popular. Check out BackMail, and if you find you use it, please register. This may be the wave of the future in messaging.

Alethic Software
2337 Princess Place
Halifax, N.S. B3K 4K5 CANADA
902-423-9860 (Voice)
$30 registration; $10 printed manual
Registration form is included in the program. You can register online by filling out the form and including a valid MasterCard or VISA number. On the form, be sure to mark whether or not you want the manual. Once completed, BackMail will do the rest.

Log

Many people need to keep track of the time they spend on various tasks or projects. This is especially true when they are billing others for the time. It's also nice to be able to print out a nice-looking bill that summarizes the work that was done. There are quite a few time and billing programs around, but many of them lack some essential features—for example, a way to add extra charges to a bill that don't involve time, such as any long distance phone calls, expenses for materials, and so on. The program, Log, by Chris Laforet, has all of the time and billing features that most people would want or need. Here's a look at what Log can do for you.

The Features You Need

To begin with, Log can handle over 32,000 individual accounts or projects. Some similar programs can only handle as few as 25. You can add new accounts, including name, address, city, state, zip code, the billing rate, a project name, and a billing increment. Figure 17-6 shows you what this New Client entry screen looks like.

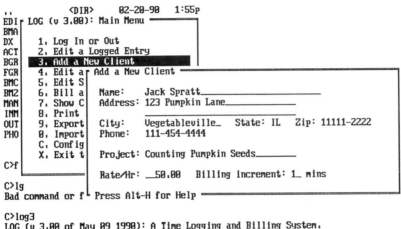

Figure 17-6

Log's New Client entry screen

```
..         <DIR>    02-20-90   1:55p
EDI┌LOG (v 3.00): Main Menu ─────┐
BMA│
DX │  1. Log In or Out
ACT│  2. Edit a Logged Entry
BGR│ ▓3. Add a New Client▓▓▓▓▓
FGR│  4. Edit a┌Add a New Client ──────────────────────┐
BMC│  5. Edit S│
BM2│  6. Bill a│ Name:    Jack Spratt_____
MAN│  7. Show C│ Address: 123 Pumpkin Lane_____
INM│  8. Print │          _____
OUT│  9. Export│ City:    Vegetableville_  State: IL  Zip: 11111-2222
PHO│  0. Import│ Phone:   111-454-4444
   │  C. Config│
   │  X. Exit t│ Project: Counting Pumpkin Seeds_____
C>f│           │
   └───────────│ Rate/Hr: __50.00   Billing increment: 1_ mins
C>lg            │
Bad command or f└ Press Alt-H for Help ════════════════════┘

C>log3
LOG (v 3.00 of May 09 1990): A Time Logging and Billing System.
Copyright (c) 1987-90, Chris Laforet Software. All Rights Reserved.
```

Log also lets you edit an existing record. If you make a mistake, you can always go back and fix it. There is also a special selection that allows you to edit information about yourself (or your company). Log gives you a host of features that let you handle your data efficiently. This is a program that has been very carefully thought out.

Log Options

When you call Log from the DOS prompt, a menu of options appears. You can select what you want to do and then exit Log. Here is a list of the Log options:

- Log in or out
- Edit a logged entry
- Add a new client
- Edit a client

- Edit self/company info

- Bill an expense

- Show current billing

- Print current billing

- Export billing logs

- Import billing logs

- Exit this program

You can use number 7 to take a look at how much work has been done on a particular project. Another excellent feature allows you to both import and export data with Log.

Let's say you have been working on a project and using Log on your main computer to keep track of the time. Now, you are going to go out in the field with a laptop, but you still want to keep track of the time accurately. All you have to do is export that logged information from the copy on your main machine and import it into a version of Log on your laptop. When you're finished in the field, you just reverse the process — export from the laptop and import into the version of Log on your main computer. The client's record is intact and accurate. When a project is finished, you can print the bill and delete the records if you like. Log also has a TSR portion that allows you to do some things with Log from anywhere on your system. Let's take a look at that.

Resident Logging Features

Log is tremendously handy for anyone who wants to bill for the time they spend working on something. Computer consultants, lawyers, and many other individuals and businesses can benefit from the features found in Log. To make Log even more convenient to use, there is also a TSR module. Using only 40K of DOS RAM, the TSR portion of Log can be popped up anywhere.

RLOG has only the most necessary features. You can log in or out, add a new client, or edit a client. Let's say that you're a lawyer and you're using an editing program to write a letter to a friend. You get a call and

---

DOCTOR'S NOTE

While Log is a great program for tracking time and billing, it can be used for other things as well. For example, if you want to keep track of how much time you spend working on a program that you are writing, you could enter a new "client" as "New Program" and log in with that. Set the hourly charge to $0.00. When you are finished, log out, and Log will keep a running history of how many hours you put into the program. One thing that I use Log for is to keep track of time and money when people are doing work for *me*. Yes, it's designed to keep track of how much money someone else owes you, but you can easily reverse the numbers and see how much you owe them. For example, say I hire a young man to do some work around my office. I set up an account for him, and for the hourly charge I enter how much I'm paying him. When he comes to do the work I log him in, and when he is done I log him out. When it's time to pay him I just have Log print out a bill and I can see exactly how much I owe him for doing work for me. Log can be used to track the time you spend on any project or to keep track of time for people who are doing hourly work for you.

---

it's a client wanting your legal advice. Without having to get out of the editing program, you can pop up RLOG and log that client in. When you're finished you can log that client out and go back to your letter. No wasted time and no missed fee. The RLOG module can also be loaded into high memory on systems that take advantage of it.

Built-In Help System

Although Log is a very easy program to use, the author has still included a full help system complete with index. Just about any question you have about Log and its usage is answered in the help screens. Figure 17-7 shows the Help Index found in Log.

From here you can move through the help screens and get help on any aspect of using Log, whether it be command line parameters or editing functions. This is another feature that isn't provided by similar programs.

Log Equals Versatility

Log can have multiple functions depending on what you need it to do. It can be used to simply track how much time you spend doing different

---

Figure 17-7

Log's help screen index

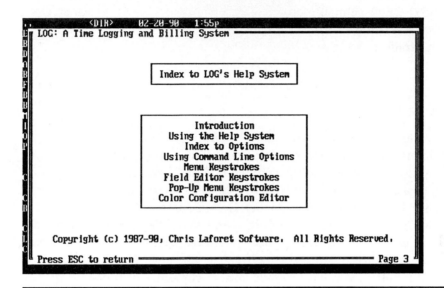

```
..          <DIR>     02-20-90   1:55p
L┌ LOG: A Time Logging and Billing System
B│
D│
A│
B│               ┌─────────────────────────────────┐
F│               │   Index to LOG's Help System    │
B│               └─────────────────────────────────┘
B│
M│
I│               ┌─────────────────────────────────┐
O│               │          Introduction           │
P│               │      Using the Help System      │
 │               │        Index to Options         │
 │               │    Using Command Line Options   │
 │               │         Menu Keystrokes         │
C│               │      Field Editor Keystrokes    │
C│               │       Pop-Up Menu Keystrokes    │
B│               │     Color Configuration Editor  │
 │               └─────────────────────────────────┘
C│
L│     Copyright (c) 1987-90, Chris Laforet Software.  All Rights Reserved.
C│
 └ Press ESC to return ═══════════════════════════════ Page 3
```

things on the computer, for example, communications, word processing, playing games, and so on. You can also use it to keep track of how much time someone has spent working for you and how much you owe them. Whether you have a large business or are a one-person consulting firm, you can use Log to track over 32,000 projects. Records can be edited, imported, and exported easily. The reports generated by Log have a nice appearance, and they include information on you and the client, and a breakdown of the work that was done. Using RLOG, you can pop up log at any time, which is a real convenience. Throw in features like online help, configurability of the colors, and being able to view a current billing, and you have a really complete time and billing program. I use Log all the time and I recommend it.

Chris Laforet
Chris Laforet Software
511D Poplar Street

Graham, NC 27253
76120,110 CompuServe ID
laforet BIX (E-mail)
XTX74591 GEnie (E-mail)
919-226-6984 (BBS)
$25 registration

Back & Forth

Simply defined, Back & Forth is a *task switching* program. It allows you to have many programs loaded at the same time. This is done by creating windows, or partitions, using your DOS RAM, expanded memory, disk space, or a combination of these. For example, you could have your word processor loaded in window number 1, your communications program in window 2, a spreadsheet in window 3, and so on. Back & Forth saves you time and effort and maximizes your system resources. For example, if you are using your word processor and realize you have to call a BBS to get some information, you have to save your document, exit the word processor, and load your communications program. You make your call and get what you need. Now you have to exit the communications program, load your word processor, and go back to what you were doing. With Back & Forth, it's much easier. You have the word processor in one window and your communications program in another. When you need to call the BBS you simply toggle over to the communications program, which is waiting for you in another window, make your call, log off, and then go back to your word processor. Look at the number of steps you've saved. Sound good? Well, Back & Forth can do much more besides.

Back & Forth Features

There are several commercial task switching programs, but they don't offer all of the things that you get with Back & Forth. Back & Forth has an excellent setup menu where you can define memory usage, disk usage, the hot keys to be used, and how many windows to open. Figure 17-8 shows the setup menu of Back & Forth.

You control how much RAM, how much EMS, how much disk space, and what drives to use. This puts you in full control of your system resources. Back & Forth only uses an average of 14K of DOS RAM, and it can be loaded into high memory. For defining the hot keys, you get a true

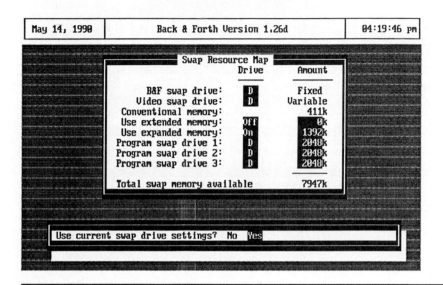

Figure 17-8

Back & Forth's memory setup screen

| May 14, 1990 | Back & Forth Version 1.26d | 04:19:46 pm |

```
                    Swap Resource Map
                                Drive      Amount
             B&F swap drive:      D        Fixed
           Video swap drive:      D        Variable
        Conventional memory:               411k
        Use extended memory:    Off          0k
        Use expanded memory:     On        1392k
       Program swap drive 1:      D        2048k
       Program swap drive 2:      D        2048k
       Program swap drive 3:      D        2048k

       Total swap memory available         7947k
```

| Use current swap drive settings?   No Yes |

representation of the keyboard, and as you select keys they are high-lighted. To make your work easier, Back & Forth also has a very nice cut and paste feature that lets you cut data from one window and paste it into another. Let's take a quick look at that.

The Cut and Paste Option It's always nice to be able to take some information from one program and put it into another one. Back & Forth's Cut and Paste function allows you to alter the format so that data can be transferred more easily. Figure 17-9 shows you Back & Forth's Cut and Paste control screen.

For example, you can cut a block of cells from a spreadsheet and store it, and then cut text from a database and store it in word processor format. If you were to then paste the cut buffer into a word processor, the spreadsheet cells would be in a rectangle format and the word processor could format the text from the database into paragraphs.

Figure 17-9

Back & Forth's Cut and Paste control screen

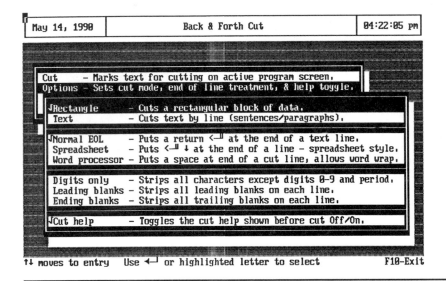

Many Extra Features
Commercial task switching programs do the job of task switching and that's about it—not so with Back & Forth. This is a task switcher plus a lot more. Some of Back & Forth's other standard features include

- Ability to add a keyboard click
- DOS command line editor
- Keyboard accelerator
- Ability to load into high memory
- Automatic recognition of and compatibility with 4DOS
- Compatibility with UltraVision by Personics
- Configurable colors
- Enhanced mouse support
- Screen blanker

- Map of already defined hot keys
- Ability to use EGA/VGA 25/43/50 line modes
- Auto-loading of programs

Another feature of Back & Forth not found in the commercial programs is that it will "clean up" EMS behind itself. Thus, when you close a Back & Forth window, any EMS it was using is reclaimed for your use.

Other task switching programs require a great deal of RAM or disk space to swap out screens if you have an EGA or VGA graphics adapter. Back & Forth can handle these types of screens easily and use approximately 66 percent less RAM or disk space than its closest competitors. This is just another way that Back & Forth optimizes the use of your system's resources. Nothing is wasted. The total amount of swap space that Back & Forth can use is 16 megabytes, and you can have up to 20 Back & Forth windows open at one time. Back & Forth's full support of the popular program, UltraVision makes it even more appealing.

Moving Forward with Back & Forth

If you are looking for a way to be more productive and do things more efficiently, you might want to look into a task switching program. Compare Back & Forth to both its Shareware and commercial competition. For the low amount of RAM it uses, the many extra features it offers, and its configurability, it can't be beat. The authors, Shane and Sandi Stump, work constantly to improve the program and actively solicit the input of users. This is another program that's on the move and rapidly gaining popularity among all levels of users. Be sure to take a good look at Back & Forth.

Shane and Sandi Stump
Progressive Solutions, Inc.
P.O. Box 276125
San Antonio, TX 78227
800-833-4400 (Orders)
512-670-1061 (Voice)
512-670-0954 (BBS)
512-670-1061 (Fax)
$50 registration includes printed manual, latest version of the program on 5.25-inch disk, and phone support

Anarkey

Anarkey is a DOS command line editor that does much more than just let you edit past DOS commands. It assists you in command line completion and execution, and it also supports powerful synonyms called AKAs. *AKAs* let you define a single word or key sequence that can represent a whole string of commands. Anarkey was the first DOS command line editor to take advantage of EMS, thereby giving it a very small overhead. If EMS is used, Anarkey will generally use less than 1K of your precious DOS RAM. That's a real benefit, as similar programs generally take 12K or more. Anarkey can reduce the number of keystrokes that you have to type in. Let's take a look at some of its features.

Anarkey—Loaded with Power

Anarkey will help you when you are working at the DOS prompt, and it can make it much easier to run programs. You can type in part of a command and Anarkey will complete it for you. If you like, Anarkey also has an option whereby it will not only complete the command for you, but will execute the command immediately. Ever wish you could alter one of your DOS environment variables? There are some utilities that are designed just to do that, but Anarkey has that function included. You can easily edit any environment variable, change your path and your prompt, and much more. Here is a listing of Anarkey's functions, taken from the manual.

- Command line editing features comparable to those found in expensive word processors
- Storage and retrieval of past command lines
- Sequential access of retrieved commands
- Character matching where you enter a portion of the line and have Anarkey search through the buffer for a matching completion
- A text substitution capability called an AKA
- Multiple commands per line (even from a batch file)
- A 255-character command line
- Filename completion, including directory and program names
- Environment variable editing

- Storing Anarkey in expanded memory

- A non-blinking cursor

- Configurable keystroke assignments

- A Mega-Completion-Key that analyzes the input line, determines the type of completion operation you are attempting, and does it for you automatically

- Writing the command line history buffer and AKA definitions to disk files

- Loading the history buffer and AKA definitions from disk files at any time

- Comprehensive UNIX switchar conventions

- Invoking Anarkey functions from a batch file

It's easy to see that Anarkey gives you a wide range of functions that can make your daily tasks a lot easier. Let's examine some of the things that Anarkey can do in a bit more detail.

History Buffer Functions

Anarkey's *history buffer* provides the ability to retrieve any command that you've entered previously from the keyboard. You can then edit the line or simply execute it again. In the course of a day, this feature can save you a lot of extra keystrokes. The lines that you enter from DOS are stored in the history buffer for later recall. If you have lines that are made up of multiple commands, they are filed in the buffer as just one line. This lets you reexecute a complicated command line over and over. You can determine how large the history buffer should be. Lines are stored in sequence, ranging from top to bottom. When the buffer is filled, the first lines stored will be moved out of the buffer to make room for new ones. The history buffer gives Anarkey some very powerful possibilities.

Retrieving Characters

Anarkey's ability to match characters is extremely powerful. You can enter just a few characters of a command line and Anarkey will search the history buffer for a line whose first characters match the ones you've entered. When Anarkey finds a match, the entire line is then retrieved and put up on the screen. It might help to point out that when Anarkey searches through its history buffer, the search is not case-sensitive. Thus, you could enter **AN** and it would still find "an" in a stored line. There are times when Anarkey might find a line that is not the one you had in mind, but one that has similar characters at the beginning. No problem. You can continue the search, and Anarkey will find other lines that match. You can enter one character and Anarkey can find the line and complete it.

Getting Directory Names for You

The default key for the function that completes directory names is F7. When you use F7, Anarkey searches for a directory name rather than a command. When it finds a match, it will put the directory name at the cursor position. If Anarkey hasn't found the directory name you want— for example, if you have four directories that start with the letter "D"— you can use F7 again. When you do this, Anarkey will bring up one of the other directories that match. You'll find yourself using this command over and over.

Lines with Multiple Commands

By default, DOS only lets you enter one command on a line. Anarkey lets you enter multiple commands on one line because it has a way of knowing where one command ends and another begins. The only restriction is that you can't have a line that is longer than 255 characters. By default, Anarkey uses the semicolon (;) as a command separator. An example might be in order. Let's say you want to clear the screen, change to the C:\WORD directory, load the VDE editor with the file TEST.DAT, and when you're finished, erase any .BAK files. Using the multiple command line option of Anarkey, you'd have something that looks like this:

```
CLS ; CD \WORD ; VDE TEST.DAT ; DEL *.BAK
```

As you can see, this is like generating a batch file that doesn't take up disk space. Lines like these can be included in Anarkey's AKAs—letting one tiny command stretch out into a complex series of multiple commands.

Editing the Environment

There are times when you'd like to change one or more of your environment variables, which can be a hassle. With Anarkey you can look at your environment variables and edit them. One very handy advantage to this feature is being able to alter your DOS PATH. How do you do it? Easy! The default key to activate this feature is F9. Let's say you use DSZ (for Zmodem), and you want to change the directory where the DSZLOG is located. You could enter this at the DOS prompt:

```
C>SET DSZLOG<F9>
```

You enter the variable and press the F9 key where <F9> is shown. When you hit F9, Anarkey searches the environment and finds the current value of DSZLOG and displays it for you on the screen. Now you can edit it and change it to the new setting. When you've finished, simply hit ENTER and your new environment variable is set. You can do this with any environment variable—PATH, for example. All you'd have to enter is,

```
C>PATH<F9>
```

and your entire PATH would appear on the screen, ready for you to edit and save. This is a nice feature to have available if you use a lot of environment variables.

The AKAs of Anarkey

Anarkey's AKA function lets you define your own commands. The commands you define can be as simple as shortening something like the COPY command to "CO" or as complex as multiple command lines that accept variables. Here are just a few of my Anarkey AKAs, showing some of the things you can do with them.

```
:ACC dx a:\%1 /copy:C:\%2
:BCC dx b:\%1 /copy:C:\%2
:ACD dx a:\%1 /copy:D:\%2
:BCD dx a:\%1 /copy:D:\%2
:CAP cd \caplus
:CK chkdsk /f;
:CL cls
:CMA dx %1 /move:a:\
:CO C:dx /v- /p- %1 /copy:C:\%2 %3 %4 %5 %6 %7 %8 %9
:CT cd \ ; cls
:CTC dx %1 /move:c:\%2
:DRA dir a:
```

```
:DRB dir b:
:DCM cd \dcom;cls
:DCMIN dcom /M /A /EMM /L /mf=MAIN
:DELV dx  %1 %2 %3 %4 %5 %6 %7 %8 %9 /del
:DN cd \dnld;cls
:DP dx /p
:DR dx
:DRS dx/single
:DRF cd \drffbk;cls
:E cd \work\edit;cls
```

Once you start defining your own AKAs, you won't know what to do without them. You may find yourself using someone else's computer and wonder why a command doesn't work. Why won't it? Because it's one of your AKAs and it isn't on that machine. Note that by typing a single **E**, I can change to my C:\WORK\EDIT directory and clear the screen. Thus, through the power of multiple command lines, your AKAs can not only reduce the number of keystrokes that you have to enter, but give you a great deal of extra power and flexibility.

Have Order with Anarkey

Anarkey has evolved into the premier program of its type. By using EMS, it uses so little RAM that it's hardly worth mentioning. It gives you the flexibility of defining AKAs, and the ability to edit your environment and easily complete command lines and retrieve directory names. Anarkey reduces the number of keystrokes that you have to enter by keeping track of them, storing them, and quickly finding them.

You'll find a copy of Anarkey on one of the disks that are available free with this book. In order to fit the program on the disks, some of the auxiliary programs that go with Anarkey had to be left out. This includes things like the ANARKED program, which lets you change Anarkey's default keys. You'll have all of the basic things you need to use Anarkey, but at some time in the future you might want to obtain a copy of the program that contains all of the Anarkey files. Anarkey version 4.0, which I'm currently beta-testing, will be available soon. Give Anarkey a try, and I think you'll find that you won't want to be without it.

Steven Calwas
Moderne Software
P.O. Box 3638

Santa Clara, CA 95055
$25 registration plus $3 shipping and handling; for credit card order information, see the CREDIT.CRD file

Directory eXtended

According to its author, Directory eXtended (DX) was born out of the desire to have a double column directory display. Since that time, the program has grown into a very powerful disk and file management tool. Robert Blaine, the author, says in his documentation, "Even if you never use the advanced features of DX, you will find the output much more informative than that of DOS's DIR command."

DX, however, is now much more than just a directory program. It is a very complex utility program that you can use to do many things on your system: move, copy, delete, and rename files, change file attributes, find files, and much more. DX is a program that appeals to the large number of people who like to work from the DOS prompt. DX commands can be included in the AKAs of Anarkey or the aliases of 4DOS. The commands in DX are enhanced. Thus, the COPY command in DX is much more flexible and intelligent than its DOS counterpart. How about a closer look at this extremely useful and powerful program?

DX—Extending Your Capabilities

DX will replace many of the other utilities that you might have on your system for disk and file management. You can customize the DX defaults so that the program displays things the way you want to see them. Once you've learned the command syntax, DX will make a variety of functions much easier to perform. Here is a summary of what DX can do:

- Provide full path and hard disk support
- Specify multiple files
- Search all directories, list all directory names, and test whether a set of files can fit on a different disk
- Search any and all archives and libraries
- Specify exactly which file attributes to display and see any hidden or system files

- Select files between (or outside) a specified range of file sizes and/or dates and times

- Suppress the annoying "." and ".." entries that are always present in directories

- Sort files by any combination of filename, extension, size, date/time, or file attributes

- Sort in ascending or descending order

- Move, copy, compare, delete, and rename files across disks and directories; append files to preexisting files

- Change file attributes and date/time stamp

- Verify special processing on a file-by-file basis (default) or performed automatically

- Produce either a cyclic redundancy check (CRC) or checksum of your files for data integrity checking—useful in detecting Trojan horses

- Choose from an extensive set of output formatting options including colors, printer formatting, upper, lower or initial caps cases, 12- or 24-hour time formats, and screen width, height, and screen-handling options

Let's take a look at some of the functions listed above so you can get an idea of just what DX can do for you.

Many Ways to Do Things
To begin with, you configure DX to have the defaults you want. Once you've set these up, you never have to do it again. You can select colors, time format, whether you want verification on all file functions, and so on. DX is fast and gives you a great deal of information. Like 4DOS, the commands in DX are enhanced so that you can see what's going on. DX will prompt you about overwriting files, moving files, and deleting files. Want to see a listing of all your directories and how much disk space they are taking up? That's not a problem for DX. If you entered the command **DX/LD** (list directories), this is what the display would look like:

```
c:\ (root)    ... 130,424 bytes in 36 files in this directory.
c:\ato    ... 283,932 bytes in 10 files in this directory.
c:\bnf    ... 345,474 bytes in 10 files in this directory.
c:\dcom    ... 251,008 bytes in 20 files in this directory.
c:\dmsdir    ... 657,710 bytes in 18 files in this directory.
c:\dnld    ... 374,835 bytes in 10 files in this directory.
c:\dos    ... 763,301 bytes in 39 files in this directory.
c:\drffbk    ... 0 bytes in 1 file in this directory.
c:\drffbk\files    ... 24,833 bytes in 9 files in this directory.
c:\dv    ... 480,667 bytes in 62 files in this directory.
c:\light    ... 544,287 bytes in 12 files in this directory.
c:\memo    ... 453,884 bytes in 15 files in this directory.
c:\mym    ... 1,507,913 bytes in 29 files in this directory.
c:\qemm    ... 238,122 bytes in 19 files in this directory.
c:\qmodem    ... 1,001,593 bytes in 50 files in this directory.
34 directory(s) found (14,738,106 bytes in 654 files).
```

As you can see, DX can produce some valuable output. You can easily change file attributes and the time and date stamps on files, and even make new directories. Directory eXtended can also use many variations of the DOS wildcards ? and * for doing things with files.

DX has so much versatility that it would be impossible to go over all of its commands here. It can find files anywhere on your system and then perform a certain operation on them. DX can locate files that fall within a size range that you define, or files that have certain dates. DX can even write batch files for you. This is a flexible and powerful tool that is easy to learn to use. Here is a listing of the DX commands.

```
12          ALign     ALTernate ANgle    ANSI      APpend    ARCDT
ATtr        Batch     BColor    BEfore   CAse      CDir      CKsum
Command     COMPare   COPy      CRC      DColor    DEfer     DELete
DOTstar     EXec      FAttr     FColor   FDate     FFind     FSBlink
FSize       Full      GOBak     HEader   INfo      Ldir      LIst
LOGTarget   MDir      MOve      MSP      NETaccess NLines    NONstd
Output      OVerwrite Pause     PRint    PRMArgin  PRMode    Quiet
RDir        REName    ROnly     RUn      SINce     SINGle    SIze
SOrt        STats     SWatch    TAttr    TDate     Totals    Verify
VIDeo       VIew      VLevel    Wide
```

You can see this listing on your screen by entering the following command at the DOS prompt:

```
C>DX /INFO
```

You'll find a copy of DX on the disks free to you by mailing the coupon at the back of this book. DX can make many file operations easier, and you can use batch files or synonyms to help you automate the DX commands you use most. Give DX a try and if you like it as much as I do, be sure to register.

Robert K. Blaine
ECONO-SOFT
P.O. Box 181030
Austin, TX 78718
800-367-7590 or 512-832-1675
73267,1664 CompuServe ID
ROB.BLAINE GEnie ID
$49.95 registration and printed manual
$24.95 for updates

dCOM—Directory Commander

Directory Commander, or dCOM, by Dave Frailey, is many programs and utilities all in one smoothly functioning package. dCOM is a DOS shell, so it could have been discussed in Chapter 14. dCOM is also an excellent menu program, so it could also have been discussed in Chapter 13. Not only does dCOM combine the functions of a DOS shell and a menu but it has many utility functions as well. Thus, dCOM is truly a special program. It has alarms, a print spooler, and a quick disk reformatter, just to name a few. Because Directory Commander does all of the things it does so well, I consider it to be a very unique program—here's why.

dCOM—Getting the Job Done
MS-DOS can be intimidating to the novice user and a pain in the neck to the experienced one. As a result, programmers have been looking for a substitute that would increase efficiency while cutting down on the learning curve. Generally speaking, two possibilities exist: Graphical User Interfaces (better known as GUIs) that mimic, to an extent, the Apple and Macintosh icons, and DOS shells.

In response to the need for a better way to navigate on a DOS-based system, quite a number of DOS shells and DOS utilities have emerged over the years. Most of them, however, have only served to turn users against DOS shells in general. dCOM, on the other hand, is one of the friendliest of the DOS shell programs around. A good DOS shell should, at its most basic, reduce keystrokes, without requiring the use of an overwhelming variety of unrelated commands, menus, and submenus that need to be remembered.

Like all good DOS shells, dCOM provides a simple way for a new user to learn and use a hard disk while at the same time providing flexibility and sophistication enough for the more experienced user. For really giving a friendly interface and tremendous flexibility, there is no greater development tool than dCOM's programmable macro keys and high-powered text editor.

A Full-Featured Program

The initial concept of dCOM was to provide the hard disk user with a quick, convenient, easily-manageable way to move through subdirectory structures, run programs, and perform housekeeping chores. The author listens to what users want and constantly improves the program. dCOM is still a window into your hard disk, capable of navigating around your system, changing directories, and running programs quickly and easily, and it has become so much more. Figure 17-10 shows the Utilities screen of dCOM.

dCOM's main screen displays the directories and files in your root directory. Moving to another directory is a simple matter of moving your cursor or pointing with your mouse to the directory of your choice. In a split second you are in the subdirectory with its files and subdirectories. From any of these screens, you can run files, read text files and edit them with the built in editor, delete directories whether they contain files or not, move directories, and tag files for block copying, moving, deleting, printing, or attribute changing. Copying can span multiple target diskettes. Optional caching for floppy accesses to track 0 improves copying to floppy disks by as much as seven times. All this alone would be enough, but there's much more.

You can sort a directory in a variety of modes including one with executable files first. You can see hidden and system files (which can then be protected with an access password). You can hide and rename individual files or entire subdirectories. You can even create a new subdirectory simply by moving files to it. dCOM will tell you that the subdirectory is new and ask if you want to create it. dCOM will even move an entire directory for you from one drive to another.

Figure 17-10

dCOM's Utilities display

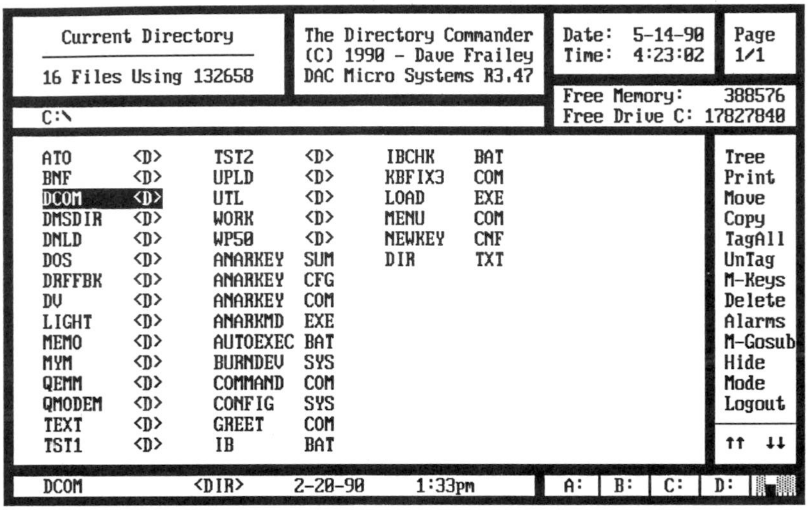

```
┌─────────────────────────┬──────────────────────────┬─────────────────┬──────┐
│    Current Directory    │ The Directory Commander  │ Date:  5-14-90  │ Page │
│    ─────────────────    │ (C) 1990 - Dave Frailey  │ Time:  4:23:02  │ 1/1  │
│  16 Files Using 132658  │ DAC Micro Systems R3.47  ├─────────────────┴──────┤
│                         │                          │ Free Memory:    388576 │
│  C:\                    │                          │ Free Drive C: 17827840 │
├─────────────────────────┴──────────────────────────┴─────────────────┬──────┤
│ ATO     <D>   TST2    <D>   IBCHK    BAT                               │ Tree   │
│ BNF     <D>   UPLD    <D>   KBFIX3   COM                               │ Print  │
│ DCOM    <D>   UTL     <D>   LOAD     EXE                               │ Move   │
│ DMSDIR  <D>   WORK    <D>   MENU     COM                               │ Copy   │
│ DNLD    <D>   WP50    <D>   NEWKEY   CNF                               │ TagAll │
│ DOS     <D>   ANARKEY SUM   DIR      TXT                               │ UnTag  │
│ DRFFBK  <D>   ANARKEY CFG                                             │ M-Keys │
│ DV      <D>   ANARKEY COM                                             │ Delete │
│ LIGHT   <D>   ANARKMD EXE                                             │ Alarms │
│ MEMO    <D>   AUTOEXEC BAT                                            │ M-Gosub│
│ MYM     <D>   BURNDEV SYS                                             │ Hide   │
│ QEMM    <D>   COMMAND COM                                             │ Mode   │
│ QMODEM  <D>   CONFIG  SYS                                             │ Logout │
│ TEXT    <D>   GREET   COM                                             │        │
│ TST1    <D>   IB      BAT                                             │ ↑↑  ↓↓ │
├───────────────────────────────────────────────────┬─────┬─────┬─────┬────────┤
│ DCOM          <DIR>    2-28-90     1:33pm          │ A:  │ B:  │ C:  │ D: ▓▒░ │
└───────────────────────────────────────────────────┴─────┴─────┴─────┴────────┘
```

If you are like me and still prefer using DOS commands, dCOM has simplified that too. Simply by pressing the TAB key, a DOS prompt appears at the bottom of the screen. Pressing TAB again will bring down the .EXE or .COM file you want to run, or you can type in a DOS command or the name of a TSR program to run. For example, press TAB, type **LIST**, and press TAB again and a highlighted text file will appear next to LIST. Press ENTER and LIST will run and show the file you indicated. If you want to unpack three or four files, use the tagging feature of dCOM to tag the archived files. Press TAB and type in the appropriate unarchiving program, press TAB again to bring down all the tagged file names, and press ENTER. You have to see it to really appreciate it. dCOM gives you the benefits of a shell program and still lets you have the feel of the DOS prompt.

dCOM Menus

If you like a menu-driven system, dCOM can provide that also. The program has its own macro language that is easy for even a novice to learn. High-powered macros that are similar to batch files can be programmed to function keys. The first time they are run, they are automatically compiled and *tokenized* to a memory buffer for instantaneous response times and efficient use of memory. All batch commands are supported plus an additional subset of commands like nestable IF blocks, DO blocks, looping, and so on. Figure 17-11 shows my main dCOM menu popped up over the Utilities screen.

Extensive menuing systems can be built using the macro keys. The menu mode can be configured to pop up automatically, and it fully supports password protection for each selection or for access to dCOM's utility functions. Thus, you can configure it so you have access to everything in dCOM, but less experienced users are restricted to the menus. The powerful macro command set lets you build menu selections that can even display a menu of files to select from before running a program. Here's an example of using a dCOM macro to simplify using QEdit.

Figure 17-11

A menu display in dCOM

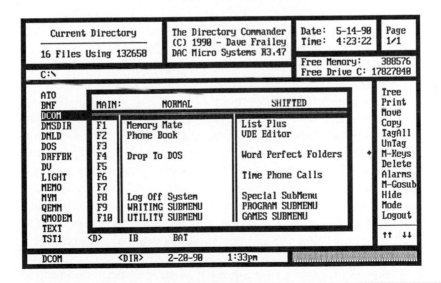

```
[F1] Qedit
SELECT C:\*.* Pick Directory Name:/D
SET %1=%SE
cd \%1
SELECT *.* Enter Filename:/N
SET %2=%SE
Q %2
cddo
```

What would this do? It would show you a window that contains the names of all your directories on drive C. You pick the one you want with mouse or keyboard. The macro then changes to that directory and shows you another window that contains all of the files in the selected directory. Select the one you want to edit, and it is loaded into QEdit. This is a wonderful feature for new users and a very desirable one for experienced ones.

dCOM—Making Life Easier

dCom includes a high-performance, full-featured, multiwindow, multi-buffer text editor with PC line drawing and enhanced video options. Buffer sizes are limited only by available memory. You can mark blocks, copy and move them, and more. In the utilities mode, a powerful visual tree, which is fully mouse driven, is available. Copy and move actions can easily invoke the tree for use in selecting the destination drive and directory. Most file-oriented commands can be performed with the mouse. Fully configurable color, with snow inhibited automatically on CGA, and with support for EGA/VGA extended colors, is an added attraction. Figure 17-12 shows the main Configuration menu of dCOM.

dCOM can run any file with a .COM, .EXE, or .BAT extension. In addition, file extensions other than .COM, .EXE, or .BAT can be config-ured as executable by having another program run and passing it the selected filename. One of the most outstanding features is a high-performance, resizeable print spooler with hot keys for clearing the spooler's buffer, sending form feeds, and sending line feeds to the printer. Printer output for the system and the spooler is easily redirected to another LPT port or a COM (RS232) port. Some additional features are: a keypad + key, which can be configured to emulate a RETURN key, which can then be toggled on-the-fly with a hot key; a screen saver configurable from 1 to 59 minutes, which is mouse-sensitive; and a hot key that blanks

Figure 17-12

dCOM's Configuration menu

```
┌────────────────────────────────┐    ┌──────────────────────┐
│  CONFIGURATION   Current  Default │    │  GENERAL COLORS      │
│                                   │    │                      │
│ Directory Sort Mode..  NONE  NONE │    │ Background...   1     │
│ Show Hidden Files....  --    --   │    │ Foreground...  31     │
│ Wait After Execute...  AUTO  AUTO │    │ dCOM Lines...  46     │
│ Keypad Plus = Ret....  --    --   │    │ Menu Lines...  46     │
│ Single Key Prompts...  --    --   │    │ Misc Lines...  18     │
│ Advance After Tag....  --    --   │    └──────────────────────┘
│ Overwrite Warnings...  ON    ON   │
│ Printer Output To....  LPT1  LPT1 │    ┌──────────────────────┐
│ Sound Suppression....  --  :::::::│    │  FILE AREA COLORS    │
│ Show File Attributes.  --  :::::::│    │                      │
│ Use Solid Lines......  ON  :::::::│    │ Background...   1     │
│ EGA Palette Mode.....  ON  :::::::│    │ Directory....  46     │
│ Cache Floppy I/O.....  --  :::::::│    │ Exec File....  62     │
│ Screen Saver Minutes.  --  :::::::│    │ Other File...  19     │
│ Save Scn out of dCOM.  --  :::::::│    │ Selec Bar....   8     │
└────────────────────────────────┘    └──────────────────────┘
```

E-Edit, C-Colors, M-Mouse, D-Drives, X-Exit:

the screen and locks the keyboard. If the system password is active, it is required to reactivate the screen and keyboard.

Alarms, Logging, and Still More

dCOM has an elaborate yet easy-to-use alarm and reminder feature. The extensive alarm clock system can hold 38 different alarms based on daily or calendar events. If you set a time for the reminder, an alarm box will appear on your screen at the designated time wherever you are, no matter what program you are in, and will remain there until removed with the touch of a key.

An optional activity log can keep track of every program run, when it started, when it stopped, how many minutes it was active, and what parameters, if any, were used. You can also set up a list of users, giving each the ability to access only certain functions in dCOM. The logging facility will also track who ran each program. This makes dCOM a great program for use both in the home and in business. dCOM can use both conventional and expanded memory. It is also compatible with both multitasking and task-switching software like DESQview, TopView, Back & Forth, and others.

Summarizing dCOM

In summary, dCOM is a full-screen, high-performance, interactive DOS shell and utility. You can change directories, sort directories, and execute, edit, print, copy, move, rename, and delete files with a single correlating keystroke. You can selectively tag files to be copied, moved, deleted, or printed. Entire directory contents can be copied, moved, and deleted. Subdirectories can be renamed or hidden. The copy command has the ability to span several destination diskettes when multiple files are involved.

Directories can be sorted in many different ways. You can put all of the executable files in alphabetical order, before the other files that the program needs to run but that you don't need to be concerned with. Your files can be sorted based on their filename extensions, or, of course, on date/time or size, in ascending or descending order. Hidden and system files can also be seen with the touch of a key. dCOM's user interface provides you with a command set that is functional, making it easy to learn and remember. All destructive commands prompt for confirmation first before proceeding.

dCOM's macro (function) key facility gives it power and flexibility that I have not found in any other program. Because the macros are compiled, they execute almost instantaneously, and no temporary batch files are used nor do they invoke a second copy of COMMAND.COM (unless programmed to do so, or a resident DOS command is used). The program has been so carefully thought out that if you load a TSR *after* dCOM, you can tell dCOM to remove the TSR when you return to dCOM, thus saving you memory. With the macro keys, you can program dCOM to perform any of your most commonly used MS-DOS commands, run programs, change directories, compile source code, and more. Thus, the macro keys can be used to build extensive menuing systems. dCOM also includes a high-powered print spooler that tunes itself to your computer and printer and can be resized or disabled at will. It is supported with a hot key that will clear its contents and any internal buffer in the printer. When its output is configured to talk directly with the printer port, CPS rates exceeding 5200 have been noted during graphics or font downloads to a laser printer.

A Personal Comment on dCOM

You should have the feeling that dCOM is a truly comprehensive program—and it is. It has a wide range of features and yet they are features that most users want: no fluff, no flashy things that you won't ever use, but good, solid, full-featured utilities and accessories. The program works beautifully and continues to get better and better. This is one program that I personally will not be without. The macro language gives me the power and flexibility that I want in menus. The shell portion of dCOM makes it easy to work with lots of files, and that is very important to me.

You'll find a copy of dCOM on the disk included with this book. In order to include it, the documentation had to be abbreviated. You'll find the number for the dCOM Support BBS in Appendix C. As a help to you, I will make sure that there are full copies of dCOM's documentation on all of the systems that are tagged in Appendix C as places where you can leave me notes. Take a look at dCOM, and if you use it, be sure to register.

Dave Frailey
DAC Micro Systems
40941 176th Street E.
Lancaster, CA 93535
805-264-1700 (Voice)
805-264-1219 (BBS)
$50 registration plus $2.50 shipping and handling; includes manual

WRAPPING THINGS UP

This chapter discussed some programs that I consider to be special in what they do and how they do it. BackMail, Anarkey, and DX are on disks you can send for free with the coupon at the back of the book. dCOM is on the disk included with this book. Perhaps now you know why. (*smile*)

## CHAPTER EIGHTEEN

Databases

While there are tens of thousands of Shareware programs to be found in The Wires, they all can be grouped under a few major headings: communications programs, word processing programs, spreadsheets, utilities, graphics, and databases. In this chapter, we'll consider the wide range of database programs available as Shareware.

Before any of us ever used a computer, we used a form of database—the familiar library card catalog. We used it to search for a book by subject, author, or title. The records were stored in drawers alphabetically to make searching easier. As new books were received, the librarian added cards to the file.

Like a computer database, the card catalog performed several functions—a way to search for data, a system for sorting data, and a method for adding data to the files. Most computerized library systems still operate on the same principles, and because the data is identical in form, this works very well. Since the cataloging system has no provision for creating another format, no other types of data such as names and addresses can be entered.

A good general purpose database program, on the other hand, allows you to set up one data file for your address book and another data file for the books in your personal library, both accessible with the same program. Moreover, it will allow you to search for any piece of information in the file, print out reports, sort and index the information, and in general, manipulate the data.

DATABASES IN GENERAL

Before going further, let's define some terms common to all databases. Using the card catalog as a model, the drawers and the cards in them represent *data files*. Where your database's data files differ from the library's is that each of your "drawers" holds a different kind of "card." The cards in an electronic database are called *records* and each piece of information in a record is called a *field*.

In most address books, the city, state, and zip code are listed on a single line. In setting up a database however, you would create separate *fields* for each piece of information to search or sort by zip code, city, or last names. The fields can include *alphanumeric* data, which is a combination of numbers and letters, or can be restricted only to numeric data. For instance, a record's zip code field could be restricted to only numeric data.

More often, numeric fields are used for calculations. For example, if you have separate fields for state and federal taxes, the database can add them to form a Total Tax column in a report. If you have a field for annual sales, your database can calculate the percentage of that figure for a particular category of goods. Most databases also have an open-ended field for comments or other information that does not fit on one line.

Masks are limitations placed on data entry in a field. They screen what can be typed in, preventing you from accidentally entering the wrong information. For example, designating a field as numeric prevents you from typing in anything except numbers. Masks can also be used to restrict a field to uppercase letters only. Masks can be automatic. If you have a mask such as YYYYMMDD, the date will be automatically inserted in the field as 19900326, for example. You can usually change the form of the date to one that will suit your purposes.

Storing and Exchanging Information

In addition to retrieving and storing records, databases can be used in a number of other ways. You can print multiple labels, reports, graphs, and pie charts, and create form letters with information from the database inserted at selected places. The more comprehensive database programs such as PC-File, ProFile, and WAMPUM allow data to be exchanged with word processing programs such as WordPerfect, WordStar, and Microsoft Word, with other databases such as dBASE, or with spreadsheets such as Lotus 1-2-3.

Let's take a closer look at three of the best Shareware database programs available: PC-File, ProFile, and WAMPUM.

PC-FILE

PC-File has been consistently mentioned in computer magazines as one of the best database programs. Although PC-File does require at least 512K of RAM and at least 1 meg of disk storage, the number of records in any database is limited only by the amount of disk space available. Figure 18-1 shows you the Master Menu of PC-File.

Figure 18-1

Master Menu of PC-File

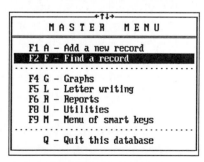

```
                                                    10:33:54 m
      PC-File 5.0, Single-user

┌──────────────────────────────────────────────────────────┐
│           C:\PCFDB\PERSONAL - Personal file                │
│         5 records.  Current index: ZIP ascending           │
│   This disk can hold approximately 38709 more records      │
└──────────────────────────────────────────────────────────┘

                    ┌────── ←↑↓→ ──────┐
                    │  M A S T E R  M E N U │
                    ├────────────────────┤
                    │ F1 A - Add a new record │
                    │ F2 F - Find a record    │
                    │ · · · · · · · · · · · · │
                    │ F4 G - Graphs           │
                    │ F5 L - Letter writing   │
                    │ F6 R - Reports          │
                    │ F8 U - Utilities        │
                    │ F9 M - Menu of smart keys │
                    │ · · · · · · · · · · · · │
                    │  Q - Quit this database │
                    └────────────────────┘

              (Alt)H - HELP (at any time)
```

As you can see from the opening menu, PC-File informs you of the number of records in the current database and how many more can be added. The databases can be compressed using a utility called PCPAK, included with the program, allowing you to keep backup copies on floppy disk.

In addition to providing the standard features of a database, PC-File has a number of unique features. It maintains a phone directory that can be set to dial your modem, and keeps a phone log for you. It can automatically import any .DBF file for processing. There are up to five data entry screens for each record. You retrieve information from other PC-File databases into the current one and index that current database on nine different fields.

PC-File provides context-sensitive online help. Help is activated with ALT-H, which can be moved to a different position on your screen as can many other PC-File windows. PC-File also provides mouse support, macros, LAN support, and password protection. You can print graphs, pie charts, and mailing labels, as well as reports on any search criteria. The search procedure can be as simple as entering enough data in any field to enable PC-File to retrieve a record, or as complex as using Boolean logic and/or comparisons.

Now that you've been introduced to some of PC-File's features, let's examine them and some other features more closely.

Features of PC-File

Since PC-File is completely menu-driven, it combines ease of use with the power of dBASE file compatibility. In addition to help screens, PC-File also has a teach mode, activated with ALT-T, which causes a Help screen to be displayed every time the program asks a question.

There are a number of other ALT and CTRL key combinations that add to the ease of use. CTRL-F, for example, duplicates information in the current field from a previously viewed record. CTRL-I will duplicate the entire record, while CTRL-C brings up the on-screen calculator. The result of the calculation can be inserted in any field using CTRL-W, the write from memory key combination. ALT-D is the key combination that lets you drop to DOS. ALT-O or CTRL-O flips data that has been designated as flip data with a tilde. ALT-P or CTRL-P activates the Print screen. (The advantage of having either an ALT or CTRL option for these last two functions is that if you have a program that uses ALT keys for other things, you can use the CTRL key to prevent conflicts.)

Moving with a Mouse

Ease of use is further enhanced by PC-File's mouse support. The program supports the most popular mice from Microsoft, Logitech, and PC-MOUSE. Once your mouse is installed using the mouse software, you don't have to configure PC-File to use it. You can use the mouse in two ways—either with the regular menus, or with a special Mouse menu. Mouse menu options include: Help, Auto-Dial, Calculator, DOS Command, Snapshot Label, Print Screen, Smart-Key (macros), View Memo, and Erase this Mouse menu. These selections replace some of the more common ALT and CTRL key combinations.

PC-File's flexibility extends to the way you choose files or fields from its menus. When you start PC-File, you are prompted for the database path you want to use. You are then presented with a list of files in that database directory. You can then either select the file by entering its number, typing the name of the file, or moving the cursor to the name of the file. By using a mouse, you can select a file by moving the cursor to the filename. You can have an unlimited number of files in any directory, but the program can only display 83.

Easy to Manage Power

PC-File uses a dBASE file structure, so any dBASE-type file is instantly compatible with PC-File. When a new database is created, files with the extension of .DBF, .NDX, and .DBT are made. .DBF files contain data, headers, and information about the field names, types, and lengths.

The .NDX file is the index or key to the database records. You can have up to nine indexes for any one database. When you add, delete, or modify a record, all of the indexes will be changed. You can rearrange your data either by switching the indexes or by sorting your database.

Files with the .DBT extension are memo files. Although you would probably only use memo fields if you need a field larger than 254 characters, PC-File does have the ability to search for data in the memo field, a capability that dBASE lacks.

Setting up PC-File is easy, even for a novice computer user. You are allowed up to 128 fields, on a maximum of five entry screens. In addition to the usual character, numeric, and date fields, you can also designate a logical field, one character long, that can contain the characters "T" for True and "F" for False, or "Y" for Yes and "N" for No.

Memo fields are a type of character field. Using an *automatic field* edit mask, you can also set up a field in which data is automatically entered for you. These are usually date, time, and duplication entries. You can also set up an automatic *unique field* that assigns the field a unique record number. If you have a field that never changes, for example, in a database of addresses from the same state, you can provide a constant for that field. Whenever you create a new record, the constant field is automatically filled in. You always have the option to change the information in the field.

A final type of field is a *calculated field*. The data is usually the result of an arithmetic calculation. A calculated field can also reflect a *relational lookup*, which is a retrieval of data from another database. You could have PC-File look up the price of an object in a price-list database and insert the price in a sales database. The length of a field can be up to 254 characters for non-memo fields and 5,000 characters for memo fields. Since the length of a display line is only 65 characters, not all the information in a field can be displayed. The field is then considered a *window field* and you need only move the cursor left or right to view the rest of the information.

PC-File Gives You Options

PC-File often provides more than one way of performing a function. Searches can be simple or complex. Reports can be defined using a free form option or using preconfigured formats for mailing labels. A new database can be defined either by the Fast method or the Paint method. These options offer you the means to decide how much control you want. If you like the quick, easy way and your database is relatively uncomplicated, choose the already-configured options; if you want or need flexibility, choose from the free form options. To give you a better idea, let's look at the Fast and Paint methods of defining a database.

Fast and Paint Methods

If you choose the Fast method, you are first presented with a screen showing four empty columns defined by square brackets. This is shown in Figure 18-2.

Type in the field names on the screen and you will be prompted for a display length, and the field length if any are window fields. If you choose the Paint method, you can still save yourself trouble. You will first be asked if you want to load an existing picture. If you have another database that is close to what you want, answer "yes" and modify the

---

Figure 18-2

The Fast method definition screen

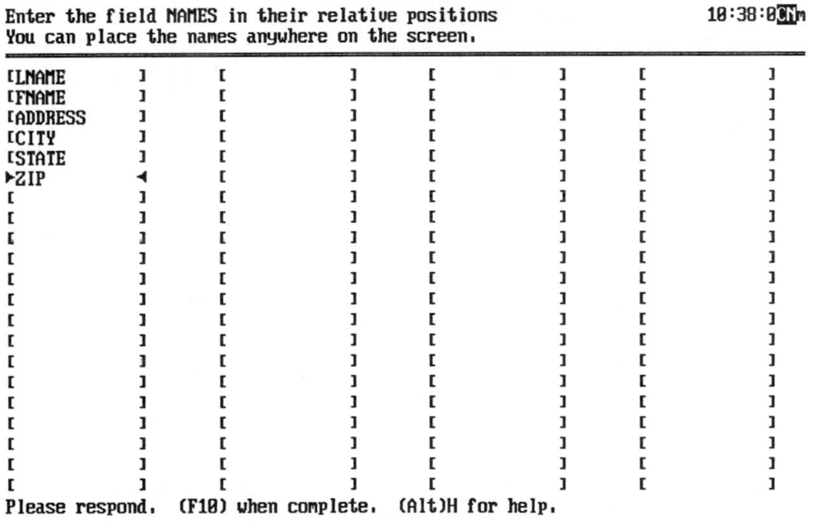

```
Enter the field NAMES in their relative positions          10:38:0   m
You can place the names anywhere on the screen.
[LNAME    ]   [          ]   [          ]   [          ]
[FNAME    ]   [          ]   [          ]   [          ]
[ADDRESS  ]   [          ]   [          ]   [          ]
[CITY     ]   [          ]   [          ]   [          ]
[STATE    ]   [          ]   [          ]   [          ]
►ZIP       ◄  [          ]   [          ]   [          ]
[         ]   [          ]   [          ]   [          ]
[         ]   [          ]   [          ]   [          ]
[         ]   [          ]   [          ]   [          ]
[         ]   [          ]   [          ]   [          ]
[         ]   [          ]   [          ]   [          ]
[         ]   [          ]   [          ]   [          ]
[         ]   [          ]   [          ]   [          ]
[         ]   [          ]   [          ]   [          ]
[         ]   [          ]   [          ]   [          ]
[         ]   [          ]   [          ]   [          ]
[         ]   [          ]   [          ]   [          ]
[         ]   [          ]   [          ]   [          ]
[         ]   [          ]   [          ]   [          ]
Please respond.   (F10) when complete.   (Alt)H for help.
```

data entry screen for the other database so it will serve for the new one. The original database won't be changed. If you answer "no," you are presented with an empty screen. Type in the field names where you want them to go and put in square brackets to mark the boundaries of the fields, adding spaces or putting default data between the brackets. Using PC-File's built-in editor, you can draw boxes or lines on a painted screen.

Accessing Fields

Whichever method you use to define the field names and lengths, you will next be asked to enter a data type for each field—for example, **C** for character, **N** for numeric, and so on. You will be asked if you want window fields. Select any field you want to become a window field. You will be shown the display length and asked to enter the field length. Another interesting option in setting up records is that you don't have to access fields in the same order you entered them. Normally, when adding or modifying records, you move from top to bottom, left to right, in the order that you entered the fields. But if you want to work from bottom to top, press Y when asked if you want to change the sequence, and number the fields in a specific order. When you add or modify a record, your cursor will move in the new sequence.

Next, you will be asked to choose a field on which to base your index and give a name for the index. PC-File will also ask for a file description for the new database. You don't have to enter one, but a description does make it easier to choose a database when you are presented with a list of names.

Adding Records

Having chosen an existing database file, or created a new one, you are then taken to the Master Menu, shown in Figure 18-1. Selections can be made either by pressing a function key or the corresponding letter command key. You can also move the highlighted bar with the arrow keys or a mouse. You'll notice that the default is Find a record. This is due to the fact that once a database has a few records, you can work with it using the default menu on the record.

Adding a record to your database is straightforward. There are, however, a few unique keys that make entering data easier. The tilde is a *flip data* character. Instead of setting up separate fields for last and first names as in dBASE, in PC-File you have a single name field. Enter the name as

Jones~William, and you can search on last name and still print in a normal order.

The two duplication keys—CTRL-D and CTRL-F—allow you to duplicate information from previous records. CTRL-D copies all data from a record, while CTRL-F duplicates only the field the cursor is on. With CTRL-R and CTRL-W, you can pick up information from a record, store it in memory, and retrieve it whenever you wish.

The Find menu can be accessed from the Master Menu and is always present on screen once a record has been retrieved. You can choose to see the first or last record in the database, the next or previous record in a sequence, or the next or previous screen full of records. After choosing one of these options, select any record from the Browse screen that you want to view in its entirety.

Searching for Your Data

There are three methods of searching for a record: *simple,* in which you fill in the blanks; *complex,* in which you type in a formula; and *global,* in which all fields are examined. Even a simple search allows you the flexibility to search in multiple fields at the same time. For instance, if you enter **Smith** in the name field and **PA** in the state field, you will only retrieve records for those Smiths who live in Pennsylvania. Even the search criteria can be entered in four different ways.

A generic search will retrieve all records starting with the search string in the selected field. You could find Tobias, for example, by entering **tob** in the name field. Generic searches do not require full names and are not case sensitive, which is convenient if you aren't sure of the spelling of a name. Scan-across searches are similar to generic searches except that if you precede the search criteria with a tilde, PC-File will search for the search string anywhere in the field. If you use a question mark instead of a tilde, you can then do a sounds-like search. Finally, you can do a wildcard search using an underscore to find an entry with characters appearing in a fixed position. For instance, **sm_th** will get you Smith, Smath, Smeth, and Smoth. The search screen is shown in Figure 18-3.

Complex searches are done in a window that is one line deep and 250 characters long. These searches use a combination of field names, search data, and parentheses for grouping items. The symbols | and & are used to indicate logical operators. Comparison operators ($=$, $\neq$, $>$, $<$) are used to symbolize equal and not equal to, and greater and less than. OR and AND can also be used. Once retrieved, a record can be modified, a new

Figure 18-3

PC-File's search screen

```
Index: Zip ascending              Enter the search data         10:35:12 m

Last_Name  ▶***************◀
First_Name [***************]
Company    [*******************************]
Street     [*******************************]
City       [*********************]
State      [**]
Zip        [*********]
Comments   [*****************************************************************]
```

```
Please respond.  (F10) when complete.  (Alt)H for help.
```

Figure 18-4

A sample record in PC-File

```
Index: Zip ascending                                           10:32:17 m

Last_Name  [Doe          ]
First_Name [John         ]
Company    [XYZ Inc.           ]
Street     [123 Main Street    ]
City       [Anytown       ]
State      [PA]
Zip        [12345-123]
Comments   [
```

search can be instituted, a record can be added, and so on. Figure 18-4 shows a sample record.

Sorting and Indexing

PC-File has remarkable sorting and indexing capabilities. You can sort up to ten fields at a time, while each database supports up to nine different indexes. Sorting and indexing can be performed in ascending or descending order, or a combination of both. The data can be sorted in random sequence, in sounds-like sequence, or by using the results of a calculation. PC-File allows any field except a memo field to be the basis for an index. These functions are accessed from a special Utilities menu shown in Figure 18-5.

The Utilities menu also allows you to make changes to an existing database, import or export a database, configure PC-File to suit your own needs and equipment, perform a series of maintenance tasks like finding duplicate records, and perform global operations.

Figure 18-5

The Utilities menu in PC-File

Presenting and Printing Data

PC-File has the ability to generate a vast number of reports, graphs, and charts. As with other functions, you can either choose a predesigned format or design your own. Every report contains six sections: a cover, which is the text to be included at the beginning of the report or on a separate cover page; headings, which include titles, page numbers, and column headings; detail, which tells PC-File what information to include in the report and where you want it printed; subtotal, which is an optional selection; total, which prints the totals for numeric fields, the number of records printed, and the selection criteria; and footing, which determines the bottom margin for the page.

Reports can be generated in either row or page format. In row format, data is lined up in columns; in page format data for each record is printed on a separate page. The Report menu is displayed in Figure 18-6.

More on Reports Although PC-File includes a stand-alone program for printing labels called PCLABEL, simple mailing labels can also be defined

---

Figure 18-6

PC-File's Report menu

10:35:52am

```
          REPORT MENU

Output to Printer, Screen, Disk  P/S/D    ►P◄
Number of copies                  1-99    [9 ]
Line spacing (0 = no detail lines) 0-9    [1]
Do Subtotals?                      Y/N     [N]
Left margin (extra spaces)        0-99    [ 0]
Page length (in "lines")                 [ 66]
Pause after each page?             Y/N     [N]
Start at which page number?              [  1]
Type size (Normal/Condensed)       N/C     [N]
Remove blank lines and spaces      Y/N     [N]
Flip~data active?                  Y/N     [Y]
Print All or Selected records      A/S     [S]
```

Press (Esc) to return to PC-File menu

Please respond. (F10) when complete. (Alt)H for help.

from the Report menu. If you choose row or page format, the six sections of information are automatically indicated in the report form. If you choose to do a free form report, you can either pattern your report after an existing report or start from scratch. This choice is similar to choosing between the Fast method and Paint method in defining a database. In setting up a report format, you can have titles on each page, multiple titles, nine different levels of subtotals, and calculated report fields where PC-File makes calculations based upon your data. You can also pull in data from related PC-File databases, and you have the option of printing to disk, printer, or file. In addition, you can print graphs and charts using information from your data in your database. Choose from horizontal or vertical bar charts, pie charts, and a variety of line charts.

Database Maintenance with PC-File

Database maintenance in PC-File is performed through the Utilities menu, which can be accessed from the Master Menu. The Utilities menu allows you to add, delete or change the name, location, size, and type of any or all fields. Most of these operations are done by making a new copy or cloning the database using either a Fast or Paint method. After making your changes, PC-File will ask you to mark the fields on which the index is to be built and will create new index files. You can clone an entire database or selected records. By cloning, you can effectively split a database in two parts, giving the cloned database a new name, path, and drive designation.

From the Utilities menu, you can search for duplicated records, list them to a report, and even delete them on the screen. You can tell PC-File to search for duplications on any field. For example, if you choose the name field to search and find you have two records for the same person but with different addresses, you will be presented with both records.

Importing and Exporting Data

One of the most powerful features of PC-File is its ability to import and export databases to and from a variety of other programs, such as other databases, word processing programs, and so on. Often, if the database to be imported saves its files with .DBF extensions, you simply tell PC-File to import it. The record setup will also be imported. You can use this feature to append one PC-File database to another if you want to combine two similar databases. The Utilities menu lets you copy, delete, or rename almost all of your files, and do global modifications and deletions.

Configurations, Smart Keys, and Indexing

Three other features of PC-File are accessed by way of the Utilities menu, including configurations, smart keys, and indexing. Since indexing is the least complicated and has already been discussed, it only remains to list the indexing operations available from the Utilities menu:

- Making a new index

- Switching indexes

- Deleting an existing index

- Renaming an existing index

Let's take a quick look at some of PC-File's configuration options.

Configuration Options

PC-File comes configured for most IBM compatible computers and the information is stored in a file called PCFILE.PRO. It is also possible to configure each database separately, saving the new configurations in a .PRO file with a unique name such as PERSONAL.PRO. If you store this new .PRO file in the same directory as your personal database, the program will read it as the default configuration. Configuration files contain information about your choice of colors and whether you are using a monochrome or color monitor. The files also contain the startup defaults, whether searches and sorts are to be case sensitive, use of European or American dates on reports, passwords, and so on. You can have a different password for each database.

You can also have PC-File automatically go to the Search menu on startup by using the Keyin option. By specifying /KEYIN,FSS, PC-File will then press F for find, S for search, and another S for simple search. If you do a lot of mailing labels, you can define the snapshot label from the Configuration menu. By inserting a series of values in a snapshot definition, you can print mailing labels by simply pressing CTRL-L while viewing a record on the screen.

Using the Phone with PC-File   PC-File will keep a log of your telephone calls through its autodialing function. Once you have set up the phone dialer from the configurations section, find the record with the phone number you want to dial, activate the dialer with ALT-J or CTRL-J, select the number from a menu box that comes up on your screen, and wait for the call to be dialed. Once the modem has dialed the number, press any key to release the modem and start the timer. Then pick up and use the telephone. If you need to use your computer while on the phone, just stop the timer by pressing any key. You can continue talking, but of course, your phone log will only show the shorter time.

Note that you can use either the ALT or the CTRL key. This is handy for preventing conflicts if you have TSR programs that use one or the other.

Using the Smart Keys

One last feature remains to be considered—PC-File's macro commands, called smart keys. Each database can have 22 different macros containing a total of 318 keystrokes. Configurable keys include the numbers from 1 through 0 at the top of the keyboard, the two adjoining - and = keys, and the ten function keys. PC-File will automatically record keystrokes to be used as a macro by pressing ALT-Y and these can be edited from the Utilities menu. Each macro can be given an identifying title, which can then be viewed along with its keystrokes in the Macro menu. The Macro menu is shown in Figure 18-7.

Figure 18-7

The Smart Key macro menu

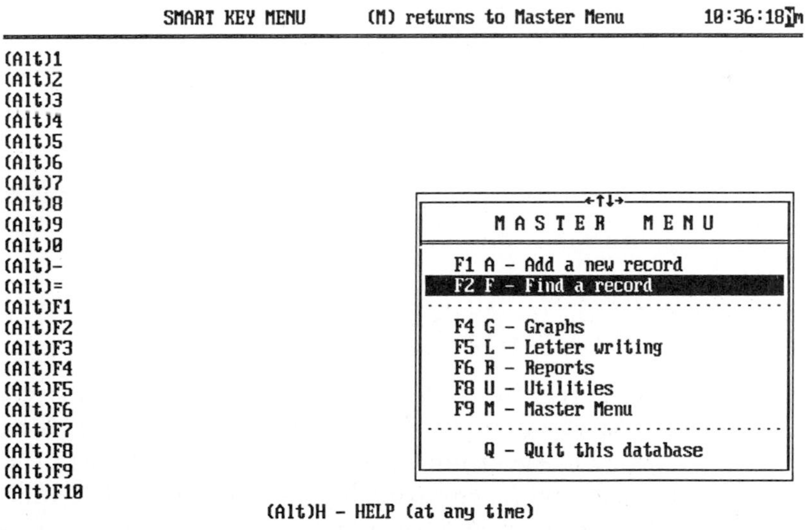

```
        SMART KEY MENU      (M) returns to Master Menu        10:36:18 m
(Alt)1
(Alt)2
(Alt)3
(Alt)4
(Alt)5
(Alt)6
(Alt)7
(Alt)8                        ┌──────────+↑↓→─────────┐
(Alt)9                        │     M A S T E R   M E N U    │
(Alt)0                        ├──────────────────────┤
(Alt)-                        │   F1 A - Add a new record    │
(Alt)=                        │   F2 F - Find a record       │
(Alt)F1                       ├ ─ ─ ─ ─ ─ ─ ─ ─ ─ ─ ─ ─ ┤
(Alt)F2                       │   F4 G - Graphs              │
(Alt)F3                       │   F5 L - Letter writing      │
(Alt)F4                       │   F6 R - Reports             │
(Alt)F5                       │   F8 U - Utilities           │
(Alt)F6                       │   F9 M - Master Menu         │
(Alt)F7                       ├ ─ ─ ─ ─ ─ ─ ─ ─ ─ ─ ─ ─ ┤
(Alt)F8                       │     Q - Quit this database   │
(Alt)F9                       └──────────────────────┘
(Alt)F10
                 (Alt)H - HELP (at any time)
```

You can use the editing feature to write macros. Certain keys, however, cannot be entered directly as keystrokes—ENTER and PGDN, for example—but can be included in the macro by enclosing the ASCII number value of the key in square brackets. Macros can be nested and can pause to accept keyboard input. A *recursive* macro can be set up so as to loop on itself, repeating the process until it is complete. Although each smart key file is limited to 22 smart keys, you can load any number of different smart key files at once.

Overview of PC-File

As comprehensive as PC-File is, ButtonWare has included in the package several companion programs: PCLABEL, which prints labels in any format on any search criteria, simple or complex; PCFIX, which repairs damaged databases; PCPAK, an editor that compresses the database for easy storage; and DBRpt, which prints out a report of your databases.

PC-File can be set up to be as user-friendly as you want. It is completely menu-driven, allowing you to choose either the predesigned option or a design-your-own option at every step. It is definitely a product to look at.

Jim Button
ButtonWare, Inc.
P.O. Box 96058
Bellevue, WA 98009
800-J-BUTTON (Voice)
206-454-2629 (BBS)
900-454-8000 (Tech Support)
$129.95 Program cost (available both as Shareware and in a commercially packaged form)

WAMPUM—PROGRAMMABLE POWER

If options is the significant word to describe PC-File, then power is the significant term for WAMPUM, or Ward's Automatic Menu Package Using Microcomputers. Unlike PC-File or ProFile, WAMPUM is a relational database incorporating the dBASE III programming language. WAMPUM differs from most database programs by being both a database management system and an applications programming tool. WAMPUM does this by

---

Figure 18-8

WAMPUM's Main Menu screen

```
WAMPUM ver. 4.0 (c) Copyright Ward Mundy, 1986-89.                 N

  ┌──────────────────────┐┌──────────────────────┐┌──────────────────────┐
  │ A - ADD a new record ││ S - SELECT utilities ││ F - FILE select      │
  │                      ││                      ││                      │
  │ E - EDIT a record    ││ R - REPORTS menu     ││ I - INDEX sel/create │
  │                      ││                      ││                      │
  │ D - DISPLAY records  ││ L - LABELS for mail  ││ B - BUILD new file   │
  │                      ││                      ││                      │
  │ M - MARK record*DEL* ││ T - FORM LETTER menu ││ G - GLOBAL replace   │
  │                      ││                      ││                      │
  │ U - UN*DEL* records  ││ W - WAMPUM PreFormat ││ # - PRINTER config   │
  │                      ││                      ││                      │
  │ P - PRINT record(s)  ││ ! - RUN ext. program ││ * - CONFIG update    │
  │                      ││                      ││                      │
  │ X - REBUILD/FileFiX  ││ Z - ZOOM/Relate File ││ C - COPY utilities   │
  └──────────────────────┘└──────────────────────┘└──────────────────────┘
HELP: Highlighted option allows you to add new record to file. HELP = Push F1.



                        NO FILE IN USE.
```

---

providing two different sets of menus. The first contains many typical database functions: adding, editing, and deleting records; printing reports and labels; selecting the index; rebuilding a damaged database; selecting reports criteria; and so on. The Main Menu is shown in Figure 18-8.

Taking a Look at WAMPUM

WAMPUM provides a second menu, accessed by typing **WAMPUM VOODOO** to start the program. This developer mode offers the same options as the Main Menu. In addition, it allows you to create new data files and indexes; set up new report, label, or print formats; and it provides access to data files that develop edit checks, data entry menus, keyboard macros, and form letters. It also allows you to browse through the records in a database. Figure 18-9 shows the browse screen.

Like most databases, WAMPUM works best if the system files are in a pathed directory and the databases are in subdirectories. This is because

WAMPUM creates supporting files for each database in the subdirectory occupied by the database. These include a main file, indexes, and report and label formats. WAMPUM also includes the files KEYS.DBF for macros; MENUS.DBF containing the data entry screen format; WAMPUM.DBF for preformatted reports, labels, and form letters; and WAMPUM.MEM containing the configuration for the database. If you have two separate databases in a single subdirectory or in a pathed subdirectory, WAMPUM will not be able to distinguish between files created for one database from those created for another. The last files created will overwrite earlier ones.

Compatible Databases

Like PC-File and ProFile, WAMPUM uses the dBASE.DBF structure for its database files, with the advantage that any similarly structured database can be imported or exported easily into any database program. The basic structure of .DBF files is sequential, meaning that as you add a record, it istacked on to the end of your database. The first part of the .DBF file defines field types, names, and lengths. If you only have a handful of

---

Figure 18-9

The browse screen in WAMPUM

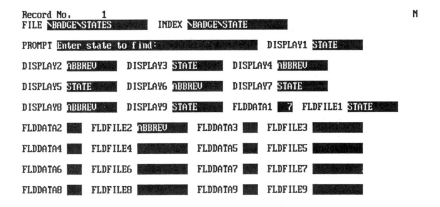

<Enter>, <PgDn>, <PgUp>, or <ESC>

records in your database, a sequential search is not a problem—the program searches each record for matching criteria. If you have a large database (WAMPUM can support databases with millions of records), then you need a way to access the information quickly rather than searching every record.

This is where .NDX files come in. An index contained in an .NDX file is nothing more than a sorted list of the keywords. You could sort the database itself, but this would be slower and you would have to re-sort each time you made changes. If you have a ZIP.NDX file, you would see a list of zip codes in ascending or descending order. The index can be on one field or on a variety of fields, depending on how you set it up. If you add a record, it is automatically entered into the proper place in the index so your index is always sorted. WAMPUM allows seven different indexes for each database.

The WAMPUM Database Files

The WAMPUM.FRM and .LBL files are templates that tell the program how to display the information once it is retrieved. You can choose the order of the records to be viewed or printed by selecting the index and the individual records.

In creating a new database for WAMPUM, you can have up to 400 fields depending on how much memory your system has. In selecting the order of the fields, put the most important ones first, since WAMPUM's browse mode can only display a single line of fields for twenty records at a time. Once you have selected the names of the fields, you must choose the type of field. WAMPUM has five different types of fields: character, numeric, date, logical, and memo. Each field has a minimum and a maximum length. For example, the minimum length of a character field is 1 and the maximum is 254 while both the minimum and maximum length for a date field is 8 characters.

Revisions Are Easy If you decide you don't like the structure of the database, revising it is very simple. After you bring up the file to be revised, select **B** for build a new file, insert an asterisk by the filename, and press ENTER. You are then presented with a screen showing the fields in the selected database. You can change the information in the database including the field name, type, and length, and delete or add additional fields. Once you have made your changes, reindex the database from the Main Menu using X for Rebuild/FileFix.

Indexing Data in WAMPUM

Indexes are the heart of the WAMPUM database function. Primarily, they provide a quick method of retrieving records for editing, displaying, or printing. As noted earlier, indexing is more effective than sorting, since indexing makes no physical changes, but does allow the program to automatically update the database constantly as new records are added or deleted. This saves time in producing reports, form letters, and labels. WAMPUM can create an index on any field in your database or on a combination of fields. For example, you can have an index of first and last names. In order to build very complex indexes, you really have to be a dBASE programmer, but usually a simple index will serve your purposes.

WAMPUM Can Link Databases

One of WAMPUM's unique features is its ability to link one database to an identical field in another database. For this to work, the second database must be in the default directory or in the DOS path. It must be indexed on a field identical in size, type, and field name to a field in the first database, although the matching field does not have to be indexed. When a report, label, or form letter is run while a related file and index are set, you can access data in any of the fields of the matching related file. This is done by typing the name of the related file, a right angle bracket, and the field name.

You can relate the second file in one of two ways. You can either press z for the Zoom/Relate File option from the Main Menu and enter the name of the file and index to be related, or use the WAMPUM preformatted output file. This last option allows you to specify all the components of a report, label, or form letter in advance. The components are stored in a separate database file called WAMPUM.DBF and can be called up as needed. This database is created much like any other WAMPUM database and can be edited or added to.

When the data entry screen appears, you will be prompted for certain information. For DATAFILE, enter the name of the primary file. For SORTINDX, enter the sort index by entering the name of the index file. If you leave this field blank, the output will be produced in the order of the records in the primary file. For RPTLBLFRM, press either R for Report, L for Label, or F for Form Letter. For OUTFILE, enter the name of the actual report form. For FONT, enter a number between 0 and 9 to identify the font you will be using.

WAMPUM allows you to embed font codes in reports, labels, and form letters to control printing. You select a set of fonts for your printer from the Printer config option on the Main Menu, which presents you with a list of .MEM files, or you can create your own .MEM file. For CRITERIA, enter the selection criteria for the report or label. DESCRIP is a brief description of the file just designed and appears on the menu when you select preformatted output. RELFILE1 is the filename for the second-ary file. RELINDX1 is the name of the index to be used in relating the secondary file to a primary field.

The Configuration Files

WAMPUM's .MEM files contain much more than just the printer configu-rations; they contain all of the configurations for the program. You can change the name that appears above the Main Menu, designate the default main file drive, disable any of 21 menu choices, set the margins for form letters, set the date format by country, and toggle networking on. In addition, the .MEM configuration saves the names of the current file, related file, indexes, and default printer template; the range of available data entry menus; and the browse mode default setting. You can have up to nine different configurations.

Configuring WAMPUM

Using the configuration option, you can change many of the WAMPUM defaults. This screen is shown in Figure 18-10.

HEADING is the name that appears at the top of the Main Menu, while Main File Drive, Related File, and DEFAULT are used if your data-bases are not stored in the default directory. Menu # is a listing by number of all of the menu choices. You can disable any of these by deleting the appropriate number.

Form Letter Margins specifies the left and right margins for form letters. PrinterOutput is available for those using a network, or for redi-recting the printer output to a file rather than a printer. AUDIT TRAIL file can be toggled to enable the audit trail, which verifies the accuracy of posted data by keeping a record of all additions and changes to the database. Confirm field entries is a toggle forcing the user to confirm each field entry before the cursor will move on. Network provides for file locking and Country determines the format of dates, including American

---

Figure 18-10

WAMPUM's configuration screen

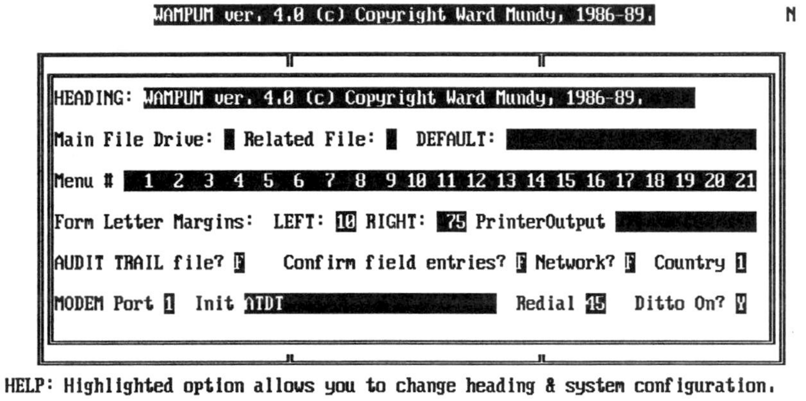

WAMPUM ver. 4.0 (c) Copyright Ward Mundy, 1986-89.   N

```
HEADING: WAMPUM ver. 4.0 (c) Copyright Ward Mundy, 1986-89.

Main File Drive: ▌ Related File: ▌ DEFAULT: ▐▐▐▐▐▐▐▐▐▐▐▐▐

Menu #  1  2  3  4  5  6  7  8  9 10 11 12 13 14 15 16 17 18 19 20 21

Form Letter Margins:  LEFT: 10 RIGHT: 75 PrinterOutput ▐▐▐▐▐▐▐▐▐

AUDIT TRAIL file? █    Confirm field entries? █ Network? █  Country ▌

MODEM Port ▌  Init ATDT                       Redial 15   Ditto On? Y
```

HELP: Highlighted option allows you to change heading & system configuration.

(MDY), ANSI (YMD), and British/French/Italian (DMY). You can also specify the width of the memo field in lists and reports, and update all memory variables.

WAMPUM's Programmable Side

If you have enough memory, you can run other executable external programs from developer mode, do global replacements of data in a file, and import or export data from a variety of formats. You can also do global deletes and undeletes.

WAMPUM allows for several unique kinds of fields. The LASTTIME field is a character field in which WAMPUM will automatically insert the current time when a record is added or edited. The LASTUPDT field is a date field in which the current date is inserted. Neither of these require any user input. A LASTUSER field is a character field to which WAMPUM will automatically post the current userid if you have included a SET USERID=X line in your AUTOEXEC.BAT file. In order for this to work however, you must first set up a USERS database, indexed with the names and passwords of authorized users.

Formatting Reports

The formats for reports, labels, and form letters are created and revised in developer mode, although they are usually run in the end user mode. Figure 18-11 shows the report generation screen. The cursor is in the highlighted bar, where you enter your heading text.

In most cases you can simply use the default settings. There are similar screens for creating label templates and form letter templates. In building form letters, you can use WAMPUM's macro creation facility, creating up to 39 keyboard macros for each database stored in its own subdirectory. The macro file, KEYS.DBF, is created and maintained like any other database with each record representing a corresponding keystroke. F2 through F10 would be records 2 through 10, SHIFT-F1 through SHIFT-F10 would be records 11 through 20, and so on. Record number one is always reserved for help since F1 is the help key. Each record in the KEYS file must be a character string that is enclosed in single or double quotation marks.

Figure 18-11

One of WAMPUM's report generator screens

Date: 04/18/34   Nantucket Report Generator   New file: test.frm]
                       P A G E   H E A D I N G:

```
            Enter page width        88
            Enter left margin        8
            Enter right margin       8
            Enter no. lines per page 58
            Double spaced report?    N
            Page eject before printing Y
            Page eject after printing N
            Plain page               N
```

Summarizing Developer Mode

Up to this point, we have been discussing some of the developer functions in WAMPUM that are available when you type **WAMPUM VOODOO** at the command line. While we have not discussed all of the developer options and functions, these should give you an idea of how WAMPUM operates. Essentially, these developer functions are performed when setting up or customizing a new database, and creating the supplemental files that WAMPUM needs to run effectively. Once the database has been created, the only functions that need concern you are end user functions. These functions enable you to add or change information in an existing database through input functions and retrieve information from that database through output functions. Let's move on to take a look at the end user side of WAMPUM.

Using the Power of WAMPUM

Input functions include adding, editing, and deleting or undeleting records. Output functions include viewing or printing what is in the database and can be further divided into single record output or multiple record output. Single record output is the fastest because it involves only the retrieval of a single record by entering the indexed key for that record. Multiple record output is more complex, slower, but more useful since it involves a search of the entire database and presents the information in a more meaningful format. To do a multiple record search, first pick the lead index to specify the order in which the records will be presented. You then have to select the group of records using Boolean logical operands. Finally, select the type of output desired—a list, report, mailing label, or form letter.

Data Input Options

The first of the input functions to master is adding new records to the database. In order to do that you must first check to see that the file you want to work with has been selected. The bottom of the Main Menu has a line that shows the file in use. If none is showing, you have to select the file you want to use by pressing F for File select while in developer mode. This is shown in Figure 18-12. An index is also indicated on the bottom line. If none appears, then you have to create or open one by selecting I for the Index sel/create option in developer mode.

Figure 18-12

The WAMPUM Main Menu with File select on

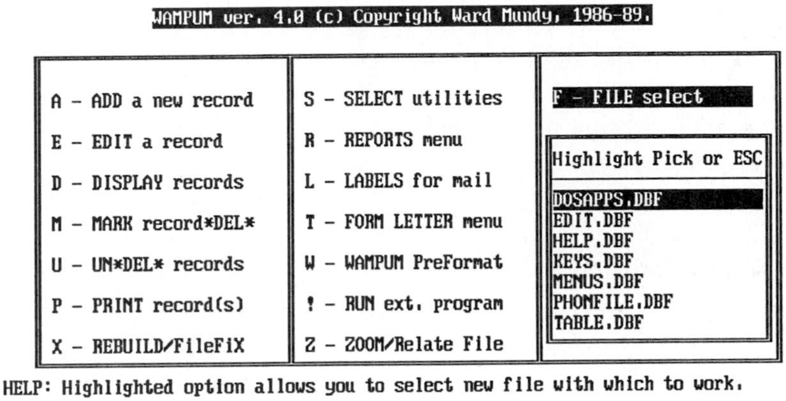

```
WAMPUM ver. 4.0 (c) Copyright Ward Mundy, 1986-89.

 ┌─────────────────────┬──────────────────────┬──────────────────────┐
 │ A - ADD a new record│ S - SELECT utilities │ F - FILE select      │
 │                     │                      │                      │
 │ E - EDIT a record   │ R - REPORTS menu     │                      │
 │                     │                      │ Highlight Pick or ESC│
 │ D - DISPLAY records │ L - LABELS for mail  │                      │
 │                     │                      │ DOSAPPS.DBF          │
 │ M - MARK record*DEL*│ T - FORM LETTER menu │ EDIT.DBF             │
 │                     │                      │ HELP.DBF             │
 │ U - UN*DEL* records │ W - WAMPUM PreFormat │ KEYS.DBF             │
 │                     │                      │ MENUS.DBF            │
 │ P - PRINT record(s) │ ! - RUN ext. program │ PHONFILE.DBF         │
 │                     │                      │ TABLE.DBF            │
 │ X - REBUILD/FileFiX │ Z - ZOOM/Relate File │                      │
 └─────────────────────┴──────────────────────┴──────────────────────┘

HELP: Highlighted option allows you to select new file with which to work.
```

You can now add a new record by pressing A for Add and filling in the information on the form that appears. The new record is saved by pressing ENTER while the cursor is on the last field of the last data entry screen. You can also save a new record by completely filling in the last field, pressing CTRL-W at any point, or pressing PGDN in the last data entry screen of a record. To update a memo field, you have to set the logical field to either true or yes. The memo editor will display any memo field marked true and allow you to update it.

Editing and Displaying Data

You must enter data exactly as it is in the database (WAMPUM does not do case-insensitive searches on fields). Once you have retrieved the record, either type over the existing data, delete data by pressing CTRL-Y and typing in the new data, or use the INS key to insert new data into a field.

CTRL-W saves the current record and prompts you for the next record to be found; PGDN saves the current record and displays the next record in the file. If you are using an index for any of these three functions, you are prompted for search criteria based on the index. For example, if the index is a ZIP index, you will be asked to enter the zip code. If you aren't using an index, you will be prompted for a record number. You can move backwards and forwards through the database using PGUP and PGDN. Using the options on the Main Menu and the same procedure, mark records to be deleted or undeleted, or retrieve records to be printed. In selecting records to be printed, enter a **T** in the lower right hand corner box for the records you want to print.

The WAMPUM Utilities

The Select utilities option on the Main Menu gives access to a submenu that performs a number of useful functions. The first, and most important, is record selection using a combination of relational operands and the principle of Boolean logic. The syntax for a search would be "Field-NameOperandValue". For example, LASTNAME< >Smith would return all records in which the data in the LASTNAME field was anything other than Smith. Two additional options are .AND. and .OR.. A search for LASTNAME="Smith" .AND. CITY="Denver" would turn up all of the Smiths in your database who live in Denver. Keep in mind that .AND. means that both expressions must be true and .OR. means that either can be true. To select from logical fields, the Boolean expression is the field plus either $ or .NOT.$, logical fields being those that have a true or false option only. The complete list of operands is

=	Equals; matches; begins with
< >	Not equals
>	Greater than; more than
> =	Greater than or equal; at least
<	Less than
< =	Less than or equal; at most
$	Is contained in
.NOT.$	Is not contained in

The last two operands are very powerful since they enable searches for matching text strings. WAMPUM provides a helping hand in selecting search criteria through the select assist option, either by entering an asterisk in the record selection field or picking the list file contents option

Figure 18-13

The browse menu in WAMPUM

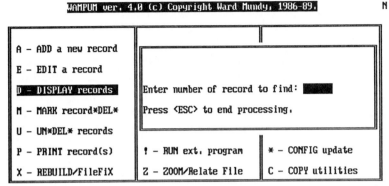

```
WAMPUM ver. 4.0 (c) Copyright Ward Mundy, 1986-89.

 A - ADD a new record     ║
                          ║
 E - EDIT a record        ║
                          ╟──────────────────────────────────────────
 D - DISPLAY records      ║ Enter number of record to find:
                          ║
 M - MARK record*DEL*     ║ Press <ESC> to end processing.
                          ║
 U - UN*DEL* records      ║
                          ╟───────────────────────────╥───────────────
 P - PRINT record(s)      ║ ! - RUN ext. program      ║ * - CONFIG update
                          ║                           ║
 X - REBUILD/FileFiX      ║ Z - ZOOM/Relate File      ║ C - COPY utilities

HELP: Highlighted option allows you to display information on existing record.
```

from the browse menu. This menu is shown in Figure 18-13. WAMPUM will prompt for the proper selection criteria.

Help in Finding Data

Once Select assist is started, it displays a screen showing the name of the first field in the database. You can page down through the field using the cursor keys. When you find the one you want, press ENTER. If you have a lot of fields in your database, you can also type enough of the beginning characters in the field name so WAMPUM can begin searching for a match. After the field name is selected, you then must choose the relational operand. The default is equals, but using the cursor keys, you can page down through them.

When the desired operand is displayed, press ENTER again and you will be prompted for the value specification. With other than character fields, the value selection is limited; with character fields, simply type in, without quotation marks, the search criterion. The final piece of information you will be asked to provide is the connector. This is optional and indicates how this selection is to be linked to the next selection, if any. The options are AND, OR, or NO CONNECTOR. Choosing one of the first two will take you to the next line to enter a second selection criterion beginning with a different field name. The next time you choose the Select option from the Main Menu, you will find that your search criterion is entered in its proper place. Select assist is very handy if you understand the Boolean search theory but have difficulty with the actual syntax.

Another feature of Select assist is to enable you to perform a List File Contents procedure if you do not enter any search criteria. Instead of the screen asking for the search criteria, you will be presented with a screen showing the field names. You will be asked to enter a number beside each field you want to include in your display. You can then either print the listing that appears, output all records—thereby bypassing any search criteria already in place—or print records marked for deletion.

Moving Around in WAMPUM

From the Selection menu you can change data entry menus. WAMPUM provides the capacity for creating up to nine customized data entry menus to match different data entry stages for any given database. These menus are created in developer mode and can be automatic, semiautomatic, or user-defined. They are stored in a file called MENUS.DBF and like the KEYS file are a special database, in this case, of alternate menus. In end user mode, you will then be able to select an alternate menu from the range shown on the screen. A selection is available for picking a new lead index, which is a simple way of switching one index from the lead index to another. Before doing this, however, you must have used the Index option from the Main Menu and selected all of the indexes.

WAMPUM's browse mode can be accessed via the Selection menu or invoked with ALT-B. In browse mode you are prompted for the key field value to find. Instead of the usual single record, you will see a table showing the first 20 records in key order beginning with the first matching key value. You can then request the next 20 records by pressing PGDN. Highlight one of the records, and the full record will appear on the screen. While you cannot change any of the data while in browse, it does enable you to select a single record when you have a number of records, for example, when last names are the same. Deleted records will also show up on the browse list, marked with an asterisk.

Figure 18-14

The List File Structure display

WAMPUM FILE STRUCTURE REVISION MODULE - Press <ESC> when done.

Fld Name	Type	Length	Dec	DELETE?	Fld Name	Type	Length	Dec	DELETE?
FILE	C	20	0	N	FLDDATA5	N	3	0	N
INDEX	C	20	0	N	FLDFILE5	C	10	0	N
PROMPT	C	40	0	N	FLDDATA6	N	3	0	N
DISPLAY1	C	10	0	N	FLDFILE6	C	10	0	N
DISPLAY2	C	10	0	N	FLDDATA7	N	3	0	N
DISPLAY3	C	10	0	N	FLDFILE7	C	10	0	N
DISPLAY4	C	10	0	N	FLDDATA8	N	3	0	N
DISPLAY5	C	10	0	N	FLDFILE8	C	10	0	N
DISPLAY6	C	10	0	N	FLDDATA9	N	3	0	N
DISPLAY7	C	10	0	N	FLDFILE9	C	10	0	N
DISPLAY8	C	10	0	N					
DISPLAY9	C	10	0	N					
FLDDATA1	N	3	0	N					
FLDFILE1	C	10	0	N					
FLDDATA2	N	3	0	N					
FLDFILE2	C	10	0	N					
FLDDATA3	N	3	0	N					
FLDFILE3	C	10	0	N					
FLDDATA4	N	3	0	N					
FLDFILE4	C	10	0	N					

Listing File Structures The final item in the Selection menu is List File Structure, shown in Figure 18-14. This is a handy listing of all of the fields in the database, for example, or sizes that can be printed to screen or sent to the printer.

Reports, Labels, and Form Letters There are three options on the Main Menu (Figure18-12) for generating reports, labels, and form letters. Option T for form letters allows you to run preexisting form letters or create new ones. The other two options, R and L, require you to first select criteria by pressing S for Select utilities. You must then enter the record selection criteria and specify the lead index. When you select reports or labels, you will be presented with a list of preset templates and prompted for the printer font. Finally, you will see a Printer Selection screen that lets you choose whether to print or display the information. Figure 18-15 shows the Form Letter screen.

Figure 18-15

The Form Letter display in WAMPUM

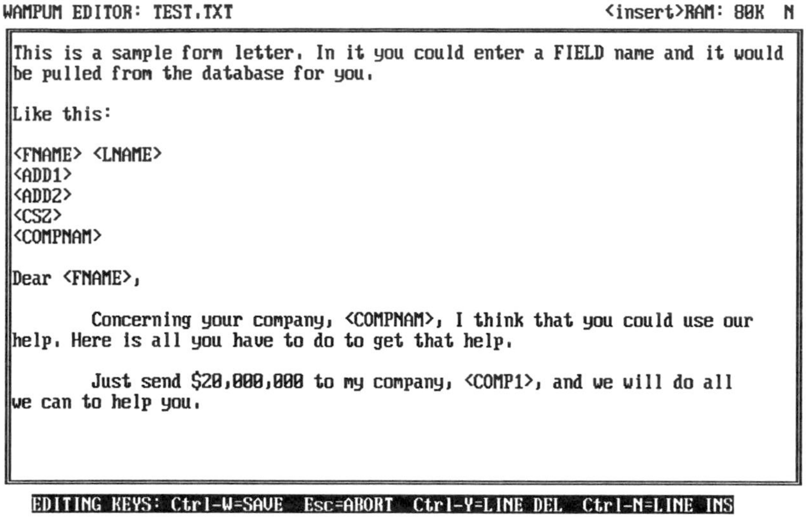

```
WAMPUM EDITOR: TEST.TXT                              <insert>RAM: 80K  N

┌──────────────────────────────────────────────────────────────────────┐
│This is a sample form letter. In it you could enter a FIELD name and it would│
│be pulled from the database for you.                                    │
│                                                                        │
│Like this:                                                              │
│                                                                        │
│<FNAME> <LNAME>                                                         │
│<ADD1>                                                                  │
│<ADD2>                                                                  │
│<CSZ>                                                                   │
│<COMPNAM>                                                               │
│                                                                        │
│Dear <FNAME>,                                                           │
│                                                                        │
│       Concerning your company, <COMPNAM>, I think that you could use our│
│help. Here is all you have to do to get that help.                      │
│                                                                        │
│       Just send $20,000,000 to my company, <COMP1>, and we will do all │
│we can to help you.                                                     │
│                                                                        │
│                                                                        │
└──────────────────────────────────────────────────────────────────────┘
 EDITING KEYS: Ctrl-W=SAVE  Esc=ABORT  Ctrl-Y=LINE DEL  Ctrl-N=LINE INS
```

High-Powered, Low-Priced

WAMPUM's most exceptional feature is the last to be discussed. Earlier, in the section on developer mode, we discussed the way in which you setup a WAMPUM.DBF file, which is a master file that includes preformatted output options. This option allows you to run up to 80 predefined reports, labels, and form letters, each with its own predefined selection criteria, sort order, and related file if desired. To access this feature from the end user menu, press **W** for PreFormat from the Main Menu. You will then see a two-column listing of all reports, labels, and form letters available for automatic production. Each description will be followed by the letter R, L, or T, indicating the type.

Mark your choices with a **Y** for yes in the logical field provided. At the bottom of the screen, you will see a range of dates if the output selected requires one. The default setting is the beginning and end of the current month. This is handy for producing monthly reports, although the dates can be changed to suit your needs. Once you have made your choices, you will be presented with a Printer Selection screen. Answer the prompts and that's all there is to it.

In summary, while WAMPUM may be a little more difficult to set up than some of the other databases, both the manual and on-line help screens take you through the developer mode. The end result is a relational database with all the power of many of the much more expensive commercial databases.

Ward Mundy
Ward Mundy Software
4160 Club Drive
Atlanta, GA 30319
$50 registration fee

PROFILE

ProFile is an exceptionally powerful program allowing for an unlimited number of database files. Up to four databases can be linked together— one primary database plus three referenced databases. You can create calculated fields in a data entry form incorporating other fields, constants, and functions. Nine options, far more than most databases allow, are available to perform mathematical functions, including:

- Sine
- Cosine
- Square
- Square root
- Log

ProFile lets you manage large databases with more than two billion records per database file and ten index files per database. Each record can support four database files per form, 3,000 characters per record, 150 fields per database, and 100 lines for the database entry form.

Getting into ProFile

ProFile supports four field types: text, numeric, lookup, and calculation. The text field attributes can include any character or alpha characters only, numbers only, auto-date or date, phone number, and social security number. Most databases support only alphanumeric, numbers, date, and alpha characters only. Number field attributes can be any number or currency, and the number field is an incrementing field that automatically increments as new forms are added.

ProFile can enforce entry rules for fields such as must fill, required, unique, force uppercase, and range checking. There is even a minimum or maximum for numeric fields, so incorrect data cannot be entered. For those who tend to forget to back up their data, ProFile automatically saves it. At every fifth record you enter, the program closes the database files, and then reopens them, putting the information permanently on your disk. This doesn't mean you can exit ProFile sloppily but it is a help. The program also offers a backup function in its Utilities menu.

Searching with ProFile

ProFile's powerful search capabilities include alphabetic, numeric and date range searches; AND; OR; partial; exact; and combination matches. In addition, you can optimize the search and sort speeds. You can index on any field, view your database in index order making use of ten index fields per database, and find any indexed record in less than two seconds. A powerful one-step global search and replace capability allows you to replace information globally, add information to the beginning or end of field data, delete partial information, or substitute partial data in a field.

Reports, Labels, and More

ProFile sorts reports or labels on up to ten fields and includes an even more innovative feature allowing you to sort reports and labels or mail merge in third class bulk mail order. Reports can be up to 64 columns or 255 characters wide. You can customize column calculations to show a running balance, percentages, spreadsheet formulas, and so on. Column summaries can display totals, averages, counts and subtotals, subaverages, and subcounts. You can have invisible columns for intermediate calculations and perform scientific calculations such as sine, cosine, square root, and so on. Once reports have been created, they can be previewed on screen before printing. Once you are satisfied with the reports, you can save an unlimited number of report formats for future use.

In addition, you can print labels up to four across, or print in third class bulk mail order with dividers and summaries, making use of an easy-to-use label creation option with 31 predefined labels and an "any-style" selection option. ProFile supports almost all popular printers.

Working with ProFile

While very powerful, ProFile utilizes pop-up and Lotus spreadsheet style menus that are easy to use. You can create help lines for any field, although ProFile has over 150 screens of context-sensitive help. The free form database design allows you to change the design of the record easily without losing data and a quick entry *ditto* key allows you to copy information from a previous form with a single keystroke. ProFile works well with other programs. A dialer function lets you automatically dial any number in your database. You can import or export ASCII data in comma-delimited, standard data format, or in a one field per line format. You can also easily convert dBASE II, III, or III Plus files to ProFile format; create a mail merge file for most popular word processing programs; and copy data between different ProFile databases.

Unlike other programs, ProFile does not default to the Main Menu on starting the program. Instead, it brings up a Load File screen, which is a file manager, shown in Figure 18-16. In addition to an automatic display of all databases available, which can be selected by moving the highlighted bar and pressing ENTER, there is also an option to enter a filename if you want to create a new database. The function keys, listed at the bottom of the screen, allow you to view files in another directory, copy a highlighted file to a new directory, or delete or rename a highlighted file. Once you have selected the database you want to work with, you are presented with the Main Menu, displayed in Figure 18-17.

This menu has a set of pull-down menus that cover all of the options you will need to enter data, print it out, maintain your files, and so on. Most are self-explanatory. Two of the selections, Print and Utility, will be

Figure 18-16

The Load File screen in ProFile

```
Load File- Form Definition
Directory Listing
BOOKS.FRM    BROKER.FRM   BUSINESS.FRM  BUSI_EXP.FRM  BUSI_INV.FRM
CHURCH.FRM   CLUB.FRM     HOME_INV.FRM  INVOICE.FRM   MAGAZINE.FRM
MUSIC.FRM    PART.FRM     PERSONAL.FRM  PRSNL.FRM     REAL_EST.FRM
RESIDENT.FRM SAMPLE.FRM   XMAS.FRM




```

The Form Definition File is where the specifications for your database are stored. Use the arrow keys to pick an existing file or, if you have not yet designed a form, choose a name for the Form Definition File and enter it here.

File Name ..: _____

F1- Help F2- New Dir F4- Copy F5- Delete F8- Rename Esc- EXIT

Figure 18-17

ProFile's Main Menu

```
Main Menu
  Form  Data  Print  Exchange  Utility  Quit
  ┌─────────────────┐
  │ Select          │
  │ Layout          │
  │ Options         │
  │ Default Values  │
  └─────────────────┘


              ProFile

        Professional Filing System

            Version 2.0e
```

Figure 18-18

The Add Records display in ProFile

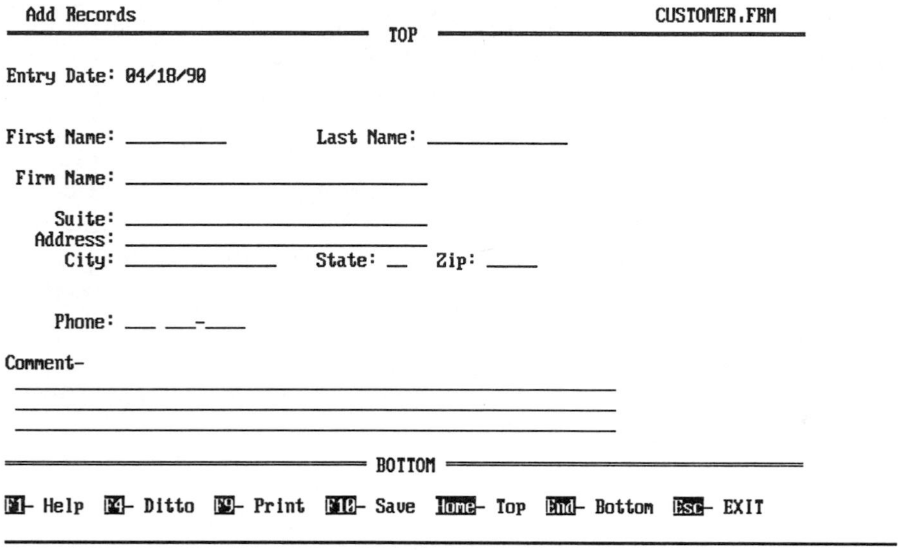

```
Add Records                                              CUSTOMER.FRM
============================================ TOP ===================

Entry Date: 04/18/90

First Name: _____        Last Name: _____

 Firm Name: _____

    Suite: _____
  Address: _____
     City: _____  State: __  Zip: _____

    Phone: ___ ___-____
Comment-
           _____
           _____
           _____
           _____

=========================================== BOTTOM ================
F1- Help  F4- Ditto  F9- Print  F10- Save  Home- Top  End- Bottom  Esc- EXIT
```

discussed later in the appropriate place. For now, the primary concern is designing a database form or adding information to an existing database.

Manipulating Data

In working with an existing database, you can either add records or edit. If you choose the add function from the Main Menu, a blank form appears, which is shown in Figure 18-18.

Adding data requires that you enter data in the proper field and press ENTER. ProFile has some unique field characteristics; for example, required fields must always have information entered to them. Unique fields like a customer number field, for example, must appear only once in a database. ProFile automatically checks to see if the information has been previously entered so there can be no duplicate customer numbers. In the case of a must-fill field, it must be completely filled or left completely empty before the record can be saved.

In addition, a range can be specified for numeric fields, meaning that in creating the database, you have specified a range of numbers that can be entered. ProFile checks to make sure that the number you have entered in that field falls within the allowable range. If any of the fields are lookup fields, you need only enter a name, for instance, and the program will check the related database and insert the correct address. If it can't find the data, it will give you a sorted list that most closely matches the information that you entered.

Some Added Flexibility and Help

When entering a large number of records, if some of the information in a field is identical on all the records, you can use F4 to copy the information. For instance, if all records are for the same state, you can automatically insert the state name in the appropriate spot. If you run into problems, every line has a help screen, and you can also create special help lines that appear when you are adding information. This could tell the user what information a field should contain and what codes or abbreviations are permitted. The help screen is shown in Figure 18-19.

Figure 18-19

Help screen to design a new form

Next Page   Previous Page   General Topics   Advanced Topics

Default Form Values

You can assign a default value to any field in your form. When you add new information to your database, the default value appears in the information blank next to the field label.

To enter Default Values:

1)   Select Default from the Form Menu. Your Form Design will appear.

2)   Move the cursor to the field where you'd like to enter a default value. Enter in the value just as if you were filling in a new form. Repeat until all values have been entered.

3)   If you want to delete a default value, move the cursor to the value you'd like deleted and press ^[Home] (Control-Home).

4)   When all changes have been made press F10.

5)   At the "Make any changes permanent" prompt, answer Yes to save your changes to disk, or No to make them applicable to this session only.

Taking Care of Business

In editing an existing record, a new menu appears at the bottom of the screen and a few additional pieces of information are provided. The Edit screen is displayed in Figure 18-20.

At the top left-hand corner of the record you will see "Ttl=12" and "Rec=7." This tells you the total number of records in the database and the current record number. Most of the editing functions don't need further explanation. Count lets you count the records that meet the Selection Spec you have chosen. Select and index lets you select a different index for the database from among those chosen when the database was created.

Power That's Easy to Handle

Selection Spec is the heart of the program. Use it to select a group of records from your database for viewing, printing reports and labels, and making changing. It's based on Boolean theory, but ProFile uses menus

---

Figure 18-20

The Edit Records screen

```
   Edit Records                                          CUSTOMER.FRM
Ttl=   12 Rec=     7                   TOP

Entry Date: 11/22/89


First Name: Greg_____        Last Name: Grouper_____

  Firm Name: Support Shareware Group_____

     Suite: Suite 10_____
   Address: 197 Village St._____
      City: Villageville____    State: MD   Zip: 21030


     Phone: 555 111-2222

Comment-
     _____
     _____
     _____
========================== BOTTOM =======================
Suite number or PO Box
F1- Help  F4- Ditto  F9- Print  F10- Save  Home- Top  End- Bottom  Esc- EXIT
```

and English terminology to help you build a Selection Spec, so you need not be familiar with any symbols. Instead of having to type **City="Pittsburgh"**, all you would have to do is go to the Selection Spec screen, shown in Figure 18-21.

From here you can toggle through the options. You can have up to four different selection criteria for any search. The fields for the database are shown at the top of the screen. Move the cursor to the one you want and press ENTER to select it. Once you press ENTER, the comparison option appears at the top of the screen next to the chosen field. There are seven ways to compare information: equal, not equal, greater than, equal or greater than, less than, equal or less than, and contains. Contains will work on any field except number or calculated fields and will search across the line. The search is not case sensitive. You can do greater than and less than searches on characters; ProFile treats the alphabet as if it were numerical.

Figure 18-21

ProFile's Selection Spec screen

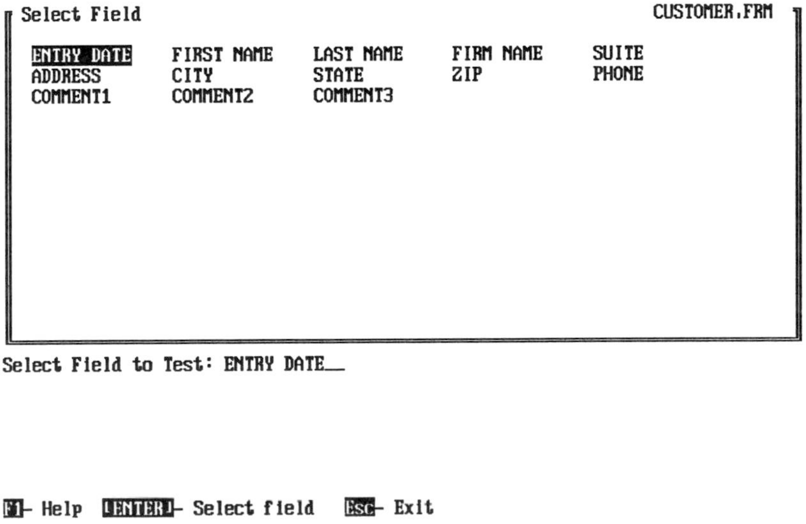

```
┌ Select Field                                          CUSTOMER.FRM ┐

  ENTRY DATE    FIRST NAME    LAST NAME    FIRM NAME    SUITE
  ADDRESS       CITY          STATE        ZIP          PHONE
  COMMENT1      COMMENT2       COMMENT3




└                                                                    ┘
Select Field to Test: ENTRY DATE__
```

F1- Help   [ENTER]- Select field   ESC- Exit

Searching Made Easy—in English

At this point all you need enter is the information to be compared. Your final selection might read "City Not Equal:Pittsburgh" and the search would turn up all entries for every city *except* Pittsburgh. You can fine-tune the search even more if you wish, or select END to conclude the process. You can also add up to four additional search criteria by using the AND/OR options. The AND means that both criteria must be satisfied; OR means that either one must be. For instance, you can have "City Not Equal:Pittsburgh OR Name Equal:Jones" and pull up only the Joneses in any city but Pittsburgh. A search for "Name Equal:Jones AND City Equal:Pittsburgh" would turn up only Joneses in Pittsburgh. Any Selection Spec can be edited using F9 from almost any screen.

Designing Databases

Designing your own database can be almost as easy as adding to or editing an existing database. From the Load File screen, type in the name of the database you wish to create. If it doesn't exist, you will be asked if you want to create it. The next question is if you want to use an existing database as a model, shown in Figure 18-22.

Let's first try typing in the name of the existing form and pressing ENTER. You will then be presented with the form for the existing database and you can edit it to suit your needs. Creating a new form from scratch is almost as easy. Here you are presented with a blank screen. Move the cursor to where you want to place a field, type in the field name followed by a colon, and draw a line using the underline character the length of the space you need for information, up to 78 characters per line. If you make the lines not long enough or too long, you can always go back and change the field length later. If you make a mistake, ProFile will beep and not let you continue. A form can be up to 100 lines long and 80 characters wide. You can insert, delete, or copy lines. If you want to draw boxes on the form to make it easier to enter data, a series of ALT keys makes it easy to do.

After you press F10 to indicate you have finished designing the form, you will then see the Field Attributes definition screen at the bottom of your screen and a part of your newly designed form at the top. To set the attributes for a field, move the cursor to the field and press ENTER. The Attributes screen will open. Figure 18-23 shows you what this looks like.

Defining Fields

The default for all fields is text. From here, you can change to any one of three other fields—numeric, lookup, or calculated—by pressing a single key. You can also enter a mask type for text and numeric fields. The default is "X," which indicates that anything can be entered. The other masks are

N	Number	Only valid numbers may be entered.
$	Money	Only valid amounts are allowed. The amount is automatically formatted with two decimal places.
I	Increment	Numeric fields that automatically increase as you add new records.
C	Alpha	Only alphabetical characters are allowed.

──────────────── **Figure 18-22** ────────────────

A form layout using a model

```
   Form Layout                                        PART.FRM
   Copy Buffer Empty ──────────── TOP ────────────────────────

   Part Number: AA_

   Description: AB_____

   Cost: AC_____




                           ═══ MORE ═══
                                              Line 1   Col 1
   ▨- Help  ▨- Insert  ▨- Copy  ▨- Delete  ▨▨- Continue  ▨- EXIT
```

9	Digits	Only numbers are allowed. Handy for zip code fields.
D	Date	Dates only.
A	AutoDate	Dates automatically filled in with today's date.
O	Soc.Sec#	Formats the field for Social Security numbers.
P	Phone #	Formats the field for phone numbers, including area code.

As the table shows, ProFile provides flexibility in the use of masks. Other options in the Attributes box include length of field; decimal places; whether this is to be an index field; and whether the information entered is required, must fill, unique, or must be in uppercase. For numeric fields, the range of numbers allowed must be specified. The help line option includes a convenient feature allowing you to type in a brief instruction line that appears when adding a record.

Figure 18-23

The Define Field Attributes display

```
 Define Field Attributes                                    CUSTOMER.FRM
━━━━━━━━━━━━━━━━━━━━━━━━━━━━━━━━━━━━━━━━ TOP ━━━━━━━━━━━━━━━━━━━━━━━━━━━━━━

 Entry Date: __/__/__

 First Name: _____        Last Name: _____

 Firm Name: _____
╔══════════════════════════════ MORE ══════════════════════════════════╗
║Field Type: Text                                                      ║
║    Prompt: ENTRY DATE__  Mask Type: A   Length: 8   Decimal: 8  Index: N
║ Help Line: _____ ║
║                                                                      ║
║          Entry Rules                           Range                 ║
║         ─────────────                         ───────                ║
║    Required: N      Unique: N             Low: 8_____             ║
║    Must Fill: N   UpperCase: N           High: 8_____             ║
╚══════════════════════════════════════════════════════════════════════╝

 F1- Help    ENTER- Attributes    F10- Save    Esc- Form Layout
```

Linking and Calculations

If you choose to have one of your fields as a lookup field, the box containing the attributes will reflect this by having spaces for the lookup filename field, the lookup match field, the lookup retrieve field, and the search field. In each case, the form in the top half of the screen is replaced by a window. From this window you can select the database to be linked, fields in that database containing the proper records to be used for matching and where the found information is to be inserted, and the field in the current database that you want to use to find the proper record in the lookup database.

Spectacular Calculations

ProFile's calculated field turns your database into a spreadsheet. The formulas used are similar to those in spreadsheets. To reference a field for a calculation, enter **F** followed by the field number. For example, **F9 + F10** will give the total of fields 9 and 10. ProFile uses certain rules to determine what parts of a calculation are done at what time. Formulas in parentheses, ( ), are calculated first; division, /, multiplication, *, and raising a number to a power, ^, are done next; and addition, +, and subtraction, −, are done last. In addition, ProFile has a series of functions that can be used in formulas in a calculated column. The syntax is *fnc(value)*, where *fnc* is the function and *value* is either a constant or a field number. Here are some examples.

ABS(n)	Absolute	Returns the absolute value of N.
SQRT(n)	Square Root	Square root of N.
SQR(n)	Square	Returns the square of N.
SIN(n)	Sine	Returns the sine of N. N is expressed in radians and the result is a real number.
COS(n)	Cosine	Returns the cosine of N. N is expressed in radians and the result is a real number.
ARCTAN(n)	Arc Tangent	Returns the angle, in radians, whose tangent is N.
LN(n)	Natural	Returns the natural logarithm of N.
LOG(n)	Logarithm	Returns the logarithm of N.
EXP(n)	Exponential	Returns the exponential of N.

You won't believe the things that you can do with calculations using ProFile.

Using the Data

After mastering the ins and outs of inputting data, it's important to be able to retrieve data in a meaningful form. Generally, that form consists of reports, mailing labels, and form letters. These items are accessed from the pull-down Printer menu at the Main Menu. This menu is seen in Figure 18-24.

Reports are generated in three basic steps that include designing the report, setting page and report options, and printing. You can either use an existing report format or design your own using the Report Layout menu. Specify options from a Report menu by entering in the selection specs you want. This is shown in Figure 18-25.

Let's take a closer look at how to create and generate a report in ProFile.

Working with Reports

Designing a report is much like designing a record since you choose information from a window and set the Selection Spec criteria you want

---

Figure 18-24

The Main Menu with Print menu pulled down

Main Menu   CUSTOMER.FRM
    Form Data Print Exchange Utility Quit
                    ┌──────────────────┐
                    │ Reports   │
                    │ Labels   │
                    │ MailMerge   │
                    │ Printer Setup   │
                    │ Ordering Labels │
                    └──────────────────┘
                            ProFile

                    Professional Filing System

                        Version 2.0e

---

included. First, you can add to a report. This lets you add columns, which you select from a listing in a window at the top of the screen. After adding each column, you are then shown another screen with the column number, field name, and length of field filled in. The total width and total number of columns are in the upper right-hand corner. You can then fill in the details for the column or choose the defaults.

In addition to length, these details include the decimal position in numeric fields, whether you want data wrapped, as in a word processor, or truncated, numeric format (numbers, currency, or percent), and whether data in a column should always be printed or only when the value changes. For example, you might want a zip code field printed only if the zip code changes. When you press F10 to show that you have finished, the program will prompt you for another column or ask if you wish to quit. If you have made an error, you can always go back and edit the column definitions. If any of the columns are to be the result of a

---

Figure 18-25

The Report Layout display

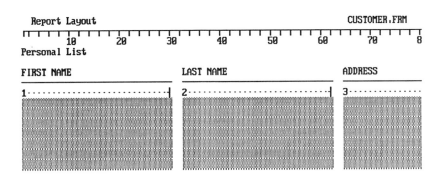

calculation, enter column calculation codes. The final results will appear at the end of the report beneath the column on which the calculation was performed.

Calculations in Reports

You can also create calculated columns by creating columns and specifying calculation as the field. Note that this is the first entry in the list of fields to select from. Invisible columns are calculated columns you don't want to appear in the final report. Create them just as you create any other column except that they are given a length of zero. This feature can be used for intermediate calculations for other calculated columns.

When you have either selected a preexisting report format or designed a new one, you will then see another Report menu. This is shown in Figure 18-26.

You have several options on the Report menu. Format allows you to change margins and insert printer control codes and printer destination;

Figure 18-26

Headers and Footers Report screen

```
┌─ Report Headers and Footers                              CUSTOMER.FRM ─┐
│                                                                        │
│                               Report Header                            │
│                                                                        │
│   FILE: @FILENAME                                          PAGE: @PAGE  │
│                            Printed On @TODAY                            │
│                                                                        │
├────────────────────────────────────────────────────────────────────────┤
│                                                                        │
├────────────────────────────────────────────────────────────────────────┤
│                               Report Footer                            │
│                                                                        │
│                                                                        │
├────────────────────────────────────────────────────────────────────────┤
│                                                                        │
│                                                                        │
└────────────────────────────────────────────────────────────────────────┘
  @PAGE = Page Number    @TODAY = Today's Date    @FILENAME = Database Name

  F1- Help      F10- Done      Esc- EXIT
```

Layout lets you make changes to the report form; Select is used to create or change the Selection Spec; Sort is used to change or create the Sort Spec; Hdr/Ftr lets you create headers and footers for reports; and New lets you choose a new report format. The Selection Spec for a report is exactly like the one you used to edit a file. Once these options are chosen, they become part of the report format, but can always be changed using Select.

Sort Spec controls the way information is printed in a report. Ten sort fields, one primary and nine secondary, are available. Fields can be sorted in ascending or descending order. You can enter page breaks between sections by entering a **P** next to the sort number. By entering an **L** and a number you can tell ProFile to skip that number of lines when the value of the sort field changes.

ProFile's Bulk Mail Option

ProFile has what it calls bulk mail sort for third class bulk mail. When you do a bulk mailing, ProFile arranges the data first by state, then by a five-digit and three-digit count, and then by a mixed state sort.

To use this option, select the Bulk Sort feature on the Sort menu, and then select the zip code field from a list. Once the bulk mail sort is complete, ProFile prints your database in bulk mail order. When you print mailing labels sorted in bulk mail order, ProFile creates a text file called BULKMAIL.TXT, which contains a summary of the counts for each five-digit, three-digit, state, and mixed state bundle. It also includes a count of the total number of pieces in the mailing. As the labels are printed, ProFile inserts dividers to mark the end of each group of labels. You can print this listing to create bag labels and to provide a summary sheet for the post office.

To create a label format, first choose the label size from 15 standard label sizes or the free form label option. ProFile provides an additional 16 NEBS (New England Business Systems) forms that include postcards, rotary file cards, laser labels, and file cards. Once you choose a label size, a template will appear on screen that is the exact size of the label chosen. You can enter information by first typing in the field name or number. If you can't remember them, pressing F9 will display your database form with the numbers after the field names. Next, enter either a colon to print only the field data or a right angle bracket to print the field data exactly where you want it. You can also add an additional message on your label, like "Save the Whales." Once the label layout is completed, press Y at the prompt to continue to the Label menu. The Label menu is exactly like the Report menu. It controls how the label is printed and allows you to create a Selection Spec or a Sort Spec, do bulk mail sort, and so on.

Summarizing ProFile

ProFile is an impressive program with a number of features more expensive Shareware database programs don't offer. The sophisticated calculation functions, the variety of masks, the flexibility of its design functions, and especially its ease of use make it a program well worth looking into.

Lee Raesly
National Software Design
12505 Fostoria Way
Darnestown, MD 20878
301-921-4283 (Voice)
76464,303 CompuServe ID
$49.95 cost includes disk and manual

OTHER KINDS OF DATABASES

Most database programs are structured with records, forms, files, fields, and so on. Free form databases have the potential to be even more useful. One reason is that all you need do is install the program—there is no setting up of forms, fields, indexes, and so on. While free form databases resemble text editors, what sets them apart from conventional databases are sensitive search capabilities, cut-and-paste operations, and the variety of uses to which they can be put.

Using a Free Form Database

If you are a programmer, you can use a free form database to store program information lying around your desk or in notebooks. You can save frequently used information from reference books such as ASCII tables, interrupt conventions, process definitions and assumptions, BIOS and

DOS calls, and interrupts. You can also keep notes on program documentation, variables and variable relationships, bug reports, version release notes, and lists of planned program enhancements.

Lots of Business Uses

Small business applications for free form databases are equally varied. A company could store employee records, lists of suppliers and customers, product information, prices, or colors. Order or delivery deadline reminders can be stored in a calendar. If you are a teacher, you can keep your lecture notes, student progress and grade notes, and reminders of faculty meetings, student conferences, or research notes in your database. You might keep a library of test questions for future reference. Your students, on the other hand, could keep a set of homework and test date reminders, their notes for your course, a select bibliography, and a calendar of due dates for papers and assignments.

Lawyers can keep time billing records, telephone and case notes, a calendar of court dates and legal due dates, meeting reminders, bibliography and law reference information, or a client and business associate address book. Accountants can keep case notes, records of tax law reference information, tax rules and tables, time billing records, as well as an address book of clients, IRS, and business contacts.

Free form databases gain in versatility whatever they may lose in power or supplementary features. Let's take a closer look at Instant Recall and NoteBook, two of the best free form databases.

Instant Recall/Memory Mate

Instant Recall can still be found on bulletin boards, but Broderbund Software now markets a commercial version under the name of Memory Mate. You can't register for Instant Recall even though you *can* download it from a BBS. Look at Instant Recall and decide if you'd like to purchase Memory Mate. Instant Recall is an excellent program and Memory Mate is even better. Memory Mate was used to keep notes while writing this book. First, we'll cover the features of Instant Recall, and then discuss the enhancements included in Memory Mate, with the kind permission of Broderbund Software.

Checking Out Instant Recall

Instant Recall is a free form, memory resident database program. You can use it to store information needed throughout the day and it doesn't get in the way of your work flow or your other programs. Instant Recall can be thought of as an electronic file cabinet. Since it indexes every word in every record, you don't need to worry about the organization of the records.

You can enter data in any form you want—lists, tables, paragraphs of text, and so on. The only minor restriction is that everything must be in ASCII text. If you want to import a paragraph from your word processor, you will have to convert it. For instance, if you have a list of birthdays, a list of phone numbers, and a note to yourself that Cousin Mildred likes Godiva chocolates, enter **Mildred** as the search criterion and all three lists will pop up for you.

Since Instant Recall is memory resident, you can pull it up while working in a document. This allows you, for example, to get a set of notes you had previously written or add a note without worrying about connecting it to other notes. As long as all the notes contain a common word, like Shareware, they will all be available. The primary difference between a structured database and a free form database is that a free form database handles data in a multitude of forms. It functions as a place to keep all those little notes to yourself that tend to clutter up your work space.

A TSR Database

To make Instant Recall even more useful, you might want to include a line in your AUTOEXEC.BAT file that will automatically invoke it at startup so you can check the day's to-dos or reminders. After you exit, you can reenter the program by pressing ALT-Z. You will reenter in the same place that you left. This is handy since it lets you toggle back and forth between, for example, your word processor and Instant Recall notes pertaining to work you are currently doing.

When you retrieve a record in Instant Recall, notice a message in the upper right-hand corner that says, for example, "Page 1 of 2." In order to see the next page, press the grey plus sign on the numeric keyboard. At the bottom of the screen is a status line that shows when the record was created, when it was last modified, and the date you selected to be reminded. On that date, the record will be automatically displayed as the first record when you enter Instant Recall. This is an especially nice feature for keeping track of to-dos since Instant Recall does not delete the list when the reminder date has passed. It will continue displaying the list until you either delete it or change the reminder date to a later one. If you set a reminder for Cousin Mildred's birthday, you will be reminded of it until you finally send that card.

At the top of the screen is the command line. To the right is a reminder that F1 will bring up a help screen and a notation that this is "Page # of #," as shown in Figure 18-27. If this is a new blank screen, the page notation will be replaced with a working record. On the left is the command line menu. An arrow pointing to ESC tells you that all of the commands do not fit on the line and you should press ESC to see more. All of the commands can also be invoked by using the control key in combination with the first letter of the command. CTRL-S will save a record and you will be prompted for a reminder date that can be left blank.

Entering Data into Instant Recall

There are three ways to enter data into a record—type it in directly; import it from other programs using the Cut, Ditto, and Paste commands; or import a complete file using Input. You can also use Cut, Ditto, and Paste to move blocks of material from one record to another. The difference between Cut and Ditto is that Cut will delete the information from

Figure 18-27

Record screen in Memory Mate

```
Find  Narrow  Reject  Cut  Ditto  Paste  Jump  Go  | F1 for Help
Save  View  Type  In   Out  Hyper  Zap  Undo  Exit |           1 of 1 Found
```

```
With Borderbund's Memory Mate, you can find any kind of
information you want -- and NEVER have to format it. The
Memory Mate program can be loaded from DOS as a standalone
program -- it can be loaded as a TSR (resident) program.
Memory Mate can use EMS so that it uses very little DOS RAM
while resident. If you try "Instant Recall" that you can find
on bulletin boards, and like it, then look for Broderbund's
Memory Mate in fine software stores around the country.
```

```
Created: 4/18/90   Modified:          Reminder: 4/18/90  Row: 2   Col: 30 Ins
```

the original place while Ditto will make a copy of it in the new place whether in Instant Recall or in another program. Cut can also be used to delete a part of a record by using it alone without the Paste feature.

Searching for Data and More

To delete a record, use the Kill command. To find a record or a group of records, use Find followed by any text. You can also find records by the date created, modified, or set to remind using the Boolean symbols for equals, greater than, less than, and so on. Being able to find records by these dates is useful in finding forgotten records. Set the find criterion as "Created > 1/1/80" and every record in the database will be available for viewing.

Instant Recall supports the Boolean AND/OR commands mentioned previously. The searches are not case-sensitive. If your search turns up too many records, use Narrow to define the search even further. For example, you could type **find names** and **narrow Colorado**, and that would bring up only those records mentioning both names and Colorado anywhere in the text. Once you have retrieved the record, you can print it using the Type command. The Window command is used when you are in another application. When Instant Recall starts and you are in another program, it covers over the other program's screen. The other screen is still there and you can see it by using the Window command. Your screen will seem to split in two, with Instant Recall in the top window and your other program in the bottom. You can move the Instant Recall window if it covers a part of the other program you need to see. Just keep using the Window command and the Instant Recall window will change size and position. In order to use the Cut, Paste, or Ditto command, open a window into Instant Recall from the program you want to move data to or from.

Memory Mate Is Instant Recall

In the truest sense, Instant Recall is no longer a Shareware program, but was chosen for this chapter since it was an excellent Shareware program that has moved on into the commercial arena as Memory Mate. The program has been enhanced with *hypertext,* a way to attach records to other records even if they don't have common keywords. Memory Mate also supports multiple databases and can use expanded memory. Some of the names of the commands have been changed, but the functions are much the same. You can look at Instant Recall, which can be found as IR164F.ZIP. If you like it, you can find Memory Mate in software stores around the country.

NoteBook

The last of the databases to be discussed, NoteBook, is also the smallest and least cluttered. Each phase of NoteBook is accessed from the Main Menu shown in Figure 18-28.

The database is divided into folders and notes. Access to any of these can be password-protected but the password is case-sensitive. If you select Access or Create a Folder, a list of available folders appears in a box at the top of the screen. One can be chosen by moving the highlighted bar and pressing ENTER. You can also enter a new name for a folder to create a new file. The database can be sorted on two criteria, a primary and a secondary sort field, and according to keywords, title, or the date the note was created or updated.

Figure 18-28

The Main Menu of NoteBook

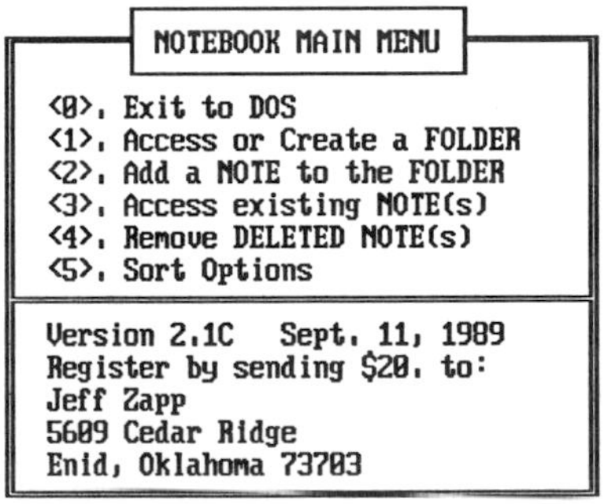

```
┌────────────────────────────────────────┐
│      ┌─ NOTEBOOK MAIN MENU ─┐           │
│      │                      │           │
│   <0>. Exit to DOS                      │
│   <1>. Access or Create a FOLDER        │
│   <2>. Add a NOTE to the FOLDER         │
│   <3>. Access existing NOTE(s)          │
│   <4>. Remove DELETED NOTE(s)           │
│   <5>. Sort Options                     │
│ ─────────────────────────────────────── │
│   Version 2.1C   Sept. 11, 1989         │
│   Register by sending $20. to:          │
│   Jeff Zapp                             │
│   5609 Cedar Ridge                      │
│   Enid, Oklahoma 73703                  │
└────────────────────────────────────────┘
```

The bottom box on the Main Menu tells you the name of the open folder, the number of notes in that folder and the number of deleted notes, the date it was created, and the date it was updated.

Using NoteBook

NoteBook doesn't have many extra functions, but if you need an easy-to-use, uncomplicated way of keeping notes and retrieving them, NoteBook is just what you want.

In using any free form database, you might benefit from a few tips. Always put a good title line at the start of any record. NoteBook will prompt you for one. This makes searching for a specific record much easier. Since free form databases will search for any text, if you can't recall, for example, the name of a company but do remember the city, you can use the city as the search criterion. NoteBook is a great database for keeping a personal journal, diary, or notes.

Jeff Zapp
5609 Cedar Ridge Avenue
Enid, OK 73703
405-233-7790 (Voice)
$20 program cost

SUMMING IT ALL UP

Databases can help you file, sort, find, print, and perform countless functions with data and information. Free form databases are handy for keeping track of less formal notes and messages. If you are looking for a database program, you will find few commercial databases that rival the power and low cost of the Shareware programs described here. Let's move on to examine some programs designed for use by programmers.

## CHAPTER NINETEEN

Programming Utilities and Patches

While the majority of computer users are not programmers, many nonprogrammers are fascinated by programming. Their curiosity is aroused by the fact that many programmers often seem to be off in a world of their own—talking about interrupts, vectors, PSP blocks, memory segments, and other mysterious things. Other people are fascinated because they too would like to learn how to write a program.

For anyone interested in programming, there is a wealth of material available in The Wires. There is so much, in fact, that planning this chapter was a difficult task. Not only are there utilities for programmers in general, but there are programs specifically designed for languages like C, Turbo Pascal, BASIC, QuickBASIC, Assembler, Prolog, and more. A partial list of the types of programs available is shown in Figure 19-1.

For those of you who are not programmers, it is my hope that a little background on what an assembler or a debugger is will help you to enjoy this chapter a bit more. To start off, let's take a very brief look at some of the items listed in Figure 19-1.

Figure 19-1

What is available from The Wires for programmers

Assemblers	Hex dump programs
B-tree sorting	Hex to decimal and back
Bubble sort	Hypertext tools
Compiler writing tutors	LZH and ARC
Conversion from ASCII to other	Macros from programmer's text editors
formats	Menus
CRC checks for 8 and 16 bit	*PC-Tech Journal* highlights
CRC checks for 32 and even 80 bit	Pop-up help screens for programmers
CRC checks for .ZIP	Program source code documenters
Debuggers	Programmer's DOS technical reference
Extracts from *Computer Language*	manual
Extracts from *Dr. Dobb's Journal*	Programmer's guides
File comparison programs	Read ROMs and save to disk
File encryption	Read/Write to PROMs
File format information	Screen designers
Flowcharters	Source libraries
Formulas	Subroutines
Functions	Text file search programs
Heap sort	TSR tools
Hex calculators	Window routines

INTRODUCTION TO PROGRAMMING

It is often hard for those who aren't involved to listen to "techie talk," even when they have an idea of what is being talked about. When you have no idea at all, it can be very frustrating. Most of us can identify with these feelings of inadequacy because after all, everyone started at the beginning. As with everything else in life, the more time you spend on a subject, the more knowledge you acquire. I'm not a programmer, but after working with so many programmers, I can say with confidence that Interrupt 8 is the clock interrupt.

The important thing to remember is that the more you work with your computer and with programs, the more you will understand. To give you some help, here are some simple definitions.

Some Programming Terminology

The brief definitions that follow are designed to give you a general understanding of what a particular programmer's tool does. When you next see these terms in file listings on bulletin boards, in online networks, or in catalogs, they will probably not seem so foreign or so mysterious. Part of feeling comfortable with computers or any subject comes with learning the terminology. With that in mind, let's examine these terms.

Pop-Up Help Screens
A number of TSR programs have been developed to create pop-up help screens to check command syntax while programming. Some of these products, such as Norton's Guide, are available commercially, but many of them are available through Freeware and Shareware. Programmers use these help screens to keep track of programming tools that they may not use very often, just as you might keep help files available for some of the Shareware programs that you don't use frequently.

Assemblers
An assembler takes assembly language source code and compiles it so that it can be used by the computer. Assembly language source files have a file extension of .ASM. A good assembler is essential to an assembly language programmer.

The number of assembly language programmers is still relatively small, and many started out using Freeware and Shareware assemblers. Programmers with only casual interest in assembly language programming also find Shareware to be a good source for assemblers.

Debuggers
Debugging is simply an interesting way of saying that one is trying to find errors, mistakes, or other problems. Some of the most talented and

experienced programmers become overwhelmed by the laborious task of debugging their code. In the world of programming, a missing semicolon can cause problems.

Interactive debuggers that point directly to errors can be real time savers. There are also a number of programming languages or environments that lack a suitable debugger. Freeware and Shareware debuggers can be an excellent source for just the help needed. They make it easier to find those errors, or "debug the code" as programmers say.

Shareware Language Libraries

Many programming languages support add-in modules or libraries developed to give enhanced commands and functions to the application program you are writing. Using libraries may increase your code size and increase the difficulty of debugging, but it is a quick and easy way to increase programming capability. For example, there is an excellent Shareware library for the C programming language, called Window BOSS, which contains programs that rival other expensive, highly touted commercial products.

Program Patches

There are times when certain bugs go undetected until after a program is released. In some cases, the program's author can determine a way to *patch* the problem through a series of programming techniques. Just as you can stick a patch over a leaky inner tube, often a patch can be used to fix a bug in a program. For example, SideKick can be modified to not make the annoying *.BAK files when using the editor.

It is often better for the programmer and the users to release a patch for a problem than it is to release a whole new version. For one, a patch is generally quite small, whereas a whole new version might be quite large. Thus, a program patch can save you time and money. For example, Procomm has about a dozen patches available to tweak it in one direction or another. These patches may be used to solve a compatibility problem or to add to or change the program's operation. You will find patches for everything from application programs to almost every version of DOS ever released.

Functions

A function is like a miniature program or subroutine that accepts arguments and returns a value. Functions are often complex mathematical formulas and are commonly used in many programs. Creating and using functions reduces code size, avoids repetition, and offers increased speed, performance, and capabilities to your code. Using functions supplied by others can make it possible for you to accomplish programming tasks that may exceed your level of programming skill.

Formulas

There are tens of thousands of formulas for calculating figures in statistics, engineering, physics, geometry, economics, finance, business, and more. Finding the formula you need in books is tedious enough, but converting it into a format to fit your programming language can be even harder. The formulas in the public domain simplify the process of incorporating them into your program.

Window Routines

Since the introduction of the Macintosh in 1984, the interest in graphically oriented user interfaces has grown steadily and is gaining momentum. There are programming tools available that aid in the development of these graphic interfaces. Like an assortment of Fourth of July fireworks, there are all sorts of tools for creating pull-down, pop-up, and pop-down menus, dialogue boxes, scrolling light bars, and shadowed and exploding windows. Many of these features that would ordinarily require a great deal of coding can be done easily with the right set of tools.

Subroutines

A *subroutine* is a programming unit that can be called from other program units. A friend of mine once wrote an enormous medical office management program that only had 12 lines of code and thousands of subroutines.

When invoked, subroutines perform a series of executive statements, and then return control to the statement that immediately follows the statement it was called from. When you use subroutines, make sure you use descriptive names for your variables. For example, *A22* is not the best designation for "Gross Earnings" unless you are in the alphabet soup business. Good subroutines help programmers write better programs more efficiently.

Read or Write to PROMs

PROMs (Programmable Read-Only Memory) are read-only memory chips designed to have programs permanently burned into them. PROM-based programs provide increased DOS memory and faster execution. With PROMs, the programmer doesn't have to worry about unauthorized copies of his program. The only difficulty lies in writing the code to the PROM. A special PROM burner and a PROM eraser are required. Many PROM burners are low-cost PC add-on cards produced by foreign companies, which lack adequate documentation and software. There are many utilities that you can use to read, modify, and save to disk the code found in PROMs. Software for PROM burners is harder to come by, but is available if you are willing to take the time to look for it.

Read ROMs and Save to Disk

When programs have been permanently burned into the PROM chip, it is called a *ROM* (Read-Only Memory). The name for the actual programs that are burned into the ROM is *firmware*. This code cannot be changed. There are many utilities that can be used to read the code in ROMs and save it to disk. Although you can't change what is burned into a ROM chip, you can write a patch that writes over portions of the ROM code or inserts a piece of programming code to make a jump to another area of memory. In other words, you put a bridge over the part that you want to avoid.

PC-Tech Journal Highlights

On many bulletin boards you can find files containing highlights of *PC-Tech Journal* articles. The articles offer a wealth of information that you can access easily, sparing you the expense and time of maintaining a library of your own. One of the best features of these text files is that in many cases they offer an historical file of information about products and methods you may find useful that have faded from the media's spotlight. Sometimes a publication may be defunct and the only way to access this information is from BBSs and disk vendors. (We'll cover more on text files of interest in Chapter 22.)

   Note: It isn't clear whether many of the text articles and extracts posted on BBSs are authorized by the holder of the copyright. If you believe a file you got from a BBS or disk vendor isn't proper, you should notify the people you got it from so they can stop distributing it.

Hex to Decimal and Back

Programmers must usually work with both decimal and *hexadecimal* number systems. Hexadecimal code is found in DOS and many programming languages. Reference material may provide only the decimal value for a key code, for example, and the programmer may need to know the value of the key code in hexadecimal. There are Shareware programs that offer the facilities to work between hexadecimal and decimal numbers.

Hex Calculators

Hex calculators come in handy for calculating memory addresses, file lengths, sizes, and so on. Since hex uses a 16-digit numbering system, it can be a real chore for beginners to do hex math without the aid of a calculator. These calculators are a valuable programming tool.

Sorting

One of the hardest tasks for a programmer to master is sorting. The bubble sort is one of the most common and basic sorts, while the B-tree sort is one of the most advanced and complex in use today. Programming utilities can be found that will simplify these sorts for the programmer.

CRC Checks

You may recall from Chapter 7, "Protocols," that cyclical redundancy checks (CRCs) are used to check the accuracy of file transfers. Code for CRCs can be difficult to write for an inexperienced programmer. CRC code started as an 8 bit calculation and has grown to 16, 32, and now even 80 bit. There are also tools to perform CRCs on a file, block by block, and special formatted files like ZIP, ARC, and LZH.

File Encryption

Data encryption is another complex programming chore that is best left to the experts. You can incorporate data encryption into your programs from one of the programming tools available with little or no encryption experience. Remember to take care when using data encryption. If you lose or forget your password, your data cannot be recovered and will be lost forever.

Macros from Programmers' Editors

Just as a macro can help you run a spreadsheet program, load a particular worksheet, and move to a certain place in that worksheet, so too can a good macro aid in programming. Macros take some of the tedium out of programming and make using programs faster.

Hypertext

Some people say when Apple released HyperCard stacks, hypertext on the PC was born. Others say HyperCard was derived from hypertext. Regardless of the origin, free-form graphic/text database systems are here to stay, and there are many useful tools on The Wires to aid you in creating, modifying, and using them.

Other Programming Files

It would be next to impossible to include definitions for all of the various programming terms and tools, but now at least you have an idea of what some of these items are. As you work with programs more, you'll learn others. Always keep in mind that learning is a gradual process. Each of us works not only from a different level of experience, but at a different level of interest as well. Some aspects of computer use, like programming, may never be of great interest to you. For others, programming is a way of life.

The best way to learn is to ask questions, and your questions *will* be answered. It's just one of the wonderful things about the conferences, forums, round tables, and so on, that you can find online. People are always willing to answer questions—the questions just need to be asked. For now, let's move on and examine programming in general and some particularly useful programmers' utilities.

PROGRAMMING—FROM THE GROUND UP

Like a builder, a good programmer is able to combine skill and the right tools to produce works of quality. Like craftspeople, some programmers may concentrate in one area, honing skills with a single set of tools, while others will branch out, becoming adept with various tools and skills. Neither approach is better than the other; it's a matter of personal taste, focus, and inclination. Since both approaches have limits, it's also a matter of balance.

With that said, let's acknowledge another fact—too many programmers let themselves be limited by the tools at hand. It's a shame because the quantity and quality of tools available in The Wires is astonishing. Some programmers spend years working with only a single set of tools. They go from project to project with a single tool kit, reinventing wheels that have been available, often free, for years.

Friends who do a lot of programming tell me it sometimes amazes them how skills picked up in one area will "cross-fertilize" into others. Writing a program, they say, involves problem solving, like doing a crossword puzzle or solving a brain teaser, but that's only at the simplest level. At a deeper level, programming is more like designing a solid, stable building. Tools and techniques that were on the cutting edge only a few years ago are interesting now mostly as museum pieces.

Since changes to programming languages occur so quickly, it makes life tough for commercial vendors of programming tools. They charge a lot of money for their products and their products keep getting out of date. Updating your tool kit with commercial products quickly gets expensive. That's one reason some programmers who use commercial products tend to limit their purchases to only key items.

Programmers who branch out into multiple languages and application areas aren't simply being "general practitioners"; they're gaining valuable skills. If they roam The Wires from time to time, they're also enlarging their tool kits. This chapter will talk about how programmers can use their modems to broaden their horizons and strengthen their art.

Keeping Up to Date

Staying current with a scene that's as fast-changing as computer programming is not just a headache for the hapless programmer. It's just as much a problem for BBS sysops and other Shareware distributors. Both the programming languages and libraries shift and change as new routines appear and new updates arrive. Sometimes a highly sought after routine, a library, or add-on product, will become a standard feature in the next version. Occasionally, a better way comes along a week or two later and the sought after routine sinks back into oblivion.

The programming scene shifts and adjusts so constantly that no one person could possibly keep up with it. The commercial vendors simply cannot afford the cost of constant updates and library revisions. If they do venture a guess at what's about to become significant, they can't afford to be wrong. It's safer to move conservatively, to wait until a commercial product is either almost out of date or faces some new, tough competition. A commercial developer can then justify the expense of issuing a new release, complete with fanfare and celebration.

Shareware distributors have an opposite view—keeping everything up to date makes their segment of the market more vital, not more risky. The sysops and disk vendors get confused too. The language updates tend to get complex and hard for nonprogrammers to understand. Updates often come as small, multiple files with nondescriptive filenames that are diffi-cult to identify or classify. It's a highly technical field, well outside the expertise of all but a very few sysops.

The Professionals' Guild Hall

How then does the programming world progress? The answer is almost, but not quite, like a runaway engine. The reason the engine doesn't just run away is that it's self-governing. This market is so technical and so highly specialized that almost anything on the market tends to be good. The reason? If you can write a program, you already know enough to tell if it's good, and if it isn't good you won't release it. This has led to higher expectations where Shareware (and free) programmers' tools are con-cerned—and the higher expectations are usually justified.

As you can see, this kind of cycle can feed upon itself and that's exactly what has happened. There are thousands of people trading pro-gramming tools, tips, and expert help. Some of the best tools available were simply fed into the BBS networks as Freeware and were refined and enhanced. Eventually, someone broadened the scope or made it central to a major application, and another Shareware product hit the market.

BBS networks are like a meeting place for professional-level program-mers, a kind of modern-day "guild hall."

New Tools Always Needed
The quality of the tools "guild members" produce are a real surprise to people who either don't know about or have lost touch with The Wires. Tools include everything from the mundane to the fiendishly clever and often make the difference between an everyday program and something

superior. At times, only fellow programmers might recognize their importance—like small, seemingly simple tools or routines to count words or strings or process a text file with Boolean logic, for example. Other examples include routines to convert uppercase to lowercase, or to do mixed-case conversions, like capitalizing only the first letters of words or the beginnings of sentences.

Programmers always need more powerful block operations. Screen design is a problem. More and more, users expect an application to include windows and menus. Mouse support is also becoming more important. There are also file formats—more of them every day—and communications protocols, archiving formats, debuggers, compilers, and so on. No one can keep up with them all, but as a member of the guild, if you don't know the answer, it's a good bet someone else will.

Shopping for Tools

One of the best ways to find the tool you're seeking is to step into the guild hall. Turn on your modem and check out what's available as Shareware, or even as free routines. It costs next to nothing, and the tool room is full to overflowing. Many of these free routines and Shareware files can only be found in The Wires and are the only sources for critical bits and pieces that aren't mainstream enough for commercial distribution.

For example, for years the only source of programming information on DOS was a programmer's technical reference manual available only through BBSs and Shareware disk vendors. Finally, after eight long years, Microsoft published the *MS-DOS Encyclopedia* that has much of the same material, but it costs $150! You may want to download yours.

Who Visits the Guild Hall?

Many of my programmer friends say they only use the commercial programming tools that they have purchased for their work. After probing a little more, though, it turns out they still use a routine or disassembler they ran across on GEnie or CompuServe.

What's happened is they've come to take for granted all the free and Shareware programming materials they accumulated through the years. They've used them for years but forgotten where they got them. Sometimes programmer friends, reminded of where some of their tools came from, are prompted to rediscover the wealth of materials in The Wires—tools to program a ROM chip, for example, or tools to create a hypertext system.

Some of the most useful material is the source code. Source code examples are how most programmers first learned, and continue to learn, their craft. There's source code available in The Wires for thousands and thousands of programs, much of it fully commented. Sometimes, it seems like everybody contributes something to the tool bin, once they start visiting the guild hall on a regular basis.

Who are these multitudes who visit the free and Shareware programmers' files? They're an extremely diverse group, including

- Beginners who want to learn from the experiences of others and get ideas for applications and techniques

- Intermediate and experienced programmers who are stuck on a problem and need some expert advice

- Anyone who needs programming information and tools quickly and inexpensively

- Experienced programmers who want to share their expertise and knowledge with others

- Programmers at varying levels of experience who want to get feedback or help

It's the interplay among these different people that gives programmers' forums and BBS topics the stimulating, guild hall feeling. If you're set on learning how to program, or just want to hone your skills, you're missing something wonderful if you don't check out The Wires. You can get good Shareware programs from any number of places. There are PC user groups and disk vendors. For the most part, however, they don't offer what programmers need and are looking for. You'll be able to understand why these things aren't offered by user groups and disk vendors as we continue on. There is simply too much to offer!

Taking Your Source Code Public

While there's an enormous amount of free, high quality code and Shareware, programmers need to think carefully before adding their own source code to the mix. There have been some high-profile disputes over authorship and copyrights, with some authors even accusing others of violating copyright laws. Nearly all of these incidents, and the hard

DOCTOR'S NOTE

Coauthor Nick Anis' first programming class was in 1973, and the resources or tools were limited to a cryptic textbook and a deck of punched cards. One day, while Anis was trying to squeeze his way off a crowded bus, a couple of football jocks helped him expedite the process. Anis flew off the bus, and his books and deck of punch cards went with him, landing in the wet New York snow. The loss was minimal; Anis had to spend that evening at the computer lab rekeying his program.

In contrast, today's programs have a lot more "horsepower" and offer complex features like graphical interfaces, complex hardware interfacing, database management, calculations, and so forth. When you write programs, regardless of language, you will have to come up with a bag of tricks to pull off this magic. If you are lucky enough to find or create the tool you need, you should make this treasure a part of your programmer's resource library. You can avoid a lot of duplication of effort and reduce bugs by creating and maintaining your own resource library.

Rich Levin, author of the popular Checkup program, who writes in BASIC and Assembler, estimates his programmer's resource library, which has taken him over ten years to accumulate, to be worth $75,000. Dan Parsons, author of RoboComm, who writes in Clipper, feels he would be lost without his programming tools and source code.

Besides the essential elements of the programming environment, such as compilers, debuggers, and editors, there are many parts of a programmer's resource library that you can't purchase at Egghead Software. For instance, your source code, functions, formulas, programming experiences, documentation, and notes are not replaceable. Your organization of this material is also important.

Shareware is an excellent source for developing most of your resource library. If you are a programmer and don't have a resource library, start one today. If you do have one, guard it carefully as you would any treasure. If you are behind in the filing and organizing department, take the time to get your materials in order. The time you take will be well spent. You will end up with useful tools and materials that will help you turn out crisp, clean code and save time and aggravation.

feelings and controversy they caused, could have been avoided if the original authors had not made their source code public.

Releasing source code does not invalidate your copyright, if you've placed one on your work. You have every right to expect people to honor your rights. Trouble, however, can enter into the picture when others misunderstand their own rights. Someone may use your source code, not realizing it's proprietary, copyrighted material, or they may not realize they're using portions of it. Misunderstandings occur. People make mistakes.

For years, people have contributed to the controversy, just for the satisfaction of joining the fray. But as major media, corporations, and others have come to realize the quality and prices available in programs like Procomm, PC-File, and others, the stakes have gone up.

Why Go Public?

If you're wondering at this point why you'd want to release source code at all, it's understandable. No one ever wants to get involved in disputes of the sort just mentioned, but there are some major advantages to going public, aside from potential recognition from others in your field of choice.

First and foremost, there's absolutely no better way to learn a craft than to invite comment from the masters. It may be occasionally humbling, but you're guaranteed to learn a lot unless you shut your ears and turn your back.

Second, if you're taking a serious professional look at the pros and cons, your program stands a much better chance of becoming a de facto standard if you provide other developers with the source code. There are always people eager to develop related support products if you're offering a good major application. You may lose licensing fees but you'll gain a host of power-enhancing side utilities, and every one of these expands your potential market.

Similarly, programmers willing to offer their source code to other developers tend to capture the loyalty and active support of users in identifying bugs and making enhancements. There's no better beta test than one that draws honest assessments, suggestions, and evaluations from hundreds of computer enthusiasts.

There's also the value of word of mouth advertising, especially when your users become fiercely loyal to you. Whether or not this has ever been measured, the key to successful businesses through the ages has been word of mouth promotion.

Make Your Position Clear

If you've decided to release some of your source code, there are ways to safeguard your rights. First, and maybe most important, be sure to make it clear what portions of it are copyrighted. Better yet, go a step further and encourage people to contact you by BBS, mail, information service membership number, or even voice phone. (Don't worry about being overwhelmed by long-distance phone calls about source code—it's too specialized a field.) While you're giving a struggling programmer a chance to

---
DOCTOR'S NOTE

Satisfying as recognition from fellow experts may be, do remember that sometimes the stakes are high, and the disputes never happen until the dollars start to roll in.

There are times when you should *absolutely not release your source code!* If you've just made a new software discovery that will revolutionize the world of Shareware, think twice before telling anyone. Whatever your earthshaking discovery is, don't lose it to a disk crash; make sure you have a complete backup in a safe place.

If you need to demonstrate it to prospective buyers or publishers, use a nondisclosure agreement. You can find standard agreements in the library. Once you clearly understand the potential effects of your discovery on the marketplace, you should talk it over with others to get an idea of whether the discovery is actually as significant as you believe it is.

Remember, an idea cannot be copyrighted or patented. If the bulk of the value in your discovery is a clever idea, don't be surprised if others like it appear on the market shortly after, or even before yours. Since people often invent the same thing at around the same time, independently of each other, some people believe that there comes a time for certain ideas, or that they're "floating around" for anyone to notice. With nearly six billion people in the world, it isn't surprising that more than one would have the same idea as someone else.

talk over a problem, you can make your copyright policy clear and avoid problems later. You may get some great ideas from such callers.

PROGRAMMERS' TOOLS AND PATCHES

There are enough programming materials available as public domain and Shareware to fill a book of several volumes. Rather than trying to cover them all here and now, the next section will just offer a mini-list of some of the major functions and languages where you can find programming support on The Wires. It's far from an exhaustive list. To really get the flavor of what's available, you'll have to wander around.

The major sources available to a wire-wanderer are the same for applications, and have been covered earlier. For an area as specialized as programming, however, here are a few things to keep in mind.

Patches

While a number of independently produced patches exist for major applications, it's wise to stick with patches approved by the authors themselves unless you're technically very competent. A surprising number of vendors, both commercial and Shareware, are willing to supply patches to their products for users technically sophisticated enough to know how to use them.

Vendor-Supplied Patches

A recent browse of the Borland support forum on CompuServe turned up vendor-approved or -supplied patches to perform the following things on SideKick (original version):

- *ASTPOU.PAT* allows use of ASTerisks (*) and POUnd signs (#) as part of Dialer phone numbers.

- *SK9.PAT* forces the SideKick (SK) Dialer to prefix all numbers with phone trunk access digits (typically "9W").

- *LASERJ.BIN* uses SideKick to send LaserJet setup command strings to your LaserJet printer directly.

- *COM34.ARC* is a group of files to patch the SideKick Dialer to work with a Leading Edge modem addressed as COM3 or COM4.

- *LE.PAT* is a patch for the Dialer to work with Leading Edge internal modems.

- *ADDCHR.PAT* allows the use of up to four extra symbols in a phone number.

- *DATFMT.PAT* is a patch to change the Notepad Time/Date format.

- *CALC.PAT* is a patch for SideKick's Calculator, for use on some 80286-based machines.

- *NOBAK.PAT* prevents the automatic creation of those annoying *.BAK files in the SideKick Notepad.

- *3INCH.DOW* is three steps to download SideKick to the 3.5-inch disk for use on IBM compatibles using DEBUG.

Not all applications are as generous with their program patches, but any major application is likely to offer a few. Datastorm, makers of Procomm, for example, offered HOSTFX.ARC to let users shell to DOS from Host Mode in Procomm 2.4.2 when using DOS 3.2 and below.

Sample from BBS Listing

Any sizeable BBS will also offer a variety of patches, often distributed by Shareware authors as bug fixes, to help their customers stay up to date. You can also run into patches that change the default screen color on booting, fix assembler/disassembler program bugs, extend the lives of characters in games, or allow games to be run on specialized or discontinued machines like the PC Convertible. A listing from a small BBS recently included these patches, among others:

```
TC_PAT09.ZIP    09-04-87  Latest patches for Turbo C
BCOM30.ZIP         0588  Get this! QB 3.0 fatal error bypass patch
T300PAT2.ZIP    08-09-88  Patch #2 for Telix 3.00 (from PTel)
T300PAT.ZIP     08-09-88  Patch #1 for Telix 3.00 (from PTel)
```

PATCH11A.ZIP	09-10-88	Current patches for PCPLUS 1.1a
DTPALL.ZIP	09-10-88	Patches for Procomm Plus - Reg. Users
PATCH-B.ZIP	11-28-88	Patches for Procomm + v1.1B
QF300PAT.ZIP	12-31-88	Patches to fix bugs in QFONE300.ZIP
QB45DTR.ZIP	12-21-89	Patch for BCOM45.LIB . *GREAT*
PUMAFIX.ZIP	02-02-90	Patch for ID and Serial# in PUMA 100
DTRPATCH.ZIP	08-09-86	Patches to Qbasic for exit to "DOORS"
DTRPTCH4.ZIP	11-16-87	DTR Patch docs from 2.X to 3.XX
CLKSYS.ZIP	11-27-87	A fix for midnight date change problem
QB40FIX.ZIP	12-05-87	Debug fix for QuickBasic 4.0
QB40PTCH.ZIP	12-13-87	Another QuickBasic 4.0 patch for DTR drop
DOS31.ZIP	05-02-87	IBM patches for DOS 3.1 and DOS 3.0
DOS3X.ZIP	08-20-86	Another DOS 3.0 and 3.1 patch
PAT32_87.ZIP	05-27-87	Patch DOS 3.2 to fix 8087 problem
DOS33PAT.ZIP	06-06-87	Patches for PC-DOS 3.30
BORINT.ZIP	06-06-87	Patches fixes for Borland products
PATCH33.ZIP	05-15-88	Patch MS-DOS 3.3 for 3.5" drives
ZAPCOMIC.ZIP	01-27-89	Debug patch for unlimited lives in COMIC
DSPTCH.ZIP	05-13-89	Microsoft patch for MS-DOS 4.01
DSPTCH41.ZIP	01-27-90	New MS patch for MS/PC DOS 4.01
FIXCOLOR.ZIP	01-07-90	Patch ANY ver. of DOS for BOOT up color
STARFL.ARC	12-08-87	Patch STAR FLIGHT to run on PCJr or on EGA

Programmers' Tools

A good place to start looking for programmers' tools is with the Association of Shareware Professionals. In this specialized field, their offerings are definitely worth trying. The most recent edition of the ASP Shareware catalog is always available on CompuServe in the IBM Applications Forum, Library 8, as CATLOG.ARC. The catalog is updated each quarter.

After looking through the ASP catalog, you can search for more programs on just about any bulletin board. A list of representative programmers' tools follows, first from the ASP, and then as culled from various bulletin boards.

ASP Catalog Offerings

In the Spring 1990 edition of the ASP catalog, the section on programming covered six pages and included some of the most powerful tools available anywhere. Some of these, like the A86 and D86 assembly language tool kits by Eric Isaacson and the EasyCASE software engineering program, are discussed in detail, just to give a taste of the quality of what's available.

Those will be followed by shorter descriptions of both ASP and non-ASP offerings. You shouldn't consider this section a complete catalog of what's available. It's offered just to help point the way.

A86

A86 is short for Assembler for the 86 family of microprocessors. The original Assembler for Intel Corporation, ASM86, was written by A86 author Eric Isaacson, then a junior engineer at Intel. He is now a seasoned microprocessor expert at the ripe old age of 41.

A86 is the finest assembler available, at any cost, for the 86 family of microprocessors. It is two to four times faster than competing commercial assemblers, much easier to use, and offers more language features. For example, A86 can assemble code to object files, which can be altered by other programmers, or directly to COM files for the end user. It has convenient programming features like local labels and it boasts a slew of enhanced instruction forms for the entire family of IBM compatible CPUs.

There are many assemblers available commercially and through Shareware, such as Microsoft's MASM, Borland's TASM, and the original Shareware assembler CHASM, which stands for cheap assembler. One assembler may have advantages over another, but many professionals settle on A86 because of its overall quality, its performance, and its terrific author support.

Shareware assemblers do have a job cut out for them in terms of being compatible with the commercial assembler, MASM, widely considered the industry standard. Although A86 may have a problem or two, it is the most compatible Shareware assembler available.

Isaacson recently translated 61 *PC Magazine* utilities from MASM source files into A86 source files. He is also distributing a tool kit to help programmers make the same changes themselves and run their MASM source files with A86. The net result at the time of this writing was over two megabytes of publicly available A86 source code. It's a true source code mother lode.

D86—The Debugger

D86 is an associated symbolic debugger with the principal advantage that it's easy to use. D86 automatically generates exactly the information you need to debug your A86 programs. You always get a display of registers, flags, and stacks, plus a symbolic disassembly of program code in the vicinity of the instruction pointer. You can set up windows into memory, with your choice of display types, including mixed types for structures.

You can instantly access some of the best, most context-sensitive help screens you have ever seen. The function keys let you step your program by one instruction or a whole procedure at a time. You can type assembly language statements to be executed immediately, just as you would in BASIC.

D86 is extremely effective for learning assembly language. If you want to know what an instruction does, you can simply go into D86 and experiment with it. Registration for A86 or D86 is $50 for each; you can register both for $90 and get a printed manual. For more information contact

Eric Isaacson Software
416 East University Avenue
Bloomington, IN 47401
812-339-1811 (Voice) MasterCard and VISA accepted

EasyCASE

EasyCASE provides transformation schema, data flow diagrams, structure and relationship diagrams, and data dictionary support.

EasyCASE is a limited function CASE (Computer Aided Software Engineering) tool intended to simplify automated generation of data/control flow diagrams such as transformation graphs, state transition diagrams, and structure charts.

If you are a CASE programmer, you may want to take a look at EasyCASE. EasyCASE uses the methodologies of Yourdon-DeMarco, Ward-Mellor, and Hatley-Pirbhai (also known as the Boeing-Hatley method). It also uses Yourdon-Constantine representations, analysis, and design methodologies. EasyCASE is automated and, according to its author, easier to use than Lotus Freelance, Micrografx Designer, Windows Draw, or Gem Draw.

The drawing functions are limited to symbols, connections, annotation, and relationships required for the specific chart types implemented. EasyCASE is also easier to use than most of the full-featured CASE tools since it provides only the basic functions (charts) necessary for structured systems analysis and design.

When you add and manipulate chart objects, EasyCASE will maintain information about each object and its relationships with other objects on the chart. Objects can also be deleted, labeled, identified, and referenced to another chart. Another nice feature is when you move or delete an object, EasyCASE will also take care of all objects associated with or connected to the object you're working with. EasyCASE is a Shareware product with an $85 registration and a $5 shipping and handling fee. For information, contact

Evergreen CASE Tools
11025 164th Avenue N.E.
Redmond, WA 98052
206-881-5149 (Voice)

The Window BOSS

The Window BOSS is an extensive library of C and assembly functions from Star Guidance Consulting, Inc. This system is designed to allow painless creation of windows in any application without snow, flicker, or screen delay. The Window BOSS is used by many C programmers to produce those dazzling windows that many people like so well. An excellent set of window routines, it comes highly recommended by a large number of C language programmers.

C-Windows

C-Windows is a library of Turbo C functions designed to help nonexperts handle screens, windows, keyboards, and file access. It provides window stacking, tiling, and other advanced functions. It also provides pull-down or pop-up menus.

Pull TC and TP

Pull TC and TP is a Turbo C and Turbo Pascal multilevel pull-down and pop-up menu environment. The program provides execute, single, and multiple choice menus with slide-up, slide-under, and other sophisticated menu building tools. This product is from Eagle Performance Software.

TesSeRact

TesSeRact contains libraries of routines for creating TSR programs, including a much-discussed proposed standard for RAM-resident program interaction. The program is available in versions designed for different languages. Some of the popular TesSeRact utilities will be discussed in later chapters.

$UPER

Pronounced "super," this TSR program gives programmers useful pop-up functions while using only 12K of RAM. $UPER is for experienced programmers but beginners may also find it useful. According to its author, Duane Bowen, $UPER functions include

- ASCII table and color chart
- Box drawing character code display
- Interactive keyboard scan code and ASCII value display
- Memory peek and poke capability
- Screen ruler
- User selectable printer port
- Printer setup capability for Epson FX and compatible printers
- Printer page eject hot key for most printers

You can custom configure $UPER. It also has the ability to remove itself from installation, freeing the memory space it occupied for other programs to use.

DOS.LST

DOS.LST is a disassembly and analysis of IBM PC-DOS 3.30 compiled by Ray Smith. The disassembly was performed on an IBM PS/2 Model 80-071 running IBM PC-DOS 3.3. DOS's segment addresses may differ for your system but the offsets will be the same.

For example, IBMBIO.COM usually has a segment address of 0070h. On my machine, IBMDOS.COM begins at segment 0275h. This segment may be higher or lower on your system depending on the buffers statement, drivers loaded, and so on. However, offsets in the IBMDOS segment are the same, so as an example, the DOS critical section flag will always be at *xxxx*:02CFh, where *xxxx*: is your IBMDOS segment address.

Ray Smith has discovered several undocumented features that exist in all IBM PC-DOS releases except where noted. This listing will show you otherwise unknown features, functions, and data areas. If you decide to experiment with any of the disk related data areas, the Doctor recommends you exercise extreme caution!

PAD.EXE

This Super Programmers' Calculator can be run from the command line or used as a TSR. PAD.EXE supports color and hot key customization and is capable of doing octal, decimal, hex, and floating-point math. Other features include the ability to set the value in the accumulator, shift right or left 1 bit, print results, and even move the pop-up window around the screen.

SWAP

This set of programs by Nico Mak and Mansfield Software Group provides an application-independent method of switching from one MS-DOS application to another. If you are using a large application or TSR programs, SWAP will free conventional memory by transferring your application or TSRs to extended or expanded RAM, or even to a disk drive. It is especially handy in program development because you can use memory-hungry compilers, linkers, or debuggers and use SWAP to keep from losing your place in a programming session while running another application.

SYSID

SYSID, by Steve Grant, is an incredible program that can tell you everything you need to know about your system. A 16-page report provides system information on BIOS revision level, DMA channel used, machine type, and keyboard.

SYSID requires DOS versions 3.0 and later and was written in Turbo Pascal 5.0 and Assembler. The source code is provided with commentary and the executable file. Grant has released the program and source code to the public domain and provides all his sources for standard system calls and other "undocumented" calls. The program is a great diagnostic tool and is useful for those who want to learn their way around programming at the system level.

TechnoJock Turbo Toolkit

TechnoJock's Turbo Toolkit is an outstanding set of programming tools for Turbo Pascal. The primary developer of TechnoJock's Turbo Toolkit is Bob Ainsbury.

TechnoJock's Turbo Toolkit comes complete with source files and a 100-page abridged version of the manual that you get with the package's registered version. The documentation includes two introductory chapters offering full and exhaustive procedure references. The registered version has full unit descriptions and graphic screen images that can't be included in ASCII text files.

TechnoJock Software also supplies, free of charge, a comprehensive online help system based on the Norton Guides' engine. Single user registration is $49.95 plus $5 shipping and handling. For more information contact

TechnoJock Software, Inc.
P.O. Box 820927
Houston, TX 77282
713-493-6354
74017,227 CompuServe ID
Registration by credit card is available through Public Software Library at 800-242-4775 and 713-665-7017 (outside the U.S.)

Programmer's DOS Technical Reference Manual
Some say before DOS was officially released to the public, a technical reference manual on disk was in the public domain, complete with commented source code. These files probably originated from the painstaking disassembly of the thousands of lines of DOS's object code by highly motivated techies. Many of today's popular software applications would not be able to do the tricks they do without the information documented in these files.

PC-TAGS
PC-TAGS is a useful source code retrieval system for DOS and OS/2 that locates and retrieves function and procedure definitions from text files written in C, Pascal, BASIC, dBASE, Assembler, Modula-2, and other languages. Once a source file is located, PC-TAGS loads it into your editor and places the cursor at the retrieved function or start of the procedure.

You can use PC-TAGS with almost any text editor or programming environment. PC-TAGS can also be easily integrated into your facility or version-control system.

You can use PC-TAGS to find out what a function or procedure does by simply placing the cursor anywhere under the function's name and pressing a key. PC-TAGS locates the source file that contains the function and loads it into the editor. The cursor will be positioned at the start of the function. If you stored the source file in a version-control library, PC-TAGS will extract the file from the library before loading it into the editor. PC-TAGS makes it very convenient to determine the purpose of a function or procedure.

Along with PC-TAGS' ability to recognize function and procedure definitions, it will also recognize certain data structures such as records and macros in some of the supported languages. According to the author, Steven Calwas, PC-TAGS will support all existing compilers and interpreters that run under DOS and OS/2 including the following systems:

- Borland Turbo C
- DeSmet DC88
- Ecosoft Eco-C88
- Lattice C
- Manx Aztec C
- Mark Williams C and Let's C
- MetaWare High C
- Microsoft C and QuickC
- Mix Power C
- Rational Systems Instant C
- Watcom C
- Borland Turbo Pascal
- MetaWare Professional Pascal
- Microsoft Pascal and QuickPascal
- Borland Turbo BASIC
- Microsoft BASIC and QuickBASIC
- Ashton-Tate dBASE, all versions
- Fox Software FoxBASE+
- Nantucket Clipper

- All other dBASE clones
- Jensen & Partners TopSpeed Modula-2
- Logitech Modula-2
- Stony Brook Modula-2 and QuickMod
- Borland Turbo Assembler
- Microsoft Macro Assembler and QuickAssembler
- SLR Systems OPTASM Assembler

PC-TAGS also supports other programming languages indirectly by working with any language that supports the use of comments. You can also use PC-TAGS to retrieve other information besides function and procedure definitions.

Registration is $34.95 for the DOS version and $69.95 for the DOS-OS/2 version. For more information contact

Steven Calwas
Moderne Software
P.O. Box 3638
Santa Clara, CA 95055

More Recommended Tools

In addition to the programmer's tools that have already been discussed, there are a few others that received high marks from programmers around the country. If you're a new programmer, some of these tools may be helpful. Let's take a look at the other programmers' tools that were recommended most often.

ASMTUTOR

ASMTUTOR is the file IBM Personal Computer Assembly Language Tutorial, by Joshua Auerbach. This is an assembly language tutorial for programmers interested in learning Assembler or just getting started. The file is formatted for printing and includes topics such as why you should learn Assembler, with five steps to becoming Assembler-literate.

1. Learn the 8086 architecture and instruction set.

2. Learn DOS function calls.

3. Learn about the MACRO assembler and the LINKer.

4. Learn tools and concepts (DEBUG, Addresses, and so on).

5. Read the technical reference and examine the BIOS listing.

There's a great deal of helpful information in this file if you haven't successfully written assembly language programs before. Discussions are included on other sources of information combined with step-by-step examples. Auerbach is from Yale University's Computer Center, and this document was created as part of a project by the Communications Group at Yale. For more information contact

Joshua Auerbach
Yale University, Yale Computer Center
175 Whitney Avenue
P. O. Box 2112
New Haven, Connecticut 06520

ENVUNIT

ENVUNIT.PAS is the program file EnvironmentUnit by Mike Babulic. EVNUNIT is a collection of handy routines to simplify using the DOS environment string.

The source code is provided and the program is in the public domain. Provided with ENVUNIT is ENVTEST, which is a program that demonstrates the use of ENVUNIT. Both programs come in the file ENV.ZIP and are in the public domain. For more information, contact

Mike Babulic
3827 Charleswood Drive N.W.
Calgary, Alberta, Canada, T2L 2C7
72307,314 CompuServe ID

BAS2MASM

BAS2MASM is a text file prepared in November 1989 by Microsoft explaining how to pass parameters between Microsoft compiled BASIC programs and Microsoft Macro Assembler (MASM) programs. You will need a general understanding of BASIC and assembly language to use this file.

The BAS2MASM document explains the syntax for the support of Microsoft's Macro Assembler of calls to FORTRAN, Pascal, and C, and contains a series of examples complete with source code. With the growing number of multi-language programmers, this information is another good piece of reference material for a resource library.

Complete C

Complete C is an object-oriented tool kit for C programmers offered by Complete Computer Corporation. Complete C has earned a reputation for rapid prototyping and timely completion of bug-free final applications. According to the author, Seth Goldstein, the package includes all the files necessary to create serious applications in Complete C.

The interest in object-oriented programming (OOP) is growing and programs with graphic interfaces are becoming more common. Like Smalltalk, Complete C's object-oriented paradigm offers true encapsulation, inheritance, and message passing. Complete C offers the flexibility of typeless objects, as well as the advantages of speed and safety that a hybrid system allows. The helpful program INSTALL.EXE is included. It prompts you for the destination drive and subdirectory for the Complete C program files.

The Shareware release includes a driver, a translator, a logical debugger, and foundation classes. There is also a production messenger for the small memory model and source code for a complete library of foundation classes.

The Translator The Complete C Translator can translate Complete C programs into ANSI standard C. The translation process and learning curve is easy because of the simple syntax for creating objects and sending messages. In fact, most of the Complete C program will still be written in ANSI C. In addition to standard C data types, Complete C allows variables to be typed as either generic objects or objects of a specific class. The Translator offers dynamic binding for rapid prototyping and an optimal mix of dynamic and static binding for final executables.

The foundation classes include fully developed "classes" for a wide range of applications and offer a rich OOP environment and good error handling and memory management. I/O classes provide directory management and data conversion tasks. Collection classes offer a number of collection strategies with a common method interface to the application. The collection classes include collection, array, dictionary, string dictionary, set, and linked list.

The Logical Debugger   A logical debugger is included and is program structure-sensitive, allowing the user to thread through the hierarchy and trap messages and display objects. The Shareware release is limited to the small memory model, and the commercial release supports all models. The high-level debugger operates at the message or object level and allows a walkthrough of memory-tracing pointers, links, and objects. You can use the logical debugger to inspect any object and all of its components.

Lots of Features   Complete C can help programmers overcome the problems of C++, Objective C, and C_talk. Some good features include flexible typing, application management, a logical debugger, fast dynamic binding, true generic objects, and an extensive foundation library. Code written using Complete C will interface seamlessly with ordinary C code or libraries of C functions.

Registration   The manuals included with Complete C are straightforward. They provide programming examples and are formatted for printing. Program registration is $15. The Complete C BBS (212-956-4535) also provides more complicated programming examples that fully explore class definition files. For more information contact

Seth Goldstein
The Complete Computer Corporation
111 West 57th Street, Suite 1400
New York, NY 10019
212-582-2635 (Voice)
212-397-1580 (Fax)

SUMMING UP PROGRAMMING UTILITIES

The number of programming utilities is astounding and well beyond the scope of this chapter. It is my hope that you now at least have an idea of the programming utilities available in The Wires. The programs discussed were recommended by a number of Shareware programmers. There are many other excellent programmers' tools available. To give you an idea of the scope of material, here is a listing of some of those programs.

$UPER300.ZIP	23437	Programmer's Pop-up Reference Tool
0929REF.ZIP	168036	Programming Technical Reference Manual
1216REF.ZIP	157010	DOS programmers referance 12-16-88
555.ZIP	2559	555 timer calculations
@LAST200.ZIP	10255	Programmer's Pop-Up Util; useful TSR
ADAMAKE.ZIP	59225	Source code control program
ADDR.ZIP	4108	Debugging aid for finding bugs
ALPHAHEX.ZIP	3411	Program to convert ascii to hexadecimal.
ASCIFY13.ZIP	16936	Binary/ASCII conversion
ASCII1.ZIP	12649	POPUP ASCII TABLE;
ASMED.ZIP	31022	An integrated editor for TASM, MASM.
BA_AB.ZIP	4419	CONVERT BINARY TO ASCII FILE
BCALC.ZIP	5752	Binary/octal/hex calculator
BINARY.ZIP	14590	Displays Binary Code for 32,768 integers
BINCOM.ZIP	1755	Binary File Compare program
BLED21.ZIP	83091	Batch Line EDitor.. compare/merge source
BOAH.ZIP	5622	Binary, Octal, ASCII, Hex calculator
BOXSCREN.ZIP	52499	Creates entry screens and menus
BRIK.ZIP	45260	Highly portable CRC-32 file verifier
CB114.EXE	256395	Fantastic programmer's editor
CODEVIEW.ZIP	186610	Microsoft Codeview Demonstration
CPE41.ZIP	64712	General Purpose Compiler Environment
CRC32.ZIP	12218	32-bit Federal Standard CRC of files (src.)
CSPATCH.ZIP	4630	Debug/patch aid for .exe files
DIFSSED.ZIP	27970	Unix-style file comparer/stream editor
DOSREF14.ZIP	158114	MS-DOS Programmer's Technical Reference
EFILE.ZIP	26377	Binary file editor
FASTZAP.ZIP	43122	Latest Disk/Mem. Utility - VERY NICE!
FILEPEEK.ZIP	4801	View file in Hex & Ascii
FORMAT83.ZIP	17371	create intel hex files from .obj
GUIDE1.ZIP	27046	Nelson Ford's Programmers Guide pt.1
GUIDE2.ZIP	49544	Programmers Guide pt.2
HC.ZIP	60771	hex calculator
HEAPANIM.ZIP	7637	Graphic of binary-tree + heap sort...
HEXSRCH.ZIP	8391	search files for hex values
HIMEM.ZIP	70273	XMS v.2 intel standard
HLBENCH.ZIP	256143	PCTECH worlds best bench marking program
HLPSCRN1.ZIP	12195	POPUP CUSTOM MULTIPLE HELP SCREENS 1 OF 4

HLPSCRN2.ZIP	6170	POPUP CUSTOM MULTIPLE HELP SCREENS 2 OF 4
HYPER-T.ZIP	32496	Simple Hypertext with Pascal source w/Poker
HYPERH.ZIP	64318	HyperHelper v1.5 -Create/view hypertext
HYPIT.ZIP	81251	Hypertext library for Turbo-C
INT489.ZIP	145275	Documented & Undocumented Interupts for IBM
IPEEK.ZIP	9932	Looks inside .OBJ files and gives stats! OK!
K9-831.ZIP	20042	K9: TSR services & programmers toolkit
KERNEL.ZIP	17473	Little kernel for multitasking
LEX.ZIP	25172	Complete UNIX lex for DOS
LIBRA13.ZIP	23534	Manage Microsoft LIB files - V1.3
MAGIC13A.ZIP	158439	Full Implementation of Hypertext programming
MAKEOBJ.ZIP	9630	Make Microsoft OBJ file out of any data
MCBTRC2.ZIP	20875	Trace the MCB chain. Update on MCBTRACE.
MEMLOOK.ZIP	14874	Examine Memory at any address. EXCELLENT!
MONITR.ZIP	7999	Debugging tool for use on 80386 PC
MOUSEREF.ZIP	2136	mouse interrupt ref card - INT 33h
OBJSCAN.ZIP	5452	Scan OBJ files.
OS2DEVEL.ZIP	278433	Unix-like development tools
PATCH101.ZIP	11622	Dunford's non-interactive zapper
PC-MAG-C	3072	PC MAG"S TSR programmer's calc
PCTECHJ1.ZIP	124671	PC-Tech Magazine utilities - Disk1
PJ(V6_5).ZIP	27035	Programmer's Journal Files Volume 6.5
RAID.ZIP	50217	full screen debugger (advanced users only)
RES86-30.ZIP	35041	RES86 3.0: debugger by Ward Christensen
RS232DD.ZIP	38602	Source code for a RS 232 Device Driver
S370INST.ZIP	2905	IBM S/370 "yellow card" for assembler pgmming
SB-SHAR2.ZIP	128313	Screen Builder -- Like Bricklin's Demo
SCCS100.ZIP	17639	SOURCE CODE CONTROL SYSTEM
SD289.ZIP	79398	Programmer's screen designer v2.89
SNIFFEXE.ZIP	24310	Verify .EXE files
STAY332.ZIP	30876	Make Mem-Res pgs w/Turbo Source
TEN.ZIP	2931	Ten Commandments for shareware authors.
TESS110.ZIP	217782	Complete TesSeRact v1.10 distributed author
U16.ZIP	7971	16 bit LZW uncompress program
UNIX.ZIP	28849	Reference to UNIX
VECTORS.ZIP	6555	Lists out your INT vector locations and bytes
VGATOOLS.ZIP	61933	VGA tools for programmers
XARGS.ZIP	13161	Unix xargs(1) for MS-DOS with C source

If you are a programmer or are studying programming, my advice is simple. Join some of the excellent programming conferences that are available on commercial networks and bulletin boards. As your skills increase, use the available commercial tools, but never forget that there is an almost limitless supply of material available in The Wires.

It's time to move on and examine some of the best Shareware spreadsheets and some proven templates that can aid you in working with this important application.

## CHAPTER TWENTY

Games and Educational Programs

Americans have always been fascinated with games—board games, games on television, trivia games, card games, and computer games. There are games for all occasions. There are games for parties, games for outdoors, games for indoors, games to play in teams, and games to play by yourself. Games are a way of distracting yourself, challenging your mind, and having some fun. Since the early days of the microcomputer revolution, games have been on computers, starting with something as simple as the "pong" game. The pong game was just two paddles and a ball (which happened to be square) that was knocked back and forth across the screen.

Games for the computer have come a long way since then. You can now get games that have 256 colors, great sound effects, animation, and the feeling of three-dimensional space. The first part of this chapter is going to discuss some of the games that are available in Shareware. The last portion of the chapter will deal with educational programs and what you can find in that area. To start off, let's take a look at games on the computer and how they have evolved.

FROM SIMPLE TO COMPLEX

Only a few years ago a discussion of Shareware computer games would have been relatively simple. Why? For one thing the games themselves tended to be simpler. They were cute and easy to play. In the beginning nearly all games used the keyboard for moving objects in a game: cursor keys to lock in on the target, the SPACEBAR to fire your shot, and so on. This was satisfactory, but, as noted previously, people are never content with what they have. Using the keyboard could be slow and awkward. Gradually, joysticks came into the picture and were finally followed by the mouse. With these two devices available, games became more complex.

Games also became more interesting because of the development of new programming languages. Many of the first games were done in BASIC, which is somewhat limited. With the advent of languages like Turbo Pascal, programmers could incorporate better graphics, sound, and movement into their games. As programming techniques got better, so did the games. Things were going along fairly well, and then some other factors were introduced into the game arena.

─────────────── **DOCTOR'S NOTE** ───────────────

You can find many games that are written in BASIC. In order to use these, you have to load them into the BASIC Interpreter that comes with your DOS program disks. BASIC programs will have a file extension of .BAS. If you are running PC-DOS, it will only run on IBM machines. IBM has a proprietary ROM chip that works with its version of BASIC. If you try using the IBM BASIC program on a clone, it won't work. Look for any of these files if you want to run a BASIC program on your machine: BASIC.EXE, BASICA.COM, BASIC.COM, or GWBASIC.EXE. If you have GWBASIC, for example, you could run a BASIC program called TEST.BAS by entering the following line at the DOS prompt:

```
C>GWBASIC TEST
```

The BASIC Interpreter would come up and run the program for you. BASIC programs are nice because if you have some knowledge of BASIC you can customize or personalize a program. Just keep in mind that if you have PC-DOS on a clone, you'll need a copy of GWBASIC.EXE, found with MS-DOS, in order to run any BASIC programs you obtain.

Resolve Yourself to Resolution

Just a few years back all Shareware computer games could be lumped into two basic classifications: games for monochrome monitors and games for CGA monitors. To put it simply, you either had color or you didn't. Many games that began as strictly monochrome games eventually evolved into CGA games. After all, what good was all this improved graphics if everything on the screen was either green or amber? For the user, however, the choices were easy. If you had a monochrome monitor you got monochrome games, whereas if you had a color monitor you could use the CGA games. Things remained fairly easy for both programmers and users for several years. Then the EGA monitor was introduced, and within a short time some "EGA-only" programs appeared in catalogs and on bulletin boards. Not long after that, the VGA was introduced and the area of games began to get more complicated. Now "VGA-only" games began to appear. What games you could play depended on what games you could display. Of course, these new graphics displays affected many other programs as well.

Graphics-Dependent Games

Now, the selection of Shareware games is widely varied. There are games that are specifically for monochrome, CGA, EGA, and VGA monitors. Some games will support several different types of graphics displays. If your machine can't support the type of graphics a game requires, you are wasting your time and money getting it. It simply won't run. Another new trend in games is that often a mouse or joystick is required. In the past it was generally an option, but many of the newer games have eliminated the keyboard control options and made a joystick or mouse a necessary part of playing the game. Here again, if you don't have the necessary equipment, don't bother getting the game—you'll only be disappointed. In this portion of the chapter you'll take a look at games that can be played on the various types of graphics adapters. There are many games available and many that are of excellent quality. Let's take a look.

THE KROZ SERIES

The KROZ games, by Scott Miller, are excellent ASCII text arcade-style adventure games that can be played in monochrome *or* color. These games have been carefully planned and are fun to play. They feature a host of "bad guys" and many ways for you to make your way through a series of mazes. Each of the games has levels for the novice, intermediate, and advanced player. The games have great sound effects and are full of surprises. The KROZ series is one of the most successful and popular game packages ever marketed under the Shareware concept. Kingdom of KROZ, the first KROZ game, won "Best Game" in a national contest sponsored by *Big Blue Disk,* a monthly disk magazine. Since then, seven more KROZ games have been created, but only two have been released as Shareware: Return to KROZ and Kingdom of KROZ II. The KROZ games (in order of creation) are

- Kingdom of KROZ

- Caverns of KROZ

- Dungeons of KROZ

- Return to KROZ

- Temple of KROZ

- Final Crusade of KROZ

- Lost Adventure of KROZ

- Kingdom of KROZ II

- Great Empire of KROZ (coming January 1991)

Exploring the World of KROZ

Kingdom of KROZ II, the most recent KROZ game, is not just a mindless game. Like all of the other games in the KROZ series, you have to *think* your way through the mazes. Each game has 25 unique levels. There are traps, creatures, and some very clever puzzles to overcome. You have a whip to protect yourself, and you can pick up more whips as you journey through KROZ. You can also use the whips to knock down some walls. One of the tricks of the game is not to let yourself run out of whips. The "scenery" is filled with lakes, forests, flowing lava, rivers, bottomless pits, treasure chests, gems, spells, boulders, tunnels, and much more. The KROZ games work on all computer systems, even laptops and other nongraphics systems.

Talking with the Author

The author of the KROZ series, Scott Miller, had this to say about the tremendous success of his games, "There's a huge following of KROZ fans that eagerly awaits each new release. There's a contest associated with each new KROZ game, for example, finding the secret message. Master Kroz Player certificates are awarded to contest winners. I have thousands of letters stating that my KROZ games are the best games available in Shareware, and in many cases even more fun than commercial games. It's all been a bit overwhelming to me—I just try to make games that are fun."

There are several reasons for the success of the KROZ games. To begin with, the games are good and fun to play. They are offered at prices that are very fair; in fact, they are low-priced. You can try out the two Shareware games, and then if you want to continue playing the rest of the series, you can order the other six directly from the author.

Why Stop at KROZ?

As if eight games in the KROZ series weren't enough, Scott Miller also has some other interesting games available.

Word Whiz This is an addictive quiz game that rates your vocabulary ability. It updates your current ranking after each multiple choice question, from Word Wimp to College Graduate to Dictionary Dude or eight others. Bonus Facts are awarded for each question that is correctly answered.

Trek Trivia This is the perfect game for fans of the original "Star Trek" television series. Bonus Facts, two skill levels, colorful screens, and sound effects make this a hard game to stop playing. I can vouch for that—this chapter almost didn't get finished because of Trek Trivia (*smile*), but I did get 98 out of 100.

Supernova Explore a galaxy and save a planet from an exploding star. An epic adventure rated by *Shareware* magazine as one of the best games ever. This advanced game has graphics, sound effects, a clue command, and dozens of unique features.

Beyond the Titanic   This game is a fantastic adventure of exploration and survival. What really happened aboard the Titanic? It has sound effects and 16-color screens.

These games are all very good for any member of the family. You can play them on monochrome or color display adapters, and on various machines. Check them out.

Scott Miller
Apogee Software
4206 Mayflower
Garland, TX 75043
214-240-0614
$7.50 registration for each game, any 3 for $20, series of 6 for $35; registration includes a code to make the games easier to complete

SHOOTING GALLERY

Shooting Gallery is just one of several excellent games written by program author Nels Anderson. Like Scott Miller, Anderson is a programmer who just happens to be very good at writing games. Shooting Gallery requires MCGA graphics and a mouse. If you like to try your hand at hitting a target amidst some great scenery, you'll like Shooting Gallery. As author Anderson puts it, "Most people seem to enjoy trying to hit a target. Whether it's tossing a ball through a hoop, trying to shoot cans off a fence, or blasting space aliens on a computer screen, there's something about it that's fun! Shooting Gallery is an attempt to recreate a shooting range on a computer screen. It originally started as a target shoot like those you might find at a carnival, but even before I had that done I had ideas for other rounds. This first version has six rounds (well, actually two different variations on each of three ideas). I still have more ideas for rounds, so later versions of the game will undoubtedly have more rounds. I wanted to get the game out to you, the player, because past experience shows that some of the best new ideas come from the people actually playing the game."

Anderson has done a beautiful job of recreating a shooting gallery as well as outdoor skeet shooting, and the graphics are great. Let's take a quick look at the various rounds.

Making the Rounds

Naturally, the object is to get as high a score as possible. You make your way through the six rounds, trying to hit as many of the targets as possible. Another factor that is considered in your score is how fast you hit the targets. Thus, on a round like Quick Draw, your reaction time will affect your score. The first round is just like a shooting gallery that you might see at a state fair or carnival. The targets go by, in several directions, and each target has different point values. Two special targets give you either more time or more ammunition. The rows move at different speeds, and you get more points for hitting things on the fastest moving row. If the action is getting too furious, you can pause the game by hitting the SPACEBAR, and then resume by clicking a mouse button.

The second round is like a skeet shoot, and the graphics are amazing. You'd swear you were standing out in the middle of a field. If you've never been skeet shooting, what happens is that the target, the "clay pigeon," is thrown up and out, and you have to try to hit it. As it moves away from you it gets smaller and more difficult to hit. How fast you hit the target will affect your score. The third round is the Quick Draw portion. You face a target, and to one side is a Christmas tree of lights that begins a countdown. When it gets to the green light, you draw and try to hit the target as quickly and accurately as possible. Your score is based on how fast you react and on how close you get to the exact center of the target.

The Final Rounds

In round four, there are different targets, the point values have increased, and you get a few surprises. For example, the targets will change direction without notice. Round five takes you back to the skeet shooting range, only this time you have to shoot at two targets at once. Two clay pigeons go up, and you have to try to hit both of them. Here again, your total score is based on how long it takes you to make two shots, so how fast you react makes a difference. Finally, in round six, you are returned to an enhanced version of the Quick Draw contest. Now you have two targets to draw and fire at. Shooting Gallery is fun and very well done.

Warning: For those of you who like shooting games, this one can be addictive.

Because his games are very good, let's take a look at some of the others created by Nels Anderson.

EGATREK

EGATREK is a game written specifically for EGA graphics. There have been many "Star Trek" games written over the years. In fact, some of the first games played on minicomputers were based on the "Star Trek" TV series. EGATREK, takes full advantage of the color and graphics supported by EGA. The sound effects are also very good. In each game, you accept a mission commanding a starship in which you have so many days to wipe out some invading Klingons. It isn't always easy because it's a big universe. Here is a quick overview of the game.

Playing EGATREK

As the captain of your starship, you have access to all of the ship's resources: long and short range scanners, phasers, photon torpedoes, the ship's computer, and so on. Using scanners, you determine a galaxy where the Klingon ships are located. Using either impulse or warp engines, you move around that galaxy. When you come under attack, you may have to divert more power to the shields. The computer can help you lock on to your targets with photon torpedoes. You receive Damage Control reports and may have to stop off at a star base for repairs. Some planets in the galaxy have raw dilithium crystals that you can use for power in emergencies. When you find such planets, you can beam up the crystals using your transporters or send a shuttlecraft. The action can get furious and the situation can often become critical. You may even have to use the self-destruct sequence.

EGATREK is a game that requires some planning and thinking. As with many things, practice will help you improve. At the end of each game, win or lose, your performance is rated by Star Fleet. You can even get your name in the Hall of Fame. If you like space action-adventure games, you'll like EGATREK.

MAHJONGG

Mah-jongg is an ancient game from China that is played with tiles. The electronic version can be played on EGA and Hercules graphics systems. Mahjongg can be played with a mouse, but does not require it. The object of the game is to remove as many of the tiles from the playing board as possible, following the rules of the game. Tiles are always removed in pairs and can only be removed from the left or the right edges. Any tile that is not on a left or right edge is considered blocked and cannot be removed. There are many different *suits* of tiles, and the suit of a tile determines the rule used for matching tiles that can be removed together. There are a total of 144 tiles on the board. The game board is a grid marked by letters and numbers. You select tiles by entering a letter for the column and a number. While this game appears simple, it can be quite addictive. The use of EGA color and resolution gives Mahjongg a nice appearance, and the game is very well done.

CIPHER

Cipher is a word game in which quotations are encrypted using a code that you have to figure out. The left side of the screen gives you the alphabet, and the right side of the screen is occupied by the scrambled puzzle. You select a letter from the left side and place it where you think it belongs in the puzzle. When you do this, all of the occurrences of that letter in the puzzle also change to match the letter you selected. Figure 20-1 shows the display of Cipher.

This is not a game for the faint of heart or the weak of word. It is extremely challenging. If you like crossword puzzles, anagrams, and other word games, Cipher might just be for you. It supports a mouse as well as EGA and VGA graphics and text mode.

All of the games done by Nels Anderson are of excellent quality and very inexpensive. You could buy all of his games for less than the cost of one commercial game. I enjoy them and I think you will too.

Nels Anderson
Arcanum Computing
92 Bishop Drive
Framingham, MA 01701

508-875-3618 or 617-449-7322 (BBS)
$10 registration for each of the programs, Shooting Gallery, EGATREK, Mahjongg, and Cipher

BASS TOUR

Bass Tour is a fascinating game that simulates a bass fishing tournament. Even if you're not a fisherperson, you'll enjoy this game. Bass Tour can be run on CGA, EGA, MCGA, VGA, and Hercules graphics systems. This is an extremely realistic game. You start out with a boat that is fully equipped for going bass fishing. You have an outboard motor, a trolling motor, a selection of rods, a fully loaded tackle box, and even a life preserver. You'll find out that if you don't put on the life preserver while the boat is moving, you may get a citation and a fine. At the beginning of the game, you select the lake or body of water where the tournament will take place—with six to choose from. From that point on, Bass Tour offers many challenges, and it's fun.

Figure 20-1

The display of Cipher

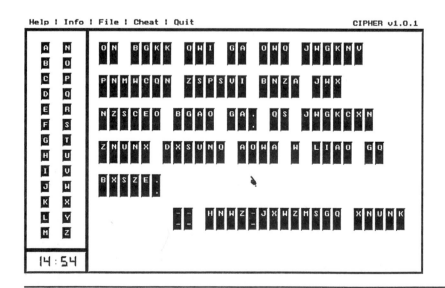

The Bass Tour Challenge

You have six hours to go out in your boat and catch the five biggest bass that you can. You have to monitor the amount of gas you have for your outboard motor as well as the battery power available for your trolling motor. Your boat has an aerator that keeps your catch alive, but you have to remember that it also uses the batteries. You move out onto the lake and select the rod of your choice. Then you can select a lure from a realistic tackle box. In Bass Tour, you not only get to select exactly what kind of lure, but even what color(s) it will be. (I did quite well with a "spoon" lure that was "frog" colored. Sorry, Kermit.)

Catching On to the Game

The fish you catch must be at least 12 inches long; otherwise, they will be thrown back. Once you get five fish in your aerator, you can keep fishing and hope to catch some that are bigger than the five that you have. For example, if you catch another bass that weighs 1.81 pounds, and it is heavier than the lightest fish in your aerator, then that fish will replace the lighter one. The idea is to get the most poundage out of five fish. As you move around the lake, you have to be careful of shallow spots, logs, and rocks where you might run aground. You get penalized for running into things by having some of your time taken away. You can lose lures, which costs you $3. You have to keep your eye on the clock because you have to weigh in before time runs out. The entire game is three days of fishing, with a running total that is kept to determine the winner. You are competing against some of the best bass fishermen alive.

No Fishing for Compliments

Bass Tour is a great game with very good graphics. It was so much fun to play that I got hooked. :) The game, like so many others, can be habit-forming. You'll want to keep at it, always trying to land a fish that's just a little bit bigger. The only advice I can offer is to take your time when coming into dock for the weigh-in at the end. You don't have to be facing a certain direction (I assumed you did), just end up close to the flag that marks the start/finish point. As far as I can tell, you can't kill yourself by sinking either. I tried crashing into several objects, and though I had time deducted, the boat didn't sink.

For those who get really serious about their Bass Tour fishing, there is another program that will let you create your own lakes (and you'll take just a brief look at that next). Enjoy the rest of the chapter; I'm going fishing. I came in *third* in my last tournament.

Dick Olsen
68 Hartwell Avenue
Littleton, MA 01460
$10 registration

BassMap

BassMap is another program by Nels Anderson, who happens to be a friend of Dick Olsen, the author of Bass Tour. Many people wanted a way to alter some of the existing lakes for Bass Tour or to create some lakes of their own. BassMap allows you to do just that. You can start from scratch and create a lake that you can call your own. Make it as different as you want. Put in islands, weed beds, logs, rocks, docks, and more. You should see Lake File Finder—it's treacherous. (*smile*) Another approach is to "edit" an existing lake. Take out some things that you may not want and add a few that you do.

KLONDIKE SOLITAIRE

Klondike, by Eduardo Martins, is a great game of solitaire that takes full advantage of EGA graphics, colors, and music. Klondike can be played with keyboard or mouse. There are several other similar games that also call themselves "Klondike," but they are not all the same. This program can usually be found with a filename like KLONDK??.ZIP, where ?? is the version number. This is the best game of solitaire for the computer that I have ever seen. Let's take a look at how it's played.

Playing Klondike

One regular deck of 52 cards is used for Klondike, and the cards are dealt in a manner that is familiar to anyone who has played solitaire. A total of 28 cards are dealt into seven piles. The first pile at the left has one card, the second two, and so on. The top card of each pile is face up, while all of the others are face down. From there, you build on the piles of cards in either an ascending or descending sequence. As you would expect, the sequence of colors alternates—black on red or red on black. A black Queen can only go on a red King, for example. If you like, you can move all of the cards that are face up on one pile to another one. When you uncover an ace, it is moved to an area of the game called the Foundation. This is the area where you build the cards into suits, the object of basic solitaire.

You also have the rest of the deck, 24 cards, in a pile. These are turned over one at a time, and if they can be played you do so. If not, they go into a discard pile called the waste pile. Playing the game with a mouse is really fun. You can sit back in your chair and just move cards by clicking buttons. If you make a mistake or try to cheat, the game tells you so, and it will not allow you to make an illegal move. There are, however, some variations on the basic game.

Klondike Variations
Playing by the basic rules of the game, it's not very easy to win. Quoting the documentation, "It has been estimated that the chances of winning are one in every thirty games"—not a very optimistic forecast. To help you out, Klondike has two variations that help increase the odds of winning. Under the one variation, cards are moved from the pack to the waste pile in groups of three, and you can go through the pack as many times as you wish. With the second variation, cards are turned up from the pack one by one, instead of three at a time, but you can still go through the pack as many times as you like. You can also move portions of a stack of cards that are face up. This lets you manipulate the cards so you have a better chance of winning. You can select which variations, if any, you would like to use at the start of each new game.

The use of graphics, color, and music in Klondike are excellent. The ability to use a mouse adds to the ease of play. You can look at a lot of Shareware card games, but I doubt that you'll find one that tops Martins' Klondike in any respect. A highly professional job, I would rate Klondike as better than many commercial card games that I have tested.

POKER SOLITAIRE

Before giving you the registration information about Klondike, you should know about another card game done by program author Eduardo

Martins. Poker Solitaire has the same level of quality that Klondike has. Once again, Martins has used a wonderful blend of graphics, color, and sound to bring you a high-quality game that's a steal. Let's take a quick look at this addictive game.

Playing Poker Solitaire

Once again, one regular deck of cards is used. On the left side of the screen is a 5 × 5 grid. You deal the first 25 cards from the deck, placing each card one at a time. Once a card is placed, you cannot move it again. The object is to get as high a score as possible by making good poker hands both horizontally and vertically. The game can use either an American or English scoring system. The *American* scoring system is based on the way hands are ranked in poker. Thus, a royal flush would be the best hand. The *English* system is based on how difficult it is to make each hand. A listing of the two systems is shown so you can compare them.

Hand	American	English
Royal flush	100	30
Straight flush	75	30
Four of a kind	50	16
Full house	25	10
Flush	20	5
Straight	15	12
Three of a kind	10	6
Two pairs	5	3
One pair	2	1

A flush is only worth 5 points in the English system because a flush is so easy to make, whereas a straight is more difficult and gets 12 points.

There are several variations available in Poker Solitaire, giving you a total of six different games in one. This game also has a Top Ten scoreboard where the best players can enter their names. This is another fine game by Eduardo Martins, author of Klondike and Pyramid. Try it!

Eduardo Martins
Station A, P.O. Box 2052

Champaign, IL 61825

$15 registration each for Klondike, Poker Solitaire, and Pyramid. For $20 (for each program) you get the latest version of the program on disk along with a printed manual.

THE MICROLINK GAMES

The MicroLink Personal Computer User's Group has a series of games written by Bob Lancaster. The games have good color and sound effects. Four discussed here are Yaht, Shut-the-Box, Otra, and Loyd. Lancaster produced the games for his user group as one way to call attention to the group. All four of these games are well worth the low cost (a $5 donation) and will provide you and your family with hours of fun.

Yaht

Yaht is modeled after the classic game of Yahtzee. The game can be controlled with keyboard, joystick, or mouse, and you can use a combination of one or all of them at the same time. Thus, if you were playing against someone, he or she could use the keyboard while you use the mouse.

If you've never played Yahtzee, here's how the game is played. When you start the game, you can enter the names of those who are playing. If you want, you can play against the computer or elect to stick it out alone. The basic idea of Yaht is to make poker hands out of the dice and get the highest score. You roll the dice. You can select dice that you want to keep and roll again, but not more than three times. After you've elected to keep a group of dice, you have to enter a score under one of the poker hand categories, or take a zero in one of them. The game proceeds until all of the categories have been filled and someone has the high score. You can then elect to play another game. Yaht is fun for all ages and easy to play.

Shut-the-Box

Shut-the-Box requires some thinking as well as a little luck. You have a box with numbers 1 through 9 across the top. Two dice are rolled. You total the dice, and then you have to start making decisions. You can break up the total in any way that you want and "pull" down numbers from the top. The idea is to pull down all of the numbers and "shut the box." It's not as easy as it might sound. The combinations are strictly up to you. For example, say you rolled a 6 and a 3. That totals 9. Using the 9, you could pull down 1, 2, and 6; 7 and 2; 4 and 5; and so on. Just when you think you've got the game licked, you get a roll of the dice and there is *no* way to break it up. What happens? You start over. This is challenging fun for children and adults.

Otra

Otra is similar to the popular game "Simon." You are faced with a screen of colored boxes. When you start the game, one box will blink and a particular tone will sound. You have to match it. Then, two boxes blink and two different tones sound, and again you have to match it. The game progresses until you hit a wrong key or simply can't remember the pattern. A little tip: the average player will do fairly well for the first six to seven patterns. This is why phone numbers consist of seven numbers. Once you get beyond that, you may have to concentrate harder.

The game can be played with keyboard or mouse. This is another game that both children and adults will find challenging and entertaining. Give it a try.

Loyd

Loyd is a game that might drive you a bit crazy, but it certainly is a challenge. You have a 4 × 4 box, which gives you 16 squares. Inside the box are 15 cubes that are numbered 1 through 15. You have to move the cubes around until you get the cubes in numerical sequence. Games like this have been popular for years. It takes some analytical thinking and logic to gradually maneuver the cubes into the proper positions. You can always make a move, it just might not be the one you want to make. Keep at it until you win or give up and start over. Loyd will have you scratching your head, but it's a good test of reasoning skills.

Look for these games written by Bob Lancaster for the MicroLink Computer User's Group. They are a great value for the money.

Bob Lancaster
P.O. Box 5612
Hacienda Heights, CA 91745
818-961-7903 (BBS)
$5 donations appreciated; the author welcomes any comments, questions, suggestions, or complaints.

THE EXPANDING WORLD OF GAMES

These are just a few of the huge number of games that are available in Shareware. There are many more to choose from: adventure games, war games, and games like cribbage, Uno, and Wheel of Fortune. You can also find computer versions of popular board games like Monopoly, Risk, checkers, chess, and many others. Many of these games are highly sophisticated and extremely detailed. Power Chess, distributed by New-Ware, is a dynamic chess game, which has competed successfully against the best commercial chess games, but it has a Shareware price. If you like games, you won't lack variety in the world of Shareware.

Because there is only room to discuss a small number of game programs, I'd like to give you some more things to look at. In this way, when

---

DOCTOR'S NOTE

As you read through this listing, there are a few things to note. For one thing, users will often indicate special requirements of a game. For example, "C/G" stands for color graphics, indicating that you need a CGA display adapter. There are also some "unprotects" for commercial game programs. Many commercial games have copy protection, which can limit your ability to use the program in exactly the way you would like to. These "unprotects" or "patches" are designed to work around these copy protection problems.

Note also that users often place the solutions for commercial games on bulletin boards. Program listings may also indicate if a program is written in BASIC, if it needs a joystick or a mouse, and other helpful information. Abbreviations are often used because space for a description is limited. These are all things that you might want to look for as you peruse this listing.

---

you visit a user group, read a catalog from a disk vendor, or call into a bulletin board or commercial network, you might have an idea of something that you'd like to get. This is the reason for providing listings from bulletin boards in various chapters. It gives you the chance to read over the lists and to check out what's available. It also gives you a filename to look for. Here is a listing of some of the game programs available. There are *many* more.

0ADV.ARC	32768	Simple adventure for XENIX or DOS
15PUZZLE.ZIP	2208	Challenging tile moving game;
2ON2.ARC	72576	Excellent basketball game, req color.
3-DEMON.ARC	34901	PACMAN from inside the maze; (C/G)
3DTICTAC.ZIP	25417	A three dimensional tic-tac-toe game.
747.ARC	24236	FLY A BOEING 747 SIMULATOR
7STUD.ZIP	67755	Play America's favorite poker
AAALIFE.ZIP	72882	Strictly for Conway's LIFE nuts. Color.
ABM.ARC	29209	MISSILE COMMAND GAME; (C/G)
ACCORD1S.ARC	38767	A solitare game - accordian style.
ADVENT.ARC	56960	Very addictive adventure game.
ADVENTR.ARC	13130	TEXT ADVENTURE GAME
ADVENTUR.ARC	63363	DESIGN YOUR OWN ADVENTURE
AFSFLY1.ARC	7552	Stunts to try with Chuck Yeager's AFT.
AIRTRAX.EXE	31104	AIR TRAFFIC CONTROLLER
ALIEN.ARC	27307	BATTLE THE WIMPS; (C/G)
ALIENVGA.ZIP	148492	Shareware space game mapped for VGA
AMS.ZIP	148537	Apollo Mission Simulator - very complex
ANTIX.ARC	21439	Game from makers of tetris.
APOLLO.ARC	148480	A simulation of the Apollo moon flights.
ARCHERY.ZIP	22428	A archery game.
ARKANOID.ZIP	111616	*EGA* breakout type game.
ASP.ARC	29485	Arcade-type game ASP ATTACK, CGA
AV2.ZIP	25708	Arcade volleyball, fun and easy to play
AXORU57.ZIP	119563	Advanced XORU v5.7 -- Role playing game
BANANOID.ZIP	51773	VGA(only) breakout type game. Excellent!
BASGAM-1.ARC	19349	BASIC text games - TRADE, TRUCKER
BASGAM-2.ARC	13056	BASIC board games - Backgammon, Yahtzee
BASGAM-3.ARC	5102	Mastermind & Space Shooter BASIC Mono
BASSLAK1.ZIP	4930	Three new lakes for BASSTOUR.
BASSLAK2.ZIP	4868	Six more lakes for BASSTOUR.
BASSLAK3.ZIP	1692	More maps for BASSTOUR.
BASSMAP.ZIP	79881	Companion program for BassTour.
BATTLE.ZIP	61977	EGA/VGA 16 color BATTLE SHIP game!
BBALL.ARC	36224	Basketball game

BBCHESS.ARC	19968	CHESSGAME FOR MONOCROME MONITORS.
BCHILD.ZIP	32235	BrainChild-Learn physics while you play
BEAST.ARC	10552	An interesting arcade style game.
BEM.ARC	37413	Bug-eyed-monster pinball game
BEYOND.ARC	29312	BEYOND COLUMNS game (TETRIS LIKE)
BIGRIG.ARC	66560	Drive a semi truck cross country
BIGTOP.ARC	39936	Circus fun arcade game.
BIO300D.ZIP	34497	BIORYTHMS TO SCREEN OR PRINTER - GOOD
BIOCOLOR.ARC	25375	Plot your biorythms for the new year.
BIRDSONG.ARC	18084	Play or create birdsongs w/BASIC. Neat!
BIZERK.ARC	20803	KIND OF LIKE THE ARCADE VERSION - FOR IBM
BJ-EGA.ARC	225280	BlackJack supports HiRes VGA/EGA.
BJ15.ZIP	155677	Professional EGA BlackJack Tutor/Game.
BLAMO.ARC	82432	Good 2-player game for EGA or CGA
BLIMP.ARC	1280	Scrolling titles on a blimp.
BLK11.ARC	46970	BLOCK ELEVEN V 2.0. Solitaire card game.
BLKJCK.ARC	63097	Blackjack game in casino style.
BLOCKADE.ARC	4396	2-person game played over modems
BLUEBALL.ZIP	35446	VGA. Verson of slither. done nice.
BOMBER.ARC	22984	A simple "bombs away" game.
BORIS.ZIP	47543	Cute supposedly Russian game.
BOWL101.ARC	97745	Maintain bowling league stats
BREAKO.ARC	24576	EGA version of Breakout - excellent
BRIDGE-H.ZIP	143486	Shareware computer Bridge game.
BTTLSHP.ARC	42460	Interesting battleship game
BUCK.ARC	32384	A fast "Buck Rogers" arcade game.
BUGFRY.ZIP	27854	Animation of bugs getting zapped...
BUGS.EXE	24064	CENTIPEDE, A GOOD MONO GAME
BUSHIDO.ARC	67712	Martial arts game.
BUZZARD.ARC	17545	A shootem em up with different twist
BZONE.ARC	66304	Battlezone game - Tanks
CALIFGAM.ARC	1050	Unprotect California Games by Epyx.
CANASTA.ARC	67970	Game of Canasta.
CASTLE.ARC	53248	GOOD GRAPHIC ADVENTURE GAME - MONO & C/G
CAVEQUES.ARC	76061	An text and graphics adventure game.
CAVERNS.ARC	36520	Caverns of Gink (fun); (C/G)
CCHESS.ARC	27064	Chinese Chess game in Turbo Pascal
CDRAGON.ARC	45056	GRAPHIC SUBMARINE ADVENTURE
CENTIP.ARC	11654	Another Centipede - good!; (C/G)
CFB21.ARC	120192	Action EGA football game
CFB23.ZIP	100757	Cunning Football v.2.3 EGA.
CHESS.ARC	113701	3-D CHESS GAME
CHESS35.ARC	128394	Excellent chess game. Best on EGA's
CHKRS.ARC	31232	Two-player checker game. VGA required.

CIBOX.ZIP	73344	Coins in a Box childrens educational game
CIPHER11.ZIP	62209	Word puzzle game EGA/VGA and mouse GOOD.
CLIMBER.ARC	36096	A public domain version of Lode Runner.
CLONINV.ZIP	106668	Space Invaders - for CGA,EGA,VGA - vg.
CLUE122.ZIP	34816	The game of CLUE
COLLIDE.ARC	68608	*EGA* shoot em up game.
COMIC3.ZIP	134528	Captain Comic ver 3.0 EGA very Good!.
CONQEGA.ZIP	44354	Game of Conquest for the EGA
CRIB-EGA.ARC	40087	A cribbage game for EGA.
CSHUF1.ZIP	106019	Good memory game for kids and adults.cga.
CYRUS.ARC	129321	Very good 3D Chess game for EGA.
DBLOCKS.ZIP	28198	Another clone of Tetris - very good
DEPTHCHG.ARC	6136	SINK THE SUBS - GOOD MONO BASIC GAME
DND.ARC	102658	public domain dungeons and dragons
DRAGONS.ARC	21259	Medieval Breakout-type game; (C/G)
DRAGRACE.ARC	2560	HIGH OCTANE MACHINES!
DRED3.ZIP	102417	City of Madness - The Showdown.
DRIVER.ARC	47206	KEEP IT ON THE HIGHWAY.
DRMYSTIK.ARC	48243	Dr. Mystik v2, the mysterious sooth-sayer
DROIDS.ARC	47638	Arcade game--blast out the rubble.
DSKCRASH.ARC	26766	Steer your floppy through magnets (C/G)
DULLES.ARC	115545	Air traffic control simulation/game.
EAGLERIV.ARC	32723	A good MEAN-18 golf course.
EAGLES.ZIP	83080	Eagle's Nest a good arcade game. CGA req.
EC2.ARC	93184	Second release of Enchanted Castle.
EG09303.ZIP	46197	Fantastic EGA version of tetris (try it).
EG93M.ZIP	54442	Great EGA version of Teteris
EGACONES.ARC	5751	Circular Kaleidoscope for Ega (Nelson).
EGAINT.ZIP	48208	Very nice EGA version of Tetris.
EGAMAZE.ARC	22037	Creates a maze and solves it. EGA ONLY.
EGAMT2.ARC	40209	Fractal mountain landscapes for the EGA.
EGAPOKER.ARC	46221	Greate EGA Poker game - mouse required.
EGAROIDS.ARC	40596	Asteroids game; EGA Version.
EMPIRE.ARC	99200	War game of the century.... Very Good.
EXERCISE.ARC	47232	Develop weight lifting program v1.0.
F19FS02.ARC	10697	Unprotect F19 Stealth Fighter
FA21.ZIP	34589	Flash Attack v2.1 game by Galacticomm.
FIRE.ARC	23240	BATTLE THE FOREST FIRE; (C/G)
FLYT.COM	25472	Excellant fight biplane game. C/G
FOOTBALL.ZIP	18296	Run your own football pool
FORDSIM.ARC	178176	Drive a real Ford or just check one out.
FORTUNE.ARC	12228	Good Wheel of Fortune Program
FOWLPLAY.ARC	39843	Can you make the chicken cross the road?
FRAC.ZIP	54904	3D Tetris Games With Fractal Images -

FREDDY.ARC	33664	Freddy the Fish swims again!
FREECE.ARC	24310	Freecell solitare from Canada very nice.
FREESTYL.ZIP	25921	a nice pinball game.
FRIGATE.ARC	96000	Missile frigate vs. Soviets game
FROGGER.EXE	37760	FROGGER; (C/G)
FS4NEW.ZIP	14777	Compuserve thread about Flight Simulator
FSEGAPAT.ARC	9707	Patch Flight Simulator v2.1 for EGA use.
FUNFACE.ZIP	78848	FaceMaker-like program-Most for kids-Fun.
FUUTBALL.BAS	35189	Football against your PC
GALAXIAN.ARC	19332	An Arcade game some will find familiar
GAPPER.ARC	34288	Maze/chase type of game; good graphics.
GEMINI.ARC	69632	Game to be played over modem
GHOST.ZIP	3829	Checkers-like game against
GIF2TGA.ARC	13969	Convert GIF images to Targa 16 format.
GIN.ARC	118470	GOOD COMPUTER GIN RUMMY GAME
GINRUMMY.ARC	113101	Gin! Play gin rummy against computer
GO.EXE	32768	ANCIENT CHINESE GAME, LIKE CHECKERS
HACK.ARC	164962	Great fighting adventure, but difficult.
HAUNTED.ARC	59769	Escape from the Haunted House, Adv. game.
HEARTS6.ARC	73432	New version of HEARTS, the old card game.
HELPHIM.ARC	7471	Help the guy trapped in computer.
HOCKEY.ZIP	117027	Anyone for Ice Hockey - supports EGA.
HOLDEM.ARC	48411	Plays poker variant "Holdem" and others.
HOPLOG.ARC	53248	A simple game similar to frogger.
HOSTAGE.EXE	43520	FREE THE HOSTAGES FROM THE BUILDING
HUGO.EXE	226688	Graphics and text interactive game -
HUGO.ZIP	235639	Haunted house adventure game --CGA.
HURKLE.ZIP	6782G	Arcade-type game, VGA required.
IBMTREK.ARC	87123	Old classic trek game... Good version.
ICBM.ARC	52224	GOOD MISSILE GAME
INTELGNT.ARC	61967	HANGMAN FOR THE SUPER INTELLIGENT!
JOTTO.ZIP	53870	Interesting word-logic game.
JOUST.ARC	28778	Tilting, anyone?; (C/G)
JOYCAL.ARC	30631	Professional joystick calibrator; 1 or 2
KARNOV.ZIP	303104	Nice arcade game (fun but kinda weired).
KENO.ARC	20399	A simple version of the casino game.
KILLER.EXE	45696	Get the Killer Bees; (C/G)
KO.ARC	109121	A boxing game with great graphics.
KONG.BAS	15488	DONKEY KONG TYPE GAME; (C/G)
KQ3.ARC	9189	Run King's Quest III on the hard disk.
KQ4DFIX.ARC	2614	Unprotect Kings Quest IV.
LABELLE.ZIP	45512	A solitare game from France, unique.
LARN.ARC	150528	Rogue or Hack type game, different feel.
LARNV12A.ARC	147299	Dungeons & Dragons type game. Good.

LAWN2.ARC	60888	Arcade style mow the lawns game.
LORD.ZIP	215750	Lord of the Rings Game.
LOTTO649.ARC	191179	The Complete Lotto Pick System CA 6/49
LSL2PAT.ARC	1845	Unprotect for Sierra's Leisure Suit Larry
LSL2PHN2.ZIP	76869	Phone #'s of girls in Leisure Suit Larry
M18NEW.ARC	3429	Unprotect Mean 18 11/87 vers.
MARS.BAS	12928	Adventure Game on the order of FIFI
MAZEGAME.EXE	56704	CHALLENGING MAZE GAME; (C/G)
MBV41.EXE	115100	Mille Bournes Version 4.01
METAPIN.ZIP	22777	Another nice pinball game.
MILLE.ARC	82731	EGA/The French card game Mille Bornes.
MILLE40.ZIP	108674	Mille Bornes game for VGA- nice graphics!
MLSHUT11.ARC	36881	Nice CGA game; good graphics; kids fun.
MONOP2.ARC	66641	GOOD MONOPOLY GAME
MONOP68.ARC	70656	Another Monopoly game, pretty good. C/G
MONOPOLY.ARC	63616	Play Monopoly against the computer.
MOONBUG.ARC	28891	Moonbuggy arcade game; (C/G)
MOONPRTL.ARC	31419	A fast arcade game--may seem familiar
MORAFF.ZIP	173024	Moraff's Revenge Role Playing game.
MOTOMAN.ARC	22058	Motorcycle Arcade Game; (C/G)
MOUSEWAR.ZIP	55168	Zap the hurkle with many levels of play
MPACKMAN.EXE	41600	Great monochrome PAC-MAN
MS-TREK.ARC	78334	Great DOS version of old StarTrek game
MSPACMAN.ARC	28672	Ms. PAC Man (Atari) works on IBM - decent
NAVALWAR.ARC	34069	Game similar to BATTLESHIPS
NINJA.ARC	29417	Martial arts arcade fun; (C/G)
NIOSA.ZIP	110495	Graphic (CGA) adventure game shareware
NITEFIRE.ARC	26828	Tank artillery duel; (C/G)
OILWELL.ARC	33962	Run your own Oil company
ORBIT.ARC	68088	Orbital Flight Simulator.
OTHELLO.ARC	23333	The game Othello
PAC-GAL.EXE	39296	PAC-PERSON GAME
PACMAN.ARC	35840	Good original type pacman. Color
PARA.ARC	9402	PARATROOPER WIPEOUT; (C/G)
PC-RR.ARC	63655	Run Your Own PC-Railroad (C/G)
PCBB104.ARC	169196	Kubek'S Prochallenge baseball; shareware
PCBOWL.ARC	64779	Let'g go bowling; (C/G)
PCCASINO.ZIP	107156	Three different casino card games
PCDARTS.ARC	21504	A simple game of darts.
PCHESS.EXE	125427	PowerChess 5.3. Powerfull chess program.
PCLANDER.ARC	28160	Graphic Lunar Lander (tricky); (C/G)
PCMAN.ARC	30542	Nice PACMAN arcade game; reqs. 286 & EGA.
PCNTBBAL.ZIP	48296	PERCENTAGE BASEBALL, fast, easy,
PCPOOL.ARC	37376	Good pool game. CGA required

PEGOUT.ARC	38016	Good solitaire-type game, challenging.
PENTE.ARC	25600	Pente, same as board game, C/G
PETE11.ZIP	34816	Excellent EGA kalidescope; good control
PIANOMAN.ARC	130596	Play/Record/Edit/Compile Music.
PINBALL.COM	64512	PINBALL IN YOUR PC GOOD C/G
PINBALL5.ARC	155953	Play pinball.
PIRATE.ARC	57084	OLD-STYLE PIRATE ADVENTURE GAME
PITFALL.ARC	24132	ARCADE GAME; (C/G)
POKER.ARC	37060	Good draw poker against six opponents.
POLYGOT.ZIP	37031	Spelling game, all leevls. CGA.
POOLMSTR.ARC	81024	Football pool program
PQ2.ARC	1823	Unprotect Police Quest II.
PRISONER.ZIP	56448	Good puzzle - can you solve it?.
PROTON.ARC	15364	PROTON STYLE ARCADE GAME
PYLON.ZIP	39680	Air Racing! works on dos 2.1 but not 3.2.
PYRSOL.ZIP	25790	Pyramid solitaire card game - GREAT!
QUADVGA.ZIP	85124	Vga Arcade Game - Great Graphics !!!
QUANTOID.ARC	100605	Game- shoot those nasty MBAs. CGA.
QUBERT.EXE	55296	BERT & THE SNAKE-GOOD ARCADE GAME (C/G)
REACTOR.ARC	108714	Run a nuclear reactor - game.
RISKEGA.ARC	44412	Game of Risk requires EGA.
RLOGIC.ARC	30481	Use logic to cross the minefield
ROBOTS.ZIP	65798	Robots from Hell. VGA required.
ROCKETS.ARC	48188	Fast action arcade game; (C/G)
ROULETTE.EXE	64256	CASINO GAME OF ROULETTE
ROUND42.ARC	37381	Space Invaders with 42 variations (C/G)
RUBIK10.ZIP	68616	Solve Rubik's cube or let computer do it.
SAILING.ARC	57227	Bermuda Triangle sailing game. Graphics.
SCRABB.ARC	62460	Scrabble board game. Mono or color.
SCRABBLE.ARC	123493	Good Scrabble game--hard to beat.
SCRAMBL2.ARC	69519	An EGA scramble type of game.
SEA126.ZIP	95542	SEAHUNT v1.26 Battleship game.
SEADRGN.ARC	40963	Subs in caves-good & fast; (C/G)
SEAHNT.ARC	102744	Seahunt v. 1.23. Neat game!
SIERANEW.ARC	271360	A demo for new sierra games. Nice.
SKULL.ZIP	75098	Skullduggery - Adventures in Horror.
SKYRUN.ARC	28144	Fly your jet through the trees.
SLOT.ZIP	46080	Las Vegas machine. Requires EGA.
SNIPE.ARC	21255	A shoot em up/maze game, needs CG.
SOPWITH.ARC	40191	NEAT AIRPLANE GAME
SOPWITH2.ZIP	33375	New SOPWITH v2.0 game, fly WWI fighter,
STARFIR.EXE	24320	RULE THE UNIVERSE. UP TO 8 CAN PLAY.
STARSHIP.ARC	63488	Starship game -- kinda like star trek.
STATES.ARC	90112	Interesting quiz on states.

```
SUB.EXE          67584   SUBMARINE ADVENTURE GAME-USES FUNCT. KEYS
TANK.ARC         47249   Tank wars      C/G
TBRIDGE.ARC      44032   Turbo Bridge game, with source
TEED-OFF.ARC     75480   Pretty good golf game, with C/G graphics
TERROR.ARC       32745   Terror in the Ice Caverns, Adventure
THIEVE.ARC       40192   Interesting card game.  Challenging.
THINGS.BAS        5504   A graphics game in basic.
THREEDEE.ARC     39168   3D handball game.
TIMEADV.ARC       9553   Adventure in time   (BASIC)
TIMEWARP.ARC     32080   A new pinball game.
TTT444.ARC       12969   A 4x4x4 Tic-Tac-Toe variant, enjoyable.
TWILIGHT.ZIP     31900   Dive for buried treasure cga game.
TWIT.EXE         64512   TWILIGHT ZONE PINBALL GAME-SOMETHING
ULARNEXE.ZIP    128275   Ultra Larn, a DND type game
ULTIMA2.ZIP      11870   Hints for finishing Ultima II.
UNO11.ARC        43054   The card game uno--runs with mono or CGA.
VEGASEGA.ARC     82219   Casino games: slots,poker,blackjack.
VOLLEY.ZIP       27648   A good game of volley ball.
VOLYBALL.ZIP     32289   A neat little volleyball game for two.
VPJOKER.ZIP      80182   Vegas Pro(tm) JOKER'S WILD ver 1.0 game
WANDERER.ZIP    145181   Work your way through 60 mazes
WARRIOR.ARC      56522   Shoot-em-up game, needs joystick.
WHEEL.ARC       148132   The Wheel of fortune game, Very GOOD!
XIANGQI.ZIP      23505   The Chinese Game of Chess; Version 2
XO.ARC           30239   A SPACE SHOOT-EM-UP ARCADE GAME
XTETRIS2.ZIP     80402   Tetris game with a twist.
```

The commercial online networks and many bulletin boards have special areas for games. Commercial networks like GEnie and CompuServe have games that can be played online. Bulletin boards often have "door" games that users can play. Thus, you will find no shortage of games and diversions in the world of Shareware. For now, we'll leave games behind and take a look at some of the educational programs that Shareware provides.

EDUCATIONAL PROGRAMS IN SHAREWARE

Not only does Shareware offer comparable software in nearly every category of commercial software, but it offers many things that commercial software does not. Educational programs are no exception. In the world of Shareware, every age group is covered and covered well. There are programs for children in preschool, elementary school, middle school, high school, and even college. The programs range from something as simple as teaching your child colors to something as complex as constructing molecular models. There are programs for math, biology, chemistry, physics, geography, history, statistics, typing . . . shall I go on? For young children, there are programs to teach colors, counting, and much more. Let's begin by taking a look at educational software in general.

Children today, in many cases, get to work with computers in school. My own children started fooling with computers at home when each was around the age of four. Children catch on to computers much faster than adults do and they adapt quickly. With the help of good software, your children can have better performance in school. If they are having trouble with math, for example, you can obtain some excellent Shareware math programs to help strengthen their skills.

There are several advantages to using the educational software you can find in Shareware rather than commercial programs. First, although companies have removed copy protection from many of their products, two notable exceptions are games and educational programs. These types of commercial programs still tend to have some form of copy protection. Shareware programs do not. Another advantage is the diversity of Shareware software. You can often find tutorial programs in Shareware that you cannot find commercially.

A final advantage, and an important one, is the price. The educational programs found in Shareware are much less expensive and, in some cases, free.

Funnels and Buckets

Funnels and Buckets is an excellent math program that handles addition, subtraction, multiplication, division, or a mix of all four. Set up like an arcade-style game, Funnels and Buckets uses colors and sound. Children can select the types of problems they want to work on. Problems "fall" from the top of the screen, and players "shoot" down the problem by supplying the correct answer. If they miss a problem, it lands in one of the "buckets" at the bottom of the screen. When all the buckets are filled, the session is over. The program automatically monitors progress so that as players do better the problems become more complex. If they are having trouble, on the other hand, the problems will get easier.

Data Sage
210 Prospect Street
New Haven, CT 06520
$10 registration for individuals; $25 for schools (per building)

PC-FASTYPE

Typing programs are particularly useful, since typing is a must when using computers—at least for the time being. PC-FASTYPE is one of the best overall typing tutors I have tried. It has exercises for the beginner, intermediate, and advanced typist. There are drills to practice your familiarity with the "home" keys, drills to practice typing a series of words, and much more.

The program comes in two versions, one for monochrome systems and one for color systems. Figure 20-2 shows the main screen of PC-FASTYPE. The program gives you many options, and even more choices are contained on submenus. What is so nice about PC-FASTYPE is that you can customize your sessions to meet your needs: add more letters to the drills, move up from beginner to intermediate, and so on. All the while, PC-FASTYPE computes your progress, letting you know how you're doing. You can gradually add more and more letters to your drills until you are doing it all.

Trendtech Corporation
P.O. Box 3687
Wayne, NJ 07474
$25 plus $3 shipping and handling for single-user registration

KwikStat

For the ultimate in statistics, no program I've seen beats KwikStat. This program is a complete statistical data analysis package with all the features that you could possibly want. KwikStat handles various statistical calculations such as:

- T-tests

- ANOVA

- Non-Parametrics

- Simple and multiple linear regressions

- Crosstabulations

- Frequencies

- Chi-square

KwikStat also gives you a range of printing options so you can display your data in a number of ways, using histograms, scatterplot graphs, pie charts, time series plots, box plots, pictographs, and three-dimensional plots.

For those interested in statistics, KwikStat is an excellent program. It does simple statistics like standard deviation from the mean, determining the mean, variance, median, and so on. For crosstabulations it can use Chi-square, Yates, and the Fischer extract test. Despite the complexity of

---

Figure 20-2

Main screen of PC-FASTYPE

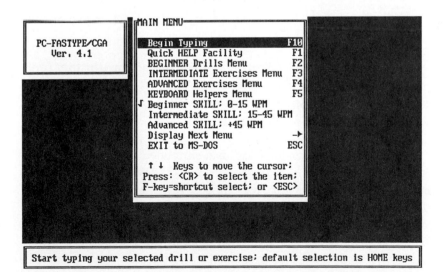

what the program does, it's easy to use. The data is stored in dBASE III format, which can also be used by other programs. KwikStat is a complete package and it's inexpensive. If you work with statistics, take a good look at KwikStat.

TexaSoft
P.O. Box 1169
Cedar Hill, TX 75104
214-291-2115
$49 registration plus $4 postage and handling includes latest version and bound manual; MasterCard and Visa accepted; special bulk pricing available.

Just to Give You an Idea

When it comes to educational programs, each person's needs vary greatly. Shareware has programs for all ages, for teachers, for the study of foreign languages, and so much more. It is very difficult to address this topic with any hope of satisfying the curiosity of a large number of readers. I just want to assure you that Shareware is filled with a full range of educational software. Whether you have a 2-year-old who is trying to learn letters or a 22-year-old who is having trouble with calculus, there is a program that will help. Here are just a few more varied programs that you might find of interest.

MATHPAR   This is an excellent program that generates math story problems using objects that the player selects. MATHPAR will break down a problem into simple steps, showing where the player made a mistake. It is generally found as MATHPAR.ZIP.

WPK   This "Word Processor for Kids" is a simplified program that gives children an introduction to word processing. It is easy to use and easy to understand, helping children to "see" how to insert text, delete text, and so on. It is usually found as WPK.ZIP.

STATES   This program helps anyone learn all of the states in the United States and their capital cities. Done in color, you first identify the highlighted state. The second portion of the program highlights a state and tells you what state it is, and you have to supply the name of the capital city. This is great for students. It can be found as STATES.ZIP.

TEACHTOT   This program teaches ABCs, numbers, and more to very young children. It can be found as TEACHTOT.ZIP.

Computerized Grade Book   This useful tool for teachers handles multiple classes, calculates grades, and much more. Hailed as "the best" by many teachers, it can be found as CGB12.ZIP.

To give you some more ideas and to show you just a tiny fraction of the kinds of things that are available in educational Shareware, a bulletin board listing follows. Take a good look at the variety found on just this one short listing.

123TUTOR.ZIP	28,862	Tutorial for LOTUS 123 - has 2 Cases
ACE1.ZIP	176,696	Great astronomical program
ACE2.ZIP	139,291	Great Astronomical program
ANIMALS.ZIP	20,444	Pre-school math game using animals.
ASTRO2SS.ZIP	31,440	Solar System simulator. Requires EGA or
ASTROL81.ZIP	95,259	Serious astrology charting
ASTROL82.ZIP	80,391	companion to astrol81.arc...GOOD
BLAST.ZIP	5,753	Calculate effect of nuclear blast!
CALCULUS.ZIP	144,961	Calculus Tutor (with Business)
CHEMICAL.ZIP	186,869	MOLECULAR MODELING PROG 3D VERY GOOD
CLOCKGAM.ZIP	12,966	Great game to teach kids to tell time.
COLLEGE.ZIP	107,815	College Probe -Program to help select a college that offers what you need
COSMOS.ZIP	96,329	Great shareware planetarium program!
CREATIV1.ZIP	108,905	Creativity Package -
CRYPTO.ZIP	41,378	Create, save, and Solve CRYPTOGRAMS!!
DPSPACE3.ZIP	173,943	Deep Space Star Charting Program
EARLYGAM.ZIP	12,565	Teaching games for small children
EDUCATE.ZIP	16,679	Three educational games for young & old
EDUGAME.ZIP	33,910	Assortment of teaching games for children - mostly math drills
ESIE.ZIP	74,706	ARTIFICIAL INTELLIGENCE-V.G.
FACTS50.ZIP	14,375	Educational game concerning all of the 50 states. Good facts learned in it.
FAMILY.ZIP	38,912	Family tree - traces your roots
FAMTIES.ZIP	172,178	Excellent geneology program
FLASHCRD.ZIP	3,558	Flash card program - 10 levels
FRENCH1.ZIP	35,020	French language tutorial

FRENCH2.ZIP	30,610	French language tutorial
GAMES.ZIP	123,431	COLLECTION OF GAMES FOR YOUNGSTERS
GEOCHRON.ZIP	45,035	World map showing time zones
GEOMNO34.ZIP	135,168	Geographic Clock. Shows day/night
GERMAN.ZIP	54,057	German language tutor
IQ.ZIP	39,936	Various IQ tests
ITALIAN.ZIP	33,580	Italian tutor program
JAPAN.ZIP	102,984	Japanese business language tutorial
KIDSTUFF.ZIP	12,273	A collection of educational kids games.
KINDGART.ZIP	45,673	Great pre-school learning game.
LOGIC2TR.ZIP	74,574	Logic tutor
MATHPAR.ZIP	7,656	Teaches math with story problems
MATLAB.ZIP	186,368	A GREAT Matrix Math Program.
MAXIT.ZIP	3,013	Games with numbers in BASIC
MOSAIC.ZIP	16,485	Teaches size and pattern relationships
MVSP.ZIP	50,043	A multivariate statistical procedure
OMNIGAME.ZIP	188,286	Excellent group of children's games helps become comfortable with computer
PCOFCAKE.ZIP	29,502	Educational math puzzles for children -
PLANETS.ZIP	27,153	Solar System Graphing Good! A lot of information on each planet
PROGEN.ZIP	63,480	Create family trees - 3 reports
REACTOR.ZIP	81,843	Nuclear reactor simulator
RECALL13.ZIP	138,752	Smart, menu-driven flash cards.
SPANISH1.ZIP	33,737	Spanish tutor - multiple choice format
SPANISH2.ZIP	31,335	Advanced Spanish tutorial
STARFIND.ZIP	71,401	Nice star finding program.
STARS.ZIP	45,783	STAR & PLANET PLOTTER ACC. TO TIME, DATE
SUJU.ZIP	29,020	Excellent word puzzle game
TELLTIME.ZIP	1,792	Teach junior to tell time.
WORLDX.ZIP	104,317	Latest version (2.6) of WORLD Map
WPK.ZIP	17,531	Word Processor for Kids.
WXRDR40.ZIP	141,472	EGA/VEA weather Super RADAR plotting

This has been an overview of some of the games and educational programs that you can find in The Wires. The variety will amaze you, and if you want something, the odds are good that you will find what you need. Whether it is a particular type of game or a program for learning Japanese, you will find that Shareware offers a wide range of programs to help you. Let's move on now and take a look at the area of business, finance, and spreadsheets.

## CHAPTER TWENTY-ONE

Business and Finance

This chapter will consider two broad areas of computer application, business and finance programs. It is difficult to look at all of the programs available in these two areas due to the wide differences in business structures and finance considerations. Most Shareware programs for these two areas are written with the small businessman and/or financial investor or entrepreneur in mind. Since businesses can range from service to manufacturing and finance considerations can range from personal budgets and investing in real estate, stocks, and bonds to small business bookkeeping, hundreds of programs could be reviewed in this chapter. However, the real foundation of business and finance is contained in only two categories of programs: databases and spreadsheets. Add to these a full-featured accounting package and a general-purpose "electronic desk," and you have pretty much everything you can productively use in these areas.

DATABASE PROGRAMS

There are a number of good database programs available as Shareware, and several have been reviewed in detail in Chapter 18. The important thing to remember in selecting one for business use is to be sure that it has the facility to convert the commercial database programs (generally dBASE-compatible) into a format that is usable in the Shareware package. (Some of the newer Shareware database releases, such as ButtonWare's PC-File DB and PC-File Version 5.0, are now using the dBASE structure in their files directly.) If you have a compatible database, you are ready not only to create your own custom applications that fit your business but also to use some of the database templates that are available on bulletin board systems. You will also be able to trade database structures with your friends, who may have solved a problem in their business that will be beneficial in yours.

Among the most common database applications in business are the following:

- Inventory control
- Price lists
- Mailing labels
- Personalized mass mailings
- Client tracking
- Prospect development
- Personnel records
- Vacation schedule tracking
- Accounting—simple or elaborate
- Recording/TV library
- Diskette catalog
- Political campaign contributions
- Personal ideas and thoughts
- Name and address directory
- Telephone directory
- Magazine/clippings library
- Scholarly publications and articles

- Organization records and management
- Travel expense records
- Consulting time and expense billing

Well, you get the idea: a database application can be made of anything that you need to have in an organized and easily accessible listing.

The Benefits of a Database

As you read over the preceding list, it's a fair bet that you thought of an application you use in your business that wasn't mentioned. That's why the use of a database program is a basic business tool. No matter how knowledgeable commercial programmers are, they will never be able to meet all of the special nuances that make your business uniquely your own. With a good database program, you can construct any number of applications that do things "your way" and even link them together with a menu system for easy use.

Since a major discussion of databases and their structure appears elsewhere in these chapters, no further discussion of their "hows and whys" is needed here. However, if you call bulletin board systems, be sure to check for dBASE and other database templates. Even if they do not meet your specific needs, the way in which the programmer put them together may help you construct something that will be exactly what you need in your application.

SPREADSHEET PROGRAMS

A spreadsheet program is absolutely essential to the financial end of business and to any investment analysis task. These financial workhorses serve as the carriers for everything from pro forma financial construction, to budget control and forecasting, to stock and bond trend analysis, and anything else having to do with the control, analysis, and tracking of dollars and cents. The business and finance use of spreadsheets is limited only by the imagination and ingenuity of the business executive. To more clearly understand the workings of a spreadsheet, here is some background on their development and a brief review of some full-featured Shareware programs.

Some History on Spreadsheets

VisiCalc is acknowledged by almost everyone as the first electronic spreadsheet. It was originally written in BASIC for the Apple II computer. Another program, called SuperCalc, was also around before Lotus 1-2-3. It was originally written for CP/M, and ported over to DOS. The first DOS spreadsheet wars consisted of SuperCalc, 1-2-3, and VisiCalc, and 1-2-3 was the winner. Later came Multiplan, Twin, VP Planner, and Excel.

Bricklin and Frankston—The Founding Fathers

In 1978, Dan Bricklin and Bob Frankston teamed up to create a product that would contribute to turning Apple Computer from a garage operation to a multibillion-dollar corporation. Bricklin and Frankston created the first electronic spreadsheet program, which they called "Visible Calculator" or VisiCalc. Before long, Bricklin and Frankston and their firm, Software Arts, entered into a marketing agreement with another firm, VisiCorp. Software Arts grew to a 15-million-dollar company with 130 employees, while VisiCorp grew even larger and became one of the leading software companies in the industry.

Between 1978 and 1982 Software Arts and VisiCalc were growth companies, and VisiCalc was the spreadsheet program to have. Just about every Fortune 500 firm had an arsenal of Apple II systems with a fresh copy of VisiCalc.

Breaking New Ground

VisiCalc broke new ground as the first spreadsheet program. Many marveled at the wonders of columns and rows magically recalculating in an instant. In 1981 the IBM PC began to capture significant market share. A version of VisiCalc was quickly developed for IBM compatible systems—some say too quickly. VisiCalc needed more features and better data integration. An upgrade was needed badly and VisiCalc's sales began to decline. VisiCorp filed suit against Software Arts and things began to go from bad to worse.

Lotus Leaps to the Front

One of the key people at VisiCorp, Mitch Kapor, left to form a new company called Lotus. He announced his new product, Lotus 1-2-3, with much fanfare at Fall COMDEX in Las Vegas in 1982. Kapor was a master showman. The roll-out for Lotus 1-2-3 was in a rented airplane hangar complete with champagne, slick literature, and demonstrations. Soon the industry was ablaze with the catchy phrases used at the unveiling:

1 for spreadsheet
2 for database
3 for graphics

Although it was an integrated package by the standards of the time, 1-2-3 version 1/1A would not fare too well by today's standards. Marketed aggressively to fill the needs of the quickly growing numbers of corporate personal computer users, 1-2-3 became the most successful software package for the IBM PC.

Spreadsheets — The Mainstay of Business

You can use a spreadsheet program in place of a piece of columnar paper, a pencil, and a calculator. Spreadsheets are the perfect "what if" tool for complex calculations. In 1978 when VisiCalc was released, one person

DOCTOR'S NOTE

The impact on VisiCalc of Kapor's marketing strengths and Lotus 1-2-3's integration was quickly apparent. VisiCorp and Software Arts suffered huge financial losses and layoffs, and eventually Software Arts was purchased by its slayer, Lotus.

For a time Bricklin did some consulting for Lotus and then took a stab at publishing a new product, Dan Bricklin's Demo Program, which was also a success. In 1988 Bricklin sold his program, called Dan Bricklin's Demo II, to Peter Norton Computing for an undisclosed sum. Bricklin, who has always been active in the computer industry, fared much better this time.

Although Frankston dropped out of sight a long time ago, Bricklin has been active with computer user groups, trade shows, and publications. He is highly regarded for his accomplishments and contributions to the industry.

with a computer, printer, and VisiCalc could do the same work as a dozen clerks with columnar paper. Erasers, liquid paper, and frustrated secretaries trying to organize and type from scratchy pencil notes became a thing of the past.

Like the columnar paper they supplant, electronic spreadsheet programs work with columns and rows. Each section is called a *cell*, and the column width can be set for a single column or a group of columns. The titles can be locked horizontally or vertically or both. The screen can be split horizontally or vertically, and multiple windows of one file or a group of files can be opened.

Commercial Versus Shareware Spreadsheets

Spreadsheet programs are RAM intensive. Shareware spreadsheet programs take about 250K of RAM to execute and leave under 300K of RAM for calculations in a typical 640K system. You should have enough memory for a 5-to-10-page spreadsheet if you design it right. While all commercial spreadsheet programs can load spreadsheets or worksheets into expanded memory, most Shareware spreadsheet programs lack this feature. Expanded RAM support is a mixed blessing. The added code will use more of the conventional memory, and users who don't have expanded memory will end up with less workspace than they would have had. There are also some compatibility problems associated with expanded memory support for spreadsheet programs.

Shareware authors have concentrated their efforts on integrity of calculations and improved user interfaces. There are some extraordinary Shareware programs that rival the ones you'll see in three-page advertisements in leading computer magazines. People used to say "a spreadsheet is a spreadsheet," but Bricklin and Frankston can tell you differently. You can find out for yourself by test driving some of the Shareware spreadsheet programs available. I'll help you get started by telling you about a few of my favorites.

The Evolution of Shareware Spreadsheets

No one is sure which Shareware spreadsheet was first. The popular Shareware spreadsheet programs of today have been around for a long time. Most Shareware spreadsheet programs were originally written in either compiled BASIC or Turbo Pascal, and not much has changed in that regard. What has changed is the addition of assembly code in critical areas, the implementation of more efficient algorithms, and better user-interface design.

The development of commercial spreadsheets has not directly affected the way Shareware spreadsheets have changed. Consider, for example, the fact that while the big guys were working on developing bigger, more powerful spreadsheets, Shareware authors were looking at development from a different angle, as in QubeCalc (a three-dimensional spreadsheet) and PC-Calc (reconfigurable size).

In the Shareware spreadsheet wars, there has been no clear-cut winner, possibly because each sheet offers something different for users (QubeCalc offers three dimensions, InstaCalc is a TSR, As-Easy-As is compatible with 1-2-3, and PC-Calc offers good interaction with the popular PC-File).

Spreadsheets have changed quite a bit since VisiCalc. To give you a better understanding of spreadsheets, let's take a look at these changes. The most significant changes are listed first and will be discussed further.

- Sparse matrix storage

- Spreadsheet macros

- Intelligent recalculation

- Selective recalculation

- Manual recalculation

- Goal seeking

- Direct file import/export

- Split-screen graphics

- Worksheet auditing

- Database input forms

Now, let's see what all of these changes have meant to the ways in which spreadsheets work.

Sparse Matrix Storage

In early spreadsheets memory was allocated for every cell, whether it contained data or not (like a big array). This meant that memory limited the number of rows and columns you could use. *Sparse matrix storage* means that memory is allocated only for those cells that contain data (not for every cell in between).

Spreadsheet Macros

Early spreadsheets did not have any macro capabilities. One of the factors in 1-2-3's success was that its macro language allowed users to customize their worksheets. Besides basic macro capability spreadsheets, macro recording is now offered.

Intelligent Recalculation

Using *intelligent recalculation,* when a cell is changed, only cells that are directly or indirectly related to it are updated. This results in a tremendous increase in spreadsheet recalculation speed, since only a few cells need to be recalculated and updated most of the time. Should there be another way? One of the leading Shareware spreadsheet programs, As-Easy-As, has used this method since 1986.

Selective Recalculation

In many cases, even intelligent recalculation would result in long recalculation times, due to the fact that some of today's worksheet templates have become so sophisticated and complex. For these situations, *selective recalculation* will force calculation of only a specified range in the worksheet.

Manual Recalculation

There are situations where a template model can get so complex that recalculation should occur only when the user specifically requests it. For those occasions, the *manual recalculation* mode is useful. In this mode, worksheet cells are intelligently recalculated when the user presses the recalculate key.

Goal Seeking

Goal seeking is a joint solution to a problem. Set up a model, specify what you want the output to be, and this option will calculate the required input. This spreadsheet capability lets you work with different options or scenarios. You can speculate or you can decide what you want the outcome to be, and the spreadsheet will tell you what you have to do first in order to accomplish your goal.

Direct File Import/Export

At the touch of a key, you can go between popular file formats including Lotus releases 1, 2.2, and 3, dBASE, DIF, ASCII, and others. This ability to import and export spreadsheet data has made spreadsheets much more flexible. The ability to import allows users to utilize spreadsheets created by others. Exporting lets you share your work with someone else.

Split-Screen Graphics

Display two totally independent graphs in two half-screen windows at the same time. This feature lets you compare data and look for trends or mistakes. By being able to look at the contents of two different graphs at the same time, you can often get a better feel for the situation.

Worksheet Auditing

Worksheet auditing lets you search for references to a particular cell, check for circular references, get an overview of the worksheet usage, and so forth. This lets you better manage a worksheet, to use it to its maximum capability. You might think of it as a bank audit. The spreadsheet audits itself, looking for things that might be amiss.

Database Input Forms

Database input forms help improve productivity. You can design input forms in a hurry, define criteria ranges using forms, and permit date entry using the natural mm/dd/yy format (internally converted to the correct worksheet format for proper manipulation).

The Main Parts of a Spreadsheet Program

To break it down into its simplest terms, there are three main parts to a worksheet program. These are

- User interface
- Linked list
- Calculation engine

The *user interface* is what the user sees and, in most cases, is what the user bases his opinion about the program on. The *linked list* is the portion that keeps tabs on the contents of each cell and its references, and decides what cells need to be recalculated, if any.

The *calculation engine* is the heart of the spreadsheet. After everything is said and done, required calculations need to be done so that appropriate cells can be updated. This is generally the toughest portion to develop, and the bottleneck when it comes to establishing the overall speed of a spreadsheet.

Having looked at the history of spreadsheets, the spreadsheet wars, the way spreadsheets work, and the major improvements that have been added, let's take a look at a couple of Shareware spreadsheet programs.

QUBECALC—A THREE-DIMENSIONAL SPREADSHEET

QubeCalc was released in mid-1986 after six months of development. Version 2, which was the first popular version of QubeCalc, was released in February 1987. Version 3, which later won *PC Magazine*'s Editor's Choice for low-cost spreadsheets, was released in January 1988. QubeCalc is still supported as a Shareware product, although FormalSoft has released a commercial 3D spreadsheet called ProQube, which provides greatly enhanced capabilities.

QubeCalc's main advantage over other spreadsheets is that it is a true 3D spreadsheet. QubeCalc provided this 3D capability three years before it was available in Lotus 1-2-3. QubeCalc provides up to 64 pages in each worksheet, and formulas can reference any cell on any page, providing instant consolidation. In addition, QubeCalc's 3D worksheets can be rotated to view and enter data from different perspectives. This allows a user to view data on several different pages together on the same screen.

The program is started by simply typing **qubecalc** at the DOS prompt. QubeCalc uses overlays, so you'll need the overlays in the current directory when you execute it. You can use the Setup program to configure QubeCalc in different ways, for example, when you're using floppies.

The QubeCalc Display

The top line of the QubeCalc screen is called the status line (see Figure 21-1). The first item on the status line [A] tells you which of the six (A...F) faces of the spreadsheet (like the panels on a Rubik's cube) is current. The E18;1: tells you the name of the current cell. The E18 part is just like any other spreadsheet. The 1: tells you what page you are on. The word NUMBER indicates the current cell has a number in it. Cells can be BLANK, TEXT, NUMBER, FORMULA, or ERROR. The (9) is the width of the cell. The next item displayed is the default directory followed by the filename in use.

Figure 21-1

The QubeCalc screen with its status line

```
[A]E18;1: NUMBER (9)        Dir: C:\TST1                      File: TEST
159.62
        A       B       C       D       E       F       G       H
   1   12.95
   2   15.84
   3
   4                           120.94
   5
   6
   7   TEST    TEST2   TEST3   TEST4   TEST5   TEST6   TEST7
   8   10.25   14.69   18.88   14.92   10.11     0       0
   9                                           87.45   20.88
  10                                   22.22
  11
  12           88.45   99.9
  13                                   85.22
  14
  15
  16           29.55
  17
  18                                  159.62
  19
  20
1=HELP  2=EDIT  3=BLOCK  4=ABS  5=GOTO  6=FIND  7=STAT  8=MACRO  9=CALC  0=GRAPH
 206784 Bytes              AutoCalc ON:A1;1..BL64;64
```

The second line displays the contents of the current cell. As you reenter a value for a cell, the original value will be displayed in the actual cell while the new value will be displayed on this line.

Moving Around in QubeCalc

Moving around the spreadsheet is quick and easy with the arrow keys, HOME, and END. PGUP and PGDN move from page to page in the 3D worksheet. QubeCalc doesn't use TAB, but you can use CTRL-LEFT ARROW and CTRL-RIGHT ARROW to move one screen at a time (the same convention used by Lotus).

At the bottom of the screen QubeCalc displays the function keys. Below this are the available RAM and the calculation mode, AUTO or MANUAL, and the range set for recalculation. QubeCalc, like several spreadsheet programs, supports selective recalculation. QubeCalc's publisher, FormalSoft, has implemented a more advanced minimal recalculation in their commercial product, ProQube, which curiously doesn't support selective recalculation.

QubeCalc's Help System

QubeCalc's context sensitive help system consists of nearly 100 pages and is well organized. The help system, similar to Hypertext, may be all you need to use the program. The Shareware edition of QubeCalc also comes with a 50-page manual, which is a bridge to the full documentation (110 pages) that comes with the registered version. FormalSoft provides technical support for all registered users and will also answer basic questions from anyone. The combination of the enhanced documentation and support are more than enough incentive for users to register the product.

Bruce Buzbee
FormalSoft
P.O. Box 1913
Sandy, UT 84091
801-565-0971
$69.95 registration plus $5 shipping and handling; VISA, MasterCard, and American Express accepted

AS-EASY-AS — CLEVER NAME AND CLEVER PROGRAM

As-Easy-As was released in January 1988. Version 3.01 was declared the best Shareware spreadsheet in *Computer Shopper* magazine in January 1989. Versions 3.0 and 4.0 have received several awards from computer publications in England. As registration screens go, As-Easy-As has one of the most informative. The opening screen displays information about Shareware, Trius (the program's publisher), and key features of the program. It's a bit crowded but nicely done. There are no death threats if you don't register. *<grin>*

As-Easy-As is not only a popular spreadsheet program, it's one the leading Shareware programs available. A few years back, my coauthor Nick Anis sold some Shareware disks to his students and had a tough time convincing the school authorities that As-Easy-As was Shareware. "Are you trying to tell us that students can get copies of this program for $3 per disk?," they asked. A quick call to Trius saved Anis from being kept after school. Since then, the features and interface of As-Easy-As have improved substantially. In fact, disk vendors and Shareware articles frequently highlight As-Easy-As as an example of quality Shareware.

The As-Easy-As Package

The files necessary to run As-Easy-As are ASEASY.EXE and ASEASY.MSG. The files HTREE.EXE and ASEASY.HLP are optional, but you'll need them to access the online help. The ASEASY.CFG will be generated automatically and is needed if you wish to change the default setting. The optional ASEASY.PRT file is a printer control file that contains printer setup codes. This file is pure ASCII and can be examined with the DOS TYPE command or Vern Buerg's LIST program. You can access the control codes in this file by pressing /F1 when you're in the program.

Trius also distributes an assortment of sample worksheet files with As-Easy-As, along with a couple of sample add-ins. One add-in makes rudimentary sideways printing possible, and the other will allow you to set up a LaserJet in graphics mode. Trius also offers related stand-alone products with more horsepower.

Running As-Easy-As

You start As-Easy-As by typing **aseasy**. You should have all the files you need on a 360K floppy or preferably in a single subdirectory on your hard disk. There are also several command line options. You can default most of the options in the .CFG file but some must be done on the command line. For instance, /E is needed to force EGA mode, /V1 will force VGA mode, and /Q will speed up screen updates (at the possible expense of video snow on older CGA systems).

As-Easy-As has a program loading message when you start the program, although loading only takes two seconds or so on an AT system.

As-Easy-As Keeps You Informed

As-Easy-As is more like one of today's mega-spreadsheets than a clone of the old Lotus 1.0-style program. There is a lot of detail in the screen design including use of lines, symbols, and colors. Neophytes may find the screen confusing at first, but users of Excel, Quattro Pro, or Lotus Release 3 will be right at home. The top line of the main screen of As-Easy-As is called the function key area. Besides a template for the function keys, there is also a mode indicator. The mode indicator messages include READY!, CALC, WAIT, MACRO, COMPOSE, and ERROR. There is also a separate message window that opens in the middle of the screen when errors occur.

As-Easy-As Features

The F7 key invokes the word processing mode. This is a useful way to perform word processing/text editing while in a spreadsheet. Word processing bypasses the columns and treats each row as a line in your document. The word processing mode even supports ragged or right-justified word wrap. You can set the right margin by invoking the ruler while in the word processing mode. Built right into the standard commands is a powerful search and replace feature. The /WTR (worksheet, text, replace) works like a charm across your entire spreadsheet or from the point of the cursor to the end of the file. There are even options that allow you to ignore case, (U)pper, and stop and confirm replacements, (P)ause.

If you have invoked the windows command, the F6 key will allow you to toggle between the two views of the spreadsheet. If you only have one window active, F6 is useful to switch between the current and the last locations of your cursor. With F6 you can leave and then go back where you came from.

Lines two and three of As-Easy-As are the panel area. Line two displays the contents of the current cell along with the formatting options for the cell. Line three echoes any keyboard input during data entry. When you press ENTER, the contents of line three are moved into line two and into the actual cell. If you press the F2 key, the contents of the current line are placed on line three and you'll be in the cell edit mode. You can back out of this mode and others by successively pressing the ESC key.

The level of detail given by the program's authors, David Schulz and Paris Karahalios, is impressive. For instance, the cursor is carefully placed right where you would expect it to be during all the phases of data entry. The cursor starts out in the current cell, when you begin data entry it jumps to line three (data entry line), and when you press ENTER it returns to the cell. As-Easy-As also has a unique column and row pointer system that helps you quickly identify the current cell. Of course, current cell location is also identified on line two of the panel area.

The As-Easy-As pull-down menus were designed with much more than just aesthetics in mind. Common sense and practicality went into this portion of the spreadsheet, as in all other portions. Each pull-down menu is divided into two portions. The bottom portion displays the commands available at the current menu level, while the top portion displays a history of how the user arrived at this level (that is, the commands that led to this level).

Like most spreadsheet programs, the main menu of As-Easy-As can be invoked with the / (slash) key although you might need to press ESC to back out of an operation first. You can choose from three locations for the menus: the left, right, and top portions of the screen. The . (period) key is used to toggle the menu from left to right, and the ! (exclamation point) key will toggle the menu from the top of the screen to one of the sides. I like my menus to be on the left (the default). You should experiment a bit and decide which style you prefer.

The Status Line

The bottom line of the screen is the status line. Here you will not only find the available RAM (a common feature of spreadsheets) but you will also find the percentage free (a not-so-common feature). The As-Easy-As status line also displays the filename of the current worksheet, the key status for CAPS, NUMLOCK, and INS, and the recalculation mode setting. Recalculation can be set to MANUAL or AUTOMATIC. As-Easy-As does not support selective recalculation but does support the more advanced intelligent recalculation. During macro execution, if you are in the macro step mode, the status line will also display the actual line of the macro being executed. There is also a clock complete with sweeping seconds to remind you to eat lunch or to give up on balancing your checkbook.

As-Easy-As and Lotus Compatibility

For the most part, As-Easy-As will execute Lotus's macros, but you may need to use the macro step execution in As-Easy-As to refine them. You can't use Lotus add-ins, but As-Easy-As comes with a few and others are about to be released. You can't compile or protect your macros, but you can hide them and make them resistant to nosy users who aren't authorized to view them. Another form of protection offered by As-Easy-As macros is the ability to disable the ESC key during macro execution. Unauthorized users will then only be able to exit a macro sequence by completing it or selecting an exit permitted by the macro author.

Summarizing As-Easy-As

The documentation with the Shareware version of As-Easy-As is about 50 pages long and is available by printing the online help files using a Trius-developed and -supplied formatting and printing program. If you haven't gotten around to learning how to use spreadsheet programs yet, you'll be pleased to know that unlike most word processors, spreadsheets all share common features and commands. Once you have learned one program you should be able to get others up and running with a minimum of effort. As-Easy-As is an extremely well-thought-out program with many advanced features. Be sure to give it a good look.

Trius, Inc.
231 Sutton Street, Suite 2D-3
North Andover, MA 01845
508-794-9377

$50 registration fee includes shipping and handling and a 300-page printed manual, along with the latest version of the program, three months of technical support, and a subscription to Trius's quarterly newsletter. Additional support can be purchased separately. Trius will also answer basic questions from anyone, but users are expected to register to receive regular, in-depth support.

SPREADSHEET TEMPLATES ON BULLETIN BOARD SYSTEMS

As with the selection of a database program, be sure that the Shareware program you select can be converted or used directly with the file structure of commercial programs such as Lotus 1-2-3, SuperCalc, and so forth. You will find that many spreadsheet templates that have been developed on these commercial packages are available on bulletin board systems and from business associates. By selecting a well-designed Shareware spreadsheet, you will be able to use these templates for your own business applications. Once again, look at any template that seems to come close to what you want to do. It may not exactly fit your needs, but you may be able to modify an existing template to fit your needs. Never reinvent the wheel when it only needs a retread! Here is a brief list of some spreadsheet templates that appear on many systems (extensions may vary):

```
123CALEN.ZIP    - Calendar Formats on LOTUS 1-2-3
123WS1.ZIP      - Variety of Example Worksheets on LOTUS 1-2-3
AMORT.WKS       - Loan Amortization Worksheet
BANKRUPT.ZIP    - Format for Predicting Bankruptcy
BUDGET1.WKS     - Personal Budget Development
CASHFLOW.ZIP    - Business Cash Flow Analysis
CPATOOLS.ZIP    - Several Worksheets for CPAs
DIETWKS.ZIP     - Worksheet for Diet Planning
EXPENSRP.ZIP    - Expense Reports
FEECALC.ZIP     - Calculate Fees for Consulting
HUSELOAN.ZIP    - House Expense Analysis
INVEST1.ZIP     - Several Investment Analysis Applications
INV_COMP.ZIP    - Several Investment Computation Worksheets
IRACALC.ZIP     - Analysis of an IRA
MGMT_FRM.ZIP    - Real Estate Property Management Worksheet
PERFINST.ZIP    - Construction of a Personal Financial Statement
RATIOHGD.ZIP    - Calculation of Investment Ratios
```

This is only a sampling of hundreds of worksheets/templates that others have prepared and you can use. Virtually all of them are available without charge other than your download time. A few are done by professionals in the finance field who may ask for a small contribution; but most are free.

Some Extra Help

Most computer stores and many of the better stocked bookstores now carry spreadsheet self-help publications. These often deal with a single subject, such as building an accounting program with your spreadsheet. Others deal with numerous financial programs and stock/bond topics such as mortgage amortization and analysis, stock puts and calls, stock sensitivity indexes, and statistical analysis of various types. Again, even if these do not exactly fit your business and personal needs, the experience of constructing a template gives you needed skills in understanding spreadsheet development and formula techniques.

Accounting Packages

While a number of very good accounting programs are built on the foundation of a database or spreadsheet package, the simplest approach for most businesspeople is to select an accounting program that is already completed and whose modules of General Ledger, Accounts Receivable, Accounts Payable, and Payroll are either integrated or are easily maintained at month's end. By using such a program, there is a continuity of user interface (each part of the program works like the other parts, menus are similar, editing commands are the same, and so forth), and the format for data entry is the same. Using bits and pieces of accounting programs and attempting to link them together can be both frustrating and fiscally disastrous!

Select a Program Carefully

Some accounting packages also contain an Inventory module in addition to the General Ledger. Usually these inventory programs do little for the average businessperson (unless the business is truly average). It is difficult to set up an inventory tracking system that meets even general requirements. If the program is set to take a six-digit part number, yours will inevitably be seven digits. If part prices are carried at even cents ($.22), you will carry parts at a price of $.2187, or need three or four pricing levels for the same part. The special needs of individual businesses go on and on. For that reason, the accounting package reviewed here has no Inventory module with it. Inventory value is entered manually into the General Ledger at the first and last of the month. Actual inventory records can be much better kept in a database file that can be customized for your specific business requirements.

PC ACCOUNTING — THE MEDLIN ACCOUNTING SHAREWARE

The Medlin Accounting package is usually found on bulletin board systems as PC-ACCT.ZIP (extensions may vary), which is the full accounting package, or as

Module Name	Module Content	Current Version
PC-GL.ZIP	General Ledger module	3.4
PC-AR.ZIP	Accounts Receivable module	3.9
PC-AP.ZIP	Accounts Payable module	1.4
PC-PR.ZIP	Payroll module	1.8

The advantage of having a program such as this available in a modular form is that if there is a module or two that you don't use in your business operation, you don't have to spend money registering it. For example, many small businesses use a CPA or accounting service to issue their payroll. The Payroll module would obviously not be needed. On the other hand, you may wish to do your accounting by journal entry to a General Ledger only. In that case, you have only one of the modules to register for use.

A Strong History of Performance

Medlin Accounting programs have been in use for over six years as of this writing and have been continually refined and updated by the author. The program and its documentation are written in a way that makes it easy for even nonaccountants to use the package. It can be used as either a double- or single-entry system and retains data for twelve accounting periods with the ability to generate reports at any time and as often as desired.

Hardware required is an IBM PC or compatible computer with one disk drive and at least 256K of memory. Reports require an Epson compatible printer. Use of a laser printer is provided by the configuration program available only to registered users.

The program can be run on floppy disk or on hard disk and, depending upon system RAM and disk space, can handle up to an absolute maximum of 6,000 transactions per accounting period. A system with 256K of memory, for example, will only record about 500 transactions per period. The number is subject to the limitations of your system's RAM and/or disk space available.

Integration of the System

The General Ledger and Accounts Payable modules are integrated, but Accounts Receivable and Payroll are not. It is a simple matter at the end of each month to make a journal entry to the General Ledger for these two accounts. It is faster and simpler this way and eliminates a large number of General Ledger entries. The General Ledger manual contains a section on posting the sales data and payroll information.

A configuration program, available to registered users, allows permanent configuration of the data path and colors for each of the four modules of the program. These can also be specified on the command line at program startup. For example, if the General Ledger module is started with this line,

```
PC-GL B: 3 14 10 1
```

the program will look for data on drive B and will use cyan borders, yellow data, light-green prompts, and a blue background. With the configuration program, these can be set along with some other parameters used in the programs, such as check stub placement, margins, and so forth.

The General Ledger Module—PC-GL

The heartbeat of all accounting programs is the General Ledger with its Chart of Accounts (COA). An extensive standard COA is provided with the General Ledger program, thus saving a great deal of time in setting up accounting codes. Any of these can easily be changed, deleted, or added to make the COA conform to your business operation. The COA allows 800 items, which should be adequate for even the largest of the small businesses.

Each time the program is run, the following menu is displayed for operator selection:

```
Enter or Change Chart of Accounts
Enter or Change Transactions
Print Chart of Accounts Listing
Print Transaction Listing
Print General Ledger
Print Income Statement
Print Balance Sheet
Print Account Summary Report
Year End Update
End of Processing
```

Make a selection by using the UP ARROW or DOWN ARROW key to highlight the desired function; then press RETURN.

Information required for the Chart of Accounts includes

Account number	A unique three-digit number used in posting
Account code	A two-digit number for report inclusion
Prior year %	Automatically generated by the program
Account description	Up to 27 characters describing the category
Current amount	Current balance in this category
YTD amount	Year-to-date entries in this category

Working with PC-GL

Once the Chart of Accounts has been edited to your satisfaction with the first menu choice, you are ready to enter transactions. You can also edit your entries as needed with the second menu choice. The following information is entered for each transaction:

Description	Up to 21 characters
Check number	Five-digit check or reference number
Date	MODA form
Account number	Three-digit account number conforming to COA
Amount	Dollar amount of the transaction

This done, you are ready to print reports. Reports can be printed at any time during the accounting period and as many times as you need for good fiscal control. No description of report content will be given here; the report titles are self-explanatory. The only report that must be printed at the end of each accounting period is the General Ledger report. This provides an audit trail and also resets the program for the next accounting period.

Providing for Many Needs

Provision is made in the program for entering beginning and ending inventory via journal entry. The manual thoroughly explains this, as well as the posting of sales data.

While accounting is usually done on a monthly basis, this accounting program allows you to use any accounting period that makes sense in your business. However, a maximum of twelve periods will be stored by the program. By storing data on a library of floppy disks or transferring them to other hard disk subdirectories, the accounting periods stored could be extended almost indefinitely if necessary.

A great deal of flexibility is built into the General Ledger report programs. They can be formatted and totaled in a number of ways to make reports more easily understood.

The Accounts Receivable Module — PC-AR

This is the accounts receivable and sales analysis program for the Medlin Accounting Shareware. Upon program startup (configurable on the command line as discussed in PC-GL), the following menu is displayed for operator selection:

```
Enter or Change Sales Codes
Enter or Change Customers
Enter or Change Charges or Payments
Print Mailing Labels
Print Charges & Payments Listing
Print Accounts Receivable Ledger
Print Statements
Print Customer Activity Report
```

```
Start a New Month
Print Customer Listing
Save Data and End
```

The program allows for a maximum of 2,000 customers and 4,000 charges and payments per month with 512K of memory. With 256K, this is reduced to approximately 200 customers and 200 charges and payments.

Using PC-AR

The program will handle up to 200 sales codes consisting of a three-character sales code and up to 21 characters for a description. New sales codes can be entered at any time as the accounting period goes on. One or more codes can be reserved for payments on account. Customer records contain the following information:

Customer name	Two lines of 31 characters each
Customer code	Ten-character code for selective sorting
Street address	One line of 31 characters
City, state, zip	One line of 31 characters
Telephone	Up to 12 characters
Late charge %	Percent to charge customer for late fees
Auto bill amount	Charges here will be automatically made to the customer account each new period
Balance due	30-, 60-, and 90-day balances due

Reports can be printed as desired; their titles are self-explanatory. The Print Statements selection will be used at the end of each accounting period, and output is formatted for a standard statement form available from the New England Business Services (NEBS). Style numbers are included for easy ordering of these forms.

As with the General Ledger program, registered users receive a configuration program to set various data drive, screen color, and output formatting commands.

The Accounts Payable Module—PC-AP

This program tracks accounts payable and writes checks for a maximum of 2,000 vendors with a maximum of 2,000 invoices per period. After starting the program, the following menu is displayed for operator selection:

```
Enter or Change Vendors
Enter, Change or Select Invoices
Print Checks for Invoices Selected
Print Check Listing
Print Invoice Listing
Print Vendor Activity Report
Print Mailing Labels
Print Vendor Listing
Start a New Accounting Period
Export Vendor Data to ASCII File
Save Data and End
```

The vendor file contains the following information:

Vendor name	Two lines of 31 characters each
Vendor code	Ten-character code for selective sorting
Street address	One line of 31 characters
City, state, zip	One line of 31 characters
Auto invoice amount	Automatic fixed monthly charge entry
Default account number	The PC-GL account number to be posted
Auto invoice date	Day of the month for automatic charge entry
YTD invoices	Total to date
YTD checks written	Total to date

Invoice data stored by the program includes the following:

Vendor code	Ten-character sort code
Invoice date	Date invoice was received as MODA
Due date	Date payment is due (can be sorted)
Invoice number	Up to 14 characters
Account number	PC-GL COA number
Amount	Amount of the invoice

With this information entered into the program, checks can be written and reports printed as needed. Checks are formatted for standard New England Business Services forms. Check style and order numbers are included in the program documentation. The PC-AP program has a configuration program for registered users that sets data drive, screen color, and certain configurable check writing elements such as stub at top or bottom and other limited options.

Some Flexible Options

Reports available are self-explanatory in the menu listing. As you use the program, you will find that PC-AP assumes that you are on a cash basis of accounting. If you are on an accrual basis, the configuration program will let you modify the program to reflect this accounting option. PC-AP is interfaced with the General Ledger program and will post all checks written to PC-GL.

The menu choice for exporting the vendor file to an ASCII file is for transporting this data file to a spreadsheet or database program. Most spreadsheet and database programs will both import and export an ASCII file as one of their conversion options.

The Payroll Module — PC-PR

The payroll program is capable of handling a maximum of 500 employees and 1,000 payroll checks per accounting period. The PC-PR program is updated annually to include any changes in the federal or state income tax levels and information and/or format changes in the federal W-2 forms. PC-PR must be ordered for the specific state in which it is to be used. Both the federal and state tax tables and formulas are written directly into the payroll program. There is no need for the user to do the tedious setups for state and federal tax that are required by many programs. PC-PR is available with the following state tax schedules:

AL	AR	CA	CO	DE	GA	HI	IA	ID
KS	KY	LA	MA	MD	ME	MN	MO	MT
NC	NE	NM	NY	NJ	OH	OK	OR	SC
UT	WI	VA	WV					

States not in this list either have no state income tax or use a formula based on a percentage of the federal tax. Complete instructions are included in the program documentation concerning the proper setup for these states. Upon entering the program, the following menu is displayed:

```
Enter or Change Employee Data
Enter or Change Payroll Checks
Print Employee Listing
Print Payroll Check Listing
```

```
Print Payroll Ledger
Print Quarterly Payroll List
Federal Liability by Paydate
Start a New Quarter or Year
Enter or Change Employer Data
Export Employee Data
End Processing
```

The following information is required for each employee's file:

Employee name	Up to 25 characters
Street address	Up to 25 characters
City, state, zip	Up to 25 characters
Sort by	Ten-character code for sorting
Social security	Nine characters; program adds dashes
Status	Marital status
Allowances	Number of dependent allowances; can also mark as exempt from federal tax
Rate	Employee's hourly rate or period salary
Dept	Department number for payroll summary

These items are permanently stored as the employee's database. Certain areas are then specified when entering payroll information for each pay period as follows:

Date	Check date—beginning of the payroll period is maintained by the system
Employee name	Entered with scroll keys
Check number	Up to four digits, sequential after the first entry by pressing +
Total hours	Total hours worked this period
Overtime hours	Overtime hours worked this pay period
Other income	Any additional income, tips, bonuses
Nontaxable	Payment added to check that is nontaxable, such as travel reimbursement, and so on

At this point, all deductions are calculated, and you are prompted for the entry of any deductions that are not calculated by the program. Upon release by the operator, the check is printed.

Reports available from the menu are self-explanatory. Export of the employee database is available in this program as in PC-AP for conversion to use in a spreadsheet or database application.

Providing for Deductions and More

Payrolls become very complicated in some companies that provide fringe benefits, deductions for retirement programs under tax deferred plans, and other miscellaneous deductions. Due to these complications, PC-PR has a few limitations on use. This program will not work for you if certain conditions exist. These conditions are outlined in the next paragraph.

FICA wages are different from taxable wages as in a tax deferred retirement plan. Tips can be handled, but the tax summaries will always include the tips, which may not always be correct. If there are different payroll periods for different employee groups (weekly payroll for some, bi-weekly for others, for example), the program will not work for you. If you employ family members, FICA must be entered manually to change this deduction to zero. There is no provision for application of earned income credit. If an employee wants an additional amount added to withholding, you must enter it manually. Considering the large number of things PC-PR will do, these few limitations will affect very few small business operators.

Some Configurable Options The configuration program provided for registered users of PC-PR not only configures the drive, screen color, and check printing format but also is a print program for W-2s at the end of the year. Payroll checks and W-2 forms are available from New England Business Services for both dot matrix and laser printers. The program documentation contains style and order numbers.

Summary of Medlin Accounting Shareware

Medlin Accounting is an excellent package, well thought out and easy for even an accounting novice to use. Telephone support is courteous and friendly and the program is continually upgraded. For small businesses, this is a good accounting package choice.

Jerry Medlin
1461 Sproul Avenue
Napa, CA 94559
707-255-4475
$35 registration per module, $140 total; MasterCard and VISA accepted

POWER DESK

A final fundamental program of value to business and finance people is a good desk management tool. There are a number of commercial and Shareware programs available that take care of a variety of desktop administrative requirements. A full-featured program that seems to combine almost all of an executive's daily desk requirements is Power Desk by Wade Dowdle. The program offers a complete office environment with the following features:

Full-featured word processor	Sort/select names
Spell checker/corrector	Mail-merged letters
Four-million-name database	Labels
Duplicate name checker	Custom reports
Autodialer	Envelopes
Phone log	Import/export files
Phone directories	Backup/restore
Timekeeper	Shell to DOS
Calendar/reminder	Screen blanking
TO DO list	Automatic alarms
DONE list	Run other programs
DOS file functions	Print-to-file
Calculator	Printer restart
ASCII table	Context-sensitive help
Pull-down menus	Database file protection
User selectable parameters	Global edit
Encrypt/decrypt text	Lock system
Boldface/underline text	Printed letterhead
Supports all printers/modems	Browse files
On-screen time and date	Color/monochrome

Repetitive labels	Variables in text
Page 2 notes	Automatic install
Ditto key	Automatic date stamp
Log callbacks	Macro keys

Here is a system that can take notes, remind you of appointments, set multiple reminder alarms, hold your complete file of addresses and phone numbers, and with a modem can even dial the phone for you.

Many Advantages of Power Desk

With a program like this, at the beginning you feel that you could do it faster with the old scraps of paper; but once you get into the habit of turning to your computer for note-taking and reminders, you'll find that it is faster and more efficient, and you never forget your wedding anniversary or your "significant other's" birthday. You don't have to paw through mountains of papers in a sequential search for that important phone number you wrote on the cocktail napkin! With Power Desk you can even encrypt private notes and company secrets like the recipe for that wonderful barbecue sauce your company sells.

Well Worth the Space

Because desk organizer programs like this depend on a number of files, most of them require a computer with a hard disk. In fact, Power Desk, with its 37 files, occupies about 845K of disk space. It must be emphasized that this is disk space well spent. A desktop environment of this type can keep you on track and well organized.

Registration of the program includes detailed, printed documentation, free updates, free telephone support, and a copy of the most recent version of Power Desk. The current Shareware version is 1.26SW and can be found on most BBSs as PDESK1.ZIP and PDESK2.ZIP (the extension may vary).

Wade B. Dowdle
8516 Sugarbush
Annandale, VA 22003
703-978-2339
$49 registration plus $5 shipping

SPECIFIC BUSINESS AND FINANCE APPLICATIONS

As mentioned earlier, it is difficult to single out program applications that will be valuable to all business and finance people. Be that as it may, there are a variety of good programs that can be found on a business-oriented BBS. Some of these are Shareware, others are in the public domain. The best approach is to download some programs that look like they might be helpful for your purposes. Yes, you'll get some junk—in fact, some real "good-for-nothing" junk! But most of these programs are short and download quickly. Every now and then you find a real gem that makes the effort worthwhile.

With that caveat, here is a short list of programs you might find of interest (extensions may vary):

General Business Aids

```
BUSPLAN.ZIP   - Text file of business plan by Price-Waterhouse
BLAKBOOK.ZIP  - Phone/address book - pocket size
CHK-DATE.ZIP  - Appointment checker
CMS.ZIP       - Church Management System
FORM33.ZIP    - Forms generator - design your own forms
FORMLTRS.ZIP  - Ready to edit and use form letters
GANTT.ZIP     - Prepare GANTT charts
JIGGLE.ZIP    - Examples for GANTT.ZIP
INVOICE.ZIP   - Design and print invoices for your business
LEGAL1.ZIP    - Ready to use legal forms
LEGAL2.ZIP    - Ready to use legal forms
LEGAL3.ZIP    - Ready to use legal forms
RES-SHOP.ZIP  - Resume building program
REVIEW.ZIP    - Employee performance review
SPRSTAT1.ZIP  - Complete statistical analysis/report program
SPRSTAT2.ZIP  - Complete statistical analysis/report program
SPRSTAT3.ZIP  - Complete statistical analysis/report program
SURVEY30.ZIP  - Logs and analyzes survey responses & demographics
TIMEKEEP.ZIP  - Logs time/client computer usage
TOOLBOX.ZIP   - Management decision making guide
VAC-SC.ZIP    - Schedule staff vacations
```

General Financial Tools

```
BANKTOOL.ZIP  - Finance tool for professionals
FA.ZIP        - Complete set of finance analysis utilities
```

```
FINANCE.ZIP    - Complete time value of money calculations
FMII-11.ZIP    - Finance manager
FMIIDOC.ZIP    - Finance manager documentation
IRR&NPV        - Allows up to 100 in/out flows for IRR & NPV
RETIRE.ZIP     - Retirement planner
RRR.ZIP        - Realized rate of return calculator
TAKEHOME.ZIP   - Calculate pay for withholding exemptions
```

Investment Analysis—Stocks and Bonds

```
BAYSIAN.ZIP    - Classic stock analysis method
BOND.ZIP       - Bond yield to maturity
HAMMER.ZIP     - Stock options analysis
MFUND.ZIP      - Mutual fund tracking
MY-IRA.ZIP     - Analysis of your IRA account
SHARPMOD.ZIP   - The Sharp stock evaluation model
STKVAL.ZIP     - Stock calculator - 11 functions
TEKSTOCK.ZIP   - Stock graphing program
```

Real Estate Tools

```
ANALYSIS.ZIP   - Property value analysis
APPROACH.ZIP   - Text file re: 3 appraisal approaches
BID.ZIP        - Bid out construction jobs
CLOSING.ZIP    - Loan closing on a LOTUS Worksheet
COMLEASE.ZIP   - Commercial Lease Form
L-BROKER.ZIP   - Mortgage loan analyzer
LANDLORD.ZIP   - Real Property Management Package
LEGALRE.ZIP    - Variety of real estate legal forms
MORT100.ZIP    - Mortgage loan calculator
MORTPLAN.ZIP   - Mortgage loan forecasting and calculation
REALTOR.ZIP    - Tools for real estate professionals
RES.ZIP        - Real estate office management
STREETS.ZIP    - Professional street & route mapper
TOTAL.ZIP      - Appraisal program
```

These lists are meant only to be a beginning. There are hundreds of programs related to business and finance on bulletin boards. Perhaps this brief listing will give you an idea of what to look for among the very wide variety of programs that are available.

## CHAPTER TWENTY-TWO

Text Files of Interest

In this chapter you will examine an aspect of Shareware that is rich and varied in material. Text files can be one of the most interesting categories of files available through Shareware, Freeware, and the public domain. These files range in size from a sentence or two, to thousands of pages. Their authors may be the equivalent of literary geniuses who are masterful craftspeople of the written word. Then again, they may be talentless and unable to write a readable note to the milkman. Sometimes the results are so funny it hardly matters.

Like snowflakes, no two text files are alike. One may contain congressional testimony on UFOs while another may be a manual on how to make paper airplanes. There are text files that can tell you how to use Zmodem or how to make cookies or explain what MNP is. No two bulletin boards will have the same selection of text files, but if you look hard enough you'll be able to find a good text file on just about anything under the sun.

VARIETY YOU WON'T BELIEVE

Writers and storytellers have planted their files in the Shareware garden and seen them spread across the nation and even around the world. It's the ultimate form of self-publishing, since all you have to do is put your ideas, stories, humor, or anything else you'd like into an ASCII file and upload it to a few bulletin boards. If people like it, they'll spread it around. For example, there's a file sometimes named ACCIDENT.TXT, usually attributed to a 1977 edition of the *Toronto Star* newspaper, with a list of excuses supposedly offered to the police after automobile accidents. Some samples include

- Coming home, I drove into the wrong house and collided with a tree I do not have.

- The guy was all over the road. I had to swerve a number of times before I hit him.

- I saw a slow-moving, sad-faced old gentleman as he bounced off the hood of my car.

- The indirect cause of this accident was a little guy in a small car with a big mouth.

- I pulled away from the side of the road, glanced at my mother-in-law, and headed over the embankment.

You'll find the accident file on bulletin boards all over the world. Other files reach a smaller audience. In general, people only pass on a text file they enjoyed or found useful.

People are often surprised to learn there are more text files than programs in the public domain. There's a wealth of computer-related text files in the public domain, but they are only a fraction of what's available. The range of topics is limitless and probably exceeds the mix found in your town's public library. Below are just a few of the subject areas you will find

Astrology	Chainletters
Astronomy	Childcare
Automobiles	Computers
Boating	Cooking
Bonds	Electronic

English   "New Age" topics
Farming   Nutrition
Foreign languages   Occult
Game hints   Politics
Geography   Programming
Ham radio   Real estate
Health   Religion
History   Sales
Investments   Science
Law   Sex
Literature   Social commentary
Love   Sports
Marketing   Stocks
Mathematics   Travel
Medicine   War

When you look over some of these text files you may feel like you are looking inside a time capsule. Some text files are from a different era (in computer terms, at least) and can give you all the flavor and insight of a time gone by. While preparing for this chapter, my coauthor came across an old copy of *Time* magazine from December 1983. We both marveled at the advertisement for the TSR80 III for $995, and the photos of Adam Osborne, with his Osborne computer, and Steve Jobs, who was developing his Macintosh. In that same issue, *Time's* "Man of the Year" was instead a Machine of the Year, the computer!

Looking Them Over

There are many advantages to having text files in machine readable format. Reading them with text listers like LIST or a text editor like QEdit can make it easier to find things or to gather up sections of interest. You can always print a hard copy and read it later the way you would any newspaper or book. There's enough material available to make up a good tutorial on computer-related subjects or a fair collection of jokes.

Some Unique Text

Besides the occasional historical significance and the diversity offered by these files, there's another facet that can make them priceless. A lot of this material simply isn't available anywhere outside of BBS distribution. In highly specialized fields, hanging around a specialty BBS or Information Service forum may be the only way to keep abreast of the latest developments.

One thing is certain. The text files available in The Wires often give more information than you can get through conventional sources, and they are usually more direct. Reading them can be like talking to a friend who is giving you the straight scoop without pulling any punches. On the other hand, you'll find a fair share of the material is crammed with personal opinions and misinformation. I'd recommend you keep in mind while reading these files that just because someone took the trouble to commit something to writing doesn't mean it's true. Take into account who the author is, when the piece was written, and even regional and cultural biases. Then make up your own mind.

Enjoy the Variety

In the meantime, enjoy yourself, reading and learning about all sorts of things. There are food recipes to create tasty dishes. There are instructions for canning fruits and vegetables, building barns, and making home brew. There are files about collecting coins, stamps, antiques, comic books—you name it. There are love stories, mysteries, amusing anecdotes, personal accounts, legal briefs, reports, reviews, manuals, and more. You'll find fascinating local histories, technical treatises and political diatribes, crackpot schemes, and thoughtful business proposals. You'll encounter announcements that the world will end tomorrow and, no doubt, announcements that the world did end yesterday. There is the equivalent of several lifetimes' worth of accumulated wisdom and crooked grins worthy of Dave Barry or Art Buchwald.

Let's take a look at a few examples of the huge number and diversity of text files available through Shareware distribution. This is just a representative sampling of what you can find.

AIDSINFO

AIDSINFO is the file AIDS (Acquired Immune Deficiency Syndrome) Information Packet, which gives basic information on AIDS from the U.S. Department of Health and Human Services. AIDSINFO includes facts from the Surgeon General's Report and trends, testing, and blood information. It's a file of particular interest today.

CONSTIT

CONSTIT is pure public domain material. This file contains the Constitution of the United States, including the preamble. You can print it out with some fancy fonts and have a nice-looking duplicate of this famous document.

COOKBK

COOKBK has three volumes that I know of and is an encyclopedic recipe collection from USENET, submitted over several years by callers. The new electronic melting pot includes dishes like "Andy's murgh kurma," beets in mustard sauce, chickpea soup, fango pie, Greek Christmas poultry stuffing, Aztec soup, X-rated melon balls, maple syrup souffle, Black Forest pie, Grammy's dark rolls, Challah, valley grape pie, Armenian rice, black-eyed peas, and hundreds more.

COPYRITE

COPYRITE is the document "Copyrighting Public Domain Programs," by June Moore, a member of the California State Bar since 1987. COPYRITE gives an analysis of the current statutes that provide copyright protection to authors.

DECLARAT

DECLARAT is public domain text of the Declaration of Independence of the United States. You might not expect to find this kind of thing on a bulletin board, but it's there just the same. You can print it and put it up next to your copy of the Constitution.

DECWARS

DECWARS is dated 03-04-89 and is a text file story similar to *Star Wars*. Told by programmers, this is a hilarious classic—some truly nerd humor. Here is a brief excerpt:

```
"THE CONTINUING SAGA OF THE ADVENTURES OF LUKE VAXHACKER"
```

```
"As we enter the scene, an Imperial Multiplexer is trying to kill a consu-
late ship. Many of their signals have gotten through, and RS232 decides it's
time to fork off a new process before this old ship is destroyed. His
companion, 3CPU, is following him only because he appears to know where he's
going... 'I'm going to regret this!' cried 3CPU, as he followed RS232 into
the buffer. RS232 closed the pipes, made the sys call, and their process
detached itself from the burning shell of the ship."
```

EPA86

EPA86 is a transcript of the Electronic Communications Privacy Act of 1986, which is the primary federal statute governing PC telecommunications. You will find this file posted on many bulletin board systems. Often, it may be one of the first screens you see or it may appear as a bulletin. Generally, the portion displayed on bulletin boards is just that segment that deals with the privacy of electronic mail. EPA86 is the complete text. This is a file that everyone who enjoys telecommunications should read.

ETHINV

ETHINV is an interesting collection of information about the employment and ethics records of major U.S. and multinational corporations. ETHINV lists the best places for women and blacks to work, community loan funds, companies doing business in South Africa, and much more. ETH-INV is a Shareware almanac that provides extensive reference material on socially responsible investing. It was originally published as a disk and is available by writing to Jerry Whiting, P.O. Box 20821, Seattle, Washington 98102.

GOODCRED

GOODCRED is a file that explains how to establish a good credit rating. GOODCRED was written by Jay Anderson, who is a loan broker. Anderson uses a step-by-step approach explaining exactly what to do.

GUIDE2

GUIDE2 is the *Programmer's Guide* written by one of the early pioneers of Shareware, Nelson Ford. The *Programmer's Guide* was first released in January 1985 and is updated frequently. The last update was in December 1989. GUIDE2 contains information about how to market Shareware, where to get equipment and supplies, and how to handle documentation. It even includes sample forms and legal tips. Readers will learn how to make programs user-friendly with help screens, logical program flow, and custom configuration. The file is an 80K ASCII text, formatted for printing, and its level of writing is much better than you would expect of a Shareware text file.

Nelson Ford started the Public Software Library in 1982, which now has over 2,000 disks and is still growing. Ford has also written about a dozen Shareware programs himself, including DISKCAT and MY-DESK. You can contact Nelson Ford and Public Software Library at 800-242-4PSL (4775) for orders or a free newsletter; or call 713-524-6394 for more information.

KARPOV

KARPOV is a chilling account of the Karpov versus Deep Thought chess game on February 2, 1990, by Fred Hapgood, who was there. This is a really interesting text file, relating the battle between a great chess master and a computer program designed to beat him.

KJV-PGM

KJV-PGM is actually a series of files. KJV-OT, numbered 1 through 5, contains the complete text of the Old Testament. You can also find

KJV-NT 1 through 3, which contains the entire New Testament. These are done by chapter and verse as in the printed Bible. There is even a Bible Search Concordance program included.

MAGCARTA

MAGCARTA is a no-frills public domain document that is the complete text of the Magna Carta—a document considered by many to be the foundation of democracy as we know it in the U.S.

NASA1990

NASA1990 is a text file collection of NASA information reports on the Hubble Space Telescope, Magellan, Galileo, and other astronomical topics, compiled from weekly NASA press releases. NASA1990 has interesting, up-to-date information on the NASA space program.

NOSTRA

NOSTRA is a file that contains Nostradamus' sixteenth century predictions for the twentieth century. It was summarized by Mike Brown from *Nostradamus Predicts the End of the World* by Rene Noorbergen.

PRIVACY

PRIVACY is the article "Computer Electronic Mail and Privacy" from *The Computer Law and Security Report,* a British publication. In it, author Ruel Hernandez discusses the U.S. federal statute, the Electronic Communications Privacy Act of 1986, and raises some interesting questions about the inadequacies of the statute.

PYTHON

PYTHON is a text collection of Monty Python sketches. Humor circulates in many forms on BBSs, including these playlets: *Argument Clinic, Australian Table Wines,* and *The Barber Shoppe.* If you're a Monty Python fan, you'll want to look for this one.

SS#-INFO

SS#-INFO is a public domain file by Barbara Bennett that explains how a social security number is keyed to regions. It includes some history on how the numbers have been assigned. If you're curious about how your social security number is assigned, this is a good place to look.

USACON.COM

USACON.COM is another public domain file of the Constitution of the United States. Unlike the text file CONSTIT noted earlier, USACON is in a special .COM file format that is easy to search through. It is excellent if you want to study the Constitution.

USEFUL, OFFBEAT, AND ENTERTAINING TEXT FILES

While the subject of many of the text files listed previously are serious in nature—for example, the Constitution and the Bible—there are others that are less serious. You can find text files that are informative, others that are a bit offbeat, and some that are just entertaining. Here are some brief descriptions of files that fall into these categories.

800-AIR

800-AIR is a file that lists all domestic and most international airlines' toll-free reservation numbers. This file is especially useful now that the phone company charges 50 cents for directory assistance for 800 numbers.

8088

8088 is a cute file that describes the three-letter assembly language acronyms with original, humorous redefinitions. For example:

OBU	Overheat and Burn if Unattended
SDJ	Send Data to Japan

This file was originally taken from the November 1985 edition of *Computerpeople Monthly* by Bruce Tonkin.

AA-TEXT

AA-TEXT is a complete text of the Alcoholics Anonymous publications, a collection of more than 20 text files. They contain information about alcoholism, testimonials, steps to recovery, how Alcoholics Anonymous works, and much more. This file was assembled in 1988.

ALCHEMY

ALCHEMY is a brief history of alchemy from *An Encyclopedia of Occultism* by Lewis Spence. Originally published in 1920, it is considered to be one of the most complete texts on the subject.

ANSMACH

ANSMACH is a file of funny sayings to put on your answering machine, collected from a Coast Guard weather station in Wales. One example from this file is "Epicentre of the Universe; God speaking."

ANSTUTOR

ANSTUTOR is a good tutorial on how to use ANSI.SYS and the ANSI escape codes to set colors, assign strings to function keys, and much more.

If working with ANSI codes is something strange to you, this file will be well worth getting. It tells you what you really need to know about ANSI. On a personal note, I used an earlier version of this same file to learn about ANSI and its powerful escape codes. It was well written.

ATOMBOMB

ATOMBOMB is an article that stirred a bit of controversy a decade ago. ATOMBOMB details how to build your own nuclear device and was taken from the *Journal of Irreproducible Results,* Vol. 25, No. 4, 1979.

BOOZE

BOOZE is a listing of hundreds of recipes for drinks and how to make them. This file is a classic. If you have aspirations of becoming a bartender or just learning how to mix up some nifty concoctions for your friends, this file might be of interest to you.

CIATEXT

CIATEXT is a neat file brought to us by the wondrous Freedom of Information Act. CIATEXT is the text of the April 25, 1956 memorandum by J. Edgar Hoover on the subject of brainwashing. This file was made public in the 1980s and is a complete "how to" document.

CONDOMS

CONDOMS is a file that seems to be getting more popular. It was written by William Safire and reprinted from *The New York Times Magazine,* December 14, 1986. It gives a complete history of the word and its usage.

CONFIG

CONFIG is an excellent tutorial on CONFIG.SYS and AUTOEXEC.BAT files. It gives tips on how to make the best use of these files when starting your computer. For those who are new to computers, this file will be very informative.

COOKIES

COOKIES is the recipe for authentic Mrs. Field's Cookies. Well, it's not guaranteed authentic, because the recipe is a closely-guarded trade secret. Since the recipe calls for placing golfball-sized cookies 2 inches apart on a cookie sheet, its total authenticity is questionable, but I understand the cookies are quite good.

DIVORCE

DIVORCE is a file prepared in March 1987 for the do-it-yourself crowd. It gives a sample divorce agreement for Washington state and an article on joint-custody arrangements with a critical view. If you want an inexpensive divorce, this file is worth checking out.

EDITORIA

EDITORIA is the article "Requiem for a sysop," which was excerpted from an article in *PC Week,* November 20, 1984. This article gives a sysop's experience fielding 12,000 messages over two years. This one can also be found as REQUIEM on many bulletin board systems. It gives you an interesting view of what being a sysop is like—at times.

ESTONIA

ESTONIA is a file written in January 1990 that explains how to telephone the Eesti #1 BBS in Tallinn, USSR. It tells you what it is like and how much it will cost, and explains the USENET connection from Moscow. In view of recent developments in the Soviet Union and between the Soviet Union and the United States, you might want to try it, comrade! (*smile*)

FOREVER

FOREVER is a file of original poetry written in 1989 from Alphaville, which is electronically published and distributed. The file includes "A Victory of Love," "Summer in Berlin," "Big in Japan," and other poems by Gold/Mertens/Lloyd.

GOURMET

GOURMET is a file of 100 recipes from a gourmet cook in Wisconsin—Donna Endreson, 4053 W. College Avenue, Milwaukee, Wisconsin 53221. I wonder if Phil Katz goes to Donna's for dinner?

JACKSON

JACKSON is an article, or a "Michael Jackson discography," which lists all of the records Michael Jackson has made with and without the other members of the Jackson family, from the first in 1969 through 1988. If you are a big Michael Jackson fan, or have children who are, you might want to check this one out. It's a thriller.

MADSAY

MADSAY is the text file quoter, "What me worry?" that displays 69 different quotes from Alfred E. Neuman. For those who have never gotten over *Mad Magazine* and its star, this is a must-have kind of file.

MHERBS

MHERBS is the file "Herbs and their Magical Uses," which gives a line-by-line listing of hundreds of herbs. It offers some interesting reading on spices that you may have never heard of, and some uses that you may not have heard of, either.

MNP

MNP is a text file that explains what MNP is and gives a description of how it works. If you are thinking about getting an MNP modem and are wondering about its advantages, then this file will be of help to you.

PICKUP

PICKUP is a file of lines to use when you find yourself at a loss for words when you're trying to meet someone. For example: At the laundromat— "How much bleach should I put in with my best suit?" These lines may or may not work; the file doesn't guarantee anything. If nothing else, you might get a few laughs out of it—maybe a date?

PEARLS

PEARLS is an unusual file. What is it? It's a text quoting file that displays 350 pearls of wisdom in random colors in VGA. It was written by Roy Stewart, 14130 Pinerock, Houston, Texas 77079.

POVERTY

POVERTY is an original proposal "to bring dignity and self esteem and a greatly improved standard of living to our nation's poor." It was written by Pat Rankin, 867 N. Lamb #180, Las Vegas, Nevada 89110. Read it and see what you think.

REALBUSH

REALBUSH is the serious article, "Will the Real George Bush Stand Up Please!," by Charles A. Burris, with a bibliography from the Libertarian Party of Oklahoma, P.O. Box 6438, Norman, Oklahoma 73070. It's an interesting look at our current president.

RODNEY

RODNEY is a text file quoter that displays some of Rodney Dangerfield's best one-liners. "Good crowd...good crowd. I'm telling you I could use a good crowd. I'm ok now, but last week I was in rough shape... Why? I looked up my family tree and found out I was the sap."

ROONEY

ROONEY is the article "A Few Minutes with Andy Rooney" by Frank Walters. "...did'ja ever notice those silly twirling cursors on some bulletin boards..." This is an interesting look at a somewhat controversial figure who is a mystery to many.

SSWBC1

SSWBC1 is the article "Sourdough Software Presents Bear Creek Bob's Alaska Stories and Recipes," a sample from the complete cookbook. It is from Sourdough Software, P.O. Box 202141, Anchorage, Alaska 99520. Recipes include: Whale's Tail, Spicy Moose, Bob's Moose Stew, and Map of Alaska. If you have any interest in some exotic dishes and some good stories, check this one out.

STTOS

STTOS is a reference guide to all of the original "Star Trek" television episodes, in order, with a brief description of each one. STTOS has the biography of each of the characters and is formatted for printing. It was compiled by Mark Schey in 1989.

WHOS-ON

WHOS-ON is the full transcript of Abbot and Costello's "Who's On First?" skit. If you've ever tried to fake your way through this famous comedy routine, you won't have to fake it anymore. Get this file and know exactly "who" is where.

ZMODEM

ZMODEM is a file that explains exactly how Zmodem works. It also details the DSZ parameters that are used with Zmodem, which will be most effective under what conditions, and much more. It's a good tutorial for those who are new to Zmodem and DSZ.

SUMMARIZING TEXT FILES

The files discussed above are just a tiny sampling of the kind of text files you can find in The Wires. In general, you can find a file on virtually any subject you can think of. There are short stories, jokes, tutorials, dissertations, essays, lectures—the list goes on and on.

The primary goal of this chapter is to make you aware of the wealth of text files available to you simply for the downloading. Some bulletin boards have special file areas reserved just for text files. On other systems, the text files will be scattered around the system, generally in areas that seem appropriate. For example, the text file on Zmodem might be found in the same directory as DSZ itself or with communications programs. You might also look in a miscellaneous files directory for good text files. Since the variety is so large, sysops often have a hard time classifying these files.

Below is a typical BBS directory listing of text files. As you take a look through the list, you will notice the diversity of the files.

```
100FORMS.ZIP    53367    Misc. business forms and letters
1040.ZIP       223963    1988 Tax forms
144DISK.ZIP      4217    Text file - how to make 720K disks   take 1.44m
1955.ZIP         1399    Top songs for the year 1955
1957.ZIP         1421    Top songs for the year 1957
1958.ZIP         1532    Top songs for the year 1958
1ANSIDRV.ZIP     5760    Using ansi to redefine fcn keys
32SNAFU.ZIP      2156    Incompatibilities of DOS 3.2 & other versions
353-352.ZIP       576    List of local prefixes to this BBS
386DXBUG.ZIP     2260    Comments regarding bugs in the 386 DX
386PCBDV.ZIP     8353    DESQview 386 setup sysop notes rev.
4STRMOV.ZIP      7389    Over 500 4-star movies - 1930s to 1987
800BBS.ZIP       4706    Lots of BBSs with 800 numbers
800HELP.ZIP      8448    List of national help- and hot-lines
80486.ZIP        1470    Description of the 80486
87TAXLAW.ZIP    12660    Describes effects of 1987 tax laws
9600-01.ZIP      6012    Info, comparison of 9600 mdms;V32,V42,MNP5
96BB1189.ZIP    45456    9600 baud BBS list over 1300 boards
ABBOTT.ZIP       2435    Abbott & Costello's "Who's on First"  routine
ABDUCT.ZIP       8014    Text file on alien abductions
```

ACCUWTHR.ZIP	1224	Get weather descriptions for all over the USA
ADATUTR1.ZIP	108294	Part 1 of 2 of Ada description
ADATUTR2.ZIP	69797	Part 2 of 2 of Ada description
ALERTTTT.ZIP	1527	WARNINGS for all users and sysops
AMNSTY02.ZIP	8770	Amnesty Int'l USA Freedom Writers Bulletin
AMTRACK.ZIP	4898	Text description of Amtrak scenic routes
APE.ZIP	2153	APE announced for MS-Windows (comm pgm)
AQUACONF.ZIP	2312	Text file about UFOs
AQUARIUS.ZIP	23678	A text file about UFOs - very interesting!
ARC_V_PK.ZIP	4701	Information about SEA vs PKARC dispute
ASP1701.ZIP	15665	Association Shareware Profession catalog 5/89
AUTONEWS.ZIP	23676	Info on buying a new car
AUTONWS2.ZIP	10238	Tips on buying and selling a car
AUTONWS4.ZIP	13952	Dec 89 newsletter for car owners & buyers
BAKETXT.ZIP	5317	About "Bakers Dozen" BAKE12-1,-2 (Button util.)
BASRPT.ZIP	5554	"Basic REPORTing" (Technotes, 8/88)
BATHINTS.ZIP	32413	Text file on making interesting batch files
BATUTOR.ZIP	58726	Tutor for making .BAT files
BBMMVU21.ZIP	53249	Info about device that reboots locked-up BBSs
BBS-BILL.ZIP	1493	Newspaper story on modem addict phone bills
BBS0390.ZIP	73291	National BBS list for 3/90
BBS0689.ZIP	82800	National BBS listing as of 6/89
BBSCOM.ZIP	14086	CompuServe's Thread BBS forum sysop pros/cons
BBSINFO.ZIP	1012	What's a BBS? What's a modem? What's protocol?
BBSJOB01.ZIP	3153	List of employment/job search related BBSs
BBSSTING.ZIP	2662	Text file on police using BBS for sting
BILLGCON.ZIP	5038	Bill Gates "in conference" on GEnie (text)
BIOANTH.ZIP	28822	Class notes for biol. anthropology course
BITCMHLP.ZIP	1329	Using BITCOM with THE LEDGE
BITS0189.ZIP	7194	January LAMLUG newsletter, ASCII text
BLOCKERS.ZIP	10346	Info about phone company blocking BBS NBRS
BLT02.ZIP	36344	Disease control statistics incl. AIDS
BRAINWSH.ZIP	20992	Professional hypnotist explains principles
BRONCOS.ZIP	3963	The Denver Bronco's 1990 schedule - good fun!
BRWNBAG3.ZIP	44240	More comments re BrownBag and PowerMenu
BUG-JOKE.ASC	3072	This one is funny; however it has some truth
CABLE.ZIP	10213	Text files on making a cable TV decoder
CALCULUS.ZIP	144929	Review of month to prepare for calculus
CCITT389.ZIP	3629	Text file re March CCITT meetings
CD_MIDI.ZIP	3060	Info regarding insertion MIDI data on CDs
CEDWARS2.ZIP	65706	Use to get the best from CED10D
CENSTORE.ZIP	38029	25 censored news stories of 1987
CHARTS.ZIP	1512	Where to get our navigation charts
CIVILWAR.ZIP	61418	Partial history of Civil War

CLASSICS.ZIP	71507	Classic text files from BBSs
CLEAR_C.ZIP	5168	Some ideas on writing clear C source code
CLIP5.ZIP	6059	Good desc. of upcoming Clipper 5.0 features
CLIP50.ZIP	2412	Information on Clipper version 5.0
CMPRSN.ZIP	6144	Background of lharc [H.Okumura]
CMPTRNSE.ZIP	2077	Glossary of nonsensical computer terms
CMS8807.ZIP	27022	Msgs from Revelation BBS for Revelation users
CNTRABND.ZIP	20422	Great TXT files for school-going teens
COMPAT.ZIP	3833	Install 386 motherboard in clones
COMPRES8.ZIP	34215	Comparison of compression progs. (inc. PKZIP)
COMSUM.ZIP	23161	All files on CompuServe IBM Comm forum 11/88
COMSUM08.ZIP	22260	10-01-88 list of files on CIS Communication forum
CONFIG.ZIP	1846	Tutorial: how to use config.sys
COPCODES.ZIP	6656	Scanner listening codes for police & fire
CORDLESS.ZIP	622	Frequencies used by 46/49 MHz telephones
CR1.ZIP	1267	Dealer cost of Nissan 4x4 PUs - Consumer Reports
CR2400E.ZIP	7363	Information about U.S. Robotics' 2400e
CR3.ZIP	4563	Dealer cost of Chevy S10 extended cab pickup
CULINARY.ZIP	17492	A small collection of recipes
DATASHAK.ZIP	564	New BBS w/3lines and >100mb @ 773-0372
DB4.ZIP	4900	Ashton-Tate's press release on dBaseIV
DB4TIPS.ZIP	49079	Collection of help articles on various db4 tx
DIRTYD9B.ZIP	78102	Latest release of the "Dirty Dozen" list
DISABKS.ZIP	48051	Disabled/Blind - this is a very good book
DIVEPROD.ZIP	2811	Review of several dive products
DOC2COM.ZIP	2633	Convert text files to .COM files
DOS400UN.ZIP	2752	Undocumented features of DOS 4.0
DOS40MSG.ZIP	3887	Microsoft announces DOS 4.0 - features, etc.
DOS40NEW.ZIP	1619	New/enhanced features of IBM DOS 4.0
DOSTECH.ZIP	166937	Technical manual on MS-DOS
DRIVEDES.ZIP	45161	Design plastic gear & sprocket drives
DRUGMAN.ZIP	241540	Drug dose & interactions hypertext
DRUGS.ZIP	2454	Interesting info about illegal drugs
DRVPINS.ZIP	2446	Learn how to set up hardware on drives
DRYFILL.ZIP	4649	Why you shouldn't wet your scuba when filling
DTAREV1.ZIP	18051	Review of SpinRite and Disk Technician
DTPBBS11.ZIP	5120	List of desktop publishing BBSs
DTP_BBS.ZIP	4443	Desktop publishing BBS
DVCOMMO.ZIP	4570	DESQview communications advice
DVORAKT.ZIP	4663	John C. Dvorak - dvorak?.txt 1,2,3,4 files
DVPROTEC.ZIP	1293	Notes on DESQview protection selection in PIF
E-I-T.ZIP	32243	Earth in trouble - ecological text files
EAGLEWR.ZIP	2175	Virus warning that SCANC doesn't catch

File	Size	Description
EMTRULES.ZIP	5302	Funny EMT rules and regulations
ESC_CODE.ZIP	1834	HP escape codes
EXCELNEW.ZIP	2314	Microsoft press release detailing new Excel
EXCHANGE.ZIP	24799	Cities->Nodes->Prefixes for PC Pursuit users
FARMER.ZIP	1134	A farmer's definitions of computer terms
FBICOMP.ZIP	2866	Text file w/info on FBI computer system
FENWICK.ZIP	56627	Text file on UFOs
FREEPHON.ZIP	1052	List of some interesting 800 numbers to call
FRENCH.ZIP	1941	French scientific accomplishments
FUSION.ZIP	285297	Comments, curses, by the experts (cold fusion)
FYFFEALA.ZIP	1262	Text file about UFO sightings in Fyffe, Alabama
GANGS.ZIP	1792	A thought worth hearing
GATES.ZIP	1664	Bill Gates lecture at CalTech
GOVTBBS.ZIP	2331	Government BBS list
GOVTFREE.ZIP	17345	Services/pamphlets/films available from the government
GRAIL.ZIP	22278	Unofficial script to Monty Python's Holy Grail
GREYS.ZIP	11296	Information on types of alien beings
HACKER.ZIP	40201	Dictionary of computer slang
HARDDISK.ZIP	9569	Data on hard disks (best for install info)
HB-LIB.ZIP	1895	Info on modem access to Huntington Beach Library
HD-DRIVE.ZIP	10812	Tech specs & tips for installilng hard drives
HDINFO10.ZIP	39160	Info on over 200 hard drives
HDPAT2.ZIP	2347	Text file showing how to change cluster sizes
HOF1289.ZIP	20608	Hall of fame for authors of free programs
HOW-TO.ZIP	31731	How to unprotect disk - discusses int13 prot.
HWSUM08.ZIP	30450	10-01-88 list of files on CIS Hardware forum
IBM33TXT.ZIP	13298	Features of DOS 3.3
IBMCODES.ZIP	2656	List of IBM DOS error codes w/ explanations
IBMERROR.ZIP	4611	Complete error codes for IBM PC, XT, & AT
IBMERRS.ZIP	2394	List of IBM error codes (handy)
IBM_SEZ.ZIP	2647	Interesting IBM notes on various 3.5" formats
ILCONF03.ZIP	12151	Description of all InterLink conferences
ILDOC.ZIP	36777	InterLink policies and procedures explained
ILINK002.ZIP	7454	Listing of all InterLink BBSs
INTAIR.ZIP	1654	List of international airline frequencies
INTERRUP.ZIP	19715	Text on IBM's Interrupt coded for XT/AT/PS-2s
KQ4SOL.ZIP	7187	Solutions for King's Quest IV - perfect score!
LAMLUG_5.ZIP	14110	LAMLUG Nov. newsletter - ASCII text format
LANG.ZIP	4616	Info on new Turbo Pascal 5.0 & Turbo C 2.0
LANHELP.ZIP	4353	Help for setting up PC Board under LANtastic
LASVEGAS.ZIP	14292	A guide to Las Vegas from Vegas natives
LAUGH.ZIP	35171	Great jokes downloaded from various BBSs
LE-BBS.ZIP	2091	Law enforcement BBS, USA & Canada

LEAR.ZIP	21247	Unbelievable docs on UFOs
LEBBS2.ZIP	8924	Leading Edge BBS dir LEWP print driver list
LEDGE-X.ZIP	68449	Discussion about X-rated files on BBSs
LEGAL2.ZIP	18433	Some real estate transaction forms
LEGAL3.ZIP	25032	Sample legal documents
LEGAL4.ZIP	8883	Legal forms for the personnel industry
LGLFORMS.ZIP	64540	Some forms to save on attorney fees
LH.ZIP	5149	President of Nantucket reponds to CW article
LOBSTER.ZIP	902	Great lobster recipe
LOCKPICK.ZIP	6013	Learn to pick locks
LOGITDIR.ZIP	3489	Logitech BBS directory of downloads available
LOSTID.ZIP	1145	How to replace your lost scuba c-card
LOTTOBUX.ZIP	2377	How to play out-of-state lotteries - excellent
LYNXNEWS.ZIP	4809	Lynx support msg. from author
MAXIWARN.ZIP	1869	Read this if you use MaxiForm
MB640K.ZIP	2205	How to install 640K on motherboard
MCAPAPER.ZIP	21935	Paper from IBM about The Micro Channel Adapt.
MEDBBS.ZIP	6406	Medical-oriented BBS listing
MENSA.ZIP	3038	Mensa mini IQ test with corrections
MICROHIS.ZIP	10229	Text, 1st ten years of microcomputing
MIDIPRIM.ZIP	14708	Paul Tauger's excellent primer
MINITEL.ZIP	1706	Find out how to access French CompuServe type
MM-TIPS.ZIP	2141	Good tips on using MARKMAIL
MNP-9.ZIP	5156	Description of MNP protocols (levels 1-9)
MOBY.ZIP	1582	Information on Zmodem Mobyturbo
MODEMDOC.ZIP	3286	Info packet for M.O.D.E.M.
MONSANTO.ZIP	85025	Data on thermally conductive fluids
MOREDOS.ZIP	1455	Description for setting up DOS partition
MOUSEBAL.ZIP	1187	Official IBM memo on replacing mouse balls
MSFTQC20.ZIP	13756	Microsoft releases Quick C version 2.00
MURPHY.ZIP	2798	Murphy's Law for computers; make great sigs.
NASA87.ZIP	20708	NASA news 1987, 88 updates, text file
NBAUGRVW.ZIP	44763	Shareware review in August
NBJULRVW.ZIP	39203	Good Shareware review (July)
NBJUNRVW.ZIP	24425	Good Shareware review (June)
NBMAYRVW.ZIP	30206	Good Shareware review (May)
NDD-TEXT.ZIP	2596	Comments from Peter Norton re Disk Doctor
NEWBBS.ZIP	2048	Great new BBS
NEWTEST.ZIP	402857	New Testament on disk
NO-ARC.ZIP	13446	Late developments in SEA vs PK (still at it)
NOISE-3.ZIP	4934	Text on building a phone line filter
NOSMOKE.ZIP	1563	New L.A. city ordinance on public smoking
NTO-PROG.ZIP	37785	Programs to word search the text in NT01 and NT02
NT01.ZIP	233509	KJ Bible (New Testament) Part 1 in ASCII

NT02.ZIP	170405	KJ Bible (New Testament) Part 2 in ASCII
OBSCENE.ZIP	8375	Violation of your 1st and 4th amend. rights
PART97.ZIP	36570	Text of new FCC rules relating to ham radio
PCB0126.ZIP	101242	International PC Board BBS list
PCBLINFO.ZIP	7549	PCB information on LANtastic network
PCDOS40.ZIP	13779	IBM DOS is here! This is the announcement
PCPRSUIT.ZIP	13435	Telenet U.S. telephone directory dated May
PERCOMB.ZIP	34800	Series of articles about Perstor HD Controllers
PERF300.ZIP	125403	Provides specs for perfect speaker enclosure
PERSTOR.ZIP	20470	Text file explaining Perstor Controller cards
PERSTOR3.ZIP	3868	Article about Perstor 16-bit HD Controller
PHILQUOT.ZIP	31588	Some memorable philosophical quotes/utterers
PICS.ZIP	22794	Catalog of files available CIS "GO PICS"
PICS01.ZIP	2049	Catalog of all files in CIS library 1
PIXBBS01.ZIP	11643	List of BBSs specializing in graphics
PK36BAD.ZIP	2920	Some possible problems with PK36.EXE
PKATZ.ZIP	14833	CompuServe discussion of ZIP with P. Katz
PKPOLICY.ZIP	7155	Discussion on BBS ZIP conversion
PKTROJAN.ZIP	1008	WARNING! Yet ANOTHER Trojan program
PLANETX.ZIP	1767	Text file of the mysterious Planet X
PM414THD.ZIP	16800	Thread of comments re PowerMenu ver. 4.14
POLICY.SEA	4385	SEA's official policy regarding ARC
PRISM11.ZIP	74265	Interesting electronic magazine - Vol.11
PRNTSHP.ZIP	898	How to unprotect the newest vers. of PRINTSHOP
PROGSIBM.ZIP	9925	A list of CIS picture file viewers
PROKEY.ZIP	4093	About ProKey protection
PROV.ZIP	50449	Book of Proverbs - King James version
PRST1024.ZIP	3048	New Perstor Controller -- 8/16 bit versions
PSCPRINT.ZIP	43615	Use to speed up IBM PC-XT (hardware)
PURS01.ZIP	22669	PC Pursuitable BBS list by area code
PURTIPS.ZIP	8216	PC Pursuit tips
QBNEWS1.ZIP	14336	New "free" newsletter for QuickBasic fans
QCOMP.ZIP	9528	Quick compiler for use with source code
QEMM.ZIP	1305	Tips on getting more RAM with QEMM
QM40NEW.ZIP	7804	Info on Qmodem 4.0 coming soon
QUIKBBS1.ZIP	83092	New PRISM BBS list - 5000 boards nationally
REBBS037.ZIP	8123	Real estate BBSs from Betty Wheaton
REBBS045.ZIP	11393	Betty Wheaton's real estate BBS list May '89
REBBS046.ZIP	10759	Betty Wheaton's real estate BBS list
REBOOTER.ZIP	3147	Schematics for building a device to reboot
RECALL$$.ZIP	866	How to profit from the currency recall
RECIPES.ZIP	89718	A compilation of excellent recipes
RESETSWT.ZIP	1414	Text on installing a reset switch in your PC
ROBOINFO.ZIP	3027	Press release and fact sheet for Robocomm 1.0

RVPRIMER.ZIP	4663	Using Racal Vadic mode with PC Pursuit
SAMIZDAT.ZIP	44160	BBS writing - an interesting collection
SAMIZDT2.ZIP	35584	BBS writing, vol. 2
SCANLIST.ZIP	7168	Latest list of scanner frequencies in SFV
SCIENCE.ZIP	3215	Funny science student bloopers (text file)
SEAGATE.ZIP	1331	Info & specs on Seagate HD drives
SEAVSPK.ZIP	18911	Info on lawsuit between ARC and PKARC
SECRET.ZIP	18284	Secret government radio frequencies
SETI.ZIP	3951	Search for extraterrestrial intelligence info
SFBBS.ZIP	2890	Recent list of San Francisco area BBSs
SHARELAW.ZIP	7808	Discussion on enforcing legal rights
SHELL.ZIP	2290	How to polish those old abalone shells
SHILOH.ZIP	62168	Text: all the facts you need to live - maybe
SHRRVW01.ZIP	70120	Shareware reviews by national net author
SHRRVW02.ZIP	59825	Shareware reviews - 11/89 reviews of 20
SHRRVW03.ZIP	29819	Shareware reviews - 12/89 -- concise, yet fun
SHRRVW04.ZIP	31005	The latest Shareware reviews - 2/90
SIMISFT.ZIP	20106	Catalog for Simi Valley Software - great prices
SOCAL059.ZIP	8066	So. Calif. BBS list [Mike Heffernan]
SPACEPRG.ZIP	4252	U.S. space program archives - all missions
SPINRV.ZIP	7432	Negative review of SpinRite
SSINFO2.ZIP	2692	Info on social security numbers
START-BB.ZIP	14045	Help file for starting a BBS
STOLLMAN.ZIP	2924	Complete text Horowitz forced to read on air
STS26KIT.ZIP	1753	Press kit for Discovery shuttle mission
STTNGKIT.ZIP	64614	Star Trek - The Next generation - press kit
SYSID.ZIP	58969	PC XT/AT and compatible systems desc. ver. 3.2
SYSID30.ZIP	42074	Great system description of IBM XT/AT
SYSOPS-2.ZIP	37138	Report on sysop liability
TABLE.ZIP	2048	Periodic table of the chemical elements
TCBN.ZIP	641	Info on a financial BBS
TDD2.ZIP	3983	Information on modems for the deaf
TECHBBS.ZIP	1227	Text phone listing of technical support BBSs
TELESYS.ZIP	39262	Censorship attempt on a San Diego BBS (text)
TELX-RVW.ZIP	2851	Review of Telix 3.0 by Hawaiian sysop
TENANT.ZIP	231050	Tenant rights
TGT1022.ZIP	9216	TGT tech. price/product list for 10/22/89
THROBNET.ZIP	3503	Info on adult message network
TLXST02.ZIP	7551	Text on souping up Telix com program
TOLLFREE.ZIP	4711	A national list of toll-free bulletin boards
TONER.ZIP	3049	Rebuild your own LASER printer cartridges
TOPBRD.ZIP	5628	One sysop's selection of best BBSs
TOPBRD5.ZIP	6343	The top boards in the country to call

TOPPAW.ZIP	1549	An unbelievable memo from the U.S. military
TVBRDFEB.ARC	30720	A very interesting BBS list writers broadcast
TWILZONE.ZIP	15955	Credits listing of '85-86 TZ episodes
UINSTALL.ZIP	6420	Info from Seagate on installing hard disks
UNUSUAL.ZIP	1277	List of unusual BBSs
UP2386SX.ZIP	7439	Text re upgrading XTs to 386s with ATI
USAFCHAP.ZIP	16401	Chapter from USAF training manual on UFOs
USBBS69.ZIP	43346	Darwin's national BBS list for 2/90
USRDUAL.ZIP	6491	Info on new USR Dual Standard modem
VESCO.ZIP	10535	Text file on UFOs - interesting!
VIR-ALRT.ZIP	4358	Warning about a recent virus
VIRDOC.ZIP	6504	Virus info from anti-viral company
VIRUS!.ZIP	1596	Warning about a virus in COMMAND.COM
VIRUS.ZIP	1015	AP article about a virus
VIRUS1.ZIP	1899	L.A. Times editorial of 4/24/88 on viruses
VIRUSD.ZIP	26580	IBM staff paper on computer virus defense
VIRUSKIT.ZIP	37123	Info on the virus from the East
VITAMINS.ZIP	25561	Information on various vitamins
VT.ZIP	90491	Calif. driver exam
W9ZRX89.ZIP	138170	Amateur radio BBSs and zip codes
WARPTEN!.ZIP	6243	Information on warp factors
WC20DESK.ZIP	15426	Setup for DV 2.2/386 with Wildcat 2.0n & 2.0p
WD2.ZIP	12932	Lists HD specs: formats, access time, cyls.
WHOS-ON.ZIP	2386	Abbott & Costello's famous comedy routine
WINTER.ZIP	1631	What a scuba diver can do in the winter
WINXTALK.ZIP	4417	Crosstalk for Windows announced
WS4.ZIP	2092	WordStar 4.0 comments
XTGUIDE.ZIP	65536	Smart guide for buying a computer
YUPPI.ZIP	565	The prayer said by Yuppies at night
YZMODEM.ZIP	64485	Official Xmodem, Ymodem, Zmodem protocol desc.
ZAPPA.ZIP	13816	Los Angeles Times Magazine interview
ZIP-2-3.ZIP	38266	A pretty fair "magazine" for home MS-DOS user
ZIPGUIDE.ZIP	11618	California zip codes in numerical order

This listing was taken from Channel 1, which was discussed in Chapter 4. As you can see, Channel 1 has a large selection of text files, and they are all located in one file area. As mentioned earlier, however, you will find different text files on every system that you visit. Use them to your advantage—for information, for your homework, for a good story, or just for a good laugh. Enjoy!

The next chapter will take a close look at some programs and DOS commands that you should use with care.

## CHAPTER TWENTY-THREE

Programs and Commands to Use with Care

Whether you're new to DOS or an old hand, there are many ways to lose your way when working at the DOS prompt level. Unexpectedly, files may accidentally be changed or erased. Program settings seem to change mysteriously from one use to the next. A utility program that promised to increase your efficiency results instead in a disk that delivers one error message after another. A handy memory resident program creates havoc on your monitor every time you use it.

If you like to experiment, you're going to run into such events, and if you're using this book to help explore the world of Shareware, you probably do like to experiment. That's okay, it's how the human race advances. But it also means you'll occasionally run into trouble.

Having tested so many thousands of programs, I love to experiment and I've learned to accept some of the problems and conflicts as an inherent part of the way things are. You also can't expect to find really good Shareware programs if you aren't willing to unpack and run them. In running some of them you may experience problems. We'll take a look at some of these potential problems shortly. It makes sense, however, to first consider for a moment what to do when things do go wrong. What's the best action to take?

WHEN THINGS GO WRONG

During the past eight years or so, nearly 42 million people have been tapping away at their keyboards trying to do things ranging from running Flight Simulator to making a backup copy of their employer's accounting data. Pressing the ENTER key at the wrong time is like missing a freeway exit during a long commute—it happens from time to time.

As programmers have developed sophistication in DOS—and as their customers have become more demanding—they have made much progress toward safeguarding data. There are safety nets everywhere now. But sometimes data misses the net.

The best preventive medicine is to get to know your programs. Know where the manuals are kept so you can refer to them to help you get out of unexpected trouble. If your best efforts don't solve your problem, *don't start punching keys at random!* You are your own best judge of your expertise, and if a problem goes beyond you, don't be shy about seeking help. Your dealer or a consultant may charge some money, but it's worth it. By trying to go farther on your own, you could turn a $40 problem into a $750 one!

SEEDS OF DISASTER

There are many ways to lose data in a system as powerful and flexible as DOS. To most of us, the power is worth the occasional system freeze-up. For users who don't want to deal with the potential problems, programmers have created menu systems. (Those of us who enjoy such projects will wind up installing the menu systems, of course.) But nothing will ever make computing completely safe for files, as long as simply copying a file over another file accidentally can destroy essential data.

Most experienced users greatly respect the hundreds of high-powered utilities and applications available in the Shareware world. With very few exceptions, Shareware offerings are as good as or better than the best and most high-priced commercial programs. But sometimes a bug escapes the testing process, or a creative user invents a new way to use a program with startling results. Powerful programs are great, but if that power is misapplied, it can cause all sorts of problems.

Luckily, there are some things you can do to minimize trouble. They all boil down to two principles—be reasonably careful, and do your best to get acquainted with a program before you load it up and use it. The rest of this chapter will discuss how to apply those two principles.

TAKE REASONABLE CARE

Being an "old hand" is no guarantee of smooth sailing—far from it. But most experienced users discover one overriding principle of safe computing—it pays to be careful. Being cautious won't always keep you out of trouble, but being careless is guaranteed to cause problems. A friend who served on submarines says the first lesson the Navy teaches its new submariners, the lesson that gets pounded over and over into their heads, is simple. If you don't know what a button does, *don't press the button.* The same principle applies to computers. Pushing buttons at random will have unpredictable results, and often not the best for a submarine or a computer.

Okay, so it pays to be careful. But what if you really, simply don't yet know what you're doing? Well, it is hard to acquire the skills of a new art without making mistakes. That's basic to how we human beings learn. When you come right down to it, it's not all that easy to physically damage your computer, short of dropping it or abusing it in other ways.

Being careful means more than just not taking chances. It means paying attention to what you're doing (not spilling coffee on the keyboard, for example). I destroyed one keyboard with a can of soda, and from that time on I've always been very conscious about where my can of soda is in relationship to the keyboard. Here are some things you can do to avoid trouble.

Read the Documentation

Nine times out of ten, when you get into trouble using a program, the answer is in the manual. Yes, some of the manuals produced today are very thick and you may not like reading them. If you lack the patience or inclination to go over the whole manual, at least skim the standard sections of any program guide. Somewhere in there you're probably going to find out what is causing your problem.

Compatibility Section

If your new program manual has a section labeled "Compatibility," here's a section to pay attention to. Such sections are the program author's attempt to warn you off if, for example, you're using an XT clone manufactured in Albania before 1986, or any other machine that has specific incompatibilities with IBM machines.

Heed the warnings in your program's manual. It's important to understand that misusing software can damage your hardware! For example, if a program warns you, "Do not run with any TSR programs," and you forget to disable or remove a cache program, or if you leave SideKick installed, you could damage your hard disk partition. Another possibility is that your system could lose its setup information.

At the most basic level, be sure the program you're trying to run is designed for the operating system you're using. Many BBSs have sections designed for systems other than MS-DOS or PC-DOS (CP/M, for example). You can't mix and match programs and operating systems.

Also, be sure you have the version of DOS that is compatible with your software. Many programs require you to have DOS 3.x in order to run properly. Programs designed for DOS 2.1 may do things the author never intended in DOS 3.x. Often, especially in the early days, programmers used accesses to DOS that IBM had seemingly forgotten. Then, in the next upgrade, programmers would discover DOS reclaimed the "forgotten" interrupt for some basic service like writing to a hard disk. In recent times, programmers no longer assume that an unused DOS function is free for the taking. But it's safest to stick with programs that specifically say they'll work with your version of DOS.

Other likely areas for compatibility problems depend upon the program. If it's a graphics display program, check for compatibility with your type of graphics display—monochrome, CGA, EGA, VGA, LCD, and so on. If it's a disk-oriented program like a disk organizer, check that it's designed for your type of hard disk. If you're not sure what type of hard disk you have—MFM, RLL, ESDI, or SCSI—take the trouble to find out.

Minimum Memory Requirements

Most program documentation will tell you the minimum amount of memory required to run the program. These days, if you're using a machine with 256K of memory, some of the best Shareware programs (or commercial programs, for that matter) will refuse to run on it.

If you find yourself in this kind of situation, here's a small suggestion.

When you're considering adding new hardware items to your machine, establish some logical priorities. Yes, you might like to get a hard disk or perhaps a bigger hard disk. You might want to get a 3.5-inch high density drive, or a VGA card and monitor.

If, however, you can't run a lot of programs because you don't have enough DOS RAM, what good would any of these things really do? Think about it. You can get by for a while longer without a hard disk, or with a smaller one, and you can make do with a CGA or monochrome monitor for the time being, but if you don't get more RAM, you will continue to be limited.

After all, isn't your main objective to run some good programs? Plenty of disk storage and colorful graphics are very nice, but they're meaningless if the selection of programs you can run is limited because you don't have enough RAM. So, think of RAM as your top priority. RAM is what makes programs run. All the other items are just the icing on the cake.

Memory Resident Loading Order

Many utility programs are designed to be loaded into memory, where they sit and wait for you to call them using a hot key. Some TSR programs behave better than others. If you're trying out a TSR, be sure not to load it into memory after another program that insists on being loaded last, for example, SideKick. Memory resident programs are touchy. If you violate their loading order your computer may "freeze up," leaving you wondering what happened. Some TSRs that are better behaved don't care what order they are loaded in, so this gives you some flexibility.

What happens if you have two or more programs that all want to be loaded last? Experiment. You'll either find that you hit on a loading order that makes them all happy, or something has to go. If you encounter a situation where, for example, two TSRs just won't work together no matter what you do, leave me a note. (Details on doing that are in Appendix C.) I'll try to get in touch with the authors and see if we can work out the conflict. Another nice thing about Shareware authors is they willingly work together to solve problems once they are aware of them.

Be Careful with "Fancy" Programming

There are virtuoso programmers out there in The Wires who can do just about anything with a computer except make it wash their backs in the shower. (If such a master reads that last sentence and takes it as a challenge, you may soon see a program to wash your back in the shower.) These are the same programmers who figured out how to modify disk interleaves in a flash, change CMOS setups without rebooting, and modify a system's built-in CPU refresh rates. There are programs that can double your screen display speed, change hard disk partitions, and move or even encrypt file allocation tables. There are even programs that can tweak UART buffers to allow continuous file downloads on one side while the computer writes captured data to the disk on the other.

As a rule, if you don't know, for example, what an *interleave* is, you should probably stay away from programs that change it, at least until you've had a chance to study the subject. If you go ahead and the program says, "Changing Interleave to 6:1," that may sound just fine to you. It will not be just fine for your computer, as you will eventually find out. There are other areas where deft programming can cause daft effects, so let's take a look at some of them as well.

Screen Mode Manipulation

Programs that change your screen's operating modes can cause real problems. For example, some programs sensing an EGA graphics card assume you have an auto-switching or "multisynch" type of monitor, and try to force the screen to a higher mode. This can result in strange looking screens and even damage your graphics card.

If you have a choice, it's always worth it to pay a little more for an auto-switching video card. Failing that, try to use programs that let the user select the video mode. Most good programs do.

Data Encryption Programs

As you roam around The Wires, you'll find there are quite a few programs that can be used to *encrypt* your data. What do these programs do? Basically, they take your data, use a password that you supply, and then turn your data into a jumbled bunch of nonsense. Without the password to *unencrypt* the data, no one can look at it, read it, or access it.

When I say no one, I mean no one! That includes you. If you forget the password that you used to encrypt a file, there is no way to get the data back. The information in that file is lost to you. Unless you think that there is some hope of your remembering the password, you might as well erase the file.

In some areas of computer use, data encryption is truly necessary. Various branches of the federal government use it to protect highly sensitive data from prying eyes. Some large companies use it for the same reason. These kinds of programs are enticing, especially to new users. They bring out the "secret agent" in all of us. Before you use a data encryption program, however, ask yourself these two questions.

1. Does this data really need to be encrypted?

2. Am I prepared to lose it forever?

If you decide to go ahead and encrypt data, be sure that you keep a copy of the password on something tangible and not just in your memory. If you encrypt many files, then you'd better keep a list of the filenames and the passwords that go with them. If the data was that sensitive to begin with, you then have the task of keeping your list of filenames and passwords safe. Find a suitable hiding place for it or use a safety deposit box. Just remember that these programs are designed to do their job well, and if you forget the password, you are out of luck.

Directory Killers

Another variety of program that you should be wary of are those that say they can "kill" or erase a directory. Using some fancy programming, these programs can remove a directory and all of the files in it. Normally, DOS is not set up to perform such a radical step.

If such a program appeals to you, just remember to use it with great care. When you erase an entire directory, it is gone and I do mean gone! The same is true, of course, if you remove a DOS directory in the conventional manner. The difference is that using the conventional manner, you at least have the opportunity to change your mind before you erase all of the files in that directory. You have another chance to change your mind before you remove the directory itself. You might be able to go in and unerase a file that you really didn't want to get rid of.

With the programs that kill directories, those options, or extra chances, are taken away from you. So be forewarned. If you elect to *kill* a directory, it will be *dead* and there will be no turning back.

DOCTOR'S NOTE

Under the normal influence of DOS, you cannot remove a directory unless all of the programs have been removed from it. There may be times when you've erased all of the files from a directory and DOS says that you still can't remove it. In a case like that, here's a little tip, gained from experience.

Use a Shareware program like DX (Directory eXtended) and have it show you just hidden files (the DX command is DX /AT:!H). The odds are good that the program that you erased from the directory had created at least one hidden file. If so, that's why you can't remove the directory. You can use DX to change those hidden files so they can be erased. You will then be able to remove the directory.

Multitasking Programs

Window-type programs that let you keep different application programs in different areas of memory can hang your machine for subtle reasons. It can be very frustrating to try to nail down what's wrong when your machine freezes every ten minutes, for example, for no apparent reason. Sometimes, such problems can disappear as mysteriously as they appeared, leaving you scratching your head and wondering what it was all about. The cause may have been one small utility program that you've stopped using, and you may never figure out the reason.

In general, multitasking programs like DESQview and Windows are safe, but do take a lot of care to install them correctly. Like telecommunications programs, they need to do a lot of things all at once. One small mistake in the parameters during installation and you're in the midst of a sea of problems, with no obvious cause. When using telecommunications programs with multitasking software, remember this:

Never allow a communications program to be swapped out!

If a communications program is swapped out while it is transferring a file, the results could be disastrous. Pay close attention to the documentation any time you intend to try a window or multitasking environment on your machine.

Expanded Memory Programs

When expanded memory became available, it was intended to let everyone finally break that 640K DOS barrier. The microcomputer giants, Lotus, Intel, and Microsoft, even got together long enough to generate a standard. Unfortunately, expanded memory requires a manager—and not all programs are compatible with the same managers. This is improving as the market settles down, but programs designed to work outside the normal 640K limit are still likely to create problems.

Conflicting Interrupts

TSR programs, device drivers, utilities, and other programs can develop a case of conflicting interrupts. That means two sets of software are trying to use the same DOS functions at once. The results can be bizarre.

Several programs can help you identify interrupt conflicts. For example, MAPMEM (which comes with MARK and RELEASE as part of the classic memory management program TSRCOM) produces a report. Figure 23-1 shows the report that MAPMEM displays. Studying this report,

---

Figure 23-1

MAPMEM report

```
d:\inset>mapmem
Allocated Memory Map - by TurboPower Software - Version 2.9

 PSP  blks bytes owner    command line          hooked vectors
 ----  ---- ----- -----    ------------          -------------
 0008   1   4272 config
 0CB0   3   6000 command  /S:E /E:2048 /A:...  2E
 0E43   3   5296 4DOS                           22 2F
 0F97   1    400 N/A      N/A                    14
 0FB6   2 125232 INSET                           09 10 17 20 21 E9 EC EF F1
                                                 F3
 2E4B   2 465744 free

 block   bytes    (Expanded Memory)
 -----   -----
    0    589024
    1     81920
 free   2785280
 total  3457024

d:\inset>
```

or showing it to someone who understands it better, can often help you solve your problems. Remember, there is a lot of help available on bulletin boards and online networks. If you are experiencing a problem now, the odds are good that others have had the same problem before you. Seek out their help.

The program CHECKINT, which comes with the Shareware classic CED, produces a report on unused vectors or interrupts. Figure 23-2 gives an example of what this output looks like. Several commercial programs, such as Quarterdeck's MANIFEST and Golden Bow Systems' VTSR, produce similar reports. These can help you interpret problems. If it's too technical, definitely get someone to help you—interrupt problems can be very troublesome.

Figure 23-2

CHECKINT report

The following vectors appear to be unused:

60	62	63	64	65	66	78	79	7A	7B	7C	7D
7E	7F	80	81	82	83	84	85	86	87	88	89
8A	8B	8C	8D	8E	8F	90	91	92	93	94	95
96	97	98	99	9A	9B	9C	9D	9E	9F	A0	A1
A2	A3	A4	A5	A6	A7	A8	A9	AA	AB	AC	AD
AE	AF	B0	B1	B2	B3	B4	B5	B6	B7	B8	B9
BA	BB	BC	BD	BE	BF	C0	C1	C2	C3	C4	C5
C6	C7	C8	E0	E1	E2	E3	E4	E5	E6	E7	E8
E9	EA	EB									

WARNING: Some of these may be reserved by your hardware or operating system. Check your documentation!

DOCTOR'S NOTE

You might ask yourself, "What is DOS, exactly?" DOS, or *Disk Operating System*, is the master system used by the computer to control operations like memory, storage, keyboard, monitor, and printer. It is the central control panel for the entire system, used by almost all other application programs.

Using DOS allows application programs to avoid having to reinvent the wheel. Instead of doing everything directly, they can just tell DOS what to do. DOS lets all the components of your system work together. But it goes deeper than that. DOS also lets you, the user, directly control what the system does. At the DOS level, called the DOS prompt, you can do all your basic file and disk management chores. You can copy disks and files, create a system startup disk, even list and print out text files.

If you have a handle on hardware and software compatibility, both you and your applications can use DOS without much trouble. But some of the DOS commands can really be troublemakers. It will pay you well to learn about these commands from other people's mistakes, not your own!

POWERFUL DOS COMMANDS

Let's not forget one of the most powerful programs on any DOS-based machine—the DOS operating system itself. Experts in DOS, the so-called "DOS Jocks," wouldn't trade it for all the menus and shells in America. It is truly a powerful and flexible operating system.

It's also, of all the "power programs," one of the least concerned with the hapless nonexpert user. It simply lacks safety features. These errors are so common that if you could get a nickel for every file accidentally erased by the DEL command, or every hard disk accidentally formatted when a user forgot to specify the right target drive, you'd be able to retire to your own island somewhere.

If you're not DOS adept, you may find it worthwhile to get a shell to mediate between you and the operating system. Or you may want to switch to a program like 4DOS, with its greater concern for the user. In any case, here are some commands in particular—not all of them obvious—that can cause endless trouble. But one DOS utility program in particular merits special caution, so we'll start with that one.

RECOVER

RECOVER is one of the worst utility programs ever put out for general consumption, and the worst news of all is that it comes with DOS itself. This program attempts to recover damaged files. If you use it on your hard drive by mistake without specifying a filename, it will try to recover everything on the disk.

Sadly, it only handles the first 512 files. It also considers subdirectories to be files, so it moves your subdirectories (and all files it finds within them—the first 512, anyway) into your root directory with generic names such as FILE0000.REC. It does all this in memory, so you don't even get a blinking drive light warning you that something is going on. When it's done, all of Norton's utilities and all of CHKDSK's tricks can't put your files back together again.

It's worth trying the Norton Disk Doctor program, which has an option called "Recover from DOS's Recover"—it may do the trick. Another good defense is an up-to-date backup. But the best defense of all is to get rid of this ill-conceived program. Do yourself a real favor: delete this awful utility program from your system.

COPY and XCOPY

These commands—the first an internal function of COMMAND.COM and the second an external utility program—carry out truly necessary functions. XCOPY in particular is a fine utility, with options to use archive flags, dates, and other variables to determine what to copy. It will prompt you before copying. But use the copy commands carefully—copying over the wrong file has lost more data than any other command but DEL (delete). Here are some things that can go wrong when using the COPY command.

Copying over Things

Copying one file on top of another of the same name is a common mistake. If you type

```
C:COPY C:\FILE.TXT C:\DNLD\FILE.TXT
```

and there is already a file called FILE.TXT in the C:\DNLD directory, then the one in the C:\DNLD directory is going to be overwritten. If there was different data in that file, it's gone now.

Mixing Things Up

Another common error is mixing binary files with ASCII files accidentally when adding one file to another. Using the form of the COPY command like this,

```
C:COPY FILE1 + FILE2  FILE3
```

adds the contents of FILE1 and FILE2 and puts them in FILE3. If FILE1 happens to be a binary file and FILE2 is an ASCII file, then FILE3 is junk.

Oops! The Wrong Path

Another frequent mistake made by users is misspelling a path directory. DOS, obedient servant that it is, does not question what you instruct it to do—it just does it. Let's say that you are trying to copy all of the files in the current directory to the C:\DOS directory. If you type

```
C:\COPY *.* \DOSS
```

instead of

```
C:\COPY *.* \DOS
```

you'll get one, huge file in the root directory named DOSS. Shareware programs like DX, 4DOS, and PCOPY can all be made to prompt you to see if what you entered is what you really wanted. If you're paying attention, you can easily avoid such a problem.

Copying Without Enough Room

You may be getting the idea that the COPY command is not very smart. Here's further proof. Let's say that you want to copy several files to a floppy disk on drive A. If you copy a file and there isn't enough room on the destination disk to hold it, you're likely to wind up with an unintended 0-byte file instead. If you then erase the original, you might find out much too late that you never actually made the copy you thought you made. And the file? It's gone for good.

You Forgot to Shift

If, when you type a drive letter designation, you type a semicolon (;) instead of a colon (:) you can wind up with strange results. For example, take a look at the following command:

```
COPY C:\COMMAND.COM A;
```

Because you entered a semicolon instead of a colon, this command will copy COMMAND.COM into a file named A in the current default directory. DOS simply isn't very smart about such things. There are some Shareware alternatives, like Norm Patriquin's PCOPY program, that ask you if you really mean what you said. Those alternatives are much safer than the DOS version. Here are some more common problems.

The REPLACE Command

The REPLACE command, like XCOPY, has a great deal of built-in flexibility. But it can copy over the wrong files if you're not careful. Before you even attempt using the REPLACE command, make sure that you've studied its syntax carefully in your DOS manual.

DELete

The DELete command is one of the classic mischief makers. For some reason, Microsoft never thought it necessary to allow a pause or a warning, except when you're trying to delete everything with "DEL *.*." Too many people learn too late that if you tell DOS to DEL a filename, and if that filename happens to be a directory name, DOS thinks you're telling it to DEL every file in that directory.

So if you get that odd message, "Are you sure? (Y/N)" when you don't expect it—especially if you just used the DEL command—*don't* automatically answer **Y**. Always find out what's happening first. Better yet, use

DOCTOR'S NOTE

When you delete a file, you don't actually write over all the data the file contains. Rather, you replace the first letter of the file's name with the delete character, a lowercase Greek omega character. Because the contents of the file are not erased, programs like UNDELETE or the Undelete function in the Professional Master Key utility can often retrieve a file when you accidentally erase it. How successful they are depends upon which version of DOS you use (it's harder with DOS 2.1 than with DOS 3.x) and on how fragmented the file was.

Fragmented files are stored in separate little pieces here and there on the disk. Unfragmented files are stored in a single place on the disk. With highly fragmented files, there's a tendency to lose pieces here and there when you try to retrieve them after erasing. Also, if you've done a lot of disk writing between erasing a file and trying to unerase it, you probably won't be successful. The reason is that, once you erase a file, DOS considers the space it occupied to be empty and is likely to use it for other data.

The lesson is one of preventive medicine—keep your hard disk organized. If you accidentally erase the wrong file, use your unerase utility to get it back right away. The most important thing to remember is not to write anything to disk before you try to unerase. Copying another file to the disk could easily cause it to occupy some of the space that was occupied by the erased file. If you do this, your chances of unerasing the file go down dramatically.

a Shareware or public domain utility like VDEL that shows what you're about to delete and lets you back out if you change your mind.

FORMAT

Once you start formatting, it's too late to back out. There are utilities to recover most of your files if you use FORMAT by mistake, but it was not always so. For the same reason that unerase utilities don't always work, you probably won't be able to recover completely from an accidental FORMAT command if your disk is highly fragmented.

It's easier than you might think to format your own hard disk. All it takes is to enter FORMAT instead of FORMAT A: or FORMAT B:, and at least with DOS 2.1, your C drive is erased. Later versions of DOS ask for confirmation if a hard disk is about to be formatted. Your best bet is to use any of several outstanding alternatives to DOS FORMAT, such as John Newlin's Format Master program. Such DOS alternatives are much safer, faster, and more flexible than the DOS utility.

ASSIGN, JOIN, and SUBST

ASSIGN, JOIN, and SUBST do some sophisticated stunts that involve fooling DOS into thinking it's dealing with a different disk drive. They can be very handy when used wisely, but they can cause a lot of trouble too. The reason is that you've fooled DOS into thinking one disk or directory is actually another. So DOS gives you misinformation. If you must use these commands, use them from a batch file, not on the fly at the DOS prompt. That way you're less likely to make careless errors.

DEBUG

DEBUG can write directly to your hard disk, modifying .COM and .EXE files. It can also cause problems with your CMOS, and directly address board-mounted memory. Unless you know what you're doing, stay away from DEBUG. Instead, use one of the many menu-driven track and sector editors that at least ask for user confirmation before they write directly to the disk.

CHKDSK

CHKDSK is a diagnostic program that is the first thing turned to when someone has a disk or file problem. That's fine; it's what the program is intended for. But if CHKDSK reports a problem, too many people run it again right away using the /F parameter. That tells CHKDSK to fix whatever problems it found. You will end up with some (usually useless) files in the root directory, but no lost clusters and no major problems.

Sometimes all that was needed was a reboot. What CHKDSK reports is not necessarily what's happening; it's just a sign of some sort of trouble. *Always* reboot your system before telling CHKDSK to fix any file, cluster, or lost chain manipulations on your disk.

Redirection Symbols

Misusing the redirection commands < and > can trash existing files or create 0-byte files. (Sometimes long or complex batch files use tiny 0-byte files to track their progress.) And there are other uses—for example, the command REM > QUIT.BAT creates a 0-byte batch file that lets you QUIT in the middle of a long batch file procedure without hunting for an :EXIT label. But too many users only find out about redirection symbols when an accidental > sign writes a 22-byte error message over a 97K data file.

OTHER SAFE COMPUTING PRACTICES

To round out this chapter, here are some recommended practices involving both software and hardware. They add up to helping you to be reasonably careful with your equipment.

Don't Experiment with Original Program Copies

Vendors *always* have a notice that reads: "Copy these files onto another diskette and store the original in a safe place." There's a simple reason—if Murphy hadn't already existed we would have had to invent him just to account for an observation made by just about every computing old-timer in the world.

The only disks that ever get erased or damaged are the ones you only have one copy of. One major vendor cut down disk returns 90 percent by removing the FORMAT.COM program and using write-protected diskettes without a notch. This problem is particularly annoying—it has genuine Murphy's Law status—because it is so easily avoidable. Simply make a backup and a working copy, and use the working copy. If the disk gets ruined, make another working copy and try again. Never use the backup copy!

Make the Right Connections

Don't plug your computer and peripherals into a "spaghetti factory" of four-way plugs or power strips plugged into power strips. If your wall outlets are faulty or the power cords seem to come loose for no reason, replace the outlets immediately. Keep your power cords off the floor and out of the way of dogs, vacuum cleaners, and people's feet. Use a separate power circuit if you can—preferably one with its own 15-amp breaker. In an area with brownouts, it pays to invest in a reliable uninterruptable power supply. It will keep your chips away from surges, noise, spikes, and sudden power failures.

Don't Abuse Your Equipment

Never remove or add printed circuit cards while the power is on. It can cause sparks or even short out other cards. It will void your warranty since service centers can easily spot "toasted" components.

Be gentle with your equipment. The old saying, "If it doesn't work, get a bigger hammer" won't work with a computer. All it takes is one good bump from a chair you're moving across the room, or from your foot if you keep the machine on a floor stand, and *poof*—your files are gone.

Take Care with Diskettes

Being portable, diskettes are vulnerable to problems that don't usually affect a hard disk. For example, don't open your drive door when the light is still on. You could be interrupting a DOS operation and lose your data. Look out for diskettes that have been exposed to heat, cold, cigarette smoke, and other hazards of transport. Defective or damaged disks can act like sandpaper, grinding down your disk drive's read/write heads.

Don't reformat your diskettes to densities they're not designed for. Some careless technicians try to get more storage by formatting double-density diskettes in high-density drives. Aside from having to listen to the disk drive grind away at unreadable sectors, you're guaranteed to lose data. The reason is that marginal sectors are readable one time, unreadable the next.

SOME CONCLUDING REMARKS

Nothing you can do will eliminate all problems with a system as complex as your computer. A small amount of thinking ahead, however, can go a very long way toward eliminating that most frustrating of problems—lost or ruined files that took hours of effort to create.

Keep current backups of the files and programs that are on your hard disk. If a program, such as a word processor, editor, or spreadsheet, offers you the option of automatically saving data every few minutes, take advantage of it. In the course of writing this book, I was saved a lot of work on several occasions because I had my work saved automatically every five minutes. In a few cases it meant the difference between losing several hours of work and losing only a few minutes of work.

That's what I mean about thinking ahead. Think before you delete. Don't automatically answer **Y** to a "Y/N?" prompt. When in doubt, answer **N**. Check out the situation first—it may save you a lot of grief. The computer only does what you tell it to do. Remember, when your bank says, "Oh, we're so sorry about the mixup, but the computer made a mistake," you can interpret that to mean that someone hit the wrong button on the computer.

As for compatibility problems with programs, those are just a fact of computing life. Some programs are going to conflict with others, and often in strange and unusual ways. In the course of testing and evaluating so many programs, I have had all of the following things occur:

- Screen goes blank

- Keyboard is locked

- Machine reboots by itself

- Screen fills with a colorful display of graphics garbage

- Strange sounds screech out of the speaker

- All my directories seem to disappear

What do you do? Reboot the machine! If it's a new program, don't load it again until you've had a chance to think about what might have caused the problem; a TSR conflict, for example. If the new program was a TSR, loaded from your AUTOEXEC.BAT file, either try to abort the AUTOEXEC.BAT file with a CTRL-C before that TSR loads, or boot from another disk. Everyone should have a specially prepared boot disk for occasions such as these.

There is one point that I cannot emphasize enough—just because a program blows up, and your machine locks or other bizarre things happen, this does not, repeat not, mean you have encountered a so-called Trojan horse program, bomb, or worm. It simply means that you have encountered a conflict between programs and that you may have to do a little work to get the programs to work well together. Perhaps, you can also take some solace from the next section.

A Special Comment About Viruses

Because I have been asked this question so many times in the past, I want to let you know the answer too. The question is: "With all of the programs and files that you have downloaded, tested, and handled, how many 'harmful' programs have you encountered?" (Harmful refers to Trojan horse programs, bombs, and worms. Unfortunately, it is a fact that viruses do exist.) The answer is this: in over seven years of being online—having unpacked and tested thousands of programs from all over the United States, so that my collection of Shareware consumes well over a gigabyte of space—I have never encountered even one program that was intentionally designed to do harm.

I am not saying that such programs do not exist, but if they do, by some miraculous coincidence I have never encountered one. I have encountered many minor program conflicts, but in nearly all cases they were easily remedied with just a little thought and work. Thus, my advice is not to jump to conclusions when trying out new programs. When using your computer, try to think ahead; don't become too automatic in your actions or in your responses to prompts. Take advantage of all of the safety nets you can. By doing these things you'll gain more enjoyment from your computer and the Shareware programs that you use.

It's time to move along now and take a look at some of the programs that have been designed to help protect your data. Since viruses do exist, it is important that you know about them and about the programs that can help you protect your system, or at least tell you if a virus has invaded your system.

## CHAPTER TWENTY-FOUR

Disk Protection Programs

In various sections of this book, references have been made to Trojan horse programs and viruses. Trojan horse programs are credited with destroying file allocation tables on hard disks, performing low-level formats, and more. Reports of these programs peaked around 1986.

It was noted earlier that after many years of handling thousands of files and programs, I have never encountered a Trojan horse program, and I can neither verify nor deny that such programs really exist. It is important to remember that even a well-written program with a serious bug can destroy the file allocation tables. The term "Trojan horse" implies that a program was *intentionally* written to cause harm. Virus programs, on the other hand, are known to exist. They have been well documented and isolated. Let's examine this topic in more detail.

A SHIFTING OF FOCUS

As reports of Trojan horse programs filtered through The Wires, program authors began writing software to thwart such programs. One fairly popular TSR program was called BOMBSQAD, which would halt any process that might harm your system, such as a command to format your hard disk. BOMBSQAD worked very well and could also detect a command to write to the disk. When the first virus attack was verified, the focus on Trojan horse programs gradually diminished. Once again, programmers began developing ways of detecting and removing viruses from infected systems. As of today, the people creating viruses continue to develop more clever ways of infiltrating systems while those who develop software to detect viruses must adapt as well, creating new ways of isolating the newer strains.

VIRUS DETECTION PROGRAMS

Rather than go into a full discussion of how viruses work and how they are designed, a few of the programs for detecting viruses in your computer system will be discussed in this chapter. For a complete discussion of viruses, I refer you to *The Computer Virus Handbook* by Richard Levin (Osborne/McGraw-Hill, 1990).

DOCTOR'S NOTE

Before examining anti-virus programs, I'd like to make a comment about Shareware software and viruses. I have seen articles in some publications claiming that viruses are spread through Shareware. It is a well-documented fact, however, that in the majority of computer virus infections, the carrier was traced to a commercial program, usually a *pirated* copy.

People who create viruses seem to want two things—publicity and to damage major systems. To inflict real damage, virus developers will attempt to infiltrate large national databases, government agencies, and big corporations. These are the kinds of places that tend to use high-profile commercial software and run extensive networks where viruses can spread easily and quickly.

Another fact to consider is that the Shareware and online communities were among the very first to start policing themselves. Before viruses arrived on the scene, bulletin board sysops were checking each uploaded file and unpacking programs looking for Trojan horses. When viruses entered the scene, anti-virus programs began to appear on bulletin boards almost immediately.

Shareware authors have devised programs to validate files, ensuring that they have not been altered in any way. PKWARE's version 1.10 of PKZIP and PKUNZIP now includes a way to show that each file inside a .ZIP file is exactly the same as it was when it was packed by the original author. Some Shareware authors are including special checking programs with their software to ensure that the program has not been modified. These and other methods have made Shareware programs much safer than their commercial counterparts.

My advice is to get the facts from a reliable source, consider the motivations of those who create viruses, and arrive at your own conclusions.

CHECKUP

The virus detection program CHECKUP is one of the most popular programs of its kind and is used by government agencies and large corporations. CHECKUP uses techniques that are not employed by some of the other virus-checking programs. The author, Richard Levin, has done an intensive study of viruses. The following section is excerpted from the documentation for CHECKUP.

"Well-written computer viruses are difficult to detect using modern file management and anti-Trojan techniques. They are ingenious yet simple programs, polluting systems by inserting copies of themselves into, appending viral clones onto, or creating shells around ordinary executable files. Expertly engineered viruses will not change file date or time stamps, nor will they alter attributes, sizes, or checksums. Converting the attributes of potential viral targets (such as COMMAND.COM, IBM-BIO.COM, and IBMDOS.COM) to read-only may prevent inadequately designed viruses from infecting them. Most viruses, however, can check file attributes, reset them if necessary, infect, and then return the attributes to their original state. As you will learn in the following sections, there are no sure-fire ways to prevent viruses from infecting your systems. The only practical solution is to isolate and eradicate infections immediately after they occur using virus detection software stored off-line.

"CHECKUP detects viral infections by comparing target file sizes, incremental cyclic redundancy checks (CRCs), and total file CRCs to previously stored baseline values. CHECKUP examines files by dissecting them into randomly sized blocks of data, using dynamic block size allocations that allow files as small as one byte to be accurately checked. CHECKUP then scans and compares every byte of the target files on a block-by-block basis. If the recorded file sizes, any of the block CRC comparisons, or the CRC totals do not match, CHECKUP alerts users that the target files have been altered. CHECKUP's incremental block CRC technique is superior to simply calculating files' sum-of-the-bytes and comparing past and present checksum totals. Future viruses may be able to compute checksums prior to infections, pad their viral code with characters that maintain checksum integrity, and then infect.

"Even more alarming is the knowledge that viruses can effortlessly exchange bytes within data files—a potent form of data destruction ordinary checksum programs cannot detect. For example, the checksum of both 1 + 2 and 2 + 1 is 3, yet the order of operators (the numbers 1 and 2) is different. This kind of viral activity would defeat other checksum calculation programs, but not CHECKUP."

The Theory Behind CHECKUP

To help you understand why CHECKUP is considered by many to be one of the very best virus-detecting programs, it will help if you see the reasoning employed in its design. Levin talks about what makes CHECKUP unique.

"We believe it is impossible for a virus to maintain an accurate intra-file (inter-block) CRC. This is especially true when the checked block size varies from one byte to near total file size, when the method for calculating the CRC is unknown and the results encrypted. To survive CHECKUP's scrutiny, a virus would need to know the block size, the exact calculation entry point, the CRC algorithm, and the encryption key used at initialization. The virus would then have the difficult, if not impossible, task of padding its code with dummy characters, since adjustments would have to occur every few hundred bytes. Even if a virus were able to achieve this high degree of adaptability, it would nevertheless be unable to operate in such an internally scrambled condition."

How To Run CHECKUP

The best way to run CHECKUP is from a clean diskette that you create. The documentation gives complete instructions for this procedure. By maintaining a clean and secure set of CHECKUP files, you ensure the program's ability to accurately assess your system. After creating the special diskette, you can check your system at any time by booting the machine, and CHECKUP will begin its work. It compares the existing files on the hard disk with its own copies. If it finds that a file has been altered, it alerts you. When CHECKUP has finished, it erases files created during the check procedure. In summary, CHECKUP is an excellent way of screening your system for viruses.

Richard B. Levin
P.O. Box 14546
Philadelphia, PA 19115
$24.95 Home use registration; $49.95 Office use registration; $74.95 Deluxe registration includes printed manual; $99.95 Premium registration includes Deluxe version plus *The Computer Virus Handbook*; site licenses available; all versions include manual on disk.

SCAN

The SCAN series of programs by John McAfee Associates has become quite popular. There is both a stand-alone and TSR version of SCAN, which acts as a continuous monitor for viruses. SCAN also tests itself each time it is loaded, and if the program is altered by a virus, it will alert you to that fact.

At the time of this writing the current version of SCAN was 6.1. Beginning with version 4.8, SCAN came packaged with VALIDATE.COM, a program that validates the integrity of the SCAN file itself. From the DOS prompt, you would use VALIDATE by entering:

```
C>VALIDATE SCAN.EXE
```

VALIDATE checks the file size and date of creation, and then provides two numbers that are verified within the documentation. Figure 24-1 shows what the VALIDATE display looks like.

How SCAN Works

SCAN can identify 82 different strains of viruses and many subvarieties. According to McAfee Associates, 10 of the 82 viruses account for over 95 percent of all infections. Some viruses have been modified, so there may be more than one variety. SCAN works based on the fact that all of the known viruses attack or infect only certain areas of a system. To quote from the documentation for SCAN (version 6.1):

"All known viruses infect one of the following areas: The hard disk partition table; the DOS boot sector of hard disks or floppies; or one or more executable files within the system. The executable files may be operating system programs, system device drivers, .COM files, .EXE files, overlay files, or any other file that can be loaded into memory and executed."

SCAN can be used to test an entire drive, a directory, or a single file. It systematically checks all files that are subject to infection. McAfee Associates will also help you learn how to get rid of a virus should your system become infected.

What If You're Infected?

In addition to SCAN and SCANRES (the TSR version), McAfee Associates produces VIRUSCAN. VIRUSCAN is used when you *know* your system is infected. The program notes each file or area of the disk infected and tells you the exact name of the offending virus. VIRUSCAN can be put to work on a system, subdirectory, individual file, or floppy diskette.

Figure 24-1

Using SCAN's VALIDATE program

```
c:\dnld>validate scan.exe
VALIDATE 0.3 Copyright 1988-89 by McAfee Associates,  (408) 988-3832

            File Name:  scan.exe
                Size:  43,277
                Date:  3-31-1990
File Authentication:
    Check Method 1 - EA5F
    Check Method 2 - 15E7
```

If your system is infected, McAfee Associates has special disinfecting utilities that can be used to eliminate infected portions of files and restore infected programs.

Currently Known Viruses

With each version of SCAN, McAfee Associates provides a list of currently known viruses. The list includes the name of each virus, programs for eradication, the degree to which their programs alter file sizes, and the areas of the system each virus attacks. A slightly modified copy of this list is seen in Table 24-1.

For the most current version of SCAN look for SCANV??.ZIP, where ?? is the version number. SCAN is an excellent virus-detection utility that is quick, thorough, and updated frequently.

McAfee Associates
4423 Cheney Street
Santa Clara, CA 95054
408-988-3832 (Voice)
408-988-4004 (BBS)
408-970-9727 (Fax)
$25 registration each for SCAN, SCANRES, and VIRUSCAN

FLU_SHOT PLUS

FLU_SHOT PLUS by Ross Greenburg is another popular virus detection program. This program has gone through serveral changes to its name, but it is now called FLU_SHOT PLUS. It is driven by a file in the root directory called FLUSHOT.DAT that allows you to write-protect (or read-protect) different file groups. For example, the program can write-protect all your .COM and .EXE files.

FLU_SHOT PLUS at Work

You can also have FLU_SHOT PLUS do a check each time you execute a program. If something triggers FLU_SHOT, a window appears on your screen with information explaining why the program was activated. You

Table 24-1

Currently Known Viruses as of April 1990

Virus	Disinfector	Size Increase of Infected Program	Damage
XA1	CleanUp	1539	F,O,P,L
1392	CleanUp	1392	O,P,L
1210	CleanUp	1210	O,P,L
1720	CleanUp	1720	F,O,P,L
Saturday 14th	CleanUp	685	F,O,P,L
Korea	M-DISK	N/A	B,O
Vcomm	CleanUp	1074	O,P,L
ItaVir	CleanUp	3880	O,P,L,B
Solano	CleanUp	2000	O,P,L
V2000	CleanUp	2000	O,P,L
1554	SCAN/D	1554	O,P,L
512	SCAN/D	none	O,P,L
EDV	M-DISK	N/A	B,O
Joker	CleanUp		O,P
Icelandic-3	CleanUp	853	O,P
Virus-101	CleanUp	2560	P
1260	CleanUp	1260	P
Perfume	CleanUp	765	P
Taiwan	CleanUp	708	P
Chaos	MDISK	N/A	B,O,D,F
Virus-90	CleanUp	857	P
Oropax	CleanUp	2773	P,O
4096	CleanUp	4096	D,O,P,L
Devil's Dance	CleanUp	941	D,O,P,L
Amstrad	CleanUp	847	P
Payday	CleanUp	1808	P
Datacrime II-B	CleanUp	1917	P,F
Sylvia/Holland	CleanUp	1332	P
Do-Nothing	CleanUp	608	P
Sunday	CleanUp	1636	O,P
Lisbon	CleanUp	648	P
Typo/Fumble	CleanUp	867	O,P
Dbase	CleanUp	1864	D,O,P
Ghost Boot Version	MDISK	N/A	B,O

Table 24-1

Currently Known Viruses as of April 1990 (continued)

Virus	Disinfector	Size Increase of Infected Program	Damage
Ghost COM Version	CleanUp	2351	B,P
New Jerusalem	CleanUp	1808	O,P
Alabama	CleanUp	1560	O,P,L
Yankee Doodle	CleanUp	2885	O,P
2930	CleanUp	2930	P
Ashar	CleanUp	N/A	B
AIDS	CleanUp		Overwrites program
Disk Killer	CleanUp	N/A	B,O,P,D,F
1536/Zero Bug	CleanUp	1536	O,P
MIX1	CleanUp	1618	O,P
Dark Avenger	CleanUp	1800	O,P,L
3551/Syslock	CleanUp	3551	P,D
VACSINA	CleanUp	1206	O,P
Ohio	MDISK	N/A	B
Typo (Boot Virus)	MDISK	N/A	O,B
Swap/Israeli Boot	MDISK	N/A	B
1514/Datacrime II	CleanUp	1514	P,F
Icelandic II	CleanUp	661	O,P
Pentagon	MDISK	N/A	B
3066/Traceback	M-3066	3066	P
1168/Datacrime-B	CleanUp	1168	P,F
Icelandic	CleanUp	642	O,P
Saratoga	CleanUp	632	O,P
405	CleanUp		Overwrites program
1704 Format	CleanUp	1704	O,P,F
Fu Manchu	CleanUp	2086	O,P
1280/Datacrime	CleanUp	1280	P,F
1701/Cascade	CleanUp	1701	O,P
1704/CASCADE-B	CleanUp	1704	O,P
Stoned/Marijuana	CleanUp	N/A	O,B,L
1704/CASCADE	CleanUp	1704	O,P
Ping Pong-B	CleanUp	N/A	O,B
Den Zuk	MDISK	N/A	O,B
Ping Pong	CleanUp	N/A	O,B

Table 24-1

Currently Known Viruses as of April 1990 (*continued*)

Virus	Disinfector	Size Increase of Infected Program	Damage
Vienna-B	CleanUp	648	P
Lehigh	CleanUp		Overwrites P,F
Vienna/648	M-VIENNA	648	P
Jerusalem-B	CleanUp	1808	O,P
Yale/Alameda	CleanUp	N/A	B
Friday 13th COM	CleanUp	512	P
Jerusalem	CleanUp	1808	O,P
SURIV03	CleanUp		O,P
SURIV02	CleanUp	1488	O,P
SURIV01	CleanUp	897	O,P
Pakistani Brain	CleanUp	N/A	B

Damage fields
B - Corrupts or overwrites boot sector
O - Affects system run-time operation
P - Corrupts program or overlay files
D - Corrupts data files
F - Formats or erases all/part of disk
L - Directly or indirectly corrupts file linkage

Size increase
The length, in bytes, by which an infected program or overlay file will increase

determine exactly how FLU_SHOT PLUS will work on your system depending on what you include in the FLUSHOT.DAT file. This program is designed more to detect possible symptoms of a viral infection than the actual virus itself. It is also effective against the Trojan horse type of program.

Ross M. Greenberg
Software Concepts Design
594 Third Avenue

New York, NY 10016
212-889-6438 (BBS)
$10 registration

OTHER VIRUS DETECTION PROGRAMS

There are other virus and Trojan horse detection programs available, which use a variety of methods for detecting viruses. Some work by actually scanning for viruses while others work by trying to catch abnormal system behavior. Programs such as SCAN and CHECKUP are specifically used to test for the presence of viruses. Other programs, such as FLU_SHOT PLUS, BOMBSQAD, and SCANRES, are designed to monitor your system at all times. To give you an idea of some of the programs available, here is a bulletin board listing.

!TROJAN!.ZIP	6154	Textfile on Trojan programs
12TRICKS.ZIP	6125	Trojan Alert/Analysis from USENET
AIDS!.ZIP	4573	Documentation on a dreaded virus.
ALERT13U.ZIP	65609	Menu driven virus protection program
BALLVIRS.ZIP	1867	Describes the bouncing ball virus.
BBPSCAN3.ZIP	27461	The ByteBrothers' Paranoid Scan System
BITVIRUS.ZIP	2325	Description of the Bitnet Virus
BNDAID.ZIP	6621	PD version of commercial virus blocker
BOMB-SQD.ZIP	15765	Anti-Trojan ascii string lister
BOMBCHK2.ZIP	18744	BOMBSQAD, CHK4BOMB, with color control
BS200.ZIP	37657	BSearch file-size database/virus checker
CAP.ZIP	45510	Controlled Access Program password
CHK4BOMB.ZIP	8953	Anti-Trojan prgm: Searches files
CHKANSI2.ZIP	25742	Check files for harmful ANSI codes
CHKSUM.ZIP	16430	do checksum check in autoexec-anti-flu
CHKUP36.ZIP	91178	RBLevin's CHECKUP v.3.6 virus detection
CIPHER12.ZIP	28172	Encrypt / decrypt rapidly and safely
CKOT11.ZIP	49337	Checkout: checks for virus within

CLEANP61.ZIP	46767	Heals/Removes ALL Viruses - from McAfee
CNC-V11.ZIP	36030	Virus checking program
CONFIDEN.ZIP	67846	Encryption program --- protect data
COP.ZIP	2567	A Virus protector for COM/EXE files
CRCDOS.ZIP	32146	A new generation of virus checking
CRYPTO.ZIP	28725	Public key code encryption programs -
CU14.ZIP	39672	Checks your programs for virus
CYPHER1B.ZIP	55601	Utility to selectively Password protect
DAYCHEK.ZIP	2391	a bat file that daily chk's system files
DDOZ10A.ZIP	27043	Dirty Dozen list of trojans. Issue 10a
DESCRYPT.ZIP	17295	Encrypt / decrypt files. Protect data.
DETECT2.ZIP	23856	VIRUS CHECKUP USING 2 CRC
DETECT31.ZIP	34273	The Detective r3.1 file tracking/virus
DPROT102.ZIP	4011	Protect hard drive against writes/format
DPROTECT.ZIP	3488	protect hard disk from trojan horses.
DVIR1701.ZIP	13340	A cure for the 1701 (Cascade) virus.
EGA_BTR.ZIP	3236	A tale about the EGABTR trojan
ENCIPHER.ZIP	50738	encipher text files on a PC
EPW.ZIP	4891	Put a password in any .exe or .com file
ESC-TROJ.ZIP	2203	Description of Escape Key Trojan
EXRUN10A.ZIP	21510	add password protectn to any program
FICHECK5.ZIP	89939	Newest version of virus protect.
FILE-CRC.ZIP	55580	Does a checksum on files - anti-virus
FIND1701.ZIP	19504	Detect and eliminate 1701 virus
FREEZE.ZIP	911	computer protection utility
FRI13WRN.TXT	1768	Friday the 13th virus - security
GUARD11.ZIP	10684	Program to make your system safe
HARDOFF.ZIP	2788	Turn off/on HD for write/trojan
HDLOCK.ZIP	15770	GREAT PASSWORD UTILITY FOR HARD DRIVES
IBM-SCAN.ZIP	195448	IBM virus scanner
IBMPAPER.ZIP	26995	IBM research paper on viruses
INOCULAT.ZIP	6056	Innoculate your System against a Virus !
JIV_31.ZIP	18550	virus detector/immuniser from Israel
JLOCK.ZIP	11752	Control access to a list of files
KEY-150.ZIP	10519	KEY v1.50: binary/ASCII
K_I_L_L_.ZIP	2698	SEXSHOW.ZIP is a VIRUS!!!!!
LOCKERUP.ZIP	2042	Lock up your keyboard
LOCKOUT.ZIP	5109	lockout unwanted keyboard users
LOCKUP11.ZIP	6735	Security system for Hard Disk
LOG8905A.ZIP	16977	Virus-l log for 1st week May.
LOG8910D.ZIP	86750	Virus-l digest 4th week, October, 1989
M-1704.ZIP	14421	Removes 1701/1704 virus versions A & B
M-1704C.ZIP	14414	Find 1704-C Virus
M-3066.ZIP	11000	M-3066 Virus Detector

M-DAV.ZIP	14912	Heal/remove Dark Avenger Virus
M-VIENNA.ZIP	11494	Vienna Virus Detector
MAKEPASS.ZIP	3608	Makes up passwords for you.
MATHTROJ.ZIP	1384	Mathkids is PCBoard trojan!!
MCAFEE.ZIP	1488	Warning on bogus VALIDATE in SCANV58
MD40.ZIP	5748	An anti-virus program from CA.
MYTHS-3.ZIP	8992	"Computer Virus Myths" treatise
MYTHS.ZIP	8725	Discussion of Computer Virus Myths
NASA.ZIP	2177	***TROJAN ALERT !!!***
NETP21.ZIP	24933	Net Goat Network Virus Checker
NETSCN60.ZIP	33899	VIRUSCAN Network Version V60 (03-18-90)
NEWVIRUS.ZIP	4151	Warning on New virus
NOBRAIN.C	19343	Cure brain virus - in C source code
NOTROJIS.ZIP	4271	Coombes' essay on NOTROJ.COM
NOVIRUS3.ZIP	33870	NOVIRUS V3, sent by author to SPACE BBS
NOVIRUSC.ZIP	8674	Virus checker. .C source
OCT13VIR.ZIP	8709	Text file on viruses
PASS.ZIP	34338	OK PC PASSWORD PROTECTION
PASSWORD.ZIP	4783	Locks your computer from unwanted users.
PASSWRD.ZIP	10209	Computer Access Security System, v.1.42S
PCLOK22A.ZIP	61189	hard disk protection system
PCPASS12.ZIP	46461	Password protect your PC with this one!
PCPROTCT.ZIP	5412	Reviews of anti-virus software
PCRYPT20.ZIP	18035	ProCrypt v2.0: text file encryption
PENECILN.ZIP	12321	Prevent Viruses on Atari ST's.
PIRATED.ZIP	3057	List of all known pirated files on bbs's
PKSCRYPT.ZIP	31395	Public key crypto program
PKTROJAN.ZIP	1769	trojan alert doc.
PROCRC11.ZIP	14115	Sam Smith's CRC Checker version 1.1
PSK306.ZIP	94259	PassKey v3.06: PC Security system
PSWRD.ZIP	6383	simple password program w/source
RACK_F.ZIP	57599	AT security pgm v1.00;EGA/VGA & ANSI
SCANRS61.ZIP	29651	Resident Version of VIRUSCAN (03-18-90)
SCANV61.ZIP	44482	VIRUSCAN System Scanner (03-18-90)
SEELY.ZIP	36965	Paper on the Unix worm, with some source
SENTINEL.ZIP	11494	Virus checker
SENTRY02.ZIP	11519	Virus detector
SM.ZIP	53671	Secure Menu 1.0 password protect your
SNOOPER.ZIP	7730	Uncover messages hidden in program
STOP.ZIP	6269	Virus protection w/ ASM source
STOP1.ZIP	4329	trojan stopper software
SUG-TROJ.ZIP	3671	SOFTGUARD UNPROTECT IS REALLY A VIRUS!
SUGWARN.ZIP	1107	Warning about very dangerous program
SYSCHK11.ZIP	9733	Check CRC of sys & command files on boot

SYSLOCK.ZIP	15770	A SYSTEM PROTECT PROGAM
TIMELOCK.ZIP	38171	Locks keyboard after settable time
TL151.ZIP	46913	TimeLock your keyboard after inactivity
TPL603.ZIP	75548	File encryption to keep data private
TPSCHK11.ZIP	17142	Make TP 4+ Programs Viral Aware 2/5/90
TRAPDISK.ZIP	5584	GREAT VIRUS DETECTION..
TRICK12.ZIP	6737	Some ways trojans get into your systems
TROJ2.ZIP	2638	Trojan Uploader gets caught redhanded
TROJHI-Q.ZIP	6143	Another Softguard trojan? HI-Q program
UNIXWORM.ZIP	13417	Arpanet mail describing the worm/virus
UNVIRUS.ZIP	19401	Remove around 7 known viruses.
UNVIRUS6.ZIP	19738	Israeli program to fight Israeli viruses
VACINE13.ZIP	14349	Anti-viral precautionary
VALIDAT3.ZIP	3385	VALIDATE v0.3:file authentication pgm
VB_110.ZIP	26643	Israeli VirusBuster program v1.10
VC101.ZIP	4764	Virus protection for DOS
VGUIDE.ZIP	9326	guide to computer viruses - ray glath
VIR-ALRT.ZIP	4655	New virus Alert -- The WOW virus
VIRPAPER.ZIP	14691	Scholarly report on viruses by S. Kiel
VIRSCAN.ZIP	8293	IBM Virus Scan program
VIRUS.ZIP	5432	Info on Virus-programs
VIRUSCAN.ZIP	16490	Virus detector from J. McAfee.
VIRUSCK.ZIP	18510	Checks for viruses
VIRUSDOC.ZIP	5548	interesting discussion on "viruses"
VIRUSST2.ZIP	7334	Good TSR virus stopper pgm -ver 2.
VIRUSTXT.ZIP	12227	IEEE Paper on Viri
VIRUSX16.ZIP	12235	New version of the BEST virus checker
VIRZIP12.ZIP	17596	Check for virus inside of Zip files
VL3-3139.ZIP	98151	Virus-L Digest, vol3, nos 31-39.
VL8903E.ZIP	21000	Virus Log, March 1989
VSTOP54.ZIP	30247	stop virus infections from occuring
VSUM9002.ZIP	28354	Merry Hughes' Virus summary
VSUM9003.ZIP	28966	Current Virus Information Summmary
VTAC41.ZIP	21245	VTAC v4.10: a TSR environment security
VTECH.ZIP	33747	Virus protection
WARN.ZIP	2290	Warning text on TROJAN file NORTSHOT
XSNOOP.ZIP	15794	Security utility that's disguised as DOS

These are just some of the many programs in The Wires designed to keep track of harmful programs. In addition, there are text files that make people aware of new viruses, suspect programs, and the like. The online community is very alert and news travels fast. When a new virus is discovered, the word is spread from system to system, making users aware of programs to be wary of. Whatever program or system you might elect to use, be aware that while viruses do exist, there are Shareware programs available to help you avoid infecting your system.

## CHAPTER TWENTY-FIVE

Dr. File Finder's Personal Picks

Throughout this book you have encountered the phrase, "software is a matter of taste." How you view a piece of software will depend on your point of view, your needs, and expectations you may not even be aware of consciously. In a telephone conversation with John Dvorak about the VDE editor, for example, we bantered excitedly back and forth about the "neat" things it could do. Another friend, however, didn't seem to share in our excitement and, instead, cited some features he thought were missing.

In discussing software programs I have tried to maintain my objectivity. All the programs mentioned are excellent. There is no one product that is the best in a category, since what is best will always depend on what you think is best. With that in mind, let me clarify the purpose of this chapter.

MAKING A CAREER OUT OF SOFTWARE

Over the course of the last seven and a half years, much of my time has been dedicated to studying Shareware as well as commercial software. This research has included finding, testing, and comparing programs that perform similar functions, as well as promoting the exceptional programs so people can be aware of them. This research has also involved visiting thousands of bulletin boards to determine what other users want or feel they need in a program. This information is passed on to numerous Shareware programmers so new and better programs can be created, benefiting all of us. Since no one pays me, I consider my work to be as unbiased and honest as I can make it. I test programs thoroughly and I'm very proud that computer users around the world have come to respect my opinions, particularly on Shareware. In the course of reviewing programs, I am frequently asked one question: "What program do you use?"

Many people often want to know what Shareware programs I use personally—which utilities, editor, communications program, and so on. If it happens that I don't use a certain type of program, people want to know which one I *would* use if I were going to use such a program. Since I am asked this question so often, this chapter will address this topic. In almost every category, the programs in this chapter have been discussed or mentioned elsewhere in the book. Here I will simply note the programs with an explanation as to why I chose them over others. In a few instances, there are types of programs mentioned that I do not personally use. In these cases, I recommend the ones I would use based on features, ease of use, and so on. When it comes to good Shareware, you have to decide for yourself which program is best for you.

APPLICATIONS PROGRAMS

This first section discusses application-type programs: communications, editors, databases, and so on. You'll recognize many of the programs I use, but some smaller ones are covered here for the first time.

Communications Program—Qmodem

Having tried all of the programs in the communications category, in my opinion Qmodem has the most solid internal file transfer protocols. This conclusion is based on testing and experience. Qmodem is a fine program that is constantly being improved by John Friel, who is dedicated to his program.

Many new features were added with the release of version 4.0 and still more with version 4.1. Version 4.2 introduced internal Zmodem, the BEW (batch entry window) for doing uploads, dynamic configuration options, and complete online help. Since I'm a Qmodem alpha tester, I do know that Friel is steadily working toward the exciting release of Qmodem 5.

Editing Chores

For some time I have used QEdit by Sammy Mitchell because of its configuration capabilities. Unlike other editors, with QEdit you can define keys to be what you want them to be. It also has other excellent features including a built-in menu, column blocks, box drawing, multiple windows, and now even a TSR version. QEdit is a good, solid editor with features that most people want. I have used QEdit to work with thousands of notes and documents.

Another program I use is VDE by Eric Meyer. By default, VDE uses the WordStar command set. It is the only Shareware editor that I have ever seen that can create double-spacing inside a document. I also like the fact that printing codes can easily be inserted into text so italics, bold, and underlining can be added. Instead of loading a word processor to add special touches to quick letters, I now use VDE, which has macros, windows, special formatting, and printing options.

Database — PC-File

After trying both commercial and Shareware databases, I prefer PC-File, by ButtonWare. It is easy to use, supports a mouse, and provides a variety of options. PC-File allows users to perform quick and simple procedures or design a fancy input screen. PC-File is easy to use and gently guides you through the program.

Spreadsheet Programs

I have used and evaluated both commercial and Shareware spreadsheets but at the present time have no need for a spreadsheet program. In the past I used As-Easy-As by Trius, which is simple to use yet filled with features. In many cases, the program can use Lotus .WKS templates that are often found on bulletin boards and commercial online networks. As-Easy-As can perform complex calculations and it is fast.

Menu and Shell Programs

By nature I am not one to use a program with a menu or shell, although I recognize the usefulness of such programs. My experience with these programs was strictly from the standpoint of testing and evaluating, but I never had either a menu or a shell program for personal use. After letting other people use my Northgate 386 computer on occasion, I have seen more of a need for a menu. (*smile*) A good menu makes it easy for others to access programs while making it easy for you to keep them away from things you don't want them to access.

A good shell program can also be useful when working with large numbers of files. As noted in the course of the book, there are programs that are strictly menu programs, others that are strictly DOS shell programs, and a few that are a combination of each. To be fair, I'll tell which one I use in each of these three categories.

4DOS

4DOS stands alone as a menu and shell program, which has many features missing from DOS. For example, 4DOS lets you see the names of files as they are deleted, giving you a chance to see if you deleted a file you hadn't intended to delete. You can also see if files are being copied or moved to where you want them to be moved.

The 4DOS "aliases" are spectacular, as are the enhanced batch file commands, built-in log function, and timer. You can also alter colors, create menus, and more. 4DOS picks up where DOS leaves off, giving you a complete package, including online help. If only half of its functions are used, you're still ahead, which is why I use it.

Menu Program—HDM IV

In the category of menu programs I like HDM IV by Jim Hass. It has a nice presentation, many configurable options, and usage logging. I appreciate its ability to run programs at designated times, making it very handy for optimizing drives while you're sleeping. HDM is fast, easy to use, and has good mouse support. The author is constantly improving the program and giving it more features. It is an excellent menu system for both home or business use. I have HDM IV running on two of my machines.

Shell Program—The Director

For a straight DOS shell program the modular approach of The Director, by Dan Baumbach, in my opinion provides the most flexibility. The main module, DL, is an excellent DOS shell. It's configurable, has mouse support, and offers all of the things that most people would want in a DOS shell. The small module, DB, is great for working in individual directories. For those times when I want an overview of everything on my system, the DA module provides that. The Director appears to have been carefully thought out and its author works to keep improving it. In one way or another, The Director is used on all my machines.

Menu and Shell—dCOM

On my frequently used Northgate 386, I use dCOM. The Directory Commander, or dCOM, by Dave Frailey, is in my opinion the best possible combination of a shell and menu program. Because dCOM has its own powerful macro language, it's extremely flexible when creating menus. This makes it easy to set up menus that can be used by someone who knows nothing about computers. I can track usage with dCOM's logging abilities. Another likable feature is that you can lock anyone out of the shell functions, thus eliminating the possibility of someone logging in and accidentally wiping out a directory.

The power of the menus is astounding. The macro language lets you prompt for input, gives a list of possible selections, and much more. Since the functions have been carefully integrated, you can tag and move files one second and select an item off a menu the next. For my needs, dCOM provides everything in one great package.

Background Mail

In this busy world we often spend our time playing phone tag with one another. BackMail, by Alethic Software, has eliminated this problem for me by handling electronic mail and files. Friends and associates who also use BackMail can send me messages while I keep on working. You don't need a multitasking environment to take advantage of BackMail since it's designed to work in the background. You can pop into BackMail, read a message, write a quick reply, and go back to what you were doing while BackMail takes care of delivering your reply. If you leave your machine for awhile and a message comes in, you'll see the message "You have new mail" on the screen. It's a complete "point to point" mail system that is excellent for use among friends or in any business environment.

Personal Notes

For keeping notes or jotting down random thoughts, I use Notebook. You can keep multiple folders that can be password protected. Whenever a password is used, the folder is encrypted upon closing. You can even use it as a place to store your passwords for other files, so the only password you need remember is the one to access your Notebook folder. (*smile*)

UTILITY PROGRAMS

The last section of this chapter deals with some of the utility programs that I use. Once again, the utility programs you use will be governed by the things you do. The utilities I use suit my needs the best, based on features and performance.

PSEARCH—for Finding Text in Files

There are times when I want to find text located within files and see the text in context. PSEARCH, by Norm Patriquin, suits my needs in this area. I can search multiple drives, look for multiple strings of text, all very quickly. PSEARCH can also be made to search the entire system, to do a case-sensitive search, and to exclude certain types of files. I have used PSEARCH for years, and it performs all the important search functions while retaining speed.

File Finding—DFF

For finding files quickly anywhere on my system, I use DFF by Dan Doman. I've tested and timed all of the other find programs and DFF is consistently faster. To be fair, DFF does *not* look inside packed files, which is one factor that slows down other utilities in the same category. On programs where this feature can be toggled off, DFF is still a bit faster. For a find utility that can look into packed files, the two fastest seem to be PKZoom by Douglas Hay and NJFIND by Nifty James (Mike Blaszczak).

Compression Programs

It is difficult today to get by with just one of the file compression programs. My personal favorites are PKZIP and PKUNZIP by Phil Katz's PKWARE. The ZIP programs offer very good compression and excellent speed. I also keep PAK, by NoGate Consulting, for unpacking .PAK and .ARC files, and to create self-extracting (SFX) files. The same is true for LHarc, which I use to unpack .LZH files and occasionally for creating SFX files. I have a copy of the latest version of ZOO on a floppy disk just in case I have to unpack a .ZOO format file. For daily use, however, I use PKZIP and PKUNZIP.

Viewing Compressed Files—FV

To determine the contents of a compressed file, I use Vern Buerg's FV (File View). FV is fast and tells you what program was used to pack the file. In addition, FV is used by LIST PLUS for the ViewArc function, so you can view the contents of packed files from within LIST PLUS.

Compressed Files—Viewing Documentation

For scanning the documentation of compressed files without having to unpack them, I use ZIPTV by Samuel Smith. ZIPTV lists the contents of a compressed file and allows you to read through the files. You can scan through READ.ME, .TXT, and documentation files without having to unpack a compressed file. In working with so many programs, I find this a particularly handy and timesaving program.

Keyboard Enhancer — KBFIX

To enhance a keyboard, I haven't found anything better than KBFIX by Skip Gelbrecht. KBFIX will increase the typematic rate, repeat rate, amount of delay, and more. KBFIX can adjust the function of the CAPS LOCK key, increase the size of the keyboard buffer, and be loaded into high memory. KBFIX is a solid utility that combines the functions of several utilities and still only uses about 2K of RAM. It does everything I need and does it well without compatibility problems.

Remind/Prompt Program — LCG/Remind

As a reminder to back up the hard disks, or for prompting me to load a program, I use LCG/Remind by the Levin Consulting Group. I like the way LCG/Remind displays its reminders and the information about my system it provides in conjunction with a reminder, such as how much disk space is free, percentage of files not backed up, and so on. If only 3 percent of the files on your system aren't backed up, for example, you may not want to take the time to do a full backup. LCG/Remind lets you make the choice.

Formatting Program — FormatMaster

For formatting disks of all sizes, I use FormatMaster by John Newlin and New-Ware. FormatMaster has an agreeable interface, is configurable, and formats 360K disks to 800K on a 1.2 meg drive. Other options include making a system disk, putting on a volume label, "cycling" a drive while you format several disks, and so on. FormatMaster works on a wide variety of machines, is fast, has excellent error checking, and even has mouse support. Carefully programmed, FormatMaster is upgraded to keep pace with new BIOS and DOS versions.

DOS Command Editor — Anarkey

Anarkey 3.0, by Steve Calwas and Moderne Software, is an excellent DOS command line editor that offers AKAs and other features like command line completion and execution, a history buffer, and now, mouse support. It can also use EMS, which allows Anarkey to use almost no DOS RAM, while similar programs may use 10K to 12K or more.

Anarkey also lets you change the default command sequences, write the history buffer to a file, and more. From the standpoint of features and lack of RAM consumption, I feel that Anarkey 3.0 is the one to beat.

DOCTOR'S NOTE

In the course of this chapter, you may have noticed what seems to be a contradiction. I stated earlier that I use 4DOS, which has aliases, and now I've also said I use Anarkey, which has AKAs—in essence, the same thing. (Aliases, AKAs, and synonyms are commands that you define to carry out complex operations. These are discussed in Chapter 17.) I generally test programs without the presence of 4DOS, however, I still like to have my "aliases a la AKAs" on my system. Thus, when I remove 4DOS to test programs, I use Anarkey 3.0 to provide me with its AKA functions and DOS command line editing. When I reinstall 4DOS to test programs in its environment, I use the 4DOS alias feature. The alias file and the AKA file are nearly identical in content, but are formatted to meet the needs of the individual programs. You have to be flexible. (*smile*)

Overall Utility—Professional Master Key

When it comes to editing disk sectors and individual program sectors, and erasing stubborn files, I use Professional Master Key (PMK) from Public Brand Software. I like PMK's interface and find it easy to use. It's also excellent for altering file attributes, undeleting files, and so on. I use PMK primarily for its Disk Edit and File Edit functions and occasionally to remove a file from my system.

Another part of the PMK package I use is the Full Screen File Sort, which puts files in a specified order on the disk and eliminates erased files through a command similar to:

```
C>FS C:\ /PACK
```

Once I've sorted the files in the root directory of drive C and have written the changes to disk, the directory is "packed." This means that all erased files have been removed.

LIST PLUS

Vern Buerg's LIST is a program I've used for years. I really don't know how I'd get along without it. I use LIST for searching through documentation to find items in a hurry. Now, with LIST PLUS, I can delete the file when I'm finished, or move it off to another directory to examine later in more detail. When one considers that nearly every Shareware program has documentation and other supplementary text files, I don't know how anyone can get by without a copy of LIST. It's excellent for finding information in any file by searching forward or backward. It can view files with high bit characters, filter out junk characters, and it has mouse support. Considering the volume of text I read each day, I can't imagine using DOS's TYPE command to do it. In my opinion, LIST is a must-have utility.

General Printing—PPRINT

For printing with either the Panasonic KX-P1124 dot matrix printer or the Panasonic KX-P4450 laser printer, I use Norm Patriquin's PPRINT. This printing utility has so many options that Patriquin suggests you only bother learning the ones you need. You can format text to be printed, make it double-spaced, put it in bold print, and much more. PPRINT may well be the best overall printing utility available supporting dot matrix and laser printers. Its flexibility is the reason I use it.

Keyboard Macros—NewKey

In creating keyboard macros, I use NewKey by Frank Bell and FAB Software. NewKey supports multicharacter macros, fixed fields, variable fields, pauses, and descriptions for each macro you define. NewKey is as powerful as any of the commercial macro programs and more powerful than any other Shareware macro program. With three modules, you have your choice of features depending on how much RAM you have available.

NewKey helped me create some spectacular macros that were of great help to me in writing this book. You can even call up macros from within batch files, which you can't do with any other macro program. NewKey is efficient and offers me everything I could want from a macro program.

Organization—The Folders System

When using PC-Write by Quicksoft, I use The Folders System written by Robert Allen. There is also a Folders interface for WordPerfect and Microsoft Word. What I like best about The Folders System is that I can enter a meaningful description for a new file. DOS filenames can be strange, especially if you try to give them some meaning. With The Folders System, I can enter something like "Letter to Lisa of 04/24/90 re:book" and never have to guess about the contents of a file. The Folders System has an easy-to-use format, keeps like files in individual folders of your choosing, and makes it easy to find exactly the file you want to work with. I've used the WordPerfect and Microsoft Word versions of The Folders System and both work very well. Programs like The Folders System can save you a lot of headaches when working with documents.

Screen Blanker—BURNOUT

To protect my monitor screens, I use BURNOUT. I like this program because, unlike most screen blankers, BURNOUT is a device driver that is loaded from the CONFIG.SYS file. Its parameters can be changed using a .COM file that comes with the package. This gives me flexibility—I can turn the blanker off, extend the time before the screen blanks, and so on.

For Sorting Data—SORTF

To sort the contents of files I use SORTF by Vern Buerg. SORTF is fast and allows for a wide range of sort criteria on many fields. SORTF will automatically prompt for an input filename and an output filename. It's the best sort program I've found thus far.

For Filling Diskettes — FILL

For getting the most from my floppy disks I use FILL, by Jean LaLonde, which fills each disk to its maximum capacity. FILL will calculate the space that a given number of files will require and then copy them to floppies so all the disk space is utilized. I often end up with disks that have 0 bytes free. Since I have so many programs in storage on floppies, it's important to me not to waste any space. FILL takes care of that for me and does a great job.

STACKEY

I use STACKEY, by Barry Simon and Rick Wilson, for a number of tasks including loading the keyboard buffer with keystrokes that I want passed to another program. With STACKEY I can insert pauses or delays and pass just about any keyboard key to a program. I can also halt the processing by pressing a hot key. STACKEY can reboot the computer and control the cursor, the EGA and VGA palettes, the length and tone of a beep, and much more. STACKEY does so many useful things that I can't describe them all here. I use it on my machine many times a day to make my work easier.

SUMMING IT ALL UP

These are some of the Shareware programs that are on my system. As mentioned earlier, the ones you decide to use will depend in part on your needs and on your own personal tastes. There are many excellent programs available in Shareware, many of which you simply won't find in the commercial arena. Shareware programs provide good quality software at good prices. Now you know some of the Shareware programs that I use. Take a good look at the abundance of quality programs that are available. Test and compare them. When you find those that meet your needs, remember to register them with their authors.

## CHAPTER TWENTY-SIX

Some Personal Thoughts and Observations

This wraps up our survey of the world of Shareware. Although each and every program Shareware has to offer has not been covered, you have taken a look at some of the latest and greatest. There are many more exciting things Shareware has to offer, and I hope you will continue to read and learn about them. I hope that you've enjoyed this trek as much as I have enjoyed being your guide.

The tens of thousands of Shareware programs are greater in number and diversity than any other source of programs for your system. Besides being a lot cheaper, they are much more fun and of excellent quality. Think of this book on Shareware as a journey and yourself as a traveler. You've followed the road and looked at some of the interesting things closest to the roadside; there is much more to explore beyond.

It is my sincere hope that this book will be one of the catalysts needed to get Shareware the recognition it deserves in the media and user community. At the same time that this book was completed, a nationwide survey of thousands of Shareware users indicated that a high percentage of them read the leading computer magazines, yet most of the leading computer magazines do not have regular columns on Shareware.

Many sources for information on Shareware, such as catalogs from disk vendors, don't provide enough coverage about Shareware's history and what Shareware is and isn't. I've made a point of filling in these gaps for you, while pointing out some of Shareware's most interesting aspects and offerings.

From its simple beginnings, Shareware has continued to grow. Shareware has become one of the fastest growing segments of the computer industry. As Shareware becomes more and more a part of mainstream computing, users will need to know more about it. You can now join me in showing the others the way.

A BRIEF LOOK BACK

In the course of the book, you've also seen the various ways in which you can obtain Shareware software: through disk vendors and PC user groups, or via online networks and bulletin boards. Your travels actually took you into The Wires. Here you examined the process of going online, from logging onto GEnie to visiting a bulletin board. The most popular file transfer protocols, uploading, and downloading were also discussed. Along the way, you learned a few tricks and some ways to save time and money. In another part of your journey you saw some of the very best programs that are available in Shareware, in a wide range of categories.

You examined editors, communications programs, file utilities, hard disk programs, DOS shells, and a large number of utility programs. You looked at compression programs, databases, programming aids, games, educational programs, spreadsheets, business and financial programs, interesting text files, files to use with care, and disk protection programs. Yet, from the very beginning, I did not want this to be a "catalog"—with a few lines about each program. You not only looked at the key features and functions of a program, but what the programs are and why you might want them. For just a moment now, I'd like to share a few personal thoughts with you.

THOUGHTS ON SHAREWARE

While it has been a tremendous amount of work, I'm glad I was given the opportunity to do this book. Each of us can look at our lives and see certain high points—things that stand above all the rest. Working on this project has been one of those high points for me. Having studied, compared, and promoted Shareware programs for so many years, I wanted to share that knowledge with you.

As was mentioned very early in the book, there are so many Shareware programs available that it can be difficult to decide what to get. With so many programs to choose from in so many categories, it can be overwhelming. You can waste a lot of time and money obtaining programs that are not as good as they might be. All of the programs you've looked at here are good. They are of good quality and contain the features and functions that most users want. The authors of Shareware programs take pride in their work and provide quality products. The variety is so great that you can often find things in Shareware you will not be able to find anywhere else. Remember that when you need a program to do a particular task. In the long run, Shareware can save you money while providing you with what you need.

On the Lighter Side

For you trivia buffs out there it occurred to my coauthor, Nick Anis, and me, that you might like to know about some of the more trivial things involved in doing a book of this size. Here are a few trivial facts.

In the course of doing the book I went through four printer ribbons on the Panasonic KX-P1124 printer, which was used primarily for printing out the screens that were used as figures in the the book. Those figures take a lot of ink. The Panasonic laser printer printed out most of the chapters and is still on its first bottle of toner. Over 2,500 sheets of paper were used to do all of the printing involved. I had to have a workstation built that is 14 feet long, complete with cupboards, in order to organize everything in my office. Our phone bills stopped coming in the regular envelopes and started coming in large manila ones instead. We believe that the value of phone company stock has risen at least four percentage points because of this. (*smile*)

I have received hundreds of Shareware programs in the mail. These arrived in floppy mailers, Federal Express envelopes, U.S. post office

"Next Day" mail envelopes, manila envelopes, and even in boxes. Some authors took no chances, packing their programs and manuals with styrofoam peanuts to protect them. The disks are being filed in a special disk box—I may recycle all of the paper through a company that buys paper.

Out in The Wires, I have received thousands of messages on bulletin boards and online networks. My office is now referred to, quite affectionately, as "The Cave" by all who know me. I only eat once a day, but I do drink a lot of Pepsi. Nick eats a lot of fast food. For those who want to know, I shave off my beard every April and start growing it again in August. The picture on the cover was taken on April 2, 1990, and I shaved off the beard, leaving the moustache, on April 4th. We hope some of these facts will be of interest to you, or at least make you smile. Some of it seems pretty funny to us, now that it's over.

Accessibility

I want to know what you think. I want to be accessible to you. If you have questions about Shareware software, I want you to be able to ask me those questions. If you have comments about the book, I'd like to hear those too. If you are a programmer with a program you'd like me to look at, I'd like to see it.

Once again I'll refer you to Appendix C. There you'll find some bulletin boards that are marked as places where you can leave me notes. I will answer your notes. Another excellent place to leave messages for me is on GEnie. My GEnie mail ID is DR-FF. If you ever visit GEnie's Chat Lines my handle is < =Guitarman= >. If you see me there, stop by and say "Hi." If you are a Shareware programmer and would like me to see your work, you'll need an address. If you just want to write to ask a question or to make a comment about the book, you'll need one too. I do not assume that everyone has a modem. (*smile*) You can write me at the following address:

Dr. File Finder
P.O. Box 591
Elizabeth, CO 80107

I can't promise I will answer all my mail because I don't know how much mail I'll get. (I've never broken a promise, so I never make a promise unless I know I can keep it.) I *can* promise that I will try to answer all of it. I will read all the mail I receive, and if I can, I'll send out a reply.

Final Thoughts

I hope you've enjoyed what you've read and have learned a few things. It has truly been a labor of love for me. The enthusiasm in the computer community has been gratifying. The response of Shareware authors and users alike has been a real motivation and an inspiration. I'll leave you to explore the world of Shareware. Be well . . . and take care.

## PART FIVE

Appendixes

Hardware and Software Used

In Chapters 10 through 26, a wide variety of good Shareware programs was discussed. Each program was examined in some detail so you'd have an idea of how it should run. I say "should" because software can sometimes be very temperamental, depending on the environment under which it's run.

In the course of beta testing many different programs over the years, mysterious problems have always been a source of wonder to me. For example, a group of us might be testing Program X and none of us will have any problems with the program except one person. As it usually turns out, that one person was running a TSR no one else had, or had a system that was configured a bit differently. On rare occasions, it turned out that he or she was running an unusual version of DOS. In the end, these problems are always resolved.

What makes a problem like this particularly frustrating is that none of the other beta testers can duplicate the problem. The solution is generally reached by determining what the one person with the problem has that is different from the rest of us.

You will most likely be able to run every program discussed in this book without any problems. If you do have problems, the first thing to do is check to make sure that you are meeting the requirements of the program. Look at the documentation carefully. If a program says that it needs DOS 3.*x* and above to run, then it will not work with DOS 2.1. With some programs—games, for example—you may need a specific type of graphics card. When a program's documentation says it needs at least 256K of RAM to run, it probably won't work with just 175K. If it does, you may run into problems because there isn't enough RAM for the program to do all that it's supposed to do. This may cause your machine to lock up or other problems. The majority of problems related to running programs can be attributed to the user not reading the documentation. Save yourself headaches by at least skimming through the documentation. As you do, look for answers to some of the following questions:

- Does the program specify a version of DOS?

- Do any environmental variables need to be set?

- Do you need a specific graphics adapter?

- Does the documentation mention a minimum amount of RAM?

- Is there a configuration file that needs to be in the same directory as the executable program (usually a .CFG or .CNF file)?

- Does the program have to be in the DOS PATH?

These are just some of the more common program requirements. As you gain more experience, you'll know what to look for. How can I be so sure that you will be able to use the programs I've discussed (assuming, that is, that your system meets the requirements of the program)? Because I've tested these programs under a wide range of conditions including different versions of DOS, on various machines, and with a variety of display adapters. I want you to know what hardware and software was used so you'll be able to eliminate as many factors as possible if you have problems.

SPEAKING OF DOS

I have used several versions of DOS including:

- MS-DOS 2.11
- PC-DOS 3.10
- MS-DOS 3.21
- MS-DOS 3.30
- PC-DOS 3.30
- MS-DOS 4.01

To clarify how programs were tested, let me give an example. If a program required DOS 3.10, it was tested with every version of DOS greater than 3.10. As an example, the Professional Master Key (PMK) program, version 3.0, worked with every version of DOS *except* 4.01. Meanwhile, the author of PMK released version 3.10, which does work with DOS 4.01. Since Professional Master Key 3.10 became the current version, it was the version chosen to be discussed. Since PMK 3.10 requires DOS 2.*x* and above, it was tested with every version of DOS greater than the version the program requires.

This is true of every program discussed in this book. In each case, the most current version of a program was used, tested under several versions of DOS, and also tested on a variety of machines.

Hardware Configurations

Another factor to consider when running software is the kind of machine that it will run on. I used machines with different kinds of BIOS and also with different clock speeds to see how the programs performed. Many games, for example, aren't as much fun on a 386 because the games move too fast. In battle games, for instance, the target may move too quickly to shoot at it. Programs designed to slow down faster machines as you play can be found in Shareware.

The next section describes the machines used for testing and what I think of each machine as well. The machines that were used include

- Tandy 1000 with 4.77 MHz clock, monochrome and CGA monitors

- Tandy 1000 with SX 7.18 MHz clock, CGA monitor

- AT clone with 12 MHz clock, monochrome and VGA monitors

- GRiD 386 laptop with 12 MHz clock, gas plasma display, and CGA monitor

- Northgate 386 with 20 MHz clock, 4 megabytes RAM, VGA monitor

These machines represent a fairly wide range of capabilities, from clock speed to processor type. Note how the speeds range from 4.77 MHz on the Tandy 8088 machine all the way to 20 MHz on the Northgate 386. In discussing these machines, I've included my opinions to help you in selecting equipment to run your software.

THE TANDY 1000s

Tandy 1000s are IBM PC clone machines, and very few difficulties were experienced with either of the Tandys used. The Tandy 1000 with a 4.77 MHz clock is one of the original 1000 series machines and is still running with all of its original equipment. Considering the price paid for it nearly eight years ago, and the beating it has taken in testing programs, it has held up remarkably well. The same can be said for the Tandy 1000 SX, which is four years old. To date, there has been no program written for the IBM that could not be run on either of the Tandy machines.

It should be noted that there is a difference in the Tandy BIOS, and the biggest effect is on the Tandy keyboard. Some programs specifying certain BIOS functions on the IBM will alter some of the keys on the Tandy keyboard. This is extremely rare today, but a few programs, written around 1985, will cause this problem. Once a fairly large number of Tandy 1000s came into use, programmers altered their programming styles to accommodate the small differences in the Tandy BIOS.

THE NORTHGATE 386

The Northgate 386, produced by Northgate Computer Systems, is an excellent machine. The one used for testing is a 386 with a 20 MHz clock. It has 4 megabytes of RAM on the motherboard and is expandable up to 16 megabytes. A VGA graphics card and monitor complete the system.

The machine comes packed as if it could withstand a nuclear blast. Directions accompanying the machine are clear and concise. From packing carton to desk, the Northgate machine was very easy to set up, and it came configured exactly the way I ordered it.

Northgate advertises that they have good technical support and they aren't kidding. I know because I called them and pretended to be a new user. I spoke with Tim Paterson in tech support and told him I wanted to repartition a large drive into two equal size drives. He was understanding and patient in walking me through the steps from beginning to end. He told me not only what to do, but even what prompts to expect and how to respond to each one. A novice would have had no problems following his clear and concise directions. A hearty *bravo* for Northgate's tech support—it's the best I've found to date.

A Close-up of the Northgate 386

The instructions and manuals that accompany the Northgate machine are concise and easy to read. The machine itself is solidly built; an inside examination shows you it was assembled with care. Cables are tucked out of the way, yet separated enough so you can easily trace their origins and points of insertion. A small manual with a map of the motherboard is the best I've ever seen, and it made it easy to find every switch and chip. Sets of DIP switches are clearly labeled, and there is no fine print to read. The entire machine exudes a sense of quality.

What About Performance?

What is there to say about the performance of the Northgate 386 except that it runs smoothly and is a superb machine? The OmniKey Plus keyboard is superior in quality and has an excellent feel. You can even adjust the typematic rate from the keyboard. You can speed it up or slow it down, until it's exactly the way you want it. The action is crisp and makes other keyboards feel like typing on oatmeal.

The machine has been on continuously since the day it arrived. It has been rebooted, but never powered down. The hard disk came formatted with the version of DOS I requested. There was a C:\DOS directory with all of the DOS files included, and another directory containing some good utility programs. Considering the price of Northgate systems, the quality of the machines, the high level of performance, the high level of technical support, and the special touches Northgate provides, it is easy to say that they are a good, solid investment. I like this one so well that I plan on getting another one. If you're in the market for a computer, check out the product line from Northgate Computer Systems—I highly recommend it!

THE PANASONIC KX-P1124 PRINTER

Panasonic's KX-P1124 dot matrix printer is a real workhorse if you're doing a lot of printing. It has both the Epson and IBM character sets available, as well as 13 international character sets. There are six basic printing pitches available:

- Pica (10 cpi)

- Elite (12 cpi)

- Micron (15 cpi)

- Compressed (17 cpi)

- Elite compressed (20 cpi)

- Proportional

The KX-P1124 averages 192 characters per second in Draft-Elite pitch. The overall speed is increased by bidirectional printing and has a quiet mode. Paper can be loaded from the front, the back, or underneath the printer. With all of the printing styles available, you can combine fonts, pitches, and features such as double height, double width, and so on, to create more than 5,500 different print styles.

The KX-P1124 in Action

The KX-P1124 has what is called a "small footprint" so it fits easily on a workstation. It features both push and pull tractor feed, memo load, perforation cut, and micro line feed. This printer from Panasonic can use continuous fanfold paper or single sheets, and does envelopes easily. You can even print envelopes without having to remove the fanfold paper.

This printer also comes with a 6K internal buffer you can upgrade to a 32K buffer, giving you a total buffer size of 38K. All of the printer functions, pitches, and so on, are easily accessible from the panel on the front. There are also several Shareware printer control programs available supporting both the Epson and IBM modes. These programs are found as PAN1124E.ZIP, PAN1124I.ZIP, and PAN4.ZIP. The manual says that the print head is good for 100 million characters in draft mode.

Impressions of the KX-P1124

In comparison to similar printers, this printer is rugged and durable, and sells for a good price. I know it's durable because I've really put it through its paces in writing this book. Besides printing the manuscript, it was also used to print the graphic images that were submitted as the figures for this book. I've used many other printers and I'm sold on the line of printers from Panasonic.

THE GRID 386 LAPTOP

The 386 laptop, from GRiD Systems Corporation, is a powerhouse. The one used for testing has a 12 MHz clock, a 20 megabyte hard disk, and a 1.44 meg floppy drive. The machine has 640K of conventional RAM and 384K of extended memory. Using QEMM by Quarterdeck Office Systems, I was able to not only "back fill" the DOS RAM so I had 652K of conventional memory, but I also had 800K of expanded memory besides.

GRiD'S Features

The GRiD 386 laptop has a battery pack as well as an AC converter. GRiD provides some special MODE commands so you can reduce power usage while running on batteries. For example, if you were going to edit a document, you could set a MODE command that would shut down the hard disk after so many minutes. There is another MODE command so the machine runs at a slower speed, thereby conserving power. Finally, there is a special screen *blanker* for the gas plasma display, which will clear the screen after a number of minutes of inactivity.

The GRiDCASE, Model 1530, has every kind of adapter you could possibly want. It comes with two phone jacks for use with the internal modem, serial and parallel ports, a video display port for attaching an external monitor, a keyboard port for an external keyboard, and a spot to plug in the AC power supply. For office use, you could hook it up to a full-size monitor and keyboard. If you want to work outside, just unplug it, pick the unit up, and go. It's a convenient way to have a desktop and portable system all in one.

Above and Beyond the Call

When I had some questions regarding the GRiDCASE 1530, the people at the GRiD office in Denver gave me superb service. Maynard Kealiher, a systems engineer, went above and beyond the call of duty. Learning that my home was such a long distance from their office, he actually met me at a location that was less than half the distance I would have had to drive. Kealiher was very helpful, answered all my questions, and gave me some handy tips on using the machine. I told him that I would not forget his extra special service and I haven't. So, "Thanks, Maynard!"

Evaluating the GRiD

The GRiD is a rugged machine with all the features anyone could want in a portable computer, or for that matter, in a full-sized computer. With all of its many ports, it can easily be used for both. Its case is tough enough to withstand banging around in airports or the trunk of a car.

The GRiD laptop is easy to use and the keyboard has a nice feel to it. Once I got used to some of the various key combinations, I could type as fast on the GRiD as I could on any of my other machines. The gas plasma display is very clear and easy on the eyes. The display even has a brightness control. The manual is quite detailed, and whenever necessary, pictures are used so you fully understand where everything is located on the machine. All of your options are clearly explained.

If you are looking for a solid, dependable laptop, with many add-on options, take a look at the machines offered by GRiD Systems Corporation. I wouldn't be without mine.

THE U.S. ROBOTICS MODEMS USED

As you know, I spend a great deal of time online. In a sense, I live in The Wires, so my modem is important to me. When it comes to modems, I only use U.S. Robotics because they are solidly built and dependable. For example, my first U.S. Robotics 2400 baud modem (external) is still working perfectly and it's five years old. It has seldom if ever been turned off in that time and has never needed service. For the tests in this book I used both the U.S. Robotics 9600 HST and the U.S. Robotics HST Dual Standard. Let's take a quick look at these two outstanding modems.

Going for Speed and Accuracy

In the chapters dealing with communications, it was pointed out how faster modems can greatly decrease your overall cost. The U.S. Robotics 9600 HST gives you that high speed along with MNP error correction. With protocols like Ymodem-G, 1K-Xmodem/G, BiModem, and MPt, you can expect to average about 1,150 cps. That means you can download a 256K file in about 3.8 minutes. At 1200 baud the same file would take you approximately 38.2 minutes.

The U.S. Robotics HST Dual Standard has the added benefit of being able to do transfers with any modem using the V.32 standard. Using the same transfer protocols mentioned above, you could expect to average around 1,550 cps and as high as 1,800. That same 256K file, at 1,550 cps, takes only 2.7 minutes to transfer. At 1,800 cps it takes only 2.3 minutes. With MNP error correction, you can have clean, fast, accurate file transfers. The U.S. Robotics HST modems cost more than other U.S. Robotics modems, but in the long run they pay for themselves many times over.

Taking a Stand

I have used several modems in the U.S. Robotics line, including the 2400, the 2400E (with MNP), the 9600 HST, and the HST Dual Standard. All of them have served me well in the past and continue to do so. I have two 2400Es on my bulletin board and they have been on continuously for over three years without a single problem. If you are looking for a high-quality modem that is durable, reliable, and backed up by a technical support group that is very knowledgeable and courteous, look for a U.S. Robotics modem.

THE WILLOW PERIPHERALS VGA-TV CARD

One of the graphics cards used while testing programs was the VGA-TV card by Willow Peripherals. The Willow VGA-TV card gave me excellent resolution in all modes.

The Willow graphics card has a feature that might be of particular interest to businesses and consultants. On the back of the card is a standard RCA jack that can be connected to a VCR. You can do graphical presentations on your computer and the output will also go to the VCR. When you want to do a presentation for a client, you needn't drag a computer, monitor, and so on with you. Take your tape, put it in any VCR, and your client will see the same thing on their television that you display on your computer.

The Willow VGA-TV card used for this book has 512K of RAM. The VCR option is excellent for showing others your work, doing presentations, and so forth. If you haven't upgraded to a VGA card and are thinking about it, give Willow Peripherals a call.

THE PANASONIC KX-P4450 LASER PRINTER

Like the KX-P1124 mentioned earlier, the Panasonic KX-P4450 laser printer is well built and durable. It has both an upper and lower paper tray, and optional trays available for printing labels and envelopes. A control panel on the top lets you control the number of copies, font used, emulation, and so on. The printer comes with a good selection of standard fonts, and others are available simply by adding an expansion card. The KX-P4450 is quiet, and that's a great feature when you're printing something and trying to talk on the phone.

Printing with the KX-P4450

What dazzled me about the KX-P4450 was not only its print quality, but its speed. I've used other laser printers, but none that matched the production of the KX-P4450.

Panasonic advertises that the KX-P4450 does 11 pages a minute and this is not an exaggeration. While printing chapters, where each page is an original, I consistently averaged between 11 and 12.5 pages per minute. In one session the printer did 100 pages in just slightly over eight minutes and the print quality was very good. I could toggle easily, if necessary, between the lower and upper paper trays. The Panasonic performed flawlessly and not once did I have a paper jam.

Overview of the KX-P4450

I've used other laser printers, but comparing price and performance, I'd recommend the Panasonic laser. It's a quality piece of equipment that outperforms many of its competitors while beating their prices. If you are in the market for a laser printer, give the Panasonic laser printer a good, long look.

DESQVIEW

My Northgate 386 has 4 megabytes of RAM, so I used DESQview to give me multitasking capabilities while working on this book. Except when noted, every program discussed in the book was run under DESQview version 2.26. I feel that DESQview helped increase my productivity a great deal by helping me download and upload files even while writing. If it weren't for the capabilities of DESQview, I'd be doing one or the other, but certainly not both! The QEMM package and Manifest program that came with DESQview allowed me to use the memory on my Northgate 386 to its maximum potential.

It's handy to be able to toggle back and forth when you are online as much as I am. I can toggle to another DESQview window and look something up, move a file, run another program, and still be online in the original window. If you are busy and want to maximize your productivity, take a look at DESQview by Quarterdeck Office Systems.

MONITORS BY NEC

In the course of writing this book both the NEC 2A and 3D monitors were used. Both have excellent clarity and displays that are extremely steady. Colors are vibrant and the text is clean and crisp. I tested other monitors that did not display colors nearly as well as the ones from NEC, and often other screen displays had a grainy quality. If you're going to invest in a better graphics display, take the time to check out the variety of quality monitors produced by NEC.

A FINAL NOTE

I hope that this appendix has given you an understanding of the DOS versions, equipment, and software used while testing and evaluating the software discussed in this book.

It is my hope that my opinions will make you aware of good equipment you might have overlooked before. They are simply my opinions based on working with equipment between 14 and 18 hours a day. I can't tolerate equipment that isn't both reliable and affordable. (*smile*)

PC and DOS History and Compatibility

In 1974, a good, if arbitrary year to pick for the beginnings of the personal computer industry, PCs were little more than gadgets for hobbyists and toys for techies. They attracted the same sort of people who, a couple of generations earlier, took joy in putting together unamplified crystal radio receivers.

Whereas the radio builder might have read *Amazing Stories,* computer tinkerers tended to watch "The Twilight Zone" and "Star Trek" on television. One of the earliest PCs, the Altair, borrowed its name from a Star Trek episode. For that matter, so did dBASE, the database program, which the author originally named "Vulcan" after everyone's favorite pointy-eared alien.

The Altair was the logical and spiritual ancestor of today's PCs. It came as a do-it-yourself computer kit from Micro Industry Telemetry Systems.

THE FAMILY TREE

There's not much in common between that early Altair and today's 386 machines. The Altair's heart was an 8080 microprocessor chip, an ancestor of the 80386. The Altair had 256 bytes (that's bytes, not kilobytes) of memory, no permanent storage, and no keyboard. Input was done in straight binary by manual switches at the front of the panel. You almost had to be a computer to operate this computer.

How did things change in the PC world so quickly? That's what this appendix will cover. In the process, some of the reasons for PC limits and compatibility issues will become clear.

Enter Bill Gates & Paul Allen

A youngster named Bill Gates, just out of high school, went into the traffic measurement business with a friend named Paul Allen. Their company, Taf-O-Data, used Intel microprocessors to count how many cars passed over a rubber hose that stretched across the street and connected to one of their machines. Not a bad first try at business for a couple of teenagers with no experience. But the business did not have a lot of promise.

Gates and Allen decided to give up a career in car-counting in favor of working with the Altair microcomputer. Specifically, they decided to enhance Altair's BASIC to support disk storage. This would give the little machine a method of storing processed information in nonvolatile form, making it more useful. Maybe they remembered their own experience with the Taf-O-Data machine, which was useful precisely because it kept its data after the hose was reeled in. In any case, they changed their small company's name to Microsoft and set about enhancing Altair BASIC.

Gary Kindal and CP/M

At about the same time, an Intel programmer named Gary Kindal developed a small computer operating system named CP/M, for *Control Program/Microprocessors*. This scaled down version of the PL/1 mainframe programming language could accept and interpret operator commands using less than 4K of memory. It was quite a feat, but Intel didn't see much future in it. It seemed interesting but useless. So they turned over all rights to Kindal, presumably with a smile and hearty good wishes.

Kindal took CP/M and founded Digital Research with it. He has presumably smiled quite a bit since then.

A Family Resemblance

If you look closely, you'll see many similarities between CP/M and early versions of PC-DOS and MS-DOS. Both use a single program command processor. Both use two input/output data handler files whose names even look alike—CP/M with BDOS and BIOS, DOS with MSDOS.SYS and IO.SYS. Both started as 8 bit systems. The only main thing they didn't have in common was system overhead—DOS 1.0 used nearly 10K and has been gobbling up memory ever since.

OTHER FAMILIES, OTHER TREES

During this period the Apple computer was also coming into being, ably assisted by Steve Jobs and Steve Wozniak. The Apple was based on the Motorola 6502 8 bit microprocessor instead of the Intel 8080, and the differences resulted in very different machines. Also about this time— moving now into the late 1970s—Radio Shack's TRS-80 came into being.

The Apple II, with help from a spreadsheet named VisiCalc that businessmen just couldn't resist, was having a strong influence on the economy just south of San Francisco. It wasn't yet called Silicon Valley, and apricot orchards still grew in Cupertino, but rumblings of the future could be heard clear into the boardrooms at IBM.

ENTER THE GIANT

In 1980, responding to the overwhelming success of the Apple II computer, IBM decided to get involved. "Big Blue" did not expect tiny computers to be the wave of the future, but it did want a piece of the action. So IBM designed a personal computer with off-the-shelf parts. It had a price and features that wouldn't lock horns with IBM's highly profitable mini- and mainframe computers. In a scant nine months—still considered a record—IBM produced the first IBM PC.

The machine had no operating system nor could it handle full BASIC, which had been designed with mainframes in mind. So IBM approached Digital Research for a workable operating system and Microsoft for a micro-sized BASIC interpreter.

Meanwhile, in Seattle

During this period, Tim Patterson of Seattle Microcomputer Products had been working on a 16 bit operating system for the Intel 8088 and 8086 chip family. Patterson figured 16 bit processing, offering twice the data throughput, would be the next stage of development.

The result of Patterson's work was QDOS, which later evolved into SCP-DOS. It was a true 16 bit operating system. Microsoft fully agreed with Patterson that 16 bit processing was the wave of the future and offered Patterson's firm $50,000 for the new system. It was a wise purchase. In November 1980, IBM and Microsoft agreed that DOS would be included in the new IBM personal computer. The stage was set.

In August 1981, IBM finally announced the IBM PC. It would use a new operating system called PC-DOS, which IBM said would be compatible with a multitude of operating systems and programs. By "compatible," they meant compatible with the then-dominant CP/M operating system of Digital Research; and in fact, various add-in cards were quickly produced to interface IBM PCs with CP/M systems.

There was a huge base of CP/M software out there after all, which made it very attractive as an alternative operating system. But the die was cast. By 1983, a special 8088/8086 version of CP/M called CP/M-86 was the chief rival of PC-DOS as a PC operating system. It had only an estimated four percent of the PC market. CP/M-86 was a powerful system, coming as an add-in board with both serial and parallel printer support, a programmable or "smart" screen driver with horizontal scrolling, screen line editing, page control, and 193K disk drive capacity. It was quite a system. But four percent of the market couldn't carry CP/M-86 for long. To be successful, products such as CP/M-86 must reach a point where software developers start paying attention, but CP/M-86 and the other systems never got there. The programmers ignored them. As a result, these "alternative systems" quickly fell by the wayside, leaving the field clear to Microsoft.

A SHORT DOS TIME LINE

The initial DOS release, version 1.0, had a rather experimental character and was both buggy and limited. Within a year, by June 1982, version 1.1 replaced it. Version 1.1 fixed many of the bugs and also supported IBM's new double-sided floppy disk drives. This was the first clear instance of

---

DOCTOR'S NOTE

The original Microsoft DOS, released in August 1981 as DOS 1.0, was a direct descendant of Tim Patterson's 86-DOS system. In fact, IBM had considered the impact on sales when they decreed CP/M compatibility for their new operating system. At that time, the few microcomputer software packages that weren't written for the Apple II were written for CP/M. This meant that making it easy for programmers to convert programs from CP/M to PC-DOS was given a high priority.

The DOS CP/M heritage shows very clearly that many of the features that drive users and programmers crazy are hand-me-downs from Gary Kindal's original CP/M system, from which Tim Patterson developed the 86-DOS 16 bit system. Parallel features included

- Eight-character file names
- Three-character file extensions
- The A> prompt
- No progress reports from commands like DEL
- Use of File Control Blocks (FCBs)
- Program Segment Prefixes (PSPs)

DOS did change some of CP/M's quirks. File lengths were now reported precisely instead of being rounded off. Commands that used a destination/source syntax got turned around to the more logical format of source/destination, and DOS was the first operating system to employ a file allocation table (FAT) that tracks where all the pieces of a file are stored. The FAT also allows more than one piece of data to be written at one time. Even in the early 1980s, the steady evolution of DOS had begun toward more power and flexibility.

---

what was to become a steady march toward greater power and flexibility, since the DSDD format doubled the storage capacity of DOS 1.0 diskette systems. Microsoft also released a generic version of DOS at this time, called MS-DOS 1.25.

The next major release of DOS, version 2.0, came in March 1983. Like 1.1, it added support for a new IBM option, the fixed disk drive (now called hard disks). DOS 2.0 introduced the directory tree. It also supported various peripheral devices by using a CONFIG.SYS file. MS-DOS added many new enhancements including commands built into the COMMAND.COM command processor. It used file handles, could label diskettes, and included a printer spooler. It used environment variables and further increased floppy diskette storage by increasing the number of sectors from eight to nine per track.

All these innovations made a maintenance release inevitable. It appeared in March 1984, as DOS 2.1, which incidentally supported the new IBM PC jr. Oddly enough, DOS 2.1 was noticeably slower than DOS 2.0. This was due to the fact that DOS had to slow down the system in order to accommodate the slower PC jr disk drives. Microsoft produced several generic versions of 2.1, including 2.05, 2.11, 2.2, and 2.25.

The Upgrade Track

If you have an older version of DOS, especially DOS 2.1, you'll enjoy significantly better performance if you upgrade to a more recent version like DOS 3.30 or 4.01. DOS now comes in nearly 70 different languages, including Japanese. Table B-1 shows the various versions of DOS and what each contributed.

Table B-1

Versions of DOS

Number	Year	Purpose
1.0	1981	Original Disk Operating System
1.1	1982	Support for double-sided disks
2.0	1983	Support for subdirectories
2.01	1983	Support for international symbols
2.25	1983	Bug fixes
3.0	1984	Extended character set, support for larger hard disks
3.1	1984	Support for PC networks, plus bug fixes
3.2	1986	Support for 3.5-inch diskettes (microfloppies)
3.3	1987	Support for PS/2 computers
4.0	1988	Support for large partitions
4.01	1989	Bug fixes

Many people, especially those who are relatively new to computers, are curious about the earlier machines, when they were released, what versions of DOS they ran, and so on. Table B-2 shows the history of PCs and the DOS versions they used.

Essential DOS Commands

To use any DOS version you only need to know how to use a very few basic commands. But you'll benefit greatly from taking the time to gain what some people call "DOS fluency." There are several excellent DOS

Table B-2

Versions of IBM Machines

Model Name	CPU	Speed (MHz)	ID Byte	BUS I/O (Bits)	Max. RAM	DOS Version	Release Date
PC	8088	4.77	FF	8	640K	1.0	8-12-81
XT	8088	4.77	FE	8	640K	2.0	3-08-82
PC Portable	8088	4.77	?	8	640K	3.0	11-01-83
PC jr	8088	4.77	FD	8	640K	2.1	2-14-83
AT	80286	6/8	FC	16	15Mb	3.0	8-14-84
PC Convertible	80c86	4.77	F9	8	640K	3.0	8-02-86
XT-286	80286	6	FC	16	15M	3.0	8-14-86
PS/2	8088	4.77	FB	8	640K	3.0	5-07-87
PS/2 Model 30	8086	8	FA	8	640K	3.0	5-07-87
PS/2 Model 50	80286	10	FC	16	16M	3.3	5-07-87
PS/2 Model 60	80286	10	FC	16	16M	3.3	5-07-87
PS/2 Model 80	80386	16/20	F8	32	4G	3.3	5-07-87
PS/2 Model 25	8086	10?		8	640K	3.3	8-04-87
PS/2 Model 50Z	80286	10?		16	16M	4.01	6-02-88
PS/2 Model 70	80386	16?		32	16M	4.01	6-02-88
PS/2 Model 30 286	80286	10?		16	16M	4.01	9-13-88
PS/2 Model 55 SX	80386SX	16?		16	16M	4.01	5-09-89
PS/2 Model P70	80386	20?		32	16M	4.01	5-09-89
PS/2 Model 486/25	80486	16?		32	16M	4.01	6-20-89

guides available, among which I can recommend *DOS: The Complete Reference*, Second Edition by Kris Jamsa (Berkeley, California: Osborne/McGraw-Hill, 1990).

If you're not familiar yet with the basics of DOS, pick up a DOS guide. It will help you understand how to use the great programs included with this book. In particular, DOS 3.3 has many new and expanded commands that will greatly enhance your ability to use and enjoy Shareware.

Dr. File Finder's BBS List

Earlier in this book, the main ways to obtain Shareware were listed and discussed. You can get good Shareware programs from commercial online networks, disk vendors, PC user groups, and bulletin boards. Chapter 4 gave you the necessary information you need to get accounts on a number of commercial online systems. Catalogs from disk vendors will come to you in the mail, or you can send for those offered by the vendors listed in Appendix D. PC user groups are something that you'll find in your local area. Finding bulletin board numbers, however, is not so easy—especially if you have no place to start. That problem will be remedied in this appendix.

Another factor that is very important to me is that I *want* to be accessible to you. I'd like to be able to interact with you, and I want you to be able to find me so that you can ask questions, make comments, and so on. I've included two different lists of bulletin boards. Some of my favorite bulletin boards are in the first list. Many of them also happen to be the "homes" of various Shareware programs. The ones marked with *** are places where you can leave me messages. I visit all of these systems regularly. Don't hesitate to leave me a message with questions about software, comments about the book, or whatever. The second, much longer listing consists of PC Board and Wildcat! systems bulletin boards found in almost every area code in the United States and Canada. The PC Board systems are separate from the Wildcat! systems so that you can know what kind of system you'll be calling. I hope that these numbers provide you with places you can call locally.

DR. FILE FINDER'S FAVORITE BULLETIN BOARDS

If you log on to any of these systems, take the time to leave a comment to the sysop and say, "The Doc sent me." If nothing else, they'll appreciate your stopping by, and I will answer your message as quickly as possible.

*** *Dr. File Finder's Black Bag*   901-753-7213
   The Doc's "home" system, visited by many program authors

*** *The Forbin Project PCBoard*   319-233-6157
   Home of Qmodem

*** *Cheers PCBoard*   901-373-5941
   Home of the InterLink EchoMail system

*** *Prof BBS*   606-269-1565
   Specializing in business, real estate, and finance

***Channel 1*   617-354-8873
   Excellent conferences; 3 gigabytes of files, and more

New-Ware BBS   619-450-3257
   Home of ArcMaster, Scout, FormatMaster, CopyMaster

*** *Lans PCBoard*   219-884-9508
   An excellent PC Board system

Valley of the Sun   602-979-5720
   Home of BiModem

Three R's BBS   503-582-4860
    Home of BiDor14, for using BiModem on PC Boards

*** *Dcom Support BBS*   805-264-4986
    Home of dCOM (Directory Commander)

NoGames RBBS   919-364-7378

RE/BBS   703-590-1441
    Home of MOTU, Sequel, and other "Door" games

Qmail Support   901-382-5583
    Home of Qmail and QPro Reader

Cam's Wildcat! House   404-461-5947

RoboComm BBS   213-556-3894
    Home of RoboComm

Menu Commando BBS   512-670-0954
    Home of Menu Commando, File Commando, Back and Forth

Coastal DOS Users   207-797-4975
    An excellent system—well organized

***VOR BBS *(public)*   707-778-8944
    Public node of Vern Buerg's system—The Buerg Utilities

Programmer's Oasis   919-226-6984
    Home of LOG—Time/Cost tracking program

The Ledge PC Board   818-352-3620
    An excellent system and very well organized

PKWare BBS   414-352-7176
    Home of PKZIP/PKUNZIP, PKFIND

***Patriquin BBS*   714-369-9766
    Home of Pcopy, Pmove, Palert, PPrint, and more

Doorway BBS   615-966-3574
    Home of Doorway

Tool Shop   602-279-2673
    Home of Prodoor and other fine programs

Dan Doman BBS   212-427-1805
    Home of DFF, Dmove, and other fine utilities

NoGate Consultants   616-455-5179
    Home of PAK

Exec-PC   414-789-4210
    An excellent system, discussed in Chapter 4

Galaxy BBS   206-385-6667
    Home of the Galaxy Word Processor

GT Power Comm   713-772-2090
    Home of GT Power Comm

Boyan Support BBS   919-682-4225
    Home of the BOYAN communications program

Nels Anderson (Games)   508-875-3618
    Home of Shooting Gallery, EGA Trek, and more

As-Easy-As BBS   508-794-0762
    Home of the As-Easy-As spreadsheet

Telix BBS   416-284-0682
    Home of the TELIX Communications program

Omen Technologies   503-621-3746
    Home of Zcomm and DSZ

PC BOARD AND WILDCAT!
SYSTEMS – BY AREA CODE

PC Board

201-214-8896	Software Society South	North Brunswick, NJ
201-239-1331	MicroSellar BBS	Verona, NJ
201-256-4509	Passaic Valley BBS	Little Falls, NJ
201-265-7364	CCSBoard	Emerson, NJ
201-273-0345	The Summit PCBoard	Summit, NJ
201-278-9044	The Final Frontier	Paterson, NJ
201-279-7048	The Dean's Office	Clifton, NJ
201-291-2302	Phantasm BBS	Leonardo, NJ
201-297-7399	Micro-Server	North Brunswick, NJ
201-298-9098	Just Programs BBS	Roselle Park, NJ
201-299-7914	Designed Letters BBSNet	Boonton, NJ
201-308-9048	The IBM Connection BBS	Freehold, NJ
201-328-3918	Gray Seas PCBoard	Randolph, NJ
201-332-6098	Edgelight On-Line BBS	Jersey City, NJ
201-333-4099	Bill's Bar & Grill	Jersey City, NJ
201-334-2555	The Hacker Central BBS	Montville, NJ
201-334-7846	Designed Letters BBSNet	Boonton, NJ
201-338-5265	The Golden*Dane BBS	Bloomfield, NJ
201-342-1105	The Wall	River Edge, NJ
201-359-1628	The Land of the Lost	Belle Mead, NJ
201-373-8020	The Mighty One BBS	Irvington, NJ
201-377-2526	Stocks and Such BBS	Madison, NJ
201-391-2052	Saddle River BBS	Saddle River, NJ
201-391-7743	Montvale BBS	Montvale, NJ
201-423-4258	The Computer Nookery	Hawthorne, NJ
201-446-5736	Cat's Lair	Englishtown, NJ
201-471-6391	Passaic BBS	Passaic, NJ
201-546-1468	Token Ring BBS	Clifton, NJ
201-548-0436	Mortgage Money BBS	Metuchen, NJ
201-580-9493	SBT Enhancements	Millington, NJ
201-613-7350	The Jersey Shore	Sayreville, NJ
201-627-3409	Micro One BBS	Rockaway, NJ
201-652-2169	The Fish Market	Glenrock, NJ
201-652-6628	Phoenix BBS	Ridgewood, NJ

201-654-3178	No Nonsense BBS	Westfield, NJ
201-664-1059	Poor George	Hillsdale, NJ
201-666-3262	NJPC	Hillsdale, NJ
201-667-2504	Nutley N.J. BBS	Nutley, NJ
201-675-2154	Deans Info Center	East Orange, NJ
201-680-1336	Arc Exchange BBS	Bloomfield, NJ
201-680-9178	Ultimate Link	Bloomfield, NJ
201-694-7133	Ric's Place	Pequannock, NJ
201-729-1494	No-Frills BBS	Sparta, NJ
201-729-2602	Chuck's Attempt	Sparta, NJ
201-729-7410	The Software Society	Lake Mohawk, NJ
201-729-9538	The New World BBS	Sparta, NJ
201-730-7328	Arrakis BBS	Annadale, NJ
201-746-0614	ASCRS Research Foundation	Glen Ridge, NJ
201-771-1642	The Summit PCBoard	Summit, NJ
201-783-3298	Hacker Central BBS	Montclair, NJ
201-791-7471	Blue Ribbon BBS	Fair Lawn, NJ
201-792-0626	The Hoboken City Lights	Hoboken, NJ
201-796-0619	Ken's Cavern	Elmwood Park, NJ
201-797-5562	The Exchange Board	Elmwood Park, NJ
201-821-8015	Kendall Park PCBoard	Kendall Park, NJ
201-827-6441	The Vernon BBS	Vernon, NJ
201-831-8152	Sail Board BBS	Wayne, NJ
201-875-8324	Empty Warehouse BBS	Sussex, NJ
201-891-3721	530 Hudson Street BBS	Wyckoff, NJ
201-905-8015	Top Gun	Lakewood, NJ
201-906-6968	DataPort	Edison, NJ
201-916-1725	Lightning Bolt BBS	Clifton, NJ
201-943-5419	The Data-Base	Ridgefield, NJ
201-974-8317	Right Choice BBS	Spring Lake Heights, NJ
201-984-6574	The Odyssey	Morris Plains, NJ

Wildcat! Systems

201-254-8117	Cop Shop	Sayreville, NJ
201-347-3780	Twilight BBS	Stanhope, NJ
201-354-6979	Computer Junction	Elizabeth, NJ
201-385-2874	Menti's Bay BBS	Dumont, NJ

201-398-1582	The Bermuda Triangle	Andover, NJ
201-525-9440	The Fortress	Parlin, NJ
201-697-9656	PC 6300 WHSE	Vernon, NJ
201-825-8624	Kratos Users BBS	Ramsey, NJ
201-831-6828	Rob's Wildcat BBS	Wanaque, NJ
201-895-4452	The Lounge	Randolph, NJ
201-974-9819	Hi-Tek Trader	Spring Lake Heights, NJ

PC Board

202-280-5423	Capital Connection	Washington, DC
202-426-8644	ATR-200	Washington, DC
202-433-6639	DC Information Exchange	Washington, DC
202-475-7885	Nardac Washington	Washington, DC
202-574-8423	Silent Service	Washington, DC
202-581-1422	Jim's Dream	Washington, DC
202-586-5406	InfoLink PCBoard Node 1	Washington, DC
202-586-9359	LaserNet PCBoard Node 2	Washington, DC
202-646-2887	Salemdug	Washington, DC
202-842-8580	Mailbag	Washington, DC

Wildcat! Systems

202-646-6497	NASA HQ ITC	Washington, DC

PC Board

203-274-1416	Excalibur BBS	Watertown, CT
203-355-2920	Pirate's Island BBS	New Milford, CT
203-496-8666	Conn-Quest BBS	New Hartford, CT
203-522-3460	The Majic Land	Hartford, CT
203-536-9549	Mystic Software Network	Mystic, CT
203-584-1798	Computer PlayRoom	Bristol, CT
203-635-7118	Emperor's Roost BBS	Cromwell, CT
203-637-0502	The Last Crusade	Old Greenwich, CT
203-649-5611	The Ivory Tower	Manchester, CT
203-738-0342	Hounds Haven BBS	New Hartford, CT
203-746-1275	Bluemoon PCBoard	New Fairfield, CT

| 203-798-9651 | Star Stuff | Bethel, CT |
| 203-878-9705 | Excalibur IV | Milford, CT |

Wildcat! Systems

203-257-8885	The Next Generation	Wethersfield, CT
203-568-0132	Northway FIDO	East Hartford, CT
203-644-1835	N.E. Photo I	South Windsor, CT
203-667-1484	The Logical Connection	Newington, CT
203-698-0588	Starport	Old Greenwich, CT
203-747-5105	Conn Hubo BBS Center	Southington, CT
203-747-5313	Central CT Wildcat	Plainville, CT
203-763-0016	Endeavor BBS	Somers, CT
203-875-6400	NE Photo II	South Windsor, CT

PC Board

204-253-1342	Pokey's Place	Winnipeg, Manitoba, Canada
204-488-3866	Hyman Industries BBS	Winnipeg, Manitoba, Canada
204-943-6508	Muddy Water	Winnipeg, Manitoba, Canada

Wildcat! Systems

| 204-275-0637 | Info-Motion Board | Winnipeg, Manitoba, Canada |
| 204-728-6615 | Brandon Univ. Cont. Educ. | Brandon, Manitoba, Canada |

PC Board

205-221-3327	Fear and Loathing Vegas	Jasper, AL
205-244-7053	HOT-DOS & Beer BBS	Montgomery, AL
205-281-9335	The Board Walk	Montgomery, AL
205-342-7866	The SuperSystem '88	Mobile, AL
205-442-3078	Southside BBS	Gadsden, AL
205-547-4936	Zenith BBS	Gadsden, AL
205-553-5322	The Lighthouse	Tuscaloosa, AL

205-592-8042	The Bus System	Birmingham, AL
205-598-1938	The Killer BBS	Fort Rucker, AL
205-598-1987	Ideas Unlimited	Daleville, AL
205-598-8770	The Killer BBS	Fort Rucker, AL
205-626-7447	Pep's Data System	Daphne, AL
205-664-9609	The Point of NO Return	Helena, AL
205-674-1851	American BBS	Birmingham, AL
205-681-7739	Chances-R	Birmingham, AL
205-734-8053	Stereo Center's Force BBS	Cullman, AL
205-744-6120	Joker's Castle	Pleasant Grove, AL
205-745-4515	The Lightning Board	Opelika, AL
205-785-7417	Channel 8250	Birmingham, AL
205-821-4664	Xignals PCBoard	Auburn, AL
205-821-8114	Xignals PCBoard	Auburn, AL
205-836-9311	The ST BBS	Birmingham, AL
205-853-6144	Sperry	Birmingham, AL
205-853-8718	ProSoft Systems	Birmingham, AL
205-854-4694	The Players Network	Birmingham, AL
205-854-6407	Magnolia	Birmingham, AL
205-854-9662	Pinson Valley PCBoard	Birmingham, AL
205-870-7770	LZ Birmingham	Birmingham, AL
205-887-5802	The Alabama PCBoard	Auburn, AL
205-956-2738	The Water Line	Birmingham, AL
205-979-0194	Sparta PCBoard	Vestavia Hills, AL

Wildcat! Systems

205-258-4624	LYNX 2	Gunter AFB, AL
205-264-0513	Smitty House	Montgomery, AL
205-277-6323	THE QUEUE	Montgomery, AL
205-351-8706	ALACOMM BBS	Decatur, AL
205-353-3278	Tom's Swap Shop	Moulton, AL
205-355-2983	Byte Swap	Decatur, AL
205-452-3897	Pro-Tech	Chickasaw, AL
205-553-0715	Halls of Valhalla	Tuscaloosa, AL
205-773-9600	The "Fence Post"	Hartselle, AL
205-774-7453	The Grey Zone	Ozark, AL
205-871-5551	Nouveaux BBS	Birmingham, AL
205-974-5123	Cyclone BBS	Moulton, AL
205-983-6283	The Wildcat! BBS	Midland City, AL

PC Board

206-232-1763	Poverty Rock	Mercer Island, WA
206-235-8760	Omniverse Network	Renton, WA
206-277-1689	Starfinder I	Renton, WA
206-296-5277	KCSS BBS	Seattle, WA
206-323-9411	The Unknown Mountain	Seattle, WA
206-328-7876	CardioBoard	Seattle, WA
206-343-9710	FHU The Objective State	Seattle, WA
206-373-1346	The Sports Complex	Bremerton,WA
206-373-5863	Pegasus Data Line	Bremerton, WA
206-373-6702	Little Bulletin Board	Bremerton, WA
206-377-3365	Omega BBS	Bremerton,WA
206-377-5883	Dragonhawk	Bremerton, WA
206-377-7289	The Sports Complex	Bremerton,WA
206-391-2339	Futzer Avenue	Issaquah, WA
206-398-7512	Micro Quest BBS	Lynden, WA
206-478-7188	Olympic College BBS (OCBBS)	Bremerton, WA
206-535-6762	PC Link	Tacoma, WA
206-674-2013	Friendly Service Bureau	Port Orchard, WA
206-675-1600	Whidbey Winds BBS	Oak Harbor, WA
206-676-5787	Barbequed RiBBS	Bellingham, WA
206-692-3002	Cloud Dancer BBS	Bremerton, WA
206-746-2509	FHU The Objective State	Seattle, WA
206-789-9302	Home DBA	Seattle, WA
206-838-1166	Evergreen Exchange	Federal Way, WA
206-865-0806	The Loft	Bellevue, WA
206-868-9384	SSE Surf Board	Redmond, WA
206-876-6735	The Wings BBS	Port Orchard, WA
206-881-8119	Microrim Technical Support	Redmond, WA

Wildcat! Systems

206-253-0006	Ken's Place	Vancouver, WA
206-289-3552	UTOPIA Software BBS	Ocean Shores, WA
206-324-4259	501 Wildcat Plaza	Seattle, WA
206-423-3730	Fire Mountain BBS	Kelso, WA
206-459-4609	KTOL "Radio Point"	Lacey, WA

206-488-0924	The Night Shift	Woodville, WA
206-488-4309	A.F.I.M.S. BBS	Bothell, WA
206-523-9897	THE GAMES BBS	Seattle, WA
206-524-7025	S.M.H.I.S.	Seattle, WA
206-532-4818	PC-MAJIC	Aberdeen, WA
206-532-9220	Techline	Montesano, WA
206-533-2179	Iceburg	Aberdeen, WA
206-547-0167	The Signpost	Seattle, WA
206-566-1155	Amocat BBS	Tacoma, WA
206-577-5238	Columbia Valley Gardens	Longview, WA
206-581-7876	Mike Force South	Tacoma, WA
206-588-5442	The Boardwalk!	Auburn, WA
206-692-7301	The Exchange of Bytes	Bremerton, WA
206-693-5477	Alacrity	Bellevue, WA
206-693-6095	Dataway BBS	Vancouver, WA
206-698-0338	Data by Night BBS	Bremerton, WA
206-698-1044	The Jimby BBS	Poulsbo, WA
206-745-4694	ProTech	Everett, WA
206-771-1730	The French Connection	Edmonds, WA
206-820-9073	Bandwagon Express	Kirkland, WA
206-839-8055	The Maintenance Man	Kent, WA
206-840-2357	Eagles	Puyallup, WA
206-854-8360	Time-Out	Kent, WA
206-869-8032	The Bleeding Edge	Redmond, WA
206-883-2670	Overbyte Software BBS	Redmond, WA
206-885-3537	Fred's After Hours	Bellevue, WA
206-922-2872	Pacific Northwest Archive	Tacoma, WA
206-939-0788	The Bull Board	Pacific, WA
206-941-0317	PRO STAR	Auburn, WA

PC Board

207-284-5740	The Addiction BBS	Biddeford, ME
207-325-4120	The Great Northern BBS	Limestone, ME
207-766-2467	Northern Lights	Portland, ME
207-783-0517	Med-Net	Auburn, ME
207-797-4975	Coastal DOS Users BBS	Portland, ME
207-799-3547	Technical Connection	Portland, ME
207-854-1015	Maine PC Connection	Westbrook, ME

Wildcat! Systems

207-581-1595	UMaine BBS	Orono, ME
207-693-3431	Nix Pix East	Naples, ME
207-989-3737	The Witch	Brewer, ME

PC Board

208-322-5227	Greater Boise BBS	Boise, ID
208-342-1379	Aviator's BBS	Boise, ID
208-343-8815	Gotham City BBS	Boise, ID
208-746-1709	Confluence BBS	Lewiston, ID

Wildcat! Systems

208-357-5887	THE SILVER PALACE	Shelley, ID
208-664-2983	Third Millennium	Coeur D'Alene, ID
208-683-2434	Don's Main Menu	Athol, ID
208-786-7211	GB-BBS	Kellogg, ID
208-882-6809	Strategic & Critical Mat.	Moscow, ID
208-885-7812	C.O.M.E.R. BBS-1	Moscow, ID

PC Board

209-357-1910	Elegant Applications BBS	Winton, CA
209-521-7484	PLATO	Modesto, CA
209-825-3103	CrossRoads BBS	Manteca, CA
209-943-1880	The Wrong Number	Stockton, CA
209-957-8762	The Outer Limits BBS	Stockton, CA

Wildcat! Systems

209-226-3993	PO's BBS	Fresno, CA
209-228-5382	VA-OSH	Fresno, CA
209-383-6417	Merced Wildcat!	Merced, CA
209-463-5842	Marlin's Super Wildcat!	Stockton, CA
209-478-7164	Crickets BBS	Stockton, CA
209-632-8944	Logarithmatic Jello	Turlock, CA
209-795-1785	Sierra's Cabin	Arnold, CA

PC Board

212-219-8824	Gateways	New York, NY
212-340-9666	The Machine	New York, NY
212-409-2671	Friends!Z	Bronx, NY
212-409-4194	Softlaw Legal BBS	New York, NY
212-410-7173	NDR Software Remote DBase	New York, NY
212-415-3500	HyperCube Systems Comm	New York, NY
212-431-1194	Invention Factory	New York, NY
212-432-1992	Zooman's Zoo BBS	New York, NY
212-496-7946	DataCom Software	New York, NY
212-519-1791	The Running Board	New York, NY
212-662-8597	The Doctor's Office BBS	New York, NY
212-721-1204	Novus Elect, Mail System	Great Neck, NY
212-769-4799	Hi Tech BBS	New York, NY
212-781-4723	Friends!	New York, NY
212-799-2123	Novus BBS	New York, NY
212-828-3989	Friends!Z BBS	Bronx, NY
212-865-2596	Virtuoso Think Tank BBS	New York, NY
212-865-7043	The Double Helix	New York, NY
212-869-3880	IDBUG	New York, NY
212-869-3923	IDBUG	New York, NY
212-924-1138	The Village Inn	New York, NY

PC Board

213-202-0710	Czar's Asylum	Los Angeles, CA
213-204-6158	Camelot	Culver City, CA
213-306-3530	LMI Forth Board	Los Angeles, CA
213-320-2924	GS-BUG BBS	Torrance, CA
213-325-1608	Impeesa's Path	Lomita, CA
213-387-5901	Little Angels PCB	Los Angeles, CA
213-421-1041	CompuCentre	Long Beach, CA
213-423-5797	Digital Diversions	Long Beach, CA
213-427-5980	Oil Patch PCBoard	Signal Hill, CA
213-432-3592	The Electric Newspaper	Long Beach, CA
213-434-2933	Planet Zed	Long Beach, CA
213-435-3757	Flag Ship	Long Beach, CA

213-494-1243	Intelligent Solutions	Long Beach, CA
213-495-2053	The Windes Country	Long Beach, CA
213-496-2369	Thunder Mountain	Lakewood, CA
213-531-3890	Holistic BBS	Lakewood, CA
213-594-5528	The Rall Computer BBS	Seal Beach, CA
213-615-0528	PC Consultant's BBS	El Segundo, CA
213-822-1804	Network Advantage Support	Venice, CA
213-859-9334	Sleepy Hollow	Los Angeles, CA
213-863-3742	Free Bytes II	Norwalk, CA
213-937-9788	Nostradamus 1	Los Angeles, CA

Wildcat! Systems

213-223-9285	PHOTO PRO	Los Angeles, CA
213-276-5263	Virus Infor Palladium	Simi Valley, CA
213-306-1447	Sportsworld	Venice, CA
213-348-2395	EpStar	Los Angeles, CA
213-394-6862	CFA Southwest Region	Santa Monica, CA
213-399-0172	LifeLine	Los Angeles, CA
213-419-4757	Night Line	Inglewood, CA
213-470-6457	Fly-In French Connexion	Los Angeles, CA
213-478-8581	DWIRE SYSTEMS	Los Angeles, CA
213-495-2053	WINDES COUNTRY	Westminster, CA
213-595-1488	Casus Belli	Long Beach, CA
213-596-9467	Ocular Skisis BBS	Los Alamitos, CA
213-609-2176	The Maverick	Rancho Dominguez, CA
213-761-8284	Kenwood U.S.A.	Long Beach, CA
213-867-1216	Night Owl	Bellflower, CA
213-938-6579	Christ's Corner	Los Angeles, CA
213-943-3082	LUV EXCHANGE BBS	Whittier, CA

PC Board

214 530-4129	The Nightcrawler	Garland, TX
214-217-0400	The Magic Mansion BBS	Ovilla, TX
214-231-0248	Shy Guy's PCBoard	Richardson, TX
214-271-8899	Trojan City	Garland, TX

214-279-3406	CDS Bulletin Board System	Garland, TX
214-291-0031	Unknown BBS	Dallas, TX
214-422-2387	The Ministry BBS	Plano, TX
214-423-6705	The Ministry BBS	Plano, TX
214-424-6446	Data Tech PCBoard	Plano, TX
214-470-2206	ESI-Richardson	Richardson, TX
214-492-5695	User-To-User	Dallas, TX
214-515-5058	The Magic Mansion BBS	Ovilla, TX
214-642-1234	GAP Software	Grand Prairie, TX
214-642-9508	Double AAce	Grand Prairie, TX
214-680-2693	PC-Help	Richardson, TX
214-709-5127	THRAX SS (HQ)	Dallas, TX
214-783-9431	After Hours	Dallas, TX
214-855-1347	ARTIST	Dallas, TX
214-931-5792	Career Board	Dallas, TX
214-980-7745	The Back Room BBS	Dallas, TX

Wildcat! Systems

214-237-2742	LTC-BBS	Longview, TX
214-328-6909	Omni-Net	Dallas, TX
214-398-0159	Hal's Byte Box	Dallas, TX
214-484-1408	Cyclop's	Farmers Branch, TX
214-534-1918	Tyler Open Forum	Tyler, TX
214-561-5697	Software Syst. "WILD-CAT"	Tyler, TX
214-680-2693	PC-HELP	Richardson, TX
214-885-5334	"Timothy's" Place	Sulphur Springs, TX
214-885-7815	Quikdraw BBS	Sulphur Springs, TX

PC Board

215-279-9722	Starbase 10	Norristown, PA
215-348-1983	A Step Beyond...	Doylestown, PA
215-356-8623	N.T.S. PCBoard	Newtown Square, PA
215-367-4053	ESA Tech Support BBS	Gilbertsville, PA
215-372-8113	Unit Systems Unit One	Reading, PA
215-399-1328	RunWay BBS	West Chester, PA

215-425-0713	Graphics Array BBS	Philadelphia, PA
215-430-6166	Asgard BBS	West Chester, PA
215-449-8381	ONLINE Systems	Drexel Hill, PA
215-463-4173	Mega-Bytes BBS	Philadelphia, PA
215-493-5242	Bucks Telematics	Yardley, PA
215-544-3757	Pats All American PCBoard	Springfield, PA
215-563-8109	The Philly Exchange	Philadelphia, PA
215-639-3242	RATS BBS	Bensalem, PA
215-674-5358	Warminster PCBoard BBS	Warminster, PA
215-674-8146	The Satalink BBS	Warminster, PA
215-678-9334	The File Cabinet	Wyomissing, PA
215-755-8799	Megabytes Super BBS	Philadelphia, PA
215-867-0164	4th Net	Bethlehem, PA
215-867-1396	4th Net	Bethlehem, PA
215-939-3615	The Explorer's Outpost	Reading, PA

Wildcat! Systems

215-333-5669	Demons Lair	Philadelphia, PA
215-376-9965	Bloom County BBS	Bethlehem, PA
215-383-7245	Fisherman's Wharf	Thorndale, PA
215-423-9628	3C Design & Data BBS	Philadelphia, PA
215-437-7085	AVI BBS	Allentown, PA
215-449-4051	Star Ship	Drexel Hill, PA
215-547-2809	J.A.D.E. Trading Post	Levittown, PA
215-569-4745	QuikLink!	Philadelphia, PA
215-626-3862	Camelot	Drexel Hill, PA
215-637-0474	"Last Chance BBS"	Philadelphia, PA
215-657-8731	Silverwood/MCS	Philadelphia, PA
215-672-5762	Nightlife Adult BBS	Horsham, PA
215-676-0810	D PLACE	Philadelphia, PA
215-692-0762	PATCHWORKS	West Chester, PA
215-752-4009	Bensalem BBS	Bensalem, PA
215-770-1858	The Trading Post BBS	Allentown, PA
215-787-6843	Temple	Philadelphia, PA
215-867-8761	Cat's Castle	Bethlehem, PA
215-943-3246	The Disk Dispatcher	Bristol, PA

PC Board

216-349-4515	Infoguide PCBoard	Solon, OH
216-366-1935	Hacker's Unlimited	Elyria, OH
216-381-3320	PC-Ohio	Cleveland, OH
216-526-9480	AMCOM	Cleveland, OH
216-529-0121	Signal BBS	Cleveland, OH
216-662-4407	The Rock -N- Roll BBS	Maple Heights, OH
216-726-2620	Rusty & Edie's BBS	Boardman, OH,
216-726-4983	Ask Fred's BBS	Boardman, OH
216-779-5669	Connections 2	North Olmsted, OH
216-951-4287	Eastlake PCBoard	Eastlake, OH

Wildcat! Systems

216-224-0163	CONK	Conneaut, OH
216-264-5116	Tri-Way	Wooster, OH
216-334-4145	Ohio Software Exchange	Cuyahoga Falls, OH
216-476-2907	Royal Flush B.B.S.	Cleveland, OH
216-499-0775	Midwest Exchange	North Canton, OH
216-729-6543	After Hours	Chesterland, OH
216-745-9355	Kenmore Clone Conn.	Akron, OH
216-864-2948	Rick's ADG II	Fairlawn, OH
216-868-6342	Pirates Cove	Minerva, OH
216-896-9500	Data Base BBS	Greensburg, OH

PC Board

217-328-4500	Big City Lights	Urbana, IL
217-888-3929	Greenwood Connection	Greenwood, IL

Wildcat! Systems

217-224-3920	Liberty BBS	Champaign, IL
217-359-3257	The Edge	Champaign, IL

PC Board

218-727-3808	Micro Simulations	Duluth, MN

PC Board

219-234-9403	Indiana Data Managers	South Bend, IN
219-269-9459	Lakeside User's Group	Warsaw, IN
219-277-0809	Capt'n Jacks Rookery	South Bend, IN
219-287-3358	River City Network	South Bend, IN
219-293-1149	"1149" BBS	Elkhart, IN
219-325-0033	The 'Planar' Board	La Porte, IN
219-533-3053	The *Star* BBS	Goshen, IN
219-594-2261	Gar Xariti	Pierceton, IN
219-636-3153	Chain O' Lakes BBS	Albion, IN
219-762-5620	Dune HighTech Express	Portage, IN
219-762-7415	Last Chance BBS	Portage, IN
219-763-4908	"Port of Call" Shakey Board	Portage, IN
219-887-6331	The Lan BBS # 4	Gary, IN
219-923-2377	Datacom of Highland Super	Highland, IN
219-929-4254	The Crystal Palace	Porter, IN

Wildcat! Systems

219-356-1212	Spirit in the Sky	Huntington, IN
219-436-2302	NEI BBS	Fort Wayne, IN
219-447-3011	The Fire Department	Fort Wayne, IN
219-456-5881	Data Management	Fort Wayne, IN
219-482-4383	Astro Bytes BBS Node 1	Fort Wayne, IN
219-636-2434	THE RAVEN'S LOFT	Albion, IN
219-693-6126	Opini/on	Fort Wayne, IN
219-825-7947	Organ Masters	Elkhart, IN
219-923-7611	EXCALIBUR BBS	Griffith, IN

PC Board

301-217-9544	Advanced Data Services	Frederick, MD
301-251-9206	Darwin BBS	Gaithersburg, MD
301-270-2638	Photo*Life	Takoma Park, MD
301-299-8667	The Market	Potomac, MD
301-353-9793	USA Board	Germantown, MD
301-444-0551	The Science Lab	Baltimore, MD

301-521-3107	Midnight Express	Baltimore, MD
301-551-5419	American Veterans BBS	Gambrills, MD
301-567-5144	Riverwatch	Ft. Washington, MD
301-621-9864	Condor	Gambrills, MD
301-654-3157	The Main Frame BBS	Bethesda, MD
301-663-3882	S.Y.S.C.O.M.	Frederick, MD
301-695-4821	Microware BBS	Frederick, MD
301-695-9130	Advanced Data Services	Frederick, MD
301-698-0212	The New Micro Connection	Buckeystown, MD
301-737-0342	Extraordinaire	Great Mills, MD
301-757-9075	The Saloon BBS	Arnold, MD
301-761-1292	Comp-U-Type BBS	Glen Burnie, MD
301-831-4650	Advanced Data Services	Frederick, MD
301-831-5954	W3JP Exchange	Mt. Airy, MD
301-840-0227	CONTECH	Gaithersburg, MD
301-843-1548	The Waldorf Connection	Waldorf, MD
301-862-8048	GPETE BBS	St. Inigoes, MD
301-884-8549	KEEPASM- Knowledge Exchange	Mechanicsville, MD
301-933-5007	Capital Express	Silver Spring, MD
301-942-5616	NETWORK East	Rockville, MD
301-997-1918	Columbia-Online	Columbia, MD

Wildcat! Systems

301-253-6705	The Starlite BBS	Laytonsville, MD
301-272-2594	Mythical Barn	Aberdeen, MD
301-334-1852	Continental BBS	Annapolis, MD
301-459-2864	Blue Hawaii	Hyattsville, MD
301-498-8502	Numis Net	Laurel, MD
301-530-5962	The Electronic Shopper	Bethesda, MD
301-570-9099	DEATH METAL	Olney, MD
301-599-0036	Dave's Place	Upper Marlboro, MD
301-604-2953	Midnight Madness	Laurel, MD
301-621-9864	CONDOR	Gambrills, MD
301-676-0208	Computer Connection	Edgewood, MD
301-689-8753	TOPCAT	Frostburg, MD
301-843-1548	THE WALDORF WILD-CAT!	Waldorf, MD

301-843-9033	Computer Classifieds	Waldorf, MD
301-843-9266	L.E.S.I.X.	Waldorf, MD
301-924-1582	Agora BBS	Gaithersburg, MD
301-932-2082	Country Ranch	Newburg, MD
301-942-5571	Private Corner	Wheaton, MD
301-945-1540	Writers Block	Baltimore, MD

PC Board

302-475-7598	Genesis First State PCBoard	Wilmington, DE
302-737-6041	Fatherboard North	Newark, DE

Wildcat! Systems

302-368-4843	Utilities Unlimited	Newark, DE

PC Board

303-236-9812	Yucca Mountain Project Group	Denver, CO
303-241-1966	Colorado West	Grand Junction, CO
303-242-7977	Squirrel's Nest BBS	Grand Junction, CO
303-423-4710	Cheyenne Social Club	Wheat Ridge, CO
303-939-8174	Computer Repeats BBS	Boulder, CO

Wildcat! Systems

303-482-8777	MRA BBS	Fort Collins, CO
303-632-8380	Cougar's Run	Colorado Springs, CO
303-673-9470	Micromanic	Lafayette, CO
303-790-7024	The Bit Bucket	Denver, CO
303-920-1263	NixPix	Aspen, CO

PC Board

304-599-6083	The Full Spectrum BBS	Margantown, WV
304-675-3745	The Electronic Point	Point Pleasant, WV

Wildcat! Systems

304-429-6838	The Secret Service BBS	Huntington, WV
304-455-1544	Tek-nician Tip Board	New Martinsville, WV
304-522-1912	Harry's Place	Huntington, WV
304-522-6454	WAMX AM/FM RADIO	Huntington, WV
304-863-3077	Peergramming	Parkersburg, WV

PC Board

305-295-2749	Computer Connections	Orlando, FL
305-297-1977	The Exchange!	Orlando, FL
305-322-8330	The Phone Booth	Longwood, FL
305-432-2223	Sunshine BBS	Pembroke Pines, FL
305-536-8678	Tamri-Net	Miami, FL
305-621-7534	Miami PC User's Grp	Miami, FL
305-641-4945	The Twilight Board][	Lake Worth, FL
305-660-6300	The Death Star	Orlando, FL
305-786-0189	The Private Collection	Pompano Beach, FL
305-791-9325	The Cross Roads	Fort Lauderdale, FL
305-831-0588	MedCom Systems BBS	Orlando, FL
305-831-0788	MedCom Systems BBS	Orlando, FL
305-894-8119	Comp. Util. RMS	Orlando, FL
305-940-3045	Florida NetWare BBS	Miami, FL
305-981-1409	The 1000 BBS	Hollywood, FL

Wildcat! Systems

305-223-6334	The Golden Eagle	Miami, FL
305-262-1787	The Miami Connection	Miami, FL
305-285-1293	The Software Pit	Coconut Grove, FL
305-344-6056	Cocoland II	Coral Springs, FL
305-383-5471	"What Ever" BBS	Miami Springs, FL
305-432-3308	The Point After	Pembroke Pines, FL
305-467-6712	"Nightmare" BBS	Fort Lauderdale, FL
305-523-1717	DrawBridge	Fort Lauderdale, FL
305-557-5357	The Road-Runner	Hialeah, FL
305-558-3945	Soft Unlimited	Hialeah, FL
305-824-0531	Mercy's Place BBS	Hialeah, FL

| 305-854-2135 | Gold BBS | Miami, FL |
| 305-944-4037 | Software Galore! | Miami, FL |

PC Board

| 306-267-3220 | SouthSide BBS | Coronach, Saskatchewan, Canada |

PC Board

| 307-856-3601 | The Mizer Board | Riverton, WY |

PC Board

| 309-682-2748 | S.S. Starglider BBS | Peoria, IL |
| 309-764-2025 | Quad Cities PCBoard | East Moline, IL |

Wildcat! Systems

309-274-2200	Burco BBS	Chillicothe, IL
309-347-1268	Space Walker	Pekin, IL
309-482-0530	Hacker A	Peoria, IL
309-797-6191	Dragon's Egg	Moline, IL

PC Board

312-231-6193	The Mystery Zone	Carol Stream, IL
312-232-1250	Windmill BBS	Geneva, IL
312-267-4749	Executive Region BBS	Chicago, IL
312-276-4159	Ye Olde Archive	Chicago, IL
312-293-1021	West Chicago Express	West Chicago, IL
312-307-9514	The Bloomingdale BBS	Bloomingdale, IL
312-323-4711	In the Dog House South	Hinsdale, IL
312-342-1866	Publisher Info Service	Chicago, IL
312-350-7863	MicroSource	Wood Dale, IL
312-390-6594	R.C.S. The Defender	Mount Prospect, IL
312-426-3279	Fox River Valley BBS	Algonquin, IL
312-465-2478	Maverick House	Chicago, IL
312-469-4850	LaserStuff BBS	Glen Ellyn, IL

312-513-1202	MidWest BBS	St. Charles, IL
312-535-2761	Rebel's Retreat	Chicago, IL
312-588-1003	Rick's BBS	Chicago, IL
312-599-8089	Oak Lawn BBS	Oak Lawn, IL
312-639-8654	Star 9	Cary, IL
312-665-9876	The Dog House North	Carol Stream, IL
312-674-1638	Bill's PCBoard	Lincolnwood, IL
312-683-3666	The Great Cavern	Hampshire, IL
312-697-1606	RichWare Software	Elgin, IL
312-758-1136	Foolish Pleasure BBS	Glenwood, IL
312-776-5561	N9CSA Heath/Zenith Ham	Chicago, IL
312-872-8086	Lakes Region BBS	Zion, IL
312-888-4821	Ye Olde Board	Elgin, IL
312-925-8854	Flowers	Chicago, IL
312-963-5496	Midwest PCBoard Exchange	Westmont, IL
312-964-0526	Logician's BBS	Darien, IL

Wildcat! Systems

312-232-6339	P.S. Meeting Room	Geneva, IL
312-253-6224	M.P.P.L. BBS	Mount Prospect, IL
312-359-9346	The Central Command	Palatine, IL
312-470-1691	Cache/Nicol Chicago BBS	Morton Grove, IL
312-636-4485	Fertech Systems	Evergreen Park, IL
312-736-0228	The Phone Company	Chicago, IL
312-827-0229	IBEW Locak 1220	Park Ridge, IL
312-858-4469	AmeriType	Glen Ellyn, IL
312-906-0698	D/831 MIS BBS	Downers Grove, IL
312-960-3425	Orchard Hill BBS	Palos Hills, IL
312-968-9050	West. Suburban Wildcat	Darien, IL
312-973-3551	The African	Chicago, IL

PC Board

313-230-8433	F.A.C.E. PCBoard BBS	Flint, MI
313-232-1905	The Ultimate Connection	Flint, MI
313-322-8966	Application Resources	Allen Park, MI

313-434-9756	The Dog House	Ypsilanti, MI
313-455-3977	Tandy Harbour	Canton, MI
313-474-4987	Auto. Res. Prem. PCBoard (#2)	Framington Hills, MI
313-476-6212	Randco MOS Info. System	Livonia, MI
313-635-2050	Eagle Junction	Swartz Creek, MI
313-661-0726	The Business Board Node 1	Framington Hills, MI
313-679-2408	Black River Systems	Croswell, MI
313-771-8786	The Western C Board	Roseville, MI

Wildcat! Systems

313-226-4423	Federal Job Info Center	Detroit, MI
313-278-0266	APA BBS	Dearborn Heights, MI
313-357-7273	Slipped Disk	Southfield, MI
313-398-3078	Atari Advocate	Madison Heights, MI
313-425-6173	The Blue Light Special	Garden City, MI
313-439-7286	Milan Connection	Milan, MI
313-478-9647	The College Board	Livonia, MI
313-482-4436	Someware In Time	Ypsilanti, MI
313-483-1359	The Builders Workshop	Ypsilanti, MI
313-537-3174	Detroit Metro Amiga	Redford, MI
313-543-2911	Armed Forces Main	Madison Heights, MI
313-546-9454	Top Gun BBS	Royal Oaks, MI
313-582-4072	PC-Palace	Dearborn, MI
313-764-7842	Wolverine IBM Info Exch.	Ann Arbor, MI
313-894-2923	Rick's Corner	Detroit, MI

PC Board

314-298-8363	Computer Assistance Network	St. Louis, MO
314-434-1378	True Blue BBS	St. Louis, MO
314-442-6023	Charlie's BBS	Columbia, MO
314-625-4054	Travel Online	St. Louis, MO
314-961-2242	Epson News Line	St. Louis, MO

Wildcat! Systems

314-329-5376	Ramwood	Fort Leonard Wood, MO
314-436-0730	Boatmen's Bank BBS	St. Louis, MO
314-443-2847	Excalibur	Columbia, MO

PC Board

315-245-3815	Kadet PCBoard	Camdem, NY
315-593-8860	Rad BBS	Fulton, NY
315-866-1725	Sierra PCBoard BBS	Herkimer, NY

Wildcat! Systems

315-697-2298	Technicians Net	Cazenovia, NY

PC Board

316-522-0051	Eagles Nest South (Node 1)	Wichita, KS
316-684-3010	Midwest Genealogical BBS	Wichita, KS
316-684-8744	The Information Booth	Wichita, KS
316-686-4501	Midwest BBS	Wichita, KS

Wildcat! Systems

316-421-9210	Parsons Computers BBS	Parsons, KS
316-662-8966	Data 1 - PC	Hutchinson, KS
316-681-6374	Dragonflight	Wichita, KS
316-686-4286	The Silent Hammer	Wichita, KS
316-788-6013	The Crossroads	Derby, KS
316-938-2627	Crawford Services BBS	Chase, KS

PC Board

317-243-0755	The Circle-City BBS	Indianapolis, IN
317-251-3356	The TECH BBS	Indianapolis, IN
317-291-7287	The Direct Access BBS	Indianapolis, IN

317-351-4981	NACNet BBS	Indianapolis, IN
317-462-1461	The Gold Mine	Indianapolis, IN
317-576-0261	Software Etc. Exchange	Indianapolis, IN
317-654-6555	The Friendly BBS	Frankfort, IN
317-782-1996	Design-Aire BBS	Indianapolis, IN
317-844-9633	PCBoard of Indianapolis	Indianapolis, IN
317-846-6182	The Northside BBS	Carmel, IN
317-862-5966	PC-User's Group	Indianapolis, IN
317-882-5575	IBM-Net Connection	Indianapolis, IN
317-897-8914	The Systems Branch	Indianapolis, IN
317-899-0929	Comm. Exchange Ser.	Indianapolis, IN
317-925-9633	The Professional's Choice	Indianapolis, IN

Wildcat! Systems

| 317-563-3713 | R.E. Frost & Associates | Brookston, IN |
| 317-825-6521 | Atec | Connersville, IN |

PC Board

| 318-783-5126 | Satellite Systems | Crowley, LA |
| 318-988-4509 | Hill Street Blues | Lafayette, LA |

Wildcat! Systems

318-348-0333	WestWind Software	Leesville, LA
318-443-1065	PVMA Wildcat	Alexandria, LA
318-463-2123	The Small Byte	DeRidder, LA
318-783-5126	Fred's Computer	Crowley, LA
318-994-2495	Home-Port	Sarepta, LA

PC Board

319-234-3527	C-Shift Phoenix	Waterloo, IA
319-235-6716	Blackhawk BBS	Waterloo, IA
319-236-0834	The Stock Exchange BBS	Waterloo, IA
319-399-8497	The Gamer's Connection BBS	Cedar Rapids, IA
319-849-2129	Power Tower Pro BBS	Center Point, IA

| 319-849-2191 | Power Tower Pro BBS | Center Point, IA |

PC Board

401-333-5912	Information Exchange BBS	Lincoln, RI
401-463-6451	Tiger's Private BBS	Warwick, RI
401-539-8636	Information Resource System	Carolina, RI
401-683-1015	The Penguin's Home BBS	Portsmouth, RI
401-724-2281	PC Heaven	Lincoln, RI
401-783-2996	The Bird Dog BBS	Peace Dale, RI
401-828-1329	Eagles Nest NetWork	Warwick, RI
401-849-2215	The Dungeon BBS	Middletown, RI
401-949-2565	Cloud Nine	Chepachet, RI

Wildcat! Systems

401-232-7734	Programmer's Paradise	Smithfield, RI
401-331-0592	PC Professional	Providence, RI
401-438-3952	Beta Days II	East Providence, RI
401-461-4223	Prometheus	Cranston, RI
401-737-4587	The Yankee Clipper	Warwick, RI
401-739-2338	Copy-Print BBS	Warwick, RI
401-739-6137	The Ocean State BBS	Warwick, RI
401-821-1546	The Arcade	Hope, RI

PC Board

402-292-6187	The Hyper Channel	Omaha, NE
402-391-3102	CBM Computer Center	Omaha, NE
402-391-5178	The Omaha Clipper	Omaha, NE
402-554-8488	The Edge	Omaha, NE

Wildcat! Systems

402-291-7497	Ripplin' Waters	Omaha, NE
402-292-2989	Hitchhikers Guide	Offutt AFB, NE
402-393-8584	"Lost Boys" BBS	Omaha, NE

| 402-734-1671 | The Hotel California | Omaha, NE |
| 402-896-6050 | WizardNet BBS | Omaha, NE |

PC Board

| 403-271-2122 | Calgary's CD-ROM BBS | Calgary, Alberta, Canada |
| 403-791-5285 | Downtown Fort McMurray | Fort McMurray, Alberta, Canada |

Wildcat! Systems

403-255-6383	Wildcat! Canada	Calgary, Alberta, Canada
403-672-8055	Camrose Computer Support	Camrose, Alberta, Canada
403-934-5832	The Pet Shoppe	Calgary, Alberta, Canada

PC Board

404-242-6952	One of a Kind BBS	Atlanta, GA
404-261-1312	System Support BBS	Atlanta, GA
404-263-8772	The Software Link	Norcross, GA
404-277-1977	Marketing Services	Dalton, GA
404-433-0689	Conference System BBS	Smyrna, GA
404-435-8122	Westfield Express BBS	Smyrna, GA
404-442-9305	Atlanta Macintosh U/Group	Atlanta, GA
404-446-6650	The Big Peach	Norcross, GA
404-455-4707	InSight Financial BBS	Chamblee, GA
404-458-3268	The Southern Mansion	Atlanta, GA
404-476-0847	The Left Place	Duluth, GA
404-476-2607	The Right Place	Duluth, GA
404-493-9421	Interthink BBS	Clarkston, GA
404-564-1256	AESC BBS	Lilburn, GA
404-565-0846	The Sword In The Stone BBS	Atlanta, GA
404-569-9651	PC-Valley	Columbus, GA
404-695-1889	The Front Porch BBS	Chattsworth, GA
404-641-1803	Crosstalk Mk.4 BBS	Roswell, GA

404-751-9231	Atlanta Macintosh U/ Group #2	Atlanta, GA
404-874-5492	Atlanta's Water Drop	Atlanta, GA
404-889-5199	Help Net	Cumming, GA
404-921-4395	The Atlanta Exchange	Atlanta, GA
404-924-3397	The Candy Store	Acworth, GA
404-934-4515	Flagship BBS #1	Stone Mountain, GA
404-938-0724	The Dreams	Tucker, GA
404-948-4584	The Clubhouse BBS	Austell, GA
404-962-5670	Georgia BBS	Atlanta, GA
404-964-4483	Software Shop #2	Fayetteville, GA
404-968-9755	Spaceport DEVA	Rex, GA
404-977-6686	PC-Exchange	Marietta, GA
404-993-5310	The Invisible BBS	Marietta, GA

Wildcat! Systems

404-226-4388	North Georgia BBS	Dalton, GA
404-349-6378	Archiver	Atlanta, GA
404-361-8431	Time Lock	Forest Park, GA
404-461-5947	Cam's Wildcat! House	Fayetteville, GA
404-498-4214	Micropolis Online 24 hrs.	Stone Mountain, GA
404-542-7873	Educator's Exchange	Athens, GA
404-548-1330	Classic City	Athens, GA
404-548-9434	Writers Online	Winterville, GA
404-624-7971	Wildside BBS	Fort Oglethorpe, GA
404-742-7736	Express Line	Winterville, GA
404-879-9223	Paul's Place BBS	Stone Mountain, GA
404-926-0905	Woodstock BBS	Marietta, GA
404-994-1279	Share a Byte BBS	Riverdale, GA

Wildcat! Systems

405-321-0642	The Family Tree	Norman, OK
405-390-4338	Discovery BBS	Choctaw, OK
405-477-2152	My Place	Altus, OK
405-482-5624	Dudley's Software Ex.	Altus, OK
405-691-3437	Recovery BBS	Oklahoma City, OK

405-733-3812	Mac Desktop Publishing BBS	Midwest City, OK
405-769-5226	Electric Dreams	Oklahoma City, OK
405-787-0033	Libra	Oklahoma City, OK

PC Board

| 406-251-4781 | The Montana Cafe | Missoula, MT |
| 406-454-0543 | Midnight Computing Service | Great Falls, MT |

Wildcat! Systems

| 406-756-8296 | MO's Back Door | Kalispell, MT |

PC Board

407-249-0212	Falcon's Nest	Orlando, FL
407-260-5675	Prestige Comp, BBS	Longwood, FL
407-260-6397	Black Hole BBS	Longwood, FL
407-650-7763	The American Dream BBS	West Palm Beach, FL
407-682-3417	Star Gate 2 BBS	Longwood, FL
407-737-9072	The Second Take	Boynton Beach, FL
407-788-3690	Star Gate One BBS	Longwood, FL
407-831-9130	Treasures-BBS	Longwood, FL
407-833-8692	Amiga Beach	West Palm Beach, FL
407-850-3983	The DataGate Connection	Orlando, FL
407-884-8505	INFONET	Apopka, FL
407-969-1884	The Bug Shop	Lake Springs, FL

Wildcat! Systems

407-338-8486	PC LOGIC	Boca Raton, FL
407-439-0341	The FireHouse BBS	Lake Worth, FL
407-633-6209	Apollo BBS	Cocoa, FL
407-642-7426	Allied-Flight	Greenacres, FL
407-683-7351	Flight Biz BBS	Cloud Lake, FL
407-694-1008	The Court of Last Resort	Palm Beach Gardens, FL

PC Board

408-247-6909	Higher Power BBS	San Jose, CA
408-253-7310	Dark Domain BBS	Cupertino, CA
408-257-5134	Bountiful Life BBS	San Jose, CA
408-270-4084	PDS-SIG BBS (Node 3)	San Jose, CA
408-286-8332	Comp-U-Ease	San Jose, CA
408-371-7654	Brown Bag Software BBS	Campbell, CA
408-373-3773	The Cricket BBS	Pacific Grove, CA
408-374-4620	Programmer's Source BBS	Campbell, CA
408-394-6234	Westlog Premium BBS	Seaside, CA
408-425-4608	The WebWorks	Santa Cruz, CA
408-649-0300	The Board of Directors	Monterey, CA
408-655-1096	Nitelog BBS	Monterey, CA
408-728-5598	Night Modulator	Watsonville, CA
408-732-1814	The Tropical BBS	Sunnyvale, CA
408-972-9516	Far Star BBS	San Jose, CA
408-972-9750	Dynamic C.M.I.	San Jose, CA

Wildcat! Systems

408-224-4853	Murphy's Law	San Jose, CA
408-226-0970	Chuck & Ginger's Board	San Jose, CA
408-227-4818	Ventura Publishers Forum	San Jose, CA
408-238-9621	SERVU	San Jose, CA
408-243-2938	After Midnight	Santa Clara, CA
408-246-0164	Pathfinder BBS	Santa Clara, CA
408-255-5810	PC-Connection	Campbell, CA
408-453-3326	Ring-of-Fire	San Jose, CA
408-688-9639	Digital Designs	Aptos, CA
408-730-5512	B&C Microsystems	Sunnyvale, CA
408-899-5728	Utility Shop Plus	Seaside, CA
408-985-1137	OTHER WORLD	San Jose, CA
408-998-8927	Enable BBS	San Jose, CA

PC Board

409-297-1634	Gulf Coast BBS	Lake Jackson, TX
409-832-8745	MSC Superboard	Beaumont, TX

409-835-9899	The Exoteric Exchange	Beaumont, TX
409-842-5449	Graphics Unlimited	Beaumont, TX
409-866-3530	The Night Light	Beaumont, TX
409-899-3360	Lunatic Fringe	Beaumont, TX

Wildcat! Systems

| 409-560-0546 | Gateway | Houston, TX |

PC Board

412-225-8682	Washington PA PCBoard	Washington, PA
412-463-1347	Cave Man BBS	Indiana, PA
412-627-3009	Greene County PCUG BBS	Waynesburg, PA
412-795-0730	Falcon Professional BBS	Pittsburgh, PA

PC Board

413-562-0274	The Wall BBS	Westfield, MA
413-567-1822	Top Cat BBS	Longmeadow, MA
413-583-6167	The Valley BBS	Ludlow, MA
413-783-2379	Larry's Shareware PCB-BBS	Springfield, MA

Wildcat! Systems

413-283-6505	BallPark BBS	Palmer, MA
413-549-8387	The Micro Shuttle BBS	Amherst, MA
413-743-7044	Berkshire Hills BBS	Adams, MA

PC Board

414-466-4039	Faxs BBS	Milwaukee, WI
414-634-5776	PC Access	Racine, WI
414-728-5818	Farmer's Daughter	Whitewater, WI
414-734-0889	PC Access	Racine, WI
414-796-8408	Top Gun][BBS	Brookfield, WI

Wildcat! Systems

414-383-9229	Fantasy Quest	Milwaukee, WI
414-426-1135	The Lakefly Connection	Oshkosh, WI
414-739-2905	Definitive Image	Appleton, WI
414-762-0286	C.A.T.C.H.	Oak Creek, WI
414-771-3032	Second Opinion BBS	Wauwatosa, WI

PC Board

415-226-9422	The Fleet Landing	Fremont, CA
415-284-9151	ComOne	Lafayette, CA
415-327-4591	KORTEK BBS	Palo Alto, CA
415-337-5599	The PC GFX Exchange	San Francisco, CA
415-343-5904	SeaHunt BBS	Burlingame, CA
415-349-6576	The CHARISMA BBS	Foster City, CA
415-352-5411	Boot to the Head	San Leandro, CA
415-438-9826	Speed Thrills	Fremont, CA
415-441-0616	Transporter	San Francisco, CA
415-471-3776	The Express Stop	Union City, CA
415-474-0227	NETwork 2000 BBS	San Francisco, CA
415-482-3402	The Pixel Penguin	Oakland, CA
415-530-0181	Pyramid of Power BBS	Oakland, CA
415-572-8219	KAYFUN HINTS BBS	San Mateo, CA
415-574-3663	Toad Hall	San Carlos, CA
415-587-9664	Midnight Mechanics Inc.	San Francisco, CA
415-595-5079	TECHNET BBS	San Carlos, CA
415-644-6806	The Guardian	Berkeley, CA
415-653-3243	Echelon BBS	San Leandro, CA
415-657-4299	Emerald City BBS	Fremont, CA
415-745-9898	The Crow's Nest BBS	Newark, CA
415-778-5929	Infolinc PCBoard (Node 1)	Antioch, CA
415-792-3210	The Midnight Express	Fremont, CA
415-794-9624	SDA	Fremont, CA
415-825-4613	InterCom	Concord, CA
415-829-6027	Easy Access BBS	San Ramon, CA
415-837-4610	The Transfer Station	Alamo, CA
415-858-0188	Software Zone	Palo Alto, CA

415-895-6159	The Knowledge Connection	San Leandro, CA
415-947-6609	Tass	Walnut Creek, CA
415-967-3484	Sailors Refuge	Mountain View, CA
415-969-4356	BayNet BBS	Mountain View, CA

Wildcat! Systems

415-255-7040	Art/Online	San Francisco, CA
415-359-6985	COASTSIDE BBS	Pacifica, CA
415-361-1847	Emerald Lake/MPG BBS	Redwood City, CA
415-365-9079	Running Wyld	Redwood City, CA
415-370-1003	Tiger's Cave	Martinez, CA
415-537-1777	Combat Arms	Castro Valley, CA
415-651-9496	Earth-Rite	Fremont, CA
415-656-7783	The Final Approach	Fremont, CA
415-683-9560	Freedom BBS	Fremont, CA
415-764-9066	NEXUS	Berkeley, CA
415-797-9590	Jet Print BBS	Fremont, CA
415-966-8533	Tiara Support	Mountain View, CA

PC Board

416-229-4295	PC Express	North York, Ontario, Canada
416-236-3209	One Thousand BBS	Toronto, Ontario, Canada
416-277-8253	The Winning Edge BBS	Mississauga, Ontario, Canada
416-372-9390	The Phantom BBS	Cobourg, Ontario, Canada
416-432-1631	Canadian Data Communications	Oshawa, Ontario, Canada
416-458-7214	The Greaf Greff BBS	Brampton, Ontario, Canada
416-467-8912	Asylum BBS	Toronto, Ontario, Canada
416-498-5962	The Seed Sowers Friendly BBS	Toronto, Ontario, Canada
416-588-0877	Port BBS	Toronto, Ontario, Canada
416-629-0168	CRS Limited	Toronto, Ontario, Canada
416-661-8064	Desktop Pub. Forum	Toronto, Ontario, Canada
416-699-1846	Media Shack PCBoard	Toronto, Ontario, Canada

416-733-2285	Rose Media PCBoard	Toronto, Ontario, Canada
416-878-5935	MCS BBS	Milton, Ontario, Canada
416-961-2477	Toronto Sports Board	Toronto, Ontario, Canada
416-977-6193	CMIX	Toronto, Ontario, Canada

Wildcat! Systems

416-274-8563	Affairs!	Ontario, Canada
416-358-8473	The Power Station	Ontario, Canada
416-358-9096	Dragon's Lair	Ontario, Canada
416-450-5672	Info/Access	Ontario, Canada
416-527-5461	The Last Unicorn	Ontario, Canada
416-646-0263	T-C-II	Ontario, Canada
416-684-4687	The Cutting Edge	Ontario, Canada
416-684-7710	Doctor On Board	Ontario, Canada
416-685-5658	Compro Systems	Ontario, Canada
416-788-0667	Panther II BBS	Ontario, Canada
416-892-4689	Zeus II	Ontario, Canada
416-937-2920	HAM BBS	Ontario, Canada
416-937-7365	PC Pipeline	Ontario, Canada

PC Board

417-649-7761	The Fortress PCBoard	Carl Junction, MO

PC Board

419-473-8651	NW Ohio Info. & S/W Exchange	Toledo, OH

Wildcat! Systems

419-423-6656	Findlay BBS	Findlay, OH
419-524-3959	DK Jet-Works	Mansfield, OH
419-526-6166	Video Fax	Mansfield, OH
419-935-0245	The Clone Connection	Willard, OH

PC Board

501-364-3282	The Five 'n' Dime	Crossett, AR

501-364-6163	KompuTek BBS	Crossett, AR
501-575-0722	CSEG BBS	Fayetteville, AR
501-646-4071	ThunderDome	Fort Smith, AR
501-750-2410	Ozark Cross-Roads BBS	Springdale, AR
501-756-2411	Ozark Cross-Roads BBS	Springdale, AR
501-767-1015	Arkansas Communications Ex	Hot Springs, AR
501-853-2209	Hamburger BBS	Hamburg, AR

Wildcat! Systems

501-224-5233	Wheels of Fire	Little Rock, AR
501-228-9194	The Fortran Fortress	Little Rock, AR
501-268-0412	The Connection BBS!	Searcy, AR
501-532-6212	McScott's BBS	Blytheville, AR
501-565-8220	Omega Systems	Little Rock, AR
501-646-0543	Ark/Ok PC Users	Fort Smith, AR
501-763-8568	Pioneer BBS	Blytheville, AR
501-851-6637	Command-Line	North Little Rock, AR
501-888-8437	Sequoyah	Hensley, AR

PC Board

502-227-2384	The Electric Voice	Frankfort, KY
502-227-9783	Kentucky Trans. Cab. BBS	Frankfort, KY
502-267-6532	The Doctor's Inn	Louisville, KY
502-423-8654	The Fifth Dimension	Louisville, KY
502-452-0443	Wheelmen's Bench	Louisville, KY
502-561-0742	LegNet	Louisville, KY
502-564-8777	DIS Connection	Frankfort, KY
502-684-9855	Pegasus	Owensboro, KY
502-886-7664	Pennyrile BBS	Hopkinsville, KY

Wildcat! Systems

502-754-1390	The Coal Mine	Central City, KY
502-778-1714	Tandy 1000 BBS	Louisville, KY
502-782-0260	Rasputin's Play Ground	Bowling Green, KY
502-894-0614	Louisville Showcase	Louisville, KY

PC Board

503-226-3341	Ma Fergusons	Albany, OR

Wildcat! Systems

503-284-5130	CFS BBS	Portland, OR
503-389-5209	MOCC BBS	Bend, OR
503-459-2430	The Short Circuit	Roseburg, OR
503-640-5225	Aqua Terra Software BBS	Hillsboro, OR
503-659-9691	MC3	Portland, OR
503-883-3893	Pelican Bay BBS	Klamath Falls, OR

PC Board

504-947-8216	Port O' Call	New Orleans, LA

Wildcat! Systems

504-275-8213	The Millennium Falcon	Baton Rouge, LA
504-335-5555	CRYSTAL CAVE	Baton Rouge, LA
504-356-3252	The Restaurant	Baton Rouge, LA
504-861-1945	INFO MASTER BBS	New Orleans, LA

PC Board

505-287-8212	Grants Area PCBoard	Grants, NM
505-437-4670	Alamo-PC	Alamogordo, NM
505-836-9576	Midnight Express PCBoard	Albuquerque, NM
505-846-8459	Navy Nuclear Safety BBS	Albuquerque, NM

Wildcat! Systems

505-488-5558	KBBS	Roswell, NM
505-523-4528	Waterfront West Wildcat	Las Cruces, NM

Wildcat! Systems

506-459-0973	Omni-Net	Fredericton, New Brunswick, Canada
506-849-6506	Hinchey Computer Products	New Brunswick, Canada

PC Board

508-285-7240	TEABBS	Norton, MA
508-346-4317	Merrimac PCBoard Systems	Merrimac, MA
508-435-4656	AVATAR BBS	Hopkinton, MA
508-653-5124	Mass. Mac & Electric	Natick, MA
508-675-5493	Data CENTRAL	Fall River, MA
508-677-9493	Data CENTRAL	Fall River, MA
508-757-3983	DataCore Information Ser.	Worcester, MA
508-757-8622	DataCore Information Ser.	Worcester, MA
508-833-0508	Auto Exec BBS	Plymouth, MA
508-875-3618	)(evious BBS	Framingham, MA
508-927-7520	The Godfathers Den	Beverly, MA
508-949-3590	The Ham Shack	Webster, MA
508-975-9779	AEG Modicon BBS, N.	Andover, MA

PC Board

512-255-0615	Speeders BBS	Round Rock, TX
512-491-9034	Diversions	San Antonio, TX
512-493-9337	Code Bleu	San Antonio, TX
512-578-3500	Victoria Online BBS	Victoria, TX
512-590-6036	Abbey Road PBBS	San Antonio, TX
512-623-2210	Rick's Place	San Antonio, TX
512-648-4689	PC-Network	San Antonio, TX
512-653-0407	U-Com	San Antonio, TX
512-681-1303	Software Connection	San Antonio, TX
512-694-4601	The Super System	San Antonio, TX
512-696-1270	Computer Aspects BBS	San Antonio, TX
512-822-8882	Telstar Communications	San Antonio, TX
512-829-4533	Telstar Communications	San Antonio, TX

Wildcat! Systems

512-270-4169	SAPD PC User's Group BBS	San Antonio, TX
512-298-3247	TLC BBS	Del Rio, TX
512-358-2828	Eilean Donan Castle	Beeville, TX
512-366-3410	Traffic Central BBS	San Antonio, TX
512-383-6176	The Computer Police Dept.	Edinburg, TX
512-590-2720	The West Coast Connection	San Antonio, TX
512-595-0491	BuckBoard Bulletins BBS	Kingsville, TX
512-595-4525	Anchor	Kingsville, TX
512-654-8349	The Gathering	San Antonio, TX
512-659-2687	The Stadium	Randolph AFB, TX
512-664-7637	Al-Tex BBS	Alice, TX
512-673-6402	Computer Ventures	Haltom City, TX
512-675-6363	2400 Archive Place	San Antonio, TX
512-684-3416	The Nightline Comm System	San Antonio, TX
512-826-2679	The Executive Board	San Antonio, TX
512-826-5026	Amicom BBS	San Antonio, TX
512-883-6419	B10S II	San Antonio, TX
512-924-0889	The Shadow Taker	San Antonio, TX

PC Board

513-274-0821	The Annex	Dayton, OH
513-424-7529	Modem Zone	Middletown, OH
513-522-3076	InterSteller Software	Cincinnati, OH
513-528-0505	The Cathouse III	Cincinnati, OH
513-528-0707	The Cathouse III	Cincinnati, OH
513-661-4533	The Rivercomm BBS	Cincinnati, OH
513-821-9703	S/W Unlmtd. Elect. Shop. Mart	Cincinnati, OH
513-851-9207	The Silver Bullet BBS	Cincinnati, OH
513-868-8911	The COLONEL'S PCBoard	Hamilton, OH

Wildcat! Systems

513-233-6353	Larry's Place	Dayton, OH
513-236-7085	KYLE'S BBS	Huber Heights, OH
513-253-0645	Gizmo's Place	Kettering, OH
513-429-7780	CDS On-Line	Dayton, OH
513-474-6325	O.I.C. Computers & Acces.	Cincinnati, OH
513-621-1538	Micro-Council	Cincinnati, OH
513-753-9428	SQUIRREL'S NEST	Cincinnati, OH
513-866-6435	Bible Study BBS	West Carrollton, OH

PC Board

514-277-0371	Micro-Care Online	Montreal, Quebec, Canada
514-284-2467	BBS GAI of Montreal	Montreal, Quebec, Canada
514-389-5146	Direct Connect BBS	Montreal, Quebec, Canada
514-389-6352	Direct Connect BBS	Montreal, Quebec, Canada
514-443-8033	DAT-A-REA BBS	St-Hubert, Quebec, Canada
514-486-0519	Input Montreal	Montreal, Quebec, Canada
514-524-8982	Rencontres Du Village	Montreal, Quebec, Canada
514-583-4239	Info-Tel Systems	Montreal, Quebec, Canada
514-583-5449	Info-Tel Systems	Montreal, Quebec, Canada
514-596-0657	Montreal Systems Group	Montreal, Quebec, Canada
514-655-5069	Power Comm	Bloucherville, Quebec, Canada
514-656-6292	Dat-A-Rea	St-Hubert, Quebec, Canada
514-670-5428	The Escape	Longueuil, Quebec, Canada
514-761-1267	XeneC BBS	Montreal, Quebec, Canada
514-935-7285	Easy Access	Montreal, Quebec, Canada
514-989-1567	Le Systeme OnLine (5 Nodes)	Montreal, Quebec, Canada

Wildcat! Systems

514-431-5287	Amigabytes BBS	Bellefeuille, Quebec, Canada

514-474-0629	The Wild BBS	Quebec, Canada
514-527-9924	Alley Cat	Quebec, Canada
514-696-6937	The Silicone Wasteland	Quebec, Canada

PC Board

516-286-1033	The New Line BBS	Medford, NY
516-286-7842	NYCONN	Long Island, NY
516-331-4353	The Mother Board BBS	Terryville, NY
516-358-2815	WGM Computer Consult. BBS	Franklin Square, NY
516-374-6045	The Software Palace	East Rockaway, NY
516-422-1483	The Sounding Board	North Babylon, NY
516-473-5438	The Elco Base PCBoard	Coram, NY
516-475-5625	The Teacher Link	Medford, NY
516-483-3783	Unicorn BBS	Garden City, NY
516-536-6819	The Sound of Music #2	Oceanside, NY
516-567-8267	Connection-80	Bohemia, NY
516-679-1641	NY State Society of CPA's	Wantagh, NY
516-689-6839	Dr. Jerry	Strongs Neck, NY
516-735-8414	Central Headquarters	Seaford, NY
516-737-2731	The Silicon Sysop	Lake Ronkonkoma, NY
516-795-7784	Atlantis BBS	Massapequa, NY
516-796-7296	Beginnings BBS	Levittown, NY
516-796-7686	The Hard Disk Cafe	Seaford, NY
516-798-4091	The All American BBS	Massapequa, NY
516-822-7396	The World BBS	Hicksville, NY
516-842-6231	CNS Computing Services	Amity Harbor, NY
516-864-1387	The Nuclear Site	Commack, NY
516-867-4446	Intelec Business Network	Freeport, NY
516-867-4447	Intelec Business Network	Freeport, NY
516-921-6806	The Sailor's Port	Syosset, NY
516-921-8026	The Far Side	Syosset, NY
516-928-4986	East Coast MIDI BBS	Coram, NY

Wildcat! Systems

516-223-5180	SunShine II	Merrick, NY
516-295-2097	Atlantic Janus	Woodmere, NY
516-493-0186	The Game Peddler BBS	Commack, NY

516-679-0674	Modem News Online	East Meadow, NY
516-735-8414	Sunshine BBS	Seaford, NY
516-737-8217	Logylink	Lake Ronkonkoma, NY
516-751-6619	Charlies Place	Centereach, NY
516-795-5874	PC BBS	Massapequa, NY
516-842-4259	Infosys	Copiague, NY
516-935-2027	The Ancient Pond	Hicksville, NY

PC Board

517-686-8300	W&WNET BBS	Bay City, MI
517-773-6479	Vixen BBS	Mount Pleasant, MI
517-790-0598	Charlie	Saginaw, MI

Wildcat! Systems

517-332-3148	Chip's Place	East Lansing, MI
517-548-4548	Total System Support BBS	Howell, MI
517-629-2012	Lil' BBS	Albion, MI
517-631-9637	Royal Crown BBS	Midland, MI
517-754-7454	Pete's Perverted Playgr.	Saginaw, MI
517-772-5394	TOLENKAR'S LAIR	Mount Pleasant, MI
517-783-2547	NICK AT NITE	Jackson, MI
517-790-1002	Chatter Box	Saginaw, MI

PC Board

518-283-4855	ESN News-State Capital	Albany, NY
518-785-4189	Night Flight	Latham, NY

PC Board

519-469-3028	Haley's BBS	Woodstock, Ontario, Canada
519-539-0523	Wildfire BBS	Woodstock, Ontario, Canada
519-681-3113	Canadian-Micro S/W BBS	London, Ontario, Canada
519-821-6389	Hillside Systems	Guelph, Ontario, Canada

519-824-9226	RGB Computing	Guelph, Ontario, Canada
519-973-7340	SouthWest Connect	Windsor, Ontario, Canada

Wildcat! Systems

519-451-8196	Jolly Miller	Ontario, Canada
519-461-0178	The HMS Botany Bay	Thamesford, Ontario, Canada

PC Board

601-268-8871	Camelot BBS	Hattiesburg, MS

Wildcat! Systems

601-234-2963	The Tech-Link (TTL)	Oxford, MS
601-485-8022	The Queen City BBS	Meridian, MS
601-943-6903	THE TWILIGHT ZONE	Carson, MS

PC Board

602-279-2673	The Tool Shop #1 (2 Nodes)	Phoenix, AZ
602-375-0641	First Board BBS	Phoenix, AZ
602-458-1155	Bed-Pan BBS	Sierra Vista, AZ
602-569-0350	The Trading Post BBS	Phoenix, AZ
602-649-0260	SkId RoW	Mesa, AZ
602-757-1125	Primetime Network	Kingman, AZ
602-786-9131	Technoids Anonymous	Chandler, AZ
602-795-5874	The Party Scene	Tuscon, AZ
602-821-4297	EDIF User's Group BBS	Chandler, AZ
602-827-0280	Genesis II	Mesa, AZ
602-877-2969	The Wish Book	Phoenix, AZ
602-897-6459	Measurement BBS	Phoenix, AZ
602-899-3406	David & Goliaths BBS	Chandler, AZ
602-899-5233	Technoids Anonymous	Chandler, AZ
602-943-6962	The Cursory BBS	Phoenix, AZ
602-957-0631	Inn on the Park	Scottsdale, AZ
602-968-2814	ASU Underground BBS	Tempe, AZ

| 602-971-2454 | The Courier Connection | Paradise Valley, AZ |

Wildcat! Systems

602-230-1464	Baron's Data Exchange	Phoenix, AZ
602-242-2462	Bible Foundation BBS	Phoenix, AZ
602-378-1164	Boonie	Herford, AZ
602-438-8489	The Newsroom	Tempe, AZ
602-565-3941	Golden Valley BBS	Kingman, AZ
602-581-9258	Realistic BBS	Phoenix, AZ
602-623-4470	Venus BBS	Tucson, AZ
602-747-2737	Clearwater BBS	Tucson, AZ
602-840-4752	Nat'l Congress for Men	Phoenix, AZ
602-843-8187	Double Density BBS	Glendale, AZ
602-848-1249	$oftware Rental, Etc.	Phoenix, AZ
602-890-0552	The On-Line! BBS	Mesa, AZ
602-899-9539	U.S. Registry	Chandler, AZ
602-996-9488	The Retreat	Phoenix, AZ

PC Board

603-431-1021	Portsmouth PCUG	Portsmouth, NH
603-432-6711	Nor'Easter BBS	Londonderry, NH
603-886-5722	The Toy Room BBS	Hudson, NH

Wildcat! Systems

603-432-2517	Leo Technology BBS	Londonderry, NH
603-525-4636	The Fire House BBS	Hancock, NH
603-641-2017	Computer Solutions	Manchester, NH
603-641-2171	Queen City Software Xchng	Manchester, NH

PC Board

604-370-2660	The White Rabbit	Victoria, BC, Canada
604-478-0254	The Christian BBS	Victoria, BC, Canada
604-479-0418	ConpuSpec	Victoria, BC, Canada
604-521-0886	Comstar BBS	Burnaby, BC, Canada

604-595-7423	InfoPool PC-Board BBS	Victoria, BC, Canada
604-727-2291	IMARCO Network	Victoria, BC, Canada
604-727-6779	Southern Cross BBS	Victoria, BC, Canada
604-785-7688	Points-North, Fort	St. John, BC, Canada
604-962-9401	The Golden Kingdom	Prince George, BC, Canada

Wildcat! Systems

604-270-7207	Inkwell	British Columbia, Canada
604-270-8331	Pinetree Software BBS	Burnaby, BC, Canada
604-380-0297	Ivo Andric Memorial BBS	British Columbia, Canada
604-434-3434	Vancouver PC User Society	Vancouver, BC, Canada
604-573-4294	Erin Valley BBS	Kamloups, BC, Canada
604-594-8180	Heiko's BBS	British Columbia, Canada
604-826-6607	Ebenezer Christian BBS Mission	British Columbia, Canada
604-949-9732	Midnight Express BBS	British Columbia, Canada

PC Board

605-256-2812	The "Dakotan" BBS	Madison, SD

Wildcat! Systems

605-642-8605	The Urban Hideout	Spearfish, SD

PC Board

606-257-1597	Electronic Maint. BBS	Lexington, KY
606-271-3809	Lexington Board of Exchange	Lexington, KY
606-293-0154	Cen. KY Comp. Soc. BBS	Lexington, KY
606-432-0879	Strawberry Patch (Node 1)	Pikeville, KY
606-745-6044	The Eastern Gate BBS	Winchester, KY
606-781-4478	Ruppel-Set][	Southgate, KY

Wildcat! Systems

606-248-7519	Captain's Wildcat	Middlesboro, KY
606-269-1565	THE PROF-BBS	Richmond, KY
606-325-1983	The Bent Diver	Ashland, KY
606-623-7951	The Digital Gallery	Richmond, KY

PC Board

607-687-4346	OFA-PC	Oswego, NY
607-754-3420	OFA-PC	Oswego, NY

Wildcat! Systems

607-324-2931	Norberts	Hornell, NY
607-687-2793	PAL-BBS	Oswego, NY
607-732-4565	Sugar Mountain	Elmira, NY

PC Board

608-251-7734	CooperWorks	Madison, WI
608-273-2123	Madison PC User's Group BBS	Madison, WI
608-781-3451	Computerland of La Crosse	La Crosse, WI
608-785-7159	The Silicon Zone	La Crosse, WI

PC Board

609-228-2358	Compu-Data	Turnersville, NJ
609-327-5553	Union Lake BBS	Millville, NJ
609-392-5953	Polymath One-Node 2	Trenton, NJ
609-435-7598	The Sports Connection	Voorhees, NJ
609-455-6365	Info-Tech BBS	Bridgeton, NJ
609-530-1116	The Death Star BBS	Trenton, NJ
609-530-1506	The Red Storm BBS	Ewing, NJ
609-645-9449	The Casino	Atlantic City, NJ
609-652-0135	Go Software BBS	Smithville, NJ
609-652-4923	Stockton State College	Pomona, NJ

609-667-5652	Liberty Bell BBS	Cherry Hill, NJ
609-678-8723	Tri-State Info Systems II	Pennsville, NJ
609-692-1502	Alpha Omega BBS	Vineland, NJ
609-692-5843	Tri-State Info Net III	Vineland, NJ
609-692-9366	Alpha Omega BBS	Vineland, NJ
609-825-1046	Harred On-Line	Millville, NJ
609-825-4418	Lakeside BBS	Laurel Lake, NJ
609-884-1086	Wulihan PCBoard BBS	Cape May, NJ
609-921-0354	The Twilight Zone	Rocky Hill, NJ

Wildcat! Systems

609-228-6596	The Online Catalog	Deptford, NJ
609-435-6689	The Boardroom	Laurel Springs, NJ
609-468-1348	DATALINE	Wenonah, NJ

PC Board

612-456-9450	American Data Terminals	Eagan, MN
612-553-0150	The Plymouth BBS	Plymouth, MN
612-871-1151	RRCA BBS	Minneapolis, MN

Wildcat! Systems

612-379-3961	The Real Estate System	Minneapolis, MN
612-425-3408	The Friendship Express	Maple Grove, MN
612-426-9357	TMS White Sheet	White Bear Lake, MN
612-489-8303	Portal	St. Anthony, MN
612-522-2026	The U.S. Veterans BBS	Robbinsdale, MN
612-588-3301	Star View Connection	Minneapolis, MN
612-738-3655	Shadow Fax BBS	Maplewood, MN

PC Board

613-233-1879	Canada's Capital BBS	Ottawa, Ontario, Canada
613-236-1730	Oasis PCBoard	Ottawa, Ontario, Canada
613-521-1267	Shadow RAM BBS	Ottawa, Ontario, Canada
613-738-1793	Source Code Central BBS	Ottawa, Ontario, Canada
613-824-0059	The Role-Players Haven	Ottawa, Ontario, Canada

Wildcat! Systems

613-238-4288	LOCAL 34 BBS	Orleans, Ontario, Canada
613-749-2174	KOMKOR	Vanier, Ontario, Canada

PC Board

614-335-3972	Odie Link	Washington Court House, OH
614-442-6695	Utilities Exchange BBS	Columbus, OH
614-457-0944	Little Italy Elite	Columbus, OH
614-553-9585	MIDNIGHT EXPRESS	Columbus, OH
614-574-6516	F.R.E.D.'S. BBS	Wheelersburg, OH
614-594-2285	Software Solutions BBS	Athens, OH
614-742-2275	Peanuts Guard D-O-G BBS	Pomeroy, OH
614-855-2659	Information Exchange II	Columbus, OH
614-875-1360	The Eagle's Nest	Grove City, OH
614-889-0387	The Satellite Computer Net	Worthington, OH
614-891-2972	Skyline BBS	Westerville, OH
614-895-7209	The Badlan	Westerville, OH
614-895-7759	The Badlan	Westerville, OH

Wildcat! Systems

614-263-9775	Northland BBS	Columbus, OH
614-353-1932	The Jungle!	Portsmouth, OH
614-423-7879	OEC-BBS	Belpre, OH
614-439-0310	SOCS	New Concord, OH
614-439-7451	The Other Board	Cambridge, OH
614-442-6703	TBS BBS	Columbus, OH
614-453-6494	Problem Solvers! BBS	Zanesville, OH
614-454-6063	Grab Bag!	Zanesville, OH
614-461-6943	NightLine	Columbus, OH
614-474-9130	Starry Night	Circleville, OH
614-478-7385	Timeclock	Columbus, OH
614-654-3910	Proteam	Lancaster, OH
614-794-3143	Your Basic BBS	Westerville, OH

614-837-3896	Aspencade BBS	Pickerington, OH
614-837-7428	NCC-1701	Columbus, OH
614-848-5971	THE MICRO GALLERY	Columbus, OH
614-855-2776	Turbo BBS	Westerville, OH
614-861-1287	THE WANT ADS	Columbus, OH
614-863-9611	THE PLTOENIX	Columbus, OH
614-864-0775	The Citadel BBS	Reynoldsburg, OH
614-864-2673	C.O.R.E.	Reynoldsburg, OH
614-885-4004	Nightmare BBS	Worthington, OH
614-889-0387	Satelite Computer Netwo	Worthington, OH
614-890-7043	Mariner's Coven	Westerville, OH
614-891-2972	THE RAVENS NEST	Westerville, OH

PC Board

615-239-3073	Poor Boy's BBS	Gray, TN
615-242-7909	Troll's Cave PCBoard	Nashville, TN
615-266-0015	Freestyle BBS	Chattanooga, TN
615-339-0350	Skyline BBS	Cleveland, TN
615-377-9122	Computer Partners	Brentwood, TN
615-386-9186	The Digital BBS	Nashville, TN
615-472-8925	The Far Side BBS	Cleveland, TN
615-476-2874	PC Solutions of Cleveland	Cleveland, TN
615-531-1823	Syd's IBM-BBS	Knoxville, TN
615-574-5529	MMES IandC	Oak Ridge, TN
615-586-8260	The Talbott BBS	Morristown, TN
615-624-1442	Freestyle BBS	Chattanooga, TN
615-675-3244	Premier BBS	Knoxville, TN
615-675-3282	Data World BBS	Knoxville, TN
615-691-9073	Syd's IBM-BBS	Knoxville, TN
615-966-3574	Data World BBS	Knoxville, TN
615-970-7418	DataComp BBS	Alcoa,TN
615-974-7484	SPARAT BBS	Knoxville, TN

Wildcat! Systems

615-246-3016	TEE-PEE	Kingsport, TN
615-254-9350	TennSpot BBS	Nashville, TN
615-262-3231	Micro Scope	Nashville, TN

615-320-2887	SHIPWRECK	Nashville, TN
615-331-9710	Micro Stuff	Antioch, TN
615-333-6223	Wet Paint BBS	Nashville, TN
615-356-3226	Lions Head BBS	Nashville, TN
615-360-9179	Nashville Underground	Nashville, TN
615-363-2361	The PUB	Knoxville, TN
615-366-4371	The Cargo Bay	Nashville, TN
615-391-5771	Kerygma BBS	Hermitage, TN
615-432-4308	Generic BBS	Cookville, TN
615-432-4622	KING'S CORNER	Cookville, TN
615-566-1792	Neutron Bomb	Maryville, TN
615-698-1456	The Candy Shop	Chattanooga, TN
615-791-4532	The Top Secret BBS	Franklin, TN
615-821-9453	Pyramid	Chattanooga, TN
615-834-8329	The Night Shift	Antioch, TN
615-875-3853	The High Seas	Hixson, TN
615-889-0813	Alph & Omega	Nashville, TN
615-889-1446	Crazy Horse	Nashville, TN
615-892-1031	The Golden Retriever	Chattanooga, TN
615-926-6476	The Byte Bucket	Johnson City, TN
615-983-8232	The Disk Fix	Maryville, TN

Wildcat! Systems

616-327-8703	Night Light!	Portage, MI
616-372-5595	KVCC CBT	Kalamazoo, MI
616-530-0821	Trillion	Wyoming, MI
616-964-4562	The Computer Express	Battle Creek, MI

PC Board

617-227-4170	Future Technology	Boston, MA
617-227-6260	Future Technology	Boston, MA
617-235-6303	BOSTON GAS	Wellesley, MA
617-237-1511	Heath User's Group	Wellesley, MA
617-262-7611	Atlantis	Boston, MA
617-274-7196	MAC's Place	Bedford, MA
617-326-0259	BINEX II Systems	Westwood, MA

617-344-4758	Cloud Nine BBS	Stoughton, MA
617-346-4317	Merrimac PCBoard	Merrimac, MA
617-354-2171	Viking Magic BBS	Cambridge, MA
617-354-2505	Channel 1	Cambridge, MA
617-454-3864	Dave's PCBoard	Lowell, MA
617-469-0192	The DigiCom BBS	Chestnut Hill, MA
617-475-5371	The New Wyverns Nest	Andover, MA
617-498-4553	Harvard BBS	Cambridge, MA
617-545-9131	Turbo Source Search	Scituate, MA
617-665-3796	Information Exchange	Melrose, MA
617-667-8905	Exodus	Billerica, MA
617-720-1330	Future Technology	Boston, MA
617-721-7360	Base 10	Winchester, MA
617-769-4966	Synergy (Node 3)	Norwood, MA
617-769-5309	Synergy	Norwood, MA
617-782-2457	The Edge of Insanity	Brighton, MA
617-786-8282	The Razor's Edge	Quincy, MA
617-889-0777	Jabba's PC-HUT	Chelsea, MA
617-975-9779	Gould Electronics BBS	North Andover, MA

Wildcat! Systems

617-266-7507	The Emerson Wall	Boston, MA
617-336-4243	Hotel California	Seekonk, MA
617-366-9141	KING INSTRUMENT BBS	Westboro, MA
617-433-2702	The Demon's Den	Pepperell, MA
617-481-4659	The Little Builder	Marlboro, MA
617-568-8110	CHAOS	Hudson, MA
617-772-3977	Silicone City BBS	Fort Devens, MA
617-772-6373	DENIS'S WILDCAT!	Ayer, MA
617-772-7199	THE DARK SIDE	Ayer, MA
617-796-6802	MEDMUG	Fort Devens, MA
617-898-6433	The Crash Cart BBS	Andover, MA

PC Board

618-233-2315	The Phoenix	Belleville, IL
618-398-2305	Wizard's Lair	Fairview Heights, IL

Wildcat! Systems

618-251-5747	Harbor Sales	East Alton, IL
618-254-6961	Plato's Place	East Alton, IL
618-397-7687	Magic Isles	Belleville, IL
618-576-9218	Calhoun System BBS	Hardin, IL
618-624-2963	METRO - EAST EX-CHANGE	O'Fallon, IL
618-684-6158	The Midnight Connection	Murphysboro, IL

PC Board

619-222-9483	La Verne & PC Street AGAIN	San Diego, CA
619-241-3564	ATMC Premium Remote BBS	Victorville, CA
619-270-2042	Forum Board	San Diego, CA
619-282-1211	The Rasta Think Tank	San Diego, CA
619-298-2023	Scanline Remote BBS	San Diego, CA
619-298-4027	MediaLine BBS	San Diego, CA
619-375-2306	Computing Technology	Ridgecrest, CA
619-433-8564	Data Trax	Oceanside, CA
619-436-2617	Dream Castle	Encinitas, CA
619-439-2159	The Cheshire Cat	Oceanside, CA
619-446-7255	The Sharper Image	Ridgecrest, CA
619-447-1422	My House BBS	El Cajon, CA
619-447-2307	The Fleet Landing	El Cajon, CA
619-448-0743	Eagle's Flight	Santee, CA
619-462-1732	The Aquarium BBS	La Mesa, CA
619-465-0327	Long Shot BBS	San Diego, CA
619-470-0771	CASINO West PCBoard	Spring Valley, CA
619-535-9580	Mushin BBS	San Diego, CA
619-560-2996	StarBase 23	San Diego, CA
619-561-2999	The Flare Path	Lakeside, CA
619-565-0785	SCANIS	San Diego, CA
619-584-0338	San Diego PCBoard	San Diego, CA
619-586-0703	Scripps Ranch BBS	San Diego, CA
619-586-7973	Kingdom Age BBS	San Diego, CA

619-693-4446	Cipher's Technical Info BBS	San Diego, CA
619-696-2568	The Information Center	San Diego, CA
619-698-2416	The Musical Chair (Node 1)	San Diego, CA
619-728-4318	The File Bank	Fallbrook, CA
619-789-6377	Back Country PCBoard	Ramona, CA
619-944-1804	California Computer Connection	Cardiff, CA

Wildcat! Systems

619-226-2822	King Kobra	San Diego, CA
619-279-9021	Christ Line	San Diego, CA
619-287-6006	The Computer Room	San Diego, CA
619-294-7480	The General BBS	San Diego, CA
619-321-0588	Dimensions 2000	Cathedral City, CA
619-367-0133	Creative World!	Twenty-Nine Palms, CA
619-367-9208	Data Byte Computer Serv.	Twenty-Nine Palms, CA
619-390-7328	Lakeside Wildcat Board	Lakeside, CA
619-421-4922	The Beach	Chula Vista, CA
619-435-8070	Coronado WILDCAT! BBS	Coronado, CA
619-447-3944	The Third Wish	El Cajon, CA
619-455-5226	Shareware	San Diego, CA
619-461-6642	RPC Library	Lemon Grove, CA
619-482-8926	Sharkey's BBS	Chula Vista, CA
619-483-0107	Facts Online	San Diego, CA
619-560-7713	Pacific Rim Information	San Diego, CA
619-561-4681	Perpetrators! BBS	Lakeside, CA
619-562-8735	Santee Micro	Santee, CA
619-565-1728	Plain Vanilla	San Diego, CA
619-566-1745	Classified Connection	San Diego, CA
619-566-1745	Classified Connection	San Diego, CA
619-572-0473	Boot Strap On-Line	Winterhaven, AZ
619-588-6941	D.J.M. BBS	La Mesa, CA
619-589-0339	THE .ARC MODEM	Lemon Grove, CA
619-673-1440	Waduki's Graphics Pad	San Diego, CA
619-789-4391	High Country East	Ramona, CA

PC Board

701-852-3996	The KAT BBS of MINOT	Minot, ND

Wildcat! Systems

701-245-6537	HAK BBS	Westhope, ND
701-663-1330	Bit-Board	Mandan, ND
701-838-1714	The American BBS	Minot, ND
701-838-2664	Graphics 'R' Us	Minot, ND
701-852-2002	MID CONTINENT BBS	Minot, ND
701-873-6282	The Gas Station	Beulah, ND

PC Board

702-641-6795	The Home Place BBS #2	Las Vegas, NV
702-882-9305	M & M Video and Computers	Carson City, NV
702-972-6111	C.O.M.Base-Nevada	Reno, NV

Wildcat! Systems

702-294-1817	BBS Titanic	Boulder City, NV
702-364-8721	RCBBS	Las Vegas, NV
702-366-9107	Western Type BBS	Las Vegas, NV
702-438-3625	THE OTHER BBS	Las Vegas, NV
702-438-6051	RAIDERS OF THE LOST .ARC	Las Vegas, NV
702-459-8378	Project Six	Las Vegas, NV
702-642-2278	Firth of Fifth	Las Vegas, NV
702-645-0761	Tech One BBS	Las Vegas, NV
702-877-3930	Compu-Lex	Las Vegas, NV
702-883-9264	THE ZERO-D BOARD	Carson City, NV
702-972-4682	THE RENO CONNECTION	Sparks, NV

PC Board

703-239-0685	The Oasis BBS	Burke, VA
703-242-8129	Turner Technologies	Oakton, VA
703-243-4820	Kwibble	Arlington, VA
703-280-9647	Special Systems Inc. BBS	Fairfax, VA
703-342-6386	The Sixteen Bit Exchange	Roanoke, VA
703-343-5106	Easy Street	Roanoke, VA
703-349-0135	Santa Software Assoc. BBS	Warrenton, VA
703-360-1463	TeleCommunication's BBS	Mount Vernon, VA
703-362-7647	Sparkies Machine BBS (Node 2)	Roanoke, VA
703-366-4299	Sparkies Machine BBS (Node 1)	Roanoke, VA
703-370-0018	Data Bit (Node 1)	Alexandria, VA
703-370-9832	Data Bit (Node 2)	Alexandria, VA
703-373-6377	Fredericksburg PC Users BBS	Falmouth, VA
703-425-5824	The Hallucination	Fairfax, VA
703-425-8762	The Crossroads	Burke, VA
703-435-7240	Digital Exchange BBS	Herdon, VA
703-442-8695	East Coast Forth Board	McLean, VA
703-444-1732	The Medium of Exchange	Herndon, VA
703-450-7807	The Circus	Vienna, VA
703-450-9693	The TSCA Orderwire	Sterling, VA
703-455-1873	The Video Pro	Burke, VA
703-455-7204	MCAAVPO BBS	Springfield, VA
703-471-4653	Washington Connection (Node 2)	Herndon, VA
703-471-8667	Washington Connection (Node 1)	Herndon, VA
703-476-1243	FastComm Data Board	Reston, VA
703-478-9850	TeleCommunications BBS	Reston, VA
703-525-4066	The Questor Project	McLean, VA
703-532-5568	The Arlington Software Exc	Arlington, VA
703-552-6427	The Vector Vale	Blacksburg, VA
703-552-8427	The Next Generation	Blacksburg, VA

703-552-8767	The MBT	Blacksburg, VA
703-556-0266	Tech-Connect BBS	McLean, VA
703-558-3711	The Warped Board BBS	Arlington, VA
703-569-8612	The Overdrive BBS	Burke, VA
703-590-4629	Lytep BBS	Woodbridge, VA
703-620-2022	The Power Supply	Oakton, VA
703-644-9662	CableComm BBS	Springfield, VA
703-648-1841	The Virginia Connection	Reston, VA
703-659-2845	The Conventions Gaming BBS	Stafford, VA
703-659-3033	The Escape Hatch	Stafford, VA
703-659-3677	Virginia Data Exchange	Stafford, VA
703-689-1357	The Lincoln Legacy	Leesburg, VA
703-690-7462	ITS TEK-NET	Woodbridge, VA
703-742-6279	Corvette Drivers BBS	Reston, VA
703-759-5321	The Online	Great Falls, VA
703-764-9297	The Beltway Bandits BBS	Fairfax, VA
703-768-8637	Scotland the Brave	Alexandria, VA
703-774-4667	PhotoStar BBS	Roanoke, VA
703-841-0959	Fred's Board	Arlington, VA
703-890-5733	Bedlam BBS	Vinton, VA
703-893-8262	The Beda Board	Falls Church, VA
703-898-6929	Burleigh's BBS	Fredericksburg, VA
703-941-5815	Springfield ByPass	Springfield, VA
703-961-1253	Betelgeuse BBS	Blacksburg, VA
703-968-9438	ZED-88 BBS	Centreville, VA
703-989-9263	Roanoke Software Exchange	Roanoke, VA

Wildcat! Systems

703-266-9459	Com-Dat	Centreville, VA
703-269-4802	Helpline	Keezletown, VA
703-342-1800	The Star City BBS	Roanoke, VA
703-451-0457	The Final Option	Springfield, VA
703-527-2062	The 370 Connection	Arlington, VA
703-620-3271	Abbey Road	Reston, VA
703-662-1503	System 7	Winchester, VA
703-671-8923	The Byrd's Nest	Arlington, VA

703-689-3821	Electronic "In Search Of"	Herndon, VA

PC Board

704-256-9500	The Foothills BBS	Hickory, NC
704-342-6507	International Trade Ed. Net	Charlotte, NC
704-366-2349	The Pyramid	Charlotte, NC
704-527-0469	The Programmer's Workshop	Charlotte, NC
704-527-3379	The Tholian Web	Charlotte, NC
704-527-3656	The DOJO	Charlotte, NC
704-542-5135	The Scorpio BBS	Charlotte, NC
704-545-6290	Simplified Computer BBS	Charlotte, NC

Wildcat! Systems

704-456-4366	PC - 8000 BBS	Waynesville, NC
704-667-8021	Armed Forces Reunion BBS	Enka, NC

PC Board

705-424-7570	Essa Color Comp, Club	Angus, Ontario, Canada
705-682-4423	The Jailhouse PCBoard BBS	Copper Cliff, Ontario, Canada
705-743-7296	'The BBS' Bulletin Board	Peterborough, Ontario, Canada

PC Board

707-252-1429	Adventure	Napa, CA
707-488-8955	Poverty Comp	Vacaville, CA
707-552-0462	N. POINTE VISTA POWER STN	Vallejo, CA
707-552-8659	The K.O.R Connection BBS	Vallejo, CA
707-646-2265	Pixels	Vallejo, CA
707-746-0827	The Computer Center	Benicia, CA

707-746-5820	Decor Computer Consultant	Benicia, CA
707-964-7114	MCAB	Fort Bragg, CA
707-664-1639	911 Emergency Services BBS	Cotati, CA
707-778-2341	Carenet	Petaluma, CA
707-778-8841	MotherBoard (Node 1)	Petaluma, CA
707-778-8944	MotherBoard (Node 2)	Petaluma, CA

PC Board

709-489-3187	FoxNet	Grand Falls, Newfoundland, Canada
709-489-4758	FoxNet	Grand Falls, Newfoundland, Canada
709-643-3462	The Stray Bit BBS	Stephenville, Newfoundland, Canada

PC Board

713-332-3355	Whovian Trading Post	League, TX
713-347-2143	The Keyboard	Houston, TX
713-353-5289	MicroLogic	Spring, TX
713-354-4915	Strange Brew	Porter, TX
713-422-3146	The Doghouse BBS	Baytown, TX
713-440-7364	LINX	Houston, TX
713-520-1569	Ye Olde Bailey	Houston, TX
713-530-7722	The After Dark Network, #1	Houston, TX
713-530-7790	The After Dark Network, #2	Houston, TX
713-681-1920	TEJAS	Houston, TX
713-771-2802	The Abend BBS	Houston, TX
713-782-5454	Ed Hopper's BBS	Houston, TX
713-870-1508	PC Consultant	Houston, TX
713-937-9097	Broadcast Computer DataBase	Houston, TX
713-961-1604	SANDS PCBoard	Houston, TX
713-996-5432	The BAPCO BBS	Houston, TX

| 713-997-1419 | The Innovator | Pearland, TX |

Wildcat! Systems

713-242-6370	Bulldozer's BBS	Sugarland, TX
713-338-2053	Serendipity	League City, TX
713-370-0814	The Firehouse	Houston, TX
713-370-6224	Synergy-I	Houston, TX
713-453-0472	Disk-N-Dat	Houston, TX
713-479-7006	FAST - 8088	Deer Park, TX
713-482-7080	The Roost	Friendswood, TX
713-488-7117	Gateway	Houston, TX
713-537-0435	Road Block Solutions	Houston, TX
713-784-2554	Space City BBS	Houston, TX
713-946-1158	The Mother Lode	South Houston, TX
713-980-7733	KING'S THRONE!	Sugarland, TX
713-984-0206	The Words & Works BBS	Houston, TX

PC Board

714-240-7459	GRASP/Pic Swap Line	San Juan Capistrano, CA
714-242-3495	Locksoft	Moreno Valley, CA
714-248-0809	Brass Tacks PC-Board	Dana Point, CA
714-359-4965	Aries Computer PCBoard	Riverside, CA
714-359-6240	FunHouse BBS	Riverside, CA
714-364-2931	Saddleback College BBS	Mission Viejo, CA
714-369-9766	Patriquins Util Support BBS	Riverside, CA
714-373-1509	Cumberland Mines BBS	Westminster, CA
714-472-4127	The Void	El Toro, CA
714-522-3980	The Punkin Duster BBS	Buena Park, CA
714-529-8460	The Sandcastle BBS	Fullerton, CA
714-530-8645	Triad Brokerage Co	Garden Grove, CA
714-536-4460	The Dark Castle BBS	Huntington Beach, CA
714-539-9374	The Black Pine	Garden Grove, CA
714-548-4836	Network XXIII	Costa Mesa, CA
714-581-0567	Video Image Library	El Toro, CA
714-636-2667	The Kandy Shack	Garden Grove, CA
714-643-3066	Laguna Hills BBS	Laguna Hills, CA

714-654-8547	The Keep	San Jacinto, CA
714-657-6804	Outlaw BBS	Perris, CA
714-674-4745	Lake County BBS	Lake Elsinore, CA
714-677-0570	The ESCape	Murrieta, CA
714-693-7126	CompuStar Network	Anaheim, CA
714-693-8755	The Gambler's Den BBS	Yorba Linda, CA
714-731-3946	ClipBoard	Tustin, CA
714-738-0841	PC Treasure Chest	Fullerton, CA
714-739-4256	The Business BBS	Buena Park, CA
714-760-3265	CHIPS+ Connection BBS	Newport Beach, CA
714-768-6256	The Barn BBS	Mission Viejo, CA
714-771-4573	Free Bytes BBS	Orange Hills, CA
714-784-0472	The Rubidoux BBS	Riverside, CA
714-821-5014	BBS-Buena Park	Buena Park, CA
714-822-2999	The Fountainhead	Fontana, CA
714-822-4003	The Low Desert Inn	Fontana, CA
714-823-3184	Bloomington BBS	Bloomington, CA
714-837-4408	Toshiba America Laptop Support	Irvine, CA
714-837-4458	Toshiba America Laptop Support	Irvine, CA
714-839-9580	PC-LAIR	Westminster, CA
714-840-1732	The Home Place	Banning, CA
714-847-7475	Compufix Tech, BBS.	Huntington Beach, CA
714-860-3213	Castle of the Four Winds	Diamond Bar, CA
714-861-1549	Diamond Bar BBS	Diamond Bar, CA
714-879-4052	N S T T Z	Fullerton CA
714-882-6199	The Computer Store	San Bernardino, CA
714-882-7181	Comland PCBoard	San Bernardino, CA
714-924-6701	The Sunny-PC BBS	Moreno Valley, CA
714-943-4301	The Billboard DOOR SupportS	Lakeview, CA
714-943-7943	Not Another BBS!	Mead Valley, CA
714-956-4878	PC Network II	Anaheim, CA
714-956-5468	PC Exchange	Anaheim, CA
714-964-1369	1139/South!	Fountain Valley, CA
714-965-3745	Barons Byte BBS	Huntington Beach, CA
714-968-5405	Shadow World Industries	Huntington Beach, CA
714-974-3730	The Tax Board	Anaheim, CA

714-982-2200	National Council Exchangers	Upland, CA
714-989-7595	Vervan's War Board	Cucamonga, CA
714-989-7596	Vervan's War Board	Cucamonga, CA
714-996-0805	The Archivist's Scroll	Yorba Linda, CA

Wildcat! Systems

714-255-9508	Colossus Galactica	Brea, CA
714-351-9029	NBS Services & Repair	Riverside, CA
714-499-1579	Pension Information Exch.	South Laguna, CA
714-526-2387	AXIOS BBS	Fullerton, CA
714-539-8644	12 & 12 Board	Garden Grove, CA
714-545-0409	Jade BBS	Costa Mesa, CA
714-551-2974	Cyborg	Santa Ana, CA
714-599-5028	Cyber Space	San Dimas, CA
714-676-6739	Temecula Valley BBS	Temecula, CA
714-678-2664	Valley Software BBS	Wildomar, CA
714-685-8380	I.D.S.	Riverside, CA
714-686-1522	Mel's Diner	Riverside, CA
714-738-4331	Astronomay BBS	Fullerton, CA
714-760-0765	International Trade Res.	Nevada City, CA
714-768-2096	Paper Chase	Mission Viejo, CA
714-772-0816	Classic Vehicle Exchange	Perris, CA
714-785-9176	Solid Rock	Riverside, CA
714-836-0190	Mistress's Digs	Santa Ana, CA
714-837-9677	Solar System	Mission Viejo, CA
714-899-2088	Everett/Charles	Fontana, CA
714-927-7566	Valle Vista BBS	Hemet, CA
714-968-3997	Car-Puter!	Huntington Beach, CA
714-980-3697	Data Comm	Alta Loma, CA

PC Board

715-726-9584	The FOG PCBoard	Chippewa Falls, WI
715-835-0880	Voyage BBS	Eau Claire, WI
715-836-2146	The Underground Connection	Eau Claire, WI

Wildcat! Systems

715-234-5499	Rice Lake PC Users Group	Webster, WI

PC Board

716-235-4336	HOBIE'S FUN HOUSE	Rochester, NY
716-272-0330	ASYST Software Technologies	Rochester, NY
716-272-0546	Mohawk Premium BBS	Rochester, NY
716-328-3844	Data Comm Network	Rochester, NY
716-342-5520	Jim's Place	Rochester, NY
716-395-2173	PAD BBS	Brockport, NY
716-482-2592	Crystal Palace	Rochester, NY
716-544-8327	Station Rochester PCBoard	Rochester, NY
716-627-3299	Data Express BBS	Lake View, NY
716-648-4477	Tech Plus Systems	Orchard Park, NY
716-681-0765	Info World BBS-MIPS 150+	Buffalo, NY
716-876-6908	Night Owls BBS	Buffalo, NY
716-877-7610	Night Owls BBS	Buffalo, NY
716-885-6604	TechPlus Systems	Buffalo, NY
716-894-7386	Apollo III	Buffalo, NY

Wildcat! Systems

716-229-2898	Bristol Specialties BBS	Canandaigua, NY
716-229-2898	Bristol Specialties BBS	Canandaigua, NY
716-272-1517	Accu	Rochester, NY
716-392-4755	The Executive Washroom	Hilton, NY
716-482-5073	Logic Systems	Worcester, NY
716-586-9335	The Bit Twiddler	Pittsford, NY
716-668-6029	BBS Enterprise	Buffalo, NY
716-735-9625	Tandy Town BBS	Middleport, NY
716-833-2852	Raven's Nest	Cheektowaga, NY
716-834-0636	OCS BBS	Cheektowaga, NY

| 716-865-9339 | Hands On Computer System | Rochester, NY |
| 716-933-7919 | Hotel California | Portville, NY |

PC Board

717-226-1943	The Software Safari	Hawley, PA
717-232-2031	Sanctuary BBS	Harrisburg, PA
717-274-3651	Data Express BBS	Lebanon, PA
717-346-4211	Federation BBS	Scranton, PA
717-346-8583	The Electric City BBS	Scranton, PA
717-563-1279	The Outer Perimeter	Dalton, PA
717-586-0221	The Encyclopedia Galactica	Clarks Summit, PA
717-757-1471	CRA Access	York, PA
717-761-4612	The Cumberland Connection	Lemoyne, PA
717-992-2631	PennSoft PCBoard	Stroudsburg, PA

Wildcat! Systems

717-252-4543	Microbe II BBS	York, PA
717-265-6104	J & R Software	Towanda, PA
717-429-1529	St. Clair BBS Systems	Pottsville, PA
717-845-5623	Staying In Touch	York, PA

PC Board

718-217-0898	PharmStat	Bayside, NY
718-252-0534	Olympic BBS Services	Brooklyn, NY
718-336-8148	The Outer Lair	Brooklyn, NY
718-358-3340	L & P Dynamic BBS	Fresh Meadows, NY
718-377-0524	Data Link	Brooklyn, NY
718-381-5616	The Dog House BBS	New York, NY
718-392-8836	Thunder Road BBS	Sunnyside, NY
718-417-1761	The WPC Comm. Center	Ridgewood, NY
718-417-9885	The Orphan BBS	Ridgewood, NY
718-441-1262	Wishbone BBS	Kew Gardens, NY

718-457-1752	Friends! Too	East Elmhurst, NY
718-457-4603	NIS BBS	New York, NY
718-458-5835	Programmer's BBS	Elmhurst, NY
718-680-2928	LaserNet	Brooklyn, NY
718-680-5852	Big Blue BBS	Brooklyn, NY
718-680-6016	Big Blue BBS	Brooklyn, NY
718-692-2498	MoonDog's Free BBS	Brooklyn, NY
718-720-7673	Nova Labs	Staten Island, NY
718-786-4191	Thunder Road BBS	Sunnyside, NY
718-836-7272	BobKat Information Systems	Brooklyn, NY
718-837-3236	The Consultant BBS	Brooklyn, NY
718-932-3757	Franklins Tower	Astoria, NY
718-961-7233	Phantom's Quarters BBS	Flushing, NY
718-962-2628	White Tiger BBS	New Hyde Park, NY
718-972-6099	Star-Link Net BBS	Brooklyn, NY
718-984-4511	Sylvia's Den BBS	Staten Island, NY

Wildcat! Systems

718-335-4874	Keyboard Arcade	Jackson Heights, NY
718-363-9806	Computron HQ	Brooklyn, NY
718-468-4797	The Bayside Board II	Bayside, NY
718-987-3063	SPEECH & HEARRING BBS	Staten Island, NY

PC Board

719-593-2232	D.I.L.L.I.G.A.F.	Colorado Springs, CO
719-599-3474	Vector Space	Woodland Park, CO
719-634-4591	The Bargain Basement	Colorado Springs, CO
719-634-5801	Kings Guild BBS	Colorado Springs, CO

PC Board

801-261-8974	Salt Air BBS (Node 1)	Salt Lake City, UT
801-261-8975	Salt Air BBS (Node 2)	Salt Lake City, UT
801-261-8976	Salt Air BBS (Node 3)	Salt Lake City, UT

801-261-8977	Salt Air BBS (Node 4)	Salt Lake City, UT
801-261-8979	Salt Air BBS (Node 5)	Salt Lake City, UT
801-261-8981	Salt Air BBS (Node 6)	Salt Lake City, UT
801-261-8987	Salt Air BBS (Node 7)	Salt Lake City, UT
801-224-9713	The Band Wagon	Orem, UT
801-225-1444	'55 CADdy	Orem, UT
801-225-2823	After 5:00!	Orem, UT
801-225-2834	After 5:00!	Orem, UT
801-225-3856	Atis Communications	Orem, UT
801-225-4031	Hacker's Haven (Node 1)	Orem, UT
801-225-7358	Hacker's Haven (Node 2)	Orem, UT
801-226-8467	The Shadow Taker	Orem, UT
801-261-2008	Micropolis BBS	Holladay, UT
801-261-3858	The Graphics Connection	Salt Lake City, UT
801-263-2887	The Jewelers Hotline	Salt Lake City, UT
801-268-0069	The Adventurer's Keep	Salt Lake City, UT
801-269-9575	Score Board BBS	Murray, UT
801-298-0190	BEACONetwork	Centerville, UT
801-298-5662	FBN Online	Bountiful, UT
801-321-5030	LDS Hospital PC-Users Group	Salt Lake City, UT
801-328-0621	INFOCAD BBS	Salt Lake City, UT
801-355-6575	MicroShare BBS	Salt Lake City, UT
801-359-6014	Center Point PCBoard	Salt Lake City, UT
801-378-5032	CCC-Info	Provo, UT
801-392-4657	StoneAge BBS	Ogden, UT
801-392-6188	The Part Time BBS	Ogden, UT
801-393-1067	Mega Board	Ogden, UT
801-393-6944	Mutant Clone BBS	Riverdale, UT
801-466-7170	NAI's Bulletin Board	Salt Lake City, UT
801-485-7646	Berserker	Salt Lake City, UT
801-487-9715	Nostradamus BBS	Salt Lake City, UT
801-522-4778	Night Hawk BBS	Dougway, UT
801-531-1162	Information Techologies	Salt Lake City, UT
801-561-1643	The Last Byte!	Sandy, UT
801-561-5025	The Rat Trap Premium BBS	West Jordan, UT
801-565-1416	The Planetary System BBS	Sandy, UT

801-583-4541	Sanctuary	Salt Lake City, UT
801-756-5204	Rampage Premium BBS	Alpine, UT
801-756-6165	Rampage Premium BBS	Alpine, UT
801-768-4617	Data-Line BBS	Lehi, UT
801-778-4400	Iomega Tech. Support BBS	Roy, UT
801-782-7755	The Construction Connection BBS	Ogden, UT
801-942-7926	Horizon BBS Premium Service	Salt Lake City, UT
801-943-2354	The Circuits BBS	Salt Lake City, UT
801-965-1678	Satellite Switchboard BBS	Salt Lake City, UT
801-965-9534	A Million Miles Away	Salt Lake City, UT

Wildcat! Systems

801-226-8467	The Shadow Taker	Orem, UT
801-298-2812	Acheron	Bountiful, UT
801-298-8311	TIPS on CHIPS	Centerville, UT
801-392-4657	Stoneage BBS	Riverdale, UT
801-451-7626	The Fast Lane	Farmington, UT
801-485-6349	WOS BBS	Salt Lake City, UT
801-485-6349	WOS BBS	Salt Lake City, UT
801-583-3028	Mtn West Media GRAPEVINE	Salt Lake City, UT
801-621-3371	Armadillo Brothers	Ogden, UT
801-964-1889	Nick At Nite BBS	Kearns, UT

PC Board

802-257-4583	DECX*NET	Brattleboro, VT
802-748-8380	Grey Goose	St. Johnsbury, VT
802-773-0799	Search for Intelligent Life	Rutland, VT
802-888-7218	The Beehive BBS	Morrisville, VT
802-933-2417	Black Creek BBS	Sheldon, VT

Wildcat! Systems

802-527-1683	St. Albans BBS	St. Albans, VT
802-655-7461	Green Mountain Boys	Winooski, VT

PC Board

803-223-3802	The True Blue BBS	Greenwood, SC
803-425-5331	Odyssey BBS	Camden, SC
803-591-3920	Spartanburg IBM PCUG	Spartanburg, SC
803-722-7099	Charleston Computer Club	Charleston, SC
803-736-6066	Southern Hospitality	Columbia, SC
803-736-9178	SC Barr Assoc, BBS	Columbia, SC
803-738-2966	The Clearing House	Columbia, SC
803-744-8275	The Q-107 Q-Board, WKQB-FM	Charleston, SC
803-792-5806	Charleston Computer Club	Charleston, SC
803-792-5807	Charleston Computer Club	Charleston, SC
803-797-8673	'CARD CAGE' BBS	Charleston, SC
803-828-4444	SCTC BBS	Myrtle Beach AFB, SC
803-828-4445	SCTC BBS	Myrtle Beach AFB, SC
803-871-3710	Turbo-88	Summerville, SC
803-871-8197	Summerville 80	Summerville, SC
803-967-3286	Door to the South	Simpsonville, SC

Wildcat! Systems

803-494-9404	Night Phantom	Jackson, MS
803-524-5056	The Low Country	MCRD Parris Island, SC
803-524-5655	The Lobby Shop	Burton, SC
803-552-4979	Pro-Files! BBS	Charleston, SC
803-552-5781	GRAPHIC INTERPRETA-TIONS	North Charleston, SC
803-572-3353	The Unknown BBS	Goose Creek, SC

803-797-7667	SPORTS PAGE BBS	Goose Creek, SC
803-879-4364	THE COMAX GROUP BBS	Greer, SC

PC Board

804-220-0533	The Blues Exchange	Williamsburg, VA
804-253-0747	The Great OutDoors BBS	Williamsburg, VA
804-266-5390	The Star-Glider	Richmond, VA
804-363-9263	Software Link of VA Beach	Virginia Beach, VA
804-397-0077	Spectrum 007 VIP	Portsmouth, VA
804-424-0416	The No Name BBS	Virginia Beach, VA
804-471-3360	Tidewater Amt. Radio/ Comp.	Virginia Beach, VA
804-471-4837	Software Central	Virginia Beach, VA
804-481-1824	Computer Connection	Virginia Beach, VA
804-482-4854	Polar Bears Premium	Chesapeake, VA
804-523-0230	The No Name BBS	Virginia Beach, VA
804-587-9241	ME BBS	Norfolk, VA
804-674-1907	Southern Knight	Richmond, VA
804-826-4315	The Connection (Node 2)	Hampton, VA
804-826-7419	The Connection (Node 1)	Hampton, VA
804-924-4326	TJU-BBS	Charlottesville, VA
804-973-5639	Central Virginia BBS	Charlottesville, VA
804-973-8235	Broadcasters BBS	Charlottesville, VA
804-977-8369	A Nickel's Worth	Charlottesville, VA
804-978-1376	Central Virginia BBS	Charlottesville, VA

Wildcat! Systems

804-266-2644	Side Track	Richmond, VA
804-323-6768	Jaybird BBS	Richmond, VA
804-346-9446	Future Systems	Richmond, VA
804-353-4893	South Anna Wildcat BBS	Rockville, VA
804-423-1338	The C.F.I. BBS	Norfolk, VA
804-451-1933	The U.S.S. Enterprise	Norfolk, VA
804-463-3724	Back Acres BBS!	Virginia Beach, VA
804-473-8345	Seabee BBS	Virginia Beach, VA

804-480-3038	The G.H.	Norfolk, VA
804-489-3733	The Free BBS	Norfolk, VA
804-490-5878	Pleasure Dome	Norfolk, VA
804-491-0857	Bob's BBS	Fort Myer, VA
804-793-6094	J.F.F.-Just For Fun	Danville, VA

PC Board

805-274-0696	AVMUG BBS	Lancaster, CA
805-484-4088	RTCS Tech Support #1	Camarillo, CA
805-484-4270	RTCS Tech Support Node # 2	Camarillo, CA
805-494-4405	Ventura Wave	Thousand Oaks, CA
805-498-3500	Nomad PCBoard	Thousand Oaks, CA
805-985-1254	Felix BBS	Port Hueneme, CA

Wildcat! Systems

805-238-1058	Paso Robles BBS	Paso Robles, CA
805-242-4046	THE HILL	Frazier Park, CA
805-264-1219	DCOM Support	Lancaster, CA
805-265-8445	FAA*ARA BBS	Palmdale, CA
805-298-6142	SEV PC Group BBS	Canyon Country, CA
805-322-3839	Wiz Kid's BBS	Bakersfield, CA
805-388-4914	CW-BBS	Camarillo, CA
805-395-0650	Mustang's WILDCAT Support	Bakersfield, CA
805-395-1880	AHI Computer Hotline	Bakersfield, CA
805-489-6714	The Amiga PC Connection	Grover City, CA
805-498-3530	RAM-NET	Newbury Park, CA
805-541-8505	CYGNUS X-1 BBS	Los Osos, CA
805-644-4573	GLOBAL EXCHANGE	Oxnard, CA
805-644-8515	GOLDMINE	Ventura, CA
805-647-8273	The Motherboard	Ventura, CA
805-648-7833	Codename: Lorraine	Ventura, CA
805-831-1618	Lottonet By USA-LOTTO	Bakersfield, CA
805-831-6025	Game Board	Bakersfield, CA
805-947-9031	Desert BBS	Lancaster, CA

805-983-0281	Bastille BBS	Port Hueneme, CA

PC Board

806-293-1901	Data Link '87	Plainview, TX
806-352-2482	The Radio Board (Node 1)	Amarillo, TX
806-352-9365	The Radio Board (Node 2)	Amarillo, TX
806-355-5157	Panhandle MS-DOS Grp. Lib.	Amarillo, TX
806-355-9600	Top of Texas BBS	Amarillo, TX
806-373-3953	Aerie BBS	Amarillo, TX
806-381-2932	The Attic	Amarillo, TX
806-792-5947	The Windmill Company	Lubbock, TX
806-792-6116	The Windmill Company	Lubbock, TX
806-792-6447	The Windmill Company	Lubbock, TX

Wildcat! Systems

806-376-1419	XPRESS BBS	Amarillo, TX

PC Board

808-487-7267	Computer Clinic BBS	Aiea, HI
808-547-5897	Hawaii PC-Law Board	Honolulu, HI
808-842-0453	TEC Information Network	Honolulu, HI
808-845-1303	Program Library & Exchange	Honolulu, HI
808-847-0313	Program Library & Exchange	Honolulu, HI

Wildcat! Systems

808-335-6091	Bill's-Board	Hanapepe, HI
808-734-7616	THE HAWAII SPACE CONNECTION	Honolulu, HI

PC Board

809-756-8863	Cyclone BBS	Rio Piedras, Puerto Rico

Wildcat! Systems

809-756-7137	RHODES BBS	Hato Rey, Puerto Rico
809-773-3001	PARADISE BBS	St. Croix, Virgin Islands
809-774-8204	Global Weather	St. Thomas, Virgin Islands

PC Board

812-275-4689	HST ExPress	Bedford, IN
812-335-5803	PC-Link Central (Node 2)	Bloomington, IN
812-335-5804	PC-Link Central (Node 3)	Bloomington, IN
812-335-7252	PC-Link Central (Node 1)	Bloomington, IN
812-378-4673	The Wolf's Lair	Columbus, IN
812-477-5343	NationServ Network	Evansville, IN

Wildcat! Systems

812-284-1321	The Geneva Convention	Clarksville, IN
812-331-3065	Connecting Point BBS	Bloomington, IN
812-425-6950	The Eagle's Nest	Evansville, IN
812-597-4091	The Labor Board	Morgantown, IN
812-876-3925	Small Town	Ellettsville, IN

PC Board

813-299-8778	Micro-World BBS	Winter Haven, FL
813-442-4286	Microwave Research BBS	Clearwater, FL.
813-526-1265	Computronics Comm Link	St. Petersburg, FL
813-526-3388	Micro-Vision	St. Petersburg, FL
813-526-7621	Nite-Owl	St. Petersburg, FL
813-527-5666	St. Pete Programmer's Exch	St. Petersburg, FL
813-545-8050	Meganet	Pinellas Park, FL
813-549-3043	Southern Lights	Cape Coral, FL
813-578-0347	The Tradin' Post	St. Petersburg, FL
813-646-6640	P.C.S.O.	Lakeland, FL
813-683-9354	J & M Marine	Lakeland, FL
813-734-1747	The Other Side	Dunedin, FL

813-747-2081	Action-Link System's	Brandenton, FL
813-787-1639	Coastland Dat Res. BBS	Palm Harbor, FL
813-793-2392	Tamiami	Naples, FL
813-796-3230	Everyware BBS	Clearwater, FL
813-796-5627	The DataCOM Super System	Clearwater, FL
813-894-6402	Litigator BBS	St. Petersburg, FL
813-938-8086	The Dreamland Express	Palm Harbor, FL
813-968-6196	The Computer Archives (Node 2)	Tampa, FL
813-968-6220	The Computer Archives (Node 1)	Tampa, FL
813-968-9480	The Computer Archives (Node 2)	Tampa, FL
813-995-5034	PConnection of SW Florida	Fort Meyers, FL

Wildcat! Systems

813-264-0073	Data Exchange-UTK Ware.	Tampa, FL
813-272-5631	Hillsborough County BBS	Tampa, FL
813-377-2346	Compulsive BBS	Sarasota, FL
813-425-4379	Boss Man	Mulberry, FL
813-441-4770	The Cat House	Clearwater, FL
813-467-0745	Big Lake BBS	Okeechobee, FL
813-521-3664	Jay Hawk BBS	St. Petersburg, FL
813-576-2562	Comp-U-Call	St. Petersburg, FL
813-585-7082	F.R.E.E.	Largo, FL
813-676-7549	Crown Jewel BBS	Lake Wales, FL
813-685-0175	Compu-Tech	Tampa, FL
813-725-4452	Crossroads Christian Info	Safety Harbor, FL
813-789-2607	Asian's Roar	Palm Harbor, FL
813-832-4133	SoftCopy BBS	Tampa, FL
813-856-7926	Gulf Coast BBS	Brooksville, FL
813-988-5889	Else World BBS	Tampa, FL
813-989-2539	Mantis Empire BBS	Temple Terrace, FL

PC Board

814-231-2568	The ICS Round Table	State College, PA
814-339-6042	Lifesaver BBS	Osceola Mills, PA
814-355-5559	The Blue & White Lion	Bellefonte, PA
814-371-5881	Random Access BBS	Dubois, PA
814-455-9860	Lake Erie Vineyard (Node 2)	Erie, PA
814-456-2767	Pyramid	Erie, PA
814-459-4631	Lake Erie Vineyard (Node 1)	Erie, PA
814-696-1146	Portage Railroad BBS	Altoona, PA
814-742-7695	Bellwood Christian BBS	Bellwood, PA
814-944-6588	Portage Railroad BBS	Altoona, PA

Wildcat! Systems

814-371-9298	Whitey's Wildcat BBS	Indiana, PA
814-664-9197	Corry's BBS	Corry, PA

PC Board

815-385-5031	The McHenry BBS	McHenry, IL
815-397-3210	Un-Named Board	Rockford, IL
815-727-9111	Midnight BBS	Joliet, IL

Wildcat! Systems

815-429-3533	The Alternative Universe	Donovan, IL
815-633-0094	Bloomford BBS	Loves Park, IL
815-965-5606	PRIMETIME	Loves Park, IL

PC Board

816-229-1841	KCM Passport	Blue Springs, MO
816-429-6245	Desert Highlands BBS	Warrensburg, MO
816-436-4516	Sound Advice BBS	Gladstone, MO
816-436-8029	Sound Advice BBS	Gladstone, MO

816-454-4448	The US-BBS	Kansas City, MO
816-454-4485	The US-BBS	Kansas City, MO
816-459-7327	Kitty Hawk PCBoard	Gladstone, MO
816-537-7675	"The Data Bank"	Kansas City, MO
816-637-4183	The Bedroom	Kansas City, MO
816-637-4185	The Bedroom	Kansas City, MO
816-734-5202	Computer Shoppe	Kansas City, MO
816-833-3410	Artificial Insanity	Independence, MO

Wildcat! Systems

816-453-0954	Shilo BBS	Kansas City, MO

PC Board

817-261-2010	The Taj Mahal	Arlington, TX
817-284-0794	Ft. Worth Heath U/Group	Fort Worth, TX
817-531-4761	Dept. of Electronics Tech	Fort Worth, TX
817-532-2459	The Computer Connection	Fort Hood, TX
817-532-2509	The Computer Connection	Fort Hood, TX
817-572-0749	DFW COM Shop	Arlington, TX
817-572-6027	Skara Brae Systems	Arlington, TX

Wildcat! Systems

817-261-6061	Mandelbrot's Chaotic BBS	Arlington, TX
817-287-8411	DOIM BBS	Fort Hood, TX
817-288-2990	Hell On Wheels	Fort Hood, TX

PC Board

818-334-5635	VIP Data Exchange	Azusa, CA
818-352-3620	The Ledge PCBoard	Tujunga, CA
818-363-7612	Leisure Time PCBoard	Northridge, CA
818-701-1021	The Programmer's Forum	Northridge, CA
818-709-1583	The Hidden Corner	Chatsworth, CA
818-709-6978	Wizard of Oz	Chatsworth, CA
818-713-0610	Hard Ball PCBoard	Canoga Park, CA
818-718-1401	CloneBoard	Chatsworth, CA

818-718-9219	Skeleton Crew	Chatsworth, CA
818-762-6161	The Hotline	North Hollywood, CA
818-764-4538	MIDIum BBS	North Hollywood, CA
818-772-0384	Moonbeams BBS	Northridge, CA
818-891-4049	Xeon's Magic Shop	Arlete, CA
818-894-0741	Lunacy PCBoard	Sepulveda, CA
818-894-1248	Lunacy PCBoard	Sepulveda, CA
818-894-1470	Lunacy PCBoard	Sepulveda, CA
818-957-6020	The 42 BBS III	La Crescenta, CA
818-963-3537	Color America MS/DOS SIG	Glendora, CA
818-966-8959	Covina Trading Post	Covina, CA
818-989-0310	You Bet Your Ascii	Van Nuys, CA
818-992-4128	Crystal Castle BBS	Woodland Hills, CA

Wildcat! Systems

818-237-6340	THE ENTITY	Placentia, CA
818-240-0280	The Proboard	Glendale, CA
818-358-2871	Eureka! BBS	Monrovia, CA
818-366-1238	THE MOG-UR'S EMS	Granada Hills, CA
818-369-6992	L A ON LINE!	La Puente, CA
818-447-6437	Get Smart BBS	Arcadia, CA
818-571-0718	MY OTHER BBS	Monterey Park, CA
818-577-9452	Digital Support	Pasadena, CA
818-710-0478	Beyond Support BBS	Woodland Hills, CA
818-773-0372	DataShack	Simi Valley, CA
818-795-8101	The Pasadena Missing Link	Pasadena, CA
818-831-9226	LOGIX Development BBS	Granada Hills, CA
818-882-7323	ICAN	Canoga Park, CA
818-915-2708	Firehouse BBS	Covina, CA
818-968-2461	VALDOCS SUPPORT WC RBBS	Valinda, CA

PC Board

819-561-5268	Synapse BBS	Gatineau, Quebec, Canada
819-770-5163	SuperByte BBS	Hull, Quebec, Canada

PC Board

901-753-7213	The Black Bag	Memphis, TN
901-363-7301	Stillwater BBS	Memphis, TN
901-365-0407	Unusual Situations	Memphis, TN
901-373-5941	Cheers!	Memphis, TN
901-386-3530	The Micro Images BBS	Memphis, TN
901-642-5657	T.S. Microline	Paris, TN
901-757-5753	Radio Free Memphis	Memphis, TN
901-873-2324	Gateway	Munford, TN
901-873-2328	The Party Line	Millington, TN

Wildcat! Systems

901-274-0797	The Knight Light!	Memphis, TN
901-358-4255	Star Dot Star	Memphis, TN
901-584-2579	Express	Camden, TN
901-587-5841	The Pacer Network	Martin, TN

PC Board

902-868-2475	VE1EI BBS	Halifax, Nova Scotia, Canada

Wildcat! Systems

902-465-4618	Halifax Wildcat! BBS	Halifax, Nova Scotia, Canada

PC Board

904-223-3536	The Hospital	Jacksonville, FL
904-246-6476	Mike's BBS	Jacksonville Beach, FL
904-249-4390	The Graveyard	Neptune Beach, FL
904-260-4728	Interstellar Comm.	Jacksonville, FL
904-260-9283	Tech's Warehouse BBS	Jacksonville, FL
904-269-7942	Joe's Barr & Grill	Orange Park, FL
904-276-5417	Computer Source Inc	Orange Park, FL
904-368-6945	Smokey's Place BBS	Ocala, FL
904-373-5864	Bob's Corner Board	Gainesville, FL

904-377-8169	Enchanted Forest (2 Nodes)	Gainsville, FL
904-384-4049	Choo Choo PCBoard	Jacksonville, FL
904-389-1792	Traders Remote BBS	Jacksonville, FL
904-562-3659	Tallahassee PCBoard	Tallahassee, FL
904-641-8167	StarGate/Clipper BBS	Jacksonville, FL
904-725-7755	Comp. Comm. Connection	Jacksonville, FL
904-737-0458	AeroStar	Jacksonville, FL
904-744-8596	Night-Time	Jacksonville, FL
904-751-3970	Excalibur BBS	Jacksonville, FL
904-777-2224	StarGate/Clipper BBS	Jacksonville, FL
904-777-2912	Freedom Lounge	Jacksonville, FL
904-777-3351	The Caboose BBS	Jacksonville, FL
904-777-5648	Inter-Coastal BBS	Jacksonville, FL
904-777-8757	The Eagles Nest	Jacksonville, FL
904-778-5116	Master Jet Base	Cecil Field, FL
904-863-2510	Flashbacker BBS	Fort Walton Beach, FL
904-878-7704	Home of Czar Wars	Tallahassee, FL

Wildcat! Systems

904-268-4400	The Wrong Number	Jacksonville, FL
904-441-5723	Fun Time BBS	Ormond Beach, FL
904-630-2245	Cop Shop	Jacksonville, FL
904-644-2853	Small Business Network	Tallahassee, FL
904-644-5463	FEDC BBS	Tallahassee, FL
904-646-2775	IPTM COP SHOP	Jacksonville, FL
904-646-9367	The Drafting Board	Jacksonville, FL
904-673-7931	Bag O' Tricks	Holly Hill, FL
904-771-3402	Marquis Manor	Jacksonville, FL

PC Board

907-258-4756	Alaska Information Net	Anchorage, AK

PC Board

912-352-0169	Southern Software Exchange	Savannah, GA

912-354-8014	MMC II	Savannah, GA
912-427-7605	Clipper Connection BBS	Jesup, GA
912-673-3516	SUBase BBS Naval Sub. Base	Kings Bay, GA
912-882-5740	Southern Honeywell UGroup	St. Marys, GA
912-923-8180	Georgia Board BBS	Warner Robins, GA
912-929-2946	The Keep	Warner Robins, GA
912-953-2817	Proto-Call BBS	Centerville, GA

Wildcat! Systems

912-328-6121	TallyBoard	Warner Robins, GA
912-436-3616	Albany Shareware	Albany, GA
912-474-6171	Dad's Only Sin. . .DOS!	Macon, GA
912-729-7789	Subsailors BBS	Kingsland, GA
912-745-5680	Capture BBS	Macon, GA
912-897-7348	Malfunction Junction	Savannah, GA
912-897-7508	The Ivy League	Savannah, GA

PC Board

913-341-4553	KC Regional HP U/Group	Overland Park, KS
913-469-4401	Johnson Cnty. Comm. College	Overland Pk, KS
913-469-4402	Johnson Cnty. Comm. College	Overland Pk, KS
913-469-4403	Johnson Cnty. Comm. College	Overland Pk, KS
913-469-4404	Johnson Cnty. Comm. College	Overland Pk, KS
913-469-4405	Johnson Cnty. Comm. College	Overland Pk, KS
913-469-4406	Johnson Cnty. Comm. College	Overland Pk, KS
913-539-9356	Software Warehouse	Manhattan, KS
913-762-4841	Members Only BBS	Junction City, KS
913-780-5539	Mod-America BBS	Olathe, KS
913-842-1129	The Pink Flamingo Cafe	Lawrence, KS

Wildcat! Systems

913-233-1057	COMPU-TRONICS SUPER BBS	Topeka, KS
913-251-5315	R-Squared	Satanta, KS
913-267-7111	The Wheat Wave	Topeka, KS
913-267-7259	The Computer Post	Topeka, KS
913-354-4466	Wildcat Information Serv.	Wakarusa, KS
913-478-9642	The Software Connection	Topeka, KS
913-651-7959	LUG & Computers ASP BBS	Fort Leavenworth, KS

PC Board

914-235-4957	The Stand	New Rochelle, NY
914-238-5833	Programmer's Workshop	Chappaqua, NY
914-238-8195	The Works	Chappaqua, NY
914-271-9366	Croton Computer Club	Hudson, NY
914-277-8030	Somers BBS	Somers, NY
914-297-5616	Software City BBS	Wappingers Falls, NY
914-338-8837	Spectrum 007 BBS	Port Ewen, NY
914-353-2157	PC Rockland PCBoard	So. Nyack, NY
914-376-2657	The Tycoons's Tabernacle	Yonkers, NY
914-485-8320	Wizard's Demise	Poughkeepsie, NY
914-562-4621	The Land of Dementia BBS	New Windsor, NY
914-562-7837	AlterLink BBS	New Windsor, NY
914-636-1455	Advanced Computer Concepts	New Rochelle, NY
914-667-1841	Access Data Connectivity	Mount Vernon, NY
914-667-4567	Executive Network	Mount Vernon, NY
914-667-4759	Executive Network	Mount Vernon, NY
914-681-1769	Kashmir BBS	White Plains, NY
914-682-1965	Silver Arrow BBS	White Plains, NY
914-779-4273	Activity BBS - ABBS	Scarsdale, NY
914-783-0343	Hillside BBS	Chester, NY
914-835-1315	The Brentwood BBS	Harrison, NY
914-948-2349	Over the Edge BBS	White Plains, NY
914-961-8749	Hardgoods-East	Eastchester, NY

Wildcat! Systems

914-428-0518	THE EVIL EMPIRE	Wilmington, NY
914-462-8128	Hudson Valley BBS	Wappingers Falls, NY
914-564-3342	Micro-Mania	Newburgh, NY
914-633-2019	Programmer's Forum	New Rochelle, NY
914-668-0515	The Open Door BBS	Mount Vernon, NY
914-684-8530	KAB BBS	White Plains, NY
914-737-7942	This New House	Montrose, NY
914-835-1315	Brentwood BBS	Harrison, NY

PC Board

915-363-0958	The Pipe Line BBS	Odessa, TX
915-592-0734	Randy's Basement	El Paso, TX
915-821-1856	Phantasia Castle	El Paso, TX
915-949-8578	The Kingdom	San Angelo, TX

Wildcat! Systems

915-544-4203	Imagine!	El Paso, TX
915-677-5008	THE PC-EXPRESS	Abilene, TX
915-695-2560	THE MASTERS DEN	Abilene, TX
915-821-4259	The Story Cellar	El Paso, TX

PC Board

916-222-3413	CAL-STAR Communications (Node 1)	Redding, CA
916-223-2046	CAL-STAR Communications (Node 2)	Redding, CA
916-427-0324	The City Lights PCBoard	Sacramento, CA
916-753-6053	California Attorneys Conf	Davis, CA

Wildcat! Systems

916-327-1208	CDMG Online	Sacramento, CA
916-661-6187	CYCLOPS	Woodland, CA
916-663-5920	KAO	Loomis, CA

916-671-1678	Computers-R-Us	Yuba City, CA
916-722-7423	BEAR'S BYTE	Citrus Heights, CA

PC Board

918-252-9137	SoftStop BBS	Tulsa, OK
918-628-0543	Horner's Corner	Tulsa, OK
918-747-3560	Integrated Micro Systems BBS	Tulsa, OK
918-825-4847	DesignCAD Bulletin Board	Pryor, OK

PC Board

919-281-5849	Hoke Co. Communications	Raeford, NC
919-386-9778	The County Seat BBS	Dobson, NC
919-471-6255	HotLine Mall	Durham, NC
919-573-2648	Star Base I	Eden, NC
919-728-2420	The Phoenix Systems	Havelock, NC
919-776-7980	Den's BBS	Sanford, NC
919-886-8826	Public Safety Officer's	High Point, NC
919-929-0974	Homestead BBS	Chapel Hill, NC
919-967-9464	Connection BBS	Chapel Hill, NC

Wildcat! Systems

919-266-7312	The Business System	Raleigh, NC
919-282-3110	The Village Square	Greensboro, NC
919-282-8460	The Village Square	Greensboro, NC
919-294-1770	PC-Technologies (Node 2)	Greensboro, NC
919-299-7935	PC-Technologies (Node 1)	Greensboro, NC
919-444-1473	Asahi BBS	Havelock, NC
919-636-5341	Mirror Image BBS	New Bern, NC
919-733-0486	The SCONC Works	Raleigh, NC
919-739-1063	BecknerVision Communication	Lumberton, NC
919-768-3043	dBoard BBS	Winston-Salem, NC

919-778-9600	Pirate's Cove BBS (2 Nodes)	Goldsboro, NC
919-779-9758	The Wits End BBS	Garner, NC
919-822-4968	Fayetteville Amateur Radio	Fayetteville, NC
919-864-0118	The CITIDESK	Fayetteville, NC
919-893-5206	Frolic & Detour BBS for Law	Buies Creek, NC

The ASP Membership for 1990

To preface this appendix I would like to thank the members of the ASP (Association of Shareware Professionals) for their support and enthusiasm. From across the country and around the world, they overwhelmed me with software to review for this book. One final note to keep in mind is that just because a program was created by an ASP member does not mean it is a great piece of software. It does mean that the program's author shares a belief in the code of ethics and policies established by the ASP. For more on these policies, see Chapter 1. My special thanks to my friend Barry Simon, President of the ASP for 1989-1990, and also to Paul Mayer, the current President of the ASP, for their help and assistance.

ASP MEMBERS: PROGRAMMERS

The following are the programmer members of the Association of Shareware Professionals for 1990.

George Abbott
PRO DEV Software
545 Grover Road
Muskegon, MI 49442

Marc Adler
Magma Software Systems
15 Bodwell Terrace
Millburn, NJ 07041

Bob Ainsbury
TechnoJock Software, Inc.
P.O. Box 820927
Houston, TX 77282

Michael Allen
Natural Software
19 South Fifth Street
St. Charles, IL 60174

Nels Anderson
92 Bishop Drive
Framingham, MA 01701

Pat Anderson
5420-324th Place S.E.
Fall City, WA 98024

Victor Baron
GTX
5419 Dahlia Drive
Los Angeles, CA 90041

John P. Bauernschub, Jr.
14809 Clavel Street
Rockville, MD 20853

Dan Baumbach
Helpware
100 Bayo Vista Way #6
San Rafael, CA 94901

James Beebe
59 Picadilly Court
Kent, OH 44240

Frank Bell
FAB Software
P.O. Box 336
Wayland, MA 01778

Lee-Jeff Bell
Rubicon Computer Labs
2 Rue Des Pommiers
Hull, QUE J8Z 2M2
CANADA

Howard Benner
OMNI Information Resources, Inc.
P.O. Box 1996
Wilmington, DE 19899

David Berdan
Expressware Corporation
P.O. Box 1800
Duvall, WA 98019

Carlos Berguido
Carlos & Star
1722 Capella Court
Petaluma, CA 94954

Robert K. Blaine
ECONO-SOFT
P.O. Box 181030
Austin, TX 78718

Mike Blaszczak
112 Verlinden Drive
Monroeville, PA 15146

C. Robert Blum
Crofton Binary Concepts
1722 Golden Court
Crofton, MD 21114

J. Anthony Borras
ComSoft
P.O. Box 5054
Playa del Rey, CA 90293

Tim Bougan
Custom Technologies
P.O. Box 62118
Colorado Springs, CO 80962

Donald K. Bowen
Bowen Software
126 Devron Circle
East Peoria, IL 61611

Karl Brendel
Sunflower Systems
5683 Dekalb Lane
Norcross, GA 30093

Dave Briccetti
Dave Briccetti & Associates
P.O. Box 1713
Lafayette, CA 94549

Derrick Burgess
Thesaur Plus
23311 Schoolcraft Street
West Hills, CA 91307

Michael Burton
Michael Burton Software
15540 Boot Hill Road
Hayden Lake, ID 83835

Jim Button
ButtonWare, Inc.
325 118th Avenue S.E., Suite 200
Bellevue, WA 98005

Bruce Buzbee
The FormalSoft Company
P.O. Box 1913
Sandy, UT 84091

Timothy Byers
Shareable Software
7507 Plum Tree Forest Court
Houston, TX 77095

Ronald Bryan Byxbe
Sonshine Software, Inc.
P.O. Box 4761
Dublin, GA 31021

Steven Calwas
Moderne Software
P.O. Box 3638
Santa Clara, CA 95055

Barry L. Campbell
47-677 Hui Kelu Street #3
Kaneohe, HI 96744

Frank Canova
Seaware Corp.
P.O. Box 1656
Delray Beach, FL 33444

Yves Charier
64, Rue de Charenton
75012 Paris
FRANCE

Richard J. Cherry, Jr.
Cherry Tree Software
2108 Birchview Road
P.O. Box 964
Reynoldsburg, OH 43068

Eric Cockrell
Thumper Technologies
P.O. Box 471012
Tulsa, OK 74147

Frank J. Condron
Contech Systems
P.O. Box 87542
Canton, MI 48187

Rex Conn
JP Software
P.O. Box 4190
Annapolis, MD 21403

Ed Croson
Business Automation Co.
P.O. Box 1575
Ojai, CA 93023

Richard Crouch
Careware
10217 Ridge View Drive
Grass Valley, CA 95945

Don Cuthbert
PC ASSIST LTD
4/4 Carubbers Close
Edinburgh EH1 1SJ
SCOTLAND

Gene P. Davis
DataMicro, Inc.
Unit F1, 1825 Tamiami Trail
Port Charlotte, FL 33948

Michael Davis
Newtools
2629 Church Street Station
New York, NY 10008

James T. Demberger
PC-*.* Shareware
9862 Lake Seminole Drive West
Seminole, FL 34643

Jim Derr
2425 Santa Cruz Court
Santa Rosa, CA 95401

Michael E. Devore
403 West Charles
Champaign, IL 61820

Kurt H. Diesch
Applied Micro Systems Technology
219 N. Franklin
Ames, IA 50010

Gary Elfring
Elfring Software
P.O. Box 61
Wasco, IL 60183

Alan C. Elliott
Mission Technologies
812 Penn Place
Cedar Hill, TX 75104

Jeffery Gene Elwood
2809 Lordshire Road
Madison, WI 53719

Harold J. Endresen
Quid Pro Quo Software
P.O. Box 1248
Cedar Rapids, IA 52406

Russell Clark Eskew
P.O. Box 8117
Austin, TX 78713

Steve Estvanik
Cascoly Software
4528 36th N.E.
Seattle, WA 98105

Bob Falk
Falk Data Systems
5322 Rockwood Court
El Paso, TX 79932

Gregory Allan Fay
Allan Computer Products
7814 Jared Way
Littleton, CO 80125

Kenn Flee
Jamestown Software
2508 Valley Forge Drive
Madison, WI 53719

Peter Richard Fletcher
P R Fletcher (Software)
1515 West Montgomery Avenue
Rosemont, PA 19010

Nelson Ford
Public (Software) Library
6111 Lake Street
Houston, TX 77005

Steve Fox
Associated Info Services
2705B Juan Tabo N.E. #197
Albuquerque, NM 87112

John M. Franck
No Sweat Software
1200 Jefferson Davis Road
Martinsville, VA 24112

Ted Freeman
MicroNet PCBoard
P.O. Box 83401
Oklahoma City, OK 73148

George Freund
7088 Culver Blvd.
Mentor, OH 44061

Doug Fricke
Disston Ridge, Inc.
4915 22nd Avenue North
St. Petersburg, FL 33710

John Friend
Softworks Development
750 Stierlin Road, #150
Mountain View, CA 94043

Reginald Gage
RPG Software Farm
Box 9221
Columbus, MS 39705

Jim Gallagher
Eagle Performance
P.O. Box 292786
Lewisville, TX 75029

Miklos Garamszeghy
Herne Data Systems, Ltd.
P.O. Box 714, Station C
Toronto, ONT M6J 3S1
CANADA

Mark W. Geisinger
Simple Solutions, Inc.
3433 East Loyola Drive
Kenner, LA 70064

Tony Gentile
Prodigy Technologies
14611 Carmel Ridge Road
San Diego, CA 92128

Donald W. Gibbard
Progressive Data Systems
6938 W. Old Sauk Road
Middleton, WI 53562

Phillip R. Glassel
P. R. Glassel & Associates, Inc.
30255 Fir Trail
Stacy, MN 55079

Donald Gloistein
DGWare Consulting
P.O. Box 669
Alvin, TX 77512

Donald L. Granger
Glencoe Computing
1100 Highway C
Glencoe, MO 63038

David P. Gray
Gray Design Associates
P.O. Box 333
Northboro, MA 01532

Ross M. Greenberg
Software Concepts Design
594 Third Avenue
New York, NY 10016

Steve Griffiths
SG Engineering
2308 Barbara Drive
Camarillo, CA 93010

David Groome
Micrometric
98 Dade Avenue
Sarasota, FL 34232

Douglas C. Gruver
Creative Computer
8868 Continental Drive
Riverside, CA 92504

Gordon R. Haff
3205 Windsor Ridge Drive
Westborough, MA 01581

Donald G. Harbaugh
771 Blanchard Way
Sunnyvale, CA 94087

Joel P. Harper
Computing Systems Design, Inc.
6712 E. 102nd Street
Tulsa, OK 74133

Richard Harper
RGH Software
777 Roth Street Norfolk #4
Reed City, MI 49677

Jim Harrer
Mustang Software, Inc.
915 17th Street
P.O. Box 2264
Bakersfield, CA 93301

Mark Harris
Granny's Old-Fashioned Software
Route 4 Box 216
Boone, NC 28607

Dennette Arthur Harrod, Jr.
Wiz Worx
83 Parkhurst Road #166
Chelmsford, MA 01824

Jim Hass
Microfox
3310 Fox Run
P.O. Box 447
Richfield, OH 44286

Rick Hawkes
Hawk Software
335 Westwood Drive
P.O. Box 1737
Kitchener, ONT N2M 2L3
CANADA

Donald S. Higgins
6365-32nd Avenue N.
St. Petersburg, FL 33710

Fred C. Hill
Micro System Solutions
5417 S. Cimarron Road
Littleton, CO 80123

Rick Hillier
405 Barrington Lane
Waterloo, ONT N2T 1
CANADA

Michael J. Himowitz
Federal Hill Software
8134 Scotts Level Road
Baltimore, MD 21208

Van Hooper
Hooper International
P.O. Box 50200
Colorado Springs, CO 80949

John Intorcio
4B Beacon Village
Burlington, MA 01803

Eric Isaacson
Eric Isaacson Software
416 E. University Street
Bloomington, IN 47401

William A. Jackson
6529 Matilija Avenue
Van Nuys, CA 91401

Stephen W. Johnson
Greater Europe Mission
330 S. Schmale Road
Carol Stream, IL 60188

Dennis Jones
Software Innovations
18631 North 19th Avenue #128-240
Phoenix, AZ 85027

Scott Jones
Austin Software Design
P.O. Box 3282
S. Pasadena, CA 91031

Brad Kaenel
PC Help-Line
35250 Silver Leaf Circle
Yucaipa, CA 92399

Paris Karahalios
Trius, Inc.
231 Sutton Street #2D-3
North Andover, MA 01845

E. Kasey Kasemodel
Parados Technical Services
401 Snyder Avenue
Ann Arbor, MI 48103

Joe Kasser
11421 Fairoak Drive
Silver Spring, MD 20902

Phil Katz
PKWARE, Inc.
7032 N. Ardara Avenue
Glendale, WI 53209

Walter Kennamer
Ernst & Whinney
2000 National City Center
Cleveland, OH 44114

David V. King
Vision Unlimited
8 Glover Road
P.O. Box 43
Wayland, MA 01778

Jim Korenthal
Korenthal Associates, Inc.
230 West 13th Street
New York, NY 10011

Kenneth Kronblum
Dataphile Software
7058 Sandpiper
Kalamazoo, MI 49002

John D. Lake
Data Solutions
1529 Thistledown Drive
Brandon, FL 33510

Justin Langseth
American On-Line Systems
12 Thirteenth Avenue
Warwick, RI 02886

Frank LaRosa
Searchlight
P.O. Box 640
Stonybrook, NY 11790

James H. LeMay
Eagle Performance Software
6341 Klamath Road
Fort Worth, TX 76116

William J. Letendre
Trendtech Corporation
14 Ella Lane
Wayne, NJ 07470

Richard Levey
151-28 22nd Avenue
Whitestone, NY 11357

James E. Levin
Levin Consulting Group
P.O. Box 41050
Cincinnati, OH 45241

Robert L. Lloyd
191 Via De La Reina
Merritt Island, FL 32953

Dennis C. Lozen
Software Expressions
P.O. Box 301002
Houston, TX 77230

Gary Lundgren
Parytech Associates
16559 Quincy Street N.E.
Ham Lake, MN 55304

Ralph B. Mace
Information Technology, Ltd.
5 Park Boulevard
Lincoln, RI 02865

Andrew F. Mackie
19 Rockwood Drive
Ottawa, KS 66067

Randy MacLean
Formgem Corp.
#3-64 Healey Road
Bolton, ONT L7E 5A4
CANADA

W. G. Madison & Associates
P.O. Box 898
Greenbelt, MD 20770

Marshall Magee
Magee Enterprises
P.O. Box 1587
Norcross, GA 30091

Matthew G. Maier
19019 Capehart Drive
Gaithersburg, MD 20879

David R. Malmberg
Softworks
43064 Via Moraga
Mission San Jose, CA 94539

Steve Mannes
Roxy Recorders, Inc.
648 Broadway, Third Floor
New York, NY 10012

Robert S. Marshall
Kindred Spirits
Finntown Road RFD 2, Box 291
Waldoboro, ME 04572

Eduardo Martins
2083-C Orchard Street
Urbana, IL 61801

Paul Mayer
ZPAY Payroll Systems
3516 Ruby Street
Franklin Park, IL 60131

Judson McCranie
Software Solutions
2406 Orlando Drive
Valdusta, GA 31602

R. Scott McGinnis
Caber Software
P.O. Box 3607/Merchandise Mart
Chicago, IL 60654

Terry McGuire
1127 12th Street #306
Santa Monica, CA 90403

Graeme W. McRae
P.O. Box 16
Monmouth Junction, NJ 08852

Jerry Medlin
Medlin Accounting Shareware
1461 Sproul Avenue
Napa, CA 94559

Stephen Meredith
Data del Mar
10423 Byrne Avenue
Cupertino, CA 95014

Kenneth E. Merker
Prologic Software & Services
P.O. Box 71
Loveland, OH 45140

Carl F. Miescke
FOTO 64, Inc.
816 Borden Rae Court
San Jose, CA 95117

Frank K. Milano
Alternative Decision Software
11 Greencastle Lane
Williamsville, NY 14221

Kevin Miller
Universal Business Concepts
169 Edgewood Avenue
Longmeadow, MA 01106

Larry B. Miller
FBN Software
10861 Northoak Square
Cupertino, CA 95014

Caroline Minori
Todaro
RD 3, Hathaway Pt. Road
St. Albans, VT 05478

Louis M. Miranda
6033 E. Northwest Highway #1106
Dallas, TX 75231

Sammy Mitchell
SemWare
730 Elk Cove Court
Kennesaw, GA 30144

Michael L. Mohle
Princeton-Galax Systems
9 Grover Avenue
Princeton, NJ 08540

Philip A. Mongelluzzo
Star Guidance Consulting
273 Windy Drive
Waterbury, CT 06705

William Moore
Morsoft
9859 IH-10 West, 107/811
San Antonio, TX 78230

G. Allen Morris III
Soft Gam's Software
P.O. Box 1311
Mendocino, CA 95460

Ward Mundy
Ward Mundy Software
4160 Club Drive
Atlanta, GA 30319

Joseph F. Murphy
Structural Reliability Consultants
P.O. Box 56164
Madison, WI 53705

Scott Musser
White Harvest Software, Inc.
P.O. Box 97153
Raleigh, NC 27624

Nassib Nassar
SoftBrush
4035 Livingstone Place
Durham, NC 27707

Mike Neuhaus
NoGate Consulting
1494 Hidden Valley
Kentwood, MI 49508

John J. Newlin
New-Ware
8050 Camino Kiosco
San Diego, CA 92122

Robert L. Obenchain
Software Prescription Co.
4102 Colville Road
Durham, NC 27707

Bob Ostrander
Public Brand Software
3750 Kentucky Avenue
Indianapolis, IN 46241

Gregory Parcell
Parcell Software
307 Greenfield Circle
Geneva, IL 60134

Norm Patriquin
Patri-Soft
P.O. Box 8263
San Bernardino, CA 92412

Blair D. Peery
Peery Data
P.O. Box 12235
Charlotte, NC 28220

Marc Perkel
Computer Tyme
216 South Glenstone
Springfield, MO 65802

Gordon E. Peterson II
Noah Systems
P.O. Box 40476
San Antonio, TX 78229

Mark Pfeifer
Bonsai Technologies
P.O. Box 6296
Rochester, MN 55903

Carley Phillips
Longhorn Systems, Inc.
3202 W. Anderson Lane, #208-513
Austin, TX 78757

Larry D. Phillips
Larry Phillips Studios
801 Marie Park N.E.
Albuquerque, NM 87123

Mike Potter
PAS Software
720 South 333rd, Suite 203
Federal Way, WA 98003

Donald Prescott
P.O. Box 165133
Miami, FL 33116

Bob Pritchett
New Dimensions Software
23 Pawtucket Drive
Cherry Hill, NJ 08003

Robert Pritt
Evergreen Case Tools
11025 164th Avenue N.E.
Redmond, WA 98052

Chip Rabinowitz
Innovative Data Concepts
3084 Woodlawn Avenue
Glenside, PA 19038

Lee Raesly
National Software Design
12505 Fostoria Way
Darnestown, MD 20878

J. C. Ratjen
2126 Glebe Avenue
Bronx, NY 10462

Tom Rawson
JP Software
P.O. Box 1470
E. Arlington, MA 02174

L. John Ribar
CDS Group
3161 Honey Run Drive
New York, NY 17404

Bill Rittenhouse
WR Software
P.O. Box 4819
Walnut Creek, CA 94596

Charles D. Robertson
Unique Software
208 Dunigan Court
Fort Worth, TX 76126

Bruce E. Robey
Alphabytes, Inc.
111 8th Street S.E.
Washington, DC 20003

Max S. Robin
Cheat River Engineering
23 Richwood Place
Denville, NJ 07834

Tom Rodman
Rodman Software
1544 Lighthouse Drive
Naperville, IL 60565

Rob J. Rosenberger
Barn Owl Software
P.O. Box 74
O'Fallon, IL 62269

Neil J. Rubenking
86 Midcrest Way
San Francisco, CA 94131

Hans Salvisberg
Froeschmattstr. 40
CH-3018 Berne
SWITZERLAND

Andrew M. Saucci, Jr.
727 Barkley Avenue
East Meadow, NY 11554

Guy Scharf
Software Architects, Inc.
2163 Jardin Drive
Mountain View, CA 94040

Martin Schiff
Custom Data Solutions
820 Driver Avenue
Winter Park, FL 32789

Russel L. Schnapp
Schnapp Software Consulting
7671 Northrup Place
San Diego, CA 92126

David Schreck
145 East Windsor Road
North Vancouver, BC V7N 1J9
CANADA

David A. Schulz
Trius, Inc.
231 Sutton Street #2D-3
North Andover, MA 01845

Peter Schulz
PCX
13734 Boquita Drive
Del Mar, CA 92014

William C. Scott
22 Cary Annex
Coalgate, OK 74538

Irene M. Senderson
System Enhancement Associates
21 New Street
Wayne, NJ 07470

Barry Simon
CTRLALT Associates
112 N. Formosa Avenue
Los Angeles, CA 90036

Tom Simondi
Computer Knowledge
P.O. Box 91176
Los Angeles, CA 90009

Orest W. Skrypuch
217 Terrace Hill Street
Brantford, ONT N3R 1G8
CANADA

Doug Slocum
DLS Development
One Gale Road
Brick, NJ 08723

Gus Smedstad
NoGate Consulting
1447 Hidden Valley
Grand Rapids, MI 49508

Tom Smith
Datastorm Technologies, Inc.
P.O. Box 1471
Columbia, MO 65205

John Steed
6907 Childsdale Road
Rockford, MI 49341

Don Strenczewilk
Rochester Heritage
72 Knapp Avenue
Rochester, NY 14609

Roger Stringer
Marietta Systems, Inc.
2917 Ashebrooke Drive
Marietta, GA 30007

Douglas C. Swallow
Software Environments, Inc.
7927 Clubhouse Estates Drive
Orlando, FL 32819

Robert C. Tellefson
RCT Design
663 S. Bernardo #7
Sunnyvale, CA 94087

John Tengwall
Tengware Enterprises
28162 Amable
Mission Viejo, CA 92692

Matthew Thomas
MPt Software Co.
P.O. Box 4694
Racine, WI 53404

Mark Tigges
P.O. Box 3694
Castlegar
CANADA

Robert Tolz
PAL Software NY
51 Cedar Lane
Ossining, NY 10562

William V. Torbert
Torbert Data Systems, Inc.
3916 Plum Lane
Chesapeake, VA 23321

Lemuel D. Turner
Turbosystems Co.
P.O. Box 165
Roy, UT 84067

Peter Volpa
Circuit Systems
418 Church Road
Sicklerville, NJ 08081

Bob Wallace
Quicksoft
219 First N. Suite 224
Seattle, WA 98109

Gordon Wanner/Bob Foster
Omniverse Software Corp.
923 Washington Street
Port Townsend, WA 98368

Iram J. Weinstein
XD Systems
1014 Shipman Lane
McLean, VA 22101

Mark J. Welch
Softworks
P.O. Box 2969
Dublin, CA 94568

Rosemary West
RK West Consulting
P.O. Box 8059
Mission Hills, CA 91346

Bill White
Westford Systems, Inc.
P.O. Box 57
Still River, MA 01467

Roger E. Wilkes
Wilkes Software, Inc.
5231 Longwood Drive
Memphis, TN 38314

Dave Williams
111 Pulaski Drive
P.O. Box 181
Jacksonville, AR 72076

Peter Williams
280 Leedom Way
Newtown, PA 18940

Richard A. Williams
1006 Butler Drive
P.O. Box 9311
Crystal Lake, IL 60014

Morrie Wilson
Wilson WindowWare
3377 59th S.W.
Seattle, WA 98116

Richard M. Wilson
CTRLALT Associates
260 S. Lake Avenue, Suite 133
Pasadena, CA 91101

Chris Wolf
CrossCourt Systems
1521 Greenview Avenue
East Lansing, MI 48823

Jeannine Wolf
Wolf Software Design
6369 Caminito Flecha
San Diego, CA 92111

Mike Woltz
Buffalo Creek Software
913 39th Street
West Des Moines, IA 50265

Emery D. Wooten
MRE Software
150 Jones Street
West Point, MS 39773

Brenton L. Worrell
6404 Mornay Drive
Tampa, FL 33615

Mark Wyatt
Sandd Software
P.O. Box 3587
Reston, VA 22090

Eric Zuck
Logistique LMM
6577 First Avenue
Montreal, QUE H1Y 3B2
CANADA

ASP MEMBERS: DISK VENDORS

The following listing contains all of the ASP member disk vendors for 1990. These disk vendors support the Shareware concept and meet the qualifications of the ASP guidelines regarding disk vendors.

Lynne Adams
Adams PC-Software
801 Henryetta, Suite 2
Springdale, AR 72764

Maxine Ajala
Megamicro Computer Center
17 Bellevue Avenue
Penndel, PA 19047

Constantine G. Alikes
Victor Video
2 West Main Street
Victor, NY 14564

T. Teken Backhaus
Mike Rowe Services
306-2722 Fifth Street
Victoria, BC V8T 4B2
CANADA

Paul Baerman
Natl. Collegiate Software Clubhouse
6697 College Station
Durham, NC 27708

Edward L. Bailey
SOFTEC PCL
880 6th Street
Maryville, MI 48040

David Banko
PC Arcade
276 Morehouse Road
Easton, CT 06612

Kenneth Ray Bellew
1st Bank Of Shareware
6944 Hudson Boulevard N.
St Paul, MN 55119

Thomas Bookhamer
Shareware Outlet
713 110th Avenue N.E., Suite 207
Bellevue, WA 98004

Chuck Bregzeale
Peoples Choice
P.O. Box 171134
Memphis, TN 38187

Judith Brown
Fox Valley Technical College
1825 N. Bluemound Drive
Appleton, WI 54913

Bob Burns
Public Brand Software
3750 Kentucky Avenue
Indianapolis, IN 46241

Frank Burr
Oasis Shareware
P.O. Box 1558
Temple City, CA 91780

James Carvin
CWI Information Services
P.O. Box 4851
Anaheim, CA 92803

David Chambers
Chambers Consulting Group
P.O. Box 59137
Philadelphia, PA 19102

Hal Chapman
BL Software, Inc.
P.O. Box 13474
Chesapeake, VA 23325

Lawrence Chiabai
Dinsdale Industries
2032 Merivale Road
Nepean, ONT K2G 1G6
CANADA

Sylvio Chin
Premium Software
24 Station Road
Barton Halsall NR O.
LANCS L39 7JN
ENGLAND

Mike Coffey
Paragon PC Software
P.O. Box 187
Moravian Falls, NC 28654

Michael C. Comish
Software Excitement
P.O. Box 5069
Central Point, OR 97502

Mark A. Connor
Software Shoppe
P.O. Box 785
Ayer, MA 01432

Leo D. Covas
Ocean State Shareware
26 Jade Road
Coventry, RI 02914

Ted Croft
Printers Shareware
5019-5021 West Lovers Lane
Dallas, TX 75209

Carole J. Cruz
PC Shareware
1943 Felspar Street
San Diego, CA 92109

Herbert Davis
Best Bits & Bytes
P.O. Box 8245
Van Nuys, CA 91409

Lawrence Delaney
$ave On $oftware
P.O. Box 2837
Wilkes Barre, PA 18703

Wilfred E. Desaulniers, Jr.
Bright Futures, Inc.
18 Iroquois Road
Enfield, CT 06082

John Dibble
D-K Distributing
1057 W. Philadelphia #243
Ontario, CA 91762

Cliff Drumfeller
General Computer Systems
22612 Foothill Blvd #200C
Hayward, CA 94541

Geraldine Eby
Computer Bin
P.O. Box 1826
Perris, CA 92370

Lawrence C. Falk
Flasoft, Inc.
9509 U.S. Highway 42
Prospect, KY 40059

Kenneth Finto
Finto Software
Route 2, Box 44
Rosebud, TX 76570

Mark S. Foster
Quanta Press, Inc.
2239 Carter Avenue
St. Paul, MN 55108

J. Cagney France
Next Stop Computing
P.O. Box 1467
San Carlos, CA 94070

Frank Goodyear
OS/TECH DBA PC-LIB
2414 Fairview, Suite 201
Santa Ana, CA 92704

Frank E. Gray III
Grayson Resource Center
P.O. Box 465
Union City, GA 30291

Jeff Green
Advantage Business Systems
56 Bath Road, Cheltenham
Gloucestershire GL53 7HJ
ENGLAND

Christine Harris
PD Software House
312 H Street
Grants Pass, OR 97526

John Hatch
Shareware Express
27601 Forbes Road, Suite 37
Laguna Niguel, CA 92677

Alan C. Heiner
Winners Edge Computer Software
P.O. Box 233
Roy, UT 84067

R. E. Hermann
Generic Software Place, Inc.
P.O. Box 1177
Carmel, IN 46032

Dr. P. A. Hickling
Shareware-Elite
25 Cades Park
Helston, Cornwall TR13 8QS
ENGLAND

Paul Jacobson
SoftSource
4241 Southport Circle
Okemos, MI 48864

Richard Johnson
Tabs, Inc.
609 Edwards Avenue
Kinston, NC 28501

Patti Jones
Shareware To Go
P.O. Box 574575
Orlando, FL 32857

Nane Jurgensen
Die Deutsche Software Biblioth
Ysenburgstrasse 10
8000 Munchen 19
WEST GERMANY

Bob Kelly
Rainware Software, Inc.
P.O. Box 1194
Mercer Island, WA 98040

Donald Kiely
Olympus Software Concepts
2110 E. Katella Avenue
Anaheim, CA 92803

Joe P. Kiene
GF Stores, Ltd.
RR #1, Davis Bay Road
Sechelt, BC V0N 3A0
CANADA

Margaret Killeen
California Freeware
1747 East Avenue Q, Unit C-1
Palmdale, CA 93550

Paul K. Kirk
Elite Shareware Labs, Inc.
1724 Springhill Road #C
Staunton, VA 24401

Michael R. Kopp
First Choice Software Etc.
425 Revere Avenue
Ventura, CA 93004

Stephen Lee
Shareware Marketing
Beer EX12 3HW
ENGLAND

Carter F. Levick
CCS, Inc.
P.O. Box 312
Lafayette Hill, PA 19444

Alex Lin
Micro Mart
792 Hamilton Street
Somerset, NJ 08873

Floyd Littrell
JF Company's Software Source
10058 Dove Oak Court
Cupertino, CA 95014

Alvin Lowe
AFL Industries
213 Ward Circle
Brentwood, TN 37027

Ian Mackay
Manaccom PTY LTD
1/9 Camford Street
Milton 4064 QLD
AUSTRALIA

Michael P. Mason
Diskkey Shareware
1100 East North Boulevard
Leesburg, FL 34748

Joanne A. McMullin
Alternative Choice Computing
77 Main Street
Shelbourne Falls, MA 01370

Michelle Menard
Software Kingdom
P.O. Box 555
Auburn, NH 03032

Joseph Mendez
The Original Software Company
P.O. Box 8472
Redlands, CA 92375

Rouce Metcalfe
Generic-Ware
3900 Richland Road
Dothan, AL 36303

William Mitchell
Mitchell Disk
P.O. Box 96
Bradford, MA 01835

Paul Mullen
PC Independent User Group
87 High Street
Tonbridge, Kent TN9 1RX
ENGLAND

John A. Nazimek
Phoenix Computer Services
P.O. Box 4129
Linden, NJ 07036

Judson Newell
Canada Remote Systems
1331 Crestlawn Drive #D
Mississauga, ONT L4W 2P9
CANADA

John H. Notor
Notor Engineering Services
1548 Arata Court
San Jose, CA 95125

Clark Oden
Rainbow Software
P.O. Box 3908
Ontario, CA 91761

Rick Olson
Advantage Plus Distributors
7113 Halifax Court
Tampa, FL 33615

Daniel W. Opperman
Opperman Associates, Inc.
191 Washington Avenue
Clifton, NY 07011

Fred Owens
Fred's Software
8310 Carmel Place
Tampa, FL 33615

Arthur A. Pagano, Jr.
AD-JP Enterprises
P.O. Box 399
Islip, NY 11751

Phil Palmer
New England Software Library
9 Davis Avenue
Shelburne, VT 05482

Charles S. Percherke
Computer Bug
4110 Brownsville Road #150
Pittsburgh, PA 15227

Mervyn Elston Perkins
Alphon Edugames
221 Ridley Road
Bridgeman Downs 4035
AUSTRALIA

Richard Petersen
PC-SIG
1030D East Duane Avenue
Sunnyvale, CA 94086

Ralph Peterson
Compu-Tech Software Library
P.O. Box 393
Tennille, GA 31089

John Queen
BudgetBytes
P.O. Box 2248
Topeka, KS 66601

Gary Rambo
Smuggly Systems
2824 Myrtle Avenue
Granite City, IL 62040

Robert A. Reid
Del-Com Services
884 164th Street
White Rock, BC V4A 4Y5
CANADA

James C. Richards
Simple Series
168 Plaistow Road
Plaistow, NH 03865

W. R. Richardson
Prairieware
3101 1st Avenue N.
Great Falls, MT 59401

Marc Routhier
3431, De La Dauversiere
Sainte-Foy, QUE G1X 2H6
CANADA

David Alan Ryan
DKR Software
9 Raymond Grove
Warradale SA 5046
AUSTRALIA

George Ryan
Florida PC Library
P.O. Box 2878
Leesburg, FL 32749

Robert Scruggs
Circle Software
P.O. Box 383
Belleville, IL 62222

Soliman Shebani
ACL Shareware
1621 Fulton Avenue #35
Sacramento, CA 95825

Arthur Silvergate
CBUG
P.O. Box 125
Columbia, MD 21045

Gordon Simmonds
Sim-Com Services
35158 High Drive
Abbotsford, BC V2S 4P6
CANADA

Rod Smith
Public Domain Software Library
Winscombe House, Beacon Road
Crowborough, Sussex TN6 1UL
ENGLAND

Donald Spero
Data Outlet Software
P.O. Box 776
Macon, GA 31202

C. Y. Stapleton
The Printer
3200 S. John Rabbitt
Lufkin, TX 75901

Ernie Starchuk
ThriftyWare Software/Hardware
82 East 39th Avenue
Vancouver, BC V5W 1J7
CANADA

Wesley A. Stratton, Jr.
SFIP
75 Nachilly Drive
New Britain, CT 06053

Liz Summerill
Advantage Business Systems
56 Bath Road, Cheltenham
Gloucestershire GL53 7HJ
ENGLAND

Charles J. Tekippe, Ph.D.
SizzleWare Shareware Library
P.O. Box 6429
Lake Charles, LA 70606

Jim Thompson
Jim Thompson Enterprises
150 S. Magnolia Avenue, Suite 248
Anaheim, CA 92804

Ronald Van Hoose
RVH Publications
4291 Holland Road, Suite 562
Virginia Beach, VA 23452

Tommy E. VanHoozier
T&Z Software
P.O. Box 780217
Sebastian, FL 32978

Linda Walker
Family Software
687 N. Summit Street
Barberton, OH 44203

Art Wengell
Princeton Software, Inc.
177 Wall Street
Princeton, NJ 08540

Chris Williams
Accusoft
740 Brittingham Court
Columbus, OH 43214

Gregory N. Wilson
Big Byte Software
2111 W. Arkansas Lane #207
Arlington, TX 76013

Steven Woas
Celestial Press
114 Valencia Drive
New Port Richey, FL 34652

Archie Young
Young's Software
P.O. Box 8214
Glen Ridge, NJ 07028

Karen Young
Argus Computerized Exchange
20 Mall Road, Suite 210
Burlington, MA 01803

A

AA-TEXT text file, 806
A86 assembler, 721
    registration address, 722
Accounting. *See also* PC Accounting and
   Medlin Accounting
Ad bulletins, Channel 1, 141
Advanced mode, 197
Advertisement, logoff, 141
Advertising, Channel 1, 140-141
AIDSINFO text file, 800-801
AIDS information text file, 800-801
Airline reservations, telephone numbers
   for, (text file), 805-806
Aladdin (GEnie navigator), 90-92, 209
   features, 92
ALCHEMY text file, 806
ALF Quick Copy unit (disk copier), 71
Allen, Paul, 892
Analog loopback, 168
Anarkey DOS command editor, 632-637,
   864-865
     altering DOS path in, 635
     author of, 636-637
     defining commands in, 635-636
     directory names, 634
     editing, 635-636
     functions, 632-633
     history buffer function, 633
     multiple commands for, 634
     power, 632-633
     retrieving characters in, 633-634
Anderson, Nels, 740, 742, 743-744
ANSI text file, 806, 807
ANSMACH text file, 806
ANSTUTOR, 806, 807
Antiqueware, defined, 10-12
Apple Computer, 59

Applications programs, 858-862
ARC program, 151, 578-581, (illus., 152,
   578, 580, 581)
     author of, 580
     format, 127, 128
     test performance, 579-580
Archive bit, 496
Archive 3.0 program, 453-454, (illus., 454)
     interim backups with, 454-455
     restoring files with, 455
Archives, 151
     computer, 130-132
     Mahoney Collection, 130-131, 132
     unpacking with PKARC, 153
ARCMASTER program, 497, 604-607,
   (illus., 605, 606)
     author of, 607
     compression programs, 604
     features, 607
     online help, 606
As-Easy-As spreadsheet program, 777-780,
   860
     author of, 780
     executing Lotus macros with, 780
     features, 778-779
     keeping informed with, 778
     running, 778
     status line, 779-780
ASCII
     exporting files in, 681
     in PC-Write, 312
     saving in, 344
     uploads and downloads in Procomm,
     388
ASCII Upload Script, 205-206, (illus., 206,
   207)
ASMTUTOR assembler, 728-729
ASP. *See* Association of Shareware Profes-
   sionals

4DOS—Power at the DOS Prompt

4DOS helps you get the most out of your PC. It replaces COMMAND.COM, the command interpreter that comes with all versions of DOS. You'll find *4DOS* provides many capabilities COMMAND.COM can't, including

- On-line help for all *4DOS* and DOS commands
- Command line editing with full cursor key support
- Recall, editing, and reexecution of previous commands
- Shorthand names (*aliases*) for commonly used sequences of commands
- Enhanced internal commands, including vastly more powerful COPY and DIR commands
- Over 40 new internal commands, including COLOR, LIST, MOVE, TIMER, and many more
- Descriptions of up to 40 characters for any file
- A rich batch file language, including IF / THEN / ELSE capability, box and line drawing, and prompted user input
- Batch file processing up to five times faster than COMMAND.COM
- Point-and-shoot file selection for any command
- Swapping to XMS, EMS, or disk to reduce resident memory requirements

4DOS is compatible with COMMAND.COM, and requires less than 3K of DOS memory while your applications are running—as little as 256 bytes if your system has "load high" capability!

4DOS is a trademark of J.P. Software.

4DOS ORDER FORM

See for yourself—try the shareware product that won finalist honors in *PC Magazine*'s 1989 Technical Excellence Awards! *4DOS* is just $40 with this coupon—a 20% discount off the regular price of $50. Shipping and handling: $4 U.S., $5 Canada, $10 others.

Name _____

Company _____

Address _____

City _____ State _____ Zip/Postal Code _____

Phone (_____) _____ Disks: _____ 5.25″ _____ 3.5″ (add $5)

_____ Check or money order enclosed _____ VISA _____ MasterCard
_____ American Express

Acct. no. _____ Exp. date _____

Signature _____

Print name on card _____

To order by phone, call 617-646-3975

J.P. Software
P.O. Box 1470
East Arlington, MA 02174

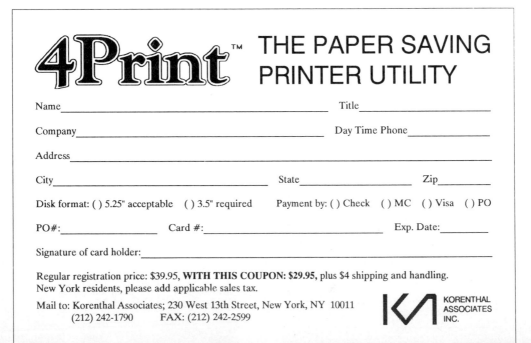

4Print™ THE PAPER SAVING PRINTER UTILITY

Name_____ Title_____

Company_____ Day Time Phone_____

Address_____

City_____ State_____ Zip_____

Disk format: ( ) 5.25″ acceptable   ( ) 3.5″ required   Payment by: ( ) Check   ( ) MC   ( ) Visa   ( ) PO

PO#:_____ Card #:_____ Exp. Date:_____

Signature of card holder:_____

Regular registration price: $39.95, **WITH THIS COUPON: $29.95,** plus $4 shipping and handling. New York residents, please add applicable sales tax.

Mail to: Korenthal Associates; 230 West 13th Street, New York, NY 10011
    (212) 242-1790   FAX: (212) 242-2599

KA KORENTHAL ASSOCIATES INC.

BATUTIL/STACKEY Special Offer

Special Order Form

AS-EASY-AS...® Diskette with Bound User's Manual, $40.00   _____
Add **$5.00** Shipping & Handling in U.S., **$8.50** International

                                                        TOTAL   _____

Name:_____   Company:_____

Street Address:_____

City:_____ State:_____ Zip:_____ Country:_____

        ____ Check or Money Order Enclosed   ____ Charge my VISA or MASTERCARD

Acct. # _____   Exp. Date:_____

Signature _____   Phone:_____

                              TRIUS, Inc.
          Send Your Order to: 231 Sutton Street, Suite 2D-3
                              North Andover, MA 01845

        (Please Allow 10 days for Delivery in the U.S.A. and 15 days for International Orders)

Mail this coupon to:

Support Group, Inc.
P.O. Box 130
McHenry, MD 21541

The Personal Electronic Bulletin Board System

Now you can be the SysOp of your own full-featured bulletin board system. Rich Levin's BBSX (tm) self-installs and is easy to configure, use and maintain. With features like single- or multi-user access, unlimited SIG and library support, powerful message entry and retrieval facilities (including true message "thread" navigation), X/Y/Zmodem support, external protocols, "doors," automated maintenance, host mode, complete documentation, free support and more, BBSX is a bulletin board you can start with today and grow with tomorrow. Join the country's fastest growing group of System Operators--those running Rich Levin's BBSX software.

To order Rich Levin's BBSX (tm) Bulletin Board System, photocopy, complete and mail this form to:

Richard B. Levin
Levin & Associates
BBSX Mail-In Offer
Dept. 90-DFFG
P. O. Box 14546
Phila., PA 19115

Please make all checks and money orders payable in United States currency to "Richard B. Levin." Site license and other information available on request. Prices, terms and conditions subject to change without notice. Please allow six weeks for delivery. For customer service inquiries, please call (215) 333-8274 or call our BBS at (215) 333-8275/8774.

Ship-to name and address: _____

_____

_____

Telephone number: (   )   -

1.   HOME editions are available ONLY to users running the BBSX system on their personal computers in their homes. All other use is prohibited.
2.   OFFICE editions must be purchased by all non-home users of the BBSX system. HOME editions may NOT be used in a non-home environment.
3.   DELUXE editions include a bound volume of the BBSX system documentation and are available to all users.
4.   PREMIUM editions include one DELUXE edition and one copy of Rich Levin's Osborne/McGraw-Hill book, "The Computer Virus Handbook." PREMIUM editions are available to all users.

```
       HOME editions ordered:  [#      ] x $  49.95 = $        .00
     OFFICE editions ordered:  [#      ] x $  99.95 = $        .00
     DELUXE editions ordered:  [#      ] x $ 149.95 = $        .00
    PREMIUM editions ordered:  [#      ] x $ 174.95 = $        .00
-----------------------------------------------------------------
Total copies ordered:         [#      ]
Subtotal:                                          $        .00
Shipping and handling (see table*, below):         $        .00
Pennsylvania residents add 6% sales tax:           $        .00
-----------------------------------------------------------------
Amount enclosed:                                   $        .00
=================================================================
* Shipping charges:  HOME and OFFICE editions:  $2.00 per copy
                            DELUXE editions:  $4.00 per copy
                           PREMIUM editions:  $6.00 per copy
```

International orders please add $2.00 to the above charges for foreign shipping charges.

[Rich Levin's]

CHECKUP

The Leading, Critically Acclaimed, User-Supported Virus Detection System

The featured virus detection system in John Dvorak's and Nick Anis'
Osborne/McGraw-Hill book, "Dvorak's Guide to PC Telecommunications"

The Virus Detection System Preferred by Educated Users World-Wide

To order Rich Levin's CHECKUP (tm) Virus Detection System, photocopy, complete and mail this form to:

Richard B. Levin
Levin & Associates
CHECKUP Mail-In Offer
Dept. 90-DFFG
P.O. Box 14546
Phila., PA 19115

Please make all checks and money orders payable in United States currency to "Richard B. Levin." Site license and other information available on request. Prices, terms and conditions subject to change without notice. Please allow six weeks for delivery. For customer service inquiries, please call (215) 333-8274 or call our BBS at (215) 333-8275/8774.

Ship-to name and address: _____

_____

_____

Telephone number: (   )   -

1. HOME editions are available ONLY to users running the CHECKUP system on their personal computers in their homes. All other use is prohibited.
2. OFFICE editions must be purchased by all non-home users of the CHECKUP system. HOME editions may NOT be used in a non-home environment.
3. DELUXE editions include a bound volume of the CHECKUP system documentation and are available to all users.
4. PREMIUM editions include one DELUXE edition and one copy of Rich Levin's Osborne/McGraw-Hill book, "The Computer Virus Handbook." PREMIUM editions are available to all users.

```
      HOME editions ordered:  [#      ] x $ 24.95 = $          .00
    OFFICE editions ordered:  [#      ] x $ 49.95 = $          .00
    DELUXE editions ordered:  [#      ] x $ 74.95 = $          .00
   PREMIUM editions ordered:  [#      ] x $ 99.95 = $          .00
   ----------------------------------------------------------------
   Total copies ordered:      [#      ]
   Subtotal:                                         $          .00
   Shipping and handling (see table*, below):        $          .00
   Pennsylvania residents add 6% sales tax:          $          .00
   ----------------------------------------------------------------
   Amount enclosed:                                  $          .00
   ================================================================
   * Shipping charges:   HOME and OFFICE editions:  $2.00 per copy
                                 DELUXE editions:   $4.00 per copy
                                PREMIUM editions:   $6.00 per copy
```

International orders please add $2.00 to the above charges for foreign shipping charges.

Please send me all of your software for $88:

Name_____

Company_____

Address_____

City_____ State_____ Zip_____

Phone_____

_____ Check enclosed   _____ Charge my Visa or MasterCard

Card No._____

Signature_____

Send your order to: Biologic Company
                          P.O. Box 1267
                          Manassas VA 22110-2839
                          703-368-2949   703-361-8251 (fax)

BIX Subscription Discount

Special three-month subscription for $19.95!

Join the BIX on-line community for three months and download thousands of shareware programs from our extensive software libraries.

With your subscription, you'll have access to: special-interest exchanges on Amiga, IBM, Mac, Product Support and Telecommunications; BYTE Magazine articles and benchmarks; Jerry Pournelle; daily computer industry news from the MicroBYTES news service; and much more.

You can reach BIX through Tymnet for a low hourly rate of $3/hr. during off-peak hours, or $6/hr. during peak hours. We also offer a special rate of $20 per month for unlimited off-peak usage. Tymnet charges are in addition to the BIX subscription fee. You can also call us directly in Boston Massachusetts at 617-861-9767 and pay no hourly rates.

Log-on instructions are on the reverse.

BOARDWATCH MAGAZINE
Online Information Services and Electronic Bulletin Boards

Since March 1987, Boardwatch Magazine has been the leading monthly publication covering the emerging cottage industry in electronic bulletin boards (BBS) and shareware software. Each issue is packed with info on hundreds of specialized low cost systems where you can download the latest shareware software, access unique information databases, and participate in hundreds of topical discussions spanning the globe by modem. Reviews of successful online services, hardware and software, profiles of industry players, tips, success stories, and ideas for new services you can use to start your own online business at home.

In each issue, Boardwatch reviews the latest in available shareware software, what it can do for you, and where to get it. Mike Callahan continues his Dr. File Finder quest in his regular Boardwatch column. To keep abreast of the latest developments in shareware programs as well as the BBS systems that carry them, mail this card today for a FREE SAMPLE COPY of Boardwatch Magazine.

Name _____

Address _____

City _____ State _____ Zip _____

BIX Log-on Instructions:

You can subscribe immediately by dialing our toll-free registration number at 800-225-4129. When you see the "please log in:" prompt, type in **bix** and when you are prompted for "Name?" type in this code word:

bix.shareware

Then simply follow the instructions that will appear. Be sure to have your Visa, American Express, or MasterCard ready. (BIX subscriptions are also available via company purchase order. Call customer service at 800-227-2983 for details.) After you complete registration, we will automatically send you the BIX User Manual free of charge. Limit one special three-month subscription per person.

BOARDWATCH MAGAZINE
5970 South Vivian Street
Littleton, CO 80127

CALIFORNIA SOFTWARE DESIGN

SHEZ THE COMPRESSION COMPANION

SHEZ is the user friendly shell for all your compressed file needs. Shez can process all popular compressed file formats using one common easy to learn menu shell. With Shez you can View, Modify, Extract, Add, Update, Delete, and Freshen files that are contained in compressed files. ZIP, LZH, PAK, ARC, and ZOO formats are supported. Normal registration price is $25.00

FILEFINDER PROGRAM PACKAGE

The FILEFINDER program pack consists of two programs designed to find files on a hard disk. The FF2 program is line oriented and the output can be redirected. The FFF program is full screen oriented and presents a scrollable list of files that were found. In addition FFF can search the hard drive and report on duplicate files that were found. Both program can also look inside compressed files when searching. Normal registration price if $10.00

SPECIAL BOOK OFFER -- Register both programs for only $25.00

Protect Your Data From A Computer Virus

You never know when a hard disk catastrophe might strike. Or when you could pick up a computer virus from an electronic bulletin board or public domain software.

You Need Protection

That's why you need the protection of our Jumbo Tape Backup System. Jumbo stores as much as 120 MB of data on a cartridge about the size of a deck of playing cards.

It works with almost all IBM computers and compatibles, including 386 and 486 based machines. Jumbo installs easily and can backup an entire 40MB drive in less than 20 minutes.

Jumbo comes complete, too, with the drive and all software, along with installation and operation manuals. Find out how easily you could protect your vital data. Just fill out the other side of this coupon, and mail it for a free demo diskette and complete details.

Here's a special bonus from

CompuServe®

CompuServe is pleased to offer CompuServe members who read *Dr. File Finder's Guide to Shareware* a usage credit worth $12.50. To take advantage of this offer, simply complete the coupon on the opposite side and mail it to

CompuServe
Consumer Billing Department
P.O. Box 20212
Columbus, OH 43220

Conditions: One coupon redemption per User Id number. Coupon not transferable. Send the original only—no photocopies will be accepted.

Disc Director

The Professional Hard Disk Management Tool for Larger Hard Disks

Disc Director is the complete hard disk management tool specifically designed to help you manage larger hard disks (40MB and up.) The first layer, a visual branch manager, lets you move, copy, delete, query, and search branches of directories. This is truly an amazing new approach to tree management. The second layer is a full directory manager that allows you to copy, remove, erase, wipe, comment, move, and tag directories. The third layer is a very complete file manager.

The fourth layer is a powerful search utility that lets you search by 14 different criteria, including duplicate filenames, date ranges, attributes, and text contents. In addition, Disc Director features a virtual work area called a *Phantom Directory* that lets you manipulate the files found during a search as though they were in one directory.

The fifth layer is a powerful document manager that lets you attach comments onto any file or directory. Comments may be up to 78 characters long. Never again will you wonder what a file contains or why a directory exists. Comments may be searched for key words or phrases, thereby allowing you to index your hard disks with practically no overhead!

Disc Director runs on DOS version 2.0 and higher and requires 384K of RAM. It includes an application and utility menu system. Disc Director supports Mono, Herc, CGA, EGA and VGA, and includes 43- and 50-line support for EGA/VGA. It also supports (but does not require) a mouse.

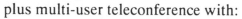

Disc Director includes a complete manual, dual-media diskettes, and technical support. **All this for just $35!**

Disc Director was awarded 3.98 out of 4.00 by PUMA, an independent BBS testing service. Just read what these people have to say about it:

"I have not even scratched the surface of this handy utility's capabilities — I really like it!" —Andy Seybold, *ASCII*

"Disc Director certainly gives XTreePro Gold and its kin a run for their money. If you're trying to squeeze as much as possible out of your hard disk (and who isn't), give Disc Director a go." —Lori Grunin, *PC Magazine*

"Very impressive was Disc Director's capability to search an entire drive for duplicate files." —Jeff Eckert, *InfoWorld*

"Disk Director's interface is well-designed, with a screen that displays plenty of information without becoming unreadable." —Lincoln Spector, *PC World*

To order: Athena Software
4915 Twin Lakes Road #19
Boulder, CO 80301
Phone: 303-530-0693 Fax: 303-530-0727 VISA/MC
Cost: $35 plus $4 shipping and handling. Normally $99.
Offer available only through *Dr. File Finder's Guide to Shareware*.

DOWNLOAD MULTI-PLAYER ONLINE GAME SHAREWARE!

To download the Shareware component of our multi-player online tank battle game, FLASH ATTACK, call our demo system by modem at 305-583-7808 (8 data bits, no parity). After creating a free BBS account for yourself online, select the File Library Edition from our Main Menu, and download the file FA22.ZIP. (Speed tip: if you call using Telix or the new QMODEM with built-in ZMODEM, enter **F F D FA22.ZIP Z** at the BBS Main Menu to zoom straight into downloading the file.)

You can play FLASH ATTACK in multi-player mode on hundreds of major BBS nodes around the nation running the Entertainment Edition, Release E or later, including:

Pro Star Plus	.206-941-0317	*The Palace Gates*	.516-698-6182
City Lights BBS	.212-645-2176	*Sho-tronics*	.602-495-0000
Hot Chat BBS	.215-887-6600	*Farwest BBS*	.604-381-3934
Moonshae Isles	.305-321-2410	*Argus*	.617-229-2345
Somewhere Online	.313-928-9353	*Multi-Comm*	.702-362-9224
Viewline	.403-467-8509	*LiveLine*	.718-332-1330
Atlanta Chatline	.404-922-2937	*MEGANET*	.813-447-4625
Inferno	.408-395-3721	*Magic Gateway*	.815-877-0061
Metropolis	.416-292-8757	*USA-Link*	.818-358-6968

GALAXY
+ THE WORD PROCESSOR

GALAXY is easy to learn and easy to use, yet it delivers the power and sophistication you demand. Whether you're new to computers, or an experienced user, you're in for a treat with GALAXY.

Special offer from Omniverse Software Corp.

As a purchaser of *Dr. File Finder's Guide to Shareware*, you are entitled to a special offer from Omniverse Software Corp.

Regular registration price: $99.95
With this coupon: $79.95

Order Form

GALAXY Word Processor

Includes 100,000-word SpellFinder™ dictionary and 220,000-word WordFinder™ thesaurus, 200-page manual, 3.5″ and 5.25″ disks.

Include $5.00 shipping and handling ($15.00 outside U.S. and Canada).

Name _____

Address _____

City _____ State _____ Zip _____

☐ Check or money order enclosed

☐ Charge my VISA, MasterCard, or American Express (circle one)

Acct # _____ Exp. Date _____

Signature _____

Send your order to:

Omniverse Software Corp.
Box 1570
Port Townsend, WA 98368

Order Form

☐ **GRAB Plus with LaserLabel complete with printed manual, $29.95.**
  Add $2.00 shipping and handling inside U.S., $10.00 outside. _____

☐ **GRAB Plus with LaserLabel Shareware Diskette. Evaluation version**
  of GRAB Plus with LaserLabel, $5.00 (S&H included) _____

☐ **5.25 size or** ☐ **3.5 size diskette** **TOTAL** _____

Name_____ **Company**_____

Street Address_____

City_____ **State**_____ **Zip**_____

☐ **Check or money order enclosed** ☐ **Charge my VISA or MASTERCARD:**

Acct. No._____ **Exp. Date** _____

Signature_____

Send your order to:
(Offer only good with return of this coupon.)

TPAY Payroll Systems Inc.
P.O. Box 445
Franklin Park, Illinois 60131

Get Started NOW!

Shareware Starter Kit from Glossbrenner's Choice

You've read about the programs in *Dr. Filefinder's Guide to Shareware*. Here's how to get started right away! By special arrangement with GLOSSBRENNER'S CHOICE, readers of this book can get three of the most popular personal computer applications for only $2 a disk ($3 for 3 1/2-inch format).

Here's what's available:

- **PC-WRITE** (3 disks) -- for word processing and desktop publishing. Fast, powerful, and loaded with features (there's even a 50,000 word spelling checker!) and online help, PC-WRITE is considered by many to be the best word processing program available -- at any price.

- **FILE EXPRESS** (2 disks) -- to get a handle on your data. Use it to keep track of virtually anything, generate mailing lists in moments, control inventory, produce invoices, or do anything else that requires the monitoring and manipulation of information. You'll love "FE's" friendly, intuitive interface and "natural language" query power.

- **AS-EASY-AS** (1 disk) -- As easy as "you know what." A clone that is so good it must be seen to be believed. Ideal for creating spreadsheets and performing other "number-crunching" chores like budgets, projections, and any "what if?"-style questions.

These programs are a terrific value at the normal Glossbrenner's Choice price of $5 per disk ($6 for 3 1/2-inch format). But with this special offer, you'll pay only $2 per disk ($3 for 3 1/2-inch), and that includes shipping and handling.

To take advantage of this offer, just complete the coupon on the back of this page and mail it with your check or money order to Glossbrenner's Choice, 699 River Road, Yardley, PA 19067.

About Glossbrenner's Choice

And just what is "Glossbrenner's Choice?" It's shareware with a difference. Every program in the collection has been personally selected by computer writer Alfred Glossbrenner (Most recent book: *Glossbrenner's Complete Hard Disk Handbook*; Osborne McGraw-Hill) as the best in its category. Glossbrenner's Choice cuts through the clutter -- and saves you time and money in the process. With Glossbrenner as your guide, you'll spend your time sampling software instead of plowing your way through catalogues. Truly, this is shareware at its best!

Please see reverse side for ordering details.

GLOSSBRENNER'S CHOICE COUPON
[Please Print Clearly]

Name:_____

Address: _____

Address: _____

City: _____ State: _____ ZIP: _____

Phone: _____

Please send me the following Glossbrenner's Choice disks:

Shareware Starter Kit -- 5 1/4-inch format (A $30 value -- yours for only $12.)

- PC-Write   (3-disk set for $6)   _____

- File Express (2-disk set for $4)   _____

- As-Easy-As   (1 disk for $2)   _____

Shareware Starter Kit -- 3 1/2-inch format (A $36 value -- yours for only $18.)

- PC-Write   (3-disk set for $9)   _____

- File Express (2-disk set for $6)   _____

- As-Easy-As   (1 disk for $3)   _____

             TOTAL ENCLOSED   _____

[   ] Please send me a FREE CATALOGUE of other great shareware available from Glossbrenner's Choice.

Make check payable to Glossbrenner's Choice. Check or money order must be denominated in U.S. dollars and drawn on a U.S.-based bank. Mail to:

Glossbrenner's Choice
699 River Road
Yardley, PA 19067

Osborne **McGraw-Hill** assumes NO responsibility for the fulfilment of this offer.

Hard Disk Director Order Form

Hard Disk Director. A $35 dollar value. With this coupon $25........_____
Orders outside of continental US, pleas add $5.00............................_____
California residents, please add 6 1/4% sales tax............................._____

Diskette size   5 1/4"_____   3 1/2"_____

Name_____
Company_____
Street Address_____
City_____ State_____ Zip_____

Check or Money Order _____   Visa/MC_____
Credit Card #_____ Exp Date_____
Signature_____

Send Order to: Helpware
                        1537 Fourth Street
                        San Rafael, CA 94901

HDM IV Order Form

☐ **Registered HDM IV disk with printed manual, $30**   _____

☐ **HDM IV Shareware Sampler (disk only), $5**   _____

   · **S&H $3 in U.S.A., $4 in Canada, $7 for all others**   _____

   · **In Ohio, add 5.5% sales tax**   _____

   All orders must add S&H charges.   <u>TOTAL</u>   _____

Name   _____

Company   _____

Address   _____

          _____

          _____

Disk _____ **5.25"** _____ **3.5"**   **Phone** _____

LINK-UP

143 OLD MARLTON PIKE
MEDFORD, NJ 08055-9936

**MEDLIN
ACCOUNTING
SHAREWARE**

$10.⁰⁰ OFF each Program! (with this coupon)

Order Form

NOW

❑	PC-GL General Ledger Version 3.4	Reg. 35.⁰⁰	$25.⁰⁰
❑	PC-AR Accounts Receivable Version 3.9	Reg. 35.⁰⁰	$25.⁰⁰
❑	PC-PR Payroll Writing Version 1.8	Reg. 35.⁰⁰	$25.⁰⁰
❑	PC-AP Accounts Payable Version 1.4	Reg. 35.⁰⁰	$25.⁰⁰

In CA add 6.25% sales tax

Total $_____

(Each Program registration includes limited phone support and configuration Program.)

Name _____ Company _____

Street Address _____

City _____ State _____ Zip _____

(Disk includes copies of all four programs plus configuration program for each registered program)

❑ Check or money order enclosed   ❑ Charge My VISA or MASTERCARD

Acct. No. _____   Exp. Date _____

Signature _____

Make checks payable to: Jerry Medlin
and send your order to: Medlin Accounting Shareware
                              1461 Sproul Ave. Napa, California 94559

MPt Protocol

by Matthew Thomas, MPt Software Company

"An easy-to-use speed demon."
— *PC World*

The MPt Protocol is a powerful tool for getting your data from one computer to another through a serial port. Whether downloading or uploading files on a BBS, or moving files between PCs over a serial cable, MPt will do the job, and will do it quickly and accurately.

MPt offers many advanced features:

- Full-color screen display of transfer status
- Setup program for changing command options and screen colors
- Baud rates up to 115,200bps
- Full support for 8250, 16450, 16550, and 16550A UARTs
- Call Data Standard (CDS) logging of file transfers
- Multitasking Video Buffer-compatible screen access
- Optional auto-start of MPt Protocol receiver
- RLE data compression

Newkey

Selected *Editor's Choice* in PC-Magazine's last major review of keyboard macro processors, Newkey makes life easier by:

Reducing typing
 - Assign complicated command strings to single keys
 - Use Newkey's shorthand mode to define your own customized abbreviations that expand as you type!

Making your software easier to use for yourself and others
 - Build your own customized help system
 - Build your own custom menu system

Speeding up data entry
 - Assign common data values to single keys or menu selections

Enhancing your computing environment in many ways
 - Eliminate the annoying buffer full beep by expanding the keyboard buffer
 - Speed through your spreadsheet or wordprocessor by increasing cursor movement speed
 - Protect your screen from phosphor burn-in by using Newkey's screen blanker

Regular registration price: $43   **WITH THIS COUPON: $30.00**

The MPt Protocol Order Form

To receive your registered copy of the MPt Protocol, send a check or money order for $20 U.S. or $25 Canadian to:

MPt Software Company
P.O. Box 4694
Racine, WI 53404

Name _____

Address _____

_____

_____

(Add $1 for 3.5″ disk.)

ORDER FORM

Yes, send me Newkey at $30.   _____
Add $7 for foreign shipping+handling.   _____
                          TOTAL   _____

Name _____

Address _____

City _____ State_____ Zip _____

Visa [ ] MasterCard [ ] Check [ ]
Card#_____ Exp. Date _____
Signature_____

Return this form to: FAB Software
                              P.O. Box 336
                              Wayland, MA 01778

PAK - The File Compression Utility
(Special Offer - Save up to 33%)

Pak is a utility for the PC that creates and maintains file archives in compressed form. There are several advantages to compressing files. On a hard disk, most files are accessed infrequently. Compressing infrequently used files frees hard disk space, and allows easier access to these files than if they were backed up on floppy disks and deleted.

PAK is available in three different editions. All three editions can read and write files created by PKZIP (© PKWARE, Inc.) and ARC (© System Enhancement Associates).

- *Command Line Edition* Using this version is much like using DOS commands such as COPY or RENAME. You can compress files, expand them, or sort them in order of date, size, or file name.

- *Full-Screen Edition* (Includes a copy of the command line edition.) This version is much like DOS shells. There are two windows on the screen, a DOS window, and an archive window. The DOS window displays all of the files in any DOS directory. You can tag these files individually or in groups for compression or viewing. Similarly, the archive window allows you to view files within an archive or tag them for expansion.

- *Toolkit Edition* (Includes copies of the full-screen and command line editions.) The toolkit is for programmers who want to include data compression in their own programs. The toolkit works with any compiler that supports OBJect files, and includes example programs in Turbo Pascal and C and Microsoft Pascal and C.

PC-Draft-CAD -
Affordable, Easy, Powerful.

PC-Draft-CAD™ • Easy to use vector based Computer Aided Drafting • Has features usually found in expensive CAD systems, including:

• Intuitive user interface with a choice of pop up menus or single keystroke commands • Context sensitive help, and mouse support, make learning easy while being unobtrusive to expert users • Supports high resolution EGA, VGA, Super VGA & Hercules • "Virtual Memory" automatically uses extended or expanded memory or disk space for drawing sizes up to 32 Megabytes • Supports unlimited layers and multiple font styles • Automatic dimensions expressed in US decimal, fractional or Metric • Draw circles, ellipses, boxes, arcs, curves and lines with varying line widths & styles • Macros automate repeated drawing sequences • Named objects may be stored in libraries for use in multiple drawings • Objects can be copied, cloned, rotated, stretched, mirrored, scaled • Save and restore multiple views • Pan and Zoom • Full Undo and Redo • Imports WordPerfect WPG and AutoCAD DXF files • Exports WPG, HPGL, and GEM Draw format.

Try before you buy: PC-Draft-CAD is available for trial from Compuserve (Go IBMAPP), most shareware disk vendors and many local BBS's.

PAK - Order Form*

Qty.

____	Command Line Edition of PAK	@ $10 each (33% Savings)	$ _____
____	Full-Screen Edition of PAK	@ $20 each (33% Savings)	$ _____
____	Toolkit Edition of PAK	@ $65 each (13% Savings)	$ _____
	Add $5.00 shipping & handling inside U.S. ($10.00 outside)		$ _____
	(Michigan residents, please add applicable sales tax)	Total	$ _____

Name _____ Company _____

Address _____

City _____ State _____ Zip _____

Phone _____ Bus. _____

Payment: [   ] Check or money order enclosed [   ] Charge my VISA, MasterCard, or American Express

Credit Card # _____

Expiration Date _____ Signature _____

Send your order to:

NoGate Consulting   P.O. Box 88115   Grand Rapids, MI 49518-0115

For faster service, order by phone: (616) 455-6270 (credit card orders only)
       or send a fax to: (616) 455-8491

*Offer applies to release 2.5 of PAK. Allow 15 days for delivery.

Registration is normally $65.00 for illustrated manual, 2 disks, complete object libraries & file conversion utilities.

PC-Draft-CAD runs on: IBM PC, XT, AT, PS/2 and "true compatible" PC's with 384k of memory, DOS 2.0 or later; CGA, EGA, VGA, or Hercules graphics display; Microsoft compatible mouse is supported but not required; Printers include IBM and Epson dot matrix, HP LaserJet+, IIP, III, and HP DeskJet and plotters compatible with the HPGL plotter language.

Special! With this card, register for $45! ● Save $20

Name _____

Company _____

Address _____

City _____ State _____ Zip _____

Card # _____ Exp _____

Signature _____

Send your order to:

Natural Software
19 South Fifth Street
St. Charles, IL 60174
(708) 377-7320

Visa/MC accepted.

Introducing:

PC-FASTYPE™

The *BEST* Shareware typing instruction program for IBM-PCs and compatibles running MS-DOS.

All computer keyboards are different. Sure, they all have the usual QWERTY layout, but some of the keys you depend on all the time are not in the place where you'd like them to be. The old-style IBM-PC keyboard had the shift keys one key farther away from where you expected them to be; and the ENTER key is too far to the right. The AT-style keyboard corrected some of these problems; now the "enhanced" 101-key keyboard changed all the rules.

Wouldn't it be nice if you had a typing tutor that took these keyboard differences into account, and wouldn't it be nice to have a detailed image displayed on the screen of the exact keyboard layout you were learning to type on? Sure it would—and PC-FASTYPE is the answer.

PC-FASTYPE can help teach you the basic skills of touch-typing on computers. Whether you are a beginner, a "hunt 'n peck'r", or a typewriter typist who needs to refresh your skills for computer typing, you can use PC-FASTYPE to improve your typing speed and accuracy by following the self-paced drills and exercises.

If you are a professional or a student, you need the skill of touch typing to successfully use your computer in a productive manner for your profession or field of study. It's easy to learn the necessary skills of touch typing to successfully use your computer in a productive manner for your profession or field of study. It's easy to learn the necessary skills of touch-typing on IBM computers and close compatibles with PC-FASTYPE.

Best of all, PC-FASTYPE is Shareware. That means that you can *try-before-you-buy* by evaluating the program first. If you find the program useful and plan to use it regularly, you must register your use of it with the author.

Trendtech Corporation
P.O. Box 3687, Wayne NJ 97474-3687
201-694-8622

Shareware Registration   Registration gives you many benefits: You will receive a brand new copy of PC-FASTYPE, your special registration code, and a typeset and printed comprehensive User Guide. You will also get an express money-back guarantee if you are not satisfied with the program. The registered package will be sent to you directly from the program author.

YES!   Please register me as a PC-FASTYPE user:

Name _____ Title _____

Company _____

Address _____

City _____ State _____ Zip _____

Telephone _____

[ ] PC-FASTYPE/MONO   [ ] PC-FASTYPE/CGA

Please specify disk size: [ ] 5.25"   [ ] 3.5"

PC-FASTYPE/CGA requires CGA graphics and includes the AT-style and 101-key keyboard images
Additional keyboard images, $5.00 each: [ ] Old Style PC [ ] Tandy-1000

PC-FASTYPE/MONO is for any monitor type and includes the PC-style keyboard.

[ ] Please send information about site licensing and volume discounts

PC-FASTYPE registered packages cost only $25.00 plus $3.00 for shipping and handling. NJ residents add 6% sales tax.

Payment: [ ] MasterCard [ ] VISA [ ] Check [ ] Money Order [ ] COD [ ] PO

Credit Card Account Number   Expiration Date

| | | | | | | | | | | | | | | | | | | | | | |

Cardholder signature: _____

MAIL THIS CARD with payment to: Trendtech Corporation
                                  PC-FASTYPE Registration
                                  P.O. Box 3687
                                  Wayne, NJ 07474-3687

Site licenses, network licenses, right-to-copy licenses, and custom versions are available; call 201-694-8622 anytime.

PC-File 5.0

Over 700,000 people enjoy this powerful, friendly database manager

Why do non-programmers and business professionals prefer PC-File? You don't have to be a computer programmer to use it! The simple menu system and context-sensitive online help let you get the job done quickly and easily. You'll be up and working in minutes.

- Customer and address filing
- Lists
- Inventory
- Business graphics
- Custom reports
- Mailing labels

PC-File can do it all easily!

Now we'll make it easier than ever to buy PC-File—save $30 off the regular price! See back of coupon for details.

Offer ends 12/92

SPECIAL OFFER!

PC-File regularly sells for $149.95. However, when you send in this coupon, you can buy PC-File for $119.95. That's $30 off! Call ButtonWare today at 800-JBUTTON for more information.

ButtonWare
P.O. Box 96058
Bellevue, WA 98009

ProFile Order Form

☐   ProFile Registered Version with disks and manual **$39.00**. _____
      Add $10.00 shipping for international orders

☐   ProFile Evaluation Disks **$9.00**. _____
      Add $5.00 for international orders

Save 20%   TOTAL   _____

Name: _____

Company: _____

City: _____ State: _____ Zip: _____

Send check or money order in U.S. funds to:
National Software Design, 12505 Fostoria Way, Darnestown, MD 20878

Software Order Form

Enter Disk Numbers You Wish To Order:

✳ ☐☐☐☐☐ **Free Disk** (with purchase of five disks or membership)

1. ☐☐☐☐☐
2. ☐☐☐☐☐
3. ☐☐☐☐☐
4. ☐☐☐☐☐
5. ☐☐☐☐☐
6. ☐☐☐☐☐
7. ☐☐☐☐☐
8. ☐☐☐☐☐
9. ☐☐☐☐☐
10. ☐☐☐☐☐
11. ☐☐☐☐☐
12. ☐☐☐☐☐
13. ☐☐☐☐☐
14. ☐☐☐☐☐
15. ☐☐☐☐☐
16. ☐☐☐☐☐
17. ☐☐☐☐☐
18. ☐☐☐☐☐
19. ☐☐☐☐☐
20. ☐☐☐☐☐
21. ☐☐☐☐☐
22. ☐☐☐☐☐
23. ☐☐☐☐☐
24. ☐☐☐☐☐

Please send: (USA Prices Only)

☐ **$39 Super Saver Membership Special** — Includes 2 years of *Shareware Magazine* (12 issues), *The Encyclopedia of Shareware*—Vol's I & II, One free disk of your choice, free technical support, periodic mailings on the newest and most popular shareware, and special member pricing on future purchases @ $39 .... $ _____

☐ _____ Disks @ $6 each (non-members) _____

☐ _____ Disks @ $4 each (members) _____

☐ $1 per disk surcharge for 3.5" disks _____

☐ CD ROM @ $495 (entire Library on disc) _____

☐ *Encyclopedia of Shareware*, Vol.'s I and II @ $22.95 _____

☐ Other _____ _____

Subtotal _____
CA residents add 7.25% sales tax _____
Shipping and Handling $4.00

Payment by: ☐ Check   ☐ Visa   ☐ MC   **TOTAL** _____

Card No _____
Exp. Date _____ Sig. _____
Name _____
Address _____
_____

1030 D East Duane Ave., Sunnyvale, CA 94086, FAX: 408-730-2107

Visa/MasterCard Phone Orders: 800-245-6717 Ask for Operator #2197

☐ **1278 Fun With Letters and Words** *Req. CGA.* Colorful graphics and personalized scripts make it fun to learn reading and spelling. For children ages 2-5.

☐ **1278 Trek Trivia** One hundred questions to test your knowledge of the universe of Kirk, Spock and the Enterprise. Call when you're done and Scotty will beam you up!

☐ **1319 Basstour** *Req. 512K RAM and EGA, VGA, CGA or Hercules.* Captain a fully-rigged bass fishing boat in this colorful tournament that will put all your fishing skills to the test.

☐ **1330 PKPAK, PKUNPAK, and PKSFX** A set of archiving utilities for the most efficient use of disk space.

☐ **1336 StupenDOS** Display and manipulate files with ease. Provides sorted directory trees, file tagging, mouse interface, file move, copy files to disk and fill in with smaller files, and find files.

☐ **1364 PKZIP, PKUNZIP, PKSFX** Call it the "Amazing Shrinking RAM". Cram many more programs and data onto the precious, crowded real estate of your hard disk by scrunching, squeezing and otherwise smooshing your files!

☐ **1544 Klondike** *Req. EGA.* Klondike is a traditional gambling game similar to a card game most of us know as "Solitaire."

☐ **1544 Slot** *Req. EGA.* A slot machine so realistic you'll forget that you're playing at home.

☐ **1577 Instant Access Menu System** *Req. Epson compatible printer.* Control all of the software in your computer from a main menu with a minimum of keystrokes and hassles. Other functions include a screen dimmer, a time log, a notepad and a text editor.

☐ **1651, 1652 TechnoJock's Turbo Toolkit** *Req. Turbo Pascal 4.0 (or greater), or Quick Pascal, and unarchiving program.* TechnoJock's Turbo Toolkit (TTT) is a comprehensive set of procedures and functions for Turbo Pascal and Quick Pascal programmers. The Toolkit is designed for professional programmers, as well as newcomers.

☐ **1686 WordMaster** WORDMASTER offers a full function wordprocessor for computer beginners a those who just want a no-nonsense approach to writing.

☐ **1706 Scout-EM** An EM version of SCOUT, the memory-resident disk/directory/file manager DOS shell. Execute extensive DOS functions from within your other applications while only using 15.4k of normal memory.

☐ **1738 Power Desk** *Req. Hard disk.* POWER DESK gives you great power and handling in a desk utility. Use it as a complete desk organizer, personal time manager and as a super pess book with mail merge and wordprocessing capabilities.

☐ **1757 PC-Draft-CAD** *Req. Hercules or better, an IBM, Epson, HP LaserJet or HP DeskJet printer.* PC-DRAFT-CAD is an object oriented CAD program for drawing or drafting on a PC. PCD-CAD is different from most drawing packages in that PCD-CAD can store drawings as basic elements in a database.

☐ **1769 LaserLabel** *Req. HPLaserJet, DeskJet, or compatible printer, and PC-SIG disk #1145.* LASER LABEL has been created to allow users of the GRAB Plus Envelope Printer (PC-SIG disk #1145) to turn their data files into a powerful label printing system.

☐ **1769 Download** *Req. HP LaserJet, HP DeskJet, or compatible printer.* DOWNLOAD is an utility program that manages the process of downloading soft fonts to a Hewlett Packard LaserJet, DeskJet, or compatible printers.

☐ **1791 Match-Maker** MATCH-MAKER — a utility that finds new space on your hard disk drives by locating and deleting duplicate files.

☐ **1791 MDTS - Member and Donation Tracking System** The DOOR program is designed for the busy Shareware author or dealer who wants to help users find and read the text files on a disk.

☐ **1862 Gradease** Spend your time teaching and let GRADEEASE do the bookkeeping for you. Calculate grades, print out class lists, print seating charts and gradebook pages, grade summaries and progress reports.

☐ **1867 LCG/Remind** LCG/REMIND is a tickler program that can display a message or execute a program at a specified time interval, certain day of the week or on a day of the month.

☐ **2011 PC-Tags** PC-TAGS is a DOS and OS/2 source-code retrieval system that will locate and retrieve a function or procedure definition from a text file written in C, Pascal, BASIC, dBASE, Assembly, Modula-2 or any other language.

☐ **2018 LHarc & Utilities** LHARC and other compression utilities will give you greater compression power with all the popular compression formats.

☐ **2029 Find Duplicates** *Req. Hard drive.* FIND DUPLICATES will locate all duplicate files on your hard drive.

☐ **2029 CopyCon** COPYCON is a program designed to take the place of the DOS command "COPY CON" commonly used to create BATCH files.

☐ **2029 gBlink** gBLINK is a screen-blanking utility with on screen clock.

☐ **2031 TSR Download** *Req. HP LaserJet+, Series II, DeskJet, or compatible laser printer.* TSR DOWNLOAD is a memory-resident soft font manager that performs in any non-graphic mode application. Supports 32 fonts.

☐ **2082, 2083, 2084 PC-File** *Req. 512K RAM, and a hard drive.* PC-FILE — A flexible database with the unbeatable combination of ease of use, power and versatility.

☐ **2160 Remind** A lean and mean date reminder. Just put REMINDER into your AUTOEXEC.BAT and always knew when a holiday will occur and never forget another birthday or anniversary.

☐ **2160 Calendar25** CALENDAR25 is a unique perpetual calendar that gives you famous dates and most major holidays for any givem month and year. It's half history lesson and half calendar.

☐ **2176 FormatMaster** *Req. A 1.2M floppy disk.* FORMATMASTER exploits your 1.2M high capacity 5-1/4" drive to get the most of your 360K low capacity floppies — it will format them to 800K.

☐ **2176 CopyMaster** COPYMASTER makes file and disk copying fast, easy, and effective through dual directory viewing, mouse driven file moves across drives, batch tagging, file verification, pop-up data entry windows, and more.

☐ **2207 Stackey** STACKEY is a keyboard stacker that lets you automate feeding of keystrokes to applications. You'll no longer have to wait for your favorite program to load itself before you tell it which file to open.

☐ **2207 Batutil** BATUTIL is a program with two purposes: to give you power inside your batch files and to give you more control over the DOS environment. It is non-resident and has almost 100 commands.

☐ **2224 Shooting Gallery** *Req. 450K RAM, VGA or MCGA, and mouse.* SHOOTING GALLERY is a colorful arcade game with several different rounds to test your shooting skill.

☐ **2236 Zapcode** The ultimate printer control utility. Use ZAPCODE to select fonts, reset the printer, change margins, advance the page, and anything else your printer is capable of doing.

☐ **2239 Systems Manager** *Req. Hard disk.* SYSTEMS MANAGER manages the DOS and hard disk systems. A fast point-and-Shoot one-screen menu system of up to 60 entries.

☐ **2245 Swapdos** SWAPDOS provides a method for one DOS application to run another, even if both would normally not fit in memory at the same time.

To order use the order form above or call Toll Free 800-245-6717 and ask for operator #2197.

PC-SIG
1030 D East Duane Ave.
Sunnyvale, CA 94086

"Back & Forth delivers stable, easy context-switching.
Given its low price, it is an outstanding value."

—Jonathan Matzkin, *PC Magazine*

SPECIAL OFFER

The Most Useful Utilities You Will Ever Use

Commando Series	Regular Price	Special Price
File Commando	$39.95	$30.00
Menu Commando	$49.95	$40.00
Back & Forth	$69.95	$50.00

Order all three for one low price of $75.00

Back & Forth Net (Networking version— one per file server)	$495.00	$395.00

See reverse side for order form

If You Like QubeCalc You'll Love ProQube

(And now you can get it for free)

PC Magazine awarded our Shareware 3D spreadsheet QubeCalc "Editor's Choice", and called it *"extremely impressive"*.

But we didn't stop there. We created an even more powerful 3D spreadsheet called ProQube, which Jim Seymour says *"is one of the best -- and best implemented -- new ideas in spreadsheets in a long time. (Today's Office)"*

And you can receive ProQube for FREE, just by registering QubeCalc (*we'll even throw in a $10 discount*). ProQube provides all of the capabilities of QubeCalc, plus much more! ProQube gives you 512 pages in each 3D worksheet, plus presentation graphics, an integrated programming language, macro recorder, point & shoot file manager, mouse support, search & replace, file encryption, the ability to directly import and export 1-2-3 and dBase files, 104 @functions, expanded memory support, and much more!

ORDER FORM

Name _____

Company _____

Address _____

City _____ State _____ Zip _____

Phone _____

Send coupon to:

		Qty.		Amount
Progressive Solutions, Inc.	File Commando	____	x $ 30.00	_____
131 Washington Street	Menu Commando	____	x $ 40.00	_____
Lodi, NJ 07644	Back & Forth	____	x $ 50.00	_____
	Combo (all three)	____	x $ 75.00	_____
Phone: 1-800-833-4400	Back & Forth Net	____	x $395.00	_____

Phone: 1-800-833-4400
1-201-473-2000
Fax: 1-201-473-1082

Subtotal _____

$5.00 S/H U.S. and Canada _____
$16.00 S/H elsewhere _____
NJ residence add 7% sales tax _____
Total _____

____ Check or money order enclosed ____ VISA ____ M/C ____ AMEX

Account # _____ Exp. date _____

Signature _____

Free 3D Spreadsheet ProQube

Purchase our award winning 3D Shareware spreadsheet QubeCalc at a $10 discount, and we'll send you a *FREE* copy of our commercial 3D spreadsheet ProQube (a $99 value).

Mail to: FormalSoft
P.O. Box 1913
Sandy, UT 84091

Phone: 801-565-0971
800-962-7118

☐ QubeCalc + Free ProQube ($59.95)
☐ QubeCalc Shareware disk & ProQube demo disk ($5)

Name _____

Company _____

Address _____

City _____ State _____ Zip _____

Bill: ☐ Visa/MC   ☐ AMEX   ☐ Check

Card Number _____ Exp date _____

Signature _____

SAVE $5 ON *QANALYST*

Qanalyst disk & manual   @ ~~$22.50~~ $17.50 $_____

Illinois residents add 6.5% sales tax $_____

TOTAL $_____

Name: _____ Date: _____

Company: _____

Address: _____

_____

Check _____   Mastercard _____   Visa _____

Number: _____ Date: _____

Expires: _____   Day phone: _____

Signature: _____

Form DFF01

Qmail DeLuxe

The Original Offline Mail Reading System

Save $$$ and time with Qmail DeLuxe.

If you call any PCBoard (tm) bulletin board system using our Qmail System then you need Qmail DeLuxe. Instead of reading messages "online" Qmail DeLuxe lets you quickly receive your messages, hangup and then read them at your own pace.

Regular price $25.   With coupon $17.50

SHEZ
THE COMPRESSION COMPANION

Special Book offer. Register SHEZ using this coupon and receive the current Small and Large version of SHEZ. The large version can be configured to handle up to 2000 files per directory. In addition you will receive the FileFinder program that can locate files that are contained within archive files. This represents a **$10** savings over the normal registration fees.

Qmail Order Form

All orders must include this original coupon

☐   Please send me _____ copies of Qmail DeLuxe
at the special price of $17.50 (US Funds) each.

☐   I operate a PCBoard(tm) BBS and would like to
purchase The Qmail System at the special price
of $40.00. I also receive Qmail DeLuxe free!

Name_____

Address_____

City_____ State_____ Zip_____

☐ Check or money order enclosed   ☐ Charge my VISA or MASTERCARD

Account number_____ Exp Date_____

Signature_____

Send your order to: **Sparkware**
P.O. Box 605
Call our PCBoard at (901) 382-5583   **Cordova, TN 38018**

Send your registration fee along with this coupon to:

CALIFORNIA SOFTWARE DESIGNS
P.O. BOX 15248
SANTA ROSA, CA. 95402

Name: _____

Address: _____

City: _____

State: _____

Zip: _____

Phone: _____

Is "Ma Bell" breaking your back with long distance charges?

Does the "other service" leave something to be desired?

Sign up for StarLink Outdial Service now and start saving money as well as enjoying the ability to communicate with BBSes in over 160 U.S. Cities.

StarLink is as low as $1.50 per hour for night time and weekend connections.

Our members report as much as 240 cps data transfer rate.

Use this coupon to save $25.00 on your StarLink Registration Fee!

To order *StupenDOS*™, return this card with check or money order to:

Eclipse Technologies
7733 North 80th Street
Milwaukee, WI 53223

Regular price:	$35.00
Special discount for readers of this guide:	$10.00
	$25.00 *
Shipping and handling:	$ 3.50
Total	$28.50

* Includes 1 free upgrade when available. Quantity discounts & site licenses available.

Name _____ Phone _____ ext. _____

Company _____

Address _____

City _____ State ____ Zip _____

Disk size: ❏ 5 1/4" ❏ 3 1/2"

SWAPDOS

SwapDos allows you to run two separate DOS applications, by swapping the first application to extended/expanded memory or disk. It then loads the second application into DOS memory. SwapDos will swap both applications and TSRs using its *Long Swap* capability ensuring that virtually all of the memory used by installed applications and TSRs is made available except for 3,000 bytes.

THE SWAP UTILITIES

The SWAP Utilities swap entire resident portions of TSR programs to extended or expanded memory or to disk, and use less than 7K bytes of DOS memory. The SWAP Utilities can be loaded into high DOS memory using a memory manager like 386MAX or QEMM 386. The benefit to users is the recovery of the DOS memory formerly used by the TSR for other applications. Currently available SWAP Utilities include:

Borland's SideKick and SideKick Plus
Micro Logic's Tornado
Lotus Development's Metro/Express
Broderbund's Memory Mate
Symatec/Norton Computing's Norton Guides
Central Point Software's PC Tools Desktop and Shell

SWAP UTILITIES ORDER FORM

Get the SWAP Utilities for $20 each—20% below the regular price of $25

SideKick	_____	SideKick Plus	_____
Express	_____	Metro	_____
Tornado	_____	Memory Mate	_____
Norton Guides	_____	SwapDos	
		Total	_____

Name _____

Address _____

City _____ State _____ Zip _____

Phone (_____) _____

_____ Check or money order _____ VISA or MasterCard

Acct. no. _____ Exp. date _____

Signature _____

OR Call 1-800-926-4551
Innovative Data Concepts
1657 The Fairways, Suite 101
Jenkintown, PA 19046

Order Form

☐ Sydex Diskette "Disk-Set" with documentation, **$55.00.**
Add **$5.00** shipping+handling inside U.S., **$10.00** outside.   _____

☐ The Sydex Shareware Sampler. Evaluation versions of
the "Disk Set" programs--and more! **$5.00** (S/H incl.)   _____

TOTAL   _____

Name_____ Company _____

Street Address _____

City_____ State_____ Zip_____

☐ Check or money order enclosed ☐ Charge my VISA or MASTERCARD:

Acct. No._____ Exp. Date _____

Signature_____

Send your order to: **Sydex**
153 North Murphy
Sunnyvale, CA 94086
Allow 15 days for delivery.

Order Form

Kwikstat Latest Version, $39.00 x ___ = $_____
PC-CAI Latest Version, $39.00 x ___ = $_____
Info. Please, Latest Ver., $39.00 x ___ = $_____
Spell Games, Practice Spelling in an
Olympic-type setting, Normally $19.00
Special price, Spell Games $12.00 x ___ = $_____
Bannerific, Make Vertical or Horizontal
Banners on any printer, Normally $15.00
Special Price, Bannerific $10.00 x ___ = $_____
SUB TOTAL $_____
Texas Residents add 7.25% tax $_____
All orders add $4 domestic shipping $_____
Overseas add $10 shipping
GRAND TOTAL $_____

Thanks! All programs come with a 30 day money back
guarantee. Quantity and site license available. Phone
orders (MC and VISA) call 214-291-2115. Mention
Dr. File Finder Special.

Mail to:_____
Address:_____
City/St/Zip_____
Phone:_____Country_____

____Check or MO enclosed or ____ Visa or MC
____Purchase Order Number:_____

If Credit Card, Name on Card_____
Account no._____
Expiration date:_____
Signature:_____

Send Order to:
TexaSoft
P.O. Box 1169
Cedar Hill, Texas 75104

Order Today!

Elfring Soft Font's Order Form

Printer: ☐ LaserJet +, II, IIP, III ☐ DeskJet / Plus
Disk Media: ☐ 5-1/4 360K, ☐ 3-1/2 720K *(add $2)*

Payment: ☐ Check, ☐ VISA [VISA], ☐ MC [MC]
Make all checks payable to: Elfring Soft Fonts

Card Number: _____ _____ _____ _____
Expiration: _____
Signature: _____

Name: _____
Company: _____
Address: _____
City/State/Zip: _____
Country: _____
Phone: _____

Quan	Product	Price	Total
	TSR Download	$45	
	TSR Download & LaserJet fonts	$75	
	TSR Download & DeskJet fonts	$75	
	Coupon discount		-$15
	3-1/2 disk	$2	
	Illinois orders 6.5% tax		
	US shipping	$4	
	Canada shipping	$5	
	Foreign shipping	$8	
	Total		

Elfring Soft Fonts
PO Box 61
Wasco, IL 60183
Offer expires December 31, 1991

Phone Orders: 708-377-3520
FAX Orders: 708-377-6402

Send in this coupon when you join The WELL and get five hours free!

When you register for the WELL, send in this coupon and get five hours of on-line time free. That's a savings of $15. The WELL is a unique on-line meeting of minds with a real "sense of place."

NAME _____

ADDRESS _____

CITY _____ STATE _____ ZIP _____

The WELL
27 Gate Five Road
Sausalito, CA 94965

Registration Forms for Software on Disks

ANARKEY
Registration Form

☐ Anarkey Registration $29.95

Number of copies   _____

Subtotal   _____

CA residents add sales tax   _____

Shipping & Handling   _$4.00_
(outside U.S. $8.00)

Total   _____

Specify Disk Size: ☐ 5.25   ☐ 3.5

Make check or money order payable to **Moderne Software**

Moderne Software
P.O. Box 3638
Santa Clara, CA 95055-3638

BlackBeard Shareware License

To register BlackBeard it is necessary to return this form with a check or money order for $ 20.00 (U.S.) to:

BlackBeard
P.O. Box 638
San Bernardino, CA 92402

Complete and return this registration card to be granted a single-user license. Licensed users will be entitled to a copy of the complete documentation on disk.

After signing and returning this registration card, you may make copies of BlackBeard for backup purposes and operate the program on any computer, provided only one user and one copy of the program are in use at any one time.

ANARKEY
Registration Form

Please register my copy of Anarkey and send me a registered disk of the latest version. Enclosed is my registration fee.

_____
Name

_____
Address

_____
City, State, Zip

_____
Country

Send to: **Moderne Software, P.O. Box 3638, Santa Clara, CA 95055-3638**

Single-User Registration

I am enclosing my fee of $20.00 for registration of BlackBeard. Please send the latest documentation.

Name _____

Company _____

Street address _____

City _____

State _____ Zip _____

I agree to the terms and conditions of this software license.

Signature _____ Date _____

dCOM Registration Form

To receive your registered version of dCOM - The Directory Commander, at a special price of $47.00 (20% off the regular retail price), complete this form and return it with your check or money order (U.S. Banks only) to:

DAC Micro Systems
40941 176th St E.
Lancaster, CA 93535

Voice: 805/264-1700
Modem: 805/264-1219

Registered users receive a complete, 150 pg, type-set quality manual, quick reference cards, and special access to the dCOM Support Bulletin Board.

dCOM Registration Form

Name: _____

Company: _____

Address: _____

City:_____ State: _____ Zip: _____

Home Phone: _____ Work Phone: _____

Comments: _____

Diskette type: [ ] 5.25"   [ ] 3.5"

Purchase Amount ($47.00 per copy): _____

California Residents add 6.75% Sales Tax: _____

Shipping & Handling: _____ 3.50

Total Purchase Amount: _____

[ ] Amount is Enclosed

[ ] Bill my Visa/MC# _____ Exp: _____

　　　Signature: _____

Orders Only: 1-800-367-7590

Information: 1-512-832-1675

CompuServe: [73267,1664]

Name_____

Address_____

　　　　_____

City/State_____

Zip/Country_____

Phone_____ Code: DFFGS

☐ Check/MO (US Funds)　☐ Visa/MC　☐ COD

Visa/MC_____

Expires_____　Signature_____

	Price	Qty	Amount
DX-Directory eXtended v2.5	$49.95	___	_____
Upgrade from earlier version*	$24.95	___	_____
In Texas, add 8% sales tax			_____
International shipping add	$10		_____
(*Use original name on upgrades.)		TOTAL:	_____

ECONO-SOFT
P.O.Box 181030
Austin, TX 78718-1030

DOC v1.x Shareware License

To register DOC v1.x it is necessary to return this form with a check or money order for $10.00 (U.S.) to:

J. Knauer Consulting
P.O. Box 747
Brookfield, CT 06804

Complete and return this registration card to be granted a single-user license. Licensed users will be entitled to a copy of the complete documentation on disk.

After signing and returning this registration card, you may make copies of DOC v1.x for backup purposes and operate the program on any computer, provided only one user and one copy of the program are in use at any one time.

IFF v5.0A Shareware License

To register IFF v5.0A it is necessary to return this form with a check or money order for $15.00 (U.S.) to:

J. Knauer Consulting
P.O. Box 747
Brookfield, CT 06804

Complete and return this registration card to be granted a single-user license. Licensed users will be entitled to a copy of the complete documentation on disk.

After signing and returning this registration card, you may make copies of IFF v5.0A for backup purposes and operate the program on any computer, provided only one user and one copy of the program are in use at any one time.

Single-User Registration

I am enclosing my fee of $10.00 for registration of DOC v1.x. Please send the latest documentation.

Name _____

Company _____

Street address _____

City _____

State _____ Zip _____

I agree to the terms and conditions of this software license.

Signature _____ Date _____

Osborne/McGraw-Hill assumes no responsibility for the fulfillment of this offer.

Single-User Registration

I am enclosing my fee of $15.00 for registration of IFF v5.0A. Please send the latest documentation.

Name _____

Company _____

Street address _____

City _____

State _____ Zip _____

I agree to the terms and conditions of this software license.

Signature _____ Date _____

Osborne/McGraw-Hill assumes no responsibility for the fulfillment of this offer.

Hard Disk Tutor or Modem Tutor License

The Hard Disk Tutor and the Modem Tutor are commercial products, NOT Shareware, and may not be distributed in any form without express written consent of Computer Business Services. These versions are being distributed by special arrangement with Computer Business Services.

Purchasers of *Dr. File Finder's Guide to Shareware* who complete and return this registration card will be granted a single user license. Licensed users are entitled to technical support and notification of future updates and new products.

After signing and returning this registration form, you may make copies of the Hard Disk Tutor or Modem Tutor for backup purposes. You may operate the program on any computer, provided only one user and one copy of the program are in use at any one time.

We support our software. Many Hard Disk Tutor and Modem Tutor features are the result of user input. If you have suggestions or comments, feel free to drop us a line:

Computer Business Services
Hard Disk/Modem Tutor Ideas
1125 Bramford Court
Diamond Bar, CA 91765
(714) 860-6914

GET A DISK FULL OF UTILITIES WITH
PPRINT!

PPRINT, as featured in this publication, is a professional quality replacement for the DOS PRINT command. Giving support to virtually every printer and printer feature available, PPRINT allows you to use one print utility regardless of the number of printers you may use.

PPRINT FEATURES...

- o Laser Support
- o Support for Every Standard Font
- o Features That You Customize to Fit Your Printer
- o Much, Much More...

PPRINT Is One of Many Fine Products from Patri-Soft. To order your copy, fill out the order form on the other side. We will send you PPRINT, and a disk full of our other utilities.

Hard Disk Tutor ☐ or Modem Tutor ☐ (check one or both)
User Registration   Serial No.:

Name: _____

Company: _____

Address: _____

City: _____ State: _____ Zip: _____

Phone (day): (____) ____ - _____ Phone (eve): (____) ____ - _____

CPU Mfgr: _____ Signature: _____

PC   XT   286   386   486   PS2   (circle one)

MGA   CGA   EGA   VGA   (circle one)

Comments: _____

Computer Business Services - Hard Disk Tutor or Modem Tutor Registration
1125 Bramford Court • Diamond Bar, CA 91765 • 714-860-6914

Osborne **McGraw-Hill** assumes NO responsibility for the fulfillment of this offer.

PPRINT ORDER COUPON

Please Send PPRINT to:

_____ Program and Printed Documentaion $15.00
_____ All 8 Patriquin Utilities and bound manual $45.00

Name: _____

Address: _____   Send to:
                                                              Patri-Soft
             _____   P.O. Box 8263
                                                              San Bernardino CA,
             _____   92412

City/State: _____

Qmodem 4.2 Shareware License

To register Qmodem 4.2 it is necessary to return this form with a check or money order for $30.00 (U.S.) to:

The Forbin Project
P.O. Box 702
Cedar Falls, IA 50613

Complete and return this registration card to be granted a single-user license. Licensed users will be entitled to a copy of the complete documentation on disk.

After signing and returning this registration card, you may make copies of Qmodem 4.2 for backup purposes and operate the program on any computer, provided only one user and one copy of the program are in use at any one time.

Single-User Registration

I am enclosing my fee of $30.00 for registration of Qmodem 4.2. Please send the latest documentation.

Name _____

Company _____

Street address _____

City _____

State _____ Zip _____

I agree to the terms and conditions of this software license.

Signature _____ Date _____

Osborne/McGraw-Hill assumes no responsibility for the fulfillment of this offer.

The Dr. File Finder Shareware Collection

Many excellent programs were discussed in *Dr. File Finder's Guide to Shareware*, and a few of them were included with the book. Because we want everyone to be able to access as many of these programs as possible, my coauthor, Nick Anis, and I want to take the time to make the following special offer:

Get a 6-pack or a 12-pack from the Doc!

All disks will be filled to capacity. You will get a mixture of applications programs and utility programs that have been discussed in the various chapters of the book. "The Doc" sends only the very latest version of each program. With any disk order you'll get two FREE issues of "Dr. File Finder's Newsletter," or if you like, you can order the newsletter without disks. The choice is yours, and you can pay by check or credit card. Put a check mark by the item(s) you want. (*Note*: If you order the newsletter AND the disks, you will get 14 issues of the newsletter!)

Upon receipt of your order, you will receive the very next release of the newsletter. The newsletter will contain tips on the latest *hot* programs, reviews of excellent computer-related books, special offers, program reviews, hardware reviews, and more.

Get more of the programs that you read about in the book from the people who wrote the book! Your satisfaction is guaranteed. And, when the next release is available, you'll get the latest catalogue of the Dr. File Finder Shareware collection, which features only the BEST Shareware programs available.

ORDER FORM

6-Pack - 6 disks plus two free issues of the newsletter _____ $25.00
12-Pack - 12 disks plus two free issues of the newsletter _____ $35.00
Newsletter - 1 year subscription, six issues _____ $12.00

Please add $3.00 for shipping and handling

Name _____

Address _____ Apt. # ____

City, State, Zip _____

Circle method of payment:

Check   VISA   MasterCard   Optima   American Express

Card number _____ Exp. date _____

American Express only: membership since _____

Make checks payable to: FF&P Enterprises

Put this form in a stamped envelope and mail it to:

Dr. File Finder Shareware Collection
FF&P Enterprises
P.O. Box 591
Elizabeth, CO 80107